Organizational Behaviour

Pearson

At Pearson, we have a simple mission: to help people make more of their lives through learning.

We combine innovative learning technology with trusted content and educational expertise to provide engaging and effective learning experiences that serve people wherever and whenever they are learning.

From classroom to boardroom, our curriculum materials, digital learning tools and testing programmes help to educate millions of people worldwide – more than any other private enterprise.

Every day our work helps learning flourish, and wherever learning flourishes, so do people.

To learn more, please visit us at **www.pearson.com/uk**

Organizational Behaviour

David A.
Buchanan

Andrzej A.
Huczynski

Edition

 **Pearson**

Harlow, England • London • New York • Boston • San Francisco • Toronto • Sydney • Dubai • Singapore • Hong Kong
Tokyo • Seoul • Taipei • New Delhi • Cape Town • São Paulo • Mexico City • Madrid • Amsterdam • Munich • Paris • Milan

PEARSON EDUCATION LIMITED
KAO Two
KAO Park
Harlow CM17 9SR
United Kingdom
Tel: +44 (0)1279 623623
Web: www.pearson.com/uk

First edition published by Prentice Hall International (UK) Ltd 1985 (print)
Second edition published by Prentice Hall International (UK) Ltd 1991 (print)
Third edition published by Prentice Hall Europe 1997 (print)
Fourth edition published by Pearson Education Ltd 2001 (print)
Fifth edition published in 2004 (print)
Sixth edition published in 2007 (print)
Seventh edition published in 2010 (print)
Eighth edition published in 2013 (print and electronic)
Ninth edition published in 2017 (print and electronic)
Tenth edition 2019 (print and electronic)

Contains public sector information licensed under the Open Government Licence (OGL) v3.0. http://www.nationalarchives.gov.uk/doc/open-government-licence/version/3/.

The screenshots in this book are reprinted by permission of Microsoft Corporation.

Pearson Education is not responsible for the content of third-party internet sites.

ISBN: 978-1-292-25157-8 (print)
       978-1-292-25158-5 (PDF)
       978-1-292-25159-2 (ePub)

British Library Cataloguing-in-Publication Data
A catalogue record for the print edition is available from the British Library

Library of Congress Cataloging-in-Publication Data
Names: Buchanan, David, author. | Huczynski, Andrzej, author.
Title: Organizational behaviour / David A. Buchanan, Andrzej A. Huczynski.
Description: 10 edition. | Harlow, England ; New York : Pearson, 2019. |
  Includes bibliographical references and index. | Summary: "Our target
  readers are students who are new to the social sciences and to the study
  of organizational behaviour. This is a core subject on most business and
  management degree, diploma and masters programmes. Accountants,
  architects, bankers, computer scientists, doctors, engineers, hoteliers,
  nurses, surveyors, teachers and other specialists, who have no
  background in social science, may find themselves studying
  organizational behaviour as part of their professional examination
  schemes"— Provided by publisher.
Identifiers: LCCN 2019025259 | ISBN 9781292251578 (print) |
  ISBN 9781292251585 (PDF) | ISBN 9781292251592 (ePub)
Subjects: LCSH: Organizational behavior.
Classification: LCC HD58.7 .H83 2019 | DDC 302.3/5—dc23
LC record available at https://lccn.loc.gov/2019025259

10 9 8 7 6 5 4 3 2
23 22 21 20

Front cover image © Shutterstock Premier/IM_Photo

Print edition typeset in 9/12pt ITC Slimbach Std by SPi Global
Print edition printed in Slovakia by Neografia

NOTE THAT ANY PAGE CROSS REFERENCES REFER TO THE PRINT EDITION

From David

To Lesley, Andrew, Mairi, Rachel, Séan, Charlie, Ciara, Archie, Leila, Harry and Hudson

From Andrzej

To Janet, Sophie, Gregory, Tom, Magnus, Freya, Rosa, Leo and Ivy

Preface

Why study organizational behaviour?

Let's put it this way: if you have a limited understanding of organizational behaviour (OB), then you have a limited understanding of one of the main sets of forces that affect you personally, that affect the society and the culture in which you live, and which shape the world around you. Think about it: organizations are involved in everything that you do – sleeping, waking, dressing, eating, travelling, working, relaxing, studying – everything. This book explores how organizations influence our views and our actions, and how we can explain the behaviour of people in organizations.

What is our approach?

Our target readers are students who are new to the social sciences and to the study of organizational behaviour. This is a core subject on most business and management degree, diploma and masters programmes. Accountants, architects, bankers, computer scientists, doctors, engineers, hoteliers, nurses, surveyors, teachers and other specialists, who have no background in social science, may find themselves studying organizational behaviour as part of their professional examination schemes.

Social science perspective   We draw on a range of social science disciplines. Other texts adopt managerial, psychological or sociological perspectives.

Critical approach   Many OB issues are controversial. But we don't identify the 'correct answers' or 'best practices'. We want to challenge assumptions, and to stimulate critical thinking. In a world flooded with information, some of which is 'fake news', critical thinking is critically important.

Self-contained chapters   The understanding of one chapter does not rely on others. You can study the chapters in any sequence. Designed for introductory-level courses, our *Springboard* feature suggests advanced reading. Many chapters are also relevant to courses in human resource management.

Let's pull it together

If you are new to OB, the subject can seem to be wide ranging and fragmented. To show how it all fits together, here is our 'field map'. First, organizations function over time and in a context. Second, individual, group, management and leadership factors influence organizational effectiveness, and quality of working life. You can easily locate the book's parts and chapters on this map.

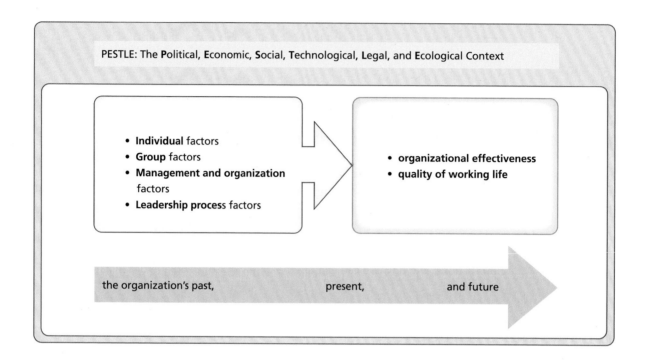

PESTLE: The **P**olitical, **E**conomic, **S**ocial, **T**echnological, **L**egal, and **E**cological Context

- **Individual** factors
- **Group** factors
- **Management and organization** factors
- **Leadership proces**s factors

- **organizational effectiveness**
- **quality of working life**

the organization's past,   present,   and future

What's new in this edition?

New features

Critical thinking	Invitations to question, challenge assumptions, consider other options
Cutting edge	Summaries of recent key research findings
What did they find?	Descriptions of research studies, asking you to predict the results
Employability check	Relating chapter content to employability competencies
Audio box	Short podcasts exploring topical issues
Video box	Brief videos exploring chapter themes in more depth
Stop and search	Suggestions for YouTube content exploring key topics

New content (a selection)

Big data and human capital analytics: How will the human resource management function be operating in 2030?

Multigenerational workforce: Why are age-diverse teams more satisfied and productive?

Ageing workforce: What are the benefits of employing older 'unretired' people?

Agile working and holacracy: Who needs managers, leaders, and hierarchies?

Artificial intelligence: Will it steal your job?

Future-proof your career: Skills that are still going to be in demand in a digital world

Gastronomic bonding: Team building by members preparing and eating food together

Learning to learn: An indispensable skill in a rapidly changing world

Neurodiversity: The extraordinarily valuable, but underutilized skills of employees with autism spectrum disorders, dyspraxia, and dyslexia

Neuroplasticity: How we are able to go on learning throughout our lives

Multicultural brokers: Their role in making diverse team members effective

Tattoo or not tattoo: How attitudes towards body art are changing

Social networks: How they affect team creativity and company performance

Do women make better leaders than men? Do women have the right personality traits?

Cybervetting: How potential employers now screen you without your knowledge

Dark personality traits: How these can damage your career

HEXACO: The Big Six model of personality

Introverts: Can they become effective and successful senior leaders?

Self-determination theory (SDT): A new way to understand, and manage, work motivation

We need to talk about organizational change: Why do 75 per cent of programmes fail?

Detroit, Estée Lauder, McDonald's, Thai Union: Case studies of successful organizational change

Political skill: Why are politically skilled women are more successful in male-dominated organizations?

Outline contents

Full contents

PART 2   Individuals in the organization   145

PART 4   Management and organization   451

PART 5   Leadership processes   **607**

Acknowledgements

A large number of friends, colleagues, students, and staff at Pearson have contributed their ideas, criticism, advice and support to the development of this new edition. Special thanks in this regard are extended to Vinay Agnihotri, Lesley Buchanan, Janet Huczynska, Antonia Maxwell, Andrew Müller, Suzanne Ross, and Vicky Tubbs. We would also like to thank the many researchers and authors who have allowed us to use their portrait photographs alongside our descriptions of their work.

Publisher's acknowledgements

We are grateful to the following for permission to reproduce copyright material:

Front Matter

Creators Syndicate Inc.: Rubes By Leigh Rubin xxxii.

Part Opener 1 (Chapter 1 to 4): Dizanna/123RF 1, **Part Opener 2 (Chapter 5 to 9):** Elenabsl/123RF 145, **Part Opener 3 (Chapter 10 to 13):** Rawpixel/123RF 313, **Part Opener 4 (Chapter 14 to 17):** PopTika/Shutterstock 451, **Part Opener 5 (Chapter 18 to 22):** Dusit/Shutterstock 607.

Portraits

Ed Hess xxxiv, **Andrew Scott** 49, **Lynda Gratton** 49, **Annie McKee** 60, **Christopher McLaverty** 60, **Frank Yu** 63, **Henrik Cronqvist** 63, **Melanie Arntz** 88, **Carl Frey** 89, **Michael Osborne:** Oxford Martin School 89, **Amir Goldberg:** Nancy Rothstein 117, **Sameer Srivastava** 117, **Vicki Taylor:** Bill Smith 119, **André Spicer** 122, **Sujin Jang** 134, **Monika Hamori:** Kerry Parker 148, **Jie Cao** 148, **Carol Dweck** 151, **Marie-Hélène Budworth** 160, **Songqi Liu** 164, **Stephane Kasriel** 181, **Todd Buchholz** 187, **Youyou Wu** 190, **Tomas Chamorro-Premuzic** 192, **Herminia Ibarra** 195, **Natalie Shefer** 196t, **Ethan Bernstein** 218t, **Stephen Turban** 218b, **Alison Wood Brooks** 220t, **Leslie John** 220b, **Elizabeth McClean** 222, **Chad Murphy** 236t, **Jonathan Clark** 236b, **Andrew DuBrin** 248t, **Laura Little** 248b, **Andrew Timming** 265, **Michele Kaufmann** 266, **Chia-Jung Tsay:** Neal Hamberg 268, **Edward Deci** 283t, **Richard Ryan** 283b, **Erik Gonzalez-Mulé** 285t, **Bethany Cockburn** 285b, **Todd Bridgman** 287, **Steven Kramer** 293t, **Teresa Amabile** 293t, **David Guest** 299b, **Gudela Grote** 299t, **Min-Ho Joo** 317t, **Vanessa Dennen** 317b, **Mark Mortensen** 331b, **Heidi Gardner** 332l, **Sunken Lee** 336, **Bret Scanner:** Josephine Cardin 350l, **Stuart Bunderson** 350r, **Martine Haas** 355, **Tomas Chamorro-Premuzic** 357r, **Erica Dhawan** 357l, **Selma van der Haar** 360, **Stefan Volk** 365, **Michael Watkins** 368c, **Chris Lam** 390t,

Wayne Neu 391, **Giada Di Stefano** 393l, **Deanna Paulin** 396t, **Barbara Griffin** 396b, **Kevin Kniffin**: JesseWinter 407t, **Laura Jones** 423l, **Amy Edmondson**: Evgenia Elseeva 424, **Soo Jeoung Han** 427, **Nina Magpili** 433t, **Pilar Pazos** 433b,**Trevor Young-Hyman** 437, **Christa Gibson** 439r, **Sharon parker** 453b, **Douglas Martin** 465, **David Graeber** 469l, **Harry Pits** 469r, **Paul Thompson** 469c, **Peter Ikeler** 473b, **Knut Laaser** 481, **Peter Gloor:** David Sella 509, **David Garvin:** Russ Campbell 538, **Samina Karim** 542b, **Stéphanie Girod** 542t, **Marcia Lensges** 555, **James Harter** 570, **Michael Lee** 589, **Martin Kornberger** 596tl, **Raffaella Sadun** 613, **Elena Lytkina Botelho:** Matt Mendelsohn 615, **Herman Aguinis** 616, **Lars Glaso:** Linn de Lange 618b, **Oyvind Martinsen** 618c, **Dame Vivian Hunt** 619b, **Laura Morgan Roberts** 621, **Alexander Haslam** 622b, **Michelle Ryan** 622t, **Jasmine Vergauwe** 632, **Karina Nielsen** 633l, **Kevin Daniels** 633r, **Mansour Javidan** 635, **Peter Gronn** 634, **Jeroen Stouten** 648, **Rene Weidner** 654, **Alannah Rafferty** 655t, **Charis Rice** 656b, **Rosalind Searle:** Adam Scoll 656t, **Amy Edmondson:** Evgenia Elseeva 669, **Joaquin Navajas** 696t, **Marcia Hagen, Alan Bernard, Eric Grube:** 701, **Lindred Greer** 727t, **Ginka Toegel** 728t, **Jean-Louis Barsoux** 728b, **Michele Gelfand** 738b, **Dacher Keltner** 758, **Janneke Oostrom** 759t, **Richard Ronay** 759b, **Jeremy Heimans:** Michael Creagh 768b, **Henry Timms:** Michael Creagh 768b, **Susan Ashford** 771l, **James Detert:** Tom Cogill 771r, **Gerald Ferris** 773l.

Photographs

(Key: T-top; B-bottom; C-Center; L-left; R-right)

123RF: Bloomua 15, Keith Bell 111, Lightwise 128, Rommel Canlas 161, John Takai 180t, Jörg Schiemann 212, Andrew grossman 214, Wang Tom 228t, Imagehit Limited 234tl, Dmitriy Shironosov 294, Mark Bowden 333, Yomogi 366, Sergey Ilin 383, HONGQI ZHANG 385, Adamson 429, Mark Bowden 502, Alena Saklakova 507, Racorn 552, lculig 719, Dirk ercken 735t, Kzenon 667, Vitaliy Vodolazskyy 672, Lightwise 692. **Andrews McMeel Syndication:** © Betty, United Feature Syndicate 224, © Dilbert United Features Syndicate 279. **Alamy Stock Photo:** US Coast Guard Photo 8, Charles Robertson 52, 360b 111tl, Chris Hennessy 111tr, Ian Paterson 256, ITAR-TASS News Agency 319b, David R. Frazier Photolibrary, Inc. 464b, Matthew Horwood 477l, Mint Photography 583, PAUL J. RICHARDS/AFP 579, Media World Images 671. **Anna Gordon:** Used with permission of Anna Gordon 57. **AT&T Archives and History Center:** Courtesy of AT&T Archives and History Center 327, 328. **Cartoon Stock:** Bob Eckstein 11, Fran 47, 611, mbcn1358 166, Seddon Mike 226b. **Craig Swanson**: Used with permission of Craig Swanson 154. **Dr Haze:** Used with permission of Dr Haze 630. **Getty Images:** T3 Magazine/Future 75, Fabrice Dimier/Bloomberg 326, JUAN MABROMATA/AFP/Stringer 418, IPC Magazines. Picture Post 459, Bettmann 463l, Bloomberg 477r, Robin Marchant 513, DEA/ICAS94 646, Mansell/The LIFE Picture Collection 768t. **Geek Culture:** Used with permission of Geek Culture 780. **Glasbergen Cartoon Service:** Used with permission of Glasbergen Cartoon Service 127, 707. **Jens Pagotta:** Used with permission of Jens Pagotta and Diala Ghassan 612. **Jim Haas:** Used with permission of Jim Haas 92. **Joe Mirachi:** © Joseph Mirachi, reproduced with permission 626. **Mark Weinstein:** Used with permission of Mark Weinstein 200. **National Museum of American History:** Used with permission of The University of National Museum of American History 460. **Pearson Education, Inc.:** Naki Kouyioumtzis 91, JOHANNES EISELE /AFP 227l, Mandel Ngan-Pool/Getty Images News 227r, Bettmann 231l, Library of Congress/Handout/Archive Photos 231r, Rob Lewine 234bl, HL Studios 359. **Rethink Robotics, Inc.** Used with permission of Rethink Robotics, Inc 77. **Reuters:** Edgar Su/REUTERS 76. **Roger Beale:** Used with permission of Roger Beale 623t. **Royal Brunei Airlines:** Used with permission of Captain Czarena Hashim 618t. **Shutterstock:** Alphaspirit 6, KlektaDarya 16, Poznyakov 23, 28, Rawpixel.com 30, Robert paul van beets 41, Sean K 45, JuliaGrin 48, Levent Konuk 74t, Karen Roach 74b, Sundry Photography 77, Zapp2Photo 83, SS_FOTO 86, Cartoon Resource 93, Brian A Jackson 96, Mypokcik 106, Casimiro PT 112l, 360b 112r, Joycolor 114, Hadrian 116, Deborah Kolb 122, Cartoon Resource 123t, Dennis Cox 123b, Paolo Bona 129, Stuart Jenner 134, Marekuliasz 151, Amir Ridhwan 180b, Tomasz Trojanowski 196b, Jason Batterham 199,

Christophe BOISSON 215t, Iqoncept 215b, Antonio Guillem 221, Paul Vasarhelyi 225, M-SUR 226t, Viorel Sima 228b, Pathdoc 233, DenisProduction.com 234tr, Gornostay 237, Christos Georghiou 250, Kathy Hutchins 257, Ilin Sergey 259, Sanyalux Srisurin 261, YAKOBCHUK VIACHESLAV 262, CoraMax 263, Eldirector77 264l, Daxiao Productions 264r, TierneyMJ 277, Goodluz 278, Daisy Daisy 280, Dusit 281, Kheng Guan Toh 284, Fotovika 293b, Erwinova 298, Marekuliasz 300, Arka38 301, Cartoon Resource 315,318, Jesadaphorn 319t, Ivanko80 322, Sirtravelalot 325, Dmitry Kalinovsky 330, TarikVision 331c, Hobbit 332r, Graphic farm 334, Tyler Olson 335, America365 346, Cartoonresource 348, Carlos E. Santa Maria 349, ESB Professional 352, Milles Studio 354, Denis Cristo 358, ESB Professional 362, Kom_Pornnarong 367, Fred Ho 368t, 368b, Kent Weakley 370,Stokk 371, America365 374, Bruce Rolff 381, Angela Waye 384, Trueffelpix 386, Iurii 387, Nejron Photo 389, Cartoon Resource 390b, Artesania Digital 393r, Wavebreakmedia 397, Cartoon Resource 402, Photographee.eu 403, 407b, Cartoon Resource 419, Vaju Ariel 422t, Shahjehan 422b, Wavebreakmedia 423r, Yulia Glam 425, MSSA 428, Arsel Ozgurdal 438, Justaa 439l, Radu Razvan 440, Cartoon Resource 442, Poznyakov 453t, Everett Collection 455,457,474t, Everett Historical 456, Rick Ray 462, Vladimir salman 463r, Zdenek Sasek 464t, TotallyBlond 467, Pressmaster 471, Chesky 477c, Zelena 491t, Michael D Brown 491b, Nito 496, Pixsooz 497t, John T Takai 497b, Cartoon Resource 498,500,520, Pressmaster 508t, Sergey Nivens 508b, Mert Toker 510, Adam Gregor 511, Lisa S 512, Kaspars Grinvalds 515, Ondrej Schaumann 519, John Dory 529, CREATISTA 531, Theerasak Namkampa 536, Media_works 537, Phipatbig 539, Dusit 541, Pixelbliss 543,549, Wally Stemberger 546t, Melinda Nagy 546b, 547t, Cartoon Resource 547b, Ksenica 566, Cartoon Resource 567, Brian A Jackson 571, StockLite 572t, Robuart 572b, Darren Brode 574, Iqoncept 576, AlesiaKan 585, Teguh Jati Prasetyo 586, Sari Oneal 590t, Fotosenmeer 590b, 360b 591, OpturaDesign 592, Tanuha2001 596tc, Hilch 596b, Bakhtiar Zein 597t, PLRANG ART 597b, Michael D Brown 598, Marco Lacobucci EPP 609, Savvapanf Photo 610, Igor Bulgarin 619t, Casimiro PT 623b, Aisyaqilumaranas 625, Robert Blaga 629, Morphart Creation 645, Iqoncept 647,649, Atomazul 650t, Gerald Bernard 650b, Cartoon Resource 653,655b, Sorbis 659, Suchatbky 660, Tupungato 662, Cineberg 665, Sashkin 666, Kheng Guan Toh 681t, Migren art 681b, Cartoon Resource 682,699, Gustavo Frazao 684, ImageFlow 685, Bakhtiar Zein 686, Franck Boston 687, Juergen Priewe 688, PhoelixDE 690, Newart-graphics 693t, Andy Dean Photography 693b, Citybrabus 694, KlektaDarya 696bl, Pedrosek 696br, Ogieurvil 698, LittleWhale 700, Julie Dreamcatcher 702, Lightspring 709, Poznyakov 720t, ProStockStudio 720b, Ljupco Smokovski 721, Idraw 722, Sharaf Maksumov 723, Michaeljung 724, Cartoon Resource 725,727b,737b,738t, Pressmaster 726,739, Photobank Gallery 729t, Matthias Pahl 729b, Airone 732, Sangoiri 734, Iqoncept 735b,740t, Carsten Reisinger 740b, ESB Professional 741, MaximP 743, Sirtravelalot 748, Everett Historical 757t, DiskoDancer 757b, Gregg Brekke 761t, Andy Dean Photography 761b, Sam72 762, Pedrosek 763, Dusit 764, SvetaZi 765, Ryan Jorgensen – Jorgo 767, ESB Professional 769, Lev Radin 772, Eyeidea 773r, ESB Basic 775, Wjarek 776, TierneyMJ 777t, Rawpixel.com 777b,778, Christopher Halloran 779. **Superstock:** Johner 234br. **The Financial Times Ltd.:** "Can a robot do your job?" by Robin Kwong, Joanna S Kao, Claire Manibog and Toyoki Nakanishi, © 2017, Used with permission of The Financial Times Ltd. 474b. **The University of Akron:** Used with permission of The University of Akron 518. **The Psychonomic Society:** © The Psychonomic Society 1998 252. **Times Union:** Used with permission of Will Waldron 165.

Text Credits

xxxi Sage Publications: Anderson, Marc H. ,'Why are there so many theories?', Journal of Management Education, 31(6): 757–76, ©2007, Sage Publications; **10 Crown Copyright:** Speech in Parliament by an MP, Tony Benn, in 1995 Retrieved from https://api.parliament.uk/historic-hansard/commons/1995/nov/22/the-economy, Crown copyright, All content is available under the Open Government Licence v3.0, except where otherwise stated; **22 The Academy of Management:** Rousseau, D.M., Is there such a thing as 'evidence-based management' ?, ©2006, The Academy of Management; **22 Kogan Page Publishers:** MacRae, Ian. and Furnham, Adrian, Myths of Work: The Stereotypes and Assumptions Holding Your Organization Back, ©2018, Kogan Page Publishers; **27 Chartered Institute of Personnel and Development:** John Purcell, Nick Kinnie, Sue Hutchinson, Bruce Rayton and Juani Swart (2003), Understanding the people and performance link: unlocking the black box. London: CIPD, Page 7. **27, 28 Raconteur:** Frary, Mark, A glimpse of the future of human resources, ©2017, Raconteur. Used with permission; **40 HRD Press:** Ansoff, Igor, 'Measuring and managing for environmental turbulence: The Ansoff Associates approach', in Alexander Watson Hiam (ed.), The Portable Conference on Change Management ©1995, Human Resource Development. Used with permission; **41 McKinsey & Company:** Hausmann, Ludwig, du Rausas, Matthieu Pellissie and Weber, Mathieu, Air Freight 2025: Agility, Speed, and Partnerships. Munich and Paris, ©2017, McKinsey & Company. Used with permission; **45 McKinsey & Company:** Hirt, M. and Smit, S. ,Economic Conditions Snapshot ©2017, McKinsey & Company; **46 Chartered Institute of Management Accountants:** Houghton, Edward, and Spence, Peter, People Measurement and Reporting: From Theory to Practice © 2016, Chartered Institute for Personnel and Development; **51 Financial Times Limited:** Groom, Brian, Remodelling roles helps ceramics company retain older workers © 2016, Financial Times Limited; **55 Chartered Management Institute:** Management 2020: Leadership to Unlock Long-Term Growth © 2014, Chartered Management Institute. Used with permission; **57 Financial Times Limited:** Conboye, Janina, When the manager is a millennial © 2017, Financial Times Limited; **59 Academy of Management:** Cavanagh, Gerald F., Moberg, Dennis J., and Velasquez, Manuel ,'The ethics of organizational politics' © 1981, Academy of Management; **60 Harvard Business Publishing:** McLaverty, Christopher and McKee, Annie, 'What you can do to improve ethics at your company', © 2016, Harvard Business Publishing; **61 Financial Times Limited:** Harris, Bryan, Jung-a, Song and Buseong, Kang , 'Korean cover-ups hide deadly work ' © 2017, Financial Times Limited; **73 McKinsey & Company:** Illanes, Pablo, Lund, Susan, Mourshed, Mona, Rutherford, Scott and Tyreman, Magnus ,Retraining and Reskilling Workers in the Age of Automation © 2018, McKinsey & Company; **76 Harvard Business Publishing:** Morse, Gardiner, 'High fidelity: Ivor Tiefenbrun on tapping talent', © 2006, Harvard Business Publishing; **76 Financial Times Limited:** Vasagar, J., 'Robots deliver service with a smile', © 2016, Financial Times Limited; **77 Chartered Institute of Personnel and Development:** Fletcher, Sarah, 'What makes a good robot co-worker?', People Management © 2018, Chartered Institute of Personnel and Development. Used with permission; **79, 473 Financial Times Limited:** Waters, Richard, 'Wearable robots help human workers challenge the machines', © 2018, Financial Times Limited; **79, 81, 87 RSA Action and Research Centre:** Dellot, Benedict, and Wallace-Stephens, Fabian, The Age of Automation: Artificial Intelligence, Robotics and the Future of Low-Skilled Work © 2017, RSA Action and Research Centre. Used with permission; **82 Harvard Business Publishing:** Davenport, Thomas.H. and Ronanki, Rajeev,'Artificial intelligence for the real world', Harvard Business Review © 2018, Harvard Business Publishing; **84 Financial Times Limited:** Waters, Richard,'The impact of cobots on workers' wellbeing', ©2017, Financial Times Limited; **87 Deloitte:** Stewart, Ian, De, Debapratim and Cole, Alex, Technology and People: The Great Job-Creating Machine © 2015, Deloitte. Used with permission; **88, 89 Oxford Institute of Population Ageing:** Frey, Carl, Benedict and Osborne, Michael A.,'The future of employment: how susceptible are jobs to computerization?', Technological Forecasting & Social Change, 114 (C): 254–80, ©2017, Oxford Institute of Population Ageing. Used with permission; **90 Citigroup Centre:** Frey, Carl, Benedict, Osbourne, Michael A. and Homes, Craig, Technology at Work v2.0: The Future Is Not What It Used to Be ©2016, Citigroup/University of Oxford. Used with permission; **94 McKinsey & Company:** Chui, M., Manyika, J., Bughin, J., Brown, B., Roberts, R., Danielson, J. and Gupta, S., Ten IT Enabled Business Trends for the Decade Ahead, ©2013, McKinsey & Company; **96 Financial Times Limited:** Noonan, Laura and Ram, Aliya, 'Social media use fuels rise in sexual harassment', © 2018, Financial Times Limited; **102 Cengage Learning:** Marcic, Dorothy, Old McDonald's Farm, ©1995,

Cengage Learning. Used with permission; **79 The Economist:** Bass, A.S., 'Gralt expectations', Non-tech businesses are beginning to use artificial intelligence at scale ©2018, The Economist. Used with permission. **91 Deloitte Touche Tohmatsu:** Knowles-Cutler, Angus and Lewis, Harvey, Talent for survival Essential skills for humans working in the machine age, Deloitte; **107 Financial Times Limited:** Tett, Gillian, 'Gillian Tett asks if banking culture has really changed', © 2018, Financial Times Limited; **109 Pearson Education Inc.(Harlow):** Adapted from Rollinson, Derek, Organizational Behaviour Analysis: An Integrated Approach, © 2008, Pearson Education Inc., 9780273711148. Used with permission; **112 Hachette UK:** Bock, L, Work Rules © 2015, Hachette UK; **112 Elsevier:** Warrick, D.D., Milliman, J.F. and Ferguson, J.M.,'Building high performance cultures', Organizational Dynamics, 45(1):64–70, © 2016, Elsevier; **113 Pearson Education Inc.:** Robbins, Stephen P., Judge Timothy A., Organizational Behaviours, 15th, © 2013. Printed and electonically reproduced by permission of Pearson Education, Inc.; **115 American Psychological Association:** Chao, G.T., O'Leary-Kellt, A.M, Wolf,S., Klein,H.J.& Gardner, P.D. Organizational socialization: Its content and consequences. Journal of Applied Psychology, Vol.79 No.5, pp.730–743, © 1994,American Psychological Association(APA), Reprinted with Permission; **115 McGraw Hill:** Colquitt, J.A., Le Pine, J.A. and Wesson, M.J., Organizational Behaviour: Improving Performance and Commitment in the Workplace © 2009, McGraw Hill; **116 Gibson Square Books:** Stenebo, J., The Truth about IKEA, © 2010, London: Gibson Square Books; **123 BBC:** Kellaway, L., 'Kellaway's history of the office: Why did offices become like home?', © 2013 ,BBC Radio; **125 Harvard Business School Publishing:** Groysberg, B., Lee, J., Price, J. and Cheng, J.Y-D ,'The leader's guide to corporate culture', Harvard Business Review, 96(1): 44–52, p. 47, © 2018, Harvard Business School Publishing; **130 Pearson Education Inc.:** Brooks, I., Organizational Behaviour: Individuals, Groups and Organization, © 2003, Pearson Education Inc. Reprinted with permission; **131 Pearson Education Inc.:** Griffin, Ricky W; Pustay, Michael W., International Business, 5th Edition, © 2007, p.102. Reprinted by permission of Pearson Education Inc; **133 Financial Times Limited:** 'Corporate culture of Japan Inc put on trial', © 2018, Financial Times Limited; **134 Financial Times Limited:** 'The rise of intercultural managers', © 2015, Financial Times Limited; **135 Harvard Business Publishing:** Meyer, Erin,'Getting to si, ja, oui, hai and da: how to negotiate across cultures, Harvard Business Review, © 2015, Harvard Business Publishing; **107 Crown copyright:** UK Parliamentary Committee on Banking Standards, Crown copyright, All content is available under the Open Government Licence v3.0, except where otherwise stated; **161 Chartered Institute of Personnel and Development:** Calnan, M.,'Long reads The future of L&D is virtual', People Management, © 2017, Chartered Institute of Personnel and Development; **163 Sage Publication:** Ibarra, H.,'Provisional selves: experimenting with image and identity in professional adaptation', Administrative Science Quarterly, 44(4): 764–91, ©1999, Sage Publication; **165 American Psychological Association:** Allen, T.D., Eby, L.T., Chao, G.T. and Bauer, T.N.,'Taking stock of two relational aspects of organizational life: tracing the history and shaping the future of socialization and mentoring research', Journal of Applied Psychology, 102 (3): 324–37 ©2017, American Psychological Association; **162 Consulting Psychologists Press:** Weiss, H.M. (1990) 'Learning theory and industrial and organizational psychology', in M.D. Dunnette and L.M. Hough (eds), Handbook of Industrial and Organizational Psychology, Consulting Psychologists Press; **181 Harvard Business Publishing:** Kasriel, Stephance, 'How I did it: Upwork's CEO on how an introverted engineer learned to lead', Harvard Business Review, 94 (5): 35–38, © 2016, Harvard Business Publishing; **186 Chartered Institute of Personnel and Development:** Chartered Institute of Personnel and Development. (2018) Stress in the workplace [online]. Factsheet. London:CIPD; **194 American Psychological Association:** Rogers, Carl R., 'Some observations on the organization of personality', American Psychologist, 2(9): 358–68 © 1947, American Psychological Association; **198 Academy of Management:** Kim, Y. and Ployhart, R.E. ,'The strategic value of selection practices: antecedents and consequences of firm-level selection practice usage', Academy of Management Journal, 61 (1): 46–66, © 2018, Academy of Management; **235 Ashgate Publishing/Taylor & Francis:**

Quirke, Bill, Making the Connections: Using Internal Communication to Turn Strategy into Action, p. 236, © 2008, Ashgate Publishing. Used with permission. **231 The Economist Newspaper Limited:** 'Debating the debates', Lexington, 11 October, p.62, © 2008, The Economist Newspaper Limited. Used with permission; **252 New Scientist:** How much of the world do we really see? © 18 November 2000, New scientist. Used with permission; **267 Crown copyright:** Ashley, L., Duberley, J., Sommerlad, H. and Scholarios, D. (2015) A Qualitative Evaluation of Non-Educational Barriers to the Elite Professions. London: Social Mobility and Child Poverty Commission, All content is available under the Open Government Licence v3.0, except where otherwise stated; **292 The Financial Times Limited:** Ibarra, Herminia, 'Tech tools that track how we perform need monitoring too', 14 April, p.12 © 2015, The Financial Times Limited; **296 Sage Publications:** Hackman, J.R., Oldham, G., Janson, R. and Purdy, K. 'A new strategy for job enrichment', California Management Review, 17(4): 57–71, © 1975, Sage Publications; **299 Sage Publications:** Grote, Gudela, and Guest, David, 'The case for reinvigorating quality of working life research', Human Relations, 70(2): 149–67, ©2016, Sage Publications. Used with permission; **300, 301 Crown copyright:** Macleod, David and Clarke, Nita, engaging for Success: Enhancing Performance Through Employee Engagement. London: Department for Business, Innovation and Skills. P.3, ©2007, All content is available under the Open Government Licence v3.0, except where otherwise stated; **287 Academy of Management:** Bridgman, T., Cummings, S. and Ballard, J., 'Who built Maslow's pyramid?: a history of the creation of management studies' most famous symbol and its implications for management education', ©2018 ,Academy of Management Learning & Education; **317 SAGE Publications:** Min-Ho Joo, Vanessa P. Dennen, Measuring University Students' Group Work Contribution: Scale Development and Validation. Small Group Research, 48(3), 288–310. © 2017, SAGE Publications; **318 Financial Times Limited:** 'What men can learn from women', © 2014, Financial Times Limited; **320 SAGE Publications:** Mesmer-Magnus, J. R., Carter, D. R., Asencio, R., & DeChurch, L. A., Space Exploration Illuminates the Next Frontier for Teams Research. *Group & Organization Management*, 41(5), 595–628. © 2016, SAGE Publications; **327 Pearson Education, Inc:** Data from Roethlisberger and Dickson (1939). From Behaviour in Organizations, 6/e by Greenberg/ Baron, © 1997. reprinted by permission of Pearson Education, Inc. Upper Saddle River, NJ; **330 The Financial Times Ltd:** Murphy, Hannah., 'The office as somewhere you enjoy', Financial Times, 10 March, 2015. © 2015, The Financial Times Ltd; **331 McGraw-Hill:** Likert, Rensis., New Patterns of Management. © 1961, McGraw-Hill Education; **333 Journal of Public Administration Research and Theory, Inc:** Comfort, Louise K. "Self-Organization in Complex Systems." *Journal of Public Administration Research and Theory: J-PART*, vol. 4, no. 3, 1994, pp. 393–410. © Journal of Public Administration Research and Theory, Inc.; **589, 342 SAGE Publications:** McCollum, Janet., & Barber, Catherine. R. *It's a Puzzle: A Self-Organizing Activity.* Management Teaching Review, 2(3), 166–178. © 2017, SAGE Publications; **359 Holt, Rinehart and Winston:** Bales, R.F., 'Task roles and social roles in problem solving groups ' in Maccoby, E.E, Newcomb, M. and Hartley, E.L. (eds.), Readings in Social Psychology, third edn,. © 1959, Holt, Rinehart and Winston; **361 SAGE Publications:** Van der Haar, Selma, Koeslag-Kreunen, Mieke., Euwe, Euwe. and Segers, Mien, 'Team leader structuring for team effectiveness and team learning in command-and-control teams', Small Group Research, 48(2) 215–248. © 2017 SAGE Publications; **362 Financial Times Limited:** 'Wearables and work - who wins?', © 2015, Financial Times Limited; **363 The Society for the Psychological Study of Social Issues:** D. Benne, Kenneth., Sheats, Paul., Functional Roles of Group Members. Journal of Social Issues, 4: 41–49. © 1948, The Society for the Psychological Study of Social Issues; **366 Academy of Management:** Pearsall, Matthew J., Christian, Michael S., and Becker, William J., Chronotype Diversity in Teams: Toward a Theory of Team Energetic Asynchrony Stefan Volk, Academy of Management Review 2017 42:4, 683–702. © 2017, Academy of Management; **371, 470 Financial Times Limited:** O'Connor, Sarah, 'The changing world of work', © 2018, Financial Times Limited; **376 Crown Copyright:** Boddy, D. and Buchanan, D.A. (1987),

Management of Technology. The Technical Change Audit. Action for Results: 5: The Process Module, pp. 32–35, Manpower Services Commission, Moorfoot, Sheffield, Manpower Services Commission. © Crown Copyright; **382, 395 Pearson Education Inc.:** Guirdham, Maureen., Interactive Behaviour at Work, Financial Times Prentice Hall, © 2002. Reproduced by permission of Pearson Education Inc.; **388 Pearson Education Inc.:** Managing Behavious in Organizations, (second edition) by Jerald Greenberg, © 1999. Reproduced by permission of Pearson Education Inc.; **396 SAGE Publications:** Paulin, Deanna., & Griffin, Barbara. Team Incivility Climate Scale: Development and Validation of the Team-Level Incivility Climate Construct. *Group & Organization Management*, *42*(3), 315–345. © 2017 SAGE Publications; **399 Academic Press:** *Advances in Experimental and Social Psycology,* Volume 15, L. Berkowicz (ed.), Socialization in small groups: temporal changes in individual – group relations by Moreland, Richard L., Levine, John M., pp.137–92. © 1982, Academic Press, with permission from Elsevier; **400 Pearson Education Inc.:** Gordon, Judith R., A diagnostic approach to organizational behavior, 4th edition, Allyn and Bacon. © 1993, Pearson Education Inc.; **403 Pearson Education Inc.:** Self-awareness and deindividuation' in Hogg, M.A and Vaughan, G.M. (2018), Social Psychology, 8th edition, Pearson Australia, © 2018. Reproduced by permission of Pearson Education Inc.; **411 SAGE Publications:** Fender, C. Melissa., Stickney, Lisa. T. When Two Heads Aren't Better Than One: Conformity in a Group Activity. *Management Teaching Review, 2*(1), 35–46. © 2017, SAGE Publications; **412 SAGE Publications:** Seltzer, Joseph. Teaching About Social Loafing: The Accounting Team Exercise. *Management Teaching Review, 1*(1), 34–42. © 2016, SAGE Publications; **419 Houghton Mifflin Harcourt:** Edwards, Douglas, I'm Feeling Lucky: The Confessions of Google Employee Number 59, HMH. © 2011, Houghton Mifflin Harcourt; **420, 436 American Psychological Association:** Sundstrom, Eric., De Meuse, Kenneth. P., Futrell, David., Work teams: Applications and effectiveness. American Psychologist, 45(2), 120–133. © 1990, American Psychological Association; **427 SAGE Publications:** Han, Soo. Jeoung., & Beyerlein, Michael. Framing the Effects of Multinational Cultural Diversity on Virtual Team Processes. *Small Group Research, 47*(4), 351–383. © 2016 SAGE Publications; **430 Cengage Learning, Inc.:** Daft, Richard L. & Noe, Raymond A., Organizational Behavior, 1st Edition, © 2001. Reproduced by permission of Cengage Learning, Inc.; **432 Lakewood Media Group, LLC:** Industry Report, 'What self-managing teams manage', Training, October, 1996. © 1996, Lakewood Media Group, LLC. Used with permission; **435 CIPD:** Bos-Nehles, A.C., Renkema, Maarten. and Bondarouk, Tanya. (2018), 'Is it possible to management without managers? People Management, 5 January, London: Chartered Institute of Personnel and Development. Used with permission; **446 SAGE Publications:** Chapman, Kenneth. J., Meuter, Matthew. L., Toy, Daniel., & Wright, Lauren K., Are Student Groups Dysfunctional: Perspectives From Both Sides of the Classroom. Journal of Marketing Education, 32(1), 39–49. © 2009, SAGE Publications; **447 Springer Nature:** Bratton, John., Callinan, Militza., Forshaw, Carolyn & Sawchuk, Peter., Work and Organizational Behaviour, Palgrave Macmillan. © 2007, Springer Nature; **454 Academy of Management:** Parker, Sharon K. and Van den Broeck, Anja and Holman, David, Work Design Influences: A Synthesis of Multilevel Factors that Affect the Design of Jobs, Academy of Management Annals, 11 (1), 267–308. © 2017, Academy of Management; **458 The Economist Newspaper Limited:** The Economist, 'Free exchange: Better, stronger, faster', 3 March, 2018, The Economist. © 2018, The Economist Newspaper Limited. Used with permission; **461 SAGE Publications:** Grey, C., A Very Short, Fairly Interesting and Reasonably Cheap Book about Management, 2nd Edition. © 2009, SAGE Publications. Used with permission; **462 Shutterstock:** Ray, Rick, 'Ford's Model T assembly plant, circa 1908'; **471 The Financial Times Ltd:** Kwong, Robin., Kao, Joanna. S., Manibog, Claire. and Nakaniski, Toyoki., *'Can a robot do your job?'*, 7 April, 2017, Financial Times. © 2017, The Financial Times Ltd; **472, 475 McKinsey & Company:** Manyika, James., Chui, Michael., Miremadi, Mehdi., Bughin, Jacques., George, Katy., Willmott, Paul. & Dewhurst, Martin., McKinsey Global Institute, A Future That Works: Automation, Employment, And Productivity, Jan 2017, Executive summary. © McKinsey & Company

hype', Harvard Business Review, 94 (7): 38–49. © 2016 Harvard Business School Publishing. Used with permission; **609:** The FA Coach. Gareth Southgate: My Coaching Approach, The Boot Room, Issue 26, 6 June, 2017. Retrived from: http://www.thefa.com/get-involved/coach/the-boot-room/issue-26/gareth-southgate-coaching-approach-060617. © 2017 The Football Association; **612 Financial Times Limited:** 'Leaders under pressure: Bill McDermott', © 2018, Financial Times Limited; 617 30% Club: 'Mark Wilson explains why he signed up to The 30% Club's commitment', © 2019, 30% Club; **619 McKinsey & Company:** Focusing on what works for workplace diversity, Video, Apr 2017. © 2017, McKinsey and Company; **620 The Equality Lounge:** 'The Equality Lounge @ Davos 2018: Delivering Through Diversity', © 2018, The Female Quotient; **620 Financial Times Limited:** 'Leaders under pressure: Ursula Burns', © 2018, Financial Times Limited; **627 Harvard Business School Publishing:** Tannenbaum, Robert, & Schmidt, Warren H. How to Choose a Leadership Pattern, Harvard Business Review, May–June 1973. © 1973, Harvard Business School Publishing. Used with permission; **628 Financial Times Limited:** 'Leaders under pressure: Cynthia Carroll', © 2018, Financial Times Limited; **647 McGraw-Hill Education:** Palmer, Ian., Dunford, Richard., Buchanan, David., Managing Organizational Change: A Multiple Perspectives Approach, 3rd Edition. © 2016, McGraw-Hill Education; **651 MCB UP Ltd:** Elrod II, P. David & Tippett, Donald D. 'The "death valley" of change', Journal of Organizational Change Management, 15(3), 273–291, © 2002 MCB UP Limited; **667 McKinsey & Company:** Sull, Donald, 'The simple rules of disciplined innovation', McKinsey Quarterly, Article, May 2015. © 2015, McKinsey & Company; **669 Wiley:** Kanter, Rosabeth.M. 'Creating the culture for innovation', in Frances Hesselbein, Marshall Goldsmith and Iain Somerville (eds), Leading for Innovation And Organizing For Results. San Francisco: Jossey-Bass, pp.73–85. © 2001, Wiley; **670 Harvard Business School Publishing:** Edmondson, Amy.C., Strategies for learning from failure, Harvard Business Review, 89(4), pp. 48–55, 2011. © 2011, Harvard Business School Publishing; **670 CIPD:** Lewis, Grace 'Women over 55 best suited to lead transformational change, finds PwC', People Management, 18 May, 2015. © 2015, Chartered Institute of Personnel and Development; **689 Elsevier Science, Inc.:** Organizational Dynamics, 28(4), Vroom, Victor .H., Leadership and decision making process, pp.82–94, © 2000, with permission from Elsevier; **695 Pearson Education Inc.:** Gordon, J.R, Diagnostic Approach to Organization Behaviour, 4th Edition, Prentice Hall, Inc. © 1993, Pearson Education Inc.; **698 Houghton Mifflin Company:** Lester Janis, Irving, Victims of Groupthink: A psychological study of foreign-policy decisions and fiascos, © 1972, Houghton Mifflin Company; **692 Financial Times Limited:** 'Richard Thaler: father of behavioural economics wins Nobel Prize', © 2017, Financial Times Limited; **704 McKinsey & Company:** Aaron De Smet, Gerald Lackey, and Leigh M. Weiss, Untangling your organization's decision making, McKinsey Quarterly, Article, June 2017. © 2017 McKinsey & Company; **708 Massachusetts Institute of Technology:** Tingling, Peter M. & Brydon, Michael J., Is Decision-Based Evidence Making Necessarily Bad? June 26, 2010. © From MIT Sloan Management Review / Massachusetts Institute of Technology. All rights reserved. Distributed by Tribune Media Services; **710 Financial Times Limited:** 'Thai football team rescue underway', © 2018, Financial Times Limited; **712 Springer:** Werner, Andrea. "'Margin Call': Using Film to Explore Behavioural Aspects of the Financial Crisis." Journal of Business Ethics 122, no. 4 (2014): 643–54. © 2014 Springer; **713:** Sashkin, M. and Morris, W.C. (1987), 'Decision types', Experiencing Management, 1987, Addison Wesley, pp. 73–74. © 1987 Pearson Education Inc.; **730 Pearson Education Inc.:** Ashleigh, Melanie and Mansi, Angela, The Psychology of People in Organizations, Harlow, ©2012, **Pearson Education Inc.** Used with permission; **731 Harvard Business School Publishing:** Shapiro,Benson, S., 'Can marketing and manufacturing coexist?' , Harvard Business Review © 1977 by the Harvard Business School Publishing Corporation. Reprinted with permission; **736 Elsevier:** Ruble, Thomas. and Thomas, Kenneth W., 'Support for a two-dimensional model of conflict behaviour', Organizational Behaviour and Human Performance, vol.16, no.1, pp.143–55,© 1976, Elsevier. Used with permission; **736 Pearson Education Inc.:** Whetton, David A., Woods, Mike, Developing Management

Skills for Europe Hardcover ©1999, Pearson Education Inc. Used with permission; **740 Pearson Education Inc.:** Robbins, Stephen P., Judge, Timothy A., Organizational Behavior, 17th Edition, ©2017, Pearson Education Inc. Used with permission. **744 Academy of Management:** Cropanzano, Russel, Bowen, David E. and Gilliland, Stephen W. (2007), 'The management of organizational justice', Academy of Management Perspectives, 21(4), 34–48, ©2007, Academy of Management. Used with permission; **751 Sage Publications:** Quijada, Maria Alejandra, 'Heavy metal conflict management', Management Teaching Review, 1(3): 155–163, ©2016, Sage Publications. Used with permission; **753 Sage Publications:** Caza, Arran, Caza, Brianna Barker and Lind, E.Allan, 'The Missed Promotion: An exercise demonstrating the importance of organizational justice', Journal of Management Education, 35(4): 537–563, ©2011, Sage Publications. Used with permission; **767, 774, 780 Sage Publication:** Buchanan, David A. and Badham, Richard J. Power, Politics, and Organizational Change: Winning the Turf Game, 2nd edition, ©2008, Sage Publication. Used with permission; **782 Times Newspapers Limited**: Furnham, Adrian, 'Seven steps to the stars: how to fly up the career ladder', The Sunday Times Appointments Section, ©2015, Times Newspapers Limited. Used with permission; **785 Sage Publication:** Barbuto, John, E., 'Power and the changing environment', Journal of Management Education, 24(2), pp.288–96 © 2000, Sage Publication. Used with permission.

Introductory briefing

The aims of this text are to:

Introduce the subject   To bring the study of behaviour in organizations to undergraduate and postgraduate students who have little or no social science background.

Stimulate debate   To encourage a critical perspective, observing that the 'correct' answers to organizational questions, and solutions to problems, rely on values, judgements and ideology, as well as on evidence.

Link to practice   To show how organizational behaviour concepts, theories and techniques can be applied in practice.

Recognize diversity   To raise awareness of the variety of social and cultural factors that affect behaviour in organizations.

Too many theories?

Students who are new to OB often complain about the number of different theories. You will see this, for example, in our discussion of motivation, culture, leadership and power. Does this mean that the field is immature? How can all of these theories be 'right'? It does not help that many organizational behaviour theories were first developed decades in the past.

Marc Anderson (2007) argues that different theories are valuable because they help us to fill our 'conceptual toolbox'. We live in a complex world, and we need a variety of tools and perspectives to deal with the many, and changing, issues and problems that we face. This means that one theory could be helpful in one context, but a different perspective could be useful in another setting. An idea that appears to be of limited value today may help us to deal with tomorrow's challenges.

There are no 'right or wrong' theories, or 'one best way'. There are only theories that are more or less useful in helping us to deal with different issues in different settings at different times. We benefit from having 'too many theories'. This is not a problem.

Anderson, M.H. (2007) 'Why are there so many theories?', *Journal of Management Education*, 31(6): 757–76.

Aids to learning and critical understanding

We use the following features to encourage an *active and questioning approach* to the subject. We want to challenge you, by inviting you to confront real, practical and theoretical problems and issues for yourselves. You are invited regularly to stop reading and to consider controversial points, on your own, or in group discussion. We want to alert you to the significance of organizational behaviour in everyday life. The study of this subject is not confined to the lecture theatre and library. Eating a pizza in a restaurant, joining a queue at a cinema, returning a faulty product to a store, purchasing a train ticket, arguing with a colleague at work, taking a holiday job in a hotel, reading a novel – are all experiences related to aspects of organizational behaviour.

In-chapter features

Learning outcomes	Chapters open with clear learning outcomes
Key terms	Chapters open with a list of key terms, which are also in the glossary
Critical thinking	Invitations to question, challenge assumptions, consider other options
Cutting edge	Summarizing recent key research findings (with researcher portraits)
What did they find?	Describing research projects, asking you to predict the results
Employability check	Relating chapter content to employability competencies
Audio box	Short podcast exploring topical issues
Video box	Brief video exploring chapter themes in more depth
Home viewing	Movies which illustrate topics in graphic and memorable ways
Stop and search	Suggestions for YouTube content exploring key topics
Cartoons	To make the subject memorable, to change the pace, rhythm, and appearance of the text

End-of-chapter features

OB Cinema	Recommended movie clips for classroom use
Exercises	Chapters have two learning exercises for tutorial and seminar use
Revision	Sample examination questions, for personal study and tutorial use
Research assignment	A focused information-gathering project involving either a website search, library exercise, or interviewing, or a combination of methods
Recap	Summaries linked to learning outcomes

Critical thinking, critical questioning

In his own mind, Jerry quickly mastered the art.

A perspective that encourages criticism, debate and challenge means asking these kinds of questions, when presented with a theory, an argument, evidence, or with a recommendation for action:

- Does this make sense, do I understand it, or is it confused and confusing?
- Is the supporting evidence compelling, or is it weak?
- Does a claim to 'novelty' survive comparison with previous thinking?
- Is the argument logical and coherent, or are there gaps and flaws?
- What biases and prejudices are revealed in this line of argument?
- Is a claim to 'neutrality' realistic, or does it conceal a hidden agenda?
- Are the arguments and judgements based convincingly on the evidence?

- Whose interests are served by this argument, and whose are damaged?
- Is the language of this argument designed to make it more appealing?

Employability and OB

Understanding OB will improve your employability and career prospects. What do employers look for, and what can you offer them? A qualification alone is not enough. Organizations are looking for qualities, skills and attributes that they think will help you to perform well. The following table lists these competencies: *personal qualities*, *leadership qualities*, *practical skills* and *other key attributes*. What are your strengths and limitations as far as potential employers are concerned? To help you to increase your value to employers, we will ask you to pause occasionally, for an **Employability check**. These checks will relate to the chapter content, and will ask you to assess your competencies in a specific area, and to consider how you can improve and demonstrate those competencies.

Competencies that will improve your employability

Personal qualities	Leadership qualities
Self-management	Leadership
Work ethic/results orientation	People management
Appetite for learning	Leading and managing change
Interpersonal skills	Project management
Creativity and innovation	General management skills

Practical skills	Other key attributes
Commercial/business acumen	Critical thinking
Customer service skills	Political awareness
Communication skills	Understand cross-cultural issues
Problem-solving skills	Understand how organizations work
Teamworking skills	Prioritizing, decision making

The New Smart

Ed Hess

Ed Hess (2018), from the University of Virginia Darden School of Business, argues that career success in the future will depend on what he calls 'the new smart'. This is defined by the quality of one's skills and attributes in the following areas: thinking, learning, curiosity, open-mindedness, problem solving, emotional intelligence, collaboration.

Quantity – how much you know – is less important, because machines already know more. Your most important skill is *iterative learning*: constantly unlearning and relearning, and adapting quickly as technology advances. Students, he suggests, should consider taking courses in various disciplines – psychology, philosophy, creative arts, systems engineering, design thinking – in order to learn different modes of thinking.

Hess, E. (2018) 'An MBA student's toolkit for the smart machine age', *Financial Times*, 16 January, https://www.ft.com/content/9d9f76c0-422e-11e7-82b6-896b95f30f58

Part 1 The organizational context

PESTLE: The **P**olitical, **E**conomic, **S**ocial, **T**echnological, **L**egal, and **E**cological context

- **Individual** factors
- **Group** factors
- **Management and organization** factors
- **Leadership process** factors

- **Organizational effectiveness**
- **Quality of working life**

The organization's past,   present,   and future

CHAPTER 1

Explaining organizational behaviour

Key terms

organizational behaviour

organization

controlled performance

organizational dilemma

fundamental attribution error

organizational effectiveness

balanced scorecard

quality of working life

positivism

operational definition

variance theory

constructivism

process theory

evidence-based management

human resource management

employment cycle

discretionary behaviour

big data

data analytics

human capital analytics

Learning outcomes

When you have read this chapter, you should be able to define those key terms in your own words, and you should also be able to:

1. Explain the importance of understanding organizational behaviour.

2. Explain and illustrate the central dilemma of organizational design.

3. Understand the need for explanations of behaviour in organizations that take account of relationships between factors at different levels of analysis (individual, group, organization, context).

4. Understand the difference between positivist and constructivist perspectives on organizational behaviour.

5. Understand the difference between variance and process theories of organizational behaviour.

6. Explain the development and limitations of evidence-based management.

7. Recognize the range of applications of organizational behaviour theory, and contributions to human resource management policy and practice.

8. Assess how the human resource management function can use big data and human capital analytics to improve individual and team performance, and organizational effectiveness

What is organizational behaviour?

Why did that happen?

It was a bad experience. You ordered a soft drink and a sandwich. The person who served you was abrupt and unpleasant. They didn't smile or make eye contact, and continued their conversation with colleagues, instead of asking if you wanted anything else. They slapped your change on the counter rather than put it in your hand, then turned away. You have used this café before, but you have never been treated so badly. You leave feeling angry, deciding never to return.

How can you explain the unusual behaviour of the person who served you?

Let's put it this way: if you have a limited understanding of organizational behaviour, then you have a limited understanding of one of the main sets of forces that affect you personally, that influence the society and culture in which you live, and which shape the world around you. Through the products and services that they provide, organizations affect everything you do – sleeping, waking, dressing, eating, travelling, working, relaxing, studying – everything. We live in an organized world.

This chapter explores how we can explain the behaviour of people in organizations. First, let's define what organizational behaviour means. The definition of a field of study sets out the issues, questions, and problems that it explores. Organizational behaviour covers environmental (macro) issues, organizational and group (meso) issues, and individual (micro) factors.

Organizational behaviour the study of the structure and management of organizations, their environments, and the actions and interactions of their individual members and groups.

Some organizations are big and powerful. Table 1.1 lists the ten largest private sector employers in the world in 2017 (www.Wikipedia.org). Half of these organizations are Chinese. Some non-corporate organizations are also big employers. For example, in 2017, the US Department of Defense had 3.2 million employees; the Chinese People's Liberation Army 2.3 million; the UK National Health Service and the Indian Railways 1.4 million each. The study of organizational behaviour thus has practical implications for those who work in, manage,

Table 1.1: The ten largest private sector employers in 2017

Organization	Country	Number of employees (million)
Walmart	USA	2.30
China National Petroleum	China	1.51
China Post Group	China	0.94
State Grid	China	0.93
Hon Hai Precision Industry	Taiwan	0.73
Sinopec Group	China	0.71
Volkswagen	Germany	0.63
United States Postal Service	USA	0.57
Compass Group	UK	0.53
Agricultural Bank of China	China	0.50

seek to subvert, or interact in other ways with organizations, whether they are small and local, or large and international.

As a subject, organizational behaviour is quite new, dating from the mid-twentieth century. The term was first used in an article in the *American Sociological Review* by Philip Selznick (1948, p.25). The Labor and Management Center at Yale University began publishing its *Studies in Organizational Behaviour* series in 1954. In the late 1950s, Fritz Roethlisberger used the term because it suggested a wider scope than 'human relations' (Wood, 1995). In 1957 the Human Relations Group at Harvard became the Organizational Behaviour Group. Organizational behaviour was recognized as a subject at Harvard in 1962, with Roethlisberger as the first area head (Roethlisberger, 1977).

How can we explain your experience in the café? Was it because of the personality and skills of the individual who served you? Perhaps, but there are other explanations:

- Poor staff training
- Staff absences leading to increased work pressure
- Long hours, fatigue, poor work–life balance
- Equipment not working properly
- Anxiety about organizational changes
- Domestic difficulties – family arguments, poor health
- Low motivation due to low pay
- An autocratic supervisor
- A dispute with colleagues creating an uncomfortable atmosphere
- Timing – you came in at the wrong moment.

Blaming the individual is often wrong. Your experience could also be explained by contextual, group, structural and managerial process factors, in and beyond the workplace. The explanation could come from any one of those factors. In many cases, a combination of factors explains the behaviour in question. The customer walks away. As a member of the organization, you have to live with those issues. As a manager, you have to solve the problem.

✓✓✓   **EMPLOYABILITY CHECK (problem-solving skills)**

In a job interview, you are asked about the following problem:

You are supervising a team of six people. The performance of one of your more experienced and long-serving team members has started to fall sharply: poor timekeeping, slow responses to requests for assistance, careless work, not sharing information. You can see no obvious reason for this. How will you approach this problem in order to find a solution?

The relationship between organizational behaviour and management practice is controversial. Are we studying this subject in order to understand, or to advise, or both? And who do we want to advise? Most American and many British texts adopt a managerialist perspective. However, the focus on management is seen by some commentators as unhelpful, for at least four reasons, concerning power inequalities, the subject agenda, multiple stakeholders, and fashion victims.

- *Power inequalities:* Management is an elite group, with privileged access to information and resources. The Equality Trust found that, in 2017, chief executives in the UK's largest 100 companies had earnings 386 times that of a worker on the National Living Wage, 312 times more than a care worker, and 165 times more than a nurse (equalitytrust.org.uk). The Chartered Institute for Personnel and Development found that, in 2018, the average employee would have to work for 167 years to earn the annual salary of a chief executive of a FTSE 100 company (Kirton, 2018). Should academic research support only the affluent and powerful?

- *The agenda:* A managerialist perspective focuses on issues of importance to managers, concerning control and performance. Issues that are significant to individuals and groups, theories that have limited practical use, and criticisms of the managerial role are pushed aside.

- *Multiple stakeholders:* Management is only one group with a stake in organizational behaviour. An understanding of this subject is of value to employees, trade unions, customers, suppliers, investors, and the wider community. Organizational behaviour is a subject of individual, social and economic significance.

- *Fashion victims:* Managers follow the latest trends in thinking and technique, to improve personal and organizational effectiveness. A managerialist perspective encourages a focus on fashion. Some fashions survive while others fade. As some fads are old ideas with new packaging, we can only make an informed assessment if we understand the history of the subject.

We adopt a 'multiple-stakeholders-inclusive-agenda' view of organizational behaviour, with a broad social science perspective. This does not mean that practical applications are ignored, but readers are encouraged to adopt a critical, challenging approach to research, theory and practice, rather than to accept a managerial or a social scientific point of view without question.

Organizations do not 'behave'. Only people can be said to behave. Organizational behaviour is shorthand for the activities and interactions of people in organizations. Organizations populate our physical, social, cultural, political and economic environment, offering jobs, providing goods and services, creating our built environment, and contributing to the existence and fabric of communities. However, we tend to take organizations for granted precisely because they affect everything that we do. Familiarity can lead us to underestimate their impact. Through their products and services, with how many organizations have you interacted in some way *today*?

CRITICAL THINKING

Why should the term 'organization' be difficult to define? Which of the following are organizations, and which are not? Explain your decision in each case.

- A chemicals processing company
- A WhatsApp group
- King's College Hospital
- The local street corner gang
- Clan Buchanan

- Your local football club
- A terrorist cell
- A famine relief charity
- The Azande tribe
- The Jamieson family next door

Organization a social arrangement for achieving controlled performance in pursuit of collective goals.

What is an organization? Why are you uncomfortable about calling some of the items on that list 'organizations'? Perhaps you considered size as a deciding factor? Or the sale of goods and services? Or the offer of paid employment? Our margin definition is *one* way to define an organization, but this should explain why you found it awkward to describe a street corner gang as an organization, but not a hospital, a company, or a club. Let us examine this definition more closely.

Social arrangement

To say that organizations are social arrangements is simply to observe that they are groups of people who interact with each other because of their membership. However, all of the items on our list are social arrangements. This is not a distinctive feature.

Collective goals

Common membership implies shared objectives. Organizations are helpful where individuals acting alone cannot achieve outcomes that are considered worthwhile pursuing. All of the items on our list are social arrangements for the pursuit of collective goals, so this is not a distinctive feature either.

Controlled performance

Organizations are concerned with controlled performance in the pursuit of goals. The performance of an organization as a whole determines its survival. The performance of a department determines the resources allocated to it. The performance of individuals determines pay and promotion prospects. Not any level of performance will do, however. We live in a world in which the resources available to us are

Controlled performance setting standards, measuring performance, comparing actual with standard, and taking corrective action if necessary.

not sufficient to meet all of our desires. We have to make the most efficient use of those scarce resources. Levels of performance, of individuals, departments and organizations are therefore tied to standards which determine what counts as inadequate, satisfactory, or good.

Performance has to be controlled, to ensure that it is good enough, or that action is taken to improve it. An organization's members have to perform these control functions as well as the operating tasks required to fulfil their collective purpose. The need for controlled performance leads to a deliberate and ordered allocation of functions, or division of labour, between an organization's members.

Membership of organizations is controlled, usually with reference to standards of performance: will the person be able to do the job? Failure to perform to standard means loss of membership. The need for controlled performance leads to the creation of authority relationships. The controls only work where members comply with the orders of those responsible for performing the control functions.

To what extent are a family, a Azande tribe, a street gang, or a WhatsApp group concerned with performance standards? To what extent does their existence depend on their ability to meet targets? To what extent do they allocate control functions to their members, programme their activities, and control their relationships with other members? The way in which you answer these questions may explain your readiness or reluctance to describe them as organizations.

It can be argued, therefore, that it is the *preoccupation with performance* and the *need for control* which distinguish organizations from other social arrangements.

CRITICAL THINKING

In what ways could the Jamieson family be concerned with performance and control?

How is membership of a street gang determined? What do you have to do to become a member? What behaviours lead to exclusion from gang membership?

Are organizations different from other social arrangements in degree only, and not different in kind? Are *all* social groupings not concerned with setting, monitoring and correcting standards of behaviour and performance, just defined in different ways?

How you define something affects how you look at it. Organizational behaviour takes the view that organizations should be studied from different perspectives. In other words, it is not worth arguing about which is the 'correct' definition. One author who has popularized this view is the Canadian academic Gareth Morgan. In his book *Images of Organization* (2006), he offers eight metaphors which invite us to see organizations through a series of different lenses. These are:

- Machines
- Biological organisms
- Human brains

- Cultures or subcultures
- Political systems
- Psychic prisons
- Systems of change and transformation
- Instruments of domination.

Metaphors are ways of thinking about, 'reading', and evaluating organizations. The 'machine' metaphor suggests an analysis of how component parts interact. The 'psychic prison' metaphor suggests looking at how an organization shapes the thinking and intellectual growth of its members. Morgan argues that by using different metaphors we can identify new ways in which to design and manage organizations.

If we destroy this planet

If we eventually destroy this planet, the underlying cause will not be technology or weaponry. We will have destroyed it with ineffective organizations. The main limitation to human aspiration lies not with intellect or equipment, but in our ability to work together. The main cause of most man-made disasters (Bhopal, Three Mile Island, Challenger, Columbia, Chernobyl, Deepwater Horizon) has been traced to organization and management factors.

Groups can achieve more than individuals acting alone. Human beings are social animals. We achieve psychological satisfaction and material gain from organized activity. Organizations, in their recruitment and publicity materials, want you to think that they are 'one big happy family'. Everyone is a team player, shooting at the same goal. Organizations, of course, do not have goals. People have goals. Collectively, the members of an organization may be making biscuits, treating patients, or educating students, but individual members also have personal goals. Senior managers may decide on objectives and try to get others to agree by calling them the 'organization's mission' or 'corporate strategy', but they are still the goals of the people who determined them in the first place.

The Macondo Well blowout

On 20 April 2010, when the blowout preventer failed a mile under water, the explosion and fire on the 33,000-ton *Deepwater Horizon* drilling rig in the Gulf of Mexico killed 11 of the 126 crew members (their bodies were never found), and seriously injured 17 others. Oil poured from the well-head on the sea bed, drifting towards the Louisiana coast 50 miles away, threatening wildlife, and local fishing and tourism industries. Around 230 million gallons of crude oil spilled into the Gulf before the flow stopped on 15 July. This was the biggest environmental disaster in the US since the Exxon Valdez spilled 750,000 barrels of crude oil in Prince William Sound in 1989. The rig's operator BP has paid over US$60 billion in fines, clean-up costs and compensation.

Was this disaster the result of a technology failure? No. A National Commission on the oil spill found that it was due to organization and management failures (*Deep Water*, and *Macondo: The Gulf Oil Disaster*, both reports published in 2011).

The rig's 'responsible operator' was BP, whose partners Anadarko Petroleum and MOEX Offshore were to share costs and profits. BP leased *Deepwater Horizon* from Transocean, whose staff operated the rig. Another company, Haliburton, was contracted to cement the pipe from the well to the rig. So the rig was manned by BP site leaders, Transocean managers, engineers, supervisors, drillers and toolpushers, and Haliburton cementers and mudloggers. BP paid US$34 million in 2008 for the lease to drill in Mississippi Canyon Block 252. Macondo was its first well on the MC 252 lease, estimated to produce at least 50 million barrels of oil.

By April 2010, drilling at Macondo was six weeks behind schedule and $58 million over budget, costing BP $1 million a day to run; it was known as 'the well from hell'. Drilling for oil is risky. Since 2001, the Gulf workforce of 35,000 people, on 90 drilling rigs and 3,500 production platforms, had already suffered 1,550 injuries, 60 deaths, and 948 fires and explosions.

The cement that Halliburton pumped to the bottom of the Macondo Well did not seal it. Test results indicating problems with the cement formula were ignored. But as

→

the cementing went smoothly, a planned evaluation was skipped. The following pressure test results were misinterpreted, and signs that the well had a major oil leak (or 'kick') were missed. Kicks must be detected and controlled in order to prevent blowouts. By the time the *Deepwater Horizon* crew realized that they were dealing with a kick, it was too late for the blowout preventer to stop an explosion. Oil was already in the riser pipe, and heading for the surface.

To create this disaster, eight factors had combined, all involving aspects of management.

1. Leadership

There was conflict between managers and confusion about responsibilities. After a BP reorganization in April 2010, engineering and operations had separate reporting structures. This replaced a project-based approach in which all well staff reported to the same manager.

2. Communication

Those making decisions about one aspect of the well did not always communicate critical information to others making related decisions. The different companies on the rig did not share information with each other. The BP engineering team was aware of the technical risks, but did not communicate these fully to their own employees or to contractor personnel.

3. Procedures

BP did not have clear procedures for handling the problems that arose. The last-minute redesign of procedures in

response to events caused confusion on the rig. It would have been more appropriate to stop operations temporarily to catch up.

4. Training and supervision

BP and Transocean had inadequate personnel training, supervision and support. Some staff were posted to the rig without prior assessment of their capabilities. Individuals made critical decisions without supervisory checks. BP did not train staff to conduct and interpret pressure test results. Transocean did not train staff in kick monitoring and emergency response.

5. Contractor management

Subcontracting was common industry practice, but with the potential for miscommunication and misunderstanding. In this case, information about test results and technical analyses did not always find its way to the right person. BP's supervision of contractors was weak, and contractors did not feel able to challenge BP staff decisions, deferring to their expertise.

6. Use of technology

The blowout preventer may have failed, in part, due to poor maintenance. Drilling techniques were much more sophisticated than the technology required to guard against blowouts. Well-monitoring data displays relied on the right person looking at the right data at the right time.

7. Risk management

BP and Transocean did not have adequate risk assessment and management procedures. Decisions were biased towards saving costs and time. The Macondo Well risk register focused on the impact of risks on time and cost, and did not consider safety.

8. Regulation

The Minerals Management Service was responsible for safety and environmental protection, and for maximizing revenues from leases and royalties – competing goals. MMS revenues for 2008 were $23 billion. Regulation had not kept pace with offshore drilling technology development. MMS lacked the power to counter resistance to regulatory oversight, and staff lacked the training and experience to evaluate the risks of a project like *Deepwater Horizon*.

Organization and management failures caused this disaster. This pattern can be seen in other serious events, accidents, and catastrophes in different sectors. (See Boebert and Blossom, 2016, for another analysis of the technological, managerial, and organizational causes of this disaster.)

Organizations can mean different things to those who use them and who work in them, because they are significant personal and social sources of:

- Money, physical resources, other rewards
- Meaning, relevance, purpose, identity
- Order, stability, security
- Status, prestige, self-esteem, self-confidence
- Power, authority, control.

Organizational dilemma how to reconcile inconsistency between individual needs and aspirations, and the collective purpose of the organization.

The goals pursued by individual members of an organization can be different from the purpose of their collective activity. This creates an organizational dilemma – how to design organizations that will achieve overall objectives, while also meeting the needs of those who work for them.

Home viewing

One of the features of 'high reliability organizations' is *deference to expertise,* which means giving decision rights to those closest to the action regardless of their seniority. What happens when the organization does not defer to 'on the spot' expertise? Starring Mark Wahlberg, Kurt Russell and John Malkovich, the disaster movie *Deepwater Horizon* (2016, Director Peter Berg) tells the story of the BP oil exploration platform in the Gulf of Mexico in 2010, when a blowout and fire killed 11 crew. The movie shows BP management more concerned with maintaining production than with safety. In one scene, a junior control room operator decides to seal the oil well which is fuelling the fire. But her colleague prevents her from doing this because 'We don't have the authority'. This also happened during the *Piper Alpha* oil platform disaster in the North Sea in 1988, where the fire would have burned out if it were not being fed by oil from two neighbouring platforms – which continued pumping as their staff did not have company permission to shut down; 167 died in that incident.

BP management criticized the movie, arguing that it did not accurately represent the character of the company, and that 'It ignores the conclusion reached by every official investigation: that the accident was the result of multiple errors made by a number of companies' (Ward and Crooks, 2016, p.17).

Health service management dilemmas

The UK National Health Service (NHS) held a boat race against a Japanese crew. After Japan won by a mile, a working party found the winners had eight people rowing and one steering, while the NHS had eight steering and one rowing. So the NHS spent £5 million on consultants, forming a restructured crew of four assistant steering managers, three deputy managers and a director of steering services. The rower was then given an incentive to row harder. They held another race and lost by two miles, so the NHS fired the rower for poor performance, sold the boat and used the proceeds to pay a bonus to the director of steering services.

Source: https://api.parliament.uk/historic-hansard/commons/1995/nov/22/the-economy

Organizations are social arrangements in which people control resources to produce goods and services efficiently. However, organizations are also political systems in which some individuals exert control over others. Power to define the collective purposes of organizations is not evenly distributed. One of the main mechanisms of organizational control is the hierarchy of authority. It is widely accepted (often with reluctance) that managers have the right to make the decisions while lower-level employees are obliged to comply, or leave.

A concern with performance leads to rules and procedures, and to jobs that are simple and repetitive. This makes it easier to plan, organize and coordinate the efforts of large numbers of people. This efficiency drive, however, conflicts with the desire for freedom of expression, autonomy, creativity and self-development. It seems to be difficult to design organizations that use resources efficiently, and which also develop human potential. Many of the 'human' problems of organizations arise from conflicts between individual needs, and the constraints imposed in the interests of collective purpose. Attempts to control and coordinate human behaviour are thus often self-defeating.

That is a pessimistic view. Organizations are social arrangements, designed by people who can also change them. Organizations can be repressive and stifling, but with thoughtful design, they can also provide opportunities for self-fulfilment and expression.

How eighteenth-century pirates solved the organizational dilemma

Martin Parker (2012) notes that life on navy and merchant ships in the early eighteenth century was vicious and unsanitary. Sailors had poor food, their pay was low, and they enjoyed highly unequal shares of the treasure. Discipline was cruel, violent, and often sadistic. A voyage could be regarded as successful if half the crew survived.

Pirates, on the other hand, developed a radical alternative approach to work organization based on more democratic, egalitarian principles.

On pirate ships, written 'articles' gave each man a vote, and most had an equal share of the stores and the plunder, apart from senior officers. Crew members could earn extra rewards for joining boarding parties, and pirate vessels operated injury compensation schemes.

There were clear rules, with graded punishments for theft, desertion and fighting on board: 'being set ashore somewhere where hardships would ensue, slitting the nose and ears, a slow death by marooning on an island or a quick death on board' (p.42). Weapons were to be kept clean, and no boys or women were allowed on board. In addition, authority depended on consent. Pirate captains had to win a vote by their crew for their position, and only had absolute authority during a conflict. Contrary to the popular image, pirate ships often cooperated with each other in pursuit of a prize. For seafarers, therefore, piracy could be a more attractive alternative than the legitimate alternatives. While naval and merchant ships often had to 'press' their crew members into service by force, many pirates were ex-merchant seamen.

Parker thus argues that the boundaries between legitimate and illegal organizations and activities (including outlaws and the mafia) are not always as clear as they appear to be. Eighteenth-century pirates solved the organizational dilemma, and could meet both individual and organizational needs more effectively than the 'legal' competition.

The organizational behaviour field map

How can behaviour in organizations be explained? To answer this question systematically, we will first develop a 'field map' (Figure 1.1). Organizations do not operate in a vacuum, but are influenced by their wider context, represented by the outer box on the field map. One approach to understanding context is 'PESTLE analysis', which explores the **P**olitical, **E**conomic, **S**ocial, **T**echnological, **L**egal and **E**cological issues affecting the organization and its members.

The map explains two sets of outcomes; organizational effectiveness, and quality of working life. There are four sets of factors which can explain those outcomes. These concern individual, group, management and organization, and leadership process factors. Organizations are not static. They and their members have plans for the future which influence actions today. Past events also shape current perceptions and actions. We need to explain behaviours with reference to their location in time.

As well as helping to explain organizational behaviour, this field map is an overview of the content of this book. You will see this field map again at the beginning of each Part of the book, to help you to locate each topic in the context of the subject as a whole.

Remember the person who served you in the café at the start of this chapter? In these situations, we often assume that the person is to blame, and we overlook the context in which they work. Our tendency to blame individuals is called the fundamental attribution error by Lee Ross (1977). In some cases, the individual could be at fault. But if we are not careful,

Fundamental attribution error the tendency to explain the behaviour of others based on their personality or disposition, and to overlook the influence of wider contextual influences.

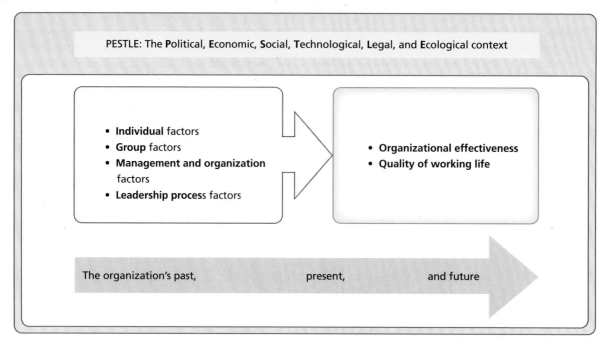

Figure 1.1: The organizational behaviour field map

the fundamental attribution error leads to false explanations for the behaviour of others. We need to be aware of how context affects behaviour, through less visible and less obvious influences. Here are some possibilities:

- *Context factors:* The café has new competition, sales have fallen, they are closing next month, and staff are angry about losing their jobs (economic factors). Perhaps closure is threatened because sales are falling because the local population is in decline (social issues).

- *Individual factors:* The café staff are not coping with the demands of the job through lack of training (learning deficit). Maybe some staff do not like dealing with a demanding public (personality traits). Or they find the job boring and lacking in challenge (motivation problem).

- *Group factors:* The café staff are not a cohesive team (group formation issues). Maybe this staff member is excluded from the group (a newcomer, perhaps) and is unhappy (group structure problems). The informal norm for dealing with awkward customers like you is to be awkward in return, and this person is just 'playing by the rules' (group norms).

- *Structural factors:* The organization is bureaucratic and slow, and staff are anxiously waiting for a long-standing issue to be resolved (hierarchy problems). Maybe there is concern about the way in which work is allocated (work design problems). Perhaps the café manager has to refer problems to a regional boss (decision making issues), who doesn't understand local issues.

- *Management process factors:* The autocratic café manager has annoyed the person serving (leadership style), or this person is suffering 'initiative fatigue' following a restructuring (change problems). Perhaps staff feel that management has made decisions without consulting employees who have valuable ideas (management decision making problems).

These are just some examples. Can you think of other contextual, individual, group, structural and management process factors? This analysis of your experience in the café illustrates four features of explanations of organizational behaviour.

First, we almost always need to look beyond the person, and consider factors at different levels of analysis: individual, group, organization, management, the wider context.

Second, it is tempting to look for the single main cause of behaviour. However, behaviour can be influenced by many factors at the same time.

Third, while it is easy to address these factors separately, in practice they are often linked. Our employee's rude behaviour could be the result of falling sales which jeopardize job security (context), and encourage an autocratic supervisory style (management), leading to changes in working practices (process), which affect existing jobs and lines of reporting (structure) and team memberships (group), resulting in increased anxiety and reduced job satisfaction (individual). These links are not shown in Figure 1.1 because they can become complex (and make our diagram untidy).

Organizational effectiveness a multi-dimensional concept that can be defined differently by different stakeholders.

Fourth, we need to consider what we want to explain. One of the terms on our field map, organizational effectiveness, is controversial. Stakeholders have different ideas about what counts as 'effective'.

CRITICAL THINKING

Consider your current educational institution. Who are the internal and external stakeholders? How you think these stakeholders each define organizational effectiveness for this institution. Why are there differences? Could these lead to conflict between stakeholders?

Organizational effectiveness can be defined in different ways. For commercial companies, effectiveness often means 'profit', but this raises other issues. First, timescale is important, as improving short-term profits can damage future performance. Second, some organizations forgo profit in order to increase market share, or to secure survival and growth. Shareholders want a return on investment, customers want quality products or services at reasonable prices, managers want high-flying careers, employees want decent pay, good working conditions, job security, and development and promotion opportunities. Environmental groups want to protect wildlife, reduce carbon dioxide emissions and other pollution, reduce traffic and noise levels, and so on.

Balanced scorecard an approach to defining organizational effectiveness using a combination of quantitative and qualitative measures.

One approach to managing organizational effectiveness is the balanced scorecard. This involves deciding on a range of quantitative and qualitative performance measures, such as environmental concerns, employee development, internal operating efficiencies, and shareholder value.

Quality of working life an individual's overall satisfaction with their job, working conditions, pay, colleagues, management style, organization culture, work–life balance, and training, development and career opportunities.

The phrase quality of working life has similar problems, as we each have different needs and expectations. Quality of working life is linked to organizational effectiveness, and also to most of the other factors on the left hand side of our map. It is difficult to talk about quality of working life without considering motivation, teamwork, organization design, development and change, human resource policies and practices, and management style.

Let's go back to Figure 1.1. What kind of model is this? The 'outputs' overlap with the 'inputs'. The causal arrow runs in both directions. High motivation and group cohesiveness lead to organizational effectiveness, but effectiveness can increase motivation and teamwork. The 'outputs' can influence the 'inputs'. Can an 'effect' influence a 'cause'? Logically, this is the wrong way around.

Home viewing

Management at the Belgian manufacturing company Solwal need to cut costs due to competition from Asia. This is the setting for *Two Days, One Night* (2014, directors Jean-Pierre and Luc Dardenne) which explores the consequences of the global financial crisis. Sandra Bya (played by Marion Cottilard) has been off work with depression. In her absence, Mr Dumont, the manager, decides that in Sandra's section they need only 16 workers and not 17. He calculates that the company can either pay the €1,000 annual bonuses for 16 employees, or cancel the bonuses and Sandra can stay. The staff vote 13 to 3 in favour of their bonuses. Sandra learns about this on the Friday before returning to work. However, one of Sandra's colleagues persuades Dumont to hold another ballot on Monday morning. Sandra is married with two children, and needs her job. Her husband persuades her to speak to those who voted for the bonuses, to ask them to change their minds. She has two days in which to do this. Sandra soon discovers that her colleagues have financial problems of their own.

How do you feel about Dumont's decision to let his employees decide whether to keep their bonuses, or to keep Sandra? At the end of the movie, how do you feel about Dumont's proposal to give Sandra her job back? Is it inevitable that, in a financial crisis, organizational and individual needs cannot both be satisfied? What else could management do in this situation?

The problem with social science

What can social science offer to our understanding of organizational behaviour? The contribution of social science to the sum of human knowledge is often regarded with scepticism. The natural sciences do not have this problem. What is the problem with social science?

Natural science has enabled us to make self-driving cars, send movies to our phones, genetically engineer crops, perform 'keyhole' surgery, and so on. It has also given us technology with which we can do great damage. Texts in computing, electrical engineering, naval architecture, and cardio-vascular surgery tell readers how things work, how they go wrong, and how to fix them. Students from these disciplines often find psychology, sociology, and organizational behaviour disappointing because these subjects do not offer clear practical guidance. Instead, social science often raises more questions than it answers, focusing on debates, conflicts, ambiguities and paradoxes. Natural science gives us material technology. Social science has not given us a convincing social engineering which, perhaps, would reduce car theft, or eliminate terrorism. Nevertheless, managers expect organizational research to help solve organizational problems.

CRITICAL THINKING

You discover that one of your instructors has a new way to improve student performance. She gives students poor grades for their first assignment, regardless of how good it is. This, she argues, motivates higher levels of performance in later assignments.

This is an attempt at 'social engineering'. To what extent is this ethical?

The goals of science include description, explanation, prediction and control of events. These four goals represent increasing levels of sophistication. Social science, however, seems to have problems in all of these areas (see Table 1.2).

These problems only arise if we expect social science to copy natural science practices. If the study of people and organizations is a different kind of business, then we need different procedures. Social science is just a different kind of science.

YOU ARE BEING WATCHED

Description

Natural and social science differ in what they want to describe. Natural science describes an objective reality. Social science describes how people understand and interpret their circumstances. Objective reality is stable. People's perceptions change.

The first goal of science, however, is description. To achieve this, social science has only three methods: observation, asking questions, and studying documents. Documents can include blogs, podcasts, emails, texts, websites, diaries, letters, company reports, committee minutes and other publications. Physicists and chemists use only one of these methods – observation. Metals, chemicals and interstellar objects do not respond well to questioning, or send text messages.

We can observe in many different ways. The researcher can observe an informal discussion in a cafeteria, join a selection interview panel, follow candidates through a training programme, or take a job with an organization to find out what it is like to work there. Our understanding of the role of managers, for example, is based largely on observation. But observation has limitations. What can we say about someone's perceptions and motives just by watching them? We can shadow somebody for a day or two, and make guesses. Eventually we will need to ask them questions.

How do we study phenomena that cannot be observed directly, such as learning (**Chapter 5**)? We do this through inference. As you read this book, we would like to think that you are learning about organizational behaviour. However, if we could open your head as you read, it would be hard to find 'the learning process' (neurophysiology has now begun to understand memory processes). The term 'learning' is a label for an invisible (to a social scientist) activity whose existence we can assume.

Table 1.2: Goals of science and social science problems

Goals of science	Practical implications	Social science problems
Description	Measurement	Invisible and ambiguous variables People change over time
Explanation	Identify the time order of events Establish causal links between variables	Timing of events not always clear Cannot always see interactions
Prediction	Generalizing from one setting to another	Uniqueness, complexity and lack of comparability between settings
Control	Manipulation	Ethical and legal constraints

We can study learning by simple inference. We can examine your knowledge before you read this book, and repeat the test afterwards. If the second set of results is better than the first, then we can infer that learning has taken place. We can also study the effects of different inputs to the learning process – characteristics of the teachers, learners, physical facilities, and the time and other resources involved. We can study variations in methods, materials and timing. In this way, we can develop our understanding of the learning process, and suggest improvements.

 EMPLOYABILITY CHECK (problem-solving skills, critical thinking)

The manager of a major high street retail store in your area has asked you, a researcher, to assess the level of job satisfaction among sales staff. You cannot speak to staff, because that would affect sales. Can you do this assessment by observation? What will you look for?

Questions can be asked in person in an interview, or through self-report questionnaires. The validity of responses, as a reflection of the 'truth', is questionable for at least three reasons.

First, our subjects may lie. People planning to defraud the company, or who simply resent the intrusion of a researcher, may give deliberately misleading answers.

Second, our subjects may not know. We are not always consciously aware of our motives. Do you constantly ask yourself, 'why am I here?', and 'what am I doing?'. The researcher gets the answers of which the person is aware, or which seem to be appropriate in the circumstances.

Third, our subjects may tell us what they think we want to hear. People rarely lie to researchers. They create problems by being helpful. Easier to give a simple answer than a complex story of intrigue and heartbreak. The socially acceptable answer is better than no answer at all.

Explanation

A second goal of science is explanation. If your test score is higher after reading this book than before (and you have not been studying other materials), then we can infer that this book has caused your score to improve. The cause, of course, should come before the effect. We might assume that high job satisfaction causes higher job performance. However, we also know that good performance makes people more satisfied. Which comes first? Which way does the causal arrow point?

The laws that explain human behaviour are different from those that govern the behaviour of natural phenomena. Consider the meteorological law, 'clouds mean rain'. This law holds good around the planet. The cloud does not have to be taught about the business of raining. Compare this with the social law, 'red means stop'. A society can change this law, to 'blue means stop'. The human driver can deliberately jump a red light, or pass the red light accidentally. Clouds cannot vote to change the laws that affect them, nor can they break these laws, or get them wrong by accident.

We are not born with pre-programmed behavioural guides. We have to learn the rules of our society at a given time. Different cultures have different rules about relatively minor matters, such as how close people should stand to each other; how and when to shake hands; for how long the shake should last; about the styles of dress and address appropriate to different occasions; about relationships between superior and subordinate, between men and women, between elderly and young.

We therefore cannot expect to discover laws that explain human behaviour consistently across time and place. Social and cultural norms vary from country to country, and vary across subcultures in the same country. Our individual norms, attitudes and values also vary over time and with experience, and we are likely to answer a researcher's questions differently if approached a second time.

Prediction

A third goal of science is prediction. Social science can often explain events, but without making precise predictions (Table 1.3). We may be able to predict the rate of suicide in a given society, or the incidence of stress-related disorders in an occupational group. However, we can rarely predict whether specific individuals will try to kill themselves, or suffer sleep and eating disorders. This problem is not critical. We are often more interested in the behaviour of groups than individuals, and more interested in tendencies or probabilities than in individual predictions and certainties.

There is a more fundamental problem. Researchers often communicate their findings to those who have been studied. Suppose you have never given much thought to the ultimate reality of human existence. One day, you read about an American psychologist, Abraham Maslow, who claims that we have a basic need for 'self-actualization', to develop our capabilities to their full potential. If this sounds like a good idea, and you act accordingly, then his claim has become true, for you.

Some predictions are thus self-fulfilling. Simply saying that something will happen can either make it happen, or increase the likelihood of it happening. A statement from a government spokesperson that 'there is no need for motorists to start panic-buying petrol' always triggers panic-buying by motorists, thus creating the fuel shortages that the statement was designed to avoid. Some predictions are intentionally self-defeating. Many of the disastrous predictions of economists, about budget deficits and interest rate movements, for example, are designed to trigger action to prevent those prophecies from coming true. In an organization, one could predict that valuable employees will leave if a given management style continues, in the hope that this will lead to a change in management style.

Table 1.3: **We can explain – but we cannot confidently predict**

We can explain staff turnover in a supermarket due to the repetitive and boring work	but we cannot predict which staff members will leave, or when they will choose to do so	**Individual** factors
We can explain the factors that contribute to group cohesiveness in an organization	but we cannot predict the level of cohesion and performance of particular groups	**Group** factors
We can explain why some types of organization structure are more adaptable to change than others	but we cannot predict the performance improvements that a given structure change will bring	**Structure** factors
We can explain how different management styles encourage higher or lower levels of employee commitment and performance	but we cannot predict which managers will achieve the highest levels of commitment and performance in a given setting	**Management** factors

Control

A fourth goal of science is control, or the ability to change things. Social science findings are often designed to encourage change. The natural scientist does not study the order of things in order to be critical, or to encourage that order to improve itself. Is it good or bad that gas expands when heated? Is the number of components in a strand of DNA correct? Social scientists, in contrast, are often motivated by a desire to change aspects of society and organizations. To do that, we need to understand the strengths and weaknesses of the way things currently work. Such understanding, therefore, is not just an end in itself. Social science can be critical of the social and organizational order that it uncovers, because that order is only one of many that we are able to create.

As we said earlier, we do not have a social technology that enables us to manipulate other people. Perhaps we should be grateful for this. However, Table 1.4 identifies organizational interventions that are designed to control aspects of employee behaviour.

✓✓✓   **EMPLOYABILITY CHECK** (communication and problem-solving skills, political awareness)

You are a management consultant studying repetitive clerical work in an insurance company. The staff are bored, unhappy, and demotivated. Your study shows how some simple work redesign would increase the variety and autonomy in their jobs. However, managers claim that their system is cost-effective, and provides the service which customers want, while allowing them to keep their staff under control.

As the management consultant with the evidence, how would you persuade management to accept your recommendations? What do you think are your chances of success?

Table 1.4: Interventions to control organizational behaviour

Organizational intervention	Attempts to control
Staff training and development programmes (**Chapter 5**, Learning)	Employee knowledge and skills
Psychometric assessments (**Chapter 6**, Personality)	The types of people employed
Employee communications (**Chapter 7**, Communication)	Employee understanding of and compliance with management-inspired goals
Job redesign (**Chapter 9**, Motivation)	Employee motivation, commitment and performance
Teambuilding (**Part 3**)	Levels of team cohesion and performance
Reorganization – structure change (**Part 4**)	Ability of the organizational to respond to external turbulence
Organizational change (**Chapter 19**, Change)	Speed of change and reduction of conflict and resistance
Organization culture change (**Chapter 4**, Culture)	Values, attitudes, beliefs and goals shared by management and employees
Human resource management (**Chapter 1**, Explaining OB)	high employee performance
Leadership style (**Chapter 18**, Leadership)	Commitment to an overarching vision

Explaining organizational behaviour

Positivism a perspective which assumes that the world can be understood in terms of causal relationships between observable and measurable variables, and that these relationships can be studied objectively using controlled experiments.

The natural sciences are based on an approach known as positivism. The term 'scientific' is often used to mean a positivist approach that is objective and rigorous, using observations and experiments to find universal relationships.

Heat a bar of metal, and it expands. Eat more salt, and your blood pressure rises. The factor that causes a change is the independent variable. The effect to which it leads is the dependent variable. These are also known as the causal and outcome variables. Salt is the independent (causal) variable; blood pressure is the dependent (outcome) variable. Those variables can be measured, and those causal relationships are universal and unchanging. To measure something, you need an operational definition – a method for quantifying the variable.

Operational definition the method used to measure the incidence of a variable in practice.

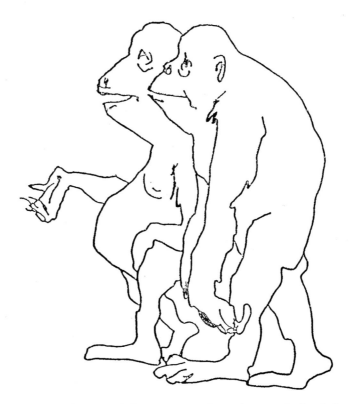

... and then he raises the issue of, 'how many angels can dance on the head of a pin ?', and I say, you haven't operationalized the question sufficiently – are you talking about classical ballet, the two-step, country swing . . .

Variance theory an approach to explaining organizational behaviour based on universal relationships between independent and dependent variables which can be defined and measured precisely.

The operationalization of temperature and blood pressure involves thermometers and monitors. Questionnaires are often used as operational definitions of job satisfaction and management style. With those measures, we can answer questions about the effects of different management styles on employee satisfaction, and job performance. That assumes that human behaviour can be explained with the methods used to study natural phenomena.

Our field map (Figure 1.1) can be read as a 'cause and effect' explanation. Manipulate the independent variables on the left, and you alter the values of the dependent variables – organizational effectiveness and quality of working life – on the right. This kind of explanation is known as a variance theory; do variations in management style cause varying levels of job satisfaction; do varying personality traits cause variations in levels of job performance?

Positivism and variance theory have been successful in the natural sciences. Many social scientists, however, argue that this approach is not suitable for the study of society and organizations. Positivism assumes that there is an objective world 'out there' which we can observe, define and measure. In contrast, constructivism argues that many aspects of that so-called objective reality are determined by us. 'Reality' depends on how we and others see it, on how we construct it socially (Berger and Luckmann, 1966).

Constructivism a perspective which argues that our social and organizational worlds have no ultimate objective truth or reality, but are instead determined by our shared experiences, meanings and interpretations.

What does it mean to say that 'reality is socially constructed'? Suppose you want to measure aggression at student functions. As a positivist, you first have to decide what counts as 'aggression'. Your *operational definition* could be an 'aggression index' which you use to count observable behaviours such as raised and angry voices, physical contact, pain and injury, and damage to property. You might find, for example, that some functions are more aggressive than others, that aggressiveness is higher later in the evening, that female students are just as aggressive as male students, and so on.

Now, suppose you observe one male student shout at and punch another on the arm. The second student responds angrily and pushes the first student away. A table is shaken, drinks are spilled, glasses are broken. Your 'aggression index' just went up by five or six points. When you speak to the students, however, they describe their actions as friendly, fun, playful: a typical Friday night. The other members of their group agree. This *socially constructed* version of events, for actors and observers, actually involves friendship. Your operational definition is misleading. What matters is how those involved interpret their own actions. Of course, in a different social or organizational setting, raised voices, physical violence, and damaged property will be understood as aggression. The interpretation of those behaviours is not consistent from one context to another. Temperatures of 45 degrees Celsius, or blood pressure of 180 over 90, will always be 'high', wherever you are.

Constructivism argues that we are self-interpreting beings. We attach meaning and purpose to what we do. Chemical substances and metal bars do not attach meaning to their behaviour, nor do they give interviews or fill out questionnaires. So, human behaviour cannot be studied using methods that apply to natural objects and events. As a constructivist, our starting point must lie with how others understand, interpret and define their own actions, and not with definitions that we create for them. The organizational behaviour variables in which we are interested are going to mean different things, to different people, at different times, and in different places.

Process theory an approach to explaining organizational behaviour based on narratives which show how several factors, combining and interacting over time in a particular context, are likely to produce the outcomes of interest.

Variance theory, therefore, is not going to get us very far. To understand organizational issues, we have to use Process theory (Mohr, 1982; Langley et al., 2013). Process theory shows how a sequence of events, in a given context, leads to the outcomes in which we are interested. Those outcomes could concern individual satisfaction, the effectiveness of change, organizational performance, the resolution of conflict. Outcomes are often generated by combinations of factors interacting with each other. If salt raises your blood pressure, half that salt will reduce the pressure by a measurable amount. If leadership is necessary for the success of organizational change, it does not make sense to consider the implications of half that leadership.

The Macondo Well blowout described earlier is a good example of a process explanation. This disaster was caused by a combination of factors over time: confused leadership structures, poor communication, lack of procedures, mismanagement of contractors, poor maintenance and use of technology, inadequate risk management and an ineffective regulatory system. No single factor was to blame as they all contributed to the sequence of disastrous events and to the tragic outcomes.

Process theory is helpful when we want to understand:

- Complex and messy social and organizational problems
- Situations that are affected by many different factors which are difficult to define and measure, and which change with time and context

- Factors which do not have independent effects, but combine and interact with each other
- Sequences of events where the start and end points are not well defined
- Interesting outcomes which are themselves difficult to define and measure.

Variance theory offers *definitive* explanations where the links between causes and outcomes do not change. The values of the causal variables always predict the values of the outcome variables (this temperature, that volume). Process theories offer *probabilistic* explanations. We can say that combinations of factors are more or less likely to generate the outcomes of interest, but not always.

CRITICAL THINKING

Hospital managers are concerned that patients with serious conditions wait too long in the emergency department before they are diagnosed, admitted and treated.

How would a positivist study this problem? How would a constructivist study this problem? Which approach will lead to a better understanding of the problem, and why?

Table 1.5 summarizes these contrasting ways of explaining organizational behaviour. What are the implications for our field map? Seen from a *positivist* perspective, the map encourages the search for consistent causal links: this organization structure will improve effectiveness and adaptability, that approach to job design will enhance performance and quality of working life. The positivist is looking for method, for technique, for universal solutions.

Table 1.5: Positivism versus constructivism

	Perspective	
	Positivism	**Constructivism**
Description	Accepts information that can be observed and quantified consistently	Accepts qualitative information, and relies on inference; studies local meanings and interpretations
Explanation	Uses variance theories	Uses process theories
	Relies mainly on observable quantitative data and measurements	Relies mainly on qualitative data and self-interpretations
	Seeks universal laws based on links between independent and dependent variables	Develops explanatory narratives based on factors combining and interacting over time and in context
Prediction	Based on knowledge of stable and consistent relationships between variables	Based on shared understanding and awareness of multiple social and organizational realities
	Predictions are deterministic	Predictions are probabilistic
Control	Aims to shape behaviour and achieve desired outcomes by manipulating explanatory variables	Aims at social and organizational change through stimulating critical self-awareness

Seen from a *constructivist* perspective, our field map suggests other questions: how do we define and understand the term 'organization', and what does 'effectiveness' mean to different stakeholders? What kind of work experiences are different individuals looking for, and how do they respond to their experience, and why? The constructivist argues that explanations may apply only to a small part of the social and organizational world, and that explanations may have to change as the context changes, with time. Constructivists seek to trigger new ideas and change by stimulating self-critical awareness.

This field map, therefore, does not set out straightforward causal links. This is just one way to picture a complex subject quickly and simply. We hope that it also gives you a useful overview, and helps you to organize the material in this book. It also serves as a reminder to consider the range of interacting factors that may explain what we observe, and that it is often helpful to look beyond what may appear to be the main and obvious explanations.

Research and practice: evidence-based management

Ian MacRae and Adrian Furnham (2018) argue that managers rely on too many out of date assumptions about work and organization, such as:

- Women are not as competitive as men
- Millennials are changing the workplace
- Working from home reduces productivity
- The use of social media at work damages performance
- A Google-style 'fun' office environment will make staff more innovative
- The best way to motivate people is to pay them more
- Open-plan offices are always better.

These are all myths. When we look at the research evidence, we find that these assumptions are false (women *are* as competitive, social media use *does not* lower performance, pay rises *do not* improve performance), or that they are too simple (open-plan offices do not suit all work, some people like ping pong and video games in the office, others see this as a management trick to keep them at work).

There is a well-known gap between academic research and organizational practice, and it is not difficult to explain why. Researchers publish their work in academic journals. Most managers do not read much, and few read academic publications. Many researchers follow lines of enquiry that do not focus on the problems that organizations and their managers are facing. Research and practice also work on different timescales. A manager with a problem wants to solve it today. A researcher with a project could take two to three years to come up with some answers.

What does evidence-based management look like?

'Here is what evidence-based management looks like. Let's call this example, a true story, 'Making Feedback People-Friendly'. The executive director of a health care system with twenty rural clinics notes that their performance differs tremendously across the array of metrics used. This variability has nothing to do with patient mix or employee characteristics. After interviewing clinic members who complain about the sheer number of metrics for which they are accountable (200+ indicators sent monthly, comparing each clinic to the 19 others), the director recalls a principle from a long-ago course in psychology: human decision makers can only process a limited amount of information at any one time. With input from clinic staff, a redesigned feedback system takes shape. The new system uses three performance categories – care quality, cost and employee satisfaction – and provides a summary measure for each of the three. Over the next year, through provision of feedback in a more interpretable form, the health system's performance improves across the board, with low-performing units showing the greatest improvement' (from Rousseau, 2006, p. 256).

In this example a *principle* (we can process only a limited amount of information) is translated into *practice* (give feedback on a small number of performance metrics using terms people understand).

MacRae and Furnham (2018) suggest that management decisions should be based on evidence, rather than on habit, bias or false assumptions. Here is another example of a myth in practice. The UK government once decided to pay hospital surgeons according to their success in their operating theatres. This approach assumes that (a) performance depends on motivation, (b) staff are motivated by money, (c) performance can be measured in a consistent and reliable way, and (d) employees work alone, and do not rely on the contributions of others. These assumptions are all false (or too simple).

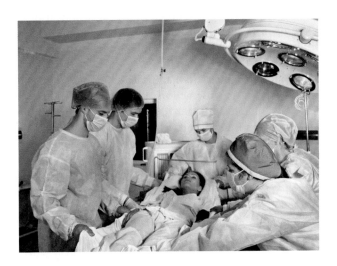

Jeffrey Pfeffer and Robert Sutton (2006) are critical of such 'pay for performance' schemes. 'Performance' can have several dimensions, some of which are subjective ('quality of care'). The emphasis on pay overlooks the importance that most of us attach to intrinsic rewards and doing a good job. The surgeon in an operating theatre is dependent on the cooperation of many colleagues, whose efforts also affect the patient's wellbeing. Paying some members of staff more than others is divisive if the scheme is seen as unfair, and that will lower everyone's performance. Pfeffer and Sutton (2006) argue that, while pay for performance schemes are popular, there is no evidence that they work. Research evidence shows that these schemes actually reduce performance. Managers aware of this evidence can find better and less expensive ways to motivate staff (see **Chapter 9**).

Evidence-based management systematically using the best available research evidence to inform decisions about how to manage people and organizations.

Inspired by evidence-based medicine, these ideas have led to an evidence-based management movement (EBMgt). There is a Center for Evidence-Based Management based in The Netherlands. EBMgt has a Wikipedia entry (check it out). EBMgt is a seductive idea. It is attractive to researchers who want to influence practice, and is attractive to managers looking for independent legitimation for their decisions and actions. But does it work as intended?

The similarities between medicine and management are exaggerated. Medicine can often advise with confidence, 'take pill, cure headache', but there are few simple solutions to

✋ **STOP AND SEARCH**   YouTube for *Evidence-based management.*

organizational problems. There is no such thing as 'best practice' because solutions depend on local circumstances. Usually, a number of initiatives or solutions are implemented at the same time. It is rare to see one solution aimed at one problem. Medical and managerial decisions differ in other ways, too; doctors treating a headache do not have to consider the impact of their decisions on other patients.

Best practice or next practice?

Susan Mohrman and Edward Lawler (2012, p.42) argue that:

'The major challenge for organizations today is navigating high levels of turbulence. They operate in dynamic environments, in societies where the aspirations and purposes of various stakeholders change over time. They have access to ever-increasing technological capabilities and information. A key organizational capability is the ability to adapt as context, opportunities, and challenges change.'

Evidence-based best practice means doing what worked in the past. To respond effectively to new challenges, we need to focus on 'next practice'.

Christine Trank (2014) sees two other problems with EBMgt. First, academic articles are designed to persuade. They are open to interpretation and are not simply neutral ways of sharing information. Different readers can come to different conclusions from the same evidence. Second, she criticizes the prescriptive 'what works' approach of EBMgt because, 'It points towards a more technocratic than professional practice: one in which scientific research is translated to narrow action rules that are applied as routines, rather than one in which considerable autonomy is granted to knowledgeable practitioners using judgement and values to decide on action' (Trank, 2014, p.384). Those involved in professional work, she argues, must be able to use their judgement and to ignore 'action rules' based on what worked in the past, and elsewhere, but which may not work here and now.

David Denyer and David Tranfield (2009, p.687) prefer the terms 'evidence-informed' and 'evidence-aware'. Rob Briner et al. (2009) note that research evidence is only one factor in most professional decisions, and may not be the most important; stakeholder preferences, context, and judgement are also involved. If the term is used rigidly, EBMgt may *underestimate* the contributions of research to practice. For Alan Bryman and David Buchanan (2009, p.711) these research contributions include:

- Developing new perspectives, concepts and ideas
- Suggesting how current arrangements could be redesigned
- Confronting social and organizational injustices
- Highlighting significant issues, events and processes
- Surfacing issues that might remain hidden
- Broadcasting voices that might remain silent
- Demonstrating the potential consequences of different actions.

Organizational research can shape practice by suggesting, in creative and positive ways, how problems are understood in the first place, and how they are approached. We can rarely say, 'here is the solution to your problem'. But we can often say, 'here is a way to understand your problem, and to develop solutions that will work in this context'.

Human resource management: OB in action

Human resource management the function responsible for establishing integrated personnel policies to support organization strategy.

Employment cycle the sequence of stages through which all employees pass in each working position they hold, from recruitment and selection, to termination.

One area where organizational behaviour (OB) contributes to evidence-based practice is human resource management (HR – or personnel management). These subjects are often taught separately, but there is overlap. OB is concerned with micro- and macro-organizational issues, at individual, group, corporate and contextual levels of analysis. HR develops and implements policies which enhance quality of working life, and which encourage commitment, engagement, flexibility and high performance from employees.

In designing those policies, HR is 'organizational behaviour in practice'. This applies to the stages of the employment cycle (Figure 1.2) – stages that you will experience at various points in your career.

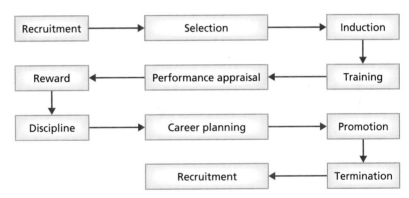

Figure 1.2: **The employment cycle**

The basic model of HR (Figure 1.3) says that, *if* you design your people policies in a particular way, *then* performance will improve. In terms of the concepts we introduced earlier, HR policies are *independent variables,* and the quality of working life and organizational effectiveness are *dependent variables.* However, as we will see, a process perspective offers a better explanation for the relationships between HR policies and organizational outcomes. Table 1.6 shows the links between HR practice and the OB topics covered in this text.

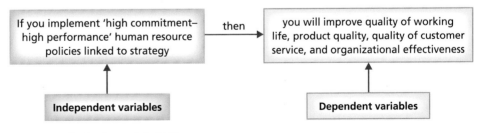

Figure 1.3: **The basic model of HR**

Table 1.6: Human resource management and organizational behaviour

HR functions	Issues and activities	OB topics
Recruitment, selection, induction	Getting the right employees into the right jobs; recruiting from an increasingly diverse population; sensitivity to employment of women, ethnic minorities, the disabled, the elderly	Environmental turbulence; PESTLE analysis; personality assessment; big data; human capital analytics; communication; person perception; learning; new organizational forms
Training and development	Tension between individual and organizational responsibility; development as a recruitment and retention tool; coping with new technologies	Technology and job design; new organizational forms; learning; the learning organization; motivation; organizational change; artificial intelligence, cobots
Performance appraisal and reward	Annual appraisal; pay policy; fringe benefits; need to attract and retain staff; impact of teamwork on individual pay	Motivation; expectancy theory; equity theory; group influence on individual behaviour; teamworking
Managing conduct and discipline	Sexual harassment, racial abuse, drug abuse, alcohol abuse, health and safety; monitoring misconduct; using surveillance; formulation and communication of policies	Surveillance technology; learning; socialization; behaviour modification; organizational culture; managing conflict; management style
Participation and commitment	Involvement in decisions increases commitment; design of communications and participation mechanisms; managing organizational culture; tap ideas, release talent, encourage loyalty	Communication; motivation; organization structure; social media at work; engagement and employee voice; organization culture; flexible organization; organizational change; leadership style
Organization development and change	The personnel/human resource management role in facilitating development and change; flexible working practices	Organization development and change; motivation and job design; organization culture and structure; leadership

The Bath model of HR

The Bath People and Performance Model (Purcell et al., 2003) is shown in Figure 1.4. This model focuses on the *processes* through which HR policies affect employee behaviour and performance. For people to perform beyond the minimum requirements of a job, three factors are needed: Ability, Motivation and Opportunity (AMO):

Factor	Employees must
Ability	have job skills and knowledge, including how to work well with others
Motivation	feel motivated to do the work, and to do it well
Opportunity	be able to use their skills, and contribute to team and organizational success

Discretionary behaviour freedom to decide how work is going to be performed; discretionary behaviour can be positive, such as putting in extra time and effort, or it can be negative, such as withholding information and cooperation.

If one of these factors is weak or missing, then an individual's performance is likely to be poor. You may have the ability and the motivation, but if your supervisor prevents you from sharing ideas with colleagues and insists on 'standard procedure', then you will probably not 'go the extra mile'.

Most employees have some choice over how, and how well, they perform their jobs. This is known as **discretionary behaviour**.

Sales assistants, for example, can decide to adopt a casual and unsympathetic tone, or they can make customers feel that their concerns have been handled in a competent and friendly way. Negative, uncaring behaviours are often a response to an employee's perception that the

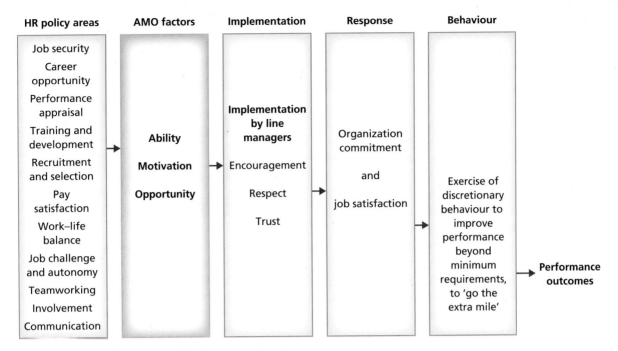

Figure 1.4: The Bath People and Performance Model

Source: adapted from Purcell et al. (2003, p.7). Reprinted by permission of the Chartered Institute of Personnel and Development

organization no longer cares about them. When one member of staff annoys a customer, and management finds out, then that employee has a problem. If all staff withdraw their positive discretionary behaviours, this affects the performance of the organization, and management has a problem.

What encourages employees to 'go the extra mile'? The answer lies in the model's *process theory*, which explains performance outcomes in terms of a combination of factors:

1. Basic HR policies are required to produce the Ability, Motivation and Opportunity that are key to any level of performance.

2. The line managers who 'bring these policies to life' have to communicate trust, respect and encouragement, in the way that they give directions, and respond to suggestions.

3. HR policies and line management behaviours must lead to feelings of job satisfaction and commitment, or the policies will have little impact on behaviour and performance.

4. People tend to use positive discretionary behaviours when they experience pride in their organization, and want to stay there.

Looking ahead: human resource management in 2030

Mark Frary (2017) predicts what human resource management will look like in the coming decades:

- Management roles are not likely to be replaced, but administrative tasks such as payroll and time-keeping will be taken over by technology.

- A higher proportion of older people – many with health conditions – will continue in work as life expectancy increases and the retirement age is raised.

- Business travel will no longer be a perk for the young, and companies will have to consider emergency planning and higher travel insurance premiums for older employees.

- With 20 to 30 per cent of the working population already 'gigging', or working 'on demand', the job-for-life culture is gone; organizations will struggle to encourage company loyalty.

→

- The ability to adapt to rapid change becomes a core competency, with faster business cycles and more disruptive technology.
- Individuals and organizations will need to commit to continuous skills development and lifelong learning.
- The workforce will be more diverse, and people skills will be more important as technology becomes pervasive; cross-cultural and cross-generational teams are the new normal.
- Your CV is obsolete, 'replaced by a sort of LinkedIn on steroids' – an online record of your experience, skills, competencies and potential, drawing from several sources such as past and current employers and your social connections.
- Pressure on property values makes large central offices too expensive, encouraging more remote working; teleworkers will use immersive virtual reality headsets to interact with colleagues around the world.
- The growth in number of smart connected products (SCPs) will allow organizations to monitor employees in detail.

'Those employees whose roles have not been automated will be monitored in real time to ensure they are happy; it could be a case of monitoring inflexions in their voices for stress as they carry out a search that would have been typed in earlier years. Behind the scenes, an algorithm will note this and automatically provide them with a different task more suited to their current state of mind' (p.16).

The *process* of implementing those policies is also important. The same policies, with inconsistent or half-hearted management, can lower commitment and satisfaction, and positive discretionary behaviours will be withdrawn. The 'high performance' HR policies in this model are:

1. *Recruitment and selection* that is careful and sophisticated
2. *Training and development* that equips employees for their job roles
3. *Career opportunities*
4. *Communication* that involves two-way information sharing
5. *Involvement* of employees in management decision making
6. *Teamworking*
7. *Performance appraisal* and development
8. *Pay* that is equitable and motivating
9. *Job security*
10. *Challenge and autonomy*
11. *Work–life balance.*

This suggests that a *positive bundle* of policies which reinforce each other will have more impact than the sum of individual policies. On the other hand, a *deadly combination* of other policies can compete with and weaken each other; for example financial rewards based on individual contributions, with appraisal and promotion systems that encourage teamworking.

Big data and the HR contribution

Big data information collected, often real-time, from sources such as internet clicks, mobile transactions, user-generated content, social media, sensor networks, sales queries, purchases.

There is compelling evidence for the link between 'high performance' human resource management and organizational performance. On commercial grounds alone, surely this evidence has made an impact on practice? Stephen Wood et al. (2013) report the findings from a survey of 87,000 UK businesses. They found that adoption of high performance practices varied from sector to sector, and between larger and smaller employers. Innovative organizations, and those in competitive markets for premium quality goods and services were more likely to be adopters than those producing basic goods. In the UK, the use of all high performance practices declined between 2007 and 2011. These 'best practices' are not as common in practice as they are in textbooks.

CRITICAL THINKING

There is evidence to show that 'high performance' HR practices do work, and can improve financial returns. They have been widely publicized in management journals. So why do you think these management practices are not more widely used?

Data analytics the use of powerful computational methods to reveal and to visualize patterns and trends in very large sets of data.

Human capital analytics an HR practice enabled by computing technologies that use descriptive, visual and statistical analyses of data related to HR processes, human capital, organizational performance and external economic benchmarks to establish business impact and enable evidence-based, data-driven decision-making.

The low impact of HR policies may now change, due to the development of big data. The digitization of services and processes allows organizations to capture large amounts of information concerning those who use them. This information allows organizations to explore and to predict patterns and trends in individual and group behaviours, such as consumer choices, traffic patterns, or the outbreak and spread of diseases. To reveal those patterns and trends, statistically and visually, more powerful computational tools have been developed, known as data analytics. Applied to HR, human capital analytics can provide insights into an organization's workforce, the HR policies and practices that support them, and workforce characteristics such as knowledge, skills and experience (see Houghton, 2017, p.24).

Big brother is not just watching you; it is logging your lifestyle through your digital traces. Send a text message; that act is recorded. Buy a book from Amazon; that purchase is recorded. Check a website; recorded. Book a holiday online; recorded. Send a Tweet; recorded. Smartphones and vehicles with GPS record your location. The Amazon home help voice-activated devices Echo and Alexa are not just speakers; they are microphones that record and transmit what you say back to Amazon. Data generated by online customers of a well-known retailer is passed on to a number of advertisers, marketing companies, data analytics groups, and other 'selected partners' who are unknown to consumers (Thompson, 2018). Some American employers are implanting staff with microchips which can be used to pay for meals in the cafeteria, open office doors, and use the photocopier, with a wave of the hand. These chips also allow the company to log staff activity and movements. Capturing big data is fast, simple and inexpensive because it is based on internet clicks, mobile transactions, calls and messages, wearable technology, user-generated content, social media, sales queries, product purchases – and the wave of a hand at a security barrier.

CRITICAL THINKING

Should we be concerned about privacy? Does big data mean more surveillance and control? Most of us are probably aware that organizations collect our personal data. But do we really know what information we reveal online, such as our social network friends, location, web searches, communication history, fitness regime, IP address or web surfing history?

Big data is contributing to human resource management by providing objective information on which to base decisions and solve HR problems. Bruce Fecheyr-Lippens et al. (2015) describe how a leading healthcare organization improved employee engagement, saving more than US$100 million. Analysis showed that pay discrepancies had caused job dissatisfaction which led to high staff turnover. Using predictive analytics, another company saved $20 million on bonuses while cutting staff turnover by half. Analysis showed that the main reasons why staff left concerned lack of investment in training and inadequate recognition. Expensive retention bonuses were having no impact. The consulting company McKinsey believed that staff defections were due to performance ratings or compensation. Analytics showed, however, that the key factors were a lack of mentoring and coaching. The 'flight risk' across the company fell by up to 40 percent once coaching and mentoring were improved (Fecheyr-Lippens et al., 2015, p.2).

Human capital analytics is transforming HR. Why? In the past, HR relied on soft, subjective, qualitative information to support policy and practice, job satisfaction, engagement, culture, commitment, and so on. Now, with the availability of large amounts of work-related data, it is possible to analyse the drivers of employee behaviour and performance. HR advice can be based on hard, objective, quantitative data. This leads to another benefit. Relying on subjective judgement, HR has lacked power compared to other management functions, especially finance (see **Chapter 22**). By measuring the impact of policy and practice on organizational performance, HR becomes a more 'hard-edged' function. Human capital analytics will increase the influence of HR in the boardroom.

Human capital analytics

Why are some employees more likely to leave an organization? Will reorganization improve productivity? Why are some groups more creative and productive than others? Will our new rewards strategy improve customer service? The answers to questions such as these traditionally draw on experience, judgement and intuition. However, big data and human capital analytics enable HR professionals to demonstrate, with quantifiable measures, the impact HR policies and practices have on individual and group behaviour and performance. HR analytics can thus identify cause and effect relationships, and predict the consequences of introducing new policies and practices.

The benefits of HR are illustrated by Henri de Romrée et al. (2016):

1. A bank faced the problem of identifying high-potential employees. What employee profile, they wanted to know, best predicts performance? Analytics revealed that branch and team structures were the best predictors. This challenged traditional assumptions about the importance of factors such as academic achievement.

2. A professional services company developed automated CV (résumé) screening to reduce the costs of processing large numbers of job applicants. However, they also had a policy of hiring more women. The HR algorithm successfully identified candidates most likely to be hired, and rejected those with little or no chance of being recruited. Costs were reduced, and the algorithm proved that achieving gender diversity did not depend on human screening.

3. An insurance company with high staff turnover offered bonuses to encourage staff to stay, but these had little effect. Data analytics were then used to profile high-risk staff. This showed, contrary to traditional assumptions, that those in small teams with longer periods between promotions, and with lower performing managers, were most likely to leave. The solution involved scrapping the bonuses and spending that money instead on offering more opportunities for development, combined with support from stronger managers. Performance and retention both improved.

EMPLOYABILITY CHECK (practical skills)

The *Financial Times* newspaper asked employers in 2018 what skills they looked for when recruiting Masters graduates from business schools. The top five were all 'soft' skills: ability to work in a team, ability to work with a wide variety of people, ability to solve complex problems, ability to sustain and expand a network of people, and time management and ability to prioritize (Nilsson, 2018). How do you rate yourself on those five skills? What actions do you need to take to develop those soft skills?

RECAP

1. *Explain the importance of an understanding of organizational behaviour.*

   - Organizations influence almost every aspect of our daily lives in a multitude of ways.

   - If we eventually destroy this planet, the cause will not lie with technology or weaponry, but with ineffective organizations and management practices.

2. *Explain and illustrate the central dilemma of organizational design.*

   - The organizational dilemma concerns how to reconcile the inconsistency between individual needs and aspirations, and the collective purpose of the organization.

3. *Understand the need for explanations of behaviour in organizations that take account of combinations of, and relationships between, factors at different levels of analysis.*

   - The study of organizational behaviour is multidisciplinary, drawing in particular from psychology, social psychology, sociology, economics and political science.

   - Organizational behaviour involves a multi-level study of the external environment, and internal structure, functioning and performance of organizations, and the behaviour of groups and individuals.

   - Organizational effectiveness and quality of working life are explained by a combination of contextual, individual, group, structural, process and managerial factors.

   - In considering explanations of organizational behaviour, systemic thinking is required, avoiding explanations based on single causes, and considering a range of interrelated factors at different levels of analysis.

4. *Understand the difference between positivist and constructivist perspectives, and their respective implications for the study of organizational behaviour.*

   - A positivist perspective uses the same research methods and modes of explanation found in the natural sciences to study and understand organizational behaviour.

   - It is difficult to apply conventional scientific research methods to people, because of the 'reactive effects' which come into play when people know they are being studied.

   - A constructivist perspective assumes that, as we are self-defining creatures who attach meanings to our behaviour, social science is different from natural science.

   - A constructivist perspective believes that reality is not objective and 'out there', but is socially constructed.

   - A constructivist approach abandons scientific neutrality and seeks to stimulate social and organizational change by providing critical feedback and encouraging self-awareness.

5. *Understand the distinction between variance and process explanations of organizational behaviour.*

   - Variance theory explains organizational behaviour by identifying relationships between independent and dependent variables which can be defined and measured. Variance theories are often quantitative, and are based on a positivist perspective.

   - Process theory explains organizational behaviour using narratives which show how many factors produce outcomes by combining and interacting over time in a given context. Process theories can combine quantitative and qualitative dimensions, and can draw from positivist and constructivist traditions.

6. *Explain the development and limitations of evidence-based management.*

- The concept of evidence-based management is popular, but the links between evidence and practice are complex; evidence can shape the ways in which problems are understood and approached, rather than offering specific solutions.

7. *Recognize the breadth of applications of organizational behaviour theory, and contributions to human resource management practice.*

- The Bath model of human resource management argues that discretionary behaviour going beyond minimum requirements relies on having a combination of HR policies.

- High performance work practices increase organizational profitability by decreasing employee turnover and improving productivity, but they are not widely adopted.

8. *Assess how the human resource management function can use big data and human capital analytics to improve individual and team performance, and organizational effectiveness*

- Extremely large and complex sets of data – 'big data' – can be captured easily, stored cheaply, and analysed rapidly, due to developments in data storage and data processing capabilities.

- Human capital analytics applies sophisticated analytical tools and techniques to big data sets in order to generate fresh HR insights that can improve organizational performance.

- Human capital analytics can complement (or replace) experience, judgement and intuition as bases for HR decision making, with quantified metrics that can help to establish causal relationships between HR policies and practices and performance outcomes.

Revision

1. How is organizational behaviour defined? What topics does this subject cover? What is the practical relevance of organizational behaviour?

2. Describe an example of organizational *mis*behaviour, where you as customer were treated badly. Suggest possible explanations for your treatment.

3. Hospital managers are concerned that patients with medical emergencies wait too long in the casualty department before they are diagnosed and treated. Which approach, positivist or constructivist, is more likely to resolve this problem, and why?

4. Using your own examples, explain how removing each element in turn from the Bath model – ability, motivation, opportunity – can reduce employee performance. For each of the three elements, suggest how the performance problem could be solved.

5. What contribution can big data and human capital analytics make to organizational performance in general, and to the human resource management function in particular?

Research assignment

Organizations affect all aspects of our lives. Buy a small notebook. Starting on Friday morning when you wake up, and ending on Sunday night when you go to bed, keep a list of all the organizations with which you have contact over this period.

'Contact' includes, for example, a radio programme that you listen to at breakfast, a television station that you watch, the shops that you visit, the bank with whose card you make payments, the companies who run the buses, trains and taxis that you use. Which companies make the food and drinks that you consume? Also, which cinemas, bars, nightclubs, sports and social clubs did you visit? Religious and educational establishments? Medical facilities or emergency services that you have used (you never know)? Check your mail: which organizations have written to you? Do you have any utility or council tax bills to pay, and from which organizations do you get these services? Have you dealt with any charity requests? Have you checked your internet service provider and social networking organizations? What companies made your computer and mobile phone? Which companies designed the browser and other software that you are using? Whose advertisements have you watched?

Every time you do anything or go anywhere over these three days, stop and ask, which organizations am I interacting with in some way? Record the names in your notebook. Then on Sunday night, or first thing Monday morning:

1. Total the number of organizations with which you have had contact on each of the three days – Friday, Saturday and Sunday.

2. Remove any duplicates and assign a number to each organization on your remaining list.

3. Devise a categorization scheme for your numbered organizations, including as many of them as possible: private-public; profit-charitable; goods-services. Use as many categories as you need. Some organizations may not 'fit' your scheme, but this is not a problem. How many organizations were in each category?

4. Consider what this list of organizations reveals about you and your lifestyle. Be prepared to share your conclusions with colleagues.

Springboard

Stella Cottrell (2017) *Critical Thinking Skills: Developing Effective Analysis, Argument, and Reflection*. Basingstoke: Palgrave Macmillan. Best-selling students' guide to nature and use of critical thinking.

Edward Houghton (2017) *Human Capital Analytics and Reporting: Exploring Theory and Evidence*. London: Chartered Institute for Personnel and Development. Reviews the evidence on human capital analytics, noting that practice is restricted to larger and more affluent organizations. Finds that HR professionals still rely on personal judgement, and that there is scope for HR analytics insights.

Lyman W. Porter and Benjamin Schneider (2014) 'What was, what is, and what may be in OP/OB', *Annual Review of Organizational Psychology and Organizational Behavior*, 1: 1–21. Fascinating account of the history of organizational behaviour from the mid-twentieth century; reviews current status, with recommendations for the future.

Patrick Wright and Michael Ulrich (2017) 'A road well traveled: the past, present, and future journey of strategic human resource management', *Annual Review of Organizational Psychology and Organizational Behavior*, 4: 45–65. Review of research focusing on the links between HR policies and practices and organizational performance.

OB cinema

Antz (1998, directors Eric Darnell and Tim Johnson). This clip (7 minutes) begins immediately after the opening credits with Z (played by Woody Allen) saying 'All my life I've lived and worked in the big city', and ends with General Mandible (Gene Hackman) saying, 'Our very next stop Cutter'. This is the story of a neurotic worker ant, Z 4195, who wants to escape from his insignificant job in an authoritarian organization – the ant colony.

1. Using the field map of the organizational behaviour terrain as a guide, identify as many examples as you can of how individual, group, structural and managerial process factors influence organizational effectiveness and quality of working life in an ant colony.

2. What similar examples of factors affecting organizational effectiveness and quality of working life can you identify from organizations with which you are familiar?

Chapter exercises

1: Best job – worst job

Objectives

1. To help you to get to know each other.

2. To introduce you to the main sections of this organizational behaviour course.

Briefing

1. Pair up with another student. Interview each other to find out names, where you both come from, and what other courses you are currently taking.

2. In turn, introduce your partner to the other members of the class.

3. Two pairs now join up, and the group of four discuss:

   What was the worst job that you ever had? What made it so bad?
   What was the best job that you ever had? What made it so good?

4. Appoint a scribe to record the recurring themes revealed in group members' stories about their best and worst jobs. Appoint also a group spokesperson.

5. The spokespersons then give presentations to the whole class, summarizing the recurring features of what made a job good or bad. As you listen, use this score sheet to record the frequency of occurrence of the various factors.

Factors affecting job experience		
Factors	**Examples**	**(✓) if mentioned**
Individual factors	Pay: reasonable or poor Job training: comprehensive or none Personality: clashes with other people Communication: frequent or little	
Group factors	Co-workers: helping or not contributing Conflict with co-workers Pressure to conform to group norms Staff not welded into a team	
Structural factors	Job tasks: boring or interesting Job responsibilities: clear or unclear Supervision: too close or little Rules: too many or insufficient guidance	
Management factors	Boss: considerate or autocratic Decisions: imposed or asked for opinions Disagreements with managers: often or few Changes: well or poorly implemented	

2: Management versus workers

Rate each of the following issues on this five-point scale, in terms of whether you think managers and workers have shared, partially shared, or separate interests (from Noon and Blyton, 2007, p.305):

share identical interests   1   2   3   4   5   have completely separate interests

- Health and safety standards
- Basic pay
- Introducing new technology
- Levels of overtime working
- Designing interesting jobs
- Bonus payments
- Flexible working hours
- Equal opportunities
- Company share price
- Developing new products and/or servicee
- Redundancy

Explain why you rated each of these issues in the way that you did.

References

Berger, P. and Luckmann, T. (1966) *The Social Construction of Reality.* Harmondsworth: Penguin Books.

Boebert, E. and Blossom, J.M. (2016) *Deepwater Horizon: A Systems Analysis of the Macondo Disaster.* Cambridge, MA: Harvard University Press.

Briner, R.B., Denyer, D. and Rousseau, D.M. (2009) 'Evidence-based management: concept cleanup time?', *Academy of Management Perspectives,* 23 (4): 19–32.

Bryman, A. and Buchanan, D.A. (2009) 'The present and futures of organizational research', in David A. Buchanan and Alan Bryman (eds), *The Sage Handbook of Organizational Research Methods.* London: Sage Publications, pp.705–18.

Denyer, D. and Tranfield, D. (2009) 'Producing a systematic review', in David A. Buchanan and Alan Bryman (eds), *The Sage Handbook of Organizational Research Methods.* London: Sage Publications, pp.671–89.

de Romrée, H., Fecheyr-Lippens, B. and Schaninger, B. (2016) 'People analytics reveals three things HR may be getting wrong', *McKinsey Quarterly,* July (3), pp.70–73.

Fecheyr-Lippens, B., Schaninger, B. and Tanner, K. (2015) 'Power to the new people analytics', *McKinsey Quarterly,* 1 (March), pp.61–63.

Frary, M. (2017) 'Fast forward for a glimpse of the future', *Raconteur: Future of HR, The Times Supplement,* 30 November, p.16.

Houghton, E. (2017) *Human Capital Analytics and Reporting: Exploring Theory and Evidence.* London: Chartered Institute for Personnel and Development.

Kidd, P. (2014) 'Ben's bum steer', *The Times,* 30 December, p.13.

Kirton, H. (2018) 'Average worker must toil for 167 years to earn a FTSE 100 leader's annual pay', *People Management Online,* https://www.peoplemanagement.co.uk/news/articles/average-worker-toil-167-years-earn-ftse-leaders-annual-pay

Langley, A., Smallman, C., Tsoukas, H. and Van de Ven, A.H. (2013) 'Process studies of change in organization and management: unveiling temporality, activity, and flow', *Academy of Management Journal,* 56 (1): 1–13.

MacRae, I. and Furnham, A. (2018) *Myths of Work: The Stereotypes and Assumptions Holding Your Organization Back.* London, New York, and New Delhi: Kogan Page.

Mohr, L.B. (1982) *Explaining Organizational Behaviour: The Limits and Possibilities of Theory and Research.* San Francisco, CA: Jossey Bass.

Mohrman, S.A. and Lawler, E.E. (2012) 'Generating knowledge that drives change', *Academy of Management Perspectives,* 26 (1): 41–51.

Morgan, G. (2006) *Images of Organization.* London: Sage Publications, (third edn).

National Commission on the BP Deepwater Horizon Oil Spill and Offshore Drilling (2011) *Deep Water: The Gulf Oil Disaster and the Future of Offshore Drilling.* Washington, DC: National Commission.

National Commission on the BP Deepwater Horizon Oil Spill and Offshore Drilling (2011) *Macondo The Gulf Oil Disaster: Chief Counsel's Report.* Washington, DC: National Commission.

Nilsson, P. (2018) 'What employers want from MBA graduates', *Financial Times,* 3 September, p.12.

Noon, M. and Blyton, P. (2007) *The Realities of Work.* Basingstoke: Palgrave, (third edn).

Parker, M. (2012) *Alternative Business: Outlaws, Crime and Culture,* London and New York: Routledge.

Pfeffer, J. and Sutton, R.I. (2006) *Hard Facts, Dangerous Half-Truths, and Total Nonsense: Profiting from Evidence-Based Management.* Boston, MA: Harvard Business School Press.

Purcell, J., Kinnie, N., Hutchinson, S., Rayton, B. and Stuart, J. (2003) *Understanding the People and Performance Link: Unlocking the Black Box.* London: Chartered Institute of Personnel and Development.

Roethlisberger, F.J. (1977) *The Elusive Phenomenon: An Autobiographical Account of My Work in the Field of Organizational Behaviour at the Harvard Business School.* Boston, MA: Harvard University Press.

Ross, L. (1977) 'The intuitive psychologist and his shortcomings: distortions in the attribution process', in L. Berkowitz (ed.), *Advances in Experimental Social Psychology.* New York: Academic Press, pp.173–220.

Rousseau, D.M. (2006) 'Is there such a thing as 'evidence-based management'?', *Academy of Management Review,* 31(2): 256–69.

Selznick, P. (1948) 'Foundations of the theory of organization', *American Sociological Review,* 13 (1): 25–35.

Thompson, B. (2018) 'Business fears online revolt after personal data shake-up', *Financial Times,* 6 January, p.3.

Trank, C.Q. (2014) 'Reading evidence-based management: the possibilities of interpretation', *Academy of Management Learning and Education,* 13 (3): 381–95.

Ward, A. and Crooks, E. (2016) 'BP joins ranks of reluctant Hollywood stars', *Financial Times Weekend,* 1/2 October, p.17.

Wood, J. (1995) 'Mastering management: organizational behaviour', *Financial Times Mastering Management Supplement* (part 2 of 20).

Wood, S., Burridge, M., Green, W., Nolte, S., Rudloff, D. and Ni Luanaigh, A. (2013) *High Performance Working in the Employer Skills Surveys.* London: UK Commission for Employment and Skills.

Environment

Key terms

environment	PESTLE analysis
stakeholders	scenario planning
environmental uncertainty	globalization
environmental complexity	unretirement
environmental dynamism	multigenerational workforce
environmental determinism	ethics
strategic choice	corporate social responsibility
environmental scanning	

Learning outcomes

When you have read this chapter, you should be able to define those key terms in your own words, and you should also be able to:

1. Understand the need for 'fit' between the organization and its environment.
2. Appreciate the strengths and limitations of PESTLE analysis and scenario planning tools.
3. Explain the challenges and opportunities created by an ageing, multigenerational workforce.
4. Apply utilitarianism, theory of rights and theory of justice to assess whether or not management actions are ethical, and recognize the limitations of those criteria.
5. Understand the concept of corporate social responsibility, and the practical and ethical implications for organizational behaviour.

Why study an organization's environment?

This chapter looks at the world outside the organization. We consider the need for an organization to 'fit' with its external environment, and describe environment analysis tools. We then examine trends in the wider business context, and explore the impact of demographic pressures arising from an ageing, multigenerational workforce. We finish by examining the increasingly important issues of individual ethical behaviour and corporate social responsibility. Technology developments are a key feature of the environment of most organizations today; we will explore these issues further in **Chapter 3**.

Environment issues, trends and events outside the boundaries of the organization, which influence internal decisions and behaviours.

Few organizations are immune from technological, political, socio-economic and demographic trends. Self-driving vehicles, changes in international trade policy, mass immigration, an ageing population, a multigenerational workforce, artificial intelligence, automation, robots, the internet of things – these are just some of the developments reshaping global businesses and the nature of work. Many organizations face competition from companies that are not even in the same business sector. How many camera manufacturers in the twentieth century predicted that in the twenty-first century their main competitors would be companies that made mobile phones? The world outside the organization has become more volatile, uncertain, complex and ambiguous: VUCA. Organizations – in both the public and private sector – need to be aware of what is happening in their wider environment.

Those developments create risks – to jobs and political stability, for example. But they also bring benefits. Immigration can compensate for an ageing workforce and help organizations to cope with skills and labour shortages. New technology creates new products and services for consumers, and creates jobs for those who provide them. Some tasks may be done by machines, but automation can also take over heavy, dirty and dangerous work. 'Cobots' (collaborative robots) work alongside humans. Artificial intelligence can augment as well as automate human capabilities. New technology brings with it both threats and benefits – an organization's survival and effectiveness depend on understanding these challenges and opportunities, and on responding to them appropriately.

Stakeholders anyone who is concerned with how an organization operates, and who will be affected by its decisions and actions.

Organizations are constantly involved in exchanges with their environment, in terms of suppliers, customers, regulatory agencies and other stakeholders, including employees. Organizations can also affect their physical environment, by generating pollution, for example, or building attractive offices. These wider impacts have come under increasing scrutiny, in particular how organizations treat their stakeholders. Acting to benefit one group of stakeholders (e.g. owners and managers) at the expense of others (e.g. child labour employed by suppliers) is now often seen as unacceptable.

CRITICAL THINKING

What trends and developments in the environment of retail food stores – e.g. Aldi, Whole Foods, Waitrose, Walmart – are affecting their management behaviour and staff working practices?

What are the main factors in the environment of your college or university? How are those factors influencing management actions – and how are these affecting you?

Figure 2.1 outlines the approach in this chapter: explaining how 'the world out there' influences 'the world in here'.

Social science texts annoy readers from other disciplines by first presenting a model, and then showing that it is wrong. We will do this here. There are three reasons for using this approach. First, it helps to start simple, then work up to complex. Second, if we build an

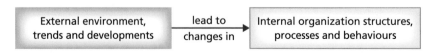

Figure 2.1: External environment organization links

argument with basic assumptions, then introduce more complex and realistic assumptions, the thinking behind the model becomes clearer. Finally, models like Figure 2.1 are 'one point of view', and are open to criticism.

Understanding the dynamics of the environment is central to organizational survival. Organizations that are 'out of fit' with their environment have to change, or go out of business: those that are still making CDs now that we have subscription-based music streaming, or still printing books now that e-book readers are commonplace, or still machining components when we have 3-D printers, will have to rethink. As the complexity and pace of environmental change increases, organizations that are able to adapt quickly to new pressures and opportunities are likely to be more successful than those that are slow to respond. The organization that jumps in the wrong direction – improving existing products and services, for example – may be in trouble. However, it is interesting to note that vinyl records ('LPs'), once seen as obsolete, are now popular again, and traditional radios are still selling well.

The search for environmental 'fit'

Environmental uncertainty the degree of unpredictable turbulence and change in the political, economic, social, technological, legal and ecological context in which an organization operates.

Environmental complexity the range of external factors relevant to the activities of the organization; the more factors, the higher the complexity.

Environmental dynamism the pace of change in relevant factors external to the organization; the greater the pace of change, the more dynamic the environment.

It seems reasonable to suggest that the internal structures and processes of an organization should reflect, or 'fit', the external environment. What does this mean in practice? One factor that affects most organizations is environmental uncertainty.

Most managers feel that the pace of events is increasing, and that they lack a clear view of the way ahead, the nature of the terrain, obstacles, or the final destination. How can organizations be adaptable enough to cope with continuous and unpredictable change? Robert Duncan defined uncertainty as the lack of adequate information to reach an unambiguous decision, and argued that environmental uncertainty has two dimensions (Duncan 1972; 1973; 1979). One dimension concerns the degree of *simplicity* or environmental complexity. The other is the degree of *stability* or environmental dynamism:

Simple–complex	The number of different issues faced, the number of different factors to consider, the number of things to worry about
Stable–dynamic	The extent to which those issues are changing or stable, and whether they are subject to slow movement or to abrupt shifts

External factors include customers, suppliers, regulatory bodies, competitors and partners in joint ventures. Duncan argued that the 'stable–dynamic' dimension is more important in determining environmental uncertainty. Complexity means that you have many issues to consider. Dynamism, on the other hand, is more difficult to manage because you don't know what is going to happen next. Plotting these two dimensions against each other gives us the typology in Figure 2.2. This typology can be applied to the whole organization, or to specific business units and departments.

CRITICAL THINKING   Which type of environment would you prefer to work in: stable–simple or dynamic–complex? Which would be better in terms of your personal development and career prospects? You will have to consider this question every time you apply for a job.

External environments do not *determine* internal structures and processes. Our *perception* is selective, paying attention to some factors and filtering out others. The same environment may be perceived differently by different managers, even in the same sector. It is management perceptions that affect decisions about organization strategy, structures and processes. Igor Ansoff (1997) developed this argument in a way that is still relevant today, summarized in Table 2.1.

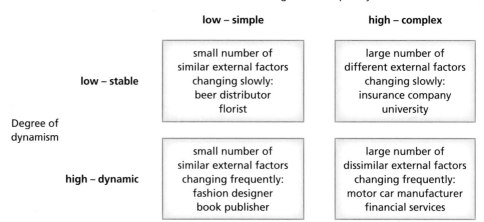

Figure 2.2: Duncan's typology of organizational environments

Table 2.1: Ansoff's typology of organizational environments

Level	Environmental change	Organization strategy	Management attitude
1	**Repetitive** Little or no change	**Stable** Based on precedent	**Stability seeking** Rejects change
2	**Expanding** Slow incremental change	**Reactive** Incremental change based on experience	**Efficiency driven** Adapts to change
3	**Changing** Fast incremental change	**Anticipatory** Incremental change based on extrapolation	**Market driven** Seeks familiar change
4	**Discontinuous** Discontinuous but predictable change	**Entrepreneurial** Discontinuous new strategies based on observed opportunities	**Environment driven** Seeks new but related change
5	**Surprising** Discontinuous and unpredictable change	**Creative** Discontinuous new and creative strategies	**Environment creating** Seeks novel change

Ansoff identifies five types of environment based on the turbulence being experienced, from 'repetitive' at one extreme, to 'surprising' at the other. Read the first two columns of his table *vertically,* working up and down the scale from 'repetitive' at one extreme to 'surprising' at the other. Go to level 1, the repetitive environment, and read the table *horizontally.* Ansoff argues that we can identify the most appropriate strategy and management attitude for that environment. In a stable environment, strategy should be based on precedent. What worked in the past will work in future. In a repetitive environment, the management attitude concerns stability. Change could ruin the business:

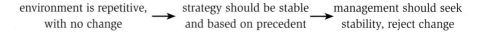

environment is repetitive, → strategy should be stable → management should seek
    with no change   and based on precedent   stability, reject change

Now go to level 5, to the surprising, discontinuous and unpredictable environment, and again read across the row. As you might expect, the recommended strategy is creative, based on new approaches, and not on what the organization has done in the past. The management attitude has to be novelty-seeking, seeking to influence the environment in creative ways. Holding on to past precedents in this context will ruin the business:

surprising environment, unpredictable change → novel strategies should be based on creativity → management should embrace change, seek novelty

Now read the other three middle rows, again working *across* the table, noting the strategy and management implications for each of the other levels of change. Once that argument and the practical implications are clear, try reading the organization strategy column *vertically*. This can be read as a strategy scale, from stability (precedent driven) at one extreme to creativity (novelty driven) at the other. The final column works in the same way, with a management attitude scale, from stability (rejecting change) to creativity (embracing novelty).

Ansoff (1997) distinguishes between *extrapolative* and *discontinuous* change, shown by the separation in Table 2.1 between levels 3 and 4. Where change is extrapolative, the future can be predicted, more or less, following (extrapolating from) current trends. When change is discontinuous, our ability to predict is limited. Most managers today would probably claim that their organizations operate in discontinuous and/or surprising environments.

CRITICAL THINKING

You might think of air freight as an established, unchanging business. But consider the following:

'Although some uncertainty surrounds the future of international trade flows, demand for air cargo has been set for change, above all, because shippers are redesigning their global production networks. These companies are now ready to take full advantage of advanced robotics: from a network of central manufacturing plants, they will ship semi-finished goods to locations near their end customers, where they will finish or customize these products. Their new networks will introduce automated warehouses, predictive shipping, and drones for deliveries. Powerful forecasting algorithms will manage and monitor end-to-end performance in networks. All players in the supply chain will need very strong IT backbones to enable this new transparency and these big, continuous data flows.

'In a world where data and connectivity are the keys to the kingdom, new entrants could easily disrupt an air-cargo sector that all too often clings to legacy technologies. The disruption could well come from e-commerce players, with their strong data-handling capabilities. Consider the case of Amazon. Ten years ago, the company was

known for shipping books and other kinds of media. Then it created an additional business by selling its spare computing capacity and eventually became the leading provider of computing power in the cloud, with a market share bigger than its nearest three competitors combined' (Hausmann et al., 2017, p.1).

Using Ansoff's typology, how would you assess the level of environmental change facing the air freight business? Does it face extrapolative or discontinuous change? Based on this assessment, what attitude should management in the air freight sector adopt? What organization strategy should air freight organizations pursue?

Environmental determinism
the argument that internal organizational responses are primarily determined by external environmental factors.

Figure 2.3 shows our updated model. The stimulus of external change prompts organizational responses. The scale, dynamism and complexity of environmental stimuli encourage adaptive, environmentally responsive arrangements – the 'post-bureaucratic' organization (Hales, 2002). Bureaucracy, macho managers and boring jobs are replaced by flexible structures with participative, supportive managers, and interesting, multiskilled jobs.

We promised at the start of this chapter that, having built a model, we would knock it down. While broadly correct, there are four problems with the reasoning in Figure 2.3. The first concerns environmental determinism.

CRITICAL THINKING

Have you experienced, or observed, a flexible, boundary-less, post-bureaucratic organization with multiskilled, autonomous employees and caring managers? Have you seen the opposite – a bureaucratic organization with low-paid, boring, unskilled jobs and autocratic managers?

So, from your experience, is bureaucracy dead – or not?

We know that internal organizational arrangements are affected by many factors: the dynamics of the senior management team, their approach to decision making, employee suggestions and past experience. We also know that, whatever the reality 'out there', what really matters is how the environment is understood and interpreted 'in here'. This means that an environmental 'stimulus' is just one stimulus among many. This stimulus is not guaranteed either a response, or the expected response.

The second problem concerns assumptions about organizational boundaries. Can we say clearly what is 'out there' and what is 'in here'? Organizations are involved in a constant process of exchange with their environment, importing staff and resources, exporting goods and services. Employees are members of the wider society, whose values and preferences are thus 'inside' the organization. Many organizations collaborate with suppliers and competitors, to share product development costs, for example. Some organizations – e.g. gymnasiums, motoring assistance – treat customers as 'members'. The boundaries between organizations and their environments are often blurred.

Strategic choice
the view that an organization's environment, market and technology are the result of senior management decisions.

The third problem is one of interpretation. We are considering 'environment' and 'organization' as separate domains. However, an organization chooses and influences its environment; this is a matter of strategic choice (Child, 1997). European motor car companies can choose whether or not to manufacture and sell their cars in China. A restaurant changes its environment (customers, suppliers, competitors) when the owners choose to stop selling fast food and move into gourmet dining. In other words, the external environment is *enacted*: the organization creates and to some extent even becomes its own environment, rather than being 'given' or 'presented with' that environment.

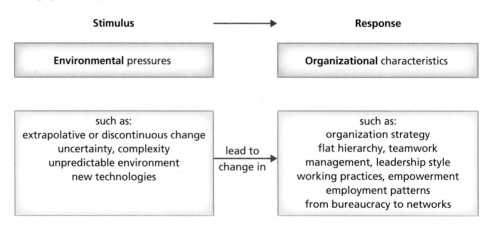

Figure 2.3: The search for environment–organization 'fit'

The final problem concerns continuity. The model suggests a picture of rapid change. However, we can see many continuities. Still a popular tourist attraction, Sean's Bar in Athlone, in Ireland, was founded in 900. The German Weihenstephan Brewery was founded in 1040, the Swedish company Stora in 1288, Oxford University Press in 1478, Beretta in 1526, Sumitomo in 1590, Lloyd's in 1688, Sotheby's in 1744, Guinness in 1759, Royal Dutch Shell in 1833, Nokia in 1865. There are over 3,000 companies in Japan that are 200 or more years old (Simms, 2017). We are familiar with the case for constant change. However, organizations that live long and prosper are also valuable: they establish community links, provide continuity of employment across generations, and create a sense of social cohesion. Organizations can adapt to their environments, or reinvent themselves: the telecommunications company Nokia began by making paper, and has since been involved in making rubber boots, raincoats, cables, television sets, and studded bicycle tyres (Skapinker, 2015).

Environment analysis tools

Environmental scanning techniques for identifying and predicting the impact of external trends and developments on the internal functioning of an organization.

How do we identify the many current and future factors 'out there' which could affect the organization? When we have identified these, we then need to assess their potential impact. The tools that are used to analyse the environment are known as environmental scanning techniques.

Environmental scanning involves collecting information from different sources: government statistics, websites, newspapers and magazines, specialist research and consulting agencies, demographic analysis, market research and focus groups – and any other potentially useful sources.

Pestle analysis

PESTLE analysis an environmental scanning tool identifying Political, Economic, Social, Technological, Legal and Ecological factors that affect an organization.

PESTLE analysis is a popular environmental scanning method. This is a structured tool which helps to organize the complexity of trends in technology, globalization, demographics, and other factors. Pestle analysis is used to inform strategic planning, human resource strategy, marketing, product development, and organizational change (Morrison and Weeks, 2017).

Figure 2.4 is an example of a PESTLE analysis for a UK retail sector organization. The factors that are listed need detailed explanation: for example, how will movements in exchange rates affect the company's retail pricing and profitability? However, this illustrates the basic method. The best way to understand environmental scanning is to do your own analysis for an organization with which you are familiar. This usually shows that the model's neat categories overlap in an untidy way in practice. Many legislative changes have political motives. Ecological concerns reflect changing social values. Some technology developments (electric cars) are encouraged by ecological and economic concerns (pollution, fuel costs). However, the aim of the analysis is to identify environmental factors, their interrelationships, and their impact. It is less important to get them into the correct boxes.

CRITICAL THINKING	Choose an organization with which you are familiar, for example a hospital, supermarket, university or college, or the place you worked last summer. Make a list of the political, economic, social, technological, legislative and ecological factors that affect that organization.
	Based on your understanding of those factors, what advice would you give to the management of this organization? How would you assess the practical value of this PESTLE analysis to the organization?

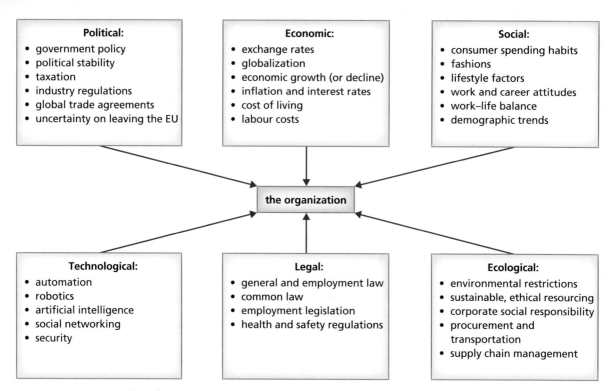

Figure 2.4: PESTLE Analysis for a UK retail organization in 2017–18

PESTLE analysis raises a number of issues.

First, it is difficult to escape from the argument that the organization must pay attention to external trends and developments. The organization which fails to respond to those factors will quickly run into difficulties.

Second, a long list of external factors can be intimidating. Identifying which are most significant, and then predicting their impact, can be difficult.

Third, a full understanding of external factors can involve the analysis of a substantial amount of different kinds of information, and this takes time.

Fourth, environmental complexity makes prediction difficult. We can predict demographic trends with some accuracy, with respect to mortality, and gender and age profiles. We can sometimes accurately predict economic trends in the short to medium term, say two to three years. Trends in social values and lifestyles, politics, or new technology, cannot be predicted with much confidence – although that does not stop journalists and others from trying to do so. Environmental scanning can mean a lot of informed guesswork and judgement.

PESTLE analysis has two strengths, and four weaknesses:

Strengths

1. The analysis focuses on 'the big picture', identifying the range of external factors affecting internal organizational arrangements and business planning.

2. This is a convenient framework for ordering a complex and bewildering set of factors, helping an organization plan for future opportunities and threats.

Weaknesses

1. The analysis may identify many factors which may not be significant. It is difficult to strike a balance between identifying all factors, and focusing on those which are important.

2. It is difficult to anticipate 'defining events', such as wars, terrorist attacks, new discoveries, economic collapse, and major political or financial crises which shift country boundaries or radically change government policies.

3. The analysis can involve the time-consuming and expensive collection of information, some of which may have to be researched, and some of which may simply be unavailable.

4. The time spent in information gathering and analysis may inhibit a rapid and effective response to the very trends being analysed.

Environmental scanning in a high-risk world

What aspects of the world economy and domestic business conditions are causing the most concern? A global survey by the management consulting firm McKinsey in 2017, involving 1,700 executives, found that the main perceived risks affecting world economic growth, in priority order, were:

1. Geopolitical instability and conflict
2. Transitions of political leadership
3. Changes in trade policy
4. Slowdown in global trade
5. Slowdown in China's economy
6. One or more countries leaving the Eurozone
7. Social unrest
8. Asset bubbles
9. Rising interest rates
10. Increased economic volatility

For the individual organization, the five most significant challenges were changes in business regulations, falling demand, changing consumer needs and expectations, changes in the trading environment, and scarcity of talent (Hirt and Smit, 2017).

Scenario planning
the imaginative development of one or more likely pictures of the dimensions and characteristics of the future for an organization.

Environmental analysis with PESTLE is used for scenario planning, a technique developed by Pierre Wack at the oil company Royal Dutch/Shell in the 1970s (Wilkinson and Kupers, 2013) and also known as the 'Shell method'. Scenario planning became unfashionable as the economic climate seemed to be stable. However, renewed concern with geopolitical risk has led to a revival of the technique, which is now popular as a way to help managers to think about and plan for future uncertainties. Scenarios are not predictions, but 'plausible stories' about the future, designed to challenge the assumption that the future will look much like the present, and to encourage creative discussion of issues that might otherwise be overlooked (Bowman, 2016).

Scenario planning combines environmental scanning with creative thinking, to identify the most probable future scenario as a basis for planning and action. In the field of corporate strategy, scenario planning is used to explore 'best case, worst case' possibilities, and to encourage creative 'out-of-the-box' thinking. You can see an example of this in the 'Work in 2022' box below.

We can now update our model. Figure 2.5 shows the links between external environmental pressures and internal organizational responses in more detail.

This model relies on a number of basic assumptions:

- That all the relevant data can be identified, collected and analysed.
- That the analysis will lead to accurate forecasts, and to realistic future scenarios.
- That the analysis will be consistent, and not pull the organization in different directions.
- That the kinds of internal organizational responses indicated by the analysis can be implemented at an appropriate pace.

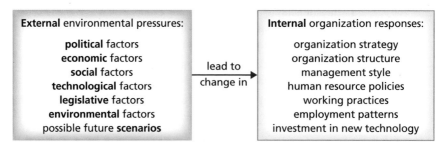

Figure 2.5: External environment–organization link detailed

Work in 2022: colourful scenarios

The consultancy company PricewaterhouseCoopers used scenario planning to explore the future of work (Houghton and Spence, 2016). They developed three possible scenarios for 2022:

Orange world **Small is beautiful**: big companies are replaced by networks of small specialized enterprises. People work on short-term contracts exploring job opportunities online through portals developed by craft guilds.

Green world **Companies care**: demographic change, climate and sustainability are key business drivers. Employment law, employee relations, and corporate responsibility are vital in this heavily regulated environment.

Blue world **Corporate is king**: large corporations are like mini-states providing staff with housing, health, education and other welfare benefits. Human capital metrics are sophisticated, and people management is as powerful as finance.

If none of these models turns out to be correct, will this have been a waste of time? No, because those who are used to thinking in innovative, lateral ways about the future are likely to be able to respond more quickly to what does actually happen.

The wider business context

Globalization the intensification of worldwide social and business relationships which link localities in such a way that local conditions are shaped by distant events.

Do you use an electric toothbrush? This gadget relies on 35 different metals, some of which are rare (neodymium, dysprosium, boron), and are used in very small quantities. China, the Democratic Republic of Congo, Chile, Russia, South Korea, Indonesia, and Turkey, were probably all involved in bringing the toothbrush and its component parts to your bathroom (Abraham, 2016). The supply chains for many everyday products – and less well-known items – draw on the combined resources of many countries in a similar way. This is a consequence of globalization (Giddens, 1990).

In the early twenty-first century, Western economies saw both threats and opportunities in the economic development of countries such as Brazil, Russia, India and China – the so-called BRIC economies. Less developed economies have lower labour costs, and are therefore attractive locations for manufacturing operations, and customer service call centres. The consulting company McKinsey (Dobbs et al., 2014) estimates that half of world economic growth between 2010 and 2025 will come from organizations based in over 400 cities in emerging markets – cities that few people in the West have heard of: Tianjin (China), Porto Alegre (Brazil), Kumasi (Ghana).

Once seen as inevitable and beneficial, globalization has become controversial. Most economists agree that, overall, globalization has contributed to rising global wealth and the increased availability of products and services for consumers. However, 'offshoring' manufacturing and service operations to low-cost countries has meant that many workers in Europe and North America have lost their jobs, and few new jobs have appeared. The benefits of globalization have not been equally shared. In 2016, the anger generated by these job losses may have contributed to the result of the UK referendum to leave the European Union, and the election of the populist American President Donald Trump, who promised to pursue a protectionist trade agenda to bring jobs back to the US.

Globalization is an uneven process. Many people around the world do not have access to the goods and technologies that contribute to the experience of globalization for affluent members of developed economies. Many societies reject the dislocation that globalization can bring, and object to the spread of Western culture. Western organizations (from fast food outlets to national embassies) have become terrorist targets, as well as focal points for demonstrations against perceived attempts to impose Western values on other cultures. Some commentators suggest that the world has moved beyond globalization, and moved to a regional emphasis, on the ICASA economies: India, China, Africa and Southeast Asia (Greenberg et al., 2017). We may be entering a period of deglobalization.

CRITICAL THINKING

How does globalization affect you personally?

In what ways could globalization influence your working life and your career?

What are the personal benefits and disadvantages of globalization?

Barbie is a globalization icon

were low at the time), and has since been made in other low-wage countries in Asia. The only components of Barbie which come from America are the cardboard packaging, and some paints. Her body and wardrobe come from elsewhere across the planet:

Component/ manufacturing stage	source
Designs, pigments, oils, moulds	United States
Cardboard packaging	made in United States with pulp from Indonesia
Oil for her plastic parts	Saudi Arabia
Refined oil and PVC plastic pellets	Taiwan
Injection moulding	China, Indonesia, Malaysia
Nylon hair	Japan
Cotton dresses	China
Distribution	Hong Kong

Barbie is one of the most profitable toys in history, selling at a rate of two per second, and generating over US$1billion in annual revenues for the Mattell Corporation based in Los Angeles (Giddens and Sutton, 2009, p.135). Sold in 140 countries, she is a global citizen, but she is global in another sense, too. Although she was designed in America, she has never been made there, and was first manufactured in Japan in 1959 (where wages

The sign on the box may say 'made in China', or Indonesia or Malaysia, but Barbie crosses many geographical boundaries on her journey from the designer's sketchpad to the customer. Look at the products that you own and use. Where do they come from? Choose one of your favourite items and see if you can find out where in the world its component parts were made.

Demographic trends

Demographic trends pose difficult challenges for management in the twenty-first century. Life expectancy is increasing, and the population is ageing. This is a global phenomenon, affecting most countries, apart from sub-Saharan Africa. At the same time, birth rates are falling, and fewer young people are joining the workforce. This means that the proportion of the population who have retired is growing relative to the proportion of those still working. How should organizations respond? Should older workers be encouraged to stay in employment? How should we manage an age-diverse workforce with different generations who may have different needs and expectations?

Other demographic trends include global migration, triggered in part by wars and famine, improved communications and transport. Migration creates social and political tensions, but also contributes to a richer ethnic, cultural and religious mix in a given workforce. An ageing population is leading to labour and skill shortages, which migrants can help to address. There is now a premium on the ability to manage this diversity of values, needs and preferences.

CUTTING EDGE Will you live to be 100?

Lynda Gratton

Lynda Gratton and Andrew Scott (2016; 2017) explore the consequences of increasing longevity for employment. Living to 100 is not unusual any more. In Britain, people who reach 100 get a message from the Queen. At the turn of the twenty-first century, one assistant sent these cards; now seven people do this job. In Japan, the government gives a silver sake dish to those who reach 100. In 1963, 153 people got one; in 2014, 29,350 did (Skapinker, 2016).

Those who reach 60 have one third of their life left. But many of us in future will not have enough savings or an adequate pension to retire in comfort at 60 or 65. We will need to generate more income to pay for our retirement. It may become normal to work until you are 70 or 80. One in five Americans over 65, and one in 12 over 75, still works, as do one in ten in the UK.

Andrew Scott

Gratton and Scott argue that many employers are not ready for the challenges and opportunities that these trends will bring. Age discrimination is common, older workers are seen as costly and less effective (blocking opportunities for younger employees), and are expected to go quietly at 65. But older workers are already creative in this respect: retraining, taking different roles, adjusting their work-life balance, starting businesses.

Gratton and Scott argue that, as well as financial assets, three intangible assets will become more important as working lives become longer:

1. Productive assets: skills, knowledge, reputation, professional networks
2. Vitality assets: mental and physical health, work–life balance
3. Transformational assets: self-knowledge, diverse networks that support personal transitions

The traditional three-stage career involved education, work, then retirement. This is changing, as more people develop portfolio careers, moving between employment and self-employment, combining paid and unpaid work. Employers will struggle, the researchers predict, with older workers' desires for personalization, their need for flexibility, and their resistance to being stereotyped because of their age. Human resource management policies will need to change to resolve these tensions. Gratton and Scott suggest providing flexible, lifelong learning, encouraging older employees to transfer their skills to other areas, and allowing flexible working and sabbaticals – to 'recharge'. The most important step is to rethink age-related stereotypes, to see those over 60 as assets, not liabilities:

> 'The early adopters celebrating the experience and wisdom of the over-60s are often found in the retail sector, selling to older customers, or in sectors such as engineering, where there is a dearth of younger talent. For example, at B&Q PLC, a home improvement and home gardening supply retailer based in Chandler's Ford, England, more than one quarter of the company's workforce is over 50. Among other things, the company considers older workers more experienced with do-it-yourself home projects and more empathic with homeowners. At Vita Needle Co., a manufacturer of stainless steel tubing and fabricated parts based in Needham, Massachusetts, about half of the employees are aged 75 or older' (Gratton and Scott, 2017, p.69).

Population trends: the statistics

The statistics of population change paint a consistent picture (Chand and Tung, 2014; CIPD, 2015; Calnan, 2017a):

- Around half of all the human beings who have ever been over 65 are alive today, and by 2035, over 1.1 billion people – 13 percent of the world's population – will be over 65.

- For most of human history, those over 65 have not exceeded 3 or 4 per cent of the population. In developed economies, those over 65 now make up about 15 per cent of the population. This this will reach 25 per cent on average by 2050, and 40 per cent in Japan, Korea and Singapore.

- In the UK, the old-age dependency ratio – the number of those aged 65 and over as a percentage of the labour force – is expected to rise from 27.6 per cent in 2015 to 35 per cent in 2030; in Japan, this ratio will be around 74 per cent by 2050.

- In the UK in 2010, there were 10 million people aged 65 or over. Over 30 per cent of the workforce was over 50 in 2015.

- In 2017, a UK survey found that half of older employees expect to work beyond the traditional retirement age of 65, to remain mentally fit, and to generate income.

CRITICAL THINKING   Are there many older workers (over 60) in your organization? Are they valued, or not? Are they as creative and productive as their younger colleagues? Are they satisfied with their jobs and motivated to work? Or are they 'marking time' until retirement? What more could your organization do to maintain the motivation and skills of its older workers?

An ageing population has social consequences. The generation born after the Second World War (which ended in 1945), have been celebrating their 60th birthdays, and considering retirement, since around 2006. These 'Baby Boomers' have been called a 'silver tsunami'. *Boomsday*, a novel by Christopher Buckley (2007), is about the anger of younger generations whose taxes pay for the pensions, health and welfare of retired Boomers. However, not everybody retires when they reach 60 or 65. In the UK, 25 per cent of retirees return to work within five years, at least in part due to the additional costs of living longer. We are seeing a new phenomenon – unretirement (Jacobs, 2017).

Unretirement having retired, then later taking full-time work, or starting full-time work after partial retirement.

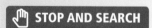 **STOP AND SEARCH**   Watch the video and take the 'intangible assets' diagnostic at www.100yearlife.com

Managing an ageing workforce

What management issues does an ageing workforce create? Let's start with the negative stereotype. Older workers are seen as expensive, poor performers, less motivated, lacking technology skills, with a limited ability to learn and resistant to change. Age discrimination is therefore widespread, discouraging organizations from recruiting and developing older workers. Another problem is that younger managers find it difficult to manage older, more experienced workers. Older employees may resent being told what to do by youngsters, and performance may suffer (Kunze and Menges, 2017).

Research shows that this stereotype is false, and that the business case for employing older workers – the unretired – is strong. In comparison with younger colleagues, older workers tend to be better than, or at least as good, in the following areas (Marvell and Cox, 2016, pp.8–9):

- Practical skills and knowledge
- Experience, insights, judgement

- Eager to share their expertise with and to mentor others
- Communication skills
- Problem-solving ability
- Handling difficult situations
- Engaged, committed, reliable, lower turnover
- Understanding the needs of older customers or clients
- Contributing to age-diverse teams, combining perspectives, encouraging innovation.

✓✓✓ **EMPLOYABILITY CHECK** (leadership, people management)

You are a 30-year-old woman. You have been given responsibility for supervising a team of 15 people. They are mostly male, and in their 50s and 60s. What are your main problems likely to be in managing this group? How will you approach your challenging new role?

See the box, 'When the manager is a millennial', later in the chapter.

From research using online focus groups with employees, and surveys of over 2,000 managers, Zheltoukhova and Baczor (2016, p.13) found that older workers (55+), due to their accumulated experience and skills, were seen as the most talented and employable of all underrepresented groups in the workforce:

> 'Older workers were seen to have a more positive attitude to work, but lower potential to develop, compared with young people. They were also rated the highest on their ability to hit the ground running, levels of relevant experience and skills, and being highly networked and connected.'

With regard to resistance to change, a study of 3,000 workers in 93 companies in Germany found that older employees were *less* resistant than their younger colleagues (Kunze et al., 2013). This may be because older workers have better strategies for coping with and adapting to changing environments.

Older employees may have motives for working that are different from younger generations. It has been suggested that the unretired (or 'returners') come back to work for many reasons: money, stimulation, intellectual challenge, meaning, to continue adding value and social contact. This may be correct, but don't most of us look for those outcomes from work? One motive that does distinguish older workers is the desire for flexible working arrangements, to allow them to care for elderly parents and grandchildren, and in some cases to manage their own health.

Remodelling roles helps maintain traditional skills

Adjusting job descriptions has helped a pottery company to retain valued workers, says Brian Groom. For some industries with ageing workforces, such as ceramics, it is vital to hold on to those with traditional skills. Nowhere does this matter more than in Stoke-on Trent's pottery industry, where Steelite International is in the forefront of the sector's recent revival.

Steelite, which makes tableware for the hospitality industry, is shortlisted for the Championing an Ageing Workforce category of the Responsible Business Awards. Other shortlisted companies include Barclays Bank, which has revamped its apprenticeship schemes to appeal to older workers.

→

At Steelite, policies include flexible working and phased retirement, continuous training, removal of upper age limits from apprenticeships and graduate programmes and sometimes redeployment to less physically arduous roles.

'These are the demographics that a lot of companies are dealing with today', says Louise Griffin, group head of human resources. 'We haven't got the same number of young people coming up. There are going to be more people working for longer and it's recognizing what skills you need and then matching that, rather than thinking about the age of the person.'

Of Steelite's 876 UK employees, 360 are aged 50 or over. Its eldest worker is 69 years and its youngest 17. Its managers believe that the mix of ages enables older workers to train apprentices and pass on knowledge that is needed for the company's future. Steelite says older workers are less likely to change jobs than younger colleagues and often have a stronger commitment to the company.

Most jobs are manual, including shovelling clay, sponging, pot-throwing or operating kilns. In some cases, help is at hand to allow people to do their jobs for longer, such as the use of electric trucks. One former shop floor worker is now a health and safety auditor while another is team leader of the cleaners (Groom, 2016a).

FT   *Source*: B. Groom (2016, p. 10)
© Financial Times, 19 April 2016, reproduced with permission

Home viewing

The Intern (2015, director Nancy Meyers) is about 70-year-old Ben Whittaker (played by Robert de Niro). Bored with retirement, he applies to be a 'senior intern' at an online fashion retailer. The company's ambitious founder, Jules Ostin (Anne Hathaway) gives him the job, but doesn't explain that he is just there for show, as part of an 'outreach program'. Why did Ben take this job? Are his younger colleagues uncomfortable having him around? What contribution does Ben make to the running of the organization? How does he contribute to the well-being and work performance of Jules and other members of staff? Is this a romantic 'Hollywood' view of older workers? Or do you think that this is a realistic picture of the value of seniors?

To attract and retain the skills and knowledge of older workers, research from the Chartered Institute for Personnel and Development (CIPD, 2016) makes these simple, low-cost recommendations:

- Carry out accurate workforce planning and age-diversity monitoring
- Build an age-diverse culture that values all age groups, with inclusive recruitment
- Support employee health and well-being; some older workers have long-term health conditions
- Help employees to balance work and caring responsibilities
- Allow more flexibility in working time
- Provide training and development based on potential, not on age
- Tailor the retirement process to individual needs, e.g. phased retirement
- Tailor job roles to suit individual needs and expectations
- Train line managers to deal with the needs of an age-diverse workforce

Managing a multigenerational workforce

Multigenerational workforce an employee group which includes up to five different generations, each with potentially different expectations of work

Figure 2.6 shows the make-up of today's multigenerational workforce, from Veterans to Generation Z (included for completeness, Alphas are too young to work). It is possible to find all five working generations in the same organization. Some commentary uses other dates to identify the generations, but these details are not significant. The point is that each generation seems to have its own approach to work. (In this discussion, we will overlook the Veterans, because their numbers are now so low.)

The differences between the generations are shaped by social context – the defining events and conditions to which we are exposed and which shape our attitudes, core beliefs and work values. When Baby Boomers were born, for example, there were no televisions or mobile phones. In contrast, Gen Z have never have known a world without touch-sensitive screens and the internet. Traditionally, management policies and practices have been applied consistently to all employees. With an age-diverse workforce, that consistency may no longer be appropriate.

> **CRITICAL THINKING**
>
> Many commentators claim that the generations are different from each other, and that each generation has its own attitudes and approach to work. Management should take this into account, managing Millennials in one way, for example, and Gen Z in another. But is this correct? Isn't everybody motivated by the same things? What does your experience tell you?

> *Veterans*: born 1925–1942; also known as the silent generation, matures, traditionalists
>
> *Baby Boomers*: 1946–1964; also just called Boomers
>
> *Generation X*: 1965–1979, also known as post boomers, baby busters
>
> *Generation Y*: 1980–1994; also known as Millennials, nexters, echo boomers
>
> *Generation Z*: 1995–2010/2015; also known as Gen C – Connected, Communicating, Clicking
>
> *Generation Alpha*: 2010–; the first generation to all be born in this century, surrounded by technology

Figure 2.6: **The six generations**

Baby boomers

The children of Veterans, Baby Boomers started to think about retirement from around 2006. However, many are still active members of the workforce, never having left, or unretired. Boomers are said to be decisive, leading, motivating, and persuasive. Research also suggests that the rewards which they regard as important include (Hewlett et al., 2009):

1. High-quality colleagues
2. An intellectually stimulating workplace
3. Autonomy regarding work tasks
4. Flexible work arrangements
5. Access to new experiences and challenges
6. Giving back to the world through work
7. Recognition from the company or the boss

How to handle 'grumpy boomers'

We tend to think of each generation as having a distinct set of attitudes and values. A study of Canadian knowledge workers, by Linda Duxbury and Michael Halinski (2014), suggests that this picture is too simple; there can be as much diversity within a generational group as between generations. Boomers (born 1946 to 1964) will retire between 2010 and 2030. But with an ageing population, Boomers will leave the workforce just as the numbers of employees to replace them is falling. How should employers respond? The Canadian study identified four categories of Boomers:

Disengaged-exiters	Organizations will benefit if they quit
Engaged-high-performers	Organizations want to retain their services
Retired-on-the-job	Organizations could benefit if they were 're-engaged'
Exiting-performers	Organizations want to retain their skills and experience

Disengaged-exiters and engaged-high-performers are not problems. There is no loss if the former leave, and the latter continue to perform well. The problems lie with those who are retired-on-the-job and are not contributing as much as they could, and the exiting-performers who are costly to replace. The main difference between exiting-performers and engaged-high-performers was workload. Those who were planning to exit worked longer hours, and worked more often at home, reporting higher levels of overload than any other group. Those who were retired-on-the-job had moderate levels of job satisfaction, and had mixed views of management and organization culture.

What are the practical implications? Organizations that want to discourage committed but grumpy Boomers from leaving need to address workload issues: reduce hours and overtime, and introduce flexible working. On the other hand, a focus on skills development, supportive management and organization culture is necessary to renew the commitment of those who have retired-on-the-job.

Generation X

Gen X are now in their 40s and 50s. Birth rates had fallen by the time they came along, so they are known as 'baby busters' (after the phrase 'boom and bust'). They have also been called 'the lost generation' because less attention has been paid to them than to the Boomers and to subsequent generations. They play a major role in the workforce, and have had a significant impact on today's social and technological climate:

'This is the generation that grew up on a diet of MTV, that remembers clunky mobile phones and painfully slow internet, that created MySpace and YouTube. Generation X created and provided the cultural and technical revolution upon which the economy now pivots' (Hudson Consulting, 2014, p.11).

Gen X is seen as being ambitious, strategic, autonomous, persuasive, people-oriented, socially confident, and as drivers for change. And they will not start to retire until around 2030.

✋ **STOP AND SEARCH**   YouTube for *Meet Generation X.*

Generation Y

Gen Y – Millennials – are the children of the Boomers. Do Boomers and Millennials want different things from work? A survey by Deloitte, a management consultancy, found that for Millennials the top reasons for choosing to work for an organization (excluding salary) were work–life balance, opportunities to progress, flexibility, sense of meaning, professional development, and impact on society (Groom, 2016b). Perhaps these generations are not so different after all.

The motivational profile of Generation Y

Generation Y, or 'Millennials', were born in the 1980s and 1990s. By 2025, they will comprise 75 per cent of the global workforce. Managers need to understand their values and expectations:

- Gen Y looks for ethical employers, opportunities for progression, a good work–life balance, and interesting work; almost half choose workplace flexibility over pay.

- More than half of Gen Y in the UK intend to leave their jobs within one or two years of joining.

- They tend to be independent and resist micromanagement, but they want feedback and coaching.

- They are comfortable with technology and social networks, creative and open-minded, multiculturally aware, confident, able to collaborate and ethical.

- More than three quarters (77 per cent) of Gen Y view formal management qualifications to be the most effective method of learning and development.

- Many want to be entrepreneurs; more than a quarter of 16- to 30-year-olds in the UK claimed in a study in 2012 that they were considering setting up a business.

- They can have a strong sense of entitlement, poor interpersonal communication skills, poor decision-making skills, a weak work ethic, and can appear overconfident.

Gen Y lacks a global mindset: just one UK student studies abroad for every 15 international students in the UK (Chartered Management Institute, 2014, pp. 20–23).

Boomers and Gen Y both want to serve a wider purpose, want opportunities to explore their interests and passions, and say that flexible working and work–life balance are important. They also share a sense of obligation to the wider society and the environment. Gen Xers are far less likely to find those obligations important. It is also interesting that Boomers and Gen Y agree that financial gain is not their main reason for choosing an employer. They are interested in other forms of reward: teamwork, challenge, new experiences, recognition. Management practices thus need to emphasize teamwork and collaboration, flexible working, phased retirement, project work, short-term assignments, opportunities to support external causes and eco-friendly work environments.

Generation Z

Gen Z was born between 1995 and 2010/2015 (there is disagreement about this). Most of the student readers of this book will be Gen Z. As this generation is connected, communicating, content-centric, computerized, community oriented, and always clicking, they have also been called Gen C. This is the first generation to have grown up with the internet, social media and mobile computing, for whom 24/7 mobile and internet connectivity are taken for granted, and freedom of expression is the norm. These technologies encourage flexible forms of working, and less hierarchical organizations, and they blur the boundaries between work and personal life. By 2020, Gen Z will make up over 40 per cent of the population in America, Europe and the BRIC countries (Friedrich et al., 2011). Gen Z are:

- *On the grid 24/7:* Connected around the clock is normal.
- *Social animal 2.0:* As personal relationships rely on social networks, online groups, blogs, and messaging platforms, this creates fast-moving business and political pressures as information and ideas spread more widely, more quickly.

Technology and teamwork are particularly important to this generation. Gen Z bring their own devices (smartphones, tablets) to work rather than use clumsy corporate resources. This means more work can be done by virtual project groups, with fewer face-to-face meetings, and less frequent travel. A survey by the telecoms company Vodaphone UK found that Gen Z placed more value in their workplace team than other generations, and want to use technology (such as messaging platforms) to support teamwork. They prefer high-quality technology, but do not think that flexible working makes them more productive (Calnan, 2017b).

CRITICAL THINKING

Those born after 2010 have been called *Generation Alpha* – the first (and thus 'alpha') generation to have been born entirely in the twenty-first century (McCrindle, 2014). It is estimated that, globally, 2.5 million Alphas are born every week, and that by 2025 there will be around two billion of them. How might they differ from previous generations? How do you think their approach to work will be shaped by their experience of technology, their longevity, and by other social trends? What new management problems do you think they will create?

Demographic trends: roundup

There are two issues we need to look at before we leave this section.

First, having many generations in the same workforce may be beneficial. Research by the fast-food chain McDonald's UK found that employees in age-diverse teams had higher job satisfaction and performed better. McDonald's surveyed 32,000 staff, and found that multigenerational teams were 10 per cent happier than those working in their peer group.

A survey of 1,000 customers found that over 80 per cent liked to see a mix of ages in a restaurant team, because it improved the atmosphere. Older workers deliver better service, and mentor younger staff; levels of customer service were 20 per cent higher in restaurants with staff aged 60 and over.

Claire Hall, McDonald's UK chief people officer said, 'Teams that bring a mix of people of different ages and at different life stages are fundamental to creating a happy and motivated workplace and to delivering a great customer experience'. The age range of staff at McDonald's in the UK is an incredible 75 years - from 16 to 91 (see Clarke, 2016; and www.mcdonalds. co.uk/ukhome/Aboutus/Newsroom/news_pages/Bridging_The_Generation_Gap_Is_The_Key_To_A_Happier_Workforce.html).

Second, does it make sense to 'generationalize' the workforce? We know that different generations share common characteristics. Although born into different eras, and with different experiences, their motives and attitudes to work seem to be similar. Can we really assume that everyone born within a particular set of dates will have similar characteristics and thought processes? Many Boomers are just as 'tech savvy' as Gen Y or Gen Z. Millennials do not have a monopoly on wanting work to give them challenge, teamwork, recognition, and opportunities to contribute to society. Rudolph et al. (2018) argue that 'generationalized thinking' is too simple. Many other factors affect an individual's attitudes to work, motivation and behaviour. They suggest instead using a 'lifespan developmental perspective' which looks at how individuals develop and change with age and experience.

The differences between the generations may thus have been exaggerated. From a management viewpoint, it may be more useful to pay attention to differences between individuals, and to how individual motives and expectations change over time.

When the manager is a Millennial

Kerri Rogan is head of reliability improvement for London Underground. She is 30, and manages a team of 16 people, who are mostly male, and in their 40s and 50s. Her advice for young managers in this situation is:

- Ensure you take the time to build personal relationships. Get to know people and find out what makes them tick.
- Engage older workers as partners and seek their advice when making a decision.
- Recognize older subordinates have a great deal of expertise and that you are not there to challenge their knowledge.
- Be upfront about what you do not know.
- Do not be afraid to stand your ground.
- Have a meeting with older employees about what you expect from them and what they expect from you.

Provide opportunities for the continual updating of tech skills, especially for those who may feel intimidated by technology, so they remain relevant in the workplace (Extracts from Conboye, 2017).

FT *Source*: J. Conboye (2017)
© Financial Times, 30 August 2017, reproduced with permission

Ethical behaviour

Ethics the moral principles, values and rules that govern our decisions and actions with respect to what is right and wrong, good and bad.

For the Institute of Business Ethics (IBE), **ethics** means behaviour based on values such as fairness, honesty, integrity and openness – treating colleagues and customers fairly, with dignity and respect, paying suppliers on time, and recognizing the organization's responsibilities to the wider society. This means 'doing the right thing because it is the right thing to do' (Russell, 2017, p.3).

Ethical behaviour has become important for two reasons. The first concerns the publicity given to high-profile corporate scandals (e.g. bribery at Samsung, cheating on vehicle emissions tests at Volkswagen). The second concerns media scrutiny of management practices, focusing on environmental issues, bribery, the use of child labour, and other potentially unethical behaviours. These concerns are not new, but they attract more attention than in the past. News about corporate misbehaviour spreads rapidly through social media. Unethical behaviour by an individual can put an end to their career. Organizations suffer reputational damage and lose customers if they are seen to be acting unethically. As such behaviour becomes more transparent, organizations need to be able to show clearly how they do business. A survey of public perceptions by the IBE found that, in 2016, less than half the British public believed that business was behaving ethically (Russell, 2017).

There is no consensus, however, on what constitutes 'ethical' behaviour. Different commentators use different criteria to decide what is right and wrong. Gerald Cavanagh, Dennis Moberg and Manuel Velasquez developed a template to help distinguish ethical from unethical management actions (Cavanagh et al., 1981; Velasquez et al., 1983). Their perspective is based on three ethical frameworks: utilitarianism, individual rights, and natural justice (Table 2.2).

Utilitarianism

A utilitarian perspective judges behaviour in terms of the outcomes, or consequences (and is also known as consequentialism). This is the classic 'ends justifies means' argument. This approach considers the 'balance sheet' of benefits and costs for those involved. Behaviour is ethical if it achieves 'the greatest good for the greatest number'. However, in even modestly complex settings, with several stakeholders, and actions with a range of consequences, assessing the costs and benefits can be challenging.

Rights

A rights perspective judges behaviour on the extent to which fundamental individual rights are respected. This includes the right of free consent, the right to privacy, the right to freedom of conscience, the right of free speech, the right to due process in the form of an impartial hearing. The ethical decision depends on whether or not individual rights have been violated.

Justice

A justice perspective assesses behaviour on whether or not the benefits and costs flowing from an action are fairly, equitably and impartially distributed. Distributive justice states that rules should be applied consistently, those in similar circumstances should be treated equally, and individuals should not be held responsible for matters beyond their control. As with the utilitarian view, these issues are awkward to resolve in practice, as judgements of consistency, similarity and responsibility are subjective and vary from one setting to another.

Table 2.2: **Ethical frameworks**

	Strengths	**Weaknesses**
Utilitarianism	Encourages efficiency	Impossible to quantify variables
	Parallels profit maximization	Can lead to unjust resource allocation
	Looks beyond the individual	Individual rights may be violated
Rights	Protects the individual	May encourage selfish behaviour
	Establishes standards of behaviour independent of outcomes	Individual rights may become obstacles to productivity and efficiency
Justice	Ensures fair allocation of resources	Can encourage a sense of entitlement that discourages risk and innovation
	Ensures democratic operation, independent of status or class	Some individual rights may be violated to accommodate justice for majority
	Protects the interests of the under-represented in the organization	

These three perspectives produce a 'decision tree' for deciding whether an action is ethical or not (Figure 2.7). First, 'gather the facts', then ask about benefits, rights and justice. The framework also introduces circumstances which could justify unethical behaviour in some settings. 'Overwhelming factors' are issues that justify setting aside ethical criteria. Some actions may have 'dual effects', with positive and negative outcomes, and the negatives may be acceptable if they are outweighed by the positives. 'Incapacitating factors' may prevent the decision maker from applying ethical criteria. For example, managers can be constrained by the views and actions of colleagues. Individual managers may not have enough information on which to reach a judgement. Finally, the individual may doubt the relevance of one or more ethical criteria to a given setting. The right to free speech may not apply if this involves information that would be damaging to others.

The result is that we have several escape routes which allow actions that would be prohibited by the three criteria. The urgency of the case, time pressures, resource constraints, penalties for inaction, and so on, can all be called upon as overwhelming, dual or incapacitating factors.

CRITICAL THINKING

Sam and Bob are research scientists in the General Rubber product development laboratory. Sam, who is introvert, quiet and serious, is more technically proficient; her patents have earned the company around $6 million over the past ten years. Bob does not have the same expertise, his output is 'solid but unimaginative', and he is extrovert and demonstrative. The rumour is that Bob will be moved into an administrative role. The lab offers a $300,000 fund each year for the best new product idea. Sam and Bob both submit proposals, which are assessed as having equal merit. Sam takes no further action, but Bob conducts a publicity campaign (about which he tells Sam in advance), promoting the advantages of his proposal to those who can influence the final decision. Informal pressure builds and the decision is made in Bob's favour.

Is Bob's behaviour ethical? Does the ethical decision tree help you to reach a decision?

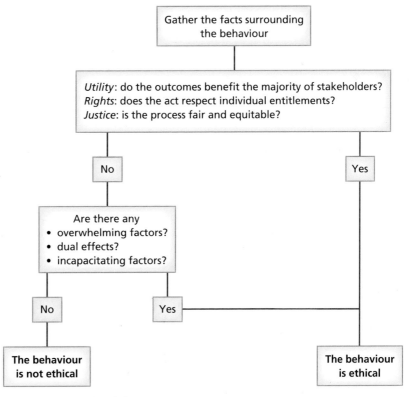

Figure 2.7: The ethical decision tree

The decision tree suggests that Bob's actions are unethical. From a utilitarian perspective, the outcome is acceptable, as both proposals had equal merit. From a rights perspective, Sam had the same opportunities, and she knew about Bob's informal campaign. However, by introducing 'irrelevant differences' between the proposals based on personal lobbying, Bob's behaviour breached the principles of justice, and was unethical.

How do you feel about this judgement? Ideas in most organizations do not make progress on merit alone. Bob recognized that ideas benefit from good publicity. Should we praise Sam for her ethics and criticize Bob for his unfair practices? Or should we regard Sam as naive and lazy, and praise Bob for his enthusiasm and understanding of the context? Bob's actions were not secret, and he won the prize. For the company that wants to encourage innovation, Bob seems to be the better role model. This decision tree offers contradictory assessments, and can lead to judgements that are controversial.

Frameworks such as this one can highlight the issues, but they cannot always make the decision for us. That is a matter of personal judgement.

CUTTING EDGE   The barriers to ethical behaviour

Christopher McLaverty

Annie McKee

Christopher McLaverty and Annie McKee (2016) asked 30 senior executives in India, Columbia, Saudi Arabia, the United Kingdom and the United States about the ethical dilemmas they had faced at work. In total, they remembered 85 major dilemmas, most of which had happened in the previous five years. The study identified three barriers to acting ethically at work:

1. *Change:* Change is often driven rapidly from the top of the organization, and leads to conflicts of interests, especially when staff numbers have to be reduced and business units closed. Managers reported having to act against their personal values in these situations.

2. *Incentives:* Managers are typically rewarded for hitting targets. This encourages decisions and actions that have immediate benefits, but which can damage the business in the long term.

3. *Culture:* Making ethical decisions is complex when different cultures have different 'rules'. Compared with Western practice, there are different cultural and ethical aspects of, for example, closing a sales office in Japan, breaking an informal promise made outside working hours in China, or overlooking 'sleeping partners' in a Saudi Arabian business deal.

How can leaders improve their organization's ethical climate? First, be aware of what is important to you, personally. Rules, codes of conduct, and ethics training are not always helpful in managing ethical dilemmas. 'Companies become ethical one person at a time, one decision at a time' (p.4). Second, understand what really matters in the organization. Watch how people are paid, who gets promoted, and how people feel about the company. Be ready to challenge unwritten rules. Third, build a wide network of people you can go to for advice. Finally, have the courage to speak out when something is not right. The researchers conclude that:

'The leaders in the study were clear about the consequences of taking these actions: increased self-respect, improved confidence in their ability to address future dilemmas, and a more ethical work climate. And perhaps more importantly, taking brave action made them happier at work' (p.5).

Corporate social responsibility

Business ethics has stimulated a lot of interest and debate. Unethical behaviour, allowing financial institutions to take unacceptably high risks, contributed to the global financial crisis triggered by the collapse of Lehmann Brothers in 2008 (Archer, 2010). Senior management and engineers at the German car manufacturer Volkswagen were accused of unethical behaviour in 2015 for cheating vehicle emissions tests. United Airlines staff were filmed dragging a passenger off an overbooked flight in 2017. Uber was accused, also in 2017, of having a company culture of sexual harassment and gender discrimination; Uber's founder and chief executive, Travis Kalanick, resigned. In 2017, Bill O'Reilly, a commentator at Fox News, resigned when it was revealed that he paid women to keep quiet about their claims of sexual harassment.

South Korea has a particularly bad history of unethical behaviour. Samsung had had a dispute with 240 employees in its semiconductor division, concerning a claim that exposure to chemicals triggered diseases such as leukaemia, lymphoma, and brain tumours. Hankook Tire, another large South Korean company, has been accused of putting profit before safety, violating labour laws, and covering up accidents and illness linked to working conditions and chemicals used in tyre manufacturing. One expert said, 'Accidents are repeated because of the rigid hierarchical corporate culture that prevents workers from raising their voice about safety' (Harris et al., 2017).

Corporate social responsibility the view that organizations should act ethically, in ways that contribute to economic development, the environment, quality of working life, local communities, and the wider society.

Should organizations support social and environmental issues? This can be good for business, if it attracts customers. The economist Milton Friedman (1970) once argued that, 'The business of business is business'. His view is now unfashionable. We now expect organizations to promote social and environmental or 'green' issues. This has become a key environmental pressure, combining Political, Ecological, Social and Technological aspects of PESTLE analysis. Many organizations are addressing these issues, to build their reputation as 'responsible corporate citizens'. We have explained a framework for exploring the ethical dilemmas facing individuals. We also have to consider ethical behaviour at an organizational level, or corporate social responsibility (CSR).

Organizations are expected to act in ethical and socially responsible ways. Those who do not are quickly exposed through social media. Organizations can be criticized even when their own activities are ethical, but those of their suppliers are not. The reputation of Apple was damaged in 2017 when it was revealed that its supplier Foxcomm employed school-age interns who were working illegal overtime. The International Labor Organization, based in Geneva, estimates that one in ten children worldwide – around 152 million aged between 5 and 17 – are employed as child labour (Flood, 2017). Modern supply chains can spread across several countries and tiers of suppliers. It has therefore become difficult for organizations to monitor all of those operations and to avoid unethical practices.

Companies which are seen to have a poor corporate social responsibility record may have problems in recruiting and retaining staff. Investors and consumers have also begun to adopt socially responsible views and behaviours, not only in relation to working practices and manufacturing operations, but also with regard to the social and political issues that organizations support. When the United States withdrew from the Paris climate agreement in 2017, the chief executives of Disney and Tesla resigned from the US President's business advisory council, as 'a matter of principle', because they did not want their organizations to be associated with an environmentally damaging policy (Bond, 2017).

Values-based purchasing

In a survey of 14,000 consumers in 14 countries, 60 per cent said that they decide whether to buy or to boycott products because of a company's views on political or social issues (Bond, 2017). Nearly a quarter said that they would buy the products of companies that shared their beliefs on particular issues even if they had to pay more. In February 2018, the shooting which killed 17 students at Marjory Stoneman Douglas High School in Florida, triggered a fresh debate about gun control in America. As a result, many companies cut their ties with the National Rifle Association, cancelling special discount deals for NRA members, to signal their disagreement with the Association's pro-gun values (Edgecliffe-Johnson, 2018). The investment management company BlackRock announced that it was excluding gun makers and retailers from its socially responsible investment funds. Investors will also be able to screen gun stocks from their endowments, and include gun-free index funds in employee pension plans. The chief executive of BlackRock, Larry Fink, said that the company must 'make a positive contribution to society' (Masters, 2018).

Socially responsible investment

Socially responsible investment (SRI) means avoiding companies that are seen to be doing harm, and investing in those that do measurable good (impact investing). The social benefits that count are broad, and can relate to climate change and product packaging, for example. The US Forum for Sustainable and Responsible Investment claims that over one-fifth of the professionally managed funds in America are based on SRI criteria, and that this proportion is rising. Goldman Sachs manages US$10.5 billion in 'ESG' investments, in companies which meet environmental, social, and governance standards (*The Economist*, 2017). 'Gender lens' investing is a growing trend, which considers what companies are doing that benefits or harms women. Is there diversity in the executive team? Do company projects benefit poor women in developing countries? Does a company have a 'toxic' management culture that condones sexual harrassment (*The Economist*, 2018)?

Traditional financial reporting focuses on revenues, profits and returns for shareholders. This approach does not take into account the contributions that a business potentially makes to 'the triple bottom line', concerning people, planet and profits. Now, around 200 companies in Europe, mostly from Austria, Germany and Switzerland have adopted the 'common good balance sheet', which assesses ethical behaviour as well as finances. The common good balance sheet has a scoring system, with a maximum of 1,000 points. Points are awarded for acting in a humane, cooperative, ecological and democratic way, and points are deducted for actions such as violating employment legislation, causing pollution, unequal pay for men and women, using tax havens, and hostile takeovers.

CRITICAL THINKING

Let's examine your own shopping habits. Does corporate social responsibility affect your purchasing behaviour? Research evidence suggests that it does:

'According to a recent report, 94% of GenZ consumers (the age of traditional college students currently) believe companies should help address social and environmental issues and 89% would rather buy from a company supporting social and environmental issues. Additionally, both Millennial and Generation Z consumers overwhelmingly agreed that they are willing to pay more for products and services produced by companies that are committed to social and environmental causes' (Beitelspacher and Rodgers, 2018, p.2).

You may have to look beyond the organization and consider its suppliers, too. Is child labour, for example, involved in the manufacturing of the company's products? What are working conditions like in the company's manufacturing plants, warehouses and call centres? What is this organization doing to limit its environmental impact: cutting pollution, waste, use of plastics and carbon emissions?

Now let's imagine that you can get the item that you want from a company with a strong reputation for corporate social responsibility. However, you can buy the same item more cheaply from a company which has a reputation for not acting in a responsible manner. What will you do?

What did they find?

Knowing that family environment affects individual behaviour, Henrik Cronqvist and Frank Yu (2017) wanted to find out whether family affected the decisions of chief executives. In particular, would having a daughter make chief executives more sensitive to issues such as diversity, the environment, employee relations, and other aspects of corporate social responsibility? They studied 416 chief executives of large, well-known American companies, collecting information on how many children they each had (2.5 on average), the gender of those children, and the gender of their first-born child. Only 3 per cent of these chief executives were female. Cronqvist and Yu then compared those family profiles with a standard measure of organizational corporate social responsibility.

What did they find? Did organizations score more highly on corporate social responsibility issues when the chief executive had a daughter? Or did having a daughter make no difference? Why should having a daughter in the family make any difference at all to chief executive decision making? **(Answers in chapter Recap.)**

Henrik Cronqvist

Frank Yu

One of the problems facing companies operating in countries where corruption is high concerns the expectation that bribes will be involved if business deals are to be agreed. However, a new Bribery Act came into force in the UK in 2010, and the defence of 'normal business practice' no longer applies. America has had a similar US Foreign Corrupt Practices Act since 1977, aimed at companies dealing with state and public sector contracts; UK legislation covers all business dealings. The penalties for corporate offences include unlimited fines for the organization and its directors, and a maximum ten-year jail sentence for individuals involved in bribery. Corporate hospitality is an unresolved problem. Hospitality is an accepted element of business, but lavish hospitality could be seen as bribery; deciding what is lavish or not is a matter of interpretation. Corporate anti-bribery policies and practices, including whistleblowing procedures, codes of conduct, and employee training, become important in this context, and may be seen as aspects of corporate social responsibility.

The actions of large, wealthy, powerful organizations can have a major impact on local communities and national economies, world trade, the environment, employment, job security, and employee health and pensions. Surely organizations must behave 'responsibly', and promote social and environmental issues? Along with management ethics, the importance of corporate responsibility has been highlighted by recent corporate scandals at Wells Fargo, Volkswagen, Samsung and Petrobras.

Be good, or else

It appears that many people still believe that 'greed is good', and that 'flexible ethics' are required to succeed in business. Reporting the findings from the Dow Jones State of Anti-Corruption Compliance Survey of 350 companies around the world, Jeremy Hazlehurst (2014) notes that 45 per cent claimed to have lost business to unethical competitors in 2013. At an individual level, 63 per cent of managers said that they had been asked to do something against their 'personal code', and 10 per cent said that they had resigned as a result. Several companies, however, appear to have achieved the ideal combination of 'doing well and doing good':

- *Walmart:* plans to use 100 per cent renewable energy and create zero waste by 2020, and will tie executive pay to meeting compliance targets and anti-corruption obligations.

→

- *Unilever:* aims to double the size of its business between 2010 and 2020 while halving its greenhouse gas emissions and waste and water usage, and source all raw agricultural products sustainably, while bringing clean water to 500 million people.

- *Marks & Spencer:* Plan A, launched in 2007, has helped the company to cut waste sent to landfill to zero, cut CO2 emissions by 23 per cent, reduce waste by 28 per cent and water use by 27 per cent – saving £320 million.

- *Nestlé:* to ensure good supplies of high-quality coffee, works with non-governmental organizations to provide over 50,000 small coffee producers and coopera-

tives in eight Latin America countries with loans, plant stock, fertilisers and pesticides, and technical advice and training - thus supporting its supply chain, and benefiting farmers.

- *Coca-Cola:* similar to Nestlé, has projects to increase the number of mangoes that can be grown from 40 to 600 an acre, securing the company's supply chain, and making farmers richer.

- *Johnson & Johnson:* helped employees to quit smoking, saving the company $250 million in healthcare costs; this project produced a return of $2.71 for every dollar spent.

Source: based on Hazlehurst (2014, p.18)

CRITICAL THINKING

Consider the CSR policies and practices described in the box 'Be good, or else'. What behaviours would you like to add to that list? What benefits would you expect those to produce?

CSR sounds desirable, but it has its critics. The concept is vague, and can mean different things in different settings. Managers who pay for community projects and make charitable donations are giving away money that belongs to shareholders, and which could be reinvested in the business, or used to improve pay and working conditions. Another objection is that, if you are acting legally, then by definition you are acting morally, so what's the problem? It is hard to distinguish between 'responsible' actions that reflect a concern for society, and actions designed to enhance the reputation of the company. It is also important to recognize that business laws and customs vary between countries and cultures. What constitutes fair and just ethical conduct depends on where you are in the world. Finally, CSR seems to overlook the benefits of competition, which leads to better quality products and services, and to reduced costs for consumers. Critics of CSR also argue that furthering social and environmental issues is the job of governments.

The popularity of CSR

Interest in the social impact of business dates from the early nineteenth century, with Robert Owen, who managed New Lanark Mills (Glasgow, Scotland) from 1800 to 1825. In contrast with other employers at the time, Owen wanted to give his workers good living and working conditions, education, and healthcare. It was not until the late 1960s, however, that corporate social responsibility and business ethics were taken more seriously. CSR has become popular for three main reasons.

1. *CSR as self-defence:* If we don't do it ourselves, we'll have it done to us. While operating within the law, organizations are still self-regulating in many respects. However, there is always the danger that a high-profile corporate scandal will create demand for new regulation. Enron and other similar fraud cases, for example, led to the introduction of new regulations affecting corporate governance in America (the infamous Sarbanes-Oxley Act, 2002). Expensive and cumbersome to implement, that legislation was designed to restore public confidence by improving corporate accounting controls. CSR can be seen as a strategy to demonstrate corporate concern with ethical behaviour and impact on the community.

2. *CSR as a result of increased affluence:* If we don't do it, they'll stop buying from us. Affluence encourages us to assess the behaviour of the companies from which we buy

products and services. If we feel that a company is not behaving in a socially responsible manner, then we withdraw our custom. Patterns of customer demand can affect corporate actions, for example by focusing on healthy eating, the promotion of ethical investment, and concern for the environment. CSR can soften criticism and maintain customer support.

3. *CSR as impression management:* Greenwashing: If we tell people how responsible we are, our reputation will improve profits. Every CSR initiative gets media attention, and free publicity. The company that makes visible contributions to society may find that sales and market share increase. False or exaggerated claims, however, can damage reputation. CSR can be seen as a strategy to manage the impression that the consuming public has of the organization, and as a result to get good public relations and free advertising.

CSR, sustainability and innovation

Many companies have linked CSR to product design and supply chain management, appointing chief sustainability officers to run sustainability units which employ sustainability consultants. Sustainability means making the most of scarce resources, reducing costs through lean production and 'tight' supply chains. Nike, which makes shoes, has a Materials Sustainability Index that tells designers about the environmental impact of products. The delivery company UPS uses a 'carbon calculator' to track the carbon footprint of individual packages. Strategies to improve sustainability can trigger innovation. Nike is making more clothes from polyester derived from recycled bottles, and has made a shoe with an 'upper' knitted from a single thread, replacing many wasteful components. Starbucks holds 'coffee cup summits' at the Massachusetts Institute of Technology to find ways to reduce the environmental impact of disposable cups. As companies become more frugal and imaginative, CSR contributes to profits as well as to reputation (*The Economist*, 2012).

 **RECAP**

1. *Understand the need for 'fit' between the organization and its environment.*

   - To survive, organizations have to adapt their internal structures, processes and behaviours to cope with complexity and the pace of external change.

   - External pressures on organizations come from the globalization of business, developments in information technology, and social and demographic trends.

   - Ansoff argues that bureaucratic organizations are effective in stable environments, but that fluid structures are more effective in 'turbulent' environments.

   - Duncan argues that what counts is the management perception of environmental uncertainty; perception determines the management response.

2. *Appreciate the strengths and limitations of PESTLE analysis and scenario planning tools.*

   - PESTLE analysis provides a comprehensive framework for identifying and planning responses to external factors that can affect an organization.

   - PESTLE analysis generates vast amounts of information, creating a time-consuming analysis problem, and making predictions based on this analysis can be difficult.

   - Explain the challenges and opportunities created by an ageing, multigenerational workforce.

   - Increased life expectancy and declining birthrates are a global phenomenon, and organizations face the challenges of managing an ageing, and age-diverse workforce.

   - Contrary to the negative stereotype, older workers have valuable experience and abilities, in communication, problem solving, and handling difficult situations, for example.

   - Creating an inclusive, age-diverse culture and tailoring job roles to suit older workers can be straightforward, inexpensive, and help to retain and transfer skills and knowledge.

   - It is possible for a workforce to have up to five generations represented at the same time: Veterans, Baby Boomers, Generation X, Generation Y, and Generation Z.

   - Boomers value stimulating colleagues, challenge, autonomy, flexibility, recognition, and being able to give back to society. Gen X are ambitious, strategic, people oriented, and autonomous, and do not share the sense of obligation to society of other generations. Gen Y and Boomers want to serve a

→

wider purpose; financial gain is not a main reason for choosing an employer. Gen Z are motivated by teamwork, personal development, and leading-edge technology.

- Age-diverse teams can increase job satisfaction and performance.

- Management practices need to reflect individual employee needs as well as the company's goals. This means emphasizing, in different ways for each generation, teamwork and collaboration, flexible working, phased retirement, project work, technology, short-term assignments, opportunities to support external causes and eco-friendly work environments.

- Generational differences may be exaggerated. Expectations of work may be more common than is widely assumed. Variation in approach to work within generations suggest that individual differences are as important as generational differences, and perhaps more so.

3. *Apply utilitarianism, theory of rights, and theory of justice to assess whether or not management actions are ethical, and recognize the limitations of those criteria.*

- The utilitarian perspective argues that behaviour is ethical if it achieves the greatest good for the greatest number.

- The theory of rights judges behaviour on the extent to which individual rights are respected, including right of free consent, right to privacy, right to freedom of conscience, right to free speech, right to due process in an impartial hearing.

- The theory of justice judges behaviour on whether or not the benefits and burdens flowing from an action are fairly, equitably and impartially distributed.

- These criteria produce different assessments of the same behaviour; circumstances can involve other factors, making the application of these criteria inappropriate.

4. *Understand the concept of corporate social responsibility, and the practical and ethical implications of this concept for organizational behaviour.*

- Businesses and their managers are expected to act in responsible and ethical ways, contributing to the triple bottom line – people and planet as well as profits.

- Responsible practices include, for example, the business contribution to the community, the sustainable use of resources, ethical behaviour in relationships with suppliers and customers, and 'common good balance sheet' reporting to complement financial reporting.

- Companies are encouraged to act responsibly by consumers adopting values-based purchasing, and investors adopting socially responsible investment practices; companies seen to be acting irresponsibly can have their reputations damaged rapidly through social media.

- Critics argue that it is government's job to deal with social and environmental issues. The role of business is to maximize profits while operating within the law. Managers who donate company funds to 'good causes' give away shareholders' money.

RECAP: What did they find?

Cronqvist and Yu (2017) found that organizations scored 12 per cent higher than the median on corporate social responsibility (CSR) issues when the chief executive had a daughter – about one third of the effect of the chief executive herself being female. Sons made no difference. Companies whose chief executive had a daughter spent 13 per cent more of corporate net income on social responsibility programmes, and scored above the medium in every other category of CSR that was measured:

CSR category	Score above median	Explanation
Diversity	+13.7%	Work–life benefits, women and minority contracting, employment of the disabled, gay and lesbian policies
Community	+6.5%	Charitable giving, support for housing and education
Employee relations	+6.3%	Union relations, profit sharing, employee involvement, retirement benefits, health and safety
Product	+6.0%	Quality, R&D, innovation, benefits to economically disadvantaged
Environment	+4.6%	Beneficial products and services, pollution prevention, recycling, clean energy
Human rights	+1.0%	Indigenous people's relations, labour rights

The researchers explain their results by pointing to a 'female socialization effect'. Women may care more about the well-being of others, and fathers may internalize those values. Fathers may have seen their daughters face discrimination in the labour market, thus affecting their attitudes to equality.

Revision

1. Explain the concept of *organizational stakeholder*. Choose an organization with which you are familiar. List its stakeholders. What expectations will they have of that organization?

2. What are the strengths and weaknesses of PESTLE analysis? Illustrate your answer with reference to issues and organizations with which you are familiar.

3. What are the benefits of employing older workers, and what are the benefits of an age-diverse workforce?

4. Why do organizations implement corporate social responsibility policies which cost money, but have no immediate or visible return on that investment?

Research assignment

Research by the fast-food chain McDonald's suggests that an age-diverse workforce is happier, gives better customer service, and improves business performance. You will find a report of their study on their website (search for 'McDonald's UK newsroom', and find 'Bridging the generation gap is the key to a happier workforce). This is the restaurant business. Are there aspects of this business that make age-diversity an asset to the company, and attractive to employees? Would you expect similar results concerning the benefits of age-diverse teams in other sectors – shipbuilding, insurance, rail transport, a bakery, a university department? Ask friends and relatives who have jobs about the other generations with whom they work. Do they like working in an age-diverse organization? Do they think that age-diversity increases job satisfaction and performance? How easy or difficult do you think it is to work closely with someone who is much older, or much younger, than you are? What do you conclude about the effects of age diversity in organizational settings?

Springboard

Stephen Bevan, Ian Brinkley, Zofia Bajorek and Cary Cooper (2018) *21st Century Workforces and Workplaces*. London: Bloomsbury. An informed review of the contemporary trends affecting organizations and the nature of work, assessing the evidence rather than the hype.

Alison Beard and Richard Hornik (2011) 'It's hard to be good', *Harvard Business Review*, 89 (11): 88–96. Profiles five companies with exemplary approaches to responsible business practices: Royal DSM (Netherlands), Southwest Airlines (US), Broad Group (China), Potash Corporation (Canada), and Unilever (UK).

Masud Chand and Rosalie L. Tung (2014) 'The ageing of the world's population and its effects on global business, *Academy of Management Perspectives*, 28 (4): 409–29. Explores the nature and implications of the rapid ageing of the world's population, and the implications for organizations in general, and for human resource policies in particular.

David and Jonah Stillman (2017) *Gen Z @ Work: How the Next Generation is Transforming The Workplace*. New York: HarperBusiness. Argues that Gen Z are different from Millennials. Technologically sophisticated, independent, pragmatic, competitive, suffering from FOMO (fear of missing out), accustomed to a sharing economy with no hierarchies.

OB cinema

Thank You for Smoking (2005, director Jason Reitman) DVD track 18: 1:13:39 to 1:20:26 (7 minutes). This is the story of a tobacco company spokesman and lobbyist for cigarettes. In this clip, Nick Naylor (played by Aaron Eckhart) testifies before a Senate hearing where issues of free choice and 'bad products' are discussed. As you watch this, identify:

1. Who are the cigarette companies' stakeholders?
2. What corporate social responsibility issues are raised here?
3. Where do you stand on the issue of freedom of choice for consumers?

Chapter exercises

1: Ethical conduct

Objectives
1. To explore the nature of ethical and unethical work behaviours.
2. To identify what makes some behaviour ethical, and some behaviour unethical.
3. To explore individual differences in reaching ethical judgements.

Briefing
The following table lists examples of behaviour at work (De Jong et al., 2008). Are these actions ethical? Tick your response in the column that best describes your opinion. Share your answers with colleagues. Note the *differences* in your responses. Explore and explain *why* you hold different views on these issues. What makes some behaviours ethical and some behaviours unethical? Are differences between individuals linked to age, sex, experience, culture, religion, or to other factors? What are the implications of these differences for you personally and for your relationships with others? What are the implications for managing a diverse multi-cultural workforce?

Behaviour	Always ethical	Ethical in some contexts	Always unethical
1 claim credit for the work of others	❏	❏	❏
2 withhold information to slow others down	❏	❏	❏
3 call in sick so that you can have the day off	❏	❏	❏
4 make a false time report	❏	❏	❏
5 pad your expenses claims	❏	❏	❏
6 accept gifts for favours	❏	❏	❏
7 use friends as sources of confidential information	❏	❏	❏
8 deliberately make your boss look bad	❏	❏	❏
9 use company materials for your own purposes	❏	❏	❏
10 report colleagues who violate company rules	❏	❏	❏
11 make friends with the power brokers	❏	❏	❏
12 give others gifts or bribes in return for favours	❏	❏	❏
13 deliberately make a colleague look bad	❏	❏	❏
14 conduct personal business on company time	❏	❏	❏
15 divulge confidential information to others	❏	❏	❏
16 deliberately take your time to complete a task	❏	❏	❏
17 drink alcohol during working hours	❏	❏	❏
18 buy company products, not those of competitors	❏	❏	❏
19 vote for issues because they support this company	❏	❏	❏
20 work for more than one employer at a time	❏	❏	❏

2: Profits versus people

Objectives   1. To explore the nature and implications of management views of ethical issues.

Briefing   In the late 'noughties' (2005–10), a lot of companies and managers found themselves accused of making a lot of money through 'suspect' business practices. Observers and commentators always say that, if they had been in charge, this would not have happened.

Individual ranking (1): Consider the following business values, and rank them in order of importance according to your own beliefs and principles:

1. Career development of employees
2. Concern for employees as people
3. Concern for the environment
4. Customer orientation
5. Efficiency
6. High quality of products and services
7. Integrity
8. Managerial and organizational effectiveness
9. Profit-making
10. Social responsibility

Individual ranking (2): Now rank these items again, this time according to the importance that you believe are actually given to them by practising managers.

Groupwork   In groups of three:

1. Develop a consensus ranking (from the most to the least important) of these business values based on the *personal sentiments and values* of your group's members.

2. Calculate the *practising managers'* rankings using the average of your group members' rankings (give 10 points to the top ranked item, 9 to the second, and so on).

Discussion   How does your group's consensus ranking of personal values compare with the practising managers' ranking? Is there a difference? If so, why?

References

Abraham, D. (2016) *The Elements of Power: Gadgets, Guns, and the Struggle for a Sustainable Future in the Rare Metal Age.* New Haven, CT and London: Yale University Press.

Ansoff, I. (1997) 'Measuring and managing for environmental turbulence: the Ansoff Associates approach', in Alexander Watson Hiam (ed.), *The Portable Conference on Change Management*: HRD Press Inc., pp.67–83.

Archer, P. (2010) 'Business ethics', *The Times Raconteur Supplement,* 18 May, p.1.

Beitelspacher, L. and Rodgers. V.L. (2018) 'Integrating corporate social responsibility awareness into a retail management course', *Journal of Marketing Education* (published online early) http://journals.sagepub. com/doi/10.1177/0273475318754933   [accessed January 2019].

Bond, S. (2017) 'Shoppers buy or boycott brands based on values', *Financial Times,* 19 June, p.18.

Bowman, G. (2016) 'The practice of scenario planning: an analysis of inter- and intra-organizational strategizing', *British Journal of Management,* 27 (1): 77–96.

Buckley, C. (2007) *Boomsday,* London: Allison & Busby.

Calnan, M. (2017a) 'Half of older employees plan to work past 65, says CIPD survey', *People Management,* 28 February https://www.peoplemanagement.co.uk/news/articles/half-of-older-employees-plan-to-work-past-65 [accessed 13 January 2018].

Calnan, M. (2017b) 'Generation Z more motivated by teamwork than the average worker', *People Management*, 17 August, [accessed January 2018] http://www2.cipd.co.uk/pm/peoplemanagement/b/weblog/archive/2017/08/17/generation-z-more-motivated-by-teamwork-than-the-average-worker.aspx

Cavanagh, G.F., Moberg, D.J. and Velasquez, M. (1981) 'The ethics of organizational politics', *Academy of Management Review*, 6(3): 363–74.

Chand, M. and Tung, R.L. (2014) 'The ageing of the world's population and its effects on global business', *Academy of Management Perspectives*, 28 (4): 409–29.

Chartered Management Institute (2014) *Management 2020: Leadership to Unlock Long-Term Growth*. London: Chartered Management Institute.

Chartered Institute for Personnel and Development (2015) *Avoiding the Demographic Crunch: Labour Supply and the Ageing Workforce*. London: Chartered Institute for Personnel and Development.

Chartered Institute for Personnel and Development (2016) *Creating Longer, More Fulfilling Working Lives: Employer Practice in Five European Countries*. London: Chartered Institute for Personnel and Development.

Child, J. (1997) 'Strategic choice in the analysis of action, structure, organizations and environments: retrospect and prospect', *Organization Studies*, 18(1): 43–76.

Clarke, R. (2016) 'Employees are happier in age-diverse teams, says study', *HR Review*, 7 September, http://www.hrreview.co.uk/hr-news/employees-happier-age-diverse-teams-says-study/101053 [accessed January 2019]

Conboye, J. (2017) 'When the manager is a millennial', *Financial Times*, 30 August, https://www.ft.com/content/2bda8436-34c2-11e7-99bd-13beb0903fa3 [accessed January 2018].

Cronqvist, H. and Yu, F. (2017) 'Shaped by their daughters: executives, female socialization, and corporate social responsibility', *Journal of Financial Economics*, 126(3): 543–62.

De Jong, P., Lancaster, J., Pelaez, P. and Munoz, J.S. (2008) 'Examination of correlates of ethical propensity and ethical intentions in the United States, Australia, and the Philippines: a managerial perspective', *International Journal of Management*, 25 (2): 270–78.

Dobbs, R., Ramaswamy, S., Stephenson, E. and Viguerie, S.P. (2014) 'Management intuition for the next 50 years', *McKinsey Quarterly* (3): 12–24.

Duncan, R.B. (1972) 'Characteristics of organizational environments and perceived environmental uncertainty', *Administrative Science Quarterly*, 17(3): 313–27.

Duncan, R.B. (1973) 'Multiple decision making structures in adapting to environmental uncertainty: the impact on organizational effectiveness', *Human Relations*, 26(3): 273–91.

Duncan, R.B. (1979) 'What is the right organization structure?: decision tree analysis provides the answer', *Organizational Dynamics*, 7(3): 59–80.

Duxbury, L. and Halinski, M. (2014) 'Dealing with the "grumpy boomers": re-engaging the disengaged and retaining talent', *Journal of Organizational Change Management*, 27 (4): 660–76.

Edgecliffe-Johnson, A. (2018) 'US companies cut corporate ties with National Rifle Association', *Financial Times*, 26 February, p.4.

Flood, C. (2017) 'Use of child labour fuels fear of reputational risk', *Financial Times*, 27 November, p.10.

Friedman, M. (1970) 'The social responsibility of business is to increase its profits', *New York Times Magazine* (13 September).

Friedrich, R., Peterson, M. and Koster, A. (2011), 'The rise of Generation C', *Strategy + Business Magazine*, issue 62, Spring, pp.1–6.

Giddens, A. (1990) *The Consequences of Modernity*. Cambridge and Oxford: Polity Press and Blackwell.

Giddens, A. and Sutton, P.W. (2009) *Sociology*, Cambridge: Polity Press.

Gratton, L. and Scott, A. (2016) *The 100-Year Life: Living and Working in an Age of Longevity*. London: Bloomsbury.

Gratton, L. and Scott, A. (2017) 'The corporate implications of longer lives', *MIT Sloan Management Review*, 58(3): 63–70.

Greenberg, E., Hirt, M. and Smit, S. (2017) 'The global forces inspiring a new narrative of progress', *McKinsey Quarterly*, 2: 33–52.

Groom, B. (2016a) 'Remodelling roles helps maintain traditional skills', *Financial Times*, 19 April, p.10.

Groom, B. (2016b) 'Inside the mind of a millennial', *Work*, Spring, pp.29–35.

Hales, C. (2002) 'Bureaucracy-lite and continuities in managerial work', *British Journal of Management*, 13 (1): 51–66.

Harris, B., Song, J-A. and Buseong, K. (2017) 'Korean cover-ups hide deadly work condition', *Financial Times*, 7 December, p.17.

Hausmann, L., du Rausas, M.P. and Weber, M. (2017) *Air Freight 2025: Agility, Speed, and Partnerships*. Munich and Paris: McKinsey & Company.

Hazlehurst, J. (2014) 'Be good', *Work*, June, pp.14–21.

Hewlett, S.A., Sherbin, L. and Sumberg, K. (2009), 'How Gen Y and Boomers will reshape your agenda', *Harvard Business Review*, 87(7/8): 71–76.

Hirt, M. and Smit, S. (2017) *Economic Conditions Snapshot 2017.* London: McKinsey & Company.

Houghton, E. and Spence, P. (2016) *People Measurement and Reporting: From Theory to Practice.* London: Chartered Institute for Personnel and Development.

Hudson Consulting (2014) *The Great Generational Shift: Why The Differences Between Generations Will Reshape Your Workplace.* New York and London.

Jacobs, E. (2017) 'The "unretired": coming back to work in an office near you', *Financial Times,* 4 December, p.14.

Kunze, F. and Menges, J.I. (2017) 'Younger supervisors, older subordinates: an organizational-level study of age differences, emotions, and performance', *Journal of Organizational Behavior,* 38 (4): 461–86.

Kunze, F., Boehm, S. and Bruch, H. (2013) 'Age, resistance to change, and job performance', *Journal of Managerial Psychology,* 28 (7/8): 741–60.

McCrindle, M. (2014) *The ABC of XYZ: Understanding the Global Generations.* Bella Vista NSW: McCrindle Research.

McLaverty, Christopher and McKee, Annie (2016) 'What you can do to improve ethics at your company', *Harvard Business Review* (online), 29 December: 2–5 https://hbr.org/2016/12/what-you-can-do-to-improve-ethics-at-your-company [accessed January 2019]

Marvell, R. and Cox, A. (2016) *Fulfilling Work: What do Older Workers Value About Work and Why?* London: Institute of Employment Studies and Centre for Ageing Better.

Masters, B. (2018) 'BackRock's gun-free funds show ethical investing is a good bet', *Financial Times,* 11 April, p. 11.

Morrison, M. and Weeks, A. (2017) *Pestle Analysis Factsheet,* Chartered Institute for Personnel and Development, London.

Rudolph, C.W., Rauvola, R.S. and Zacher, H. (2018) 'Leadership and generations at work: a critical review', *The Leadership Quarterly,* 29 (1): 44–57.

Russell, T. (2017) *Business Ethics and the Role of HR Factsheet.* London: Chartered Institute for Personnel and Development.

Simms, J. (2017) 'Don't jump the shark', *Work,* Summer, pp.44–55.

Skapinker, M. (2015) 'What helps companies endure longer than others?', *The Times,* 8 April, p.7.

Skapinker, M. (2016) 'Planning on living to 100?: prepare for a fight at work', *Financial Times,* 9 June, p.12.

The Economist (2012) 'Schumpeter: good business, nice beaches', 19 May, p.66.

The Economist (2017) 'Generation SRI', 25 November, pp.75–76.

The Economist (2018) 'Gender and investing: the power of money', 10 March, pp.71–72.

Velasquez, M., Moberg, D.J. and Cavanagh, G.F. (1983) 'Organizational statesmanship and dirty politics: ethical guidelines for the organizational politician', *Organizational Dynamics,* 12(2): 65–80.

Wilkinson, A. and Kupers, R. (2013) 'Living in the futures: how scenario planning changed corporate strategy', *Harvard Business Review,* 94 (5): 118–27.

Zheltoukhova, K. and Baczor, L. (2016) *Attitudes to Employability and Talent.* London: Chartered Institute for Personnel and Development.

Technology

Key terms

second machine age

computerization

technological determinism

organizational choice

socio-technical system design

robots

cobots

artificial intelligence

augmented reality

replacement effects

compensatory mechanisms

social matrix

Learning outcomes

When you have read this chapter, you should be able to define those
key terms in your own words, and you should also be able to:

1. Understand the nature and organizational implications of 'the
    second machine age'.

2. Explain criticisms of technological determinism from a socio-
    technical systems point of view.

3. Understand the capabilities of advanced robotics and the
    implications for the nature of work and employment.

4. Understand the capabilities of artificial intelligence and the
    implications for the automation of knowledge work.

5. Understand the capabilities of augmented reality and how these
    systems will affect the nature of work.

6. Assess the impact of new technologies on employment – mass
    redundancies, or job creation?

7. Understand the nature of 'the social matrix', the potential
    organizational uses of social media technologies, and the risks
    involved.

Why study technology?

Changing jobs

'The world of work is facing an epochal transition. By 2030, according to a recent McKinsey Global Institute report, as many as 375 million workers – or roughly 14 per cent of the global workforce – may need to switch occupational categories as digitization, automation and advances in artificial intelligence (AI) disrupt the world of work. The kinds of skills companies require will shift, with profound implications for the career paths individuals will need to pursue' (Illanes et al., 2018, p.1).

Technology affects most aspects of your life: how you communicate and share information; how you buy goods and services; how you find places and travel; how and what you study; how you discover and apply for job vacancies; how you spend your leisure time. Technology also affects the work that you do, and the skills and knowledge that you need to do it. But in future, if some predictions come good, your job could be done just as well by a machine. Traditionally, automation has only affected simple manual tasks. However, developments in artificial intelligence and machine learning mean that the jobs of professional knowledge workers are no longer safe from automation. What are the management implications of these radical changes to the world of work? How can you avoid being replaced by a machine? How will you future-proof your own career?

Second machine age a twenty-first-century phenomenon based on computing developments which will affect tasks previously considered impossible to automate.

We are now in the second machine age. The new technologies that we are seeing are powerful and widespread. As with the first machine age, these developments will reshape our economy, society, culture, organizations, and the nature of work. The first machine age began with the steam engine, which led to the Industrial Revolution in the eighteenth century. Erik Brynjolfsson and Andrew McAfee (2014) argue that the second machine age is based on computerization, which has three properties:

Computerization job automation by means of computer-controlled equipment.

1. *Exponential growth in computing power:* computers are performing more functions, faster, on smaller and cheaper devices.

2. *Big data and powerful analytics:* everything that we do online leaves a digital trace, which is recorded, thus producing vast amounts of information about your behaviour.

3. *Innovations that can be combined and recombined with other innovations:* if you design a new app, you do not have to first invent the internet and the smartphone – they are already there.

This age is also called the Fourth Industrial Revolution. The first three relied on steam, electricity and computing. The fourth is now being driven by robotics and artificial intelligence. There are few sectors, and few organizations, that will not be affected.

STOP AND SEARCH YouTube for *Microchipping employees* (5:12) to find out how the Wisconsin software company Three Square Market is using implants, between the thumb and forefinger. Using near-field communication (NFC) technology, these chips can be used to pay for food in the canteen, open doors, log into computers and use the photocopier (DelMonaco, 2017). What concerns does this development raise for employees?

Computerizing Lego

Lego, the highly profitable (and privately-owned) Danish toy manufacturer, famous for its coloured bricks, is not immune from computerization. The company's traditional business model is simple, transforming plastic that costs $1 a kilo into Lego box sets which sell for $75 a kilo. However, children increasingly play games on iPads and smartphones, and Lego's sales growth slowed after 2010. How can Lego compete in the evolving digital world?

Lego's first experiment with the online game, *Lego Universe,* was not successful. They then developed a partnership with a Swedish company, Mojang, which designed *Minecraft,* a popular computer game based on virtual landscapes resembling Lego building blocks. Lego now sells sets based on the game. Another partnership involved TT Games, to develop video games based on Lego ranges such as *Star Wars* and *Legends of Chima. The Lego Movie,* made in collaboration with Warner Bros in 2014, generated $500 million when it was released. In partnership with Google, *The Lego Movie* was accompanied by a video game, new construction sets (the Giant Sea Cow pirate ship and the hero Emmet Brickowski), and a website (**www.buildwithchrome.com**). The movie sequel appeared in 2017. Another innovation was *Lego Fusion.* Items built with Lego bricks are captured using a smartphone or tablet which imports them into a 3D digital online world where users can play using their own

designs. Lego was one of the most-watched brands on YouTube. Emphasizing the continuing importance of the physical brick, and physical play, Lego's chief executive, Jørgen Vig Knudstorp, explained that, 'I see digital as an extra experience layer' (Milne, 2014). With record sales and earnings, Lego became the world's most popular and most profitable toymaker in 2015; the company estimates that, on average, every person on earth owns 102 Lego bricks (Milne, 2015).

CRITICAL THINKING   How will the second machine age affect you? Can a robot do your job? Find out here: https://ig.ft.com/can-a-robot-do-your-job/

The pace of innovation is such that there is probably more change and disruption to come. Computers can forecast property prices, teach students, grade exams, and design beer bottles – better and cheaper than we can, meaning better and cheaper products and services. But there are problems. First, the scale and pace of automation may create mass redundancies. Second, while those in routine office jobs and manufacturing were traditionally under threat, computerization is now affecting knowledge workers: accountants, doctors, lawyers and managers. This could create a 'two tier' society with a well-paid elite, and everybody else – who either have no jobs, or who perform simple routine 'screen-sitting' or menial manual work. Third, widespread computerization may lead to higher levels of cybercrime.

Determinism or choice

We first have to consider a fundamental question: to what extent does technology determine the nature of work? Compare a hospital with a call centre. Their different technologies seem to determine the kinds of tasks that need to be done, the knowledge and skills required, how work is organized and the organization structure. The argument that

Technological determinism the argument that technology explains the nature of jobs, skill and knowledge requirements, and organization structure.

technology has predictable outcomes for work and organization is called technological determinism.

Does technology really determine these factors? Does work have to be organized to meet the demands of the technology? Many studies (notably in coal mining, textile manufacturing, and car assembly), from the 1940s onwards, have shown that this is not the case (Trist and Bamforth, 1951, is a classic example). Whatever the technology, jobs can be designed with different levels of variety, autonomy, responsibility, and interaction with others. These are job design choices.

For example, it is important to note that, just because a job can be automated, does not mean that it will be. This too is a matter of choice. People may be cheaper than equipment, and may produce similar outputs. For some tasks, human judgement may be desirable, to monitor a process, solve problems, avoid breakdowns and maintain continuity of operations. In the provision of some services, customers may prefer to interact with a person rather than a machine.

Organizational choice the argument that work design and organization structure depend on decisions about how and why technology is used, and not by the technology itself.

Determinism is an oversimplified perspective, which overlooks the importance of organizational choice. Choice involves the design of equipment and systems, such as how much control is built into a machine, and what human intervention and discretion are allowed or required. There are choices concerning the goals that a technology is being used to pursue: reduce costs, improve quality, generate management information, or enhance employee surveillance and control. There are choices in how work is organized and how jobs are designed: see box, 'How to make hi-fi'.

These choices are based on assumptions about human capabilities and organizational characteristics. They rely less on the capabilities of particular items of equipment. These are called 'psychosocial assumptions', concerning beliefs about individuals and groups. To consider the 'impact' of a technology, therefore, is to consider the wrong question. Technological innovations trigger decision making and negotiation processes which are driven by the perceptions, goals and assumptions of those who are involved. The outcomes of those processes influence the 'impact' of technology.

Socio-technical system design an approach to job and organization design which tries to find the best fit between the social and technological dimensions

To help understand these issues, researchers at the Tavistock Institute in London (Emery and Trist, 1960) developed the concept of socio-technical system design. An organizational system that is designed to satisfy social needs, ignoring the technical system, will run into problems. But a system designed to meet only the demands of the technology will create social and organizational problems. The aim, therefore, has to be 'joint optimization' of the social and technical dimensions.

How to make Hi-Fi

Linn Products, based in Glasgow (Scotland), makes top-of-the-range audio equipment. Despite the engineering sophistication and complexity, every product is assembled by hand, by a single employee. The company's founder and executive chairman, Ivor Tiefenbrun, explains why he abandoned the traditional assembly line in favour of 'single-stage build':

'Early on, we did use an assembly line and tried to operate like a mini General Motors. But try as I might, I couldn't get all the manufacturing processes to synchronize efficiently. So, one day, I asked one of the women on the turntable assembly line to collect all the parts of the product, assemble it, and bring it to me. She looked at me a little strangely, went and gathered the components, and assembled the turntable in 17 and a half minutes – a process that took 22 and a half minutes on the line.

'That was an 'aha' moment for me. We reorganized the factory to accommodate a single-stage build model, using computer-controlled vehicles to distribute materials to work positions, and taught everyone in the plant how to build any product we made. That way, we could do real-time manufacturing, let customer orders

→

pull, reconfigure the factory, and shift resources as needed to produce what customers wanted that day.

'When one person builds a product from start to finish, they feel responsible for it and can see the connection between what they do and how the product performs. And since the people who build the products are often responsible for servicing them later, those employees interact with customers and see how happy – or unhappy – they are. So, they're learning a lot more than just how to assemble a product. They start to spot connections that no engineer, service technician, or assembly-line worker ever would, and bring skills developed in one area to bear on what they do somewhere else. As a result, they can contribute to product quality with improvements and innovation' (Morse, 2006; Everard, 2013).

Is there a position between determinism and choice? Technology must have some influence on work and organization. As we will see, technological innovations in the second machine age mean that more manual tasks can be automated. In addition, many tasks requiring complex cognitive skills can now be performed by clever computer systems. Paradoxically, we could see more demand for creative, problem-solving, management and leadership skills. Jobs for graduates in the STEM subjects – science, technology, engineering, mathematics – are likely to grow in number faster than non-STEM subjects. Rather than determining the outcomes, however, our smart new technologies have *enabling* properties. They open up fresh choices and possibilities. The outcomes will depend on how we use our socio-technical system design choices.

CRITICAL THINKING

The online retail company Amazon has patented a wristband that is designed to collect information about the location and movements of workers in its warehouses. The wristband can also vibrate in order to guide workers' actions and to maximize efficiency (*The Economist,* 2018). Is this a good way in which to use the technology – or is this an inappropriate choice? Explain your view.

The second machine age

Service with a (robotic) smile

Singapore restricts the number of foreigners who can work there. This creates staff shortages, and companies are using automation to solve the problem. For example, at the Chilli Pad Nonya café, a robot waiter moves between the tables saying, 'Could you help me to clear your table?'. Customers put their used dishes on a tray which the robot takes back to the kitchen. The restaurant manager says that:

'In Singapore it's very difficult to get manpower from overseas, so it's very helpful to get a robot. The customers are coming back because of the robot. They like to see it.'

These service robots are expensive, costing over US$30,000, but government subsidies cover a high proportion of this. Pizza Hut in Asia is also using robots to

take customer orders and process card payments, giving waiting staff more time to interact with customers.

Source: based on Vasagar (2016)

The three technologies that are probably going to have the greatest impact on work and employment in the next decade are advanced robotics, artificial intelligence (AI) and augmented reality. What are the capabilities of these technologies? What impacts will they have?

Advanced robotics

Robots physical machines that move within an environment with a degree of autonomy

For most of the twentieth century, robots were simply articulated arms, located in one place and often behind screens or in cages to protect human operators. Such robots are good at performing routine manufacturing tasks. This changed with the turn of the millennium. We now have humanoid robots that walk on two legs, mobile robots that shuttle pallets around warehouses, and autonomous vehicles. The main feature that these developments have in common is *mobility*. This is due to advances in hardware (sensors and materials), software, and large datasets or 'big data' (see **Chapter 1**).

Cobots collaborative robots that work alongside and help human workers

Moving around and working alongside humans, cobots (collaborative robots) are now used to handle jobs that used to need human dexterity and eyesight, and to deal with the problems of labour shortages and rising wages. Cobots can do things that humans find physically difficult or unpleasant. They are light and easy to move between tasks, and do not require specialist programming skills. This means they can be used by smaller organizations, which could not afford more expensive traditional robots.

One example is Sawyer, one of a new generation of cobots designed to work safely alongside and assist employees. They are also known as service robots. Made by an American company, Rethink Robotics, Sawyer has a single arm, and can perform a range of tasks in electronics manufacturing such as machine tending and circuit board testing. Another cobot, from Universal Robots, a Danish company, is called UR3, and is a small table-top device that can assemble, polish, glue and screw components and pack eggs. Rather than threaten job security, cobots can work with and help employees in various ways. With an ageing workforce, cobots could help companies to retain the services of older workers. Research by MIT and BMW found that robot-human teams were 85 per cent more productive than either working alone (Hollinger, 2016).

Sawyer the cobot

Showing how the technology has developed, Benedict Dellot and Fabian Wallace-Stephens (2017) identify the five different kinds of robots shown in Figure 3.1: articulated robots (with which we are probably most familiar), assistance robots, humanoid robots, mobile robots and serpentine robots. Expect to see more of these pieces of equipment coming into use, in factories, offices, hospitals, shops, schools – and elsewhere – in the coming years. The question to which everybody wants an answer is – will a robot steal my job? We will explore this possibility shortly.

Robots not welcome?

Robots may not always deliver the benefits they promise. Sarah Fletcher (2018) describes the experience of an animal charity in San Francisco that had security problems, with break-ins and vandalism, and local drug users who made staff and visitors feel unsafe. They employed a 1.5 metre tall Knightscope security robot. The robot patrolled nearby car parks and alleyways, taking video recordings, and saying 'hello' to passers-by. However, it was accused of harassing homeless people. Calls for retribution appeared on social media, and the charity suffered more vandalism. The Knightscope was regularly tripped over, was covered by a tarpaulin, and smeared with barbecue sauce (and worse). Other robots have been tripped up by angry office workers, and a robot in another city in America accidentally knocked over a toddler.

Robots with artificial intelligence routinely provide care for children and the elderly, they work in hospitals, perform surgery, deliver customer care, and play a range of analytical roles in offices. But Fletcher sees the spread of workplace robots as a major challenge.

How far are we willing to – or should we at all – let robots into the workplace? What kinds of roles are acceptable and which are not? Most importantly, who sets the rules for how they behave, and how they decide on priorities when interacting with people?

Knightscope security robot patrolling a shopping mall

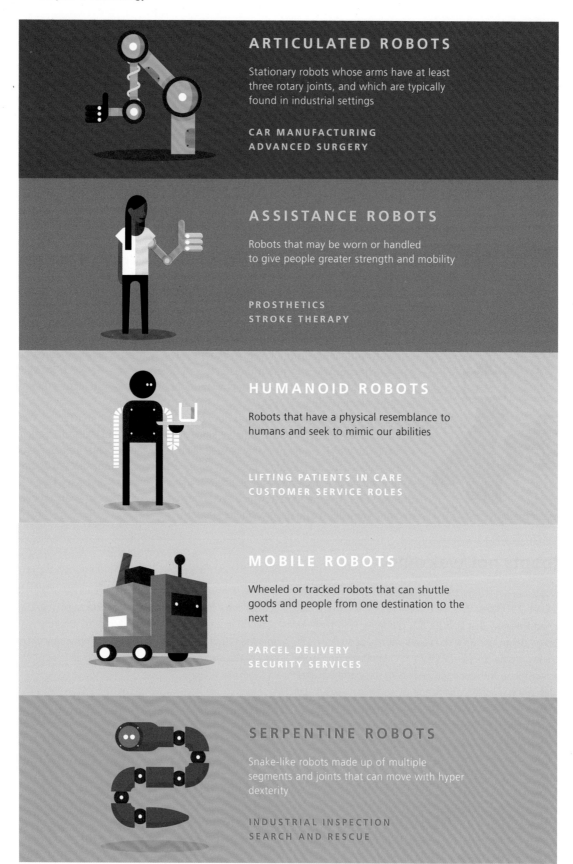

Figure 3.1: An overview of robots
Source: Designed by Nic Hinton, © RSA reproduced with permission from Dellot, B. and Wallace-Stephens, F. (2017) *The Age of Automation: Artificial Intelligence, Robotics and the Future of Low-Skilled Work*. London: RSA Action and Research Centre, page 25.

Wearable robots help human workers challenge the machines

Richard Waters, West Coast editor for the *Financial Times*, demonstrates the latest exoskeleton technology, designed to help older workers in particular.

Artificial intelligence (AI) and intelligence augmentation (IA)

Artificial intelligence tasks performed by computer software that would otherwise require human intelligence

Some reports have suggested that artificially intelligent systems could turn against us and take control, steal jobs and make humans obsolete, erode privacy, and dehumanize the world. This makes interesting reading, but the evidence suggests that these predictions are exaggerated. The concept of artificial intelligence (AI) dates from the 1950s. AI development was initially funded by the US government Defense Advanced Research Projects Agency. But the research made limited progress, and funding was cut back in the 1970s. With developments in computing power and the availability of 'big data', artificial intelligence is now evolving rapidly. AI can now be found in autonomous vehicles, machine translation, automatic speech recognition, face recognition, spam filters, search engines, digital assistants and AI-enabled drones which are used in disaster relief operations.

AI everywhere

'Johnson & Johnson, a consumer-goods firm, and Accenture, a consultancy, use AI to sort through job applications and pick the best candidates. AI helps Caesars, a casino and hotel group, guess customers' likely spending and offer personalized promotions to draw them in. Bloomberg, a media and financial information firm, uses AI to scan companies' earnings releases and automatically generate news articles. Vodafone, a mobile operator, can predict problems with its network and with users' devices before they arise. Companies in every industry use AI to monitor cybersecurity threats and other risks, such as disgruntled employees' (Bass, 2018, p.3).

Two main developments are reshaping AI today. The first is machine learning, which involves 'training' algorithms how to operate using existing data. Machine learning programmes use pattern recognition to create generalized rules which make sense of future inputs. Advanced machine learning systems, given enough data, can teach themselves and improve their own performance. The second development is deep learning, which uses layers of pattern recognition based on complex neural networks which are designed to simulate our brain functions. A study at King's College London found that deep learning methods more than doubled the accuracy of brain age assessments when using data from MRI scans (Dellot and Wallace-Stephens, 2017, p.20).

Artificial intelligence (AI) is a contemporary buzzword. It is often associated with computers that can beat humans at complex board games such as chess and Go. These technologies, however, can do much more than play games. Figure 3.2 explains the components of artificial intelligence: expert systems, machine learning, deep learning, reinforcement learning and transfer learning.

There are three types of AI: narrow, general and super (Brockhaus et al., 2018, p.13):

Narrow AI: Systems that can perform discrete tasks with strict boundaries, such as:

- *Image recognition*: used in self-service desks at passport control, and automatic name tagging on Facebook photos
- *Natural language processing*: used in voice recognition for AI assistants like Amazon Echo and Google Home
- *Information retrieval*: used in search engines
- *Reasoning using logic or evidence*: used in mortgage underwriting and determining the likelihood of fraud

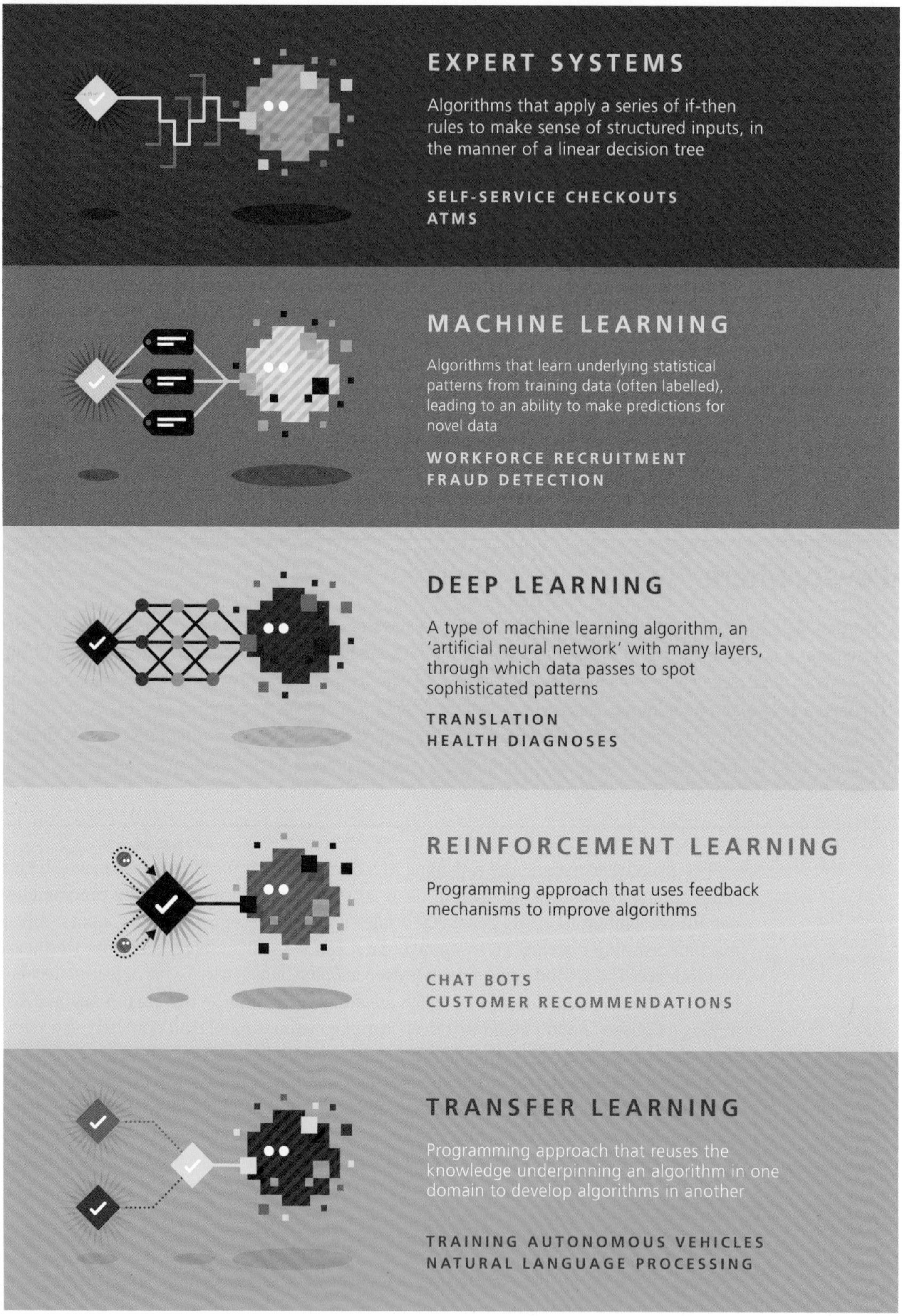

EXPERT SYSTEMS

Algorithms that apply a series of if-then rules to make sense of structured inputs, in the manner of a linear decision tree

SELF-SERVICE CHECKOUTS
ATMS

MACHINE LEARNING

Algorithms that learn underlying statistical patterns from training data (often labelled), leading to an ability to make predictions for novel data

WORKFORCE RECRUITMENT
FRAUD DETECTION

DEEP LEARNING

A type of machine learning algorithm, an 'artificial neural network' with many layers, through which data passes to spot sophisticated patterns

TRANSLATION
HEALTH DIAGNOSES

REINFORCEMENT LEARNING

Programming approach that uses feedback mechanisms to improve algorithms

CHAT BOTS
CUSTOMER RECOMMENDATIONS

TRANSFER LEARNING

Programming approach that reuses the knowledge underpinning an algorithm in one domain to develop algorithms in another

TRAINING AUTONOMOUS VEHICLES
NATURAL LANGUAGE PROCESSING

Figure 3.2: An overview of artificial intelligence
Source: Designed by Nic Hinton, © RSA reproduced with permission from Dellot, B. and Wallace-Stephens, F. (2017) *The Age of Automation: Artificial Intelligence, Robotics and the Future of Low-Skilled Work*. London: RSA Action and Research Centre, page 26.

General AI: Systems which can understand their environment, and reason and act accordingly, carrying out tasks such as greeting customers, and creating works of art; these kinds of systems are still in development

Super AI: Systems that are smarter than the best human brains, and which can make deductions about unknown environments; whether and how these systems will be developed is the subject of intense debate.

General and super AI are still in their infancy. In contrast, applications of narrow AI are common, based on three types of intelligence: sensing, reasoning, and communicating. These were once considered to be beyond the capabilities of machines. This is no longer the case.

Automation began with simple routine tasks in manufacturing and office administration. It is more difficult to automate tasks where adaptability, flexibility, judgement and sophisticated cognitive skills are required, such as legal writing, driving a car and managing people. However, there have been breakthroughs in situational awareness, and the ability of robots to grasp objects and replicate hand-eye coordination. Those 'difficult' tasks are now easier to automate.

Will knowledge workers be replaced by machines, like manual workers before them? We can use AI to automate jobs and replace people, but we can also use 'intelligence augmentation' (IA) systems, which do not replace individual expertise but enable us to work faster and more effectively. This means that knowledge workers have more time to deal with interesting, complex and challenging tasks, making them more productive. For example, automated decision support for air traffic controllers increases their accuracy and performance. A study of an automated dispensing system in a hospital found that this reduced the amount of time pharmacists spent in the dispensary, and allowed them to spend more time with patients on wards (Hislop et al., 2017). IA systems are also used to aid medical diagnosis, and by law firms to search documents for litigation and due diligence purposes.

Other current applications of AI and robotics include (Dellot and Wallace-Stephens, 2017):

- Cancer detection: using a deep learning algorithm
- Media reports: based on quarterly corporate earnings
- Construction: bricklaying
- Utility repairs: such as failed pipes
- Parcel delivery: autonomous wheeled robots
- Patient care: lifting and moving patients
- Fraud detection: machine learning spots fraudulent behaviour in financial transactions
- Housing inspections: tracking unlicensed landlords, protecting vulnerable tenants
- Online shopping: learning customer preferences, offering personalized recommendations

Why should organizations invest in artificial intelligence? A survey of 250 executives identified the business benefits shown in Table 3.1 (Davenport and Ronanki, 2018, p.112):

Would you let a computer write job ads?

An American company, Textio, uses artificial intelligence to analyse millions of job advertisements, looking for words and phrases that are statistically proven to be more likely to attract applications from men or from women. Terms that attract men include: exhaustive, enforcement, fearless, wickedly, fast-paced, and ruthlessly. Women are more likely to be attracted by terms such as: transparent, catalyst, in touch with, our family, storytelling, and building alliances. Textio can tell an organization if its job advertisements are biased. It can also use artificial intelligence to write better, unbiased job ads (Frean, 2018).

Table 3.1: Business benefits of artificial intelligence

Benefits	% of executives citing as AI benefit
Enhance features, functions and performance of products	51
Optimize internal business operations	36
Free up workers to be more creative by automating tasks	36
Make better decisions	35
Create new products	32
Optimize external processes such as marketing and sales	30
Pursue new markets	25
Capture and apply scarce knowledge where needed	25
Reduce head count through automation	22

The main objective was to make existing products better. Only 22 per cent mentioned reducing head count, but 36 per cent mentioned freeing up workers to be more creative. The same survey found a number of challenges facing companies seeking to develop AI:

- Problems integrating AI with existing processes and systems
- Expensive technologies and expertise
- Lack of management understanding of AI and how it works
- Lack of people with appropriate expertise
- Immature technology
- Technology that has been 'oversold'

As decisions come to rely more on 'big data', will 'thinking machines' take over top management jobs? Kirkland (2014) argues that data analytics software with pattern-matching capabilities may be able to solve some problems better than managers who rely on intuition and personal experience. However, he concludes that, because computers are not good at innovating, top executives will still be required for their creative abilities, leadership skills and strategic thinking:

> 'I've still never seen a piece of technology that could negotiate effectively. Or motivate and lead a team. Or figure out what's going on in a rich social situation or what motivates people and how you get them to move in the direction you want. These are human abilities. They're going to stick around' (Kirkland, 2014, p.72).

 **STOP AND SEARCH**   YouTube for *Ask the AI experts* (short videos by the consulting firm McKinsey; 2:00 to 4:00).

The work of chief executives and other senior managers requires a high degree of social intelligence, dealing with senior colleagues and other officials to discuss future plans and strategies, coordinate activities, resolve problems, and to negotiate and approve contracts and agreements. Consequently, most (but not all) management, business and finance occupations where social intelligence is necessary face a low risk of being affected by computerization, as with many jobs in education, healthcare, the arts and media. (See 'Replaced by an algorithm' below, which describes how one finance job was automated.) Engineering and science occupations where creative intelligence is required are also low risk. Lawyers are low risk, but paralegals and legal assistants are high risk. In general, high-skill/high-wage occupations are least susceptible to computerization.

Replaced by an algorithm

'Tom Gordon was 45 when his lucrative career as an oil trader suddenly faced a new threat. Electronic trading, which originally had been introduced to expand trading capacity overnight, was now operating head-to-head with Gordon and his colleagues on the floor of the exchange during the day. Gordon says he used to handle between 500 and 750 trades a day. In his nearly 25 years as a trader he recalls recording only two months of losses. But even the high volumes that a successful trader like Gordon could handle were quickly overshadowed by the volumes electronic systems were capable of processing.

'For Gordon, working alongside the electronic market was like being hit by a truck. "I saw the transition was coming and knew [traders] were going to get run over," he says. He eventually left and retrained as a social worker. He was wise to do so, because a few years later, in 2016, CME Group, which owns the New York Mercantile Exchange (Nymex), closed the last of its remaining commodity-trading pits. Gordon says some of his former colleagues have struggled to cope in their new lives. "Some have done quite well, but for many of the people it really broke their lives and their spirit." Losing a job to a machine or algorithm carries a unique psychological burden, says Marty Nemko, a psychologist and career counsellor.' (Extracts from Waters, 2017)

FT   *Source:* R. Waters (2017)
© Financial Times, 13 September 2017, reproduced with permission

Augmented reality

Augmented reality technology that superimposes digital information and images on the physical world through a screen, such as a smartphone, iPad or television.

You already know something of what augmented reality (AR) can do, with smartphone apps such as *Pokémon Go* and *Zombie Shooter*. Using your phone's camera, these games superimpose three-dimensional moving images onto the real world around you, and allow you to interact with them (capturing the creatures, killing the walking dead). With *Ikea Place,* you can see how a piece of furniture will look in your home, as you walk

around it, and change its position in a room. The 'heads-up' displays that show navigation and collision warning information on the screen in the car driver's line of sight are further examples of AR.

These are examples of intelligence augmentation. Augmented reality systems will improve the performance of individuals and teams, and are likely to have a limited effect on job numbers.

Virtual reality is a different technology, which replaces physical reality with a computer-generated environment. However, AR and VR can be combined for entertainment and training purposes, and to enable collaboration and teamwork in dispersed employee groups. Ford Motor Company uses VR to create a virtual workshop where engineers from different locations can collaborate in real time on life-size holograms of vehicle prototypes, walking around and inside to explore design options.

Most of the information that we use, including this page, is two-dimensional. However, we live in a three-dimensional world. AR creates a new kind of interface between people and machines, bridging the gap between 2-D and 3-D information. AR thus promises not only to augment reality, but also to complement and enhance human capabilities. Michael Porter and James Heppelmann (2017, p.48) note that 'AR allows people to process the physical and digital simultaneously, eliminating the need to mentally bridge the two. That improves our ability to rapidly and accurately absorb information, make decisions, and execute required tasks quickly and efficiently'.

Porter and Heppelmann argue that the impact of AR will spread with the growing number of smart connected products (SCPs), also known as 'the internet of things'. AR is currently available mainly through mobile devices, but these are being complemented by wearable technologies such as head-mounted displays and smart glasses. Many factories, for example, are experimenting with wearable AR devices that superimpose production, assembly, and servicing instructions directly onto real objects and manufacturing environments, replacing traditional paper manuals and training methods.

AR has three main capabilities: visualization, instruction and guidance and interaction.

Visualization

AR applications allow users to see inside objects in ways not previously possible. The medical device manufacturer AccuVein uses AR technology to convert the heat signature of a patient's veins into an image that is superimposed on the patient's skin. This makes the veins easier to find, and reduces the mistakes that are often made when taking blood. Workers at the BMW plant in Shenyang in China wear exoskeletons, smart gloves, and augmented reality glasses that allow them to see inside a virtual reality engine and chat online with the plant's AI bot called Xiao Bao (Clover and McGee, 2017).

> 'AR is making advances in consumer markets, but its emerging impact on human performance is even greater in industrial settings. Consider how Newport News Shipbuilding, which designs and builds US Navy aircraft carriers, uses AR near the end of its manufacturing process to inspect a ship, marking for removal those steel construction structures that are not part of the finished carrier. Historically, engineers had to constantly compare the actual ship with complex 2-D blueprints. But with AR, they can now see the final design superimposed on the ship, which reduces inspection time by 96 per cent from 36 hours to just 90 minutes. Overall, time savings of 25 per cent or more are typical for manufacturing tasks using AR' (Porter and Heppelmann, 2017, pp.48–49).

Instruction and guidance

AR provides real-time, step-by-step visual guidance on how to perform tasks, such as product assembly or machine operation. Traditional 2-D drawings and manuals are replaced by interactive holograms. Boeing uses AR to train employees in the 50 steps involved in assembling an aircraft wing section which has 30 components. This reduces the training time by more than a third, and the number of inexperienced trainees who can perform the operation correctly the first time has increased by 90 per cent. AR can transmit what a user sees to a remote expert, putting the expert at the user's side. This improves performance, and cuts costs. The parcel delivery company DHL relies on hiring and training temporary staff to cope with occasional sharp increases in demand. AR is used to train newcomers on navigating warehouses, sorting items and packing materials. The company now needs fewer traditional instructors, and new staff become productive more quickly.

Interaction

AR can superimpose a virtual control panel directly onto an SCP, such as a machine, which can then be operated using an AR headset or smart glasses, voice commands, hand gestures, or direction of gaze. This removes the need for knobs and levers and touchscreens. For example, a factory worker wearing smart glasses can walk along a line of machines, see how they are performing, and make any necessary adjustments without having to touch them.

In contrast with the apocalyptic forecasts of the impact of artificial intelligence and robots, Porter and Heppelmann (2017, p.57) see AR and its implications in a more positive light:

> 'While the advances in artificial intelligence and robotics are impressive, we believe that combining the capabilities of machines with humans' distinctive strengths will lead to far greater productivity and more value creation than either could generate alone. What's needed to realize this opportunity is a powerful human interface that bridges the gap between the digital and physical worlds. We see AR as a historic innovation that provides this. It helps humans enhance their own capabilities by taking full advantage of new digital knowledge and machine capabilities. It will profoundly change training and skill development, allowing people to perform sophisticated work without protracted and expensive conventional instruction – a model that is inaccessible to so many today.'

Augmented reality is a developing technology, with many organizations still trying to work out how to use it effectively. Gardiner Morse (2017) sees three areas where AR will be applied in future. First, to provide operators with accurate information in dangerous environments such as refineries, chemical plants and construction. Second, to provide those working in remote locations such as offshore wind farms and oil rigs with the appropriate skills and knowledge. Third, giving guidance to people working with extremely complex products or machines, where automation is difficult or impossible, such as servicing an industrial 3-D printer.

Will new technology steal our jobs?

Our heading for this section is misleading. Automation does not take over jobs; it takes over *tasks*. This is an important distinction. Most jobs are made up from bundles of different tasks (Arntz et al., 2016). It may not be possible to automate an entire job; but some tasks could be done (and done better) by machine. Few people will complain if automation does work that is dangerous, boring or strenuous. The problem is that automated systems can now perform a much wider range of tasks.

Automation anxiety and a workless future?

'Our findings suggest that, while a significant proportion of jobs could be fully displaced by new machines (15 per cent of private sector jobs over the next 10 years, according to our YouGov poll), grim predictions of mass automation and widespread economic strife do not stand up to scrutiny. Machines are still incapable of performing many tasks, and very few can comprehensively automate whole jobs. Occupations are more likely to evolve than be eliminated, and new ones will emerge in the long run. Low-skilled workers will probably face the greatest disruption, but sectors vary significantly in their automation potential and we are likely to see a continued growth in human-centric roles in health care, social care and education' (Dellot and Wallace-Stephens, 2017, p.42).

Replacement effects processes through which intelligent machines substitute for people at work, leading to unemployment.

Compensatory mechanisms processes that delay or reduce employment replacement effects, and which lead to the creation of new products, services and jobs.

The answer to the jobs question also depends on two sets of opposing factors – replacement effects and compensatory mechanisms. New technologies create unemployment through replacement effects, substituting equipment for people, such as self-service checkouts in supermarkets.

Historically, those who have been replaced by technology have (sooner or later) found work in other sectors, supplying the new products and services generated by those new technologies. It was predicted in the 1980s that developments in computing would lead to technological unemployment. Widespread automation would lead to redundancies, and we would have to worry about how to use our new leisure time. The economist John Maynard Keynes made a similar prediction in the 1930s. These predictions have never come true. Although people in some jobs are indeed replaced by smart machines, a number of compensatory mechanisms come into play.

There are many compensatory mechanisms. New products and services need new infrastructure (factories, offices, distribution chains), which create jobs in those areas. The reduced costs from technological innovation lead to lower prices which increase demand for other goods and services – creating more jobs. New technologies are not always implemented rapidly;

Where have the people gone?

Nike uses advanced automation to manufacture its Flyknit Racer trainers. This trainer, made with a special knitting machine, uses less labour and fewer materials than most running shoes; automation can halve labour costs and cut material costs by a fifth. Nike plans to use more automation, and is experimenting with laser-cutting and automated gluing in its factory in Mexico. Nike employs almost half a million people making footwear in 15 countries, and takes pride in being an ethical and sustainable business.

What impact will automation have on the workforce? The company expects growing sales will allow it to automate further while keeping its current employees. The main motive for automating production is not cost cutting, but the need to adapt the company's products to meet changing consumer tastes. Shoe manufacturing is complex, involving around 200 pieces (across 10 sizes) which traditionally were cut and glued manually. Lead times for new products could run to several months. With automation, Nike can get a new trainer to market in three or four weeks. If the company continues to grow, jobs will be created, and not lost (Bissell-Linsk, 2017). For similar reasons, Mercedes-Benz replaced robots with humans on some production lines, because the machines were not agile enough to keep up with demand for customized products (Hollinger, 2016).

it takes time to solve technical and organizational problems, and scrapping existing facilities can be costly. The benefits of new technologies may not at first be clear, and organizations often experiment with and introduce new systems gradually, to hedge the risks. Investment in new technologies is based on the expectation that the organization's market will expand, in which case the existing workforce may be retained, if not increased. Finally, new technologies do not always live up to their promise, and may not be able to do everything that the 'old' technology could do. This explains why many homes still have traditional landlines, and there is still a demand for vinyl records, compact discs, printed books, and radios. Autonomous vehicles could replace truck drivers. But it will take time to replace the fleet of conventional trucks, and the self-driving kind will still have to be loaded, programmed with their destinations, unloaded, cleaned, maintained, and serviced. They will have to be manufactured and distributed to customers in the first place. The net effect on job numbers is thus difficult to predict.

Emphasizing the role of compensatory mechanisms, Ian Stewart et al. (2015, p.10) argue that:

'The stock of work in the economy is not fixed; the last 200 years demonstrates that when a machine replaces a human, the result, paradoxically, is faster growth and, in time, rising employment. [. . .] The work of the future is likely to be varied and have a bigger share of social interaction and empathy, thought, creativity and skill. We believe that jobs will continue to be created, enhanced and destroyed much as they have in the last 150 years'.

The impact of new technology thus depends on the interplay between replacement effects and compensatory mechanisms. The latter have ensured that computerization has created more jobs than have been replaced. But with so many clever new technologies – advanced robotics, artificial intelligence, augmented reality – is the balance between replacement and compensation changing? Technology may be developing so rapidly that those who are displaced may not be able to 'reskill' themselves fast enough. New technology has created many new business models. Banks, taxi drivers, camera makers, music and book publishers, and universities have seen their traditional business models undermined by faster-moving and cheaper competitors whose products and services are more appealing to internet-savvy consumers. Let's look at the evidence.

CRITICAL THINKING	Do different generations have different attitudes towards new technologies such as self-service supermarket checkouts, self-driving taxis, automated bank deposit terminals, and the intelligent personal assistant on your phone? Are older generations less comfortable using these devices?

Work can be classified as routine (repetitive) or non-routine (varied, requiring flexibility). The former follows explicit rules or procedures. The latter is more difficult to codify because of the many exceptions. Work can also be classified in terms of whether manual (physical) or cognitive (intellectual) capabilities are more important. In the past, work that was more easily codified was more readily automated. Today, computerization can handle non-routine work as well. Table 3.2 (based on Frey and Osborne, 2017, p.258) lists some of the non-routine manual and cognitive tasks that can now be computerized.

Table 3.2: How computerization will affect non-routine tasks

Non-routine work that can now be computerized	
Manual tasks	**Cognitive tasks**
Elderly care	Driving a car in city traffic
Equipment maintenance	Deciphering poor handwriting
Maintaining wind turbines	Financial trading
Quality screening vegetables	Fraud detection
Hospital surgery	Medical diagnostics

What did they find? Automation and jobs

Melanie Arntz and colleagues (2016) explored whether automation would result in a jobless future. Some studies have reached pessimistic conclusions. For example, Frey and Osborne (2013) estimated that 47 per cent of American workers were in jobs that could be taken over by machines and algorithms within the next 10 to 20 years. That study, however, used an occupation-based approach, which Arntz and her colleagues argue is too simple. Most jobs are made up of bundles of tasks, and workers in the same job can have different task structures. So, we need to look more closely at which tasks in a job can be done by machines, and which cannot. Using this task-based approach, Arntz and her colleagues studied jobs in 21 OECD countries.

Melanie Arntz
(photo © ZEW)

What did they find? Were even more jobs at risk than Frey and Osborne predicted? Or did they reach similar conclusions to that earlier study? Are there differences in the potential for automation across different countries, and if so, why should this be the case? **(Answers in chapter Recap.)**

🤚 **STOP AND SEARCH**   YouTube for *What the research can teach us about automation* (1:30:01).

✓✓✓   **EMPLOYABILITY CHECK** (business acumen, how organizations work, managing change)

Whose jobs will be replaced by self-driving vehicles, and what new jobs will this technology create?

New technology has created more jobs in the past, but will history be a guide to what happens to jobs in the second machine age? The pace of automation may be faster than the pace of job creation. Those who are displaced may not have the skills and knowledge required for newly created jobs. The pace of retraining for displaced employees may not be fast enough – and some may be unwilling or unable to be retrained. New jobs may not be in the same locations as those who become unemployed.

Given these uncertainties, it is difficult to make confident predictions about the impact of technology on jobs. However, a survey of over 230 organizations produced the findings summarized in Figure 3.3 (Frey et al., 2016, p.5). This shows that there are more 'techno-optimists', who believe that new technology will create jobs, than there are 'techno-pessimists', who expect mass redundancies.

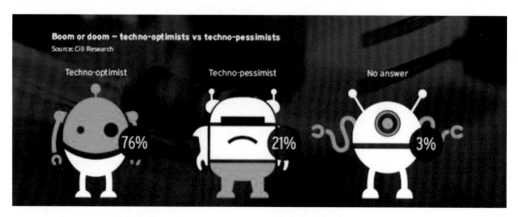

Figure 3.3: Boom or doom?

CUTTING EDGE

Automation potential

Carl Frey

Michael Osborne
(photo © Oxford
Martin School)

Carl Frey and Michael Osborne (2017) analysed over 700 occupations, assessing their automation potential – given the rapid advances in computing technology which mean that more tasks can now be automated. Their analysis was based on the distinctions between routine and non-routine tasks, and between manual and cognitive tasks. Computerization in the past has been applied to routine manual and cognitive tasks that involve explicit rule-based activities. New technologies, however, with the aid of 'big data', improved sensors, machine learning and pattern recognition, can handle non-routine tasks as well, widening the scope for automation. This now applies even to tasks where 'subtle judgement' is required, where the unbiased decision of an algorithm may be better than a human choice.

Their analysis also took into account three 'engineering bottlenecks'. These concern the problems that machines have with complex perception and manipulation tasks, creative intelligence tasks, and social intelligence tasks. Occupations that rely on those kinds of tasks are less susceptible to automation. As this diagram shows (Frey and Osborne, 2017, p.263), the task of a dishwasher, which requires little social intelligence, has a high probability of computerization. The probability of computerizing fashion designers and surgeons is low as their work requires complex perception and manipulation skills and creativity. Court clerks and telemarketers are more likely to be replaced by machines.

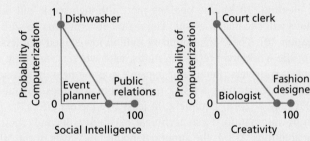
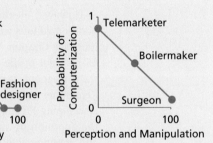

Occupations were given a probability score between zero (low automation potential) and one (high automation potential) based on the nature of the tasks of the job.

Occupations with low scores were mainly in healthcare, education and creative roles, such as recreational therapists, dieticians, choreographers, surgeons, school teachers and set designers.

Occupations with a middling score (around 0.5) included dental assistants, embalmers, shoe and leather workers, commercial pilots, teacher assistants, advertising sales agents and computer programmers.

Occupations with a high automation potential included insurance underwriters, watch repairers, cargo and freight agents, umpires and referees, legal secretaries, and real estate brokers – and telemarketers.

Frey and Osborne conclude that: 'recent developments in machine learning will put a substantial share of employment, across a wide range of occupations, at risk in the near future' (p.266). The main barriers to further automation will continue to be those bottlenecks.

> ✓✓✓ **EMPLOYABILITY CHECK** (how organizations work, managing change)
>
> In a job interview you are asked what factors should be taken into account when considering whether or not to invest in automation. How will you answer this question?

An RSA/YouGov survey of business leaders in 2017 (Delot and Wallace-Stephens,2017) suggested that only 15 per cent of private sector jobs in the UK could be fully automated in the next decade. But there was wide variation in views; one-fifth saw no prospects for job automation in their sector, almost 40 per cent said the impact would be low, and only 13 per cent predicted a high impact. Peter Fleming (2018) also argues that robots and artificial intelligence will not create mass redundancies. Computerization has done this in the past and there is no reason to believe that the current wave of automation is different. Fleming also argues that the question of whether robots will steal your job depends not just on the technology, but on organizational factors which affect which tasks are automated. These factors include:

The nature of the task	Most customers want to talk to a human being when they contact a call centre for help – and how many of us are prepared to fly in a fully automated aircraft that has no pilots?
The cost of labour	It is cheaper to pay people to clean your home than it is to buy a robot.
Power relations	Trade unions and prominent professional groups can resist the implementation of new technologies.

However, Fleming (2018) also predicts that, although work will not disappear, more poorly paid jobs will become available. The main concerns thus lie with low-skill, low-pay jobs (see **Chapter 10**). There are around 14 million low-skilled workers in the UK – about 45 per cent of the workforce: retail assistants, care workers, teaching assistants, waiting staff, cleaners, taxi drivers. Retail and logistics may be heavily affected by automation. Remember that, just because a task can be automated does not mean that it will be. Developing Fleming's (2018) argument, at least five factors affect the pace and extent of the adoption of automation. First, technical feasibility. Second, the cost of developing and applying solutions. Third, the supply, demand, and costs of the labour that could be replaced. Fourth, the economic benefits. Finally, legal, regulatory and social acceptance may require human presence in some work (Bughin et al., 2017). There are many tasks, especially in personal service settings (hospitality and leisure, medical and health services, education), where we will not feel comfortable interacting with a machine (Berriman and Hawksworth, 2017).

If pessimistic predictions concerning the impact of technology on low skill jobs are correct, this could lead to the creation of a two-tier workforce:

Tier one	Highly educated, skilled professionals, highly paid, immune from automation
Tier two	Less well-educated, unskilled manual workers, poorly paid, susceptible to automation unless employing them is cheaper than using machines

Those who are unskilled and poorly paid are already at a disadvantage. Cribb et al. (2018) argue that the minimum wage ('national living wage') in the UK affects many employees in routine occupations, such as retail cashiers and receptionists, whose work tends to be easier to automate. As the minimum wage rises, employers will have more incentive to automate those jobs. The social implications of a two-tier workforce could be worse if the two tiers were located in different parts of the country. The UK think tank Centre for Cities (2018) argues that, although automation will create jobs, it will also create deep economic and political divisions. Cities in the North and Midlands of England (Mansfield, Sunderland, Wakefield) have a higher concentration of factories and warehouses, with repetitive work that is susceptible to automation. Those regions are thus likely to experience high levels of job losses. In contrast, the more affluent cities in the South of England (Oxford, Cambridge, London) will not be so badly affected. Their report estimates that 3.6 million jobs are at risk between now and 2030, mainly in retailing, administrative roles, and warehousing. This will be offset by jobs growth. However, jobs created in Northern and Midlands cities will be mainly in low skilled occupations. Southern cities are more likely to attract highly skilled and better paying jobs. If this were to happen, the resulting inequality in income and living standards could lead to social unrest.

CRITICAL THINKING	New technology could create a two-tier workforce and also create greater inequality between different parts of the country. Why should these trends concern an organization's management?

In summary, AI and robotics will create a mix of 'bad news' and 'good news'. The good news will probably outweigh the bad (Lawrence et al., 2017; Wisskirchen et al., 2017).

The bad news is:

- AI and robotics will transform many jobs and destroy others in the short term.
- Employees in jobs that require low to medium skill and qualifications will be most affected.
- Those who are displaced may lack sufficient training and may not readily find other work.
- Income inequality between those in 'lovely' and 'lousy' jobs could lead to social conflict.

The good news is:

- New technologies will create new organizational opportunities and new jobs.
- Sudden mass redundancies are unlikely.
- Time saved with the use of intelligent IT systems will reduce production costs.
- New technologies will take over dangerous, monotonous tasks.
- AI and robotics free up time for employees to do more interesting and valuable work.
- Older employees and those with disabilities can be integrated.
- New job models will encourage the creation of personalized working conditions.
- Employees will supervise rather than participate in production.
- AI and robotics will contribute to a growth in prosperity.

Technology transforming work

The gigantic baggage handling systems at Dubai's international airport – the world's largest such system – demonstrate how robots are remixing workforce skills. In 2015, the airport handled 78 million passengers. Its 17 kilometres of conveyor belts, 46 kilometres of high-speed sorting systems and 800 Radio Frequency Identification (RFID) read/write stations can automatically sort 15,000 pieces of luggage every hour. Yet the entire operation is managed by a team of just 400 IT and maintenance specialists using sophisticated software (Knowles-Cutler and Lewis, 2016, p.14).

→

The social matrix

Everything is social

'Social technology is a massive technological and social phenomenon – but its power as a business tool is still being discovered. Never before has a communications medium been adopted as quickly or as widely as social media. It took commercial television 13 years to reach 50 million households, and Internet service providers took three years to sign their 50 millionth subscriber. But it took Facebook just a year and Twitter even less time to reach the same milestone.

'Socially enabled applications will become ubiquitous, allowing liking, commenting, and information sharing across a large array of activities. We will live and conduct business in a social matrix, where virtually all resources can be found – collaborators, talent, customers, funders. The social matrix will enable new forms of organization that are only just becoming apparent' (Chui et al., 2013, p.3).

Social media are one of the defining features of our lives. These are 'low friction' tools: they are everywhere, they are flexible, and you don't need any training. These tools have changed the way in which we interact with each other, how we share information, the kinds of information that we share (ideas, pictures, music, videos), and how we form opinions. They potentially shift power and decision-making responsibility to front line staff who can now have access to the same information as everybody else. The mobile internet and cloud storage mean that we can interact and share where and when we want, without having to rely on corporate computing. For many people, social media are now the main source of news about what is going on in the world.

These technologies have spread rapidly. The social networking service Facebook was launched in 2004. In 2017, Facebook had over 2 billion users; WhatsApp had 1.2 billion; Twitter 330 million; Snapchat 255 million. WeChat, the Chinese mobile text and messaging service, had 940 million users – three times the population of the United States, 15 times the population of the UK.

We now live and work in a **social matrix** in which any interaction or activity can become social. Crowdsourcing solves problems. Crowdfunding supports new business ideas. Social networks encourage collaboration, knowledge sharing and co-creation. Customers can be attracted by the 'social' features of new products and services, which they can help to improve. Facebook 'likes' can identify what products people are buying, and thus improve retail merchandising and marketing.

Social matrix
an environment in which any online activity can be social, influencing actions, solving problems, innovating, and creating new types of organizations that are not constrained by traditional boundaries

---

CRITICAL THINKING

What social media tools do you use? Do you think that using social media at work could make you more productive? Why do some organizations prohibit the use of social media at work? Would organizations benefit if they allowed employees to use social media? What problems and risks can social media create for an organization?

Employees seem to be more sophisticated in the use of social media tools in their private lives than are employers with regard to organizational uses. Organizations have been slow to adopt these tools, even prohibiting employees from using social media at work, and not allowing them to connect their personal devices to organizational IT networks. Organizations using social media have been more interested in how they can interact with and gather information from their customers, than interacting with their employees (Gifford, 2013). This may now be changing. Traditionally, employees were introduced to new technologies by their employers. With social media, this is being reversed. We use social media routinely in our personal lives, and employees may use social media for work purposes whether their employers are aware of this or not.

There are many possible reasons for the poor organizational uptake. Perhaps senior (older) managers neither use nor understand the technology and its potential. The links between social media and corporate goals may not be obvious. The benefits of social media are difficult to quantify. Jobs may not be designed to make good use of social media. Management may feel that using social media at work encourages 'cyberloafing' or 'cyberslacking'. Cybersecurity is also a growing concern; one fifth of cyberattacks involve insiders (employees, contractors, third-party suppliers) who have easy and legitimate access to an organization's systems, and more opportunities to disrupt operations and steal intellectual property. Employees can be targeted through social media.

The list of organizational applications of social media tools, however, is long (Gifford, 2014):

- Facilitating employee voice
- Supporting corporate communications
- Getting the right information to the right people
- Creating interconnections and networks
- Improving employee relations
- Building shared purpose and workplace community
- Developing collaboration, cooperation and information sharing
- Drawing on insight and experience from across the organization
- Strengthening advocacy of the organization
- Strengthening the employer reputation and brand
- Widening the recruitment pool
- Transforming learning and development
- Encouraging distributed leadership
- Increasing top team visibility
- Shaping organization culture
- Encouraging openness, egalitarianism, and a lack of rigidity

"The internet brings everyone closer."

With regard to recruitment, social networking sites can reveal (to potential employers) information about candidates' abilities and characteristics, and display (to potential employees) an organization's culture, goals, and priorities, such as attitude to corporate social responsibility.

A study by the McKinsey Global Institute concluded that social media could increase the productivity of knowledge workers by 20 to 25 per cent, by reducing the time spent looking for information. McKinsey also predicts that social media could save companies $1.3 trillion, through improvements in intra-office collaboration (Chui et al., 2013). Paul Leonardi and Tsedal Neeley (2017) cite a study of 4,200 American organizations which found that over 70 per cent used social media tools. The reported benefits included promoting collaboration and knowledge sharing, speeding up decisions, developing innovative ideas for products and services, increasing employee engagement, establishing relationships between employees in different locations, and avoiding the duplication of work. However, they argue that organizations can fall into four traps:

1. Assuming that Millennials want to use social media at work; they see social media as tools for self-expression and communication with friends and family.

2. Prohibiting informal discussion of non-work topics on internal organization sites; personal interactions make it easier to access other people and work-related information.

3. Not recognizing the difference between *direct learning* (knowing *how* to do something, like solve a problem) and *metaknowledge* (learning *who* has the expertise that you need); informal communication is important in developing metaknowledge.

4. Treating visible information as the most valuable; staff with technical skills may be more highly valued than those with cultural and political skills – but the latter are just as useful.

When we think of social media, we think of the online platforms that are available to everyone. However, the potential of these technologies may rely on *enterprise-specific* networks (Gifford, 2014). Facebook launched its corporate social network platform *Workplace* in 2016. Other popular enterprise networking platforms include *Yammer, Chatter, Jive* and *Slack*. With these tools, employees can be involved in two-way discussions using a secure 'gated' corporate networking platform, for incubating ideas and feeding these to senior management. This can also be used to facilitate communication and collaboration. Social networking can be a more engaging medium than traditional organization communication tools, to send corporate messages, quickly capture employee reactions, to check that messages have been understood, and for information-sharing in general. A corporate social network can strengthen the sense of shared purpose, by celebrating achievements, reinforcing mission and values, and fostering identification with the organization.

Employee voice

Employee voice
the ability of employees to express their views, opinions, concerns and suggestions, and for these to influence decisions at work.

One valuable application of social media concerns encouraging employee voice, 'where everyone in an organization feels they have a say, are listened to and have their views taken into account' (Simms, 2018, p.41). Unlike the annual staff satisfaction survey, social media can capture real-time information, continuously.

Joe Dromey (2016) reports research by the Advisory Conciliation and Arbitration Service (ACAS) which studied the extent to which employers in the UK are making use of social media to promote and access employee voice. The study found that half of employers were using social media tools, but mainly for marketing and customer engagement purposes. Only one in six had internal enterprise social networks, and these were used mainly to provide organizational updates rather than to collect employee views. Dromey suggests that high levels of personal use of social media could promote its organizational adoption. But where enterprise social networks were in use at work, few employees said that this was effective in sharing knowledge and ideas, or to encourage employee voice. Interestingly, employees in organizations with enterprise networks said that they felt less able to influence decisions than in organizations not using social networks. Dromey concludes that the benefits of these technologies are not being fully exploited.

Antisocial media

One large UK bank had a company intranet, which gave staff the opportunity to give feedback to senior management. During a major reorganization, which involved cutting costs, and the closure of many branches with job losses, the bank's human resources director decided to assess staff morale. He posted an intranet article which praised employees' commitment and flexibility. Staff were asked to leave comments, and hundreds responded. Most of the feedback was negative:

'If you want promotion do every extracurricular task that you can. Don't worry about the quality of the work as it is irrelevant.

.'Either execs are lying, or somewhere down the line people are misrepresenting what is being communicated from above.

'Why should we trust you after what you did on pensions?'

Most complaints concerned the decision to close the generous final salary pension scheme. This happened at the same time as the chief executive was awarded a large pension contribution as part of his multi-million pound annual package, and was seen as showing double standards. Staff also criticized the excessive bureaucracy and lack of top management support. The corporate intranet makes it easy for management to capture staff feedback. That feedback, however, may be unfavourable, particularly when management actions are seen as inconsistent, or unfair. (See the discussion of the website **glassdoor.co.uk** in **Chapter 21**.)

Peter Holland et al. (2016) explore the implications of social media for employee voice in Australia. They also argue that 'The understanding and management of social media at work are not well developed' (p.2629). Their research examined the relationship between social media use and job satisfaction, and found that social media were not commonly used to voice concerns about work. They suggest that this is an untapped resource for workplace communication, which could give management 'real time' feedback on workplace issues. They conclude that:

'The challenge for management is whether to embrace this form of communication which is now ubiquitous outside the workplace and harness the ability to increase knowledge and understanding of workplace issues and improve the employment relationship in real time. The alternative is to ignore the opportunity such a medium provides and potentially allow social media to develop its own culture with the potential to be a focus for negative issues in the workplace and about the organization' (p.2630).

CRITICAL THINKING

Is the increased use of social media by organizations inevitable, as employees are using these tools anyway? Do you see more benefits to come from this development? Or do you see more problems and risks? If the latter, what are the problems and risks? And how can these be managed?

Many failures and scandals might have been avoided had managers listened to and acted upon what employees were saying. The employee engagement movement, Engage for Success (2018), claims that employee voice is 'the cheapest smoke alarm you can ever install in an organization'. Engage for Success also found that over 60 per cent of employees say that they have more to give to their organizations, but no one is asking them (see **Chapter 9**). Research has demonstrated that people who feel that their opinions matter are more likely to be satisfied and productive (Bosak et al., 2017). Employees have to feel that it is safe to voice their opinions, even with gated enterprise social networks, so employee feedback has to be managed carefully. Simms (2018, p.42) describes two cases where management ignored psychological safety:

'When Google engineer James Damore posted a memo about the firm's diversity initiatives last year to highlight what he saw as a left-wing bias that was silencing alternative views, he was fired. Similarly, at a town hall meeting at a technology company in Ireland, the chief executive claimed he wanted people to ask him questions, but when a male employee stood up and asked a question, he was asked: 'Are you still here?'. The next day, he wasn't.'

Simms (2018) cites a positive example. The food company Danone UK encourages employee voice through three channels: Workplace by Facebook, its own intranet, and live events. Facebook – which is popular with younger staff – is especially effective, with over 90 per cent of employees being active on Workplace every week, to share documents, minute meetings and exchange other information.

The dark side of social media

Social media have many useful organizational applications, for communicating, sharing information and collaborating. An investigation by the *Financial Times* newspaper, however, found that social media are contributing to sexual harassment in the workplace (Noonan and Ram, 2018). Employees share personal details through social media, and some organizations have their own internal enterprise networks, such as Workplace by Facebook, that allow potential stalkers to track the location of their colleagues in real time, through their online calendars. A financial service sector employee said:

'It's great to connect people across the world to form cross-border teams and share expertise. But if some guy at the company is persistently trying to ask you out on a date, or pressuring you into sex, it means he has loads of tools to stalk you online, get tons of information about you and find your whereabouts, which is really scary.

'And because all these systems are company mandatory, you can't block the guy, switch messenger off, or hide your profile from him. At least if you're harassed on Twitter or Facebook, you can block people or close your account.'

One employee was hounded on Facebook after she made a complaint about sexual harassment – a complaint that was widely publicized through the social network. Organizations may need to set up and enforce 'acceptable use' policies that prohibit misuse of social media. Privacy controls and blocking functions can be introduced to allow individuals to protect themselves, although these steps could reduce the networking and collaboration benefits of social media. A participant in this study pointed to one benefit of sexual harassment through social networks: 'It gives a great trail of the abuse should a person choose to report it'. (Extracts from Noonan and Ram, 2018)

In future

How will these technologies develop in future? The current pace of innovation is so rapid, that much of this chapter is likely to be out of date before the text is published. However, we can make some predictions about future trends. For example, Frey and Osborne (2017) identify three bottlenecks that are preventing or delaying further computerization. These concern the problems that computers have with tasks that involve perception and manipulation, creative intelligence, and social intelligence:

Complex perceptual and manipulation tasks	Identifying objects and their properties in a cluttered environment
Creative intelligence tasks	Music, sculpture, jokes, recipes, creative writing
Social intelligence tasks	Negotiating, persuading, caring, counselling, therapy

These bottlenecks suggest that many non-routine professional tasks cannot be automated. That may not be the case, as Frey and Osborne (2017, p.261) observe:

> 'Beyond these bottlenecks, however, we argue that it is largely already technologically possible to automate almost any task, provided that sufficient amounts of data are gathered for pattern recognition. Our model thus predicts that the pace at which these bottlenecks can be overcome will determine the extent of computerization in the twenty-first century.'

For those who fear being left behind, the answer is not to compete, but to develop capabilities that complement new technologies. So how can you 'future-proof' your career against increasingly smart machines? Frey et al. (2016, pp.51–2) identify ten skills which are going to continue to be important and in demand in future:

1. *Sense-making*: understanding the deeper meaning of what is being expressed.
2. *Social intelligence*: understanding others and the effect you have on them.
3. *Novel and adapting thinking*: taking creative approaches to new situations.
4. *Cross-cultural competency*: understanding different cultural norms and expectations.
5. *Computational thinking*: especially the ability to apply machine learning methods creatively.
6. *New media literacy*: understanding how to use mobile, multimedia, online information.
7. *Transdisciplinarity*: understanding concepts across several different disciplines.
8. *Design mindset*: able to develop tasks and processes to achieve desired outcomes.
9. *Cognitive load management*: ability to decide which information is important.
10. *Virtual collaboration*: the ability to work effectively as a member of a virtual team.

 **EMPLOYABILITY CHECK** (interpersonal skills, creativity, problem solving, cross-cultural issues)

What evidence can you cite concerning at least two of the ten skills listed above? What other skills will you need to develop in your chosen career? How will you acquire those skills?

RECAP

1. *Understand the nature and organizational implications of 'the second machine age'.*

   - The second machine age is based on a combination of growth in computing power, the availability of big data and data analytics, and innovations which can build on each other.

   - We now have the ability to automate many more tasks using computerized equipment.

   - Computerization could create a 'two tier' society and greater income inequality, with a highly-skilled and well-paid elite, and others who will have poorly paid jobs, if they are employed.

2. *Explain criticisms of technological determinism from a socio-technical systems point of view.*

   - Technology does not determine the nature of jobs and organization structures. Work can be organized in different ways. The degrees of variety, responsibility and interaction in work are design choices.

   - Socio-technical system design attempts to meet the needs of both the social and technological aspects of work; focusing on the demands of one aspect alone creates problems.

   - Technology should be seen as having enabling properties, opening up fresh possibilities.

3. *Understand the capabilities of advanced robotics and the implications for the nature of work and employment.*

- There are five main categories of advanced robot: articulated, assistance, humanoid, mobile, and serpentine robots. Many of these are mobile, unlike traditional static caged robots.

- Robots have successfully automated manual work. Cobots – collaborative robots – are being developed to work safely alongside employees, to augment rather than replace human skills.

- Routine tasks have traditionally been easier to automate than non-routine tasks. That is changing. Non-routine manual tasks that can now be computerized include elderly care, equipment maintenance and hospital surgery. Non-routine cognitive tasks that can now be computerized include driving cars in city traffic, financial trading and medical diagnosis.

- To adapt to new technology, employee training and development will have to focus on abilities that machines cannot handle, such as social skills, creativity, leadership and motivation.

4. *Understand the capabilities of artificial intelligence and the implications for the automation of knowledge work.*

- There are five main components of artificial intelligence: expert systems, machine learning, deep learning, reinforcement learning and transfer learning. These systems can now perform many tasks that were once thought to be uniquely human, and beyond the ability of machines.

- Tasks that require cognitive skills, adaptability and judgement have been difficult to automate. However, artificial intelligence and machine learning can computerize professional knowledge work. AI can also be used for intelligence augmentation, to support human capabilities.

- Computers struggle with tasks that require complex perception and manipulation, creativity and social intelligence. Also, machines are not good at leadership, motivation, complex problem solving, creativity, negotiating and managing people.

5. *Understand the capabilities of augmented reality and how these systems will affect the nature of work.*

- Augmented reality (AR) systems superimpose digital information and images on the physical world through a screen, such as a smartphone, iPad or television.

- AR can be combined with virtual reality for entertainment and training purposes, and to enable collaboration and teamwork in dispersed employee groups.

- AR works through mobile devices, head-mounted displays and smart glasses. An AR device can superimpose production, assembly and servicing instructions onto manufacturing environments, replacing traditional paper manuals and training methods.

- AR enhances human capabilities, allowing people to perform sophisticated tasks without lengthy and expensive instruction.

- AR is a developing technology with applications that will support those working in dangerous environments, in remote locations, and with extremely complex equipment.

6. *Assess the impact of new technologies on employment – mass redundancies, or job creation?*

- New technology in the past has not led to unemployment, as the development of new products and services has created new demand, and thus new jobs. However, the pace of change in the second machine age is such that many of those who are displaced may not be able to catch up.

- The impact on jobs may not be as dramatic as predicted because there are many things that machines still cannot do, such as work involving social intelligence, complex manipulation, and creativity.

- Tasks may not be automated even where this is possible. Automation may be more expensive than human labour in some regions. Regulatory requirements may require human presence and judgement. It may not be socially acceptable to have some tasks performed by machines.

- Management will have to pay more attention to: managing resistance to new technology; leadership capabilities for managing skilled knowledge workers; frequent retraining and redeployment to enable workers to function alongside intelligent machines; finding ways of using new technology to assist older workers.

7. *Understand the nature of 'the social matrix', the potential organizational uses of social media technologies, and the risks involved.*

- We live and work in a social matrix. Any online activity can now be social, involving others in sharing information and solving problems, and creating new types of organization.

- Social media provide easy-to-use 'low friction' tools. For organizations, they can improve external and internal communications, strengthen employee voice, support learning and development, and streamline recruitment.

- Employees should be allowed to exchange personal information through social media, as this helps to form relationships and develop metaknowledge – knowing who to ask for help when needed.

- The corporate development of social media for internal purposes has been poor, perhaps due to a lack of understanding of the technology, weak links to corporate goals, work that is not designed to make use of these tools, and concerns about cyberslacking and cybersecurity.
- One approach to overcoming those concerns is to develop enterprise-specific social networks, which are 'gated' and limit communications to employees, at all levels.

- Organizations resisting these developments may be encouraged, or forced, into social media adoption by employees who will use these technologies anyway.
- Social media involve risks; employee voices can be critical of management, and social media can be used as a tool for sexual harassment and stalking.

RECAP: What did they find?

Arntz et al. (2016) found that:

- Only 24 per cent of clerks could avoid group work and interpersonal interaction – tasks with which robots struggle, and where humans have comparative advantage. According to Frey and Osborne (2013), in contrast, the probability of automation replacing clerks in accounting jobs was 98 per cent. For the same reason, where Frey and Osborne put the probability of replacing retail salespeople at 92 per cent, Arntz et al. estimate the automation potential of this job to be only 4 per cent.

- 9 per cent of occupations in OECD countries are at risk of automation, not 47 per cent as Frey and Osborne predict for America.

- In Korea and Estonia, only 6 per cent of jobs were at risk of automation, and in Germany and Austria 12 per cent. These contrasts reflect differences in workplace organization, differences in investment in automation, and differences in worker education.

- Automation is not likely to create mass redundancies. However, those in low-skill jobs are at greater risk, and retraining will be necessary to avoid growing inequality.

Revision

1. Why is technology such an important aspect of organizational behaviour?
2. Will robots steal our jobs? What does the evidence say?
3. Will artificial intelligence automate knowledge work, including management? What capabilities will you need to develop in order to avoid being replaced by a machine in your chosen career?
4. What are the organizational applications of augmented reality systems? In what ways will these technologies replace or complement human capabilities?
5. What does it mean to say that we live and work in a social matrix? What are the implications of the social matrix for you, personally, and for organizations?

Research assignment

The second machine age is based on a number of technologies – robots, cobots, artificial intelligence, machine learning, augmented reality, virtual reality, social media. As these technologies are constantly evolving, there is a lack of academic research concerning their implications for organizational behaviour. To update yourself, choose a technology that you find interesting. What more can you find out about that technology using Google, YouTube, other online resources, and traditional print media (magazines, newspapers)?

- What can you discover about the benefits of this technology for individuals, organizations and society as a whole?
- What can you discover about the problems and risks with this technology?
- As an employee, how do you assess the implications of this technology for you?
- As a manager, how do you assess the implications of this technology for your organization?

Springboard

Martin Ford (2015) *The Rise of the Robots: Technology and the Threat of Mass Unemployment.* London: Oneworld Publications. Artificial intelligence will automate knowledge work, not just simple manual jobs. However, this new technology will do what new technology in the past has done – facilitate more highly skilled and better paid jobs.

Andrew McAffee and Erik Brynjolfsson (2017) *Machine, Platform, Crowd: Harnessing the Digital Revolution.* London and New York: W.W. Norton & Co. Explores how artificial intelligence will transform business and the nature of work, also emphasizing the role of platforms (Uber, Airbnb) and the 'crowd' – informal, decentralized, self-organizing participants.

James Wilson and Paul R. Daugherty (2018) 'Collaborative intelligence: humans and AI are joining forces', *Harvard Business Review,* 96(4): 114-123. Explores examples of the performance gains achieved when humans and smart machines collaborate; artificial intelligence will have the most significant impact when it augments human workers instead of replacing them.

OB cinema

Modern Times (1936, director Charles Chaplin). DVD track 2: 0:01:10 to 0:06.00 (5 minutes). Clip opens with flock of sheep, and ends when the scene cuts from the assembly line to the manager's office. Despite the date, this sequence is still one of the most powerful movie illustrations of the human being treated as a machine, of the worker caught in the cogwheels of capitalist production.

1. Are employees still subjected to such treatment in organizations today? Give examples.

2. Can you identify instances where new technology has liberated workers from this kind of treatment?

3. Chaplin's movie was set in a factory; do office workers escape from the effects of technology?

DVD track 3: 00:06:07 to 00:12: 57 (6 minutes). Clip begins in the manager's office as the salesmen bring in a piece of equipment, and ends with the manager saying, 'It's no good – it isn't practical'. This is a disastrous demonstration of the Billows Feeding machine which is designed to feed employees while they work, thus improving productivity.

1. What does this scene reveal about management objectives in the use of technology?

2. What does this scene tell us about management values in relation to employees?

Chapter exercises

1: Into the matrix

Objectives

1. To encourage breadth of thinking about a topic, in this case the social matrix.

2. To develop skills in producing a wide-ranging and balanced assessment.

3. To consider the extent to which technology determines or facilitates the outcomes or impacts that it produces.

Briefing

The issue for debate is: What are the individual, organizational, and social benefits and dangers of living and working in a social matrix?

Divide into groups of three. Your group's task is to think of as many relevant points as you can concerning the issue for debate. List these points on a flipchart for presentation. Time allowed: 10 to 15 minutes.

Present your points in plenary. Your points will be awarded 'quality marks' for relevance, importance, plausibility and creativity. If your argument for a point is particularly impressive or original, you can win more quality marks. The group with the highest quality marks will be declared the winner. Time allowed depends on the number of groups: up to 45 minutes.

Consider two of the main benefits and two of the main dangers that you have identified. To what extent are these inevitable consequences of the social matrix? To what extent do these consequences depend on how individuals and organizations decide to use the technologies that are involved?

2: Old McDonald's Farm

Objective To explore the integration of social and technical aspects of an organization.

Briefing Organizations are sociotechnical systems. This means that technology – equipment, machines, processes, materials, layout – has to work alongside people – structures, roles, role relationships, job design. You can't design an organization to suit the technology while ignoring the people, because that would be ineffective. Similarly, designing an organization just to suit the people, while ignoring the technology, would be equally disastrous. The concept of sociotechnical system design means that the social system and the technical system have to be designed so that they can work with each other.

Old McDonald's Farm Let's consider Old McDonald's Farm. On this farm, he had no pigs, cows or chickens. He had only corn, planted in long rows that grew all year round. McDonald had a perfect environment for growing corn. The soil was rich, and the climate was perfect, twelve months every year.

McDonald's rows were so long that at one end of the row, the soil was being prepared for planting, while the next section on that row was being planted, the next section was growing, and the next was being harvested. McDonald had four of these long rows.

McDonald is a progressive and scientific farmer. He is concerned about both productivity and quality. He had an industrial engineer study the amount of effort required to complete the work in each function on each row. He found that two employees were required per section, on each row, fully employed in that function all year round. Therefore, he employed eight workers on each row.

Initially, Mr McDonald had only four rows, A, B, C and D, and a total of 32 people. But he decided to expand, adding two more rows. This added 16 more workers. Now he had 48 employees. Until this time, he had only one supervisor responsible for directing the work of all 32 employees on the initial four rows. Now he decided that there was too much work for one supervisor. He added another. Mr McDonald now had to decide whether to reorganize the work of his managers and employees. He spoke to his two supervisors, Mr Jones and Mr Smith, who had very different ideas.

Mr Jones insisted that the only intelligent way to organize was around the technical knowledge, the functional expertise. He argued that he should take responsibility for all employees working on the first two sections, soil preparation and planting, on all rows. Mr Smith, he acknowledged, had greater expertise in growing and harvesting, so he would take responsibility for all employees in the last two sections. They would each have an equal number of employees to supervise.

→

Mr Smith had a different idea. He argued that, while some specialized knowledge was needed, it was more important for the employees to take responsibility for the entire growing cycle. This way, they could move down the row, seeing the progress of the corn. He argued for organizing the employees into teams by row.

	soil prep	planting	growing	harvesting
row A				
row B				
row C				
row D				
row E				
row F				

Mr McDonald has hired you as a consultant to help him with his organization design. The questions that he wants you to answer are:

1. How will you organize employees on the farm, and how will you assign responsibility to Smith and Jones? You can recommend any assignment that you like, but the numbers of employees that are required will stay the same.

2. What sociotechnical principles support your recommendations? Why is your approach better than the alternatives?

If you were one of Mr McDonald's employees, which approach to organization design would you prefer, and why?

References

Arntz, M., Gregory, T. and Zierahn, U. (2016) *The Risk of Automation for Jobs in OECD Countries.* Paris: Organization for Economic Co-operation and Development.

Bass, A.S. (2018) 'GrAIt expectations', *The Economist Special Report AI In Business,* 31 March.

Berriman, R. and Hawksworth, J. (2017) 'Will robots steal our jobs?: the potential impact of automation on the UK and other major economies, in *UK Economic Outlook.* London: PricewaterhouseCoopers, pp.30–47.

Bissell-Linsk, J. (2017) 'Robotics in the running', *Financial Times,* 23 October, p.23.

Bosak, J., Dawson, J., Flood, P. and Peccei, R. (2017) 'Employee involvement climate and climate strength: a study of employee attitudes and organizational effectiveness in UK hospitals', *Journal of Organizational Effectiveness: People and Performance,* 4 (1): 18–38.

Brockhaus, J., Deichmann, J., Pulm, J. and Repenning, J. (2018) *Artificial Intelligence: Automotive's New Value-Creating Engine.* Düsseldorf: McKinsey & Company.

Brynjolfsson, E. and McAffee, A. (2014) *The Second Machine Age: Work, Progress, and Prosperity in a Time of Brilliant Technologies.* New York and London: W.W. Norton & Company.

Bughin, J., Manyika, J. and Woetzel, J. (2017) *A Future that Works: Automation, Employment, and Productivity.* San Francisco and London: McKinsey Global Institute.

Centre for Cities (2018) 'The rise of the robots could compound Britain's North/South divide', http://www.centreforcities.org/press/rise-robots-compound-britains-northsouth-divide-1-4-jobs-risk-cities-outside-south/ [accessed January 2019]

Chui, M., Manyika, J., Bughin, J., Brown, B., Roberts, R., Danielson, J. and Gupta, S. (2013) *Ten IT-Enabled Business Trends for the Decade Ahead.* New York: McKinsey & Company/McKinsey Global Institute.

Clover, C. and McGee, P. (2017) 'China emerges as engine of BMW strategy', *Financial Times,* 1 June, p.17.

Cribb, J., Joyce, R. and Keiller, A.N. (2018) 'Will the rising minimum wage lead to more low-paid jobs being automated?', *Institute for Fiscal Studies,* https://www.ifs.org.uk/publications/10287 [accessed January 2019]

Davenport, T.H. and Ronanki, R. (2018) 'Artificial intelligence for the real world', *Harvard Business Review,* 96 (1): 108–16.

Dellot, B. and Wallace-Stephens, F. (2017) *The Age of Automation: Artificial Intelligence, Robotics and the Future of Low-Skilled Work.* London: RSA Action and Research Centre.

DelMonaco, P. (2017) 'Is it legal to microchip employees?', *People Management,* 7 August, https://www.peoplemanagement.co.uk/experts/legal/microchipping-employees# [accessed January 2019]

Dromey, J. (2016) *Going Digital?: Harnessing Social Media for Employee Voice.* London: ACAS [51 pages].

Emery, R.E. and Trist, E.L. (1960) 'Socio-technical systems', in C.W. Churchman and M. Verhulst (eds), *Management Science, Models and Techniques, Volume 2.* London: Pergamon Press, pp.83 97.

Engage for Success (2018) http://engageforsuccess.org/employee-voice [accessed January 2019]

Everard, A. (2013) 'Linn celebrates 40 years exakt-ly – but it's still developing its first product', *Words and Music* blog, https://andreweverard.com/2013/10/05/linn-celebrates-40-years-exaktly-but-its-still-developing-its-first-product/ [accessed January 2019]

Fletcher, S. (2018) 'What makes a good robot co-worker?', *People Management,* 15 January, https://www.peoplemanagement.co.uk/voices/comment/good-robot-worker [accessed January 2019]

Fleming, P. (2018) 'Robots and organization studies: why robots might not want to steal your job', *Organization Studies,* published online early.

Frean, A. (2018) 'How to attract the best people?: ask a computer to write your job ads', *The Times,* 21 February, p.41.

Frey, C.B. and Osborne, M.A. (2013) 'The future of employment: how susceptible are jobs to computerization?', Oxford: University of Oxford Department of Engineering Science.

Frey, C.B. and Osborne, M.A. (2017) 'The future of employment: how susceptible are jobs to computerization?', *Technological Forecasting & Social Change,* 114 (C): 254–80.

Frey, C.B., Osbourne, M.A. and Homes, C. (2016) *Technology at Work v2.0: The Future Is Not What It Used To Be.* London and Oxford: Citigroup/University of Oxford, Oxford Martin School.

Gifford, J. (2013) *Social Technology, Social Business?* London: Chartered Institute for Personnel and Development.

Gifford, J. (2014) *Putting Social Media to Work: Lessons From Employers.* London: Chartered Institute for Personnel and Development.

Hislop, D., Coombs, C., Taneva, S. and Barnard, S. (2017) *Impact of Artificial Intelligence, Robotics and Automation Technologies on Work.* London: Chartered Institute for Personnel and Development.

Holland, P., Cooper, B.K. and Hecker, R. (2016) 'Use of social media at work: a new form of employee voice?', *International Journal of Human Resource Management,* 27 (21): 2621–34.

Hollinger, P. (2016) 'Meet the cobots: humans and robots together on the factory floor', *Financial Times,* 5 May.

Illanes, P., Lund, S., Mourshed, M., Rutherford, S. and Tyreman, M. (2018) *Retraining and Reskilling Workers in the Age of Automation.* New York: McKinsey & Company.

Kirkland, R. (2014) 'Artificial intelligence meets the C-suite', *McKinsey Quarterly,* September, pp.66–75.

Knowles-Cutler, A. and Lewis, H. (2016) *Talent for Survival: Essential Skills for Humans Working in the Machine Age.* London: Deloitte.

Lawrence, M., Roberts, C. and King, L. (2017) *Managing Automation: Employment, Inequality and Ethics in the Digital Age.* London: Institute for Public Policy Research.

Leonardi, P. and Neeley, T. (2017) 'What managers need to know about social tools', *Harvard Business Review,* 96 (5): 118–26.

Milne, R. (2014) 'Lego: King of the castle', *Financial Times,* 10 July, p.13.

Milne, R. (2015) 'Lego shores up title of most profitable toymaker', *Financial Times,* 26 February, p.18.

Morse, G. (2006) 'High fidelity: Ivor Tiefenbrun on tapping talent', *Harvard Business Review,* 84(11): 28.

Morse, G. (2017) 'One company's experience with AR', *Harvard Business Review,* 95 (6): 60–61.

Noonan, L. and Ram, A. (2018) 'Social media use fuels rise in sexual harassment', *Financial Times,* 3 January, p.14.

Porter, M.E. and Heppelmann, J.E. (2017) 'Why every organization needs an augmented reality strategy', *Harvard Business Review,* 95 (6): 46–57.

Simms, J. (2018) 'Is anybody actually listening?', *People Management,* February, pp.40–43.

Stewart, I., De, D. and Cole, A. (2015) *Technology and People: The Great Job-Creating Machine.* London: Deloitte LLP.

The Economist (2018) 'Free exchange: better, stronger, faster', 3 March, p.72.

Trist, E.L. and Bamforth, K.W. (1951) 'Some social and psychological consequences of the longwall method of coal-getting', *Human Relations,* 4(1): 3–38.

Vasagar, J. (2016) 'Robots deliver service with a smile', *Financial Times,* 20 September, p.14.

Waters, R. (2017) 'The impact of cobots on workers' wellbeing', *Financial Times,* 13 September, https://www.ft.com/content/a0b8e562-3734-11e7-99bd-13beb0903fa3 [accessed January 2019]

Wisskirchen, G., Biacabe, B.T., Bormann, U., Muntz, A., Niehaus, G., Soler, G.J. and von Brauchitsch, B. (2017) *Artificial Intelligence and Robotics and Their Impact on the Workplace.* London: International Bar Association Global Employment Institute.

Key terms

organizational culture

surface manifestations of
    organizational culture

organizational values

basic assumptions

organizational socialization

anticipatory stage of socialization

accommodation stage of
    socialization

role management stage of
    socialization

role modelling

integration (or unitary)
    perspective on culture

differentiation perspective on
    culture

fragmentation (or conflict)
    perspective on culture

strong culture

weak culture

internal integration

external adaptation

social orientation

power orientation

uncertainty orientation

goal orientation

time orientation

Learning outcomes

When you have read this chapter, you should be able to define those
key terms in your own words, and you should also be able to:

1. Account for the popularity of organizational culture among
    managers and researchers.

2. List, describe and give examples of Schein's three levels of
    organizational culture.

3. Distinguish the stages of organizational socialization.

4. Contrast managerial and social science perspectives on
    organizational culture.

5. Distinguish between different types and traits of organizational
    culture.

6. Contrast different dimensions of national culture.

7. Compare different national negotiating styles.

Why study organizational culture?

Organizations are affected by culture in two different ways, internally by their organizational cultures, and externally by the national cultures of the countries within which they exist. Beginning with organizational culture, this chapter discusses what it consists of; where it comes from; how it affects employees; and what different forms it takes. Then, we move on to consider national cultures and think about how nations differ in terms of their cultural characteristics and how these affect human processes such as communicating, decision making and negotiating.

In recent years, defective organizational culture has been invoked to explain successive national scandals. Those relating to banks and financial institutions have been the most prominent. However, organizational culture has also been cited as a cause contributing to negative actions of police, the media, hospitals and local government councils. Culture is seen to have played a role in company problems including bribery, worker exploitation, sexual misconduct and car emissions data manipulation. The 'culture explanation' has been proposed as a counter to the individualistic justification of the 'one bad apple'– a single person's unethical behaviour representing an irrational departure from ethical organizational norms.

Banks have been accused of rash lending, tax evasion, financial mis-selling, attempts to manipulate the London Interbank Offer Rate (Libor) and the foreign exchange (forex) markets, and even of money laundering. In the UK, fines for mis-selling include over £10 billion for pensions, £2.6 billion for endowment mortgages, and over £16 billion for payment protection insurance (Brannan, 2017). Since 2010, the world's largest banks have spent over $300 billion on litigation (Shotter, 2015). Some have admitted their misdemeanours and have been fined, sued, forced to make reparations, or all three. When challenged by the media or an investigating parliamentary committee, their senior managers claim that the problem was caused by a small group of staff or an isolated individual employee ('a bad apple') who has now resigned, been dismissed or else is being retrained.

Home viewing

The opening scene of *Margin Call* (2011, director J.C. Chandor) shows a large number of company employees, who have been laid off, leaving their office building. Their surviving colleagues do not show any emotion or sense of loss. At the end of this scene, the character of Sam Rogers explains to his staff that this event should sharpen their focus on their own individual survival and success. He tells them it's 'Your opportunity'. The scene demonstrates the impersonal, instrumental culture of the bank, and provides an example of the 'individualizing effect' of companies' disciplinary processes. These processes are carefully designed to align employees' actions with the bank's short-term profit goals, and prevent them from caring about anything other than their own, self-interested contribution to these corporate goals (Werner, 2014; Roberts, 2001).

Peter Day (2012) argued that the banking industry's culture had changed from doing 'what is right' to doing what is OK by the lawyers and compliance officers or, as he puts it, 'doing what you can get away with'. A study by André Spicer and colleagues (2014) concluded that the 'toxic' and 'aggressive' culture inside British banks which led to the aforementioned scandals would take a generation to change. If banking culture is the problem, then changing that culture has to be the solution. Hill (2018) was concerned that the fading of the institutional memory of banks since the 2007 crisis could result in the repetition of the same problems. Others argue that such a repetition is more likely due to the same senior management being in place, denying responsibility for what had happened, and recruiting similar new staff to a fundamentally unchanged culture.

Two culture change solutions have been proposed, both involve changing people.

First, having more women – the UK Parliamentary Committee on Banking Standards reported that 'The culture on the trading floor is overwhelmingly male'. A better gender balance would reduce the amount of male testosterone that fuels greater risk taking (Thompson and Jain, 2013). Second, by training employees more, so as to reinforce company work codes, values, desired staff behaviour and positive corporate culture. Managers would then monitor, measure and maintain adherence to corporate values, especially when competitive pressures mounted (Hill, 2013).

 EMPLOYABILITY CHECK (creativity and innovation, people management, leading and managing change)

The government is frustrated at the slow speed of change in bank cultures. They are planning to legislate to force bank chiefs to implement changes to counter the potential for future mis-selling. They have asked you to recommend new, radical measures in areas of human resource management, compensation and job design that will lead to significant differences within a year. What suggestions would you make?

Has banking culture really changed?

 In this video, Gillian Tett discusses the 'flaw' in Alan Greenspan's thinking and how culture has been overlooked at the cost to the global economy ten years on from the financial crisis. By understanding the role of culture in banking, can we become more resilient to the next crisis? (14:50)

Organizational cultures

Organizational culture the shared values, beliefs and norms which influence the way employees think, feel and act towards others inside and outside the organization.

Organizational culture can be thought of as the personality of an organization. It is also often referred to as corporate culture. It deals with how things are done in a company on a daily basis. It affects how employees perform their work; how they relate to each other; to customers, and to their managers. Organizational culture affects not only task issues (how well or badly an organization performs), but also emotional issues (how workers feel about their work and their companies), as well as ethical issues (how companies behave in society).

Organizational culture has been increasingly discussed and written about since the early 1980s. First used by management consultants as a quick-fix solution to virtually every organizational problem, it was later adopted by researchers as an explanatory framework with which to understand behaviour in organizations (Alvesson, 2001). Ann Cunliffe (2008) states that organizational culture is important because it:

- shapes the image that the public has of an organization
- influences organizational effectiveness
- provides direction for the company
- helps to attract, retain and motivate staff

Some writers argue that just as one can talk about French culture, Arab culture or Asian culture, so too it is possible to discuss the organizational culture of the British Civil Service, McDonald's, Microsoft, or of Disney. It is generally recognized that organizations have 'something' (a personality, philosophy, ideology or climate) which goes beyond economic rationality, and which gives each of them their own unique identity. Organizational culture has been variously described as: 'the way we do things around here' (Deal and Kennedy, 1982), and 'how people behave when no one is watching' and 'the collective programming of the mind' (Hofstede, 1980, 2001). Some writers think that organizational culture can be created and consciously managed by company founders and chief executives, while others believe it spontaneously evolves and just has to be tolerated.

Originally introduced to managers by consultants, it was not long before researchers started to take an interest in organizational culture as well. Edgar Schein (1983), a business school professor, was amongst the first to refine the concept, seeking to measure it for research purposes. Research attention turned to the meanings and beliefs that employees assigned to organizational behaviour, and how these influenced the ways in which they themselves behaved in companies (Schultz, 1995). Writers agree that organizational culture possesses four key attributes (Groysberg et al, 2018a):

- *Shared:* resides in the shared behaviours, values and assumptions of groups and is experienced through their norms and expectations which are their unwritten rules.
- *Pervasive:* permeates the organization and is manifested in surface manifestations such as collective behaviours, physical environments, group rituals, physical symbols, stories and legends.
- *Enduring:* directs the thoughts and actions of employees over time. Culture becomes self-reinforcing as individuals are attracted to characteristics similar to their own, and companies select applicants who will 'fit in'. Culture becomes self-reinforcing and resistant to change.
- *Implicit:* despite its subliminal nature, individuals are hardwired to recognize and respond to culture instinctively as it acts like a silent language.

Culture: surface manifestations, values and basic assumptions

Edgar Schein's (2004) model is widely accepted and considers organizational culture in terms of three levels, each distinguished by its visibility to, and accessibility by individuals (Figure 4.1).

Surface manifestations

Surface manifestation of organizational culture culture's most accessible forms which are visible and audible behaviour patterns and objects.

Schein's first level of organizational culture is surface manifestations (also called 'observable culture'). It refers to the visible things that a culture produces. It includes both physical objects and also behaviour patterns that can be seen, heard or felt. These all 'send a message' to an organization's employees, suppliers and customers.

The surface level of culture is the most visible. Anyone coming into contact with it can observe it. Its constituent elements are defined below and illustrated in Table 4.1:

1. *Artefacts* are material objects created by human hands to facilitate culturally expressive activities. They include tools, furniture, appliances and clothing.
2. *Ceremonials* are formally planned, elaborate, dramatic sets of activities of cultural expression, e.g. opening events, prize-givings, graduations, religious services.
3. *Courses* and workshops are used to instruct, induct, orient and train new members in company practices.
4. *Heroes* are characters, living or dead, who personify the cultural values and beliefs; who are referred to in company stories, legends, sagas, myths and jokes; and who represent role models that current employees should emulate.
5. *Jokes* are humorous stories intended to cause amusement, but their underlying themes carry a message for the behaviour or values expected of organizational members.
6. *Language* is the particular form or manner in which members use vocal sounds and written signs to convey meaning to each other. It includes both specialist technical vocabulary related to the business (jargon), as well as general naming choices.

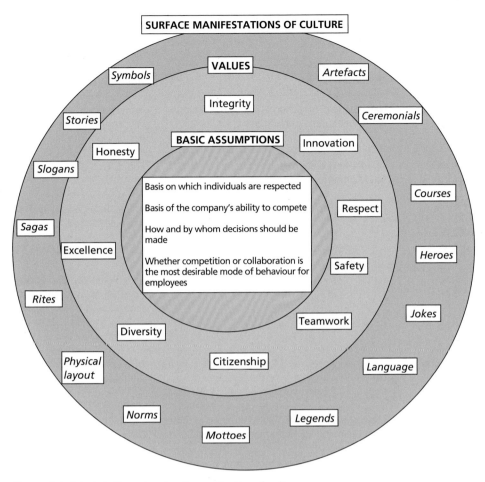

Figure 4.1: Schein's three levels of organizational culture

Source: adapted from Rollinson, D. (2008) *Organizational Behaviour and Analysis: An Integrated Approach*, Pearson Education Limited, © Pearson Education Limited 2008.

7. *Legends* are handed-down narratives about wonderful events based on company history, but embellished with fictional details. These fascinate employees and invite them to admire or deplore certain activities.

8. *Mottoes* are maxims adopted as rules of conduct. Unlike slogans, mottoes are rarely, if ever, changed.

9. *Norms* are expected modes of behaviour that are accepted as 'the company's way of doing things' thereby providing guidance for employee behaviour.

10. *Physical layout* concerns things that surround people, providing them with immediate sensory stimuli, as they carry out culturally expressive activities.

11. *Rites* are elaborate, dramatic sets of activities that consolidate various forms of cultural expression into one event. They are formally planned events such as annual staff performance reviews.

12. *Sagas* are historical narratives describing the unique accomplishments of groups and their leaders. They usually describe a series of events that are said to have unfolded over time and which constitute an important part of an organization's history.

13. *Slogans* are short, catchy phrases that are regularly changed. They are used for both customer advertising and also to motivate employees.

14. *Stories* are narratives describing how individuals acted and the decisions they made that affected the company's future. Stories can include a mixture of both fact and fiction.

15. *Symbols* refer to any act, event, object, quality or relationship that serves as a vehicle for conveying meaning.

Table 4.1: Examples of surface manifestations of organizational culture at Motorola and Rolls Royce

Manifestation	Examples	
	Motorola	*Rolls Royce*
1 Artefacts	Name badges, stationery, T-shirts, promotional items, celebratory publications	Name badges. Standard work wear, issued to all staff levels in the organisation. Each polo shirt is customised with the wearer's name.
2 Ceremonials	Annual service dances, annual total customer satisfaction competition	Fun days, sporting events, commemorative shows
3 Courses	Basic health and safety course	Induction courses to orientate new starts to RR principles
4 Heroes	Paul Galvin, Joseph Galvin – founders	Henry Rolls, Charles Royce – founders
5 Jokes		'The Right Way, The Wrong Way and the Rolls-Royce Way' – humorous, self-deprecating comments about the evolution of certain ways of going about things, but also a reminder of the importance of individuality and identity.
6 Language	Employees known as 'Motorolans'. Role-naming conventions and communications remind everyone of their responsibilities as Motorolans.	Divisional / departmental naming- job roles defined within particular naming structures
7 Legends	The first walkie-talkies. First words communicated from the moon via Motorola technology	Commemorative window in tribute to the Rolls-Royce Spitfire's contribution to World War II.
8 Mottoes	Total Customer Satisfaction, Six Sigma Quality, Intelligence Everywhere, Engineering Intelligence with Style	Centre of Excellence Trusted to Deliver Excellence
9 Norms	Ethics, Respect, Innovation	Code of Business Conduct – Quality, Excellence, Ethics, Respect
10 Physical layout	Semi-open plan – cubed group set-up. Junior managers have separate offices beside staff; senior managers have corporate offices distanced from most employees.	Open-plan layouts – applies to both offices and work cells where possible
11 Rites	Badges – initially the identity badge, but then the service badge, given at five-year intervals, has a great deal of kudos	Length of Service Acknowledgement – rite of passage.
12 Sagas	Motorola's time-lined history used repeatedly to demonstrate its influence on the world.	The 1970s bankruptcy saga.
13 Slogans	*Hello Moto* – modern re-invention of how the Motorola name came into being – a fusion of 'Motor' (representing a car) plus 'Hola' representing Hello in Spanish, to emphasise communications on the move.	
14 Stories	About a particular vice-president who fell asleep at a very important customer meeting. A cautionary tale about what not to do!	Impact of a particular shop floor visit and how the feedback to quality managers changed thinking and processes. The tale is cautionary about how misunderstandings can generate unnecessary panics.

Manifestation	Examples	
	Motorola	*Rolls Royce*
15 Symbols	Motorola 'M' brand – known as the *emsignia*	The Rolls-Royce brand – RR
	![Motorola logo]	![Rolls Royce logo]

Source: Personal communications.

> ✋ **STOP AND SEARCH**   YouTube for *Jay Wilkinson's TED talk, Company culture* (21:10).
> Wilkinson discusses whether an organization's culture is
> determined by design or by default.

Organizational values

Organizational values the accumulated beliefs held about how work should be done and situations dealt with, that guide employee behaviour.

Schein's second level of organizational culture is organizational values. These are the accumulated beliefs held about how work should be done and situations dealt with that guide employee behaviour. They can be consciously or unconsciously held; they are often unspoken, but guide employees' behaviours. They can be encapsulated either in phrases or in single words. These values:

- represent something that is explicitly or implicitly desirable to an individual or group
- influence employees' choices from available means and ends of action
- reflect their beliefs as to what is right and wrong, or specify their general preferences.

Values are said to provide a common direction for all employees, and to guide their behaviour. 'People way down the line know what they are supposed to do in most situations because the handful of guiding values is crystal clear' (Peters and Waterman, 1982, p.76). Motorola has two core values – 'uncompromising integrity' and 'constant respect for people'. The Central Intelligence Agency's (CIA) core values, shown on its website, state that 'quiet patriotism is our hallmark'; 'we pride ourselves on our extraordinary responsiveness to the needs of our customers'; staff 'embrace personal accountability'; put 'country first and agency before self', and they learn from their mistakes because they 'reflect on their performance'. Additionally, CIA employees 'seek and speak the truth', but they add, only 'to our colleagues and our customers'. You can go to the website of any large, private, public or voluntary organization (e.g. Microsoft, the British National Health Service or Amnesty International) and locate their values in their vision or mission statement. Two well-known companies' values, Google and Zappos, are listed in Table 4.2.

> ✋ **STOP AND SEARCH**   YouTube for *Zappos is a weird company – and it's happy that way.* (10:03)

Sources of values

Values distinguish one organization from another, but where do they come from? One source of values is the views of the original founder, as modified by the company's current senior management (Schein, 1983). Originally, a single person or group of people has an idea for a new business, and brings in other key people to create a core group who share a common vision. This group then creates an organization, recruits others, and begins to build a common history. Stephen Robbins and Timothy Judge (2017) suggest that a company's current top management acts as its 'culture carriers'. Thus 'organizational values are really always the values of the current company elite (senior managers). This is similar to the way that 'organizational goals' actually represent the preferred aims of chief executives and their management teams (see Figure 4.2).

In a sense, therefore, organizational values are always backward looking, despite being developed to contribute to the future development of the company. For an organizational culture to form, a fairly stable collection of people need to have shared a significant history, involving problems, which allows a social learning process to take place. Organizations that

Table 4.2: **Corporate values**

Google's 10 things we know to be true	Zappos' 10 practised core values

1 Focus on the user and all else will follow	1 Deliver WOW through service
2 It's best to do one thing, really, really well	2 Embrace and drive change
3 Fast is better than slow	3 Create fun and a little weirdness
4 Democracy on the web works	4 Be adventurous, creative and open-minded
5 You don't need to be at your desk to need an answer	5 Build open and honest relationships with communication
6 You can make money without doing evil	6 Pursue growth and learning
7 There's always more information out there	7 Build a positive team and family spirit
8 You don't need a suit to be serious	8 Do more with less
9 The need for information crosses all borders	9 Be passionate and determined
10 Great just isn't good enough	10 Be humble

Source: based on Bock (2015, p.31) and Warrick et al. (2016, p. 66)

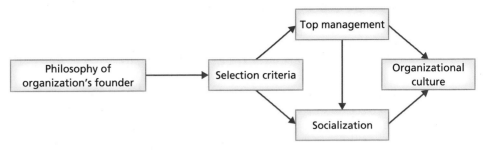

Figure 4.2: Where does organizational culture come from?
Source: Robbins and Judge (2017, p.579)

have such histories possess cultures that permeate most of their functions (Schein, 2004). Company values come in lists. They are to be found printed in company reports, framed on company walls, and published on organizational websites.

Discussing the relationship between junior level employees and corporate values, Chris Grey recounted the experience of one of his MBA students, a senior manager in a supermarket chain, a company known to be an exemplar of successful culture management. The staff had been subject to a multi-million pound culture training initiative, and he wanted to discover the extent of their 'buy-in' to the company's culture values. To what extent did front line staff subscribe to these corporate values? Not only did he find that staff did not believe in these values, but three-quarters of them claimed never to have even *heard* of these values! (Grey, 2009, p.74)

Basic assumptions

Basic assumptions
invisible, preconscious, unspoken, 'taken-for-granted' understandings held by individuals within an organization concerning human behaviour, the nature of reality and the organization's relationship to its environment.

Schein's third level of organization culture is basic assumptions. These are the invisible, preconscious, unspoken, 'taken-for-granted' understandings held by individuals within an organization concerning human behaviour, the nature of reality and to an organization's relationship to its environment. Basic assumptions are located at the deepest level of culture, and are the most difficult to comprehend. They are the set of shared but unspoken suppositions about the best way to do things within a company. They relate to the nature of reality and the organization's relationship with its environment.

Towards the start of the animated film *Chicken Run* (2000), Mrs Tweddie the farmer, responds to her husband's suspicion that the chickens are planning to escape, by saying 'They're chickens you dolt! Apart from you, they're the most stupid creatures on this planet. They don't plot, they don't scheme, and they are not organized!' Here, Mrs Tweddie's 'basic assumptions' are blinding her to reality and preventing her from taking appropriate action – her husband's suspicions are correct! (Ambrosini et al., 2012).

Over time, a company's values, beliefs and attitudes become so ingrained and well-established, that they cease to be articulated or debated by employees. Instead of being discussed, they become 'baked' into the fabric of an organization's culture. These basic assumptions begin with the founder's thinking, and then develop through a shared learning process. A company's basic assumptions often relate to:

Quality	Economy	Predictability
Stability	Excellence	Responsibility
Morality	Profitability	Innovativeness

As employees act in accordance with company values, beliefs and attitudes, these actions become embedded as basic assumptions. Because they are invisible, they are difficult to pin down (Notter and Grant, 2011). Staff who are judged not to share these basic assumptions come to be regarded as outsiders, are ostracized, and may even be 'performance managed' out of the company.

Dress rules at UBS and Google

Employee workwear is a key aspect of every organization's corporate image and reflects its organizational culture. Companies are therefore keen to ensure that their employees wear appropriate clothing when working alongside colleagues and meeting clients. However, how detailed the rules concerning appropriate dress in the workplace are, varies considerably between companies. At one extreme, there is UBS, a Swiss bank, which once issued a 42-page employee dress code to its staff. It required female staff not to wear tight, revealing shirts; ankle chains; flashy jewellery; or to let their underwear show. Male bank employees were informed that they should not wear socks with cartoon motifs or a three-day beard on their faces. Moreover, their ties should match the bone structure of their face. Other useful advice included avoiding tight shoes, as they cause a strained smile.

The UBS dress code was an attempt aimed at improving the bank's image which suffered after it accepted Europe's biggest bailout – £37 billion during the 2008 financial crisis. A UBS spokesperson said staff and clients had responded well to the rules which were being implemented in five offices in Switzerland. Staff appearance is important said one financial PR consultant, 'If banks are spending money on plush carpeting and flowers in vases, then you don't want people romping around in jeans'. In contrast, there is Google's four-word, official office dress code: 'You must wear clothes' (Schmidt and Rosenberg, 2017; Wachel, 2011).

 **STOP AND SEARCH** YouTube for *company dress code.*

Organizational socialization

Organizational socialization the process through which an employee's pattern of behaviour, values, attitudes and motives is influenced to conform to those of the organization.

The ultimate strength of a company's culture depends on the employees' shared agreement on their company's core values and their emotional attachment to them (Gordon and DiTomaso, 1992). One learns about these through organizational socialization. This is the process through which an employee's pattern of behaviour, values, attitudes and motives are influenced to conform to those of the organization's (see Figure 4.3). It includes the careful selection of new company members, their instruction in appropriate ways of thinking and behaving; and the reinforcement of desired behaviours by senior managers.

Socialization is important because, as John van Maanen and Edgar Schein (1979) argue, if the culture of the organization is to endure, new organization recruits have to be taught to see the organizational world the same way as their more experienced colleagues do. Socialization involves newcomers absorbing the values and behaviours required to survive and prosper in an organization. It reduces the variability of behaviour by instilling employees with an understanding of what is expected of them, and how they should do things. By providing both internal guidance and a shared frame of reference, socialization standardizes employee behaviour making it predictable for the benefit of senior management.

Richard Pascale (1985) distinguished seven key steps in the process of organizational socialization:

1. *Select*: carefully choose entry-level candidates whose traits predispose them towards accepting the firm's culture.

2. *Humiliate*: provide humility-inducing experiences to foster self-questioning of prior behaviour, belief and values; lower their self-comfort and self-complacency; and thus increase their acceptance of the organization's norms and values.

3. *Train*: provide front-line training that leads to mastery of one of the core disciplines of the business and tie to a proven track record.

Figure 4.3: Dimensions addressed in most socialization efforts

Source: Colquitt et al. (2009, p. 558) from Chao, G.T., O'Leary-Kelly, A.M., Wolf, S., Klein, H.J. and Gardner, P.D., 'Organizational Socialization: Its Content and Consequences', *Journal of Applied Psychology*, Vol. 79, No 5, pp. 730–43, American Psychological Association, (APA), reprinted with permission

4. *Evaluate*: measure results, reward desired behaviour, and punish undesired ones.

5. *Adherence*: ensure identification with the company's transcendent values. This allows them to reconcile the personal sacrifices that membership of an organization entails.

6. *Reinforce*: use stories and legends to interpret watershed events in the company's history to validate its culture and its aims. This provides the new employee with a code of conduct of 'how we do things around here'.

7. *Role model*: have peers or superiors, who are recognized as winners and who share common qualities, to teach by example. The protégé watches the role model and copies the traits and behaviours that they display.

David Feldman (1976) distinguished three stages in the process of socialization which he labelled anticipatory, accommodation and role management.

The anticipatory stage of socialization describes expectations that a newcomer has about the job or organization before starting work. These expectations come from learning about the firm from the media or, in the case of students, attending graduate recruitment fairs and reading the company's recruitment literature. If the individual finds that the company's values do not fit in with their own, they may withdraw from the application process. This stage is also referred to as *pre-arrival*.

The accommodation stage of socialization involves the newcomer learning about their organization, making sense of what is going on around them, and adjusting to the new norms, values and behaviours. Once inside, the organization encourages new entrants to adopt the company's beliefs and values. It can do this by having them attend induction courses; assigning them to an existing employee who 'shows them the ropes' (buddy system), or by rotating them through different departments to familiarize them with the organization's work. This stage has also been labelled *encounter* (as when the new recruit actually encounters the organization proper), and also *onboarding* (as when the individual is brought onto the 'deck' of the company).

The role management stage of socialization involves fine-tuning the lessons that newcomers have learned from the accommodation stage, and adding responsibilities expected of fully fledged organizational members . New company entrants also learn about their organizations through role modelling. They are shown employees who are judged by the company to be 'winners'. These are employees who possess the required traits, demonstrate

Anticipatory stage of socialization the expectations that a newcomer has about the job or organization before starting work.

Accommodation stage of socialization period during which newcomers learn about company norms, values, behaviours and expectations, and adjust themselves to them.

Role management stage of socialization fine-tuning newcomers' learning and adding those responsibilities expected from fully fledged organizational members.

Role modelling a form of socialization in which an individual learns by example, copying the behaviour of established organizational members.

the required behaviours, achieve the required results, and who are thus recognized and valued by the firm. The learner observes these 'winners' and acquires a mental picture of the act and its consequences (rewards and punishments), and then copies them, acting out the acquired image. This stage is also labelled the *metamorphosis* stage as the individual transforms from being a member of the public to company employee.

As individuals begin new jobs or join new organizations across a lifelong career, these three stages are re-experienced, with new lessons interpreted with the benefit of knowledge from previous socializations.

Do you speak IKEA?

IKEA is a private company founded by Ingvar Kamprad in 1943. When he died in 2018, it had 411 stores in 49 countries; 194,000 employees; and revenues of over €35 billion. Its catalogue has gone through 52 editions, and

each year, 208 million copies of it are printed in 30 languages, in 62 different versions, for 43 countries.

Language is an important part of every organizational culture. Two decades ago, it was decided to make English the working language of the group. IKEA-Swenglish is a form of pidgin English that is a living and developing language, with a limited vocabulary and a fluid grammar. It has to be learned by anyone seeking to make a career within the company. During his life and in his presence, all IKEA staff, irrespective of their position in the hierarchy, referred to Ingvar Kamprad, as 'Ingvar', while in his absence, he was to be called 'IK' or 'the founder'; but never as 'Kamprad' in the third person. The new IKEA employee also needed to become familiar with some other IKEA words and phrases which are explained below.

IKEA speak	Translation
Co-worker	IKEA employee
Retailer	Store
Visitor	Person visiting an IKEA store
Customer	Visitor who picks up an IKEA item
Advantage	Price difference below that of competitors
Swedish money	Swedish kroner (SEK)
'straight into the woodshed'	Product achieving bestseller status
BTI – breath-taking item	Product so cheap it makes customers gasp
PIJ – punch-in-the-jaw item	Cheap alternative to a competitor's product
Ingvar's bag	Blue bag with the yellow-handled lettering that customers carry around the shop
Ingvar-cakes	Biscuits served at IKEA headquarters in Älmhult in Sweden
'Open-the wallet' item	Item so cheap that it is designed to be bought on impulse.
'False nose'	Taking an inefficient decision
'I have no confidence in you any longer'	'You will be dismissed'

Source: based on Stenebo (2010)

STOP AND SEARCH   YouTube for *IKEA values.*

CUTTING EDGE   Language and cultural embeddedness

Sameer Srivastava

Amir Goldberg
(photo credit:
Nancy Rothstein)

Sameer Srivastava and Amir Goldberg (2017) studied how employees communicated with their work colleagues. Language offers a way to study organizational culture. How employees use language sheds light on how well they fit into their organization's cultural environment. The authors analysed 10 million electronic messages exchanged between the 600 staff of a US technology company over a five-year period. Word choice provided a window into company culture. Both language form and content transmit culture, and each company has its own linguistic conventions. For example, the choice of opening salutation ('Hi', 'Dear John'); use of 'I' and 'we'; how disagreement is expressed; frequency of words like 'would' and 'should'; the extent of written swearing and cursing; and so on. The film, *Margin Call* (2011) provides a good example of the prevalence of spoken profanity within a bank.

Shared linguistic patterns reinforce group solidarity while individualized ones that deviate from company conventions create symbolic barriers. The authors used an algorithm to assess how closely an individual's linguistic style matched that of others in their workplace. This was used as an indicator of cultural embeddedness which was defined as the degree to which an employee internalizes their firm's common culture and accepts group norms. It indicates their degree of person–organization culture fit. Srivastava and Goldberg found that non-managerial employees with high cultural fit were 1.5 to 2.7 times more likely to be promoted to a management position than their medium- to low-fit peers. Additionally, low-fit employees were four times more likely to leave the firm after three years than their medium-fit co-workers. In addition to current employees, these linguistic measures of cultural compatibility can also be used to identify and select job applicants who have the greatest potential to adapt themselves quickly and thoroughly to their new organization's culture.

Perspectives on culture contrasted

The debate about organizational culture takes place between two camps – managerial and social science. The managerial camp contains writers and consultants who believe that there is a relationship between a strong culture and organizational performance. They hold that, 'A well-developed and business-specific culture in which management and staff are thoroughly socialized . . . can underpin stronger organizational commitment, higher morale, more efficient performance, and generally higher productivity' (Furnham and Gunter, 1993). Ranged against them is the social science camp, home to those academics who believe that organizational culture is a term that is overused, over-inclusive and under-defined. The description of organizational culture on the preceding pages has taken a managerial perspective. Its distinguishing feature is that it is both prescriptive and normative, that is, it recommends what a company's culture *should* be. The managerial–social science debate about organizational culture can be considered under four headings:

Managerial		Social science
1. Culture *has*	*versus*	Culture *is*
2. Integration	*versus*	Differentiation/fragmentation
3. Culture managed	*versus*	Culture tolerated
4. Symbolic leadership	*versus*	Management control

1. Culture 'has' versus culture 'is'

The *has*-view holds that every organization possesses a culture which, along with its strategy, structure, technology and employees, is part of the organizational machine that can be controlled and managed. It sees organizational culture as constituting an objective reality of artefacts, values and meanings that can be quantified and measured. The culture is 'given' to new hires who have not participated in its formation. From this perspective, culture is acquired by employees. It is seen as capable of definition, intervention and control, representing a 'tool for change' that can be used by managers. The writers most associated with this view, which is still current, are the management academics and consultants mentioned earlier in the chapter (Peters and Waterman, 1982; Deal and Kennedy, 1982; Pascale and Athos, 1982).

The alternative is the *is*-view. It sees organizational culture as something that the organization *is*. Culture emerges as a matter of course as executives work to update strategy and improve processes (Lorsch and McTague, 2016). From this standpoint, individuals do things, and work together in certain ways. Thus, they create a culture which evolves spontaneously and is therefore not capable of being managed. It holds that culture cannot be easily quantified or measured, and that researchers must study it the way that anthropologists study other societies. Culture is produced and reproduced continuously through the routine interactions between organizational members. Hence organizational culture exists only in, and through, the social (inter) actions of employees. This approach seeks to understand social relations within organizations, and holds that a company's culture may not necessarily conform to what management wants. Writers associated with this view include Gagliardi (1986), Knights and Willmott (1987), Ogbonna (1993) and Smircich (1983).

 **STOP AND SEARCH**   YouTube for *Kim Hoogeveen's TED talk, Work Culture – Why the Gap?* (16:38). Hoogeveen explores why companies and leaders fail to live up to their ideals and how to correct that situation.

2. Integration versus differentiation/fragmentation

Joanne Martin (1992) distinguished three perspectives on culture which she labelled integration differentiation and fragmentation. These have formed the basis of research and writing on this topic.

Integration (or unitary) perspective on culture regards culture as monolithic, characterized by consistency, organization-wide consensus and clarity.

The managerial integration (or unitary) perspective on culture holds that an organization possesses a single, unified culture, consisting of shared values to which most employees subscribe. These integrating features lead to improved organizational effectiveness through greater employee commitment and employee control, as measured by productivity and profitability. It also includes the controversial notion of a 'strong' culture, which is defined by three characteristics: the existence of clear set of values, norms and beliefs; the sharing of these by the majority of members; and the guidance of employees' behaviour by those same values, norms and beliefs.

Differentiation perspective on culture sees organizations as consisting of subcultures, each with its own characteristics, which differ from those of its neighbours.

In contrast, social science emphasizes two perspectives – differentiation and fragmentation. The differentiation perspective on culture regards a single organization as consisting of many groups, each with their own subcultures. Each subculture possesses its own characteristics which differ from those of its neighbours. It therefore sees organizational culture as differentiated or as a plurality rather than as a single unified whole. Within an organization, there are diverse interest groups which have their own objectives (e.g. management versus labour; staff versus line; marketing versus production). Thus, the differentiation perspective sees 'cultural pluralism' as a fundamental aspect of all organizations; seeks to understand the complexity and the interaction between frequently conflicting subcultures; and therefore stands in direct contrast to the managerial integration (unitary) perspective on culture.

Martin Parker (2000) argued that subcultures are the way in which employees distinguish themselves within companies – by their occupation or profession; by the function they perform; by their geographical location in the firm; and by their age (e.g. senior members of the engineering department in the research building). These subcultures overlap and contradict each other. Thus the neat typology of types of organizational culture, which is presented later in this chapter, may understate the complexities of organizational life. These subcultures act to obstruct management attempts to develop a unified culture which might be used to control staff.

Fragmentation (or conflict) perspective on culture regards it as consisting of an incompletely shared set of elements that are loosely structured, constantly changing and which are generally in conflict.

The other social science perspective is the fragmentation (or conflict) perspective on culture. It assumes an absence of consensus; stresses the inevitability of conflict; focuses on the variety of interests and opinions between different groups; and directs attention to the power differences in organizations. The fragmentation perspective sees organizations as collections of opposed groupings which are rarely reconciled. It is critical of managers and management consultants who underplay the differences that exist between individuals, groups and departments within a company. It sees conflict rather than consensus as the norm within organizations and challenges the notion of the existence of a single unified organizational culture.

CUTTING EDGE   Frames of organizational culture

Vicki Taylor (photo credit: Bill Smith)

Vicki Taylor and Nathan Goates (2017) used a survey and interviews to assess the degree of integration, differentiation and fragmentation surrounding staff perceptions of their organization's culture. They investigated 124 employees who were located in six different offices of the same engineering company. They asked them about aspects of their company's culture and received three sets of comments.

Integrationist comments were consistent with management's espoused values with no dissent or ambiguity from individuals. Staff were asked what the company's three most important values were. The value around which there was the greatest degree of consensus was *detail-oriented* ('we are good at checking things before they go out of here'), followed by *integrity* ('we are consistently honest and, and if there's an error made, we will come clean').

Differentiation presumes the presence of subcultures which co-exist in harmony, conflict or indifference to each other. Staff were asked whether the culture of their local office or that of the entire organization was more important to them. The answers revealed differences between offices in terms of their formality and their access to management. Employees described their firm as a 'collection of six different fiefdoms' suggesting differentiation around some of the values.

→

Fragmentation focuses on conflict and ambiguity and looks for inconsistencies, contradictions and conflicting interpretations. Staff were asked if they saw a difference between formal policy and informal practice. Inconsistencies were highlighted in how the staff appraisal process was administered; how employees and clients were treated; and how the operation of standard procedures differed between offices. This suggests that each employee sees the culture differently.

The authors' findings challenge the simplistic idea that a company's culture is one set of shared meanings, ideas and values communicated by senior management. They conclude that instead, it should be understood from the parallel perspectives of consensus, subculture differentiation, and ambiguity.

3. Culture managed versus culture tolerated

Since the managerialist perspective sees culture as something that an organization *has,* it further assumes that it is capable of being managed by corporate leaders. Some companies even have a 'Director of Corporate Culture'. This has sparked three debates. First, concerning how managers can change their company's culture from 'weak' to 'strong'. Second, how culture can help a company innovate and adjust rapidly to environmental changes. Third, the part played by leaders' visions and styles of management in managing their cultures. This view assumes that senior company executives can and should exercise cultural leadership which maintains, promotes and develops their company's culture (Trice and Beyer, 1984; 1993). Some 'culture managed' writers, such as Fred Luthans (1995), argue that strong cultures can be created by management's use of rewards and punishments. In contrast, the 'culture tolerated' academics argue that employees' deeply held values and beliefs cannot be modified in the short term using such external stimuli.

Chris Grey was critical of culture management programmes. In his view, they had an ambitious desire to shape individuals' beliefs. This search for shared values (between the company's and the employees') entailed, in his view, an aggressive approach which focused primarily on employees rather than upon their work. He stated that, 'Culture management aspires to intervene in and regulate [employee] being, so that there is no distance between individuals' purposes and those of the organization for which they work' (Grey, 2009, p.69).

In general, he felt that culture management programmes achieved this by selecting those staff amenable to organizational values; sacking employees who were less amenable; using training and communication to expose staff to organizational values through videos and mission statements; having core values printed on pocket-sized cards and distributed to staff; and using company slogans, company songs, group exercises and, in the case of one UK bank, having, 'a parade of employees in animal costumes chanting the virtues of the bank as a fun place to be!' (Grey, 2009, p. 69).

4. Symbolic leadership versus management control

Symbolic leadership (or the management of organizational culture) is one way of encouraging employees to feel that they are working for something worthwhile, so that they will work harder and be more productive. Burman and Evans (2008) argue that it is only those managers who are also leaders who can impact culture in this way. This view treats leader-managers as heroes who symbolize the organization both internally to their employees, and externally to customers, governments and others (Smircich and Morgan, 1982). These leaders said Carol Ray (1986, p. 294) 'possess direct ties to the values and goals of the dominant elites in order to activate the emotion and sentiment which may lead to devotion, loyalty and commitment to the company'. The managerialist view holds that employees can be helped to internalize organizational values.

Home viewing

The film *Steve Jobs* (2015, director Danny Boyle) is a biographical drama based on life of the co-founder of Apple Inc. It depicts the launches of three iconic company products – Macintosh, Next and the iMac. As you watch the film, look out for examples of Jobs' values and beliefs. How might these have influenced the development of Apple's organizational culture?

In contrast, the social science perspective, argues that symbolic leadership represents management's attempt to get employees to direct their own behaviour themselves towards senior management's goals. People enter organizations with different motivations, experiences and values. These natural individual differences tend to direct their behaviours in numerous, often divergent directions. Managers have always sought ways to control their employees, ensuring that they behave in relatively uniform and predictable ways. Carol Ray (1986) distinguished three different types of management control through history

From the 1870s	*Bureaucratic control (Frederick Winslow Taylor, Max Weber)*
	Detailed rules and procedures, jobs and roles specified, use of rewards to encourage compliance
From the 1920s	*Humanistic control (Elton Mayo)*
	Emphasis on work as a group activity, group membership as a human need, and directing employees through group norms and sanctions
From the 1980s	*Culture control (Deal and Kennedy, Edgar Schein)*
	An organization's culture is managed to encourage employees to identify with their company and its goals

Ray noted the move away from *bureaucratic control* towards *humanistic control*. The former focuses on external, overt control of employees through rules, procedures, close supervision, appraisal and rewards. Frederick Taylor, Henry Ford, Max Weber and Henri Fayol, all recommended this approach to direct the behaviour of employees towards organizational goals. It was expensive in terms of the supervisory manpower required, frequently caused resentment, and elicited grudging compliance from the workers. In contrast, humanistic control sought to satisfy employees' needs by providing a satisfying work task or a pleasant working group life to promote internal control. Pioneered by Mayo (1933, 1945), the hope was that by using this approach, workers would willingly meet organizational goals by achieving their own personal needs and objectives.

CRITICAL THINKING

A study by the Boston Research Group into governance, culture and leadership asked employees from all hierarchical levels about their company's culture. Some saw their employer's culture as being top-down, but with skilled leadership, many rules and a mixture of carrots and sticks – 'the informed acquiescence approach'. Others described their company's culture as being based on command-and-control, top-down management or leadership-by-coercion – the 'blind obedience approach'. Still others, reported a culture where employees were guided by a set of core principles and values that inspired them to align their behaviour with their firm's mission – 'the self-governance approach'. Into which of these three categories would you place your own organization's culture? (*The Economist*, 2011).

The next change was from *humanistic control* to *culture control*. It was an attempt by management to regulate organizational members' thoughts, values and emotions. It involves shaping the internal worlds and identities of the employees in their workplaces. Carol Ray suggested that managers saw organizational culture as an effective control tool. It sought to affect what employees thought, believed, felt and valued. She said that 'control by corporate culture views people as emotional, symbol-loving and needing to belong to a superior entity or collectivity' (Ray, 1986, p. 295). This form of control had previously only been attempted by religious organizations. A manager at a high-tech US company summarized the approach: 'Power plays don't work. You can't make 'em do anything. They have to want to. So you have to work through the culture. The idea is to educate people without [their] knowing it. Have the religion and not know how they got it' (quoted in Kunda, 1992, p.5).

Work or play?

André Spicer

Peter Fleming and André Spicer (2004, 2007) researched what they termed the social geography of self and identity. They studied a call centre company that they named Sunray, which emphasized a culture of fun, epitomized in the slogan 'Remember the 3Fs – Focus, Fun, Fulfilment'. Their study demonstrated how the company attempted to blur the traditional boundaries that typically divided work life and private life, in an effort to extend its control over employees. It disrupted and reorganized the traditional inside/outside boundary by holding team meetings before or after work at city centre cafés or nearby parks. Its team-building meetings involved participants bringing personal items from home into the workplace. Sunray used the private lives of workers as a training strategy to get them to invest more of themselves in their work.

It also encouraged inside-the-organization activities that normally took place outside work, e.g. wearing pyjamas, drinking alcohol; bringing home-made food to share with colleagues; decorating a work area with personal items; dressing casually – to be 'free to be themselves'. Additionally, it encouraged activities-at-home

which were more appropriate inside the organization e.g. the memorizing of the company slogan; attending company training sessions on Sundays. These actions challenged the social geography of work and non-work.

The researchers found that Sunray's cultural techniques evoked in employees' feelings and identities traditionally associated with outside work, but not normally found inside it. The cultural message was that all the experiences that employees normally looked forward to after work, such as having fun, partying, joy, fulfilment, exhilaration and friendship could be obtained inside the company. The aim of this consciously blurring of the boundary between private life and working life was to maximize the productive demands of the company. It was the 'whole' person that the company now desired, not just the uniform corporate self, since employee creativity and innovation were now linked to staff 'being themselves'. Sunray had a conscious recruitment strategy of employing young people who they found 'can be themselves and know how to have fun'. The major corporations around the world seek to absorb the lifestyles, consumption patterns and social activities of their employees by importing the positive experiences and emotions associated with non-work into the workplace.

Other researchers have picked up these themes. Fleming and Sturdy (2011) studied the fun culture in a call centre and showed how management's compulsory sociability and organized fun events acted as distractions from their punishing Tayloristic control regimes. Costas (2012) investigated the culture of friendship in a large, global professional services firm and Ramarajan and Reid (2013) considered how much of our own self was defined by our work and how this came about.

The use of organizational culture to control and direct employees' behaviour involves the selective application of rites, ceremonials, myths, stories, symbols, and legends by company managers to direct the behaviour of their employees. It is called symbolic management. It involves encouraging employees to internalize desired company values and norms. External control is thus replaced by self-control, such as that used by professionals such as doctors, teachers, lawyers and priests (Willmott, 1993). This approach appeals to managers because it is cheaper, avoids resentment, and builds employee commitment to the company and its goals.

CRITICAL THINKING

Consider the organizational approach to culture as described in the research on Sunray. What are the costs and benefits of it to (a) the company and (b) the employees?

'Dress down Friday' – employee democracy or management control?

In Lucy Kellaway's radio programme about work in offices, Professor Chris Grey noted that superficially a relaxed corporate dress code such as 'Dress down Fridays', appeared to be something that was humanizing and which allowed employees to demonstrate their individuality. However, he argued that it sent the message to staff that there was no difference between their being at work and their not being at work. It said to each employee, there is no 'real you' that is separate from work. The 'real you' is there, always present, at work. The relaxed corporate dress code, along with a company's access to all its staff through their mobile phones at all times and everywhere, symbolized and enacted the idea that home and work exist together and that employees should no longer think of themselves as '9-to-5ers' even if they officially work these hours. The dress code symbolized the view that work life and home life are one. Thus, in Grey's view, the real importance of informal clothing at work was not that it denoted a freer, more democratic atmosphere within the workplace, but rather the opposite, it was an example of greater control being exerted over employees by their senior management (Kellaway, 2013).

Types and traits of organizational cultures

An individual can be described in terms of either the personality type that they fit or the traits that they possess –'you fit a type, you have a trait' (**Chapter 6**). The personality of an organization – its culture – can be described in a similar way. In the past, type approaches to culture have been favoured with an entire company being labelled as having a *power, role,* *person* or a *task culture* (Handy, 1993); or a *communal, networked, mercenary* or *fragmented culture* (Goffee and Jones, 2003) depending on the variables considered to be crucial by the researchers.

In recent years however, a traits approach to culture has been favoured. Authors like Cameron and Quinn (2011) have argued that an organization's culture is made up of a blend of four competing traits which they call 'value sets', and label *clan, hierarchy, adhocracy* and *market culture.* They suggest that while a company may have a dominant value set at a given time, the other value sets are also present to a lesser degree (Figure 4.4). Thus both complementary and opposing value sets co-exist within a single firm in a symbiotic relationship with each other.

Boris Groysberg and his associates (2018a) developed this traits approach to culture. Using surveys, they studied the leadership styles and values of 1,300 executives and 25,000 employees in 230 organizations of various types in different industries and regions. The crucial variables that they believed distinguished firms were:

- *How people interact:* This dimension relates to an organization's orientation towards people interactions. It ranges from highly independent to highly interdependent. Independent ones emphasize employee autonomy, individual action and competition. In contrast, interdependent ones stress integration, collaboration, managing relationships and coordinating group effort.

- *How people to respond to change:* This dimension concerns an organization's orientation towards change. It ranges from flexibility to stability. A flexibility culture stresses adaptability, innovation, openness, diversity and long-term orientation. In contrast, a stability culture will prioritize consistency, predictability and maintenance of the status quo. It follows rules, reinforces hierarchy and strives for efficiency.

Using these dimensions, the authors identified eight styles which distinguish both organizational cultures and the individual values of its leaders and employees. These styles are mapped along the two dimensions shown in Figure 4.5.

Each culture style had its own characteristics and advantages and disadvantages for both employees and their managers. Table 4.3 lists these together with an example company. Groysberg et al. argue that a single company's culture can be made up of a combination of these styles.

Implicit in this research is the belief that culture and leadership are linked; that founders are capable of creating distinctive cultures; and that managers, through their conscious actions, can shape those same cultures. Like Cameron and Quinn (2011) before them, Groysberg et al. (2018a) argue that several styles or cultures can co-exist within a single organization and its employees. For example, they assert that while styles located within a single quadrant such as *safety* and *order* (Figure 4.5) can co-exist, those located in different quadrants such as

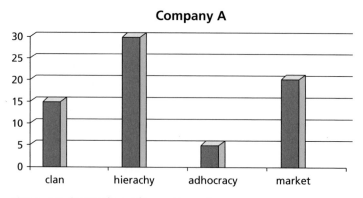

Figure 4.4: Competing culture value sets

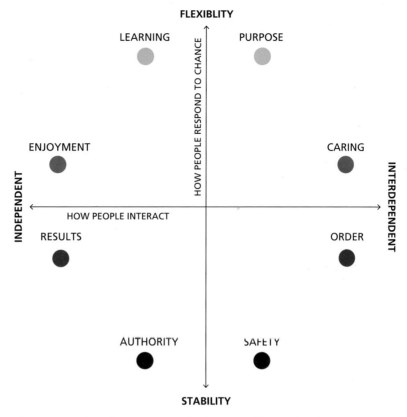

Figure 4.5: Styles of organizational cultures and leadership framework
Source: Groysberg et al. (2018a, p. 47)

Table 4.3: Styles of organizational cultures and leadership

Culture style	Style description	Advantages	Disadvantages	Company example
CARING Warm, sincere, relational	*Caring* focuses on relationships and mutual trust. Work environments are warm, collaborative, and welcoming places where people help and support one another. Employees are united by loyalty; leaders emphasize sincerity, teamwork, and positive relationships.	Improved teamwork, engagement, communication, trust and sense of belonging	Overemphasis on consensus building may reduce exploration of options, stifle competitiveness, and slow decision making	Disney
PURPOSE Purpose-driven, idealistic, tolerant	*Purpose* is exemplified by idealism and altruism. Work environments are tolerant, compassionate places where people try to do good for the long-term future of the world. Employees are united by a focus on sustainability and global communities; leaders emphasize shared ideals and contributing to a greater cause.	Improved appreciation of diversity, sustainability, and social responsibility	Overemphasis on a long-term purpose and ideals may get in the way of practical and immediate concerns	Whole Foods

(Continued)

Table 4.3: *Continued*

Culture style	Style description	Advantages	Disadvantages	Company example
LEARNING Open, inventive, exploring	*Learning* is characterized by exploration, expansiveness, and creativity. Work environments are inventive and open-minded places where people spark new ideas and explore alternatives. Employees are united by curiosity; leaders emphasize innovation, knowledge and adventure.	Improved innovation, agility and organizational learning	Overemphasis on exploration may lead to a lack of focus and an inability to exploit existing advantages	Tesla
ENJOYMENT Playful, instinctive fun-loving	*Enjoyment* is expressed through fun and excitement. Work environments are light-hearted places where people tend to do what makes them happy. Employees are united by playfulness and stimulation; leaders emphasize spontaneity and a sense of humour.	Improved employee morale, engagement and creativity	Overemphasis on autonomy and engagement may lead to a lack of discipline and create possible compliance or governance issues	Zappos
RESULTS Achievement, driven, goal-focused	*Results* is characterized by achievement and winning. Work environments are outcome-oriented and merit-based places where people aspire to achieve top performance. Employees are united by a drive for capability and success; leaders emphasize goal accomplishment.	Improved execution, external focus, capability building, and goal achievement	Overemphasis on achieving results may lead to communication and collaboration breakdowns and higher levels of stress and anxiety	GSK
AUTHORITY Bold, decisive, dominant	*Authority* is defined by strength, decisiveness, and boldness. Work environments are competitive places where people strive to gain personal advantage. Employees are united by strong control; leaders emphasize confidence and dominance.	Improved speed of decision making and responsiveness to threats or crises	Overemphasis on strong authority and bold decision making may lead to politics, conflict and a psychologically unsafe work environment	Huawei
SAFETY Realistic, careful, prepared	*Safety* is defined by planning, caution and preparedness. Work environments are predictable places where people are risk-conscious and think things through carefully. Employees are united by a desire to feel protected and anticipate change; leaders emphasize being realistic and planning ahead.	Improved speed of decision making and responsiveness to threats or crises	Overemphasis on strong authority and bold decision making may lead to politics, conflict and a psychologically unsafe work environment	Lloyds of London
ORDER Rule abiding, respectful, cooperative	*Order* is focused on respect, structure and shared norms. Work environments are methodical places where people tend to play by the rules and want to fit in. Employees are united by cooperation; leaders emphasize shared procedures and time-honoured customs.	Improved operational efficiency, reduced conflict, and greater civic-mindedness	Overemphasis on rules and traditions may reduce individualism, stifle creativity, and limit organizational agility	SEC

Source: adapted from Groysberg et al. (2018a, p. 49)

"I want the public to think of us as 'The Company With A Heart'. But I want *you* to think of us as the company that will chew you up, spit you out and smear you into the carpet if you screw up."

safety and *learning* are unlikely to be found together within a single company. The authors recommend their framework as a tool to help managers to:

- Orient new employees to the culture that they are joining
- Understand their organization's culture and its consequences
- Design an aspirational culture and communicate changes to achieve it
- Identify the existence of subcultures which might affect group performance
- Measure the degree of consistency in employees' views of their company's culture
- Assess the match between an executive's leadership styles and their organizational culture

---

CRITICAL THINKING   Consider the two approaches towards organizational culture – 'culture *is*' and 'culture *has*'. Given the vested interests of chief executives, management consultants and business school academics, which one would each favour and why?

Strong, weak and appropriate cultures

Strong culture one in which an organization's core values and norms are widely shared among employees, intensely held by them, and which guide their behaviour.

Weak culture one in which there is little agreement among employees about their organization's values and norms, the way things are supposed to be, or what is expected of them.

The task of measuring organization culture, using various survey methods, is itself problematic. Denison et al. (2014) have critically reviewed the various attempts that have been made to do this.

Strong and weak cultures

The research literature distinguishes between strong culture and weak culture organizations (Gordon and DiTomaso, 1992; Chatman et al., 2014). A strong culture is defined by O'Reilly (1989) as one which possesses:

- *Intensity:* organizational members have a strong emotional attachment to the core values and norms of the organizations and are willing to display approval or disapproval of fellow members who act in certain ways.
- *Sharedness:* there is widespread agreement among employees about these organizational values and norms.

In contrast, a weak culture is one in which employees neither agree upon nor are emotionally attached to their organization's core values.

✓✓✓   **EMPLOYABILITY CHECK (how organizations work, critical thinking)**

A company's senior management team has read in a business magazine that developing a strong company culture is the key to improving organizational performance and achieving financial success. It is considering hiring an international consultancy to implement a 'culture change programme'. Before embarking on this long and expensive 'culture strengthening' venture, the team has asked you to assess the likelihood of its success. What recommendations would you make?

Denison et al. (2004) noted that models linking organizational culture and organizational performance have to deal with the contradiction of companies attempting to achieve both internal integration (getting all their departments and staff to work in tandem) and external adaptation (responding quickly and effectively to environmental changes). They write that organizations that are market-focused and opportunistic have problems with internal integration. In contrast, those that are well-integrated and over-controlled can have difficulties of external adaptation responding to their changing environments.

A strong culture may impede success if it encourages conformist attitudes. Miller (1994) suggested that it can cause inertia (clinging to past recipes); immoderation (foolish risk taking); inattention (selective perception of signals) and insularity (failure to adapt to the environment). Strong cultures are slow to develop and difficult to change. Strong cultures may not necessarily be 'good' cultures if they result in employees holding inappropriate attitudes and managers making wrong decisions. They can also impede attempts at successful mergers between companies whose different cultures do not 'fit' together. Thus one can compare the advantages and disadvantages of strong cultures as shown in Table 4.4.

> **Internal integration** the process through which employees adjust to each other, work together, and perceive themselves as a collective entity.

> **External adaptation** the process through which employees adjust to changing environmental circumstances to attain organizational goals.

Appropriate culture

This line of argument leads us away from a 'one best culture' for organizational effectiveness viewpoint and towards having an appropriate culture. Rob Goffee and Gareth Jones (2003) take this contingency approach to culture which holds that 'it all depends'. The most appropriate culture for any organization is one that 'fits' the organization's environment, that is, it meets the challenges facing the company. Developing this theme, Groysberg et al. (2018b) identified five internal and external company factors to be considered:

- *Strategy:* Culture must support the business strategy. If a company has a low-cost corporate strategy, then an *order* and *authority* cultural style can maintain efficiency and keep costs low. If it has an innovation strategy, then *enjoyment* and *learning* styles can stimulate new ideas.

- *Leadership:* Culture can constrain or facilitate the performance of a chief executive. A lack of cultural fit between a company and the leadership style of an incoming chief executive can lead to failure at senior management level.

- *Organizational design:* Structure usually follows culture. Companies stressing teamwork and cooperation may emphasise *caring* and *enjoyment* cultural styles. However, a long-established structure can generate its own company culture.

Table 4.4: Advantages and disadvantages of a strong culture

Advantages	Disadvantages
Creates and supports the company mission, vision and values	Difficult to adjust at times of environment change
Helps create a unique company brand image	May be resisted by some employees with resultant effects on their performance
Guides all members, directing them towards common goals	Common view reduces critical thinking among employees resulting in unethical behaviour.
Promotes a healthy relationship between employees, uniting those from different backgrounds	Creates difficulties when a company merges or is acquired by another with a different culture.
Attracts and retains the best applicants, reduces turnover	Reduces diversity by attracting similar-minded applicants thereby reducing creativity.
Reduces need for detailed policies and procedures because the 'way things are done around here' is well understood and accepted	

- *Industry:* Cultures need to adapt to meet the demands of different industries with their own regulations and customer needs. Governmental financial regulations of banks may stress *safety* and *order* cultural styles in the future, while charities may emphasize *caring* and *purpose* styles.

- *Region:* Organizational culture is affected by national culture. Companies operating in countries which have a collectivist social orientation which values equity have cultural styles that emphasize *order* and *safety* like France. Those which are oriented to uncertainty, such as the USA emphasise *learning, purpose* and *enjoyment* styles.

Culture change

Since 2014, under the leadership of Satya Nadella, Microsoft has de-emphasized Windows and promoted Azure, its Windows-based cloud computing platform. This has allowed Nadella to change the firm's culture to one which permits staff to constantly renew themselves, to keep learning and improving. The company's new service is its global computing cloud consisting of 100 data centres serving-up web-based applications. This shift in corporate strategy has been accompanied by

a more open and less abrasive organizational culture. Specific strategic, staff and symbolic changes have included:

- Allowing Microsoft Office to be run on mobile devices that use competing operating systems.

- Restructuring to become more of a vertically integrated technology firm. It not only writes its own software, but also designs its own hardware; develops some of its own chips; and builds its own data centres.

- Employees are no longer graded along a curve, with those at the bottom receiving no bonus or promotion.

- Microsoft's annual retreats are now attended by the heads of recently-acquired companies, and not just by long-time executives.

Well regarded firms find it easier to attract top-rated employees who are highly mobile and who can choose their preferred employer. They are likely to avoid firms with a culture that has a reputation for aggression. Such a culture can also attract the attention of regulators, leading to a public backlash. Mr Nadella has given Microsoft a new Gestalt or personality that investors appear to like (*The Economist,* 2017).

National cultures

The culture of a nation is affected by many variables. Laurent (1989) argued that national culture is more powerful and stable than organizational culture. Brooks (2018) saw organizational culture being partly the outcome of societal factors, some of which are identified in Figure 4.6. National cultural stereotypes are well established: Scots are mean; Americans are brash; Germans are humourless; French are romantic; and Japanese are inscrutable. Researchers have studied how national cultures might affect organizational cultures in specific country settings. For example, there is much known about the processes and outcomes of multi-cultural teams (Stahl et al., 2010). Attempts to establish a common organizational culture in a multi-national firm can be undermined by the strength of a national culture. An organization's culture, while having unique properties, is necessarily embedded within the wider norms and values of the country in which its office and facilities are located. It is affected by the personal values that employees bring with them to work.

Vanhoegaerden (2001) felt that an awareness and understanding of national cultural differences was crucial for everybody in the organization. He suggested two reasons as to why these have been neglected. First, many people believed that, underneath, everybody was fundamentally the same. This belief is reinforced by the impression that national cultures are merging.

Figure 4.6: **Factors affecting national culture**

Source: Brooks, I. (2018) Organisational Behaviour: Individuals, Groups and Organisation, Pearson Education Limited, p.12

The success of global companies such as Disney, Coca-Cola and others can wrongly convince us that the countries in the world are becoming more alike. However, the political upheavals, economic crises, military conflicts and human suffering reported on TV screens every evening challenges this similarity view and vividly demonstrates that national cultures remain very different.

Social orientation
the relative importance of the interests of the individual versus the interest of the group – *individualism v collectivism.*

Second, the convergence that appears to exist does so at only a superficial level. Many deep national cultural differences remain. Even an archetypal global brand like McDonald's encounters cultural obstacles as it covers the world. When it opened in Japan, it found that Ronald McDonald's clown-like white face did not go down well. In Japan, white is associated with death and was unlikely to persuade people to eat Big Macs. The company also found that Japanese people had difficulty in pronouncing the 'R' in Ronald, so the character had to be renamed *Donald* McDonald. Studies have examined the impact of national culture (Taras et al., 2011).

Home viewing

Outsourced (2007, director John Jeffcoat) tells the story of Todd Anderson (played by Josh Hamilton), a 32-year-old manager of a Seattle customer call centre whose entire order fulfilment department is outsourced to India. Despite facing unemployment, he accepts a temporary job to go there to train his replacements. What does he learn about Indian culture? As you watch the film, each time you notice a culturally-specific practice, tradition, taboo, behaviour, attitude, assumption or approach, pause the film, and make a note of it. How many items do you end up with on your list? What issues does the film raise about the effect of national cultural difference at work; the relationships between employees from different backgrounds; and the global economy's impact on national and personal identity?

Power orientation
the appropriateness of power / authority within organizations – *respect v tolerance.*

Uncertainty orientation the emotional response to uncertainty and change – *acceptance v avoidance.*

At both the organizational and national levels of the cultural debate, one sees not only attempts to identify specific traits, but also attempts to classify organizations and countries into different types. This creation of trait lists and typologies parallels work in individual personality. In the 1980s, Geert Hofstede (1986, 1991) carried out a cross-cultural study of 116,000 employees of the same multi-national company located in forty countries. He distinguished national cultures in terms of five orientations – social, power, uncertainty, goal and time (Hofstede and Bond, 1988). Each cultural orientation affects the perceptions, attitudes, values, motivation and behaviours of people who live in it. Like personality assessment, each of the orientations represents a separate cultural continuum (personality trait), so each national culture can be positioned somewhere along each dimension as shown in Figure 4.7.

 **STOP AND SEARCH**   YouTube for *Hofstede.*

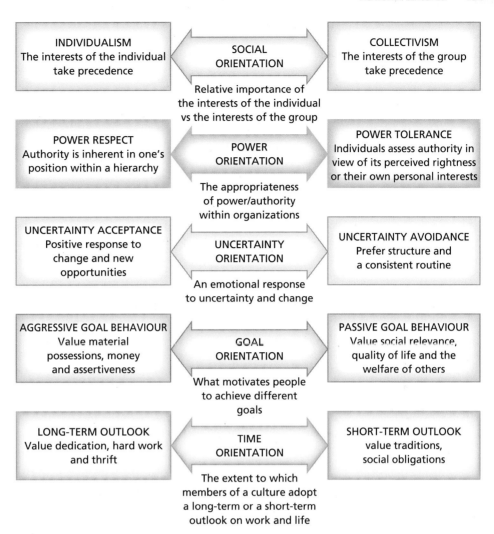

Figure 4.7: Hofstede's five dimensions of national culture

Source: Griffin, Ricky W; Pustay, Michael W., *International Business,* 5th Edition, © 2007, p.102. Reprinted by permission of Pearson Education, Inc. Upper Saddle River, NJ.

Goal orientation the motivation to achieve goals – *aggressive masculinity v passive femininity.*

Time orientation the time outlook on work and life – *short term v long term.*

The Global Leadership and Organizational Behaviour Effectiveness (GLOBE) programme has updated and extended Hofstede's pioneering work. This is a longitudinal study of leadership and organizational culture of 825 organizations located in 62 countries (Javidan and House, 2001; House et al. 2004). Whereas Hofstede's was a one-off, snapshot survey, GLOBE is a longitudinal study reporting changes over time. GLOBE contrasts national cultures on nine dimensions, which include, but also go beyond, those proposed by Hofstede. The GLOBE researchers have summarized the findings of the first two decades of their research into leadership and national culture and these are shown in Table 4.5. This shows the three highest and lowest ranking countries on each of GLOBE's nine dimensions.

Table 4.5: Cultural dimensions and GLOBE country rankings

Cultural dimension	Definition: the degree to which	Countries scoring high	Countries scoring low
Assertiveness	Individuals are bold, forceful, dominant, confrontational or demanding in relationships with others	Spain USA Greece	Sweden New Zealand Switzerland

(Continued)

Table 4.5: *Continued*

Cultural dimension	Definition: the degree to which	Countries scoring high	Countries scoring low
In-group collectivism	Individuals express pride, loyalty and cohesiveness to their organizations or families	Egypt China Morocco	Denmark Sweden New Zealand
Institutional collectivism*	Organizational and government practices encourage and reward collective distribution of resources (as under socialism) and collective action.	Greece Hungary Germany	Denmark Singapore Japan
Future orientation	Individuals engage in future-oriented behaviours planning, delaying gratification and investing in the future.	Denmark Canada Netherlands	Russia Argentina Poland
Gender differentiation	A collective minimizes different treatment of men and women, as through equal opportunities based on ability and performance.	South Korea Egypt Morocco	Sweden Denmark Slovenia
Humane orientation	A society or organization encourages and rewards individuals for being fair, altruistic, generous, caring and kind to others.	Indonesia Egypt Malaysia	Germany Spain France
Performance orientation	A society encourages and rewards group members for performance improvements, excellence, high standards and innovation.	USA Taiwan New Zealand	Russia Argentina Greece
Power distance	Members of a collective expect power to be distributed equally.	Russia Spain Thailand	Denmark Netherlands South Africa
Uncertainty avoidance	A society, organization or group relies on social norms, rules and procedures to alleviate unpredictability of future events	Austria Denmark Germany	Russia Hungary Bolivia

* *A low score indicates collectivism*

Source: based on House et al. (2004) in Hellriegel and Slocum (2009); Javidan and House (2001) and Dorfman et al. (2012)

 **STOP AND SEARCH**   YouTube for *GLOBE Project Group 2* (9:15).

Home viewing

Culture clashes are a popular genre in films allowing the misunderstandings between people from different national cultures to be explored including cross-cultural miscommunication. Amongst the best known of these movies are *French Kiss* (with Meg Ryan and Kevin Kline); *Fools Rush In* (Matthew Perry and Salma Hayek); and *Lost in Translation* (Bill Murray and Scarlett Johansson). Can you think of any other similar films?

Corporate culture of Japan Inc. put on trial

 This video discusses how quality control scandals at companies such as Nissan Motor and Kobe Steel have shaken trust in Japan's hard-earned reputation for high manufacturing quality (2:22).

What did she find? Leadership cultures

? Erin Meyer (2017) studied differences in leadership cultures in different countries. She argues that managers fail to distinguish between two important dimensions of leadership culture – authority and decision making. Cultural attitudes towards authority range from strongly hierarchical (subordinates defer to their superiors) through to strongly egalitarian (power shared among employees). Attitudes towards decision making extend from top-down (boss makes the decisions) through to consensual (decisions reached by group agreement). Following her interviews with managers from 19 countries, she was able to place each country's leadership culture into one of the four quadrants below – each had its own combination of attitude to decision making and to authority.

Top-down decision making and egalitarian authority	Top-down decision making and hierarchical authority
Consensual decision making and egalitarian authority	Consensual decision making and hierarchical authority

First try something easy. Into which boxes would you place Japan, Indonesia, Sweden and Australia? Now try something more difficult. Where would Brazil, Germany, Netherlands and the United Kingdom go? **(Answers in chapter Recap.)**

Cultural disintegration

Erin Meyer (2015a) observed that in the past, individuals worked in local organizations, occupied the same building, interacted with colleagues and clients from the same culture, and shared common ways of communicating and making decisions. However, with globalization employees have become geographically dispersed, they have lost shared assumptions and norms, and differences in how they respond to information, communicate with each other and make decisions have increased. She has noted that long-established company cultures have begun to break down. She observed a number of phenomena in relation to this:

- *Implicit communication breakdown:* In culturally and physically homogeneous organizations, messages are passed implicitly. We communicate in shorthand using unspoken cues. We read others' voice tones and their body language, picking up on subtexts. However, when employees work with colleagues from other cultures in far-flung locations, that implicit communication breaks down. This is because, as we cannot see them or read their body language, we miss the subtle meanings. The consequence is misunderstanding and inefficiency.

- *Fault lines appear:* Employees split into separate camps, creating a 'them-and-us' situation. Trust and empathy between colleagues is built by interacting over lunch and the

coffee machine. If you do not see people regularly; if they speak unfamiliar languages; have different customs; and experience the world differently, it is difficult to bond with them.

- *Corporate and national cultures clash:* Firms with strong, successful cultures seek to maintain these in their offices around the world, even when these conflict with local national cultures. This may work for companies with highly innovative products or services. However, hiring and training local employees to fit in with corporate culture may prevent them succeeding in the local, national culture.

Meyer offers five solutions to avoid cultural disintegration when expanding a company internationally:

- *Train everyone in key norms:* Train local recruits to adopt some corporate norms.
- *Give everyone a voice:* Ensure that every cultural group within the organization is heard.
- *Identify dimensions of difference:* Understand the relevant dimensions along which the two cultures differ.
- *Be heterogeneous everywhere:* Take steps to ensure national, age and gender diversity in all company locations. Spread tasks and functions around different locations. Instruct employees to build bridges of cultural understanding.
- *Protect creative units:* Before formalizing systems with detailed job descriptions and employee handbooks, protect those parts of the organization which rely on implicit communication, flexible job roles, and informal operating methods.

Rise of intercultural managers

In this video, Della Bradshaw talks to Jean-Phiippe Ammeux, director of the IESEG School of Management in France. She asks him about the way in which managers are being taught be become inter-culturally aware. What are the limitations of the approaches that Ammeux describes? What would you suggest yourself? (4:00)

Multicultural brokers and team performance

Sujin Jang

Sujin Jang (2017) addressed the well recognized problem that while teams composed of individuals from different countries can generate more creative ideas, their effectiveness is often reduced due to the presence of different cultural norms. Jang considered whether a 'cultural broker', someone who can facilitate cross-cultural interactions based on their multicultural experience, could improve the performance of culturally diverse teams.

Her experiment involved creating 83 three-person teams, each of which included two monocultural members, an American and one Indian, and one multicultural member. In approximately half of the teams, the multicultural member was a 'cultural insider' whose background overlapped with those of their fellow team members (in this case, cultural insiders were Indian American). In the rest of the teams, the multicultural member was a 'cultural outsider' whose background did not overlap with either of their team members (for example, a Chinese Australian).

Each of the 83 teams had the same task. Their members worked together in an online chat system to plan a multicultural wedding, developing ideas for rituals, music and food that integrated both American and Indian cultures. The chats were analysed to determine whether members were *eliciting* information from each other (e.g. 'What is a famous American wedding song?') or *integrating* information (e.g. 'How about a Western wedding song remixed in Bollywood style?'). A panel of experts judged the teams' ideas.

Jang found that although the performance of the different teams was similar irrespective of whether they included a cultural insider or a cultural outsider, the composition of the team did affect how they operated. She found that while cultural outsiders mainly elicited information and ideas from the different cultures in the team, cultural insiders mainly integrated information and ideas from the different cultures. Both eliciting and integrating led to enhanced team performance. The author recommends that when putting together teams, managers should identify those members who have had experience of working in multiple cultures, and be aware of how their backgrounds overlap with those of the other team members.

Negotiating internationally

In today's globalized economy, managers are negotiating with their counterparts from different countries and cultures. To succeed, they need to know how the other person is reacting, read their unspoken signals, and reach correct conclusions. Erin Meyer (2015b) grouped nationalities on the basis of how emotionally expressive and confrontational each was (Figure 4.8).

 **STOP AND SEARCH**   YouTube for *The culture map – Erin Meyer* (11.09). The author discusses how to be an effective negotiator in different countries.

She then offered five rules of thumb for negotiating with individuals with different cultural styles of communication:

1. Decide how best to express disagreement

Direct expressions of disagreement can be invitations to discussions (in Russia) or lead to a relationship breakdown (in Mexico). Listen for verbal cues called 'upgraders' and

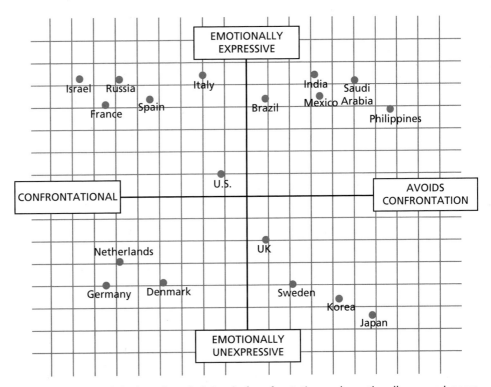

Figure 4.8: Nationalities based on their level of confrontation and emotionally expressiveness
Source: Meyer (2015b, p.78)

'downgraders'. Upgrading words strengthens disagreements (totally, completely, absolutely) and are used by French, Germans and Russians; while downgraders soften it (partially, a little bit, maybe) and are popular with Japanese, Peruvians and Ghanaians.

2. Recognize significance of emotional expressiveness

In some cultures, certain preverbal behaviours (raising voice, laughing) and non-verbal behaviour (touching counterpart's arm) are acceptable, while in others they are seen as intrusive or unprofessional. Emotionally expressive cultures (Brazil, Mexico) avoid open disagreement, while in emotionally unexpressive ones (Denmark, Netherlands) it is acceptable if done calmly and factually. Recognize what an emotional outpouring signifies in their culture and adapt your reaction accordingly.

3. Learn how other cultures build trust

In negotiations the parties are assessing whether they can trust each other. There are two types of trust. Cognitive trust comes from the head. It is based on the confidence in someone's achievements, skills and reliability. It develops through the negotiation if you show yourself to be knowledgeable, reliable, pleasant and consistent. In contrast, affective trust comes from the heart. It arises from feelings of emotional closeness, empathy and friendship. Americans separate the two types of trust, while the Chinese connect them. BRIC, Middle Eastern and Mediterranean cultures emphasise affective trust.

4. Avoid yes-no questions

In some cultures 'yes' means 'no', and in others, 'no' means 'let's discuss it further'. In some cultures saying 'no' is considered impolite and is done instead by body language and tone of voice. When needing to discover if your counterpart is willing to do something but may be unforthcoming, avoid yes-no questions, replacing them with 'How long would it take you to do this' type ones. If forced to ask that question, even if answer is in the affirmative, look for signals suggesting the negative (short silence, inhalation of breath, change of sitting posture).

5. Beware of putting it in writing

The repetition of key messages in writing is a standard Western practice and a basis for negotiation. However, in many Asian and African countries, written confirmation of verbal agreements signals lack of trust between the parties. In the West, negotiated agreements normally lead to signed, legally enforceable contracts which allow companies to do business with people whom they have no reason to trust. However, in countries with less reliable legal systems, relationships are more important than contracts, which may not be legally binding anyway. Proceed cautiously with contracts.

 **RECAP**

1. *Account for the popularity of organizational culture among managers and researchers.*

   - Culture management offers managers a route to economic success.

   - For consultants, the concept provides an appealing; easy-to-grasp, quick-fix solution to sell to managers wishing to improve their organization's performance.

   - For academics, it offers an alternative perspective with which to research and theorize about organizations and provides a new context within which to explore postmodernist ideas.

2. *List, describe and give examples of Schein's three levels of organizational culture.*

   - Schein distinguished surface manifestations of culture at level one (e.g., artefacts, rites, ceremonials); organizational values at level two (e.g. customer obsession); and basic assumptions at level three.

3. *Distinguish the stages of organizational socialization.*

   - The stages of organizational socialization are anticipatory, accommodation and role management.

4. *Contrast managerial and social science perspectives on organizational culture.*

- Organizational culture is something that a company either *has,* or what a company *is.*

- Organizational culture is a single, integrated unit or a differentiated entity consisting of multiple, different subcultures, fragmented with conflicting interests.

- An organization's culture can be managed by its leaders or it is beyond their direct control and instead has to be tolerated by them.

- Culture management signals a new era of symbolic leadership which relies on internalized forms of employee direction, or it represents old style management control in a new guise.

5. *Distinguish between different types and traits of organizational culture.*

- Groysberg and colleagues distinguished companies across two cultural dimensions – 'how people interact' (from independence to interdependence) and 'how people react to change' (from stability to flexibility).

- These dimensions produce eight culture styles: enjoyment, learning, purpose, caring, order, safety, authority and results.

- Each organization is seen has as possessing some combination of these eight styles.

6. *Contrast different dimensions of national culture*

- Hofstede suggested that national culture could be differentiated along five dimensions: social, power, uncertainty, goal and time.

- The GLOBE framework for assessing national culture incorporates and extends Hofstede's dimensions and includes the cultural dimensions of: assertiveness; in-group collectivism; institutional collectivism; future orientation; gender differentiation; humane orientation; performance orientation; power distance; and uncertainty avoidance.

7. *Compare different national negotiating styles.*

- Meyer uses the two dimensions of emotion (from emotionally expressive to emotionally unexpressive) and confrontation (from confrontation to avoids confrontation) to distinguish national negotiating styles.

- She places countries into four quadrants depending on their degree of decision making (top down or egalitarian) and authority (hierarchical or egalitarian).

RECAP: What did she find?

Meyer (2017) found that Japanese are well known for their hierarchical views towards authority; their deference towards their bosses; and their preference for waiting for instructions from above rather than taking the initiative themselves. However, they are also recognized as being consensual decision makers. They like to get group agreement before embarking on a course of action. With this combination of attitudes, they are located in the bottom-right, 'consensual decision making and hierarchical authority'. Other leadership cultures are shown in the table below. Erin Meyer argues that being able to distinguish between and adapt to different leadership cultures will lead to greater personal success in cross-cultural interactions.

Top-down decision making and egalitarian authority	Top-down decision making and hierarchical authority
Australia Canada United Kingdom United States	Brazil China France India Indonesia Mexico Russia Saudi Arabia
Consensual decision making and egalitarian authority	Consensual decision making and hierarchical authority
Denmark Netherlands Norway Sweden	Belgium Germany Japan

Revision

1. Is organizational culture capable of being managed or do chief executives have to tolerate the culture that they inherit?

2. How do culture styles described by Groysberg et al. help or hinder an organization's effectiveness?

3. What guidance does Erin Meyer's research into national culture offer managers working around the world for global corporations?

4. To what extent, and in what ways, might a national culture affect an organization's own culture?

Research assignment

First, familiarize yourself with the list of Schein's 15 surface manifestations of culture as shown earlier in this chapter. Use this list to (a) interview a manager and obtain examples of as many of the surface manifestations of culture as they are able to provide you with; (b) for each manifestation, ask your manager what purpose it serves within their organization; (c) ask them what external and internal factors have moulded the organization's culture into what it is today; (d) locate your organization on Groysberg's organizational cultures and leadership framework justifying your decision with examples from the company concerned.

Springboard

Benjamin Schneider, Cheri Ostroff, Vincente González-Romá and Michael West (2017) 'Organizational climate and culture: Reflections on the history of the constructs', *Journal of Applied Psychology*, 102(3): 468–482. The authors provide a historical account of the academic research into organizational culture and organizational climate.

Sameer Srivastava, Amir Goldberg, Govind Manian and Christopher Potts (2018) 'Enculturation trajectories: Language, cultural adaptation, and individual outcomes in organizations', *Management Science*, 64(3): 1348–1364. The authors ask how people adapt to organizational cultures and what the consequences of their adaptions are for their organizations.

D. D. Warrick, John Milliman and Jeffery Ferguson (2016) 'Building high performance cultures', *Organizational Dynamics*, 45(1): 64–70. The authors provide a case study of the culture-building efforts of the chief executive officer at Zappos, the online retailer.

Erin Meyer (2015) 'When culture doesn't translate', *Harvard Business Review*, 93(10): 66-72. The author discusses the organizational-national culture conflict. As companies globalize, their employees lose shared assumptions and norms. Those in different countries react to the same inputs differently, communicate differently, and make decisions differently.

OB cinema

Dead Poets Society (1989, director Peter Weir): DVD track 1: 0:00:53-0:04:44 (4 minutes).
To establish context, many films begin with shots of an organization to communicate its culture. The clip begins with the opening credits of the film, and ends after Mr Keating has been introduced, sits down and there is a shot of an outside scene.

1. Which surface manifestations of Welton Academy's culture are being communicated here?

2. What values can you infer about Welton Academy's organizational culture from viewing this clip?

Surface manifestation	Example from Welton Academy culture

1 *Artefacts* are material objects created to facilitate culturally expressive activities. They include tools, furniture, appliances and clothing.

2 *Ceremonials* are formally planned, elaborate, dramatic sets of activities of cultural expression.

3 *Courses* and workshops are used to instruct, induct, orient and train new members, and to recognize the contributions of existing ones.

4 *Heroes* are characters, living or dead, who personify the values and beliefs; who are referred to in company stories.

5 *Jokes* are humorous stories intended to cause amusement but whose underlying themes may carry a message about behaviour or values.

6 *Language* is the particular form or manner in which members use vocal sounds and written signs to convey meaning to each other.

7 *Legends* are handed-down narratives about wonderful events based on history, but embellished with fictional details.

8 *Mottoes* are maxims adopted as rules of conduct which are rarely, if ever, changed

9 *Norms* are expected modes of behaviour that are accepted as the company's way of doing things.

10 *Physical layout* concerns things that surround people, providing them with sensory stimuli.

11 *Rites* are elaborate, dramatic sets of activities that consolidate various forms of cultural expression into one event.

12 *Sagas* are historical narratives describing the unique accomplishments of a group and its leaders.

13 *Slogans* are short, catchy phrases that are regularly changed.

14 *Stories* are narratives describing how individuals acted and the decisions they made that affected the company's future.

15 *Symbols* refer to any act, event, object, quality or relation that serves as a vehicle for conveying meaning.

Chapter exercises

1: Surface manifestations

Objectives
1. Understand how organizational structure and processes affect organizational culture.
2. Speculate about how organizational culture might affect your views and behaviours as an employee.

Briefing
Examine the three clusters of descriptions as directed by your instructor. For each one:
1. Decide what 'message' each one sends to employees about the organization's culture.
2. Speculate on the reactions and behaviours it might encourage or discourage among employees.

Descriptions

1. Companies want their employees to have creative ideas.

   a. Company A hires only the smartest people and then, immediately after appointment, sends them on creativity workshops.

   b. Company B has a rigorous selection procedure. Its expensive and elaborate three-day assessment centre selection approach focuses on determining each applicant's level of creativity.

   c. Company C has a staff restaurant with only six-seater tables to allow different staff to meet; its rest areas have whiteboards on the walls; and there are suggestion boxes in every main corridor.

2. Companies have different approaches to employees' work spaces.

   a. Company A encourages staff to personalize their workspaces by decorating them with photos, toys and other items brought from home. Staff are free to come to work dressed as they like.

   b. Company B has open-space work areas for all staff. They wear business dress and address each other by their first names. Managers do not have their own offices or secretaries. The conference suite is used for staff meetings to which secretarial and support staff are invited. Recycling boxes are located throughout the building.

   c. Company C believes messy desks demonstrate a lack of personal organization. It operates a paperless office system and requires managers to enforce a 'clear surface' policy. Non-business related items in workspaces are considered unprofessional and are banned. 'Dress down Fridays' were introduced by senior management, after much discussion, some time ago.

3. Companies have different approaches to employees' errors.

   a. In company A, an employee's mistake is discussed at a team meeting, recorded on the employee's file, and senior management is informed for possible disciplinary action.

   b. In Company B, the manager identifies errors made by subordinates, talks to the individuals, shows them where they went wrong, and what he should do in the future.

   c. In Company C, employees discuss their mistakes with their managers. The manager assists the subordinate to analyse their error, helps them learn from it, and agrees an action plan for future improvements.

2: National culture etiquette

Objectives

1. To recognize the similar ways in which national cultural values are shared.

2. To understand differences between national cultures.

Briefing

1. Students form into small groups based on their country of origin (e.g. China, USA, Japan) or region (e.g. Scandinavia, Eastern Europe, South America, Middle East).

2. Individually, identify an experience that you had after coming to this country that you found surprising, unusual, upsetting, puzzling, irritating, pleasing or significant in some way.

3. Each group then prepares:

   (i) A list of 'student experiences' about this country.

   (ii) A Do's and Don't's guide for a person visiting their country or region for the first time, so as to avoid embarrassment or causing offence when interacting with its nationals.

Your guide should cover:

- Business situations (e.g. visiting company offices, attending business meetings) and social situations (e.g. being invited to the person's home and meeting their family)
- Verbal behaviour (e.g. choice of words, mode of speech, conversation topics) and non-verbal behaviour (e.g. dress, greetings, gifts)

Nominate a speaker and present your group members' experiences and their guide to the other class members.

 **STOP AND SEARCH** YouTube for *cultural etiquette around the world.*

References

Alvesson, M. (2001) *Understanding Organizational Culture.* London: Sage Publications.

Ambrosini, V., Billsberry, J. and Collier, N. (2012) 'To boldly go where few have gone before' in Billsberry, J., Charlesworth, J. and Leonard, P. (eds.), *Moving Images: Effective Teaching with Film and Television in Management*, Charlotte, NC: Information Age Publishing, pp. 171–91.

Bock, L. (2015) *Work Rules,* London: John Murray.

Brannan, M.J. (2017) 'Power, corruption and lies: Mis-selling and the production of culture in financial services', *Human Relations,* 70(6): 641–67

Brooks, I. (2018) *Organizational Behaviour: Individuals, Groups and Organization*, fifth edition, Harlow, Essex: Pearson Education.

Burman, R. and Evans, A. (2008) 'Target zero: a culture of safety', in R. Oddy (ed.), *Defence Aviation Safety Centre Journal.* RAF Bentley Priory, Stanmore: MoD Aviation Regulatory and Safety Group, pp.22–27.

Cameron, K.S. and Quinn, R.E. (2011) *Diagnosing and Changing Organizational Culture: Based on the Competing Values Framework*, third edition, Chichester: John Wiley.

Chatman, J.A., Caldwell, D.F., O'Reilly, C.A., and Doerr, B. (2014) 'Parsing organization culture: how the norm for adaptability influences the relationship between culture consensus and financial performance in high technology firms', *Journal of Organizational Behaviour,* 35(6): 785–808.

Costas, J. (2012) 'We are all friends here: reinforcing paradoxes of normative control in a culture of friendship', *Journal of Management Inquiry,* 21(4): 377–95.

Cunliffe, A., L. (2008) *Organization Theory,* London: Sage Publications.

Day, P. (2012) 'What's gone wrong with the bank?', *BBC News Online,* 24 July

Deal, T.E. and Kennedy, A.A. (1982) *Organization Cultures: The Rites and Rituals of Organization Life.* Reading, MA: Addison Wesley.

Denison, D.R., Haaland, S. and Goelzner, P. (2004) 'Corporate culture and organizational effectiveness: is Asia different from the rest of the world?' *Organizational Dynamics,* 33(1): 98–109.

Denison, D., Nieminen, L. and Kotrba, L. (2014) 'Diagnosing organization cultures: a conceptual and empirical review of culture effectiveness', *European Journal of Work and Organizational Psychology,* 23(1): 145–61.

Dorfman, P., Javidan, M., Hanges, P., Dastmalchian, A. and House, R. (2012) 'GLOBE: A twenty year journey into the intriguing world of culture and leadership', *Journal of World Business,* 47(4): 504–18.

Feldman, D. C. (1976) 'A contingency theory of socialization', *Administrative Science Quarterly,* 21(3): 433–52

Fleming, P. and Spicer, A. (2004) 'You can checkout anytime, but you can never leave: spatial boundaries in a high commitment organization', *Human Relations,* 57(1): 75–94.

Fleming, P. and Spicer, A. (2007) *Contesting the Corporation: Struggle, Power and Resistance in Organizations.* Cambridge: Cambridge University Press.

Fleming, P. and Sturdy, A. (2011) 'Being yourself in the electronic sweatshop: new form of normative control', *Human Relations,* 64(2): 177–200.

Furnham, A. and Gunter, B. (1993) 'Corporate culture: definition, diagnosis and change', in Cary L. Cooper and Ivan T. Robertson (eds.), *International Review of Industrial and Organizational Psychology, Volume 8.* Chichester: John Wiley, pp.233–61.

Gagliardi, P. (1986) 'The creation and change of organizational cultures: a conceptual framework', *Organization Studies,* 7(2): 117–34.

Goffee, R. and Jones, G. (2003) *The Character of a Corporation: How Your Company's Culture Can Make or Break Your Business,* London: Profile Business.

Gordon, G.G. and DiTomaso, N. (1992) 'Predicting corporate performance from organizational culture', *Journal of Management Studies,* 29(6): 783–98.

Groysberg, B., Lee, J., Price, J. and Cheng, J.Y-D (2018a) 'The leader's guide to corporate culture', *Harvard Business Review,* 96(1): 44–52.

Groysberg, B., Lee, J., Price, J. and Cheng, J.Y-D (2018b) 'Context, conditions and culture', *Harvard Business Review,* 96(1): 56–57.

Grey, C. (2009) *A Very Short, Fairly Interesting and Reasonably Cheap Book About Studying Organizations,* London: Sage.

Griffin, R.W. and Pustayy, M.W. (2007) *International Business* (fifth edition), Pearson Education Inc.

Handy, C. (1993) *Understanding Organization,* fourth edition, Harmondsworth, Middlesex: Penguin Books.

Hellriegel, D. and Slocum, J.W. (2009) *Principles of Organizational Behaviour,* twelfth edition, London: South-Western Cengage Learning.

Hill, A. (2013) 'Bankers back in the classroom', *Financial Times,* 17 October, p. 16.

Hill, A. (2018) 'Amnesia dooms bankers to repeat mistakes', *Financial Times,* 17 June.

Hofstede, G. (1980) *Culture's Consequences: International Differences in Work-Related Values,* Beverley Hills, CA: Sage Publications.

Hofstede, G. (1986) 'Editorial: the usefulness of the concept of organization culture', *Journal of Management Studies,* 23(3): 253–57.

Hofstede, G. (1991) *Cultures and Organizations,* London: McGraw-Hill.

Hofstede, G. (2001) *Culture's Consequences: International Differences in Work-related Values.* second edition, London: Sage Publications.

Hofstede, G. and Bond, M. (1988) 'The Confucian connection: from cultural roots to economic growth', *Organizational Dynamics,* 16(4): 4–21.

House, R.J., Hanges, P.J., Javidan, M., Dorfman, M. and Gupta, V. (eds) (2004) *Culture, Leadership and Organizations: The GLOBE Study of 62 Societies,* Thousand Oaks, CA: Sage Publications.

Jang, S. (2017) 'Cultural brokerage and creative performance in multicultural teams', *Organization Science,* 28(6): 993–1009.

Javidan, M. and House, R.J. (2001) 'Cultural acumen for the global manager: lessons from the Project GLOBE', *Organizational Dynamics,* 29(4): 289–305.

Kellaway, L. (2013) 'Kellaway's history of the office: why did offices become like home?', BBC Radio 4, 2 August.

Knights, D. and Willmott, H. (1987) 'Organizational culture as management strategy: a critique and illustration from the financial services industry', *International Studies of Management and Organization,* 17(3): 40–63.

Kunda, G. (1992) *Engineering Culture: Control and Commitment in a High Tech Corporation.* Philadelphia, PA: Temple University Press.

Laurent, A. (1989) 'A cultural view of organizational change', in P. Evans, Y. Doz and A. Laurent (eds), *Human Resource Management in International Firms.* London: Macmillan, pp.83–94.

Lorsch, J.W. and McTague, E. (2016) 'Culture is not the culprit', *Harvard Business Review,* 94(4): 96–105.

Luthans, F. (1995) *Organizational Behaviour,* seventh edition, New York: McGraw Hill.

Martin, J. (1992) *Cultures in Organizations: Three Perspectives.* Oxford: Oxford University Press.

Mayo, E. (1933) *The Human Problems of an Industrial Civilization.* New York: Macmillan.

Mayo, E. (1945) *The Social Problems of an Industrial Civilization.* Cambridge, MA: Harvard University Press.

Miller, D. (1994) 'What happens after success: the perils of excellence', *Journal of Management Studies,* 31(3): 325–58

Meyer, E. (2015a) 'When culture does not translate', *Harvard Business Review,* 93(10): 66–72.

Meyer, E. (2015b) 'Getting to si, ja, oui, hai and da: how to negotiate across cultures, *Harvard Business Review,* 93(12): 74–80.

Meyer, E. (2017) 'Being the boss in Brussels, Boston and Beijing', *Harvard Business Review,* 95(4):70–77.

Notter, J. and Grant, M. (2011) *Humanize: How People-centric Organizations Succeed in a Social World,* Indianapolis: Indiana: Que Publishing.

Ogbonna, E. (1993) 'Managing organizational culture: fantasy or reality?' *Human Resource Management Journal,* 3(2): 42–54.

O'Reilly, C.A. (1989) 'Corporations, culture and commitment: motivation and social control in organizations', *California Management Review*, 31(4): 9–25.

Parker, M. (2000) *Organizational Culture and Identity: Unity and Division at Work.* London: Sage Publications.

Pascale, R.T. (1985) 'The paradox of organization culture: reconciling ourselves to socialization', *California Management Review*, 27(2): 26–41.

Pascale, R.T. and Athos, A.G. (1982) *The Art of Japanese Management.* Harmondsworth, Middlesex: Penguin Books.

Peters, T.J. and Waterman, R.H. (1982) *In Search of Excellence: Lessons from America's Best Run Companies*, New York: Harper & Row.

Ramarajan, L. and Reid, E. (2013) 'Shattering the myth of separate worlds: negotiating non-work identities at work', *Academy of Management Review*, 38(4): 621–44.

Ray, C.A. (1986) 'Corporate culture; the last frontier of control?', *Journal of Management Studies*, 23(3): 287–97.

Robbins, S.P. and Judge, T.A. (2017) *Organizational Behaviour*, seventeenth edition, Harlow: Pearson Education.

Roberts, J. (2001) 'Trust and control in Anglo-American systems of corporate governance: the individualizing and socializing processes of accountability', *Human Relations*, 54(12): 1547–72.

Schein, E.H. (1983) 'The role of the founder in creating organization culture', *Organization Dynamics*, 12(1): 13–28.

Schein, E.H. (2004) *Organizational Culture and Leadership*, third edition, San Francisco, CA: Jossey Bass.

Schmidt, E. and Rosenberg, J. (2017) *How Google Works*, London: John Murray.

Schultz, M. (1995) *Studying Organizational Cultures: Diagnosis and Understanding.* Berlin: De Gruyter.

Shotter, J. (2015) 'Weak markets and new regulations left Deutsche chiefs with tough task', *Financial Times*, 10 June, p.21.

Smircich, L. (1983) 'Concepts of culture and organizational analysis', *Administrative Science Quarterly*, 28(3): 339–58.

Smircich, L. and Morgan, G. (1982) 'Leadership: the management of meaning', *Journal of Applied Behavioural Science*, 18(2): 257–73.

Spicer, A., Gond, J.P., Patel, K., Lindley, D., Fleming, P., Mosonyi, S., Benoit, C. and Parker, S. (2014) *Report on the Culture of British Retail Banking*, Cass Business School and New City Agenda.

Srivastava, S. B. and Goldberg, A. (2017) 'Language as a window into culture', *California Management Review*, 60(1): 56–69.

Stahl, G.K,. Maznevski, M.L., Voigt, A. and Jonsen, K. (2010) 'Unravelling the effects of cultural diversity in teams: A meta-analysis of research on multi-cultural workgroups', *Journal of International Business Studies*, 41(4): 690–709.

Stenebo, J. (2010) *The Truth about IKEA*, London: Gibson Square Books.

Taras, V, Steel, P. and Kirkman, B. (2011) 'Three decades of research on national culture in the workplace: Do the differences still make a difference?', *Organizational Dynamics*, 40(3): 89–198.

Taylor, V.F. and Goates, N. (2017) 'Rope or elephant's tail: Different frames of culture', *Organization Management Journal*, 14(2): 76–89.

The Economist (2011) 'The view from the top and bottom', 24 September, p.86.

The Economist (2017) 'Head in the cloud', 18 March, pp. 61–62.

Thompson, J. and Jain, A. (2013) 'Female prudence back in vogue', *Financial Times*, 19 June, p.3.

Trice, H.M. and Beyer, J.M. (1984) 'Studying organization cultures through rites and ceremonials', *Academy of Management Review*, 9(4): 653–69.

Trice, H.M. and Beyer, J.M. (1993) *The Cultures of Work Organizations.* Englewood Cliffs, NJ: Prentice Hall.

Vanhoegaerden, J. (2001) *Sense and Sensitivity*, Directions – The Ashridge Journal Ashridge corporate website, August.

van Maanen, J. and Schein, E.H. (1979) 'Toward a theory of organization socialization', *Research in Organization Behaviour*, 1: 209–64.

Wachel, K. (2011) 'That crazy, 44 page long UBS dress code got ridiculed so that now it's getting revised', *Business Insider*, 18 January.

Warrick, D.D., Milliman, J.F. and Ferguson, J.M. (2016) 'Building high performance cultures', *Organizational Dynamics*, 45(1): 64–70.

Werner, A. (2014) '*Margin Call*: using film to explore behavioural aspects of the financial crisis', *Journal of Business Ethics*, 122(4): 643–54.

Willmott, H. (1993) 'Strength is ignorance, slavery is freedom', managing culture in modern organizations', *Journal of Management Studies*, 30(5): 515–52.

Part 2 Individuals in the organization

PESTLE: The **P**olitical, **E**conomic, **S**ocial, **T**echnological, **L**egal, and **E**cological context

- **Individual** factors
- **Group** factors
- **Management and organization** factors
- **Leadership process** factors

- **Organizational effectiveness**
- **Quality of working life**

The organization's past,   present,   and future

CHAPTER 5

Learning

Key terms

learning

behaviourist psychology

cognitive psychology

growth mindset

feedback

positive reinforcement

negative reinforcement

punishment

extinction

Pavlovian conditioning

Skinnerian conditioning

shaping

intermittent reinforcement

schedule of reinforcement

behaviour modification

cybernetic analogy

intrinsic feedback

extrinsic feedback

feedforward interview

concurrent feedback

delayed feedback

socialization

behavioural modelling

provisional selves

neuroplasticity

Learning outcomes

When you have read this chapter, you should be able to define those
key terms in your own words, and you should also be able to:

1. Understand the increased importance of learning, for individuals
   and organizations.

2. Explain the characteristics of the behaviourist and cognitive
   approaches to learning.

3. Explain the socialization process, and assess the practical relevance
   of this concept.

4. Explain what neuroscience can tell us about making learning more
   effective.

5. Apply the 'AGES' model to your own learning process, to help
   make your learning 'stick'.

6. Assess the practice and ethics of methods of behaviour
   modification.

Why study learning?

Staff development in many organizations is going through a profound transformation. If your employer sends you on a management training programme, you may find yourself playing a virtual reality game rather than listening to an instructor. Virtual, augmented and mixed-reality games have been designed to present topics such as leadership, cyber security and teamwork. The use of virtual environments is especially useful where remote working has become the norm. The nature of work is changing, and learning methods are changing, too (Wylie, 2018).

This means making even more use of technology. Some organizations use cloud-based learning to provide MOOCs (massive open online courses), SPOCs (small private online courses), instructional videos, learning games, e-coaching, virtual classrooms, online performance support and online simulations. One Asian company offers a digital 3-D learning environment at its virtual model factory. This lets employees 'see' and 'feel' complex equipment being used in the company's other plants. The cloud-based Danone Campus 2.0 gives employees access to the company's best practices, covering internal and external knowledge, and encouraging a culture of collaborative learning and networking (Benson-Armer et al., 2016).

Do you think that once you have finished your current degree course, you can leave formal education behind? Think again. The ability to learn – and to go on learning – has become a valuable skill in its own right. The world of work is changing fast, and you will have to keep learning in order to keep up. A report on the future of jobs by the World Economic Forum (2016) notes that in many industries and countries, the occupations or specialities that are most in demand today did not exist ten or even five years ago. In addition, 65 per cent of children going to primary school today will end up working in completely new jobs that nobody has yet heard of. In the traditional career model, your early education and qualifications equipped you for the rest of your working life. That pattern is obsolete. Advanced robotics and artificially intelligent systems are displacing some workers, and transforming the jobs of many others **(see Chapter 3)**. These technology trends affect professional roles as well as manual work. Nobody's job is entirely 'safe' from automation.

Many of us will have to deal with technology-driven changes to our work, moving from one kind of job to another many times in our working lives. This will mean continuous, lifelong learning. If the kind of work that you do changes often, then you will have to get used to 'learning at the speed of business' (Benson-Armer et al., 2016). If you are offered a job that has little or no opportunity for further learning and development, turn it down. Many employers are looking for people who are 'intellectually curious'. Completing a college or university degree is one indicator of that attribute. However, studying subjects just to get the credits for the qualification is not going to help your career. 'Cramming, passing, and forgetting' may sound like a good short-term student survival strategy. But if you are not interested in and don't learn anything about what you are studying, potential employers will not be impressed. We will explore ways to make your learning 'stick' later in this chapter.

✓✓✓   **EMPLOYABILITY CHECK** (critical thinking, appetite for learning, interpersonal skills, problem-solving, teamworking skills)

To what extent do you feel that you have the cognitive and 'soft' skills that will continue to be important in future? Do you feel that you will need to develop your capabilities in any of these areas? What will you need to do in order to develop and to maintain those skills?

CUTTING EDGE — Encourage them to learn if you want them to stay

Jie Cao

Monika Hamori
(photo by
Kerry Parke)

Jie Cao and Monika Hamori (2016) designed a study to find out if developmental assignments strengthened or weakened organizational commitment, which is defined as 'individuals' emotional attachment to, identification with, and involvement in an organization' (p.500). We know that one of the best ways to learn management skills is through challenging assignments and novel experiences. But there could be a problem. Assignments can improve leadership skills and other capabilities. They also increase the individual's value to other organizations. So, do developmental assignments encourage managers to stay, or tempt them to explore other opportunities? The study also looked at other development methods such as coaching, mentoring, training and senior management support.

The researchers surveyed over 300 skilled early-career professionals in 66 countries. They found that:

- there was no evidence that development opportunities weaken organizational commitment; in contrast, they trigger positive work attitudes
- mentoring and coaching had no effect on commitment
- to increase commitment significantly, organizations should combine challenging developmental assignments with senior management support.

The researchers conclude that, 'assignments with high-level responsibilities and support from senior management are the most important ways to increase the commitment of early-stage highly skilled employees. Specifically, people who have responsibilities for key decisions, feel that they are tested by higher management, have jobs that are visible in the organization, and receive support and guidance from senior managers will be most committed' (p.511).

Literacy, numeracy, and digital skills will always be significant. However, according to the World Economic Forum, skills which will become even more important (because machines can't handle them – yet) are cognitive and 'soft' or social skills. These include:

- Critical thinking
- Creativity
- Complex problem-solving
- The ability to absorb large amounts of information
- Interpersonal and communication skills
- Collaboration and working productively in teams.

In other words, as well as professional and technical knowledge, you will need a 'balanced scorecard' of capabilities including cognitive, social, process and problem-solving skills – and learning how to apply these in novel contexts in order to become more employable. This scorecard includes 'the fundamental skills, knowledge and abilities that workers require to interact with, understand, and communicate with other people' (Knowles-Cutler and Lewis, 2016, p.9).

The learning process

How do we learn? How do we come to know what we know, and to do what we are able to do? These questions lie at the heart of psychology, and it is not surprising that we are faced with different approaches to these questions. This variety maintains controversy, excitement and interest in the subject, and also helps to generate new thinking. The ability to learn is not unique to human beings. Animals also learn, as dog owners and circus fans can confirm. One feature that seems to distinguish us from animals is our ability to learn about, adapt to, survive in, and manipulate our environment for purposes that we ourselves define. Animals can adapt to changes in their environment, and many animals, birds and fish can learn to use basic tools. However, they appear to have little choice over their goals, and animals have developed no science, technology or engineering – or social science.

We hope that when you have finished reading this book you will be able to say that you have learned something. The test is whether or not you will be able to do things that you could not do before. You should know what the study of organizational behaviour involves, and you should be able to tell others what you know and think about it. You should be able to complete assignments and answer questions that you could not tackle before. We can describe this process as learning.

This definition of learning emphasizes durability and experience. Behaviour can be changed temporarily by many factors, in ways that do not involve learning. Other factors which change our behaviour are maturation (in children), ageing (in adults), drugs, and fatigue. Our interest is with lasting behaviour change. This can involve procedural learning, or 'knowing how', concerning your ability to carry out skilled actions, such as horse riding, or painting a picture. Or this can involve declarative learning, or 'knowing that', such as the history of our use of the horse, or the contribution of the European Futurist movement in the early twentieth century to contemporary art.

Neurological research has identified the areas of the brain that are involved in learning and memory processes. The study of learning, however, is not confined to neurology and brain surgery. We can *infer* that learning has taken place by examining changes in behaviour. If we assume that behaviour does not alter spontaneously, for no reason, then we can look for experiences that cause behaviour change. These experiences may be internal, or they may arise in our environment.

Changes in behaviour can be measured using a 'learning curve', an example of which is shown in Figure 5.1, concerning the development of manual skills. The learning can be plotted for one person, for a group of trainees, or even for a whole organization. The curve in Figure 5.1 suggests that:

1. Learning is not a smooth process, but changes in pace over time, until a stable peak performance is reached.

2. The learner's ability develops slowly at first, then accelerates and develops more quickly, before reaching a plateau.

Learning the process of acquiring knowledge through experience which leads to a lasting change in behaviour.

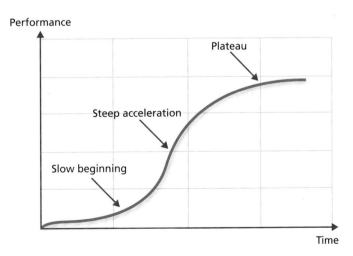

Figure 5.1: The typical manual skills learning curve

> **CRITICAL THINKING**
>
> Draw your own learning curve for this organizational behaviour course. Why is it that shape? What would be your ideal learning curve look like? How could you change the shape of your learning curve?

Behaviourist psychology a perspective which argues that what we learn are chains of muscle movements; mental processes are not observable, and are not valid issues for study.

Cognitive psychology a perspective which argues that what we learn are mental structures; mental processes can be studied by inference, although they cannot be observed directly.

Learning curves for manual skills often follow this profile, but cognitive skills can develop in the same way. The shape of a learning curve depends on the characteristics of the task and the learner. It is often possible to measure learning in this way, to compare individuals with each other, and to establish what counts as good performance. If we understand the factors influencing the shape of the curve, we can develop ways to make learning more effective.

The experiences that lead to changes in behaviour have a number of important features.

First, the mind is not a passive recorder of information picked up through the senses. We can often recall the plot of a novel, for example, but remember very few of the author's words. This suggests that we do not record experiences in a straightforward way.

Second, we are usually able to recall events in which we have participated as if we were another actor in the drama. We are able to reflect, to see ourselves 'from outside', as objects in our own experience. At the time when we experienced the events, those cannot have been the sense impressions that we picked up. Reflection is a valuable capability.

Third, new experiences do not always lead to behaviour change. Declarative learning, for example, may not be evident until we are asked the right questions. Our experiences must be processed in some way if they are to influence our behaviour in future.

This chapter examines two main approaches to learning, based on ('stimulus-response') behaviourist psychology and cognitive psychology ('information processing'). These perspectives are in many respects contradictory, but they can also be seen as complementary. Summarized in Table 5.1, these perspectives have different implications for organization and management practice.

What did they find?

? Francisco Campos and colleagues (2017) designed an experiment to explore whether you have to be born with the innate traits of an entrepreneur, or if this is something that you can learn. This is significant because many students want to start their own business after they graduate. The researchers recruited 1,500 small businesses in Lomé, the capital of Togo, in West Africa. The businesses, with an average of three employees and monthly profits of US$170, were divided at random into three groups. One group was given a training course designed by an international finance organization, covering business planning, accounting and financial management, marketing and human resources. The second group followed a psychology course focusing on personal initiative – self-starting behaviour, identifying new opportunities, goal setting, dealing with feedback, and overcoming obstacles. The third group were given no help. The researchers monitored the sales, profits and new product ideas of these businesses over two and a half years.

What did they find? Which of the three groups do you think performed best in terms of sales, profits and innovation – and why? **(Answers in chapter Recap.)**

Table 5.1: Behaviourist and cognitive perspectives

Behaviourist, stimulus-response	Cognitive, information processing
Studies observable behaviour	Studies mental processes
Behaviour is determined by learned sequences of muscle movements	Behaviour is determined by memory, mental processes and expectations
We learn habits	We learn cognitive structures
We solve problems by trial and error	We solve problems with insight and understanding
Routine, mechanistic, open to direct research	Rich, complex, studied using indirect methods

Growth mindset
the belief that you can develop your capabilities through hard work, good methods and contributions from others.

Do you have a growth mindset or a fixed mindset – and does it matter?

Carol Dweck

What is your own approach to learning? Is there scope for development, or are you limited by the abilities that you have inherited? Exploring these questions, Carol Dweck (2016; 2017) distinguishes between a growth mindset and a fixed mindset. People with a growth mindset believe that they can improve their capabilities, but those with a fixed mindset do not share this belief.

A fixed mindset, in contrast, is the belief that your capabilities are inherited, and that you can't do much to develop them further. People with a growth mindset put more energy into learning, and they achieve more. Dweck claims that organizations can encourage a growth mindset, such that employees say that they feel empowered and committed, and that they get support for collaboration and innovation. Where a growth mindset is discouraged, employees tend to complain about cheating and deception, possibly because they see those behaviours as the best way to get ahead. Dweck admits that it is difficult to change your mindset. Part of the problem lies with the 'triggers', in our own experience and at work, which encourage a fixed mindset:

'It's not easy to attain a growth mindset. One reason why is we all have our own fixed-mindset triggers. When we face challenges, receive criticism, or fare poorly compared with others, we can easily fall into insecurity or defensiveness, a response that inhibits growth. Our work environments, too, can be full of fixed-mindset triggers. A company that plays the talent game makes it harder for people to practise growth-mindset thinking and behaviour, such as sharing information, collaborating, innovating, seeking feedback or admitting errors.

'To remain in a growth zone, we must identify and work with these triggers. Many managers and executives have benefited from learning to recognize when their fixed-mindset "persona" shows up and what it says to make them feel threatened or defensive. Most importantly, over time they have learned to talk back to it, persuading it to collaborate with them as they pursue challenging goals. It's hard work, but individuals and organizations can gain a lot by deepening their understanding of growth-mindset concepts and the processes for putting them into practice. It gives them a richer sense of who they are, what they stand for, and how they want to move forward' (Dweck, 2016, pp.3 – 4).

STOP AND SEARCH   YouTube for *Carol Dweck Developing a Growth Mindset* (9:38).

The behaviourist approach to learning

When someone else's smartphone rings, with the same ringtone as yours, do you automatically check your own phone? This is an example of classical conditioning; from repeated past experience, you now associate that sound with a personal message, which you have to check. The concept of conditioning was developed by the behaviourist school of psychology, and is in widespread use today.

The American psychologist John B. Watson (1878–1958) introduced the term *behaviourism* in 1913. He was critical of the technique of introspection, a popular technique at that time, in which subjects were asked to talk about their experiences and thought processes. Watson wanted more objective insights into human behaviour, its causes and its consequences. This led him away from the intangible contents of the mind to study relationships between visible stimuli and visible responses. That is why behaviourist psychology is also known as 'stimulus-response psychology'.

Behaviourism assumes that what lies between the stimulus and the response is a mechanism that will be revealed as our knowledge of the biochemistry and neurophysiology of the brain develops. This mechanism relates stimuli to responses in a way that governs behaviour. We can thus study how stimuli and responses are related without understanding the nature of that mechanism. Behaviourism argues that nothing of *psychological* importance happens between stimulus and response.

The oldest theory of learning states that actions that are experienced together tend to be associated with each other (touching a flame, pain). We use knowledge of the outcomes of past behaviour to do better in future (don't touch flames). You learn to get higher assignment grades by finding out how well you did last time and why. We cannot learn without feedback. Behaviourists and cognitive psychologists agree that experience affects behaviour, but disagree over how this happens.

Feedback can be rewarding or punishing. If a particular behaviour is rewarded, then it is more likely to be repeated. If it is punished or ignored, it is likely to be avoided in future. This is known as the 'law of effect', which states that we learn to repeat behaviours that have favourable consequences, and avoid those that have neutral or undesirable outcomes. How have you modified your own behaviour, by repeating behaviours that have been successful, and dropping those that have not worked?

Behaviourism makes subtle distinctions relating to reward and punishment (see Table 5.2.) With positive reinforcement, desired behaviours lead to positive consequences. With negative reinforcement, the undesirable outcomes continue until the desired behaviour occurs, at which point the negative consequences stop. As punishment follows undesirable behaviour, this is different from negative reinforcement. Where behaviour has no positive or negative outcomes, this can lead to the extinction of that behaviour, as it comes to be seen as unimportant.

Feedback information about the outcomes of our behaviour.

Positive reinforcement the attempt to encourage desirable behaviours by introducing positive consequences when the desired behaviour occurs.

Negative reinforcement the attempt to encourage desirable behaviours by withdrawing negative consequences when the desired behaviour occurs.

Punishment the attempt to discourage undesirable behaviours by applying negative consequences, or withholding a positive outcome following the undesirable behaviour.

Extinction the attempt to eliminate undesirable behaviours by attaching no consequences, positive or negative, such as indifference and silence.

Table 5.2: Reinforcement regimes

	Behaviour	Reinforcement	Result	Illustration
Positive reinforcement	Desired behaviour occurs	Positive consequences are introduced	Desired behaviour is repeated	Confess, and stick to your story, and you will get a shorter prison sentence
Negative reinforcement	Desired behaviour occurs	Negative consequences are withdrawn	Desired behaviour is repeated	The torture will continue until you confess
Punishment	Undesired behaviour occurs	A single act of punishment is introduced	Undesired behaviour is not repeated	Fail to meet your scoring target and we kick you off the team
Extinction	Undesired behaviour occurs	Day's work not counted towards bonus	Undesired behaviour is not repeated	Ignore an individual's practical jokes used to gain attention

CRITICAL THINKING

Some airlines, concerned about the cost of fuel, encourage passengers to carry less luggage. One approach is to allow passengers with hand luggage only to skip the check-in queues. Another is to charge passengers extra for each item of luggage that they check in. Which reinforcement regimes are being used to teach passengers to travel light?

Reinforcement regimes in a call centre

David Boddy (2011, p.458) reports the following communication from a call centre manager:

'In our call centre, staff are rewarded when behaviour delivers results in line with business requirements. Each month, staff performance is reviewed against a number of objectives, such as average call length, sales of each product, and attention to detail. This is known as Effective Level Review and agents can move through levels of effectiveness ranging from 1 to 4, and gain an increase in salary after six months of successful reviews. Moving through effective levels means that they have performed well and can mean being given other tasks instead of answering the phone. The role can become mundane and repetitive so the opportunity to do other tasks is seen as a reward for good performance. Thus it reinforces acceptable behaviour.

'Conversely, staff who display behaviour that is not desirable cannot move through these levels, and repeated failure to do so can lead to disciplinary action. This can be seen as punishment rather than behaviour modification. People can become resentful at having their performance graded every month, particularly in those areas where it is their line manager's perception of whether or not they have achieved the desired results.'

Which reinforcement regimes does this call centre manager describe?

Pavlovian conditioning a technique for associating an established response or behaviour with a new stimulus.

Skinnerian conditioning a technique for associating a response or a behaviour with its consequence.

Associations between stimuli and responses develop in two different ways, known as Pavlovian conditioning and Skinnerian conditioning. Pavlovian conditioning, also known as classical and as respondent conditioning, was developed by the Russian physiologist Ivan Petrovich Pavlov (1849–1936). Smartphones were not available at that time, so Pavlov used dogs and food instead.

The best-known response which Pavlov studied concerned a dog salivating at the sight of food. Pavlov showed how this could be associated with a completely different stimulus, such as the sound of a bell. Dog owners are trained to use classical conditioning methods with their pets. If you show meat to a dog, it will produce saliva. The meat is the stimulus, the saliva is the response. The meat is an *unconditioned* stimulus; the dog salivates naturally, and the saliva is an *unconditioned* response. Unconditioned responses are also called reflexes. Your lower leg jerks when you are struck just below the kneecap; your pupils contract when light is shone into your eyes. These are typical human reflexes. Humans also salivate, another unconditioned response, at the sight and smell of food.

Suppose we ring a bell before we show the meat to the dog. Do this often enough, and the dog will associate the bell with the meat. Soon, it will salivate at the sound of the bell, without food being present. The bell has become a *conditioned* stimulus, and the saliva is now a conditioned response. The dog has learned from experience to salivate at the sound of a bell as well as at the sight of food. It does not have to be a bell. All manner of stimuli can be conditioned in this way. Pavlov discovered this form of conditioning by accident. His research was initially concerned with salivation, but he observed that his dogs salivated at the sight and sound of his laboratory assistants, before they were given their meat. He found this more interesting, and changed the focus of his research.

Suppose we now stop giving the meat to the dog after the bell. The dog will continue to salivate at the sound of the bell alone, expecting the bell to signal the arrival of food. If we continue to do this, however, the volume of saliva produced falls, and the association between the conditioned stimulus and conditioned response eventually suffers *extinction*.

CRITICAL THINKING   Can you recognize conditioned responses in your own behaviour, such as your response to someone else's ringtone? Is there a song, or a smell (perfume, after shave, food), that makes you think of another person, another place, another time, another experience?

Skinnerian conditioning (also known as instrumental and or operant conditioning) was discovered by the American psychologist Burrhus Frederic Skinner (1904–1990). With instrumental conditioning, new behaviours or responses become established through association with particular stimuli.

Where the consequence of a behaviour is desirable to the individual, then the frequency of that behaviour is likely to increase. In a given context, any behaviour that is rewarded or reinforced will tend to be repeated in that context. Skinner put a rat into a box (known as a 'Skinner box') with a lever which, when pressed, gave the animal food. The rat is not taught to press the lever. However, moving around the box, the rat eventually presses the lever. It may sit on it, knock it with its head, or push it with a paw. That random behaviour is reinforced with food, and so it is likely to happen again.

Skinnerian conditioning is also called instrumental conditioning because it concerns behaviours that are a means (or instruments) to getting some material reward. Skinner's rat has to be under the influence of some drive before it can be conditioned in this way. His rats were hungry when they went into his box, and their behaviour thus led to a desired reward.

Where do the terms respondent and operant conditioning come from? Respondent conditioning comes from Watson's stimulus-response psychology which stated that there was no behaviour, or no response, without a stimulus to set it in motion. One could thus condition a known response to a given stimulus. Such responses are called respondents. Knee jerks, pupil contractions and salivation are well known and clearly identified responses that can be conditioned.

Home viewing

Search YouTube for *Big Bang Theory – operant conditioning*. In this five-minute clip from the comedy series, Sheldon uses operant conditioning methods to change the behaviour of Leonard's girlfriend, Penny. Leonard complains about this, but Sheldon's tactics are working. Are you aware of your own behaviour being conditioned in this way? Can you use this method on your friends? What ethical issues are raised by such attempts to manipulate the behaviour of others?

Skinner, on the other hand, observed that animals and humans behave in the absence of specific stimuli, such as a rat wandering around in his box. He argued that most human behaviour is of this kind. Behaviours that do not have identifiable stimuli are called operants. Operant conditioning thus explains how new behaviours are established, such

Shaping the selective reinforcement of chosen behaviours in a manner that progressively establishes a desired behaviour pattern.

as pressing that lever to get food. Respondent conditioning does not alter the animal's behaviour (the dog always did salivate when it thought that food was coming), only the behaviour's timing. Skinner also developed the technique of shaping, or the selective reinforcement of desired behaviours. He was able to get pigeons to play ping-pong and to walk in figures of eight – demonstrating how spontaneous behaviours can be shaped by operant conditioning.

 **STOP AND SEARCH**   YouTube for *BF Skinner Foundation – Pigeon Ping Pong* (0:39).

Automating behaviour modification

Fogg (2009) argues that technology can be used to modify people's behaviour, by 'automating persuasion'. One persuasive technology is the fuel gauge in a Toyota Prius. This measures engine efficiency, encouraging owners to change driving behaviour to get more miles per gallon. Roadside speed monitors display happy or sad faces depending on whether or not drivers are sticking to the speed limit. Fogg's five rules for designing automated persuasion are:

1. *Target a simple behaviour.* 'Reduce stress levels' is a complex and ambitious goal; persuading people to stop and stretch for 20 seconds when prompted is more realistic, anyone can do it, and the success rate is measurable.

2. *Understand what is preventing the target behaviour.* The reason always concerns lack of motivation, lack of ability, or lack of a trigger to perform the behaviour. In other words, **B**ehaviour change depends on **M**otivation, **A**bility, and a **T**rigger.

3. *Choose the right technology channel.* Email, online video, e-commerce websites, social media, text

messages – these are simple and direct. Installed software and specialist devices can make target behaviours simpler and increase ability.

4. *Start small and fast.* Sophisticated ideas take time to design, and users may reject the complexity. Creating a simple, focused persuasive experience with a clear goal is inexpensive, can be implemented quickly, and is easy to change if it doesn't work.

5. *Build on small successes:* Getting people to stretch for 20 seconds is not a sexy project. However, Fogg's trial had a 70 per cent compliance rate, and the prompt was expanded to include relaxation techniques – again with high compliance.

The trigger, therefore, lies in the technology. Once a simple approach is working, it can be expanded. Get people to repeat the behaviour routinely, on a fixed schedule. Increase the difficulty of the behaviour. Reach more people. Target other simple behaviours. Target less persuadable groups. Automating behaviour modification is inexpensive, and it works.

 **STOP AND SEARCH**   YouTube for *Baby Steps for Behavior Change: BJ Fogg.*

Intermittent reinforcement a procedure in which a reward is provided only occasionally following correct responses, and not for every correct response.

Skinner studied variations on the operant conditioning theme. One concerned the occasional reward of desired behaviour rather than delivering rewards in a continuous and regular way. This is closer to real life than a laboratory experiment. Why, for example, do gamblers keep playing when they lose most of the time? Why do anglers continue to fish when they are catching nothing? There are many such examples of the power of intermittent reinforcement. Behaviour can be maintained without regular and consistent reinforcement every time that it occurs.

Table 5.3: Schedules of reinforcement

Schedule	Description	Effects on responses	Example
Continuous	Reinforcement after *every correct response*	Establishes high performance, but can lead to satiation; rapid extinction when reinforcement is withheld	Praise
Fixed ratio	Reinforcement after a *predetermined number* of correct responses	Tends to generate high rates of desired responses	Incentive payments
Variable ratio	Reinforcement after a *random number* of correct responses	Can produce a high response rate that is resistant to extinction	Commission on sales
Fixed interval	Reinforcement of a correct response after a *predetermined period*	Can produce uneven response patterns, slow following reinforcement, vigorous immediately preceding reinforcement	Weekly payments
Variable Interval	Reinforcement of a correct response after random periods	Can produce a high response rate that is resistant to extinction	prizes

Schedule of reinforcement the pattern and frequency of rewards contingent on the display of desirable behaviour.

The pattern and timing of rewards for desired behaviour is known as the schedule of reinforcement. The possible variation in schedules of reinforcement is limitless, and Skinner investigated the effects of a number of these (Ferster and Skinner, 1957). However, there are two main classes of intermittent reinforcement, concerning interval schedules and ratio schedules, which are described in Table 5.3 (based on Luthans and Kreitner, 1985), contrasted with continuous reinforcement.

Skinner argued that one could explain the development of complex patterns of behaviour with the theory of operant conditioning. This shows how behaviour is shaped by our environment, by our experiences, and by selective rewards and punishments. The *behaviour modification* techniques described below are also based on his ideas.

Thinking, problem solving, and learning language, he argued, are dependent on simple conditioning processes. Skinner rejected the use of 'mentalistic' concepts and 'inner psychic forces' to explain human behaviour because these were not observable, were not researchable, and were therefore not necessary to the science of psychology. Why use complicated and unobservable concepts when simple and observable phenomena provide adequate explanations?

Reinforcing desired behaviour is generally more effective than punishing undesirable behaviour. However, C.C. Walters and J.E. Grusek (1977) suggested that punishment can be effective if it meets the following conditions:

- The punishment should be quick and short
- It should be administered immediately after the undesirable behaviour
- It should be limited in its intensity
- It should be specifically related to behaviour, and not to character traits
- It should be restricted to the context in which the undesirable behaviour occurs
- It should not send 'mixed messages' about what is acceptable behaviour
- Penalties should take the form of withdrawal of rewards, not physical pain.

Behaviourism in practice

Behaviour modification a technique for encouraging desired behaviours and discouraging unwanted behaviours using operant conditioning.

Behaviourism led to the development of behaviour modification techniques. These were first used to treat mental and learning disorders, and phobias, and for psychiatric rehabilitation and accident and trauma recovery. These methods have since been used in organizational settings.

Developed by Fred Luthans (Luthans and Kreitner, 1985; Luthans et al., 1998), organizational behaviour modification, or OBMod, has five steps:

1. *Identify* the critical, observable and measurable behaviours to be encouraged.
2. *Measure* the current frequency of those behaviours, to provide a baseline against which to measure improvement.
3. *Establish* the triggers or antecedents for those behaviours, and also establish the consequences – positive, neutral and negative – that follow from those behaviours.
4. *Develop* a strategy to strengthen desired behaviours and weaken dysfunctional behaviours through positive reinforcement (money, recognition) and feedback; punishment may be necessary in some cases, for example to inhibit unsafe behaviour.
5. *Evaluate* systematically the effectiveness of the approach in changing behaviour and improving performance compared with the original baseline measurement.

Many managers today apply these techniques without being aware of their origin. Indeed, a manager may have used a variation of this method on you. Behaviour modification is attractive to managers because they can manipulate the reinforcement of employee behaviours. The method focuses on behaviour rather than on internal mental states and processes. Desirable behaviours include speaking politely to customers, helping colleagues, or in a hospital washing hands to reduce infections. Undesirable behaviours include lateness, making poor quality items, and being rude to customers. OBMod uses reinforcement to eliminate undesired behaviour and encourage desired behaviour. Suppose a manager wants work assignments completed on time, with few submitted beyond the deadline. The OBMod options are summarized in Table 5.4.

Table 5.4: Behaviour modification options

Procedure	Operationalization	Behavioural effect
Positive reinforcement	Manager praises employee each time work is completed on schedule	Increases desired work behaviour
Negative reinforcement	Unpaid overtime continues to be mandatory until work is completed on schedule, then overtime is rewarded	Increases desired work behaviour
Punishment	Manager asks employee to stay late when work is not handed in on time	Eliminates or decreases undesired behaviour
Extinction	Manager ignores the employee when work is handed in late	Eliminates or decreases undesired behaviour

---

✓✓✓   **EMPLOYABILITY CHECK** (people management, problem-solving skills, critical thinking)

In a job interview you are asked to imagine that you manage a team of eight people. A male team member has been accused by a female colleague, informally, of mild sexual harassment. If this stops immediately, no further action may be taken. What behaviour modification approach would you use to deal with this issue? What problems could arise in using this method in these circumstances?

OBMod has the following characteristics:

- It applies to clearly identifiable and observable behaviours, such as timekeeping, absenteeism, carrying out checks and repairs, and the use of particular work methods.

- Rewards are contingent on the performance of the desirable behaviours.

- Positive reinforcement can take a number of forms, from the praise of a superior to cash prizes, to food, to clothing.

- Behaviour change and performance improvements can be dramatic.

- The desired modification in behaviour may only be sustained if positive reinforcement is continued (although this may be intermittent).

OBMod, MRSA and ICUs

Adverse events cost the UK health service £2 billion a year, and hospital-acquired infections cost a further £1 billion. Human error seems to be the main cause, but research shows that organization culture and management systems can encourage undesirable behaviour. Could behaviour modification techniques be used to improve patient safety?

Dominic Cooper et al. (2005) describe a hospital OBMod programme designed to reduce infections, such as MRSA (methicillin-resistant *staphylococcus aureus*). The usual methods include screening, isolation, cleaning, monitoring, training, awareness-raising, and improved policies and protocols, but that wasn't enough to solve the problem. Two intensive care units (ICUs) were involved, employing 140 doctors, nurses, healthcare assistants, and administrative staff. The units had many visitors, including physicians, other hospital staff, family members and friends. The programme focused on two behaviours. The first was hand-washing, to reduce the spread of infection; research shows that doctors wash their hands on less than 10 per cent of appropriate occasions. The second concerned the accuracy and completeness of nursing documents which record patient' conditions.

Staff were briefed on the aims and conduct of the programme, to engage them in problem solving and in generating ideas (such as installing a sink at the entrance where visitors could wash). Staff were asked to identify their main concerns, and what they saw as the most common undesired behaviours. A project coordinator and eight observers were trained in behaviour modification methods: how to observe, how to give feedback, how to set improvement goals. A checklist of 36 desired behaviours was developed, so that observers could record compliance, which they did by standing at the central nursing station for 20 minutes at a randomly chosen time each day. Observation data were analysed weekly, posted on a feedback chart, and discussed in group feedback meetings.

The results showed significant changes in behaviour which along with other methods reduced MRSA infections by 70 per cent. With fewer MRSA patients, there was extra ICU capacity, reduced laboratory costs, less overtime and temporary staff costs, and reduced costs of complaints. These outcomes were attributed to motivation to provide quality care (goals), and to the weekly performance data (feedback) which let staff know that they were doing a good job. Apart from the time that staff spent training, observing, and in meetings, the programme costs came to only a few hundred pounds for clerical materials and cleaning items.

The cognitive approach to learning

Why should we look only at observable stimuli and responses in the study of psychology? Is it not possible to study the internal workings of the mind in indirect ways, by inference? Behaviourism seems to be unnecessarily restrictive, as it excludes those characteristics that make us interesting, different and, above all, human.

How do we select from all the stimuli that bombard our senses those to which we are going to respond? Why are some outcomes seen as rewards and others as punishments? This may appear obvious where the reward is survival or food and the punishment is pain or death. However, with intrinsic or symbolic rewards this is not always clear. To answer these questions, we have to consider states of mind concerning perception and motivation.

The rewards and punishments that behaviourists call reinforcement work in more complex ways than conditioning theories suggest. Reinforcement is always knowledge, or *feedback* (defined earlier), about the success of past behaviours. Feedback is information that can be used to modify or maintain previous behaviours. This information has to be perceived, interpreted, given meaning, and used in decisions about future behaviours. The feedback has to be processed. This is why cognitive learning theories are called information processing theories. In addition, feedback, rewards and punishments, and knowledge of results, have a *motivating* effect on behaviour, as well as a reinforcing effect. Opportunities to learn new skills and knowledge, to understand more, and to develop more effective ways of coping with our environment, can be intrinsically motivating. The American psychologist Robert W. White (1959) suggests that we have a built-in motive to develop 'competence', the 'urge towards discovery', the 'will to understand'.

The cognitive approach draws ideas from the field of cybernetics which was established by the American mathematician Norbert Wiener (1954). He defined cybernetics as 'the science of communication in the animal and in the machine'. One central idea of cybernetics is the notion of the control of system performance through feedback. Information processing theories of learning are based on what is called the cybernetic analogy.

The elements of a cybernetic feedback control system are outlined in Figure 5.2.

In a domestic heating control system, the temperature standard is set on a thermostat, and a heater (effector) warms up the room. A thermometer measures changes in temperature, which is continually compared with the standard. When the room reaches the set temperature, the effector is switched off; when the room cools, it is switched on again.

The cybernetic analogy says that this control loop is a model of what goes on in the mind. For standard, read motive, purpose, intent, or goals. The output is behaviour. Our senses are measuring devices. Our perception is the comparator which organizes and imposes meaning

Cybernetic analogy
an explanation of the learning process based on the components and operation of a feedback control system.

Intrinsic feedback
information which comes from within, from the muscles, joints, skin, and other mechanisms such as that which controls balance.

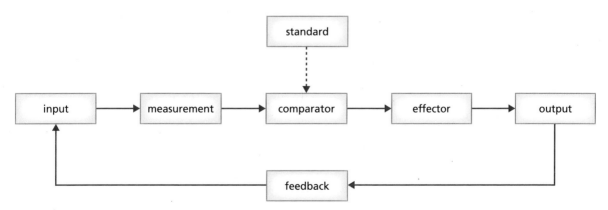

Figure 5.2: Elements of cybernetic feedback control

Extrinsic feedback information which comes from our environment, such as the visual and aural information needed to drive a car.

on the sensory data which control behaviour in pursuit of our goals. We each have an internal representation or 'schema' of ourselves and our environment. This internal representation is used in a purposive way to determine our behaviour, and is also known as your *perceptual world* (**Chapter 8**).

We can also use information on how we are doing – feedback – to update our internal representation and to refine and adapt our plans. Feedback can either be self-generated – intrinsic feedback – or it can come from an external source – extrinsic feedback.

CUTTING EDGE   Feedback – or feedforward

Marie-Hélène Budworth

Feedforward interview a method for improving employee performance by focusing on recent success and attempting to create the same conditions in the future.

Marie-Hélène Budworth and colleagues (2015) advocate an alternative to traditional staff appraisal methods: the feedforward interview. The aims of performance appraisal interviews are to give employees feedback on past performance, and to provide guidance to help them to improve in future. However, there are problems with this approach. It is often seen as an annual ritual in which the main purpose is to complete the paperwork as quickly as possible. If the feedback is negative, focusing on mistakes, shortfalls and weaknesses, this can trigger a defensive response, and reduce the motivation to change behaviour. Job satisfaction and organizational commitment are also damaged if employees feel that the feedback is biased, unfair, inaccurate or politically motivated.

A traditional appraisal focuses on what went wrong and what the employee has to do in order to improve. A feedforward interview explores what has been positive in the employee's experience, focusing on strengths and successes. The appraiser does not have to act as judge or critic, and provides no negative feedback in this process (Kluger and Nir, 2010).

A feedforward interview begins by asking the employee to describe occasions when their performance was successful. The interviewer then explores situations where the individual and the organization both benefit. The employee is then asked to identify the difference between their goals and the current state. This leads finally to the employee setting goals to reduce this discrepancy. As employees identify their own performance goals, and what they have to do to achieve them, the motivation to change is higher that it would be if those goals and behaviour changes were imposed.

Budworth et al. (2015) describe how the sales and customer service unit in a business equipment organization compared the effects of traditional appraisals with feedforward interviews. All 25 managers were randomly assigned to a traditional or a feedforward approach. Those who were to use feedforward were trained in the method, but employees were not aware of this. About half of the employees (70) were given a feedforward interview, and the other 75 had a traditional appraisal. After the appraisals, employee performance was assessed using a behavioural observation scale, with items such as 'this individual completes projects before deadlines' and 'this person actively finds ways to improve this business'. The feedforward interview not only improved performance more than traditional appraisals, but that improvement was lasting. Citing a survey of 5,000 employees which found that less than one third felt that a traditional appraisal helped them to improve performance, Budworth et al. (2015) conclude that feedforward could be more effective than feedback.

Jonny Gifford et al. (2017) tested this approach with 3,000 employees in three UK government agencies: Her Majesty's Revenue and Customs, The National Offender Management Service, and The Valuation Office Agency. Staff were allocated at random to either the 'feedforward' approach, or to a control group which had traditional appraisals. Staff were asked in the feedforward interviews to describe successes, and to explain why they had been successful on those occasions. They were then asked to apply that approach in future. Employees' performance was rated before and after the trial, over two years. The performance of the 'feedforward' group was significantly better than that of the control group. Survey replies showed that the feedforward method was seen as fairer than traditional appraisal, which explained the performance improvement.

Concurrent feedback
information which arrives during our behaviour and which can be used to control behaviour as it unfolds.

Delayed feedback
information which is received after a task is completed, and which can be used to influence future performance.

Independent of the source and nature of the feedback, timing is also important. Feedback can arrive during, or after the behaviour that we are learning: in other words, it can be either concurrent feedback or delayed feedback.

Intrinsic feedback is invariably concurrent. When you throw rings over pegs at the fair to win a soft toy, the intrinsic concurrent visual feedback means that you know immediately how well (or how badly) you are performing. Some extrinsic feedback is also concurrent; from a driving instructor, for example. However, for your next course assignment, feedback from your lecturer is going to be delayed. Instructors cannot provide concurrent feedback on your essay or project, but the longer the delay, the less effective the feedback is likely to be.

Virtual reality learning

With a virtual reality (VR) headset, you can find yourself immersed in a video game, or in a computer simulation of a real-life setting, as in a flight simulator. Until recently, VR was expensive and visual 'fidelity' was poor. As the technology has developed, however, VR is finding a wider range of applications. Marianne Calnan (2017) explores how VR is being used as an engaging, high-impact employee learning and development tool.

VR technology is already used by trainee surgeons and offshore workers in the oil and gas industry. These are 'safety-critical' settings where mistakes can be disastrous; VR allows trainees to practise and to learn from mistakes without doing any damage. Some companies use VR in leadership training, offering experience in giving virtual presentations and conference speeches, and handling

difficult situations in diversity programmes. The retail and hospitality sectors are adopting VR to help train shop floor employees. Calnan gives some specific examples:

- Best Western hotels train front-desk staff in customer service skills with a VR platform which simulates a range of guest interactions; this has improved customer satisfaction.

- McDonald's uses a VR game to help shift managers learn how to use a new on-demand food production system; the managers have to make rapid decisions on how to deal with equipment breakdowns, staff absences, and large numbers of customers turning up.

- Walmart uses VR to develop the leadership skills of front line supervisors and department managers, by allowing them to experience and to learn from difficult and unsafe situations, such as Black Friday crowds, hygiene issues, and natural disasters.

VR technology is still unfamiliar to many people, and some can experience motion sickness. The cost of headsets has fallen, but customized software can be very expensive. However, as one learning designer said, 'As adults, we're very keen to avoid embarrassment. VR provides fully immersive yet safe spaces where there are no real consequences for our mistakes. And mistakes make great learning opportunities' (Calnan, 2017, p.46).

Identify examples of each of the four types of feedback in your own experience. How should that feedback change in order to help you to improve your performance (on this course, in your favourite sport, whatever)?

Cognitive perspectives in practice

Socialization the process by which new members learn the value system, the norms, and the required behaviour patterns of the society, organization, or group which they are entering.

Behavioural modelling learning how to act by observing and copying the behaviour of others.

When people join an organization, they give up some personal freedom – the price of membership. Employees accept that an organization can make demands on their time and effort, as long as these demands are seen as legitimate. Other members of the organization have to teach new recruits what is expected of them. The process through which recruits are 'shown the ropes' is called socialization (Schein, 1968, p.3). Cognitive psychologists regard behaviour modification as simplistic, and turn to more complex social explanations and methods for organizational behaviour change.

This perspective draws on social learning theory which is based on assumptions about human psychology different from those behind OBMod techniques. One of the most influential advocates of social learning theory has been Albert Bandura (1977; 1986), who showed that we learn new behaviours by observing and copying others, through behavioural modelling. We copy the behaviour of others, and we do not need rewards or punishments to encourage us to do this. However, if the behaviours that we copy are successful (rewarded or reinforced by positive results), then we are more likely to continue to act in that way. Our capabilities for reflection and self-determination are central in this perspective. We construct, through observation and experience, internal models of our environment, and plan courses of action accordingly. The ways in which we model ourselves on others is particularly apparent in children, and we continue to copy or imitate others as adults.

Bandura's argument that we learn with social experience, through observation and modelling, does not mean that reinforcement is unimportant. Behavioural modelling involves the four processes of attention, retention, production and reinforcement shown in Figure 5.3. Suppose we choose to behave (taking a job interview, making new friends) by modelling ourselves on someone who is successful in those areas. Suppose that our new approach does not lead to the desired results; we don't get the job, we don't establish friendships. Without reinforcement, we abandon our new behaviours and look for other models. If our new methods are successful, however, we will use them again.

When we get a new job, we have to learn how to 'fit in'. This means accepting the norms and rules that are considered to be appropriate in a particular organization and work group. As a typical career in the future is likely to involve several job changes, not always in the same organization, many employees will go through repeat socialization. Formal induction or 'onboarding' processes typically use several socialization methods: a tour of the premises,

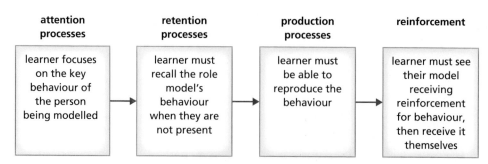

Figure 5.3: The behavioural modelling process (based on Weiss, 1990)

formal presentations, online materials including videos and podcasts, meetings with key staff and colleagues, social media to introduce new staff to colleagues before they start work, and to get to know staff in other locations (Green, 2017).

As well as formal induction processes, you can use your own tactics – proactive socialization – using your own initiative to learn how to adjust to the new environment (Song et al., 2017). Proactive socialization tactics include:

* Build a relationship with your boss
* Observe others and ask for feedback from them
* Positive framing: see things in an optimistic light
* Negotiate changes to your job or tasks
* Experiment: test the limits of what is expected
* Socialize with your colleagues
* Network more widely with other departments.

Provisional selves the personal experiments that we carry out with regard to how we act and interact in new organizational roles, based on our observations of the behaviour of others.

Research shows that use of these proactive socialization tactics can improve your task mastery, role clarity, job satisfaction, commitment and performance.

From her study of financial analysts and consultants, Herminia Ibarra (Ibarra and Barbulescu, 2010) shows how we adapt to new roles by experimenting with **provisional selves**, which are based on the role models that we see around us. This process, she found, has three stages:

Observing	We watch other people to see how they behave and respond
Experimenting	We try out some of those behaviours to see how they work for us
Evaluating	We use our own assessment and feedback from others to decide which behaviours to keep, and which to discard

Our observations of role models in a new setting can cover a range of issues: physical appearance, personal style, ways of interacting, displays of skill. This does not mean that we just copy others. We choose the behaviours that we feel are credible, and that are consistent with how we see ourselves, and also consistent with how we want others to see us – as competent, creative, enthusiastic, trustworthy. We do this by experimenting, keeping those actions that we like, and discarding those that do not work, or which are inconsistent with our self-image. Comments from Ibarra's (1999) interviewees illustrate this:

'There are a good half dozen to a dozen senior people I'd view as mentors. I think up until director, you're building your skills, you're trying on different styles, like different clothes, almost. You try and figure out what styles fit your personality and fit what you're good at. And then that's how you should try to go after business' (p.777).

'I've been out with X and watched him in action. He's very aggressive in new business – one of the best in the firm. He has a very charismatic personality, which is something you can't teach. I don't think I could really replicate his style. I'm not as outgoing, but I think the attitude and persistence are things that I have' (p.775).

'I don't have an aggressive personality. I have been told I need to improve. I have adjusted to it by becoming more assertive over time. Just watching P was good. She is very vocal, asks lots of questions, always makes sure she has a point to make, is very assertive. Now I do like she does' (p.780).

CRITICAL THINKING	Think of two people who you have observed recently – one a real person, the other a character in a movie or a television programme. How have they influenced you? Which of their behaviours have you adopted? How did that work out?

Social learning is key for new recruits. Organizations encourage different standards concerning what counts as good performance, familiarity in social interactions at work, the amount of deference to show to superiors, dress and appearance, social activities after work, and attitudes to work, colleagues, managers, trade unions, and customers. We have to learn what attitudes to take, what style of language to use, what 'dress code' to obey, where to take lunch and with whom, and so on.

Listen to this podcast on 'Rethinking staff inductions' (25 minutes)

https://www.cipd.co.uk/podcasts/rethinking-staff-inductions

The dark side of socialization

Songqi Liu

New recruits have to learn the behaviours and attitudes that will help them to 'fit in', and to perform their jobs well. Many organizations have formal induction programmes. Informal socialization – observing, and getting information and feedback from co-workers – is also important. However, as well as introducing newcomers to desired organizational norms, informal processes can encourage unsafe and risky behaviours, such as drinking alcohol at work.

Songqi Liu and colleagues (2015) studied 57 supervisors and 147 recently appointed members of sales and client service staff in two manufacturing companies in China. The roles of the service staff included contacting and visiting new and existing customers, to discuss their needs for products and services, to negotiate sales, and to resolve complaints. The researchers used interviews and questionnaires to find out about staff drinking habits in relation to clients.

The new client service staff quickly learned that 'drinking alcohol is an effective and legitimate means to improve job performance' (p.334). Why? Alcohol creates a more relaxed and friendly atmosphere, lowers inhibitions, and encourages the free and open exchange of information. Some cultures have a tradition of closing a deal with a drink. After observing existing employees and external clients, new recruits began 'performance drinking'. The consumption of alcohol in work meetings was acceptable, because it improved business relationships, increase sales, and helped individual careers. The long-term damage to health was less important than the need to conform with the job expectations.

Is alcohol an important part of working culture in the UK? Research by the think-tank Demos found that 40 per cent of young workers see drinking with colleagues as a 'rite of passage' and as 'social glue'. Not drinking alcohol was seen as a barrier to social integration at work. Almost half said that they drink with colleagues, and a further 10 per cent said that they drink alcohol with company clients. Some were concerned that their careers would suffer if they abstained, and a quarter had come under pressure from colleagues to drink. Asked about the last month, around a fifth said that they had gone to work with a hangover, and 9 per cent said that they had been under the influence of alcohol at work (Wybron, 2016).

CRITICAL THINKING

Remember when you first joined this college or university; how did you feel about the formal socialization or induction process? To what informal socialization were you exposed? Which had the greater impact on your behaviour, the formal or the informal processes?

Of course, organizations do not rely on socialization techniques alone to equip employees with appropriate knowledge and skills. Most use a combination of other formal and informal learning and development methods. A survey of 550 human resource professionals in the

UK in 2015 found that the five the most common learning and development methods in use were (CIPD, 2015a):

- On-the-job training
- In-house development and internal peer-to-peer knowledge-sharing programmes
- Coaching by line managers or colleagues
- Online e-learning courses
- External conferences, workshops and events.

These methods were expected to grow in popularity, except external events. Formal education, off-site instructor-led training, external conferences, and the use of MOOCs, were expected to decline. The survey also found that on-the-job training was thought to be the most effective learning practice. Online and mobile learning, off-site instructor-led training, and external events were considered to be the least effective (CIPD, 2015b, p.11). It is interesting that technology-based methods were thought to be among the less effective learning and development methods. However, the developments in learning technology which respondents said would have the most impact over the next five years included mobile learning, virtual classrooms, social media, and webinars.

CRITICAL THINKING

Socialization processes could be better understood, it has been suggested (Allen et al., 2017), by giving employees wearable sensors which can:

- monitor how social networks facilitate learning in the organizationoassess how and when employees interact with each other
- detect where people are located in relation to each other
- identify the dominant individuals who play major roles in socialization
- assess the strength of relationships between employees
- identify the locations where groups regularly meet
- provide objective information, without having to ask the individuals themselves.

This information could help an organization to improve its socialization processes, by providing more networking opportunities, changing workplace layouts, supporting those who offer informal socialization, and identifying which approaches work best. But is this employee surveillance ethical?

Neuroscience and learning

Neuroscience is the study of brain activity, using tools such as magnetic resonance imaging to explore how mental processes relate to emotions and behaviours. One area where neuroscience has developed fresh insights concerns the study of learning. These findings have implications for organizational practice. Paul Howard-Jones (2014) argues that neuroscience will help us to:

- understand how the brain is capable of learning continuously, at all ages
- be aware of the flexibility, or neuroplasticitity of the brain and how it can reorganize and develop with experience
- learn skills that support the development of further learning
- improve learning through exercise and other physical activity.

Neuroscience research has shown links between exercise, cognitive function and learning. The ability to learn and speed of recall, for example, are higher in teenagers and adults who are physically fit. Studies have also shown how financial rewards for completing a learning task *reduce* motivation by removing the fun and intrinsic value of the task. Contrary to popular belief, caffeine may keep you awake, but it suppresses cognitive function, and interferes with learning. Caffeine can also cause sleep disruption, and reduce the efficiency of our learning further.

"I'm afraid my brain is full and I can't learn any more. I'll need a few days off to dumb down."

One piece of bad news is that playing computer games late at night can also lead to sleep disorders and interfere with learning. However, research shows that video games can help to improve our ability to switch our visual attention, ignore irrelevant visual cues, and to infer the probable outcomes of different actions. These learning effects may be due to the way in which games stimulate the brain's reward and pleasure centres. One study found that a specially designed video game improved the performance of air force cadet pilots, and another study showed that surgeons who played video games made over 30 per cent fewer errors in a test of their surgical skills (skill using Nintendo Wii may be linked to ability to perform laparoscopic or 'keyhole' surgery). The 'gamification' of learning is not currently well understood, however, and may apply to some skills, but not to others.

Neuroplasticity the ability of the human brain to keep learning and changing throughout an individual's life; also called brain plasticity.

Neuroscience research suggests that a lot of what we think we know about learning is over-simplified. This idea is not new, but has only recently started to influence thinking and practice (Lancaster, 2017). For example, it used to be thought that our brains did not develop much beyond puberty, and that as we got older, we became more rigid in our behaviours and ways of thinking. You will be familiar with the saying, 'You can't teach old dogs new tricks'. However, advances in our understanding of how the brain functions tell us that these traditional views are not correct. As just mentioned, we have neuroplasticity, which means the ability to learn new things with experience and practice, regardless of our age; in other words, we are never too old to learn.

✋ **STOP AND SEARCH** YouTube for *Jan Hills: How can neuroscience help us to understand how we learn in organizations?* (4:25); and *Neuroplasticity* to find a TedTalk about this topic.

There are now a number of 'brain-friendly' learning models which can help to tailor the learning experience, to avoid cognitive overload, to make the learning process less intimidating or threatening, and to strengthen learning retention and transfer. For example, the SCARF model (Rock, 2008) is based on understanding how the brain responds to threat and reward, and how we approach social situations. The SCARF model predicts that we increase our engagement, making learning more effective, when threats are decreased, and when rewards are maximized. The learning process can be improved, therefore, when the following five (SCARF) conditions are present:

Status	We are more likely to learn when this will enhance our status
Certainty	Clear orderly steps increase learning, but uncertainty leads to disengagement
Autonomy	Autonomy, choice and control reduce stress and improve learning
Relatedness	Trust, empathy, and social connection in the process increase engagement in learning
Fairness	Unfairness creates hostility and threat; learning that is fair and justified is motivating

These five factors are responsible for activating our threat or reward brain circuits. When we interact with others, our motivation is influenced by the desire to minimize threats and maximize rewards. Our social experiences are thus affected by the same threat and reward brain networks that relate to our survival needs for food and water.

A perceived threat to status activates brain networks similar to those involved in a threat to one's life; a perceived increase in fairness activates the same reward circuitry as getting a financial reward. If you feel that your boss is acting in a threatening way, and undermining your credibility, you will be less likely to be able to solve complex problems, and more likely to make mistakes (Rock, 2008). This understanding can be used to design more effective learning experiences. An instructor can avoid 'micromanaging' learners, knowing that a lack of autonomy will prompt a threat response. A line manager can increase someone's autonomy as a reward for good performance.

 **STOP AND SEARCH**   YouTube for *David Rock on the SCARF model* (2:47).

How often have you learned something, later to find that you have forgotten it? Learning retention is a well-known problem, to organizations sending staff on costly training programmes, and to students studying for exams. Neuroscience research has produced the AGES model, which sets out four principles for helping new learning to 'stick' (Davachi et al., 2010; Davis et al., 2014):

Attention Learners must devote adequate undivided attention to the new material

We have an attention span of about 20 minutes, at which point we need variety and novelty. Multitasking interferes with attention and impairs learning. Davis et al. (2014, pp.4–5) note that those who think they are good at multitasking perform worse than those who do not: 'It seems that those people who spend more time multitasking across various media (e.g. computers, tablets, phones, etc. at the same time) train their brains to have a harder time focusing and remembering. [. . .] In one study, people who multitasked not only obtained poorer results, but assessed themselves as having performed better than when only carrying out one task'.

Generation Learners need to generate their own connections to their existing knowledge

In a study that has been repeated many times, asking learners to take eight seconds to generate a response (own knowledge generation), which turns out to be wrong, followed by five seconds of studying the correct response (traditional learning), led to better recall than just studying the correct response for the full 13 seconds. We retain information better when it has personal significance.

Emotion Moderate levels of emotion are necessary to stimulate interest

Emotion is key to encouraging attention and enhancing memory. Positive emotions are key to effective learning transfer. Learners are less likely to engage with the subject matter if the process is associated with a negative emotion, such as a fear of failure.

Spacing Learning is more likely to stick when the learner returns to the material regularly

Instead of cramming lots of content into a long session, learning transfer and long-term memory are more effective when the learning is distributed – spaced – between discrete 'chunks' which are each delivered over a short time period. Leaving time between sessions may sound counterintuitive, and many people believe that this will not work as well as a 'cramming marathon'. One study even found that 90 per cent of participants performed better after spacing than they did when cramming, but 72 per cent of them reported that cramming was more effective than spacing.

To see how the AGES model can be applied in practice, consider this description of a management training session (Davis et al., 2014, p.7). Which AGES principles are present, and which are not? How effective do you think this session will be, and why?

'Imagine you've been flown in from out of town, arriving at 9:00 am for a day of learning, where you're met with a laptop connection at each desk, Wi-Fi in the room, all desks facing forward, and dim but attractive lighting, so as to see the slide projections while maintaining some visibility. A speaker begins talking in front of beautiful, professional-looking slides, each one with graphs, tables, references, and paragraphs of useful text, not to mention logos and branding elements. On your laptop, you have an electronic copy of the slides and a series of paper handouts. The speaker courteously offers to plough ahead, rather than take breaks, so as to respect your time and deliver maximal content to you.'

This may sound like a well-planned session, but the AGES model suggests that every aspect of it will damage the learning of those present. How would you approach the redesign of a session like that, using the AGES model as a guide?

EMPLOYABILITY CHECK (self-management, appetite for learning)

Given the neuroscientific advice from the SCARF and AGES models, how do you plan to change your learning strategies in general, and your study habits in particular? How will these changes make you more employable, and how will you describe your approach to learning to potential employers?

Behaviour modification versus socialization

Is behaviour modification a useful approach to learning at work and the development of appropriate behaviours? The evidence suggests a qualified 'yes'; there are two qualifications.

First, behaviour modification needs careful planning to identify specific behavioural goals, and procedures for reinforcing the behaviours that will achieve those goals. The method can be effective when behaviour and reinforcement are clearly identified and linked; wear your seat belt and we'll give you cash. The method is less effective when this relationship is vague; demonstrate your commitment and we will consider you for promotion.

Second, the 'rewards for good behaviour' method appears broadly consistent with American (and perhaps Eastern European) cultural values and aspirations. The transfer of this approach to other cultures could be a problem. The most often cited practical examples are American.

CRITICAL THINKING

You are responsible for training the new shelf-stacker in your local supermarket. In particular, items have to be stacked neatly, with those which have short sell-by dates to the front. What combination of behaviour modification and socialization techniques will you use, and how will you apply these?

Behaviour modification is manipulative, often ignores internal needs and intrinsic rewards, and can be a threat to individual dignity and autonomy. It can be seen as a simplistic and transparent attempt to manipulate others, prompting cynicism rather than behaviour change. The technique thus has limitations. However, OBMod requires the communication of goals and expectations in unambiguous terms. Many would argue that such clarity is desirable. Fred Luthans and Robert Kreitner (1985) summarize the problems with behaviour modification:

1. Appropriate reinforcers may not always be available, in routine work settings, for example.

2. We do not all respond in the same way to the same reinforcers; what one person finds rewarding may be of little consequence to someone else.

3. Once started, a behaviour modification programme has to be sustained.

4. There may not be enough extrinsic motivators (healthcare benefits, bonuses) available.

They also argue, however, that the technique has made significant contributions:

1. Behaviour modification techniques put the focus on observable employee behaviour and not on hypothetical internal states.

2. The method shows how performance is influenced by outcomes that depend in turn on the individual's behaviour.

3. It supports the view that positive reinforcement is more effective in changing employee behaviour than punishment.

4. It is possible to show a clear causal link to performance, which is often hard to establish with other behaviour change methods, such as job enrichment.

Social learning is dependent on the cultural context, and is a process rather than a specific technique. Socialization, in contrast is more flexible. American socialization techniques, for example, may be quite different from Swedish, Belgian, Nigerian, Malaysian or Spanish ones. Socialization is a process that takes place anyway, planned or not. The issue concerns appropriate socialization, with respect to organization culture and behavioural preferences. Because it is a 'natural' process, with no clear financial or other benefit from investing in its operation, it may be difficult to persuade management to give socialization the attention and resource that this requires. Table 5.5 summarizes the contrasts between behaviour modification and socialization.

Table 5.5: Behaviour modification versus socialization

Behaviour modification	Socialization
Feedback needed in both approaches for behaviour to change	
Planned procedure	Naturally occurring, even if also planned
Stimulus determines responses	Individual needs determine responses
Externally generated reinforcements	Internally generated reinforcements
Focuses on observable behaviour	Focuses on unobservable internal states
Focus on tangible rewards and punishments (money, other material rewards)	Focus on intangible rewards and punishments (social inclusion, self-esteem)
Clear links between desired behaviour and consequences	Intangible links between desired behaviour and consequences
Compliance required by external agent	Conformity encouraged by social grouping

 **RECAP**

1. *Understand the increased importance of learning, for individuals and organizations.*

   - Automation will make some skills and knowledge redundant, and workers at all levels will need to learn new skills and acquire fresh knowledge in order to stay in employment.

   - The ability to learn – and to keep on learning – is a valuable skill in its own right, with a premium on lifelong learning.

   - Skills that will remain critical include critical thinking, complex problem solving, the ability to absorb information, interpersonal and communication skills, and teamworking.

2. *Explain the characteristics of the behaviourist and cognitive approaches to learning.*

   - Behaviourism argues that we learn chains of muscle movements. As mental processes are not observable, they are not considered valid issues for study.

   - Cognitive psychology argues that we learn mental structures. Mental processes are important, and they are amenable to study although they cannot be observed.

   - In behaviourist theory, feedback contributes to learning by providing reinforcement; in cognitive theory, feedback provides information and is motivational.

3. *Explain the socialization process, and assess the practical relevance of this concept.*

   - Social learning theory argues that we learn values, beliefs and behaviour patterns through experience, through observation and modelling.

   - Socialization can be informal – this happens anyway – or it can be formally organized through induction and training programmes.

   - In addition to attending formal induction programmes, new recruits can use proactive socialization tactics to learn how to fit into their new environment.

   - Socialization can have a 'dark side', encouraging behaviours such as alcohol use (and abuse) at work.

4. *Explain what neuroscience can tell us about making learning more effective.*

   - Neuroscience research reveals that much of what we once knew about learning is over-simplified.

   - Research has shown that we have neuroplasticity (or brain plasticity) which is the ability to continue learning throughout one's life.

- Learning and speed of recall are better in teenagers and adults who are physically fit.

- Financial rewards for completing a learning task reduce the motivation to learn.

- Playing computer games late at night can lead to sleep disorders that interfere with learning.

- The 'brain-friendly' SCARF model says that learner engagement is enhanced when the learning design takes into account Status, Certainty, Autonomy, Relatedness and Fairness.

5. *Apply the 'AGES' model to your own learning process, to help make your learning 'stick'.*

- Learning is more likely to be remembered if the process involves Attention (focusing on the task), Generation (learners work out the answers themselves), Emotion (interest is stimulated), and Spacing (learners return to and review the material).

- Multitasking interferes with attention and is the enemy of learning; people who believe that multitasking does not affect them perform worse than whose who focus.

- Learning that is distributed – spaced – across a number of shorter time periods is more effective, in terms of learning transfer and long-term memory, than a single 'cramming marathon'.

6. *Assess the practice and ethics of methods of behaviour modification.*

- Respondent (or Pavlovian, classical) conditioning is a method by which an established response (good work performance) is associated with a new stimulus (supervisory encouragement).

- Operant (or Skinnerian, instrumental) conditioning is a method by which a behaviour (good work performance) is associated with a new consequence (bonus payment).

- Positive reinforcement, negative reinforcement, punishment and extinction condition the target by manipulating the consequences of desirable and undesirable behaviours.

- Behaviour modification works well when rewards are linked clearly to specific behaviours, but does not work well when these links are ambiguous and vague; this manipulative approach may not be acceptable in some cultures.

RECAP: What did they find

Campos et al. (2017) found that:

- The Togolese entrepreneurs who were given the psychology training performed best. Their monthly sales increased by 17 per cent and their profits by 30 per cent, compared with the 'no help' group. They also developed more new product ideas.

- The personal initiative training had strengthened the positive 'psychological mindset' of the entrepreneurs, and encouraged them to improve their business management practices.

- The personal initiative training was particularly effective for businesses owned by women, who saw their profits increase by 40 per cent.

- The traditional training had little impact on the businesses that followed that programme, with their profits increasing by only 5 per cent over the period of the study.

This experiment suggests that you can learn what are often thought to be 'innate' attributes and behaviours of entrepreneurship, through proactive mindset training.

Revision

1. What recommendations does the AGES model make with regard to making sure that learning 'sticks' in long-term memory? How can you apply this model to your own learning habits?

2. Describe and illustrate the technique of organizational behaviour modification, and identify the advantages and disadvantages of this technique.

3. What is the difference between feedback and feedforward? With regard to performance appraisal, what are the advantages and disadvantages of these approaches?

Research assignment

Review your understanding of social learning theory, behaviour modelling, and the concept of provisional selves. How do these approaches explain the ways in which new employees learn about the organization and their job? Interview a supervisor or team leader, and a front line employee in an organization of your choice. Find out how each of those two individuals learned about the organization and their work when they first joined (and/or when they moved to a new job in another part of the organization). Collect examples of behaviour modelling, and of their experiments with provisional selves. How effective were those methods in helping the new employee to 'fit in'? What other methods and sources of information did those individuals use in order to help them to 'fit in'? From this evidence, what are the strengths and limitations of behaviour modelling and provisional selves as an explanation of how new employees are socialized by organizations?

Springboard

Kathy Beevers and Andrew Rea (2016) *Learning and Development Practice in the Workplace.* London: Chartered Institute for Personnel and Development (third edn). Comprehensive description of learning and development practice: explanation of learning models, advice on identifying needs, designing learning activities, using technology and social media, how to enhance learner engagement, and supporting collective and social learning.

Kenneth Blanchard and Spencer Johnson (1994) *The New One Minute Manager.* London: Harper Collins. Classic and influential text – which has sold over 18 million copies – on behaviour modification techniques for managers.

Stella Collins (2015) *Neuroscience for Learning and Development: How to Apply Neuroscience and Psychology for Improved Learning and Training.* London: Kogan Page. Summarizes recent research and suggests practical approaches to improve face-to-face, online, and virtual training and learning. Explains the neuroscience of attention and memory, separating evidence from myths.

OB cinema

A Clockwork Orange (1971 and 2000, director Stanley Kubrick). DVD track (scene) 19: 1:06:57 to 1:11.40 (6 minutes). Clip begins with doctor introducing herself: 'Good morning. My name is Dr Branom'. Clip ends with Dr Branom (played by Madge Ryan) saying, 'Dr Brodski is pleased with you. You've made a very positive response'.

This movie is based in a future a totalitarian state in which the Droog (thug) Alex (played by Malcolm McDowell) is subjected to aversion therapy to cure him of his addiction to violence, rape, drugs and classical music. Fiction? Aversion therapy was used to 'treat' homosexuals in the 1960s. An extremely violent film for its time, Kubrick removed it from circulation in 1974 when it was accused of triggering copycat crimes. The film was released on the anniversary of Kubrick's death, in 2000. In this clip (which contains violence and nudity):

1. To what conditioning and reinforcement regime is Alex subjected?

2. How effective is this in changing his behaviour?

3. Does society have a moral right to interfere with individual behaviour in this way?

Chapter exercises

1: Reinforcement and behaviour

Objective

To explore how positive and negative reinforcement can affect behaviour. This exercise takes about half an hour. It can be used with any size of group, but works particularly well with large classes.

Exercise overview

Two or three volunteers will get reinforcement from the rest of the class while performing a simple task. The volunteers leave the room while the class is briefed. The instructor identifies an object which the volunteers must find when they come back into the room. This object should be unobtrusive, but it should be clearly visible to the class: a piece of paper stuck to the wall, a bag in the corner, a mark on a window. The instructor specifies the reinforcement regime that will apply when each of the volunteers comes back into the room.

- *Negative reinforcement regime:* the class will hiss, boo, make sarcastic comments, and throw harmless items at the first volunteer when they are moving away from the chosen object, and sit in silence when they are moving towards it.

- *Positive reinforcement regime:* the class will smile, cheer, applaud, and make encouraging comments when the second volunteer is moving towards the chosen object, and sit silently when they move away.

- *Combined reinforcement regime:* the class will cheer when the third volunteer approaches the object, and boo when they move away from it.

Nominate one student to record the time that it takes each of the volunteers to find the object.

Exercise sequence

1. The first volunteer is brought back into the room, and told: Your task is to find and touch a particular object in the room. The class will help you, but you cannot ask questions, and they cannot speak to you. The first volunteer continues to look for the object until it is found, with the class giving negative reinforcement.

2. The second volunteer is brought back into the room, and is given the same instruction, to look for the object, with the class giving positive reinforcement.

3. The third volunteer is brought back into the room, and is instructed to find the object with the class giving a combination of negative and positive reinforcement.

Class discussion

- Ask the volunteers how they each felt during this exercise. What were their emotional responses to the different kinds of reinforcement they received?

- What effects did the different reinforcement regimes have on the behaviour of the volunteers?

- Which of these reinforcement regimes are you mostly likely to find in organizations? What effects will these regimes have on motivation and productivity?

2: Branto bakery

Branto Bakery is a large company producing a range of bakery products for major supermarkets. Analysis by the human resource management department shows that the sales and administration departments have the highest rates of absenteeism and poor timekeeping. Interestingly, each of these departments also has individuals with the best absence and punctuality records. The managing director has asked the two department

→

heads to address these absence and timekeeping problems. Alan Anderson, head of sales, has decided to adopt a behaviour modification approach. Barbara Brown, head of administration, has chosen to develop a socialization approach with current and new staff. As an external management consultant, you have been hired to give advice.

1. Design either a behaviour modification programme for Anderson, or a socialization plan for Brown, that will reduce absenteeism and improve timekeeping in their departments.

2. Explain the elements of your plan, how it will address their problems, and how it will be implemented.

3. Assess the strengths and weaknesses of your plan in the short term, and in the long term.

References

Allen, T.D., Eby, L.T., Chao, G.T. and Bauer, T.N. (2017) 'Taking stock of two relational aspects of organizational life: tracing the history and shaping the future of socialization and mentoring research', *Journal of Applied Psychology*, 102 (3): 324–37.

Bandura, A. (1977) *Social Learning Theory*. Englewood Cliffs, NJ: Prentice-Hall.

Bandura, A. (1986) *Social Foundations of Thought and Action: A Social Cognitive Theory*. Englewood Cliffs, NJ: Prentice-Hall.

Benson-Armer, R., Arne Gast, A. and van Dam, N. (2016) 'Learning at the speed of business', *McKinsey Quarterly*, May, pp.115–21.

Boddy, D. (2011) *Management: An Introduction*. Harlow, Essex: Financial Times Prentice Hall, (fifth edition).

Budworth, M.-H., Latham, G.P. and Manroop, L. (2015) 'Looking forward to performance improvement: a field test of the feedforward interview for performance management', *Human Resource Management*, 54(1): 45–54.

Calnan, M. (2017) 'Do you want virtual fries with that?', *People Management*, October, pp.44–6.

Campos, F., Frese, M., Goldstein, M., Lacovone, L., Johnson, H.C., McKenzie, D. and Mensmann, M. (2017) 'Teaching personal initiative beats traditional training in boosting small business in West Africa', *Science*, 357 (6357): 1287–90.

Cao, J. and Hamori, M. (2016) 'The impact of management development practices on organizational commitment', *Human Resource Management*, 55 (3): 499–517.

CIPD (2015a) *Learning and Development Strategy Factsheet*. London: Chartered Institute for Personnel and Development.

CIPD (2015b) *Learning and Development Annual Survey Report 2015*. London: Chartered Institute for Personnel and Development.

Cooper, D., Farmery, K., Johnson, M., Harper, C., Clarke, F., L., Holton, P., Wilson, S., Rayson, P. and Bence, H. (2005) 'Changing personnel behavior to promote quality care practices in an intensive care unit', *Therapeutics and Clinical Risk Management*, 1(4): 321–32.

Davachi, L., Kiefer, T., Rock, D. and Rock, L. (2010) 'Learning that lasts through AGES: maximizing the effectiveness of learning initiatives', *NeuroLeadership Journal*, 3: 53–63.

Davis, J., Balda, M., Rock, D., McGinniss, P. and Davachi, L. (2014) 'The science of making learning stick: an update to the AGES model', *NeuroLeadership Journal*, 5: 1–15.

Dweck, C. (2016) 'What having a "growth mindset" actually means', *Harvard Business Review Online*, January, https://hbr.org/2016/01/what-having-a-growth-mindset-actually-means [accessed 3 January 2019]

Dweck, C. (2017) *Mindset: How You Can Fulfil Your Potential*. New York: Ballantine Books.

Ferster, C.S. and Skinner, B.F. (1957) *Schedules of Reinforcement*. New York: Appleton-Century-Crofts.

Fogg, B.J. (2009) 'The new rules of persuasion', *RSA Journal*, Spring, pp.24–28.

Gifford, J., Urwin, P. and Cerqua, A. (2017) *Strengths-Based Performance Conversations: An Organisational Field Trial*. London: Chartered Institute for Personnel and Development.

Green, M. (2017) *Induction Factsheet*. London: Chartered Institute of Personnel and Development.

Howard-Jones, P. (2014) *Fresh Thinking in Learning and Development: Neuroscience and Learning.* London: Chartered Institute for Personnel and Development.

Ibarra, H. (1999) 'Provisional selves: experimenting with image and identity in professional adaptation', *Administrative Science Quarterly,* 44(4): 764–91.

Ibarra, H. and Barbulescu, R. (2010) 'Identity as narrative: prevalence, effectiveness, and consequences of narrative identity work in macro work role transitions', *Academy of Management Review,* 35(1): 135–54.

Kluger, A.N. and Nir, D. (2010) 'The feedforward interview', *Human Resource Management Review,* 20(3): 235–46.

Knowles-Cutler, A. and Lewis, H. (2016) *Talent for Survival: Essential Skills for Humans Working in the Machine Age.* London: Deloitte.

Lancaster, A. (2017) *Psychology and Neuroscience in Learning Factsheet.* London: Chartered Institute for Personnel and Development.

Liu, S., Wang, M., Bamberger, P., Shi, J. and Bacharach, S.B. (2015) 'The dark side of socialization: a longitudinal investigation of newcomer alcohol use', *Academy of Management Journal,* 58(2): 334–55.

Luthans, F. and Kreitner, R. (1985) *Organizational Behaviour Modification and Beyond.* Glenview IL: Scott, Foresman, (second edition).

Luthans, F., Stajkovic, A., Luthans, B.C. and Luthans, K.W. (1998) 'Applying behavioural management in Eastern Europe', *European Management Journal,* 16(4): 466–74.

Rock, D. (2008) 'SCARF: a brain-based model for collaborating with and influencing others', *NeuroLeadership Journal,* 1: 1–9.

Schein, E. H. (1968) 'Organizational socialization and the profession of management', *Industrial Management Review,* 9: 1–16.

Song, Y., Liu, Y., Shi, J and Wang, M. (2017) 'Use of proactive socialization tactics and socialization outcomes: a latent growth modeling approach to understanding newcomer socialization process', *Academy of Management Discoveries,* 3 (1): 42–63.

Walters, C.C. and Grusek, J.E. (1977) *Punishment.* San Francisco, CA: Freeman.

Weiss, H.M. (1990) 'Learning theory and industrial and organizational psychology', in M.D. Dunnette and L.M. Hough (eds), *Handbook of Industrial and Organizational Psychology.* Palo Alto, CA: Consulting Psychologists Press, pp.75–169.

White, R.W. (1959) 'Motivation reconsidered: the concept of competence', *Psychological Review,* 66(5): 297–333.

Wiener, N. (1954) *The Human Use of Human Beings: Cybernetics and Society.* New York: Avon Books.

World Economic Forum (2016) *The Future of Jobs: Employment, Skills and Workforce Strategy for the Fourth Industrial Revolution.* Geneva: World Economic Forum.

Wybron, I. (2016) *Youth Drinking in Transition.* London: Demos.

Wylie, I. (2018) 'Virtual reality helps students prepare for a digital future', *Financial Times Business Education Supplement,* 5 March, p.2.

Personality

Key terms

personality	idiographic
psychometrics	self-concept
chronotype	generalized other
type	unconditional positive regard
trait	thematic apperception test
nomothetic	need for achievement
Type A personality	projective test
Type B personality	predictive validity
The Big Five	cybervetting
HEXACO model	

Learning outcomes

When you have read this chapter, you should be able to define those key terms in your own words, and you should also be able to:

1. Distinguish between type, trait and self theories of personality.

2. Explain the relationship between personality and stress, and identify individual and organizational stress management strategies.

3. Compare the advantages and disadvantages of questionnaires and projective tests as measures of personality.

4. Evaluate the benefits and problems of psychometric assessment as a management decision-making tool, particularly in selection.

5. Assess your own personality.

Why study personality?

Personality the psychological qualities that influence an individual's characteristic behaviour patterns, in a stable and distinctive manner.

Personality is important for many reasons. We want to know what kind of person we are. Our personality affects how we deal with stress at work. Employers want to know whether we can do the job, work in a team, and be open to further development. Personality testing was used by the United States Army during World War I to identify soldiers who would suffer from shell shock. **Psychometrics** – the measurement of personality and other individual capabilities – is now a US$500 million industry (Harrell, 2017). Three-quarters of *The Times* newspaper's Best Companies to Work For, and 80 per cent of Fortune 500 companies, use psychometric assessments (Jacobs, 2018).

Latin roots

per sonare	to speak through	*persona grata*	an acceptable person
persona	an actor's mask; a character in a play	*persona non grata*	an unacceptable person

---

Psychometrics the systematic testing, measurement and assessment of intelligence, aptitudes and personality.

It is widely believed that that personality is related to job performance and career success. And most of us believe that we are 'good judges of character'. In a selection interview, this often means that you are not going to get the job unless 'your face fits', even if you have the capabilities. This opens up the possibility of bias. Psychometrics can support selection decisions with objective data.

This chapter explains two approaches to personality assessment: *nomothetic* and *idiographic*. Nomothetic methods form the basis for most psychometrics, using 'tick box' questionnaires which are easy to administer and to score. Idiographic methods use open-ended approaches to capture an individual's unique characteristics. These take more time, and are more difficult to score and to interpret. Quantitative, nomothetic methods also appear to be more objective.

Psychometrics include assessments of intelligence, aptitudes and personality. When measuring intelligence or aptitude, we can use the term 'test', because a high score is usually better than a low one. When measuring personality, the term 'assessment' is more appropriate. There are no 'correct' answers in a personality assessment; high scores cannot be said to be better or worse than low scores.

In addition to selecting job applicants, psychometrics have other applications:

- Assessment of suitability for promotion
- Counselling for redundancy or redeployment
- Evaluation of training potential
- Team and leadership development
- Career counselling
- Recruiting graduates with limited work experience.

Defining personality

The concept of personality helps to identify our unique characters and to measure and understand differences between individuals. Personality describes behaviours which are stable and enduring, and which distinguish one individual from others.

Stability

Personality theory deals with behaviour patterns that are consistent in different contexts, and over time. We are less interested in behaviours that occur briefly and on rare occasions.

Mood swings, and behaviours caused by illness, or drugs, are not stable and are not personality characteristics, unless they become permanent. Our stable behaviours depend on social context. For example, the manager who is loud and autocratic in the office can be caring and supportive at home. Some personality features (as with allergies) may only appear in particular social and physical settings.

Chronotype a cluster of personality traits that can affect whether someone is more active and performs better in the morning or in the evening.

Distinctiveness

Personality theory is concerned with the pattern of dispositions and behaviours unique to the individual, and is less concerned with properties that all or most other people share. You may be aggressive towards waiters, friendly with librarians, deferential to professors, and terrified of mice. You may share many of these dispositions with a friend whose hobby is breeding mice.

Are you a morning person or a night owl – and does it matter?

Christoph Randler (2010) argues that those who are most energetic and proactive in the morning (they get up early), are more likely to have successful careers than those who are at their best in the evening. You can adjust your chronotype with training, but Randler argues that it is difficult to make major changes. His research on university students showed that morning people, on average:

- get better grades in school and go to better college
- have better job opportunities
- anticipate and try to minimize problems
- perform better at work, are paid better, and have greater career success.

Morning people tend to be agreeable, optimistic, stable, proactive, conscientious, satisfied with life.

Evening people can be creative, intelligent, humorous, extraverted, pessimistic, neurotic, depressed.

Although evening people can be creative, smart, funny, and outgoing, Randler notes that, 'they're out of sync with the typical corporate schedule'. Most organizational timetables are tailored to morning people. The evidence suggests that the population is evenly split between morning and evening types, but that after age 50, most of us become morning types. Research also shows that chronotype diversity improves team performance, as long as team members take this into account when structuring their work (Volk et al., 2017).

Is your chronotype geared for career success? If not, what can you do about that?

It has been argued that our personalities are inherited, and depend on our genes. For example, evidence suggests that, because measures of job satisfaction are fairly stable over time and across jobs, a predisposition to be content with, or to be frustrated at, work may have a genetic component. In this view, your personality is given, and life's experiences do little to alter it.

It has also been claimed that our characters are shaped by environment, culture and social factors, and that our feelings and behaviour patterns are learned. Social learning theory argues that we acquire new behaviours by observing and imitating others. Every society has distinctive ways of doing things. We were not born with this local knowledge. In this view, your personality is flexible, and changes with experience. Psychological well-being may depend on such adaptability.

The controversy over the effects of heredity and environment on personality is known as the 'nature–nurture' debate. Few psychologists hold extreme views on this issue. Both genetic *and* situational factors influence behaviour. The argument concerns the emphases to be given to these factors, how to measure them, and how they interact. In the twentieth century, 'nurture' was the fashionable view. In the twenty-first century, evidence from biology, genetics and neurophysiology has shifted attention towards 'nature'. From an organization and management perspective, the question is – can personality assessment help us to make better predictions about an individual's future job performance?

EMPLOYABILITY CHECK (self-management, people management, problem-solving skills)

You and your closest colleague have not been working well together recently. You now realize that this is because you have different chronotypes. She is a morning person, and you are an evening person. Your supervisor wants your performance to improve. What action will you take?

Types and traits

Type a descriptive label for a distinct pattern of personality characteristics, such as introvert, extravert, neurotic.

The analysis of personality has used the concepts of type and trait. One of the most straightforward ways of analysing personality is to classify people in terms of personality *types*.

One of the first personality theorists was Hippocrates, ('The father of medicine') who lived in Greece around 400 BC. He claimed that personality type or 'temperament' was determined by bodily 'humours', which generated the behaviour patterns shown in Table 6.1.

Table 6.1: Hippocrates' type theory of personality

Body humour	Temperament or type	Behaviours
Blood	Sanguine	Confident, cheerful, optimistic, active
Phlegm	Phlegmatic	Sluggish, apathetic
Black bile	Melancholic	Depressed, sad, prone to ill-founded fears
Yellow bile	Choleric	Aggressive, excitable, irritable

Hippocrates' type labels are still used today. However, there is no evidence to confirm the links between body chemistry and behaviour – and there are more than four types of people in the world.

William Sheldon (1942) argued that temperament was related to physique, or 'somatotype' (Figure 6.1). Your personality type thus depends on your 'biological individuality', your body size and shape (and on how many hamburgers you eat). Once again, however, this typology is not a good predictor of behaviour. Can you think of an endomorph who is introverted and intellectual? Are you friendly with a mesomorph who is a relaxed gourmet – or an ectomorph who is sociable and artistic?

Type theory was elaborated by the Swiss psychologist, Carl Gustav Jung (1875–1961) who explored psychological preferences for extraversion or introversion, sensation or intuition, thinking or feeling, and judging or perceiving (Jung, 1953, 1971). The mother and daughter team of Katharine Briggs and Isabel Myers (Myers, 1962, 1976; Myers and McCaulley, 1985) used Jung's theory to develop the Myers-Briggs Type Indicator (MBTI). In the 1940s, Isabel became interested in organizations that were using 'people sorting' questionnaires. Lockheed Aircraft used a test to identify 'potential troublemakers', and another US company developed a test to select 'henpecked husbands' in the belief that they would make compliant employees (Ahmed, 2016). Encouraged by her mother, Isabel created her own assessment. She called it the Briggs-Myers Type Indicator because of her mother's contribution, but she was later persuaded to change it to 'Myers-Briggs'.

🖐 **STOP AND SEARCH**   YouTube for *Myers-Briggs personality types.*

Endomorph	Mesomorph	Ectomorph

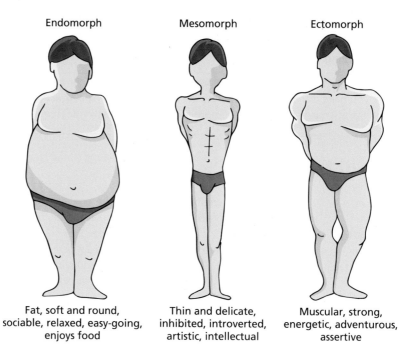

| Fat, soft and round, sociable, relaxed, easy-going, enjoys food | Thin and delicate, inhibited, introverted, artistic, intellectual | Muscular, strong, energetic, adventurous, assertive |

Figure 6.1: Somatotypes

The MBTI rates your personal preferences on four scales:

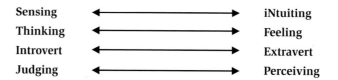

Sensing	⟷	**iNtuiting**
Thinking	⟷	**Feeling**
Introvert	⟷	**Extravert**
Judging	⟷	**Perceiving**

Individuals are assigned to one side or other of each dimension, establishing 16 personality types, each known by its letter codes (iNtuiting is known by the letter N to avoid confusion with introversion). If you are ENFP, you have been typed as Extravert, Intuitive, Feeling and Perceiving. It is useful to remember, however, that these are preferences and tendencies, not fixed categories. We may prefer impersonal analysis (T), but we can when appropriate use emotional judgements (F). We may prefer to focus on the immediate and concrete (S), and also be able when desirable to consider imaginative opportunities (N).

The MBTI is the world's most popular personality assessment; over 50 million people have completed it. It is used in many ways, such as in staff selection, and on management development programmes that explore self-awareness and personal development. It is also used with problem-solving and decision-making groups, which often need a mix of personalities: intuitive types need sensing types, feeling types need thinking types. See Belbin's (1993) theory of group composition **(Chapter 11)**.

The main benefit of the MBTI seems to lie with helping people to understand their own preferences and styles, and those of colleagues. However, MBTI scores cannot predict individual or team performance, and half of those who repeat the test get different results (Harrell, 2017). As another type theory, it can be criticized for over-simplifying the rich complexity of human personality.

Trait a relatively stable quality or attribute of an individual's personality, influencing behaviour in a particular direction.

A personality type (e.g. extravert) is a category whose members are expected to have the same pattern of behaviours (i.e. active, impulsive, risk taking, sociable). A personality trait, on the other hand, is a predisposition to behave in a particular way. Traits allow us to explore the complexity and variation in personality. Individuals belong to types, traits belong to individuals. You fit a type, you have a trait - and the traits that you have may allow us to categorize you as belonging to one broad personality type or another.

Nomothetic an approach to the study of personality emphasizing the identification of traits, and the systematic relationships between different aspects of personality.

Examples of traits include shyness, excitability, reliability, moodiness, punctuality. The study of traits in personality assessment, and of how traits cluster to form 'super traits', is associated with the nomothetic approach in psychology.

Nomothetic means 'law setting or law giving'. This approach assumes that personality is inherited and that environmental factors have little effect. This sits on the nature side of the nature–nurture debate, and uses the following procedures. First, the main dimensions on which personality can vary are identified. Trait approaches assume that there is a common set of dimensions – temperament, character, predispositions – on which we can all be assessed, and also assumes that your personality can be measured and compared with others on the same dimensions.

Second, the personalities of groups of people are assessed, using self-report questionnaires based on 'forced choice' questions: 'true' or 'false', 'yes' or 'no', or 'strongly agree' to 'strongly disagree'.

Third, your personality profile is constructed across the traits measured. Your score on each dimension is compared with the average and the distribution of scores for the whole group. This allows the assessor to identify individuals around the norm, and those with characteristics that deviate from the norm. Your personal score has little meaning beyond the scores of the population with which you are being compared. You cannot have 'high' or 'low' scores; you can only have scores that are high or low when compared with others. It may seem odd that this approach to individual personality assessment relies on studies of large groups. However, this method can show us what is normal or average – in the statistical sense – and we can then compare individuals with that.

Our understanding of personality today is based on the influential work of Hans Jurgen Eysenck (1970; 1990). He explored how personality varies on two dimensions – the extraversion–introversion or 'E' dimension, and the neuroticism–stability or 'N' dimension. However, unlike Jung, Eysenck sought to identify trait clusters. Eysenck's model offers a way of linking types, traits and behaviour, arguing that personality structure is hierarchical. Each individual possesses more or less of a number of traits – trait 1, trait 2, trait 3, and so on. Research shows how individuals who have a particular trait, say trait 1, are more likely to have another, say trait 3, than people who do not have trait 1. In other words traits tend to 'cluster' in patterns. These clusters identify a 'higher order' of personality description, which Eysenck refers to as personality types, or 'super traits'.

The result of an individual assessment using this approach is a personality profile across several traits. Eysenck's approach identified two main sets of trait clusters (or super traits, or types). The E dimension runs from extravert to introvert. The N dimension runs from neuroticism to stability.

CUTTING EDGE   Can an introvert be a successful leader?

Stephane Kasriel

Stephane Kasriel (2016) is a software engineer, and chief executive of Upwork, an online freelancing platform where businesses and independent professionals connect and collaborate remotely. Upwork has access to 10 million freelancers, with over 4 million clients in over 180 countries, and generates over $1 billion of work a year. Chief executives are expected to be cheerful and outgoing, but the Myers-Briggs assessment showed that Kasriel was introverted. He explains how his personality could have been a barrier to a leadership role.

'I recognized early on that I was an introvert, although I probably didn't know the word for it at the time. Some kids in high school clearly thrive on popularity and going out all the time – being surrounded by lots of people. In contrast, I enjoyed being with a small number of people. I liked to read books, program computers, and do things by myself. I'm not completely socially awkward - I can get by in a crowd, but it doesn't come naturally.

'A particularly difficult task for someone like me is to go to a big networking event or conference – where there's a large room filled with hundreds of people I don't know –

→

and mingle. To make that manageable, I set goals: I'm going to talk to at least 30 people, get ten business cards, and arrange five follow-up meetings. Because I'm competitive and results-oriented, those goals counterbalance the anxiety I feel about inserting myself into a random conversation and introducing myself. I've worked on the skill of starting a conversation. I've also worked on findings ways to say goodbye gracefully, because not every interaction at these events needs to be a long one' (pp.37–38).

Other successful introverted technology entrepreneurs include Bill Gates and Mark Zuckerberg. Are you an introvert? Could Kasriel's approach work for you?

Extraverts are tough-minded individuals who need stimulation. They are sociable, enjoy parties, are good at telling stories, enjoy practical jokes, have many friends, but do not enjoy studying on their own. *Introverts* are tender-minded, have strong emotions, and do not need intense stimuli. They are quiet, prefer books to people, are reserved, plan ahead, distrust impulse, appreciate order, lead careful sober lives, suppress emotions, are pessimistic, worry about moral standards, and are reliable.

Neurotics are emotional, unstable and anxious, have low opinions of themselves, feel that they are unattractive failures, tend to be disappointed with life, and are pessimistic and depressed. They feel controlled by events, by others and by fate. *Stable* people are 'adjusted', self-confident, optimistic, realistic, solve their own problems, have few health worries, and have few regrets about their past.

Most of us have a trait profile between these two sets of extremes. Is one personality more desirable than another? Extraverts may be sociable and friendly, but they can also be unreliable. Introverts, on the other hand, are more reliable, but they would rather read a book than talk to you. Those with extreme scores have what Eysenck calls an 'ambiguous gift'. It is important to be aware of your personality, and to appreciate what others could see as strengths and weaknesses.

Would you pass an integrity test?

Employers want staff who are conscientious, dependable and honest. Many companies use integrity tests to identify those who could pose risks, through dishonesty, cheating, lying, stealing, drug abuse, racism, sexism, and violent and criminal behaviour. After using integrity testing in 600 of its 1,900 stores, one American retailer reported a 35 per cent drop in the loss (or theft) of stock in its stores, while losses rose by over 10 per cent in stores that did not use integrity testing (Arnold and Jones, 2006). Paul Whitely (2012) at the University of Essex Centre for the Study of Integrity has developed a test that asks you to rate the following ten items using these scores and ratings:

1. Never justified   2. Rarely justified
3. Sometimes justified   4. Always justified

a. Avoiding paying the fare on public transport

b. Cheating on taxes if you have a chance

c. Driving faster than the speed limit

d. Keeping money you found in the street

e. Lying in your own interests

f. Not reporting accidental damage you've done to a parked car

g. Throwing away litter in a public place

h. Driving under the influence of alcohol

i. Making up things on a job application

j. Buying something you know is stolen

If your score is	This means
Up to 15	You are very honest and really want to do the right thing
15 up to 19	Your integrity is above average but you don't mind bending the rules
20 up to 24	You are relaxed about breaking the rules when it suits you
25 and above	You don't believe in rules and it's easy to break them when it suits you

A survey in 2011 found that just under 50 per cent of UK respondents scored up to 15, and only 5 per cent scored over 25. The average was 16. There was high tolerance for keeping money found in the street, exceeding the speed limit, and lying in one's own interests. Faking job applications, dropping litter, buying stolen goods, and drunk driving were condemned. There were no differences depending on affluence, education, or occupational status. Women had slightly higher scores than men.

Younger people were more relaxed about 'low level' dishonesty. For example, while 75 per cent of those over 65 regarded making false statements on a job application as never justified, only 33 per cent of those under 25 took that view, with similar views about telling lies. An earlier survey, in the year 2000, showed that the percentage of respondents saying that a behaviour is never justified had fallen for eight out of the ten indicators. Attitudes to dropping litter have not changed much, but on the whole we appear to be more tolerant of low level dishonesty than we were ten years ago.

Societies in which trust and integrity are strong have better economic performance. This effect may apply to organizations in a world increasingly sensitive to corporate social responsibility. Remember – it is easy to cheat on these tests, and to give yourself a higher integrity score, especially if you are low in integrity.

Home viewing

Glengarry Glen Ross (1992, director James Foley) is based in a Chicago real-estate office. To boost flagging sales, the 'downtown' manager Blake (played by Alec Baldwin) introduces a sales contest. First prize is a Cadillac Eldorado, second prize is a set of steak knives, third prize is dismissal. The sales staff include Ricky Roma (Al Pacino), Shelley Levene (Jack Lemmon), George Aaronow (Alan Arkin) and Dave Moss (Ed Harris). In the first ten minutes of the film, note how Blake in his 'motivational talk' fits the stereotype of the extravert, competitive 'macho' salesman (warning: bad language). How does his 'pep talk' affect the sales team? Should salespeople copy Blake's stereotype? What is Blake's view of human nature? This part of the movie shows how identity is constructed through a 'performance'. This contrasts with a view of identity as genetically determined.

 **STOP AND SEARCH**   YouTube for *Leadership Glengarry Glen Ross* (8:10; warning, bad language).

Personality types A and B

Type A personality
a combination of emotions and behaviours characterized by ambition, hostility, impatience and a sense of constant time-pressure.

Type B personality
a combination of emotions and behaviours characterized by relaxation, low focus on achievement, and ability to take time to enjoy leisure.

Another influential type theory links personality to stress. Meyer Friedman and Ray Rosenman (1974) identified two 'behaviour syndromes' called Type A and Type B personality (see Table 6.2).

Friedman and Rosenman found that Type As were three times more likely to suffer heart disease than Type Bs. Type As thrive on long hours, high workload, and tight deadlines. These are socially and organizationally desirable characteristics, as are competitiveness and a high need for achievement. However, the extreme Type A may not be able to relax enough to stand back from a complex problem to make an effective and comprehensive analysis, and may lack the patience and relaxed style required in some management roles. In addition, impatience and hostility can increase stress in those who work with them. Like the extravert, a Type A personality appears to have many desirable aspects, but this behaviour syndrome can be dysfunctional for the individual, and for others.

Friedman and Rosenman argue that a Type A can change into a Type B, with awareness and training, and they suggest a number of personal 're-engineering strategies':

- Keep reminding yourself that life is always full of unfinished business
- You only 'finish' when you die

- Learn how to delegate responsibility to others
- Limit your weekly working hours
- Schedule time for leisure and exercise
- Take a course in time management skills.

The problem, of course, is that the extreme Type A personality – the person most at risk – can never find time to implement these strategies.

Table 6.2: Type A and Type B personality characteristics

Type A personality characteristics	Type B personality characteristics
Competitive	Takes time out to enjoy leisure
High need for achievement	Not preoccupied with achievement
Aggressive, works fast	Easygoing, works at steady pace
Impatient, restless, alert	Seldom impatient, not easily frustrated, relaxed
Tense facial muscles	Moves and speaks slowly
Constant feeling of time pressure	Seldom lacks enough time
More likely to suffer stress related illness	Less likely to suffer stress related illness

CRITICAL THINKING

Are you a Type A or a Type B? Do you suffer from: alcohol abuse, excessive smoking, dizziness, upset stomach, headaches, fatigue, sweating, bad breath? If 'yes', these could be stress responses to your Type A behaviour. Expect your first heart attack before you are 45.

If you don't suffer stress-related symptoms, perhaps you are a Type B. Do you think that your relaxed, casual behaviour will damage your career prospects?

Whichever your response, what are you going to do about it?

 EMPLOYABILITY CHECK (self-management, work ethic, appetite for learning)

You now know that you have a Type A personality. Your typical Type A behaviour means that you have been successful in a number of fields – sport, education, work. You also know that if you maintain this pace, your health, and some of your close relationships, will suffer. What action will you take to limit or avoid this damage, while keeping up your success rate?

Stress and stress management

Stress is expensive. Over 12 million working days were lost in the UK in 2016–17 due to work-related stress; the Health and Safety Executive (2017) estimates that stress costs the economy over £5 billion a year. Negative emotional states such as depression, hostility and anxiety are linked to heart disease, ulcers, headaches, and respiratory disorders such as asthma. People in highly stressful jobs, in which they have little or no autonomy, have a 23 per cent higher risk of a heart attack (Boseley, 2012). Stress has individual causes: Type A personality, difficulty in coping with change, lack of confidence, poor time management, poor stress management skills.

Any condition that requires an adaptive response is known as a stressor. The pace of life and constant change generate stress by increasing the range and intensity of the demands on our time. Typical stressors that arise in organizations are:

- *Inadequate physical working environment:* noise, bad lighting, poor ventilation, lack of privacy, extremes of heat and cold, old and unreliable equipment.

- *Inappropriate job design:* poor coordination, poor training, lack of information, rigid procedures, inadequate staffing, high workloads, no challenge, little use of skills, no responsibility or participation in decision making, role ambiguity.

- *Poor management style:* inconsistent, competitive, crisis management, autocratic management, excessive time pressures.

- *Poor relationships:* with superiors, with colleagues, with particular individuals, lack of feedback, little social contact, racial and sexual harassment.

- *Uncertain future:* job insecurity, fear of unemployment or redeployment, few promotion opportunities, low-status job.

- *Divided loyalties:* conflicts between personal aspirations and organizational requirements, conflict between job and family and social responsibilities.

Stress – or pressure – can also be arousing and exciting, enhance our sense of satisfaction and accomplishment, and improve our performance. The term *eustress* describes this positive aspect of stress. The prefix 'eu' is Greek for 'good'. This contrasts with *distress,* which means the unpleasant, unhealthy side of stress.

Stress can be episodic. When dealing with life's problems, we get anxious, cope with the problem, and then relax. Some events can be extremely stressful, such as the death of a relative, or a prison sentence. Other stressful experiences include getting a poor exam grade, being fined for speeding, or arguing with a friend, but these trigger less extreme responses. Each of these episodes on its own is unlikely to cause lasting damage. However, when several of these episodes occur around the same time, the health risk is increased.

Stress can be chronic. This happens when we face constant stress, with no escape, and this can lead to exhaustion and 'burnout'. This may be due to the unfortunate coincidence of several unrelated episodes. However, chronic stress also arises from the enduring features of our personal, social and organizational circumstances. If we are always under pressure, always facing multiple unrealistic demands, always having difficulties with our work, our colleagues, and our relationships, then the health risk from stress is likely to increase.

There are three other factors moderating the impact of stressors:

Condition	You are better able to cope with stress if you are in good health.
Cognitive appraisal	If you believe that you are not going to cope with a particular event, this belief can become a 'self-fulfilling prophecy'.
Hardiness	Hardiness is an outlook on life characterized by a welcoming approach to change, commitment to purposeful activity, and a sense of being in control. This combination increases ability to deal with stress.

Table 6.3 summarizes the typical signs of stress (Ayling and Wilmott, 2017).

Stress can have emotional consequences: anxiety, fatigue, depression, frustration, nervousness, low self-esteem. Extreme stress can lead to mental breakdown and suicide. Stress also affects behaviour in other ways, from 'comfort tricks' involving alcohol and other drugs and excess eating, to accident-proneness and emotional outbursts. Stress affects our ability to think, and interferes with learning, concentration, decision making, attention span, and reaction to criticism. Physiological responses to stress include increased heart rate and blood pressure, sweating, and 'hot and cold flushes'.

The consequences of stress can be costly. The performance of stressed employees can be poor, and stress causes absenteeism, staff turnover, accidents, and sabotage. Stress damages

Table 6.3: The signs of excessive pressure and stress

Work performance	Regression
Declining, inconsistent performance	Crying
Uncharacteristic errors	Arguments
Loss of control over work	Undue sensitivity
Loss of motivation, commitment	Irritability, moodiness
Indecision	Over-reaction to problems
Lapses in memory	Personality clashes
Increased time at work	Sulking
Lack of holiday planning, usage	Immature behaviour

Withdrawal	Aggressive behaviour
Arriving late to work	Malicious gossip
Leaving early	Criticism of others
Extended lunches	Vandalism
Absenteeism	Shouting
Resigned attitude	Bullying or harassment
Reduced social contact	Poor employee relations
Elusiveness, evasiveness	Temper outbursts

Other behaviours	Physical signs
Out-of-character behaviour	Nervous stumbling speech
Difficulty relaxing	Sweating
Increased alcohol consumption	Tiredness, lethargy
Increased smoking	Upset stomach, flatulence
Lack of interest in appearance, hygiene	Tension headaches
Accidents at home or work	Hand tremor
Reckless driving	Rapid weight gain or loss
Unnecessary risk-taking	Constantly feeling cold

Source: Ayling and Willmott (2017)

relationships (poor relationships can cause stress in the first place), and commitment to work and the organization falls.

There are two broad strategies for reducing stress: *individual emotion-focused* strategies, and *organizational problem-focused* strategies.

Individual emotion-focused strategies improve resilience and coping skills and include:

- Consciousness-raising to improve self-awareness
- Exercise and fitness programmes
- Self-help training, in biofeedback, meditation, relaxation, coping strategies
- Time management training
- Development of other social and job interests.

Built to rush: pressure and stress are good for you

In his book *Rush: Why You Need and Love the Rat Race,* Todd Buchholz (2011a) argues that speed, stress and competition at work add to our health and happiness. Taking it easy makes us unhealthy and miser-able. Buchholz is a Harvard economics professor and a former White House economic adviser. He has no time for 'work–life balance', lazy vacations, or yoga retreats. Instead, he emphasizes the benefits of activ-

Todd Buchholz

ity. As we are 'built to rush', pressure and stress drive us to perform better, and competition encourages creativity and innovation.

Friedman and Rosenman (1974) argued that people with Type A personalities have problems with their health and with making good decisions. In contrast, Buchholz cites an Australian study, involving 9,000 people, which found that those with a passive lifestyle, who spent four or more hours a day 'de-stressing' in front of the television, had an 80 per cent higher chance of developing heart disease than those who spent less than two hours a day channel hopping:

'In your bloodstream is an enzyme called lipoprotein lipase. It's a friendly enzyme because it draws fat to your muscles, where it can be burned as fuel. But sitting on your bum leaves fat in your bloodstream, where it might as well clog into formations that spell out 999. We want to feel that rush of dopamine when we face a new challenge at work. We need that push of forward momentum in order to be creative. And we need it much more than we need mantras, deep breathing or the murmur that comes when we try to snooze through life' (Buchholz, 2011b, p.1).

Research has shown that cognitive abilities – speed and clarity of thought – decay in people after they retire from work. Competition is beneficial. Buchholz criticizes 'Edenists' who want a simpler, happier lifestyle. What will you do when you finish this chapter: go relax, or rush on to the next task?

Organizational problem-focused strategies deal directly with the stressors and include:

- Improved selection and training
- Staff counselling
- Improved organizational communications
- Job redesign and enrichment strategies
- Development of teamworking.

Figure 6.2 summarizes the argument of this section, in terms of the causes of stress, factors that moderate the experience of stress, stress symptoms, and coping strategies.

 EMPLOYABILITY CHECK (self-management, communication skills)

You are stressed at work – you recognize the signs. What action will you personally take to reduce your stress? How will you approach your manager about this matter? What action can they take to help reduce the stress that you – and perhaps other colleagues – are experiencing?

The Big Five (or six)

The Big Five consistent trait clusters that capture the main dimensions of personality: Openness, Conscientiousness, Extraversion, Agreeableness and Neuroticism.

Research on personality trait clusters now focuses on The Big Five (Paul Costa and Robert McRae, 1992; Sackett et al., 2017; Soto et al., 2017). This is widely accepted as a common descriptive system. Studies have reproduced these dimensions in different social settings and cultures, with different populations, and different forms of data collection. However, a sixth dimension has recently been identified. Let's explore The Big Five first, and then update the model.

The Big Five (which spell OCEAN) are not personality types. These are sets of factors, or 'super traits', which describe common elements among the sub-factors or traits which cluster together. Costa and McCrae identify six traits under each of the five headings, giving 30 traits in total. Table 6.4 summarizes The Big Five trait clusters. You can profile your own

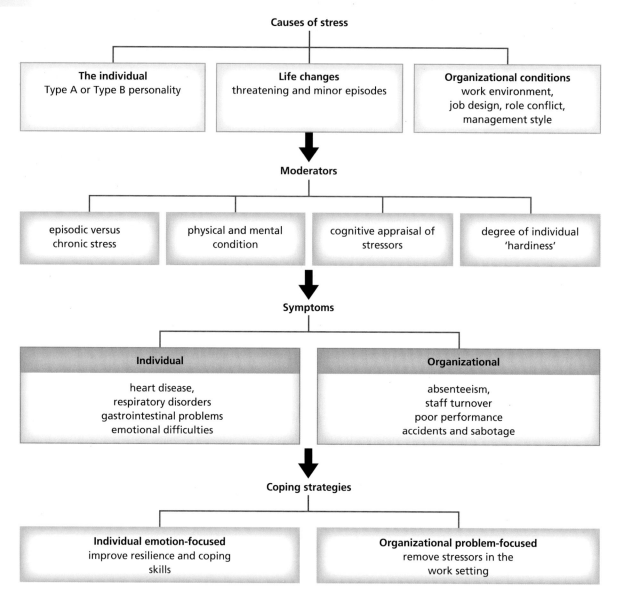

Figure 6.2: Stress causes, moderators, symptoms and coping strategies

personality using the assessment at the end of this chapter, or find online versions of the Big Five inventory at:

https://openpsychometrics.org/tests/IPIP-BFFM/
https://www.truity.com/test/big-five-personality-test

As you read the following descriptions, see if you can identify where your personality lies on each trait cluster. How open, conscientious, extravert, agreeable and neurotic are you?

- **Openness** is based on six traits: fantasy, aesthetics, feelings, actions, ideas, values. These run on a continuum from 'explorer', at one extreme, to 'preserver' at the other:

Explorer (O+) traits are useful for entrepreneurs, architects, change agents, artists and theoretical scientists. *Preserver* (O−) traits are useful for finance managers, stage performers, project managers and applied scientists. Those in the middle (O) are labelled 'moderates' who are interested in novelty when necessity commands, but not for too long.

Table 6.4: The Big Five personality trait clusters

High ←		→ Low
Explorer (O+)	**Openness**	*Preserver* (O−)
Creative, curious, open-minded, intellectual	Rigidity of beliefs and range of interests	Conventional, unimaginative, narrow-minded
Focused (C+)	**Conscientiousness**	*Flexible* (C−)
Organized, self-disciplined, achievement-oriented	Desire to impose order and precision	Disorganized, careless, frivolous, irresponsible
Extravert (E+)	**Extraversion**	*Introvert* (E−)
Outgoing, sociable, talkative, assertive	Level of comfort with relationships	Reserved, quiet, introverted
Adapter (A+)	**Agreeableness**	*Challenger* (A−)
Good-natured, trusting, compliant, soft-hearted	The ability to get along with others	Rude, quarrelsome, uncaring, irritable, uncooperative
Reactive (N+)	**Neuroticism**	*Resilient* (N−)
Anxious, depressed, self-conscious	Tendency to maintain a balanced emotional state	Calm, contented, self-assured
High ←		→ Low

- **Conscientiousness**: competence, order, dutifulness, achievement striving, self-discipline, deliberation. This continuum runs from 'focused' to 'flexible':

  Focused (C+) traits are useful for leaders, senior executives and other high achievers. *Flexible* (C−) traits are useful for researchers, detectives and management consultants. Those in the middle (C) are 'balanced', and find it easy to move from focus to being flexible, from production to research.

- **Extraversion**: warmth, gregariousness, assertiveness, activity, excitement-seeking, positive emotions. This continuum runs from 'extravert' to 'introvert':

  Extravert (E+) traits are useful in sales, politics and the arts. *Introvert* (E−) traits are useful for production management, and in the physical and natural sciences. Those in the middle (E) are 'ambiverts' who move easily from isolation to social settings.

- **Agreeableness**: trust, straightforwardness, altruism, compliance, modesty, tender-mindedness. This continuum runs from 'adapter' to 'challenger':

  Adapter (A+) traits are useful in teaching, social work and psychology. *Challenger* (A−) traits are useful in advertising, management and military leadership. Those in the middle (A) are 'negotiators' who move from leadership to followership as the situation demands.

- **Neuroticism,** or 'negative emotionality': worry, anger, discouragement, self-consciousness, impulsiveness, vulnerability. This continuum runs from 'reactive' to 'resilient':

  Reactive (emotional) or 'N+' traits are useful for social scientists, academics, and customer service professionals, but extreme reactivity interferes with intellectual performance. *Resilient* (unflappable) or 'N−' traits are useful for air traffic controllers, airline pilots, military snipers, finance managers and engineers. Those in the middle (N) are 'responsives', able to use levels of emotionality appropriate to the circumstances.

Those trait clusters may be appropriate to particular occupations (Moutafi et al., 2007):

Openness	Shown to reduce the performance of rugby referees
Conscientiousness	Positively related to salary, promotions, and job status in most occupations
Extraversion	Findings are inconsistent, linked to performance, salary, and job level in some studies, but not in others; may depend on type of work
Openness and agreeableness	Do not correlate consistently with job performance; these attributes could contribute to lower performance in some jobs
Neuroticism	Negatively related to performance, salary and status
Agreeableness	Seems to interfere with management potential

CUTTING EDGE Automating personality assessment

Youyou Wu

Youyou Wu and colleagues (2015) compared human and computer-based judgements of the personalities of 86,200 participants, who first completed a Big Five personality assessment. Most of us believe that we are good judges of personality, but this could be another skill that computers perform better. The researchers also designed a computer model using Facebook Likes, which indicate 'positive associations' with a range of issues: products, brands, websites, sports, music, books, restaurants. The participants' personalities were then rated on The Big Five by Facebook friends.

The computer model was more accurate, needing only 100 Likes in order to perform better than a human judge (300 Likes if the human assessor was a spouse). On average, Facebook users each have 227 Likes. Computers may be better judges because they can store and analyse volumes of information which are difficult for humans to retain, and their assessments are not biased by emotions and motives. Why should Facebook Likes be linked to personality?

'Exploring the Likes most predictive of a given trait shows that they represent activities, attitudes, and preferences highly aligned with The Big Five theory. For example, participants with high openness to experience tend to like Salvador Dali, meditation, or TED talks; participants with high extraversion tend to like partying, Snookie (reality show star), or dancing' (p.1037).

Automated, accurate, inexpensive personality assessment could have several uses: tailoring marketing messages, matching candidates to jobs, adjusting services to customers. However, the personal information that can be collected from your 'digital footprint' can also be used to influence and manipulate, raising questions of privacy.

In the movie *Her* (2013, director Spike Jonze), the writer Theodore Twombly (played by Joaquin Phoenix) falls in love with Samantha (Scarlet Johansson), who is his computer's artificially intelligent operating system. Samantha understands and responds to Theodore in a more helpful and effective way than his friends. The researchers conclude that their findings could turn this fiction into reality.

Is personality linked to success in management? Joanna Moutafi et al. (2007) studied 900 British managers, from ten organizations, in retailing, telecoms, manufacturing, consultancy, accounting, and legal services. They reached three conclusions:

1. *Conscientiousness* was positively related to management level. This suggests that you are more likely to be promoted if you are capable, sensitive, effective, well-organized,

thorough, dependable, reliable, ambitious and hard-working. However, it may also be the case that high-level jobs encourage the development of those characteristics.

2. *Extraversion* was positively related to management level. This implies that you are more likely to be promoted if you are dominant, confident, assertive, energetic, determined, outgoing and sociable. The researchers note that, 'Management is an extraverted activity. Managers attend meetings, give talks and socially interact all day long, which are activities more easily handled by extraverts than introverts' (Moutafi et al., 2007, p.77).

3. *Neuroticism* was negatively related to management level. This means that you are less likely to be promoted if you appear nervous, tense, anxious, stress-prone, unhappy, depressed, shy, and unable to cope. People with those characteristics may avoid jobs with high levels of responsibility, but the stress in those management roles may increase neuroticism.

This study suggests, therefore, that personality assessment could be useful in selecting people for management roles.

The H factor

Research now recognizes a sixth personality dimension, which has been labelled 'the H factor'. Identified by Michael Ashton and Kibeom Lee, the H dimension concerns Honesty–Humility (Ashton et al., 2004; Ashton and Lee, 2007; Lee and Ashton, 2012; Sackett et al., 2017). This dimension is based on four facets: sincerity, fairness, greed avoidance and modesty. The contrasts are:

High honesty–humility ⟵	⟶ Low honesty–humility
Sincere, honest, faithful, loyal, modest, unassuming	Sly, deceitful, greedy, pretentious, hypocritical, boastful, pompous

HEXACO model a model of personality based on six trait clusters – honesty–humility, emotionality, extraversion, agreeableness, conscientiousness, and openness to experience.

This creates the HEXACO model, with six trait clusters:

H Honesty–Humility
E Emotionality
X Extraversion
A Agreeableness
C Conscientiousness
O Openness to experience

Those who score highly on the honesty–humility scale avoid manipulating others, do not break the rules, are not interested in wealth, and do not consider themselves worthy of high social status. In contrast, those with low scores tend to flatter others to get what they want, break the rules when it suits them, are motivated by financial gain, and have a strong sense of their self-importance.

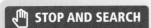 **STOP AND SEARCH**   YouTube for *Did you take the HEXACO personality test yet?* (5:30).

Take the HEXACO personality inventory, at no cost, at http://hexaco.org.
On the landing page, go to the panel on the left and click 'Take the HEXACO-PI-P'.

CUTTING EDGE — Can your personality damage your career?

Tomas Chamorro-Premuzic

Tomas Chamorro-Premuzic (2017) identifies eleven 'dark side' personality traits which can derail your career. Each of these traits has an 'upside', which is desirable. However, unless this is kept under control, the downsides of these traits can be damaging. Studies show that most of us display at least three of these dark side traits, and that 40 per cent have high scores that put their careers at risk. The eleven traits fall into three clusters. Distancing traits can push others away. Seductive traits pull people in. Ingratiating traits can be positive for followers, but negative for leaders.

Trait	Upside	Downside
Cluster 1: distancing traits		
Excitable	Passion, enthusiasm	Outbursts, volatility
Sceptical	Politically astute, hard to fool	Mistrustful, quarrelsome
Cautious	Careful, precise	Indecisive, risk-averse
Reserved	Stoic, calm under pressure	Uncommunicative, insensitive
Leisurely	Relaxed, easygoing on the surface	Passive-aggressive, personal agenda
Cluster 2: seductive traits		
Bold	Assertive, filled with conviction	Arrogant, grandiose
Mischievous	Risk-tolerant, charmingly persuasive	Impulsive, manipulative
Colourful	Entertaining, expressive	Socially insensitive
Imaginative	Creative, visionary	Wacky ideas, constant change
Cluster 3: ingratiating traits		
Diligent	Hard-working, high standards	Perfectionist, micromanaging
Dutiful	Compliant, loyal	Submissive, conflict-averse

You can manage your dark side, by taking a personality assessment, by asking colleagues for feedback, and by comparing your behaviour patterns with the traits in the table.

 EMPLOYABILITY CHECK (self-management)

Which two or three of the 'dark side' traits do you recognize as potential 'derailers' of your own career success? How will you change your behaviour in order to control those dark-side traits?

The development of the self

Idiographic an approach to the study of personality emphasizing the uniqueness of the individual, rejecting the assumption that we can all be measured on the same dimensions.

Advocates of an idiographic approach to the study of personality are critical of nomothetic methods. Idiographic means 'writing about individuals'. Psychologists using this perspective begin with a detailed picture of one person, aiming to capture their unique richness and complexity. This is a valuable way of deepening our understanding, but does not produce universal laws of behaviour. As we will see, compared with nomothetic methods, an idiographic approach appears to be a complex, untidy view of personality and its development. This perspective has influenced research, but has had little impact on contemporary psychometrics.

The idiographic approach makes the following assumptions.

First, we each have unique traits that cannot be compared with the traits of others. Your sensitivity and aggression are not necessarily the same as my sensitivity and aggression. To build a detailed picture, idiographic research uses many sources: information posted on social media, interviews, letters, diaries, biographies, what people say about themselves.

Second, we are socially self-conscious, and not mere biological machines powered by heredity. Our behaviour is shaped by our experience, reflection, and reasoning, not just by instinct and habit.

Third, we learn about ourselves through interacting with others, and we behave in accordance with the image that we have of ourselves – our self-concept. We take the attitudes and behaviours of others and use those to form our self-concept and direct our behaviour.

Fourth, as the development of the self-concept is a social process, this means that personality can change with social experiences. The development of personality is not the inevitable result of genetic inheritance. It is through interaction with others that we learn to understand ourselves as individuals. We cannot develop self-understanding without the (tacit) help of others. In this view, 'human nature' is a fluid concept. This perspective, therefore, is on the nurture side of the nature–nurture debate.

The mind's ability to reflect on its own functions is an important capability. We experience a world 'out there' and we can experience ourselves in that world, as objects that live and behave in it. We can observe, evaluate and criticize ourselves in the same conscious, impersonal way that we observe, evaluate and criticize others, and we can experience shame, anxiety or pride in our own behaviour. Our capacity for reflection allows us to evaluate past and future actions and their consequences.

The American psychologist Charles Horton Cooley introduced the concept of the 'looking glass self'. Our mirror is the other people with whom we interact. If others respond warmly and favourably towards us, we develop a 'positive' self-concept. If others respond with criticism, ridicule and aggression, we develop a 'negative' self-image. The personality of the individual is thus the result of a process in which the individual learns to be the person they are. Most of us learn, accept and use most of the attitudes, values, beliefs and expectations of the society in which we are brought up.

In other words, we learn the stock of knowledge peculiar to our society. Red means stop. Cars drive on the left-hand side of the road (in Australia and Britain). An extended hand is a symbol of respect and friendship, not of hostility or aggression. These examples, on their own, are trivial. Taken together, these make up our 'recipe knowledge' of how society works. The taken-for granted 'rules' that govern our behaviour are created, recreated and reinforced through our ongoing interactions with others based on shared definitions of our reality. We interact with each other successfully because we share this understanding. What we inherit from our parents cannot possibly tell us how to behave in a specific culture. We have to learn how to become *persona grata* through social interaction.

If we all share the same ideas and behaviours, we have a recipe for a society of conformists. This is not consistent with the evidence, and the theory does not imply this. George Herbert Mead (1934) argued that the self has two components:

I   The unique, individual, conscious and impulsive aspects of the individual

Me The norms and values of society that the individual learns and accepts, or 'internalizes'

Mead used the term generalized other to refer to the set of expectations that we believe others have of us. 'Me' is the part of self where these generalized attitudes are organized. 'Me' refers to the mental process that enables us to reflect on our own conduct. 'Me' is the self as an object to itself.

The 'I' is the active, impulsive component of the self. Other people encourage us to conform to current values and beliefs. Reflective individuals adjust their part in the social process. We can initiate change by introducing new social values. Patterns of socially acceptable conduct

Self-concept the set of perceptions that we have about ourselves.

Generalized other what we think other people expect of us, in terms of our attitudes, values, beliefs and behaviour.

are specified in broad and general ways. There is plenty of scope for flexibility, modification, originality, creativity, individuality, variety, and change.

Figure 6.3 illustrates what Carl Rogers (1947) called the 'two-sided self'.

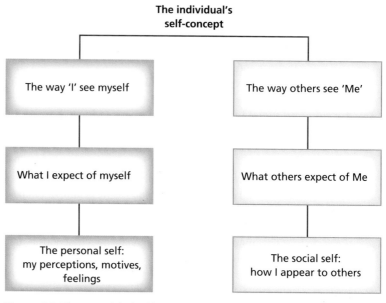

Figure 6.3: The two-sided self

CRITICAL THINKING

List the ten words or phrases that best describe the most important aspects of your identity. These features could concern your social roles, physical characteristics, intellectual qualities, social style, beliefs, and particular skills.

Then make a second list, putting what you regard as the most important feature at the top, and ranking all ten items with the least important at the bottom.

Starting at the bottom of your list, imagine that these items are removed from your personality one by one. Visualize how you would be different without each personality feature. What difference does its absence make to you?

This is the start of the process of establishing your *self-concept.* How much more or less valid is this approach than one based on forced choice questionnaires – and why?

Our self-concept gives us a sense of meaning and consistency. But as our perceptions and motives change with new experiences and learning, our self-concept and our behaviour also change. Our self-concept can be reorganized, and personality in this perspective, therefore, is not stable. We have perceptions of our qualities, abilities, attitudes, impulses and so on. If these perceptions are accurate, conscious, organized and accepted, then we can regard our self-concept as successful because it will lead to feelings of comfort, freedom from tension, and psychological adjustment. Well-adjusted individuals have flexible images of themselves, and are open to change through new experiences.

Personality disorders can be caused by a failure to bring together experiences, motives and feelings into a consistent self-concept. We usually behave in ways consistent with our self-images, but when we have new experiences or feelings that are inconsistent we either:

- recognize the inconsistency and try to integrate the two sets of understanding - the healthy response; or
- deny or distort one of the experiences, perhaps by putting the blame onto someone or something else – an unhealthy defence mechanism.

Unconditional positive regard unqualified, non-judgemental approval and respect for the traits and behaviours of the other person (a term used in counselling).

Rogers argued that at the core of human personality is the desire to realize fully one's potential. To achieve this, the right social environment is required, one in which we are treated with unconditional positive regard. This means that you are accepted for who you are, valued, trusted, and respected, even in the face of characteristics which others dislike. In this environment, we are likely to become trusting, spontaneous, and flexible, with a rich and meaningful life and a harmonious self-concept. However, this is different from the social environment in many contemporary organizations. Most of us face highly conditional regard, in which a narrow range of thoughts and behaviours is accepted.

CUTTING EDGE Should you be true to yourself?

Herminia Ibarra

Herminia Ibarra (2015) argues that a rigid self-concept is a problem when we are constantly faced with radical work and organizational changes, and where we want to change our behaviour to improve our performance. But leaders and managers are often advised to be 'authentic' if they are to be effective. What does that mean in practice? 'Authenticity' means genuine, original, not a copy. For the individual, this means behaving in ways that are consistent with one's 'true self'. However, with an increasingly diverse workforce, many of us have colleagues whose norms and expectations are different from our own. It can be difficult to choose between what is expected of us, and what feels authentic.

Ibarra (2015) describes how two contrasting psychological profiles lead to different ways of managing our self-concept:

- *Chameleons* are able and willing to adapt to the demands of different situations without feeling that they are faking. They 'try on' different styles to find a fit with the context.

- *True-to-selfers* say what they really think and feel, even if that is not consistent with the expectations and demands of the situation.

There are problems with both of those profiles. Adaptable chameleons may have fast-track careers, but can be seen as insincere and immoral. True-to-selfers may stay in their comfort zones and not change behaviour to meet new demands. Ibarra cites the example of a manager who took on a more responsible position. She believed in transparent, collaborative leadership, and openly shared her anxieties with her new staff. However, her staff were looking for a confident leader to take charge. Instead of building trust, her 'authenticity' damaged her credibility.

Instead, Ibarra (2015, p.8) advises managers and leaders to develop an *adaptively authentic* profile. This involves 'playing' with different approaches:

'When we adopt a playful attitude, we're more open to possibilities. It's OK to be inconsistent from one day to the next. That's not being a fake; it's how we experiment to find out what's right for the new challenges and circumstances we face.'

There are three ways to develop an adaptively authentic profile. First, adapt the styles and behaviours of others, by borrowing selectively from a large number of varied role models. Second, set learning goals, stop protecting our 'comfortable old selves', and do not expect to get everything right first time. Third, keep under review the personal narratives – the stories and images that we have of our selves – and edit or drop these when we find ourselves in new situations. For example, the 'friendly team player and peacekeeper' image may not be helpful in a demanding new leadership assignment, and a bolder, more adventurous narrative may be appropriate. Ibarra (2015, p.59) concludes:

'The only way we grow as leaders is by stretching the limits of who we are – doing new things that make us uncomfortable but that teach us through direct experience who we want to become. Such growth doesn't require a radical personality makeover. Small changes – in the way we carry ourselves, the way we communicate, the way we interact – often make a world of difference in how effectively we lead.'

Natalie Shefer

The concept of regard may sound vague and abstract, and unrelated to work behaviour. However, in a series of experiments and field studies, Natalie Shefer et al. (2018) found that those who received unconditional positive regard from colleagues at work displayed higher energy, organizational citizenship behaviours, and job performance. The researchers argue that work relationships tend to be seen in instrumental terms, and that we need instead to 'embrace a more humanizing approach to the ways people relate to each other'. They conclude that 'Co-workers should realize that small acts that convey positive regard can make a considerable difference in people's lives at work' (p.76).

Any approach to studying your self-understanding with questions worded by someone else is not going to work. Their wording may not be relevant to *your* self-concept. We need another route into the mind. Well, we can ask people to write and to talk about themselves. Such methods are in common use. With free association, interpretation of dreams, and the analysis of fantasies, the individual has freedom of expression, and responses are not tied to given categories. The researcher's job is to identify themes that reveal an individual's preoccupations, interests and personality. One such technique is the thematic apperception test, or TAT.

Thematic apperception test
an assessment in which the individual is shown ambiguous pictures and is asked to create stories of what may be happening in them.

This label breaks our rule about not calling personality assessments 'tests'. However, we have to be consistent with the literature. This is how the TAT works. First, you are told that you are about to take a test of your creative writing skills. Then you are shown photographs or drawings, typically including people, and asked to write an imaginative story suggested by what you see. The images do not imply any particular story. Your imaginative accounts are then assessed in various ways. One of these concerns your need for achievement. This is not a test of imaginative writing at all.

Need for achievement
a concern with meeting standards of excellence, the desire to be successful in competition, the motivation to excel.

Assessment first involves deciding whether any of the characters in your story have an achievement goal. In other words, does somebody in your story want to perform better? This could involve doing something better than someone else, meeting or exceeding a self-imposed standard of excellence, doing something unique, or being involved in doing something well. Points are scored for the presence of these features in your story. The more achievement imagery, the higher your score.

The TAT is widely used in psychological research, occupational choice, psychiatric evaluation, and screening candidates for high-stress jobs. The test was invented by Henry Murray and Christiana Morgan in the 1930s, and was later developed by David McClelland (1961; McClelland et al., 1976) as a way to measure the strength of need for achievement. The TAT is also used to measure the needs for power and affiliation, using similar scoring procedures, but looking for different imagery. In the original full test, you are asked to write stories about 31 pictures.

The question is – what can short, creative stories about ambiguous pictures tell us about your distinctive and stable personality characteristics?

Test your creative writing skills

Write an imaginative story (100 words) about what is happening in this picture:

Projective test
an assessment based on abstract or ambiguous images, which the subject is asked to interpret by projecting their feelings, preoccupations and motives into their responses.

The thematic apperception test is a projective test. The label 'projective' is used because subjects project their personalities into the stories they write. McClelland argues that it is reasonable to assume that the person with a strong concern with achievement is likely to write stories with lots of achievement imagery and themes. The evidence supports this view.

People with low need for achievement are concerned more with security and status than with personal fulfilment, are preoccupied with their own ideas and feelings, worry more about self-presentation than performance, and prefer bright Scottish tartans. People with high need for achievement tend to have the following characteristics:

- They prefer tasks in which they have to achieve a standard of excellence rather than simply carrying out routine activities.
- They prefer jobs in which they get frequent and clear feedback on how well they are doing, to help them perform better.
- They prefer activities that involve moderate risks of failure; high-risk activities lead to failure, low-risk activities do not provide opportunities to demonstrate ability.
- They have a good memory for unfinished tasks and do not like to leave things incomplete.
- They can be unfriendly and unsociable when they do not want others to get in the way of their performance.
- They have a sense of urgency, appear to be in a hurry, to be working against time and have an inability to relax
- They prefer sombre Scottish tartans with lots of blues and greens (Buchanan tartan has lots of red and yellow); unobtrusive backgrounds allow them to stand out better.

Organizations want employees with drive, ambition and self-motivation. Can the TAT be used to identify them? Unfortunately, it is not a good assessment for this purpose. Although the detailed scoring is not obvious to the untrained, the definition of achievement imagery is close to popular understanding. When you know what the 'test' is all about, it is easy to fake your score – but we also have this problem with objective questionnaires.

The TAT faces other problems as an organizational tool. The scoring procedure involves subjective interpretation, and the result is hard for the untrained eye to see as 'objective data'. Costly training is required in the full technical procedure to produce judges who can reach reliable assessments. With an objective questionnaire, anyone with the scoring key can get accurate results quickly.

McClelland argues that need for achievement can be increased by teaching you the scoring system, thus helping you to write high scoring stories, and by encouraging you to see life more clearly in achievement terms. McClelland and colleagues have used this approach with senior managers, entrepreneurs, police officers and social workers, and the first application outside America was with Indian businessmen in 1963. The TAT can thus be used to assess, and also to change personality.

The nomothetic and idiographic perspective are summarized in Table 6.5.

We can regard these perspectives as complementary rather than competing. Each is capable of telling us about different aspects of human psychology. What each alone reveals is interesting, but partial. However, contemporary employee assessment and selection methods ignore this suggestion, using mostly nomothetic methods.

Selection methods

In the early twentieth century, finding the right candidate for the job was described by psychologists as 'the supreme problem' (Ployhart et al., 2017). A century later, it still is. Organizations continue to explore ways to identify the KSAOs – the knowledge, skills, attributes, and other characteristics – that applicants have in relation to the requirements of jobs on offer. With the average cost of hiring senior managers at £6,000, and £2,000 for other staff, selection errors are costly (McCartney, 2017). The most common selection methods, one of which is personality assessment, are shown in Table 6.6.

Table 6.5: Nomothetic versus idiographic

The nomothetic approach	The idiographic approach
Positivist, based on statistical studies of large groups	Constructivist, based on intensive studies of individuals
Generalizing; emphasizes the discovery of laws of human behaviour	Individualizing; emphasizes the richness and complexity of the human behaviour
Uses objective questionnaires	Uses projective tests and other written and spoken materials
Describes personality in terms of traits, and trait clusters or personality types	Describes personality in terms of the individual's own understanding of their identity
Personality is composed of discrete and identifiable elements	Personality has to be understood as an indivisible whole
Personality is primarily determined by heredity, biology, genetics	Personality is primarily determined by social and cultural processes
Personality is given and cannot be altered	Personality is open to change through experience

Predictive validity
the extent to which assessment scores accurately predict behaviours such as job performance.

The main criterion for choosing a selection method is predictive validity; how well will this method be able to predict the candidate's performance in the job? A perfectly accurate method has a predictive validity of 1.0; a wholly inaccurate method has a predictive validity of 0.0.

Table 6.6: Common selection methods

Method	Used to assess
Personality assessment	Personality traits (e.g. The Big Five)
Intelligence test	Tests of reasoning and comprehension abilities
Job aptitude test	Cognitive capacities and candidate's suitability
Professional ability test (written)	Specific job knowledge and expertise
Traditional interview	Interpersonal and communication skills, and personality
Professional ability interview	Job-specific knowledge and expertise
Assessment centre	Individual and group skills, and problem solving
Group discussion	Problem-solving and discussion skills in a group
Practical test	Actual job ability regarding tasks
References	Candidate's standing with other employers, teachers, others
Personal statement of purpose	Candidate's achievements, career goals, writing skills
Internship	Job-related skills and abilities, and 'fit' with colleagues

Source: based on Kim and Ployhart (2017)

No single method can accurately predict how well someone will perform in a specific role. For this reason, most employers use several methods for gathering information about candidates. Employers in Britain and America rely on interviews. Graphology (handwriting analysis) is sometimes used in France. Assessment centres are popular in Britain, Germany, and The Netherlands. Blood group is a selection criterion in Japan. Graphology and blood typing have a predictive validity of zero. Aptitude and intelligence tests tend to have relatively high predictive validity.

We will consider first the use of psychometrics in general, and personality assessment in particular, before turning our attention to interviews and assessment centres. Finally, we will consider the growing contemporary use of *cybervetting* to assess job candidates.

Finding nice people

The East Midlands bus company *trentbarton* has for many years used psychometric assessment to identify suitable supervisory staff, but not bus drivers. Customer research, however, showed that there was a problem, with comments such as, 'Your drivers just take us for granted; they don't speak to us'. Jeff Counsell, the managing director, decided to use psychometric assessment to select drivers. The company looked at the profiles of drivers who were good at relationships with passengers, and wanted other drivers to match this profile. Psychometrics were used to identify drivers with people skills, who could bend the rules, and who would act on their own initiative when things went wrong. The same assessment approach was extended to administrative and engineering roles. Jeff Counsell describes the outcomes:

'We haven't paid for advertising for bus drivers for three or four years – we've got a waiting list. Invariably our applicants will say, "You've got a good reputation; your drivers are so good so I want to come and work for you". And when we ask customers why they travel with *trentbarton,* nine times out of ten they'll say, "Because your drivers are nicer, and I get a greeting every morning"' (Jacobs, 2018, p.31).

Psychometrics

Personality assessment, formal or informal, is a feature of most if not all employee selection and promotion decisions. As noted earlier employers want to know if candidates will 'fit in', as well as be able to do the job. The question of 'fit', however, is subjective. Psychometrics, the systematic testing, measurement and assessment of intelligence, aptitudes, and personality, promise to improve the objectivity of selection and promotion decisions by collecting information with predictive power.

Tests of cognitive ability can be good predictors of performance, especially for jobs that involve complex thinking. Evidence on how well personality questionnaires or work sample tests predict job performance is mixed. Personality assessments can now be administered at little cost online, or on a mobile phone app, especially where large numbers of candidates are involved.

Psychometric applications have developed rapidly since the late twentieth century, and there are now thousands of tests and assessments in use. However, critics argue that many tests, because of their design and language, discriminate against minorities and those with disabilities, including neurodiverse individuals and those with certain mental health conditions.

In personality assessment, three tests in particular have made a major impact (Harrell, 2017). The first two are the Myers-Briggs type indicator (MBTI) and The Big Five, discussed earlier. The latter claims, in some settings, to be able to predict job performance, but not as well as intelligence and specific aptitude tests. Assessments based on MBTI and The Big Five may also be able to identify personalities that are more likely to collaborate, or to come into conflict at work. A third popular personality assessment is Strengthsfinder. Based on positive psychology, strengths-based assessment has been developed since the 1990s. Strengthsfinder 2.0, developed by the American management consultancy Gallup, is completed by 1.6 million people a year, and aims to increase engagement, job satisfaction and productivity by helping organizations to design jobs that are consistent with employees' capabilities. However, critics argue that focusing on positives is not the best way to encourage improvement; criticism and realistic self-assessment can also lead to better performance.

✋ **STOP AND SEARCH**   YouTube for *Your greatest talents* (2:59).

Harrell (2017) notes that many organizations are now developing their own tailored personality assessments based on open source tools, instead of using branded products. One approach is to identify high performers in a particular role, and to base selection on their traits (see box 'Finding nice people' for an example of this).

The results of personality assessments are rarely used as the sole basis of a selection or promotion decision. While these may provide further useful information, along with other selection methods, personality assessments are not always good predictors of performance because:

- People are flexible and multi-faceted, and can develop new skills and behaviours and adapt to new circumstances; personality assessment captures a part of the whole at one point in time.

- Most jobs are multi-faceted in their demands on skill and knowledge, and traits which enhance competence in one task may not improve overall job performance.

- Job performance usually depends on many factors that are not related to personality such as luck, training, payment systems, physical facilities, supervisory style, organization structure, company policies and procedures, and organizational culture and norms.

- Most jobs change over time, so predictions based on current measures are unreliable.

- nomothetic methods work with large samples, against which individual profiles can be compared; these methods are not designed to make predictions about individuals, although that is how they are often used.

- In clinical and research settings, most people give honest answers about personality, but these assessments are easy to falsify when a job or promotion is at stake.

Despite these observations, personality assessment seems certain to remain popular. Scores can highlight issues to be discussed with candidates in greater depth, and may reveal information about someone that would not be available from other sources. Also, some organizations have used psychometrics successfully in selection for particular occupations, such as the UK bus company *trentbarton*, described in 'Finding nice people' above.

It is now widely recognized, therefore, that selection and promotion decisions should be based on a wide range of information about candidates, from different sources. These decisions should rarely if ever rely on personality assessments alone.

Interviews

Meeting someone in person, in an interview, offers an informal opportunity to assess their personality. Conventional interviews are still in widespread use by most organizations, but they are a poor way to predict future job performance. The football team manager who selected players on the basis of how well they did in the interview would not keep their own job for long. Interviews serve other purposes. The interviewer can begin to assess the candidate's experience and ability, and also how well they will fit into the organization. The interviewer can explain the job and its benefits, including development opportunities. Candidates can also find out more about the job and the organization. However, the outcome of an interview can often be influenced by the candidate's personality, and the main weaknesses of interviews include (Green, 2018):

- Questions can be unintentionally worded in such a way that initial impressions of the candidate are confirmed – the 'self-fulfilling prophecy effect'.
- The interviewer may assume that particular characteristics, positive and negative, are typical of members of a particular groups – the 'stereotyping effect' (decisions made on this basis can sometimes be discriminatory, and thus illegal).
- When an interviewer has judged a candidate as either 'good' or 'bad' in some respects, this can affect judgements of other characteristics, leading to an unbalanced decision – the 'halo and horns effect'.
- Interviewers may allow the experience of interviewing one candidate to influence how they interview subsequent candidates – the 'contrast effect'.
- Interviewers can prefer candidates who they see as being the same as themselves in some respect (background, personality, attitudes) – the 'similar to me effect'.
- Interviewers' decisions can be affected by whether or not they like the candidate – the 'personal liking effect'.

CRITICAL THINKING	At your next job interview, you are asked, 'Why should we employ you?'. The first part of your answer concerns your knowledge and skills. The second part of your answer concerns your personality. What are you going to say? Will this help you to get the job?

It is difficult to predict the future job performance of candidates using traditional unstructured interviews. Interviewees prepare, and good social skills can influence interviewers who do not have time to gather more information. Interviews can be improved by training interviewers in questioning techniques, effective probing of responses, taking notes (many interviewers do not do this), using structured rating scales, and not making any decisions until after the interviews are over.

Structured competency-based interviews can overcome many of these limitations. Questions focus on key competencies and behaviours, and the candidate's responses are matched with the requirements of the job. This can mean tailoring questions to individual candidates, which may be seen as unfair. This approach to selection interviewing is common in the UK (McCartney, 2017), being used by four-fifths of employers surveyed by the Chartered Institute for Personnel and Development. Competency-based interviews can have a high predictive validity. Candidates may be presented with work-related problems, and asked how they would respond. For example, imagine that you have applied for a job as an emergency telephone operator. Your interviewer asks you this question:

- A friend calls you. She is upset. Her child has been injured. She begins to tell you, in a hysterical manner, about how difficult it is to get baby-sitters, what the child is wearing, what words the child can speak, and so on. What would you do?

Your answer is rated for communication skills, emotional control, and judgement, and is compared with the actual behaviour of high-level performers in this occupation. It is difficult for you to cheat or to practise responses to a structured competency interview, because you do not know what behaviours are being sought by assessors. Companies using these methods report a high success rate.

Assessment centres

Assessment centres are also widely used for employee selection, and are popular with public sector organizations (McCartney, 2017). Assessment centres first were developed during the Second World War by British War Office Selection Boards. Typically, groups of six to ten candidates are brought together for one to three days. They are presented, individually and as a group, with a variety of exercises, tests of ability, personality assessments, interviews, work samples, and written and team problem-solving tasks. Their activities are observed and scored. This is useful for selection and promotion, staff development, talent spotting and career guidance. The evidence suggests that this combination of techniques improves the chances of selecting and promoting appropriate candidates.

Selection at Google

Every year, between one and three *million* people apply to work for Google, which hires several thousand of them, making it more selective than Harvard, Yale or Princeton universities. Because only 10 per cent of applicants will become top performers, Google has to separate the exceptional from the rest. Alan Eustace, Senior Vice President for Knowledge says that, 'A top notch engineer is worth three hundred times or more than an average engineer' (Bock, 2015, p.62). Selection is so important to Google that, in the beginning, it took over six months to appoint anyone; each applicant had 15 to 25 interviews. Each new recruit consumed 250 hours of employee time.

Selection aims to predict how well candidates will perform when they join a team. Google looks for five attributes: engineering ability, general cognitive ability, leadership, role-related knowledge, and 'Googleyness'. These attributes are assessed using structured interviews, and assessments of cognitive ability, conscientiousness and leadership. Each job has attributes to test for, and interview questions are designed to predict performance. Google also uses work sample tests to identify problem-solving ability: 'Write an algorithm to do this'. By 2013, despite recruiting even more staff, the amount of time spent on each hire was reduced by 75 per cent. But there is one final reviewer of every job applicant – Larry Page, the co-founder and current chief executive of Google.

Assessment centres are expensive to design and run. Qualified assessors are necessary, and a lack of top management commitment to the process can give assessors and candidates inappropriate signals. Methods must be tailored to each organization's needs. The focus on observable and measurable aspects of behaviour overlooks less easily assessed skills. Advocates argue that the information collected is comprehensive and comparable, and candidates have opportunities to demonstrate capabilities unlikely to appear in interviews. The self-knowledge gained can also be valuable to candidates. It has been claimed that a well-designed assessment centre using a variety of methods can achieve a predictive validity of 0.8 with respect to job performance (CIPD, 2013).

Cybervetting

Cybervetting covertly gathering information from informal, non-institutional online sources via social media and search engines to help decide whom to recruit, hire, promote or fire.

The widespread use of social media has given organizations access to other sources of information about potential – and current – employees. Most employers now use cybervetting, to complement traditional selection methods, and this approach is increasing in popularity, particularly for initial candidate screening, as more people post more information about themselves on social media (Berkelaar, 2017). Some employers also cybervet current employees. The information is in the public domain, and gathering this information involves no social contact with candidates, so this method saves time and money. However, information from social media sources can be misleading if used on its own.

Brenda Berkelaar (2017) found that recruiters use cybervetting as a tool to exclude applicants who display 'questionable behaviour' and other 'red flags'. Asked about the benefits of cybervetting, one employer explained how it:

> 'Adds a great depth and breadth to narrowing down the candidates and discerning who they are, what they're capable of, how they could help the company, how you might be able to help them. Facebook in particular, the first thing I'll do is just look at their profile and I'll read as much of it as is available to me. It tells me the things they're interested in, their hobbies, what movies do they like. It can to some extent cut through the social aspects of the job interview' (p.1130).

The research by Wu et al. (2015) mentioned earlier, basing personality assessment on Facebook 'Likes', opens the possibility of automating candidate profiling and personality assessment. This would be valuable for organizations faced with large numbers of applicants for vacancies. Automated screening could alert the human resources department only to those candidates whose profiles match the profiled requirements of the jobs for which they are applying (Barrett, 2017).

This approach has limits. Information is unlikely to have been posted to popular social media sites for the sole purposes of impressing potential employers, who are dependent on the volume and quality of information that candidates have decided to upload. Many candidates can in turn read about potential employers on company review websites such as glassdoor.co.uk, and not apply to organizations with poor reputations or an unfavourable culture. The implications for job-seekers are clear: think carefully about the personal information that you put into the public domain through social media.

CRITICAL THINKING	You have been given the resources to recruit two new members to your software development team. Your boss has asked you to base your interview shortlist on a thorough cybervetting of the applicants. What are the benefits and disadvantages of this approach? Do you believe that time that you have to spend cybervetting the applicants will be worthwhile?

 **RECAP**

1. *Distinguish between type, trait and self theories of personality.*

   - Type theories (Hippocrates, Sheldon, Jung) *classify* individuals using a limited number of personality categories.

   - Trait theories, based on a nomothetic perspective (Eysenck, Costa and McCrae), *profile* the individual's personality across a number of different facets.

   - Self theories, based on an idiographic perspective (Cooley, Mead), *describe* unique individual personalities.

2. *Compare the advantages and disadvantages of questionnaires and projective tests as measures of personality.*

   - Objective questionnaires are easy to score and offer quantitative rigour. But they can only be interpreted using group norms; individual scores are meaningless.

   - Projective tests capture the richness and uniqueness of the individual. But they have complex scoring, are subjective, and individual results cannot easily be compared.

3. *Explain the relationship between personality and stress, and identify appropriate individual and organizational stress management strategies.*

   - Type A personalities (competitive, impatient) are more stress prone than Type B personalities (easygoing, relaxed).

   - Individuals can develop physical and psychological resilience and coping skills.

   - Management has to reduce or remove work-related stressors (job design, management style, adverse working conditions, excessive workload).

4. *Evaluate the benefits and problems of psychometric assessment as a tool to assist management decision making, particularly in selection.*

   - Psychometrics offer objective, systematic, comprehensive and quantitative information. They are also useful in career guidance, counselling and development.

   - Intelligence and aptitude tests are better predictors of performance than most personality assessments.

   - It is usually difficult to predict job performance from a personality profile.

   - Personality assessment can identify strengths and limitations in specific areas of competence.

   - Traditional selection interviews are poor predictors of job performance, which is why many organizations now use structured competency-based interviews.

   - Most organizations use cybervetting – gathering information from social media – to screen potential job candidates.

5. *Assess your own personality.*

   - Current thinking profiles personality either on 'The Big Five' trait clusters of Openness, Conscientiousness, Extraversion, Agreeableness and Neuroticism (OCEAN), or on the HEXACO model, which adds the honesty–humility dimension to The Big Five. Self theories argue that the self-concept is what is important, not your test scores.

Revision

1. What is psychometrics, and what are the main applications? What are the benefits and drawbacks of psychometric assessment in organizational contexts?

2. What is the difference between 'type' and 'trait' theories of personality? Using at least one example of a trait theory, explain the benefits and problems associated with this approach to personality assessment.

3. How valuable is cybervetting as a selection tool for organizations? How should potential employees respond to the growth in popularity of cybervetting?

Research assignment

Interview two managers who are involved in selecting candidates for jobs in their organizations. Choose two different types of organization; large and small, or public and private sector, or manufacturing and retailing. First ask them (a) what selection methods do they use, (b) why they use those methods, and (c) what in their experience are the strengths and weaknesses of these methods. Then ask them for their judgement concerning the relative importance of personality as a predictor of a candidate's job performance. If they use psychometrics, find out the extent to which the scores influence selection decisions. Your report will cover the following issues:

1. Describe the range of selection methods used by these organizations.

2. If the two managers reported using different methods, how can this be explained? Was this due to personal preferences, to the nature of the work for which candidates were being chosen, or to the differing nature of the organizations?

3. Summarize the strengths and weaknesses of their methods. Is their experience-based assessment consistent with the evidence presented in this chapter? Based on the evidence concerning selection methods, what advice would you give to these managers?

4. Prepare a brief assessment of the importance placed on personality by those managers in their selection processes, compared with the evidence concerning our ability to predict job performance using personality assessment scores.

Springboard

Robert D. Austin and Gary P. Pisano (2017) 'Neurodiversity as a competitive advantage: why you should embrace it in your workforce', *Harvard Business Review*, 95 (3): 96–103. Make the case for taking a more inclusive approach to neurodivergent employees who often have valuable skills, but who can be overlooked or rejected by conventional selection methods.

Merve Emre (2018) *What's Your Type?: The Strange History of Myers-Briggs and the Birth of Personality Testing.* London: William Collins. History of personality testing, explaining the popularity of the MBTI despite the lack of scientific grounding.

Neal Schmitt (2014) 'Personality and cognitive ability as predictors of effective performance at work', *Annual Review of Organizational Psychology and Organizational Behavior*, 1: 45–65. Comprehensive review of research assessing the advantages and limitations of cognitive testing and personality assessment in employee selection.

OB cinema

The Imitation Game (2014, director Morten Tyldum) is based on the story of Alan Turing (played by Benedict Cumberbatch), one of the founders of computing science and artificial intelligence. During the Second World War, Turing worked as a cryptanalyst for the UK Government Code and Cypher School at Bletchley Park, where he and his team broke the German communications code, Enigma. Turing was arrogant, antisocial, literal-minded, and showed little empathy with others. These behaviours appear to be personality-based, but are often related to a neurological condition called Autism Spectrum Disorder (ASD). Around one per cent of the population has some form of ASD and the condition mainly affects men. At one end of the spectrum, ASD can be socially devastating. At the other, those with 'high functioning' autism (Asperger's Syndrome) can be extremely intelligent. People high on the spectrum are typically persistent, with excellent memory and attention to detail, and are good at mathematics, data analysis, and pattern recognition – useful skills for fraud detection, actuaries, software testers, and proof-readers (Austin and Pisano, 2017)

→

Today's equivalent of Bletchley Park, GCHQ, employs 'neurodiverse' intelligence officers for their superior skills which are useful in dealing with cybercriminals, state-led cyberespionage, and political activists (Kerjab, 2014). Most job descriptions mention good communication interpersonal, and teamworking skills, and those with ASD can be rejected as they perform badly in traditional interviews. Jo Faragher (2018) argues that organizations should be more inclusive in their approach to neurodivergent employees, to use their skills. The symptoms of ASD vary. They can include difficulty with verbal and non-verbal communication, along with restricted and repetitive interests and behaviours. Some autistic people are sensitive to levels of noise and distractions that others find normal. They often prefer routine and can become disturbed by changes in their regular habits. In this movie, consider the organizational issues that ASD raises:

1. Turing is interviewed for his job at Bletchley Park by Commander Denniston (Charles Dance). What does this reveal about the problems that can arise in selection interviews with candidates who have ASD? How can these interviewing problems be overcome?

2. Turing joins a team led by Hugh Alexander (Matthew Goode). From the evidence in this movie, what problems can arise for leaders of teams with an ASD member? What capabilities and attributes do team leaders ideally need in these circumstances?

3. What guidance and support would help an ASD member of staff?

4. What training and support would it be useful to give to the other team members?

Chapter exercises

1: The Big Five

Objectives
1. To assess your personality profile on 'The Big Five' personality trait clusters.
2. To assess the value of this kind of personality assessment in employment selection.

Briefing   To assess your personality on The Big Five dimensions, look at each of the following 15 pairs of adjectives, and tick the point on the scale that most accurately describes you or your preferences.

1	Quiet	❑ 1	❑ 2	❑ 3	❑ 4	❑ 5	Talkative
2	Tolerant	❑ 5	❑ 4	❑ 3	❑ 2	❑ 1	Critical
3	Disorganized	❑ 1	❑ 2	❑ 3	❑ 4	❑ 5	Organized
4	Tense	❑ 1	❑ 2	❑ 3	❑ 4	❑ 5	Calm
5	Imaginative	❑ 5	❑ 4	❑ 3	❑ 2	❑ 1	Conventional
6	Reserved	❑ 1	❑ 2	❑ 3	❑ 4	❑ 5	Outgoing
7	Uncooperative	❑ 1	❑ 2	❑ 3	❑ 4	❑ 5	Cooperative
8	Unreliable	❑ 1	❑ 2	❑ 3	❑ 4	❑ 5	Dependable
9	Insecure	❑ 1	❑ 2	❑ 3	❑ 4	❑ 5	Secure
10	New	❑ 5	❑ 4	❑ 3	❑ 2	❑ 1	Familiar
11	Sociable	❑ 5	❑ 4	❑ 3	❑ 2	❑ 1	Loner
12	Suspicious	❑ 1	❑ 2	❑ 3	❑ 4	❑ 5	Trusting
13	Undirected	❑ 1	❑ 2	❑ 3	❑ 4	❑ 5	Goal-oriented
14	Enthusiastic	❑ 5	❑ 4	❑ 3	❑ 2	❑ 1	Depressed
15	Change	❑ 5	❑ 4	❑ 3	❑ 2	❑ 1	Status quo

The complete Big Five personality assessment questionnaire is much longer than this short version which provides only an approximate measure of traits and individual differences.

Calculate your profile as follows:

Personality dimension	Add these item scores	Total (from 3 to 15)
Openness to experience	5 + 10 + 15 =	
Conscientiousness	3 + 8 + 13 =	
Extraversion	1 + 6 + 11 =	
Agreeableness	2 + 7 + 12 =	
Emotional stability	4 + 9 + 14 =	

Interpretation:

	A high score suggests that you	A low score suggests that you
Openness to experience	Are imaginative and intellectual with a range of interests	Prefer tradition and stability, and dislike change
Conscientiousness	Are responsible, dependable, and achievement-oriented	Easily distracted, unreliable, and disorganized
Extraversion	Are sociable, talkative, outgoing, assertive	Prefer to be alone, and that you are quiet and reserved
Agreeableness	Are good-natured, trusting, and cooperative, deferring to others	Prefer to promote your own views, to have your own way
Emotional stability	Are calm, secure, enthusiastic	Feel tense, insecure and depressed

Syndicate groups

1. How accurate do you find your personality profile from this assessment? If it was inaccurate, why do think that was the case?

2. How helpful is this personality assessment to job interviewers who need to make predictions about a candidate's future job performance? What aspects of the assessment make it valuable in this respect? What aspects make it unhelpful?

Plenary

• Why are we as individuals interested in understanding more about our personalities?

• Why are organizations are interested in the personalities of job applicants?

2: Measuring up

Objectives

1. To develop understanding of how personality characteristics and other attributes can be assessed.

2. To explore the value of different assessment strategies.

3. To identify the limitations of selection interviewing and to explore how other approaches can improve the reliability and predictive validity of the organizational selection process.

→

Introduction

The decision to select somebody for a job is always a prediction – that the chosen candidate will perform the job well, and better, than others. On what information should this prediction be based?

Almost all organizations still rely on the selection interview, at least to make initial assessments of the suitability of candidates. Most organizations have refined the selection process, using a wider range of methods, including different kinds of interview, psychometrics, and assessment centres. The choice of approach is not straightforward. Assessment centres and psychometrics can be expensive and time consuming, and need specially trained staff. Interviews can be organized quickly and cheaply, and candidates can talk to those with whom they will be working.

This exercise asks you to design a strategy for selecting five graduate management trainees from a candidate pool of 20. The company's briefing describes the attributes for which they are looking. What methods will you use to identify which five candidates best fit this specification?

Procedure

1. Review the section of this chapter that discusses different selection methods.

2. Working in groups with three to five members, you will design a selection strategy to meet the *Measuring up briefing.* You will then assess your approach, and nominate a spokesperson to explain the nature, strengths, and limitations of your strategy to the whole class.

Measuring up briefing

You are a member of the human resources department of ScotSouth Bank, a medium-sized national retail bank. Each year, the company recruits five graduate management trainees who will begin their career at the head office in Edinburgh, but who can be seconded to branches anywhere in the UK. Like other financial services sector institutions, the bank is going through a period of rapid change, requiring new management styles and processes. The bank's research has identified a number of 'high performance competencies' that managers will require in order to operate effectively in a dynamic, turbulent business climate. These competencies are:

Competency	Definition
Information search	Uses a variety of sources and information before reaching decisions
Concept formation	Uses information to detect patterns, form concepts, build models, to identify trends, and cause and effect relationships
Conceptual flexibility	Seeks out and evaluates a range of options when planning and deciding
Interpersonal search	Effective in getting good information from others through appropriate questioning, and good at seeing others' viewpoints
Managing interactions	Builds effective, cooperative teams by involving and empowering others
Developmental orientation	Helps others to develop by increasing awareness of their own strengths and limitations, and providing coaching, training and other resources
Impact	Uses influencing techniques to get support for plans and ideas
Self-confidence	Willing to commit when required, expresses confidence in success
Presentation	Good at presenting ideas in an interesting and persuasive manner
Social media-savvy	Understands organizational benefits of social media technologies
Achievement orientation	Sets high personal standards, sets ambitious but realistic goals, wants to do things better, has targets against which progress is measured

Your task

1. Design a selection strategy, using whatever combination of methods you consider appropriate, to identify the five candidates who measure up best against this list of competencies. Choosing the right candidates is important to the bank's future, and you can design your strategy on the assumption that you have no time or resource constraints.

2. Prepare a realistic evaluation of the strengths and limitations of your selection strategy. Assess the reliability and predictive validity of your methods. Indicate the level of confidence – high, medium, low – that you have in your assessment of the candidates using those methods.

3. You have just heard a rumour about the company's next quarterly financial results, due to be published shortly. The results are not good. Costs will need to be reduced. Assuming that your department will have to make cuts, design a contingency plan that would allow you to complete the selection process within a week, at a fraction of the cost of your original plan.

Prepare a realistic assessment of the strengths and limitations of your contingency plan, including the reliability and predictive validity of your methods and your confidence in the approach. Prepare to present and justify your plans in a plenary session.

References

Ahmed, M. (2016) 'The truth about Myers-Briggs', *Financial Times Weekend Magazine*, 13/14 February, pp.14–19.

Arnold, D.W. and Jones, J.W. (2006) 'Who the devil's applying now?', from www.crimcheck.com/employment_testing.htm (no longer available).

Ashton, M.C. and Lee, K. (2007) 'Empirical, theoretical, and practical advantages of the HEXACO model of personality structure', *Personality and Social Psychology Review*, 22 (2): 150–66.

Ashton, Michael C., Lee, Kibeom, Perugini, Marco, Szarota, Piotr, de Vries, Reinout E., Di Blas, Lisa, Boies, Kathleen and De Raad, Boele (2004) 'A six-factor structure of personality-descriptive adjectives: solutions from psycholexical studies in seven languages', *Journal of Personality and Social Psychology*, 86 (2): 356–66.

Austin, R.D. and Pisano, G.P. (2017) 'Neurodiversity as a competitive advantage: why you should embrace it in your workforce', *Harvard Business Review*, 95 (3): 96–103.

Ayling, L. and Willmott, B. (2017) *Stress in the Workplace Factsheet*. London: Chartered Institute for Personnel and Development.

Barrett, P. (2017) 'Social media analysis could usher in a new era of recruitment automation', *People Management Online*, 8 August, https://www.people-management.co.uk/voices/comment/new-era-recruitment-automation# [accessed January 2019]

Belbin, R.M. (1993) *Team Roles at Work*. Oxford: Butterworth Heinemann.

Berkelaar, B.L. (2017) 'Different ways new information technologies influence conventional organizational practices and employment relationships: the case of cybervetting for personnel selection', *Human Relations*, 70 (9): 1115–40.

Bock, L. (2015) *Work Rules: Insights from Inside Google That Will Transform How You Live and Lead*. London: John Murray.

Boseley, S. (2012) 'Work stress can raise risk of heart attack by 23%, study finds', *The Guardian*, 14 September, p.5.

Buchholz, T.G. (2011a) *Rush: Why You Need and Love the Rat Race*. Hudson Street Press: New York.

Buchholz, T.G. (2011b) 'Stressing the benefits', *RSA Journal*, Autumn, pp.20–21.

Chamorro-Premuzic, T. (2017) 'Could your personality derail your career?', *Harvard Business Review*, 95 (5): 138–41.

CIPD (2013) *Resourcing and Talent Planning: Annual Survey Report*, Chartered Institute of Personnel and Development: London.

Costa, P. and McCrae, R.R. (1992) *NEO PI-R: Professional Manual*. Odessa, Florida: Psychological Assessment Resources.

Eysenck, H.J. (1970) *The Structure of Human Personality*. London: Methuen, (third edition).

Eysenck, H.J. (1990) 'Biological dimensions of personality', in L.A. Pervin (ed.), *Handbook of Personality, Theory and Research*. New York: Guilford Press, pp.244–76.

Faragher, J. (2018) 'Thinking differently has made us winners at work', *People Management*, February, pp.33–36.

Friedman, M. and Rosenman, R.F. (1974) *Type A Behaviour and your Heart*. New York: Knopf.

Green, M. (2018) *Selection Methods Factsheet*. London: Chartered Institute for Personnel and Development.

Harrell, E. (2017) 'A brief history of personality tests', *Harvard Business Review*, 95(2): 63.

Health and Safety Executive (2017) *Tackling Work-Related Stress Using the Management Standards Approach*. London: Health and Safety Executive.

Ibarra, H. (2015) 'The authenticity paradox: why feeling like a fake can be a sign of growth', *Harvard Business Review*, 93 (1/2): 52–59.

Jacobs, K. (2018) 'Psychometric testing no longer meets my business needs', *People Management*, March, pp.28–32.

Jung, C.G. (1953) *Collected Works*. New York: Bollingen Series/Pantheon.

Jung, C.G. (1971) *Psychological Types, (The Collected Works of C.G. Jung, Volume 6)*. Princeton, NJ: Princeton University Press (first published 1923).

Kasriel, S. (2016) 'How I did it: Upwork's CEO on how an introverted engineer learned to lead', *Harvard Business Review*, 94(5): 35–38.

Kerjab, Richard (2014) 'Dyslexic spies sharpen GCHQ's senses', *The Sunday Times*, 21 September, p.4.

Kim, Y. and Ployhart, R.E. (2018) 'The strategic value of selection practices: antecedents and consequences of firm-level selection practice usage', *Academy of Management Journal*, 61 (1): 46–66.

Lee, K. and Ashton, M.C. (2012) *The H Factor of Personality: Why Some People Are Manipulative, Self-Entitled, Materialistic and Exploitive – and Why it Matters for Everyone*. Waterloo, Ontario: Wilfrid Laurier University Press.

McCartney, C. (2017) *Resourcing and Talent Planning 2017: Survey Report*. London: Chartered Institute for Personnel and Development/Hays UK & Ireland.

McClelland, D.C. (1961) *The Achieving Society*. Princeton, NJ: Van Nostrand Reinhold.

McClelland, D.C., Atkinson, J.W., Clark, R.A. and Lowell, E.L. (1976) *The Achievement Motive*. New York: Irvington, (second edition).

Mead, G.H. (1934) *Mind, Self and Society*. Chicago, IL: University of Chicago Press.

Moutafi, J., Furnham, A. and Crump, J. (2007) 'Is managerial level related to personality?', *British Journal of Management*, 18(3): 272–80.

Myers, I.B. (1962) *The Myers-Briggs Type Indicator Manual*. Princeton, NJ: Educational Testing Service.

Myers, I.B. (1976) *Introduction to Type*. Gainesville, FL: Centre for Applications of Psychological Type, (second edition).

Myers, I.B. and McCaulley, M.H. (1985) *Manual: A Guide to the Development and Use of the Myers-Briggs Type Indicator*. Palo Alto, CA: Consulting Psychologists Press.

Ployhart, R.E., Schmitt, N. and Tippins, N.T. (2017) 'Solving the Supreme Problem: 100 years of selection and recruitment at the *Journal of Applied Psychology*', *Journal of Applied Psychology*, 102 (3): 291–304.

Randler, C. (2010) 'The early bird really does get the worm', *Harvard Business Review*, 88(7/8): 30–31.

Rogers, C.R. (1947) 'Some observations on the organization of personality', *American Psychologist*, 2(9): 358–68.

Sackett, P.R., Lievens, F., Van Iddekinge, C.H. and Kuncel, N.R. (2017) 'Individual differences and their measurement: a review of 100 years of research', *Journal of Applied Psychology*, 102(3): 254–73.

Shefer, N., Carmeli, A. and Cohen-Meitar, R. (2018) 'Bringing Carl Rogers back in: exploring the power of positive regard at work', *British Journal of Management*, 29(1): 63–81.

Sheldon, W. (1942) *The Varieties of Temperament: A Psychology of Constitutional Differences*. New York: Harper & Row.

Soto, C.J. and John, O.P. (2017) 'The next Big Five Inventory (BFI-2): developing and assessing a hierarchical model with 15 facets to enhance bandwidth, fidelity, and predictive power', *Journal of Personality and Social Psychology*, 113 (1): 117–143.

Volk, S., Pearsall, M.J., Christian, M.S. and Becker, W.J. (2017) 'Chronotype diversity in teams: toward a theory of team energetic asynchrony', *Academy of Management Review*, 42(4): 683–702.

Whitely, P. (2012) 'Are Britons getting more dishonest', *University of Essex Centre for the Study of Integrity Working Paper*, Essex, January.

Wu, Y., Kosinski, M. and Stillwell, D. (2015) 'Computer-based personality judgements are more accurate than those made by humans', *Proceedings of the National Academy of Sciences*, 112 (4): 1036–40.

CHAPTER 7

Communication

Key terms

social intelligence

communication process

coding

decoding

perceptual filters

noise

feedback

non-verbal behaviour

power tells

high context culture

low context culture

impression management

emotional intelligence

communication climate

employee voice

Learning outcomes

When you have read this chapter, you should be able to define those key terms in your own words, and you should also be able to:

1. Describe the dimensions of social intelligence, and explain the importance of this capability.

2. Understand the components of the interpersonal communication process.

3. Identify the main barriers to effective interpersonal communication.

4. Understand different questioning techniques, conversation controls and listening skills.

5. Explain the nature and significance of non-verbal communication cues and clusters.

6. Understand the nature and mechanisms of impression management skills and techniques.

7. Assess the concept of emotional intelligence and its practical significance.

8. Explain the nature and significance of an organization's communication climate.

9. Assess how social media can improve organizational communication and strengthen employee voice.

Why study communication?

People management skills

According to research by the Chartered Management Institute, employers look at the following attributes when recruiting graduates:

- Graduates must be able to manage a project, work in a team, and communicate and persuade – both orally and in writing.

- Nearly two-thirds (65 per cent) of employers agree that graduates lack the interpersonal skills necessary to manage people.

- The ability to communicate is the most important skill that a graduate can possess, according to employers. This is followed by problem-solving, team-building and motivational skills.

   Source: Chartered Management Institute (2014, p.8)

Communication is central to understanding organizational behaviour for several reasons:

- The effectiveness of communication affects individual careers and organizational performance.

- Very few people work alone; the typical management job involves interacting with other people, often for more than 90 per cent of their time.

- Communication is seen as a problem in many organizations.

- In an increasingly diverse society, sensitivity to the norms and expectations of others is vital to effective cross-cultural communication.

- New technology has radically changed how, what, and when we communicate.

Social intelligence
the ability to understand the thoughts and feelings of others and to manage our relationships accordingly.

Everything significant that happens in an organization involves communication: hiring and training staff, giving feedback, purchasing supplies, solving problems, dealing with customers and deciding strategy. However, many factors can interfere with communication: hierarchy, power and status differences, job design, the nature of (part time, temporary) employment, physical layouts and rules.

Communications are improved if you are able to 'feel' what others are feeling. Can you 'read' what's happening in complex social settings? Do you use that understanding to manage your relationships? If so, then you have social intelligence. Despite modern communications technology, personal interactions, one-to-one, face-to-face (F2F), or 'face time' are still important, perhaps even more so. Our ability to interact effectively with others was first described as social intelligence in 1920 by Edward Thorndike, but the idea was seen then as just another aspect of general intelligence.

For Daniel Goleman (2007), social intelligence involves social awareness (what we sense about others) and social facility (how we act on that awareness). Each of these dimensions has four components (see Table 7.1). Social intelligence is crucial in a culturally diverse world. We often find ourselves working with people from other cultures. Cultures have different norms concerning how conversations are handled, appropriate greetings, degree of formality, eye contact, suitable topics for discussion, physical distance between speakers, and the interpretation of gestures.

Technology, including social media, seems to have made communication simpler. But technology-mediated

Table 7.1: Social intelligence

Social awareness	*Primal empathy*	'Reading' others' emotions intuitively from small clues, such as a brief facial expression
	Attunement	Understanding the other person through sustained attention and careful listening
	Empathic accuracy	Understanding, through observation and inference, what someone feels and thinks
	Social cognition	Knowing how the social world works, what is expected, reading the social signals
Social facility	*Synchrony*	Orchestrating our interactions with the right gestures – smiles, nods, posture, timing
	Self-preservation	Ability in interactions to trigger desired emotional responses in others, charisma
	Influence	Shaping the outcomes of interactions with tact and control, tuning actions to fit the circumstances
	Concern	Capacity for compassion, sharing others' emotions, elation or distress

communications (text messages, FaceTime, Skype) offer fewer social and non-verbal cues, and give little information about the context in which others are working. The anonymity of digital media also means that we are less aware of how our behaviour affects others.

Thomas J. Allen demonstrated in the 1970s that the frequency with which we communicate depends on distance (Allen and Henn, 2006). At that time, we were four times more likely to communicate regularly with someone who was two metres away from us than with someone who was 20 metres away, and we rarely communicated with colleagues on separate floors or in other buildings. He expressed this finding in 'The Allen curve' (Figure 7.1).

Does distance no longer matter in today's digitally connected world? Yes it does. Research by Ben Waber et al. (2014) shows that the Allen curve is still valid. Indeed, proximity has become more important as technology has developed. In one study, engineers sharing an office were 20 per cent more likely to communicate digitally than those who worked at other locations. When close collaboration was necessary, colleagues in the same location sent four times the volume of emails compared with those in other locations, leading to faster project completion times. Waber et al. (2014, p.73) conclude, 'out of sight, out of sync'.

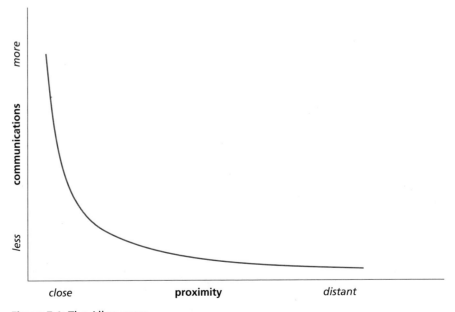

Figure 7.1: The Allen curve

"Let's work on your communication style."

Instead of making communication easier, Moser (2013, p.29) argues that, 'Virtual work requires much more frequent and elaborate communication and thus much more effort compared to traditional work settings. Things that literally work "without saying" in a face-to-face context need to be made explicit, discussed and agreed on in a virtual work context. This is only possible if there is an awareness of the central differences in working face-to-face versus virtually, and if the employees have both the motivation and the ability to engage in that extra effort'. If you rely on the apps on your smartphone to communicate with others, be aware that you are not practising – and not developing – the face-to-face skills that are needed in most jobs, and expected by most if not all employers.

✓✓✓ **EMPLOYABILITY CHECK** (interpersonal skills, communication skills)

How do you rate your communication skills – written and oral? Do you feel that you spend too much time communicating through apps and social media rather than face-to-face? What practical steps can you take in order to improve your face-to-face communication skills?

Interpersonal communication

Communication process the transmission of information, and the exchange of meaning, between at least two people.

Conversation: a competitive sport in which the first person to draw breath is declared the listener.

In most cultures, conversation is a social imperative in which silences are discouraged (Finland is different). Normally, as soon as one person stops talking, another takes their turn, following the unwritten 'no gap, no overlap' rule. The currency of conversation is information. We ask you the time. You tell us the time. Information has been transmitted. Interpersonal communication has been achieved. However, the communication process is more subtle and interesting.

We will first focus on interpersonal communication. A more detailed study would recognize the importance of other aspects of communication, including the use of different media, networks, and inter-organizational communication. The principles that we will explore, however, have wide application. For the moment, let us focus on 'one-on-one' or F2F communication.

CRITICAL THINKING

We all have experience of ineffective communication. Did you misunderstand the other person, or did they misunderstand you? The last time this happened to you, what caused that communication failure? Share this with colleagues to see if there are common causes.

We do not receive communication passively. We have to interpret or decode the message. To the extent that we interpret communication from others in the manner they intended, and they in turn interpret our messages correctly, then communication is effective. However, the communication process is prone to errors.

Interpersonal communication involves more than the transfer of information. Pay attention to the next person who asks you what time it is. You will often be able to tell how they are feeling, and about why they need to know, if they are in a hurry, perhaps, or if they are anxious or nervous, or bored with waiting. In other words, their question has a purpose, a meaning. Although it is not always stated directly, we can often infer that meaning from the context and from their behaviour.

The same applies to your response – which suggests, at least, a willingness to be helpful, may imply friendship, and may also indicate that you share the same concern as the person asking the question (we are going to be late; when will this film start?). However, your reply can also indicate frustration and annoyance; 'five minutes later than the last time you asked me!'. Communication thus involves the transmission of both information and meaning.

This process of exchange is illustrated in Figure 7.2 which shows the main elements of interpersonal communication. This model is based on the work of Claude Shannon and Warren Weaver (1949), who were concerned with signal processing in electronic systems, rather than with organizational communication. At the heart of this

Coding the stage in the interpersonal communication process in which the transmitter chooses how to express a message for transmission to someone else.

Decoding the stage in the interpersonal communication process in which the recipient interprets a message transmitted to them by someone else.

model, we have a transmitter sending a message to a receiver. We will assume that the channel is face-to-face, rather than text, phone, or email.

It is useful to think of how the transmitter phrases and expresses the message as a coding process; the transmitter chooses words, and also how the message will be expressed (loud and with exasperation, quiet and in a friendly manner, for example). The success of our communication depends on the accuracy of the receiver's decoding; did they understand the language used, and appreciate the

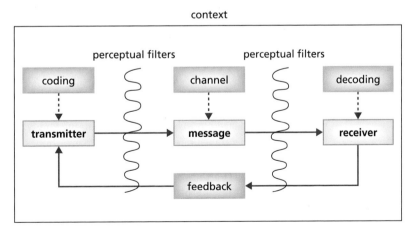

Figure 7.2: Exchanging meaning: a model of the communication process

Perceptual filters
individual characteristics, predispositions and preoccupations that interfere with the effective transmission and receipt of messages.

exasperation or friendship? We each have our own perceptual filters which can interfere with accurate decoding, such as predispositions to hear, or not to hear, particular types of information, and preoccupations which divert our attention elsewhere.

There are many ways in which coding and decoding can go wrong. For example, without a shared 'codebook', some common words can lead to misunderstandings:

Term	Popular use	Dictionary definition
decimate	devastate	cut by ten per cent
exotic	colourful, glamorous	from another country
aggravate	to annoy, to irritate	to make worse
clinical	cold, impersonal	caring, at the bedside of the sick
avid	enthusiastic	greedy

Cross-cultural communication clangers

'The most common blunders reported by international managers invariably involve communication. We have all heard the story of a Western manager who is perplexed when his Middle Eastern business partner links arms with him as they walk side by side, of the Mexican business person who did not understand that arriving "on time" in Germany meant arriving 5 minutes before the meeting's start, or an Asian manager who expresses doubt about a deal by saying "We will give this serious consideration," which the Western counterpart interprets to mean the deal is very much on track. [S]uccessful international business communication involves more than just understanding that your counterpart engages in physical contact, has a different perspective on time, or uses words in a different way. It necessitates understanding the role that the sociocultural context plays in eliciting different nonverbal communication patterns, words, and the meanings conveyed by each' (Adair et al., 2016, p.213).

CRITICAL THINKING

Research shows that listening is the workplace communication skill most valued by employers, followed by conversing (interviewing, for example), and then presenting. However, a study of business schools found that they had their priorities the other way around, concentrating on students' presentation skills, followed by conversing, and paying little attention to listening skills (Brink and Costigan, 2015).

How does your programme prioritize these skills? Do you need to speak to your instructors about this? How can you fill gaps in your skills development for yourself?

Do students 'fail' exams, or do they experience 'deferred success'? Language is used to 'soften' or to disguise unpleasant events. Employees being made redundant, for example, may be 'given the pink slip', 'downsized', 'demised', 'rightsized', 'delayered', invited to 'take gardening leave', to 'spend more time with the family', or to 'put their careers on hold'. They may also be 'transitioned out of the company', 'repositioned', invited to 'develop their careers elsewhere', but are rarely 'fired'. In some organizations, there are no 'problems and difficulties', only 'challenges and opportunities'.

The communication process is also affected by the perceptual filters which influence what we say, what we hear and how we hear it. When you asked what time it was, did you 'hear' the frustration or friendship in the response? Or did you focus on the information, because that was more important to you? The transmitter of a message has motives, objectives, personality traits, values, and prejudices, which colour the content and expression of communication. We filter which information we wish to reveal, and which to withhold from others, but our filtering is not always conscious. Similarly, at the receiving end, filtering can affect what is heard, what is decoded, what is not decoded, and the way in which the message is understood.

Our physical, social and cultural context also affect the communication process. The casual remark by a colleague in a café ('we could all be redundant by Christmas') may be dismissed. The same remark by a colleague across an office desk could cause alarm. An innocent gesture in one culture causes offence in another. The style and content of our conversation depends often on our relationships with others. Status differences colour our communication. We do not reveal to the boss what we discuss with colleagues. The style and content of communication can change dramatically when normal organizational relationships are 'suspended', such as at an office party.

Anything that interferes with a communication signal is called noise.

Noise factors outside the communication process which interfere with or distract attention from the transmission and reception of the intended meaning.

Communication suffers from noise, a term which covers more than just the sound of machinery, and other people talking. Noise includes coding and decoding problems and errors, perceptual filters, and any other factors that damage the integrity of our chosen channel, including issues arising from our relationships with others. Coding and decoding are affected by anxiety, pressure, stress, and by enthusiasm and excitement. Our motives, emotions, and health can thus generate noise.

Our past experiences also affect the way in which we see things today, and lead us to filter what we transmit and what we receive. Communication stumbles when transmitter and receiver have different frames of reference, and do not share experience and understanding, even where they share a common language. We make judgements about the honesty, integrity, trustworthiness and credibility of others, and decode their messages and act on them (or not) accordingly. People in an organizational setting may have time to reflect, or they may be under time pressure, or 'communication overload'.

There is a final aspect of our communication model which we have to consider: feedback.

Feedback processes through which the transmitter of a message detects whether and how that message has been received and decoded.

When we communicate face to face, we can usually tell if the other person likes us, if they agree with us, and if they are interested in what we have to say – or not. How do we know this? Well, they may say, 'that's interesting', or 'I disagree', or 'I have to catch my flight'. We can also tell from cues such as the tone of their replies, their facial expression, body posture, and limb gestures. We will explore the coding and decoding of non-verbal communication (body language) later in the chapter.

When we communicate face to face, we get instant feedback, from what others say, and how they say it. This helps us to exchange information more effectively. Communication can be awkward where feedback is delayed, or absent. We ask a question, see the other person look annoyed or puzzled, see that we have not worded our question correctly, and 'recode' the message. Face to face, if we pay attention, this works well. With more formal and distant forms of communication, feedback can be partial, delayed or non-existent, and we need to be more careful about our coding.

CRITICAL THINKING

With whom do you communicate often? What prevents effective communication in your experience? How can you improve the effectiveness of your communication?

The communication process is prone to errors arising on both sides of the exchange. We cannot confidently assume that receivers will always decode our messages in a way that gives them the meaning that we wanted to send. Communication is also central to organizational effectiveness, and this has practical implications. We assume that organizations function better where:

- communications are open
- relationships are based on mutual understanding and trust
- interactions are based on cooperation rather than competition
- people work together in teams
- decisions are reached in a participative way.

These features, however, are not universal, and do not feature in all countries or cultures.

Never apologize, it's a sign of weakness

How often have you said 'sorry' when someone else has bumped into you on the street? Saying 'sorry' can make us sound weak and lacking self-confidence, especially in a professional setting where directness and leadership may be required. Women seem to say 'sorry' more often than men. Tara Mohr (2015) thus advises women to stop apologizing, and to avoid other 'undermining speech patterns'. These include phrases which sound apologetic, like 'I just have a question', 'I just think', 'Kind of', 'I could be wrong, but', and 'Does that make sense?'. Other types of apology include 'Sorry, but', and 'I'm no expert, but'.

Mohr suggests that there are three reasons why women use undermining speech patterns. First, this is an unconscious habit, based on hearing other women talk that way. Second, most women want to appear likeable and are more concerned than men about sounding aggressive or arrogant. Third, our 'inner self-critic' encourages a feeling of self-doubt, which is useful, but has to be managed.

The women who Mohr has coached say that they get faster replies to their emails and find that their requests are taken more seriously. The word 'sorry' is of course sometime appropriate, but in the right context, and not in order to apologize for having an opinion or a suggestion (McMahon, 2016).

 **STOP AND SEARCH**   YouTube for *Tara Mohr.*

What did they find? Interaction in open plan offices

Ethan Bernstein and Stephen Turban (2018) studied the effects of open plan offices on employee communication. Open plan is popular due to the belief that the absence of walls and doors increases interaction, collaboration and creativity. The evidence, however, is mixed. Researching patterns of interactions at work has traditionally been difficult. However, advanced wearable devices and electronic communication servers now allow researchers to capture the data required to study how open plan offices influence face-to-face (F2F), email, and instant messaging communications.

Ethan Bernstein

Bernstein and Turban studied a corporate headquarters which conducted a 'war on walls', going from traditional cubicles to open office architecture. The aim was to increase face-to-face interactions and collaboration among staff. Interactions were measured before and after the office moves using sociometric badges which recorded face-to-face interactions, infrared sensors which recorded who they were facing, microphones which captured whether they were talking or listening, an accelerometer which sensed body movements and posture, and a Bluetooth sensor which recorded locations. This information was collected for three weeks before the office move, and for another three weeks, three months later, once staff had time to adjust to the new office layout.

Stephen Turban

What did they find? What effect did the move to the open plan office have on face-to-face and electronic interaction? **(Answers in chapter Recap.)**

The main barriers to effective organizational communication are:

Power differences	Research shows that employees distort upward communication, and that superiors often have a limited understanding of subordinates' roles, experiences and problems.
Gender differences	Men and women use different conversational styles which can lead to misunderstanding; men tend to talk more and give information while women tend to listen and reflect more.
Physical surroundings	Room size and layout affect our ability to see others and our readiness to join in conversations and discussions.
Language	Even in one country, variations in accent and dialect can make communication difficult.
Cultural diversity	Different cultures have different norms and expectations concerning formal and informal conversations; lack of awareness of those norms creates misunderstanding.

Given these barriers, communication is more effective when we are able to speak to someone directly, as we can use feedback to check the coding and decoding, and correct misunderstandings. Good communication also depends on empathy. We need to see things from the other person's point of view, try to understand how they will decode our message, and listen closely to their feedback.

Verbal communication

The word 'verbal' also causes decoding problems. Verbal means 'in words', which can be either spoken utterances, or written. 'Verbal agreement' can thus refer either to oral or to written communication, and both are different from non-verbal communication.

Questioning techniques

How do we get the information we want from a conversation? We do this with different questioning techniques. The main types of question are shown in Table 7.2.

Table 7.2: Questioning techniques

Question types	Illustration	Uses
Closed	Did you enjoy the movie?	To get a 'yes' or 'no' answer; to get factual information; to establish conversation control
Open	What did you think of that movie?	To introduce a subject; to encourage discussion; to keep the other person talking
Probe	Can you tell me more about that?	To follow up an open question; to get more information; to show interest
Reflective	You thought the acting was poor	To show interest and concern; to encourage further disclosure of feelings
Multiple	What did you think of the movie, and wasn't the star excellent in that role, and didn't you think that the ending was predictable?	Confuses the listener; gives them a choice of question to which to respond
Leading	You didn't see anyone leave the house?	To get the answer that you expect to hear (so, why ask ?)
Hypothetical	What would happen if . . . . ?	To encourage creative thinking

The first distinction in questioning strategy is between *closed* and *open* questions. Closed questions invite a factual statement in reply, or a simple yes or no. Open questions require the person responding to give us more information. Predict the different response to these two questions:

Will you have dinner with me this evening?
What are you doing this evening?

Are closed questions limited, and open questions more effective? If your aim is to get the other person to give you lots of information, then this is correct. But closed questions are useful in two settings. First, where all that is required is simple factual information: 'Are you coming to the meeting?' Second, to control the conversation. We have all had conversations where the other person took control, telling us things that we did not want to know. Closed questioning can prevent this. Consider the following sequence at the start of an interview:

What is your current job title?
How long have you been in your present position?
What was your previous position?

That sequence of closed questions establishes the conversation pattern by signalling to the other person, 'I ask the questions, you give the answers'. Usually, by the time the third or fourth closed question has been answered, your interviewee will wait for you to ask your next question, and will not start talking about some other issue instead.

CUTTING EDGE   If you don't ask, you don't get

Alison Wood Brooks

Leslie John

Alison Wood Brooks and Leslie John (2018) argue that many of us ask too few questions. Asking for information is something that we take for granted. Some people are naturally good at this. But do we ask enough questions, and do we ask them in the best way? Good questioning speeds up learning, identifies problems, and builds relationships. For example, a study of speed daters found that people were more willing to go on a second date with partners who asked more questions – and even asking just one more question made a difference.

Questioning is a skill that can be developed. Brooks and John suggest that, although the number of questions that you ask is important, the *type, tone, sequence* and *framing* of your questions also matter.

Use follow-up questions

Follow-up questions (probes) ask for more information. This lets the other person know that you are interested, that you are listening, that you care, and that you want to know more. Open questions are also useful for finding out more information. Closed questions can make a conversation feel like an interrogation, and they constrain the person answering.

Use the right tone

People are usually more willing to give information when questions are asked in a casual way, rather than in a formal, official manner. The same is true when being asked questions through websites, which can be designed to look like fun, or to appear official.

Get the sequence right

In a tense situation, asking difficult questions first can encourage the other person to give you more information, as subsequent questions feel less intrusive. However, if you want to build a new relationship, the opposite strategy is more appropriate, starting with less sensitive questions.

Pay attention to group dynamics

One-on-one and group conversations are different. The presence of others can affect willingness to answer questions. And group members often tend to follow each other's lead. If a few people are unwilling to respond, this can dampen the response from the others. But if one or two people start to 'open up', the other group members are likely to do the same.

Why don't we ask more questions? Brooks and John (2018, p.62) suggest that we may be eager to impress others with our own thoughts, that we don't really care enough to ask, that we think we already know the answers, or we are concerned that we will ask the wrong question. 'But the biggest inhibitor is that most people don't understand how beneficial good questioning can be'.

Probes are another type of open question, showing that the listener is interested. In most cases, that show of interest encourages the disclosure of more information.

The *reflective statement* is a technique for maintaining rapport and getting information, particularly about feelings and emotions. All you have to do is to mirror or reflect back to the person an emotion that they have 'given' to you. That emotion can be spoken ('you didn't enjoy your holiday') or it can reflect a non-verbal expression ('you look happy this morning'). As with probes, reflective statements signal interest and concern and encourage the other person to tell us more.

CRITICAL THINKING

Watch a police drama, a magazine programme, or a news broadcast. Watch somebody being interviewed; police interview suspect, host interviews celebrity, news reader interviews politician. What questioning techniques are used? What advice can you give to the interviewer to improve their questioning?

Replay this interview with the sound off. Can you identify any barriers which made this communication less effective; physical layout, posture, timing, non-verbal behaviours?

Multiple questions and *leading* questions are rarely used by trained interviewers. Multiples are often used when politicians are being asked about their views on topical subjects. Leading questions are especially ineffective when fresh information is required. Watch a police drama, and identify how many times witnesses and suspects are confronted with questions such as:

> So you didn't see anyone else leave the house after five o'clock?
> You're saying that the stolen televisions were put in your garage by somebody else?

Hypothetical questions can be useful in stimulating creative and innovative 'blue skies' thinking. Used in selection interviewing, however, this technique tells us how well the candidate handles hypothetical questions, and reveals little about their future job performance.

Conversation controls

We also control our conversations through a range of conscious and unconscious verbal and non-verbal signals which tell the parties to a conversation, for example, when one has finished an utterance and when it is somebody else's turn to speak. These signals reveal agreement, friendship, disagreement and dislike – emotions which in turn shape the response of the listener. The four main conversation controls are explained in Table 7.3. Note that the use of pauses depends on context. Normally, we use these signals habitually. However, awareness of these controls allows us to use them consciously. Therapists and counsellors, for example, use several methods to shape conversations in ways that allow their clients to express their problems and to identify solutions. Managers holding selection, appraisal or promotion interviews need to understand conversation control techniques in order to handle these interactions effectively.

What did they find? Speak up or pipe down

? Elizabeth McClean and colleagues (2018) studied how speaking up in meetings affects the way in which those who speak are seen by their colleagues. And can active participation in meetings influence whether you lose or gain status? The researchers focused on two kinds of participation. *Promotive voice* involves offering new ideas for improvement and change. *Prohibitive voice* involves identifying problems that need to be fixed to improve performance. Both promotive and prohibitive voices can thus make valuable contributions. So does voice matter, or is it the act of speaking up in the first place that counts?

Elizabeth McClean

First, the researchers surveyed 36 ten-member teams (men and women) at the United States Military Academy, West Point. Participants were asked about the nature of contributions in meetings, about the status of other team members, and which member they would prefer to be their team leader. Second, the researchers designed an experiment involving 196 participants recruited through the Amazon Mechanical Turk 'on demand workforce' service. Participants were given scenarios involving a sales team which used 'scripts' to sell insurance. In one scenario the person who spoke in the meeting used a promotive voice: 'I think that we should come up with a new and improved script in order to give us more flexibility in meeting customer needs going forward. My idea is for a new script that could include much more leeway around bundling products for our customers so that we can better meet their needs in the future. I think a new script will help all of us to be better.' In the other scenario the person who spoke used a prohibitive voice: 'I think that we should get rid of this ineffective script because it has restricted our flexibility in meeting customer needs in the past. My concern is that this script makes it much harder to bundle products for our customers and is harming our ability to meet their needs right now. I think getting rid of the script will fix the harm done.'

What did they find? Does speaking up affect your social standing, regardless of what you say and how you say it? Does it matter if you speak promotively or prohibitively? Are there differences between men and women in the consequences of speaking up? **(Answers in chapter Recap.)**

Table 7.3: Conversation controls

Signal	Example	Meaning
Lubricators	'uh huh'; 'mmm, mmm' and other grunts and groans	I'm listening, keep talking, I'm interested
Inhibitors	'what !'; 'really' 'oh' and similar loud interjections	I'm surprised, i don't agree, I've heard enough of this
Bridges	'I'd like to leave that and move on to ask you about . .'	I'd like to make a clean link to the next conversation topic
Pauses (1)	About two seconds silence	In normal conversation: same as lubricators
Pauses (2)	Silence of three seconds or longer	In a threat context: I'm going to wait until I get an answer
Pauses (3)	Silence of three seconds or longer	In a counselling context: I'll give you time to think

Non-verbal behaviour

Non-verbal behaviour the process of coding meaning through behaviours such as facial expressions, limb gestures and body postures.

Which part of the human anatomy can expand up to ten times in size when we are emotionally aroused? The answer, of course, is the pupil of your eye. When we look at something we find interesting – an image, a scene, a person – our pupils dilate. When we lose interest, our pupils contract. **Non-verbal behaviour** (NVB) thus gives us the 'dark limpid pools' to which romantic novelists refer. NVB is also called *body language.* We will use the term NVB for two reasons. First, the term body language suggests that we are only concerned with body movements and postures. NVB is richer than that. Second, body language also implies that gestures have specific meanings. That is not the case; the meaning of NVB also depends on context.

When we interact with others face to face, we are constantly sending and receiving messages through our signs, expressions, gestures, postures and voice. In other words, what we say – our verbal communication – is always complemented by our non-verbal behaviour. When our verbal and non-verbal signals are inconsistent, it is the non-verbal that will be believed. We code and transmit factual information mainly through verbal communication. We code and transmit feelings and emotions, and the strength of our feelings, through non-verbal communication.

Our non-verbal behaviour is extremely varied, although for most of the time, we are probably not aware that we are communicating in this way at all. Silvia Bonaccio and colleagues (2017) identify the nine categories or modes of non-verbal behaviour described in Table 7.4.

Bonaccio et al. (2017) outline five functions of non-verbal behaviour.

1. *To reveal your personal attributes:* Our NVB sends signals about our personality, intentions, and attitudes. Even the absence of NVB can be decoded as signalling an attitude. For example, you might keep a blank face, to indicate neutrality, but this could be 'read' as a sign that you are unfriendly or not interested. Others make assumptions about you based on 'thin slices' (brief observations) of your NVB. This can be a problem in selection interviews where judgements about candidates may be reached based on limited evidence.

2. *To exercise social control and establish hierarchy:* We often respond to nonverbal cues of power – such as the 'power posture' – with cues that signify submission. Other 'power tells' include talking and interrupting more, eye contact, the pitch of your voice, and facial expression. Most of these power markers are common across different cultures. However, putting your feet up on your desk is a power posture in America, but not in East Asia.

Table 7.4: Modes of non-verbal behaviour

Category	Mode of communication	Examples
Kinesics	Body movements	Facial expressions, gestures (head and hand movements), posture, synchronizing movements with those of others
Appearance	The way you look	Dress, accessories, makeup, height, weight, attractiveness
Oculesics	With your eyes	Eye contact, direction of gaze, blinking, pupil dilation, eye movements
Haptics	Through touch	Types of touch, touch avoidance
Paralanguage	Voice qualities (aka vocalics)	Pitch, volume, laughter, pauses, silence
Olfactics	Smell	Body odour, perfume, after shave
Proxemics	Physical space	Personal space, territory
Chronemics	Through the use of time	Talk time, speech rate
Environment and artefacts	Through objects	Build environment, design, landscape, objects that say something about you

3. *To promote social functioning:* Followership and social coordination can be encouraged through nonverbal displays of competence, prestige and persuasion such as smiling, and leaning towards others. People are more likely to follow those who show charisma, enthusiasm and ability. The way in which messages are delivered affect listeners' perceptions and attitudes. Speakers achieve this through eye contact, verbal fluency and tone of voice, facial expressions and body gestures that convey energy and passion.

4. *To develop good relationships:* NVB can help to establish and maintain interpersonal relationships, trust and commitment. Establishing rapport – being in harmony with others – involves paying attention, and responding to the intentions, emotional states and attitudes of others. NVB can thus affect rapport, for example through self-disclosure. We must be willing and able to reveal personally sensitive information (e.g. anxiety, stress, concern) about ourselves through non-verbal as well as verbal means.

5. *For emotional displays:* We reveal our emotions through facial expressions, gestures and tone of voice, as well as verbally. The emotions that we express at work can affect our interactions with others and our performance. Waiting staff in restaurants get bigger tips by smiling and using eye contact. But emotional displays have to be seen as authentic. Subtle variations in behaviour can tell observers that we are managing our emotional display which is then seen as fake (like the 'trained' smiles on the faces of restaurant staff). Displays of negative emotions are important in some jobs, such as debt collecting and interrogation. Managed displays of anger can help negotiators to get concessions from opponents.

Can we really 'read' somebody's attitudes and emotions from their non-verbal signals? If we are careful, yes, sometimes. We can exchange meaning with non-verbal codes, as long as we assess the verbal and non-verbal components together, and pay close attention to the context.

 **STOP AND SEARCH**   YouTube for *Amy Cuddy Ted Talk: Your body language may shape who you are* (21:03).

Reading NVB

What is happening in this picture? We don't know these characters or what their meeting is about, but can we 'read' the situation by looking at their non-verbal behaviour?

How many non-verbal behaviours can you identify in this picture? What does each of those behaviours tell you about the feelings of the characters? If you could speak to the characters about this situation, how confident would you be that your decoding of their NVB was correct?

Spot the spy

How can you tell if an overseas diplomat is also working as a spy? Is that foreign president confident about the threats he is making to a neighbouring country? To help answer questions like these, governments and security agencies turn to body language. In America, a Pentagon think-tank called the Office of Net Assessment spends $300,000 a year studying the body language of foreign leaders. Russian government agencies use Western body language experts to analyse the movement patterns of American and European leaders. The FBI has a Behavioural Analysis Programme which monitors the body language of diplomats. For example, when diplomats switch from their routine work to covert duties, they become more agitated, and this can be seen in their body movements. 'Micro-expressions' lasting fractions of a second can reveal hidden emotions (but the context is critical to making this assessment). People who are hiding important information often change their dress, facial expressions, gestures, the way they smoke, how they check the time, how close they stand to shop windows, and even the way they walk. For obvious reasons, the FBI do not publish details of these clues (based on *The Economist*, 2015).

 **STOP AND SEARCH**   YouTube for *The importance of being inauthentic: Mark Bowden at TEDx Toronto* (20:50).

Another aspect of non-verbal behaviour concerns the way in which we use distance in relationships. The study of this behaviour is known as 'proxemics'. Different cultures have different norms concerning personal space – how close we get to others before we feel uncomfortable. The British like to keep one metre away from strangers. Argentinians see that as unfriendly. Agnieszka Sorokowska and colleagues (2017) asked 9,000 people from 42 countries about their preferred interpersonal space. Argentinians like to get very close. In contrast, Romanians like to be 1.3 metres away from those who they have just met. But Romanians, Norwegians and Germans like to be physically close to their close friends. Generally, women prefer more personal space than men.

You can test the theory of personal space. At a social gathering, a party perhaps, move gradually and tactfully into someone else's space, by pretending to reach for a drink, moving aside to let someone past, leaning forward to hear better, and so on. You can move someone across a room in this way. The same result can be achieved while seated, if the chairs are easy to move.

When we are lying, we may unconsciously send non-verbal 'deceit cues', which include rapid shifts in gaze, fidgeting in our seats, long pauses and frequent speech corrections. When lying, it is important to control these cues, ensuring that verbal and non-verbal messages are consistent. Similarly, when we want to emphasize the sincerity or strength of our feelings, it is important that the non-verbal signals we send are consistent with the verbal message.

Non-verbal behaviour is a 'relationship language'. This is how we communicate trust, boredom, submission, dislike and friendship without revealing our feelings directly. For example, when someone wants to signal liking or friendship, they will turn their body towards you, look you straight in the face, establish eye contact, look away infrequently, and nod and smile a lot, keeping their hands and arms by their sides or in front of them. This pattern or combination of behaviours is called an *open or positive* non-verbal cluster.

Luckily for Karen, her management training had included a session on detecting negative body language.

The typical *closed or negative* non-verbal behaviour pattern, indicating disagreement or dislike, involves turning your body away, folding your arms tightly, crossing your legs so that they point away from the other person, loss of eye contact, wandering gaze, looking at someone else or at the door (suggesting a desire to leave), and a lack of nods and smiles. If you are observant, you can often tell that someone does not like what you are saying before they talk to you about it. The context is also important. We adopt closed postures when we are unwell, anxious, or cold.

The dilation and contraction of our pupils is beyond our direct control, unlike our hand movements, but our eyes also send non-verbal information. Our pupils dilate in low light, and when we see something or someone interesting. Dilation conveys honesty, openness, and sexual attraction. Our pupils also dilate when we are relaxed, and when consuming alcohol and other drugs. Context is again critical to accurate decoding. Contracted pupils can signify low lighting conditions, or lack of interest, distrust, hostility, stress, sorrow or a hangover. It is only possible to decode pupil dilation or contraction with reference to other non-verbal clues, and to the context.

Interpreting gesture clusters

Cluster signals	Indicating
Flexible open posture, open hands, display of palms and wrists, removing jacket, moving closer to other person, leaning forward in chair, uncrossed arms and legs, smiling, nodding, eye contact	Openness
Rigid, closed posture, arms and legs tightly crossed, eyes glancing sideways, minimal eye contact, frowning, no smiling, pursed lips, clenched fists, head down, flat tone of voice	Defensiveness
Drumming fingers, head cupped in palm of hand, foot swinging, brushing or picking lint from clothing, body pointing towards exit, repeatedly looking at watch, the exit, a book	Boredom, impatience
Small inward smile, erect body posture, hands open and arms extended outwards, eyes wide and alert, lively walk, expressive and well-modulated voice	Enthusiasm
Knitted forehead, deadpan expression, tentative nodding or smiling, one slightly raised eyebrow, strained voice, saying 'I understand' while looking away	Lack of understanding
Blank expression, phoney smile, tight posture, arms stiff at side, sudden eye shifts, nervous tapping, sudden mood shifts, speech toneless and soft or too loud and animated	Stress

Someone who is anxious usually displays 'self-manipulation': stroking lips or an ear lobe, playing with hair. Anxiety can also be signalled by shifting direction of gaze. Some friendship signals can be amusing to observe. When we meet someone to whom we are attracted, we often use 'preening gestures'; smoothing our clothes, stroking our hair, straightening our posture. Watch a group of friends and you will often see them standing, sitting, and even holding cups or glasses in an almost identical manner. This is known as 'posture mirroring'. You can often spot the 'outsider' as the one not using the posture. Friendship groups copy each other's gestures, known as 'gesture mirroring'.

Power tells non-verbal signals that indicate to others how important and dominant someone is, or how powerful they would like us to *think* they are.

We also use non-verbal communication to show how important we are with power tells (Chapter 22).

The power tells that dominant people display include using open postures and invasive hand gestures, smiling less, looking away while speaking, speaking first and dominating the conversation, and interrupting others. Signals which suggest a submissive attitude include modifying your speech to sound like the other person, hesitations (lots of 'ums' and 'ers'), close postures, and self-comfort gestures such as clasping your hands, and touching your face and hair.

Leading politicians also use non-verbal gestures to signal their dominance (Kirton, 2014). As a 'positive power gesture', Angela Merkel (Germany) grips and then pats the shoulder of political colleagues. To signal that he was confidently in control, Barack Obama (USA) held his hands in front of him, palms facing inwards, as if holding an invisible brick. Some political

leaders, including Margaret Thatcher, a previous UK prime minister) are trained to speak with a deeper voice. Other advice concerns walking with a sense of purpose to appear young and energetic (Ronald Reagan, USA), and making eye contact while shaking hands (Bill Clinton, USA).

Saying 'sorry' without saying anything

In Japan, the way in which bosses bow indicate how sorry the company is for mistakes, such as Toyota's recall of 8 million cars in 2010 due to faulty accelerator pedals.

A slight bow from the waist, not held for very long, indicates a mild apology.

A deeper bow, at an angle of about 45 degrees, and lasting for about one and a half seconds, suggests contrition, without accepting personal responsibility.

A full 90-degree bow, held for up to seven seconds, indicates personal and/or official responsibility for an incident that has caused significant damage, and for which the person is asking forgiveness.

The most extreme form of bow involves kneeling with one's head on the floor for perhaps 30 seconds. This indicates that, 'The law may punish me, but that does not cover how sorry I am'.

When Toyota recalled its cars, the company president Akio Toyoda performed a 25 degree bow, suggesting that

he was 'quite sorry': 'In bowing terms, it holds the same apology value as you might get from a waiter who had forgotten your order' (Lewis and Lea, 2010).

🖐 **STOP AND SEARCH**   YouTube for *Intercultural communication.*

Cultural differences in communication style

The use and interpretation of non-verbal communication differ from culture to culture. In Japan, smiling and nodding implies understanding, but not necessarily agreement. In Australia, raising the pitch of your voice at the end of a sentence signifies openness to challenge or question. In some Asian cultures, it is impolite to give superiors direct and prolonged eye contact; a bowed head signals deference and not a lack of self-confidence or defensiveness. People from northern European cultures prefer a lot of personal space and rarely touch each other. French, Italians and Latin Americans stand closer together and touch more often to show agreement and friendship.

Simple gestures must be used with care. Make a circle with your thumb and forefinger, extending the other three fingers. How will this be interpreted? In America, and to scuba divers, it means 'OK'. In Japan, it means money. In France, it means zero or nothing. In some Arab countries, it signifies a curse. In Germany and Brazil, it is obscene.

High context culture
a culture whose members rely heavily on a range of social and non-verbal clues when communicating with others and interpreting their messages.

Low context culture
a culture whose members focus on the written and spoken word when communicating with others and interpreting their messages.

Edward Hall (1976; 1989) distinguished between high context culture and low context culture.

High context culture	Low context culture
Establish relationship first	Get down to business first
Value personal relations and goodwill	Value expertise and performance
Agreement based on trust	Agreement based on legal contract
Slow and ritualistic negotiations	Fast and efficient negotiations

China, Korea, Japan and Vietnam are high context cultures, where people tend to take a greater interest in your position, your business card, your dress, material possessions, and other signs of status. Written and spoken communications are not ignored, but they are secondary. Agreements can be made on a handshake, on someone's word.

North America, Scandinavia, Switzerland and Germany are low context cultures, where people pay less attention to non-verbal messages. People in German organizations tend to be preoccupied with detailed written rules, and Americans like to have precise legal documents. Agreements are not made until the contract is in writing, and it is signed. If you insist on recording an agreement in writing in a high context culture, you could be accused of not trusting the other party.

These categorizations reflect tendencies and are not absolute. Most countries have sub-cultures with very different norms. In addition, men tend to be more high context than women, but this observation does not apply to all men or to all women. Nevertheless, it is easy to see how misunderstanding can arise when high and low context cultures meet, unless those communicating are sensitive to their respective differences. You can reduce these misunderstandings with the following four rules (Robbins et al., 2010, p.307):

1. *Assume that others are different,* unless you can establish otherwise; we tend to assume that others are more like us than they often are, so you are less likely to make a mistake if you assume difference until you can prove similarity.

2. *Use description and avoid evaluation,* until you have had time to observe and understand the perspectives of the other culture, or cultures, as interpretations and evaluations are based on cultural background rather than on what you observe.

3. *Practise empathy,* putting yourself in the other person's position, understanding their values, background and experience, and frames of reference.

4. *Treat interpretations as working hypotheses,* and keep testing and questioning your conclusions and explanations, using feedback and checking with colleagues.

Aboriginal culture and communication

Australian Aboriginal culture uses verbal and non-verbal communication in ways that are different from European and North American communication styles (Nelson-Jones, 2000):

- Aborigines value brevity in verbal communication rather than detailed elaboration, and simple 'yes' and 'no' replies are common.

- There is no word for 'thank you' in Aboriginal languages. People do things for you as an obligation.

- In some Aboriginal tribes, it is unlawful to use the name of a dead person.

- The terms 'full-blood', 'half-caste', 'quarter-caste', 'native' and 'part-Aborigine' are regarded as offensive by Aborigines.

- Long silences in Aboriginal conversation are common and are not regarded as awkward.

- To some Aboriginal people, it is not acceptable to look another straight in the eye.

- Some Aboriginal groups do not allow men and women to mix freely.

- Aborigines feel that it is not necessary to look at the person who is speaking to them.

- Aborigines do not feel that it is necessary to attend meetings (an interview, for example) at specific times.

How do these norms and preferences compare with the communication style of your culture?

Impression management

Impression management the processes through which we control the image or impression that others have of us.

We usually send and receive non-verbal signals unconsciously. However, it is possible to control the signals that we send, and to read the cues that others are sending to us. This level of attention and control is difficult to sustain, but it is important in organizational settings when we want to control the image or impression that others have of us. We do this through impression management techniques.

Mark Bolino and colleagues (2016) identify five impression management tactics and their uses – and suggest how these tactics can backfire if they are not used carefully:

Tactics	Used in order to be seen as	But can instead be seen as
Ingratiation: favours, conforming to others' opinions, compliments	Likeable	Sycophantic
Self-promotion: boasting, taking credit	Competent	Braggart
Exemplification: staying late at work, appearing to be busy	Dedicated	Self-righteous
Intimidation: making threats	Threatening	Bullying
Supplication: playing dumb	Needy	Incompetent

Research consistently shows that observers respond more favourably to impression management tactics that are consistent with gender stereotypes. Men are more likely to use aggressive (male) impression management tactics than women. Women who want to be seen as leaders thus tend to use male tactics like self-promotion and intimidation. However, there is 'backlash effect'. By contradicting the social norm, women who use those male tactics are usually seen as less likeable, and are not evaluated as favourably as men who use those tactics (Bolino et al., 2016, p.390).

Bolino et al. (2016) offer three pieces of advice about the best way to manage impressions. First, emphasize your genuine qualities and avoid trying to signal traits, skills and competencies that you don't have. Others prefer impression management behaviour that is authentic and not deceitful. You should therefore consider your qualities and emphasize those, and avoid trying to communicate traits, skills, and competencies that you don't have. Second, use impression management tactics in situations where this is appropriate: job interviews, speaking to customers. Third, develop awareness of when and how often to manage your impressions, through practice, self-monitoring, feedback from friends and colleagues, and developing your political skills **(see Chapter 22).**

 EMPLOYABILITY CHECK (communication skills, interpersonal skills)

At your next job interview, how will you consciously manage your appearance, speech, gestures, postures and other NVB in order to manage the impression that you want to give to the interviewers?

CRITICAL THINKING

Is impression management deceitful? What ethical problems are raised by suggesting that we should consciously manipulate the impression that others have of us through verbal and non-verbal communication?

As with conversation controls, we can use impression management to manipulate the behaviour of others. We do this, for example, by 'giving off' the impression that we are friendly, submissive, apologetic, angry, defensive, confident, intimidating, and so on. The more effectively we manage the impression we give, the greater the control we can achieve in social interaction, and the greater our power to pursue our preferred outcomes over others.

Some people regard impression management as acting. However, we manage our impression all the time. Do you dress and act the same way at a party as you do when at home? It is hardly possible to avoid sending signals through, for example, our dress, posture, facial expressions, gestures, tone and pitch of voice, and even location in a room. We can distinguish between conscious (by implication more effective) and unconscious (by implication less effective, or misleading) impression management. Conscious impression management has many advantages. Interactions run more smoothly when we give the correct signals to others who in turn accurately decode these signals of our attitudes and intent. Impression management is a critical skill in many organizational contexts, such as counselling, and in selection, appraisal and disciplinary interviews.

The ethics of impression management

At first, Richard Nixon vowed he would not debate with John Kennedy. He had little to gain from such an encounter, and much to lose. As vice-president, he was better known than the young senator and universally considered a heavyweight. But in the end his fear of appearing fearful overcame his caution. It was a mistake. The camera is unkind to men who look shifty.

At the first debate in 1960, Nixon was not feeling well. After hearing Kennedy turn down the offer of make-up, he turned it down too, although it might have covered his five o'clock shadow. Kennedy got his aides to apply make-up when Nixon wasn't looking, and presented a tanned and handsome face to the nation. Nixon looked like a sweaty corpse. Radio listeners thought he did well. But on television, Kennedy won by a mile (*The Economist*, 2008).

In your judgement, was John F. Kennedy's behaviour ethical at that debate in 1960?

Home viewing

Catch Me If You Can (2003, directed by Steven Spielberg) is a comedy drama based on the true story of the forger and confidence trickster Frank Abagnale Jr (played by Leonardo Di Caprio) and the FBI agent Carl Hanratty (Tom Hanks) who finally apprehends him, but not before Frank has committed millions of dollars' worth of fraud. Frank is a master of the art of impression management, effortlessly convincing others that he is, at various stages in his 'career' a newspaper journalist, high school teacher, airline pilot, doctor, and lawyer. He is so convincing that, when he does at one point decide to reveal the truth, his fiancé's father (Martin Sheen) does not believe him. Note examples of how Frank combines non-verbal communication, courtship techniques, avoidance of lie detection cues, paralanguage, and gesture clusters, to manage the impression that he wants to convey.

Most practical advice concerns how to make a good impression, for example in a job interview. Andrew DuBrin (2011, pp. 76–77) identifies tactics for creating a *negative* impression of yourself:

- Mumbling, putting your hand over your mouth, not using facts to persuade someone
- Writing business email messages in the style that teenagers use when texting and tweeting
- Appearing immature, unprofessional, and uninterested
- Ignoring colleagues while they are talking, looking at your watch, taking a mobile phone call, checking text messages
- Making immature excuses for being late – 'my alarm clock broke', 'the traffic was bad'
- Denying rather than apologizing for your mistakes
- Appearing unenthusiastic and bored when others talk about their problems
- When asked a job-related question, you reply, 'I don't know, I haven't googled it yet'.

Do men and women use impression management tactics in different ways? Deborah Tannen (1990; 1995) argued that girls and boys learn different linguistic styles – characteristic speaking patterns – which create communication barriers, and affect career prospects. Her research found that, while girls learn to develop rapport, boys learn that status is more important. Girls focus on a small group of friends, emphasizing similarities, and playing down ways in which someone could be better than others. Girls tend to be modest, less self-assured, and ostracize those who claim superiority. Boys play in large groups, emphasize status and leadership, display their knowledge and abilities, challenge others, take 'centre stage' by telling jokes and stories, and try to acquire status in their group by giving orders. This childhood learning follows girls and boys into adult life.

Tannen's arguments are good today. Kathryn Heath et al. (2014) studied successful and ambitious women who said that they were not being taken seriously in critical high-level meetings. They were ignored, and found it hard to break into the conversation, so their ideas were overlooked. Some men are aware of this problem. After a meeting, one male manager said to a female colleague, 'Stop acting like a facilitator. Start saying what you stand for'.

The researchers analysed feedback that had been collected on 1,100 female executives, surveyed 250 female managers in Fortune 500 organizations, and interviewed 65 top male and female executives from large multinational companies. This study found that, although men and women agreed on the problems, they disagreed on the causes. For example, men said that they were concerned that women would respond negatively to criticism. Women, on the other hand, complained that they did not get feedback, even when they asked for it. Men said that women should be more concise when making a point. Women said that they did not want to repackage old ideas or to state the obvious. Men observed that women were more emotional than men, but women said that, 'it's not emotion – it's passion'. Heath et al. (2014, pp.120–21) suggest three steps to help women become more comfortable and effective in what are still male-dominated settings.

- *Groundwork:* Ideas are tested, and decisions are taken in informal meetings that happen before the main meeting. That is why men often arrive for meetings early and leave late, to sound people out, and build alliances. Women also need to 'master the pre-meeting'.

- *Preparation:* Women prefer formal presentations, which men avoid. However, key points, relevant comments, and interesting questions can be written down in advance, and 'off-the-cuff' remarks can be rehearsed. Women should '*prepare* to speak spontaneously'.

- *Emotion control:* Passion can be persuasive, but when women felt passionate about an idea, men saw 'too much emotion'. Women must appear to be in command, speak with an even tone, accept that confrontation is not personal, and avoid signalling frustration.

The differences between women and men are not always as clear as this brief discussion suggests. Research findings are often expressed in terms of averages, tendencies, and predispositions. Many women do not fit the Tannen profile. And Heath et al. (2014, p.119) suggest that 'men with more reserved personalities' will find their advice useful, as will members of racial and ethnic minorities.

Emotional intelligence

Emotional intelligence the ability to identify, integrate, understand and reflectively manage one's own and other people's feelings.

Non-verbal communication is one way in which we display emotion. While often embarrassing, an open show of emotion can sometimes be desirable. Emotions are a key source of motivation. Inability to display and share feelings can be a handicap. Sharing feelings of frustration and anger can be as important in an organizational setting as showing positive feelings of, for example, praise, satisfaction and friendship. The ability to handle emotions can be regarded as a skill, which can be developed with training, but some regard this skill as a personality dimension **(see Chapter 6)**.

The concept of emotional intelligence (EQ) was first developed by Peter Salovey and John D. Mayer (1990) who argued that the concept of 'rational' intelligence ignores emotional competencies.

The concept was popularized by Daniel Goleman (2005; Goleman et al. 2013), who argues that EQ is more important to career success than technical skills or rational intelligence. Goleman's dimensions of EQ are summarized in Table 7.5.

Goleman claims that EQ gives us an advantage, at work and in social relationships, but that it is particularly important for top management, where conventional notions of intelligence are taken for granted. At senior levels, high EQ is a mark of the 'star performer'. There are

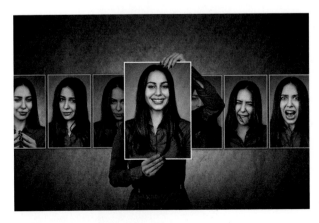

several EQ assessments, and some commentators argue that EQ can be developed with experience and training.

However, EQ is a controversial concept. Different commentators use different definitions, and there is no agreed measure, although there are lots of questionnaires which say that they do this. Even if EQ can help us to explain someone's behaviour, that is only one factor that affects an individual's job performance. We therefore need to treat exaggerated claims for the power of EQ with caution. Along with personality and functional skills, cognitive ability – traditional intelligence – is also important, even in jobs that are emotionally demanding. Take the short emotional intelligence test, 'Who is about to explode'.

 **STOP AND SEARCH**   YouTube for *It pays to have an eye for emotion,* with Jochen Menzes (8:50).

Table 7.5: The five dimensions of emotional intelligence

Dimension	Definition	Hallmarks
1 **Self-awareness**	The ability to recognize and understand your moods, emotions and drives, and the effect you have on others	Self-confidence, realistic self-assessment, self-deprecating sense of humour
2 **Regulating feelings**	The ability to control your disruptive moods and impulses; the propensity to suspend judgement, to think before acting	Trustworthiness and integrity, comfortable with ambiguity, openness to change
3 **Motivation**	A passion to work for reasons beyond status and money; a propensity to pursue goals with energy and persistence	High achievement need, optimism even in the face of failure, organizational commitment
4 **Empathy**	The ability to recognize and understand the emotional makeup of others; skill in dealing with the emotional responses of others	Expertise in building and retaining talent; cross-cultural sensitivity; service to clients and customers
5 **Social skills**	Effectiveness in managing relationships and building networks; ability to find common ground, to build rapport	Effectiveness in leading change; persuasiveness; expertise in building and leading teams

Who is about to explode?

Test your emotional intelligence. Look carefully at the microexpressions in each of these four portraits. Can you tell which one is about to 'blow'?

What clues did you use to reach that judgement?

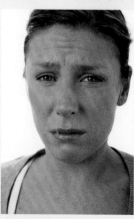

Organizational communication

Many managers regard communication as a problem, and many employees feel that they are not fully informed about management plans. Employee communication has become more important, partly due to the volume of information available through the internet, and because expectations, to be kept informed, and to contribute ideas, have increased.

Better communication is often advocated by management consultants as a cure for problems such as low morale, high absenteeism and turnover, labour unrest and conflict, low productivity and resistance to change. This advice is based on the theory that, if people understand what is going on, then they will be more likely to follow management directions. A well-presented argument supported with compelling evidence should result in consensus and compliance. Is that always the case?

Organizations have in the past used one-way-top-down ways of communicating with employees: the chain of command, management meetings, in-house newsletters, noticeboards, videos, conferences, employee reports, team briefings, email. New technologies **(see Chapter 3),** and social media tools in particular, now allow a range of two-way communication channels. Organizations are also now exposed to public criticism by their employees through websites such as glassdoor.co.uk.

How much communication is enough? Bill Quirke (2008, p.236) argues that communication depends on change. The more significant the change, the more employees need to be involved. He uses the 'communication escalator' (Figure 7.3) as a guide to designing communications strategy. Levels of involvement go from awareness, understanding, support, and involvement, to commitment. The escalator shows the communication approaches that are appropriate to each level. For commitment, the organization should consider using all of those approaches. At the awareness level, information may be enough. However, for involvement and commitment, communication needs to focus on improving the quality of relationships.

Communication climate the prevailing atmosphere in an organization – *open* or *closed* – in which ideas and information are exchanged.

Jack Gibb (1961) developed the concept of communication climate. An open communication climate promotes collaborative working; people develop self-worth, feel that they can contribute freely without reprisal, know that their suggestions will be welcome, that mistakes will be seen as learning opportunities, and they feel trusted, secure and confident in their job. In a closed communication climate, information is withheld unless it is to the advantage of the sender, and recrimination, secrecy and distrust can make life unpleasant. This distinction is summarized in Table 7.6. These extremes are not absolutes; most organizations are likely to have a climate which lies on the continuum between open and closed, and the climate may vary between sections or departments.

> **CRITICAL THINKING**
>
> How would you describe the communication climate of your educational institution? Of an organization where you have recently worked? Of your current employer? Based on your assessment, what advice can you give to the organization's management?

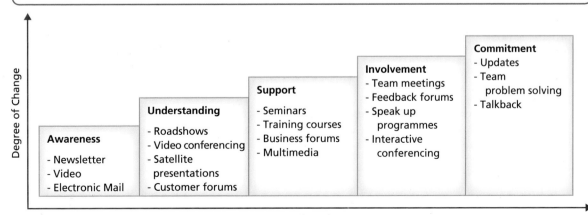

Figure 7.3: The communication escalator

Source: Quirke, B. (2008) © *Making the Connections: Using Internal Communication to Turn Strategy into Action*, Gower Publishing.

Table 7.6: Open and closed communication climates

Open, supportive communication climate	Closed, defensive communication climate
Descriptive: informative rather than evaluative communication	**Judgemental:** emphasis on apportioning blame, make people feel incompetent
Solution-oriented: focus on problem solving rather than on what is not possible	**Controlling:** conformity expected, inconsistency and change inhibited
Open and honest: no hidden messages	**Deceptive:** hidden meanings, insincerity, manipulative communication
Caring: emphasis on empathy and understanding	**Non-caring:** detached and impersonal, little concern for others
Egalitarian: everyone valued regardless of role or status	**Superior:** status and skill differences emphasized in communication
Forgiving: errors and mistakes recognized as inevitable, focus on minimizing	**Dogmatic:** little discussion, unwillingness to accept views of others or compromise
Feedback: positive, essential to maintaining performance and relationships	**Hostile:** needs of others given little importance

CUTTING EDGE The language of organizational mission statements

Chad Murphy

Jonathan Clark

The language that an organization uses to communicate its mission can affect employee commitment and performance. The problem, as Chad Murphy and Jonathan Clark (2016) argue, is that many mission statements use abstract, conceptual terms. Organizations thus tend to use the same corporate-speak: 'striving for excellence', 'delivering cutting-edge services in a global marketplace'. They cite a bank whose mission statement reads:

'The mission of People's Community Bank is to be the preferred independent community bank which meets and exceeds the expectations of our customers and communities, by providing excellent customer service, products and value, while maximizing shareholder return, along with maintaining the well-being and satisfaction of our employees.'

For a mission statement to encourage a *shared* sense of purpose, it has to use vivid concrete imagery that people can visualize and interpret in the same way. They cite the mission statement of a manufacturer of wearable robotic prosthetic devices:

'One day, our robotic exoskeletons will be a viable and accessible option for the millions of wheelchair users who want the option to stand up and walk.'

Here are examples of real company mission statements, using concrete imagery and abstractions. Which do you think will be more effective in creating a shared sense of the organization's purpose?

Statements using imagery	Statements using abstractions
To put joy in kids' hearts and a smile on parents' faces	To be the world leader in . . .
	To be the recognized performance leader in . . .
To detect a previously undetectable tumour inside a human lung by asking a patient to breathe into a device like ours	To be the most trusted provider of . . .
To make people laugh	To be a leading company delivering improved shareholder value
To ensure the security and freedom of our nation from undersea to outer space, and in cyberspace	Create a better everyday life for many people
	To create long-term value for customers, shareholders, employees
We believe in long candlelit baths, filling the world with perfume	To create a better future every day
A computer on every desk and in every home	

Social media and employee voice

Most of us use mobile technology and social media tools routinely, for our own purposes. Employers, however, have been slow to exploit the possibilities of social media. Organizational communication has traditionally been one-way, top-down, and closed. With social media tools, communication can become two-way, bottom-up, and more open. Enterprise social networks (like an in-house Facebook) could change the climate of internal organizational communications. Management can work more closely with front line staff, who can in turn can make their views known, directly and rapidly, to management and others. Social networks encourage interaction, facilitate the sharing of information across a dispersed workforce, and encourage collaboration between teams and departments. They can give management insights into issues that are affecting employees and their work (Baczor, 2017).

Employee voice the ability of employees to express their views, opinions, concerns and suggestions, and for these to influence decisions at work.

One of the main organizational applications of social media thus concerns improving two-way communications between management and employees, or employee voice.

In the UK, Joe Dromey (2016) examined the extent to which employers are making use of social media to promote employee voice. This study found that half of employers were using social media tools, but mainly for marketing and customer engagement purposes. Only one in six were using an internal enterprise network. These networks were used mainly

to provide organization and HR updates rather than to collect employee views. Dromey notes that high levels of personal use of social media could promote organizational adoption. But where enterprise social networks were in use, few employees said that this was effective in sharing knowledge and ideas, or to access employee voice. Interestingly, employees in organizations with enterprise networks said they felt less able to influence decisions than at organizations not using social networks. Dromey concludes that the benefits of these technologies are not being exploited.

Peter Holland et al. (2016) explore the implications of social media for employee voice in Australia. They also conclude that 'The understanding and management of social media at work are not well developed' (p.2629). Their research examined the relationship between social media use and job satisfaction. They found that social media were not commonly used to voice concerns about work. They suggest that this is an untapped resource, which could give management 'real time' feedback on workplace issues. Their conclusion is that, if organizations do not use this technology, that would 'allow social media to develop its own culture with the potential to be a focus for negative issues in the workplace and about the organization' (Holland et al., 2016, p.2630).

The organizational use of social media may be more advanced in the United States. Leonardi and Neeley (2017) cite a study of 4,200 American organizations by the McKinsey Global Institute, a think tank, which found that over 70 per cent reported using social media tools. The benefits included:

- Increasing employee engagement
- Promoting collaboration and knowledge sharing
- Speeding up decisions
- Developing innovative ideas for products and services
- Establishing relationships between employees in different locations
- Avoiding the duplication of work.

However, they argue that organizations can fall into four traps.

1. Assuming that younger workers (Millennials) want to use social media at work, when that is not the case. Social media are seen as tools for self-expression and communication with friends and family.
2. Prohibiting informal discussion of non-work topics on internal organizational sites. But personal interactions make it easier to access other people and work-related information.
3. Not recognizing the difference between direct learning (knowing how to do something, like solve a problem), and metaknowledge (learning who has the expertise that you need). Informal communication is important in developing metaknowledge.
4. Treating the most visible information as the most valuable; staff with technical skills may be more highly valued than those with cultural and political skills – but the latter are as valuable if not more so.

Social media can potentially strengthen employee voice, but the benefits may be difficult to quantify. These tools also allow organizations to tailor information to individuals and groups, communicate with large numbers of people at the same time regardless of location, create dialogue concerning particular topics and problems, and encourage networks and collaboration. Social networking sites can also reveal (to potential employers) information about candidates' abilities and characteristics, and display (to potential employees) an organization's culture, goals, and priorities, such as attitude to corporate social responsibility, for example.

The organizational use of social media involves some risks, including cyberloafing or cyberslacking (surfing the web for fun during working hours). Data security and the possibility of cyber attacks are growing concerns. Managers must also be aware that using social media to encourage employee voice may generate unwelcome feedback that is critical of management.

✓✓✓ **EMPLOYABILITY CHECK** (communication skills, how organizations work)

Your organization has no social media policy, and does not use social media tools for internal communication purposes. One of your senior managers asks for your view. Would you like to make more use of social media for work purposes? Should the organization develop a social media strategy? What are the benefits and risks?

 **RECAP**

1. *Describe the dimensions of social intelligence, and explain the importance of these capabilities, especially for managers.*

   - The capabilities that make up social intelligence involve a combination of awareness (what we sense about others) and facility (how we act on that awareness).

   - Managers spend lots of time interacting with others, and it becomes more important to understand the thoughts and feelings of others in a more culturally diverse population.

2. *Understand the main components of the interpersonal communication process.*

   - Communication involves an exchange of meaning, achieved through the processes of coding, transmission, decoding and feedback.

   - Face-to-face communication allows instant feedback; coding and decoding problems arise with other forms of communication where feedback is delayed or absent.

3. *Identify the main barriers to effective interpersonal communication.*

   - The main barriers to effective communication include power and gender differences, physical surroundings, language variations and cultural diversity.

   - Barriers can be overcome through face-to-face communication, by checking decoding, by paying attention to context, and by seeing things the way the other person does.

4. *Understand the effective use of different questioning techniques, conversation controls and listening skills.*

   - Getting appropriate information from someone else involves the effective use of different questioning methods: open, closed, probe, hypothetical and reflective.

   - Effective communication involves the use of a range of simple conversation controls: lubricators, inhibitors, bridges and pauses.

   - Active listening involves a range of verbal and non-verbal skills.

   - Communication methods differ between high context and low context cultures.

5. *Explain the nature and significance of non-verbal communication.*

   - Non-verbal communication includes facial expressions, eye behaviour, gesture and posture, distance between ourselves and others, and para-language.

   - If the verbal and non-verbal messages which we are sending are inconsistent, the verbal will be discounted and the non-verbal accepted.

   - Lies can be detected in non-verbal communication, but many clues are culture-specific.

6. *Understand the nature and mechanisms of impression management skills and techniques.*

   - We influence the image that others have of us through verbal and non-verbal signals.

   - We use impression management to create a favourable image through ingratiation, intimidation, self-promotion, exemplification, accounting and supplication.

   - Impression management can be seen as natural and unconscious, or as a deliberate attempt at deceit.

   - Emotional intelligence concerns the ability to identify, integrate, understand and reflectively manage one's own feelings, and the feelings of other people.

   - As with social intelligence, understanding our own emotions and the emotions of others is a key skill for all of us, particularly for managers, and its importance is heightened in culturally diverse organizational settings.

7. *Explain the nature and significance of an organization's communication climate.*

   - The communication climate in an organization can be classed as open and supportive, or closed and defensive.

   - To encourage a shared sense of purpose, organization mission statements should use concrete imagery and not vague abstract language.

→

8. *Assess how social media can improve organizational communication and strengthen employee voice.*

- One of the most valuable applications of social media concerns facilitating employee voice.

However, many organizations have still to develop the use of social media tools, which can also improve organizational communications in other ways.

RECAP: What did they find? Interaction in open plan offices

Bernstein and Turban (2018) found that:

- Employees spent 72 per cent less time in face-to-face interaction in the open plan office than they had in traditional office cubicles.

- After the move, staff sent 56 per cent more emails to their colleagues, and were copied into 41 per cent more emails from other participants in the study.

- The volume of instant messages increased by 67 per cent (more messages), and the length of messaged increased by 75 per cent (more words).

- Productivity declined after the office move.

- Instead of creating more vibrant interpersonal communication, therefore, the open architecture encouraged social withdrawal, and increased the use of email and instant messaging.

Bernstein and Turban (2018, p.6) conclude that: 'transitions to open office architecture do not necessarily promote open interaction. Consistent with the fundamental human desire for privacy and prior evidence that privacy may increase productivity, when office architecture makes everyone more observable or "transparent", it can dampen F2F interaction, as employees find other strategies to preserve their privacy; for example, by choosing a different channel through which to communicate. Rather than have an F2F interaction in front of a large audience of peers, an employee might look around, see that a particular person is at his or her desk, and send an email.'

RECAP: What did they find? Speak up or pipe down

McClean et al. (2018) found that:

- Men who spoke up with new ideas (promotive voice) were seen by others as having higher status.

- Men who spoke up with a promotive voice were also more likely to be seen as leaders.

- The status of women was not affected by speaking up, regardless of voice.

- Neither men nor women lost status by speaking up with a prohibitive voice, but saw no gains from those contributions either.

- If you are male and you want to get ahead, therefore, speak up in a way that presents positive ideas for improving your team's performance. Unfortunately, women are not likely to get the same benefits from this strategy, unless management explicitly give them credit for their ideas.

This research was carried out in the United States. From your experience, would you expect the same findings to apply in other countries and cultures?

Revision

1. What is social intelligence, and why are these capabilities now seen as ranking in importance with general intelligence, especially for managers?

2. What are the main problems affecting the communication process, and how can these problems be solved?

3. Explain, with examples, the questioning techniques which we use to obtain information from others, and the conversation control methods that we use to ensure that our interactions run smoothly, and in our favour.

4. What is non-verbal communication, and what part does it play in human interaction in general and in organizational settings in particular?

Research assignment

Choose two different television programmes which include interviews; news, political commentary, magazine programmes, chat shows. It does not matter whether the interview is about news information, or simply audience entertainment. In each case observe one interviewer or host or commentator interviewing someone, and makes notes on:

1. What questioning techniques are used, and their effectiveness.
2. What questioning techniques are not used.
3. The interviewer's use of body language.
4. Does the interviewer display social intelligence, and what evidence can you cite.
5. Does the interviewer display emotional intelligence, and what evidence can you cite.
6. Who controls the flow of conversation – interviewer or interviewee.

Write a report comparing the similarities and differences in these two interviews. Assess the skill and effectiveness of the interviewer in each case. From your assessment, what practical advice you would give to these interviewers to help them to improve their technique? What general conclusions can you reach concerning interviewing skills in general, and television interviewing in particular?

Springboard

Andrzej Huczynski (2004) *Influencing Within Organizations,* London: Routledge. Practical guide to the realities of influence, arguing that job skills alone are not enough to ensure career advancement. Chapters on verbal and non-verbal influencing and impression management.

Erin Meyer (2014) 'Navigating the cultural minefield', *Harvard Business Review,* 92 (5): 119–23. Compares business cultures on eight scales: communicating, evaluating, persuading, leading, deciding, trusting, disagreeing and scheduling. For example, Israel and Russia differ in how they prefer to lead (Russians are more hierarchical than egalitarian), and to decide (Russians prefer top-down to consensual decision making).

Mark Bolino, David Long and William Turnley (2016) 'Impression management in organizations: critical questions, answers, and areas for future research', *Annual Review of Organizational Psychology and Organizational Behavior,* 3: 377–406. Explores whether and when these tactics work, and the skills involved in using them.

OB cinema

Burn After Reading (2008, directors Joel and Ethan Cohen). DVD track 6: 0:27:13 to 0:29:08 (2 minutes). Clip opens with Linda asking for 'just a tea'; clip ends with Linda saying, 'Haven't you heard of the power of positive thinking?'

Gym employee Linda Litzke (played by Frances McDormand) is talking to the gym manager, Ted Treffon (Richard Jenkins).

1. What does Linda want to achieve in this conversation?
2. What tactics does she use?
3. Why does she not achieve her goal?
4. What advice can you give to Linda about managing this conversation more effectively?
5. What does Ted want to achieve in this conversation?
6. What tactics does he use?
7. Why does he not achieve his goal?
8. What advice can you give to Ted about managing this conversation more effectively?

Chapter exercises

1. Impression management checklist

Objective 1. To assess aspects of the way in which you deal with other people.

Briefing As you read each of the following 18 statements, ask yourself whether or not it applies to you, and answer (tick) 'yes' or 'no' accordingly. You will of course occasionally feel that you want to answer 'sometimes', but try in each case to decide where your personal preferences, strengths, and priorities really lie. You don't always get to sit on the fence. This is not a test with right or wrong answers. It is designed for personal reflection and group discussion (based on Snyder, 1987, p.179).

		yes	no
1	I find it hard to imitate the behaviour of other people.		
2	At parties and gatherings, I do not attempt to do or say things that others will like.		
3	I can only argue for ideas which I already believe.		
4	I can make impromptu speeches even on topics about which I have almost no information.		
5	I guess I put on a show to impress or entertain others.		
6	I would probably make a good actor.		
7	In a group of people, I am rarely the centre of attention.		
8	In different situations and with different people, I often act like very different persons.		
9	I am not particularly good at making other people like me.		
10	I'm not always the person I appear to be.		
11	I would not change my opinions or the way I do things in order to please someone or win their favour.		
12	I have considered being an entertainer.		
13	I have never been good at games like charades, or acting.		
14	I have trouble changing my behaviour to suit different people and different situations.		
15	At a party I let others keep the jokes and stories going.		
16	I feel a bit awkward in company and do not show up quite as well as I should.		
17	I can look anyone in the eye and tell a lie with a straight face, if for an appropriate reason.		
18	I may deceive people by being friendly when I really dislike them.		

Scoring   You get either one point or zero, depending on how you responded to each statement. Simply add up the number of points you got.

statement	score		your score
	yes	**no**	
1	0	1	
2	0	1	
3	0	1	
4	1	0	
5	1	0	
6	1	0	
7	0	1	
8	1	0	
9	0	1	
10	1	0	
11	0	1	
12	1	0	
13	0	1	
14	0	1	
15	0	1	
16	0	1	
17	1	0	
18	1	0	
		Total:	

Interpretation   A score of 13 or more implies strong impression management skills:

Awareness   You are consciously aware of your own and other people's feelings and behaviour, and of how you affect others

Flexibility   You are able to adjust what you say and do to match other people's expectations, and to achieve your goals

Control   You are able consciously to control your behaviour, and thus to control other people; you probably enjoy this

A score of 7 or less implies weak impression management skills:

Awareness   You are not always aware of your own or other people's feelings and behaviour, or of how you affect others

Flexibility   You are unable to adjust what you say and do to match other people's expectations, and to achieve your goals

Control   You are unable consciously to control your behaviour, and may feel uncomfortably manipulated at times

A score between 8 and 12 implies moderate impression management skills. Read over the interpretations, and judge your strengths for yourself. Which way would you like to go – up or down?

→

Analysis   Whatever your own score, consider the following key issues:

1. To what extent are impression management skills learnable and to what extent are we born with them?

2. Is it unethical to adjust your behaviour in order to modify the feelings and behaviours of others?

3. Regardless of your own impression management score, in what ways would it benefit you to be more aware of how other people use these skills? Give specific examples.

2. How would you respond?

Objectives   1. To analyse the practical uses of questioning techniques and conversation controls.

2. To explore appropriate management options in dealing with employee grievances.

Briefing   Individually, read each of the cases and choose your preferred responses. Then, in groups of three or four:

1. Decide the objective of the interaction with this person; what do you, as this person's supervisor, want to achieve by the end of the conversation?

2. What are the key issues relevant to the individual, team and organization in this situation?

3. Which is the best response of the four offered, and why?

4. Develop a fifth response, if you think that is desirable, and explain its strengths.

5. Plenary: Each group presents and explains its conclusions to the group as a whole.

6. Debriefing: Your instructor will lead a discussion of the implications of the different responses in each case, and of the key learning points from this exercise.

Here are statements from employees, directed at you, their immediate supervisor.

Situation A: Assistant Supervisor, age 30, computer manufacturing plant

'Yes, I do have a problem. I'd like to know more about what happened with the promotions last month. Charlie got the supervisor's job in motherboard assembly and I didn't even know he was interested. Why did you give the job to him? I would like to know more about what you think of my promotion prospects here. I've been doing this job for about three years now, and I've been with the company for almost five years. I haven't had any complaints about my work. Seems to me I've been doing a pretty good job, but I don't see any recognition for that. What do I have to do to get promoted round here?'

1. You'll make a great supervisor, Bill, but give it time. I'll do what I can to make your case. Don't be discouraged, OK? I'm sure you'll get there soon, you'll see.

2. So, you're not sure about how the company regards your work here?

3. I understand how you feel, but I have to admit it took me five years to make supervisor myself. And I guess I must have felt much the same way you do today. But we just have to be patient. Things don't always happen when we'd like them to, do they?

4. Come on, you've been here long enough to know the answer to that one. Nobody got promoted just by waiting for it to happen. Get with it, you've got to put yourself forward, make people stand up and take notice of your capabilities.

> ### Situation B: Personnel Officer, age 26, local authority
>
> 'I've just about had it. I can't put up with this kind of pressure for much longer. We just don't have the staff to service the level of requests that we're getting and still do a good job. And some of the people we have to deal with! If that old witch in administration calls me one more time about those files that went missing last week, she's going to get a real mouthful in return. How come you let your department get pushed around like this?'
>
> 1. You're not alone. Pressure is something that we've all had to endure at some time. I understand that, it comes with the territory. I think it's about developing the right skills and attitudes to cope.
>
> 2. You're right, this is a difficult patch, but I'm sure that it will pass. This can't go on for much longer, and I expect you'll see things start to come right at the end of the month.
>
> 3. Well, if you can't stand the heat, I suppose you just have to get out of the kitchen. And please don't refer to people who are senior to you in this organization in that manner ever again.
>
> 4. Let me check – this is not about Mrs Smith in admin is it? You're saying the strain is such that you're thinking of leaving us?

References

Adair, W.L., Buchan, N.R., Chen, X.-P. and Liu, D. (2016) 'A model of communication context and measure of context dependence', *Academy of Management Discoveries*, 2 (2): 198–217.

Allen, T.J. and Henn, G. (2006) *The Organization and Architecture of Innovation: Managing the Flow of Technology*. London: Routledge.

Baczor, L. (2017) *Employee Communication Factsheet*. London: Chartered Institute for Personnel and Development.

Bernstein, E.S. and Turban, S. (2018) 'The impact of the "open" workspace on human collaboration', *Philosophical Transactions of the Royal Society B*, 373: 20170239.

Bolino, M., Long, D. and Turnley, W. (2016) 'Impression management in organizations: critical questions, answers, and areas for future research', *Annual Review of Organizational Psychology and Organizational Behavior*, 3: 377–406.

Bonaccio, S., O'Reilly, J., O'Sullivan, S.L. and Chiocchio, F. (2017) 'Nonverbal behavior and communication in the workplace: a review and an agenda for research', *Journal of Management*, 42 (5): 1044–74.

Brink, K.E. and Costigan, R.D. (2015) 'Oral communication skills: are the priorities of the workplace and AACSB-accredited business programs aligned?', *Academy of Management Education & Learning*, 14 (2): 205–21.

Brooks, A.W. and John, L.K. (2018) 'The surprising power of questions', *Harvard Business Review*, 96(3): 60–67.

Chartered Management Institute (2014) *21st Century Leaders: Building Practice Into the Curriculum to Boost Employability*. London: Chartered Management Institute.

Dromey, J. (2016) *Going Digital?: Harnessing Social Media for Employee Voice*. London: ACAS.

DuBrin, A.J. (2011) *Impression Management in the Workplace: Research, Theory, and Practice*. New York and London: Routledge.

Gibb, J.R. (1961) 'Defensive communication', *Journal of Communication*, 11(3): 141–48.

Goleman, D. (2005) *Emotional Intelligence: Why It Can Matter More Than IQ*. London: Bloomsbury Publishing (first published 1995).

Goleman, D. (2007) *Social Intelligence: The New Science of Human Relationships*. London: Hutchinson.

Goleman, D., Boyatzis, R.E. and McKee, A. (2013) *Primal Leadership: Unleashing the Power of Emotional Intelligence*. Harvard: Harvard Business Press.

Hall, E.T. (1976) *Beyond Culture*. New York: Doubleday/Currency.

Hall, E.T. (1989) *Understanding Cultural Differences.* Yarmouth, ME: Intercultural Press.

Heath, K., Flynn, J. and Holt, M.D. (2014) 'Women, find your voice', *Harvard Business Review*, 92 (6): 118–21.

Holland, P., Cooper, B.K. and Hecker, R. (2016) 'Use of social media at work: a new form of employee voice?', *International Journal of Human Resource Management*, 27 (21): 2621–34.

Kirton, H. (2014) 'Reach for the brick', *People Management*, October, p.31.

Leonardi, P. and Neeley, T. (2017) 'What managers need to know about social tools', *Harvard Business Review*, 96 (5): 118–26.

Lewis, L. and Lea, R. (2010) 'Toyota chief bows to pressure over pedal defect', *The Times*, 6 February, p.13.

McClean, E.J., Martin, E.J., Emich, S.R. and Woodruff, T. (2018) 'The social consequences of voice: an examination of voice type and gender on status and subsequent leader emergence', *Academy of Management Journal*, 61(5): 1869–91.

McMahon, B. (2016) 'The new superwoman rules', *The Times*, 19 January, Times2 Supplement, pp.4–5.

Mohr, T. (2015) *Playing Big: A Practical Guide for Brilliant Women Like You.* London: Arrow Books.

Moser, K. (2013) 'Only a click away? – what makes virtual meetings, emails and outsourcing successful', *CMI Management Articles of the Year 2013.* London: Chartered Management Institute, pp.25–30.

Murphy, C. and Clark, J.R. (2016) 'Picture this: how the language of leaders drives performance', *Organizational Dynamics*, 45(2): 139–46.

Nelson-Jones, R. (2000) *Introduction to Counselling Skills: Text and Actitivies.* London: Sage Publications.

Quirke, B. (2008) *Making the Connections: Using Internal Communication to Turn Strategy into Action.* Aldershot: Gower Publishing.

Robbins, S.P., Judge, T.A. and Campbell, T.T. (2010) *Organizational Behaviour*, Harlow, Essex: Financial Times Prentice Hall.

Salovey, P. and Mayer, J.D. (1990) 'Emotional intelligence', *Imagination, Cognition and Personality*, 9 (3): 185–211.

Shannon, C.E. and Weaver, W. (1949) *The Mathematical Theory of Communication.* Urbana, IL: University of Illinois Press.

Snyder, M. (1987) *Public Appearance and Private Realities: The Psychology of Self-Monitoring.* New York: W.H. Freeman.

Sorokowska, A., Sorokowski, P., Hilpert, P., Cantarero, K. and others (2017) 'Preferred interpersonal distances: a global comparison', *Journal of Cross-Cultural Psychology*, 48 (4): 577–92.

Tannen, D. (1990) *You Just Don't Understand: Women and Men in Conversation.* New York: William Morrow.

Tannen, D. (1995) 'The power of talk: who gets heard and why', *Harvard Business Review*, 73(5): 138–48.

The Economist (2008) 'Debating the debates', Lexington, 11 October, p.62.

The Economist (2015) 'James Bond's body language', 24 January, p.40.

Waber, B., Magnolfi, J. and Lindsay, G. (2014) 'Workspaces that move people', *Harvard Business Review*, 92(10): 69–77.

CHAPTER 8

Perception

Key terms

perception

perceptual world

selective attention

perceptual threshold

habituation

perceptual filters

perceptual organization

perceptual set

halo effect

stereotype

self-fulfilling prophecy

attribution

Learning outcomes

When you have read this chapter, you should be able to define those key terms in your own words, and you should also be able to:

1. Identify the main features of the process of perception.

2. Distinguish between the bottom-up processing of sensory information and the top-down interpretation of that information.

3. Understand the nature and implications of selective attention and perceptual organization.

4. Give examples of how behaviour is influenced by our perceptions.

5. Explain and illustrate the main processes and problems in perception, including false attributions, halo effects and stereotyping.

6. Explain some less widely appreciated sources of discrimination at work arising from characteristics of the person perception and attribution processes.

7. Suggest ways to improve perceptual accuracy and avoid errors.

Why study perception?

Of all the topics covered in this text, perception is perhaps the one which most clearly sets social science apart from natural science. We attach meanings, interpretations, values and aims to our actions. Our actions are influenced by how we perceive ourselves, and on how we perceive our social and physical environment. We explain our behaviour with terms like reason, motive, intention, purpose and desire. Astronomers, chemists, engineers and physicists do not face this complication in coming to grips with their subject matter. For a natural scientist, there is a reality 'out there' to observe and study. For a social scientist, 'reality' is often what people perceive it to be.

Are you an Alpha?

Andrew DuBrin

Perception is key. How other people see you counts just as much as who you think you are. Andrew DuBrin (2011) cites research which found that three-quarters of senior executives and half of all middle managers are *alphas* – people who are ambitious, self-confident, competitive and brash. Non-alphas who want to make it to the executive suite will not get there unless they are seen to have alpha traits. To be an alpha – female or male – others have to see that you have these attributes:

1. Self-confident and opinionated
2. Highly intelligent
3. Action oriented
4. High performance expectations, of self and others
5. Direct communication style
6. Highly disciplined
7. Unemotional

Alpha females and alpha males are usually perceived positively by others, who in turn respond positively to them. However, alphas have to be careful not to exaggerate their attributes. For example, if an alpha is so self-confident that they ignore others, or focus on results at the expense of others' feelings, then the perceptions of others may be extremely negative.

Perception
the dynamic psychological process responsible for attending to, organizing and interpreting sensory data.

It is our perception of reality which shapes and directs our behaviour, not some objective understanding of it. We each perceive the world around us in different ways. If one person on a hillside perceives that it is cold, they will reach for a sweater. If the person standing next to them perceives that it is warm, they will remove their sweater. These contrasting behaviours can occur simultaneously, regardless of the ambient temperature. Human behaviour is a function of the way in which we perceive the world around us, and how we perceive other people and events in that world.

 **STOP AND SEARCH** Find on Google the TED Talk, *Frans de Waal: The surprising science of alpha males* (15:55).

Perception management

Laura Little

How do perceptions of women at work change when they become pregnant, and how do pregnant women try to maintain their professional image? Laura Little and colleagues (2015) interviewed 35 women who were either pregnant or who had just given birth to their first child, and who had worked full time during pregnancy. They were asked to describe how being pregnant had influenced their experience at work, how this affected others' perceptions of them, and what they did to influence the way in which others perceived them. The participants in the study emphasized four motives: to show that their commitment to work had not changed; to be seen as maintaining a professional image; to avoid damaging their careers; and to persuade others that they were not about to leave. Analysis of the interviews revealed six tactics for managing professional image:

Tactics	Illustrations
Managing the pace	'I still worked as hard as I did before I got pregnant'
	'I still worked an eight-hour day, or go in on a Saturday'
Not expecting concessions	'I always made sure that I was actually at work'
	'I'd say, I don't mind, I'll come in. It's no big deal'
Going the extra mile	'It made me work hard, to let them know, she can get this done'
	'I started busting my butt at work, working that much harder'
Accepting shorter leave	'I took only two and a half months leave instead of four months'
	'I told them I'd be back in ten weeks, show them I was serious'
Passing as not pregnant	'I didn't meet with people. I'd talk to them on the phone'
	'I didn't want to tell them, fear of hiring someone to replace me'
Downplaying the issue	'I try not to bring up my pregnancy in conversations'
	'I want to be seen as professional, and 'cuter' is not professional'

There may be personal costs in the use of these tactics:

'Women who devote a considerable time to the successful management of their professional images may do so at the expense of their personal lives. In addition, going the extra mile may have adverse health outcomes for the pregnant woman or the baby. A few interviewees wondered if they had pushed themselves too hard in their efforts to "prove themselves" to supervisors and others. One respondent was put on bed rest for hypertension, and another, who had a high risk pregnancy, chose not to follow her doctor's orders to reduce her hours at work' (Little et al., 2015, p.34).

However, women who are worried about how their professional image will be affected by pregnancy can take steps to change how others perceive them, and thus reduce discrimination.

CRITICAL THINKING   Choose a movie that you have seen recently, and which you particularly enjoyed. Now find a friend or colleague who has seen the same film, and who hated it. Share your views of that film. What factors (age, sex, background, education, interests, values and beliefs, political views, past experience) can you identify that explain the differences in perception between you and your friend or colleague?

We often find ourselves unable to understand other people's behaviour. People can say and do surprising things in settings where it is obvious to us that some other behaviour would have been more appropriate. If we are to understand why you behaved in that way in that context, we first need to discover how you perceive that context and your place in it. When we are able to 'see it the way you see it', to put ourselves in your position, what took us by surprise is likely to become understandable. To understand each other's behaviour, we need to be able to understand each others' perceptions. We need to be able to understand why we perceive things differently in the first place.

Selectivity and organization

We do not passively register sense impressions picked up from the world around us. We process and interpret the incoming raw data in the light of our past experiences, in terms of our current needs and interests, in terms of our knowledge, expectations, beliefs and motives.

The main elements in the perceptual process are shown in Figure 8.1. From a psychological point of view, the processes of sensation, on the one hand, and perception, on the other, work together through what are termed *bottom-up* and *top-down* processing. The bottom-up phase concerns the way in which we process the raw data received by our sensory apparatus. One of the key characteristics of bottom-up processing concerns the need for selectivity. We are simply not able to attend to all of the sensory information available to us at any given time. Bottom-up processing screens or filters out redundant and less relevant information so that we can focus on what is important.

The top-down phase, in contrast, concerns the mental processing that allows us to order, interpret, and make sense of the world around us. One of the key characteristics of top-down processing concerns our need to make sense of our environment, and our search for meaning.

This distinction between sensation (bottom-up) and perception (top-down) is demonstrated by our ability to make sense of incomplete, or even incorrect, sensory information. The missing letter or comma, or the word spelled incorrectly, is not often a problem, as you know from text messaging:

This sent nce us incorr ct, bit U wull stell B abl to understa d it.

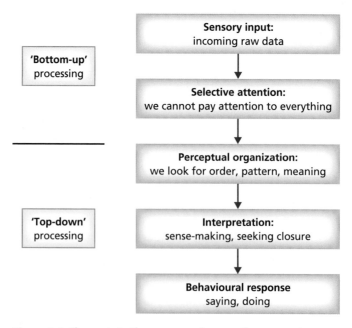

Figure 8.1: Elements in the process of perception

Our top-down conceptual processing ability means that we are able to fill in the gaps and correct the mistakes, and make sense of 'imperfect' raw data.

Perceptual world
the individual's personal internal image, map or picture of their social, physical and organizational environment.

We all have similar nervous systems and share much the same sensory equipment. However, we have different social and physical backgrounds, and different values, interests and expectations, and thus different perceptions. We do not behave in, or respond to, the world 'as it really is'. This idea of the 'real world' is arbitrary. The 'real world' as a concept is not a useful starting point for developing an understanding of human behaviour in general, or organizational behaviour in particular. We behave in, and in response to, the world as we perceive it. We each live in our own perceptual world.

Home viewing

In the movie, *The Matrix* (1999, directors Andy and Lana Wachowski) Morpheus (played by Laurence Fishburne) explains the arbitrary nature of reality to Neo (Keanu Reeves). As Morpheus reveals the nature of the Matrix, Neo exclaims, 'This isn't real'. Morpheus replies, 'What is reality?' This occurs around 35 minutes into the film.

 **STOP AND SEARCH**   YouTube for *The Matrix (1999) Construct scenes* (3:00).

Successful interpersonal relationships depend on some overlap between our perceptual worlds, or we would never be able to understand each other. Our perceptual worlds, however, are in a detailed analysis unique, which makes life interesting, but also gives us problems.

Our perceptual processing is normally carried out without much conscious deliberation or effort. In fact, we often have no effective control over the process, and fortunately, control is not always necessary. We can, however, control some aspects of the process simply by being consciously aware of what is happening. There are many settings where such control is desirable and can help us to avoid dangerous and expensive errors. Understanding the characteristics of perception can be useful in many organizational settings – with the design of aircraft instruments and displays for pilots, in the conduct of selection interviews, and in handling disputes and employee grievances.

Perception is a dynamic process because it involves ordering and attaching meaning to raw sensory data. Our sensory apparatus is bombarded with vast amounts of information. Some of this information is internal: feelings of hunger, lust, pain, fatigue. Some of this information comes from people, objects and events in the world around us. We do not passively record these sensory data. We are constantly sifting and ordering this stream of information, making sense of and interpreting it.

Selective attention
the ability, often exercised unconsciously, to choose from the stream of sensory data, to concentrate on particular elements, and to ignore others.

Perception is an information processing activity which involves selective attention.

Our senses – sight, hearing, touch, taste, smell, and internal bodily signals or 'kinaesthesia' – each consists of specialist nerves that respond to specific forms of energy, such as light, sound, pressure and temperature changes. There are some forms of energy that our senses cannot detect unaided, such as radio waves, sounds at very low and very high pitch, and infrared radiation. Our sensory apparatus has limitations that we cannot overcome without the aid of special equipment. We are unable to hear sound frequencies above 10,000 hertz, but many animals, including dogs and dolphins, can. We are unable to hear sounds below 30 hertz, but whales can. Owls have much better eyesight than we do.

Home viewing

The Sixth Sense (1999, director M. Night Shyamalan) concerns the attempts by a child psychologist, Malcolm Crowe (played by Bruce Willis), to cure a young boy, Cole (Haley Joel Osment), who is tormented because he sees dead people. Crowe spends so much time with Cole that he ignores his wife Anna (Olivia Williams). However, this film manipulates the perceptions and assumptions of the audience. Once you have watched the film, either reflect on the action, or watch it again. Notice which clues you 'saw', but either ignored or misinterpreted the first time around. Notice how your interpretation of events relied on the assumptions that you made – or the assumptions that you were *expected* to make. Only when you know the full plot of the film can you make 'correct' assumptions and interpretations, based on the same evidence you were given the first time around. What does this movie say about the ease with which your perceptions can be manipulated?

Change blindness: just how selective are we?

Picture this. You're walking across a park when a stranger asks you for directions. While you're talking to him, two men pass between you carrying a door. You are annoyed by this, but they move on and you continue with your explanation. When you're finished, the stranger tells you that you've just taken part in a psychology experiment. 'Did you notice anything change after the two men passed with the door?' he asks. 'No', you reply uneasily. He then explains that the man who first approached you walked off behind the door, leaving him in his place. The first man now comes up to join you. Looking at them standing side by side, you realize that they differ in height and build, are dressed differently, have different haircuts, and different voices.

a

b

c

d

When Daniel Simons and Daniel Levin (1998) did this experiment, they found that half of those who took part failed to notice the substitution. They had suffered what is called 'change blindness'. Instead of paying attention to every detail of what we see, we are highly selective. The notion that we see everything is just that – a notion. We extract a few details and rely on memory, or perhaps even our imagination, for the rest (Simons and Ambinder, 2005).

👆 **STOP AND SEARCH**   for *Daniel Simons: the 'door' study* on YouTube (1.37).

Perceptual threshold
a boundary point, either side of which our senses respectively will or will not be able to detect stimuli, such as sound, light or touch.

The constraints imposed by our sensory apparatus can be modified in certain ways by experience. The boundary, or perceptual threshold, between what we can and cannot detect can be established by experiment. We can explore individual differences in thresholds across the senses, and these thresholds can sometimes be altered by training and experience.

If there is a clock ticking in the room where you study, you will almost certainly not be aware of the sound, until somebody mentions it, or the clock stops. Next time you visit a library, close your eyes for few seconds and pay attention to the background noise that you do not usually hear. But surely, you must have heard it, as you must have heard the clock ticking, if your ears were working properly? Our sensory apparatus responds, not simply to energy, but to changes in energy levels. Having detected a stimulus, such as a clock, or the hum of air conditioning, the nerves concerned become tired of transmitting the same information indefinitely and give up, until the stimulus changes. This explains our surprise at the sudden silence which follows when machinery stops.

Habituation
the decrease in our perceptual response to stimuli once they have become familiar.

Once stimuli become familiar, they stop being sensed. This phenomenon, in which the perceptual threshold is raised, is known as habituation.

Our sensory apparatus has design limitations which filter out some information, such as x-rays and dog whistles. Perception involves other filtering processes, as the phenomenon of habituation suggests. In particular, information that is familiar, non-threatening and unnecessary to the task in hand is screened out of our conscious awareness.

Stand on the pavement of a busy street and pay attention to as much of the available information as you can: the noise of the traffic, the make and colour and condition of passing vehicles, the smell of rubber tyres and exhaust fumes, the pressure of the pavement on the soles of your feet, the breeze across your face, the aftershave of a passing man, that woman's perfume, the clothes of the man across the street and the type of dog he is walking, an overheard mobile phone conversation. When you think you are taking it all in, start to cross the road. If you get across safely, you will find that your heightened awareness has lapsed, dramatically. You would be mown down fairly quickly if this were not the case. Selective attention allows us to concentrate on the important and significant, and to ignore the insignificant and trivial.

We become habituated in our use of language. Read the following sentence, and then quickly count the number of Fs:

FINISHED FILES ARE THE RESULT OF YEARS OF SCIENTIFIC STUDY
COMBINED WITH THE EXPERIENCE OF YEARS

Most people who speak English as a second language see all six Fs. Native English speakers usually pick up only three or four, because they tend to miss out the Fs in 'of'. Native speakers have been habituated to skip the 'of' because it does not contribute to the meaning of the sentence.

Perceptual filters
individual characteristics, predispositions, and preoccupations that interfere with the effective transmission and receipt of messages.

The explanation is that, once we stop seeing the 'ofs', we do not see them again, even when we are looking for them. There is too much information available at any one time for us to pay attention to all of it, so we screen out that which is apparently of little value. The image of the world that we carry around inside our heads can only ever be a partial representation of what is 'really out there'. This leads to the conclusion that our behavioural choices are determined not by reality, but by what we perceive that reality to be. Our perception is influenced by what are called perceptual filters.

The internal and external factors which affect selective attention are illustrated in Figure 8.2.

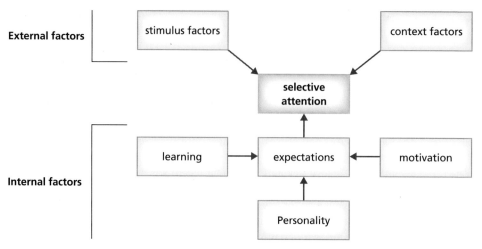

Figure 8.2: The external and internal factors influencing selective attention

The external factors affecting selective attention include stimulus factors and context factors. With respect to the stimulus factors, our attention is drawn more readily to stimuli that are:

large		small
bright		dull
loud		quiet
strong	rather than	weak
unfamiliar		familiar
stand out from surroundings		blend with surroundings
moving		stationary
repeated (but not repetitive)		one-off

Note, however, that we do not merely respond to single features, as this list might imply; we respond to the pattern of stimuli available to us.

CRITICAL THINKING

How do advertisements creatively use stimulus factors to attract our attention, on websites, magazines, billboards and television? Do you feel manipulated by these tactics?

Our attention is also influenced by context factors. The naval commander on the ship's bridge and the cook in the kitchen may both have occasion to shout 'fire', but these identical statements mean quite different things to those within earshot, and will lead to radically different forms of behaviour (the taking and saving of lives, respectively). We do not need any help to make this crucial distinction, beyond our knowledge of the context.

The internal factors affecting perception include:

- *Learning.* You've heard those instructions before (the pre-flight safety briefing), so are you going to listen to it again? Our past experience leads to the development of expectations or perceptual sets, which predispose us to pay attention to some stimuli, and to ignore others.

- *Personality.* How come you (gregarious, sociable) saw the advertisement for the party, but your friend (reserved, shy) did not? Our personality traits predispose us to pay attention to some issues and events and human characteristics and not others.

- *Motivation.* Do you get out of the shower to take a phone call, perhaps expecting a party invitation or a job offer? We are more likely to respond to stimuli that we perceive as important and motivating.

Much of perception can be described as classification or categorization. We categorize people as male or female, lazy or energetic, extrovert or shy. In fact our classification schemes are usually more sophisticated than that. We classify objects as cars, buildings, furniture, crockery, and so on, and we refine our classification schemes further under these headings. However, we are not born with a neat classification scheme 'wired in' with the brain. These categories are learned. They are social constructs. What we learn is often culture specific. The British revulsion at the thought of eating dog (classified as pet), the Hindu revulsion at the thought of eating beef (classified as sacred), and the Islamic aversion to alcohol (classified as proscribed by the Koran), are all culturally transmitted emotions based on learned values.

Problems arise when we and others act as if our culture had a monopoly on 'right thinking' on such issues. Different does not mean wrong. Different people in the same culture have different experiences and develop different expectations. The internal factors – our past experience and what we have learned, our personalities, our motivations – all shape our expectations of the world around us, what we want from it, what will happen in it, and what should happen. We tend to select information that fits our expectations, and pay less attention to information that does not.

Our categorization processes, and the search for meaning and pattern, are key characteristics of perception. This perceptual work is captured by the concept of perceptual organization.

Perceptual organization
the process through which incoming stimuli are organized or patterned in systematic and meaningful ways.

The principles by which the process of perceptual organization operates were first identified by Max Wertheimer (1880–1943) in 1923. The 'proximity principle' notes that we tend to group together or to classify stimuli that are physically close to each other and which thus appear to 'belong' together. Note how you 'see' three sets of pairs rather than six blobs here:

The 'similarity principle' notes that we classify or group together stimuli that resemble each other in appearance in some respect. Note how you 'see' four pairs here, not eight objects:

The fact that we are able to make use of incomplete and ambiguous information, by 'filling in the gaps' from our own knowledge and past experience, is known as the 'principle of closure'. These principles of perceptual organization apply to simple visual stimuli. Of more interest here, however, is the way in which these principles apply to person perception. How often do we assume that people are similar just because they live in the same neighbourhood, or work in the same section of the factory or office building (proximity principle), or just because they wear the same clothes or have similar ethnic origins (similarity principle)? How often do we take incomplete information about someone (he's Scottish) and draw inferences from this (closure principle)? This can cause the spread of false rumours in organizations through what is called 'the grapevine'.

> **CRITICAL THINKING**
>
> Are you aware of making assumptions about other people based on their backgrounds and appearance? Did you check those assumptions? Have your assumptions turned out to be correct, or not? What will you do in future to avoid making false assumptions about other people?

Perceptual sets and perceptual worlds

Perceptual set
an individual's predisposition to respond to people and events in a particular manner.

We have shown how the perceptual process selects incoming stimuli and organizes them into meaningful patterns. We have also argued that this processing is influenced by learning, motivation, and by personality – factors which give rise to expectations, which in turn make us more ready to respond to certain stimuli in certain ways and less ready to respond to others. This readiness to respond is called the individual's perceptual set.

Ways of seeing

Look at this drawing, made in 1915 by the cartoonist W.H. Hill. What do you see? Is she an old woman, or a young woman? Your answer may be influenced by what you are predisposed to see. The reactions of different individuals may not be the same, and it does not make sense to argue over whose perception is correct. Two people can see the same thing, but perceive it in different ways.

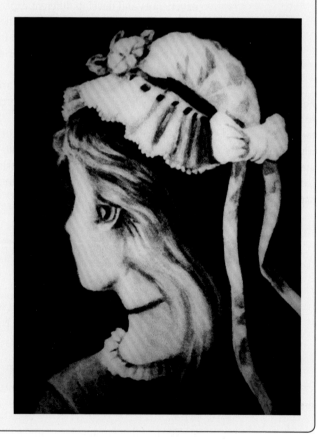

Failure to understand the importance of differences in perception creates many problems. Employees may perceive that they face chronic difficulties, while management see these complaints as trivial and temporary. The starting point for resolving such issues must lie with the recognition that different people hold different, but equally legitimate, views of the same set of circumstances. **Chapter 1** identified two views of human behaviour. The *positivist* perspective sets out to discover an objective world out there, as it really is. The *constructivist*

perspective explores how our world is socially constructed, and how we experience and interpret that world. The argument in this chapter suggests that, 'the world out there', is not a good starting point for developing an understanding of human behaviour. We each have a unique version of what is out there and of our own place in it. We each live in our own perceptual world.

How movies affect perceptions of women

 Geena Davis (2014), founder of the Institute on Gender in Media, argues that, 'Images have a profound effect on how we see the world and our role in it'. Watching children's television with her daughter, Davis was struck by the lack of female characters. This inspired her to conduct the first global study of how women appear in films. She analysed 120 family films; this is what she found:

- In these films, the ratio of male to female characters is 3:1.

- This ratio has not changed since the 1940s.

- Only 23 per cent of films had a female lead.

- Only 10 per cent had a gender-balanced cast.

- Of the characters with jobs, 81 per cent are male.

- Women make up only 17 per cent of the people in crowd scenes.

- Female characters in G-rated (family) animated movies wear the same amount of sexually revealing clothing as female characters in R-rated (adult) films.

Davis concludes that, 'If women are continually depicted as one-dimensional, sidelined, stereotyped, hypersexualized, not given leadership roles or simply absent, it sends a very clear message: women and girls are not as important as men and boys. And that has an enormous impact on business and society' (p.131).

 **STOP AND SEARCH** YouTube for *Geena Davis: Addressing Unconscious Bias* and find a video of Geena Davis embedded in a *McKinsey Quarterly* article (4:44).

We each have a perceptual world that is selective and partial, and which concentrates on features of particular interest and importance to us. Through the processes of learning, motivation and personality development, we each have different expectations and different degrees of readiness to respond to objects, people and events in different ways. We impose meaning on received patterns of information; the meanings that we attach to objects, people and events are not intrinsic to these things, but are learned through social experience and are coloured by our current needs and objectives.

Our perceptions, that is the meanings that we attach to the information available to us, shape our actions. Behaviour in an organization context can usually be understood once we understand the way in which the individual perceives that context. Figure 8.3 illustrates the links between available information based on observation and experience, the perception based on that information, and outcomes in terms of decisions with respect to actions. This example explains why employees would ignore apparently reasonable management requests to become 'team players'.

CRITICAL THINKING Have you disagreed with someone recently? What did you disagree about? How can this disagreement be explained by differences between your perceptual world and theirs?

Figure 8.3: The information–perception–actions link

To understand an individual's behaviour, therefore, we need to know something of the elements in their perceptual world, and the pattern of information and other cultural influences that have shaped that world. To change an individual's behaviour, therefore, we first have to consider changing their perceptions, through the information and experiences available to them. In the example in Figure 8.3, this would involve radical, visible and sustained changes in company performance review, and in promotion policies and practice.

Developing an understanding of our own perceptual world is difficult because there are so many influences of which we are not fully aware. Information about the perceptual worlds of others is even more elusive. Although we can in principle find out how others perceive things, a lack of mutual understanding creates barriers to interpersonal communications. Unfortunately, we often forget that our own perceptual world is not the only possible or correct one.

Do we see to know or know to see?

Fortunately, we as individuals are not as isolated from each other as the argument so far suggests. We do not live in a social and organizational world of constant disagreement and failed communication. Most of our interactions are fairly successful. Why? Fortunately, our separate individual perceptual worlds overlap. We have the same, or similar, sensory equipment. We share the same basic needs. We share much of the same social environment. Within the same society, although there are vast differences in experience, we share some of the same problems and environmental features. All this common ground makes the tasks of mutual understanding and interpersonal communication possible.

We have defined the process of perception in terms of making sense of the information available to us. We are active processors of that information, not passive recipients. However, much of that information is already processed for us. We are bombarded with sensory information, from other people, from books and newspapers and magazines, from advertising, from radio, television, and the internet, and from internal organizational sources – reports, newsletters, blogs, podcasts, briefings.

Employees at all levels have experienced major upheavals in recent years as organizations have introduced initiatives to cut costs and improve performance. These changes, which have often led to stress, burnout, initiative fatigue and work intensification, have typically been communicated using arguments like this:

In order to survive in a rapidly changing, turbulent, and highly competitive environment, we need to become more efficient, more cost conscious, more flexible and adaptable, and more customer-focused. Therefore, we need to implement the following radical changes to organization structures, procedures, and jobs.

There are two ways to read this 'turbulent world' argument. First, this is a taken-for-granted expression of contemporary organizational reality. There is nothing unusual in this argument about the need for flexibility to deal with change. People have been saying that for years. It's obvious, isn't it? This is a widely accepted view.

Second, this is an attempt to promote a particular perception of organizational reality, based on management values. After all, change is stressful and employees are likely to resist. If we can present a case that is difficult to challenge, then resistance can be avoided and the changes can go ahead more smoothly.

The key to this second reading lies with our use of language. One view of language is that we use it as a tool to communicate observations and understanding. An alternative view is that language creates that understanding, particularly through the concepts that we use. You cannot 'see' twenty different types of snow until you know what they are called and can link those labels to different visual stimuli. In other words, one view of language says that we 'see in order to know'. The alternative view is that we need to know first, before we can 'see'. The implication of this second view, that 'we know to see', is that perceptions can be influenced, or managed, through language.

Consider the 'turbulent world so we must change' argument. What kind language is typically used to support this case? Looking through job advertisements and other organizational communications, note how often the following kinds of statements appear:

- We need to become more *customer orientated*
- Our mission is *excellence*
- We believe in employee *empowerment*
- Our survival depends on *efficiency* and *cost effectiveness*
- *Initiative* and *creativity* are key competencies
- *Flexibility* is the key to competitive success
- We must strive for *continuous improvement*

The 'turbulent world' argument is hard to challenge. Communications of this kind have the potential to lead employees to internalize management values as their own, without question. It is difficult to argue that 'there is so little change in the business environment that we should be developing a rigid bureaucracy', or that 'customers don't matter, let's focus on our own staff'. However, rapid change can be personally and socially damaging; factory and office closures and relocation, loss of jobs, loss of community. An organization that ignores the well-being of its staff may find that it loses customers who feel that they have been given poor service.

Language promotes a particular set of perceptions related to a specific set of values. An organization can have 'difficulties and problems' (negative), or 'challenges and opportunities' (positive). The term 'turbulent world' creates an impression of 'the way things are', of 'it makes sense doesn't it?', of 'that's obvious'. Why experience 'failure' when you can enjoy 'deferred success'? If you can get people to accept this kind of language and these arguments, then language becomes a tool for manipulating perceptions. If we can manipulate perceptions, we can control behaviour because, as argued already, our behaviour depends not on some 'external reality' but on our perception of reality.

This 'second reading' of the 'turbulent world' argument, viewing it as an attempt to manage perception, reflects a change in our understanding of the use of language, not simply to represent the world, but also to create it. This perspective argues that 'reality out there' is not simply waiting to be discovered, but is created in social exchange through language. We don't go out and discover reality. Multiple realities are presented to us through our interactions. What matters is the version of reality in which most people come to believe. The management of perception is thus a tool for 'keeping people in their place' by inhibiting criticism. You cannot criticize something that appears to be, and is widely accepted as, natural, obvious or inevitable without appearing deviant or eccentric yourself.

This argument highlights the existence and value of differences in perception, of multiple perspectives, arguing that no single perspective should be given the privilege of being correct. This also invites us to question the obvious, and the taken-for-granted.

CRITICAL THINKING

We are often 'fed' information in language which reinforces the management definition of reality and justifies decisions in order to make employees compliant. Find examples of managers and politicians using language to make what they have to say more acceptable to their audience and more persuasive (e.g. 'It's obvious to everyone that . . . ').

Perceptual sets and assumptions

Halo effect
an overall assessment of a person which influences our judgement of their other specific characteristics.

The concept of perceptual set, or perceptual expectation, applies to the ways in which we see other people, events and objects. To understand the nature of perception is to understand, at least in part, the sources and nature of many organizational problems. There are two related features of the process of people perception: the halo effect and stereotyping.

The term halo effect was first used by the psychologist Edward Thorndike in 1920. It is a natural human response, on meeting a stranger, to 'size them up', to make judgements about the kind of person they are, and whether we will like them or not. On meeting someone, we make reasonably accurate judgements of age, sex, and emotional state, and we also automatically start to assess characteristics such as their dominance and trustworthiness, even if those evaluations are not necessary. It takes one-tenth of a second to reach these first impressions, based on aspects of appearance, such the shape of their jawline and the width of their eyebrows (Vernon, et al., 2014).

When we meet someone for the first time – the physical and social setting, their appearance, what they say, how they say it, their posture, non-verbal behaviour, how they respond to us – we must be selective. In terms of our model of the perceptual process (Figure 8.1), the halo effect can create errors at the selective attention stage. Our judgements can rely on a particular

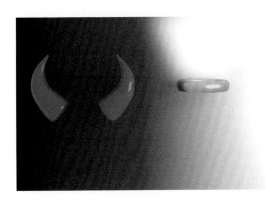

feature: a familiar accent, a perfume, dress or tie, hairstyle. If our judgement is favourable, we give that other person a positive halo. We may then overlook further information that could lead us to a different, more balanced, evaluation. If our judgement, on the other hand, is not favourable, we give the other person a negative halo (or horns). The halo effect can work in both directions.

The halo effect can act as an early screen that filters out later information which is not consistent with our earlier judgement. The problem, of course, is that what we notice first about another person is often not relevant to the judgement that we want to make. Another problem is that we tend to judge more favourably people who are similar to us. However, since when did somebody's voice, hairstyle, deodorant or clothes enable us to predict, say, their ability to design bridges, or manage a hotel? Some people feel that they can make predictions from such limited evidence, based presumably on their own past experiences.

Organizations can also benefit from the halo effect. Harrison Hong and Inessa Liskovich (2015) found that American companies with comprehensive corporate social responsibility (CSR) policies were treated more leniently following prosecutions for corrupt practices than companies with weak CSR programmes. As prosecutors had limited personal knowledge of the companies concerned, the researchers attribute these outcomes to the halo effect ('good CSR, good image, good company').

Warm and cold halos

If we have an overall positive evaluation of someone, we are more likely to perceive that their specific attributes are positive, too. This is known as the *halo effect*. Richard Nisbett and Timothy Wilson (1977, pp. 244–45) demonstrated the power of this phenomenon in a famous experiment.

Subjects in their experiment were shown an interview exploring education practices with a teacher who spoke English with a European accent. Half of the subjects saw the teacher answering these questions in a 'warm' way: pleasant, friendly, enthusiastic. The other half saw the same teacher answering the same questions, but in

a 'cold' way: autocratic, rigid, intolerant. The subjects were then asked to rate how likeable they found the teacher, and rated him on three other factors that were the same in the two experimental conditions; his physical appearance, mannerisms, and accent.

Those who had seen the 'warm' lecturer liked him much better than those who saw the 'cold' one. Most of the subjects who saw the 'warm' version also rated his appearance, mannerisms, and accent as attractive. Subjects who saw the 'cold' teacher rated those other qualities as irritating.

Stereotype
a category, or personality type to which we allocate people on the basis of their membership of some known group.

The term stereotype was first used by typographers who made up blocks of type, and was used to describe bias in person perception by Walter Lippmann in 1922. The concept refers to the way in which we group together people who seem to share similar characteristics. Lippmann saw stereotypes as 'pictures in the head', as simple mental images of groups and their behaviour. So, when we meet, say, an accountant, a nurse, an engineer, a poet, or an engineering student, we attribute certain personality traits to them because they belong in one of those groups. Everybody knows, for example, that Scots are mean, and blondes have more fun. In terms of the model in Figure 8.1, therefore, stereotyping is an error at the perceptual organization stage in the process of perception.

If we know, or assume, somebody's group membership (engineer, nurse), our quick categorization allows us to attribute qualities to them. Stereotypes are often false, but they can be helpful. By adopting a stereotyped perspective, we shortcut our evaluation process, and make quicker predictions of behaviour. We can have problems, however, with those who fall into more than one category with conflicting stereotypes: the engineer who writes poetry, for example.

The magazine *People Management* (2014) reviewed research evidence concerning a number of common stereotypes. Most turned out to be false, including 'older workers are not good with technology', 'women are not suited to manual work', and 'young people don't like being told what to do'. Age presents few barriers to learning new skills; the concept of 'women's work' is based on attitudes not on abilities; and 'Millennials' have attitudes to authority (and the need for guidance) that are similar to other generations. Only two of the stereotypes examined were supported by the evidence: 'Asians are better at mathematics', and 'good-looking people are more successful'.

Self-fulfilling prophecy
a prediction that becomes true because someone expects it to happen.

Another perceptual shortcut is the self-fulfilling prophecy. For example, if you predict an avalanche in a loud voice under a large and loose overhang of snow, your prediction is likely to come true. The quickest way to create a fuel crisis is to have a government spokesperson announce that 'motorists are advised not to start panic-buying petrol'. This phenomenon applies to other aspects of human behaviour. If we expect people to be lazy, apathetic and careless, and treat them accordingly, we are likely to find that they respond to that treatment by displaying those behaviours. The reverse can also be true; if we treat people as though we expect them to be motivated, enthusiastic, and competent, then they are likely to respond accordingly. We will meet this phenomenon again in **Chapter 9** in our discussion of motivation, in Douglas McGregor's contrast between Theory X and Theory Y.

CRITICAL THINKING

You are a student. What is the popular stereotype of a student? What characteristics are you supposed to have? What behaviours are expected of you? Is this a positive, favourable stereotype, a negative, critical one, or is it balanced? Is this stereotype broadly accurate, as far as you are concerned, or is it biased and false? How do you feel about being stereotyped?

What stereotypes do you have of other groups, occupations and people? Are those positive or negative? To what extent are they based on experience and evidence? How would you expect those others to respond if you revealed your stereotype to them?

Appearance, age and attributions

Appearance bias can cost you £1,500 a year

Short men and overweight women earn less than their taller and slimmer colleagues. Researchers at the University of Exeter collected information on 120,000 people, aged between 40 and 70, for whom height and weight data were available through the UK Biobank, along with information from the participants themselves. Men who were 3 inches (7.5 centimetres) shorter than the national average, for no other reason than genetics, were likely to have an income that was £1,500 per year less than taller colleagues. Women who were 1 stone (6.3 kilos) heavier than average were also likely to have an income £1,500 less per year than their slimmer colleagues (Tyrrell et al., 2016).

This is the result of 'appearance bias', which leads to discrimination on the basis of height, weight, and other characteristics, such as age and attractiveness – none of which are covered by legislation (as are sex and race). The bias may be unconscious, but those who are involved in recruitment and selection need to be aware of this, in order to avoid rejecting well-qualified candidates.

 **STOP AND SEARCH**   YouTube for *Short man, or overweight woman? Your size could make you poorer* (3:39).

Attribution

the process by which we make sense of our environment through our perceptions of causality.

We said earlier that the perceptual process is concerned with making sense of and explaining the world around us, and the people and events in it. Our need for explanation and understanding is reflected in the way in which we search for the causes of people's actions. Our perceptions of causality are known as attributions.

An attribution is a belief about the cause or causes of an event. Attribution theory was developed by Fritz Heider (1958) and Harold Kelley (1971). They argue that our understanding of our social world is based on our continual attempts at causal analysis based on how we interpret our experiences.

Why is that person successful? Why did that project fail? If we understand the causes of success and failure, we may be able to adjust our behaviour accordingly. Attribution is simply the process of attaching causes or reasons to the actions and events we see. We tend to look for causes either in people's abilities and personalities, or in aspects of the circumstances in which they find themselves. This distinction can be described in terms of internal causality and external causality. We may explain an individual's success, or promotion, with reference to their superior skills and knowledge (internal causality), or with reference to luck, powerful friends, and coincidence (external causality).

Research has revealed patterns in our attributions. When we explain our achievements (exam success), we point to our personal capabilities, but when we are explaining our lack of success, we blame our circumstances (poor teaching). This is known as *projection*. We project blame onto external causes that are beyond our control. However, we tend to attribute the behaviour of others to aspects of their personality and capabilities. We met *the fundamental attribution error* in **Chapter 1**. This refers to the tendency to exaggerate the disposition and personality of the individual rather than the context in which they find themselves – explaining company success in terms of the chief executive's leadership, rather than the buoyant economy.

Appearance bias

Attribution theory can explain discrimination in organizational settings. For example, sex and appearance affect how we are paid and promoted. In Britain, Barry Harper (2000) studied over 11,000 people (belonging to the long-term National Child Development Study) aged 33 to determine the effects of looks, height and obesity on pay. This study confirmed that attractive people, men and women, earn more, and that tall men earn substantially more. Height is slightly less important for women. Tall men earn 10 per cent more than men of average height, but tall women earn only 5 per cent more. Employers in China prefer taller employees, who are often paid more for the same job as shorter colleagues. Tall Chinese security guards, for example, are more highly paid because they make people feel safer than do short guards (*The Economist*, 2015).

The term 'aesthetic labour' has been used to refer to the ways in which managers sometimes try to control the appearance of employees. This can include directives concerning, for example, facial expressions (smile, use eye contact), modes of speech and accent, style of dress, the colour of clothing and shoes, hairstyles, accessories such as jewellery – and body art (piercings, tattoos). Employees can suffer discrimination based on their appearance, and managers can thus be accused of 'lookism'. Elias et al. (2018) argue that, given the widespread use of photography and social media, women in particular are increasingly required to pay careful attention to their appearance.

Unattractive men earn 15 per cent less than colleagues with average looks, while unattractive women earn 11 per cent less. Obese women earn 5 per cent less than those of average weight, but obese men are not affected. While widespread, the benefits of height and the costs of being unattractive were more common in 'white collar' occupations. For women, a 15 per cent penalty for being unattractive was most common in secretarial and clerical jobs. Attractive men in customer-facing sales roles earned 13 per cent more, while tall men in 'high touch' positions earned 25 per cent more. Some commentators are critical of 'beauty bias', putting appearance before capability, and see this as another form of unfair discrimination at work.

Why should appearance affect career progression? Our attributions are related to our stereotypes. We seem to attribute explanations of people's behaviour to aspects of their appearance. Discrimination against particular groups and individuals, on the basis of sex, sexual orientation, age or ethnic origin, is now widely recognized, but legislation addresses only sexual and racial discrimination. Social attitudes towards the LGBT community and the elderly in organizational settings do appear, slowly, to be changing. However, attribution research suggests that discrimination, based on our perceptions of causal links between sex, appearance and job performance, are more subtle, and less public.

Tattoo or not tattoo

How do you feel about people with tattoos? Body art has become popular, and many managers themselves have (often hidden) tattoos and piercings (other than in their ears). How do you think that body art will affect your job prospects? Research in the past has suggested that anyone with tattoos or piercings will be less employable, because they are seen as unreliable and aggressive. These attributions may be changing, but the stigma and prejudice persists.

Look at these images of employees with tattoos. Do you see this woman and this man as competent, reliable, conscientious – or as lacking in skill, unreliable, less conscientious? Share your assessment with colleagues. How do you think your parents and grandparents would respond to these images?

With respect to attractiveness, sex, height and weight, we are dealing with factors which cannot have any meaningful impact on performance for most jobs or occupations. The tall, attractive female computer programmer of average weight may be more effective in her job than the short, overweight male programmer with the unremarkable features. A moment's thought, however, would probably lead us to reject height, weight and attractiveness as causal factors here, and lead us to look for differences in education, experience and ability instead. The problem is that we make attribution errors by jumping quickly and unconsciously to judgements of this kind, particularly when we have little information about the other person on which to base a more careful assessment.

What did he find? Can tattoos improve your job prospects?

? Andrew Timming (2017) is interested in the role of body art in customer-facing roles. This is significant because of the sharp rise in the number of people who have tattoos. Most research suggests that visible tattoos can damage your job prospects, because they signal rebellion, aggression, promiscuity, and other negative traits which could annoy customers, especially in service sector jobs. But can tattoos sometimes be beneficial? Timming conducted two studies. First, 190 managers were asked to rate photographs of the tattooed faces of male and female applicants for a job as either a server in a fine dining restaurant or a bartender in a nightclub. Second, 20 interviews were held with managers, tattooed front line

Andrew Timming

employees, and customers in two service sector firms – a skateboard shop and a public house – whose customers were mostly under 35 years of age. Most of the customers who were interviewed had tattoos themselves.

What did he find? Does visible body art always make you less employable? Can tattoos ever be an asset? Are some tattoos more acceptable than others? Are men and women with visible body art perceived differently when seeking employment? **(Answers in chapter Recap.)**

Stereotypes and age discrimination

Organizations in most countries face an ageing population, as life expectancy increases, and fewer younger employees join the labour market (see **Chapter 2**). Many employers will thus rely on people working beyond the traditional retirement age. However, older workers are stereotyped as less motivated, poor performers, expensive, with poor technology skills and a limited ability to learn. Research has shown these perceptions to be false. One common belief is that older workers are more resistant to change. A German study found that older employees were *less* resistant to change than younger colleagues (Kunze et al., 2013). This could be because older workers have better strategies for coping with and adapting to changing organizational environments.

The stereotype of younger workers also has negative elements, as they are often perceived as being disloyal, inexperienced, unmotivated, immature, irresponsible and selfish. Younger workers are rated lower than older employees on traits such as conscientiousness, emotional stability and agreeableness, and are not seen as good 'organizational citizens' (Marchiondo et al., 2016).

But younger workers are more likely to be stronger, ready for change, eager to learn, capable with technology, and creative. Older workers tend to be more engaged, loyal, client-focused, and have better social skills. In other words, these different sets of capabilities can be seen as *complementary*. We need to look beyond the stereotypes, at the attributes of the workforce as a whole.

CUTTING EDGE   How old you look matters more than how old you are

Michèle Kaufmann

Michèle Kaufmann and colleagues (2016) wanted to know if 'facial age appearance' – how old you look, regardless of your actual age – can contribute to age discrimination. It is known that we make judgements about others based on their facial features. For example, signs of ageing, such as lines across the forehead or bags under the eyes, can lead others – mistakenly – to believe that you are tired, stressed or not coping. The researchers designed an online experiment in which 500 participants from Switzerland, Germany, and Austria were asked to assess applicants' suitability for an age- and gender-neutral job (travel agent). Some applications included the candidate's date of birth and age, but others only suggested the applicant's age with a portrait photograph. The researchers used six photographs of younger people, three male and three female. These were 'morphed' with ageing software to create an older looking version of each person ('older' in this study meant 52 to 62 years of age).

They found that candidates who *looked* older were perceived to have lower health and fitness compared to those who looked younger. Younger applicants were thus more likely to be hired. However, selection intentions for those candidates whose age was revealed only through their photograph were even less favourable than for those whose date of birth was shown. In other words, regardless of your actual age, the older you look, the less chance you have of being hired.

✓✓✓   **EMPLOYABILITY CHECK** (Self-Management, Interpersonal Skills)

Do you recognize your own biases in the assumptions that you make about other people? How can you control these? The person who is interviewing you for a job asks you for your view of older workers as suitable employees. Comments they have made lead you to believe that they have a negative stereotype of older workers. How will you respond to their question?

Any aspect of our appearance – including tattoos – is a form of *non-verbal communication* (**Chapter 7**). We cannot control our age, or height, but these factors, combined with behaviour that is under our control, send signals that others decode in the light of their experiences (age is related to reliability), expectations (tall and handsome means self-confident and knowledgeable), and prejudices (short and overweight women deter customers). This also applies to clothing, which is under our control. Dress can indicate organizational culture, and can contribute significantly to the individual's *impression management* (**Chapter 7**). The way in which we dress can tell others how we want to be seen (as formal, relaxed, creative, businesslike) rather than what we are really like. However, we may not always be aware how others perceive our attempts to manage our impression through our appearance.

Perceptual errors and how to avoid them

As we said at the beginning of the chapter, it is our *perceptions* of circumstances, events, and other people which influence our judgements, decisions and actions. However, we have seen how our perceptions can often lead to inaccurate judgements and inappropriate decisions and actions. In order to avoid perceptual errors, we need to be aware of how these can arise, and how we can be misled.

Will you pass the 'posh test'?

You may not get that job even if you have the capabilities. A lot depends on how you are perceived by the person who interviews you. A study by the UK Social Mobility and Child Poverty Commission found that elite law, accountancy and financial services organizations discriminate against working-class applicants (Ashley et al., 2015). Although a degree from an elite university was taken as a 'signal for quality', recruiters looked for a number of other characteristics including 'personal style, accent and mannerisms, adaptability, teamworking and other soft skills' (p.25). These criteria give applicants from middle and upper class backgrounds an advantage. The press accused these companies of using a 'posh test' to choose candidates (Churchard, 2015).

Asked about interviewing applicants with working-class backgrounds, one employer said, 'Is there a diamond in the rough out there? It's highly probable, but how much mud do I have to sift through in that population to find that diamond?' (Ashley et al., 2015, p.45). Another employer said, of a recent recruit, 'She's short of polish. We need to talk about the way that she articulates, the way that she chooses words and the way she pronounces them.

It will need some polish because whilst I may look at the substance, I've got a lot of clients and a lot of colleagues who are very focused on the personal presentation and appearance side of it' (p.46). It is perhaps not surprising that a successful working-class candidate admitted to covering up his background, and to adjusting his accent saying that, 'It's about having the skill to adapt to your environment. When I went home, I went back to my old slight twang. When I'm in this environment, I pretend I'm posher than I am' (p.71).

A study by Lauren Rivera (2015) uncovered the same perceptual biases in American banking, law and consulting companies, where graduates from affluent backgrounds get the best jobs. Rivera suggests how less privileged candidates can create the perception that they do fit in, by studying the organization to which they have applied, exploiting connections with 'insiders', not appearing eccentric, preferring team sports (a sign of a 'rounded character'), telling stories about how they 'triumphed against the odds', and showing self-confidence. Style is just as important as substance.

The main sources of errors in person perception include:

1. Not collecting enough information
2. Allowing visual cues to dominate our assessments
3. Seeing what we expect and want to see, and not investigating further – *selective attention*
4. Basing our judgements on particularly favourable pieces of information – *the halo effect*
5. Categorizing others on the basis of specific attributes – *stereotyping*
6. Basing our judgements on information that is irrelevant or insignificant
7. Allowing early information to colour our judgement, despite later contradictory information
8. Allowing our own characteristics to influence our judgements of others
9. Attempting to decode non-verbal behaviour outside the context in which it appears

The steps we need to take to avoid making perceptual errors thus include:

1. Take more time, avoid instant judgements, do not let visual cues dominate.
2. Collect and consciously use more information about other people.
3. Develop self-knowledge, and an understanding of how our personal biases and preferences affect our perceptions and judgements of others.
4. Check your attributions – the assumptions you make about the causes of behaviour, and the links between personality and appearance on the one hand and behaviour on the other.

It's not what you hear, it's the way that you see it

Chia-Jung Tsay (photo by Neal Hamberg)

Our perceptions (of someone's intelligence and trustworthiness, for example) can be influenced by factors that have little or no relevance (height and attractiveness). But when we are asked to judge the quality of music, surely nothing matters but the sound – the *auditory* cues. Chia-Jung Tsay (2013; 2014) argues that such judgements actually depend more on what we see – on *visual* cues.

In one experiment, 118 'novices' with no training in classical music were exposed to six-second excerpts from recordings of international chamber ensemble competitions, and asked to choose which they thought was the winning ensemble in each case. Participants were divided into three groups. One group watched the video-only version. One heard the sound-only recording. The third had video-and-sound. Questioned afterwards, over 80 per cent of participants said that, in judging these performances, the sound was critical. However, participants who only saw the recordings quickly identified the winning ensembles. Participants who were given the sound-only, or video-and-sound recordings, were less able to identify which ensembles had won. Participants who watched the full video-and-sound recordings were no better than chance at picking the competition winners.

With video, one can see the passion, the gestures, and the group interactions that produce a winning performance. Were the original competition judges influenced as much as what they saw as what they heard? Or perhaps the musical novices in this experiment relied more heavily on those visual cues. Tsay repeated the experiment, this time using 193 experienced professional musicians. Once again, over 80 per cent said that the music was the critical factor. However, as with the novices, the professionals who were shown the video-only recordings were able to identify the winning ensembles; the choices of those who were exposed to sound-only or video-and-sound were no better than chance.

These experiments demonstrate the powerful effect of visual cues on our perceptions and judgements, even in situations where we would expect auditory cues to be more important. Other research has shown that our impressions of the personalities and capabilities of others are influenced by aspects of their appearance. It is therefore important to recognize the visual bias in our perceptions, and to take this into account, particularly when making selection and promotion decisions. Tsay (2014, p. 30) concludes that, 'This research suggests that the ultimate music ensemble astounds not its listeners, but its viewers'. Does this also apply to 'the ultimate chief executive'?

 STOP AND SEARCH YouTube for *Musicians' moves matter more than their sound* (0:52), and *Try The McGurk Effect* (3:26).

 **RECAP**

1. *Identify the main features of the process of perception.*

   - People behave according to how they perceive the world, not in response to 'reality'.

   - The perceptual process involves the interpretation of sensory input in the light of past experience, and our store of knowledge, beliefs, expectations and motives.

2. *Distinguish between the bottom-up processing of sensory information and the top-down interpretation of that information.*

   - Sensation, or bottom up processing, determines the data to which we pay attention.

   - Perception, or top down processing, determines the way in which we organize and interpret perceived information in order to make behavioural choices.

3. *Understand the nature and implications of selective attention and perceptual organization.*

   - Selective attention is influenced by external factors relating to the stimulus and the context, and by internal factors such as learning, personality and motivation.

- The way in which we organize and interpret sensory data in meaningful ways, even when it is incomplete or ambiguous, is known as perceptual organization.

4. *Give examples of how behaviour is influenced by our perceptions.*

- We each have our own perceptual world, an internal mental image of our environment.

- Different cultures lead to differences in perception and consequently in behaviour.

5. *Explain and illustrate the main processes and problems in perception, including false attributions, halo effects and stereotyping.*

- An attribution is a belief about cause and effect. When speaking about ourselves, we tend to attribute success to personal factors and failure to external factors. When speaking about others, we tend to attribute success and failure to personality features.

- Making a favourable judgement of someone on the basis of a single positive characteristic is known as the halo effect, and is called the horn effect if the judgement is negative.

- Assuming that someone possesses a set of personality traits because they belong to a particular social group is known as stereotyping.

6. *Explain some less widely appreciated sources of discrimination at work arising from characteristics of the person perception and attribution processes.*

- Aspects of behaviour are attributed to appearance, leading to discrimination. You are likely to be paid less at work if you are an overweight or underweight female, a short man, and are perceived to be unattractive.

- The fundamental attribution error leads us to emphasize individual personality and ignore social and organizational context when explaining behaviour.

7. *Suggest ways to improve perceptual accuracy and avoid errors.*

- To avoid mistakes, avoid rapid judgements, take more time, collect more information, be aware of your own prejudices and biases, and develop increased self-awareness.

- To improve accuracy, expect errors to occur, use as much feedback as you can get, and take small steps rather than radical ones to reduce risks.

RECAP: What did he find? Can tattoos improve your job prospects?

Timming (2017) found that:

- Tattooed applicants were rated as less employable in the fine dining restaurant, and as more employable as a nightclub bartender.

- For the nightclub job, tattooed women were rated as more employable than tattooed men.

- The managers of the skateboard shop and the public house were both 'pro-tattoo', encouraging staff to be individualistic in their appearance. None of the study's participants expressed negative views of tattooed women, but noted the negative perceptions held by society at large.

- Skateboard shop customers thought that tattooed staff were more likely to know about the products and 'skateboarding culture'. Staff felt that their tattoos helped them to 'bond' with customers who were also mostly tattooed.

- Like the skateboard shop customers, public house customers saw the pub staff tattoos as a sign of creativity, indicating 'counter culture' values similar to their own.

- Not all tattoos are acceptable. Customers said that body art was unacceptable if it was racist, homophobic, sexual, satanic, misogynistic, fascist, nationalist, sectarian, or related to drugs and alcohol. Tattoo location is important; one respondent said, 'A face tattoo is too much'.

- Tattoos increase employability if they fit with the 'brand personality' of the business, where tattooed employees can promote relationships with mostly younger tattooed customers.

Revision

1. Explain the distinction between sensation and perception. What is the significance of this distinction?

2. What is the individual's perceptual world? What factors influence this construct, and how does an understanding of someone's perceptual world help us to understand their behaviour?

3. How can an organization's selection, appraisal, and promotion processes be affected by errors and biases in perception? How can these errors and biases be overcome?

4. How can attribution theory help us to explain whether or not people with body art (tattoos, piercings) are perceived as employable?

Research assignment

Look carefully at the style of dress and appearance of the instructors in your educational institution, across all the subjects that you are studying. How does their appearance affect your perceptions of their:

• Approachability

• Subject knowledge

• Professionalism

• Understanding of the world beyond the academic 'ivory tower'

Write a report that first identifies specific aspects of your instructors' dress and appearance that lead you to make judgements on those criteria. Conclude your report with advice to instructors on how they could change their dress and appearance to improve the ways in which they are perceived by students on those criteria – to make them appear more approachable, more professional, and so on.

Springboard

Daniel S. Hamermesh (2011) *Beauty Pays: Why Attractive People are More Successful,* New Jersey: Princeton University Press. Handsome men earn 4 per cent more than average-looking men, and unattractive men earn up to 13 per cent less. The laws of 'pulchronomics' also apply to women. Attractive workers may attract more customers, so perhaps they should be paid more. Hamermesh argues that those who are unattractive should have legal protection.

Heidi Grant Halvorson (2015) 'Managing yourself: a second chance to make a first impression', *Harvard Business Review,* 93 (1/2): 108–11. Advice on what to do if you made a *bad* first impression. Provide positive information. Compliment the person on their fairness and open-mindedness. Make yourself indispensable. Offer to help when they are under pressure.

Alexander Todorov (2017) *Face Value: The Irresistible Influence of First Impressions.* New Jersey: Princeton University Press. If you show people pictures of two politicians for only a 30th of a second, and ask them which is more competent, you can predict around three quarters of election results. Looking more capable than your opponent wins an extra five per cent of the vote. Looking more attractive adds 10 to 20 per cent. Todorov argues that, although we may think that we can judge strangers from their facial features, we are usually wrong.

OB cinema

Legally Blonde (2001, director Robert Luketic). DVD track (scene) 8; 0:21:17 to 0:22:46 (3 minutes). Clip begins with the tutor saying, 'OK, welcome to law school'; clip ends with Elle saying, 'Whoever said that orange was the new pink was seriously disturbed'.

This movie tells the story of a blonde sorority queen, Elle Woods (played by Reece Witherspoon), whose boyfriend leaves her to go to Harvard Law School. To get him back, she goes to Harvard, too. Every character in this movie plays a stereotyped role. In this clip, on the law school lawn, Elle and three of her classmates are asked by a tutor to introduce themselves. As you watch the clip, observe the five characters carefully and:

1. Decide on an appropriate stereotype label (e.g. 'absent-minded professor') for each character.

2. Explain why you have chosen that label, based on the evidence that each character provides (what they say, how they say it, appearance, non-verbal behaviour).

3. For each character, identify two adjectives that you think would describe how they would be likely to interact socially with others.

4. Think about each of those characters in an organizational context, assess what you feel would be their strengths and their weaknesses.

Chapter exercises

1. Person perception

Objective   To explore factors influencing our perception of other people. Research has shown, for example, that we assess others' characters from their faces. These assessments include how friendly, aggressive, trustworthy and creditworthy another person is. The judgements that we reach based on such apparently limited information often turn out to be correct.

Briefing   1. Break into groups of three.

2. Your instructor will give you five or six photographs of people, taken from recent newspapers and magazines. You have five minutes to work out as much as you can about each of these people, using only what you can see in the picture. Consider characteristics such as their:

   conscientiousness

   sense of humour, fun

   intelligence

   aggressiveness

   approachability

   reliability

   other characteristics suggested by the photographs

3. Prepare a presentation based on your photographs and your assumptions. Explain clearly which items of evidence from the photographs led you to make those assessments.

2. You're the interviewee: what would you do?

You are about to go for a job interview, but first you will be kept waiting in the interviewer's office. During that time, you can observe clues about your interviewer and

→

perhaps about the organization. What clues do you think are significant and revealing? What personal experiences in your own past affect how you observe and make judgements in this setting?

This exercise can be completed in class time, but is more effective if steps 1 to 3 are completed in advance. For a one-hour tutorial, time will be tight without preparation.

Step 1   Read *The manager's room description* which follows, to get a feel for the setting in which you find yourself.

Step 2   Complete the analysis sheet.

- In the *data* column, record those observations that you find significant and revealing about the kind of person who occupies this room.

- In the *inferences* column, note the perceptions or conclusions that you reach from your data.

- In the *experiences* column, record past experiences, incidents or events, recent or distant, that you think affect your inferences.

Data I observe in the room	The inferences that I make from those observations	Based on my experiences of/in (e.g. work, films, TV, online)

Step 3   Using that analysis, construct a profile of your interviewer.

Step 4   Finally, record your answers to the following questions:

1. What is the sex, marital status, and ethnic background of the managing director? Identify the data in the room that lead you to your inferences.

2. How would you describe the managing director's character? What are this person's interests? What would you expect this person's management style to be like? Once again, identify the data on which you base these judgements.

3. Given your own personality, do you think that you would be happy working for this person?

4. Explain how your analysis illustrates the concepts of selective attention, perceptual organization, perceptual world, halo effect, and stereotyping.

Step 5   Present your findings, according to your Instructor's directions.

The manager's room description

You are now in the Acme Holdings company offices, top floor, for your job interview. It sounds like your ideal position. As personal assistant, you will be working for the managing director who has asked to interview you. You have arrived on time, but the managing director's secretary apologizes and tells you there will be a delay. The managing director has been called to an important meeting which will take up to 15 minutes. The secretary tells you that you are welcome to wait in the managing director's private office, and shows you in.

You know that you will be alone here for 15 minutes. You look around the room, curious about the person with whom you may be working. The shallow pile carpet is a warm pink, with no pattern. You choose one of six high-backed chairs, upholstered in a darker fabric that matches well with the carpet and curtains, and with polished wooden arms. In the centre of the ring of chairs is a low glass-topped coffee table. On the wall behind you is a large photograph of a vintage motor car, accompanied by its driver in leather helmet, goggles, scarf and long leather coat; you can't make out the driver's face. The window ledge holds four plants arranged equal distances apart; two look like small exotic ferns and the others are a begonia and a geranium in flower.

On the other side of the room sits a large wooden executive desk, with a black leather chair. There are some papers on the desk immediately in front of the chair. A framed copy of the company's mission statement hangs on the wall behind the desk, and below that sits a black leather briefcase with combination locks. The plain grey waste basket by the wall beside the desk is full of discarded paper. There is a thick pile of what looks like committee minutes at the front of the desk, with a pad of yellow 'post-it' notes on the top, and a Mont Blanc pen with the Acme company logo on the barrel. To the side are a laptop computer and a desk lamp. In front of the lamp sits a metal photograph frame holding two pictures. One is of an attractive woman in her thirties with a young boy around eight years old. The other photograph is of a retriever dog in a field to the side of some farm buildings.

On the other side of the desk is a delicate china mug. In front of it lie what look like a leather-covered notebook or perhaps a diary, and a passport. A copy of the *Financial Times* newspaper sits beside the notebook. You see that there is no telephone on the desk. Behind the desk is a small glass-fronted display case. There are some books lined up on top of the case: *Gen Z @ Work: How the Next Generation is Transforming the Workplace, The Oxford Concise Dictionary of Quotations, Managing Difficult Interactions,* and *Win: When Business Works for Women It Works for Everyone.* Also on top of the case sits a small bronze statue, of a man sitting with his legs crossed in a Yoga position. Inside the case, there are computing systems manuals and books and pamphlets on employment law, many of which deal with race and sex discrimination issues.

You decide to get up and look out the window. There is a three-seater settee under the window, covered in the same fabric as the armchairs with matching scatter cushions in the corners. From the window you can see people shopping and children playing in the nearby park. You turn to another table beside the settee. Some magazines sit in front of a burgundy ceramic lamp with a beige shade. There are two recent copies of *The Economist,* and a copy each of *Asia Today, Classic CD* and *Fortune.* As you head back to your chair, you notice that the papers on the desk in front of the chair are your job application and curriculum vitae. Your first name, obviously indicating your sex, has been boldly circled. As the Managing Director may return at any moment, you go back and sit in your chair to wait.

References

Ashley, L., Duberley, J., Sommerlad, H. and Scholarios, D. (2015) *A Qualitative Evaluation of Non-Educational Barriers to the Elite Professions.* London: Social Mobility and Child Poverty Commission.

Churchard, C. (2015) 'Posh test bars working-class talent from top jobs, finds study', *People Management,* 15 June, http://www.cipd.co.uk/pm/peoplemanagement/b/weblog/archive/2015/06/15/posh-test-bars-working-class-talent-from-top-jobs-finds-study.aspx [no longer available]

Davis, G. (2014) 'Addressing unconscious bias', *McKinsey Quarterly,* 4: 130–31.

Dubrin, A.J. (2011) *Impression Management in the Workplace: Research, Theory, and Practice.* New York and Abingdon, Oxon: Routledge.

Elias, A.S., Gill, R. and Scharff, C. (2018) *Aesthetic Labour: Rethinking Beauty Politics in Neoliberalism.* London: Palgrave Macmillan.

Harper, B. (2000) 'Beauty, stature and the labour market: a British cohort study', *Oxford Bulletin of Economics and Statistics*, 62(S1): 771–800.

Heider, F. (1958) *The Psychology of Interpersonal Relationships.* New York: John Wiley.

Hong, H. and Liskovich, E. (2015) 'Crime, punishment and the halo effect of corporate social responsibility', Princeton University, Department of Economics.

Kaufmann, M.C., Krings, F. and Sczesny, S. (2016) 'Looking too old?: how an older age appearance reduces chances of being hired', *British Journal of Management*, 27(4): 727–39.

Kelley, H.H. (1971) *Attribution: Perceiving the Causes of Behaviour.* New York: General Learning Press.

Kunze, F., Boehm, S. and Bruch, H. (2013) 'Age, resistance to change, and job performance', *Journal of Managerial Psychology*, 28(7/8): 741–60.

Little, L.M., Major, V.S., Hinojosa, A.S. and Nelson, D.L. (2015) 'Professional image maintenance: how women navigate pregnancy in the workplace', *Academy of Management Journal*, 58(1): 8–37.

Marchiondo, L.A., Gonzales, E. and Ran S. (2016) 'Development and validation of the workplace age discrimination scale', *Journal of Business Psychology*, 31 (4): 493–513.

Nisbett, R.E. and Wilson, T.D. (1977) 'Telling more than we can know: verbal reports on mental processes', *Psychological Review*, 84 (3): 231–59.

People Management (2014) 'Are these stereotypes true?', July, p.24.

Rivera, L.A. (2015) *Pedigree: How Elite Students get Elite Jobs.* Princeton NJ: Princeton University Press.

Simons, D.J. and Ambinder, M.S. (2005) 'Change blindness: theory and consequences', *Current Directions in Psychological Science*, 14(1): 44–48.

Simons, D.J. and Levin, D.T. (1998) 'Failure to detect changes to people in a real-world interaction', *Psychonomic Bulletin & Review*, 5: 644–49.

The Economist (2015) 'The rise of China', 25 October, p.64.

Timming, A.R. (2017) 'Body art as branded labour: at the intersection of employee selection and relationship marketing', *Human Relations*, 70(9): 2041–63.

Tsay, C.-J. (2013). 'Sight over sound in the judgment of music performance', *Proceedings of the National Academy of Sciences*, 110(36), 14580–85.

Tsay, C.-J. (2014) 'The vision heuristic: judging music ensembles by sight alone', *Organizational Behavior and Human Decision Processes*, 124 (1): 24–33.

Tyrrell, J., Jones, S.W., Beaumont, R., Astley, Christina M. and others (2016) 'Height, body mass index, and socioeconomic status: mendelian randomisation study in UK Biobank', *British Medical Journal Online*, 352:i582

Vernon, R.J.W., Sutherland, C.A.M., Young, A.W. and Hartley, T. (2014) 'Modeling first impressions from highly variable facial images', *Proceedings of the National Academy of Sciences*, 111 (32): 3353–61.

CHAPTER 9

Motivation

Key terms

presenteeism

gig economy

drive

motive

motivation

self-determination theory

instrinsic rewards

extrinsic rewards

hierarchy of needs theory

self-actualization

equity theory

expectancy theory

valence

instrumentality

expectancy

total rewards

goal-setting theory

inner work life theory

job enrichment

motivator factors

hygiene factors

vertical loading factors

growth need strength

job diagnostic survey

motivating potential score

employee engagement

high-performance work system

Learning outcomes

When you have read this chapter, you should be able to define those key terms in your own words, and you should also be able to:

1. Understand different ways in which the term motivation is used.

2. Understand how motives and motivation processes influence behaviour.

3. Explain the distinction between content and process theories of motivation.

4. Apply expectancy theory and job enrichment techniques to diagnose organizational problems and to recommend practical solutions.

5. Explain contemporary interest in work motivation, with respect to presenteeism, the gig economy, employee engagement, and high-performance work systems.

Why study motivation?

Your motives – from the Latin *movere*, to move – are key determinants of your behaviour. If we understand your motives (e.g. you would like more leisure time), we can influence your behaviour (e.g. you can take a day off if you finish that assignment). A number of current trends are making the topic of work motivation more important. We have an ageing workforce and a competitive market for skilled employees. Organizations need to be able to motivate older workers to stay beyond the traditional retirement age to make up for shortages of younger workers. How should organizations motivate the Millennials who are now joining the workforce, with different expectations concerning rewards, work–life balance, flexible working, and their relationships with employers **(see Chapter 2)**? How will organizations motivate people to learn new skills and to work with increasingly sophisticated smart technologies – automation, cobots, artificial intelligence **(see Chapter 3)**?

Motivation – a central issue for individuals, organizations, and government

'Work motivation affects the skills that individuals develop, the jobs and careers that individuals pursue, and the manner in which individuals allocate their resources (e.g. attention, effort, time, and human and social capital) to affect the direction, intensity, and persistence of activities during work. At the same time, work motivation is a topic of critical importance to public policymakers and organizations concerned with developing work environments, human resource policies, and management practices that promote vocational adjustment, individual wellbeing, and organizational success. As such, work motivation stands at the nexus of society, science, and organizational success' (Kanfer et al., 2017, p.338).

The question to which most managers want an answer is – can employees be motivated without giving them more money? Douglas McGregor (1960) set out two sets of motivational propositions, which he called 'Theory X' and 'Theory Y'. (McGregor died in 1964, but his terms are still in use, and his ideas remain influential: Judge et al., 2017). To find out which propositions apply to you, complete this questionnaire. Read each pair of statements, and circle the number that reflects your view:

The average person inherently dislikes work	1	2	3	4	5	Work is as natural as rest to people
People must be directed to work	1	2	3	4	5	People will exercise self-discretion and self-control
People wish to avoid responsibility	1	2	3	4	5	People enjoy real responsibility
People feel that achievement at work is irrelevant	1	2	3	4	5	Achievement is highly valued by people
Most people are dull and uncreative	1	2	3	4	5	Most people have imagination and creativity
Money is the only real reason for working	1	2	3	4	5	Money is only one benefit from work
People lack the desire to improve their quality of life	1	2	3	4	5	People have needs to improve their quality of life
Having an objective is a form of imprisonment	1	2	3	4	5	Objectives are welcomed as an aid to effectiveness

Show me the money

Hicks Waldron, when he was chief executive of Avon, once said, 'It took me a long while to learn that people do what you pay them to do, not what you ask them to do' (Aguinis et al., 2013, p.242).

Is money a motivator? Surveys often find that money is not a major factor, but pay does affect whether or not somebody will accept a job offer from one organization, and not a competitor. Reviewing the research evidence, Herman Aguinis et al. (2013) argue that financial rewards can improve motivation and performance in some ways, but not in others.

- *Can do*: Money helps to attract and retain top performers. Financial rewards also meet basic and higher level needs, from food, shelter, and leisure, to group membership, personal development, and status (including the purchase of status symbols). Level of pay itself is often seen as an indicator of social status and achievement.

- *Can't do*: The money cannot improve job-related knowledge, skill, and abilities, unless it is invested in training and development. Paying someone more highly does not mean that they will become smarter and increase their productivity. Higher pay does not make the work itself more meaningful and interesting – which are known motivating factors. Nor does money affect other powerful motivators such as level of autonomy and degree of participation in decision making.

Finally, generous payments do not always lead to good performance. Those on high salaries may misrepresent results in order to protect their earnings. Employees can reduce their performance ('choke') due to fear of failure when they are offered large sums of money. Well-paid staff can develop a sense of entitlement and react negatively when rewards do not meet their expectations. Money can thus motivate undesirable behaviours. Aguinis et al. (2013, p.243) give this example:

'Green Giant, a producer of frozen and canned vegetables, once rewarded its employees for removing insects from vegetables. It was later found that employees began to bring insects from their homes, placed them in the vegetables, and subsequently removed them to receive the monetary rewards.'

In 2016, Wells Fargo, a multinational financial services company, fired over 5,000 staff in its retail banking division because they had created fake accounts without customers' permission. Staff were rewarded for cross-selling financial products to clients, and the fake accounts increased their bonuses. Wells Fargo paid a $185 million fine, and the chief executive John Stumpf resigned (Gray and Jopson, 2016; *The Economist*, 2016).

In making decisions about financial rewards, therefore, it is important to know when and why money will be effective in improving motivation and performance, and how rewards will affect behaviour.

Add up the numbers that you circled to give you a score between 8 and 40. If you scored 16 or less, then you subscribe to Theory X. If you scored 32 or more, then you subscribe to Theory Y. Theory X managers believe in giving orders, direct supervision, and in the motivating power of money. Theory Y managers believe in giving autonomy and responsibility, and in the motivating power of interesting jobs. As an employee, which theory would you like to have applied to you at work?

McGregor argued that Theory Y was a more accurate description of most people's attitudes to work, and that the application of Theory X demotivated people. In other words, non-financial rewards can be as powerful, if not more powerful motivators than money, as we also value recognition, jobs with a worthwhile purpose, flexible working, and personal development.

Presenteeism and the gig economy

Presenteeism working for more hours than required, even when unwell, motivated by a sense of job insecurity, and the desire to appear enthusiastic and committed.

Research into work motivation declined in the 1990s. Ideas developed in the mid- to late twentieth century, however, are still current. Organizations still use the terms and tools from that earlier research. Two other trends suggest that motivation is still an important issue. One concerns *presenteeism*: what motivates people to work more hours than they have to? A second concerns the *gig economy*: what motivates people to work freelance, finding jobs through mobile apps and the internet?

Presenteeism

Organizations have in the past been concerned with absenteeism – employees not turning up for work. Today, there is a new problem – presenteeism. Many employees work longer hours than necessary – arriving early, leaving late – even when they are unwell. This may be due to a 'long hours culture', but presenteeism is also motivated by job insecurity; you may be seen as loyal and conscientious if you spend more time at work. Working long hours can reduce performance and cause health problems, and make existing health conditions worse. A study of 300 employees in a UK utilities company by Zara Whysall et al. (2018) found that employees who come to work when they are ill cost their employers over £4,000 per person each year in lost productivity. Presenteeism accounts for between six and ten times more lost productivity than sickness absence.

Research by the Chartered Institute of Personnel and Development found that presenteeism in the UK has tripled over the past decade while absenteeism has been stable (Sinclair, 2018). In 2018, 86 per cent of 1,000 survey participants said that their organization had experienced presenteeism over the past year, compared to only 26 per cent in 2010. This survey found that 'leavism' – using annual leave to catch up with work – was also a growing problem. Almost 90 per cent of respondents said technology was responsible for staff being unable to switch off outside working hours. The survey also found that few organizations were taking action to discourage unhealthy working practices.

Can presenteeism ever be an advantage? A report by the Institute for Employment Studies argues that the workplace can often help with recovery and rehabilitation, especially for some chronic and psychological conditions (Garrow, 2016). As long as there is no risk of cross-infection, and work will not make a health condition worse, employers should recognize the potential benefits of presenteeism. Garrow also argues that presenteeism is a choice that employees make, and that this choice has a number of organizational drivers and personal motivators.

The organizational drivers of presenteeism include:

- *Concern for others:* where an individual's absence affects others (e.g. in education and healthcare) or increases the workload of colleagues.

- *Management behaviour:* supervisor presenteeism is a role model for staff presenteeism.
- *Work culture:* which encourages long hours, and the belief that taking time off is a sign of poor performance and low commitment.
- *Job insecurity:* which encourages attendance even when an employee is ill.
- *Job demands:* increased work pressure and exhaustion increase presenteeism as employees attempt to cope.

The personal motivators of presenteeism include:

- *Domestic circumstances:* difficult conditions at home.
- *Fear of isolation:* not wanting to suffer alone.
- *Financial worries:* anxiety about loss of income.
- *Individual lifestyle factors:* some people ignore symptoms and avoid medical help.

Death by overwork: presenteeism can be fatal

Parry (2017) tells the story of Miwa Sado, a television reporter in Japan, who died from a heart attack at the age of 31 after working 159 hours of overtime in one month. She had taken only two days off in the month before she died, and had worked 147 hours of overtime the previous month. When her body was discovered, she was still holding her mobile phone. In 2015, a 24-year old Japanese woman killed herself by jumping off her apartment building. She worked for an advertising company, had been pressured into working excess overtime, and suffered depression. The Japanese term for death by overwork is *karoshi.* In 2016, *karoshi* was responsible for 107 deaths in Japan, where surveys also show that 20 per cent of employees work an average of 80 hours overtime a month.

Those who are most at risk of presenteeism can be found at all organizational levels and include managers, those with high sickness absence, people with financial problems, workaholics, insomniacs, highly-skilled professionals, older workers, and people with unhealthy lifestyles (smoking, poor diet, lack of exercise, overweight, high blood pressure).

STOP AND SEARCH   YouTube for *Professor Cary Cooper explains presenteeism* (2:28).

To manage presenteeism, an organization needs a health strategy, which supports employee well-being. However, Garrow (2016) argues that line managers have an even more important role to play, offering support, role modelling healthy behaviours, encouraging employees to report problems, and establishing team cultures that reduce peer pressure for presenteeism. Paradoxically, this is a situation where managers may need to motivate employees to stop working and go home. But managers also need to consider circumstances in which presenteeism is appropriate, and how to help presentees.

The gig economy

Many jobs still need employees to be in the same place most of the time, such as in manufacturing, hospitals, schools, and many service sector jobs. But mobile technology allows many of us to work anywhere. We don't need to commute to the same place and work there from nine to five every day. As long as we have a smartphone, a tablet, or a laptop, we can choose where to work and when, finding jobs online with website such as Upwork, Elance, TaskRabbit, Toptal and Freelancer. This flexibility has created the gig economy, also known as the 'Uberification' of work.

What motivates people to choose gigging? One reason is flexibility – the freedom to decide when to work. But are workers free to choose not to gig? One study found that only 14 per cent worked in the gig economy because they could not find traditional employment (Chartered Institute for Personnel and Development, 2017a). For most workers, therefore, gigging is an individual preference. This report describes several personal experiences of gig economy workers. Mary does short-term secretarial and administrative jobs. Susan uses online platforms to find evening work as a tutor. That study also found that the proportion of the UK adult workforce that was gigging (e.g. performing tasks online, providing transport, delivering food or other goods) was just 4 per cent.

Gig economy a system of employment in which freelance workers sell their skills and services, through online marketplaces, to employers on a project- or task-basis.

Gigging benefits employers, too. Why hire a full-time permanent member of staff when you can employ just the freelance expertise that you need for a specific period of time? This cuts the cost and delay in hiring permanent staff. People working from home don't need car parking or office space. In a downturn, it is easier to stop hiring freelancers than it is to make permanent staff redundant.

The changing world of work

Listen to the *Financial Times* podcast by Sarah O'Connor (2018): 'The changing world of work' (25:00). With the development of the gig economy, is the traditional relationship between employer and employee changing – and how?

What would motivate you to work independently, without the security and social contact of the conventional organization? Well, you won't have to navigate the bureaucracy or the office politics. You will be self-reliant, and have access to a wider variety of clients and tasks than you would in a single organization. Flexibility improves work–life balance, and frees time for personal development, and for caring responsibilities. These trends have many benefits and are desirable.

The gig economy has a dark side. Flexible working, freelancing and gigging may be a lifestyle preference. But this is precarious work; insecurity is the price of flexibility. Looking for gigs can be lonely, financially risky, and leads to a blurring of work and home lives. Freelance workers do not have the same benefits as permanent employees, or the organization's protection should things go wrong. Working gigs, there is little or no prospect of a progressive career. Gigging involves a transfer of risk from employers to employees, who are more likely to deal with individual managers, without the support of a human resource management department. But it seems that, despite these disadvantages, many are motivated by the benefits and the lifestyle.

Drives, motives and motivation

Motivation can be explored from three distinct but related perspectives:

1. *Goals.* What are the motives for our behaviour? Reward, promotion, empowerment, responsibility, personal growth? This perspective views motivation in terms of our desired outcomes or goals, and is explored by *content* theories of motivation.

2. *Decisions.* Why do we choose to pursue certain goals? Why do you study hard to earn distinctions while a friend has a full social life and is happy with pass grades? This perspective views motivation in terms of the cognitive decision-making processes influencing an individual's choice of goals. This question is explored by *process* theories of motivation.

Drive an innate, biological determinant of behaviour, activated by deprivation.

3. *Influence.* How can we get you to work harder? Managers want to motivate employees to turn up on time, to be helpful to customers, 'to go the extra mile'. This perspective views motivation as a social influence process and is explored by *job enrichment* theories.

Do we inherit our goals, or are they acquired through experience? If our motives are innate, then it would be pointless to attempt to change them. If they are acquired, then they can be altered. Our behaviour is influenced by our biological equipment. We appear to have an innate need for survival. Our needs for oxygen, water, food, shelter, warmth and sex can be overpowering. These needs are triggered by deprivation and are known as drives.

Our drives may not be restricted to basic biological needs. Some psychologists claim that we are active sensation-seekers who have the innate cognitive drives listed in Table 9.1.

Table 9.1: Innate cognitive drives

Curiosity	The need to explore, to play, to learn more
Sense-making	The need to understand the nature of the world around us
Order and meaning	The need for order, certainty, equity, consistency, predictability
Effectance or competency	The need to exert mastery and control over the world around us
Self-understanding	The need to know who and what we are

Home viewing: 'good job'

The focal character in *Whiplash* (2014, director Damien Chazelle) is a young drummer, Andrew Neiman (played by Miles Teller) who enrols at the prestigious Schaffer Conservatory of Music. Andrew's goal is to become 'one of the jazz greats', like Buddy Rich. His bandleader and instructor, Terence Fletcher (J.K. Simmons) has high expectations of his students. To push Andrew and others to reach their potential, he uses fear and intimidation, abuse, insults, public humiliation, and physical violence. When a student commits suicide as a result of this pressure, Fletcher is fired by the school. However, he defends his methods:

'Truth is, I don't think people understood what I was doing at Schaffer. I wasn't there to conduct. I was there to push people beyond what's expected of them. I believe that is an absolute necessity. Otherwise we're depriving the world of the next Louis Armstrong. The next Charlie Parker. There are no two words in the English language more harmful than "good job".'

At the end of the movie, Andrew plays an outstanding drum solo. To what extent was Fletcher responsible for that performance? What are the advantages and disadvantages of Fletcher's motivational methods? How widely applicable is this approach?

 **STOP AND SEARCH**   YouTube for *Whiplash 'good job' motivational scene* (2:30).

The drives come with the body. We do not have to learn to be cold, thirsty or hungry. However, we can *override* these drives. Some religious orders inflict celibacy on willing members. Altruism can overcome personal safety needs in extraordinary circumstances. The idea that our behaviour is pre-programmed is too simple. Animal behaviour, in contrast, is triggered largely by instincts. Birds and squirrels cannot override their programming, and remain locked into their niches in nature. We in contrast seek to satisfy our drives in many different ways, which differ between individuals and across cultures. David Zweig (2014), for example, describes those who are not interested in public recognition as 'invisibles'. They are motivated instead by the anonymous reward from pride in the work that they do, such as designing airport signs, making celebrity brand perfumes, or servicing the band's gear so that concerts run smoothly.

Motive a socially acquired goal activated by a desire for fulfilment.

Motives, in contrast to drives, appear to be goals that we acquire through experience.

Polygamy is a crime in most Western cultures, but a sign of male achievement, wealth and status in parts of the Arab world. In some Muslim societies, the consumption of alcohol is punished, but gifts of alcohol are the norm in Western cultures. Our choice of goals and behaviours is influenced by the norms of our society. Those who choose not to conform are often shunned, ridiculed, and sometimes imprisoned. Table 9.2 outlines the distinction between drives (needs) and motives (goals).

Motivation the cognitive decision-making process through which goal-directed behaviour is initiated, energized, directed and maintained.

Motivation is a broad concept which includes preferences for particular outcomes, strength of effort (half-hearted or enthusiastic) and persistence (in the face of problems and barriers).

Table 9.2: **Drives versus motives**

Drives (needs)	Motives (goals)
Innate	Learned
Have a physiological basis	Have a social basis
Activated by deprivation	Activated by environment
Aimed at satiation	Aimed at stimulation

These are the factors that we have to understand in order to explain your motivation and behaviour. These are the factors which a manager has to appreciate in order to motivate employees to behave in desirable ways.

Content theories

Edward Deci

Richard Ryan

Self-determination theory a content theory of motivation which argues that we all have three equally important innate psychological needs for autonomy, competence and relatedness.

Theories of motivation based on drives and needs are known as content theories, because drives and needs are seen as part of our common 'mental luggage'. We will consider two content theories: self-determination theory, and the hierarchy of needs theory.

Self-determination theory

Developed by Edward Deci and Richard Ryan, self-determination theory argues that we have three basic psychological needs, for autonomy, competence, and relatedness (Deci et al., 2017; Ryan and Deci, 2017). These are innate needs, which are therefore not acquired through socialization or experience. Meeting these needs is essential for our psychological growth and well-being, and all three needs are of equal importance. When these three needs are satisfied, our motivation, performance and wellness are increased. Self-determination theory thus addresses the twin goals of organizational performance, and individual well-being defined in terms of life satisfaction, mental and physical health, and vitality (Kanfer et al., 2017).

Autonomy is defined as 'individuals' need to act with a sense of ownership of their behaviour and feel psychologically free' (Van den Broeck et al., 2016, p.1198). In other words, we determine our own actions, which are not controlled by external forces. This does not mean that we need to act independently of others, but that our actions are based on our own preferences and choices – and we can choose whether to meet or to comply with the desires and directions of others. Autonomy is measured by questionnaire items such as: 'The tasks I have to do at work are in line with what I really want to do'.

Competence is defined as the need to feel a sense of mastery over the environment and to develop new skills. Questionnaire item: 'I feel competent at my job'.

Relatedness – concerns the need to feel connected to others, to love and care for, or to be loved and cared for – a need satisfied when we see ourselves as a member of a group with which we have close relations. Questionnaire item: 'At work, I feel part of a group'.

 **STOP AND SEARCH**   YouTube for *Edward Deci: Self-determination theory* (8:03).

Intrinsic rewards
valued outcomes or benefits which come from the individual, such as feelings of satisfaction, competence, self-esteem and accomplishment.

Extrinsic rewards
valued outcomes or benefits provided by others, such as promotion, pay increases, a bigger office desk, praise and recognition.

It helps to distinguish between intrinsic rewards and extrinsic rewards.

Intrinsic rewards are valued outcomes within the control of the individual, such as feelings of satisfaction and accomplishment. For some of us, and for some actions, the outcome is its own (intrinsic) reward. Mountaineers, poets, athletes, authors, painters and musicians are usually familiar with the concept of intrinsic reward. Few people ever get paid for climbing hills, and there are few wealthy poets on this planet. Extrinsic rewards are valued outcomes that are controlled by others, such as recognition, promotion, or pay increases. The relationships between performance and intrinsic reward are more immediate than those between performance and extrinsic reward. Intrinsic rewards are thus more important influences on our motivation to work.

Self-determination theory makes a similar distinction between *autonomous motivation* and *controlled motivation*.

Autonomous motivation	You do something because you want to do it, because you are interested and willing, as a matter of personal choice. The (intrinsic) motivation lies in the activity itself.
Controlled motivation	You do something under pressure, because you have no choice, for financial reward or to avoid punishment. The (extrinsic) motivation lies in the context.

Self-determination theory predicts that controlled motivation leads to a narrowing of effort, a focus on short-term outcomes, low engagement and poor performance. Autonomous motivation, in contrast, is predicted to lead to greater persistence, better performance and improved well-being.

Previous research into motivation and work design has consistently found a desire for greater autonomy at work, and found links between autonomy and performance **(Chapter 14)**. Is there support today for the practical application of self-determination theory? A review of the evidence by Deci et al. (2017) concludes that:

- Autonomous work motivation leads to less stress, emotional exhaustion and burnout and higher job satisfaction and commitment, and to greater knowledge sharing and work performance.

- Indicators of job autonomy predict company profitability – a relationship that is stronger in younger companies than in those which are well-established (employee contribution is presumably more important for companies that are still trying to establish themselves).

- Management support for employee autonomy is important – acknowledging employee perspectives, giving feedback, encouraging initiative, offering challenging assignments.

Is this a Western theory, relevant to individualistic cultures, and not to collectivist cultures such as those in East Asia? Autonomy in self-determination theory is defined in terms of decision and choice, rather than in terms of independence and individualism. Research comparing

South Korea, Russia, Turkey and the United States found that in all of those cultures, when employees were more autonomous in their behaviour, they were psychologically healthier. Research has also suggested that autonomy is important for positive work outcomes in non-individualistic cultures.

What did they find? Work and wellbeing

Erik Gonzalez-Mulé and Bethany Cockburn (2017) have been exploring the effects of job characteristics on health, and in particular on mortality. Over seven years, they studied the wellbeing of over 2,300 employees in Wisconsin who were in their 60s, and still employed. As well as monitoring the health (in some cases death) of their participants, they measured two aspects of their work. The first concerned job demands, including the amount of work, time pressures, and the need for high levels of concentration. The second concerned job control, including discretion over decisions at work. The researchers were interested in the effects of different combinations of high or low demand, and high or low control in their participants' jobs.

What did they find? What effects did these job characteristics have on employee health? Were demanding jobs always unhealthy? And were the health effects small, moderate or significant? **(Answers in chapter Recap.)**

Erik Gonzalez-Mulé

Bethany Cockburn

Hierarchy of needs theory a content theory of motivation which argues that we have innate needs for survival, safety, affiliation, esteem, and self-actualization, and that we pursue higher order needs only once our lower order needs have been met.

Self-actualization the desire for personal fulfilment, to develop one's potential, to become everything that one is capable of becoming.

Self-determination theory has significant implications for organizational pay policy. It has long been known that 'eat what you kill' incentive schemes do not work well (Kohn, 1993). Self-determination theory also claims that, when part of your pay depends on your performance, that can *lower* your intrinsic motivation. Why? Money is not an overriding concern for most of us, and 'bribing' people to perform better with cash incentives can be seen as manipulative. Incentive pay schemes also discourage risk taking and creativity, and undermine interest in the job itself. Extrinsic rewards might buy compliance, but they do not encourage commitment. Pay for performance (PFP) also emphasizes short-term goals, and encourages behaviour that meets those goals whether or not that is best practice. PFP requires constant monitoring and evaluation, which can be demoralizing (Deci et al., 2017).

Hierarchy of needs theory

Self-determination theory is similar in some ways to the hierarchy of needs theory developed by the American psychologist Abraham Maslow (1943; 1954; 1971). Maslow also argued that we have innate needs, and identified nine (Figure 9.1). If our biological and safety needs are not satisfied, we die. If our needs for love and esteem are not satisfied, we feel inferior and helpless, but if these needs are satisfied, we feel self-confident. Self-actualization, Maslow argued, is our ultimate goal, and freedom of inquiry and expression is a prerequisite for this. Aesthetics and transcendence have been ignored by management writers and researchers who have focused instead on self-actualization.

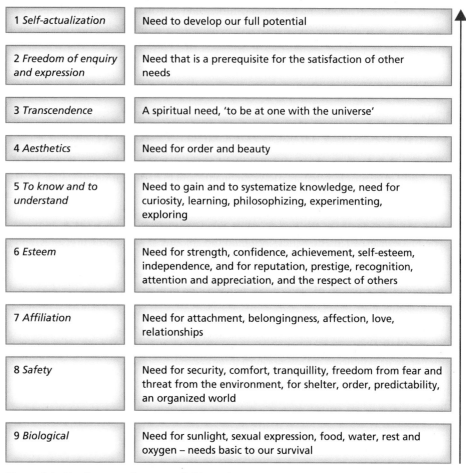

Figure 9.1: Abraham Maslow's needs hierarchy

Maslow argued that self-actualized people are rare, and that creating the conditions for us to develop our capabilities to this extent is a challenging task. Unlike self-determination theory, he argued that these needs are organized in a hierarchy, with lower order biological and safety needs at the bottom, and higher order self-actualization and transcendence needs at the top.

CRITICAL THINKING	How could you use Maslow's framework to explain a friend's preference for either the freedom and flexibility of working freelance in the gig economy, or the security and social contact provided by working in a conventional organization? Is Maslow's explanation satisfactory?

This hierarchy, Maslow argued, has the following properties.

1. A need is not a motivator until those lower in the hierarchy are more or less satisfied. A satisfied need is not a motivator. We have an innate desire to work our way up the hierarchy.

2. Lack of need satisfaction affects mental health. Loss of the respect of others, lack of self-esteem, inability to sustain relationships, and no opportunities to develop one's capabilities lead to frustration, anxiety and depression.

3. The experience of self-actualization stimulates desire for more. Maslow claimed that self-actualizers have 'peak experiences'. When you have had one of these, you want another.

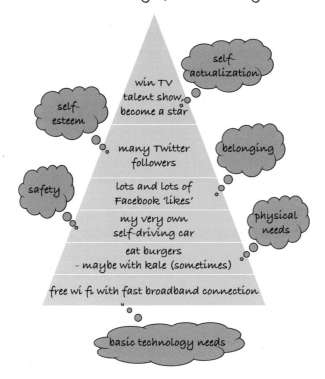

Maslow's hierarchy of 21st century needs

- self-actualization
- win TV talent show, become a star
- self-esteem
- many Twitter followers
- belonging
- safety
- lots and lots of Facebook 'likes'
- my very own self-driving car
- physical needs
- eat burgers - maybe with kale (sometimes)
- free wi fi with fast broadband connection
- basic technology needs

Abraham Maslow in the twenty-first century

Todd Bridgman

Todd Bridgman and colleagues (2018) remind us that Maslow was a psychologist, and not a management scholar or consultant. He wrote about human needs, freedom of inquiry and expression, growth and fulfilment, and about how societies constrain individual creativity. He was not writing about organizational needs. Others have translated his theory into a management tool, to improve productivity and profit. The famous pyramid is not Maslow's either.

Maslow never explained his theory in the form of a pyramid; someone else developed that graphic in the late 1950s. A ladder is a more appropriate metaphor, and closer to Maslow's thinking, because 'multiple rungs are occupied by the feet and hands', and people move up and down a ladder. The pyramid on the other hand, with horizontal lines separating the levels, suggests that we focus on one set of needs at a time as we ascend the pyramid.

Bridgman et al. argue that 'to discard Maslow completely would be a loss, because he really did practise the free and creative thinking that he believed society needed', which is largely absent today:

'Maslow's original question that spurred his motivation theory was not "how can managers motivate workers to maximize productivity and profit", but "what do we need for happiness and fulfilment in life". The test of enlightened management, he believed, was the effect of organizational policies on people's behavior outside of work, in the community. Inspiring the study of management and its relationship to creativity and the pursuit of the common good would be a much more empowering legacy to Maslow than a simplistic, five-step, one-way pyramid' (Bridgman et al., 2018, p.30).

 **STOP AND SEARCH** YouTube for *'Who built Maslow's hierarchy of needs pyramid?'*

Maslow's theory has been criticized as reflecting white American middle class values in the mid-twentieth century. However, Louis Tay and Ed Diener (2011) found that subjective well-being is associated with need fulfilment around the world. They analysed data from the Gallup World Poll which asks about six needs: food and shelter, safety and security, social support, respect and pride, mastery and self-direction. This poll covers over 60,000 people in 123 countries in eight regions: Africa, East and South Asia, Former Soviet Union, Latin America, Middle East, Northern Europe, South East Asia and Southern Europe. Need fulfilment was important for well-being in 80 per cent of those surveyed. A survey of 130 bank managers in Bangladesh also found support for Maslow's needs hierarchy (Rahman and Nurullah, 2014). It seems that the needs identified by Maslow may be universal, and independent of culture.

Maslow's ideas still have a major influence on management practice, particularly concerning rewards, management style and work design. Many techniques such as job enrichment, total quality management, process redesign, self-managing teams, 'new leadership' and engagement have been based on his thinking. Maslow's theory is particularly valuable in recognizing that behaviour depends on a range of needs, drives, and motives.

 EMPLOYABILITY CHECK (work ethic/results orientation, appetite for learning)

How would you describe your own motivation? What needs do you want to satisfy through work? What kinds of work are most likely to meet your needs? If asked, how will you explain your work motivation to a potential employer?

Process theories

Theories of motivation that focus on how we make choices with respect to goals are known as process theories. Unlike content theories, process theories give us a role in deciding our goals and how to pursue them. Individuals are motivated by different outcomes. Cultures encourage different patterns of motivation. Content theories, in contrast, are universalist – applying to everyone regardless of culture. We will explore four process theories of work motivation, *equity theory, expectancy theory, goal-setting theory,* and *inner work life theory.*

Equity theory

Equity theory a process theory of motivation which argues that perception of unfairness leads to tension, which motivates the individual to resolve that unfairness.

Several theorists have argued that we look for a just or equitable return for our efforts. The calculation of what is just or equitable depends on the comparisons we make with others. Equity theory is thus based on our perceptions of fair treatment. Stacy Adams (1963, 1965) argued that we are motivated to act in situations which we perceive to be inequitable or unfair. Inequity occurs when you get either more, or less, than you think you deserve. The theory is based on perceptions of *in*equity, but is traditionally called *equity* theory.

This theory explains behaviour using perceptions of social comparisons. Equity theory argues that, the more intense the perceived inequity, the higher the tension, and the stronger the motivation to act. Adams argues that we respond differently to 'over-reward' and 'under-reward'. We usually see a small over-reward as 'good luck', and do nothing, but a modest under-reward is not easily accepted.

How do you calculate inequity? Adams argued that we compare our rewards (pay, recognition) and contributions (time, effort, ideas) with the outputs and inputs of others. We have equity when these ratios are equal:

$$\frac{\text{my rewards (minus my costs)}}{\text{my efforts and contributions}} = \frac{\text{your rewards (minus your costs)}}{\text{your efforts and contributions}}$$

Rewards can include a range of tangible and intangible factors: pay, status symbols, fringe benefits, promotion prospects, satisfaction, job security. Inputs similarly relate to any factor that you believe you bring to the situation, including age, experience, skill, education, effort, loyalty and commitment. The relative priority or weighting of these various factors depends on the individual's perception.

How do you resolve inequity? Let's imagine that you are serving tables in a restaurant in Gamla Stan (the Old Town) in Stockholm and you discover that Annika is earning 45 Swedish kroner (about US$5.0) an hour more than you, for the same work (about US$200 a week more than you). Table 9.3 shows Adams's seven strategies for reducing this inequity.

Choice of strategy is a sensitive issue, and equity theory does not predict which strategy an individual will choose. Each option has different short and long term consequences. Arguing with your manager, reducing your input, or making Annika do the hard work, may reduce inequity in the short term, but could have long term consequences for your relationships and future employment.

The theory's predictions of behaviour for over- and under-reward are shown in Figure 9.2.

Evidence from laboratory research supports the theory, and confirms that people who are overpaid reduce their perceived inequity by working harder. Studies in real settings also broadly confirm equity theory predictions. Interestingly from a management perspective, perceived equity seems to lead to greater job satisfaction and organizational commitment (Sweeney et al., 1990).

Equity theory has some problems. A number of quantitative and qualitative variables have to be considered when calculating an equity ratio. These variables depend on individual perception, and are difficult to measure. Different people use different timescales when calculating fairness; short-term calculations may be different from long-term implications. There are individual differences in tolerance levels, and not everyone will respond in the same way to a particular level of inequity. Whether or not you believe there is a valid explanation for inequity will also moderate your response.

Table 9.3: **Strategies for reducing inequity**

Strategy	Example
1 Alter your outcomes	Persuade the manager to increase my pay
2 Adjust your inputs	I won't work as hard as Annika
3 Alter the comparison person's outcomes	Persuade the manager to cut Annika's pay
4 Alter the comparison person's inputs	Leave the difficult tasks to Annika
5 Compare with someone else	Per gets the same as I get
6 Rationalize the inequity	Annika has worked here for much longer
7 Leave	Get another job

Figure 9.2: **Equity theory – causal chains**

Equity theory also overlooks the wider context in two ways. The first concerns the basis of our social comparisons, which can be extremely varied. Some of us compare our situations with immediate colleagues, while others make comparisons with people in other organizations, sectors and countries. There is no rationale for preferring one basis of comparison to another. Second, equity theory ignores the systemic inequities in capitalist economies. Colleagues may receive the same treatment from their employing organization (perception of equity) while being exploited by senior managers in positions of wealth, influence and power (perception of inequity). However, this inequity is a 'normal' feature of capitalist society, and is thus difficult to challenge.

CRITICAL THINKING

What actions would you take if you were earning just a little more than Annika in our example from the Stockholm restaurant?

What actions would you take if you were earning very much more than Annika?

To what extent do you think equity theory can make accurate predictions of your behaviour in inequitable situations like these?

Expectancy theory
a process theory which argues that individual motivation depends on the *valence* of outcomes, the *expectancy* that effort will lead to good performance, and the *instrumentality* of performance in producing valued outcomes.

Valence the perceived value or preference that an individual has for a particular outcome, and can be positive, negative, or neutral.

Instrumentality the perceived probability that good performance will lead to valued rewards, and is measured on a scale from 0 (no chance) to 1 (certainty).

Expectancy the perceived probability that effort will result in good performance, and is measured on a scale from 0 (no chance) to 1 (certainty).

Equity theory has implications for management practice. Employees compare pay (even when it is supposed to be 'secret'), and perceived inequity generates resentment. Comparisons are often subjective and imprecise, and may be based on rumour. It is important to recognize that perceptions of inequity generate tension, even where there is actually little inequity. It may thus be important to provide accurate information about rewards, and the links between effort and rewards. Equity theory is also the basis for the distributive justice component of organizational justice **(Chapter 21)**.

Expectancy theory

A motive is an outcome that has become desirable. The process through which outcomes become desirable is explained by the expectancy theory of motivation.

Cognitive theories in psychology assume that we are purposive, and that we are aware of our goals and actions. Expectancy theory is a cognitive theory, and was developed by the American psychologist Edward C. Tolman in the 1930s as a challenge to the behaviourist views of his contemporaries. Tolman argued that behaviour is directed by the expectations that we have about our behaviour leading to the achievement of desired outcomes.

For work motivation to be high, productive work has to be seen as a path to valued goals. If you need more money, and if you expect to get more money for working hard, then we can predict that you will work hard. If you still need more money, but if you expect that hard work will only result in happy smiles from the boss, then we can predict that you will decide not to work hard (unless you value happy smiles). This theory thus assumes that we behave in ways that are instrumental (that is, will lead us) to the achievement of our valued goals.

The American psychologist Victor H. Vroom (1964) developed the first expectancy theory of work motivation, based on three concepts: valence, instrumentality, and expectancy.

Instrumentality and expectancy are both *subjective probabilities*. What is important is what the individual estimates to be the likelihood of good performance leading to valued rewards, and of effort leading to good performance, respectively.

The force (F) of your motivation to work hard is the result of the product (multiplication) of these three variables and not the sum (addition). This is because, if one of the variables is zero, then, despite the value of the other two, the product, F, will be zero, and that is what we would expect. This cumbersome explanation is expressed in *the expectancy equation*:

$$F = V \times I \times E$$

What is the effect of a low 'V' value? If you do not care what grade you get for your next assignment, then you will not be motivated to work hard for it.

What is the effect of a low 'E' value? If you believe that long hard hours in the library will not get you a high assignment grade, then you will not be motivated to work hard.

What is the effect of a low 'I' value? If you believe that a good grade will not lead to a chosen qualification, or to your preferred career, then you will not be motivated to work hard.

Only when all three of the terms in the expectancy equation are positive and high will the motivating force be positive and strong. However, behaviour often has several outcomes. Working hard affects our performance, level of fatigue, social life, today's pay and tomorrow's promotion. The expectancy equation thus has to be summed for all possible outcomes. The full expectancy equation is:

$$F = \sum (V \times I \times E)$$

The sign $\sum$ is the Greek letter sigma, which means, 'add up all the values of the calculation in the brackets'. Note that there will be only a single E value, concerning the probability that high effort will lead to high performance. However, there will be several different I values, one for each rated outcome, concerning the probability that these will be obtained.

CRITICAL THINKING

Why would a highly motivated individual perform badly? Why would an individual with a very low level of motivation be a poor performer? Why could a competent individual have a low expectancy of performing well? To what extent does expectancy theory help to answer these questions?

In summary:

- Expectancy theory states that behaviour results from a conscious decision-making process based on expectations, or subjective probabilities, that the individual has about the results of different behaviours leading to performance and to rewards.
- Expectancy theory can explain individual differences in motivation and behaviour.
- Expectancy theory measures the strength of the individual's motivation to behave in particular ways.
- Expectancy theory assumes that behaviour is rational, and that we are aware of our motives.

Expectancy theory has several management consequences:

- The link between effort and performance must be clear, but there is no point in offering rewards that are not valued.
- If employees are told to do one thing but rewarded for doing another, they will focus on behaviours that are rewarded and ignore other instructions.
- Money is only one of several extrinsic rewards; to be motivating it must be linked to performance and be seen as equitable.
- If different employees value different kinds of rewards, it may help to introduce a 'cafeteria benefits' scheme, offering a choice of fringe benefits.
- The value of different rewards may change with time and has to be monitored.

Total rewards All aspects of work that are valued by employees, including recognition, development opportunities, organization culture, and attractive work environment, as well as pay and other financial benefits.

In other words, to ensure *low* motivation and *poor* performance: (1) keep performance goals vague and ambiguous; (2) reward behaviour other than good job performance; (4) offer rewards which employees do not value; (5) concentrate on money and ignore other intrinsic and extrinsic rewards; (6) ensure that performance ratings are subjective and inconsistent.

These arguments have led many organizations to consider total rewards, which takes into account all of the intrinsic and extrinsic rewards that can be used to attract, motivate, and retain employees. This involves developing a comprehensive approach that covers pay and fringe benefits, the design of jobs and experience of work (recognition, autonomy, work–life balance, personal development), as well as the organization culture and physical work environment – everything that is of potential value to employees (Chartered Institute for Personnel and Development, 2015).

CRITICAL THINKING	Think about the job that is ideal for you, in your ideal organization. Apart from pay, what other benefits and rewards do you want that job and that organization to give you? What does your ideal 'total rewards' package contain? Is this realistic?

Goal-setting theory

Goal-setting theory a process theory of motivation which argues that work motivation is influenced by goal difficulty, goal specificity, and knowledge of results.

Goal-setting theory is another process theory of motivation, which attempts to predict and explain work behaviour. However, the main advocate of this approach, Edwin Locke (1968) once argued that 'goal-setting is more appropriately viewed as a motivational technique rather than a formal theory' (Locke, 1975, p.465). Is seems to be both a theory and a technique.

Goal theory has four propositions which are well-supported by research (Locke and Latham, 1990):

1. *Challenging goals* lead to higher levels of performance than simple and unchallenging goals. Difficult goals are also called 'stretch' goals because they encourage us to improve.

2. *Specific goals* lead to higher levels of performance than vague goals such as 'do your best'. It is easier to adjust our behaviour when we know precisely what is required of us. Goals should thus be SMART: specific, measurable, attainable, realistic and time-related.

3. *Participation* in goal setting can improve performance by increasing commitment to those goals, but managerially assigned goals that are adequately explained and justified can also lead to high performance.

4. *Knowledge of results* of past performance is necessary for effective goal achievement. Feedback contains information and is also motivational.

Management can use these propositions in order to set motivational goals that will encourage good performance. However, the theory has been tested mainly in situations where short-term targets can be expressed in clear and quantifiable terms. It is less clear if this applies to longer term goals, say over a period of years, as targets are likely to be more qualitative and to change with circumstances. It is also uncertain whether this applies where goals are difficult to measure, as in professional work. Another limitation is the focus on individual goals and performance rather than on teamwork.

Herminia Ibarra (2015) suggests that mobile and wearable devices (smartphones and Fitbits), and other technology tools, are making 'the quantified self' and goal-setting more popular. BetterWorks, in Palo Alto California (www.betterworks.com), designs performance-tracking software that allows individuals to set and share goals, log progress on the company dashboard, and get feedback ('cheers' or 'nudges') from colleagues through a smartphone app. This approach is used by Google, Twitter and Intel, and BetterWorks has 50 other customers (*The Economist*, 2015). This does not solve the problem that aspects of work which are difficult to measure (e.g. 'thinking strategically') may be overlooked by the focus on problems and activities with clear 'OKRs' – objectives and key results. Another problem is that the pursuit of goals interferes with learning; people want to look good by getting results, rather than spending 'downtime' developing new capabilities. Ibarra (2015) explains:

> 'Imagine this, not too far-fetched situation: a manager sets a goal of "becoming a better listener". Aided by polling tools that provide continual, anonymous feedback from his or her direct reports and name badges with sensors that track location, face-to-face interaction, gestures and speech dynamics – technologies that are already available – the

Steven Kramer and Teresa Amabile

manager might realise that listening is easier in the morning, and schedule accordingly. That would be a benefit. But she might also start unconsciously avoiding people with whom listening is harder, in order to keep her numbers up.'

Inner work life theory

Equity, expectancy and goal-setting theories of motivation allow us to make choices, implying a rational, logical, reasoned approach to the decisions that shape our behaviour. They do not allow for the influence of emotions. The inner work life theory developed by Teresa Amabile and Steven Kramer (2007) argues that our behaviour and work performance are influenced by the way in which our perceptions, motives, and emotions interact with each other, triggered by everyday events.

Inner work life theory a process theory of motivation which argues that our behaviour and performance at work are influenced by the interplay of our perceptions, emotions and motives.

Our private thoughts and feelings may not be visible to others, but we do not leave them at home when we go to work. So, how do the dynamics of our 'inner work life' affect performance? To find out, Amabile and Kramer asked 238 professionals from 26 project teams to complete a personal diary, in a standard format, every day for the duration of their projects. The researchers sent daily emails to each professional, asking for a description of an event that stood out in their mind that day and how that made them feel. This gave the researchers 12,000 diary entries to analyse, revealing the richness and intensity of people's inner work lives, what they call 'the reality management never sees'.

The role of emotions is central in this perspective. Neuroscience has shown that cognition (including perception) and emotion are linked. Events at work trigger a combination of perceptual, emotional, and motivational processes. The way in which these processes interact shapes our behaviour and our performance. The researchers conclude that we perform better when our work experiences include positive emotions, stronger intrinsic motivation, and more favourable perceptions of the work, the team, management, and the organization. Positive emotions, perceptions, and motivation are also linked to creativity. Productivity, commitment, and collegiality also improve when we 'are in a good mood'.

The management implications of this research differ from those of other motivation theories, which emphasize the 'daily pat on the back', and attempts to make work fun. This research suggests instead that the two most important management behaviours involve 'enabling people to move forward in their work', and 'treating them decently as human beings'.

1. Enable progress

The factor that made the difference between 'good days' and 'bad days' for the respondents in this study was a sense of being able to make progress. This could mean achieving a goal, accomplishing a task, solving a problem. The worst days – frustrating, sad, fearful – were characterized by setbacks, and even small delays could have this impact. Managers should:

- provide direct help and not get in the way
- make sure that time and other resources are adequate
- react to successes and failures with a learning orientation
- set clear and unambiguous goals (as goal theory suggests).

2. Manage with a human touch

Interpersonal relationships are also important, treating people fairly and with respect. These events had almost as much impact as 'enabling progress' on the distinction between good and bad days. Praise in the absence of real progress has little positive impact, and can arouse cynicism. Good progress without recognition leads to anger and sadness.

No play, no stay

If you have fun at work, are you less likely to leave? Michael Tews et al. (2014) studied the relationship between fun and employee turnover in a national restaurant chain in the USA. Turnover is a constant problem in this sector, which tends to employ younger workers. The researchers surveyed almost 300 recently employed staff in 20 restaurants. Fun activities included social events, teambuilding tasks, competitions, and public celebrations of achievements and milestones. Fun activities on their own, however, had little effect on staff turnover. Staff retention was improved where managers were seen to support the idea of having fun at work, and where the fun involved opportunities to socialize and to develop quality relationships with colleagues. The researchers conclude (p.931) that, 'entry-level employees in the hospitality industry appear to particularly value co-workers who are friendly, outgoing and who socialize with one another, as well as managers who allow and encourage fun on the job'. If an organization has problems retaining staff, supporting a workplace environment where staff can have fun together could help to solve the problem.

We should, however, be cautious. John Michel et al. (2018) argue that fun can be seen as a chore when workload is high, when the time involved is unpaid, and when managers do not genuinely support the activity. Also, employees may be uncomfortable with unusual 'fun' tasks if they feel that they will be asked to do something that they will find difficult to do well.

CRITICAL THINKING   Some organizations (such as Google) – and management consultants – claim that making work fun is motivational. How do you feel about this? Would you like to be employed in a fun workplace? Or is this just another fad designed to make employees more compliant with management demands?

The social process of motivating others

Motivation can also be seen as a social influence process. The advice in the previous section, about enabling progress, and 'managing with a human touch', illustrates this. The general question is, how do we motivate others to do what we want them to do? The question for management is, how do we motivate employees to perform well? Many jobs are still designed using the methods of the American engineer Frederick Winslow Taylor (1911). Taylor's *scientific management* approach to designing jobs **(Chapter 14)** is as follows:

1. Decide on the optimum degree of *task fragmentation*, breaking down a complex job into a sequence of simple steps.
2. Decide the *one best way* to perform the work, through studies to discover the most effective method for doing each step, including workplace layout and design of tools.
3. *Train* employees to carry out these simple fragmented tasks in the manner specified.
4. *Reward* employees financially for meeting performance targets.

CRITICAL THINKING

You are employed on a job in which you repeat the same simple task every fifteen seconds, perhaps wiring plugs for lamps, 9.00 am until 5.30 pm, every day (with a lunch break), five days a week. Describe your emotional response to this work.

Is it inevitable that some jobs just have to be like this, given the nature of work and technology, and the need to keep quality high and costs low?

Task fragmentation has advantages:

- Employees do not need expensive and time-consuming training
- Repeating one small specialized task makes employees very proficient
- Unskilled work gets lower pay
- Some of the problems of achieving controlled performance are simplified.

The disadvantages include:

- Repetitive work is very boring
- The individual's contribution to the organization is meaningless and insignificant
- Monotony leads to apathy, dissatisfaction and carelessness
- The employee does not develop skills that might lead to promotion.

Job enrichment a technique for broadening the experience of work to enhance employee need satisfaction and to improve motivation and performance.

Taylor's approach to job design appears logical and efficient, but it creates jobs that do not stimulate motivation or improve performance. Taylor had a simplified view of human motivation, regarding 'lower level' employees as 'coin operated' and arguing that the rewards for working as instructed should be financial. Taylor's methods are more likely to encourage absenteeism and sabotage than commitment and flexibility. Managers are thus interested in theories of motivation as sources of alternative methods for encouraging motivation and high performance. During the 1960s and 1970s, these concerns created the Quality of Working Life (QWL) movement whose language and methods are still influential today (Grote and Guest, 2017). One QWL technique is job enrichment.

Motivator factors aspects of work which lead to high levels of satisfaction, motivation and performance, including achievement, recognition, responsibility, advancement, growth, and the work itself.

The concept of job enrichment was first developed by the American psychologist Frederick Herzberg (1966, 1968). However, more recent research suggests that many employees today respond in ways that his theory predicts (Basset-Jones and Lloyd, 2005). To discover what factors affected job satisfaction and dissatisfaction, 203 Pittsburgh engineers and accountants were asked two 'critical incident' questions. They were asked to recall events which had made them feel good about their work, and events which had made them feel bad about it.

Hygiene factors aspects of work which remove dissatisfaction, but do not contribute to motivation and performance, including pay, company policy, supervision, status, security and physical working conditions.

Analysis of these incident narratives showed that the factors which led to job satisfaction were different from those which led to job dissatisfaction. Herzberg called this a 'two factor theory of motivation', the two sets of factors being motivator factors and hygiene factors, summarized in Table 9.4. Motivators are also known as (job) content factors, while hygiene factors are known as (organizational) context factors.

Herzberg (1987) claimed that this pattern of motivation had been identified in Finland, Hungary, Italy, Israel, Japan and Zambia. In South Africa, however, while managers and skilled workers, black and white, produced the expected results, unskilled workers' satisfaction appeared to be dependent on hygiene. Herzberg claimed that, 'the impoverished nature of the unskilled workers' jobs has not afforded these workers with motivators – thus the abnormal profile'. He also cites a study of unskilled Indian workers who were, 'operating on a dependent hygiene continuum that leads to addiction to hygiene, or strikes and revolution'.

According to this theory, the redesign of jobs to increase motivation and performance should focus on motivator or content factors. Improvement in the hygiene or context factors, Herzberg (1968) argued, will remove dissatisfaction, but will not increase motivation and performance. He suggested using vertical loading factors, to achieve job enrichment.

The Job Characteristics Model (Figure 9.3) describes the job enrichment strategy of Richard Hackman and Greg Oldham (1974; Hackman, Oldham et al., 1975). This model sets out the links between the features of jobs, the individual's experience, and outcomes such as

Vertical loading factors methods for enriching work and improving motivation, by removing controls, increasing accountability, and by providing feedback, new tasks, natural work units, special assignments and additional authority.

Table 9.4: Motivator and hygiene factors

Motivator factors (job content)	Hygiene factors (organizational context)
Achievement	Pay
Advancement	Company policy
Growth	Supervisory style
Recognition	Status
Responsibility	Security
The work itself	Working conditions

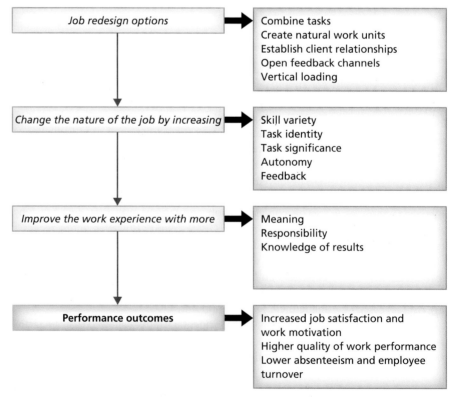

Figure 9.3: The job characteristics model
Source: based on Hackman et al. (1975, p.62)

motivation, satisfaction and performance. The model suggests that jobs can be analysed in terms of five *core dimensions*:

1. *Skill variety*: making use of different skills and abilities.
2. *Task identity*: providing a 'whole' and meaningful piece of work.
3. *Task significance*: how the job affects the work of others.
4. *Autonomy*: the degree of independence and discretion.
5. *Feedback*: providing performance information.

Growth need strength a measure of the readiness and capability of an individual to respond positively to job enrichment.

This model also takes into account individual differences in growth need strength, which is similar to Maslow's concept of self-actualization.

Growth need strength (GNS) is an indicator of your willingness to welcome personal development through job enrichment. The causal chain, from job redesign through individual experience, to performance outcomes, depends on GNS. With employees whose GNS is low, an enriched job is unlikely to improve their performance.

CRITICAL THINKING

Your instructor offers to enrich your educational experience of studying organizational behaviour, with additional classes and tutorials, further reading, and extra feedback and revision sessions. There is no guarantee, however, that this enriched experience will increase your course grades. How do you feel about this offer?

Job diagnostic survey a questionnaire which assesses the degree of skill variety, task identity, task significance, autonomy and feedback in jobs.

To assess jobs on the core dimensions, Hackman and colleagues developed a questionnaire called the job diagnostic survey (JDS).

Skill variety and autonomy are measured in the JDS by questions such as:

How much *variety* is there in your job ? That is, to what extent does the job require you to do many different things at work, using a variety of your skills and talents ?

How much *autonomy* is there in your job ? That is, to what extent does your job permit you to decide *on your own* how to go about doing the work ?

Respondents rate their answers to these questions on a seven point scale. The JDS thus provides *operational definitions* (glossary) of the variables in the model. The core job dimensions are *independent variables,* and critical psychological states and performance outcomes are *dependent variables* **(see Chapter 1)**. Growth need strength is a mediating variable in this causal chain. The JDS can be used to establish how motivating a job is, by calculating the motivating potential score (MPS), from answers across groups of employees doing the same job.

Motivating potential score an indicator of how motivating a job is likely to be for an individual, considering skill variety, task identity, task significance, autonomy and feedback.

The MPS is calculated using the values of the variables measured by the JDS:

$$\text{MPS} = \frac{(\text{skill variety} + \text{task identity} + \text{task significance})}{3} \times \text{autonomy} \times \text{feedback}$$

The first part of this equation concerns aspects of the job. The second part concerns how the work is managed. Autonomy and feedback are more important than the other dimensions. The equation reflects this by treating them as two separate components. Only the arithmetic mean of the ratings for skill variety, task identity and task significance is used. If one of the three main components – job aspects, autonomy, feedback – is low, then the MPS will be low. A near-zero rating on either autonomy or feedback, for example, would pull the score down disproportionately (five times zero equals zero). A near-zero rating on task variety, identity or significance would not have much impact on the overall score. The five core dimensions stimulate three psychological states critical to high work motivation, job satisfaction and performance. These critical psychological states are:

1. *Experienced meaningfulness*: the extent to which the individual considers the work to be meaningful, valuable and worthwhile. (Susie Cranston and Scott Keller, 2013, call this the 'meaning quotient', which inspires employees to perform at their peak).

2. *Experienced responsibility*: the extent to which the individual feels accountable for their work output.

3. *Knowledge of results*: the extent to which the individual knows and understands how well they are performing.

Jobs with high MPS are more likely to lead to the experience of critical psychological states than jobs with low scores. Expectancy theorists argue that all three critical states, and not just one or two, must be present if the personal and work outcomes on the right-hand side of the model are to be achieved. The MPS is only a guide to how motivating a job will be as different employees can have different perceptions of the same job. Those who put a low value on personal growth (revealed by a low GNS score) will not respond as the model suggests. No point, then, in offering them enriched jobs, unless one believes that the experience of personal development can in itself stimulate future growth need.

The model also shows how the motivating potential of jobs can be improved by applying five *implementing concepts*:

1. *Combine tasks*: Give employees more than one part of the work to do, to increase variety and contribution to the product or service.

2. *Form natural work units*: Give employees meaningful patterns of work, to increase individual contribution and task significance.

3. *Establish client relationships*: Give employees responsibility for personal contacts, to increase variety, autonomy, and feedback (see 'Here's looking at you, chef' below).

Here's looking at you, chef

Scott Berinato (2014) interviewed Ryan Buell, a researcher at Harvard Business School, whose study (with colleagues Tami Kim and Chia-Jung Tsay) found that chefs made better meals when they could see their customers. Using a real cafeteria, and a video-conferencing arrangement, Buell set up four different scenarios. In the first of these, chefs and diners could not see each other. Second, diners could see the chefs. Third, chefs could see the diners. Finally, chefs and diners could see each other. Customers were surveyed about the service and the food. Satisfaction with the food was 10 percent higher when the chefs could see their customers, than when they could not see them. When customers and chefs could all see each other, customer satisfaction was over 17 per cent higher.

Buell argues that seeing the customer makes employees feel more appreciated and satisfied, and more motivated to perform well. The study also showed that it was not just the customers' perception of quality that improved; the food did get better. Buell explained:

'During the experiment we had an observer in the kitchen taking notes and timing service. Normally, chefs would make eggs on the grill in advance, adding them to plates as needed and often overcooking them. When we turned on the screens and the chefs saw the customers, they started making eggs to order more often. [. . .] There's something refreshingly human about the idea that just seeing each other can make us more appreciative and lead to objectively better outcomes' (Berinato, 2014, pp.34 and 35).

The researchers conclude that 'opening up the work environment' in this way, creating a relationship with the customers, can motivate chefs to higher levels of performance, for little or no cost.

4. *Vertical loading*: Increase autonomy, by giving employees responsibilities normally allocated to supervisors, such as work scheduling, problem solving, training others, and recruitment decisions.

5. *Open feedback channels*: Give employees performance summaries and corporate information. Feedback tells people how well they are doing, and provides a basis for improvement.

 EMPLOYABILITY CHECK (people management, problem-solving skills)

Your team is not working well, and the members appear to be demotivated. As team leader, what factors will you explore in order to explain their poor performance? What changes will you consider making to their working arrangements in order to improve motivation and performance?

CUTTING EDGE   Quality of working life in the twenty-first century

Gudela Grote

David Guest

Gudela Grote and David Guest (2017) argue that the approaches to work design developed by the quality of working life movement in the 1960s and 1970s is applicable today. The nature of work is changing and we need to find ways to improve employee well-being and emancipation – involving employees in the changes that will affect them. Grote and Guest propose an updated set of quality of working life criteria:

Criteria	Description
Adequate and fair compensation	Pay meeting socially determined minimum and fair standards; equal pay for equivalent work
Safe and healthy environment	Promotion of healthy work and work environment
Development of human capacities	Jobs that promote skill development, decision-latitude and task identity
Growth and security	Jobs that promote employability and opportunities for personal development
Social integration	Positive organizational climate and psychological safety; accommodating diversity
Constitutionalism	Respect for and protection of employees' rights and mechanisms for employee representation
Consideration of the total life space	Adequate concern for balancing demands from different life domains
Social relevance	Adherence to socially responsible practices in the organization
Individual proactivity	Support for personal initiative without undue transfer of employment risks to the employee
Flexible working	Flexible working schemes to bridge organizational and employee interests

Source: Grote and Guest (2017, p.156)

To what extent do these criteria address the universal needs for autonomy, competence and relatedness that are identified by the self-determination theory of motivation? To what extent are these criteria consistent with work design techniques that aim to enrich jobs and improve the motivating potential of work?

Engagement and high performance

Employee engagement being positively present during the performance of work by willingly contributing intellectual effort, experiencing positive emotions, and meaningful connections to others.

Employee engagement is a fashionable topic, but it is not new. The idea came from William A. Kahn (1990), whose work initially had little impact on either practice or research. That is surprising because engagement is often discussed in terms of 'discretionary effort', 'going the extra mile', 'feeling valued', and 'passion for work' (CIPD, 2017b). Reviewing the history of the concept, Frank Giancola (2014) describes how engagement was promoted in the USA by management consultants, and in Europe by academics. Although the term has been defined and measured in different ways, there appear to be links between engagement, on the one hand, and job satisfaction, commitment, and performance, on the other. Engagement has thus been described as a 'bottom line issue', and as 'a must-do, not a nice-to-have' (Rayton et al., 2012, p.i).

As a way to improve individual and organizational effectiveness, engagement has attracted a lot of management attention. As a potential way to improve the nation's productivity and competitiveness, the UK government commissioned *The MacLeod Review,* which created a Task Force to promote an 'engagement movement', called *Engage for Success.* Check their website: engageforsuccess.org. Their report concluded that the UK faced an 'engagement deficit':

'We believe that if employee engagement and the principles that lie behind it were more widely understood, if good practice was more widely shared, if the potential that resides in the country's workforce was more fully unleashed, we could see a step change in workplace performance and in employee well-being, for the considerable benefit of UK plc. Engagement, going to the heart of the workplace relationship between employee and employer, can be a key to unlocking productivity and to transforming the working lives of many people for whom Monday morning is an especially low point of the week' (MacLeod and Clarke, 2009, p.3).

One definition (CIPD, 2017a) identifies three dimensions of engagement:

Intellectual	Thinking about the job and how to do it better
Affective	Feeling positively about doing a good job
Social	Discussing improvements with others.

CRITICAL THINKING

How engaged in your studies are you as a student? Does your university or college have a 'student engagement deficit'? How could the institution's management and instructors reduce this deficit?

Employees can be engaged with different aspects of work: the job itself, relationships with colleagues, the organization as a whole, and in some cases with other stakeholders (customers, suppliers). In general, women are more engaged than men, older workers are more engaged than younger colleagues, and managers are more engaged than non-managers.

The MacLeod Review identified four engagement 'enablers' (MacLeod and Clarke, 2009, p.75):

1. Leadership that gives 'a strong strategic narrative' about the purpose of the organization

2. Line managers who motivate, empower and support employees

3. Opportunities for employees to challenge the status quo and be involved in decision making

4. Integrity, through the values that are embedded in the organization culture.

 **STOP AND SEARCH**   Google for *CIPD Podcast: The Engagement Myth* (15:59).

Creating an engagement system

David Guest (2014, pp.152–53) identifies the core practices that enhance employee engagement:

1. Select staff who have a propensity for engagement.

2. Train staff for engagement, through induction and coaching.

3. Invest in human capital and employability to develop competencies and confidence.

4. Redesign jobs to increase autonomy, challenge, variety, skills use and scope for learning.

5. Provide organizational support, through supportive systems, culture and leadership.

6. Reward and promote managers for their ability to engage employees.

7. Ensure fair treatment and trust in management.

8. Ensure extensive and effective two-way communication.

9. Create a context that reinforces job security and flexible working.

10. Adopt a human resource strategy that values engagement and these other practices.

Guest notes that these practices are consistent with high performance work system models, and that an integrated engagement system should thus produce positive outcomes.

Do we still have an 'engagement deficit'? The polling organization Gallup (2017) studied employee engagement in 155 countries. They found that 85 per cent of employees worldwide are not engaged or are actively disengaged in their jobs. Engagement levels vary from country to country, but no region exceeded 40 per cent of employees engaged. The figure for Eastern Europe was 15 per cent; Western Europe 10 per cent; below 10 per cent in France, Italy and Spain; Australia and New Zealand, 14 per cent; Norway 17 per cent. The United States and Canada, 30 per cent. In the UK, only 11 per cent of employees said that they were engaged, with 21 per cent actively disengaged.

Gallup (2017) argues that these figures reflect a waste of potential. Employers with the most engaged workforces – those in the top 25 per cent, with around 70 per cent of employees saying they were engaged – were 17 per cent more productive and 21 per cent more profitable than those in the bottom 25 per cent. Reinforcing the arguments of the motivation theories explored earlier, one of the key conclusions from this research concerns the need for autonomy at work:

'In many cases, making better use of employees' strengths will require businesses to grant workers greater input and autonomy to use their strengths. This approach often requires a profound shift in management perspective, as traditional manager-employee power dynamics give way to more personalized relationships through which managers position their team members for maximum impact according to their individual strengths.

'The resulting sense of empowerment benefits both the employee and the organization. Employees who strongly agree that their opinions count at work are more likely to feel personally invested in their job. Gallup's global data suggest that without such opportunities, workers are more likely to doubt their ability to get ahead by working hard – a devastating blow to their motivation and productivity. Higher levels of autonomy also promote the development and implementation of new ideas as employees feel empowered to pursue entrepreneurial goals that benefit the organization' (Gallup, 2017, p.7).

Research in the UK found that the three factors lowering engagement were attitudes towards senior management who did not consult with employees, difficulty maintaining work-life balance, and poor relationships with line managers (CIPD, 2017a).

The need for autonomy is also reflected in techniques for improving motivation and performance, through individual job enrichment, and self-managing teams. This chapter focuses on individual motivation and jobs. **Chapter 13** explores teamworking. These approaches converge in the concept of the high-performance work system.

The 'core ingredients' of high-performance working include (CIPD, 2017b, p.21):

High-performance work system a form of organization that operates at levels of excellence far beyond those of comparable systems.

- Formal appraisal systems
- Incentives, such as performance- and profit-related pay, and share option schemes
- Consultation mechanisms: joint committees, staff briefings, surveys, suggestion schemes
- Employee autonomy and teamworking
- Continuous improvement: total quality management, problem-solving teams, accreditation
- Skills development: induction programmes, training in a range of roles
- Recruitment processes, job design, and training aligned with business strategy
- 'Family-friendly' and flexible working practices

Are the claims for high performance work systems justified? Research suggests that organizations adopting high performance practices perform better than those which do not (CIPD, 2017b). From their cross-sectoral study in The Netherlands, Karina Van de Voorde and Susanne Beijer (2015) found that high performance practices improved both organizational performance, and employee commitment and well-being, where staff felt valued and supported by the approach.

Work redesign methods and theories of motivation have seen little development since the 1980s. However, as Grote and Guest (2017) argue, the organizational context to which these theories and techniques apply has changed dramatically. The differences between the quality of working life (QWL) approach, and high performance work systems (HPWS) are summarized in Table 9.5.

Table 9.5: QWL versus HPWS

QWL in the 1970s	HPWS today
Aimed to reduce costs of absenteeism and labour turnover and increase productivity	Aims to improve organizational flexibility and product quality for competitive advantage
Autonomy improves quality of work experience and job satisfaction	Engagement improves commitment, skill, decision making, and adaptability
Focused on repetitive manual and office work	Focuses on challenging knowledge work
Had little impact on management roles	Redefinition of management roles
'Quick fix' applied to problematic groups	Takes time to change attitudes and behaviour
Most employees broadly want the same kinds of things from work	Need to cater for a wide range of individual differences in interests and expectations

The organization of your dreams

When Rob Goffee and Gareth Jones (2013) asked executives to describe their 'ideal organization', they identified six features of 'an organization that operates at its fullest potential by allowing people to do their best work' (p.99):

- People are allowed to 'be themselves': different personalities, skills, interests, perspectives, habits, and assumptions are welcomed, creating 'a culture where opposite types can thrive and work cooperatively' (p.100).

- Information is not suppressed or distorted: 'radical honesty' involves using many different communication channels, so that people know what is really happening (p.102).

- Staff are given opportunities to develop their knowledge and skills, enabling them to perform more effectively: this is done through networking, creative interaction with colleagues, stretch assignments, and training.

- The organization stands for something more than profit or shareholder value: profit is the result of accomplishing socially worthwhile outcomes, for which people feel proud to work.

- The work itself is intrinsically rewarding and meaningful – and can become a cause which encourages staff to stay: people are matched with tasks that make sense to them and which are engaging, and managers trust employees to be more innovative and collaborative.

- There are no stupid rules or arbitrary restrictions: procedures and quality controls have to be followed, of course, but the rules must be understood and seen as legitimate, and important in terms of supporting the organization's purpose.

Admitting that creating the 'dream organization' can be challenging, given other competing claims on time and resources, Goffee and Jones (2013, p.106) conclude that:

'People want to do good work – to feel they matter in an organization that makes a difference. They want to work in a place that magnifies their strengths, not their weaknesses. For that, they need some autonomy and structure, and the organization must be coherent, honest, and open.'

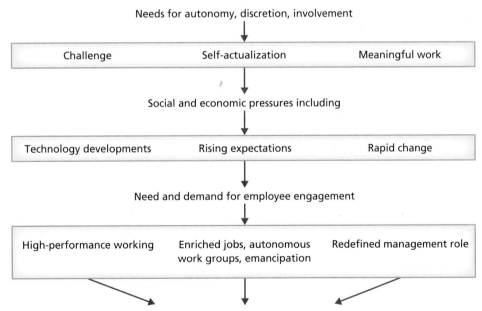

Figure 9.4: The case for high-performance work systems

The argument of this chapter is summarized in Figure 9.4. This begins with the need for involvement and autonomy in work, and with the challenge and personal development that we desire. These needs seek fulfilment in contexts facing multiple socio-economic pressures. Addressing these needs and pressures involves job enrichment, self-managing teamwork, and engagement. The emphasis on personal development and continuous improvement helps to promote adaptability, product quality and customer care, increasing organizational effectiveness and quality of working life.

🤚 **STOP AND SEARCH** YouTube for *High performance work systems examples* and find Tom Kochan describing how organizations such as Southwest Airlines, Costco, Semco and Toyota have implemented high-performance systems (7:50).

CRITICAL THINKING Some commentators argue that high-performance work systems and employee engagement are radical changes to organization design and management–employee relationships. Others argue that these are cosmetic, because they do not affect the power and reward inequalities in contemporary organizations. Given your own experience of work, which view do you support?

 **RECAP**

1. *Understand different ways in which the term motivation is used.*

   - Motivation can refer to the desired goals which individuals have or acquire.

   - Motivation can refer to the individual decision-making process through which goals are chosen and pursued.

   - Motivation can refer to a social influence process that aims to change the behaviour of others.

2. *Explain the distinction between content and process theories of motivation.*

   - Content theories of motivation explain behaviour in terms of innate drives and acquired motives. The content theories covered in this chapter are self-determination theory and hierarchy of needs theory.

   - Process theories of motivation explain behaviour in terms of individual decision-making processes rather than innate needs. The process theories covered in this chapter are equity theory, goal-setting theory, expectancy theory, and inner work life theory.

3. *Understand how motives and motivation processes influence behaviour.*

   - Motives as desirable goals can be innate (drives) or acquired (socially learned).

   - Self-determination theory argues that we have innate needs for autonomy, competence, and relatedness.

   - Hierarchy of needs theory argues that we have five main needs, for survival, security, affiliation, esteem and self-actualization.

   - Equity theory explains motivation in terms of perceived injustice or unfairness.

   - Goal-setting theory explains behaviour in terms of goal difficulty and goal specificity.

   - Expectancy theory explains motivation in terms of valued outcomes and the subjective probability of achieving those outcomes.

   - Inner work life theory explains behaviour in terms of the interactions between perceptions, motives, and emotions.

4. *Apply expectancy theory and job enrichment techniques to diagnose organizational problems and to recommend practical solutions.*

   - A job will only be motivating if it leads to rewards which the individual values.

   - Rewards motivate high performance when the link between effort and reward is clear.

- Hygiene factors can overcome dissatisfaction but do not lead to motivation.

- Content factors lead to job satisfaction, motivation, and high performance.

- Jobs can be enriched by applying vertical job loading factors.

- The motivating potential of a job can be increased by improving skill variety, task identity, task significance, autonomy and feedback.

- Job enrichment will not improve the performance of individuals with low growth need strength.

5. *Explain the contemporary interest in work motivation, with respect to presenteeism, the gig economy, employee engagement and high-performance work systems.*

   - Presenteeism – being motivated to work more hours than required, even when unwell – has become a contemporary problem, costing organizations more than absenteeism.

   - The main motive for presenteeism is job insecurity, but working long hours can lead to ill health. Paradoxically, continuing to work can benefit some health conditions.

- The gig economy – based on freelancers selling their skills online – is a new form of employment. Some individuals are motivated by the freedom and flexibility of gigging, working freelance as and when they choose, on defined tasks for different clients.

- The problems of gigging include difficulty finding assignments, insecure income, lack of development and career opportunities, and the lack of employment rights enjoyed by those in standard work.

- In a rapidly changing competitive business environment, organizations need to motivate employees to be flexible, adaptable, committed and creative – to 'go the extra mile' – and not just turn up on time and follow instructions.

- Employee engagement is linked to productivity, but levels of engagement in most countries, including the UK, are low, and this has attracted national government interest.

- Employee engagement strategies and high-performance work systems use combinations of individual job enrichment, autonomous teamworking, facilitative, coaching supervisory style, and other forms of delegation to empower and motivate lower-level employees.

RECAP: What did they find? Work and wellbeing

Erik Gonzalez-Mulé and Bethany Cockburn (2017) found that:

- Employees in high-demand, low-control jobs die younger, have a higher body mass index (i.e. are heavier) and are less healthy than those who have more discretion and flexibility in their jobs, and are able to set their own goals

- Those in high-demand, low-control jobs were over 15 per cent more likely to die, compared to those in high control jobs.

- Of those who died during the study, 26 per cent were in front line service jobs (retail sales, restaurant server), and 32 per cent were in manufacturing jobs (machine operator, welder) with high demands and low control; those in entry-level service and construction jobs had higher death rates than those in professional and office roles. Lack of control in a high-demand job encourages coping behaviours such as eating, drinking, and smoking more heavily.

- Stressful jobs can have health benefits when accompanied by freedom in decision making; for those in high control jobs, high job demands (which can be energizing) actually led to a 34 per cent decrease in the likelihood of death compared to those in jobs with low demands.

- Management can avoid working people to death by allowing employees to set their own goals, schedule their own time, and make their own decisions – in other words providing the autonomy advocated by self-determination theory.

Revision

1. What is presenteeism, and why is this a bigger problem for organizations than absenteeism?

2. The self-determination theory of motivation identifies three innate needs. What are these, and what steps can management take to ensure that these needs can be met at work?

3. How does equity theory explain motivation and behaviour. How can this theory be used to diagnose and improve employee motivation and performance?

4. What is 'employee engagement', and why has this become a popular management concept? How can organizations increase employee engagement, and what are the benefits?

Research assignment

Interview two line managers who have responsibility for managing others. Ask them how they motivate their staff. What motivational methods, techniques, or tools do they use? How effective do they think that their staff motivational tactics are? Assess their approaches using one of the motivation theories described in this chapter. Are they following recommended practice? Are there things that they could be doing to strengthen their motivational approach? What practical advice can you give to your two managers to improve their approaches to staff motivation?

Springboard

Todd Bridgman, Stephen Cummings and John Ballard (2018) 'Who built Maslow's pyramid?: A history of the creation of management studies' most famous symbol and its implications for management education', *Academy of Management Learning & Education* (published online early). Explores the history of Maslow's ideas and explains his contemporary relevance.

Ruth Kanfer, Michael Frese and Russell E. Johnson (2017) 'Motivation related to work: a century of progress', *Journal of Applied Psychology,* 102 (3): 338–55. Reviews a century of research into work motivation, covering content, process, and work design theories, noting the main developments and achievements in this field.

Sarah Kessler (2018) *Gigged: The End of the Job and the Future of Work.* New York: Macmillan. Explores the experience of individual gig workers – computer programmer, Uber driver, charity worker – exposing the realities of the new world of work.

John P. Meyer (2017) 'Has engagement had its day: what's next and does it matter?', *Organizational Dynamics,* 46 (2): 87–95. A critical review of the history of the concept of engagement and its enduring significance for organizations and for employees.

OB cinema

Enron: The Smartest Guys in the Room (2005, director Alex Gibney): DVD track 4, 0:17:00 to 0:23:00 (6 minutes). Clip begins at the start of this track; clip ends when the trader says, 'Well I'll stomp on the guy's throat'.

The collapse of Enron is one of the largest corporate scandals in twenty-first-century America. We are introduced in this clip to senior executive Jeff Skilling, hired by company president Kenneth Lay because he saw Skilling as a visionary, as 'a man with a big idea'.

1. How would you describe Jeff Skilling's management style?

2. What effect does he have on employee motivation?

3. Jeff's view of human motivation is based on competition, greed, and 'survival of the fittest'. He introduces the Performance Review Committee system which applies a 'rank and yank' (also known as 'stack ranking') approach to staff appraisals. What are the advantages and disadvantages of this system, for managers, and for employees?

Chapter exercises

1: Chris and Pat compare salaries

Objectives
1. To identify factors affecting pay decisions.
2. To understand the complexity of pay determination.
3. To distinguish between legal and illegal bases for pay decisions.
4. To distinguish between wise and unwise pay decisions.

Briefing
- Form groups of four or five.
- Read the *Chris and Pat compare salaries* briefing.
- Individually, list all the reasons you can think of why Chris and Pat earn different salaries. You can include reasons that may be legal or illegal, wise or unwise.
- As a group, combine your reasons, where possible adding to them, so that your group list contains at least 20 items.

Chris and Pat compare salaries
Chris Clements and Pat Palmer are both computer programmers. One day, they find out that Chris earns £32,750 a year while Pat earns £41,150. Chris is surprised and says, 'I can't think of any reasons why we should be paid so differently'. Pat replies, 'I can think of at least 20 reasons'.

Source: Based on Renard (2008)

2: Job characteristics model and job redesign

Objectives
1. To assess the motivating potential score (MPS) of a particular job or jobs.
2. To determine which core job characteristics would need to change to improve the MPS of that job or those jobs.

Briefing
To measure the MPS for a given job, researchers developed the Job Diagnostic Survey (JDS). For this exercise, we will use a short version of the JDS, which allows job design problems to be diagnosed, and generates ideas for job redesign.

→

Complete this analysis for a job in which you are currently employed (full or part time); or for a job that you have performed recently. (If you have never been employed, analyse the 'job' of a student.) The JDS is designed to be completed by the job holder, and not by an observer. For each of the 12 statements, decide whether this is an accurate or an inaccurate description of the chosen job, and rate it using this scale:

1 = Very inaccurate

2 = Mostly inaccurate

3 = Somewhat inaccurate

4 = Uncertain

5 = Somewhat accurate

6 = Mostly accurate

7 = Very accurate

The job chosen for analysis is: _____

Item	Rating	
1	_____	Supervisors often let me know how well they think I am performing
2	_____	The job requires me to use a number of complex high-level skills
3	_____	The job is arranged so that I have the chance to do a complete piece of work from beginning to end
4	_____	Just doing the work required by the job provides many chances for me to work out how well I am doing
5	_____	The job is not simple and repetitive
6	_____	This job is one where a lot of other people can be affected by how well the work is done
7	_____	The job does not deny me the chance to use my personal initiative or judgement in carrying out the work
8	_____	The job gives me the chance to completely finish the pieces of work I begin
9	_____	The job itself provides plenty of clues about whether or not I am performing well
10	_____	The job gives me considerable opportunity for independence and freedom in how I do the work
11	_____	The job itself is very significant and important in the broader scheme of things
12	_____	The supervisors and co-workers on this job almost always give me feedback on how well I am doing in my work

Scoring Work out the average of the two items that measure each job characteristic:

Job characteristic	Item numbers	Average score
Skill variety	2 + 5 ÷ 2 =	_____
Task identity	3 + 8 ÷ 2 =	_____
Task significance	6 + 11 ÷ 2 =	_____
Autonomy	7 + 10 ÷ 2 =	_____
Feedback		
From the job itself	4 + 9 ÷ 2	
+	= _____ ÷ 2 =	
From others	1 + 12 ÷ 2	_____

To calculate the MPS for this job, first add your scores for the two feedback items, and divide the total by two, to give a single, average, feedback score. Then put all of the scores into the MPS formula:

$$MPS = \frac{(skill\ variety + task\ identity + task\ significance)}{3} \times autonomy \times feedback$$

Reminder: the core job dimensions in this model are:

1. *Skill variety*: does the job make use of different skills and abilities?
2. *Task identity*: does the job involve a 'whole' and meaningful piece of work?
3. *Task significance*: does the job affect the work of others?
4. *Autonomy*: does the job provide independence and discretion?
5. *Feedback*: is performance information related back to the individual?

If you have completed this analysis *alone*:

- Assess the strengths and weaknesses of this job in terms of its motivating potential.
- Identify recommendations for redesigning this job to improve the MPS.
- Assess the difficulties in implementing these recommendations, given the nature of the work and the organizational context in which it is performed.

If you have completed this analysis *with colleagues*:

- Share the results of your analysis with colleagues and pick the job with the lowest MPS.
- Identify redesign options for improving the job's MPS (you will first need to ask the job holder for a detailed description of the job).
- Assess the difficulties in implementing these recommendations, given the nature of the work and the organizational context in which it is performed.

References

Adams, J.S. (1963) 'Toward an understanding of inequity', *Journal of Abnormal and Social Psychology*, 67(4): 422–36.

Adams, J.S. (1965) 'Inequity in social exchange', in L. Berkowitz (ed.), *Advances in Experimental Social Psychology*. New York: Academic Press, pp.267–99.

Aguinis, H., Joo, H. and Gottfredson, R.K. (2013) 'What monetary rewards can and cannot do: how to show employees the money', *Business Horizons*, 56(2): 241–49.

Amabile, T.M. and Kramer, S.J. (2007) 'Inner work life: understanding the subtext of business performance', *Harvard Business Review*, 85(5): 72–83.

Bassett-Jones, N. and Lloyd, G.C. (2005) 'Does Herzberg's motivation theory have staying power?', *Journal of Management Development*, 24(10): 929–43.

Berinato, S. (2014) 'Cooks make tastier food when they can see their customers', *Harvard Business Review*, 92(11): 34–35.

Bridgman, T., Cummings, S. and Ballard, J. (2018) 'Who built Maslow's pyramid?: a history of the creation of management studies' most famous symbol and its implications for management education', *Academy of Management Learning & Education* (published online early).

Chartered Institute of Personnel and Development (2015) *Strategic Reward and Total Reward Factsheet*, London: Chartered Institute of Personnel and Development.

Chartered Institute of Personnel and Development (2017a) *To Gig or Not To Gig?: Stories from the Modern Economy*. London: Chartered Institute of Personnel and Development.

Chartered Institute of Personnel and Development (2017b) *Employee Engagement and Motivation*, London: Chartered Institute of Personnel and Development.

Cranston, S. and Keller, S. (2013) 'Increasing the meaning quotient of work', *McKinsey Quarterly*, January, pp.1–12.

Deci, E.L., Olafsen, A.H. and Ryan, R.M. (2017) 'Self-determination theory in work organizations: the state of a science', *Annual Review of Organizational Psychology and Organizational Behavior*, 4: 19–43.

Gallup (2017) *State of the Global Workplace: Executive Summary*. Washington D.C.: Gallup

Garrow, V. (2016) *Presenteeism: A Review of Current Thinking*. Brighton: Institute for Employment Studies.

Giancola, F. (2014) 'Employee engagement: the unusual birth and development of an HR concept', *WorldatWork Journal*, 23(4): 71–81.

Goffee, R. and Jones, G. (2013) 'Creating the best workplace on earth', *Harvard Business Review*, 91(5): 98–106.

Gonzalez-Mulé, E. and Cockburn, B. (2017) 'Worked to death: the relationships of job demands and job control with mortality', *Personnel Psychology*, 70(1): 73–112.

Gray, A. and Jopson, B. (2016) 'Illinois suspends $30bn of business with Wells Fargo', *Financial Times Online*, https://www.ft.com/content/8e562182-8979-11e6-8cb7-e7ada1d123b1 [accessed April 2019]

Grote, G. and Guest, D. (2017) 'The case for reinvigorating quality of working life research', *Human Relations*, 70(2): 149–67.

Guest, D. (2014) 'Employee engagement: a sceptical analysis', *Journal of Organizational Effectiveness: People and Performance*, 1(2): 141–56.

Hackman, J.R. and Oldham, G.R. (1974) *The job diagnostic survey: an instrument for the diagnosis of jobs and the evaluation of job redesign projects*, Technical Report no.4. Department of Administrative Sciences, Yale University.

Hackman, J.R., Oldham, G., Janson, R. and Purdy, K. (1975) 'A new strategy for job enrichment', *California Management Review*, 17(4): 57–71.

Herzberg, F. (1966) *Work and the Nature of Man*. New York: Staples Press.

Herzberg, F. (1968) 'One more time: how do you motivate employees?', *Harvard Business Review*, 46(1): 53–62.

Herzberg, F. (1987) 'Workers' needs the same around the world', *Industry Week*, 21 September, pp.29–32.

Ibarra, H. (2015) 'Tech tools that track how we perform need monitoring too', *Financial Times*, 14 April, p.12.

Judge, T.A., Weiss, H.M., Kammeyer-Mueller, J.D. and Hulin, C.L. (2017) 'Job attitudes, job satisfaction, and job affect: a century of continuity and of change', *Journal of Applied Psychology*, 102(3): 356–74.

Kahn, W.A. (1990) 'Psychological conditions of personal engagement and disengagement at work', *Academy of Management Journal*, 33(4): 692–724.

Kanfer, R., Frese, M. and Johnson, R.E. (2017) 'Motivation related to work: a century of progress', *Journal of Applied Psychology*, 102(3): 338–55.

Kohn, A. (1993) 'Why incentive plans cannot work', *Harvard Business Review*, 71(5): 54–63.

Locke, E.A. (1968) 'Towards a theory of task performance and incentives', *Organizational Behaviour and Human Performance*, 3(2): 157–89.

Locke, E.A. (1975) 'Personnel attitudes and motivation', *Annual Review of Psychology*, 26: 457–80.

Locke, E.A. and Latham, G.P. (1990) *A Theory of Goal Setting and Task Performance*. Englewood Cliffs, NJ: Prentice Hall.

McGregor, D.M. (1960) *The Human Side of Enterprise*. New York: McGraw-Hill.

Macleod, D. and Clarke, N. (2009) *Engaging for Success: Enhancing Performance Through Employee Engagement*. London: Department for Business, Innovation and Skills.

Maslow, A. (1943) 'A theory of human motivation', *Psychological Review*, 50(4): 370–96.

Maslow, A. (1954) *Motivation and Personality*. New York: Harper & Row.

Maslow, A. (1971) *The Farther Reaches of Human Nature*. Harmondsworth, Middlesex: Penguin Books.

Michel, J.W., Tews, M.J. and Allen, D.G. (2018 in press) 'Fun in the workplace: a review and expanded theoretical perspective', *Human Resource Management Review*, https://doi.org/10.1016/j.hrmr.2018.03.001

Parry, R.L. (2017) 'Young TV reporter died of overtime', *The Times*, 6 October, p.35.

Rahman, M.H. and Nurullah, S.M. (2014) 'Motivational need hierarchy of employees in public and private commercial banks', *Central European Business Review*, 3(2): 44–53.

Rayton, B., Dodge, T. and D'Analeze, G. (2012) *Employee Engagement Task Force: 'Nailing the Evidence' Workgroup*. London: Engage for Success.

Renard, M.K. (2008) 'It's all about money: Chris and Pat compare salaries', *Journal of Management Education*, 32(2): 248–61.

Ryan, R.M. and Deci, E.L. (2017) *Self-Determination Theory: Basic Psychological Needs in Motivation, Development, and Wellness*. New York: Guilford Press.

Sinclair, A. (2018) *Health and Well-Being at Work: Survey Report*. London: Chartered Institute of Personnel and Development.

Sweeney, P.D., McFarlin, D.B. and Inderrieden, E.J. (1990) 'Using relative deprivation theory to explain satisfaction with income and pay level: a multi-study examination', *Academy of Management Journal*, 33(2): 423–36.

Tay, L. and Diener, E. (2011) 'Needs and subjective well-being around the world', *Journal of Personality and Social Psychology,* 101(2): 354–65.

Taylor, F.W. (1911) *Principles of Scientific Management.* New York: Harper.

Tews, M.J., Michel, J.W. and Allen, D.G. (2014) 'Fun and friends: the impact of workplace fun and constituent attachment on turnover in a hospitality context', *Human Relations,* 67(8): 923–46.

The Economist (2015) 'The quantified serf', 7 March, p.66.

The Economist (2016) 'Wells Fargo's boss steps down', 15 October, p.69.

Van de Voorde, K. and Beijer, S. (2015) 'The role of employee attributions in the relationship between high-performance work systems and employee outcomes', *Human Resource Management Journal,* 25(1): 62–78.

Van den Broeck, A., Ferris, D.L., Chang, C.-H. and Rosen, C.C. (2016) 'A review of self-determination theory's basic psychological needs at work', *Journal of Management,* 42(5): 1195–229.

Vroom, V.H. (1964) *Work and Motivation.* New York: John Wiley.

Whysall, Z., James Bowden, J. and Michael Hewitt, M. (2018) 'Sickness presenteeism: measurement and management challenges', *Ergonomics,* 61(3): 341–54.

Zweig, D. (2014) *Invisibles: The Power of Anonymous Work in an Age of Relentless Self-Promotion.* London: Portfolio Penguin.

Part 3 Groups and teams in the organization

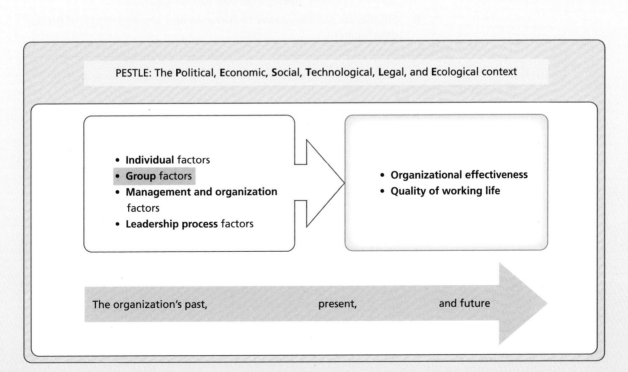

PESTLE: The **P**olitical, **E**conomic, **S**ocial, **T**echnological, **L**egal, and **E**cological context

- **Individual** factors
- **Group** factors
- **Management and organization** factors
- **Leadership process** factors

- **Organizational effectiveness**
- **Quality of working life**

The organization's past,   present,   and future

CHAPTER 10

Group formation

Key terms

team player	Human Relations approach
group	work passion
group dynamics	formal group
aggregate	informal group
additive task	group self-organization
conjunctive task	activities
disjunctive task	interactions
Hawthorne Effect	sentiments

Learning outcomes

When you have read this chapter, you should be able to define those key terms in your own words, and you should also be able to:

1. List the key characteristics of a group.
2. Distinguish between different types of group tasks.
3. Name the four research phases of the Hawthorne studies.
4. Distinguish between a formal and an informal group.
5. Outline Homans' theory of group formation.
6. Enumerate the five stages of Tuckman and Jensen's model of group development.

Why study groups?

Work groups and teams have become a ubiquitous feature of contemporary organizational practice around the world. Increasingly, companies have been organizing work around groups and teams rather assigning it to individuals. In this chapter, we discuss the benefits and challenges of group working; and identify the tasks best performed by groups. We consider the increasing popularity of group working, how groups form and how they develop (Li et al, 2014; Kozlowski and Bell, 2013; Tannenbaum et al., 2012). Diane Coutu (2009, p.99) observed that:

'. . . a cult has grown up around teams. Even in a society as fiercely independent as America, teams are considered almost sacrosanct. The belief that working in teams makes us more creative and productive is so widespread that when faced with challenging new tasks, leaders quickly assume that teams are the best way to get the job done.'

Groups have become an essential element in a modern organization's functioning. Studies show that employees at work spend an average of 54 per cent of their time in group settings. The highest percentages are in China (65 per cent) and the United States (51 per cent), while South Africa (47 per cent) has the lowest number (Ernst and Young, 2013). Marion Hampton (1999, p.113) points to the symbolic function of groups in organizations:

Groups embody many important cultural values of Western society: teamwork, cooperation, a collective that is greater than the sum of its parts, informality, egalitarianism and even the indispensability of the individual member. Groups are seen as having a motivating, inspiring influence on the individual, drawing the best out of him or her, enabling him or her to perform feats that would be beyond him or herself as a detached individual. Groups can have a healing effect on individuals, bolstering their self-esteem and filling their lives with meaning.

However, Richard Hackman, reflecting on his many years of research into groups and teams cautioned:

'I have no question that when you have a team, the possibility exists that it will generate magic, producing something extraordinary, a collective creation of previously unimagined quality or beauty. But don't count on it. Research consistently shows that teams underperform despite the extra resources that they have. That's because problems with co-ordination and motivation typically chip away at the benefits of collaboration. And even when you have a strong and cohesive team, it's often in competition with other teams, and that dynamic can also get in the way of real progress' (in Coutu, 2009, p.100).

It is possible to summarize the pros and cons of group working:

Pros	Cons
Increases possibility of creative solutions through cross-fertilization of ideas	Difficult to coordinate individuals' efforts
Reflects the values of egalitarianism	High-flying star performers in teams can be undervalued
Has an inspiring influence on members, motivating them to excel	Social loafers and free-riders are empowered
Cross-functional and multi-industry teams can improve product quality	Confusion, delay and poor decision making can result
Stresses the importance of individuals' unique contributions	Groupthink, group polarization and commitment escalation are facilitated
Can achieve goals unattainable by individuals working alone	Reduces individuals' personal responsibility autonomy and accountability
Reduced production time if tasks are performed concurrently by people in groups	Can develop their own goals which can be in conflict with those of the wider organization

Underpinning group and teamworking is the principle of collaboration. Rob Cross and his colleagues (2016) found that collaboration with internal colleagues and external contacts was increasing. In the past decade, the time spent by employees in collaborative activities had jumped by 50 per cent. Managers now spend 85 per cent of their time on email, on the phone and in meetings. While this may be beneficial, it is also costly and these costs are not evenly spread between employees. It creates workflow bottlenecks as individuals wait to be consulted and it can result in staff burnout.

The researchers recommend that leaders can improve their management of collaboration by mapping who requests information and who supplies it; by eliminating or redistributing work; and by incentivizing staff to collaborate more efficiently. Meanwhile, employees can protect themselves from collaboration overload by understanding why they take on too much work involving others; restructuring their role, network and schedule to eliminate unnecessary collaboration; and ensuring that desirable collaborative work is as productive as possible (Cross et al., 2018). Generally, companies need to decide when collaboration in the form of group working is appropriate and when it is not.

 **STOP AND SEARCH**   YouTube for *TED talks: Collaboration.*

✓✓✓   **EMPLOYABILITY CHECK** (problem solving, people management, teamworking skills)

Describe a challenge that you faced while a member of a group. This may have been at school, university or in a job. Explain the situation, the task in which the group was engaged in, your contribution to the group, and the result that it achieved. What did you learn from the experience?

Team players in organizations

Group performance affects the success of the organization as a whole. Being able to work productively with others is so important that companies place an emphasis on their recruits being good 'team players'. The Financial Times' 2018 Skills Gap survey placed 'ability to work in a team' as among the top five skills most desired by top employers from graduates (Nilsson, 2018). Researching how graduates could get a job in one of the top management consultancies, investment banks or big law firms, Lauren Rivera (2015) noted that these companies expected their employees to spend extraordinary amounts of time together – learning the ropes in boot camps, working late in the office, having constant work dinners, getting stuck together in distant airports. Recruiters told her that they looked for people who could be their friends as well as colleagues, and that selection was like 'picking a team in the playground', so as to create a 'fraternity of smart people'.

David Aguado and his colleagues (2014) observed that successful teamwork required its members to deploy specific competencies to enable them to effectively interact with each other; synchronize their contributions; deal constructively with conflict; and function as a unified whole so as to achieve the group objective. They should become an 'expert team' and not merely a 'collection of experts'. Those who possess these competences are called team players. A team player is a person who works willingly in cooperation with others for the benefit of the whole team. He or she is humble; does not pursue personal glory; values the performance of the group over individual recognition; is committed to a common goal and to achieving it selflessly. He or she works willingly in cooperation with others for the benefit of the whole team.

Team player a person who works willingly in cooperation with others for the benefit of the whole team.

CUTTING EDGE

Are you a team player?

Min-Ho Joo

Vanessa Dennen

Min-Ho Joo and Vanessa Dennen (2017) studied factors which are known to affect an individual's contribution to their group's work and which could be measured by self-assessment. They developed their *Group Work Contribution Scale* (GWCS). Group-based learning is now a common feature in universities in the form of group assignments and team projects. However, task success and effective learning cannot be guaranteed. Students need to learn how to work together effectively and be encouraged to do so. If they do not feel responsible for their group's output, they are unlikely to collaborate or contribute sufficiently to it. It requires students to work and interact well with each other. The researchers studied 458 undergraduates and found that there were four essential contributions that a student needed to make to their group:

- *Effort:* Whether the student worked to the best of their abilities. Did they participate fully in group discussions, share their opinions, make suggestions, contribute their ideas?
- *Initiative:* Whether the student became actively involved in the group activity. Did they suggest new group working processes and engage in them enthusiastically?
- *Responsibility:* Whether the student fulfilled their duty as a group member to achieve the common goal. Did they attend all group meetings, arrive punctually and complete their allocated tasks?
- *Back-up behaviour:* Whether the student's contributions extended beyond fulfilling their own group responsibilities. Did they help teammates with their duties, stand in for a member unable to fulfil their role, provide them with feedback or correct their mistakes?

How well do you work with others in groups? Are you a team player? Rate yourself using the scale below.

The Group Work Contribution Scale (GWCS)

Think about your most recent experience of working in a group at university. On a five-point scale (5= strongly agree; 1 = strongly disagree), rate yourself as a team player?

During group work, I . . .		Rate 1–5
Effort	Make the best use of my ability to accomplish a group project	
	Do my equal share of a group project	
	Am willing to undertake a task if I have the ability to perform the task	
Initiative	Actively get involved in group discussions (e.g., brainstorming and idea sharing)	
	Actively express my opinion to achieve better group outcomes	
Responsibility	Never miss a scheduled group meeting	
	Am punctual for the scheduled meetings	
	Fulfill allocated tasks	
Backing-up behaviour	Help teammates who were unable to fulfil their roles	
	Correct teammates' mistakes	
	Provide constructive feedback on teammates' work	
	Am willing to help others beyond my assigned tasks	

Source: Joo and Dennen, 2017, pp. 305–6

→

The Group Work Contribution Scale reports an individual's own assessment of their contribution to the work of their group. It does not reflect either their actions or how teammates perceive their contributions. It can be used by instructors to alert students as to what behaviours are desirable for successful group working; by individual members for self-reflection about their group contribution; and by the group as a whole (along with peer assessment) to help progress its journey through the forming, storming, norming and performing stages of the group development process.

THE TEAMMATE'S MOTTO
A teammate is productive, helpful, positive, courteous, cheerful, never way way off point and irreverent.

✓✓✓ **EMPLOYABILITY CHECK** (teamworking skills)

Companies want to hire applicants who are good team players. At your job interview, you claim to be one. What evidence would you provide to support your claim?

What men can learn from women

In this video, Della Bradshaw talks to Karl Moore of McGill University. He discusses the four areas where women appear to be more skilled than men. What are these skills? How can these skills help anyone become a better team player? (4:00)

Critics contend that the extent of employee resistance to management's attempt to establish groups has been underplayed or ignored. Employees also have been less convinced about teamworking. A study by Denise Thursfield (2015) of laboratory technicians revealed that when employees enjoy personal responsibility, individual autonomy and accountability in the performance in their work, they dislike and resist management attempts to introduce group working. More generally, David Knights and Darren McCabe (2000) reported that employees in an automobile plant:

- disliked the intrusion that group working had into their personal lives, causing them to distrust management
- claimed they did not understand the norms of group working and its protocol
- resented the move away from traditional, individual working.

Such reservations are shared by many university students. Despite the enthusiasm of both their university and its instructors for group projects and team assignments, individual students concerned with securing top course grades prefer to work and be assessed individually (Seltzer, 2016; Fiechtner and Davis, 2016). The only redeeming factor is that these students can be sure that when applying for graduate jobs, they will be asked in their application form and at their interview, if they have ever worked in a team, what problems they encountered, and how they overcame them. At least they will have some answers!

Lone introverts do the best work

Susan Cain (2012) observed that the modern workplace is all about teams, open plan offices and collective brainstorming. Schools are increasing arranged in teaching 'hubs' rather than individual desks to encourage group learning. However, she suggests that teamwork might actually be stifling the creativity it is intended to encourage. The lone wolf, who likes to sit in an office with the door closed in order to think, has become an endangered species. Lone geniuses are out, collaboration is in. However research suggests that people are more creative when they have privacy and freedom from interruption.

This is particularly true of introverts who suffer from excessive group work, team-bonding and the fashion for hyper-connectedness. Seventy per cent of American employees inhabit open plan offices. People are in each other's faces all the time, listening to each other's conversations. This constant interaction is exhausting and unproductive according to Cain. Studies show that workers who are constantly interrupted make 50 per cent more mistakes and typically take twice as long to complete tasks. Groups work better when their members are not interacting with each other all the time. 'Always on' communication stifles individual creativity and problem solving (Bernstein et al., 2018). In contrast, some of the most spectacularly creative people in many fields are introverts, who see themselves as individualistic, independent, non-joiners. That puts them out of step with the modern, team-focussed workplace. Perhaps it is time to review our approach to people working together in organizations.

STOP AND SEARCH YouTube for *Susan Cain.* The presenter argues that introverts possess extraordinary talents and abilities, and in a world, where being social and outgoing are prized above all else, introverts should be encouraged and celebrated.

Mars 500 – to boldly go . . . in groups

The prospect of sending a team to Mars by the year 2030 has motivated researchers to assess what is known and what still needs to be discovered about inter-planetary teamwork (Salas, et al. 2015). The Mars project will be a multicultural and interdisciplinary effort which involves travelling to and then living and working in uncomfortable, dangerous conditions; and in close collaboration with distant teams back on Earth. This represents as much of a psychological as a technical challenge. Perhaps the most fictional aspect of the classic science fiction TV and film series, *Star Trek,* was how well the crew members got on with each other despite being in such close proximity in the Starship Enterprise for years.

In preparation for this project, in June 2010 a Frenchman and a Columbian-Italian, together with three Russians and one Chinese, entered a set of four steel containers which they would occupy together. This was a 17-month simulated mission to Mars (called Mars 500) designed by Roskosmos and the European Space Agency (ESA) to test the physical and mental requirements of an ultra-long duration spaceflight. The cramped metal construction (see photo), which has no windows, and in which the volunteers lived, was the Mars 500 'spaceship'. It was located in the car park of Russia's Institute of Biomedical Problems (IBP). Like the contestants on the TV's show *Big Brother,* the subjects were required to complete tasks, and were monitored to determine the effects of separation and close proximity living. The Mars 500 volunteers emerged after their 17-month, 70 million mile virtual journey complaining of boredom. This study showed that teamworking within a confined was problematic and needed to be better understood.

→

To do this, Mesmer-Magnus and his colleagues (2016) interviewed NASA experts on human space exploration to identify still-unanswered questions about teamwork for effective, long-duration space exploration. They listed seven.

1. *Team context*: What aspects of a team affects a person's learning, well-being, and productivity? What might lead an individual to want to leave their team?

2. *Team task switching:* What helps and hinders a person to switch between individual and collective tasks? How does this affect overall team effectiveness?

3. *Multi-team working*: What are the costs and benefits of individuals being members of multiple teams? How does dividing effort and attention between several teams affect individuals' allegiance to team goals and outcomes?

4. *Intra- and inter-team working:* How do intra- and inter-team interactions affect the wider organization and vice-versa? What training is needed to improve intra-team and inter-team working?

5. *Team-technology:* How does members' use of technology facilitate or impede teamworking? What can be done to maintain team performance as technology develops?

6. *Teamworking changes:* How do patterns of teamworking which determines team performance change over time? How do informal behaviours emerge and affect teamworking?

7. *Team adaption:* In circumstances of extreme disruption, which team members' cognitive, motivational, affective and behavioural traits most contribute to continued team effectiveness? What are the obstacles to a team adapting to major changes?

Psychologists are unsure whether a Mars mission should be crewed entirely by women (they are less likely to commit suicide or murder each other when irritable); be mixed (the sexes would support each other); or consist entirely of psychologically robust and less libidinous robots.

Source: based on Mesmer-Magnus et al. (2016); Alliger et al. (2015); Amos (2010, 2011)

STOP AND SEARCH YouTube for *Mars 500*.

Definitions of groups

Group two or more people, in face-to-face interaction, each aware of their group membership and interdependence, as they strive to achieve common group goals.

Group dynamics the forces operating within groups that affect their performance and their members' satisfaction.

Interpersonal behaviour builds up into group behaviour that in turn sustains and structures future interpersonal relations. The term group is thus reserved for people who consider themselves to be part of an identifiable unit, who relate to each other in a meaningful fashion and who share dispositions through their shared sense of collective identity. Members of groups seek to meet their individual needs as identified by Maslow – biological, safety, affiliation, esteem and self-actualization ones (**Chapter 9**).

Groups affect the behaviour of the individuals who compose them. For this reason, researchers study internal group dynamics. They investigate how members of a group communicate with each other and coordinate their activities; how they influence each other; what roles they play in a group; what kind of relationships they have; which members lead and which follow; how they balance a focus on their task with social issues; and how they resolve conflicts (see Figure 10.1).

CRITICAL THINKING

Why would only *one* of the following be considered to be a group? In what circumstances could one of the other aggregates become a group?

(a) People riding on a bus

(b) Blonde women between 20 and 30 years of age

(c) Members of a football team

(d) Audience in a theatre

(e) People smoking outside an office building

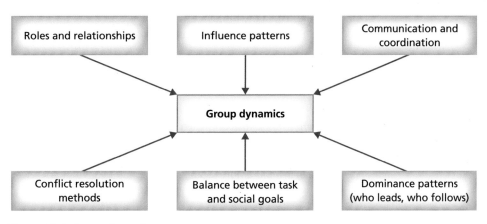

Figure 10.1: Group dynamics

It is important to maintain a distinction between mere aggregates of individuals and what are called groups. The latter are so called because they exist not only through the (often visible) interactions of members, but also in the (not observable) perceptions of their members.

In the Critical thinking example, only the football team would fulfil our criteria for a group, and we can usefully distinguish it from an **aggregate**.

Aggregate a collection of unrelated people who happen to be in close physical proximity for a short period of time.

Aggregates are individuals who happen to be collected together at any particular time. Like the bus travellers, theatre audience or the smokers, they neither relate to one another in any meaningful fashion, nor consider themselves a part of any identifiable unit, despite their temporary physical proximity. Similarly, our definition excludes classes of people defined by their physical attributes, geographical location, economic status or age, and those who do not interact with each other on a regular basis. Thus, a group is unlikely to exceed 12 or so persons. Beyond that number, the opportunity for frequent interaction between members and hence group awareness is considerably reduced.

Home viewing

The Poseidon Adventure (1972, director Ronald Neame) is the story of the attempts of ten passengers to survive the destruction of a luxury passenger liner. A tidal wave strikes the *S.S. Poseidon*, capsizing the ship. The survivors have to decide whether to remain in the ballroom, now deep in the ocean, or climb upwards towards a possible above-water exit at the hull of the sinking ship. The film illustrates the process by which these ten individuals come to identify themselves as a group and gain solidarity. Their separation from the main group, the existence of a common goal (survival), and their goal-oriented actions, all strengthen their cohesion. The omnipresent external threat and their ability to help each other, reinforces the group's unity and sense of identity. As members die, the group's role structure changes and non-leadership roles emerge, showing that all members are crucial to a group's success. The film dramatizes the unification of the group and the struggle for leadership within it; and it shows group conflict, commitment to task, the effects of external pressure on task completion and the effect of intrinsic rewards (Shields and Kidd, 1973).

It is possible for aggregates to be transformed into groups through outside circumstances. At the start of disaster movies, strangers fight for their lives on board sinking ships, hijacked aeroplanes and burning skyscrapers. The danger causes them to interact with one another, increasing their awareness of each other, and leads them to see themselves as having common problems. By the end of the film, the survivors demonstrate all the characteristics of a group as defined here. Groups differ in the degree to which they possess the five characteristics shown below. The more of them that they have, the more they will be recognized as being a group, and the more power the group will have with which to influence its members.

1. *A minimum membership of two people:* Groups can range from two people to over 30. However, the greater the number of group members, the higher the number of possible relationships between them, the greater the level of communication that is required, and the more complex the structure needed to operate the group successfully.

2. *A communication network:* Each group member must be capable of communicating with every other member. In this communication process, the aims and purposes of the group are exchanged. The mere process of interaction satisfies some of our social needs, and it is used to set and enforce standards of group behaviour.

3. *A shared sense of collective identity:* Each member must identify with the other members of their group, and not see themselves as an individual acting independently. They must all believe themselves to be participants in the group which itself is distinct from other groups.

4. *Complementary goals:* Members have individual objectives which can only be met through membership of and participation in the group. Their goals may differ but are sufficiently complementary that members feel able to achieve them through participation in the group. They recognize the need to work collectively and not as individuals.

5. *Group structure:* Individuals in the group will have different roles e.g. ideas person, suggestion-provider, compromiser. These roles, which tend to become fixed, indicate what members expect of each other. Norms or rules exist that indicate which behaviours are acceptable in the group and which are not (e.g. swearing, late coming, not contributing).

> ✋ **STOP AND SEARCH**   YouTube for *Amy Edmondson TED talk: How to turn a group of strangers into a team* (13:08). Edmondson discusses 'teaming' where people come together quickly (and often temporarily) to solve new, urgent or unusual problems.

Size matters

Technological developments have enabled organizations to create ever larger teams to tackle ever larger challenges.

The problem is how to motivate and direct their members. Susan Wheelan studied 329 work groups to assess the impact of size on their productivity and developmental processes. She concluded that 'small is better than large'. Groups of three to four were the most productive, developmentally advanced, and superior to those of five to six and nine-plus. At Google tasks are divided up into projects that can be handled by groups of between five and ten people. At Amazon, founder and chief executive Jeff Bezos limits team size numbers to those small enough to be fed with two pizzas.

Limited numbers improve accountability and goal clarity. In a small group no one can avoid pulling their weight, or claim that they do not know what their goal is. The more people there are at a meeting, the harder it is to get consensus. Once they exceed 20 members, it is difficult to reach consensus because too many sub-groups are formed. On the other hand, a meeting of eight people is the worst total for decision making as it produces neither a consensus nor a majority view, and has the highest probability of becoming deadlocked (Schmidt and Rosenberg, 2017; Taher, 2009; Wheelan, 2009).

Once formed, all groups face a number of challenges, irrespective of whether they are a government ministers agreeing a policy or university students completing a group project. The ten classic challenges facing groups are listed in Table 10.1, and have a direct affect on the group's success or failure.

Table 10.1: **Work group challenges**

Challenge	Explanation
Climate	What atmosphere should pervade a group and how should members relate to one another? e.g. in a university student project group
Objective	To what extent do members understand, accept and are committed to the group's objective? e.g. producing a project that will gain an A-grade
Contribution	Are all members expected to be equally involved in the group's activities? Who will contribute what expertise? e.g. is work to be shared equally and completed on time?
Task division	How is the group's task to be divided up and shared between its members? e.g. on what basis is work to be divided between members?
Information	How is information to be shared between members? What is the best way to inform those who need to know? e.g. regular face-to-face meetings, emails, social media?
Leadership	Should leadership be shared by the group or performed by one person? Should that person be appointed or elected? e.g. should there be a formal leader or should leadership be rotated?
Conflict resolution	How should conflict between group members be managed? Should differences be avoided, accommodated or negotiated? e.g. what happens when members express differences of view?
Decision making	How should the group make decisions? What should happen if there are disagreements? e.g. leader decisions or group voting?
Member evaluation	How should members performance be assessed? What happens when members fail to meet their obligations (social loafing)? e.g. assessment by group leader or by peer review?
Performance evaluation	How should the performance of the group as a whole be assessed and improved? e.g. regular group reviews or individual member questionnaires?

Types of group tasks

Borrill and West (2005) reported research that estimated that 88 per cent of the variation in a group's performance could be explained with reference to the task that it was being asked to perform. Thus, to fully understand group process or group performance, one has to take account of the task that a group performs. Joseph McGrath's model shown in Figure 10.2 offers a classification of group tasks. It consists of two axes. The horizontal axis reflects the degree to which a group task entails conceptual (mental) versus behavioural (doing) requirements. The vertical axis reflects the degree to which the group task is conflicted or cooperative. The degree of conflict or cooperation in a group is the result of the diversity of perspectives, values, or interests of group members that leads to differences or similarities in their preferences for alternative outcomes. McGrath proposes that groups engage in four major processes: 'generate', 'execute', 'negotiate' and 'choose'.

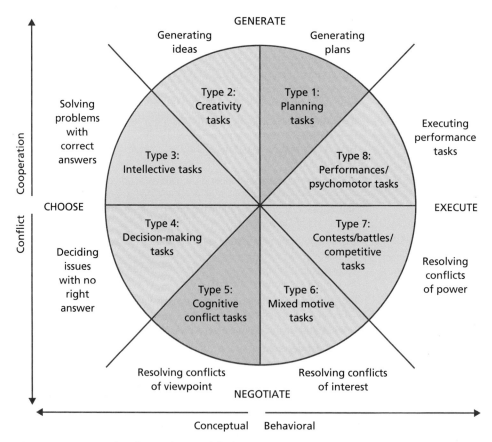

Figure 10.2: McGrath's circumplex model of group tasks
Source: McGrath (1984, p. 61)

Generating tasks requires the production of new ideas and solutions, for example, using brainstorming, blue sky thinking and scenario planning. Executing tasks involves physical movement, coordination and dexterity, for example, surgical operations, military missions, athletic contests. Negotiating tasks entails resolving conflicting viewpoints or interests, for example, in labour–management industrial disputes. Choosing tasks means choosing the best options and decision making, and necessitates option evaluation and consensus-seeking. McGrath's model goes on to identify eight different task categories. While some groups only perform one of these eight types of tasks, others will perform those from several categories (Straus, 1999).

Ivan Steiner (1972) took a different, simpler approach to classifying group tasks based on the type of interdependence that a group's task created between its members. He distinguished three types of tasks:

Additive task a task whose accomplishment depends on the sum of all group members' efforts.

- **Additive task**: With this type of task, all group members do basically the same job, and the final group product or outcome (group performance) is the sum of all their individual contributions. The final outcome is roughly proportional to the number of individuals contributing. There is low interdependency between these people. A group working together will normally perform better than the same number of individuals working alone, provided that all group members make their contribution. However, social loafing can reduce performance on an additive task. Examples of additive tasks are tug-of-war contests, crowdsourcing and cricket.

Conjunctive task a task whose accomplishment depends on the performance of the group's least talented member.

- **Conjunctive task**: In this task, one member's performance depends on another's. There is high interdependency. Thus, a group's *least* capable member determines performance. A successful group project at university depends on one member finding the information, a second writing it up, and a third presenting it. All three elements are required for success and hence coordination is essential in conjunctive tasks. Groups perform less well on conjunctive tasks than lone individuals. Examples of conjunctive tasks include climbing a mountain, playing chamber music, and running a relay race (Steiner and Rajaratnam, 1961).

Disjunctive task a task whose accomplishment depends on the performance of the group's most talented member.

- **Disjunctive tasks**: In this type of task, once again, one member's performance depends on another's. Again there is high interdependency. However, this time, the group's *most* capable member determines its performance. Groups perform better than their average member on disjunctive tasks, since even the best performer will not know all the answers, and working with others helps to improve overall group performance. Diagnostic and problem-solving activities performed by a group would come into this category. Coordination is important here as well, but in the sense of stopping the others impeding the top performers (Diehl and Stroebe, 1991). Examples of disjunctive task performers are quiz teams (*University Challenge*, pub quiz) and a maintenance team in a nuclear power generating plant.

The handover

Yves Morieux of the Boston Consulting Group observed that relay races were often won by teams whose members did not necessarily have the fastest individual times. Members of the medal-winning French women's Olympic relay team explained that, at some point, each had to decide whether to run their guts out, and literally be unable to see straight when they passed the baton, or whether they held something back, to make a better baton change, and thus enable their team mate to run a faster time. The value of this sort of decision making, and each individual's contribution to the team, was beyond measure (Hindle, 2006).

✋ **STOP AND SEARCH**   YouTube for *Yves Morieux, TED Talk: How Too Many Rules at Work Keep You from Getting Things Done* (16:39). Using the example of the women's relay team, the presenter considers the topic of productivity.

Groups will tend to outperform the same number of individuals working separately when working on disjunctive tasks than on additive or conjunctive tasks. This is provided that the most talented member can convince the others of the correctness of their answer. The attitudes, feelings and conflicts in a group setting might prevent this from happening.

World of Warcraft group dynamics

MMORGs (massive multiplayer online role-playing games) such as Activision Blizzard's *World of Warcraft* have become some of the most popular computer games in recent times.

At the start of 2015, the number of its active subscribers passed 10 million. Typically, 40 to 200 players combine into groups (or guilds), getting to know each other and forming their relationships within the game world. Members adopt different roles and responsibilities on behalf of their group which has to undertake some incredibly difficult tasks. Guild membership often changes as players/members become fed up with their colleagues or seek more attractive opportunities elsewhere. The game has become the focus of many scholarly studies which have used qualitative ethnography and quantitative census data analysis. Researchers have examined many aspects of this virtual world including its culture, economic markets and group formation. Irrespective of how strong an individual game character may be, the challenges require that the person works with others, as part of a group. These others possess complementary skills as well as weaknesses.

Leading a raiding party of 25 group (guild) members on a six-hour raid on Illidan the Betrayer's temple fortress poses many organizational challenges. These include recruiting, training, assessing, motivating, rewarding and retaining a talented and culturally diverse number of team members and coordinating their efforts. Decision making has to be done quickly but collectively, using limited information, and has long-term implications. The organization must be built and sustained with a volunteer workforce in a digitally-mediated environment. That environment features a fluid workforce; self-organized and collaborative work activities; decentralized, non-hierarchical, rotating leadership, which is changed when conditions alter. It is therefore not surprising that companies and management consultants are exploring the potential of similar online 'group management simulators' to develop managers' group leadership skills (Bainbridge, 2015; Reeves et al., 2008).

The Hawthorne studies

The famous Hawthorne studies consisted of a series of experiments conducted during the 1920–30s. Although they are approaching their centenary anniversary, they are still of relevance today. Then, as now, there was concern with poor productivity. Hawthorne reminds us that individual behaviour in the workplace is modified both positively and negatively by the group of which he or she is a member. These studies consisted of a series of experiments conducted at the Hawthorne plant of the Western Electric Company, located in Cicero, Illinois, which manufactured telephones. They formed the basis of the Human Relations School of Management. (Hassard, 2012).

The illumination experiments (1924–27)

The original experiments examined the effect of physical changes – originally illumination – on worker productivity (Gillespie, 1991). Electric light replaced natural light and candles. No correlation was found between production output obtained and the lighting provided. Production even increased when the light intensity was reduced. The conclusion was that lighting was only one of several factors affecting production and perhaps a minor one. Professor George Elton Mayo of the Harvard Business School was invited to bring an academic research team into the factory.

Relay Assembly Test Room experiments (1927–33)

These experiments focused on effect of rest pauses and the length of the working day on employees and their attitudes to their work and the company. Six, self-selected female workers were located in the Relay Assembly Test Room, along with a researcher (Figure 10.3). A total of 13 time periods were studied during which changes were made to the women's rest pauses, hours of work and refreshment breaks. The results showed a nearly continuous increase in output over those 13 periods (Figure 10.4). This increase began when employee benefits such as rest periods, served lunches and early finishes were added, but was maintained even when these privileges were withdrawn and the women returned to their normal 48-hour week. The five reasons offered for the increased output were:

1. The motivating effect of acquiring a special status through their selection for and involvement in the experiment.

2. The effect of participation as the women were consulted and informed by the researcher.

3. The effect of observer friendliness which improved their morale.

4. A different and less intensive form of supervision which reduced their stress while increasing their productivity.

5. The self-selected nature of the group creating higher levels of mutual dependence and support appropriate for group working.

Hawthorne Effect the tendency of people being observed to behave differently than they otherwise would.

The increase in output due to the increased attention paid to employees in this study is now known as the Hawthorne Effect. It is defined as the tendency of people being observed as part of a research effort, to behave differently than they otherwise would. Mayo became convinced that the women were not solely motivated by money or by improvements in their

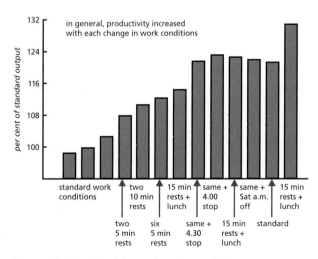

Figure 10.4: Productivity and work conditions

Source: Based on data from Roethlisberger and Dickson (1939). From *Behaviour in Organizations,* 6/e by Greenberg/ Baron, © 1997. reprinted by permission of Pearson Education, Inc. Upper Saddle River, NJ

Figure 10.3: Relay Assembly Test Room, c.1929

working conditions. Their attitudes towards and achievement of increased output seemed to be affected by the group to which they belonged. These results led management to study employee attitudes using an interviewing programme.

Interviewing programme (1928–30)

To find out more about how employees felt about their supervisors and working conditions and how these related to morale, management instituted an interviewing programme involving over 20,000 interviews which extended to include family and social issues. These interviews also revealed the existence of many informal, gang-like groups within the formal working groups. Each had its own leaders and 'sidekicks' who controlled production output. Examining this became the focus of the next experiment.

Bank Wiring Observation Room experiments (1931–32)

The interviews had revealed that groups exercised a great deal of control over the behaviour of their members. A group of 14 men were observed in the Bank Wiring Observation Room (Figure 10.5). This group was operating below its capability and its individual group members were not earning as much as they could. The norms under which the group operated were found to be (Roethlisberger and Dickson, 1939, p.522):

- You should not turn out too much work. If you do, you are a *rate-buster*.
- You should not turn out too little work. If you do, you are a *chisler*.
- You should not tell a supervisor anything that might get a colleague into trouble. If you do, you are a *squealer*.
- You should not attempt to maintain social distance or act officiously. If you are an inspector, you should not act like one.

The men were afraid that if they significantly increased their output, the piece rate would be cut and the daily output expected by management would increase. The men could be reprimanded and lay-offs might occur. To avoid this, the group members agreed between themselves what was a fair day's output (neither too high nor too low). They enforced this informal output norm through a system of negative sanctions or punishments. These included:

- Ridicule as when a group member was referred to as The Slave or Speed King
- 'Binging' which involved striking a norm-violator painfully on the upper arm
- Total rejection or exclusion of the individual by the group as a whole.

Figure 10.5: Men in the Bank Wiring Observation Room, c.1932

The social organization of the group controlled the behaviour of its individual members and protected it from management interference. These results showed that workers were more responsive to the social forces of their own peer group than to the controls and incentives of management. Mayo concluded that:

- Work is a group activity and not just an individual activity.
- The social world of the adult is primarily patterned around work activities.
- At work, within their social group, people fulfil their needs for belonging and recognition, which enhances their productivity.
- A worker's complaint is a manifestation of a more basic, often psychological problem.
- Informal groups at work exercise strong social controls over the work habits and attitudes of individual workers.
- Managers need to collaborate with these informal groups to increase cohesion for the company's benefit.

Human Relations approach a school of management thought which emphasizes the importance of social processes at work.

Those conclusions led to the Human Relations approach to management which held that work should be a source of social relationships for individuals, a way of meeting their need for belonging, for group membership, and could even be a focus for their personal identity. As Rose (1988, p.104) noted:

'Within work-based social relationships or groups . . . behaviour, particularly productivity or cooperativeness with management, was thought to be shaped and constrained by the worker's role and status in a group. Other informal sets of relationships might spring up within the formal organization as a whole, modifying or overriding the official social structure of the factory which was based on purely technical criteria such as division of labour.'

 **STOP AND SEARCH**   YouTube for *Hawthorne studies* and for *Human Relations Theory Elton Mayo.*

Group-oriented view of organizations

In his book, *The Social Problems of an Industrial Society*, Elton Mayo proposed a social philosophy which placed groups at the centre of our understanding of human behaviour in organizations (Mayo, 1945). He stressed the importance of informal groups and encouraged managers to 'grow' them. He discussed *natural groups* of three to six workers and *family groups* of between eight and thirty members. These would develop into one, large *organized group* consisting of a plant-wide network of family groups, each with its own natural groups. Mayo's vision was of a community organization in which all or most employees were members of well-knit, natural groups which were linked together in common purpose. These were not the formal groups discussed earlier. Mayo invited managers to act somewhat like gardeners rather than engineers, and to use their skills, intelligence and experience to deliberately integrate individuals within groups.

The work-as-community theory reflects the observation that many employees now spend more time at work than previous generations. For many staff, work is the most important thing in their lives. Work passion has been defined as a strong inclination towards a job that you like, and into which you invest your time and energy. Harmonious work passion results from individuals internalizing their favourite work activity into their identity and voluntarily engaging in it harmoniously, along with other aspects of their lives. In contrast, obsessive work passion, also the result of internalization, is driven by intra- or interpersonal pressures such as a person's need for self-esteem or acceptance, or a desire for rewards. Obsessive work passion is in conflict with other life activities and comes at a cost to the individual (Vallerand,

Work passion a strong inclination towards a job that you like, and into which you invest your time and energy.

2010; Astakhova and Porter, 2015). Arlie Hochschild (1997) was amongst the first to suggest that individuals work long hours not because of employers' demands but because they obtain most satisfaction from work.

Google staff perks: efficiency, innovation and community

Most people know that Google gives its staff the perk of free food at work. Lazlo Bock, Senior Vice President of People Operations, listed some of the other, lesser-known perks that contributed to the company's goals of efficiency, innovation and community.

- ATMs
- Bureaucracy busters
- Car wash and oil change
- Concierge service
- Electric vehicle loans
- Employee resource groups
- Equality in benefits
- Free food at work
- gCareer (return to work programme)
- Haircuts and salons
- Mobile libraries
- Onsite laundry machines
- Organic grocery delivery
- Shuttle service
- Subsidized child care
- Take Your Child to Work Day

Efficiency in employees' personal lives is valued by the company. To avoid their going home to perform, time-consuming mundane chores, it offers on-site services like ATMs, car washes, dry cleaning, and mobile libraries, to make life easier. A concierge system helps staff with travel planning, finding plumbers, ordering flowers and similar tasks.

Innovation is something that the company wants to encourage and uses its staff perks to increase the number of 'moments of serendipity' that spark creativity. Company cafés are laid out to allow 'casual collisions' to occur between people who might have interesting conversations and micro kitchens are scattered around the building allowing Googlers to meet, chat and compare notes.

Community helps people do their best work. Within the company, the question-and-answer section of the weekly TGIF ('Thank Goodness It's Friday') meeting allows any employee to ask a question; gTalent shows make staff aware of the personal achievements of their colleagues; and email lists of clubs and Employee Resource Groups provide networks for those with similar interests. Externally, 'Take Your Child to Work' and 'Take Your Parent to Work Days' aim to extend a sense of community to Googlers' children, spouses, partners, parents and grandparents.

Bock argues that other companies could give their employees similar perks at little or no cost. In East London, the digital start-up *GoCardless* also offers its 50 employees a similar Millennial-friendly workplace. Its founders' aim is to attract, retain and engage new recruits by creating a workplace that blends the office and home, and promotes team interaction. Work, it appears, can give us friends, lovers, identity, childcare and dry cleaning. Researchers have documented a renewed appetite for community and belonging in Western democracies and 'corporate communities' and 'company families' are developing to fill the gap. (Bock, 2015, p.52; Murphy, 2015).

Rebuilding companies as communities

Henry Mintzberg argued that companies had to re-engage their employees, and remake themselves into places where people were committed to one another and to their enterprises. Individualism (an 'it's all about me' culture) cannot promote leadership and development on its own because humans are social animals, and cannot function effectively without 'community' – a social system that is larger than themselves. Community provides the social glue that binds us together for the greater good. Community means caring about our work, our colleagues, and our communities. Some of the most admired companies such Pixar, possess a strong sense of community. The president of Pixar attributed his company's success to its vibrant community where talented people were loyal to one another and their collective work.

Everyone felt that they were part of something extraordinary, and their passion and accomplishments made their community a magnet for talented people. In our hectic, individualistic world, this sense of community has been lost in many organizations. Mintzberg suggested that we should allow a sense of community to bloom in organizations (Mintzberg, 2009; Catmull, 2008).

Rensis Likert (1961), a famous psychologist, was one of the first to recognize that most people in an organization are members of several groups at the same time. He went on to argue that organizations should be viewed and managed as a collection of groups rather than individuals. He is remembered for proposing the concept of the overlapping group membership structure. This he termed a 'linking pin' process. The overlapping works vertically by having the leaders of related subordinate groups as members of the next higher group, with their common superior as leader and so on up the hierarchy. The organization is therefore conceived as consisting of many overlapping groups. This is shown in Figure 10.6. In Likert's view, an organizational design based around groups rather than individuals, improves communications, increases cooperation, provides more team member commitment, and produces faster decision making.

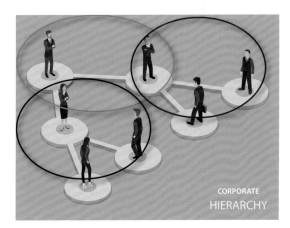

Figure 10.6: Rensis Likert's linking pin model

Multi-team working

Mark Mortensen

Mark Mortensen and Heidi Gardner (2017) studied multi-team working. Early research into teamwork assumed that people worked in only one team. However, recent studies show that in global companies between 81 and 95 per cent of employees work on three to fifteen different team projects simultaneously. Assigning people to multiple teams allows them to share their expertise across different teams and facilitates knowledge transfer through the company.

Multi-teaming is increasingly common because increasingly companies need to combine the expertise of different disciplines in order to solve complex problems quickly (e.g. cyber security); to contain costs and use resources efficiently (e.g. avoiding under-utilization of specialist

→

Heidi Gardner

staff) and to share knowledge across groups; and to attract, develop, engage and retain talented employees.

However, multi-teaming can cause problems. Projects may depend on a few individuals contributing their specialist skills all at the same time; the unpredictability of project skill requirements can cause delays as individuals are pulled off one project and assigned to another; constant member entrances and exits weaken team identity and cohesion; employees can find working on multiple projects and reporting to multiple team leaders difficult; and competing priorities and conflicts can prevent teams with overlapping memberships staying on track. Members may be so stretched that they are unable to share learning with their team colleagues so their company does not benefit. Multi-team members can experience stress, fatigue and burnout as they juggle their time and commitments to various projects.

Mortensen and Gardner offer solutions to improve the effectiveness of multi-team working. They say that team leaders should create opportunities for members to get to know each other and develop mutual trust and understanding; clarify members' role expectations and responsibilities; audit member skills and knowledge to discover the team expertise possessed so as to facilitate team learning and peer mentoring; and they should begin by discussing how members' future conflicting team priorities and deadlines will be resolved.

Company leaders in turn, should be aware that not all teams in their organization will share employees with other teams and that these 'island teams' also need to stay connected with the business and share knowledge, skills and learning. With shared team membership, one team's problem can impact on others. The most vulnerable teams should be identified, problems anticipated, and slack introduced to create 'buffers' to mitigate the consequences. Senior management should signal the importance of knowledge transfer within the company by rewarding it when it occurs. Successful multi-team working involves managing risk, competing priorities and removing obstacles to successful team learning, knowledge transfer and team member coordination.

CRITICAL THINKING

You have accepted a job and your new employer tells you that you will become 'part of the team' and a 'member of one big happy family here'. What positive expectations do you have? What are you worried about?

Formal and informal groups

Workplace behaviour can be considered as varying along a continuum from formally to informally organized. At one extreme, formal behaviour is planned to achieve the collective purpose of an organization (e.g. make a film, manufacture a car, sell insurance). To do this, the organization is structured so as to use the limited resources it has at its disposal as efficiently and effectively as possible. It does this by creating what is called a formal organization. The overall collective purpose or aim is broken down into sub-goals and sub-tasks. These are assigned to different sub-units in the organization. The tasks may be grouped together and departments thus formed. Job requirements in terms of job descriptions may be written. The subdivision continues to take place until a small group of people is given its own sub-goal which it divides it between its members. This process of identifying the purpose, dividing up tasks and so on is referred to as the creation of the formal organization and produces formal groups. A formal group is one that has been consciously created by management to accomplish a defined task that contributes to the organization's goal.

Formal group one that has been consciously created by management to accomplish a defined task that contributes to the organization's goal.

Whatever type of formal group we are interested in, they all have certain common characteristics:

- They are task-orientated.
- They tend to be permanent.
- They have a formal structure.
- They are consciously organized by management to achieve organizational goals.
- Their activities contribute directly to the organization's collective purpose.

Alongside these formal groups, and consisting of the same employees, albeit arranged differently, will be a number of informal groups. These emerge in an organization and are neither anticipated nor intended by those who create the formal organization. They emerge from the informal interaction of the members of the formal organization. These unplanned-for groups share many of the characteristics of small social leisure groups. These function alongside the formal groups.

Informal group a collection of individuals who become a group when they develop interdependencies, influence one another's behaviour, and contribute to mutual need satisfaction.

An *informal group* is a collection of individuals who become a group when they develop interdependencies. It develops during the spontaneous interaction of persons in the group as they talk, joke and associate with one another. At school, your classes were examples of formal groups. Students were assigned to classes by teachers for specific subjects. Outside classes at break times, you regularly associated with different students from different classes. These were examples of informal groups.

Group self-organization the collective process of communication, choice and mutual adjustment in behaviour based on a shared goal among members of a given system.

Between the top-down formal group and the bottom-up informal group, there has been increasing interest in the concept of group self-organization within companies (McCollum and Barber, 2018). *Group self-organization* is defined as the 'a collective process of communication, choice and mutual adjustment in behaviour based on a shared goal among members of a given system' (Comfort, 1994, pp. 397–98). It occurs when 'people and resources organize without planning into coordinated, purposeful activity. If the system is a group, leaders emerge and recede based on who is available and who has information' (Wheatley and Kellner-Rogers, 1996).

Home viewing

In the film *Mean Girls* (2004, director Mark Waters), Cady's map of North Shore High School distinguishes 11 different informal groups of students or *cafeteria tribes* as she calls them. These are reflected in their seating choices in the school cafeteria. One of these is the *Plastics*. Can you name the other ten?

Researching the social networks of informal groups

Interest in informal employee networks and productivity goes back to the Hawthorne studies. The original term *social network* refers to the informal organization developed by the workers themselves, in contrast to the formal organization created by management. Allen et al. (2007) and Cross and Prusak (2002) studied the social networks that existed within large organizations. Their research revealed a few role-players in the network whose performance was critical to the entire organization. The roles of these individuals included:

- *Central connectors* link most of the people within an informal network to one another. Despite not being

formal leaders, they know who possesses the critical information or expertise required to get the work done.

- *Boundary spanners* connect the informal organization with other parts of the company or with similar networks in other organizations. They consult and advise individuals from many different company departments, regardless of their own functional affiliations.

- *Information brokers* keep different subgroups in an informal network together. Failure to communicate

→

across sub-groups would lead to their splintering into smaller less effective segments.

- *Peripheral specialists* are those members within an informal network to whom anyone can turn for specialized expertise.

Figure 10.7 depicts four different departments (formal organization) in a company, and the informal links between individuals within each one. Some individuals are more interacted with than others. The lines demonstrate the informal linkages between individuals in each of the different departments.

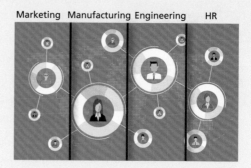

Figure 10.7: Informal links in formal organizations

More recent work by Maya Orbach and her colleagues (2015) used advances in social sensing technology to collect sensor and digital data to investigate the informal network communication structure within the sales division of a US global manufacturing company. The researchers used sociometric badges to gather data on face-to-face interactions (see **Chapter 11**) as well as email and instant messaging logs over a two-month period. They studied individuals' intra-team and inter-team communication with their colleagues to determine the structure of their informal network and its effect on task completion. Their findings showed that the management's expected inter-team workflows did not describe the actual communications that existed between the different teams in the company. It suggested that it did not have a clear idea of how its employees accomplished their tasks. Using this new, face-to-face sensing technology the company could change the spatial layout of the workplace and measure the effects of the changes on employee communications.

A formal organization is ostensibly designed on rational principles and is aimed at achieving the collective purpose of the organization. It thus limits employees' behaviour in order to be able to control and predict it. However, individuals bring their hopes, needs, desires and personal goals to their work. While the company may not be interested in these, the employee will nevertheless attempt to achieve their personal ambitions while at work by manipulating the situation to fulfil their unmet needs. Most other staff will generally be seeking to do the same so it will not be difficult to set up a series of satisfying relationships. These relationships in turn will lead to the formation of informal groups. Because of our social nature we have a tendency to form informal groups. Task-orientated, formal groups rarely meet the social needs of their members. Indeed these social needs are frequently considered to be dispensable and counterproductive to the achievement of the formal purpose of the organization.

✋ STOP AND SEARCH   You Tube for *Creating the conditions for your dream team* (1:54). This animation video offers advice on team design emphasising team diversity and appropriate team climate.

Group formation

George Homans (1951) argued that a group's environment is shaped by management decisions in three areas: physical, technological and social. His three-part model is summarized in Table 10.2, and we shall examine it in relation to management and workers in organizations.

- *Physical.* These are the surroundings within which a group functions. It includes the spatial arrangement of physical objects and location of human activities e.g. office architecture and work furniture; placement of workers on an assembly line.

Table 10.2: Homans' model of group formation

Environment of group	External system	Internal system	
Physical Technological Social	➡ Required activities Required interactions Required sentiments	➡ Emergent activities Emergent interactions Emergent sentiments	➡ Formation of a group

- *Technological.* This includes both the material technology (the tools, machinery and equipment that can be seen, touched and heard) that group members use to do their jobs, and the social technology (the methods which order their behaviour and relationships).

- *Social.* This encompasses the norms and values of the group itself, of its managers (e.g. employees as motivated solely by money) and of the organizational culture (stressing mutual support and collaboration or competition, distrust and backstabbing).

External system

Activities in Homans' theory, the physical movements, and verbal and non-verbal behaviours, engaged in by group members.

Homans' external system broadly equates to the concept of the formal organization introduced earlier. Managers have certain requirements or expectations of employees which, from the employees' perspective, are the 'givens' of their jobs. They require individuals to perform certain activities; to have certain interactions with others; and to have certain sentiments or feelings towards their work.

For example, in a supermarket, the physical, technological, social environment is represented by the design and positioning of the checkout stations, the choice of scanning equipment, and the company's 'the customer is always right' policy. The supermarket management wants its checkout operators to scan customers' purchases (activities); greet them, offer to pack their bags, and say goodbye to them (interactions). They are also expected to have positive attitudes and feelings towards their customers and their employer (sentiments). Homans prefaced each of these elements with the term 'required' (*required activities, required interactions* and *required sentiments*) and referred to them collectively as the *external system.*

Interactions in Homans' theory, the two-way communications between group members.

Sentiments in Homans' theory, the feelings, attitudes and beliefs held by group members towards others.

Each of these three elements reinforces each other. The more activities that employees share, the more frequent will be their interactions, and the stronger will be their shared sentiments (how much the other persons are liked or disliked). The greater the number of interactions between persons, the more will be their shared activities and the stronger their sentiments towards each other. The stronger the sentiments people have for one another, the greater will be the number of their shared activities and interactions. Persons in a group interact with one another, not just because of spatial or geographical proximity (called propinquity), but also to accomplish goals such as cooperation and problem solving.

Internal system

Homans' internal system broadly equates to the concept of the informal organization introduced earlier. This is another, different set of group members' activities, interactions and sentiments that emerge from the physical-technological-social environment, and as a result of the required activities, required interactions and required sentiments themselves. Homans prefaced each of these elements with the term 'emergent' (*emergent activities, emergent interactions* and *emergent sentiments*) and referred to them collectively as the *internal system.* They represent the creation of informal groups within the organization.

These emergent activities can occur in addition to, or in place of the required activities, and are not required by the organization's management. For example, if the job is repetitive (technological context), operators might see how quickly they can perform it (emergent activity) so as to give their work more challenge. If employees are in close proximity to each other (physical context) they might relieve their boredom by talking to each other (emergent interaction) even though company rules forbid it. Group members may come to view customers as a nuisance and develop anti-customer feelings (emergent sentiments). For Homans, the relationship between the external and internal systems was crucial.

- *The internal and the external systems are interdependent.* A change in one system will produce a change in the other. For example, the replacement of a management-selected team leader (external system) can impact on the activities between the group members (internal system). Similarly, the sentiments of group members (internal system) can affect the way they do their work (external system).

- *The environment and the internal and external systems are interdependent.* Changes in the environment produce changes in the external (formal) and internal (informal) work organization. Individuals and groups will modify what they do and how they do it to respond to the changes they perceive.

Homans' model of group formation established the basis for our understanding of group behaviour. First, it highlights how the environment within which a group functions (the physical dispersion of staff; the technology that they use; and their social context) helps or hinders the process of group formation. Second, it highlights how this management-created environment imposes the required activities, required interactions and required sentiments on individuals and groups in an organization, and then how these in turn stimulate the emergent activities, emergent interactions and emergent sentiments, that are not required by the external system.

What did he find? Proximity of seating arrangements

Sunkee Lee (2019) studied the effects of reconfiguring the spatial proximity of staff in the work place. He investigated a large South Korean e-commerce company that was moving into a new headquarters. Its sales employees (called merchandisers) had the job of identifying and sourcing novel products (such as electronics, appliances, food/health products) to sell on the company's online platform. These merchandisers could choose between an *exploitation* approach (repeatedly selling the same products they had sourced in the past) and an *exploration* one (sourcing novel products that had not been sold by anyone in the firm before). The latter was more desirable for the firm's long-term viability but was usually avoided by merchandisers because of the inherent risk associated with experimentation.

Sunkee Lee

The relocation caused a rearrangement of the seating of 60 merchandisers. Some sales employees' workspaces in the new headquarters were moved closer to each other. This greater physical proximity also increased their opportunity for social interaction. The workspaces of others remained at a similar distance to previously co-located peers. The former individuals were studied as the 'treatment group' and the latter ones as the 'control group'. Lee looked at 38,435 deals executed by these 60 merchandisers working in 12 product teams over 204 days. He was interested in what effect placing merchandisers closer together had on their exploration behaviour and on their sales performance. What do you think he found?
(Answers in chapter Recap.)

Group development

Many organizations rely on teams which are constantly being formed and reformed to adapt to rapidly changing business conditions. Teams therefore need to be 'up to speed' as quickly as possible. The famous model of group development developed by Bruce Tuckman and Mary Ann Jensen (1977) explains how this can be achieved, and also identifies the problems. They suggested that groups pass through five stages (Figure 10.8).

1. Forming

This is the orientation stage, at which the set of individuals has not yet gelled. The individual asks, 'How do I fit in?' and the group asks 'Why are we here?' Everyone is busy finding out about each other's attitudes and backgrounds, and establishing ground rules. Members are also keen to establish their personal identities within the group and make a personal

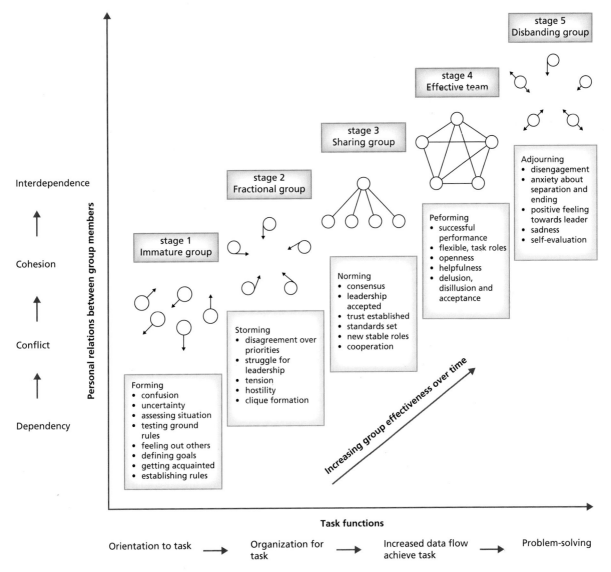

Figure 10.8: Stages of group development

Source: based on Tuckman and Jensen (1977) and Jones (1973)

impression on the others. In the personal relations area, members are *dependent* on a leader to provide them with structure in the form of ground rules and an agenda for action. Task-wise, they seek *orientation* as to what they are being asked to do, what the issues are, and whether everyone understands the task.

2. Storming

This is a conflict stage in the group's life and can be an uncomfortable period. The individual asks 'What's my role here?' and the group asks 'Why are we fighting over who's in charge and who does what?' Members bargain with each other as they try to sort out what each of them individually and as a group, want out of the group process. Individuals reveal their personal goals and it is likely that interpersonal hostility is generated when differences in these goals are revealed. Members may resist the control of other group members. The early relationships established in the forming stage may be disrupted. The key personal relations issue in this stage is the management of *conflict*, while the task function question is *organization* – how best to organise to achieve the group objective.

3. Norming

In this cohesion stage, the members of the group develop ways of working together to develop closer relationships and camaraderie. The individual asks, 'What do others expect me to do?' and the group asks 'Can we agree on roles and work as a team?' The questions of 'who will do what' and 'how it will be done' are addressed. Working rules are established in terms of norms of behaviour (do not smoke) and role allocation (Jill will be the spokesperson). A framework is therefore created in which each group member can relate to the others and questions of agreeing expectations and dealing with a failure to meet members' expectations are considered. The personal relations within the group stress *cohesion*. Members feel that they have overcome conflict, have 'gelled' and experience a sense of 'groupiness'. On the task side, there is an *increase in data-flow* as members become increasingly prepared to be more open about their goals and share information with one another.

4. Performing

By this stage the group has developed an effective structure and it is concerned with actually getting on with the job in hand and accomplishing objectives. The individual asks 'How can I best perform my role?' and the group asks 'Can we do the job properly?' The fully mature group has now been created which can get on with its work. Not all groups develop to this stage but may become bogged down in an earlier and less productive stage. In personal relations *inter-dependence* becomes a feature. Members are equally happy working alone or in sub-groupings or individually. Both collaboration and functional competition occur between members. On the task side, there is a high commitment to *problem solving* and members' roles become well defined.

5. Adjourning

In this final stage, the group may disband, either because the goal has been achieved or because the members have left. The individual asks 'What's next?' and the group asks 'Can we help members make the transition to their next task or group?' Before they do so, they may reflect on their time together, and ready themselves to go their own, separate ways.

The various group development stages need not occur in sequence. While groups do pass through these different stages, they have been found to go through more of an iterative process. They cycle back and forth between the different stages. They may pass through one stage several times or become stuck in a certain stage for a period of time. Some groups pass through certain stages more quickly than others. Moreover, progress through to any given stage is not guaranteed (Gersick, 1988; 1989). Group formation can be seen as an adaptive process as one moves from feeling and thinking as an individual (personal identity) to feeling and thinking as a member of a group (social identity).

The value of the Tuckman and Jensen framework shown in Figure 10.7 is that it can help explain some of the problems of group working. A group may be operating at half power because it may have failed to work through some of the issues at the earlier stages. For example, the efficiency of a project team may be impaired because it has not resolved the issue of leadership. Alternatively, people may be pulling in different directions because the objectives of the group have not been clarified. Members might be using the group to achieve their personal and unstated aims (so-called hidden agendas). For all these reasons, effective group functioning may be impaired.

✓✓✓ **EMPLOYABILITY CHECK** (results orientation, people management, teamworking skills)

Choose a group to which you currently belong to or are familiar with – a sports club, drama society, tutorial group, project group, etc.

- Identify which stage of development it has reached.
- What advice would you give to this group to accelerate its progress to the 'performing' stage?

Home viewing

Two films illustrate the different stages of group development. In *The Breakfast Club* (1984, director John Hughes) five American high school students spend a whole Saturday in detention under a teacher's less than watchful eye. Over the day, the individuals form and develop into a group. In *Remember the Titans* (2000, director Boaz Yakin) a very different set of students are welded into a successful American football team under the leadership of their coach played by Denzil Washington. In both cases, identify the transition between the forming, storming, norming, performing and adjourning stages of group formation (Reimers and Parsons, 2003; Smith, 2009).

 **RECAP**

1. *List the key characteristics of a group.*
   - These are: two or more people, in face-to-face interaction, each aware of his or her membership in the group, each aware of the others who belong to the group, and each aware of their positive interdependence as they strive to achieve mutual goals.

2. *Distinguish between different types of group tasks.*
   - Groups can be assigned many different tasks, many of which can be categorised under the headings of additive, conjunctive and disjunctive.

3. *Name the four research phases of the Hawthorne studies.*
   - The Hawthorne studies consisted of four major phases – Illumination experiments, Relay Assembly Test Room experiments, Interviewing programme, and the Bank Wiring Observation Room experiments

4. *Distinguish between a formal and an informal group.*
   - Formal groups can be distinguished from informal groups in terms of who creates them and what purposes that they serve.

5. *Outline Homans' theory of group formation.*
   - George Homans' theory of group formation distinguishes between background factors, and required and emergent activities, interactions, sentiments, to explain how individuals come to form groups.

6. *Enumerate the five stages of Tuckman and Jensen's model of group development.*
   - Tuckman and Jensen distinguished five stages through which groups typically proceed, which they named forming, storming, norming, performing and adjourning.

→

RECAP: What did he find?

Lee (2019) found that:

- Increasing spatial proximity between individuals did not, on its own, lead to an increase in individuals' exploration behaviour.

- However, merchandisers' exploration behaviour was increased when they were moved closer to their *previously separated* peers. They increased their level of exploration by an average of 25 per cent.

- This relationship was strongest among individuals with high levels of prior work experience (due to their abilities to better utilize ideas of newly met peers) as well as those with no previous social ties with their newly co-located peers (because social ties are channels of information flow).

- It was therefore useful to co-locate individuals who had different ideas or work processes.

- An increase in spatial proximity among previously separated peers went hand-in-hand with an increase in their exploration behaviour and an increase in their sales performance. The aggregated daily deal revenue increased on average by $16,510 for individuals in the group. This represented a 40 per cent increase compared to that of all merchandisers before the move.

Revision

1. Is having a work passion a good or a bad thing? How does it affect the career choices of university graduates?

2. How do informal groups within an organization differ from formal ones? What function do informal groups perform and which members' needs do they meet?

3. Choose a group with which you are familiar, and analyse it using the four elements of Homans model of group formation.

4. Under what circumstances should management form a group or a team to perform a task and when should it arrange for individuals to work on their own?

Research assignment

Select either a group featured in a television series or one of which you know well (e.g. sports team; scout/guide group; social club). Consider the following questions:

a. Is this a formal or informal group?

b. What stage is this group at, in terms of Tuckman and Jensen's model of group development?

c. What is your group's size, composition, function and status?

d. How do these factors affect its operation and outcomes?

e. What roles do group members play in the group and what are their relationships with one another?

f. What expectations, rights and responsibilities are attached to each of the group member roles?

g. What formal rules and informal norms does the group use to control its members' behaviour?

h. How does the group react if a member breaks its rules or norms?

Springboard

John Mathieu, John Hollenbeck, Daan van Knippenberg and Daniel Ilgen (2017) 'A century of work teams', *Journal of Applied Psychology*, 102 (3): 452–67. The authors provide a comprehensive summary of the research into groups and teams, setting this chapter's content into context.

John Hassard (2012) 'Rethinking the Hawthorne Studies: The Western Electric research in its social, political and historical context', *Human Relations*, 65(11): 1431–61. The author reflects upon the relevance of the findings to contemporary organizations.

Henry Mintzberg (2009) 'Rebuilding companies as communities', *Harvard Business Review*, 76(7/8): 140–43. The author discusses 'communityship' updating Mayo's original idea, and placing it into a contemporary context.

Amanda Sinclair (1992) 'The tyranny of a team ideology', *Organization Studies*, 13(4): 611–26. This classic article provides a critical review of the concept of team in managerial and organizational writings.

OB cinema

The Magnificent Seven (1960, director John Sturges). DVD track 6: 0:18:35 – track 12: 0:39:48 (6–11–21 minutes – sequenced).

Everybody who joins a group does so in order to meet their specific needs. In this classic American western film, a group of Mexican farmers cross the border, initially with a view to buying guns in order to defend their village against bandits. Eventually, they end up hiring gunmen. The clip begins as the three villagers enter Chris's (played by Yul Brynner) hotel room. As you watch the clip of the selection process, pause each time a gunman agrees to join the group. Speculate as to which of his Maslow needs (**Chapter 9**) he appears to meeting by joining. There may be more than one need.

	Needs				
Character (actor)	Biological	Safety	Affiliational	Esteem (self and others)	Self-actualization
Chris (Yul Brynner)					
Harry (Brad Dexter)					
Vin (Steven McQueen)					
O'Reilly (Charles Bronson)					
Britt (James Coburn)					
Lee (Robert Vaughn)					
Chico (Horst Bucholz)					

Chapter exercises

1. Group experiences

Objectives   1. Demonstrate how groups affect your work and social life.

Briefing   1. Individually
   a. Make a list of all the different groups to which you belong at the present time.
   b. Distinguish work groups from non-work groups, and formal from informal groups.

2. Form groups

    a. Share the number of groups that you each belong to. Which are face-to-face and which are virtual?

    b. Identify to which types of groups all or most of you belong. Why is this?

    c. Using examples, explain how being in a group affects your behaviour. Do you behave differently when in a group than when alone? Do you behave differently in different groups?

3. In your groups

    a. Each person shares a *positive* experience that they have had while being a member of a group.

    b. Each person shares a *negative* experience that they have had while being a member of a group.

    c. Identify any common factors in your positive experiences; and in your negative experiences

    d. What conclusions do you draw about the way that groups should be designed and managed?

2. It's a puzzle: A group self-organizing activity

Objectives
1. Students will be able to apply self-organization concepts to the puzzle activity experience
2. Students will be able to appropriately apply selected abstract self-organization concepts to their current or past organization/group experiences.

Briefing
1. Form a group of 8–15 individuals around a table.
2. Nominate two observers to make notes and report back on what happens.
3. Your instructor will place puzzle pieces, jumbled up and face up, on the table.
4. Group members place themselves around the table.
5. Your task is to put the puzzle pieces together.

De-briefing
- *Individual reflection:* Individually reflect on your group's process, their individual actions, their interaction with others in the group, and the impact their actions and interactions had on the outcome. Write down your reflections.

- *Group reflection:* Share your individual reflections with other students, and compare them with the student observers; observations.

- The instructor leads a plenary class discussion.

Source: McCollum and Barber (2018)

References

Aguado, D., Rico, R, Sánchez-Manzanares, M. and Salas, E. (2014) 'Teamwork Competency Test (TWCT): a step forward in measuring teamwork competencies, *Group Dynamics: Theory, Research and Practice,* 18(2):101–21.

Alliger, G.M., Cerasoli, C.P., Tannenbaum, S.I. and Vessey, W.B. (2015) 'Team resilience: how teams flourish under pressure', *Organizational Dynamics,* 44(3):176–84.

Astakhova, M.N. and Porter, G. (2015) 'Understanding the work passion: the mediating role of organizational identification and moderating role of fit at work', *Human Relations,* 68(8), 1315–46.

Allen, J., James, A.D. and Gamlen, P. (2007) 'Formal versus informal knowledge networks in R&D: a case study using social network analysis', *R&D Management*, 37(3): 179–96.

Amos, J. (2010) 'Cosmonauts chosen for Mars test, *BBC News*, 10 May.

Amos, J. (2011) 'Simulated Mars mission 'lands' back on Earth', *BBC News*, 4 November.

Bainbridge, W.S. (2015) 'World of Warcraft', *The International Encyclopedia of Digital Communication and Society*, Chichester: Wiley, pp.1–4.

Bernstein, E., Shore, J. and Lazer, D. (2018) 'How intermittent breaks in interaction improve collective intelligence', *Proceedings of the National Academy of Sciences*, 115(35): 8734–39.

Bock, L. (2015) *Work Rules*, London: John Murray.

Borrill, C. and West, M. (2005) 'The psychology of effective teamworking' in N. Gold (ed.), *Teamwork*, London: Palgrave Macmillan, pp.136 60.

Cain, S. (2012) *Quiet: The Power of Introverts in a World That Can't Stop Talking*, New York: Crown Publishing.

Catmull, E. (2008) 'How Pixar fosters collective creativity', *Harvard Business Review*, 86(9): 64–72.

Comfort, L. K. (1994) 'Self-organization in complex systems', *Journal of Public Administration Research and Theory*, 4(3): 393–410.

Coutu, D. (2009) 'Why teams don't work', *Harvard Business Review*, 87(5): 99–105.

Cross, R. and Prusak, L. (2002) 'The people who make organizations go – or stop', *Harvard Business Review*, 80(6): 104–12.

Cross, R., Rebele, R. and Grant, A. (2016) 'Collaboration overload', *Harvard Business Review*, 94(1): 74–79.

Cross, R., Taylor, S. and Zehner, D. (2018) 'Collaboration without burnout', *Harvard Business Review*, 96(4): 134–37.

Diehl, M. and Stroebe, W. (1991) 'Productivity loss in idea generating groups: tracking down the blocking effect', *Journal of Personality and Social Psychology*, 61(3): 392–403.

Ernst and Young (2013) *The Power of Many: How Companies Use Teams to Drive Superior Corporate Performance*, https://www.ey.com/Publication/vwLUAssets/EY-The-power-of-many/$FILE/EY-The-power-of-many.pdf [accessed April 2019]

Fiechtner, S.B. and Davis, E.A. (2016) 'Republication of 'Why some groups fail: a survey of students' experiences with learning groups', *Journal of Management Education*, 40(1) 12–29.

Gersick, C.J. (1988) 'Time and transition in work teams', *Academy of Management Journal*, 31(1): 9–41.

Gersick, C.J. (1989) 'Marking time: predictable transitions in task group', *Academy of Management Journal*, 32(2): 274–309.

Gillespie, R. (1991) *Manufacturing Knowledge: A History of the Hawthorne Experiments*. Cambridge: Cambridge University Press.

Greenberg, J. and Baron, R.A. (1997) *Behaviour in Organization*, sixth edition, Englewood Cliffs, NJ: Pearson/Prentice Hall.

Hampton, M.M. (1999) 'Work groups' in Yiannis Gabriel (ed.), *Organizations in Depth*. London: Sage Publications, pp.112–38.

Hassard, J. (2012) 'Rethinking the Hawthorne Studies: The Western Electric research in its social, political and historical context', *Human Relations*, 65(11): 1431–61.

Hindle, T. (2006) 'Take a deep breath', *The Economist, The New Organization: A Survey of the Company*, 21 January, pp.5, 6 and 8.

Hochschild, A.R. (1997) *The Time Bind: When Home Becomes Work and Work Becomes Home*. New York: Owl Books.

Homans, G.C. (1951) *The Human Group*. London: Routledge and Kegan Paul.

Jones, J.E. (1973) 'Model of group development', *The 1973 Annual Handbook for Group Facilitators*, San Francisco, CA: Jossey Bass, pp.127–29.

Joo, M-H. And Dennen, V.P. (2017) 'Measuring university students' group work contribution: scale development and validation', *Small Group Research*, 48(3): 288–310.

Knights, D. and McCabe, D. (2000) 'Bewitched, bothered and bewildered: the meaning and experience of teamworking for employees in an automobile plant', *Human Relations*, 53(11): 1481–1518.

Kozlowski, S.W.J. and Bell, B.S (2013) 'Work groups and teams in organizations' in Weiner, I.B., Schmitt, N.W. and Highhouse, S. (eds), *Handbook of Psychology, Volume 12: Industrial and Organizational Psychology*, second edition, London: Wiley, pp.412–69.

Lee, S. (2019) 'Learning-by-moving: can reconfiguring spatial proximity between organizational members promote individual-level exploration?', *Organization Science*, (published early online)

Li, N., Kirkman, B.I. and Porter, C.O.L.H. (2014) 'Toward a model of team altruism', *Academy of Management Review*, 39(4): 541–65.

Likert, R. (1961) *New Patterns of Management*. New York: McGraw-Hill.

Mayo, E. (1945) *The Social Problems of an Industrial Civilization*. Cambridge, MA: Harvard University Press.

McCollum, J. and Barber, C.R. (2018) 'It's a puzzle: a self-organizing activity', *Management Teaching Review*, 2(3): 166–78.

McGrath, J.E. (1984) *Groups: Interaction and Performance.* Upper Saddle River, NJ: Prentice Hall.

Mesmer-Magnus, J.R. Carter, D.R. Asencio, R. and DeChurch, L.A. (2016) 'Space exploration illuminates the next frontier for teams' research', *Group & Organization Management*, 41(5): 595–628.

Mintzberg, H. (2009) 'Rebuilding companies as communities', *Harvard Business Review*, 76(7/8): 140–43.

Mortensen, M. and Gardner, H.K. (2017) 'The overcommitted organization', *Harvard Business Review*, 95(5): 58–65.

Murphy, H. (2015) 'The office as somewhere you enjoy', *Financial Times*, 10 March, p.7.

Nilsson, P. (2018) 'What top employers want from MBA graduates', *Financial Times*, 3 September.

Orbach, M., Demko, M., Doyle, J., Waber, B.N. and Pentland, A. (2015) 'Sensing informal networks in organizations', *American Behavioural Scientist*, 59(4): 508–24.

Reeves, B., Malone, T.W. and O'Driscoll, T. (2008) 'Leadership online labs', *Harvard Business Review*, 86(5): 58–66.

Reimers, J.M. and Parsons, G. (2003) 'Case study: *Remember the Titans* (2000) to examine power, servant leadership, transformational leadership, followership and change', *Journal of Behavioural and Applied Management*, 5(2): 152–65.

Rivera, L.A. (2015) *Pedigree: How Elite Students Get Elite Jobs,* Princeton, NJ: Princeton University Press.

Roethlisberger, F.J. and Dickson, W.J. (1939) *Management and the Worker,* Cambridge, MA: Harvard University Press.

Rose, M. (1988) *Industrial Behaviour and Control,* Harmondsworth, Middlesex: Penguin Books.

Salas, E., Tannenbaum, S.I., Kozlowski, S.W.J., Miller, C.A., Mathieu, J.E. and Vessey, W.B.(2015) 'Teams in space exploration: a new frontier for the science of team effectiveness', *Current Directions in Psychological Science*, 24(3): 200–07.

Schmidt, E and Rosenberg, J. (2017) *How Google Works,* second edition, London: John Murray.

Seltzer, J. (2016) 'Teaching about social loafing: the accounting team exercise' *Management Teaching Review*, 1(1): 34–42.

Shields, D.C. and Kidd, V.V. (1973) 'Teaching through popular film: a small group analysis of *The Poseidon Adventure*', *The Speech Teacher*, 22(3): 201–07.

Smith, G.W. (2009) 'Using feature films as the primary instructional medium to teach organizational behaviour', *Journal of Management Education*, 33(4): 462–89.

Steiner, I. (1972) *Group Process and Productivity*, New York: Academic Press.

Steiner, I. and Rajaratnam, N.A. (1961) 'A model for the comparison of individual and group performance scores', *Behavioural Science*, 6(2): 142–47.

Straus, S.G. (1999) 'Testing a typology: an empirical validation of McGrath's (1984) group task circumplex', *Small Group Research*, 30(2): 166–87.

Taher, A. (2009) 'Number's up for 'unlucky' eight', *The Sunday Times*, 11 January, p.7.

Tannenbaum, S. I., Mathieu, J. E., Salas, E. and Cohen, D. (2012) 'Teams are changing: are research and practice evolving fast enough? *Industrial and Organizational Psychology: Perspectives on Science and Practice*, 5(1): 2–24.

Thursfield, D. (2015) 'Resistance to team working in a UK research and development laboratory', *Work, Employment and Society*, 29(6): 989–1006.

Tuckman, B.W. and Jensen, M.A.C. (1977) 'Stages of small group development revisited', *Group and Organizational Studies*, 2(4): 419–27.

Vallerand, R. J. (2010) 'On passion for life activities: the dualistic model of passion' in *Advances in Experimental Social Psychology:* Volume 42, Academic Press, pp. 97–193.

Wheatley, M. J. and Kellner-Rogers, M. (1996) 'Self-organization: the irresistible future of organizing', *Strategy & Leadership*, 24(4): 8–24.

Wheelan, S.A. (2009) 'Group size, group development, and group productivity', *Small Group Research*, 40(2), 247–62.

Group structure

Key terms

person–group fit

group structure

group process

power

reward power

coercive power

referent power

legitimate power

expert power

formal status

social status

group hierarchy

sociometry

sociogram

communication network analysis

communigram

communication pattern analysis

communication pattern chart

virtual team

interaction process analysis

task activity

maintenance activity

social role

team role

distributed leadership

networked individualism

Learning outcomes

When you have read this chapter, you should be able to define those
key terms in your own words, and you should also be able to:

1. List the six dimensions of group structure.

2. Identify the sources of power within a group.

3. Distinguish between two common uses of the concept of status.

4. Understand how emotional relationships within a group can be
   represented symbolically.

5. Distinguish between communication network analysis,
   communication pattern analysis and Interpersonal Process Analysis
   (IPA).

6. Distinguish between task, sociability and dominance roles within a
   group.

7. Differentiate between Belbin's team roles.

8. Give examples of three original leadership styles identified by
   Lewin, White and Lippitt.

9. Distinguish between a task and a socio-emotional group leader.

10. List the key dimensions of a virtual team.

11. Identify the benefits and problems associated with virtual teams

Why study group structure?

Organizations are keen to employ people who work well together. Nicky Binning, head of experienced hire and global mobility at KPMG, an international advisory firm says that:

> 'There is now such a pace of change that it almost doesn't matter what you have done in the past . . . It is the ability to understand what is in front of you, and work collaboratively that counts. You have to work together as a team because it is likely that you are facing something that you have never faced before' (cited by Tieman, 2012, p.1).

An individual from a function like marketing may be delegated to participate in various teams which can be face-to-face, project, virtual, cross-industry, cross-cultural or a combination of these. Increasingly, members of one firm may be required to create a joint team with those of another company, in order to meet a client's needs. Pam Jones, director of Ashridge Business School's Performance Through People programme, studied teamworking in 600 organizations from around the world. She found that 75 per cent of the teams were dispersed geographically; 30 per cent were spread across time zones; and half were 'virtual' and rarely met (cited in Tieman, 2012, p.1).

Person–group fit the interpersonal compatibility between individuals and the members of their immediate groups.

Person–group fit

Every company wants employees who have person–group fit which refers to the interpersonal compatibility between individuals and the members of their immediate groups. When 'fit' is achieved there is an increase in an individual's satisfaction with their job and with their co-workers and a rise in their organizational commitment and task performance. Much of the research into groups seeks to understand why individuals do *not fit,* i.e. why they have different goals, attitudes, values, perceptions from their fellow group members; do not cooperate with them; fail to perform their assigned tasks, etc. Meanwhile, much organizational effort in the form of staff selection, employee induction, training, team composition choices, and team-building activities is expended to ensure that the individual *does fit*!

Team problem

There were four team members named Everybody, Somebody, Anybody and Nobody.

There was an important job to do and Everybody was asked to do it.

Everybody was sure Somebody would do it.

Anybody could have done it, but Nobody did.

Everybody was angry about that, because it was Somebody's job.

Everybody thought Anybody could do it, but Nobody realised that Everybody wouldn't.

In the end, Everybody blamed Somebody when Nobody did what Anybody could have done.

Group structure and process

Group structure the relatively stable pattern of relationships among different group members.

A central idea in helping us to examine the nature and functioning of groups is that of structure. Group structure refers to the way in which members of a group relate to one another. When people come together and interact, differences between individuals begin to appear. Some talk while others listen; some make decisions while others accept them; some ask for information while others provide it. These differences between group members serve as the basis for the establishment of group structure. As differentiation occurs, relations are established between members. Group structure is the label given to this patterning of relationships.

Group structure carries with it the connotation of something fixed and unchanging. While there is an element of permanency in terms of the relationships between members, these do continue to change. Group members continually interact with each other and in consequence their relationships are tested and transformed. As we describe the structure of any group, it is useful to view it as a snapshot photograph, correct at the time the shutter was pressed but acknowledging that things were different the moment before and after the photo was taken.

Differences between the members of a group begin to occur as soon as it is formed. A rank order is quickly established between them. Nik Halvey and colleagues (2011) explain that this rank ordering, or the creation of a hierarchy within a group, facilitates its survival, functioning and performance and contributes to its success. This ordering occurs along not one, but several dimensions. The most important of these are:

- Power
- Status
- Liking
- Communication
- Role
- Leadership

There are as many structures in a group as there are rank ordering dimensions along which a group can be differentiated. Group members will be accorded different amounts of status and hence a group will have a status hierarchy and thus a status structure. They will be able to exert differing amounts of power and thus a power hierarchy and a power structure will emerge. While it is possible to examine each structural dimension of the group in turn, we need to remember that all are closely related and operate simultaneously in a group setting. A group's structure is determined by:

1. The requirements for efficient group performance.
2. The abilities and motivations of group members.
3. The psychological and social environment of the group.

Why does a patterning of relationships between individuals in a group occur and what purpose does it serve? Robert Bales (1950a) offered a psychological explanation based on an individual's desire for stability, 'need for order' and 'low tolerance of ambiguity'. He argued that meeting and dealing with other people within a group can cause a person stress. It is the potential uncertainty and unpredictability of the actions of others that causes this. If the behaviour between group members can be made predictable, this can reduce the tension for all concerned. This, he explained, is what group structure does.

Group process the patterns of interactions between the members of a group.

A group's structure will be affected by group process which is defined as the patterns of interactions between the members of a group. Examples of a group's process include:

- Direction of communication   (Who talks to whom)
- Quantity of communication   (Number of times each group member speaks)
- Content of communication   (Type of oral utterance made)
- Decision-making style   (How decisions are made in the group)
- Problem-solving style   (How problems are approached and solved)

The relationship between group structure and group process is two-way. The structure of a group can affect its process. For example, when an individual is appointed the leader of a formal group, they will tend to speak more often and will be listened to more closely. Being group leader will therefore determine the direction, frequency and content of their communication with others in the group. Conversely, group process can shape group structure. In an informal group, the individual who speaks most often to all fellow members may come to be liked the most. Their status will rise in the eyes of the other members, and they may be given permission to take on a leadership role within the group. If a group can become aware of its processes, and manage them better, then it is likely to achieve improved outcomes.

Power structure

Power the capacity of individuals to overcome resistance on the part of others, to exert their will, and to produce results consistent with their interests and objectives.

Individual members of a group differ in terms of how much power they each possess and hence in their ability to direct the behaviour of other members. Power is defined as the capacity of individuals to overcome resistance on the part of others, to exert their will, and to produce results consistent with their interests and objectives. For this reason, it becomes necessary for the group to have established control relations between members. This means clarifying and accepting which types of power are possessed by different members of a group. By having a power structure, the group avoids continued power struggles that can disrupt its functioning. It can also link activities intended to achieve its goals to a system of authority which is seen as legitimate by all members (Dahl, 1957).

Reward power the ability to exert influence based on the other's belief that the influencer has access to valued rewards which will be dispensed in return for compliance.

Coercive power the ability to exert influence based on the other's belief that the influencer can administer unwelcome penalties or sanctions.

Referent power the ability to exert influence based on the other's belief that the influencer has desirable abilities and personality traits that can and should be copied.

"I'm not disputing that you have a lot of power around the office. I'm just saying you need to follow the dress code."

Legitimate power the ability to exert influence based on the other's belief that the influencer has authority to issue orders which they in turn have an obligation to accept.

Expert power the ability to exert influence based on the other's belief that the influencer has superior knowledge relevant to the situation and the task.

Various writers have defined power as the ability to exert influence. Power is an aspect not only in relationships between individuals within a group, but also in leadership relations and political issues (**Chapters 18 and 22**). John French and Bertram Raven (1958) saw power as a property not of an individual, but of a relationship. These authors distinguished different types of power – reward, coercive, referent, legitimate and expert.

Saying that power is a property of the relationship and not of the individual means that, for example, what matters is not whether you actually have rewards to distribute, but rather, whether others *perceive* you to have that ability. So you have reward power when others believe that you have rewards available to give, even if you do not.

Status structure

Formal status the collection of rights and obligations associated with a position, as distinct from the person who may occupy that position.

Status is a value or prestige ranking. Status can be important because it motivates people and has consequences for their behaviour (Gould, 2002). This is particularly the case when individuals perceive a disparity between their own perception of themselves and how others perceive them to be. Each position in a group has a value placed upon it. Within a company, the value that is ascribed to a position by the formal organization e.g. chief executive officer, vice-president, supervisor, is labelled formal status. Formal status is best thought of as being synonymous with rank as in the police or the military. It signals the particular position that an individual occupies within a well-defined hierarchy (Sauder et al., 2012). In a formal group or team, individual members will be accorded formal status within it, based on hierarchical position and task ability.

Home viewing

In *The Flight of the Phoenix* (1965, director Robert Aldrich) an oil company plane crashes in the Sahara desert (do not view the 2004 version which is very different). It tells the story of the formation of a group of passengers who attempt to rebuild the plane to escape. The group has to deal with the inevitable interpersonal issues of conflict, team roles, and differences in members' values and power. There are 13 people on the plane but the story focuses on six main characters – Towns, Moran, Harris, Watson, Renaud and Dorfmann. Using French and Raven's classification, decide which person possesses which type of power (Huffman and Kilian, 2012).

The organization is made up of a number of defined positions arranged in order of their increasing authority. The formal status hierarchy reflects the potential ability of the holder of a position to contribute to the overall goals of the organization. It differentiates the amount of respect deserved and simultaneously ranks group members on a formal status scale. The outward symbols associated with formal status (e.g. size of office, quality of carpet) are there to inform other members in the organization of where exactly that person stands on the 'organizational ladder'. This topic leads ultimately to a consideration of an organization's structure (**see Chapter 15**).

In addition, value can also be placed upon an individual (not a position) by a group (not the organization). This refers to the social honour, respect or prestige that is accorded to an individual group member by its other members. In this second sense, the word 'status' is prefixed by the word 'social' to indicate that this 'person value' is informally established. The social status ranking is therefore independent of formal status or position. It is closely related to leadership because if an individual's higher status is accepted by others within a group, that person can influence, control or command those around them. Social status ranking can be thought of as a group's 'pecking order'.

Social status the relative ranking that a person holds and the value of that person as measured by a group.

While one can view social status as a sort of badge of honour awarded for meritorious group conduct, it can also be seen as a hierarchy where some members receive more respect from their peers than others. Those members with high status are seen as performing better and generally receive more group resources. Additionally, because status is used as a signal for the allocation of group resources, such as time, money, and equipment, a group functions more efficiently if all of its members have the same view of the status hierarchy within it. Generally speaking, when members do not agree on which of them has high or low status, sharing information and other resources becomes a more complex process. For these reasons, adding high status team members or those with ambiguous status to a group, reduces its performance until the group can adapt to the presence of that new member (Emich and Wright, 2016).

Status, authority and problem solving in an airplane cockpit

Commercial aeroplanes are piloted by groups not individuals. The actions needed when taxiing, taking off, flying, making the final approach and landing, all require the cockpit crew to work together. However, smooth group working can be impeded by status differences and group dynamics. Larger aircraft consist of a pilot, a co-pilot and a flight engineer. To indicate the relative social status and authority of each position, these roles are labelled captain, flight engineer and second officer. By law, the final authority on board rests with the captains who exert their authority and power in various ways. Over two-thirds

→

of air crashes involve human or pilot error rather than mechanical failure. The US National Transportation Safety Board attributed the causes of many fatal crashes to two teamwork factors – the captain's refusal to comply with the suggestions of other crew members, and the crew's excessive obedience to the captain's authority.

In one case, a near miss occurred when a captain ignored his co-pilot's warning to reduce airspeed. In the case of a DC-8 running out of fuel and crashing in Portland, Oregon, the flight recorder revealed that the captain had ignored the flight engineer's repeated reminders of their dwindling fuel. A Northwest Express Airlines co-pilot failed to correct the captain's errors on

an approach, leading to a crash. Aviation authorities have now recognized the abuse of power by captains and the negative impact of excessive obedience by flight crews. Rather than attempting to change the group structure in terms of the norms of hierarchy and cockpit deference, they have sought to improve communication between all members of the flight crew. To fly safely, team members need to engage in the behaviours of *inquiring* why one member is taking certain actions; *advocating* alternative options; and *asserting* their views on matters. The accident literature is full of examples where this had not been done (Foushee, 1984; Milanovich et al. 1998; Tarnow, 2000; Courtright et al., 2012; BBC, 2016).

 **STOP AND SEARCH**   YouTube for *Groupthink in the Cockpit (CRM Training Video)* (7:14).

One of the powers possessed by an informal group is its ability to confer status on those of its members who meet the expectations of the group. These members are looked up to by their peers, not because of any formal position they may hold in the organization, but because of their position in the work group. Many people actively seek status in order to fulfil their need for self-esteem. The granting of it by their group provides them with personal satisfaction. Similarly, the withholding of status can act as a group control mechanism to bring a deviant group member back into line. The status accorded by the group to a member is immediate in terms of face-to-face feedback. The recognition and esteem given to group members reinforces their identification with the group and increases their dependence upon it.

Group hierarchy refers to distinct differences in group members' status and power.

A group member's informal status may be the result of their ability to contribute to a group's goals. Those individuals whose contributions are most critical to group success are accorded the greatest social status. What effect does status have in groups? Alessandro Piazza and Fabrizio Castellucci (2014) showed how hierarchy emerged in groups through members' own status-conferring actions producing a self-reinforcing status ranking. Research has shown that individuals are willing sacrifice their individual performance in order to enhance their own group status (Bendersky and Shah, 2012, 2013; Bendersky and Hays, 2012).

Hierarchy in groups

Josephine Cardin

Bret Sanner   Stuart Bunderson

Bret Sanner and Stuart Bunderson (2018) argue that, contrary to popular opinion, research shows that having hierarchy in groups can help rather than hinder their creativity and innovativeness. **Group hierarchy** refers to distinct differences in group members' status and power. Hierarchy

is found in virtually every human group; is either formally designated or emerges naturally and informally; and is important to its functioning. In contrast, non-hierarchical groups can become unfocused, tumultuous and inefficient as equality prevents their expert members playing leadership roles. Using four case studies of groups in a variety of organizations and industries, the authors conclude that if a group has a hierarchy, it will help to resolve disagreements more easily and coordinate actions better; will keep the group moving in the same direction when conflicts threaten to tear it apart; and will assist it to generate, identify and select new ideas by bounding its solutions, converging its ideas and its structuring its processes.

- *Bounding solutions:* Paradoxically, individuals are more innovative when they have clear constraints (e.g. time, budget, customer requirements). A single influential group member within a hierarchy is better able to set those parameters of innovation than the whole group. Once the boundaries have been established, the group is then left free to explore options within them.

- *Converging ideas:* Once a group has generated numerous ideas and possibilities, a hierarchy can assist them in deciding which to prioritize and which to discard. The transition from the idea generation stage to the refining and implementation stages requires an objective prioritizing mechanism, and an influential member can counter others' emotional attachment to certain ideas thereby preventing endless group procrastination.

- *Structuring processes:* Group creativity involves members' proposing wild ideas and challenging established beliefs. When brainstorming, a group must have processes and norms to reduce members being ridiculed or negatively sanctioned. Without hierarchy, groups can struggle to structure such a haphazard process. Having a clear hierarchy can create a safe knowledge-sharing environment and establish 'speak-up' norms. Clarity as to who is in charge and how each member is to contribute gives everyone a structured way to engage in the creative process.

To secure the benefits of a group hierarchy while avoiding its pitfalls, Sanner and Bunderson advise groups to have a clear chain of command (clarity and agreement about who defers to whom); a performance-based culture to ensure that the most knowledgeable and least incompetent people were running the show; and a team-focused feedback system. Hierarchy promotes performance when goals and feedback are group-oriented but stifles it when they are individually-oriented.

✋ **STOP AND SEARCH**   YouTube for *Lindred Greer: Opening Keynote – Flattening the Hierarchy in Health Care Teams* (22:18).

Liking structure

Sociometry the measurement of interpersonal feelings and relationships within groups.

Within any group, individual members will like, dislike or be indifferent to other members, in varying degrees. Their combined feelings towards each other represent their group's liking structure. This can be studied using the technique of sociometry. The term derives from the Latin *socius* (companion) and the Greek *metron* (measure). Sociometry was devised by Jacob Moreno who coined the term. Moreno and his colleagues originally used the technique in their research in the New York Training School for Girls in the 1930s (Moreno, 1953). They mapped the friendship choices among girls in a reformatory.

Sociometric maps show the emotional relationships between individual members in a group on the basis of their personal choices of selection and rejection of other group members using a few standard symbols. This network of a group's interpersonal feelings is exposed by the use of a sociometric assessment using a preference questionnaire in which group members are asked with whom they would prefer (or not prefer) to work, study, play or live. These reveal the spontaneous feelings and choices that individuals in a group have and make towards each other. These are divided into three classes – attraction (liking), rejection (disliking), and indifference (neutral feeling).

After analysing the answers, Moreno calculated how many times an individual had been chosen as a comrade by the other members of the group for the activity in question. This feeling (the sociometric term for which is *tele*), may be one of attraction (positive *tele*) or repulsion (negative *tele*), alternatively there may merely be indifference. As shown in Figure 11.1, the members' choices are depicted on a sociogram, which reveals the group's likes structure by showing all the different members' positions. Sociometric assessment can reveal 'stars', 'isolates', 'neglectees', 'rejectees', 'mutual pairs' and 'mutual trios' in a group (see Figure 11.1).

Sociogram diagram showing the liking (social attraction) relationships between individual members of a group.

Sociometry (or social network analysis) continues to be applied in organizations today. Sociograms have been used to avoid personality clashes; raise group cohesion; identify

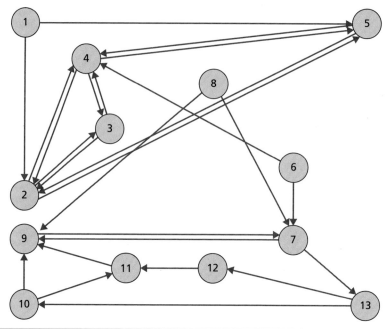

Star	Recipient of a large number of choices, sometimes described as 'over-chosen'
Isolate	Person who makes no choices at all and receives none, i.e. a relationship of mutual indifference to the remainder of the group
Neglectee	Person who, although he or she makes choices, receives none at all
Rejectee	Person who is not chosen by anyone and who is rejected by one or more persons
Mutual pair or mutual trio	Individuals who choose one another

Figure 11.1: Sociogram and sociometric positions within a group

unhappy pupil isolates who have not adjusted to their school class group; and isolate employees who have not fitted into their work teams. They can also be used in universities to build a greater sense of community in the classroom (Dunn, 2018). Comparative sociograms (social networks) of productive and unproductive teams can highlight areas where aspects of group structure require modification.

✓✓✓ **EMPLOYABILITY CHECK** (self-management, interpersonal skills, teamworking skills)

Think about a group that you are familiar with. Can you identify an individual who is a 'star', an 'isolate', a 'neglectee', a 'rejectee' or part of a 'mutual pair' or 'mutual trio'. Which are you?

Communication structure

Communication network analysis a technique that uses direct observation to determine the source, direction and quantity of oral communication between co-located members of a group.

To understand the communication structure of a group, it is necessary to know the role and status of every member and the duration and direction of communication from position to position. Each group member depends on information provided by others. Solving a problem, making a decision or reaching agreement, all require information exchange between individuals. The members of a group may work in the same building, interact frequently, and attend face-to-face meetings, or they may be geographically dispersed in offices around the country or be in different countries (globally dispersed groups) and thus interact only intermittently and communicate mainly electronically.

Communication network analysis

Communigram a chart that indicates the source, direction and quantity of oral communication between the members during a group meeting.

When group members meet face-to-face, and participate in a meeting around a table, they are said to be *co-located*. In such circumstances, a communication network analysis of their meeting can be conducted. This approach was pioneered by Noel Tichy and Charles Fombrun (1979). The observer makes a note of each participant's oral utterance and at whom it is directed. The outcome is a communigram which answers the two questions of who speaks to whom and how often (Figure 11.2).

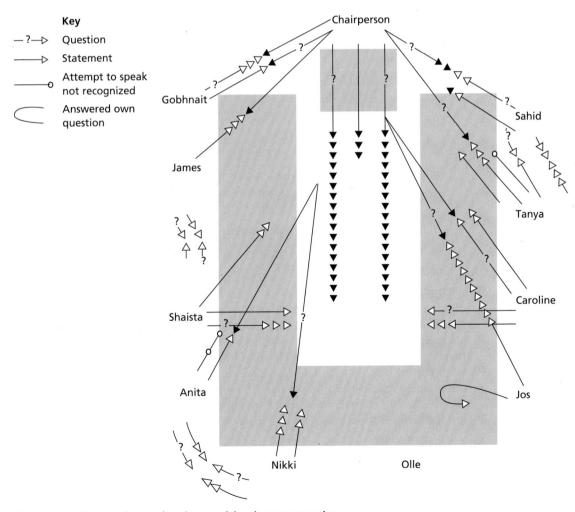

Figure 11.2: Communigram showing participation at a meeting

Communication pattern analysis

Communication pattern analysis a technique that uses analysis of documents, data, and voice mail transmission, to determine the source, direction and quantity of oral and written communication between the dispersed members of a group.

When members of a group are physically dispersed around the same building, around different buildings or are located in different countries, it is still possible to determine the source, frequency and direction of their communication with each other by using communication pattern analysis. Instead of observing the face-to-face interactions between individuals, which is impossible, the researcher would note the initiation and direction of emails, texts and voice mail between the group's members. This information is then documented in a communication pattern chart.

Virtual teams

Communication pattern chart indicates the source, direction and quantity of oral and written communication between the dispersed members of a group.

Virtual team one that relies on technology-mediated communication while crossing boundaries of geography, time, culture and organization, to accomplish an interdependent task.

The combination of market-push and technology-pull has led companies to explore new types of working arrangements and organizational forms. One such development is the virtual team. Although these differ, they tend to possess most of the following characteristics. Team members:

Spatial dispersion	Work in different geographical locations
Temporal dispersion	Work in different time zones
Organizational dispersion	Work across organizational boundaries
Cultural dispersion	Come from different countries or cultures
Altering membership	Join and leave their team frequently
Technological communication	Communicate mainly electronically

Gilson et al. (2015) reported survey results that suggest that 66 per cent of multinational organizations utilize these groups and over 80 per cent expect them to grow. Globalization has accelerated geographically dispersed teams. Drawing upon the best functional expertise from around the world, they benefit from international diversity by linking employees from different cultures with different skills, work experiences and perspectives, to address organizational challenges. However, research suggests that the more different the members of a team are, the more time they spend dealing with their diverse perspectives and interests, and less time performing their required work tasks (Harvey et al., 2017).

STOP AND SEARCH YouTube for *George Siantonas, TED talk: Challenges of Virtual Working* (19:10). The presenter discusses how virtual working impacts on the dynamics of teams in multinational organizations and how to deal with some of the challenges this causes.

CUTTING EDGE   Virtual teams

Martine Haas

Martine Haas and Mark Mortensen (2016) drew on 15 years of group and team research involving over 300 interviews and 4,000 surveys of team leaders and managers. They noted that in the past, teams had a stable membership and predictable tasks. Its members knew with whom they would be working and what they all wanted to achieve. In contrast, today's virtual teams are culturally diverse and geographically dispersed, communicate digitally and have dynamic, changing memberships. However, some things have not changed. The authors argue that what makes a team effective is the same for both face-to-face teams and virtual teams. They call these 'enabling conditions':

Compelling direction

Virtual teams cannot be inspired if they do not know what goals they are working towards. Does the team have a common goal that is clear, challenging but not impossible and that has clear consequences for the company? Team members coming from dissimilar backgrounds can hold differing views about their group's purpose.

Strong structure

Virtual teams need the correct number and mix of members, optimally designed tasks and processes, as well as clear group norms of what represents acceptable conduct. They require a good balance of skills and diversity not only in knowledge, views and perspectives, but also in age, gender and race, in order to avoid groupthink and stimulate creativity.

Supportive context

Virtual teams need a support system that provides them with the necessary resources to do their job. This includes a reward system that reinforces good performance; an information system that provides data; and an education system that offers training. This can be difficult for teams that are geographically distributed and digitally dependent.

Shared mindset

Given the 'us-and-them' thinking that virtual working can breed among members, there is a need to develop a common team identity and understanding to overcome the inevitable obstacles to cooperation and information exchange. Individuals should be publically recognized for their contributions to team goals, and time set aside to allow discussion between members about non-work matters so as to enhance inter-member familiarity and develop trust.

STOP AND SEARCH   YouTube for *Martine Haas: The Real Reason Your Multinational Team Has Trouble Communicating* (8:18) and *Mark Mortensen on Working in Global Teams* (4:11).

Just as Joo and Dennen (2017) had identified the characteristics of the ideal student project team member, Stefan Krumm and his colleagues (2016) synthesized the existing research into a comprehensive description of what an ideal virtual team player does (Krumm et al., 2016; Schultze and Krumm, 2017). The authors used Bartram's (2005) 'Great Eight' taxonomy and adapted it to fit the virtual team context (Table 11.1).

Table 11.1: Great Eight virtual team competency framework

Great Eight domain	Description	Sample items as included in the study ('for the success/collaboration of my team it is important to . . .')
Leading and Deciding	Initiates action, takes responsibility, sets goals, works autonomously	. . . set clear goals for team members. . . . work autonomously. . . . act on own initiative.
Supporting and Cooperating	Supports others, puts people first, acts with integrity	. . . share relevant information and resources. . . . display willingness to cooperate. . . . listen to colleagues actively and non-judgementally.
Interacting and Presenting	Communicates and networks effectively, successfully persuades and influences others	. . . resolve conflicts effectively. . . . maintain one's social and business networks. . . . present topics illustratively.
Analysing and Interpreting	Clear analytical thinking, quickly takes on new technology, communicates well in writing	. . . communicate in writing understandably. . . . use communication media effectively. . . . work effectively with computers and digital media.
Creating and Conceptualizing	Openness to new ideas and experience, seeks learning opportunities, drives change	. . . promote change and innovation. . . . show creativity. . . . approach problems strategically.
Organizing and Executing	Works thoroughly, plans ahead, follows instructions and procedures	. . . set oneself goals. . . . manage one's time effectively. . . . clearly organize one's tasks.
Adapting and Coping	Adapts and responds well to change, manages pressure effectively	. . . flexibly adapt to different circumstances. . . . constructively deal with criticism. . . . deal with unclear and conflicting situations.
Enterprising and Performing	Focuses on achieving work objectives, seeks career advancement	. . . motivate oneself through performance and goals. . . . work with enthusiasm and energy. . . . keep track of the organizational goals.

Source: Krumm et al. (2016, p. 126)

In general, the 'Great Eight' personality characteristics described in Table 11.1 required for effective virtual team membership are similar to those needed by successful members of traditional face-to-face teams. Others of course, are unique. For example, and unsurprisingly, the authors suggested that virtual team members should possess competencies in the areas of technology use, intercultural awareness and geographical dispersion. These findings specify in detail exactly what types of experience, knowledge, skills and motivation the ideal virtual worker needs to have. This is valuable for virtual team member selection, training programme design and offers practical guidance to managers and leaders of virtual teams. This is useful as studies have identified not only the potential benefits of virtual teams to be gained, but also potential problems to be avoided by team leaders (Table 11.2).

Given the aforementioned virtual team problems, there is a greater potential for misunderstandings to arise and for more things to go wrong. Team leaders may be skilled in dealing with members in face-to-face interaction, but they generally lack the experience and expertise to guide and facilitate interactions with those in virtual teams. As Zander et al. (2013) noted: 'Being a team leader is no longer what it used to be. Instead of discussing work face-to-face, casually interacting around the coffee machine, and probably relying on social control for work to be carried out, global virtual team leaders now have to lead from a distance' (p.228).

Table 11.2: Benefits and problems of using virtual teams

Benefits	Problems
Complete tasks quickly and efficiently	Different member cultural background can create difficulties
Enables recruitment of talented employees	Members not 'in synch' being in different time zones
Gives access to the best and cheapest people around the world.	Members and leaders lack experience of virtual teamworking and team managing
Reduces travel and cost	Unsuitable for employees with certain psychological predispositions
Promotes different geographical areas	Lowers the level of social support for, and reduces interaction between, members
Builds diverse teams	Inadequate exchange of social-emotional information between members to develop 'swift trust'
Increases task-oriented working because members have not previously met	Reduced member satisfaction with processes compared to face-to-face teams
Assists in promoting proactive employment practices for disadvantaged individuals and groups Reduces discrimination	Can stimulate the creation of sub-groups with negative consequences

Source: based on Ferrazzi, (2014), Halgin et al. (2015), Shapiro et al., (2002) and Zander et al. (2012).

Communication tips for virtual teams

Erica Dhawan

Tomas Chamorro-Premuzic

Erica Dhawan and Tomas Chamorro-Premuzic (2018) write that the digital era has ushered in a revolution in communication through texts, emails, conference calls and other digital communications. It has changed both how we speak and what we hear causing frequent misunderstandings resulting in confusion. The tone of a text or the formality of an email is left wide open to interpretation. Misinterpretations can create anxiety that can become costly, affecting morale, engagement, productivity and innovation. Remote communication can distort the normal pace of our conversations. The delay between our messages can often postpone or hide emotional reactions to our comments. The absence of an immediate response can cause us to become distracted and frustrated with our teams. The authors state that to perform at the highest levels, virtual teams have to find new and better ways to communicate which maximize their strengths and give them an advantage over co-located teams. The authors offer four 'best practice' tips:

- *Don't sacrifice message clarity for brevity*: To be efficient, a team member may use fewer words to communicate. This can result in other members wasting time trying to interpret the messages, and often misinterpreting. Writers cannot assume that others understand your signals and shorthand. Hence, communicate with the aim of maximizing the clarity of your message.

- *Don't bombard your team with messages*: Some individuals follow up a task with email, text and phone. Such 'over-communication' creates demands on the time of the receiver. Using all of them for the same message is both ineffective and annoying, so choose your 'digital volume' carefully.

- *Establish communication norms*: Virtual teams need to establish communication norms to bring clarity, predictability and certainty to virtual conversations. These norms can relate to the use of acronyms (NNTR- no

→

need to respond); the use or non-use of software (e.g. Slack, Google Docs); and to members' preferred response time, writing style, use of humour, formality level and tone.

- *Grasp the opportunities in written communications:* Virtual working offers opportunities for shy members who are less inclined to speak in face-to-face groups. Text-based communication places less importance on interpersonal skills and physical appearance, and offers an effective way to share

power and decision making. This reduces the inhibitions of introverts and can increase their contributions to the group process.

- *Virtual parties:* Creating a virtual opportunity for team celebrations that allows members to socialize online enhances their relationships, lays the foundations of their future collaboration, and improves their communications. Informal, non-task 'get-togethers' can help individuals become better acquainted with their fellow team members.

STOP AND SEARCH YouTube for *virtual teams.*

Interaction Process Analysis

Interaction Process Analysis a technique used to categorize the content of speech.

Task activity an oral input, made by a group member that contributes directly to the group's work task.

Maintenance activity an oral input, made by a group member that reduces conflict, maximizes cohesion and maintains relationships within a group.

The techniques of communication process analysis and communications network analysis provide information about the source, direction and quantity of verbal communication (oral or written) between the members of co-located and dispersed teams. However, neither of them considers the content of that communication. When we observe a congregated group in action, for example, rugby players discussing their strategy for the second half, or a group of students discussing their tutorial system, what we observe are individuals saying certain things. If we want to study the content of their oral behaviour within that group, we need a precise and reliable way of categorizing it. Robert Bales (1950b) and his colleagues at Harvard University's Laboratory of Social Relations developed a technique for categorizing the *content* of group member's oral behaviours (utterances) which he called Interaction Process Analysis (IPA).

Bales discovered that every group engaged in two types of oral activities – task activities (getting the job done) and maintenance activities (keeping the group working together). He found that when work groups were assigned a task, such as solving a problem or making a recommendation, their members inevitably engaged in 12 different types of oral interactions which are shown in Table 11.3.

One can classify or 'code' each person's oral utterance during a group discussion, into these 12 categories. For example, Category 7 is 'shows solidarity, raises others status, gives help, reward'. So, if one group member said, 'That's an excellent idea from Lucy', that would be an example of a Category 7 utterance. In contrast, Category 12 is 'shows antagonism, deflates other's status, defends or asserts self'. If another member said, 'Jill's report was pathetic!' that would be an example of a Category 12 utterance. Bales felt that with his twelve categories, one could classify most utterances that were likely to be made by individuals in a group when they engaged in oral interaction.

Bales' IPA is the most practical method yet developed which can be used to study the content of the oral communication between individuals in groups. He provided the first picture of what happens

Table 11.3: Bales' categories of oral interaction in small groups

Task

Questions

1. Asks for orientation, direction, implying autonomy for others.
2. Asks for opinion, evaluation, analysis, expression of feeling.
3. Asks for orientation, information, repeats, clarifies, confirms.

Answers

4. Gives suggestion, direction, implying autonomy in others.
5. Gives opinion, evaluation, analysis, expresses feelings, wishes.
6. Gives orientation, information, repeats, clarifies, confirms.

Maintenance

Positive reactions

7. Shows solidarity, raises others' status, gives help, reward.
8. Releases tension, asks for help, withdraws from field.
9. Shows antagonism, deflates others' status, defends or asserts self.

Negative reactions

10. Disagrees, shows passive rejection, formality, withholds help.
11. Shows tension release, asks for help, withdraws out of field.
12. Shows antagonism, deflates others' status, defends or asserts self.

Source: based on Bales (1959)

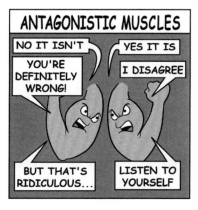

Analysing oral interactions in a group

Below is a simplified version of Bales' Interpersonal Process Analysis (IPA) oral behaviour (utterances) classification scheme. It consists of six oral categories, and each has an explanation alongside. Also provided is a chart for categorizing group members' oral contributions. There is a space for their initials along the top row. Next time you are present at a group discussion, listen to what each individual says. Every time they speak, decide in which oral category their utterance belongs, and place a dot beside that category, under their name. Continue to do this, building up a record of the whole discussion.

After you have finished observing your discussion, total up your dots in the columns (horizontally) and for each group member (vertically). Your horizontal scores total gives you an indication of the oral behaviour profile of the group as a whole. For example, is this a group whose members are cooperating or competing with each other? Your vertical scores, will contrast the contributions of the individual group members, and can provide a clue to the roles that they are playing within the group.

→

Proposing	Any utterance that puts forward a new suggestion, idea or course of action
Building	Any utterance that develops or extends an idea or suggestion made by someone else
Supporting	Any utterance that declares agreement or support with any individual or idea
Disagreeing	Any utterance that states a criticism of another person's statement
Giving information	Any utterance that gives facts, ideas or opinions or clarifies these
Seeking information	Any utterance that asks for facts, ideas or opinions from others

Oral interaction score sheet

Oral category	*Members' names*					
Proposing						
Building						
Supporting						
Disagreeing						
Giving • information • opinions • suggestions						
Seeking • information • opinions • suggestions						
TOTAL						

in face-to-face groups and developed a theory of group functioning. He argued that group behaviour could be explained by showing how groups dealt with certain recurring problems such as orientation, evaluation, control, decision, tension-management and integration.

What did they find? Leaders' oral behaviours in emergency teams

? Selma van der Haar and her colleagues (2017) investigated the oral behaviours that leaders of emergency teams used to achieve success. When motorway car crashes or terrorist attacks occur, the emergency services in the form of fire, police and medical assistance arrive. These different teams need to work together cooperatively and interdependently. The different team commanders come together under the direction of a formal leader. There is a need to define the situation, establish goals and determine actions.

The leader's oral behaviours, such as defining team tasks and encouraging members, is crucial since these facilitate constructive conflict, encourage contributions and guide critical thinking. The researchers collected data from 102 respondents from 17 multidisciplinary emergency teams. They sought to discover which of ten leaders' oral behaviours contributed most to team success. Which oral behaviour did they find was most used by effective team leaders? **(Answers in chapter Recap.)**

Selma van der Haar

Label	Oral behaviour	Example
Goal orientation	Pointing out the goal and bringing the team back to the topic when its members stray or lose focus from it.	Make statements which encourage others to share their information and interpretation of the facts.
Clarifying or sensemaking	Ensuring everyone understands statements made by members and their link to the topic, identifying crucial information and clarifying it.	Team member: 'The victims have a bad cough and I do not trust it' Team leader: 'So you imply there might be a hazardous substance present in the smoke, right?'
Question repetition	Repeating the words of a team member's question.	Team member: 'We found three casualties and I saw a big fire.' Team leader: 'So there are three casualties and there is a big fire.'
Procedural suggestion	Organizing group work activity by suggesting how to proceed in current and future meetings, indicating which topics to deal with and in which order.	'This is something that I want to postpone to the second OSCT meeting.'
Procedural question	Asking questions about how to proceed further in the meeting.	'Which discipline do you think should share his or her information first?'
Summarizing: Command	Briefly over viewing what has been said by repeating crucial information, followed by a command as to what actions members should take or what information they should gather.	'So we want to ensure the safety of the professionals on scene with respect to toxic smoke. Fire department, you will take care of that.'
Summarizing: Decision	Briefly over viewing what has been said by repeating crucial information, concluding with a decision statement concerning the topic discussed.	'Okay, as we are anticipating a national threat, we have decided that we are going to GRIP 3.'
Question: Directed to a specific team member	Asking a question directed at a specific service or team member (identified by name) while making eye contact or pointing at a specific team member.	'Fire department, what do you think?' 'Peter, what do you think?' (points to the specific person)
Question: Directed to the team in general	Asking a question directed at the team as a whole.	'How shall we approach this problem?'
Time management	Specifying how much time is needed or remains.	'I want to take 8 minutes for this first meeting.' 'We are taking longer than I suspected.'

Source: Van der Haar et al. (2017, pp. 222–23)

Badging up for measurement

Sandy Pentland (2012) and his research team at the MIT's Human Dynamics Laboratory discovered that the pattern of communication – the manner in which members communicated – was the most important predictor of a team's success. The researchers equipped team members with electronic badges that collected data on their individual communication behaviour. This included whom they talked to; how much they talked, listened, gestured and interrupted; their tone of voice; whether they faced each other, and even their levels of extroversion and empathy. These badges produce *sociometrics* – measures of how people interacted (Orbach et al., 2015).

Recent developments in AI have extended Pentland's original work. Humanyze is a firm which offers 'people analytics' and sells smart ID badges. Each is the size of a credit card and the thickness of a book of matches. It can track employees around the office to reveal how they interact with their colleagues. The badge also contains a microphone that picks up whether they are talking to one another; a Bluetooth and infrared sensor to monitor where they are; and an accelerometer to record when they move. The company merges the data from these badges with employees' calendars and emails to form a full picture of how they spend their time at work. Metrics include time spent with members of the same sex, activity levels, and speaking versus listening times.

This information can reveal which departments a team communicates with; which parts of a building are underused; how hard people are working; and which staff members work together. This can reveal inadequate communications, the need to redesign office space, change team incentives, or revamp diversity initiatives. Other companies, such as Hitachi and Workday, sell similar employee monitoring products. Thanks to the internet, smartphones and the cloud, employers can check when employees are working; who is looking at a document; whether they might be stealing company files and contacts; and which individuals are likely to quit. 'The company probably knows more about their employee than their familiy does' said one employee. The boss of Humanyze observed that 'Every aspect of business is becoming more data-driven. There's no reason the people side of business shouldn't be the same' (*The Economist,* 2018a).

Wearables and work – who wins?

This video describes how employee monitoring, facilitated by new technology, has increased. From the company perspective, what are the problems of obtaining reliable personal data using wearable monitoring devices? From the employees' perspective, would you be willing wear a workplace wearable and share your sleep data with your boss? (8:05)

Role structure

It is a short step from identifying the types of oral contributions that individuals make in their groups to determining their team member roles. The occupants of every position in a group are expected to carry out certain functions when group members interact with one another. The expected behaviours associated with a position within the group constitute the social role of the occupant of that position. Social role is the concept that relates the individual to the group. People's behaviour within an organization is structured and patterned in various ways. An understanding of role helps us to explain how this happens.

Social role the set of
expectations that others
hold of an occupant of a
position.

Social role refers to the set of expectations that others hold of an occupant of a position in an organization structure, e.g. shop manager, bishop, head of the production department, etc. These role expectations presume attitudes, relationships and behaviours. A role is similar to a script that actors are given. The same actor changes their roles and can act out different parts in front of different audiences. Different roles are played by different members of a group. By totalling the columns in the oral interaction score sheet shown earlier, you can see how group members contributed to the group discussion. Bales found that individuals played different roles within their groups, and that this was a universal feature of face-to-face interaction in groups. As the group deals with its problems, individual members begin to 'specialize' in certain types of behaviours, thereby taking on different 'roles' within their group.

Group member roles

Within a group activity, such as a staff meeting or a tutorial discussion, some individuals will show a consistent preference for certain oral behaviours and not for others. For example, expressing their opinion or asking for information from others. How an individual chooses to expresses him or herself leads them to be seen to be playing a particular role within their group. Kenneth Benne and Paul Sheats (1948) distinguished three categories of roles played by members of a group and these are shown in Table 11.4.

- *Task orientation roles:* These roles distinguish between behaviour that is oriented toward the solution of task problems versus behaviour that shirks or evades task responsibilities. It related to achieving the group goal, cooperation, and performance of the task.

- *Relationship roles:* These roles distinguish behaviour that is sociable, relationship-focused, friendly and agreeable versus behaviour that is withdrawn, unfriendly and aloof. It is related to positive social interaction, sociability, and maintenance of relations ensuring the group as a whole can work together.

- *Individual roles:* These roles distinguish behaviour that is dominant versus submissive; active versus passive; and control-seeking versus deference. It is associated with striving for recognition and aggressiveness. These behaviours can impede the group's efforts to achieve its aims.

Reviewing the subsequent group research literature, Tripp Driskell and his colleagues (2017) concluded that the three primary role dimensions described by Benne and Sheats seventy years ago, continue to satisfactorily describe the role performance of individuals and their interaction behaviours with others in small group situations including work teams.

Table 11.4: Benne and Sheats' roles commonly played by members of a group

Task roles	Relationship roles	Individual roles
Initiator-contributor	Encourager	Aggressor
Information seeker	Harmonizer	Blocker
Opinion seeker	Compromiser	Recognition seeker
Information giver	Gatekeeper and expeditor	Self-confessor
Opinion giver	Standard setter	Dominator
Evaluator-critic	Observer and commentator	Help seeker
Energizer	Follower	Special interest pleader
Procedural technician		Playboy / cougar
Recorder		

Source: based on Benne and Sheats (1948)

EMPLOYABILITY CHECK (self-management, interpersonal skills, teamworking skills)

You have been brought in to replace a team leader whose team has been performing poorly. Members are reported to have missed business deadlines and are working badly together. Senior management has asked you to 'turn this team around'. Unfortunately you inherit the team members and have to work with them in the immediate future. What actions do you take?

Belbin's team role theory

Dave Winsborough and Tomas Chamorro-Premuzic (2017) observed that individuals' personalities play a significant role in determining team performance. They wrote that:

> 'personality affects what role you have within the team; how you interact with the rest of the team; and whether your values (core beliefs) align with the team's. Importantly, the above processes concern the psychological factors (rather than the technical skills) underlying both individual and team performance. These psychological factors are the main determinants of whether people work together well . . . team members' personalities influence cooperation, shared cognition, information sharing, and overall team performance. In other words, who you are affects how you behave and how you interact with other people' (p.3).

Team role an individual's tendency to behave in preferred ways which contribute to, and interrelate with, other members within a team.

The authors go on to recommend thinking about teams as achieving the right mix of skills and personalities and consider the roles played by team members.

A widely used framework for understanding roles within a group or team was developed by Meredith Belbin (2018, 2010, 1996, 1993). He distinguished nine team roles. Each team role makes its own, distinctive contribution to the performance of the team. These are shown in Figure 11.3 and can be grouped under three headings:

Action roles	Social roles	Thinking roles
• Shaper	• Coordinator	• Plant
• Implementer	• Teamworker	• Monitor-Evaluator
• Completer-Finisher	• Resource-Investigator	• Specialist

Belbin (1996) argued that:

1. Within an organization people are generally appointed to a functional role based on their ability or experience e.g. marketing. They are rarely selected for personal characteristics that would fit them to perform additional tasks within a team.

2. The personal characteristics of an individual fit them for some roles within a team, while limiting the likelihood that they will be successful in other roles. Team roles are individual preferences based on personality and not the expectations of others, as discussed earlier in this chapter with respect to social role.

3. Individuals tend to adopt one or two team roles fairly consistently.

4. The roles that individuals are naturally inclined towards can be determined through personality assessments and a team role questionnaire.

5. In an ideal ('dream') team, all the necessary roles are represented and the preferred roles of members complement each other, thereby avoiding 'gaps', i.e. there is team role balance. A single member can 'double up' and play several roles, thereby enabling the overall size of the team to be reduced.

6. The assessment, selection, placement and guidance of individual employees by management is the way to improve team effectiveness. Once management knows employees' team role preferences, it can use them to compose balanced teams in which all the required role preferences are represented.

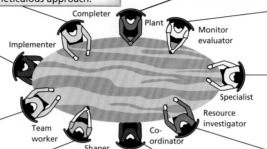

IMPLEMENTER
Practical thinker who turns theoretical ideas into workable solutions.

Disciplined, reliable efficient, and conservative. Produces processes and systems to meet team's needs.

COMPLETER-FINISHER
Searches out errors and omissions; knows if team is on track; meets deadlines; ensures quality and timeliness.

The team's 'detail person'; painstaking, conscientious, anxious; possesses analytical and meticulous approach.

PLANT
Provides creative thinking, dispassionate analysis solves difficult problems.

Creative, imaginative, unorthodox.

MONITOR-EVALUATOR
Provides critical input, a careful and objective approach, offers options, checks progress, helps team avoid mistakes.

Sober, strategic, discerning; sees options, judges accurately.

SPECIALIST
Provides team with specific, technical input.

Single-minded, self-starting, dedicated; possess rare, expert skills.

TEAMWORKER
Looks after interpersonal relationships between team members; resolves conflicts; ensures team cohesion.

Cooperative, mild, perceptive, team diplomat; listens, sensitive to others, averts friction; is sensitive to team atmosphere; helps others

SHAPER
Moulds others' ideas, pushes them to achieve, in order to obtain a result.

Challenges others; dyanamic; possesses drive; strives on pressure, overcomes obstacles.

COORDINATOR
Brings together others' inputs, clarifies goals, allocates responsibilities; ensures all contribute to discussions and decisions; articulates team conclusions.

Mature, confident, good chairperson, delegates well; concerned with fairness and equity among team members.

RESOURCE-INVESTIGATOR
Keeps others in touch, explores opportunities, shares external information; develops contacts.

Extrovert, enthusiastic, communicative, is the team's networker; can call upon connections; negotiates with outsiders.

Figure 11.3: Belbin's team roles
Source: adapted from Matthewman et al. (2009); based on Belbin (1981).

 **STOP AND SEARCH**   YouTube for *Belbin team roles.*

Are you a morning or an evening team member?

Stefan Volk

Stefan Volk and his colleagues (2017) considered the effects of chronotype diversity on team performance. The daily functioning of the human body and brain is regulated by a combination of homeostatic processes and circadian rhythms. Chronotype refers to an individual's timing of these rhythms and the related timing of daily peaks and troughs in their physical and psychological energy. Chronotype diversity means that team members differ in their biologi-cal predispositions with respect to the optimal timing of daily periods of their activity and rest. Even small differences between team members' energy peaks may have a significant effect on daily work performance and team interactions.

The authors hypothesize that if each member determines whether they are a morning or an evening person, it can lead to positive team outcomes. By knowing their own chronotype, individuals can pace their work to match their own energy peaks and those of their fellow team members. An understanding of members' energy differences can act as a team resource and increase the quality of their interactions. It allows a team to better allocate tasks and to schedule workflow throughout the

→

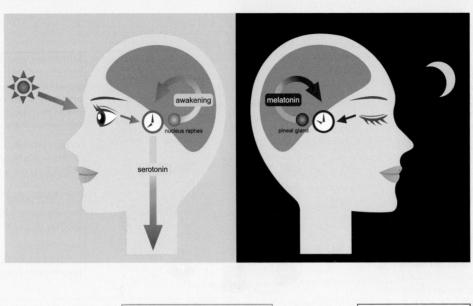

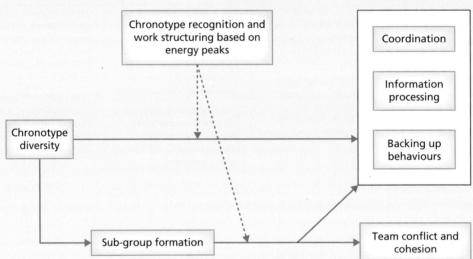

Source: Volk et al. (2017) p. 688.

day. Not understanding chronotype diversity can result in various forms of misalignment in members' energy levels resulting in negative group outcomes.

What other effects can chronotype diversity have on team functioning? The authors suggest four main group consequences:

- *Sub-group formation:* As morning people become drawn together, they begin to avoid working with evening people who have different peak performance periods. This can cause intra-team conflict and endanger the cohesion of the entire team..

- *Coordination:* Requires members to work interdependently, aligning and integrating their efforts with one another at the right time. Individuals normally anticipate others' likely actions and automatically and quickly adjust their behaviours to complete the task. Chronotype diversity can prevent their ability to do this.

- *Information-processing:* Affects a team's ability to perform complex and cognitively demanding tasks. If members have varied chronotypes and are thus out of sync with one another, each individual will have their own optimal time for learning, sharing and applying information. Thus the team as a whole will be less able to gather information, trust its accuracy or use it to make decisions.

- *Backing-up behaviour:* Team members normally help each other in response to unexpected demands or events. Before offering help, they need to recognize

that a team member requires assistance which they do by observing each other and looking out for performance errors. Chronic diversity interferes with mutual monitoring of fellow members and their ability to predict when and what backup is required.

The practical implication of this work is that companies should recognize the importance of chronotype diversity in their teams. By distinguishing morning team members from evening ones, they can create superior teams or arrange the work of existing teams differently so as to make them more effective.

Home viewing

In the film, *The Internship* (2013, director Shawn Levy), Google summer interns form themselves into small teams to compete with one another. One of these teams, 'Team Lyle', consists of six members – Lyle, Neha, Yo-Yo, Stuart, Nick and Billy. Team members have to work effectively together to meet the challenges set for them. Identify which individuals play which of Belbin's team roles, on which occasions, with what result.

Team role theory continues to generate interest, assessment and research (Aritzeta et al., 2007). According to Belbin, a balanced team, i.e. one in which all nine roles present, will perform better than an unbalanced one in which roles are duplicated or missing.

- Simona Lupuleac and her colleagues (2012) studied 32 teams containing 145 members working on development projects. They found a statistical relationship between team role balance and team motivation (preparedness to work hard and make a contribution to their team).

- Nicoleta Meslec and Petru Curşeu (2015) investigated the impact of team role balance on group processes (communication, coordination and planning) and group outcomes (group cohesion, perceived performance). They studied 459 students at a Dutch university. They concluded that although balanced teams performed significantly better in the initial phases of group development, the effect disappeared towards the end of the group project and thus did not predict group performance at later points in time.

- Nel Mostert (2015) studied 730 employees in the R&D teams of a fast-moving consumer goods company over a seven-year period. He found that:

  - each team had its own unique team innovation culture
  - all team members benefitted from knowing each other's team roles
  - most project team leaders were Shapers
  - in an R&D environment, Plants, Resource-Investigators, and Specialists produced the most creative team combination

| **CRITICAL THINKING** | Team role theory has a commonsense appeal to many managers – pick the members with the right characteristics, and your team will be successful. What are the problems with this view? What other factors, inside or outside the organization, excluding team role balance, are likely to affect the success or failure of a team within an organization? |

Leadership structure

There are many roles to be performed in a group if it is to be both productive and satisfying for its members. One of the most important of these is 'leader'. A team leader can either be appointed or can emerge. In the latter case, a group makes a leader of the person who has some special capacity for coping with the group's particular problems. They may possess physical strength, shrewdness, or some other relevant attribute. In their classic research, Kurt Lewin, Ralph White and Ronald Lippitt distinguished three distinct leadership styles (White and Lippitt, 1960):

- *Authoritarian leadership:* The leader stresses the distinction between themselves and their followers; establishes a distanced, professional relationship; believes in maintaining control; and focuses on efficiency.

- *Democratic leadership:* The leader shares decision making with group members by promoting the interests of group members and by practising social equality.

- *Laissez-faire leadership:* The leader gives followers the resources to achieve their goals; freedom to make decisions concerning their own work; allows them self-direction while simultaneously offering guidance, support and decision advice, but only if requested.

CUTTING EDGE Leading an inherited team

Michael Watkins

Michael Watkins (2016) noted that a poorly functioning group or team may have its leader replaced by someone from outside. In such circumstances, the new leader does not get to handpick those with whom they will be working. Rather, he or she inherits their predecessor's team members. In such 'legacy groups', the presence of existing team members may be essential in the short term, but not necessarily over the longer term. Watkins offers a three-step approach for taking over and transforming an existing team.

Step 1: Assess the team

Evaluate the members that have been inherited. Do you have the right people, doing the right things, in the right way? You need to clarify what qualities your team

members need to possess in order to tackle the challenges that the team faces. What member characteristics are you looking for? Do they need to work as a team all the time? How essential are their team roles in meeting your goals? On which tasks do they need to collaborate and on which ones can they work independently?

Step 2: Reshape the team

Reform the team within the constraints of the organization's culture, the leader's mandate, and the available talent, to achieve what is needed. Leaders want their members to share information freely; deal with conflict swiftly; solve problems creatively; support each other; and defend their decisions to outsiders. To achieve this, Watkins suggests focusing on four factors:

- *Composition:* When replacing and recruiting is not an option, wait for normal turnover, encourage marginal performers to seek alternative roles; groom high-potentials to take on new responsibilities; have people swap jobs; look for opportunities to transfer members out to other departments and create new positions.
- *Integration:* Establish ground rules and processes which encourage and reinforce the desired behaviours; change destructive team behaviours and foster a sense of shared purpose.
- *Alignment:* Since team members have their own vested interests, ensure they share a sense of purpose and direction; secure agreement on the questions of what the group will accomplish; why it should do so; how it will do it; and who will do what.
- *Operating model:* Rethink group working practices by changing the number of core team members; creating sub-teams; adjusting the frequency of meetings and altering the way they are run; and asking your team how it can operate more efficiently and productively within existing constraints.

Step 3: Accelerate the team

Leaders need to energize members with some early team successes which will speed up team development and performance. This reinforces people's confidence in their capabilities and reinforces the value of the new rules and processes. Once there has been a 'win', build upon it, to achieve a virtuous circle of achievement and confidence.

Distributed and shared leadership

Distributed leadership the exercise of leadership behaviours, often informally and spontaneous, by staff at all levels of an organization, with a group taking collective responsibility, or taking turns in leadership roles depending on circumstances.

There has been an increasing interest in distributed or dispersed leadership within a group as opposed to individual leadership (see **Chapter 18**). Distributed leadership refers to the collective exercise of leadership behaviours, often informal and spontaneous, by staff at all levels of an organization.

It has been found to improve both group performance and member satisfaction. One can distinguish between a leader and acts of leadership. If we accept Raymond Cattell's (1951) view that the leader is any group member who is capable of modifying the properties of the group by their presence, then we can acknowledge that any member of a group can perform acts of leadership, and not just a single, designated individual. From this perspective, leadership can switch or rotate between group members as circumstances change, rather than being a static status associated with a single individual.

Distributed leadership problems

Greg Stewart and his colleagues (2017) examined obstacles to empowering groups, delegating and sharing leadership within a Veterans Health Administration in the United States. High-status team leaders (doctors) were found to be less effective in implementing team-based empowerment than lower-status leaders such as nurse practitioners or doctors' assistants. They attributed the differences to two problems. First, to a leader identity problem where, as people experience changes in their status and prestige, they have difficulty redefining who they are. Second, to a leader delegation problem where leaders have difficulty in recognizing others' expertise and distributing work tasks accordingly.

→

The authors argue that in order for team-based empowerment to succeed, leaders had to change their perceptions of who they were, before they could change what they did. The results emphasize the general problem in any organization transformation situation when leaders in managerial roles within a hierarchy which gives them high status are asked to switch to a more egalitarian, team-based structure in which power and leadership are more widely distributed.

Focusing on the UK, Martin Beirne (2017) summarized the findings of research into distributed leadership within the British healthcare system. He discovered that doctors were highly sceptical of distributed leadership and overwhelming committed to medical hierarchies and their prerogatives. This distributed leadership style clashed with their medical thinking about the boundaries of authority and who should have the 'final word'. Front-line nurses were more accepting of the logic and benefits of distributed leadership and were more amenable to collective leadership activities than were managers, doctors or even senior nurses. However, they were aware of the limiting effects of traditional healthcare organization structures and orientations. Beirne's findings confirm those of Stewart et al.'s, illustrating the difficulty of changing leadership styles within institutionalized healthcare systems.

While low-status leaders embraced their new identity, seeing themselves as a member of a team with a larger purpose, doctors in contrast, sought to sharpen the distinction between their own higher-status identity and the identities of other team members. Doctors with high workloads struggled to delegate; remained opposed to being helped; and were reluctant to give up control, even though it would have benefitted them to do so. The results revealed a pattern of non-doctors embracing the new, team-based empowerment identity and doctors engaged in efforts to resist more equal status and to protect their previous identity.

Research by Robert Bales and Philip Slater (1956) into newly constituted groups found that two individuals regularly emerged who shared the leadership role. One was the *task leader* who specialized in making suggestions, giving information, expressing opinions and generally contributing to helping the group achieve its objective. The other was the *socio-emotional leader* who helped maintain relationships between group members allowing them to express their ideas and positive feelings. This person made jokes, and released tensions in the group, and helped to maintain the group as a functioning entity. Although there was some rivalry, the two group leaders typically cooperated and worked together well.

Lynda Gratton and her colleagues (Gratton et al., 2007) confirmed this distinction fifty years later when investigating teams which demonstrated high levels of collaboration. They found that the flexible behaviour of their team leaders, both task and relationship-oriented, was crucial. Successful group leaders changed their style. Initially, they emphasized task leadership – clarifying goals, committing members and defining individual responsibilities. Later, when tensions around the sharing of knowledge emerged, they switched to a relationship orientation. Such 'ambidextrous team leaders' possessed both task and relationship skills. The topic of multi-leader teams has continued to be of research interest (Dust and Ziegert, 2016).

Home viewing

Twelve O'Clock High (1949, director Henry King) is a classic war film set on a US Air Force in Archbury, England during the Second World War. The 918th Bomber Group is performing badly while engaging in highly risky daylight bombing raids deep into Nazi-occupied Europe. With success and morale low, General Frank Savage (played by Gregory Peck) is sent in to replace the popular Colonel Davenport (Gary Merrill). The film offers numerous leadership lessons and illustrates the difference between the task and the social emotional leader.

Networked individualism

Networked individualism
people functioning as connected individuals rather than embedded group members, moving between different sets of co-workers, using their ties to get jobs done, and relying on digital media to connect themselves with others.

Beyond the virtual team, Rainie and Wellman (2012) discuss the development of what they labelled as networked individualism. This is where in a gig economy, people function more as connected individuals and less as embedded group members or lone workers.

There are approximately 150 million people in North America and Western Europe now working as independent contractors (Petriglieri et al., 2018). These people are networked workers, moving between different sets of co-workers, using their ties to get jobs done, and relying on digital media to connect them to network members both near and far. According to these authors, networked individualism was the result of three revolutions:

- *Social network revolution:* Starting in the 1960s, people changed from being embedded in groups – family, work, community – to being involved in multiple, partial networks.

- *Internet revolution:* The provision of internet communication and information-gathering capacities has allowed networked computers connectivity over large distances. However, the computers, being personal, make the individual and not the work group, the point of contact.

- *Mobile revolution:* Digital media have become body appendages giving workers convenient access to co-workers and information. Separation by space and time has ceased to be of importance. This revolution has affected all employees from the boardroom to the shop floor.

It is this triple revolution that allows networked workers to establish relationships between different sets of fellow workers, both with other individuals and with groups, doing different jobs. *The Economist* (2018b, 2018c) estimated that the UK had around one million gig workers who operated on short-term contracts or freelanced, rather than occupying full-time, permanent positions within companies. Thus, many workers are no longer defined by their membership of a single workgroup, whether co-located or virtual, but by a multitude of intersecting networks to which they temporarily belong. They work as connected individuals in multiple teams on multiple projects, both locally and at a distance. Between 65 per cent and 90 per cent of knowledge workers participate in multiple teams simultaneously (O'Leary, 2011). Dimitrova and Wellman (2015) say that participation in such networks is 'do or die for networked workers and organizations' (p.446).

The changing world of work

In this podcast Sarah O'Conner considers the shifts in the world of work. In the gig economy the traditional relationships between employers and employees are fraying (24:20).

 **RECAP**

1. *List the six dimensions of group structure.*

   - The six main dimensions along which the members of a group differ are: power, status, liking, communication, role and leadership. A person may be placed high on one dimension and simultaneously low on another.

   - The group's structure acts to increase the predictability of behaviour between the group's members.

2. *Identify the sources of power within a group.*

   - There are six sources or types of power: reward, coercive, referent, legitimate, expert and informational.

3. *Distinguish between two common uses of the concept of status.*

   - The status structure of a group is determined by how much status an individual member possesses. There is formal status and social status.

4. *Understand how emotional relationships within a group can be represented symbolically.*

   - The liking (emotional) structure of a group is revealed through the use of sociometry, a technique developed by Jacob Moreno.

5. *Distinguish between communication network analysis, communication pattern analysis and Interpersonal Process Analysis (IPA).*

   - A communication network analysis maps the direction and quantity of oral communication of members in a co-located group. It is depicted on a communigram.

   - A communication pattern analysis maps the direction and quantity of oral communication of members of a dispersed group. It uses emails, documents, data, and voice mail transmission, to determine the source, direction and quantity of both oral and written communication between group members.

   - Interpersonal Process Analysis (IPA) classifies the content of oral communications between group members. It was developed by Robert Bales.

6. *Distinguish between task-oriented, sociability and dominance behaviours within a group*

   - Task behaviours focus on problem solutions; sociability behaviours focus on relationship issues; and dominance behaviours focus on individual member dominance or passivity.

7. *Differentiate between Belbin's team roles.*

   - Meredith Belbin's team role theory distinguishes the roles of Plant, Resource-investigator, Coordinator, Shaper, Monitor-Evaluator, Teamworker, Implementer, Completer-Finisher, and Specialist.

8. *Give examples of the three original leadership styles identified by Lewin, White and Lippitt.*

   - These researchers distinguished three leadership styles which they labelled authoritarian, democratic and laissez faire.

9. *Distinguish between a task and socio-emotional group leader.*

   - Bales and Slater suggested that a group often had both a task leader and a socio-emotional leader. The first drove the group towards task achievement, while the second focussed on relationships to keep the group working as a cooperative unit.

10. *List the key dimensions of a virtual team.*

    - Spatial dispersion – different geographical locations; temporal dispersion – different time zones; organizational dispersion – working across organizational boundaries; cultural dispersion – members coming come from different countries or cultures; altering membership: members joining and leaving; and technological communication – communicating mainly electronically

11. *Identify the benefits and problems associated with virtual teams.*

    - Virtual teams offer organizations many benefits but also create problems which need to be anticipated and managed.

    - Leading virtual teams is both similar to and different from leading face-to-face teams. It demands certain additional knowledge, skills and abilities from virtual team leaders,

    - Beyond the virtual team is the growth of networked individualism. Its effect on organizations and management is not yet known.

RECAP: What did they find?

- Van der Haar et al. (2016) found that the structuring oral behaviour of team leader's that distinguished highly effective teams from less effective teams was *summarizing* – a short repetition of what has been said – in both its forms.

- A summary followed by a command that indicated what action team members should take or what information should be collected was found to be beneficial if used in the first meeting.

- A summary followed by a decision in terms of a statement closing a raised topic or problem was valuable when used in the second meeting.

- The argument is that explicit communication supports shared problem solving which is essential for avoiding ambiguity or a lack of information that may lead to serious errors. As such, in an emergency situation involving multidisciplinary teams, summarizing, followed by a clear command or a decision supports the development of a shared understanding and contributes to team effectiveness.

Revision

1. Give three reasons all jobs should be designed around groups, and three reasons why they should not.

2. Describe situations in which (i) team role analysis and (ii) a sociogram would be relevant to improve a group's functioning. How would you apply these two techniques? How would you use the results?

3. Critically assess the strengths and weaknesses of Belbin's team role theory as a guide for the manager wishing to construct a team that will be effective.

4. Identify some of the problems of virtual teamworking for (a) the companies which establish them and (b) the individuals who work in them. How might these problems be overcome?

Research assignment

Studies suggest that employees spend many hours each week in meetings. Get invited to a real meeting that will last at least 30 minutes. Consult the box 'Analysing oral interactions in a group' and make several copies of the oral interaction score sheet that you will find there. Read and follow the instructions detailed in the box. After 30 minutes of silently observing and scoring, excuse yourself and leave the meeting quietly. After you have added up your scores, write a brief report which comments on (a) the way this group as a whole was working, (b) the roles played by its individual members, and (c) the adequacy of your scoring sheet and its underlying assumptions. Make recommendations as to how your group's members' interactions could be improved.

Springboard

Tripp Driskell, James Driskell, Shawn Burke and Eduardo Salas (2017) 'Team roles: A review and integration, *Small Group Research*, 48(4): 482–511. The authors review the history and development of the topic that is probably of the greatest interest to business management.

James Dulebohn and Julia Hoch (2017) 'Virtual teams in organizations', *Human Resource Management Review*, 27 (4): 569–74. The authors overview the latest virtual teams research and use the input-process-output framework to identify the key inputs, team emergent states, processes, moderators, and outcomes relevant to virtual team effectiveness.

Selin Kesebir (2012) 'The superorganism account of human sociality: How and when human groups are like beehives', *Personality and Social Psychology Review*, 16(3): 233–61. The author contrasts groups with beehives emphasising the role of individuals within the collectivity.

Matthias Weiss and Martin Hoegln (2015) 'The history of teamwork's societal diffusion: A multi-method review', *Small Group Research*, 46(6) 589–622. The authors assess how research on teamwork has affected what managers and companies do.

OB cinema

Network (1976, director Sidney Lumet). DVD track 16: 1:48:00–1:53:00 (5 minutes).

This film is set in the US television industry. Because of his falling ratings, the Union Broadcasting System (UBS) fires its leading news anchorman Howard Beale (played by Peter Finch). Beale's on-air behaviour then becomes increasingly bizarre, after he promises to kill himself on television. Initially, his ratings skyrocket as he becomes the 'Mad Prophet of the Airways' but they then decline, affecting UBS's other programmes and its revenue. The clip begins as network executives assemble for a meeting and ends with Diana saying 'let's kill the son-of-a-bitch'. Hackett (played by Robert Duvall) sits at the desk and begins the meeting by describing the problem.

Listen to the discussion between the six individuals in the room. Each time one of them speaks, decide into which of the six oral categories if fits, and indicate this by putting a dot, under their name. Continue scoring until the clip has finished. At the end of the discussion, total up the rows to reveal which oral categories were used most and least and then add up the columns to discover which member spoke most and least.

B	C	D	E	F
Joe	Man in chair	Man in armchair	Herb (standing)	Diana

A
Hackett

Oral interaction score sheet

Oral category	*Meeting participants*						
	A **Hackett**	**B** **Joe**	**C** **Main in chair**	**D** **Man in armchair**	**E** **Herb (standing)**	**F** **Diana**	**TOTAL**
Proposing							
Building							
Supporting							
Disagreeing							
Giving • information • opinions • suggestions							
Seeking • information • opinions • suggestions							
TOTAL							

Chapter exercises

1: Oral communication

Objectives
1. Understand the effects of group members' communication patterns.
2. Analyse group communication patterns.
3. Raise self-awareness of group communication.
4. Improve group communication skills.

Briefing
1. Form into groups of between four and five.
2. Nominate one person to be observer/scorer and provide them with an oral interaction score sheet (see above).

Your instructor will provide each group with a topic for discussion. Before speaking, a member has to pre-categorize their oral contribution before making it, e.g.

• Giving information – 'The price of these items has doubled in recent years'
• Proposing – 'I think we should make substantial cuts'.

After 15 minutes the instructor will say 'time up'. The observer/scorer will total up.

Debrief
1. The observer/scorer summarizes the individual member scores and gives their overall impression of the group discussion.
2. The group members then discuss the following questions:

• Did you find the task difficult?
• How did having to pre-categorize each of your contributions affect you?

→

- What did you learn about how a group discussion proceeds?
- What have you learned about group communication? How might you change the way that you communicate in a group in the future? What specifically will you do or not do?

2: Team roles questionnaire

Objectives
1. To introduce team role theory.
2. To identify your preferred team roles.

Instructions
Listed below are statements that describe behaviours that members use when they are participating in a team. As a student, you may demonstrate these behaviours at work, in team projects, student organizations and societies, or in interactions with your flatmates.

Use the 1–5 scale below to indicate how frequently you engage in these behaviours when part of a team. Place a number from 1 to 5 in the space to the left of each statement.

1	2	3	4	5
Very infrequently				Very frequently

_____ 1. I organize and use other people's abilities and talents productively.

_____ 2. I react strongly when meetings look like losing track of the objective.

_____ 3. I start to look around for possible ideas and openings.

_____ 4. I often produce a new approach to a long-continuing problem.

_____ 5. I analyse other people's ideas objectively for their merits and flaws.

_____ 6. I can be relied on to see that the work we need to do is organised.

_____ 7. I am always ready to support good suggestions that help us resolve a problem.

_____ 8. I notice omissions and have an eye for getting the details right.

_____ 9. I like to employ my experience, training and qualifications.

_____ 10. I often draw out contributions from other team members.

_____ 11. I am ready to make my personal views known in a forceful way if necessary.

_____ 12. A broad range of personal contacts is important to my style of working.

_____ 13. I like to use my imagination to suggest completely new approaches.

_____ 14. I like to weigh up several alternatives thoroughly before choosing, which may take time.

_____ 15. I am interested more in practicalities than in new ideas.

_____ 16. I am concerned to help others with their problems.

_____ 17. I keep a watchful eye on areas where difficulties may arise.

_____ 18. I usually only contribute when I really know what I'm talking about.

_____ 19. I am happy to take the lead when action is needed.

_____ 20. It is worth incurring some temporary unpopularity to get my views across.

_____ 21. I like to discover the latest ideas and developments as I get easily bored.

_____ 22. I can quickly see how ideas and techniques can be used in new relationships.

_____ 23. I approach the topic in a carefully analytical way.

_____ 24. Given an objective, I can sort out the concrete steps to achieve it.

_____ 25. I get on well with others and work hard for the team.

_____ 26 I like to finish my current work before I start something new.

_____ 27. My technical knowledge and experience are usually my major contributions.

Transfer the points from each of the 27 statements into the table below, placing them next to the statement number. Then add up the points in each of the nine columns. Enter these in the 'Total' row. This indicates the roles that you most frequently play in a team. The higher the score, the more you see yourself taking that role.

Coordinator	Shaper	Resource-Investigator	Plant	Monitor-Evaluator	Implementer	Team-worker	Completer-Finisher	Specialist
1.	2.	3.	4.	5.	6.	7.	8.	9.
10.	11.	12.	13.	14.	15.	16.	17.	18.
19.	20.	21.	22.	23.	24.	25.	26.	27.
TOTAL								

Briefing

1. Divide into groups.

2. Remind yourself of each of the nine team roles.

3. In your groups:

   a. Compare your top two team role scores with those of the other members of your group. Give an example of behaviours that demonstrate your performance of that role.

   b. Identify which roles are preferred among students in this group (high-scoring roles). Identify which roles are avoided, rejected or are missing (low-scoring roles).

   c. If this was a real management or project team, what could be done to cover the missing roles?

   d. Decide whether certain roles are more important in certain phases of a team's operation? For example, which two team roles are likely to be crucial in the getting-started phase of a team's work: the generating-ideas phase; the developing-the-ideas phase; and the implementing-the-decision phase?

   e. Decide to what extent your preferred team roles are a reflection of your personality.

This questionnaire was adapted from one developed by Nancy Foy, building on the work of Meredith Belbin. It appeared in Boddy, D. and Buchanan, D.A. (1987), *Management of Technology. The Technical Change Audit. Action for Results: 5: The Process Module*, pp. 32–35, Manpower Services Commission, Moorfoot, Sheffield, Crown Copyright.

References

Aritzeta, A., Swailes, S. and Seniuor, B. (2007) 'Belbin's team role model: development, validity and applications for teambuilding', *Journal of Management Studies*, 44(1): 96–118.

Bales, R. F. (1950a) *Interaction Process Analysis*, Reading, MA: Addison-Wesley.

Bales, R. F. (1950b) 'A set of categories for the analysis of small group interaction', *American Sociological Review*, 15(2): 257–63.

Bales, R.F. (1959) 'Task roles and social roles in problem solving groups ' in Maccoby, E.E, Newcomb, M. and Hartley, E.L. (eds.), *Readings in Social Psychology*, third edition, New York: Holt, Rinehart and Winston.

Bales, R. F. and Slater, P. E. (1956) 'Role differentiation in small decision-making groups' in T. Parsons and R. F. Bales (eds.), *Family, Socialization and Interaction* (pp. 259–306), London: Routledge.

Bartram, D. (2005) 'The great eight competencies: a criterion-centric approach to validation', *Journal of Applied Psychology*, 90(6): 185–203.

BBC (2016) 'From the cockpit to the operating theatre', Radio 4, 20 July.

Beirne, M. (2017) 'The reforming appeal of distributed leadership: recognizing concerns and contradictory tendencies', *British Journal of Healthcare Management*, 23(6): 262–70.

Belbin, R. M. (1993) *Team Roles at Work*, Oxford: Butterworth Heinemann.

Belbin, R. M. (1996) *The Coming Shape of Organizations*, London: Butterworth Heinemann.

Belbin, R. M. (2010) *Management Teams: Why They Succeed or Fail,* third edition, Oxford: Butterworth Heinemann.

Belbin (2018) *Great Teams Start With Belbin,* http://www.belbin.com

Bendersky, C. and Hays, N.A. (2012) 'Status conflict in groups', *Organization Science,* 23(2): 323–40.

Bendersky, C. and Shah, N.P. (2012) 'The cost of status enhancement: performance effects of individuals' status mobility in task groups', *Organization Science,* 23(2): 308–22.

Bendersky, C. and Shah, N.P. (2013) 'The downfall of extraverts and the rise of neurotics: the dynamic process of status allocation in task groups' *Academy of Management Journal,* 56(2): 387–406.

Benne, K. D. and Sheats, P. (1948) 'Functional roles of group members', *Journal of Social Issues,* 4(2): 41–49.

Cattell, R. (1951) 'New concepts for measuring leadership in terms of group syntality', *Human Relations,* 4(2): 161–68.

Courtright, S.H., Stewart, G.L. and Ward, M.M. (2012) 'Applying research to save lives: learning from health care training approaches in aviation and health care', *Organizational Dynamics,* 41(4): 291–301.

Dahl, R. A. (1957) 'The concept of power', *Behavioural Science,* 2(3): 201–15.

Dhawan, E. and Chamorro-Premuzic, T. (2018) 'How to collaborate effectively if your team is remote', *Harvard Business Review,* Reprint HO46TS, 27 February.

Dimitrova, D. and Wellman, B. (2015) 'Networked work and network research: new forms of teamwork in the triple revolution', *American Behavioural Scientist,* 59(4): 443–56.

Driskell, T., Driskell, J.E., Burke, C.S., and Salas, E. (2017) 'Team roles: a review and integration, *Small Group Research,* 48(4): 482–511.

Dunn, M.B. (2018) 'Using social network analysis in the classroom: an experiential activity and tool to enhance a sense of community', *Management Teaching Review* (published early online).

Dust, S.B. and Ziegert, J.C. (2016) 'Multi-leader teams in review: a contingent-configuration perspective of effectiveness', *International Journal of Management Reviews,* 18(4): 518–41.

Emich, K.J. and Wright, T.A. (2016) 'The 'I's in team: the importance of individual members to team success', *Organizational Dynamics,* 45(1): 2–10.

Ferrazzi, K. (2014) 'Getting virtual teams right', *Harvard Business Review,* 92(12):120–23.

French, J. R. P. and Raven, B. H. (1958) 'The bases of social power' in D. Cartwright (ed.), *Studies in Social Power* (pp. 150–167) Ann Arbor, Michigan: Institute for Social Research, University of Michigan Press.

Foushee, H.C. (1984) 'Dyads and triads at 35,000 feet: factors affecting group process and air crew performance', *American Psychologist,* 39(8): 885–93.

Gilson, L.L., Maynard, M.T., Jones Young, N.C., Vartiainen, M. and Hakonen, M. (2015) 'Virtual teams research: 10 Years, 10 themes and 10 opportunities', *Journal of Management,* 41(5): 1313–37.

Gould, R.V. (2002) 'The origin of status hierarchies: a formal theory and empirical test', *American Journal of Sociology,* 107(5): 1143–78.

Gratton, L., Voight, A. and Erickson, T. (2007) 'Bridging fault lines in diverse teams', *MIT Sloan Management Review,* 48(4): 22–29.

Halgin, D.S., Gopalakrishnan, G.M. and Borgatti, S.P. (2015) 'Structure and agency in networked distributed work: the role of work engagement', *American Behavioural Scientist,* 59(4): 457–74.

Halvey, N., Chou, E.Y. and Galinsky, A.D. (2011) 'A functional model of hierarchy: why, how and when vertical differentiation enhances group performance', *Organizational Psychology Review,* 1(1): 32–52.

Harvey, S., Currall, S.C. and Hammer, T.H. (2017) 'Decision diversion in diverse teams: findings from inside a corporate boardroom', *Academy of Management Discoveries,* 3(4): 358–81.

Haas, M. and Mortensen, M. (2016) 'The secrets of great teamwork', *Harvard Business Review,* 94(6): 7–76.

Huffman, B.J. and Kilian, C.M. (2012) 'The Flight of the Phoenix: interpersonal aspects of project management', *Journal of Management Education,* 36(4): 568–600.

Joo, M-H. and Dennen, V.P. (2017) 'Measuring university students' group work contribution: scale development and validation', *Small Group Research,* 48(3) 288–310.

Krumm,S., Kanthak, J., Hartmann. K. and Hertel, G. (2016) 'What does it take to be a virtual team player? The knowledge, skills, abilities, and other characteristics required in virtual teams, *Human Performance,* 29 (2): 123–42.

Lupuleac, S., Lupulaec, Z.-L. and Rusu, C. (2012) 'Problems of assessing team role balance – Team design', *Procedia Economics and Finance,* 3: 935–40.

Meslec, N. and Curseu, P.L. (2015) 'Are balanced groups better? Belbin roles in collaborative learning groups', *Learning and Individual Differences,* 39: 81–88.

Milanovich, D.M., Driskell, J.E., Stout, R.J. and Salas, E. (1998) 'Status and cockpit dynamics: a review and empirical study', *Group Dynamics,* 2(3): 155–67.

Moreno, J. L. (1953) *Who Shall Survive?*, second edition, New York: Beacon Press.

Mostert, N.M. (2015) 'Belbin – the way forward for innovation teams', *Journal of Creativity and Business Innovation,* 1: 35–48.

O'Connor, S. (2015) 'Wearables at work: the new frontier of staff surveillance', *Financial Times,* 9 June, p.14.

O'Leary, M.B., Mortensen, M. and Woolley, A.W. (2011) 'Multiple team membership: a theoretical model of its effects on productivity and learning for individuals and teams', *American Behavioural Scientist,* 59(4):508–24.

Orbach, M., Demko, M., Doyle, J., Waber, B.N. and Pentland, A. (2015) 'Sensing informal networks in organizations', *American Behavioural Scientist,* 59(4): 508–24.

Pentland, A. (2012) 'The new science of building teams', *Harvard Business Review,* 90(4): 60–70.

Petriglieri, G., Ashford, S. and Wrzesniewski, A. (2018) 'Thriving in the gig economy', *Harvard Business Review,* 96(2): 140–43.

Piazza, A. and Castellucci, F. (2014) 'Status in organization and management theory', *Journal of Management,* 40(1): 287–315.

Rainie, L. and Wellman, B. (2012) *Networked: The New Social Operating System,* Cambridge, MA: MIT Press.

Sanner, B. and Bunderson, J.S. (2018) 'The truth about hierarchy', *MIT Sloan Management Review,* 59(2): 49–52.

Sauder, M., Lynn, F. and Podolny, J.M. (2012) 'Status: insights from organizational sociology', *Annual Review of Sociology,* 38: 267–83.

Schultze, J. and Krumm, S. (2017) 'The virtual team player: a review and initial model of knowledge, skills, abilities, and other characteristics for virtual collaboration, *Organizational Psychology Review,* 7(1): 66–95.

Shapiro, D. L., Furst, S. A., Speitzer, G. M., and Von Glinow, M. A. (2002) 'Transnational teams in the electronic age: are teams' identity and high performance at risk', *Journal of Organizational Behaviour,* 23(4): 455–67.

Stewart, G.L., Astrove, S.L., Reeves, C.J., Crawford, E.R. and Solimeo, S.L. (2017) 'Those with the most find it hardest to share: Exploring leader resistance to the implementation of team-based empowerment', *Academy of Management Journal,* 60(6): 2266–93.

Tarnow, E. (2000) 'Self-destructive obedience in the airplane cockpit and the concept of obedience optimization' in Blass, T. (ed), *Obedience to Authority: Current Perspectives on the Milgram Paradigm,* Mahwah, NJ, Erlbaum.

The Economist (2018a) 'Special Report: AI in Business: GrAIt expectations; Smile, you're on camera', 31 March, pp. 9–10.

The Economist (2018b) 'The gig economy on trial', 23 February, pp. 23–24.

The Economist (2018c) 'Surfs up', 6 October, pp.66–68.

Tichy, N. and Fombrun, C. (1979) 'Network analysis on organizational settings', *Human Relations,* 32(11): 923–65.

Tieman, R. (2012) 'From teamwork to collaboration', *Financial Times,* Executive Appointments, 15 March, p.1.

Van der Haar, S, Koeslag-Kreunen, M. Euwe, E. and Segers, M. (2017) 'Team leader structuring for team effectiveness and team learning in command-and-control teams' , *Small Group Research,* 48(2) 215–48.

Volk, S., Pearsall, M.J., Christian, M.S., and Becker, W.J. (2017) 'Chronotype diversity in teams: toward a theory of team energetic asynchrony', *Academy of Management Review,* 42(4): 683–702.

Watkins, M.D. (2016) 'Leading the team you inherit', *Harvard Business Review,* 94(6):60–67.

White, R. and Lippitt, R. (1960) *Autocracy and Democracy,* New York: Harper and Row.

Winsborough, D. and Chamorro-Premuzic, T. (2017) 'Great teams are about personalities, not just skills', *Harvard Business Review,* Reprint H03F24, 25 January.

Zander, L., Mockaitis, A.I. and Butler, C.L. (2012) 'Leading global teams', *Journal of World Business,* 47(2): 592–603.

Zander, L., Zetting, P. and Mäkelä, K. (2013) 'Leading global virtual teams to success', *Organizational Dynamics,* 42(3): 228–37.

CHAPTER 12
Individuals in groups

Key terms

self-concept

social identity

social categorization

self-categorization

self-esteem

social representations

shared frame of reference

social influence

social facilitation

social inhibition

synergy

social compensation

social loafing

free rider

group norm

pivotal norm

peripheral norm

group sanction

ostracism

conformity

obedience

group cohesion

group socialization

organizational socialization

deindividuation

compliance

conversion

team building

Learning outcomes

When you have read this chapter, you should be able to define those key terms in your own words, and you should also be able to:

1. Explain the basic principles of social identity theory and social representation theory.

2. Distinguish between social facilitation and social loafing.

3. Understand how groups use norms to regulate the behaviour of their members.

4. Understand the process of group socialization of individuals.

5. Explain why individuals conform to the dictates of their group.

6. Distinguish between conformity and obedience, and between compliance and conversion.

Why study individuals in groups?

The enthusiasm of management for groups and teams in the workplace is tempered by researchers who believe that they possess a darker side, one which becomes evident when manifested in the behaviour of some mobs and crowds on the street. They are seen as taking over individuals' minds, depressing their intelligence, eliminating their moral responsibility and forcing their conformity. A group can cause their members a great deal of suffering and despair and can perpetuate acts of great cruelty. There is now extensive research evidence which demonstrates the ability of groups to affect the behaviour of their members.

Managements have harnessed this power by creating groups and teams which police and discipline their own members, keeping their behaviour in line with company objectives. In addition, they have taken active steps to build cohesive teams in which individuals work well together to achieve organizational goals. While the power of the group to affect the perceptions, performance and behaviour of its individual members is well established, there is also a growing body of research that shows how a lone individual can influence a majority.

The individual and the group

Henri Tajfel and John Turner (1986) argued that as long as individuals see themselves as more important than their group, then the latter cannot function effectively. Participants have to identify themselves as group members, treating the group's values as their own. Such an attitudinal 'switch' and commitment facilitates the long-term existence and success of their group. This question of how much an individual should be part of the group (for their own wellbeing, for that of their group, and for the organization) and how much separate from it (to remain creative, critical and for their own mental health) is a continuing debate in the literature.

Let us first consider concepts and theories that explain the relationship between an individual and their group. **Self-concept** refers to the set of perceptions that we have about ourselves. It is the way in which we see ourselves. It affects both how we feel about ourselves and how we act within a group. This is because joining a group lowers our self-awareness and raises our group awareness. The roles that we play within different groups, especially those that are important to us, influence and shape our attitudes and behaviours.

Self-concept the set of perceptions that we have about ourselves.

Tajfel and Turner (1986) developed social identity theory. **Social identity** is that part of an individual's self-concept which derives from their membership of groups. It holds that a person's self-concept is based not only on their individual characteristics or personal identity (*I am reserved, I am interested in music, I have blond hair*), but also on their group membership (*I am French, I work for ABC corporation, I am a member of the accounting profession*). People have a strong tendency to mentally organize things and people, including themselves, into categories. To the extent that we categorize ourselves as being members of groups, we have social identities.

Social identity that part of the self-concept which comes from our membership of groups and which contributes to our self-esteem.

Our social identities, developed through our group membership, are an important part of how we define ourselves. The groups or social categories to which we belong (e.g. student course member, management team member, parent or sports club secretary) are an integral part of our self-concept. Social identity fulfils two functions. First, it defines and evaluates a person (e.g. 'she's a member of the design team'). Such definition and evaluation is done both by others and by the person themselves. Second, it prescribes appropriate behaviour for them. They think and behave in characteristically 'design team' ways.

According to Tajfel, in order to evaluate your own opinions and abilities, you compare yourself with other individuals with whom you interact. This comparison

Social categorization
classifying the people
we meet, on the basis of
how similar or different
they are, from the way
that we see ourselves.

process is called social categorization. It involves assessing the people that we meet on the basis of how similar or different they are from the way that we see ourselves. If I see myself as motivated, I will categorize other people as being more, equally or less motivated than me. This self-categorization process means that we perceive ourselves as having the same social identity as other category members. It leads us to behave in ways that are consistent with the stereotypes of the categories to which we believe that we belong. Self-categorization transforms a number of separate individuals into a group (Figure 12.1). You then compare the group that you are in (the in-group) with similar but distinct groups of which you are not a member (the out-group). This inter-group comparison leads us to a 'we–they' view of the world.

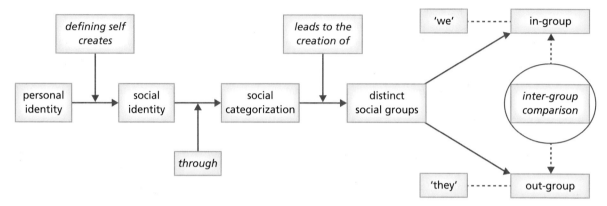

Figure 12.1: Social identity theory
Source: based on Tajfel and Turner (1986)

Self-categorization
perceiving ourselves
as sharing the same
social identity as other
category members,
and behaving in ways
consistent with that
category stereotype.

Together, social categorization and self-categorization lead to assumed similarity among those who are categorized together. They minimize the perceived differences between members of the in-group and maximize the differences between the in-group and other out-groups. When this happens, the individuals who are part of the in-group will have assumed a social identity and will view other people from this standpoint (See Figure 12.2).

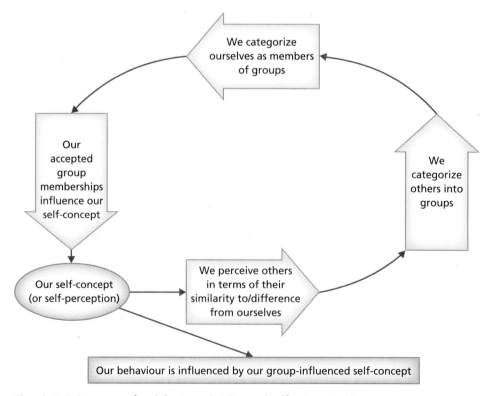

Figure 12.2: Processes of social categorization and self-categorization
Source: Guirdham, M. (2002) *Interactive Behaviour at Work*, Pearson Education Limited.

CUTTING EDGE   Trust and job satisfaction in virtual teams

Philipp Romeike and his colleagues (2016) examined the relationship between a virtual team member's degree of trust in their co-workers and their level of job satisfaction by investigating the role of social comparison processes. Comparing one's own abilities with those of others is a common response to the fundamental human need to know one's relative position in any group context. Social comparisons reduce uncertainty. Virtual teams are characterized by a high degree of uncertainty and the need for trust between members. Their members engage in ongoing social comparisons with one another. However, as these virtual team members have less information available to them on which to base their comparisons (in contrast to those in face-to-face groups), they frequently come to biased conclusions that can lead to a reduction in their trust in other group members. The authors found that almost every member considered that their own individual performance exceeded that of the group target.

A team member who considers their own performance to be superior to that of their team may either infer that the remaining team members do not adequately reciprocate her or his contributions to the team, or that they are putting in less effort than she or he is. In either case, the team member perceives the exchange relationship with the team to be unbalanced and unfair, and this erodes their attitude towards the team and decreases their level of trust in it. Team members were found to distance themselves from their team, express less trust in their co-workers, and were less satisfied with their jobs. This represents a serious threat to virtual team effectiveness. Trust is a key interpersonal process that is linked to a wide range of desirable outcomes such as knowledge sharing.

What can be done? First, the authors recommend that team leaders should clearly explain how each performance indicator is derived and what it refers to. They need to explain not only about how the team as a whole is performing, but also how each individual within it is doing. This avoids biased perceptions of individuals' own performances. If team leaders only discuss the overall team performance, and if it is below target, individuals will conclude that it is not their fault, but that it is their fellow team members who are to blame. In virtual work contexts the potential for such scapegoating is particularly high as team members almost never observe each other at work. If they do not understand the information being provided, and if they make biased social comparisons, then the consequential adverse effects on group trust and member job satisfaction are likely to occur.

Self-esteem that part of the self which is concerned with how we evaluate ourselves.

We all see ourselves as members of various social groupings which are distinguishable and hence different from other social groupings. The consequence is that by identifying with certain groupings but not others, we come to see the world in terms of 'us-and-them'. There are two benefits for us from this. First, our understanding of the world is enhanced by classifying everybody this way. Second, our self-esteem can be maintained or even enhanced. Membership of a high-status group gives us prestige, which in turn raises our self-esteem. We are highly motivated to feel proud to belong to the group of which we are members. If we cannot achieve this feeling of pride, we will either try to change the group's perceived status or will detach ourselves from it.

Categorizing people into groups and identifying with some of these groups appears to be a fundamental human characteristic which derives from the fact that human beings are social animals. However, by differentiating themselves from others and because of their need for belonging, individuals expose themselves to the control of others. Within the organizational context, we offer control to fellow group members who wish to direct our attitudes, thoughts and behaviours in line with what the group considers appropriate. We also hand control to managers who seek both to motivate and control us by instituting various forms of team working arrangements.

Group influences on individuals' perceptions

How does a group affect the perceptions of its individual members? One explanation was offered at the start of the book with the *constructivist* perspective **(see Chapter 1)**. This argued that our social and organizational surroundings possess no ultimate truth or reality, but are determined instead by the way in which we experience and understand those worlds which we construct and reconstruct for ourselves, through our interactions with others. In short, we don't see things as *they are* – we see things as *we are*. Among these important 'others' with whom we interact and with whom we experience and understand the world, are the members of the groups to which we belong.

Social representations the beliefs, ideas and values, objects, people and events that are constructed by current group members, and which are transmitted to its new members.

Social representations theory was formulated by Serge Moscovici (1984). **Social representations** are the beliefs, ideas and values, objects, people and events that are constructed by current group members and which are transmitted to its new members. When individuals join a new group, its members will construct and transmit complex and unfamiliar ideas to newcomers in straightforward ways. This process creates social representations which come to be accepted, in a modified form, by the new members of a group who may come from different backgrounds and cultures. It helps these new recruits to make sense of what is going on around them within their group. The explanation of some occurrence is simplified, distorted and ritualized by the group. It becomes a 'common sense explanation' which is accepted as orthodoxy among its members and is then communicated to new ones. Social representations are a group's theories about how the world works and are used by them to justify their actions. The prefix 'social' in both phrases, reminds us about the collective way in which reality is jointly manufactured, accepted and shared.

As a new company recruit, you discuss your role in the group with existing members. During these interactions, representations are presented, developed, adapted and negotiated before being incorporated into your own, existing, belief framework. This happens during the period of socialization, shortly after you have joined the group. It is not a matter of you, as a new recruit, being given and accepting a bundle of existing group assumptions, ideas, beliefs and opinions to absorb. Rather, Moscovici's theory emphasizes the interactive nature of the process between you as an individual, and the other group members. Once incorporated, the group representations are revealed in all group members' talk and actions (e.g. that the boss is an idiot).

Shared frame of reference assumptions held in common by group members which shape their thinking, decisions, actions and interactions, while being constantly defined and reinforced through those interactions.

Through these social representations, group members gain a shared frame of reference. Over time, new group members learn about the different assumptions, ideas, beliefs and opinions held by established group members about their common work situation. Some agreement on perception and meaning is essential if group members are to interact, communicate, agree goals and generally act in concert on a common task. Such a shared view is essential for a group to continue and to develop. Moreover, as we work in a group, we find that our views begin to coalesce with those of other members. A shared frame of reference and social representations suggest the existence of a group-level process equivalent of organizational culture forming – a 'group culture' **(see Chapter 4).** Together, the shared frame of reference and social representations processes determine the meanings that group members come to attach to events and to other people's behaviour around them.

CRITICAL THINKING	What challenges have you found when working in a tutorial or project group at university with fellow students coming from different parts of the world? In your view, does their ethnic or national background affect their behaviour within your group? In what ways?

Group influences on individuals' performance

Social influence
the process whereby attitudes and behaviours are altered by the real or implied presence of others.

Social influence refers to the process whereby our attitudes and behaviour are influenced by the presence of others. This presence can either improve or reduce our performance. Figure 12.3 indicates that having other people around us increases our arousal. The complexity of the task that we perform (easy or difficult) also determines how well we do. The explanation is that the presence of others increases arousal which acts to enhance whatever a person's 'dominant response' is. If the task is easy to complete successfully, has been frequently performed in the past, or is already well learned, then there will be an increase in the person's performance in the presence of others. In contrast, if a task is difficult to complete successfully, has rarely been performed in the past, or has been poorly learned, then the increased arousal caused by the presence of others will reduce performance.

Social facilitation the effect of the presence of other people enhancing an individual's performance.

Social facilitation refers to the effect of the presence of other people enhancing an individual's performance. Early research investigated individuals performing various physical tasks. Norman Triplett (1898) studied children winding fishing reels and cyclists racing. The children were found to turn the reels faster when other children were present, and the cyclists performed 20 per cent faster when accompanied by a pacemaker than when alone, even in a non-racing situation. Later studies focused on non-physical tasks. Floyd Allport (1920) discovered that students completed mathematical calculations faster in the company of other students than

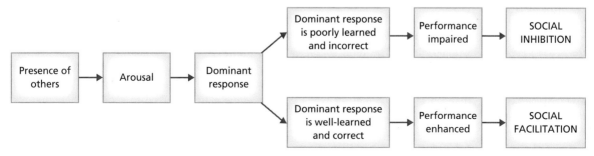

Figure 12.3: Social facilitation and social inhibition

Social inhibition the effect of the presence of other people reducing an individual's performance.

when alone. However, research also revealed the existence of social inhibition which is the effect of the presence of others reducing an individual's task performance.

Also relevant here is the concept of synergy which refers to the outcome of interactions of two or more individuals which can either be positive or negative, and which is different from the sum of outcomes of individuals operating separately. Positive synergy is a concept which underpins of all kinds of groups working in organizations. In particular, it supports the use of cross-functional and cross-industry teams. Positive synergy is the belief that the final output produced by a group of individuals working together rather than separately, will equal more than the sum of the individual members' abilities and efforts. A popular short hand term for this is 2 + 2 = 5. It has been argued that the designated purpose of group tasks should necessarily *require* more than its members are able to offer working as individuals, so as to benefit from the positive aspects of synergy.

Synergy the positive or negative result of the interaction of two or more components, producing an outcome that is different from the sum of the individual components.

The paradox of the team

Paul Gaffney (2015) recounted what a sports teacher had once told him at school: 'You never look better individually than when you play as a member of a team.' But how can you promote your own self-interest by subordinating it to the group interest? Mumford (2015) explained that taking part in a social interaction can positively affect an individual's contributions. New ideas can occur; new ways of achieving objectives might be suggested; members share experiences and encourage each other. Indeed, unspoken understandings can develop which can allow members to anticipate each other's moves, thereby enabling them to act as a single entity. A strong team is greater than the sum of its parts because it brings out the very best in individual members, through their working together.

Social compensation when group cohesion and evaluation are absent, a person who cares about the quality of the group's output will expend greater effort to compensate for others in the group who are performing inadequately.

Sometimes, when people work together as a group, they perform better than if they worked alone. The term social compensation refers to persons increasing their effort and working harder when in a group than when alone (Williams and Karau, 1991: Zaccaro, 1984). This happens when individuals place greater value upon the group rather than on the individual, or when group members are expected to achieve goals that are important to both the individuals and to the group (Guzzo and Dickson, 1996). Much of management's enthusiasm for teamworking is based on its belief (or hope) that social compensation will be triggered among employees once they are organized to work in groups (Figure 12.4).

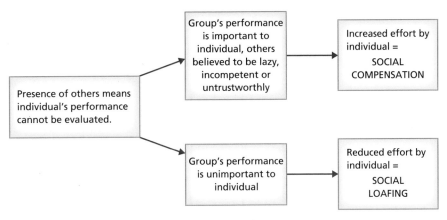

Figure 12.4: Social compensation and social loafing

✓✓✓   **EMPLOYABILITY CHECK (appetite for learning)**

Think of a time when you put a lot of effort into a group of which you were a part – a work group, sports team or social group – when you contributed far more than you would normally have been expected to. What did you learn from this experience that could help you as a team leader?

Social loafing the tendency for individuals to exert less effort when working as part of a group than when working alone.

At other times, when working in a group, individuals will expend less effort because their input, within the group, is more hidden. Social loafing is defined as the tendency of people to exert less effort when working as part of a group than when working alone. Jos Benders (2005) traced management's concern with employees working less hard than they theoretically could to the start of the twentieth century. In Europe, the famous German sociologist, Max Weber wrote about what he called 'braking' (Weber, 1924). At the same time in America, Frederick Taylor, a management consultant, was concerned with 'systematic soldiering' among the workers **(see Chapter 14)**. This shirking or withholding of individual effort can explain why group working can reduce productivity.

Max Ringelmann, a French professor of agricultural engineering, conducted the original social loafing research in the late 1920s on subjects who were arranged in a row, pulling a rope, as in a 'tug-of-war' contest (Kravitz and Martin, 1986). People in the first position on the rope pulled less hard when they thought that people behind them were also pulling. Research suggests that individual effort tends to decrease as the size of the group increases.

Ringelmann found that three people pulling together only achieved two and a half times the average individual rate, while eight pullers achieved less than a quarter of the average individual rate. Later, Ingham et al. (1974) repeated these experiments and reported that subjects expended 18 per cent more effort when pulling alone, than when pulling as part of a group (Figure 12.5). The 'Ringelmann effect' was renamed social loafing in the 1970s by Bibb Latane following investigations at Ohio University to confirm Ringelemann's original work (Latane et al., 1979).

Social loafing is an example of negative synergy. Teamwork of all kinds is fraught with tensions, conflicts, obstacles and problems. If these are not managed effectively, rather than surpassing the best member's capabilities, the total group output may actually equal *less* than its weakest members' efforts. This is caused by various 'process losses' which can hinder effective group functioning (Steiner, 1972). If group process losses exceed group process gains, then one will have a situation of negative synergy. The mathematical analogy would be 2 + 2 = 3. Suggestions have been offered at both the individual and the social level to account for social loafing (George, 1992; Karau and Williams, 1993; Latane and Nida, 1980). These are listed in Table 12.1.

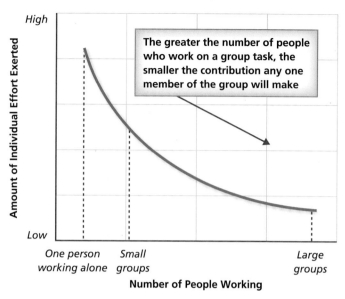

Figure 12.5: The social loafing effect

Source: from *Managing Behaviour in Organizations,* (second edition) by Jerald Greenberg, © 1999. reproduced by permission of Pearson Education Inc., Upper Saddle River, NJ, p.158

 **STOP AND SEARCH**   YouTube for *social loafing* and for the *Ringelmann effect.*

Table 12.1: Causes of social loafing with illustrative statements

Cause	Definition	What the loafer says
Lack of individual evaluation	One's effort is neither noticeable nor measurable.	'They can't identify how much I'm contributing or not contributing to getting the job done'
Dispensability of effort	As the team size increases, individual's own input is seen as being less necessary to the group's task achievement.	'With all these people, they don't need me to get the job done'
Lack of influence	Belief that group will not achieve its goals, irrespective of how great the individual's own contribution is.	'However much I do, they'll still never be able to get the job done, so why bother'
Lack of effort by others	The perception that other members are loafing.	'They others aren't making much effort, why should I?'
Individualism v collectivism	Members coming from individualist national cultures place personal interests ahead of group goals. For those coming from collectivist cultures, it is the reverse **(see Chapter 4).**	'I come from an individualistic culture, I look after myself first!'
Unmotivating task	Loafing declines if group members are performing motivating work.	'I'm not going to put any effort into doing this boring job.'
Lack of task ability	An individual who perceives that they are less competent at a task than other group members will see themselves as unnecessary.	'I'm not as good as Jane at this, so I'll just let her get on with it.'
Superior task ability	An individual who is more competent than the others, but lacks influence over the overall group outcome.	'I'm better than all the others at doing this, but they are useless, they'll slow me down, and we won't get the job done anyway, so why should I bother.'

Source: based on Comer (1995)

Undergraduates increasingly have group assignments to develop their employability skill of team working. Typically the group breaks down the task into its component parts and each member is responsible either for researching or presenting their own part or doing both. Success is premised on the expectation that each person will do their fair share of work. Regularly however, a group will include a social loafer who does not do their part well. In consequence, either the team members will have to do extra work to compensate or else the group will perform poorly and receive a low grade. It is not surprising that this problem has received much research attention (Hall and Buzwell, 2013; Jassawalla et al, 2009; Seltzer, 2016).

This phenomenon is now so common that many students now prefer individually assessed course work (Joo and Dennen, 2017; Fiechtner and Davis, 2016). This is because at university there are strong social norms preventing fellow course members from reporting their group's social loafer to the course instructor. Social loafing is also a feature of the workplace. However formal company practices such as team leader supervision and staff appraisal play a role in dealing with it. Nevertheless, being able to cope with social loafing at the work team level is an important employability skill (Ettington and Camp, 2002).

✓✓✓ **EMPLOYABILITY CHECK** (problem-solving and teamworking skills)

How would you deal with a social loafer on your university course project group?

Schippers (2014) found that if there was a high degree of consciousness and agreeableness within a group, its members compensated for social loafing tendencies and overall group performance increased. In the absence of this, the solutions offered to managers to overcome social loafing assume that it is a natural group state and that something has to be added to a situation to avoid it occurring (Greenberg and Baron, 1997). Suggestions include:

Make work more involving	Raise commitment to successful task performance and encourage members to perform at a higher level
Upgrade task	Increase the perceived importance of the task in the group members' eyes
Increase group significance	Increase the significance that the group has for its individual members
Strengthen group cohesion	Make the group size small, membership attractive and stable, establish common goals, facilitate member interaction
Identify workers	Point out each member's individual contribution in order to prevent their getting away with a 'free ride'
Reward contributions to group	Reward members for helping others achieve the common goal, and not just for their individual contributions
Threaten punishment	Fear of punishment prevents loafing and gets members to 'pull their weight' in the group

Minimizing social loafing at university

Chris Lam

Chris Lam (2015) investigated social loafing in student group projects at university. He found that communication quality and task cohesion significantly reduced social loafing.

Group members' perceptions of communication quality consisted of:

- *Group discussion value:* how effective and satisfactory discussions were

- *Appropriateness:* how applicable the group discussions were to the topic

- *Richness:* how detailed communication messages were

- *Openness:* how receptive team members were to each other's communication

- *Accuracy:* whether the group's communication was accurate and properly understood

Task cohesion referred to:

- *Commitment:* the degree to which the group was united and committed to achieving the work task

Lam found that communication quality and task cohesion accounted for more than 53 per cent of the variance in social loafing. To reduce social loafing, he recommended careful attention to setting up student project groups (e.g. choice of group size and evaluation method); providing students with communication training; agreeing a 'communication charter' that details shared expectations; assessing and developing their communication styles; and ensuring that each student member's contribution is documented.

CRITICAL THINKING

At university, social loafing and free riding are most likely to be found in the classroom among individuals doing a group project rather than out on the sports field when they are playing a match. What are the similarities and differences between these two group events and what do they tell us about the how best to reduce these two problems?

Free rider a member who obtains benefits from team membership without bearing a proportional share of the costs for generating that benefit.

Free riding is related to social loafing (Frohlich and Oppenheimer, 1970; Kerr, 1983). A **free rider** obtains benefits from team membership without bearing a proportional share of the costs for generating the benefit. Hogg and Vaughan (2008) give the example of a tax evader who uses the healthcare service, the education system and the roads. The main difference between social loafing and free riding is that although loafers reduce their individual effort on team tasks, they still contribute something to the group's goal. In contrast, free riders exploit the group product, as in the case of a team project where a student gets the same grade as all the others, without having contributed anything whatsoever to the team's final report.

Free riding dooms a team to ineffectiveness and is abhorrent to team members because it violates a(n):

- *Equity standard*: members who have contributed baulk at others who receive the same benefits, despite having contributed nothing.
- *Social responsibility standard*: everyone should contribute their fair share.
- *Reciprocity standard*: members should exchange their contributions with each other.

The basic strategy for management to counteract free-riding is to broaden the individual's concept of self-interest and arrange matters so that an individual's personal goals are attained by the achievement of the group's collective goal (Albanese and Van Fleet, 1985).

What did he find? Choosing project team members

Wayne Neu (2015, 2012) studied how university business school undergraduates chose their project group members. In the film *The Internship* (2013) the large aggregate of Google summer interns rapidly form themselves into small groups to compete with one another. The members of the winning group will be offered permanent jobs. Neu found that students wanted to find individuals who would be willing to do their share of the group's work (no free riders); who would help the group achieve a high project grade; and who would not cause them anxiety, uncertainty, anger or stress. Essentially, they wanted a person whom they could trust, and that trustworthiness was primary signalled to them by a person's reliability, communicativeness, cooperativeness and flexibility. Their personality was also held to be important, and four of the 'Big Five' traits – conscientiousness, agreeableness, extroversion and openness **(see Chapter 6)** – were sought.

Wayne Neu

However, a person's attributes such as their personality or trustworthiness can only be deduced indirectly. So how did students decide whom to invite to join their project group? The answer is that in the group member selection process, students use external, directly observable, physical and behavioural cues. What did Neu find to be the most important physical and behavioural characteristics that students looked for when choosing their fellow project members? **(Answers in chapter Recap.)**

Group influences on individuals' behaviour

Group norm an expected mode of behaviour or belief that is established either formally or informally by a group.

A group norm is an expected mode of behaviour or belief that is established either formally or informally by a group. Elton Mayo was among the first to discover the existence of group norms and their enforcement through sanctions, during the Bank Wiring Observation Room studies at the Hawthorne works. The men there restricted their output to conform to a group-agreed norm or standard. In what has now become a classic in experimental social psychology, Muzafer Sherif (1936) showed how group norms emerged.

Sherif's work showed that in a situation where doubt and uncertainty exist and where first-hand information is lacking, a person's viewpoint will shift to come into line with those of other group members. In essence this situation leads to the creation of a group norm. This occurs quickly amongst group members who have had little previous experience of the group's work. It also occurs amongst those who have had experience, although more slowly. Few of the subjects who took part in Sherif's experiments felt conscious that others had influenced their judgements. Sherif's work suggested that in order to organize and manage itself every group developed a system of norms. Norms are behavioural expectations and they serve to define the nature of the group. They express the values of the members of the group and provide guidelines to help the group achieve its goals. A group may develop its norms both consciously and unconsciously.

Sherif's study of the emergence of group norms

Muzafer Sherif (1936) placed a group of three subjects in a darkened room and presented them with a small spot of light on a wall for them to view. He then asked them to track the apparent movement of the spot, and to say, aloud, each in turn, the direction in which they thought that the light was moving. The apparent movement is an optical illusion known as the 'autokinetic effect'. The light does not move. Sherif's subjects made three series of 100 estimates on successive days. Initially, there were quite wide individual differences in the response to this situation. Some subjects saw little movement while others saw a lot. However, Sherif discovered that they started to agree on the amount of apparent movement quite quickly. Having exchanged information on their judgements their behaviour changed. They began seeing the light moving in the same direction as those who had spoken earlier.

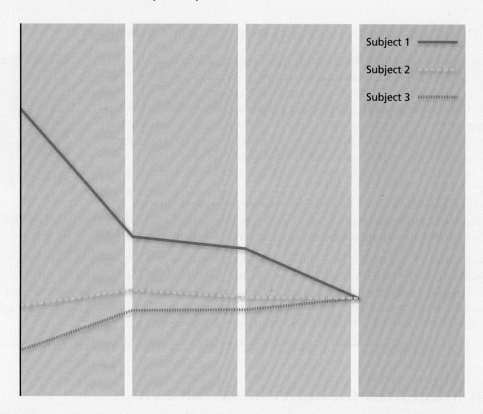

Gradually, all the members came to see the light as moving in the same direction at the same time. There was of course no 'real' movement of the light. Each individual began to see the light in the same way as the group saw it. The results Sherif obtained with two-person and three-person groups are shown in the diagram. When a group norm emerged it was found that it became the basis for subsequent judgement when subjects were re-tested independently. The group norm therefore became a relatively permanent frame of reference for individual behaviour.

🖐 **STOP AND SEARCH**　　YouTube for *Sherif conformity experiment.*

Pivotal norms socially defined standards relating to behaviour and beliefs that are central to a group's objective and survival.

Peripheral norms socially defined standards relating to behaviour and beliefs that are important but not crucial to a group's objective and survival.

Norms guide behaviour and facilitate interaction by specifying the kinds of reactions expected or acceptable in a particular situation. Not all group norms have equal importance. Pivotal norms guide behaviour which is central to the group, for example, the level of output or the amount of work preparation done. In contrast, peripheral norms guide behaviour that is important but not essential, for example, choice of clothing or break-time activities. Group members who violate pivotal norms can impede group objectives or endanger its survival. Therefore, the consequences for transgressing pivotal norms are severe. In contrast, violation of peripheral norms, although frowned upon, has fewer negative consequences for the offender.

Norms and sanctions in gourmet cuisines

Giada Di Stefano

Giada Di Stefano and her colleagues explained (2015) that norm violators had to be punished if norm-governed social exchanges between individuals were to succeed. The problem is deciding when to sanction norm transgressors. To maintain their creativity within the gourmet cuisine industry, chefs exchange their knowledge in the form of recipes of signature dishes and cooking techniques. However, if their inventive ideas are misappropriated, misused or distributed further by others, then chefs have no incentive to share them. There is no legal system of intellectual property rights covering culinary knowledge.

Norms: Gourmet cuisine industry norms regulate when and how chefs use transferred knowledge. They provide the 'mental copyrights' that encourage innovation and exchange:

- Norm 1: Colleagues will not copy exactly the recipe or the cooking technique but instead will use it as source of inspiration to develop something new.
- Norm 2: Colleagues will cite the source of the inspiration for the adapted recipe by including the original chef's name in its menu entry.
- Norm 3: Colleagues will not pass on information to a third party without previously asking for permission from the original chef.

Sanctions: When norm violations occur, three types of sanctions are commonly used:

- Sanction 1: Refusing further knowledge transfers.
- Sanction 2: Cutting off material exchanges with the transgressor such as withholding help with missing ingredients or personnel.
- Sanction 3: Sharing negative gossip about the transgressor with colleagues in the industry.

When to sanction?: The researchers' main finding was that while on the one hand chefs felt inclined to sanction significant norm violations, before acting, they considered how other community members would interpret their actions. They needed to be sure that their community members would see the transgression the way that they did; would consider their chosen sanction to be legitimate; and would see the action as a reasonable way of maintaining a valuable norm and restoring social order. What they wanted to avoid at all costs was having their sanction misinterpreted by their community and being considered to be norm violators themselves.

STOP AND SEARCH YouTube for *Giada di Stefano @HECParis: Why do we sanction norm violations?* (4:54).

Home viewing

The film *Mean Girls* (2004, director Mark Waters) is a teen comedy which examines American high school social cliques and the damaging effects that they can have on girls. Cady Heron (played by Lindsay Lohan) is a 16-year-old, home-schooled student whose zoologist parents return to the USA after a 12-year research trip to Africa. Cady attends public school for the first time and is warned to avoid the school's most exclusive clique – the Plastics – led by Regina George (Rachel McAdams). Which types of power does Regina exert over her group's members? What does Cady learn about the group norms? How does group pressure ensure that members do not transgress these norms?

Why do group norms develop? David Feldman (1984) argued that their purpose was to:

- *Facilitate group task achievement or group survival*: Groups develop norms to increase their chances of being successful and to protect themselves from outsiders.

- *Increase the predictability of group members' behaviours*: Predictability means that internally, members can anticipate and prepare for the actions of colleagues, thereby smoothing social interaction. Externally, it allows them to relate appropriately to outsiders.

- *Reduce embarrassing interpersonal problems for group members*: Knowing what to do and say in a group (and what not to) increases an individual member's comfort.

- *Express the group's core values and define their distinctiveness*: Norms allow members to gain a sense of the essence of the group.

How do group norms develop? Feldman (1984) reported that they did so in four ways:

- *Initial pattern of behaviour*: The first behaviour pattern that emerges in a group can establish group expectations. For example, if the first speaker shares his feelings and anxieties with the other group members, the discussion of emotions in a group can become a norm.

- *Explicit statement by a supervisor or co-worker*: This person may explicitly state certain expectations. The project leader may tell the newcomer that the group meetings start promptly on the hour when all members are expected to be present.

- *Critical events in the group's history*: A shop floor employee makes a suggestion for an improvement to his supervisor who criticises and ridicules him. Group members ensure that in the future none of them offer any more suggestions.

- *Transfer behaviours from past situations*: When individuals carry over behaviours from past situations they can increase the predictability of group members' behaviours in new settings. For example, instructors and students transfer constant expectations from class to class.

Research has shown that the things that happen the first time that a new group meets strongly affect how that group will operate throughout its entire future life (Coutu, 2009). The first few minutes at the start of the first group meeting are crucial as they establish not only where the group is going, but also what the relationship will be between the group's leader and its members, and what basic norms will be established and enforced. A distinguished orchestra conductor reported that he pays the greatest attention to the first few minutes of his first rehearsal with any new orchestra as, in his view its members will very quickly make an assessment about whether or not he and they are going to make great music together.

Figure 12.6 shows the process of the formation and operation of group norms. It appears that once established, group norms are difficult to change. Since the group members originally created the norms, it is they who consequently change them. Members will tend to resist any attempts by managers or any other outsiders to modify their group's norms. Some examples of norms and the reasons for their enforcement are shown in Table 12.2. To enforce its norms, a group develops a set of sanctions with which to police them. The term group sanction refers to both the punishments and rewards that are given by a group to its members in the process of enforcing group norms. Punishment is a negative sanction and a reward is a positive sanction. Some of these norms relate to how members should behave towards one another in the group to avoid incivility.

Group sanction a punishment or a reward given by members to others in the group in the process of enforcing group norms.

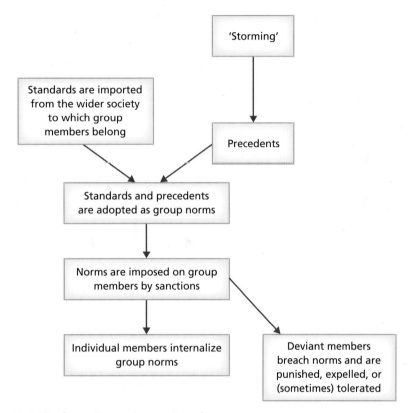

Figure 12.6: The formation and operation of group norms.

Source: Guirdham (2002, p. 465).

Table 12.2: Norms and sanctions

Norm	Enforcement reason	Examples of sanctions to enforce the norm
Members attend all group meetings regularly and arrive on time.	Group survival	Absentees or latecomers are first teased or ridiculed, and then criticized.
All members are required to prepare written work before the group meetings to avoid delay at meeting.	Group task achievement	Group members compliment individuals whose preparation has been particularly thorough.
Members listen to each other's ideas without interrupting, allowing them to fully present their thoughts and opinions	Clarification of behavioural expectations	A member who interrupts is taken aside after the meeting and asked, in future, to let the person finish speaking.
Members do not discuss their private lives with colleagues at work	Avoidance of embarrassment	Members who insist on discussing such matters are ostracized until they stop doing so.

CUTTING EDGE

How uncivil is your team?

Deanna Paulin

Barbara Griffin

Deanna Paulin and Barbara Griffin (2017) studied incivility in the workplace which they defined as rude or disrespectful behaviour that violates workplace norms for mutual respect. In addition to the business costs, workplace incivility has been shown to have detrimental effects on a range of individual outcomes including job satisfaction, organizational commitment, and work behaviours. They focused on incivility at the group level arguing that work groups and organizations differ in the extent to which their environments promote or inhibit incivility between colleagues.

Their research examined the concept of an 'incivility climate' and they developed a questionnaire – the *Team Incivility Climate Scale* (TICS) – which could be used to investigate how incivility permeated work teams. They argue that team members are influenced by ambient stimuli that saturate the work setting and potentially affect everyone present through team composition, shared norms and workplace climate. Acts of incivility between team members would be an example of ambient stimuli. Assess your own group or team in terms of its level of incivility by completing the questionnaire below and comparing it with that of a colleague.

The Team Incivility Climate Scale (TICS)

Think about your experience of working in a team. Rate it on a five- point scale (1 = *strongly disagree* and 5 = *strongly agree*) on the dimensions below.   Rate 1–5

1. My team treats one another with respect
2. People within my team shame and humiliate each other
3. General bad manners (e.g. interrupting, being late to meetings) is tolerated within my team
4. It is common for members of my team to put each other down
5. People within my team get away with being rude and disrespectful to others
6. My team members never verbally abuse one another
7. My team rarely shows anger or hostility to one another
8. There are clear policies and procedures that prohibit uncivil behaviour in this team
9. Respecting people's privacy is a strong part of my team's culture
10. There is a climate of professionalism within my team
11. The atmosphere within my team is one of consideration and courtesy
12. There is a spirit of inclusion within my team
13. On the whole, team members listen respectfully to each other's ideas
14. Invading people's personal space is the norm within my team
15. Gossiping behind people's backs is rife within my team

TOTAL

Source: Paulin and Griffin (2017, p.325).

In their study of 1,100 respondents and 50 work teams, individuals were asked to decide the extent to which incivility was encouraged in team practices, procedures, and norms (not the frequency with which uncivil incidents occurred in the group). The results showed that a team incivility climate was negatively related to job satisfaction and positively related to intention to leave. These findings indicate that employees are affected not only by their direct personal experiences of incivility, but also by the team environment and climate to which they are exposed. The research confirms that workplace incivility is a team or organizational problem, and not just the result of individual experiences. The TICS gives both team members and managers the ability to diagnose and monitor uncivil team climates.

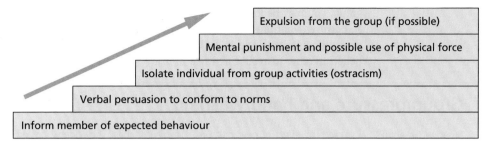

Figure 12.7: Escalating group pressure to secure individual conformity to group norms

The earliest research examples of negative sanctions exercised in groups were revealed by the Bank Wiring Observation Room phase of the Hawthorne studies. The researchers discovered that persons who broke the group norm, for example, producing either over or under the group norm were 'binged'. This involved a group member flicking the ear of the norm transgressor or tapping him painfully on the upper part of their arm. Both actions were intended to indicate physically to the man, that his behaviour was unacceptable to the other group members. Other negative sanctions can be used by the group, and can be placed in ascending order of severity as shown in Figure 12.7. If negative sanctions represent the 'stick' to enforce group norm compliance, then the positive sanctions represent the 'carrot'. Such carrots for the conforming individual include accolades from other members, emotional support, increased social status and the acceptance of their ideas by others (Doms and van Avermaet, 1981).

Ostracism an individual or a group failing to take actions that engage another organization member when it would be customary or appropriate to do so.

Isolating an individual from the group is labelled ostracism. It is defined as an individual or a group failing to take actions that engages another organization member when it would be customary or appropriate to do so (Robinson et al., 2013). Ostracism in the workplace can take many forms including having one's greetings ignored, being excluded from invitations, or others 'going silent' when the person tries to join their conversation. It involves the absence of wanted behaviour or directing non-behaviour towards the person ostracized.

Jane O'Reilly and her colleagues (2015) studied employees' perceptions of and reactions to workplace ostracism. They confirmed previous studies that it was an extremely painful and unpleasant experience. Those targeted experienced hurt feelings, sadness, anxiety, loneliness and shame. The research found that ostracism was strongly related to negative outcomes such as greater health problems, lower job satisfaction, and higher psychological withdrawal. Those who were ostracized at work were more likely to leave their organization. Because it possesses such a strong threat to an individual's need to belong at work, ostracism is a powerful tool that a group can use to secure members' conformity to its norms (De Jong et al., 2014).

Conformity a change in an individual's belief or behaviour in response to real or imagined group pressure.

Conformity is defined as a change in an individual's belief or behaviour in response to real or imagined group pressure. Conformity to norms tends to increase under certain conditions. An increase in conformity is associated with a decrease in the size of the group and also with an increase in its homogeneity, visibility and experienced stability. Members who perceive themselves to be of low status in the group will tend to conform more, and feel that they have to 'earn' the right to be deviant. High conformers are also those who feel that they are not fully accepted by the others. Diagnosing a team's norms and its members' conformity to them can help to explain group behaviour. Conformity can be contrasted with obedience, a situation in which individuals change their behaviour in response to a direction from others.

Obedience a situation in which an individual changes their behaviour in response to a direct command from another.

If you want to deviate from a group norm you have several options. You can attempt to persuade others to your viewpoint and thus alter the group norm. Of course, the other members may respond by persuading you to conform to the existing norm. The higher your status, the more power you will have in the group and the more you will be able to change the behaviours and beliefs of the other members (and the less likely they will be to change your own). What other options are there? If the group is of little importance to you, and if you are free to leave the group, you will do so. Conversely, if you are of little importance to the group, you may be forced either to conform to its norms or else be rejected by its members. If, however, your presence is important to your group (e.g. because you possess high status, power, popularity or special skills), then the group may tolerate your deviant behaviour and beliefs in order to avoid the threat of losing you as a valued member.

Group pressure and hand washing

Susanna Gallani (2017) studied the effect of peer pressure in a Californian hospital that was seeking to encourage improved hand hygiene among staff. The hospital offered a one-off cash bonus to staff if they improved their hand-washing. However, to obtain the bonus, everyone including doctors, who were not eligible for the bonus, had to improve. To encourage the doctors, the other staff members offered public applause to those doctors with good hand-hygiene habits. They openly posted their names on hand-shaped stickers and occasionally sent them congratulatory emails that the chief nursing officer called 'love notes'. Those doctors who were lax in their hand-washing received gentle private reprimands with messages such as 'We will be watching'. While providing positive feedback is cheaper and often more effective than a financial bonus, managers should also harness peer pressure as well as the desire for monetary gain.

In the film comedy *Galaxy Quest* (1999), five unemployed actors whose sci-fi TV series has been discontinued earn a living through public appearances at fan conventions, shopping mall dedications and supermarket openings. One member of the group, Jason Nesmith (played by Tim Allen) is regularly late at these events. He was the fictional captain of the Starship Protector in the TV show, and is the character most loved by the fans. Because of his popularity and fan appeal, the other group members are forced to tolerate his continued late coming. Hence, the power that a group has to influence its members towards conformity to its norms depends on four main factors:

- How important a member's presence is to the group
- The positive and negative sanctions (rewards and punishments) that the group has at its disposal
- That member's desire to avoid negative sanctions such as social and physical punishments or expulsion from the group
- The degree of attraction that the group has for an individual member and the attraction that group members have for each other. This is called group cohesion.

Group cohesion the number and strength of mutual positive attitudes between individual group members.

Group cohesion refers to the number and strength of mutual positive attitudes towards group members. Table 12.3 shows the contributors to and consequences of group cohesion (Pearce et al., 2002). The widely cited research conclusion is that cohesion has a moderating, positive relationship on group performance (Greer, 2012; Gully et al., 1995).

Table 12.3: Group cohesion – contributors and consequences

Contributors to group cohesion	Consequences of group cohesion
Small size	Group success
Past success	Member satisfaction
External threat	Higher group productivity
Common goals	Increased member satisfaction
Difficulty of entry	Greater conformity by members
Stable membership	Increased interaction between members
Opportunity to interact with others	Member's evaluations become distorted
Attractiveness of group to individuals	Increased group influence over members
Fairness of rewards between members	More cooperative behaviour between individuals
Members' agreement about their statuses	

CRITICAL
THINKING

Consider a group of which you are a member and its norms and sanctions. Reflect on a situation in which a member (perhaps yourself) broke a norm and received a negative sanction. Assess the positive and negative outcomes of this occurrence for the individual group member concerned and for the group as a whole.

Having established a set of norms and the sanctions to enforce them, a group has to communicate these to new members. The new group member 'learns the ropes' and is shown how to get things done, how to interact with others, and how to achieve high social status within the group. An important aspect of achieving such status is to adhere to the group's norms or rules. Initial transgressions will be pointed out to the new member gently. However, the continued violation of norms by a group member puts at risk the cohesion of the group. When there is disagreement on a matter of importance to the group, the preservation of group effectiveness, harmony and cohesion requires a resolution of the conflict. Hence pressure is exerted on the deviating individual through persuasive communication to conform. The name given to this 'educational' process which the new member undergoes is group socialization. It is the process whereby members learn the values, symbols and expected behaviours of the group to which they belong. It occurs within most groups in all types of organizations (Figure 12.8).

Group socialization
the process whereby members learn the values, symbols and expected behaviours of the group to which they belong.

If new recruits are thoroughly socialized, they are less likely to transgress group norms and require sanctions to be administered. However, while such pressure to go along with the majority of other members may be beneficial for the group, it also carries costs. If conformity is allowed to dominate and individuals are given little opportunity to present different views, there is the danger of the group collectively making errors of judgement, leading them to take unwise decisions. **Chapter 20** will consider the concept of groupthink which, through internal conformity and external group pressure, leads individual members to collectively make poor group decisions.

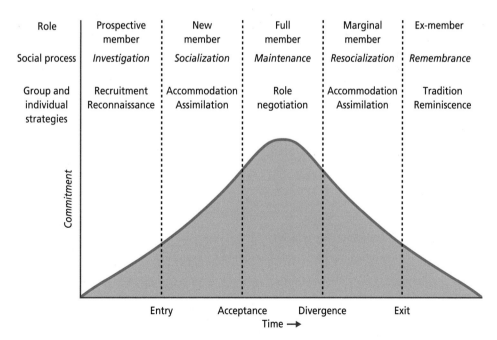

Figure 12.8: **A model of the process of group socialization**
Source: adapted from *Advances in Experimental and Social Psychology*, Volume 15, L. Berkowicz, (ed.), Socialization in small groups: temporal changes in individual–group relations by Moreland, R.L. and Levine, J.M., pp.137–92. © 1982, Academic Press, with permission from Elsevier.

Home viewing

Ratatouille (2007, director Brad Bird) is an animated film about Remy, a young rat, who wants to become a chef. It includes a short sequence which opens with a young man, Alfredo Linguini, cutting vegetables and Colette Tatou the restaurant's only female chef, immediately corrects his technique. She tells him 'keep your station clear'. It ends with the characters thanking each other for giving and receiving advice. This sequence illustrates a range of concepts in the accommodation stage of socialization. Can you identify what these concepts are? (Champoux, 2012)

Organizational socialization the process through which an employee's pattern of behaviour, values, attitudes and motives is influenced to conform to that of the organization.

It is important to remember that while a work group will be attempting to get its new member to adopt its own values, symbols and expected behaviours, the organization which recruited the person will be endeavouring to do the same (see Table 12.4).

Some companies such as Disney, are famous for investing much time, money and effort into getting their new employees to adopt the 'company way' of doing things. This equivalent process is called **organizational socialization** **(see Chapter 4)**. If the picture of company life that the newcomer is presented with by their organization is congruent with the picture held by the person's workgroup, then they will accept it. If it is not, the newcomer is more likely to adopt the picture held by their own work group as these are the people with whom he or she will spend most of their working time.

 **STOP AND SEARCH**   YouTube for *group socialization.*

Table 12.4: Comparison of group development and organizational socialization stages

	Group development	Organizational socialization
Stage 1: Orientation	1. Forming • Establish interpersonal relationships • Conform to organizational traditions and standards • Boundary testing in relationships and task behaviours	1. Getting in (anticipatory socialization) • Setting of realistic expectations • Determining match with the newcomer
Stage 2: Redefinition	2. Storming • Conflict arising because of interpersonal behaviours • Resistance to group influence and task requirements	2. Breaking in • Initiation to the job • Establishing interpersonal relationships • Congruence between self and organizational performance appraisal
Stage 3: Coordination	3. Norming • Single leader emerges • Group cohesion established • New group standards and roles formed for members	3. Settling in (role management) • The degree of fit between one's life interests outside work and the demands of the organization • Resolution of conflicts at the workplace itself
Stage 4: Formalization	4. Performing • Members perform tasks together • Establishing role clarity • Teamwork is the norm	

Source: Gordon (1993, p.184).

Why do members conform to group pressure? Group norms increase the predictability of the behaviour of others and reduce the chances of individuals embarrassing each other when interacting, for example, during group discussions. Complying with group norms may be of such personal benefit to us that we are willing to abide by them. In so doing, we suppress our own personal desires and reduce our individual freedoms. Moreover, we also punish those who violate the group's norms and reward those who do not. Additionally, individuals have a desire for order and meaning in their lives. They view uncertainty as disturbing and as something that should be reduced to the absolute minimum. Norms, and the adherence to norms, help us 'make sense' of seemingly unconnected facts and events; provide us with explanations of 'what's going on'; and allow us to feel in control of the situations in which we find ourselves. The earliest experimental studies into conformity to group norms were carried out by Solomon Asch (1951, 1952, 1956).

Asch's study of conformity

In the early 1950s Solomon Asch (1951) devised a laboratory experiment into individual conformity within groups. Seven men sat around a table supposedly to participate in a study on visual perception. Only one of the group was a real subject. The other six were Asch's paid accomplices. The task was an easy one. They had to decide which of the three lines shown below on the right, A, B or C, was equal to the one on the left.

In the experimental conditions, the accomplices had been instructed to lie about which line was correct. Under pressure, the real subjects showed signs of conflict when deciding whether to conform to the group's judgement or give the response that he or she considered to be correct. The results below show how much individuals in groups can be pressured to conform to a majority view.

The problem

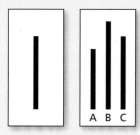

The results

Members making at least one error	76%
Times average member conformed	37%
Members who never conformed	24%
Members who conformed over 10 times	11%
Members making at least one error when tested alone	5%

STOP AND SEARCH   YouTube for the *Asch conformity experiment.*

Asch found that those subjects who yielded to group pressure did so for different reasons. He distinguished three types of yielding:

Distortion of perception

These subjects seem to have convinced themselves that they actually did see the lines the way the other group members stated their judgements. Yielding at the perceptual level was rare and occurred primarily among those who displayed a lack of trust in themselves. They were unaware that their estimates had been displaced or distorted by the majority.

Distortion of judgement

These subjects yielded either because they were unsure that they understood the task set for them or because they did not want to 'spoil the experiment'. They suffered from primary doubt and lack of confidence. The most important factor was their judgement that their own perceptions had been inaccurate and that those of the majority were correct. Distortion of judgement occurred frequently.

Distortion of action

The subjects did not suffer a modification of perception, nor did they conclude that they were wrong. They yielded because they feared being excluded, ostracized or considered eccentric. These subjects suppressed their observations and voiced the majority position with a full awareness of what they were doing.

Asch's experiment was replicated more than 30 years later, this time with five individuals using PCs who were told that they had been linked together (Doms and Avermaet, 1981). Whereas Asch had found that the number who refused to conform to the group in any trial was just 24 per cent, in the repeat study 69 per cent of the subjects made no errors. Maybe a computer-mediated communication environment reduces our tendency to conform to a unanimous group position.

CRITICAL THINKING

How difficult is it to resist the majority views in a group situation? Think of an occasion when you have supported a decision contrary to your own judgement but consistent with that of the majority of those around you. What factors played a part in your choosing between disagreeing and voicing your minority view or in acquiescing, remaining silent, and accepting the majority view?

Deindividuation

Deindividuation an increased state of anonymity that loosens normal constraints on individuals' behaviour, reducing their sense of responsibility and leading to an increase in impulsive and antisocial acts.

Social facilitation explains how groups can arouse individuals and stimulate their performance, while social loafing shows that groups can diffuse and hence diminish individual responsibility. Together, arousal and diffused responsibility combine to decrease normal social inhibitions and create deindividuation. Deindividuation refers to a person's loss of self-awareness and self-monitoring. It involves some loss of personal identity and greater identification with the group.

The writings of Gustave Le Bon led to the theory of deindividuation which was proposed by Leon Festinger, Albert Pepitone and Theodore Newcombe (1952). However, it is Marion Hampton (1999, p. 112) who neatly captures the experience of deindividuation when she writes:

'There are moments when we can observe ourselves behaving irrationally as members of crowds or audiences, yet we are swept by the emotion, unable to check it. In smaller groups too, like committees or teams, we may experience powerful feelings of loyalty, anxiety or anger. The moods and emotions of those around us seem to have an exaggerated effect on our own moods and emotions.'

The influence of the crowd

Gustave LeBon stated that the crowd is, 'always intellectually inferior to the isolated individual . . . mob man is fickle, credulous, and intolerant showing the violence and ferocity of primitive beings'. He added, 'by the mere fact that he forms part of an organized crowd, a man descends several rungs in the ladder of civilization. Isolated he may be a cultivated individual, in a crowd he is a barbarian – that is a creature acting by instinct' (LeBon, 1908, p.12).

In his book, *The Crowd,* LeBon hypothesized that humans had a two-part personality. The upper half was conscious, unique to each individual and contained dignity and virtue. The lower half, in contrast was unconscious, shared with everyone else, and contained bad desires and instincts. Observers have noted that as long as individuals are physically together as part of a collectivity they feel strong and invulnerable. Separate seating in football stadia and postal strike voting by union members have reduced football crowd hooliganism and unofficial strikes. LeBon attributed this primitive human behaviour to three things:

Anonymity   Individuals cannot be easily identified in a crowd.

Contagion   Ideas and emotions spread rapidly and unpredictably.

Suggestability   The savagery that is just below the surface is released by suggestion.

Edward Diener (1980) considered self-awareness (i.e. awareness of oneself as an object of attention) to be the crucial element in the deindividuation process. The environmental conditions which reduce self-awareness and thereby trigger deindividuation, as well the consequences of deindividuation, are summarized in Figure 12.9.

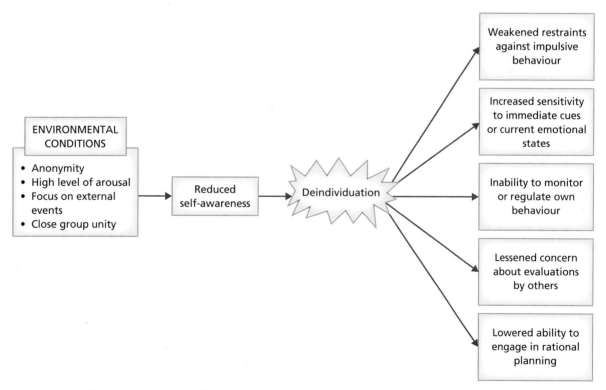

Figure 12.9: Self-awareness and deindividuation
Source: reproduced with permission from Hogg & Vaughan, *Social Psychology* © 2011 Pearson Australia, p.424.

Anonymity within a crowd or large group lessens inhibitions. Warriors in a tribe paint their faces and wear masks. When attention is drawn away from the individual in a crowd or group situation, their anonymity is increased and they are more likely to abandon their normal restraints and to lose their sense of individual responsibility (e.g. internet trolling). This can lead to antisocial behaviour such as attacking a policeman during protest demonstrations. In military organizations, members have always worn uniforms and companies now provide their staff with corporate clothing. While this may get them to identify more closely with their organizations, it can also increase their anonymity.

A great number of different factors influence conformity to norms (see Figure 12.10). The personality characteristics of individuals play a part in predisposing them to conform to group norms. The kind of stimuli eliciting conformity behaviour is also important. That people conform to norms when they are uncertain about a situation was demonstrated by the Sherif experiments. He also discovered that a person with a high degree of self-confidence could affect the opinions and estimates of other group members. Asch found that if even only one confederate in his experiment broke the unanimity with his dissenting voice, then the dramatic effects of conformity were erased, and the experimental subject felt free to give the correct answer that seemed obvious all along. Upbringing (including formal education) also plays an important part. Bond and Smith's (1996) analysis showed a steady decline in conformity since the original Asch studies. Collectivist culture countries show higher levels of conformity than individualist culture countries **(see Chapter 4).**

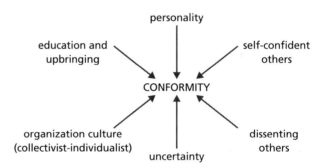

Figure 12.10: Factors influencing conformity to group norms

CRITICAL THINKING

Is conformity by the individual to their group within an organization a bad thing that should be stopped or is it a good thing that should be encouraged? Give your reasons for both positions.

Individual influences on group attitudes and behaviour

So far, the focus has been on the group influencing its members' perceptions, performance and behaviour. Does this mean that an individual can never influence their group? Clearly not, since history recounts numerous instances of individuals – revolutionaries, rebels, radical thinkers, religious zealots – who created minority groupings and who, as minorities, successfully persuaded majorities. Indeed, leadership can be considered an example of minority influence. The underpinning to the process of a minority's influence on a majority

Compliance a majority's influence over a minority.

Conversion a minority's influence over a majority.

is provided by Serge Moscovici's (1980) social influence theory. He used the term compliance to describe what happens when a majority influences a minority. It does this through its possession of various kinds of power and its ability to implement positive and negative sanctions. He applied the term conversion to describe a minority's persuasion of a majority. The concept of conversion is illustrated every time an employee persuades their company to adopt a new product or create a new division.

In their review of 143 studies of minority influence, Wood et al. (1994) found that minorities had the ability to change the opinions of those who listened to them, especially if the listeners were not required to publicly acknowledge such a change. Moscovici (1980) stressed the importance of consistency in the conversion process. The individual persuading the group had to stick unswervingly to his or her point of view. Moscovici's research provides us with an understanding of how a minority can influence a majority (Nemeth, 1986). These different writings have been summarized by Huczynski (2004) who listed what the minority influencer of a majority has to do:

Become viable	Take a position that others are aware of, make yourself heard, get yourself noticed, and generally overcome the illusion of unanimity.
Create tension	Motivate those in the majority to try to deal with your ideas.
Be consistent	Stick unswervingly to the same position. Do not take a variety of positions that disagree with the majority.
Be persistent	Restate your consistent position in the face of others' opposition to you.
Be unyielding	Being firm and unyielding involves digging your heels in and not compromising.
Be self-confident	This is conveyed by one's consistency and persistence. It raises self-doubts among the majority leading them to reconsider their position.
Seek defectors	Defections from the majority increase the self-doubt of the remaining majority and free its doubters who may have self-censored themselves to speak out, perhaps encouraging more converts.

In the classic film, *Twelve Angry Men* (1957), a jury retires to decide on the guilt or innocence of a youth from a slum background. At the outset, eleven of the twelve jurors are keen to find him guilty without further discussion. In the film, Juror 8 (played by Henry Fonda) says:

'There were eleven votes for guilty. It's not so easy for me to raise my hand and send a boy off to die without talking about it first.'

The Henry Fonda character has reservations. He successfully persuades the other eleven jurors to acquit the young defendant. As the sole juror, he has the integrity, sense of justice, persistence and courage to go against the crowd and fight for a fair deliberation. He also uses all the above techniques to achieve his objective. This is an example of conversion. Emich and Wright (2016) discuss the film and provide other examples of where a single individual influences a group. They note that the attitudes and views of one (or more) team members can spill over onto the others. The practical implication of this they say is that before adding anyone to a team, managers should consider how a new person might influence the team processes that have already been established, and whether their strength of character and strong convictions are likely to affect other group members.

STOP AND SEARCH   YouTube for *12 Angry Men*.

Team building

Companies may experience a situation in which an inappropriate teamworking atmosphere has developed and in which there is a need to align individual members around organizational goals, build effective working relationships, reduce members' role ambiguity and find solutions to team problems.

Team building a set of techniques used to help team members to understand their own roles more clearly and improve their interaction and collaboration with other members.

In such circumstances, companies utilize team building. This refers to a set of techniques used to help team members to understand their own roles more clearly and improve their interaction and collaboration with other members.

Team building is popular with companies. Team activities are designed to integrate individuals better into their groups to achieve improved person–group fit. They seek to create bonds between their members to increase collaboration between them in order to make the team more cohesive. There are many different approaches to team building. The main ones include:

Goal setting

This approach involves team members identifying individual and team goals and defining measures of success and failure. It can bring into the open individual members' personal priorities and negotiate these so that in achieving their own goals they also achieve team objectives. The purpose of this activity is to foster a sense of team goal ownership and individual motivation.

Effectiveness rating

Building on the previous activity, members rate their team on criteria such as of goal clarity, willingness to share ideas, time management, focus on achieving results, willingness to listen to others, and ability to allow all team members to contribute. Individual ratings are scored and the combined ratings are used to identify and address differences in perceptions so as to highlight problems affecting the team. This triggers discussion of how these can be overcome so as to improve team functioning.

Role clarification

Using a team role assessment questionnaire, members can identify their personal team role preferences. (e.g. Plant, Co-ordinator, Shaper). Having done so, they determine which roles are present and which are absent and how to compensate for any imbalance. Members may be invited to 'hold back' on a preferred role if it is over-represented in the group or 'cover' for roles that are not among their strong preferences but which are missing from the group's overall profile.

Interpersonal relations

These techniques seek to develop members' teamworking skills such as giving and receiving feedback providing mutual support and information sharing. They may involve outdoor training where participants engage in a series of challenges involving rock climbing, sailing, orienteering or mountain walking (preferably in appalling weather) to heighten the sense of challenge. All the activities are designed to require teamwork and to encourage the development of interpersonal trust, group decision making, communication skills and an awareness of leadership roles. In the film, *The Promotion* (2008), there is a sequence with illustrates such an activity.

🖐 **STOP AND SEARCH**   YouTube for *team building*.

Team building through eating together

(photo credit: @Jessewinter)

Kevin Kniffin

Kevin Kniffin and his colleagues (2015) investigated a cheap and simple method of team building – having members prepare and eat their food together. They labelled it *commensality*. Historically, many companies have arranged seating in their staff cafeterias to encourage serendipitous encounters (or 'collisions') between employees from different parts of the building so as to spark creativity. In contrast, commensality concerns intact working team members not only eating food together but also preparing and sharing it. This unconventional team-building approach is based on the observation that eating is a primal and meaningful human behaviour. Eating a meal involves a special intimacy between those participating in it. The authors stud-

ied 13 fire stations in a medium-sized American city and interviewed 395 fire-fighters who prepared and ate their meals during shifts. The fire stations had their own cooking and dining facilities but employees brought in their own food. They pooled their funds, worked out cooking schedules and menus, and prepared the food themselves.

The interviewees reported that eating together was an important element in keeping their fire teams working effectively. It made them feel like a family and created a common bond between them when they were not out on a job. In addition to eating, meal practices involved collecting money, planning, talking and cleaning, all of which were found to encourage cooperation and enhance team performance. The authors noted that such behaviours which, superficially appeared to be superfluous or wasteful, were in practice important for team performance.

While this research may suggest replacing the trust fall at the team awayday with a team meal, Kniffin warns about the dangers of this specific technique and about building cohesive teams in general. These include insularity – team members only socializing with each other and thus risking becoming disconnected from other groups and from the rest of the organization. Tightly bonded teams can be scary things to join and new members may feel pressured to conform to their norms. Teams may use cliquish meal practices and can ostracize or 'manage out' non-performers. Devoting resources to encourage communal eating in a company can be an effective team building investment but needs to be carefully managed.

 STOP AND SEARCH for *Mass appeal cooking with the West Springfield firefighters!* (4:19).

 **RECAP**

1. *Explain the basic tenets of social identity theory and social representation theory.*

- Social identity theory holds that aspects of our identity derive from the membership of a group.

- Groups construct social representations consisting of beliefs, ideas and values which they transmit to their new members

- Such representations, together with group socialization, lead to all members sharing a common frame of reference.

2. *Distinguish between social facilitation and social loafing.*

- Individual behaviour is variously modified by the presence of others or by being a part of a group.

- The concepts of social influence, social facilitation, synergy and social loafing distinguish the direction and nature of such modifications.

3. *Understand how groups use norms to regulate the behaviour of their members.*

- Social norms guide the behaviour of individuals in a group. They can be pivotal or peripheral.

- Social norms are established in four ways – explicit statements, critical events, initial behaviour and transfer behaviour.

- Sanctions are administered by members to those individuals who transgress or uphold the group's norms. Sanctions can therefore be negative (verbal abuse) or positive (praise). Groups possess an escalating hierarchy of ever-stronger negative sanctions.

4. *Understand the process of group socialization of individuals.*

- Groups teach new members about their norms and incorporate them into their shared frame of reference through the process of group socialization.

5. *Explain why individuals conform to the dictates of their group.*

- As individuals, we tend to conform to group norms because of the benefits to us individually if others abide by the agreed rules; our desire for order and meaning in our lives; and a need to receive a satisfying response from others.

- The cost to the person who is a member of a group is the deindividulization that membership entails. Group membership brings with it anonymity and becoming 'lost in the crowd'. This can reduce our sense of individual responsibility, lower our social constraints, and lead us to engage in impulsive, anti-social acts.

6. *Distinguish between compliance and conversion.*

- A majority's influence over an individual is called compliance.

- A minority's influence over a majority is called conversion.

RECAP: What did he find?

Neu (2015) found that the most important cues to look for when recruiting high-performing student project group members were:

Physical cues

- *Clothing attributes*: include those wearing business school casual clothing
- *Hair attributes*: include those who are well-groomed, clean cut, and clean-shaven men
- *Tool attributes*: include those who already possess tools and supplies relevant to the team's task (writing instruments, paper, planner, textbook, laptop)
- *Body art attributes*: avoid students with piercings or tattoos
- *Physique*: avoid men who are too physically fit

Behavioural cues

- *Smiling*: avoid non-smilers
- *Class behaviours*: include those who attend lectures regularly, listen to the lecturer, take notes, use a highlighter pen, write in a planner
- *Socializers*: include those who socialize with fellow students before a class
- *Participation*: include those who ask or respond to questions and comment thoughtfully

Making inferences about fellow classmates based on which social category you place them in rather than on their individual merits is stereotyping. How many of these physical and behaviour cues would you use to help you decide whom to approach or to avoid during the selection period for a student group project?

Revision

1. Is social loafing an individual issue, varying according to an individual's personality and values, or is it an organizational issue affected by management action or non-action?

2. Select any three key terms from the list at the beginning of the chapter and illustrate them with examples taken from your home or work.

3. Critically evaluate the research on individual conformity to group pressure.

4. Suggest how an individual might go about persuading a majority.

Research assignment

Choose an organization with which you are familiar, and interview some employees who work there. Ask each interviewee how their co-workers would react if they themselves:

1. Were seen being rude or indifferent to a customer.
2. Criticized a co-worker who was not performing satisfactorily.
3. Performed their work at a level noticeably higher than that their co-workers.
4. Approached management offering a solution to a problem they had identified.
5. Expressed concern to management about the wellbeing of their fellow workers.
6. Expressed concern about the poor quality of the organization's product or service.
7. Actively developed their skill and knowledge about the organization's operations and products.

Finally, ask if there are things that any employee should do or not do, if they want to get on well with their co-workers in the organization. Use the information obtained from your interviewees to determine: (a) on which topics there appear to be group norms; (b) which norms are pivotal and which are peripheral; (c) what effects these norms have on the behaviour of the individuals, the operation of the group and the performance of the department.

Springboard

Wayne Neu (2018) 'Quantitative evidence of students' use of social networks and social categorizations when self-selecting teams', *Journal of Marketing Education*, 40(3): 161–75. The author reports the findings of experiments in giving students complete freedom in choosing classmates for a group project assignment.

Nigel Nicholson (2003) 'How to motivate your problem people', *Harvard Business Review*, 81(1): 56–65. Provides useful advice on ways of dealing with social loafers and free riders.

Andreas Richter, Jeremy Dawson and Michael West (2011) 'The effectiveness of teams in organizations: A meta-analysis', *International Journal of Human Resource Management*, 22(13): 2749–69. Reviews and summarizes past research studies into whether teamworking in organizations is related to organizational effectiveness.

Cass Sunstein and Reid Hastire (2014) 'Making dumb groups smarter', *Harvard Business Review*, 92(12): 90–98. The authors consider how groups are subject to decision making errors and suggest how these might be overcome.

OB cinema

The Secret of My Success (1987, director Herbert Ross) DVD track 4: 0:17:00–0:20:00 (3 minutes).
In this film, Brantley Foster (played by Michael J. Fox) leaves his home in Kansas to make his career as an executive in New York City. However, the only job he can get is in the mailroom of the Penrose Corporation. The clip begins with the mailroom manager saying 'You can't come in here bozo, take your crap to the mail slot', and ends with Melrose saying, 'you put these things away'. On his first day, Brantley learns a great deal about the organization.

- What are the sources of his information?
- What does he learn from each source about the organization and how to behave in it?
- In your current or last job, what did you learn? How?

Chapter exercises

1: Capitals exercise

Objectives
1. Compare individual with group decision making.
2. Contrast the advantages and disadvantages of group decision making.
3. Consider the effects of conformity pressure in group activity.

Briefing
1. Everybody turns off and puts away all their internet-accessible electronic devices.
2. Individually, each student writes in the name of the country's capital city in the grid, next to its name, inserting it in the 'Your answer' column.
3. Groups of 4–5 are formed. Each group agrees on their answers, inserting them in the 'Group answer' column.
4. The instructor reveals the names of the capitals. Students insert them in the 'Correct answer' column, and total up the number of correct individual and group answers.

Class discussion   The instructor leads a discussion on the results and the dynamics of the exercise

50 Capitals

Country	Capital			Country	Capital		
	Your answer	*Group answer*	*Correct answer*		*Your answer*	*Group answer*	*Correct answer*
Albania				Lichtenstein			
Andorra				Lithuania			
Armenia				Luxembourg			
Austria				Macedonia			
Azerbaijan				Malta			
Belarus				Moldova			
Belgium				Monaco			
Bosnia and Herzegovina				Montenegro			
Bulgaria				Netherlands			
Croatia				Norway			
Cyprus				Poland			
Czech Republic				Portugal			
Denmark				Romania			
Eire				Russia			
Estonia				San Marino			
Finland				Serbia			
France				Slovakia			
Georgia				Slovenia			
Germany				Spain			
Greece				Sweden			
Hungary				Switzerland			

Country	Capital			Country	Capital		
	Your answer	*Group answer*	*Correct answer*		*Your answer*	*Group answer*	*Correct answer*
Iceland	·			Turkey			
Italy				Ukraine			
Kazakhstan				United Kingdom			
Latvia				Vatican City			
Total							

Source: adapted from Fender and Stickney (2017)

2: Accounting team exercise

Objectives
1. Understand and address social loafing in student classroom teams.
2. Generate solutions to deal with social loafers.

Briefing
1. Read the case (3–5 minutes).
2. In groups discuss the case and make a decision as to what to do about Erica and Frank.
3. Decisions are made public, followed by a brief discussion.
4. Class groups are asked to list five things to do to help the accounting team avoid the problem in the future.
5. Instructor discusses options to avoid social loafing.
6. Class groups are asked to list five things that they can do to prevent social loafing in university group projects.

Case
Alan, Beth, Cathy, Dave, Erica and Frank all work as junior accountants for Price Waterhouse in Philadelphia. Each was hired about 18 months ago to the audit department and all report to Gloria, a manager. They were assigned to work as a team to audit the manufacturing plant of ABC Industries, a medium-sized company in a small town about two hours west of Philadelphia. The plan as described by Gloria was that the team would stay in the area of the plant for five days, starting on a Monday. Each person was assigned a particular part of the overall audit (e.g. Alan would review accounts payable, Beth would examine the physical inventory of raw material and finished goods, etc.) and on Thursday, the team would meet in the afternoon to finalize their report and then deliver it to Gloria when she arrived on Friday morning. Gloria would review the report and, in the afternoon, meet with the plant manager.

Alan, Beth, Cathy, Dave, and Erica drove together from Philadelphia on Sunday and checked into the hotel. Frank who was from a nearby town, wanted to stay with his parents, so he drove himself on Friday evening. On Monday morning the five people at the hotel drove together to the plant, arrived at 8:00 am, and each met a staff member from ABC Industries and began to collect information. Frank arrived at about 10 am, saying he had had trouble with his car. At 5.00 pm, Frank left, saying that his mother had dinner waiting for him. The rest of the team stayed until about 6.30 pm before returning to their hotel. On Tuesday and Wednesday, there was a similar pattern with Frank arriving somewhat later than the rest of the team and leaving at 5.00 pm.

On Monday, Erica immediately ran into problems with the accounts receivable manager who said that their computer system had been upgraded over the previous weekend and he (the manager) was having trouble accessing the accounts receivable records. Erica was supposed to compare the computer-based records to the physical bills that had been sent with the bank deposits. She worked much of the morning trying to organize the bills, but

→

eventually ran out of things to do. At that point, she went around to other team members to see if she could help them. When the computer problem still hadn't been resolved by the end of the day, Erica called Gloria to ask for directions. Gloria said the team should continue the audit and to report back again the next day. On Tuesday, about 1.00 pm, the accounts receivable manager told Erica that he could finally access the records. She spent the rest of the day working through her tasks, reluctantly leaving at 6.30 pm when the rest of the team wanted to get back to the hotel. Wednesday, Erica was still behind schedule and stayed as late as she could.

On Thursday afternoon, when the team met as planned, both Erica and Frank had not completed their parts. The team decided to spend the afternoon finishing everything and then to meet in the evening to finalize the report. At 5.00 pm, Frank said that no one was paying attention to his ideas and announced that he was leaving. The rest of the team was angry and several said so, but Frank left anyway. The team went back to the hotel and worked until 11.00 pm finishing the project. The following week Gloria assigned the same people to do another audit for a New Jersey company. Alan, Beth, Cathy and Dave got together after work to talk about what to do for the next audit. Decide what your team should do about Erica and Frank.

Action on Erica	Action on Frank
Vote:	Vote:
A – Do nothing	A – Do nothing
B – Talk to Erica	B – Talk to Frank
C – Tell the boss about Erica's behaviour	C – Tell the boss about Frank's behaviour
D – Refuse to do the audit with Erica	D – Refuse to do the audit with Frank

Source: Seltzer (2016)

References

Albanese, R. and Van Fleet, D.D. (1985) 'Rational behaviour in groups: the free rider tendency', *Academy of Management Review,* 10(2): 244–55.

Allport, F. H. (1920) 'The influences of the group upon association and thought', *Journal of Experimental Psychology,* 3(3): 159–82.

Asch, S. E. (1951) 'Effects of group pressure upon the modification and distortion of judgements'. in H. Guetzkow (ed.), *Groups, Leadership and Men,* Pittsburgh, PA: Carnegie Press, pp. 177–90.

Asch, S. E. (1952) *Social Psychology,* Englewood Cliffs, NJ: Prentice Hall.

Asch, S. E. (1956) 'Studies of independence and submission to group pressure: a minority of one against a unanimous majority', *Psychological Monograph: General and Applied,* 9(416): 1–70.

Benders, J. (2005) 'Team working: a tale of partial participation' in B. Harley, J. Hyman and P. Thompson (eds.), *Participation and Democracy at Work: Essays in Honour of Harvie Ramsey* London: Palgrave Macmillan, pp. 55–74.

Bond, R. and Smith, P.B. (1996) 'Culture and conformity: a meta-analysis of studies using Asch's (1952b, 1956) line judgment task', *Psychological Bulletin,* 119(1): 111–37.

Champoux, J.E. (2012) 'The unique effects of animated film in teaching and learning environments' in Billsberry, J., Charlesworth, J. and Leonard, P. (eds.), *Moving Images: Effective Teaching with Film and Television in Management,* Charlotte, NC: Information Age Publishing, pp. 49–62.

Comer, D. (1995) 'A model of social loafing in real work groups', *Human Relations,* 48(6): 647–67.

Coutu, D. (2009) 'Why teams don't work', *Harvard Business Review*, 87(5): 99–105.

Di Stefano, G., King, A.A. and Verona, G. (2015) 'Sanctioning in the wild: rational calculus and retributive instincts in gourmet cuisine', *Academy of Management Journal*, 58(3): 906–31.

De Jong, B.A., Bijlsma, K.M. and Cardinal, L.B. (2014) 'Stronger than the sum of its parts? The performance implications of peer control combinations in teams', *Organization Science*, 25(6): 1703–21.

Diener, E. (1980) 'Deindividuation: the absence of self-awareness and self-regulation in group members' in P.B. Paulus (ed), *Psychology of Group Influence*, Hillsdale, NJ: Erlbaum.

Doms, M., and van Avermaet, E. (1981) 'The conformity effect: a timeless phenomenon?', *Bulletin of the British Psychological Society*, 36(1): 180–88.

Emich, K.J. and Wright, T.A. (2016) 'The 'I's in team: the importance of individual members to team success', *Organizational Dynamics*, 45(1): 2–10.

Ettington, D.R. and Camp, R.R. (2002) 'Facilitating transfer of skills between group projects and work teams', *Journal of Management Education*, 26(4): 356–79.

Feldman, D. C. (1984) 'The development and enforcement of group norms', *Academy of Management Review*, 9(1): 47–53.

Fender, C.M and Stickney, L.T. (2017) 'When two heads aren't better than one: conformity in a group activity', *Management Teaching Review*, 2(1): 35–46.

Festinger, L., Pepitone, A. and Newcomb, T. (1952) 'Some consequences of deindividuation in a group', *Journal of Abnormal and Social Psychology*, 47(2 supplement): 382–89.

Fiechtner, S.B. and Davis, E.A. (2016) 'Republication of "Why some groups fail: a survey of students' experiences with learning groups"', *Journal of Management Education*, 40(1): 12–29.

Frohlich, N. and Oppenheimer, J. (1970) 'I get by with a little help from my friends', *World Politics*, 23(1): 104–20.

Gaffney, P. (2015) 'The nature and meaning of teamwork', *Journal of the Philosophy of Sport*, 42(1): 1–22.

Gallani, S. (2017) 'Incentives, peer pressure, and behaviour persistence', Harvard Business School, Working Paper 17-070 (38 pp), https://www.hbs.edu/faculty/Publication%20Files/17-070_e2c4afab-a36c-47c6-a2a4-8f094ded4601.pdf [accessed January 2019].

George, J. M. (1992) 'Extrinsic and intrinsic origins of perceived social loafing in organizations', *Academy of Management Journal*, 35(1): 191–202.

Gordon, J. (1993) *A Diagnostic Approach to Organizational Behaviour*, Boston, MA: Allyn & Bacon.

Greenberg, J. (1999) *Managing Behaviour in Organizations*, second edition, Upper Saddle River, NJ: Prentice Hall.

Greenberg, J., and Baron, R. A. (1997) *Behaviour in Organizations*, sixth edition, Englewood Cliffs, NJ: Prentice Hall.

Greer, L.L. (2012) 'Group cohesion: then and now', *Small Group Research*, 43(6): 655–61.

Guirdham, M. (2002) *Interactive Behaviour at Work*, Harlow: Financial Times Prentice Hall.

Gully, S.M., Devine, D.J. and Whitney, D.J. (1995) 'A meta-analysis of cohesion and performance: effects of level of analysis and task interdependence', *Small Group Research*, 26(4): 497–520.

Guzzo, R.A. and Dickson, M.W. (1996) 'Teams in organizations: Recent research on performance and effectiveness', *Annual Review of Psychology*, 47: 307–38.

Hall, D. and Buzwell, S. (2013) 'The problem of free-riding in group projects: looking beyond social loafing as a reason for non-contribution', *Active Learning in Higher Education*, 14(1): 37–49.

Hampton, M.M. (1999) 'Work groups' in Y. Gabriel (ed), *Organization in Depth*, London: Sage Publications, pp.112–38.

Hogg, M.A. and Vaughan, G.M. (2008) *Social Psychology*, fifth edition, Harlow: Pearson Education Limited.

Huczynski, A. A. (2004) *Influencing Within Organizations*, second edition, London: Routledge.

Ingham, A. G., Levinger, G., Graves, J., and Peckham, V. (1974) 'The Ringelmann effect: studies of group size and group performance', *Journal of Experimental Social Psychology*, 10(4): 371–84.

Jassawalla, A., Hemant,S. and Sashittal, A. (2009) 'Students' perceptions of social loafing: Its antecedents and consequences in undergraduate business classroom teams', *Academy of Management Learning & Education*, 8(1): 42–54.

Joo, M-H. And Dennen, V.P. (2017) 'Measuring university students' group work contribution: scale development and validation', *Small Group Research,* 48(3): 288–310.

Karau, S. J. and Williams, K. D. (1993) 'Social loafing: meta-analytic review and theoretical integration', *Journal of Personality and Social Psychology,* 65(4): 681–706.

Kerr, N.L. (1983) 'Motivation losses in small groups: a social dilemma analysis', *Journal of Personality and Social Psychology,* 45(4): 819–28.

Kniffin, K.M., Wansink, B. Deveine, C.M. and Sobal, J. (2015) 'Eating together at the firehouse: how workplace commensality relates to performance of firefighters'. *Human Performance,* 28(4): 281–306.

Kravitz, D. A., and Martin, B. (1986) 'Ringelmann rediscovered: the original article', *Journal of Personality and Social Psychology,* 50(5): 936–41.

Lam, C. (2015) 'The role of communication and cohesion in reducing social loafing in group projects', *Business and Professional Communication Quarterly,* 78(4): 454–75.

Latane, B., and Nida, S. (1980). 'Social impact theory and group influence: a social engineering perspective'. In P. B. Paulus (Ed.), *Psychology of Group Influence* Hillsdale, NJ: Lawrence Erlbaum Associates, pp. 3–34.

Latane, B., Williams, K., and Harkins, S. (1979) 'Many hands make light work: the causes and consequences of social loafing', *Journal of Personality and Social Psychology,* 37(6): 822–32.

LeBon, G. (1908; first published 1895 by Ernest Benn), *The Crowd: A Study of the Popular Mind,* London: Unwin.

Moreland, R.L. and Levine, J.M. (1982) 'Socialization in small groups: temporal changes in individual-group relations' in Berkowicz, L. (ed) *Advances in Experimental and Social Psychology, Volume 15,* New York: Academic Press, pp.137–92.

Moscovici, S. (1980) 'Towards a theory of conversion behaviour' in L. Berkowitz (ed.), *Advances in Experimental Social Psychology, Volume. 13,* New York: Academic Press, pp. 209–39.

Moscovici, S. (1984) 'The phenomenon of social representations' in R.M. Farr and S. Moscovici (eds), *Social Representations,* New York: Academic Press, pp. 3–69.

Mumford, S. (2015) 'In praise of teamwork', *Journal of the Philosophy of Sport,* 42(1): 51–56.

Nemeth, C. (1986) 'Differential contributions of majority and minority influences', *Psychological Review,* 93(1): 23–32.

Neu, W.A. (2012) 'Unintended cognitive, affective, and behavioural consequences of group assignments', *Journal of Marketing Education,* 34(1): 67–81.

Neu, W.A. (2015) 'Social cues of (un)trustworthy team members', *Journal of Marketing Education,* 37(1): 36–53.

Neu, W.A. (2018) 'Quantitative evidence of students' use of social networks and social categorizations when self-selecting teams', *Journal of Marketing Education,* 40(3): 161–75.

O'Reilly, J., Robinson, S.L., Berdahl, J.L. and Banki, S. (2015) 'Is negative attention better than no attention? The comparative effects of ostracism and harassment at work', *Organization Science,* 26(3): 774–93.

Paulin, D. and Griffin, B. (2017) 'Team incivility climate scale: development and validation of the team-level incivility climate construct', *Group & Organization Management,* 42(3): 315–45.

Pearce, C. L., Gallagher, C. A., and Ensley, M. D. (2002) 'Confidence at the group level of analysis: a longitudinal investigation of the relationship between potency and team effectiveness', *Journal of Occupational and Organizational Psychology,* 75(1): 115–20.

Robinson, S.L., O'Reilly, J. and Wang, W. (2013) 'Invisible at work: An integrated model of workplace ostracism', *Journal of Management,* 39(1): 203–31.

Romeike, P.D., Nienaber, A-M. and Schewe, G. (2016) 'How differences in perceptions of own and team performance impact trust and job satisfaction in virtual teams', *Human Performance,* 29 (4): 291–309.

Schippers, M.C. (2014) 'Social loafing tendencies and team performance: The compensating effects of agreeableness and conscientiousness', *Academy of Management Learning & Education,* 13(1): 62–81.

Seltzer, J. (2016) 'Teaching about social loafing: The accounting team exercise' *Management Teaching Review,* 1(1): 34–42.

Sherif, M. (1936) *The Psychology of Social Norms.* New York: Harper & Row.

Steiner, I. (1972) *Group Process and Productivity,* New York: Academic Press.

Tajfel, H., and Turner, J. C. (1986) 'The social identity theory of inter-group behaviour' in S. Worchel and W. G. Austin (eds.), *Psychology of Inter-group Relations,* second edition, Chicago, IL: Nelson-Hall, pp. 7–24.

Triplett, N. (1898). 'The dynamogenic factors in pacemaking and competition', *American Journal of Psychology,* 9(4): 507–33.

Weber, M. (1924) 'Zur Psychophysik der industriellen Arbeit' (first written in 1908/09) in M. Weber (Ed.), *Gesammelte Aussatze zur Sociologie und Sozialpolitik von Max Weber* Tubingen: J.C.B. Mohr. pp. 61–255.

Williams, K.D. and Karau, S.J. (1991) 'Social loafing and social compensation: the effect of expectations of co-worker performance', *Journal of Personality and Social Psychology,* 61(4): 570–81.

Wood, W., Lundgren, S., Ouellette, J.A., Busceme, S. and Blackstone, T. (1994) 'Minority influence: a meta-analytical review of social influence processes', *Psychological Bulletin,* 115(3): 323–45.

Zaccaro, S.J. (1984) 'Social loafing: the role of task attractiveness', *Personality and Social Psychology Bulletin,* 10(1): 99–106.

CHAPTER 13

Teamworking

Key terms

team

group

advice team

quality circle

total quality management

just-in-time system

action team

project team

cross-functional team

production team

high-performance work system

empowerment

Japanese teamworking

self-managing team

team autonomy

external work team differentiation

internal work team differentiation

external work team integration

team performance

team viability

Learning outcomes

When you have read this chapter, you should be able to define those key terms in your own words, and you should also be able to:

1. Understand why 'team' is a contested concept in the organizational literature.

2. List the nine dimensions of team autonomy.

3. Differentiate between four major types of teams and give an example of each.

4. Discuss the types of obstacles to effectiveness experienced by each type of team.

5. Contrast Western with Japanese concepts of teamworking.

6. List the four main elements in the ecological framework for analysing work team effectiveness.

7. Understand the continuing importance of teamworking.

Why study teamworking?

The value of high-performing teams has long between recognized. Using a sporting analogy, it has been said that while individual talent may win games, teamwork and intelligence wins championships (Keller and Meaney, 2017):

> 'Teams have become the building blocks of organizations. Recruitment ads routinely call for 'team players'. Business schools grade their students in part on their performance in group projects. Office managers knock down walls to encourage team-building. Teams are as old as civilization, of course: even Jesus had 12 co-workers.' (*The Economist*, 2017, p.68)

Lencioni (2002, p. vii) commented:

> 'Not finance. Not strategy. Not technology. It is teamwork that remains the ultimate competitive advantage, both because it is so powerful and so rare.'

Deloitte, a professional services consultancy, surveyed 70 executives in over 130 countries and found that teamwork had reached a new high (Brown et al., 2015). Nearly half reported that they were in the process of reorganizing and intending to place greater emphasis on teams in their organization structure. What is driving this 'stream to team'?

- *Technological innovation:* Product development through technological innovation has accelerated product changes from five or six to one or two years. Companies have begun competing against market transitions rather than competitors. To meet this challenge, companies have had to become more agile in the modern marketplace.
- *Digital communication technology:* This allows junior staff to easily coordinate their own activities themselves. They no longer need a manager in the company hierarchy to do it for them.
- *Employee expectations:* 'Millennials' who represent an ever-greater percentage of the workforce in Western countries have been brought up to work in groups from school and expect to do so at work.
- *Failure of hierarchy:* The US Army found that its hierarchical structure impeded its progress during the Iraq war while its opponent leaders decentralized their authority to self-organizing teams (McChrystal, 2015).

The required agility cannot be achieved by traditional ways of organizing. Rigid, hierarchical organization structures which worked in the past are no longer suitable for the twenty-first century. That is why a network of teams is replacing conventional hierarchies. These cross-disciplinary teams are being allowed to manage and coordinate between themselves.

Teamworking at Copiapó

On the 14 October 2010, the last of the 33 Chilean miners who had been trapped for 69 days at the San José gold and copper mine in Copiapó in the Atacama Desert, 2,300 feet below the Earth's surface (two Empire State Buildings deep) was pulled to safety with the help of an unlikely source – the United States' National Aeronautics and Space Administration (NASA). It was a dire situation. While developing their rescue plans, the Chilean government also sought advice and information from other governments and organizations as to how to assist the trapped miners. One of the organizations that responded to the call for assistance was NASA. It quickly formed a team consisting of two medical doctors, a psychologist and an engineer. The team spent three days at the rescue site in Chile assessing the similarities between the miners' plight and life in space.

They gave advice to the rescue team at the mine site. This ranged from warning rescuers not to give the starving men too much food too quickly (which could prove fatal), to suggesting they wear sunglasses when surfacing after two months underground. Most importantly, the NASA team also provided the design for the innovative rescue capsule (nicknamed *Phoenix*) that was used to pull the miners to the surface and which ultimately saved

→

cushion the capsule's ride up reducing both the friction with the tunnel walls and the possibility of it getting stuck half way.

On the day, with remarkable speed – and flawless execution – miner after miner climbed into the capsule, and was hoisted through the rock and saw precious sunlight after the longest underground entrapment in history. Dr Michael Duncan, NASA's deputy chief medical officer stated, 'We were able to bring the knowledge we learned in space to the surface, and under the surface, to help people here on Earth'. The Copiapó incident involved not only very unusual team composition – these occupations, professions and cultures do not normally collaborate in this way; but also a very unusual team context – rescuing trapped miners – this is not something that is done routinely (National Aeronautics and Space Administration, 2011; Rashid et al., 2013).

their lives. The four-person NASA team consulted with 20 of their colleagues and came up with 50 design recommendations. For example, that exterior rollers would

✋ STOP AND SEARCH   YouTube for *NASA, Chilean Miner Rescue.*

The T-word and team work design

Team a collection of individuals who exist to achieve a shared goal; are interdependent with respect to achieving that goal; whose membership is bounded and stable over time; and who operate within a system.

Group two or more people in face-to-face interaction, each aware of their group membership and interdependence as they strive to achieve common group goals.

A **team** refers to a collection of individuals who exist to achieve a shared goal; who are interdependent with respect to achieving that goal; whose membership is bounded and stable over time; and who operate within a system. The word derives from Middle English, Fresian and Norse word for a bridle and thence to a set of draught animals, for example a team of oxen, harnessed together and then, by analogy, to a number of persons involved in joint action. The term, literally refers to a relatively small number of entities that pull together to reach a common goal (Weiss and Hoegh, 2015). **Group** refers to two or more people, in face-to-face interaction, each aware of their group membership and interdependence as they strive to achieve their goals. Team thus represents a sub-category of group.

In much of the literature, the terms *group* and *team*, are used interchangeably. Management consultants frequently use the term team metaphorically, that is, they apply this label to a collection of employees to which it is imaginatively, but not literally, appropriate. Hayes (1997) noted that the idea of team must be one of the most widely used metaphors in organizational life. These same writers also use the term to describe a collection of people as what they *should* be, or what they would *prefer* them to be, rather than as they actually *are*.

Nicky Hayes saw teams as a sporting metaphor used frequently by managers and consultants. One of the large British supermarket chains used the employee job title of 'checkout *captain*'. The metaphor stresses both inclusiveness and similarity – members sharing common values and cooperating to achieve common goals while also emphasizing

✋ STOP AND SEARCH   YouTube for *Teams versus groups* (3:11).

Teams at Google

In Douglas Edwards' (2011) account of the early days of Google, he described Urs Hölzle, as a key person on the engineering side ('Saint Urs, Keeper of the Blessed Code'):

> 'Urs's most significant accomplishment, however, was building the team that built Google. Your greatest impact as an engineer comes through hiring someone who is as good as you or better" he exhorted everybody who would listen, 'because over the next year, they double your productivity. There's nothing else that you can do to double your productivity. Even if you are a genius, that's extremely unlikely to happen' . . . If you have very good people it gives you a safety net', he believed. 'If there's something wrong, they self-correct. You don't have to tell them. 'Hey, pay attention to this. They feel ownership and fix it before you even knew it was broken' (p.36).

differences as various individuals play distinct, albeit equally valuable roles, and have different responsibilities. She wrote that:

> 'The idea of 'team' at work must be one of the most widely used metaphors in organizational life. A group of workers or managers is generally described as a 'team' in much the same way that a company or department is so often described as 'one big family'. But often, the new employee receiving these assertions quickly discovers that what was described as a 'team' is actually anything but The mental image of cohesion, coordination and common goals which was conjured up by the metaphor of the team was entirely different from the everyday reality of working life.' (Hayes 1997, p. 27)

"I love the sense of teamwork."

Home viewing

In the film *Early Man* (2018, director Nick Park) a tribe of primitive Stone Age dwellers have to defend their land from Bronze Age invaders. What distinguishes a great team from a group of great players? Whether hunting or playing football, the Stoneagers support and work for one another and share a common objective – remaining in their valley. In contrast, the Bronze Age football team members, although individually skilled, are too egotistical to work together effectively, and seek personal rewards. Despite their inferior football skills but with coaching and teamwork, the Stoneagers win their valley back – a team of individual champion players can be beaten by a champion team.

Types of team tasks

Eric Sundstrom, Kenneth De Meuse and David Futrell (1990) distinguished four types of teams – advice, action, project and production – on the basis of what each did (see Table 13.1).

Sundstrom et al.'s team typology allows you to categorize different teams in organizations; compare and contrast their processes; analyse their outputs, and suggest ways of making improvements. Advice teams provide information to management to be used in its own decision making, e.g. quality circles. Action teams execute brief performances that are repeated under new conditions, e.g. football teams. Project teams bring together employees from different departments to accomplish a specific task, e.g. new product development team. Production teams consist of individuals who share a production goal.

Table 13.1: Types of team tasks and their outputs.

Types and examples	Differentiation	Coordination	Specialization	Work cycles	Typical outputs
ADVICE Committees Review panels and boards Quality control circles Employee involvement groups Advisory councils	Low	Low	Low	Work cycles can be brief or long; one cycle can be a team life span	Decisions Selections Suggestions Proposals Recommendations
ACTION Sports teams Entertainment groups Expeditions Negotiating teams Surgery teams Cockpit crews Military platoons and squads	High	High	High	Work cycles brief, repeated under new conditions	Competitive events Expeditions Contracts Lawsuits Concerts Surgical operations Flights Combat missions
PROJECT Research groups Planning teams Architect teams Engineering teams Development teams Task forces	High	Low (for traditional units) or High (for cross-functional teams)	High	Work cycles typically differ for each new project; one cycle can be a team's life span	Plans Designs Investigations Presentations Prototypes Reports Findings
PRODUCTION Assembly line teams Manufacturing cells Mining teams Hospital receptions Data processing groups Maintenance crews	Low	High	High	Work cycles typically repeated or continuous process; cycles often briefer than team life span	Food Chemicals Components Assemblies Retail sales Customer service Equipment repairs

Source: Sundstrom et al. (1990, p.125).

Each team type can be further compared along five dimensions:

1. *Degree of differentiation from other units*: How similar (low differentiation) or different (high differentiation) is this team from others within the department or organization?

2. *Degree of coordination*: Is its work closely related to and intertwined with that of other work units within the organization (high coordination) or does it operate relatively independently (low coordination)?

3. *Degree of technical specialization*: Are members required to apply special, technical skills acquired through higher education or extensive training (high specialization) or do they draw upon their general experience and innate problem solving ability (low specialization)?

4. *Work cycles*: How much time does the team need to achieve its aims? Does it perform short, repetitive work cycles, or a single, long one?

5. *Typical outputs*: What does the team produce as its output?

<table><tr><td>**CRITICAL THINKING**</td><td>Naquin and Tynan (2003) found that when people seek to understand team performance; they often give the team credit when it is successful, but blame its individual team members when it is not. Why do you think that teams are not held accountable for their failures?</td></tr></table>

Advice teams

Advice team a team created by management to provide the latter with information for its own decision making.

Quality circle shop floor employees from the same department who meet for a few hours each week to discuss ways of improving their work environment.

An advice team is created primarily to provide a flow of information to management for use in its own decision making. Advice teams require little in the way of coordination with other work units in the company. Following a major accident or disaster, governments often set up committees of experts. The committee reviews the events that occurred and makes recommendations about improvements.

In organizations, the quality circle (also known as a Kaizen team) is the best known and most publicized advice team of recent times. The original concept was of a team of six to twelve employees from the shop floor of a manufacturing department, meeting regularly to discuss quality problems, investigate their causes and recommend solutions to management. In practice, a wide range of different arrangements were established under this label. Quality circles varied in terms of the number of members; were applied in service as well as manufacturing contexts; included supervisory staff; discussed non-quality issues; and some had authority to implement their suggestions. All these matters depended on how the quality circle was established by management in the particular organization.

Quality circles are a Japanese export. The first quality circle in the United States was introduced at the Lockheed Missile and Space Company in 1974 and the first British one appeared at Rolls Royce in 1978. Originally used in manufacturing, they are now used worldwide in the service industries, government agencies and the voluntary sector. Despite their differences, quality circles possess certain common features:

- Membership is voluntary, and members are drawn from a particular department.
- No financial rewards are given for team suggestions.
- Members receive training in problem solving, statistical quality control and team processes.
- Their problem-solving domain is defined by management (often, but not always quality, productivity and cost reduction).
- Meetings are held weekly, usually in company time, often with trained facilitators helping members with training issues and helping them to manage the meetings.
- The decision to install quality circles is made at the top of the organization, and the circles are created at the bottom.

Total quality management
a philosophy of management that is driven by customer needs and expectations and which is committed to continuous improvement.

Just-in-time system
managing inventory (stock) so that items are delivered when they are needed in the production process instead of being stored by the manufacturer.

Management's objectives for introducing quality circles vary greatly, for example, quality improvement, quality enhancement, employee involvement. Although an organization may claim to have introduced quality circles, even at the height of their popularity only a small proportion of the employees ever took part (Marchington, 1992). Quality circles represent one of the largest experiments in the use of advice teams to improve organizational performance during the 1980s. From the 1990s, quality circles begun to be superseded by the 'total quality movement' (Hill, 1991). Quality circles are now part of total quality management (TQM) and just-in-time systems (JIT).

Action teams

Action team a team that executes brief performances that are repeated under new conditions. Its members are technically specialized, and need to coordinate their individual contributions with each other.

The members of an action team are specialized in terms of their knowledge, skill and contribution to the team's objective. The 'performance' of an action team is brief, and is repeated under new conditions each time. Additionally, both the specialized inputs of the various team members and the need for individuals to coordinate with other team members are high.

If a football player sustains an injury on the field, an action team consisting of the club physiotherapists will work on him. If the injury is serious, he may be taken to hospital where another action team – a surgeon and his co-workers – operate on him. Finally, when recuperating in his private room, he may watch TV and see a Formula 1 race where an action team changes the tyres of racing cars. In all these situations, action team members have to exhibit peak performance on demand. Popular films such as the *Mission Impossible* series depict action heroes working together in action teams.

Formula 1 tyre change

When the Grand Prix racing car flicks into the pits to collect fresh tyres, it is time for the pit crew to take their brief place in the sun under the eyes of the packed grandstands and TV cameras. A pit crew can change all four tyres of an F1 racing car in under two seconds. Pit stops are a critical time as they can make the difference between victory and defeat. The speed of the mechanics practically defeats the eye. Have you seen a tyre change on a Formula 1 car? Count the number of mechanics involved.

There can be 20 or more. There are three men at each corner of the car; one with the wheel gun; another to remove the wheel; a third to put on the replacement; and the last operates the car jack. Others are positioned around these. In fact, the final member of the team is the driver himself who has to streak down the pit lane and stop 6 to 12 inches in front of where the mechanics are positioned. Moving equipment wastes valuable tenths of a second. The tyre change is fraught with danger.

One slip up, one sticking wheel nut, one man unable to fling his arms up in the all clear signal, and the race can be lost. To achieve a consistent, high level of team performance requires military precision, movement programmes (like ballet), and practised rehearsals which go on throughout the year. At present the pit stop record is held by the Ferrari team in the 2013 Japanese Grand Prix changing Fernando Alonso's tyres in 1.95 seconds.

STOP AND SEARCH   YouTube for *Fastest F1 Pit Stop.*

Another example of an action team is a *crew*. This term is frequently used to refer to employees who work on aircraft, boats, spacecraft and film sets. A distinguishing feature of a crew is that that it is technology-driven. That is why perhaps McDonald's refers to its restaurant employees as 'crew members'. If the technology changes, then so does the nature of the crew. A crew depends on its technology which transforms difficult, cognitive tasks into easy ones. The crew's 'tools' affect the division of labour among its members who use various techniques to coordinate their activities (Hare, 1992; Hutchins, 1990).

Ginnett (1993) reported how, on a Boeing 727 aircraft, the crew members' roles are determined by the location of their seats in the cockpit. The captain sits in the left seat from which he tests all the emergency warning devices. He is the only one who can taxi the aircraft, since the nose wheel gear steering is located on that side of the cockpit. The first officer who starts the engines and who communicates with the control tower occupies the right-hand seat. The flight engineer sits sideways facing a panel that allows him to monitor and control the various sub-systems in the aircraft. He is the only one able to reach the auxiliary power unit. In other transportation craft, the relationship of roles to equipment is different. Airplane personnel consist of those in the cockpit – flight crew (pilot, co-pilot, flight engineers) and those outside it – the cabin crew (flight attendants). Between 1959 and 1989, 70 per cent of all severe aircraft accidents were at least partly attributable to flight crew behaviour (Weiner et al., 1993). Thus, it is a more common cause than either pilot error or mechanical failure.

Social behaviour in operating theatres

Laura Jones

Laura Jones and her colleagues (2018) studied hospital operating theatres which are inhabited by hierarchical, mixed-gender clinical teams who engage in both technical communication and social interactions. The researchers recorded all behaviour between 400 doctors, nurses and technicians during 200 surgical procedures. In additional to professional (technical) exchanges, surgical team members were found to engage in a variety of interactions including dance (music is often played during operations). The majority of communications focused on clinicians' personal lives, current events and popular culture.

The 6,348 non-technical, social interactions observed were classified into three categories:

- *Cooperative*: affiliative behaviour and team building including chit-chat, exchanging pleasantries, bilateral joking and teaching that led to better surgical outcomes. (This represented 59 per cent of interactions.)

- *Conflictive*: team disintegrating communication including yelling, insults, being curt and disrespectful and unilateral joking. Behaviours ranged from differences of opinion to discord and distraction which could jeopardize patient safety (3 per cent).

The remaining interactions were classed as neutral (38 per cent).

The researchers found that hierarchy, social role and the gender composition of surgical teams affected cooperative and conflict behaviours. Even though rare, conflict was distracting and detrimental to the outcomes. Generally, conflicts were more common when a team consisted of more males than females. Predominantly male surgical teams led by a man were twice as likely to experience conflict as similar teams led by a woman (51 compared to 21 per cent). In female teams there were no differences, regardless of leader.

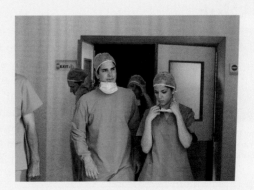

Lead surgeons initiated most of the conflicts. 80 per cent of the conflicts were directed down the hierarchy, mostly at individuals several positions down from the initiator. Circulating nurses and scrub persons were the most frequent recipients of conflict-provoking behaviours. The results confirm the prevalence of intra-sexual competition with alpha males seeking to assert their own position and status.

Cooperation increased significantly when the lead surgeon's gender differed from that of the majority of the other clinicians in the room. The highest percentage of cooperative behaviour was observed when the lead surgeon was a female-dominant in a male-dominant room or a male in a female-dominant room. Previous studies show that up to 80 per cent of surgical errors are the result of incorrect interactions between medical team members. The researchers suggest that greater gender diversity may increase cooperative behaviour in this and other work settings.

 STOP AND SEARCH   YouTube for *teamwork surgery.*

Project teams

Project team a collection of employees from different work areas in an organization brought together to accomplish a specific task within a finite time.

A project team consists of individuals who have been brought together from different parts of the organization for a limited period of time to contribute towards a management-specified task. The task may be developing a product, refining a service or commissioning a new plant. Once this has been completed, the team is either disbanded or its members are given new assignments. Project teams are created when:

- Creative problem solving is required involving the application of different types of specialized knowledge.

- There is a need to closely coordinate the work on a specific project, e.g. design and development or the production and testing of a new product.

Cross-functional team employees from different functional departments who meet as a team to complete a particular task.

Every university has hundreds of project teams who are conducting research. Most of their members are on two- to three-year contracts which span the period of the research project. Team members are recruited on the basis of their specialist knowledge and their output consists of research reports, books and journal articles.

Within the organizational context, the best known and most common type of project team is the cross-functional team. This is a collection of employees who are brought together from different departments (functions) of the company to accomplish a specific task within a finite time.

CUTTING EDGE   Cross-industry project teams

Amy Edmondson (photo credit: Evgenia Eliseeva)

Amy Edmondson (2016) studied cross-industry project teams and identified four leadership practices that lead to team success. If forming groups consisting of individuals from within the same company or university class is difficult, then doing so with people who work in different companies in different industries is an even greater challenge. These team members occupy different intellectual worlds; use distinctive technical languages; possess their own behavioural norms and values; and have their own individual and professional frames of reference. It is therefore not surprising that when these individuals form a cross-industry team, they can experience a culture clash which creates antagonisms that result in emotionally-charged disagreements and conflicts.

Cross-industry teams are being increasingly used for radically innovative projects such those involving technology and motor car companies. Managing such teams presents unique challenges. Edmondson offered advice to leaders of such teams:

- *Foster an adaptive vision*: While having a clear and unwavering goal which is normal for stable teams with well-defined outputs in these complex dynamic innovative projects, it is better for a goal to evolve. This is because at the outset it is unclear what the team is capable of. It allows members to exercise their influence over the vision. Also, it is likely that end-users' needs will change during the project. While the goal may alter, cross-industry team leaders need to explain to participants the importance of what is being attempted, framed in terms of personal, social or environmental values. They need to invite input from members from the diverse industries in developing and reshaping the project vision so as to keep all of them engaged with the project.

- *Promote psychological safety:* Creating a climate in which individuals feel able to openly disagree, offer wild ideas, and speak up without fear of retribution. Leaders do this by modelling the desired behaviours themselves – showing curiosity, acknowledging their uncertainty, highlighting their own fallibility. These are important for such teams because members may fear showing their ignorance in front of those coming from different fields. They may hold stereotypical images of these people and feel inhibited about addressing an issue. To avoid these problems, leaders need to stress that the team members' work is novel and experimental and that they expect members to take risks. This can reduce their worries about being judged to be ignorant or of making social errors. They should also foster inquisitiveness, clarify the protective legal context, and frame the team's diverse expertise and differing professional cultures as being a valuable resource.

- *Enable knowledge sharing:* A failure by team members to explain their reasoning based on their industry-specific expertise can cause misunderstanding and conflict. So too can contrasting professional goals when for example, civil engineers value reliability while software developers stress experimentation. To avoid these problems, team leaders should insist that individuals share their thought processes with others; make explicit the distinctive professional values that characterize different disciplines represented in the team; frame these differences as a source of strength and advantage for the team; encourage face-to-face interaction between members from different industries; and search for common ground, for example, by exploring

→

how engineers and developers might achieve experimentation and reliability simultaneously.

- *Cultivate execution-as-learning*: While traditional project management techniques work satisfactorily on projects where tasks and responsibilities are well specified and there is a blueprint to follow, they are likely be disastrous with innovative projects lacking a blueprint. In such situations, team leaders need to adopt an execution-as-learning approach. It involves creating narrow and deliberate experiments to gain insight into what works in an unfamiliar situation, and welcoming and considering change suggestions that surface unexpectedly.

Traditionally, organizations have been divided into functional departments. These have been dubbed 'boxes', 'silos' or 'chimneys' to stress their insularity. By forming teams consisting of people from these different boxes, organizations can break down the boundaries between their functions (e.g. accounting, marketing, research, product design, human resources); improve coordination and integration; release the creative thought of their employees; and increase the speed and flexibility of their responses to customers. Cross-functional teams are established in order to combine a wide range of employee expertise to achieve a more informed and rounded outcome than would otherwise be possible.

Cross-functional teams comprise employees who traditionally work in different departments or work areas. Sometimes, such teams also include customers, suppliers and external consultants. They are supported by their organization's structures, systems and skills which enable the teams to operate successfully as a more independent unit (less bound by functional ties) towards goals which transcend the combined abilities of individual members. Advocates of cross-functional teams claim that they are beneficial to their customers, employees, and to the organization as a whole. Customers obtain more attractive and customized products and have their needs met more rapidly. Team members benefit through having more challenging and rewarding jobs with broader responsibilities; greater opportunities for gaining visibility in front of senior management; an increased understanding of the entire processes across the organization; a 'fun' working environment; and closer relationships with colleagues. The organization gains through:

- increased productivity
- reduced processing times
- improved market and customer focus
- improved coordination and integration
- reduced time needed to develop new products
- improved communications by having boundaries between functions spanned.

Cross-functional teams differ from other types of teams in three important ways:

- *Representative*: They are representative in that their individual members usually retain their position back in their 'home' functional department.
- *Temporary*: They have a finite life, even if their end is years in the future.
- *Innovative*: They are established to solve non-conventional problems and meet challenging performance standards.

The most common application of cross-functional teams has been in new product development and in research and development (R&D). However, they have also been used whenever an organization requires an input of diverse, specialist skills and knowledge. For example, in manufacturing and production, IT development or process re-engineering initiatives. Recent years have seen the evolution of the multi-national virtual (project) team. These now permeate all levels of most large organizations, often supplementing traditional, face-to-face teams.

Since team members are departmental representatives, they owe their true allegiance to their home, functional department. These members are therefore likely to experience a high degree of pressure and divided loyalties. Their temporary nature also places strains on members who have to quickly develop stable and effective working group processes. Cross-functional teams can therefore have a negative effect on their participants. Organizations and managers need to clearly define cross-functional team assignments in order to maintain order and accountability.

CUTTING EDGE Multicultural virtual teams

Soo Jeoung Han

Soo Jeoung Han and Michael Beyerlein (2016) identified the factors that affected the processes and performance of nationally and culturally diverse project teams that worked in virtual environments. They identified eight task and socio-emotional challenges that affected team process and performance within multinational virtual teams.

Task-related challenges

Task-related communicating	Communication problems and misunderstandings; magnified task conflict; dependence on early and frequent task-oriented communication
Coordinating	Coordination difficulties due to power, culture, and communication; issues with keeping on schedule and staying on budget; different preferences for a selection of communication media
Establishing expectations	Difficulties in norming due to various standards of acceptable behaviour and cultural norms
Knowledge sharing	Difficulties in keeping goals stable; reduced information flow due to group perceptions and cultural differences; uneven distribution of information due to differences in information salience and speed of access to information

Socio-emotional challenges

Overcoming biases	Unhealthy racial and national stereotypes; lack of social information due to cultural differences; conflict due to in-group and out-group dynamics
Building relationships	Relationship conflict due to cultural diversity; lack of shared beliefs and experiences for developing interpersonal relationships
Developing trust	Little informal messaging or social information that can increase trust; greater reliance on cognitive rather than affective elements for trust
Intercultural learning	Intercultural misunderstandings: conflicts due to communication style differences; impaired decision quality

The task and socio-emotional processes were found to be interrelated, circular and iterative, and occurred simultaneously. Overcoming each challenge and moving to the next process is non-linear because changes in membership, small successes and failures, and outside influences, can all set the team back or move it forward in its mastery of challenges. Because of this, the authors recommend that the task and socio-emotional processes should be jointly optimized by managers.

STOP AND SEARCH   YouTube for *Managing multicultural teams.*

Production teams

Production team
a stable number of
individuals who share
production goals and
who perform specific
roles which are
supported by a set of
incentives and sanctions.

Typically, a production team consists of individuals who are responsible for performing day-to-day, core operations. These may be product-orientated teams such as those assembling a computer on a factory floor; construction workers placing a bridge in position across a motorway; or teams assembling sound and light systems for a rock concert. The degree of technical specialization required of the team members varies from medium to low, depending on the nature of the duties performed. However, the required degree of coordination, both between the members of each team and between the team and other work units, is high. It is these other units that are either responsible for providing support activities such as quality control and maintenance or who provide the inputs to, or receive the outputs of that team.

Experiments in the 1970s into employee participation and democracy aimed to raise productivity by providing employees with more interesting and varied work. In contrast, team-based working innovations of the 1990s represented a greater concern with efficiency and effectiveness. They were stimulated by the need for companies to remain competitive in a fiercely aggressive global environment. The rationale is that in the race to improve service quality or reduce new product cycle times, technology only gives an organization a short-term advantage and one which can be copied anyway. It is the way that human resources are organized and developed that is more critical.

Team member familiarity

Most major commercial airlines routinely rotate members of their flight crews. Senior pilots on large planes often fly with a different co-pilot on every trip during a month. Airlines do not stick to the same airplane crews because financially the airline gets most from its capital equipment and labour by treating each airplane, each pilot, and every other crew member as an individual unit, and then uses an algorithm to maximize their utilization. In consequence, pilots dash through the airports just like

passengers, since they have to fly two or three different aircraft, each with a different crew, in a single day.

Team familiarity refers to the amount of previous experience that members have had of working with one another. Robert Huckman and Bradley Staats (2013) studied corporate, healthcare, consulting, military and aviation teams. They found that the degree of familiarity greatly affected team performance and was a better predictor of it than either individual member or project

manager experience. They measured how often team members had previously worked together over time. In one study of an Indian software services firm, they found that when team familiarity increased by 50 per cent defects fell by 19 per cent and budget deviations by 30 per cent. How does team familiarity and unfamiliarity affect team performance?

- *Communication*: Differences between members in unfamiliar teams frequently result in poor communication causing conflict and confusion. Team familiarity obviates the need to learn to communicate with each other and this speeds up progress towards team goals.

- *Learning*: Unfamiliar teams often fail to tap the knowledge that their members possess as they are unaware of who knows what. Familiarity allows them to become acquainted with what expertise each individual has to help achieve the group task and encourages them to share it.

- *Innovation*: Since new solutions come from new combinations of existing knowledge, team members must not only share their own knowledge but also have to integrate it with that of other members. Team familiarity facilitates this knowledge integration process by increasing the chances of finding innovative solutions.

- *Change*: Teams may be asked to modify goals or change time frames due to outside circumstances which can cause stress and require flexibility. Familiar teams provide a more secure basis from which to meet such challenges.

Organizations develop capabilities that their competitors cannot replicate to gain competitive advantage and familiar teams are one source of that advantage. Since each team member's performance is dependent on that of the others, competitors cannot replicate an entire team's capabilities by hiring away just one individual member. The US National Transportation Safety Board found that 73 per cent of accident incidents occurred on a crew's first day of flying together, before individuals had a chance to learn, through experience, how best to operate as a team.

A NASA study found that fatigued but familiar crews made about half as many errors as rested but unfamiliar ones. Asked how long it would take for two crew members to work together well on a flight, an airlines operations staff member estimated five to six years. Clearly this is not good news from a passenger point of view. Next time you board an airplane, ask how many crew members have ever flown together before (Coutu, 2009).

Team activities

Management's interest in production teams has always been in finding ways of improving employee motivation and performance. Employee participation in decision making can take the form of increasing their autonomy. Bram Steijn (2001) distinguished between *individual* autonomy for the employee who was not part of a team, for example, in the form of job enrichment **(see Chapter 9)** and team autonomy which was the collective autonomy for the workers *as a team* to do a task. It is the latter that is considered here. In practice individual

High-performance work system a form of organization that operates at levels of excellence far beyond those of comparable systems.

Empowerment organizational arrangements that give employees more autonomy, discretion and decision-making responsibility.

Japanese teamworking use of scientific management principles of minimum manning, multi-tasking, multi-machine operation, pre-defined work operations, repetitive short cycle work, powerful first line supervisors, and a conventional managerial hierarchy.

Self-managing team a group of individuals with diverse skills and knowledge with the collective autonomy and responsibility to plan, manage, and execute tasks interdependently to attain a common goal.

and the teamworking approaches have converged in what has come to be known as the high-performance work system.

There has been confusion about the use of the concept of teamworking in different countries and in different companies. Western teamworking emphasizes enhanced employee control and job satisfaction through participation and represents an example of worker empowerment. This refers to organizational arrangements that give employees more autonomy, discretion and decision-making responsibility. However, employee empowerment in organizations is only allowed by management if it is exercised in ways that are judged to be beneficial to the organization. Daft and Noe (2001) described a range of empowerment possibilities for individuals and teams, indicating the number and range of skills needed by the employees involved (see Figure 13.1).

Teamworking does not necessarily empower workers. How work is structured and the context in which teamworking takes place, both make a great difference. Japanese teamworking, for example, operates at the other end of the empowerment continuum. It differs little from Fordism with its emphasis on direct management control, repetitive tasks and labour discipline. It uses the scientific management principles of 'minimum manning, multi-tasking, multi-machine operation, pre-defined work operations, repetitive short cycle work, powerful first line supervisors, and a conventional managerial hierarchy' (Buchanan, 1994, p.219). Japanese work teams tend to be advice teams mistaken for production teams. They meet and function as teams 'off line' (outside the production context) in contrast to autonomous work teams which function as teams 'on line' (inside the production context).

Japanese teamworking is also called lean production (or *Toyotaism*) because, compared with other mass production plants, it has higher labour flexibility by using multi-skilled employees who operate different machines; fewer workers not directly involved in product manufacture; a minimum of unfinished products (work in progress); and requires very little rectification of work already carried out. In a Toyota production system, work operations are

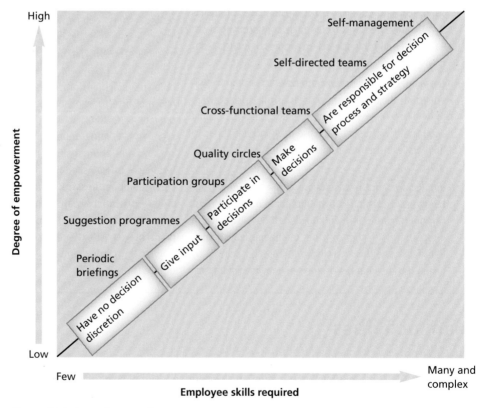

Figure 13.1: A continuum of empowerment
Source: from Daft and Noe, Organizational Behaviour, 1E. P.218 (c) 2001 South-Western, a part of Cengage Learning, Inc. Reproduced by permission www.cengage.com, p.218

highly standardized. After three days, new workers are able to perform any particular job specified on a standard operation sheet. Each highly standardized job is combined with other, similarly standardized ones, so as to extract the maximum amount of effort from employees with minimum labour input.

Team autonomy and self-managing teams

Team autonomy
the extent to which a team experiences freedom, independence and discretion in decisions relating to the performance of its tasks.

A **self-managing team** consists of individuals with diverse skills and knowledge possessing the collective autonomy and responsibility to plan, manage and execute tasks interdependently to attain a common goal. The adjectives that frequently precede this type of team in the organizational literature are *autonomous, semi-autonomous, self-managing, self-regulating* or *self-directing*. However, there are many types of teams, for example, those in the archetypal Japanese system of lean production, which are not necessarily participative, let alone self-managing. Teams range from having no autonomy to full autonomy. **Team autonomy** refers to the extent to which a team experiences freedom, independence and discretion in decisions related to the performance of its tasks. Teams differ in terms of how much autonomy management grants them.

When encountering an example of a supposed self-managing team within a company, it is necessary to ask: who decides about what, and to what extent? Jan Gulowsen (1979), a Norwegian researcher, provided a framework which allows more specific assessments to be made about team autonomy (Table 13.2). He distinguished nine 'task areas' or dimensions

Table 13.2: Team task areas, levels of team input and team autonomy levels

Team task area / dimensions

1. Team leader selection
2. Acceptance of a new member into the team
3. Distribution of work
4. Time flexibility
5. Acceptance of additional work
6. Representation outside the team
7. Production methods (choice of)
8. Production goals (output determination)
9. Production goals (quality determination)

Team input levels

1. *None*: No team participation and total management control. Managers make all the decisions and the team implements them. Team members have no input into the decision-making process; there is no element of participation, not even in the form of suggestions or requests.
2. *Some:* The team has some input into decisions concerned with its immediate working environment. It can make suggestions and requests and has discussions with management who may adopt its ideas.
3. *Joint:* A situation of co-decision making in which a team shares decision-making power with management and plays an equal role in the taking and implementing of decisions.
4. *Autonomy:* The team is fully trusted by management and is truly autonomous. It reaches its decisions with no input from management whatsoever. Management accepts the team as a full and equal partner.

Team autonomy level

Low autonomy teams	Moderate autonomy teams	High autonomy teams
Assembly line workers	Quality circles	Autonomous work groups
Supermarket checkouts teams	Semi-autonomous groups	High performance
		Self-directed team

Table 13.3: Tasks performed by self-managing teams themselves

A survey conducted of 1,456 organizations in the United States with over 100 employees, found the following:

Task	%
Set own work schedules	67
Deal directly with external customers	67
Conduct own member training	59
Setting own production quotas / performance targets	56
Deal with suppliers / vendors	44
Purchase equipment / services	43
Develop budgets	39
Do their own performance reviews on members	36
Hire co-workers	33
Fire co-workers	14

Source: Training (1996, p.69)

in a team's working which offer the potential for autonomy. Within each area, he specified four possible levels of team input. This allows different teams to be distinguished in terms of the level of autonomy that they possess.

Depending on the self-managing team, it can have autonomy to make decisions about project management, problem solving, conflict management, strategy formulation, skill development, and even performance evaluation. The results of a survey which identified the types of tasks most often performed by SMTs are shown in Table 13.3.

According to Druskat and Wheeler (2004), 79 per cent of Fortune 1000 companies and 81 per cent of Fortune 1000 manufacturing companies had self-managing teams. These teams are now a leading innovation in work structures. SMTs have many benefits. Under certain circumstances, they can:

- use individual members' skills better
- provide more scope for team innovation
- increase organizational flexibility and adaptability
- raise employees' job satisfaction morale due to empowerment
- increase employees' sense of responsibility and accountability
- increase task importance by those who have a stake in its outcome.

However, SMTs can also have negative aspects. Under other circumstances, they can:

- increase the number of meetings
- lengthen the decision-making process
- escalate conflict among team members
- reduce members' awareness of changes outside their team
- increase stress among both team members and leaders due to changes in their roles.

CUTTING EDGE

Self-managing teams

Nina Magpili

Pilar Pazos

Nina Magpili and Pilar Pazos (2018) investigated the research literature to discover the factors that influenced the successful implementation of high-performing, self-managing teams. They identified three sets of factors:

Individual factors	Team factors	Organizational factors
Individual autonomy	External leadership	Corporate culture
Individual roles	Peer control	Corporate policies
Leadership	Task characteristics	National culture
Self-management skills	Team autonomy	Organizational goals
Technical skills	Team skill diversity	Organizational structure
Teamwork skills		Training
Resistance to change		Resources
Work experience		Rewards

The most important individual level factors were members' ability to work in teams; their possession of a range of technical skills that enabled job rotation within the team; and the ability of leaders to balance the promotion of the team's autonomous state while still providing some basic guidance and structure. At the team level, shared leadership was critical with team members requiring the less conventional team skills of resilience, ability to learn from mistakes, and a risk-taking attitude. Critical organizational level factors included the corporate structure, policies, culture, reward systems and resources available.

A flat organizational structure that reduces formalization and an empowering culture that supports and facilitates autonomy provides the ideal organizational context in which SMTs can thrive. Magpili and Pazos concluded that successful implementation of SMTs required a thorough understanding of input factors and an ability to manage those factors at different levels in the organization. Implementing SMTs without consideration of these factors would almost certainly lead to failure.

✓✓✓ **EMPLOYABILITY CHECK** (interpersonal, people management and teamworking skills)

As team leader what steps would you take to convert your own traditional team into a self-managing one?

The research evidence concerning the effectiveness about SMTs is mixed and depends on which dimension is being considered. SMTs appear to have a modest impact on the performance and the attitudes of team members; a direct impact on quality; and a modest, positive impact on productivity. The vast majority of studies report improvements with respect to employee job satisfaction and their quality of working life. The effects of SMTs on staff absenteeism, safety, and health issues have been less systematically studied and the results are inconsistent (Cohen and Ledford, 1994). The main differences between traditional and self-managed teams are shown in Table 13.4.

Table 13.4: Traditional and self-managed teams compared

	Traditional team *Team supervisor . . .*	Self-managing team *Team members . . .*
Leadership	is the one, assigned leader	rotate leadership between themselves
Authority	has formal responsibility to make decisions	are given authority and responsibility to make their own decisions
Accountability	holds group members individually accountable	collectively hold each other accountable
Goals	sets the team's goals	agree goals by discussion
Work organization	determines how work is to be done	decide how work is to be done
Outputs	individual results achieved by people working on their own	collective results achieved by members' close collaboration
Information	provides required information	gather and integrate information for themselves
Direction	gives instructions	act upon information obtained, taking responsibility for their actions
Scrutiny	checks that instructions have been followed	guide their own work
Performance evaluation	by supervisor and senior management	by team members themselves and senior management
Responsibility	ensures each worker performs their specified job tasks	are cross-trained and collectively responsible for completing tasks
Performance	at first faster than a SMT as members do not have to learn how to work with each other	low at first as team learns how to work together and are cross-trained, then same rate as a traditional team
Control	uses company rules to direct workers' actions	draw upon senior management's corporate vision to guide their daily actions.
Works well with	time-pressured tasks requiring leader's knowledge to integrate various contributions	complex, challenging tasks requiring collaboration and a mix of interdependent skills

Home viewing

The film *Rumours – Classic Albums DVD* (2008) chronicles the making of one of rock music's biggest selling albums by Fleetwood Mac. The film describes the internal struggles of band members who stayed together for several years. Consider which group members performed which team roles? What was the balance between team performance and team viability? How did the interpersonal issues help or hinder their work product? What was the nature of conflict and how was it resolved? What group norms guided their behaviour? (Comer and Holbrook, 2012; Hill, 2018).

Manager-less teams

More and more organisations are choosing to get rid of layers of management, in favour of giving their teams' full autonomy. In just a few years, the concept of removing managers from their controlling and monitoring duties – and instead empowering teams to plan and manage their own day-to-day activities – has developed into the concept of self-managing teams (SMTs).

We'd expect SMTs to have no need for managers any more, meaning their role is redundant. Employees would effectively manage themselves. But is that actually happening in reality? Becoming self-managing, we have discovered, is never a simple, linear process. But to achieve a successful transition, organisations can follow a four-step implementation process that runs from *initiation* to *adoption-and-adaptation,* through to *use* and *incorporation.*

During the initiation-phase, teams have a functional leader, which implies that the power to make decisions is in the hands of their manager. An external leader tells the team what to do and how to do their tasks, and helps the inexperienced team members to acquire new skills. Managers follow a directive approach to reduce uncertainty and ambiguity among team members. In this phase, it is crucial for managers to remain functional, directive leaders by calming down members of the team and explaining what is going to happen when teams become self-managing.

In the adoption-and-adaptation-phase, managers need to transform from a directive leader to a coach. Coaching is a daily, hands-on approach that helps the employees improve their competences by slowly transferring more responsibilities to the team. Team members learn to work autonomously. During this phase, managers slowly start transferring responsibilities to team members by deciding with them who would become responsible for which tasks. Decisions are still taken by the managers, but some tasks may be devolved to individuals.

During the use-phase, the range of tasks for SMTs grows significantly. At this stage, the formal leader becomes less involved in the daily work activities of the team. They start to set their own work schedules, determine budgets, order and allocate resources and monitor service quality. The teams are already well designed and merely need help regarding unsolvable issues or disruptive events. Nevertheless, there is still need for external supervision. In this role, the manager helps team members get the necessary information to take decisions independently by connecting them with people inside and outside the organisation. During this phase, the manager is a coach who serves as a boundary spanner – supporting teams to take decisions independently but still monitoring from the outside.

Finally, in the incorporation-phase, teams become fully self-managing. Team members take over the role of managers by becoming internal leaders – either through a rotated leadership model or a peer evaluation model. This means teams either share the leadership responsibility or rotate it between members. During this last phase, it is important that managers stop taking decisions for the teams, but support and facilitate them in taking decisions and changing directions from the outside.

So can SMTs manage themselves without the help of managers? The answer depends on what we understand a manager to be. If we believe they are a directive leader, SMTs still need such a person in the beginning of the implementation process but would have no need for them when they become self-managing. However, if we believe there are other managing styles – more supportive and coaching leadership styles in which managers help team members take their own decisions by facilitating them along the way – then SMTs will always need managers. They just need a different sort of leader at the helm.

Source: Bos-Nehles et al. (2018)

Ecological framework for analysing work team effectiveness

Eric Sundstrom, Kenneth De Meuse and David Futrell's (1990) ecological framework for analysing work teamwork effectiveness provides a perspective which looks at teams as embedded within their organizations (see Figure 13.2). It holds that the effectiveness of any work team is facilitated or impeded by the team's own internal processes and the features of the organization within which it operates. The framework emphasizes the interactions between a team and the different aspects of its environment. The framework is intentionally vague about causation and timing. The spiked circular symbols in the figure stress that team effectiveness is *dynamically interrelated* with organizational context, boundaries and team development – being more of an ongoing process than a fixed end-state.

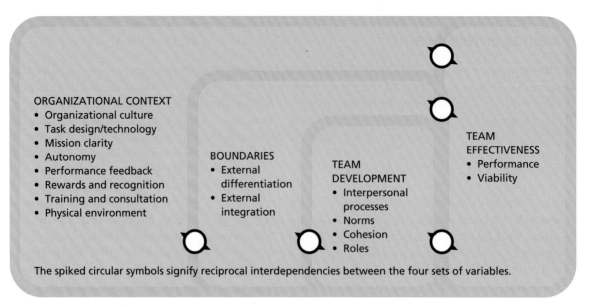

ORGANIZATIONAL CONTEXT
- Organizational culture
- Task design/technology
- Mission clarity
- Autonomy
- Performance feedback
- Rewards and recognition
- Training and consultation
- Physical environment

BOUNDARIES
- External differentiation
- External integration

TEAM DEVELOPMENT
- Interpersonal processes
- Norms
- Cohesion
- Roles

TEAM EFFECTIVENESS
- Performance
- Viability

The spiked circular symbols signify reciprocal interdependencies between the four sets of variables.

Figure 13.2: Ecological framework for analysing work team effectiveness
Source: Sundstrom et al. (1990, p. 122)

The framework also makes extensive use the concept of boundary which acts to:

- distinguish (differentiate) one team from another
- present real or symbolic barriers to the access to or transfer of information, goods or people
- serve as points of external exchange with other teams, customers, peers, competitors or other entities
- define what constitutes effectiveness for the team within its particular organization context.

The framework suggests that at any time, a team's effectiveness is the outcome of team development and the organizational context mediated by the team's boundaries. Each of these four sets of variables will be described in turn.

Organizational context

The first major variable in Sundstrom et al.'s framework is the organizational context of the work team. This refers to those features of an organization which are external to the work team, but which are relevant to the way it operates. The context consists of eight features:

1. Organizational culture

Every team operates within an organization that has its own corporate culture set within a wider, national culture. How do these values and beliefs impact on team effectiveness? Certain companies have a multi-stakeholder culture (e.g. Germany) where teamworking is more likely to succeed than in a shareholder culture (e.g. USA, Britain).

2. Task design and technology

Every team works to complete its given task in a particular way. The way that management defines the team task and specifies the technologies it will use to achieve it will affect the arrangement of individual team roles.

3. Mission clarity

If a team has a clearly defined mission or purpose within the organization it can assist those teams which are closely related to or synchronized with its work. How clear is the team's mission and how clearly has it been communicated to others?

4. Autonomy

Externally, management will determine a team's autonomy. Internally, it will depend on the role of the leader and how they delegate their authority within the team. Every effective team has to coordinate and integrate the contributions of its individual members. Which type of team leadership best achieves this?

5. Performance feedback

Does the team receive accurate, timely feedback on its performance from dependable measurement systems?

6. Rewards and recognition

These can range from financial rewards to oral praise. Are rewards sufficiently connected to performance in a way that contributes to team effectiveness?

7. Training and consultation

Training and consultation in technical skills and interpersonal processes are seen as key elements in achieving team effectiveness. Cross-training in technical skills is very often a pre-requisite for job rotation which itself can be an aspect of autonomous teamworking.

8. Physical environment

The proximity of team members to one another affects both their ability to communicate and their level of team cohesion. Whether communicating across a table during a meeting or between workstations on a factory shop floor, territories can reinforce team boundaries and encourage or inhibit exchanges. Physical environments are therefore central to group boundaries.

Organizational context affects team performance

Trevor Young-Hyman

Trevor Young-Hyman (2017) examined the organizational context of teams and in particular, how a company's formal power structure and team work structure interacted to affect cross-functional project team performance. He studied knowledge-intensive teams in a worker cooperative where power was dispersed and in a conventional engineering firm where it was concentrated in the hands of senior management. In contrast to earlier research, he found that when collective tasks were uncertain and complex, the value of cross-functional interactions depended on an organization's formal power structure. When power was concentrated, cross-functional interactions improved a team's productivity, but not when it was widely distributed among workers. He found that dispersed formal power decreased the productivity benefits of cross-functional interaction by:

- reducing status distinctions between team members which increased the time needed to resolve conflicts

- boosting participation in monitoring and coordination processes outside teams so that workers had more access to information and less need for cross-functional interactions

- increasing the distribution of knowledge management technology which increased workers' autonomy and reduced the value of cross-functional interactions.

His findings challenge assumptions about the benefits of frequent cross-functional member interaction in knowledge-intensive work. By focusing on the distribution of formal power, he illustrates how organizational resources and rules constrain or enable the actions not only of teams but also of their team members. Researchers have long argued that formal hierarchy is the best organizational form for modularized and standardized tasks and that decentralized organizational forms with distributed power are best for creativity and experimentation since workers are less constrained. Young-Hyman's findings suggest that the picture is not so clear.

Status hierarchy may actually encourage direct interpersonal knowledge exchange because areas of expertise are clearly defined and conflict is subdued through coercion. On the other hand, the equal status of team members in

→

a non-hierarchical formal power structure can stifle inter-personal knowledge exchange because of unclear roles, anticipated contentious interactions, and a lack the authority to efficiently resolve conflict. Moreover, distributed formal power encourages alternative avenues for knowledge

exchange. The key point is that the exchange required for creative work may occur through multiple avenues and different formal organizational structures facilitate different modes of knowledge exchange.

Tenerife air disaster

At 5.01 p.m. on 27 March 1977 at Tenerife airport in the Canary Islands, two 747-100 jets began taxiing along the runways, their captains in communication with the airport's traffic controllers. Four minutes later, Pan Am 1736 and KLM 4805 collided on the tarmac when the Dutch aircraft took off without permission. It led to the death of 583 people, to this day the biggest air fatality in history. A number of contextual variables came together, interrupting the routines of the cockpit and air-traffic control crews, and generating stress. These included Dutch law (pilots' work hours); difficult manoeuvres and unpredictable weather. In this stressful setting, KLM cockpit crew interaction broke down. More stress improves team performance but reduces individual performance which is lowered by task complexity. Hence the importance of a cockpit crew members coalescing into a team with a distinctive identity, rather than falling apart and acting more like individuals.

Karl Weick (1990) stated that it was unclear whether the KLM crew experienced negative synergy defined as a form of interaction between team members which caused a failure of coordination within the team so severe that nobody knew what they were supposed to be doing. It might have been that the three individuals in the cockpit acted independently and in parallel, falling back on their most familiar and well-rehearsed response routines rather than behaving as a team. The interruption of their normal operating procedures induced a high level of arousal in the crew members which reduced their cognitive information-processing abilities and led them to ignore important cues. As a result, both the cockpit crew and the air-traffic control team made the wrong responses which resulted in the deadly crash. This was an example of the context influencing individuals and teams who responded in a way that changed the context as the events unfolded. A well-functioning, high-integrated cockpit crew might have responded to the increased stress with increased performance.

🖐 **STOP AND SEARCH**   YouTube for *Tenerife air disaster.*

Work team boundaries

The second major variable in Sundstrom et al.'s framework is the set of work team boundaries. The question 'Who's in your work team?' is a simple question to ask but as Mark Mortensen and Martine Haas (2018) explain, it is now a difficult one to answer. These authors consider the blurring of team membership boundaries that has occurred in recent times. Traditionally teams have been defined as a bounded set of individuals who work interdependently to achieve a common goal. However, as teams have changed, their boundaries have become less clear. There is no longer a clear delineation between who is and is not a team member. Today's work teams look quite different from their predecessors which were composed of stable, full-time, co-located members. They are now:

- *Fluid*: individuals move in and out of them during the course of their work
- *Overlapping*: individuals work in several different teams simultaneously
- *Dispersed*: individuals work in different geographical locations and organizational units

Collectively these factors result in individual uncertainty and collective disagreement about who is a team member. A person can consider a team's membership to be composed of named individuals on a staff list; or those who label themselves team members or are so labelled by others; or those whose interaction patterns suggest membership. Individual uncertainty about team membership may arise because an individual is not sure which criterion to use in a given situation at a given point in time. Using different criteria results in different understandings of who is or is not a team member.

Collective disagreement occurs when, even if individual team members are certain in their own minds about who is and is not a team member, they may disagree with one another. Wageman et al. (2007) found that when top executives were asked to list their team members, fewer than 10 per cent were in agreement, while in Mortensen and Hinds' (2002) study of product development teams up to 25 per cent of their membership was contested.

Mortensen and Haas (2018) recommend defining teams in terms of participation rather than membership. While 'membership' is binary (you either belong or you do not), 'participation' is continuous, and can vary in terms of degree, time, roles played and colleagues worked with. They advise viewing teams as dynamic hubs of participants rather than as clearly bounded groups of members. These hubs represent centres of activity with which individuals connect in different ways at different times as they contribute to the team goal.

What did they find? Team boundary permeability

Rebekah Dibble and Cristina Gibson (2018) examined the research on team membership change and team boundary permeability. This refers to the ease with which workers can cross team boundaries. Many of today's teams are dynamic and permeable with workers moving quickly and easily in and out of them. For example, doctors, contract workers and consultants are now required to move seamlessly in and out of teams dealing with patient care, software development and corporate strategy implementation. Much collective work in companies takes place outside the realm of clearly bounded teams. Increasingly, units labelled 'teams' are less identifiable as such or remain intact for long. What factors did Dibble and Gibson find which facilitated or impeded the movement of people across team boundaries? **(Answers in chapter Recap).**

Cristina Gibson

While working to complete an assigned task (e.g. improving a procedure; designing a new product; winning a match), a team has to meet the needs of the larger organization within which it is embedded (external integration). At the same time, it has to secure enough independence to allow it to get on with its own work (external differentiation). These two features define every team's boundary. Boundary management refers to the process by which teams manage their interactions with other parts of their organization. How successfully a team manages its boundaries will affect its performance.

External work team differentiation the degree to which a work team stands out from its organizational context in terms of its membership, temporal scope and territory.

External work team differentiation refers to the team as a whole in relation to the rest of the organization (team-organization focus). For example, a temporary team may be assembled by management and given resources to deal with a crisis. This team thus stands out and hence *differs* from other work units within the company by virtue of containing an identifiable collection of people (membership); working in a specific place (territory); over a set period of time (temporal scope); on a unique task.

Four features define the team's boundary, distinguishing it from other teams within an organization:

Team membership	The identity of the individuals treated as members by both the team and the organization is crucial. Who decides the composition and size of a work team?
Team territory	A work team has to have its 'own turf' to establish its identity and manage its external relations, especially in teams whose missions demand both external integration and differentiation.
Temporal scope	The longer a work team exists and the more time its members spend cooperating, the greater will be its temporal scope and differentiation as a distinct team.
Team task	The task given to the team may be *additive* (accomplishment depends on the sum of all members' efforts); *conjunctive* (depends on the performance of the least talented member); or *disjunctive* (depends on the performance of the most talented member).

Internal work team differentiation the degree to which a team's members possess different skills and knowledge that contributes towards the achievement of the team's objective.

Internal work team differentiation refers to the degree to which a team's members possess different skills and knowledge that contribute towards the achievement of the team's objective. A team may have high differentiation with its members having special, perhaps unique skills such as the cockpit crew in an aircraft; or it may have low differentiation, when the knowledge and contributions of members tend to be similar as in a quality circle team.

Differentiation within the peloton

The Tour de France cycle race was first run in 1903 and now involves about 150 top cyclists. The racers cover over 2,700 miles during their 23-day journey and the winner receives a €400,000 prize. The competitors ride together in the *peloton* – the picturesque mob of competing teams that fly like birds in formation across the French countryside every summer. Despite the focus on individual riders, the Tour is a sport structured around the teams. The 2018 Tour involved 22 teams, 176 riders from 30 countries including Team Sky, Team Sunweb and Bahrain–Merida. During each 125-mile, five-hour stage, team members fight to put their leader in a position to win. What appears to be a random mass of bicycles is really an orderly, complex web of shifting alliances, crossed with brutal competition, designed to keep or acquire the market's most valuable currency – energy.

A cycling team consists of six to nine riders, each of whom is a specialist. The *rouleurs* are fast riders who create draughts for their team's leader over flat terrain. Riding close behind a rouleur can reduce drag by 40 per cent. *Grimpeurs* are hill specialists who create a slipstream (a field of low wind resistance) for their leader as he goes up mountains, and *domestiques* are riders who carry supplies. Towards the end of the race, team members will bunch together ahead of their sprinter, shielding him from the wind for as long as possible, while leaving a space to let him break out near the finish line (Hochman, 2006).

 **STOP AND SEARCH**   YouTube for *Tour de France guide: peloton* (1:32).

External work team integration the degree to which a work team is linked with the larger organization of which it is a part.

External work team integration refers to the degree to which a work team is linked with the larger organization of which it is a part. It is measured in terms of how its goals and activities are coordinated and synchronized with those of other managers, peers, customers and suppliers inside and outside the company. This will depend on the type of team and its task.

Team development

The third major variable in Sundstrom et al.'s framework concerns the internal development of the team. Four factors are relevant here – interpersonal processes, roles, norms and cohesion.

1. Interpersonal processes

A group of individuals passes through a series of stages before achieving effective performance at the performing stage. Tuckman's and Jensen's (1977) model describes the characteristics of each preceding stage – forming, storming and norming.

2. Roles

Roles in general are a defining feature of a team and the role of a leader is much studied. Are the required member roles being performed given the group's tasks and are the task and interpersonal aspects of the leadership role being fulfilled?

3. Norms

Are the norms and rules of behaviour which are agreed on by the team members supportive or in conflict with effective performance? Can organizational culture be used to modify team norms?

4. Cohesion

Team cohesion can engender mutual cooperation, generosity and helping behaviour, motivating team members to contribute fully. However, it can also stifle creative thinking as individuals seek to 'fit in' and not to 'rock the boat'. Small group size, similar attitudes, and physical proximity of workspaces have all been found to encourage cohesion. Does the level of cohesion aid or impede the team's effectiveness?

Team performance a measure of how well a team achieves its task, and the needs of management, customers or shareholders.

Team viability a measure of how well a team meets the needs and expectations of its members.

Team effectiveness

Team effectiveness is the dependent variable in the Sundstrom et al. framework and is measured using two criteria – performance and viability. Team performance is externally focused and concerns meeting the needs and expectations of outsiders such as customers, company colleagues or fans. It is assessed using measures such as quantity, quality and time. Meanwhile, team viability is the social dimension, which is internally focused and concerns the enhancement of the team's capability to perform effectively in the future. Team viability indicators include its degree of cohesion, shared purpose and the level of team member commitment. The two are closely related since there is a possibility that a team may get a job done but self-destructs in the process.

Google's perfect team

"On paper we have the perfect team."

In 2012 Google became focused on building the perfect team and initiated Project Aristotle to discover why certain teams succeeded while others failed. The company studied 180 teams from all over the company. However, they were unable to find any patterns. Surprisingly, they found no evidence that the composition of a team made any difference to its performance. Abeer Dubey, a manager in Google's People Analytics division stated that 'We had lots of data, but there was nothing showing that a mix of specific personality types or skills or backgrounds made any difference. The 'who' part of the equation didn't seem to matter.' Indeed, there were two teams with nearly identical member composition with overlapping memberships that had radically different levels of effectiveness.

In the end, the researchers concluded that it was psychological safety that was critical to making a team work. This is defined as a shared belief held by members that interpersonal risk-taking is safe within the team. It is a sense of confidence that the individual will not be embarrassed, rejected or punished for speaking up. It describes a team climate characterized by interpersonal trust and mutual respect in which people are comfortable being themselves (Edmondson, 1999, 2012).

For Project Aristotle, the data indicated that psychological safety was most critical to making a team work. They had to get people to establish psychologically safe environments. The two main behaviours that contributed to psychological safety were conversational turn-taking, that is, ensuring that team members spoke roughly the same amount during a meeting, and social sensitivity, that is, intuiting how others were feeling based on their tone of voice, their expressions and other nonverbal cues ('ostentatious listening'). These two behaviours are part of the same unwritten rules we turn to as individuals when we need to establish a bond with another person. This is as important at work as outside it (Duhigg, 2016).

 **STOP AND SEARCH** YouTube for *How Google builds the perfect team* (2:23) and for *Amy Edmondson: Building a psychologically safe workplace TED talk* (11:27).

 **RECAP**

1. *Understand why 'team' is a contested concept in the organizational literature.*

   - Teamworking is being increasingly adopted as a favoured form of work organization in different companies and industries around the world.

   - The different purposes and ways in which managers have introduced this innovation has meant that the term 'team' is used to describe a wide range of radically different working arrangements.

2. *List the nine dimensions of team autonomy.*

   - Gulowsen's nine dimensions of team autonomy are selection of the team leader; acceptance of new member into the team; distribution of work; time flexibility; acceptance of additional work; representation outside the team; production methods (choice of); production goals (output determination); production goals (quality determination)

3. *Differentiate between four major types of teams and give an example of each.*

   - Teams in organizations can be classified as advice (e.g. quality circles); action (e.g. surgery team); project (e.g. cross-functional team); and production (e.g. autonomous work team).

4. *Discuss the types of obstacles to effectiveness experienced by each type of team.*

   - Advice teams frequently lack authority to implement their recommendations. Action teams can fail to integrate their members' contributions sufficiently closely. Project team members can suffer 'divided loyalties' between their team and their home department. Production teams may lack autonomy for job satisfaction.

5. *Contrast Western with Japanese concepts of teamworking.*

   - The Western concept is based upon principles of empowerment and online teamworking, while the Japanese concept is based upon management principles of individual working on-line, and teams advising off-line.

6. *List the four main variables in ecological framework for analysing work team effectiveness.*

   - Team development; work team boundaries and organizational context affect team effectiveness.

7. *Understand the continuing importance of teamworking.*

   - Japanese forms of teamworking (Toyotaism) have influenced the production processes used in both manufacturing and service industries all around the world.

   - As a concept, teamworking has an appeal in a management philosophy that stresses egalitarianism, non-hierarchy and inclusiveness within organizations.

RECAP: What did they find?

Dibble and Gibson (2018) found four factors which facilitated or impeded the movement of people across team boundaries. These were team boundedness, membership model diversity, team member receptivity and inter-team integration.

- *Team boundedness:* The extent to which members are involved in a team. It depends on the extent to which members serve for the full cycle of the project as opposed to only part of the project; have full-versus part-time assignment to the team; and are assigned to core versus peripheral positions on the team. It ranges from high to low boundedness.

- *Membership model diversity:* Refers to the degree that team members share a common view as to who is a member of their group and who is not. This is indicated by formal team rosters; identification by the team members themselves or by others; or by patterns of team member interaction. When members disagree as to who is or is not in a team, it makes it easier for new members to enter and exit the team and vice versa.

- *Team member receptivity:* Refers to the ways in which a team responds to new members who join the team. It concerns a team's preparedness to adapt to the newcomer; to use that person's unique knowledge and skills to do its work; and its willingness to accept them as a full member. When a team does these things, the newcomer experiences a commitment to the team, a feeling of attachment to it and an obligation to remain in it. These factors facilitate an individual's entry into a team but make it harder for them to exit the team.

- *Inter-team integration:* This refers to the degree to which teams in different parts of an organization are integrated with each other because of overlapping memberships. When integration is high, it facilitates movement of individuals across a team boundary. In contrast, the greater the segmentation and uniqueness of the different teams whose boundaries one is required to cross, the more movement between them will be impeded.

Revision

1. Self-managing teams are heavily promoted in the literature. What are the costs and benefits of these to (a) the management that establishes them and (b) the individuals who are members of such teams?

2. What impact can technology have on the behaviour and performance of teams? Discuss positive and negative effects, illustrating your answer with examples.

3. 'Autonomous team is a relative term'. Discuss the concept of team autonomy explaining why similarly labelled teams may, in practice, operate very differently. Consider why management might have difficulty in increasing the autonomy that it gives to a team.

4. Highlight briefly the main differences between West European and Japanese-style teamworking. Then, using references to the literature, consider the positive and negative aspects of both systems for either shop floor workers or management.

Research assignment

Using your library and internet, locate any relevant research and management literature on effective teamworking and devise a list of best practice 'do's' and 'don'ts', and use it to develop a list of questions. Select an organization; interview a team member, a team leader or a manager responsible for a team. Begin by determining the team's purpose, method of working, performance and the challenges that it faces. Write a brief report assessing the team against your best practice list items from the research literature.

Springboard

Mark Mortensen and Martine Haas, (2018). 'Perspective—rethinking teams: From bounded membership groups to dynamic participation hubs', *Organization Science*, 29(2): 341–55. The authors discuss the latest thinking about the operation of groups in organizations.

Thomas O'Neill and Eduardo Salas (2018) 'Creating high performance teamwork in organizations', *Human Resource Management Review*, 28(4): 325–31. The authors review the trends in the use of teams and the challenges of achieving high performance teamwork.

Matthias Weiss and Martin Hoegl (2015) 'The history of teamwork's societal diffusion: A multi-method review', *Small Group Research*, 46(6): 589–622. The authors consider the progress of academic research on teamwork and its diffusion through society over time.

Amanda Sinclair (1992) 'The tyranny of team ideology', *Organization Studies*, 13(4): 611–26. The author criticises management's obsession with teams.

OB cinema

The Dish (2000, director Rob Sitch). DVD track 8: 0:35:55–0:53:07 (18 minutes sequenced)

It is July 1969, and Apollo 11 is heading towards the moon. On earth, the Parkes Radio Telescope in New South Wales, Australia, the largest in the southern hemisphere has been designated by NASA as the primary receiving station for the moonwalk which it will broadcast to the world. Then, due to a power cut, it 'loses' Apollo 11! Parkes' director, Cliff Buxton (played by Sam Neill) and his team of scientists – Mitch (Kevin Harrington); Glenn (Tom Long); and Al (Patrick Warburton) – all have to work hard (and quickly) to solve the problem. The clip begins with the lights going out during the dance, and ends with Al saying, 'Just enough time to check the generator'.

Identify examples of each of the elements of Sundstrom et al.'s ecological framework for analysing work team effectiveness as team members deal with the crisis.

Sundstrom framework element	Example
Organizational context	
1. Organizational culture	
2. Task design / technology	
3. Mission clarity	
4. Autonomy	
5. Performance feedback	
6. Rewards and recognition	
7. Physical environment	
8. Training and consultation	
Work team boundaries	
9. External differentiation	
10. External integration	
Team development	
11. Interpersonal processes	
12. Norms	
13. Cohesion	
14. Roles	

Chapter exercises

1. Factors affecting team performance

Objectives
1. Identify the various factors that influence a team's success or failure.
2. Reflect on students' own experiences of working in a team.

Briefing
1. Divide into groups of 3–4.
2. Individually, think about a team or group of which you have been a member. This could have been for a group assignment at university, a team at work or a leisure team such as a sports team, choir, or something similar. Assess how well this team functioned. Use the questionnaire below to rate your team. Think about your overall experience of it and its dynamics and performance.

Team Evaluation Form

Team feature	Think about a team or group of which you have been a member. Assess how well this team functioned using the four-point scale (4 = *strongly agree*; 1 = *strongly disagree*).	*Rate 1–4*
Cohesion	Members were supportive of each other.	
	Members treated each other with respect.	
	Members collaborated with each other – worked together to solve problems, make decisions, and produce results.	
	Members showed a professional attitude to their work with the team.	

→

Team Evaluation Form

Communication	Members communicated well with each other, making sure that all relevant issues were brought before the team.
	Members listened well to each other by withholding judgements until all members had spoken.
Goal orientation	Team members knew what was required of them.
	Team members all worked toward a common purpose.
Task planning and coordination	Team was well organized.
	Team managed meetings well.
	Team effectively distributed work among its members.
Accountability	Members took responsibility for tasks.
	Members met deadlines.
Leadership	Team had a leader
	Members were supportive of the team leader.
	(If your team did not have a leader, leave this rating blank)
Conflict resolution	Team overcame conflicts and interpersonal problems in order to accomplish goals and objectives.
	(If your team did not have any conflict, leave this rating blank)

Source: adapted from Chapman et al. (2010, p.47)

3. Score your questionnaire. All the statements are positive so the higher the number the better your team worked together (and vice versa).

4. Share your scores with your group members. Explain the type of team that you were rating and the reasons for its score focusing on items where you ticked 'Strongly disagree' or 'Strongly agree'. Mention any leadership or conflict blanks.

5. Once group members have shared their evaluations, prepare a list of do's and don'ts as a guide for team members and team leaders.

2. Land Rock Alliance Insurance

Objectives

1. To evaluate the advantages and disadvantages of teamworking arrangements within an organization.

2. To identify conditions favouring the introduction of different forms of working arrangements.

Briefing

1. Individually, read the case study concerning the two different proposed work arrangements for the processing of the insurance claims at Land Rock Alliance Insurance's offices in Edinburgh.

2. Divide into groups, nominate a spokesperson and:

   a. Consider the advantages and disadvantages of Eleanor Brennan's teamworking arrangements for (i) the employees and (ii) the management of the company.

   b. Consider the advantages and disadvantages of Thomas Campion's proposed work fragmentation arrangements for (i) the employees and (ii) the management of the company.

   c. Opt for one or other of the two managers' work organization solutions or suggest a solution of your own.

d. More generally, under what conditions in a company is (i) teamworking, and (ii) fragmented task working, likely to be most beneficial?

Group spokespersons should be ready to report their group's conclusions to the class.

Case study

Background

Since the 1940s, the use of asbestos in building materials and other products has led to many claims for damages as a result of personal injury or wrongful death. The procedure for those making claims is complicated and time-consuming. Insurance companies employ groups of employees trained to process the claims from each particular industry. The employees are given information on the history, use and current medical research results on the product. The processing of each individual claim application form is tedious but very important: any mistakes may affect the total amount paid to the claimant. Land Rock Alliance Insurance has successfully bid for the contract to process the claims for over 213,000 asbestosis-related chest impaired cases (ACD) and vibration white finger (VWF) victims, their partners or descendants.

The company

Land Rock Alliance Insurance's main office is based in Sheffield, England. The company has decided to open a branch office in Edinburgh to manage the new contract. It will be dedicated to processing the asbestosis and VWF claims. The plan is to hire 60 new employees including supervisors and line managers. Senior managers at head office, however, disagree on how the work should be organized at the new office.

Planning meeting

At the meeting to review how the work will be organized at the Edinburgh office, Eleanor Brennan, the HR director, suggested it would be more effective and efficient to create four teams of around 15 employees, with each team processing the claims according to geographical area: Scotland, Wales, Northern England and Southern England. She explained that each application form would be processed by team members, to enable each member to complete the whole processing task and to contribute to the recommendation of the final settlement. Presenting some of the advantages of teamworking, Eleanor commented, 'the synergy generated by teamworking and communication will enhance efficiency and motivate employees to actively participate in reaching a decision in optimum time'. She argued that there was a direct link between job enrichment and high performance.

However, the director of facilities, Thomas Campion, strongly disagreed. He informed the assembled management team that in his opinion, 'self-regulated teams were b*** s***!' Besides, work teams required a much longer training period for employees. Moreover, it was his belief that increased communication impeded decision making rather than enhanced it'. Campion, continuing to dominate the meeting, outlined an alternative work arrangement for the processing of claimants' forms. The work, he said, was to be divided into three major steps:

Step 1: Scrutinize and verify biographical details, date of birth, gender.

Step 2: Scrutinize and verify employment details, start/end/job description.

Step 3: Scrutinize and verify medical history including lifestyle (such as smoker or non-smoker, or whether there was evidence of exposure to second-hand smoke).

Of the 60 new employees, 20 would be trained to complete task one, 20 to complete task two, and 20 to complete task three. Each major step in the claim process would also have a supervisor, a technical advisor and section manager. Organizing the work this way, Campion insisted, would optimize training time, and enable the easy replacement of any employee resigning from the company. Individual employees would be assigned a target to achieve each month, which would determine an annual bonus payment. Every six months, their section manager would appraise each employee based on how quickly he or she successfully processed the application forms.

Source: Bratton et al., (2007, p. 317)

References

Bos-Nehles, A.C., Renkema, M. and Bondarouk, T. (2018) 'Is it possible to manage without managers? With the right processes in place, self-managing teams are more than just a nice idea', *People Management*, 5 January, London: Chartered Institute of Personnel and Development (CIPD).

Bratton, J., Callinan, M., Forshaw, C. and Sawchuk, P. (2007) *Work and Organizational Behaviour*, Houndmills, Basingstoke: Palgrave Macmillan.

Brown, D., Cheng, S., Melian, V., Parker, K. and Solow, M. (2015) *Global Human Capital Trends 2015: Leading in the New World of Work.* Deloitte University Press.

Buchanan, D. A. (1994) 'Cellular manufacture and the role of teams' in J. Storey (ed.), *New Wave Manufacturing Strategies: Organizational and Human Resource Management Dimensions*, London: Paul Chapman Publishing, pp. 204–25.

Chapman, K.J., Meuter, M.L., Toy, D., and Wright, L.K. (2010) 'Are student groups dysfunctional? Perspectives from both sides of the classroom', *Journal of Marketing Education*, 32(1): 39–49.

Cohen, S.G. and Ledford, G.E. (1994) 'The effectiveness of self-managing teams: a quasi-experiment', *Human Relations*, 47(1): 13–43.

Comer, D.R. and Holbrook, R.L. (2012) 'Getting behind the scenes of Fleetwood Mac's Rumours: using a documentary on making a music album to learn about task groups', *Journal of Management*, 36(4): 544–67.

Coutu, D. (2009) 'Why teams don't work', *Harvard Business Review*, 87(5): 99–105.

Daft, R.L. and Noe, R.A.(2001) *Organizational Behaviour*, San Diego, CA: Harcourt Inc.

Dibble, R. and Gibson, C.B. (2018) 'Crossing team boundaries: a theoretical model of team boundary permeability and a discussion of why it matters', *Human Relations* 71(7): 925-50.

Druskat, V.U. and Wheeler, J.V. (2004) 'How to lead a self-managing team', *MIT Sloan Management Review*, 45(4): 65–71.

Duhigg, C. (2016) 'What Google learned from its quest to build the perfect team', *New York Times*, 25 February, https://www.nytimes.com/2016/02/28/magazine/what-google-learned-from-its-quest-to-build-the-perfect-team.html?mcubz=0 [accessed January 2019]

Edmondson, A. (1999) 'Psychological safety and learning behavior in work teams', *Administrative Science Quarterly*, 44(2): 350–83.

Edmondson, A. (2012) 'Teamwork on the fly', *Harvard Business Review*, 90(4): 72–80.

Edmondson, A.C. (2016) 'Wicked problem solvers: Lessons from successful cross-industry teams', *Harvard Business Review*, 94(6): 53–59.

Edwards, D (2011) *I'm Feeling Lucky: The Confessions of Google Employee Number 59*, London Allan Lane.

Ginnett, R. C. (1993) 'Crews as groups: their formation and leadership' in E. L. Wiener, B. G. Kanki and R. L. Helmreich (eds.), *Cockpit Resource Management* (pp. 71–98). San Diego, CA: Academic Press.

Gulowsen, J. (1979) 'A measure of work-group autonomy' in L. E. Davis and J. C. Taylor (eds.), *Design of Jobs*, second edition, Santa Monica: Goodyear, pp. 206–18.

Han, S.J. and Beyerlein, M. (2016) 'Framing the effects of multinational cultural diversity on virtual team processes', *Small Group Research*, 47(4): 351–83.

Hare, A. P. (1992) *Groups, Teams and Social Interaction*, New York: Praeger.

Hayes, N. (1997) *Successful Team Management.* London: International Thompson Business Press.

Hill, A. (2018) 'When partners go their own way, the band plays on', *Financial Times*, 16 April, https://www.ft.com/content/1e7c5848-3e38-11e8-b7e0-52972418fec4 [accessed January 2019]

Hill, G.W. (1991) 'Why quality circles failed but total quality management might succeed', *British Journal of Industrial Relations*, 29(4): 517–39.

Hochman, P. (2006) 'Pack mentality', *Fortune*, 1 June.

Huckman, R. and Staats, B. (2013) 'The hidden benefits of keeping teams intact', *Harvard Business Review*, 91(12): 27–29.

Hutchins, E. (1990) 'The technology of team navigation'. In J. Galegher, R. E. Kraut and C. Egido (eds.), *Intellectual Teamwork: Social and Technological Foundations of Co-operative Work*, pp. 191–220, Hillsdale, NJ: Lawrence Erlbaum Associates.

Jones, L.K., Jennings, B.M. Higgins, M.K. and de Waal, F.B.M. (2018) 'Ethological observations of social behaviour in the operating room', *Proceedings of the National Academy of Sciences of the United States of America (PNAS)*, 2 July, 201716883.

Keller, S. and Meaney, M. (2017) 'High-performing teams: a timeless leadership topic', *McKinsey Quarterly*, June.

Lencioni, P. (2002) *The Five Dysfunctions of a Team: A Leadership Fable*, San Francisco: Jossey Bass.

McChrystal, S. (2015) *Team of Teams: New Rules of Engagement for a Complex World*, Portfolio Penguin.

Magpili, N.C. and Pazos, P. (2018) 'Self-managing team performance: a systematic review of multilevel input factors', *Small Group Research,* 49(1): 3–33.

Marchington, M. (1992) *Managing the Team: A Guide to Successful Employee Involvement.* Oxford: Blackwell.

Mortensen, M. and Haas, M.R. (2018) 'Perspective-rethinking teams: from bounded membership to dynamic participation, *Organization Science,* 29(2): 341–55.

Mortensen M. and Hinds P.J. (2002) 'Fuzzy teams: boundary disagreement in distributed and collocated teams' in Hinds P.J. and Kiesler S. (eds.), *Distributed Work,* Cambridge, MA: MIT Press, pp. 281–308.

Naquin, C. E., and Tynan, R. O. (2003) 'The team halo effect: why teams are not blamed for their failures', *Journal of Applied Psychology,* 88(2), pp. 332–40.

National Aeronautics and Space Administration (2011) 'NASA's response to mine disaster remembered', 14 October, http://www.nasa.gov/news/chile_assistance .html [accessed January 2019]

Rashid, F., Edmondson, A.C. and Leonard, H.B. (2013) 'Leadership lessons from the Chilean mine rescue', *Harvard Business Review,* 91(7/8): 113–19.

Sinclair, A. (1992) 'The tyranny of team ideology', *Organization Studies,* 13(4); 611–26.

Steijn, B. (2001) 'Work systems, quality of working life and attitudes of workers: an empirical study towards the effects of team and non-teamwork', *New Technology, Work and Employment,* 16(3):191–203.

Sundstrom, E., De Meuse, K.P., and Futrell, D. (1990) 'Work teams: applications and effectiveness', *American Psychologist,* 45(2): 120–33.

The Economist (2017) 'Schumpeter: Team spirit', 19 March, p.68.

Training (1996) 'What self-managing teams manage, 1996 Industry report, 33(10): 69.

Tuckman, B.W. and Jensen, M.A.C. (1977) 'Stages of small group development revisited', *Group and Organizational Studies,* 2(4): 419–27.

Wageman, R., Nunes, D.A., Burruss, J.A. and Hackman, J.R. (2007) *Senior Leadership Teams,* Boston, MA: Harvard Business School Press.

Weiner, E. L., Kanki, B. G., and Helmreich, R. L. (eds.) (1993) *Cockpit Resource Management.,* New York: Academic Press.

Weiss, M. and Hoegl, M. (2015) 'The history of teamwork's societal diffusion: a multi-method review', *Small Group Research,* 46(6): 589–622.

Weick, K. E. (1990) 'The vulnerable system: an analysis of the Tenerife air disaster', *Journal of Management,* 16(3): 571–93.

Young-Hyman, P. (2017) 'Co-operating without co-labouring: how formal organizational power moderates cross-functional interaction in project teams', *Administrative Science Quarterly,* 62(1): 179–214.

Part 4 Management and organization

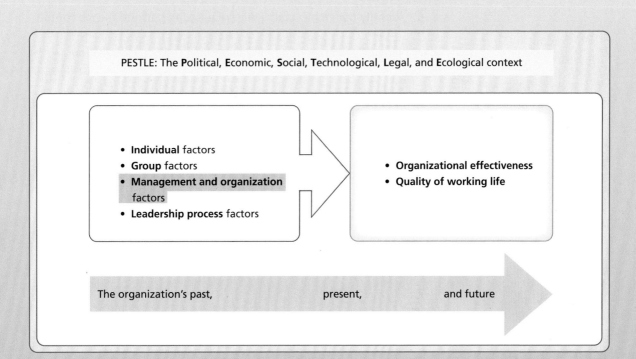

PESTLE: The Political, Economic, Social, Technological, Legal, and Ecological context

- **Individual** factors
- **Group** factors
- **Management and organization** factors
- **Leadership process** factors

- **Organizational effectiveness**
- **Quality of working life**

The organization's past,   present,   and future

CHAPTER 14

Work design

Key terms

work design

scientific management

systematic soldiering

initiative and incentive system

time-and-motion studies

Fordism

mass production

lean working

McDonaldization

technical feasibility

Learning outcomes

When you have read this chapter, you should be able to define those key terms in your own words, and you should also be able to:

1. Identify the factors that influence choices in the process of work design.

2. Describe the main objectives and principles of the scientific management approach.

3. Identify the contributions of the Gilbreths to scientific management.

4. Understand how Fordism developed out of Taylorism.

5. Explain the relationship between jobs, tasks, skills and technology changes.

6. Identify the employability skills required to perform the jobs of the future.

7. Provide examples of digital Taylorism in today's organizations.

Why study work design?

Work design the content and organization of an employee's work tasks, activities, relationships and responsibilities.

Work design refers to the content and organization of an employee's work tasks, activities, relationships, and responsibilities (Parker, 2014). High-quality work design is a key determinant of employee well-being, positive work attitudes, and job/organizational performance. It affects work stress, job satisfaction, absenteeism, accidents, team innovation, company profits and much more.

The problem is that many job incumbents are currently experiencing deskilled and demotivating work. Studying and understanding work design can help to foster the more widespread design of higher quality work (e.g. reducing low-skilled jobs in retail, personal services and call centres); improve our understanding of the effects of contemporary technological, economic and social changes on work (e.g. the 'uberfication' of the economy); and can enhance the successful implementation of work redesign (e.g. reducing the risk and complexity inherent in re-designing jobs).

Home viewing

Office Space, (1998, director Mike Judge) follows the progress of Peter Gibbons (played by Ron Livingston) an employee of the computer company *Initech.* His behaviour is driven by the nature of his work and imminent loss of his job due to downsizing. Peter shows signs of alienation, particularly feelings of powerlessness, meaninglessness and self-estrangement. He tells his hypnotherapist: 'Ever since I started working, every single day of my life, has been worse than the day before it. So that means that every single day that you see me, that's on the worst day of my life.' What aspects of the design of his job might account for this?

 **STOP AND SEARCH** YouTube for *Matthew Taylor, James Manyika: Who's in control of the gig economy [1 of 2]* (2:21).

Influences on work design

Sharon Parker

Sharon Parker and her colleagues (2017) ask the question: what causes variation in the design of individual jobs? Their answer begins with the observation that all organizations have goals to achieve and need to solve the twin problems of how to divide labour and integrate effort. Labour division involves task division and task allocation, while effort integration requires cooperation and coordination through the provision of information and rewards. How organizations solve these two problems of organizing leads to their choices about work design.

Reviewing the research literature, these authors identify four classes of influences, each with its own sub-elements which combine uniquely in each organization to produce a particular kind of job for an employee to do (Figure 14.1). Let us consider each in turn.

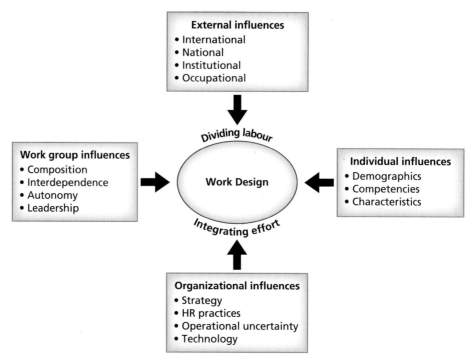

Figure 14.1: Influences on work design
Source: adapted from Parker et al. (2017a, p.270)

External influences

- *International:* Overseas competition raises job insecurity and expectations about having to work harder affects job design. An outsourcing company can coerce its suppliers to adopt a cost-minimization strategy that creates poor quality jobs.

- *National:* Countries with strong economies have jobs with lower workloads and greater autonomy, skill variety and challenge. There is little evidence that national culture affects work design.

- *Institutional:* Union resistance to job simplification, employment protection legislation, welfare provision and full employment all shape work design. National training systems increase managers' willingness to enrich jobs.

- *Occupational:* Occupations shape the formal and informal distribution of tasks, influencing the skills used in the performance of those tasks. This enables employees to perform certain activities which affect work design.

Organizational influences

- *Strategy:* Those companies with a mass production strategy making standardized products at the lowest cost adopt low-skill, low-paid work designs. Those with a quality and innovation strategy use high-involvement, enriched work designs with high employee discretion and challenging tasks.

- *HR practices:* High-involvement human resources (HR) practices like flexible working (flexi-time, home working) can directly affect work design by altering employee autonomy or indirectly by changing how employees respond to or perform their work tasks.

- *Operational uncertainty:* When the production process is unpredictable due to changing goals, inputs, tasks and outputs, operational efficiency is maximized by using enriched job designs with high job discretion and task variety allowing staff to cope with unexpected demands. When uncertainty is low, the opposite is the case.

- *Technology:* Lean production technology increases employee workloads and limits opportunities for employees to control their work. In contrast, advanced manufacturing technologies increase job variety, autonomy and interdependence.
- *Bureaucracy:* Written rules, job specialization and hierarchy reduce job discretion, task variety and skill utilization. However, they can also lessen role ambiguity and role conflict and enrich work by using formal procedures to coordinate challenging, interdependent roles.

Work group influences

- *Composition:* Heterogeneity in membership creates a richer pool of knowledge, skills and abilities for a group to draw upon to perform a wider range of tasks by increasing task variety and thereby improving work design.
- *Interdependence:* Members' need to interact and coordinate with each other to complete a group task can either have a positive effect on work design (by increasing individual responsibility and providing social interaction and mutual support opportunities) or a negative effect (as tighter coordination reduces individuals' job autonomy).
- *Autonomy:* Self-managing work teams can make their own decisions about the division of labour which impacts on individual work design. It leads to greater job discretion and task variety.
- *Leadership:* Group leaders' decisions about the division of labour and task coordination shape the individual work design of the group members.

Individual influences

- *Demographics:* An employee's age, gender and ethnicity signals to managers who design the work whether a person is competent, physically able, and trustworthy to perform it. Tasks and training opportunities are allocated on these bases.
- *Competencies:* Employee competencies encourage managers to enrich job holder's work design. Competent employees have work delegated to them because they are trusted to perform it effectively.
- *Characteristics:* Employees' personality traits can influence managers' decisions about whom to select for particular jobs thereby enabling or restricting work designs for certain classes of employees. These traits shape employees choice of occupation, increase their chances of expressing particular work behaviours, and affect their decision to adapt their work designs.

Scientific management

Between 1880 and 1910 the United States underwent major and rapid industrialization, including the creation of its first large corporations like Standard Oil Trust (Esso), General Motors and Ford. These firms used new technologies of production and employed large workforces. The workers in these new factories came from agricultural regions of America or were immigrants from Europe. The fact that they had little knowledge of the English language, possessed few job skills and had no experience of factory work, were major problems for company managers. Scientific management offered a solution, and represented one of the first organizational practices capable of being applied in different companies. It introduced a formal system of industrial discipline.

At the start of the twentieth century most products were hand-made by skilled craftsmen and women making shoes, dresses, bicycles and other goods. They used general-purpose machine tools such as lathes, sewing machines, drills and hammers. It took them years of training to acquire the necessary skills and experience.

They could read a blueprint, visualize the final product, and possessed a level of hand–eye coordination and gentleness of touch that allowed them to manufacture the required item. However, there were insufficient numbers of them to permit mass production. It was against this background that Frederick Taylor and Henry Ford developed and implemented their ideas.

Taylorism

Scientific management a form of job design which stresses short, repetitive work cycles; detailed, prescribed task sequences; a separation of task conception from task execution; and motivation based on economic rewards.

Systematic soldiering the conscious and deliberate restriction of output by operators.

Scientific management is also known as *Taylorism* and in this chapter the two terms are used interchangeably. Frederick Winslow Taylor was the world's first efficiency expert. He was born into a wealthy Philadelphia Quaker family in 1856. Taylor joined the Midvale Steel Company in 1878 where he developed his ideas, rising to the position of shop superintendent. He observed that workers used different and mostly inefficient work methods and rarely ever worked at the speed of which they were capable. He contrasted natural soldiering (i.e. the inclination to take it easy) with what he labelled systematic soldiering which was the conscious and deliberate restriction of output by operators. Taylor attributed systematic soldiering to a number of factors:

- The view among the workers that an increase in output would result in redundancies.
- Poor management controls which enabled them to work slowly in order to protect their own best interests.
- The choice of methods of work which were left entirely to the discretion of the workers who wasted a large part of their efforts using inefficient and untested rules-of-thumb.

Initiative and incentive system a form of job design in which management gives workers a task to perform, provides them with the financial incentive to complete it, but then leaves them to use their own initiative as to how they will perform it.

Systematic soldiering was facilitated by the use of the initiative and incentive system within the company. This involved management specifying production requirements; providing workers with incentives in the form of a piece rate bonus; and leaving them to use their own initiative in deciding how best to organize their work and what tools to use. In Taylor's view, not only did this result in wasted effort but also, and more importantly, workers kept their craft secrets to themselves and worked at a collectively agreed rate that was below their ability. Taylor argued that managers should exercise full responsibility for the planning, coordinating and controlling of work, including selecting the tools to be used, (management work), thereby leaving workers free to execute the specified tasks (shop floor work).

Appalled by what he regarded as the inefficiency of industrial practices, Taylor took steps to increase production by reducing the variety of work methods used by the workers. He showed how management and workforce could both benefit from adopting his more efficient work arrangements. His objectives were to achieve:

- *Efficiency* by increasing the output per worker and reducing deliberate 'underworking' by employees.

- *Predictability* of job performance by standardizing tasks and dividing them into small, closely specified subtasks.

- *Control* by establishing discipline through hierarchical authority and introducing a system whereby all management's policy decisions could be implemented.

To achieve these objectives, he implemented his five principles of scientific management (Taylor, 1911):

- A clear division of tasks and responsibilities between management and workers.

- Use of scientific methods to determine the best way of doing a job.

- Scientific selection of the person to do the newly designed job.

- The training of the selected worker to perform the job in the specified way.

- Surveillance of workers through the use of hierarchies of authority and close supervision.

Taylor applied his principles and methods in the Bethlehem Steel Company. He specified what tools workers were to use and how they were to do their jobs. His 'deal' with his workers was as follows: 'You do it my way, by my standards, at the speed I mandate, and in so doing achieve a level of output I ordain, and I'll pay you handsomely for it, beyond anything you might have imagined'. Taylor said, 'All you do is take orders, give up your way of doing the job for mine' (Kanigel, 1997, p. 214). He increased the productivity of the 75 pig iron handlers from loading $12\frac{1}{2}$ tons per man per day to 47 tons. In the process he saved the company $80,000 per annum at 1911 prices, made many workers redundant, and increased the wages of the remaining workers by 60 per cent.

Taylor's approach involved studying each work task. He chose routine, repetitive tasks performed by numerous operatives where study could save time and increase production. Many variables were measured including size of tools, location of tools, height of workers and type of material worked. He wanted to replace rules-of-thumb with scientifically-designed working methods. Taylor experimented with different combinations of movement and method to discover the 'one best way' of performing any task.

Taylor believed that the application of the principles of science would end arbitrary management decisions. Managers would plan and organize the work and workers would execute it, all in accordance with the dictates of science. He attempted to align the goals of the workers with those of management. Taylor was adamant that after the implementation of his methods, workers would be rewarded by large pay increases and managers would secure higher productivity and profits. However, workers were concerned that scientific management just meant 'work speed-up', that is, more work for less pay and increased redundancies.

✋ **STOP AND SEARCH**   YouTube for *Frederick Taylor Scientific Management* (11:02).

CRITICAL THINKING   You have travelled back through time and are able to meet Taylor. What three things would you congratulate him for, and what three things would you criticize him for?

Better, stronger, faster

'Bosses have always sought control over how workers do their jobs. Whatever subtlety there once was to this art, technology is now obliterating it. In February, Amazon received patents for a wristband apparently intended to shepherd labourers in its warehouses through their jobs with maximum efficiency. The device, were Amazon to produce it, could collect detailed information about each worker's whereabouts and movements, and strategically vibrates in order to guide their actions. Using such technology seems an obvious step for firms seeking to maximize productivity. Whether workers should welcome the trend or fear it, is harder to say.

Workplace discipline came into its own during the Industrial Revolution. As production came to depend ever more on expensive capital equipment, bosses, not keen to see that equipment sitting idle, curtailed their workers' freedom, demanding they work during set hours, in co-ordination with other employees, at a pace dictated by the firm. Technology creates new opportunities for oversight. Editors can see which of their journalists attract the most readers (though many wisely focus on other measures of quality). Referees at sporting events are subject to reviews that check their decisions within millimetres.

Workers and labour activists have often attacked strict discipline as coercive, unfair and potentially counter-productive . . . in the past, high [staff] turnover helped motivate some factory owners to share their gains from workplace discipline with workers. The '$5 day' introduced by Henry Ford in 1914 was an 'efficiency wage' . . . But high turnover does not appear to bother Amazon much. The past decade's weak labour markets have meant queues of willing workers even without the promise of above-market pay. The same technologies that monitor workers can also reduce the training time needed to prepare new employees, since the gadgets around them guide most of their activity.

And new disciplinary technologies create an additional risk for workers. Heaps of data about their activities within a workspace are gathered, while their cognitive contribution is reduced. In both ways, such technologies pave the way for automation, much as the introduction of regimentation and discipline in factories facilitated the replacement of humans by machines. The potential of automation increases the power of firms over workers. Anyone thinking of demanding higher pay or of joining a union in the hope of organizing to grab a share of the returns to increased efficiency can be cowed by the threat of robots'.

Source: from *The Economist* (2018a, p.72)

✋ **STOP AND SEARCH**   YouTube for *Phoebe Moore: quantified workplace*.

Criticisms of Taylorism

Critics of scientific management have argued that it:

- failed to appreciate the reactions of workers to new procedures and to being timed and closely supervised

- had an inadequate understanding of how individual incentives were affected by an employee's immediate work group. That group pressure could as easily keep production and morale up as down

- ignored the psychological needs of workers. The imposition of a uniform way of working can both destroy individuality and cause other psychological problems

- had too simple an approach to the question of productivity and morale. It sought to keep both of these up exclusively by economic rewards and punishments

- ignored the subjective side of work – its personal and interactional aspects, the meanings that employees give to work and the significance to them of their social relationships at work

- neglected the importance of other rewards from work (achievement, job satisfaction, recognition) which later research studies found to be as important.

> **STOP AND SEARCH**   YouTube for *David Lee: Why jobs of the future won't feel like work* (Ted Talk, 10:07). The speaker discusses designing jobs that will still be relevant in the age of robotics.

Contributions of the Gilbreths

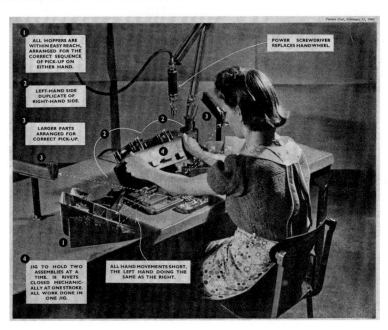

Taylor's work was developed by Frank and Lillian Gilbreth. Gilbreth's experience was in the construction industry and his most famous experiments involved bricklayers. He refined the techniques for measuring work while his wife Lillian, a trained psychologist, focused on the human aspects of work. Together they contributed in four ways:

- *Motion study*: Classifying the basic motions of the body. Gilbreth attached small electric lamps to workers' hands and left the camera lens open to track their changing positions creating *cyclographic* photographs showing their motion paths. He also used motion picture cameras to record workers' motions and times simultaneously (Gilbreth, 1911).

- *Therbligs*: Gilbreth developed a notation system for the elementary body movements which he called *therbligs* (his name spelt backwards). Each had its own symbol and colour. All the worker's body movements were noted down using therbligs notation (See Figure 14.2). Removing unnecessary body movements improved productivity.

- *Time-and-motion studies*: Gilbreth also developed a standard time for each job element, thereby combining time study with motion study. Time-and-motion studies are conducted to this day to improve occupational health, increase productivity and design wage payments systems.

Time-and-motion studies measurement and recording techniques used to make work operations more efficient.

- *Fatigue study*: Since all work produced fatigue which was remedied by rest, Lillian Gilbreth investigated the best work–rest combination to maximize productivity. She studied jobs to eliminate fatigue-producing elements; shortened the working day; introduced rest periods and chairs; and instituted holidays with pay (Gilbreth and Gilbreth, 1916).

Micro-motion studies and cyclographic models

Figure 14.2: Cyclographic photographs and therbligs

Source: Frank and Lillian Gilbreth Collection, Archives Center, National Museum of American History, Smithsonian Institution.

symbol	name	colour
	search	black
	find	grey
	select	light grey
	group	red
	bold	gold ochre
	transport loaded	green
	position	blue
	assemble	violet
	use	purple
	disassemble	light violet
	inspect	burnt ochre
	preposition	pale blue
	release load	carmine red
	transport empty	olive green
	rest for overcoming fatigue	orange
	unavoidable delay	yellow
	avoidable delay	lemon yellow
	plan	brown

Therblig symbols and colours

Home viewing

Cheaper by the Dozen (1950, director Walter Lang) is based on the real-life story of the Gilbreth family. It tells the story of Frank Gilbreth (played by Clifton Webb) and his wife Lillian (Myrna Loy) who are time and motion efficiency experts. Set in the 1920s, the film tells the story of how Gilbreth applies his unorthodox but efficient teaching methods on his 12 children which results in domestic conflict. He takes every opportunity to study motion and in order to increase efficiency in the home.

 **STOP AND SEARCH**   YouTube for *Gilbreth: time-and-motion studies.*

Stop and drink

Order a glass of beer.

Start position: Sitting at table

Movement 1: Hand to glass (2 seconds)

Movement 2: Grip glass (0.5 seconds)

Movement 3: Lift to horizontal (1 second)

Movement 4: Lift to lips (1 second)

Movement 5: Swallow 0.05 litres of drink (2 seconds)

Movement 6: More arm to horizontal (1 second)

Movement 7: Move glass to table (1 second)

Movement 8: Release grip on glass (0.5 seconds)

Movement 9: Belch (1 second)

End position: Sitting at table

Total time for operation: 10 seconds

Go to your local pub or bar with a friend and a stopwatch and check the above timings.

Source: adapted from Grey (2009, pp. 37–38).

Fordism

Fordism a form of work design that applies scientific management principles to workers' jobs; the installation of single purpose machine tools to manufacture standardized parts; and the introduction of the mechanized assembly line.

By 1920, the name of Henry Ford had become synonymous not only with his Model T motor car but also with his revolutionary techniques of mass producing it. Ford moved on from the analysis and rationalization of the *individual* production of work objects pioneered by Taylor, to the mechanization of the flow of objects between workers which represents a form of work organization designed for efficient *mass* production. This was known as Fordism and it is this that distinguishes Ford from Taylor.

Ford established his company in 1903. In the 1890s it was only skilled craftsmen who built motor cars. Ford claimed that there were not enough of them to meet the level of car production that he wanted and that was why, in his view, the deskilling of work was necessary. Others argue that deskilling made labour easier to control and replace. Ford's goal was 'continuous improvement' rather than the 'one best way'. His objective was to increase his control by reducing or eliminating uncertainty from the production system (Ford and Crowther, 1924). Among his major innovations were:

- Systematic analysis of jobs using the time-and-motion techniques.
- Installation of single-purpose machine tools to manufacture standardized parts
- Introduction of the mechanized assembly line.

Ford's Model T assembly plant, *circa* 1908

 This silent video shows clips from different parts of Henry Ford's automobile assembly plant at the start of the twentieth century. What do you notice about the technology being used and the tasks being performed by the workers? (1:46)

Systematic analysis of jobs

Ford established a Motion Picture Department and filmed work methods in different industries so as to learn from them. Employees were allocated simple tasks, all of which had been carefully designed to ensure maximum efficiency. Ford's approach was experimental and very pragmatic – try it, modify it, try it again, keep on until it is right. The Ford mechanic, originally a skilled craftsman, became an assembler who tended his machine performing only low-grade tasks. For example, the wheelwright's job was divided into almost a hundred operations, each performed by a different man using specialized equipment.

Installation of single-purpose machine tools to produce standardized parts

Ford used rigid and heavy machine tools, carbon alloy steel and universal grinding machines. This ensured that each part was exactly like the next and hence interchangeable. This facilitated the division of labour and increased certainty. The single-purpose machines that he designed for his factory were called 'farmer machines' because farm boys, coming off the land, could be quickly trained to use them. Their operators did not have to be skilled, just quick. The skill was now incorporated within the machine. This eliminated the need for skilled workers as anybody could now assemble an automobile.

Creation of the mechanized assembly line

Despite the aforementioned innovations, employees could still work at their own speed. In 1913 it still took 90 minutes to assemble a car. So, instead of moving the men past the car, the car was moved past the men. The mechanized assembly line imposed upon employees the working speed that Ford wanted. By 1914, the plant had installed a continuous automatic conveyor. The materials and semi-completed parts passed through the plant to where they were needed. The conveyor belt took radiator parts to assemblers and then carried their work away to solderers who finished them off (Gartman, 1979). Workers complained about this work intensification which they called 'job speed up' (Figure 14.3).

First moving assembly line, 1913, Ford's Highland Park factory

Modern, automated assembly line, 2018

Figure 14.3: **Old and new assembly lines**

✋ STOP AND SEARCH   YouTube for *Henry Ford assembly line.*

Mass production a form of work design that includes mechanical pacing of work, no choice of tools or methods, repetitiveness, minute subdivision of product, minimum skill requirements, and surface mental attention.

Ford's legacy was twofold. First, he created what came to be defined as the characteristics of **mass production** work:

1. Mechanical pacing of work
2. No choice of tools or methods
3. Repetitiveness
4. Minute subdivision of product
5. Minimum skill requirements
6. Surface mental attention.

While Taylorism and Fordism had many similarities, they also had some differences as Table 14.1 shows.

Critics have asserted that short cycle repetitive jobs have caused worker alienation and stress and have subjugated human beings to the machine. The assembly line is criticized for exerting an undesirable, invisible control over the workers. Other commentators observe how Fordism has shaped reforms within the British National Health Service. 'Fordism monitors the time doctors and nurses spend with each patient; a medical treatment system based on dealing with auto parts, it tends to treat cancerous livers or broken backs rather than patients in the round' (Sennett, 2008, p. 47). The debate over the balance of costs and benefits of Fordism and its precursor, Taylorism, continues to this day.

Table 14.1: **Differences between Taylorism and Fordism**

	Taylorism	**Fordism**
Approach to machinery	Organized labour around existing machinery	Eliminated labour with new machinery
Technology and the work design	Took production process as given and sought to re-organize work and labour processes	Used technology to mechanize the work process. Workers fed and tended machines
Pace of work	Set by the workers or the supervisor	Set by machinery – the speed of the assembly line

Aircraft assembly line

Boeing is the world's biggest plane maker and its factory in Everett near Seattle is the largest building in the world. Empty aircraft fuselages come in at one end and are hooked onto a moving assembly line. Nose-to-tail, they move along at a rate of two inches a minute through the final assembly process. Out at the other end, roll off complete aircraft with wings, tails, cockpits, toilets, galleys and seats. Aircraft manufacturers like Boeing and Airbus have been seeking ways of speeding up production of their planes. In 2014, Boeing and Airbus delivered 723 and 629 aircraft respectively.

Boeing is using Henry Ford's principles to create a lean manufacturing environment that resembles a Toyota car plant. It can build a 737 in six days and by using two assembly lines, the current version of its 737 is being manufactured at a record rate of 42 a month. Elizabeth Lund, a director of manufacturing, stated that: 'A moving line is the most powerful tool available to identify and eliminate waste in a production system . . . [it] drives efficiency throughout the system because it makes problems visible and creates a sense of urgency to fix the root causes of those problems' (Boeing website, 2006; Hollinger, 2015; *The Economist,* 2012).

Boeing is using Henry Ford's principles to create a lean manufacturing environment that resembles a Toyota car plant.

✋ **STOP AND SEARCH**   YouTube for *Boeing 737 assembly line.*

Lean working

Lean working a systematic method for minimizing waste within a manufacturing or service providing system that does not sacrifice productivity.

Today, Frederick Taylor's and Henry Ford's legacies are discussed in terms of lean working (or 'lean'), which has become one of the world's most influential management ideas. Its use is widely promoted in manufacturing and service industries in both the private and public sectors.

It is a term that was originally used to describe the Toyota Production System (TPS) or *Toyotaism.* TPS's aim is constant improvement and reduction in costs through the systematic elimination of waste using the assembly line system. For Womack et al. (1990), lean is a scientific discovery that will 'banish waste and create wealth'. Lean working continues to be a controversial topic with its promoters and critics making claims about its benefits and shortcomings as shown in Table 14.2. How management chooses to implement it has a major effect on employees.

Table 14.2: Plaudits and criticisms of lean working

Plaudits	Criticisms
Offers employees skill acquisition	Leads to job deskilling
Expands workers' skills repertoire	Narrows job definitions
Provides more fulfilling jobs	Intensifies work
Allows staff to initiate improvements	Reduces discretion and job autonomy
Encourages teamworking and multi-skilling	Produces narrow multi-tasking
Facilitates job rotation	Increases management's control over staff
Promotes organizational learning	Creates rigid standardization
Facilitates continuous improvement	Generates managerial bullying
Empowers employees	Increases job strain and job stress
Enlarges jobs	Increases supervisory surveillance

Source: based on Martin (2017); McCann et al. (2015); Carter et al (2011); Mehri (2006)

CUTTING EDGE   Lean working, decision making, deskilling

Douglas Martin

Douglas Martin (2017) examined the impact of lean working on the work skills of civil servants engaged in making decisions about tax and security claims which required the exercise of discretion to implement a legal process on behalf of the state. His study thus focused on the service sector (not manufacturing) and on decision-makers (not production staff). He found that the way that lean working had been introduced into the Her Majesty's Revenue and Customs (HMRC) and Department of Work and Pensions (DWP) resulted in two main changes. First, it ended 'whole case working' which involved a single tax officer managing the end-to-end process, e.g. calculating an individual's tax

→

liability, communicating with them, answering their questions and then issuing a tax notice. Second, it greatly increased the use of metrics to measure workers' performance.

The changes to their jobs restricted the scope for task variety within individual roles as staff were prevented from swopping between different decision-making disciplines. The routinization and standardization of their work gave them no opportunity to adopt distinctive working practices to suit local circumstances and it prevented managers from providing staff with a range of duties to perform. The fragmented work reduced skill variety as parts of the work were allocated to separate work locations, obviating the need to have a range of tax and benefit decision-making experts at each location. Task complexity was reduced by training staff to make decisions relating to only a single aspect of the tax or social security code. They were not trained to perform a full job role. This reduced both the range of skills required and the time needed to train them. Staff were not expected to understand how their function fitted in with the wider objectives of their department. Job autonomy was affected by assigning the now simplified decision making to staff trained in administrative processes. Decision making became an automated process which involved entering client data into a computer. The accompanying staff cuts resulted in work intensification for the remaining employees.

With respect to performance measurement, the effect of these changes was to put pressure on workers to focus exclusively on those parts of their job that linked directly to government targets. The changes led to arbitrary performance targets being established, e.g. number of calls answered taking priority over the quality of the decisions made. Staff had to compromise the legal quality of their decisions due to time pressures to meet performance targets. These became the central measure of valid decision making rather than the quality of the decisions made themselves.

In terms of deskilling, lean working removed any vestiges of discretion in decision making. It resulted in all aspects of work coming to be treated as administrative processes. Management's emphasis on workers' compliance with standardized decision making rules reduced employees' ability to interpret rules independently. Lean working emphasised the process of applying tax and social security decisions at the expense of discretion, professional judgement and expertise in decision making, all of which were devalued. The changes were symptomatic of a move away from a primarily bureaucratic rationality to a managerialist one. The implementation of lean working in the HMRC and DWP led to significant deskilling among its decision makers.

CRITICAL THINKING   Ask your lecturer how the annual monitoring of their research output has affected the kind of research they do and how they do it. How has the measurement of their research publications affected their teaching role?

McDonaldization

The principles and practices of mass production as developed by Taylor and Ford have affected many areas of our social and organizational lives. George Ritzer (2018/1993) labelled this process **McDonaldization**. He had no particular complaint against McDonald's restaurants merely using this fast food chain as an illustration a wider process which gained his attention.

McDonaldization a form of work design aimed at achieving efficiency, calculability, predictability and control through non-human technology, to enhance organizational objectives by limiting employee discretion and creativity.

For him, the new model of rationality, with its routinization and standardization of product and service as represented by McDonald's, had replaced the bureaucratic structures of the past, as described by Max Weber. He saw the McDonald's approach as possessing four key elements:

1. *Efficiency*: Every aspect of the organization is geared towards the minimization of time. The optimal production method is the fastest production method. For McDonald's customers, it is the fastest way to get from hungry to full.

2. *Calculability*: An emphasis on things being measurable. The company quantifies its sales, while its customers calculate how much they are getting for their money. McDonaldization promotes the notion that quantity is equivalent to quality, e.g. that a large amount of product delivered quickly represents a quality product.

3. *Predictability*: The provision of standardized, uniform products and services, irrespective of time or location. It is the promise that irrespective of whichever McDonald's outlet you visit in the world you will receive the same product in the same manner.

4. *Control*: Standardized and uniform employees perform a limited range of tasks in a precise, detailed manner complemented by non-human technology which is used to replace them whenever possible.

🤚 **STOP AND SEARCH**   YouTube for *Ritzer: McDonaldization.*

Ritzer's argument is that the process of McDonaldization is spreading and that while it yields a number of benefits, the associated costs and risks are considerable. His own view is that this trend is undesirable. He looks at the issue primarily from the perspective of what the consumer, client or citizen is receiving – a uniform, standardized product or service. However, to achieve this, the jobs of producers have to be deskilled. In addition to the simplified jobs that McDonald's employees perform, their work is also limited by the sophisticated technology of fast food preparation which gives them little or no discretion in how they prepare and deliver food to customers.

Hamburger grilling instructions are precise and detailed covering the exact positioning of burgers on the grill, cooking times, and the sequence in which burgers are to be turned. Drinks dispensers, french-fry machines, programmed cash registers – all limit the time required to carry out a task and leave little or no room for discretion, creativity or innovation on the part of the employee. Such discretion and creativity would of course subvert the aims of efficiency, calculability, predictability and control.

The McJob debate

The term *McJob* was coined by the sociologist Amitai Etzioni in his 1987 article in the *Washington Post* newspaper entitled 'McJobs are bad for kids' and first entered major dictionaries in 2001. Anthony Gould (2010) noted that the scholarly literature on the jobs of crew members (non-management employees) depicted the jobs as non-stimulating, low-wage with few benefits, factory-like, requiring little skill, intellectually unchallenging and often temporary. He added that academics had argued that such work occurred in an exploitative context with companies seeking to manipulate employees into believing that they had coveted jobs with great opportunities.

In contrast, other commentators, mainly although not exclusively industry advocates, took a positive perspective, arguing that such jobs offered teenage employees training; the chance to develop effective work habits and attitudes; an opportunity to observe cutting edge management practices; helped groups from minority backgrounds who might otherwise experience labour market disadvantages; and gave junior employees career progression to the company's managerial and executive positions (Allan et al., 2006).

The contrasting negative and positive opinions arise partly as a result of commentators emphasising different aspects of these jobs – the former focusing primarily on work organization, and the latter on human resource management. From an employee perspective, this implies that while the jobs are routinized and simplistic, the organization itself may operate helpful and supportive human resource management practices. This view allows for the possibility of a job's attractiveness to be multifaceted, possessing both positive and negative characteristics simultaneously. Gould's (2010) research attempted to reconcile these two aforementioned perspectives on fast-food jobs. His findings with regard to the fast-food work organization were that:

- Crew work was organized according to Taylorist principles.
- Crew members overwhelmingly perceived their duties as comprising a limited range of non-complex tasks to be performed in prescribed ways.
- Repeatedly doing the same task did not burn out or indoctrinate crew members.
- Many crew members adapted to the way the work was organized or at least did not view the job negatively.
- A large minority of crew appeared to like the way McDonald's work was organized and were satisfied with their job.

Gould's findings with regard to human resource management were that:

- Fast-food jobs offered crew members job security and the possibility of careers.
- McDonald's strategy was compatible with the needs and aspirations of industry-suitable crew.
- Managers adopted a benign developmental view of their workforce, believing that good work performance should result in promotion and advancement opportunities and continuity of employment tenure.

Gould concluded that fast-food work was a more complex phenomenon than had previously been suggested. Despite being low-paid and, in this respect unambiguously negative, crew jobs were best understood in terms of their compatibility with individual employee life styles (human resource management/employment characteristics) and in terms of a match between individuals' personalities and the company's work organization characteristics.

Through 2018, McDonald has been modernizing the restaurant experience for its customers through its 'Restaurant of the Future programme'. It has been using technology to update product delivery and revamp menus. The work changes include the introduction of new menu items, and new customer ordering through mobile apps and self-service kiosks. Using the latter, customers can now request that their meals be delivered to their table. Rather than using new technology to drive up profit margins by reducing staff count, the company have redirected its human capital resources (staff), to add value to customer interactions and improve the overall service experience. It has been reported that the modernization has changed the work experience of its employees and increased pace of work. Some staff have complained of having to perform more tasks resulting in increased work stress (Patton, 2018; Battye, 2018).

Bullshit jobs debate

David Graeber

Paul Thompson

Harry Pitts

Case for: David Graeber's (2018) bullshit job thesis (BST) is based on the twin claims that individuals hate their jobs or find no meaning or pleasure in them (but are coerced by the work ethic to do them), and that half of all jobs have no social value and could be abolished without any personal, professional or social cost. The two claims are linked by the view that these jobs are seen as pointless by those who perform them. His thesis is founded on a 2015 YouGov survey in the UK which he claims shows that 37 per cent of people said that 'they did not believe that their job needed to exist'. Meaningless employment in his view is concentrated in professional, managerial, clerical, sales and service sectors. Graeber lists five classes of such jobs:

- *Flunkies*: jobs that exist to make their bosses look good (e.g. receptionists, administrative assistants, door attendants).

- *Goons*: jobs that only exist because other companies also employ people in such roles (e.g. lobbyists, corporate lawyers, telemarketers, public relations).

- *Duct-tapers*: jobs that exist to fix organizational problems that should not have occurred (e.g. programmers rectifying incorrect code).

- *Box-tickers*: jobs that allow an organisation to claim it is doing something that it is not (e.g. performance managers, in-house magazine journalists, leisure coordinators).

- *Taskmasters*: jobs that involve supervising people who do not require supervising (e.g. middle management, leadership professionals).

Case against: Paul Thompson and Harry Pitts (2018) think that Graeber overstates the position. First they say, the 37 per cent did not say that their job 'did not need to exist' but rather that 'it did not make a meaningful contribution to the world'. These are two different things. However, another 50 per cent in the survey said it did make a meaningful contribution. Sixty-three per cent found their job very or fairly 'personally fulfilling', while 33 per cent did not. These figures, say these writers, are consistent with evidence of high levels of work attachment produced by the Work Employment Relations Survey which showed that between 2004–11, 72 per cent of employees were satisfied or very satisfied with 'the work itself', while 74 per cent had a sense of achievement. Workers are capable of disliking aspects of their jobs and how they are treated while, at the same time, finding positive meaning in their work.

What makes a job 'pointless'? While there is a high degree of academic consensus on what makes a 'good job', Thompson and Pitts say that Graeber relies too much on the testimonies of self-selected respondents. 'Pointlessness' they say is a concept with no explanatory power and that it is the equivalent of criminal or anti-social behaviour being labelled as 'mindless'. They state that Graeber does not distinguish between 'bullshit in the job' and the job itself. There are specific elements in all jobs that cause frustration (e.g. completing forms about what you have done). However, these result from external managerial and political choices and are not integral to the job itself.

This is highly controversial topic, where the opposing sides disagree over the evidence that should be considered, and how that evidence should be interpreted. However, an important benefit of this controversy is that it has stimulated discussion about the nature of the tasks that, in combination, constitute a 'job'. Do agree with Graeber or with Thompson and Pitts?

> **CRITICAL THINKING**   Anthony Gould's research revealed that many McDonald's workers were satisfied with their jobs. Do you find this surprising?

STOP AND SEARCH   YouTube for *David Graeber: Bullshit jobs.*

Jobs, tasks, skills and technology

A number of major reports have analysed the effects of automation on employment. While **Chapter 3** examined how automation, in the form of artificial intelligence (AI) and robotics, has destroyed certain jobs and occupations and created others, this chapter section considers how automation has or is likely to change parts of existing employees' jobs and work activities.

Jobs as tasks

All jobs, especially white collar ones, consist of bundles of tasks. (Arntz et al., 2016). People at work rarely do just one thing in their jobs. If you break down a job into its constituent tasks, you find that while it may not be possible to automate an entire job, some of those tasks can be done (and done better) by a machine. Consider the job of a university academic as shown in Table 14.3. It lists some of that job's constituent tasks. Can you produce a complementary list of tasks for the job of a student?

The changing world of work

In this podcast, Sarah O'Connor (2015) discusses how work is changing. She focuses on the gig economy with work flexibility, job insecurity, work-life balance, changes in labour markets, unions and collective bargaining, effects of technology, re-privatization of risk and basic incomes (26:12).

Table 14.3: Job tasks of university academics

Lecturing	Course administrating
Tutoring	Research findings promoting
Researching	Committee attending
Grant seeking	Student advising
Publishing	Staff appraising
Examining	Conference paper giving

In every shop you will find sales assistants. Their job can be broken down into 31 separate tasks as shown in Figure 14.4 (Kwong et al., 2017). Thinking of jobs in terms of constituent tasks is helpful when discussing what human skills are required to perform them and which of these skills are most and least likely to be automated.

1. Greets customers
2. Calculates costs of goods
3. Answers questions about goods and services
4. Cleans work and maintains areas
5. Demonstrates product features
6. Processes sales transactions
7. Sells products or services
8. Maintains sales records
9. Explains product information to customers
10. Reconciles records of sales transactions
11. Monitors inventories of products
12. Prepares sales
13. Trains sales personnel
14. Sets up merchandise displays
15. Issues money, credit, or vouchers
16. Gathers information on customer needs
17. Advises customers on the use of products
18. Stocks products or parts
19. Monitors work areas to provide security
20. Takes product orders from customers
21. Supervises sales or support personnel
22. Examines condition of products
23. Recommends products to customers
24. Reviews accuracy of sales
25. Monitors sales activities
26. Verifies customer credit information
27. Explains financial information to customers
28. Purchases stocks of merchandise
29. Maintains own professional knowledge
30. Arranges delivery of goods
31. Estimates costs or terms of sales

Figure 14.4: Tasks comprising a retail sales assistant's job

Source: Kwong et al. (2017)

 **STOP AND SEARCH**   YouTube for *Sales assistant job.*

✓✓✓   **EMPLOYABILITY CHECK** (how organizations work)

Consider a job that you are familiar with. List its *core work* (required, predictable tasks performed by you alone); *peripheral work* (tasks carried out by you at your discretion); *unstructured work* (where objectives are given to you but without guidance as to what tasks are needed to achieve those objectives); and *team work* (tasks performed by you working in collaboration with others).

Job tasks and human skills

For its successful performance, each task requires the job holder to apply their human skills. At work, we as human beings carry out a wide range of tasks without consciously analysing the exact skill set that we use. Everything we do, from stapling a document to interviewing a job applicant, requires a combination of innate or acquired capabilities ranging from manual dexterity to social perceptiveness.

The McKinsey Global Institute developed a list of 18 human skills or competencies (see Figure 14.5). These are divided into five core areas – sensory perception, cognitive abilities,

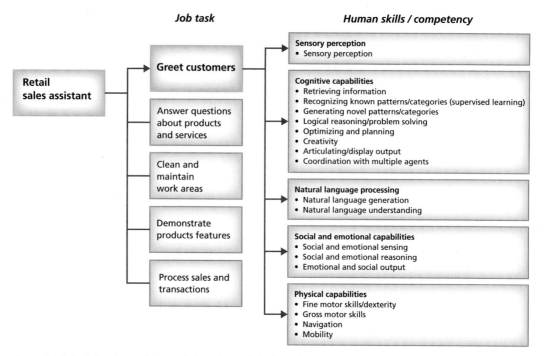

Figure 14.5: Retail sales assistant – job tasks and skills and competencies

Source: adapted from Manyika et al. (2017, p.4)

natural language processing, social and emotional capacities, and physical capabilities (Manyika et al., 2017). Using the example of the sales assistant introduced earlier, and focusing only on her first listed job task, 'Greets customers', what skills or competencies do you think are needed from among the five core areas shown in Figure 14.5 to perform this task successfully? Other job tasks, e.g. calculating costs of goods, answering questions, etc. will all require their own particular skill-competency combinations. The same principle applies not only to sales assistants, but also to software engineers, manufacturing managers, and all other jobs.

New technologies changing job tasks

Computers, algorithms and software have made it technically possible to automate many tasks within jobs that previously could only have been done by human beings. Technology, in the form of artificial intelligence and robots, can affect job tasks in four ways:

- *Remove tasks within existing jobs*: Bank ATMs relieve bank tellers from having to dispense cash over the counter; robots in restaurants deliver food and drinks to customers' tables; automated transcription software for doctors' orders does away with the need for medical secretaries to perform this task.

- *Create new tasks within existing jobs:* Technology can create new tasks to fill the gaps. For example, bank tellers can use their interaction time with customers to sell them additional financial products.

- *Augment tasks within existing jobs*: Technology assists and reinforces how employees perform their job tasks. Doctors employing algorithms to recommend appropriate patient treatments; care workers using collaborating robots (co-bots) to move patients in and out of beds. These allow workers to achieve more and do a better job.

- *Modify the balance of tasks within existing jobs:* Once tasks have been removed, added or modified, then the balance of a job changes. Typically, employees concentrate on those human-centric tasks that machines cannot do.

Robots help workers challenge the machines

This video shows how wearable robots may soon become common for ordinary workers in factories and warehouses (3:17). Companies such as SuitX, based in California, are trying to turn exoskeletons into a consumer product. A lightweight harness with counterweights and pulleys can be strapped on to enhance arm, back and leg movements. 'These exoskeleton systems for workers basically minimise the stress and strain in some particular joints,' says Homayoon Kazerooni, chief executive and founder of SuitX. 'We're looking at bionic devices as affordable consumer products such that workers can buy them'.

Costing about £12,000 for a full-body suit, the price may still be high for some, but SuitX has sold about 400 suits so far and the exoskeleton market overall is expected to accelerate. ABI Research expects global sales of exosuits to go from fewer than 5,000 units in 2017 to more than 100,000 by 2025. There is a scene in the film *Aliens* where Sigourney Weaver gets inside a exoskeleton and battles with the alien creature (*Aliens power loader*). (*Financial Times*, 2018).

STOP AND SEARCH   YouTube for *Top 10 Robot Suits in Movies* (11:49).

Current technologies can automate a large number of work tasks that people are paid to perform, and in the future many occupations will see a large percentage of their constituent job tasks removed or replaced. However, only a very small number of occupations can be fully automated, i.e. become wholly obsolete (Chui et al., 2016). A RSA/YouGov survey reported that just under half of business leaders expect new technologies to alter jobs rather than to eliminate them altogether (Dellot and Wallace-Stephens, 2017).

Retail sales assistant skills through the ages

Peter Ikeler

Peter Ikeler (2016) studied how the jobs and skills of retail sales assistants in US department stores had changed over time. He compared accounts of mid-twentieth century department store work with contemporary full-line department stores and modern discount stores. Historically, department-store labour policy had encouraged skilled selling, that is, the use of trained sales staff to increase the size and number of sales transactions through merchandise information and sales psychology. Indeed, courses were run to teach staff retailing with the intention of upgrading sales work into 'skilled labour'.

Ikeler distinguished the different management skills used in sales jobs. These include *pecuniary* skills (wrapping goods, dealing with customer payments); *prescrip-*

tive skills (locating items for customers and finding prices); *presentational* skills (making a connection with the customer, inspiring them, improvising small talk, interpreting their mood, selling by product advising); and *philanthropic* skills (using one's own personality and specialized product knowledge to help customers get what they wanted).

He found that skilled selling had been a feature of post-1945 department stores and had involved salespersons deploying nuanced, philanthropic knowledge and presentational sales styles. In contrast, contemporary full-line stores were characterized by semi-skilled selling where salespersons needed less in-depth knowledge yet still instinctively assessed customer moods, advised them individually and closed purchases. Deskilled selling was found to be a feature of modern discount stores where salespersons and cashiers only performed brief, prescriptive or pecuniary interactions

→

defined by compliance with managerial guidelines, involving little or no product knowledge or any attendant 'philanthropic' gifting.

Despite the 'soft' or human-centric skills apparently being sought by recruiters for those working in customer-facing jobs, for store sales personnel the trend is actually for a reduction in the necessity for product knowledge and interpersonal ability among new hires. This requirement went down as one moved from mid-twentieth-century department stores to modern, full-line stores (e.g. Selfridges, Nordstrom's, Karstadt) and then down again to large-format discounters (e.g. Asda, Walmart, Real).

Ease of job task automation

Technical feasibility
the potential that
a given job task or
work activity can be
automated by adopting
current technology.

A job task is judged to be capable of being automated if the capabilities required to perform it by a human being can be matched by those of a machine. This is called technical feasibility. Every job is made of multiple tasks and each task has its own degree of technical feasibility (Frey and Osborne, 2017).

Robin Kwong and his associates (2017) used McKinsey's Global Institute's data to create a tool to assess the technical feasibility of jobs. They called it the 'Can a robot do your job?' quiz.

It groups 820 occupations into 97 job categories (e.g. legal); the jobs within them (e.g. lawyers, judges); adds up the tasks that constitute each job (e.g. 23); describes each task (e.g. research legal materials, prepare legal documents); and estimates how many of the tasks could currently be performed by a robot (e.g. 5 out of 23).

✓✓✓ **EMPLOYABILITY CHECK** (self-management)

Can a robot do your current job or that of a relative? Go to the website below and find out.

The McKinsey Global Institute also identified seven categories of job tasks which they arranged in order of their increasing technical feasibility (Figure 14.6). The first four tasks on the list are the most difficult to automate (low technical feasibility) since they involve

1. *Managing and developing others*

   Tasks include motivating, training, coaching and mentoring staff. With respect to education, digital technology is transforming online learning, but the essence of teaching still requires both expertise and experience, and complex interactions with others.

2. *Applying expertise*

   Applying expertise to decision making, planning and creative tasks. It encompasses determining goals, interpreting results and checking for solutions. Such job tasks include tax decisions, coding software, creating menus, assessing students, coordinating activities, and writing promotional material.

3. *Interacting with stakeholders*

   Employees regularly interface with a wide range of stakeholders including customers, patrons and visitors. Tasks involve greeting them, explaining technical product details, providing service information, responding to complaints and questions.

4. *Doing unpredictable physical work*

   These are tasks that are performed in different ways, at irregular times, or in changing situations. Examples include providing medical care as a first responder, collecting rubbish in public areas, setting up classroom materials and equipment, making beds in hotel rooms, and operating a crane on a construction site.

5. *Collecting data*

   These are tasks that involve collecting and storing information. They include personnel staff recording job applicants' personnel histories, mortgage brokers filling in loan seekers' details, medical staff compiling patient records, and academic administrators inserting student examination results.

6. *Processing data*

   This is the collection and manipulation of data to produce meaningful information. It involves data validation, sorting, summation, aggregation, classification and reporting. The awarding of classes of student degree at examiners' meetings follows these steps.

7. *Doing predictable physical work*

   Areas such as manufacturing on assembly lines, and self-service check-outs stations in supermarkets.

Figure 14.6: **Categories of job tasks arranged in increasing ease of automation**

Source: based on Manyika et al. (2017, pp.42–46).

dealing with people or with unexpected events requiring the application of expertise In contrast, the greatest scope for automation (high technical feasibility) is for the last three types of tasks on the list – those that involve collecting or processing data and performing predictable tasks.

CRITICAL THINKING	Go into your nearest bank branch (if you still have one). Count the number of machines around the walls; count the number of staff on the bank floor; and count the number of customers in the queue waiting to be served. Who do you think benefits most and least from customer service bank automation?

The industrial sector with the greatest technical feasibility is accommodation and food services, followed by manufacturing. Also rated high is retailing. Within retail in general, 53 per cent of all tasks are automatable, ranging from 86 per cent of those done by retail bookkeepers, accountants and auditing clerks, down to 47 per cent of those performed by retail sales persons (Chui et al., 2016). Every employee's job, such as that of the retail sales assistant, is a combination of these seven categories of tasks. In the case of the retail sales assistant, Kwong et al. (2017) judged that 15 of the 31 activities could be done by a robot – all those that are even-numbered in Figure 14.4.

It is necessary to remember that jobs are dynamic in the sense that a manager of a clothing store may add or remove tasks that constitute a retail sales assistant's job. Increasingly employees are being required to focus not only on one main practice area, but also to take on several multifaceted, sometimes highly complex tasks, as required by their job, and also to perform as a member of a team.

 EMPLOYABILITY CHECK (commercial business acumen)

Just because it is technically feasible to automate a job task, there may be good reasons not to do so. Look again at the even-numbered (automatable) list of retail sales assistant's tasks shown in Figure 14.4, and identify those that could be automated but which should not be. Give reasons for your choices.

Job skill changes – past and current reductions

Technological developments have taken the debate away from the narrow deskilling–upskilling dichotomy towards a broader concern with the *pattern* of skill and competency requirements that will be needed in different jobs and industry sectors as technology develops. **Chapter 3** attempted to make generalized predictions about the numbers and types of occupations and jobs which, as a result of AI and automation, were likely to decline and disappear or increase or be created. This chapter asks the same question about possible changes in tasks *within* specific jobs. In both cases, the picture is mixed and uncertain.

The obvious, stereotyped prediction is that changes in technology will lead to low-skill jobs disappearing; robots and AI taking over many middle-skill jobs; and high-skill jobs remaining safe for the time being or having their incumbents' capabilities augmented by AI. However, while there may be some truth in this view, the overall pattern of job skill and job task changes in likely to be far more nuanced. It will depend not only on the sector, occupation, job and current skill level, but also on management choices. Jacques Bughin and his colleagues (2018) described the coming shifts in demand for workforce skills:

Low-skill jobs

Consider first low-skilled jobs. Physical and manual jobs involving equipment operation, inspection, monitoring and navigation such as driving, caring, cleaning, and waitressing are predicted to decline by 14 per cent. (Bughin et al., 2018). These jobs embody predictable and repetitive tasks that demand manual dexterity and complex manoeuvring which were previously thought of as being too difficult for machines to replicate. AI and robotics can change unskilled jobs in different ways:

- *Eliminate jobs*: Technology will wholly replace the skills of some workers. Once autonomous vehicles come onto the roads, the skills of taxi and lorry drivers will no longer be required and their jobs will become superfluous.

- *Deskill jobs*: Low-skilled jobs may be further deskilled by giving ever more precise instructions for every manner of tasks thereby reducing workers' scope and need for employee initiative. In the warehousing industry, machines tell fulfilment centre workers how big a size of box to use and produce exactly the right amount of tape for packing.

- *Upskill jobs*: As machines increasingly embed intelligence and knowledge that low-skill workers can access with a little training, knowledge-enabled jobs will become possible. For example, algorithms in healthcare could allow entry-level nurses to play a more active role in patient diagnoses.

- *Complement jobs*: technology can complement low-skill jobs as when collaborating robots (co-bots) in social care allow low-skill caring staff to spend more time comforting patients and less time lifting them and preparing their meals.

The world's population of older people is growing at an unprecedented rate. Some 8.5 per cent of the global population is aged 65 or over, and the percentage could reach 17 per cent by 2050, says the US National Institute on Aging. Caring for the elderly will be a key challenge. Japan with a quarter of its population already over 65 is at the sharp end of this trend. It has experimented extensively with using robots to perform mundane tasks in care homes (Lewis, 2017).

However, definitions of low skill overlook the emotional intensity associated with many forms of work including caring, teaching and certain forms of retail. A proportion of these low-skill jobs which involve person-to-person interaction will continue as customers or clients expect or demand a 'human touch' in sectors like hospitality, leisure, health services and education. Many low-skill jobs require certain cognitive and social skills.

Robotic warehouses

It has been estimated that In 2015 over 780,000 people in the US were employed in warehousing and storage centres, and many more around the world. Christian Frey and his colleagues (2016) discussed the increased use of robots in these warehouses. Amazon, a leader in applying technology in its fulfilment centres has 120 giant warehouses worldwide. Originally, it used a Pickers Find Items (PFI) work design. Items were stacked on shelves and a picker with a trolley travelled to its warehouse location; removed the item from the shelf, placed it in their trolley, and moved on to pick the next one needed to complete the customer's order. Wristbands tracked the hand movements of workers and vibrations were used to nudge them into being more efficient. The company has been increasingly automating its processes reducing the number of workers roaming around its warehouses (*The Economist,* 2018b).

In 2012, it acquired *Kiva Systems* (now *Amazon Robotics*), and by 2015 was using about 30,000 robots in 13 of its fulfilment centres. These robots move shelves of products across the floor to the workers, who then pick items from them. This is the Items Find Pickers (IFP) work design. Whereas before, human pickers came to the products, now the products come to the human pickers. According to Amazon, Kiva robots have reduced the order processing time down from 1.5 hours to as low as 13 minutes. Despite this, having workers pick the items off the shelves by hand is still an expensive and tedious task, and the company is attempting to replace the human pickers entirely with robots.

Frey et al. (2016) note that while Amazon is currently at the forefront of bringing the savings and scalability of robots into warehouses, logistics and distribution, Alibaba and other ecommerce companies in China are also developing their own robot logistic systems.

Pickers find items	Robot shelves	Items find pickers

| A picker collects items from storage shelves, to collate customers' orders | Shelves travel to picker station. | Picker at her station, selects an item from the robot shelves to complete a customer order |

What negative consequences can the following modern scientific management features have? For whom?

- Slicing and dicing knowledge jobs
- Measuring everything and everyone constantly
- Pushing people to their work limits
- Using employee peer review and individual rewards

 **STOP AND SEARCH**   YouTube for *Mick Mountz: Let the inventory walk and talk* (Ted Talk, 12:10).

Medium-skill jobs

According to the Resolution Foundation, jobs in the middle of the pay distribution such as secretarial, manufacturing and administrative work, have fallen markedly as a share of total UK employment. The 1990s and early 2000s saw a hollowing out of the labour market with a subsequent filling-in of middle-skilled jobs as other professions plugged the gap. Middle-skill workers whose activities have the highest technical potential for automation involve performing predictable physical tasks. Brynjolfsson and McAfee (2014) describe these workers as 'racing with the machines rather than racing against the machines'. Bughin et al. (2018) predict that these jobs which require only basic data input, literacy, numeracy and communication skills, will decline by 15 per cent. For example, the skills associated with tax collection will soon be eliminated, as from 2022 it is predicted, tax returns will be digitally processed in most Western countries (Wisskirchen et al., 2017).

High-skill jobs

Among high-skill workers, automation is likely to strip out tasks such as analyzing reports and data to inform decisions, reviewing status reports, and preparing staff assignments. Manyika et al. (2017) estimated that this would raise the productivity of CEOs and those in financial services by over a quarter. Deep learning algorithms capable of detecting cancers which enable lower skilled nurse practitioners to complete diagnoses, replace the skill that radiologists take a decade to train for and acquire, with the latter losing out as a result.

 **STOP AND SEARCH**   YouTube for *RSA Animate – Re-Imagining Work* (9:06).

Job skill changes – future increases

What skills and capabilities do you think that you will need to develop if you are to have a successful career and be in continued employment? International surveys by the McKinsey Global Institute (2017) and *Harvard Business Review* (2017) show strong agreement what these are. Unsurprisingly, the greatest requirement is for technological skills (55 per cent) and in particular, for specifically digital, programming and advanced IT skills. Next highest are social and emotional or people skills (24 per cent) including entrepreneurship, initiative taking, leadership and managing others. The third growth area is higher cognitive skills (8 per cent) that take in creativity and complex information processing and interpretation (Bughin et al., 2018).

When addressing AI/automation challenges, company managers have to decide whether it is more cost effective for them to retain and re-train their existing employees or to replace them with new ones who already possess the requisite skills. A survey identified two barriers to their making this difficult decision. First, their need to rethink and upgrade their current human resource (HR) infrastructure so as to allow the correct type of training to be performed. Second, their ignorance about how job roles are likely to change in the future and what kind of skills and types of employees will be required over the next five to ten years (Illanes et al. 2018). Bughin et al. (2018) identified five organization structure changes needed to cope with the shifts in skill requirements:

- *Mindshift change:* instilling a culture of life-long learning and providing staff training opportunities.
- *Organizational set-up*: creating agile corporate structures involving less hierarchy and more team collaboration.
- *'New collar' jobs*: creating new middle-skill posts and allocating activities to workers with different skill levels.
- *Workforce composition*: the gig economy will create a rise in the use of independent contractors and freelancers.
- *C-suite and HR changes*: CEOs will need to change their mindsets and talent recruitment strategies to facilitate the required changes.

They also offer five options for companies to build their future workforces:

- *Re-train*: raise employee skill levels by teaching them new, advanced skills
- *Redeploy*: redefine work tasks and redesign processes and shift sections of the workforce
- *Hire*: appoint individuals and teams possessing the required skills
- *Contract*: use external contractors, freelancers and temporary workers
- *Release*: remove unnecessary skills through employee attrition, retirement and redundancies.

What are the skills needed for the twenty-first-century workplace?

In this podcast, Lucy Kellaway talks to Chris Hirst (chief executive of Havas UK and Europe), Keely Woodley (partner at Grant Thornton who leads its human capital practice), and Andrew Mullinger (co-founder of Funding Circle) about what skills today's employees should possess in order to survive a career that is likely to span more than 40 years (27:03)

As noted **(in Chapter 3)**, it is impossible to predict job skill changes from an understanding of technological capabilities alone. Algorithms and robots do not have their own objectives but are directed by human beings. The consequences for future jobs and their associated job skill requirements will change depending on a series of management choices which will be influenced by a range of political, economic, social, legal and ecological factors and not just by technological considerations **(Chapter 2).** Later in the book, we contrast technological determinism with strategic choice **(Chapter 16).**

For now, we can note that there is no clear, linear impact on differently skilled jobs. Technically, the degree to which a job is deemed to be high-skilled, middle-skilled or low-skilled is based on an assessment of its technical intensity and the degree to which formal training and qualifications are required to perform it. Studies show that all workers' jobs, at all skill levels, will be affected to different degrees by automation based on currently demonstrated technologies. But exactly how, we do not yet know.

✓✓✓ **EMPLOYABILITY CHECK** (self-management, appetite for learning)

Are you currently acquiring capabilities that could just as easily be done by machines, either when you graduate or later in your career? Give one example. Or are you developing some of the skills that can future-proof your career? Give one example.

Back to the future?

The Economist (2015) noted the trend to 'Digital Taylorism', a term attributed to Philip Brown and his colleagues (2011). The distinguishing feature of this new version of an old work design was that its basic principles were being supercharged with digital technology and applied to a wider range of employees in new ways. Originally focused on manual workers, Taylorism has been extended to office, knowledge and service workers and now even to managers and other professionals. Digital Taylorism has had an impact in four main areas: work fragmentation, worker measurement, employee rewards and worker punishment.

Work fragmentation

As described earlier in this chapter, technology has allowed the division of labour to progress beyond manual and unskilled jobs to administrative and professional ones which require expertise and judgment. These have been divided into discrete, routine, measurable tasks which, after they have been 'sliced and diced', can be outsourced to lower skilled, cheaper freelancers. Gillian Tett (2018) discusses the outsourced task of removing unsuitable material from Google and Facebook websites. The people doing the actually 'cleaning' do not sit in Silicon Valley but are located in places like Manila in the Philippines. They are known as 'cleaners'.

Home viewing

The Cleaners (2018, directors Hans Block and Moritz Riesewieck) looks at the shadowy underworld of the internet where questionable content is removed. As you watch the film, focus on the job tasks of the individuals who perform this work.

Worker measurement

Today, technology allows the surveillance of employees and the measurement of their work performance at a level of detail that Taylor would never have believed to be possible. The fashionable buzzword is 'metrics'. For example:

- drones are used to measure the progress of building projects
- enhanced time-and-motion studies use sociometric badges to monitor employee interactions

- change from annual staff appraisal to continuous performance assessment and review (Williams and Beck, 2018)
- terminals strapped to warehouse workers' arms monitor their work efficiency.

The computers at Workday, a software firm, analyse 60 factors to predict which employees will leave. Those at Evolv analyse more than half a billion 'employee data points' across 13 countries seeking to identify patterns across companies and industries. They know, in real time, why employees were hired, how productive they are, and can even follow them to a new job. These data points range from how often employees interact with their supervisors to how long it takes them to get to the office. Workers unguardedly consent to surveillance when they sign their employment contracts. These big data analytics which measure workers claim to improve productivity (*The Economist,* 2018b, 2017).

Is 'metric fixation' sucking the life out of work?

 In this podcast, Isabel Berwick, and Michael Skapinker talk to Jerry Muller about his book, *The Tyranny of Metrics.* He discusses 'metric fixation' which he defines as a a a combination of the belief that standardised measures of performance can replace human judgement and the idea that people respond to incentives. 'What gets measured may get done' but setting targets often leads to people gaming the system, resulting in unexpected and undesirable consequences. Which of his points do you agree and disagree with? Give your reasons (24:32).

Research by Debora Jeske and Alecia Santuzzi (2015) revealed that close, unpredictable or continuous monitoring of individuals via cameras, data entry, chat and phone recording had significant negative effects on employees' job satisfaction, self-efficacy and commitment to the company. Cavazotte et al. (2014) found that providing legal professionals with smart phones intensified an organization's hold over their employees beyond their regular 9 to 5 working hours reaching out into new settings, time slots and social contexts.

What did they find? Performance management and co-worker relationships

Knut Laaser and Sharon Bolton (2017) studied the impact of Electronic Performance Management (EMP) on co-worker relationships in a leading UK retail clearing bank. EMP is a form of annual staff appraisal procedure that involves the methodical collection, shortage, analysis and display of information of workers' efforts by means of sophisticated technology. Promoters claim that EMP benefits both workers and employers by providing target-setting, performance monitoring and evaluation. Critics complain that in semi-routine workplaces EMP increases management surveillance and control by micro-monitoring, measuring and evaluating employees' computer, email and phone activities. It reduces job autonomy; increases down-skilling; intensifies worker-management conflict; and reduces trust between employees and their organization.

Knut Laaser

The prioritization of sales over customer service from the 1990s onwards meant that the former became a greater part of bank work. EMP assigns employees explicit sales targets that are underpinned by performance-related pay and disciplinary policies for underperformance. Each bank worker's performance was fed into a personalized balance scorecard (BSC). The technology allowed management to rank

→

employee performance; communicate it to them on a monthly or weekly basis; and advise them of its implications in terms of their bonus pay or disciplinary actions. Promoters claim that EMP was welcomed by employees as it replaced ambiguous staff assessment and reward techniques with more objective, accountable and valid management measures. Critics complain that in the banking context, it fostered work intensification, degraded the quality of the work process, and led to workers feeling devalued.

Laaser and Bolton were interested in the impact that EMP had on horizontal co-worker relationships. How you get on with colleagues affects whether you experience work as meaningful and dignified or as degrading and stressful. Social relations between co-workers rest not only on their shared concrete interest, but also on shared moral sentiments of fairness, decency and well-being. They affect how much workers care for one another and are concerned with their well-being in the workplace.

What did the researchers find to be the consequences of the implementation of the EMP on horizontal co-worker relationships? How did the pre-EMP workplace compare with post-EMP workplace? **(Answers in chapter Recap.)**

Worker rewards

A third area that Digital Taylorism has impacted is pay for performance. Frederick Taylor had always been keen that his 'first class man' should be well rewarded. Wage increases of 30 per cent were not uncommon. Today's organizations increasingly rely directly on their workers' brainpower. Bill Gates (Microsoft) has been quoted as saying that a great lathe operator commands several times the wage of an average lathe operator, but a great writer of software code is worth 10,000 times the price of an average software writer. The most talented workers command a prince's ransom. Google has been reported to have offering a star engineer $3.5m in stock so as to dissuade him from defecting to Facebook (*The Economist,* 2016). Laszlo Bock, Head of People Operations at Google, cited a situation where one employee received a stock award of $10,000 and another worker in the same area was awarded $1,000,000 (Bock, 2015, p.241)

Worker punishments

In Taylor's day, workers who did not perform their tasks as instructed, or who failed to achieve the required productivity targets were dismissed. This Darwinian 'survival of fittest' approach was popularized by Jack Welch, Chief Executive of General Electric from the 1980s. His 'vitality curve' used a 20–70–10 performance ranking system that divided the company's 300,000 employees into the top performing 20 per cent, the middle 70 per cent, and the bottom 10 per cent. The last group were fired. The approach has been dubbed 'up or out management' since, as an employee, you either moved up or were replaced. It is also known as 'rank-and-yank' or 'stack ranking' and appears to be back in fashion (*The Economist,* 2015; Hill, 2015). Laaser and Bolton (2017) reported that all the banks that they studied used a forced distribution curve placing employees in statistically predetermined categories of 'over', 'satisfactory' and 'under' performers. Irrespective of whether staff at each branch had all met or exceeded their targets, a percentage of them would be categorized as 'underperformers'.

The digital future of work: What skills will be needed?

 This video considers how robots, long having carried out routine physical activities, can now increasingly take on more sophisticated tasks (5:29).

 **RECAP**

1. *Identify the factors that influence choices in the process of work design.*

   - Four groups of factors influence work design: external (international/global, national, institutional, occupational); organizational (strategy, HR practices, operational uncertainty, technology, bureaucracy); work group (composition, interdependence, autonomy, leadership); and individual (demographics, competencies, characteristics).

2. *Describe the main objectives and principles of the scientific management approach.*

   - The objectives are efficiency (by increasing the output per worker and reducing deliberate 'underworking'); predictability of job performance (by standardizing tasks and dividing them up into small and closely specified subtasks); and control (by establishing discipline through hierarchical authority and introducing a system whereby all management's policy decisions can be implemented).

   - The principles are: a clear division of tasks and responsibilities between management and workers; use of scientific methods to determine the best way of doing a job; scientific selection of employees; the training of the selected worker to perform the job in the way specified; and the monitoring of workers through the use of hierarchies of authority and close supervision.

3. *Identify the contributions of the Gilbreths to scientific management.*

   - Frank Gilbreth's contributions were motion study; the 'therbligs' notation system; time-and-motion studies.

   - Lillian Gilbreth developed fatigue study and the beginnings of a more psychological approach to work design.

4. *Understand how Fordism developed out of Taylorism.*

   - Ford moved on from the mechanization and rationalization of work on the individual work piece or object pioneered by Taylor, to mechanizing the flow of objects between workers.

   - He developed the systematized analysis of jobs; installed single purpose machine tools to produce standardized parts; and established the mechanically paced assembly line.

5. *Explain the relationship between jobs, tasks, skills and technology changes.*

   - All jobs consist of bundles of tasks. Designing a job involves combining these different tasks, redesigning it involves adding or removing tasks.

   - Each job task requires the unique application of a combination of human skills. One skills framework groups 18 human skills under five headings: sensory perception; cognitive capacities; social and emotional capacities; physical capacities; and natural language processing.

   - New technology changes the balance between tasks within a job by removing, adding or augmenting existing tasks.

   - Job tasks can be grouped into seven types and arranged in descending order of their ease of automation (technical feasibility). Tasks requiring human-centric skill are at the top while those involving data collection and processing come at the bottom.

   - Changes in job tasks at all skill levels will be the result of management choices influenced by a range of political, economic, social, legal and ecological factors and not just by technological considerations.

6. *Identify the employability skills required to perform the jobs of the future.*

   - Research has identified a range of employability skills which will be particularly needed by future employees. These include the people skills of social networking, people development, coaching and collaboration.

7. *Provide examples of Digital Taylorism in today's organizations.*

   - Developments in technology have allowed greater work fragmentation, worker measurement, worker rewards and worker punishments.

RECAP: What did they find?

Laaser and Bolton (2017) found that:

- Before EMP's introduction the bank workplace was characterized by stability and shared employee interests. Staff experienced high levels of job discretion and engaged in various forms of teamwork. Under these conditions, they

→

shared experiences and co-workers developed trust, respect and recognition between each other. They described themselves as a 'family' where gradually and over time, caring co-worker relationships were fostered which went beyond the contractual duties of cooperation and support. Relationships were characterized by attentiveness to the vulnerability of others and a relaxed acceptance of mutual dependency.

- After EMP and BSC introduction, the single-minded pursuit of targets impoverished co-worker relationships preventing new connections being created or sustained between colleagues. The new environment fostered an individualized and instrumental approach to work, amplifying inter-worker competitiveness. Staff no longer saw their fellow workers as interdependent and vulnerable. Instead, it encouraged employees to prioritize their own self-interest; stimulated opportunism; promoted a 'me-first' personal philosophy; and encouraged employees to see their relationships with their colleagues as a means of achieving their own personal goals. As a result, antagonistic co-worker relationships developed which featured fierce competition as staff members came to see each other as threats to their own ambitions and livelihood with the obvious consequences for teamworking. The frequency of incivility increased and worker-management conflict concerning the former's performance rating become routine.

- For post-EMP employees, recruited under the performance-driven employment relationship which stressed competition and self-reliance, the system was not in conflict with their previous employment experiences or perceptions of how they should relate to their co-workers. They accepted that it was just 'the way it is', and rarely challenged what was for them merely 'normal practice' rather than the 'new order'.

Revision

1. Taylorism has been much criticized. What are these criticisms? Which criticism do you feel are valid and which are not? Give reasons for your assessment.

2. Define some of the key principles or practices of Taylorism or Fordism. Using examples, explain how these are being used in today's organizations. Discuss how these forms of work design affect employee behaviour.

3. What are the implications of the current research findings on technology and jobs for graduate career choice and training priorities?

4. Who benefits most and least from the new Digital Taylorism?

Research assignment

Visit your local fast-food restaurant. Observe and make notes on the behaviour of its employees, both those at the counter and those in the kitchen. Arrange to talk to one or two crew members – perhaps you already know someone who currently works there, or has done so in the past. Ask them about the best and worst aspects of that job. Relate their answers to the theories and research findings discussed in this chapter. Are the criticisms of fast food restaurants unfair?

Springboard

Michel Anteby and Curtis Chan (2018) 'A self-fulfilling cycle of coercive surveillance: Workers' invisibility practices and managerial justification', *Organization Science* 29(2): 247–63. The authors show how worker surveillance and control originated by Taylor and Ford has now developed into highly sophisticated forms of employee monitoring.

Christopher Elliott and Gary Long (2016) 'Manufacturing rate busters: Computer control and social relations in the labour process', *Work, Employment and Society*, 30(1), 135-151. The authors provide a detailed case study of the use of computer control over manual jobs in a distribution centre and discuss workers' attempts at resistance.

Sharon Parker, Frederick Morgeson and Gary Johns, (2017) 'One hundred years of work design research: looking back and looking forward', *Journal of Applied Psychology*, 102(3): 403–420. The authors discuss the different factors which collectively influencing work design.

Ritzer, G. (2018) *The McDonaldization of Society: Into the Digital Age*, ninth edition, London: Sage. The author brings Max Weber's rationalization thesis up to date using fast food restaurant as the model for the rationalization process in today's society.

OB cinema

The Rebel (1961, director Robert Day): DVD track 2: 0:05:00–0:11:30 (7 minutes).

In this film, the comedian Tony Hancock plays himself, as a London office worker who finds the routine of his job oppressive. The clip begins with a shot of the office, and ends with the manager saying to Tony, 'Off you go'. As you watch this clip:

1. Identify the design principles underlying the office jobs that Tony and his (all male) colleagues are performing at United International.

2. Complete this matrix, indicating the advantages and disadvantages, to management and to employees, of designing jobs in this way:

	Advantages	Disadvantages
For management		
For employees		

3. Tony's manager diagnoses his problem and suggests some solutions. How appropriate do you think his suggestions are?

4. Is this movie out of date, because management practice and office technology have changed since the 1960s? Or can you identify jobs that you have personally had, or which you have recently observed, that are designed in the same way? What would be – or what has been – your reaction to work like this?

Chapter exercises

Automating universities

Objectives
1. To distinguish different types of academic and student tasks performed in universities.

2. To assess the technical feasibility of their automation.

3. To identify opportunities for the current automation of some of these tasks and the future automation of others.

Briefing Despite being low on technical feasibility, there is still scope to automate many tasks performed in universities by its service producers and service consumers.

→

Individually   Below is a list of both student-related tasks performed both by academic staff members and by students. Add any missing ones. Working individually, suggest how existing technology could (a) automate these so that they no longer required the services of a university academic, and (b) assist the student, making their tasks faster, easier or more enjoyable. You may wish to describe a still-to-be-invented technology needed to automate a task, if none currently exists.

Group   1. Compare your individual lists to ensure any additions have been included.

2. Considering one task at a time, discuss the automation options that members have generated.

3. If implemented, what effect would your automation proposals have on (a) the jobs of academic staff members and (b) the experience of university of students?

Academics' tasks	Automation solution
Giving lectures	
Tutoring	
Examining	
Student feedback giving	
Student advising	
Course administrating	
Other tasks:	

Students' tasks	
Attending lectures	
Attending tutorials	
Reading	
Preparing assignments	
Sitting examinations	
Other tasks:	

2: Taylor Road orderfillers

Objectives   1. To recognize contemporary examples of Taylorist work design.

2. To explain the reasons for the popularity of these practices.

3. To identify the problems associated with this form of work design.

Taylor Road orderfillers   Taylor Road is a computer-controlled warehouse of a large, multinational company with over 10,000 employees around the world which distributes food products and customer orders. The non-unionized employees receive a wage that is higher than other local manufacturing facilities and twice that of comparable, low-skilled service jobs. With its strict staff selection (95 per cent were males, aged between 20 and 40), and high wages and benefits, the facility enjoys a good reputation in the area. Computer controls direct, monitor and evaluate workers' manual tasks using algorithms.

Initially, the warehouse used a Pickers Find Items (PFI) work design. The items were distributed in an unsystematic way around the shelves. This system is called 'random stack' and was found to be the most efficient way to arrange goods. Pickers with trolleys travelled to the item location points ('slots') removed the item from the shelf, placed it in their trolley and then moved on to pick the next one to complete a customer order. A central computer coordinated and individually tailored work for employees. At the start of a shift, each employee received a wireless mini-computer ('unit'), a headset, and a vehicle for moving goods. They logged onto their unit with their personalized settings and passwords.

The central computer assigned orderfillers their discrete tasks which come packaged as 'trips'. These were software-generated routes through the warehouse which they had to follow to collect the different parts of customers' orders. Orderfillers were directed to their collection slots using computer voice-guided instructions. On arrival, the employee confirmed their location by speaking a three digit code printed above the slot. Once the unit 'heard' the code, it responded with the number of cases to be collected from that slot. The orderfillers then manually transferred the cases onto their vehicles and then again spoke the correct quantities into their units. If they did not follow this behaviour sequence exactly, the orderfillers were unable to complete a trip.

If they were working at the minimum production rate, each employee would perform this behaviour sequence 1,500 to 2,000 times per shift. On average, each order weighed 18 pounds so an orderfiller would physically lift between 27,000 and 36,000 pounds of goods per shift. The company's industrial engineers developed a formula which calculated a standard time for each trip. This was based on time study, digitalized maps of the warehouse, size and weight of cases, number of required stops, and fatigue allowances. Thus, every task a worker performed was electronically dispensed and tracked. The collected data was used to maintain the desired level of employee performance. Computer coordination was so good that, in order to function, the warehouse did not require the workers to interact with each other. They might cross paths on two or three occasions during a shift. Thus, the orderfillers task was designed to be repetitive, fatiguing and isolating.

Once he had delivered his load to the dispatch dock, the computer informed the orderfiller how quickly he had completed his last trip; updated him on his cumulative shift performance up to that point; let him know the standard time for his next trip; and told him the aisle and slot that he had to go to next. To keep their jobs, employees had to maintain a rolling four week average performance of 95 per cent of standard time as specified by the formula. Failure to achieve this standard resulted in disciplinary warnings, and 3–4 weeks of underperformance led to dismissal. Employees who survived the first two months of employment generally continued to meet the standard. Each fortnight workers who had achieved between 105 and 130 per cent performance received bonuses.

A few years ago, this type of work design was replaced by one called Items Find Pickers (IFP). Here, robotic carriages containing items, arrived at picker stations. Pickers stand stationary at their work stations. Shelves of items, moved by floor robots, arrive at the picker's station, who then picks the items and packs them for customers.

1. Form into groups and discuss the following questions:

   a. Which of practices of Taylorism and Fordism can you identify here?

   b. How do these practices improve efficiency and productivity?

   c. What problems does the way that work is organized in these warehouses create for its employees?

   d. Would you prefer to work in warehouse that used a Pickers Find Items (PFI) or an Items Find Pickers (IFP) work design?

Source: case based on Elliott and Long (2016) and Frey et al. (2016)

References

Allan, C., Bamber, G. and Timo, N. (2006) 'Fast-food work: are McJobs satisfying?', *Employee Relations*, 28(5): 402–20.

Arntz, M., Gregory, T. and Zierahn, U. (2016) *The Risk of Automation for Jobs in OECD Countries*, Paris: Organization for Economic Co-operation and Development.

Battye, L. (2018) 'Why we're loving it: the psychology behind the McDonald's restaurant of the future', *Behavioural Economics*, 10 January, https://www.behavioraleconomics.com/loving-psychology-behind-mcdonalds-restaurant-future/ [accessed January 2019]

Bock, L. (2015) *Work Rules,* London: John Murray.

Boeing website (2006), 'Boeing begins use of moving assembly line for 777 jetliners', News release, 8 November.

Brown, P., Lauder, H and Ashton, D. (2011) *The Global Auction: The Broken Promises of Education, Jobs and Incomes,* New York: Oxford University Press.

Brynjolfsson, E. and McAfee, A. (2014) *The Second Machine Age: Work, Progress, and Prosperity in a Time of Brilliant Technologies*. New York and London: W.W. Norton & Company.

Bughin, J., Hazan, E., Lund, S., Dahlström, P., Wiesinger, A. and Subramaniam, A. (2018) *Skill Shift: Automation and the Future of the Workforce*, McKinsey Global Institute.

Carter, B., Danford, A., Howcroft, D., Richardson, H., Smith and Taylor, P. (2011) 'All they lack is a chain': lean and the new performance management in the British civil service', *New Technology, Work and Employment,* 26(2): 83–97.

Cavazotte, F., Heloisa Lemos, A. and Villadsen, K. (2014) 'Corporate smart phones: professionals' conscious engagement in escalating work connectivity', *New Technology, Work and Employment,* 29 (1): 72–87.

Chui, M., Manyika, J. and Miremadi, M. (2016) 'Where machines could replace humans – and where they can't (yet)', *McKinsey Quarterly,* 3: 58–69.

Dellot, B. and Wallace-Stephens, F. (2017) *Artificial Intelligence, Robotics and the Future of Low-skilled Work,* RSA Action and Research Centre, September, https://www.thersa.org/discover/publications-and-articles/reports/the-age-of-automation [accessed January 2019]

Elliott, C.S. and Long, G. (2016) 'Manufacturing rate busters: computer control and social relations in the labour process', *Work, Employment and Society,* 19(1): 153–74.

Financial Times (2018) 'Video: exoskeletons to become common for factory workers', 5 March.

Ford, H. and Crowther, S. (1924) *My Life and Work.* London: William Heinemann.

Frey C.B., Osborne M., Holmes, C,, Rahbari E,, Garlick, R., Friedlander, G., McDonald, G., Curmi, E., Chua, J,, Chalif, P. and Wilkie, M. (2016) *Technology at Work v2. 0: The Future is Not What It Used To Be,* CityGroup and University of Oxford, January, https://www.oxfordmartin.ox.ac.uk/downloads/reports/Citi_GPS_Technology_Work_2.pdf [accessed January 2019]

Frey, F.B. and Osborne, M. (2017) 'The future of employment: how susceptible are jobs to computerization?', *Technological Forecasting and Social Change*, 114: 254–88.

Gartman, D. (1979) 'Origins of the assembly line and capitalist control of work at Ford' in A. S. Zimbalist (ed.), *Case Studies on the Labour Process* (pp. 193–205). London: Monthly Review Press.

Gilbreth, F.B. (1911) *Motion Study,* New York: Van Nostrand.

Gilbreth, F. B. and Gilbreth, L. (1916) *Fatigue Study,* New York: Sturgis and Walton.

Gould, A.M. (2010) 'Working at McDonald's: some redeeming features of McJobs', *Work, Employment and Society,* 24(4): 780–802.

Graeber (2018) *Bullshit Jobs: A Theory,* London: Allen Lane.

Grey, C. (2009) *A Very Short, Fairly Interesting and Reasonably Cheap Book About Studying Organizations,* second edition, London: Sage.

Harvard Business Review (2017) 'Automation: what skills will keep you ahead of AI?', 95(2): 36.

Hill, A. (2015) 'Relegation fear works on the pitch but not in the office', *Financial Times,* 5 May, p.12.

Hollinger, P. (2015) 'Boeing beats Airbus to the title of largest jet maker in 2014', *Financial Times,* 13 January.

Ikeler, P. (2016) 'Deskilling emotional labour: evidence from department store retail', *Work, Employment and Society,* 30(6): 966–83.

Illanes, P., Lund, S., Mourshed, M., Rutherford, S. and Tyreman, M. (2018) 'Retraining and re-skilling workers in the age of automation', *McKinsey Quarterly,* January, https://www.mckinsey.com/global-themes/future-of-organizations-and-work/retraining-and-reskilling-workers-in-the-age-of-automation [accessed January 2019]

Jeske, D. and Santuzzi, A.M. (2015) 'Monitoring what and how: psychological implications of electronic performance monitoring', *New Technology, Work and Employment,* 30(1): 62–78.

Kanigel, R. (1997) *The One Best Way: Frederick Winslow Taylor and the Enigma of Efficiency.* London: Little Brown.

Kwong, R., Kao, J.S., Manibog, C. and Nakaniski, T. (2017) 'Can a robot do your job?', 7 April, *Financial Times,* https://ig.ft.com/can-a-robot-do-your-job/ [accessed January 2019]

Laaser, K. and Bolton, S. (2017) 'Ethics and care and co-worker relationships in UK banks', *New Technology and Employment,* 32:3(3): 213–27.

Lewis, L. (2017) 'Six Japanese robots that care for an ageing population', *Financial Times*, 8 December.

McKinsey Global Institute (2017) 'Creating meaningful work and driving business success amid technological disruption', https://www.mckinsey.com/global-themes/future-of-organizations-and-work/creating-meaningful-work-and-driving-business-success-amid-technological-disruption [accessed January 2019]

Martin, D. (2017) 'Making tax and social security decisions: lean and deskilling in the UK Civil Service', *New Technology, Work and Employment*, 32(2): 146–59.

McCann, L., Hassard, J.S., Granter, E. and Hyde, P.J. (2015) 'Casting the lean spell: the promotion, dilution and erosion of lean management in the NHS', *Human Relations*, 68(10): 1557–77

Manyika, J., Chui, M., Miremadi, M., Bughin, J., George, K., Willmott, P. and Dewhurst, M. (2017) *A Future That Works: Automation, Employment, and Productivity*. McKinsey Global Institute, New York, NY, September, https://www.mckinsey.com/~/media/McKinsey/Global%20Themes/Digital%20Disruption/Harnessing%20automation%20for%20a%20future%20that%20works/MGI-A-future-that-works-Executive-summary.ashx [accessed January 2019]

Mehri, D. (2006) 'The darker side of lean: an insider's perspective on the realities of the Toyota production system', *Academy of Management Perspectives*, 20(2): 21–42.

O'Connor, S. (2015) 'Wearables at work: the new frontier of staff surveillance', *Financial Times*, 9 June, p.14.

Parker, S. K. (2014) 'Beyond motivation: job and work design for development, health, ambidexterity, and more', *Annual Review of Psychology*, 65: 661–91.

Parker, S.K., Van den Broek, A. and Holman, D. (2017) 'Work design influences; a synthesis of multilevel factors that affect the design of jobs', *Academy of Management Annals*, 11(1): 267–308.

Patton, L. (2018) 'McDonald's high tech-tech makeover is stressing workers out', *Bloomberg Technology*, 13 March, https://www.bloomberg.com/news/articles/2018-03-13/worker-exodus-builds-at-mcdonald-s-as-mobile-app-sows-confusion [accessed January 2019]

Ritzer, G. (2018/1993) *The McDonaldization of Society: Into the Digital Age*, ninth edition, London: Sage.

Sennett, R. (2008) *The Craftsman*, New Have, CT: Yale University Press.

Taylor, F. W. (1911) *Principles of Scientific Management*. New York: Harper.

Tett, G. (2018) 'The low paid workers cleaning up the horrors of the internet', FT Magazine, *Financial Times*, 16 March.

The Economist (2012) 'Faster, faster, faster', 28 January, p. 59.

The Economist (2015) 'Schumpeter: Digital Taylorism', 12 September, p. 68.

The Economist (2016) 'Schumpeter: the other side of paradise', p.68.

The Economist (2017) 'Sofas and surveillance', 29 April, pp. 57–58.

The Economist (2018a) 'Free exchange: better, stronger, faster', 3 March, p.72.

The Economist (2018b) 'Special Report: AI in Business: GrAIt expectations', 31 March.

Thompson, P. and Pitts, F.H. (2018) 'Bullshit about jobs', *Royal Society of Arts*, 9 July, https://www.thersa.org/discover/publications-and-articles/rsa-blogs/2018/07/bullshit-about-jobs [accessed January 2019]

Williams, G. and Beck, V. (2018) 'From annual ritual to daily routine: continuous performance management and its consequences for employment security', *New Technology, Work and Employment*, 33(1): 30–43.

Wisskirchen, G. Biacabe, B.T., Bormann, U., Muntz, A., Niehaus, G., Soler, G.J. and Von Brauchitsch, B, (2017) *Artificial Intelligence and Robotics and Their Impact on the Workplace*, IBA Global Employment Institute, April, https://www.ibanet.org/LPD/Human_Resources_Section/Global_Employment_Institute/Global_Employment_Institute_Home.aspx [accessed January 2019]

Womack, J. P., Jones, D. T., and Roos, D. (1990) *The Machine that Changed the World: The Triumph of Lean Production*. New York: Macmillan.

Elements of structure

Key terms

organization structure

delegation

job specialization

job definition

job description

organization chart

hierarchy

organization hierarchy

responsibility time span

span of control

employee engagement

line employees

staff employees

authority

responsibility

accountability

line relationship

chain of command

staff relationship

functional relationship

formal organization

informal organization

sexuality

sex

gender

role

role conflict

rules

formalization

centralization

decentralization

Learning outcomes

Once you have read this chapter, you should be able to define those key terms in your own words, and you should be able to:

1. Explain how organization structure affects human behaviour in organizations.

2. List the main elements of organization structure.

3. Relate the concept of span of control to that of organization hierarchy.

4. Identify line, staff and functional relationships on an organization chart.

5. Distinguish between the formal and informal organization within a company.

6. Understand the nature and impact of sexuality on organizational behaviour.

Why study elements of structure?

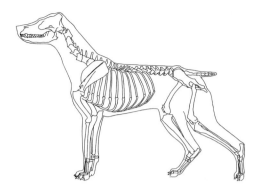

The structure of an organization is like the skeleton of an animal. The various bones link to each other in specific ways. Different animals have different skeletons. When scientists unearth the remains of an animal and examine its skeleton, they can tell what kind of animal it was. When living, you cannot directly observe an animal's skeleton. It is hidden beneath its skin. However, when a part of the skeleton becomes faulty, e.g. a broken leg, the whole animal cannot perform as normal until the bone heals or has been replaced. What an animal can and cannot do during its life is greatly determined by its skeleton. As Sacha Albers and her colleagues (2016, p.589) explain:

Formal organization structures group and connect individuals within an organization. Departments, committees, boards, teams and task forces create temporary or permanent channels for individuals to come together and interact . . . Role descriptions and task assignments typically specify reporting or supervisory duties and thus create connections among individuals. Essentially then, organization structures establish networks of ties among organizational members.

Employees' attitudes and behaviour are shaped as much by the structure of the organization within which they work as by the personalities that they possess and the groups to which they belong. The constraints and demands of the job imposed through the roles that they play can dictate their behaviour and even change their personalities. For this reason, it is impossible to explain the behaviour of people in organizations solely in terms of individual or group characteristics. Jay Lorsch described organization structure as management's formal and explicit attempts to indicate to organizational members what is expected of them. This involved the definition of individual jobs and their expected relationship to each other as indicated in organizational charts and in job descriptions. In his words, 'this was management's attempt to draw a map of whom they want to do what' (Lorsch, 1977, p.3).

✓✓✓ **EMPLOYABILITY CHECK** (how organizations work)

What information about this company does the organization chart below provide?

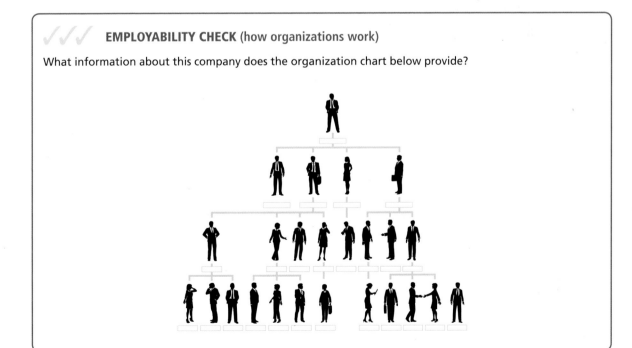

Alan Fox (1966) argued that explanations of human behaviour in organizations must consider structural factors. He was critical of those who insisted on explaining behaviour in organizations exclusively in terms of personalities, personal relationships and leadership. Such explanations are highly appealing to common sense. This is because such variables are directly observable – people say and do things. In contrast, the effects of a company's structure on its employees are generally hidden. The structural approach stands in contrast to the psychologistic approach which holds that it is the individual factors that are the main determinants of human behaviour in organizations.

While corporate strategy specifies the *goals* that a company pursues, organization structure directs the *means* by which these will be achieved. John Child (2015, p.17–22) noted that inappropriate structure can obstruct the achievement of organizational goals by causing at least five problems:

1. *Motivation and morale*: can fall if inappropriate delegation and spans of control lead to too little or too much responsibility being given to employees. Ill-defined roles and unclear priorities, work schedules and performance standards, all lead to staff not knowing what is expected of them.

2. *Decision making*: decisions may be of poor quality and will be made slowly if the company has too many hierarchical levels; if decision makers are separated from each other, and if decision making is over-centralized.

3. *Conflict and lack of coordination*: if the structure does not emphasize a single set of company-wide objectives, departmental priorities may take precedence. Conflict results from a failure to coordinate the activities of individuals, teams and departments, whose work is interdependent.

4. *Changing circumstances*: may not be responded to imaginatively if the structure lacks people performing forecasting and planning roles; if it does not give priority to innovation and change; and if there is no top management support or adequate resources.

5. *Rising costs*: due to many expensive bosses in tall hierarchies with narrow spans of control; and where additional staff are hired to administer excessive rules, procedures, paperwork and targets.

CRITICAL THINKING   Consider the behaviour of the instructor teaching this course. Identify aspects of their behaviour that you like and do not like. Decide if these positive and negative behaviours are influenced by that person's personality or by the organization structure within which they work.

Organization structuring

Organization structure the formal system of task and reporting relationships that control, coordinate and motivate employees to work together to achieve organizational goals.

At the start of the book, organizations were defined as social arrangements for achieving controlled performance in pursuit of collective goals. One aspect of these 'arrangements' is the creation of a structure. An organization structure is the formal system of task and reporting relationships that control, coordinate and motivate employees to work together to achieve organizational goals. It:

- designates the formal reporting relationships, specifying both managers' spans of control and the number of hierarchical levels

- groups together individuals into departments

- specifies systems within the firm, to ensure that the communication, coordination and integration between different departments are effective.

 **STOP AND SEARCH**   YouTube for *Organizational structure.*

Table 15.1: Elements of organization structure

Element	Topic	Question
Work specialization	Division of work tasks	Should there be high specialization or should workers do several, different jobs (low specialization).
Hierarchy	Levels of management in the organization	Should there be many layers of management (tall hierarchy) or few (flat hierarchy).
Span of control	Number of workers supervised by a single manager	Should a single manager be responsible for many subordinates (wide span of control) or a few (narrow span of control)?
Chain of command	Reporting relationships	To whom should an individual or group report with respect to their work?
Departmentalization	Grouping of jobs	Should jobs be grouped on the basis of function, task or geography?
Formalization	Extent of rules	Should many rules be used to coordinate and control the activities of employees (high formalization) or just a few (low formalization)
Centralization	Location of decision making	Should decisions be made at the top of the company by senior managers (centralized) or delegated to junior staff (decentralized)?

Delegation managers granting decision making authority to employees at lower hierarchical levels.

Because organization structure is an abstract concept, it is useful to begin by listing the seven things that it is concerned with – the elements of structure. These are shown in Table 15.1. Senior management's decisions regarding each element will have a major impact on the employees' work satisfaction and organizational performance, either positively or negatively. A recurring theme running through these decisions is delegation which refers to managers granting decision making authority to employees at lower hierarchical levels.

Home viewing

The opening scene of the film *Joe Versus the Volcano* (1990, director John Patrick Shanley) ends when Joe Banks (played by Tom Hanks) says 'I don't know'. The scene contains an example of each of the seven elements of the organization structure of *American Panascope,* the company that Hanks works for. Can you identify these?

A popular way of depicting the structure of any large organizations is as a pyramid or triangle as shown in Figure 15.1. This is only one of many possible shapes for an organization's structure. Several others will be presented later in the chapter. For the time being, we can note that the pyramidal form shows that an organization has both a vertical and a horizontal dimension. Its broad base indicates that the vast majority of employees are located at the bottom, and are responsible for either manufacturing the product or providing the service (e.g. making refrigerators, selling insurance).

In Figure 15.1, each of the six successive levels above the workers represents a layer of management. On the left-hand side of the diagram, the managerial ranks are divided into three groupings: supervisory or first-line management, middle management, and senior or top management. The diagram's right-hand side lists the commonly used job titles of managers who are members of each grouping. The layers also represent differences in status. While

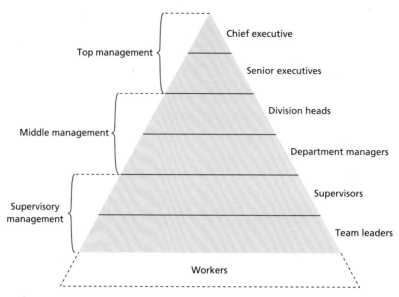

Figure 15.1: Organization structure

most people will recognize an organization structure, they are less clear about its purpose. Robert Duncan (1979, p.59) said that:

> 'Organization structure is more than boxes on a chart; it is a pattern of interactions and coordination that links the technology, tasks and human components of the organization to ensure that the organization accomplishes its purpose.'

For Duncan, the purpose of a structure was two-fold. First, it facilitated the flow of information within a company in order to reduce the uncertainty in decision making that was caused by information deficiency. Second, a structure achieved effective coordination and integration of the diverse activities occurring within different departments of a firm.

Why drug dealers live with their moms

Sudhir Venkatesh and Steven Levitt investigated the working of a Chicago-based, crack cocaine dealing organization called the Black Gangster Disciple Nation. They found that it was structured similarly to the fast food chain, McDonald's – 'if you were to hold a McDonald's organizational chart and a Black Disciple org chart side by side, you could hardly tell the difference' (Levitt and Dubner, 2005, p.87). The operation was divided into about a hundred branches (or franchises). J.T., the leader of one such franchise (gang), reported to about 20 men called (without irony) the board of directors, to whom he paid nearly 20 per cent of his revenues for the right to sell crack in a designated twelve-square-block area. The remainder of the money he distributed as he saw fit. Three officers reported directly to J.T. – an enforcer (who ensured the gang's safety); a treasurer (who watched over the gang's liquid assets) and a runner (who transported large quantities of drugs and money to and from the supplier).

Below these officers were 25–75 street-level salesmen known as foot soldiers who aspired to become officers themselves one day. At the very bottom of the hierarchy were 200 members known as the rank-and-file. These were not actually gang employees, but they did pay dues to the gang for either protection from rival gangs, or for the chance to secure a job as a foot soldier. A drug dealing organization works like a standard capitalist enterprise. You have to be near the summit to make a lot of money. The 120 men at the top of the Black Disciples organizational pyramid were paid very well (2.2 per cent of gang members took home more than half of all the money) with the top 20 bosses netting $500,000 each per annum. J.T. the gang-leader (franchise holder) earned $66 dollars an hour; his three officers each received $7 dollars an hour; and the foot soldiers made $3.30 an hour – less than the US minimum wage. The authors concluded that, except for the top cats, drug dealers don't make much money and that's why they live with their mothers (Venkatesh and Levitt, 2000; Levitt and Venkatesh, 2000).

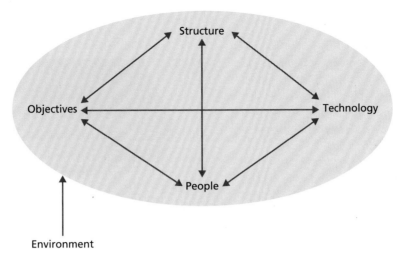

Figure 15.2: Leavitt diamond

Harold Leavitt (1965) has suggested that organizations can be viewed as complex systems which consist of four mutually interacting, independent variables: organizational objectives, technology, people and organization structure. All four of these were affected by the firm's environment such as the prevailing political, economic, social, technological and ecological situation. The differences in organization structure can be partly accounted for by the interactions of these four variables and partly by environmental factors (see Figure 15.2).

 **STOP AND SEARCH**   YouTube for *Yves Morieux: As work gets more complicated, six rules to simplify* (Ted Talk, 12:02).

Types of jobs

Job specialization the number of different work tasks that are combined within a single job.

Job definition specification of the work task requirements of a job.

An important aspect of organization structure is the choice that is made about how jobs are designed. How should the work be divided up and what should be the content of each person's job? The detailed answers will of course depend on the type of job considered, whether it is that of a nurse, engineer, car assembly worker, teacher or Member of Parliament. A key question is how well defined ought a job to be? This is the question about job specialization which refers the number of different work tasks that are combined into a single job. Specialized jobs consist of one or just a few different work tasks.

Some commentators argue that newly appointed staff should know exactly what their duties are in detail. They suggest that this high degree of job definition which specifies in detail the task requirements of a job helps to motivate employees by letting them know exactly what is expected of them. Such detail can also assist in staff appraisal when their performance is evaluated.

Specialization is a feature of all knowledge, clerical and manual jobs. After their general medical training, some doctors become paediatricians, other choose obstetrics. On the assembly line, some workers fit car wheels, while others fix on the doors. The choices concerning the extent and type of specialization depend on the criteria being used by the organization designer. These will be affected by their values, beliefs and preferences. It may be a case of trading off efficiency of production against job satisfaction. Senior management might decide to attempt to maximize both elements. Specialization can lead to demarcation disputes.

Job retitling

Alun Withey (2018) noted that pompous job titles such as hygiene technician (cleaner), media distribution officer (paper boy) and communications executives (call-centre workers) are not a twenty-first- or even a twentieth-century invention. Pretentious and outlandish job titles, he explains, date back to the nineteenth century and were created to promote trades and inflate the importance of tradesmen. They included a tripocoptontic perruquier (washable wig maker), Delineator of the Natatorial Science (swimming instructor) and couranteer (journalist). Job titles not only indicate a person's work activities but can also reduce staff burnout and increase work satisfaction.

Research by Adam Grant and his colleagues (2014) concluded that creative job titling could improve employees' attitudes and boost recruitment. The researchers argue that titles are powerful symbols of what an employee is, what they can do, and what can be expected of him or her. They studied the Make-a-Wish Foundation in Michigan whose chief executive invited her employees to create their own unique fun job titles to complement their official ones. The finance director became 'minister of dollars and sense' and the office manager was the 'keeper of keys'. Results revealed that their new, self-reflective job titles made their jobs more meaningful and helped them to cope with the emotional challenges of supporting families with sick or dying children. They concluded that the initiative reduced stress by helping staff to focus on the most critical aspects of their work. Why be a student when you can be a 'scholastic end-user unit'? (*Harvard Business Review,* 2016; Grant et al., 2014).

Others commentators believe that, far from being motivating, a high level of job definition acts to control people's behaviour and sets minimum performance standards. What is needed, they argue, is for the employee to create their own job. In practice, a detailed job definition is provided to those doing low level manual and clerical jobs, while at more senior levels there is a greater degree of own job-making. The physical manifestation of the choice about how much to define the job is the piece of paper on which is written the job description. A job description will usually contain the following information:

Job description a summary statement of what an individual should do on the job.

- Job title and the department in which it is located
- Job holder's position in the hierarchy
- To whom the job holder is responsible
- The objectives of the job
- Duties required of the job holder (regular, periodical and optional)
- Liaison with other workers, staff, supervisors and managers
- Authority to exercise own judgement in carrying out the job

Organization chart a diagram outlining the positions in an organization's structure and the relationships between them.

The specialization of work activities and the consequent division of labour is a feature of all large complex organizations. Once tasks have been assembled together they are allocated to individuals in the form of jobs. A job can be seen as consisting of one or more tasks. Persons carrying out the jobs occupy positions in the organization's hierarchy. Particular levels of responsibility and authority are allocated to these positions. The division of labour and the relationship of one position to another is shown on an organization chart which is a diagram outlining the different positions in an organization's structure and the relationships between them.

An organization chart graphically depicts an organization's structure. It shows how the work of different people in the organization is coordinated and integrated (Chandler, 1988). The first organizational chart, that of the Union Pacific and Southern Pacific Railway in the USA, was published in 1910 (*Harvard Business Review,* 2014).

Let us consider the organization charts in Figures 15.3a and 15.3b, since they clarify some of the basic aspects of an organization's structure that are introduced in this chapter. These include chain of command; formal communication channels; division of labour; departmentalization; span of control and levels of hierarchy.

Hierarchy distinct differences between individuals in terms of their status and power.

Hierarchy in an organization refers to the number of levels of authority to be found within a company. Each level is shown in a different colour below. Hierarchy is a coordinating and integrating device intended to bring together the activities of individuals, groups and departments that were previously separated by the division of labour and function.

Regional Corporate Hierarchy & International Support Systems

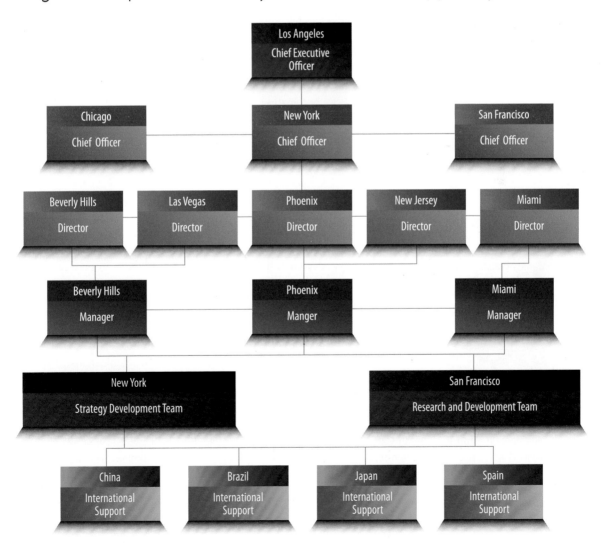

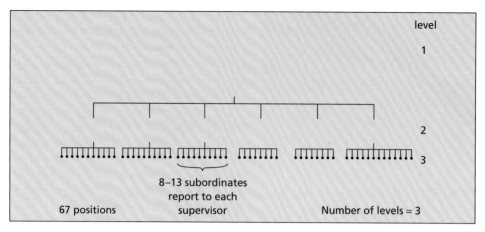

Figure 15.3a: Flat organization structure

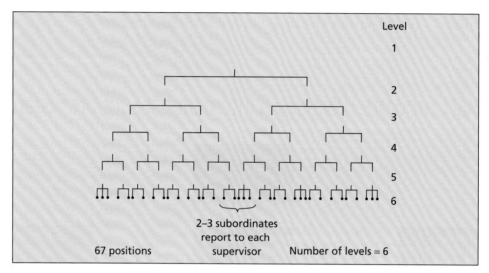

Figure 15.3b: Tall organization structure

"What we've done is make it dramatically easier to navigate the corporate hierarchy."

Organization hierarchy differences in status and power in an organization reflected in the number of levels of authority shown on an organization chart.

In a company that has a flat organization structure such as that shown in Figure 15.3a, only one level of hierarchy separates the managing director at the top from the employees at the bottom. In contrast, the organization hierarchy depicted in Figure 15.3b, has four levels in between the top and the employees at the bottom. Google has opted to have four levels of hierarchy – vice president, director, manager and individual contributor (Bock, 2015). Hierarchy has both costs and benefits for an organization and its employees (Anderson and Brown, 2010).

It is useful to distinguish between organizations which have many levels in their hierarchy, such as the military, the police and the civil service (referred to as having a 'tall' hierarchy), and organizations which manage to operate with relatively few levels of hierarchy (referred to as possessing a 'flat' hierarchy) such as small businesses and the Roman Catholic Church. In his classic article, Edward Lawler (1988) examined the functions of hierarchies in organizations and discussed what companies needed to do if they wanted to reduce or replace them.

Elliott Jaques believed that a well-designed, hierarchy 'can release energy, creativity, rationalize productivity and . . . improve morale' (1990, p. 127). He argued that the level of responsibility in every organizational role could be objectively measured in terms of the target completion time of the *longest* task, project or programme assigned to that role. He called this

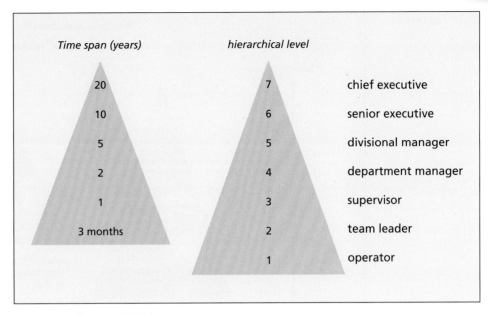

Figure 15.4: Responsibility time span

Responsibility time span target completion time of the *longest* task, project or programme assigned to that role.

the **responsibility time span** (Figure 15.4). Moreover, break points in hierarchical responsibilities time spans occurred at three months, one year, two years, five years, ten years and twenty years.

He argued that positions in an organizational hierarchy should be based on the length of time needed to complete the longest task. In an effective hierarchy, every layer would be associated with its own responsibility time span. The layer above would have a longer one and the one below would have a shorter one.

Span of control the number of subordinates who report directly to a single manager or supervisor.

Span of control refers to the number of subordinates who report to a single supervisor or manager and for whose work that person is responsible. Comparing the two organization charts in Figure 15.3, it can be seen that in the one with the flat hierarchy, there are many employees reporting to each supervisor. Hence, that person has a wide span of control. In a tall organization structure, fewer employees report to each manager and hence the span of control of each of the managers is therefore narrow. The larger the number of subordinates reporting to one manager,

The army's span of control

Every army in the world is hierarchically organized with its own chain of command and span of control (SOC). This ensures that every commanding soldier in that line directs the actions of no more than seven to twelve subordinates. Similarly, every soldier in a section, platoon, company or battalion reports to only one senior officer.

	Form	Commanded by one	SOC	Total soldiers
12 men	1 section	corporal/sergeant	12:1	12
3 sections	1 platoon	lieutenant	3:1	30
3 platoons	1 company	major/captain	3:1	150–200
3 companies	1 battalion	lieutenant colonel	3:1	500–1,000
3 battalions	1 brigade	brigadier	3:1	3,500–4,000
3 brigades	1 division	major-general	3:1	16,000
3 divisions	1 corps	lieutenant general	3:1	45,000
3 corps	1 army	general/field marshal	3:1	135,000+

Thus in a battle, a general or field marshal does not control 135,000 soldiers directly; he or she controls the three lieutenant generals and so on down. The underlying principle of organization in both armies and companies is to split the task up into manageable proportions and not to have an excessive span of control so that real control is lost.

Source: based on National Army Museum (2019)

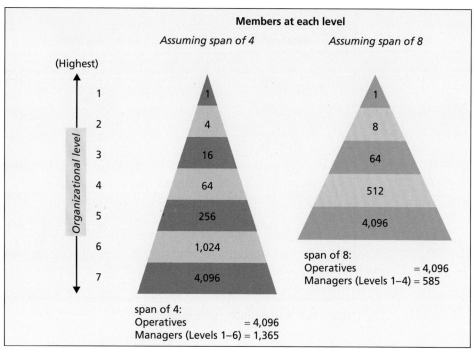

Figure 15.5: Contrasting spans of control
Source: Robbins et al. (2017, p. 434)

the more difficult it is for her to supervise and coordinate them effectively. General Sir Iain Hamilton once said that, 'No one brain can effectively control more than 6 or 7 other brains'.

Harold Koontz (1966) wrote that if an organization with 4,000 employees widened its span of control from 4-to-1 to 8-to-1, it could eliminate two hierarchical layers of management, which translated into nearly 800 managers. Robbins et al. (2017) explain the simple arithmetic involved. Figure 15.5 shows an organization with 4,096 workers at the shop floor level – level 7. All the levels above this represent managerial positions. With a narrow span of control of

 **STOP AND SEARCH**   YouTube for *span of control.*

4-to-1, 1,346 managers are needed (levels 1–6). However, with a wider 8-to-1 span of control, only 585 would be required (levels 1–4).

The concepts of span of control and hierarchy are closely related. The narrower the span of control, the more intense the degree of supervision employees receive. However, it also means that there are many more steps in the promotion ladder, and thus more career progression opportunities for staff. In contrast, the wider a span of control is, the fewer the number of levels that there will be in the hierarchy. At each level, the contact between the manager and each of those reporting to him will be reduced. A supervisor responsible for eight operatives will have less contact with each operative than if she was responsible for only four.

This wide span of control, with few levels of hierarchy produces a flatter organization structure with fewer promotion steps for employees to climb. However, it is likely that the communication between the levels will be improved as there are fewer of them for any message to pass through. It also forces managers to delegate their work to others if they are not to be faced with an intolerable workload. Evidence suggests that individuals with high self-actualization needs prefer flat hierarchies, while those who emphasize security needs tend to gravitate towards

Table 15.2: Factors determining the choice of span of control

Factors encouraging wider work spans

Similarities of tasks: The more similar the tasks carried out by subordinates are . . .

Subordinate characteristics: The more subordinates are competent, responsible and able . . .

Interaction requirements: The lower the interaction required with subordinates . . .

Standardized procedures: The more standardized procedures there are . . .

Planning and coordination: The less planning and less coordination that is required of subordinates' work . . .

. . . the wider the span of control

Factors encouraging narrower work spans

Geographic proximity: The more physically dispersed subordinates are . . .

New problems: The higher the frequency of new problems experienced by subordinates . . .

Knowledge gap: The greater the gap between the manager's and subordinates' expertise . . .

Task complexity: If the work activities to be performed by employees are complex . . .

Manager's job: The greater the non-supervisory element in a manager's job . . .

. . . the narrower the span of control

CRITICAL THINKING

Can a lecturer's span of control (class size) ever be too narrow or too wide? What factors determine the number of students that a single instructor can deal with in terms of teaching, assessment and course administration? What are the effects of high and low class sizes on (a) lecturers and (b) students?

Span of control at Google

The engineers at Google believed that managers did not matter. They thought them to be a necessary evil, but they got in the way, created bureaucracy and messed things up. In consequence, all manager roles were eliminated and all 130 engineers reported directly to Wayne Rosing, head of engineering. Bureaucracy and hierarchy had been removed and the engineers became independent entities, linked only to the other members of their teams and to the product managers in the central organization. It worked reasonably well for some time, and then it did not. In January 2002, Wayne announced that the company's flat structure could not scale much further. Google intended to recruit another hundred engineers that year and they could not all report to Wayne. The new goal would be to reduce the span of control to thirty-five to one. The 'no managers' experiment at Google lasted six months (Schmidt and Rosenberg, 2017; Bock, 2015).

---

organizations with tall hierarchies. Many factors affect the choice of a span of control. The main ones are listed in Table 15.2.

However, research by Theobald and Nicholson-Crotty (2005) suggests that due to negative consequences of a narrow span, it is a moderate span of control that maximizes productivity, as shown in Figure 15.6.

The graph in Figure 15.6 shows that organizational performance and span of control both increase to the point at which the supervisor or manager is unable any longer to coordinate or monitor the large number of subordinates who report to her. Companies differ, and each seeks to find the span that is best for it. For example, a supermarket chain can set different spans of control in its different departments – narrow for store managers so as to ensure standardization and wide for merchandizing managers at headquarters in order to implement best practices.

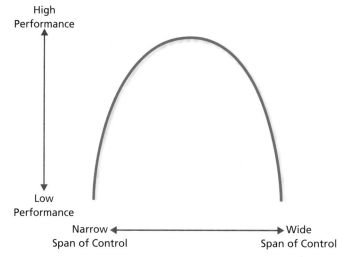

Figure 15.6: Relationship between organizational performance and span of control
Source: based on Theobald and Nicholson-Crotty (2005).

Employee engagement being positively present during the performance of work by willingly contributing intellectual effort, experiencing positive emotions, and meaningful connections to others.

What did they find? Span of control and employee engagement

Deb Cathcart and her colleagues (2004) studied the relationship between span of control and **employee engagement** (see **Chapter 9**) in a large US integrated healthcare system. A common cost-reduction strategy in many organizations has been the removal of management positions. It is based on the belief that this can reduce overhead costs without affecting service quality. The general research literature supports managers having narrow spans of control ranging between 8 and 12 direct reports, and up to 20–30 direct reports when 'simple' operations are being managed. These same studies have recommended flattening organizational hierarchies and broadening spans of control in order to empower employees and gain efficiencies.

The nursing management literature identified three variables affecting span of control. These were the frequency and intensity of the relationship between manager and subordinates; the complexity of the work being performed; and the capabilities of the manager and her staff. The research suggested that the less frequent and less intense the relationships, the less complex the work; and the more capable the manager and staff were, the wider the span of control that could be accommodated. However, there was no research into how span of control affected employee engagement in healthcare.

Within the healthcare system studied by Cathcart, nurses managed teams whose span of control varied widely – between 5:1 and 100:1. Thirteen per cent of all managers had more than 40 direct reports, and 86 per cent of these were nurse managers of patient care areas. Senior nursing leaders received complaints about wide variations in span of control. They acknowledged inconsistencies in how span of control was defined and decided. A team of middle managers was asked to assess whether span of control affected employee engagement in their healthcare system. Using a survey questionnaire, they studied 651 work groups, matching group size with the level of employee engagement of its members measured on a five-point scale.

What do you think they found? Was there a link between a group's span of control and the engagement of its members? Did span of control matter? **(Answers in chapter Recap).**

Line, staff and functional relationships

Line employees
workers who are directly responsible for manufacturing goods or providing a service.

Staff employees
workers who occupy advisory positions and who use their specialized expertise to support the efforts of line employees.

Authority the right to guide or direct the actions of others and extract from them responses that are appropriate to the attainment of an organization's goals.

Responsibility the obligation placed on a person who occupies a certain position in the organization structure to perform a task, function or assignment.

Accountability the obligation of a subordinate to report back on their discharge of the duties for which they are responsible.

Within an organization, one can distinguish two classes of workers. First, there are the line employees who contribute directly to the provision of goods or services to the customer. In a motor car company this refers to those who assemble the car (production) and those who sell the car (sales). These are considered to be the primary organizational functions. Line employees are shown on an organization chart which depicts their positions in the organization's structure and shows the relationships between them. The line structure is the oldest and most basic framework for an organization and all other forms are modifications of it. It is indispensable if the efforts of employees are to be coordinated. It provides channels for upward and downward communication and links different parts of the company together with the ultimate source of authority.

The second class of workers are called staff employees. They contribute indirectly to the provision of goods or services to the customer. These individuals occupy advisory positions and use their specialized expertise to support the efforts of line employees. Staff employees work in departments such as purchasing, human resources, information technology and legal. These are considered to be secondary organizational functions. A firm may provide line managers with advice by establishing a separate department headed by staff specialists. This is a modification of the basic line structure, and is referred to as a *line-and-staff structure*. The staff departments and the staff employees within them, perform their tasks through the line structure and not independently of it.

Within any organization structure, individuals occupying different positions will have different relationships with one another. These relationships can be labelled *line, staff* and *functional*.

To explain the differences between these types of relationships, it is first necessary to introduce and define the concepts of authority, responsibility and accountability. You cannot be held accountable for an action unless you are first given the authority to do it. In a situation where your manager delegates authority to you, they remain responsible for your actions to senior management. Authority is vested in organizational positions not in the individuals who occupy them. Military personnel salute the rank, not the person holding it. Authority is accepted by subordinates who comply because they believe the position holder has a legitimate right to exercise the authority. Authority flows down the vertical hierarchy of the organization, along the formal chain of command.

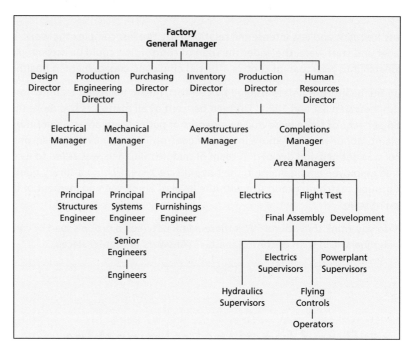

Figure 15.7: Line relationships
Source: Boddy (2016, p.317)

Line relationship one in which a manager has the authority to direct the activities of those in positions below them on the same line.

A **line relationship** is one in which a manager has the authority to direct the activities of those in positions below them on the same line on an organization chart. Line managers can 'tell' their subordinates on their own line, what to do. Such relationships are depicted with vertical lines on the chart, and these connect positions at each hierarchical level with those above and below it. It is this set of manager–subordinate relationships that are collectively referred to as the organization's chain of command. Using the analogy of a river, the line relationships are the designated channels through which authority flows from its source at the top of the organizational pyramid, through the middle management ranks, down via the supervisors, to employees at the desk or on the factory floor. Thus the most junior employee has some linkage to the most senior manager. All non-managerial employees have some authority within their jobs which may be based on custom-and-practice or formally defined in their job descriptions.

Every organization possesses line relationships if it has formally appointed managers who have subordinates who report to them. All individuals in an organization report to a manager from whom they receive instructions, help and approval. Thus in the organization chart shown in Figure 15.7, the Completions Manager has the authority to direct the activities of the four area managers. The Completions Manager in turn, can be directed by the Production Director. All the aforementioned individuals are in the same line relationship. The line relationships in a company are found within departments and functions. Line managers are responsible for everything that happens within their particular department.

Chain of command the unbroken line of authority that extends from the top of the organization to the bottom and clarifies who reports to whom.

Given the pyramidal nature of companies, managers located towards the top of an organization have more authority to control more resources than those below them. For this reason, lower level managers are forced to integrate their actions with those above them by having to ask their bosses to approve their actions. In this way, managerial control is exercised down through the organization by the chain (or line) of command. Figure 15.8 shows 17 'links' in the chain of command of the British Royal Navy

Staff relationship one in which staff department specialists can recommend, advise or assist line managers to implement their instructions concerning a particular issue, but have no authority to insist that they do so.

A **staff relationship** is one in which staff department specialists provide a service to line managers. Normally they can only recommend, advise or assist line managers to implement their instructions concerning a particular issue, but have no the authority to insist that they do so. Usually they have to 'sell' their recommendations to line managers. Thus the human

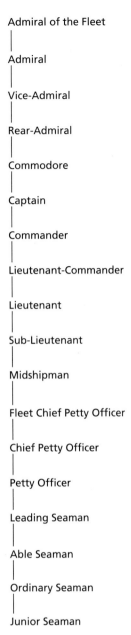

Figure 15.8: British Royal Navy: Chain-of-command
Source: from Royal Naval Museum website. http://www.royalnavalmuseum.org/info_
sheets_nav_rankings.htm

Functional relationship one in which staff department specialists have the authority to insist that line managers implement their instructions concerning a particular issue.

resources department cannot direct shop floor workers, even when dealing with a personnel problem. It has to work with or through the line manager of the employees concerned. Staff authority is usually subordinate to line authority and its purpose is to facilitate the activities being directed and controlled by the line managers.

The exception to this is when a staff department is in a functional relationship with a line department. In such circumstances staff department specialists, such as human resources, have the authority to insist that line managers implement their instructions concerning a particular issue, e.g. redundancy procedures. So, in a functional relationship, staff specialists can also 'tell' line managers who to do, but only within their prescribed area of expertise. A functional relationship is shown in Figure 15.9.

The different relationships between the various positions on an organizational chart – line, staff and functional – are summarized in Figure 15.9 and depicted in Figure 15.10 using various types of lines.

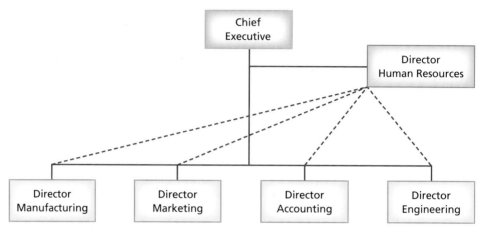

Figure 15.9: Functional relationship

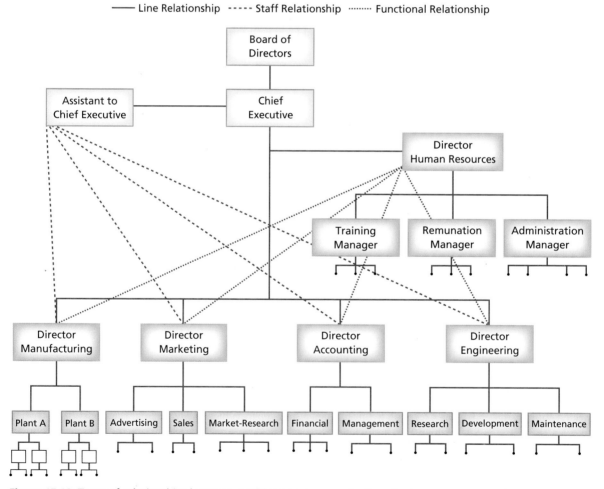

Figure 15.10: Types of relationships between positions on an organization chart

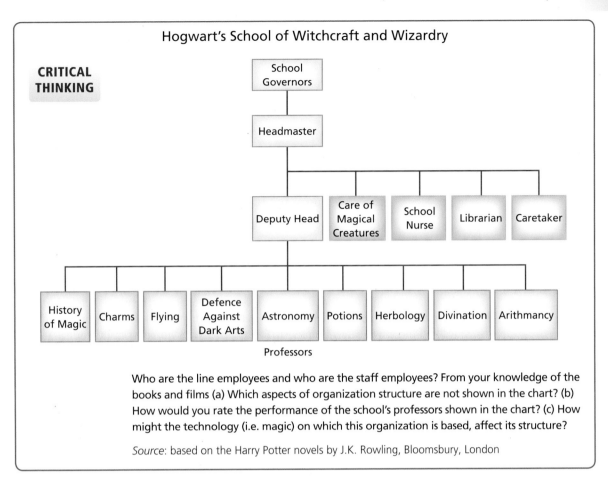

Hogwart's School of Witchcraft and Wizardry

Who are the line employees and who are the staff employees? From your knowledge of the books and films (a) Which aspects of organization structure are not shown in the chart? (b) How would you rate the performance of the school's professors shown in the chart? (c) How might the technology (i.e. magic) on which this organization is based, affect its structure?

Source: based on the Harry Potter novels by J.K. Rowling, Bloomsbury, London

🤚 **STOP AND SEARCH**   YouTube for *line and staff relationships*

Decisions about division of labour, levels of hierarchy, job descriptions, organization charts and types of authority all constitute the process of designing the formal organization. Senior management carefully plan the relationships that they wish to exist between different positions within the company. This enables the activities of different employees to be coordinated so as to achieve the organizational goal. These relationships between employees are all written down and can be checked and modified as required. However, to understand and explain the behaviour of people in organizations, it is also necessary to become familiar with the informal organization.

The informal organization refers to the undocumented relationships that arise spontaneously between individuals in the workplace as they interact with one another, not only to do their jobs, but also to meet their psychological needs (**Chapter 9**). These interactions lead to the creation of relationships between individual employees and to the development of informal groups, each with their own values and norms of behaviour. These groups are separate from those specified by the formal organization.

Formal organization
the documented, planned relationships, established by management to coordinate the activities of different employees towards the achievement of the organizational goal.

Informal organization
the undocumented relationships that arise spontaneously between employees as individuals interact with one another to meet their own psychological and physical needs.

Compared to the formal organization, the informal organization has a more transient membership, making it looser and more flexible, with interactions between individuals being more spontaneous and more emotional, resulting in their relationships being less clearly defined and their involvement more variable. The relationship between the formal and the informal organizations is shown in Figure 15.11.

However, the informal organization created by employees can come into conflict with the formal organization established by management. Together, the two affect the human behaviours that occur within an organization. Some of the differences between the two are shown in Table 15.3. Research by Knoche and Castrogiovanni (2015) examined the effects of informal social structures on individual actions and organizational outcomes. They concluded that in order to improve individual effectiveness and organizational efficiency, it would be beneficial for senior managers to examine the fit between the informal social structures of the groups and the formal structures and strategies of the organization.

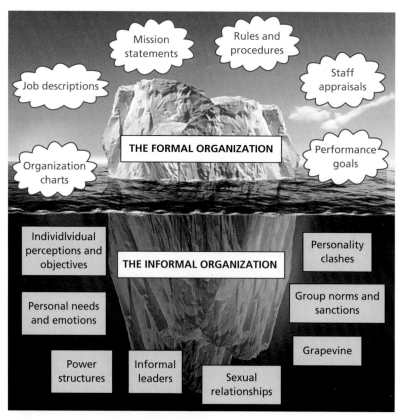

Figure 15.11: The formal and the informal organization

Table 15.3: The formal and the informal organization compared

	Formal organization	Informal organization
A structure		
(a) origin	planned	spontaneous
(b) rationale	rational	emotional
(c) characteristics	stable	dynamic
B position terminology	job	role
C goals	profitability or service to society	member satisfaction
D influence		
(a) base	position	personality
(b) type	authority	power
(c) flow	top down	bottom up
E control mechanism	threat of firing or demotion	physical or social sanction (norms)
F communication		
(a) channels	formal channels	grapevine
(b) networks	well defined, follow formal lines	poorly defined, cut across regular channels
G charting	organizational chart	sociogram
H miscellaneous		
(a) individuals included	• all individuals in work group	• only those 'acceptable'
(b) interpersonal relations	• prescribed by job description	• arise spontaneously
(c) leadership role	• assigned by organization	• result of membership
(d) basis for interaction	• functional duties or position	• personal characteristics status
(e) basis for attachment	• loyalty	• cohesiveness

Source: Based on *Organizational Behaviour: Concepts and Applications,* by Gray/Strake, © 1984. Reprinted by permission of Prentice-Hall, Inc., Upper Saddle River, NJ., p.412.

CUTTING EDGE   Social networks in organizational settings

photo credit: David Sella

Peter Gloor

Peter Gloor (2016) mapped the social networks found in various organizational settings including R&D organizations, bank marketing departments, high-tech sales teams and hospitals. He studied informal communication by measuring email archives, tweets and blog links. He sought to understand what distinguished innovative teams from less creative ones, and high-performing companies from underperforming ones.

His research identified how effective collaborative communication worked and thus offered guidance to managers as to how their groups should be organized and led; what the optimum level of group member participation should be; how quickly members should respond; and what tone of language they should use. His research findings relate to five topics:

- *Leadership*: Creative people work more effectively if they have strong leaders. Moreover, teams with rotating leadership, where different individuals took turns to lead the group, were found to be more creative than those in which one person was constantly in charge.

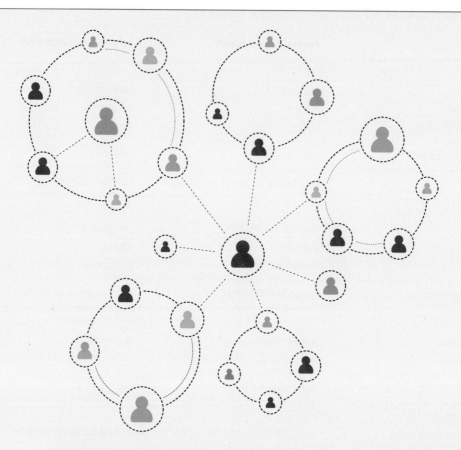

- *Participation level*: Information-consumers can be distinguished from information-producers or 'contributors'. Creative teams were characterized by their core members contributing similar numbers of email messages and by senior and junior members taking turns to contribute.

- *Response time*: While speed of email response is an indicator of employee and customer satisfaction as well as mutual respect, the study found no direct link between employee response speed and customer satisfaction. However, they found that happy customers answered their emails faster.

- *Language tone*: An evaluation of the sentiment and emotionality of email messages (though not their content) revealed the state of various relationships. For example, employees who are about to resign became less emotional in their language and contributed less leadership in rotational settings.

- *Shared context*: New word usage was considered from the perspective of the frequency of use of rare words (the more complex the language salespersons used, the more dissatisfied the customer become) and the diffusion of new words in the community (successful word introducers became most influential).

Information about collaboration obtained from electronic communication records can allow managers to optimize communication for improved employee collaboration and innovation.

STOP AND SEARCH YouTube for *Peter Gloor: Collaboration Innovation Networks* (7:17).

Sexuality and the informal organization

In contrast to the formal organization just described, the informal organization includes personal animosities and friendships, prestige and power structures, relationships between managers and subordinates, as well as emotional feelings, needs and desires. Sexuality is an important feature of the informal organization. It has been defined as the expression of our social relations to physical, bodily desires, real or imagined, by or for others, or for oneself, together with related bodily states and experience (Hearn et al., 1989). It is useful to contrast the concept of sex, which refers to the basic physiological differences between men and women, with gender, which refers to culturally specific patterns of behaviour which may be attached to either of the sexes (Oakley, 1972). For example, who should mow the lawn? Who should change the nappies? Most people now say gender when they actually mean sex.

Many of the themes of this chapter – such as jobs, hierarchy, authority and roles – are significantly influenced by sexuality, an issue that has hitherto been ignored in management and organization behaviour textbooks. This past neglect can be ascribed to organizations treating sexuality as something that should not occur within them. However, recent revelations in the media about sexual misconduct in a wide range of different organizations including banks, charities and in parliament, has radically changed this view. It has clearly demonstrated that sexuality is an integral part of every employee's personality and identity, and affects their interactions with other workers (Riach and Wilson, 2007). *Sexuality* refers to the way that a person goes about expressing themselves as a sexual being. Sexuality surrounds people in every way and in many forms.

Various commentators have written that organizations are a complex of web of work and play; that when you enter most organizations, you are entering a world of sexuality; and since human beings are sexual, so too will be the places where they work. Moreover, sexuality is closely related to power – the first reinforces the second. Both shape, control and maintain human interaction between employees, and therefore their behaviours. Power can be expressed through sexuality, and sexuality can be used to subordinate others to a lower status. Rosabeth Moss Kanter (1977) suggested that what may look like sex differences may, in reality, be power differences. Sexuality affects employees' work experiences, job performance, as well as the organizational balance of power (Fleming, 2007). Taking a historical perspective on men and women in the workplace, Julie Berebitsky (2012) argued that what actually goes on between men and women in the workplace has changed little, but what is acceptable has changed a great deal.

Fiona Wilson (2010) wrote that at work, sexuality refers to sex roles, sexual preference, sexual attractiveness and notions of masculinity and femininity. According to Michel Foucault (1979), notions of masculinity and femininity are based on social meanings that have been socially and culturally constructed. These meanings therefore are not fixed, but are subject to a process of ongoing revision through which sex is used to shape and control human relationships. Within organizations, sexuality manifests itself in issues such as sexual attractiveness; gender stereotyping; sex typing of jobs; the glass ceiling; office romances; sexual harassment and emotional labour (Table 15.4).

Since the 1960s, women have increasingly joined men in organizations. In Western societies, most people will spend more than a third of their adult life in the workplace, working in close proximity to one another. This, plus the social trends for later marriage and the long-hours culture, means that the boundaries between work and home have become blurred. Much courtship and mate selection now occurs at work. It is not surprising that about 30 per cent of workers will date a co-worker at some point in their careers (Nardi, 2008). Many relationships begin (and end) in the workplace even though some companies have policies banning office romances. The #Me Too campaign around the world has brought the issue of sexual behaviour in the workplace to the forefront of all organizations' attention. However, as Aquino et al. (2014, pp.233–34) noted:

> What we do know from reading the literature is that there are many ways that human sexuality reveals itself at work and that not all of them should or even can be entirely eliminated. We also know that there are many reasons social sexual behaviour occurs, and this behaviour is not always driven by ignoble motives. As in many other arenas of life where human sexuality finds expression, people engage in these behaviours at work because they feel lonely or daring or playful or bored or curious or distressed or excited or anxious or, perhaps more often than management scholars want to admit, simply because they are possessed by that most primordial and mystifying of human emotions, a state which James Joyce once described with characteristic eloquence as the 'deep unending ache of love!'

Table 15.4: Issues of sexuality in organizations

Issue	Description
Sexual attractiveness	Men and women using their physical appearance to influence outcomes, e.g. decisions on appointments, promotions, pay.
Gender stereotyping	Assumption that men and women possess different personality traits, e.g. men are strong, rational and firm; women are caring, emotional, passionate.
Sex-typing of jobs	Stereotyped attitudes towards men's and women's abilities, so that jobs are sex-typed e.g. 'male jobs' e.g. (engineering) or 'female jobs'(nursing).
Glass ceiling	Limitation of the seniority level to which women can rise – percentage of women occupying chief executive officer positions; on boards of directors; in top leadership positions.
Office romances	Emotional, physical or sexual involvement with another employee affecting organizational behaviour: includes daydreaming; flirting; handholding; sexual intercourse in the office.
Sexual harassment	Unwanted sexual attention that is perceived as threatening or offending; can be physical, verbal or non-verbal.
Emotional labour	The management of feelings to create publicly observable facial and bodily displays.

Sexuality and organizational image

Sexuality is also present in the way that a company may wish to be perceived by others. Virgin Atlantic Airlines' 2009 campaign for their 25th year anniversary had the slogan 'Still Red Hot'. Their television commercial featured a male pilot as well as female cabin crew wearing glamorous and sexy red suits while walking through an airport. As they do so, mostly men ogle the group of attractive air hostesses, and one man inadvertently squirts hamburger filling over himself. The 90-second commercial caused an uproar (which perhaps it was designed to do), and complaints were sent to the Advertising Standards Authority. It was claimed that this advertisement was insulting to all women, especially those working in the aviation industry, as the all-female cabin crew members were being promoted as the main reason for choosing the airline. The ASA responded by saying that even though some viewers might have found the representation of the women and men in the advertisement distasteful, it was unlikely to be seen as sexist towards men or women, or to reinforce those stereotypes (Sweney, 2009a, 2009b).

 **STOP AND SEARCH**   You Tube for *Virgin Atlantic Still Red Hot after 25 Years* (1:01).

Sexual harassment: the hidden costs for employers

Kate Greene (name changed), 25 describes how a male colleague, more than twice her age and with whom she had no working relationship, walked across their open-plan office and began to stroke the young journalist's long hair. 'I felt a hand on the back on my neck; somebody playing around with my hair and feeling my skin'. He put his hand underneath the ponytail, picked it up and started pretending to cut it off with his fingers as scissors and then swinging the end of the ponytail around. It came completely out of the blue and I was really shocked by it. I said: 'Oh my God, don't do that. Don't touch me,' and he took his hands off and slunk back to his desk'. After confiding in a friend and telling her manager, Ms Greene was sent home and stayed off work for two days. The harasser was temporarily moved to a different office, while the human resources department encouraged her to resolve the incident informally. 'The HR manager read out an apology the colleague had written: 'Sorry if you were upset . . . I didn't mean to cause offence'. The kind of shit apology that nobody really wants'. She has since began the process of making a formal complaint but is also contemplating leaving her job.

→

The consequences of sexual harassment on the workplace are well documented. Sexual harassment is defined in the Equality Act 2010, as 'unwanted conduct of a sexual nature which has the purpose or effect of violating someone's dignity, or creating an intimidating hostile, degrading, humiliating or offensive environment for them'. Sexual harassment leads to poor morale and performance, lost productivity, greater levels of stress and risk of stress-related illness, lack of respect for management and reputational damage. $45m is the amount 21st Century Fox paid to settle allegations of sexual harassment. The costs to business are far harder to quantify, but Matteo Winkler, assistant professor in international law at HEC business school in Paris, believes the existing legal tools 'will only be effective when organisations understand the [financial] consequences of such misbehaviours'. 'It is very hard to measure the cost of sexual harassment at work. Sexual harassment is an under-reported problem, but companies also enforce a code of silence through non-disclosure agreements' Prof Winkler says.

Reporting by large firms gives us a glimpse into some of the financial costs. 21st Century Fox, for example, paid $45m in the first quarter of 2017 to settle allegations of sexual harassment. In the same year, it received a $90m insurance payment for investor claims arising from the sexual harassment scandal at Fox News. There are high profile cases now coming to light in virtually every industry, reflecting survey results that show that harassment is commonplace. A report by the Trades Union Congress and the Everyday Sexism Project in 2016 found that more than half of the women polled had experienced some form of sexual harassment in UK workplaces but four out of five of them did not report the harassment to their employer.

ACAS, the UK workplace conciliation and advice service, recommends involving employees in policy design, and supplementing that with guidance training sessions and seminars. Small companies, which may not have HR departments, and where the impact of sexual harassment can feel disproportionately large, are advised to develop clear policies and designate people to deal with issues as they arise. Still, Prof Winkler cautions against seeing the framework of the law and having robust corporate sexual harassment policies as a solution in themselves: 'When you talk about the law, it's not only what you find in the statutes. It's what you find applied everyday in people's lives'. Good policy application comes down to corporate culture and, in particular, the role of management. Ben Willmott, head of public policy at the CIPD, the professional body for HR and people development, says: 'Have a clear policy, but lead by example. It is the perspective of the victim that matters, not the harasser, and management needs to take that very seriously. Policies are only of use if applied in practice'.

FT *Source:* E. Anyangwe (2018)
© *Financial Times,* 14 March 2018, reproduced with permission

Sexuality through informal relationships between employees in organizations can have both negative and positive aspects. The negative consequences for individuals and their fellow employees include creating jealousies; distractions from work; decreased productivity; increased errors; reduced professionalism; and exposure to sexual harassment. For the organization, the dangers include having to fire an employee; losing valuable talent; staff replacement costs; law suits; as well as bad publicity.

However, there are positive consequences as a good work atmosphere can develop when informal relationships are encouraged. Rather than being a limitation on bureaucracy, sexuality can actually contribute to efficient operation. It can make work more fun and exciting for employees, thereby reducing their absenteeism and late coming, increasing their motivation and job satisfaction, and raising overall company performance. Some commentators have treated sexual behaviour as inappropriate, and as having nothing to do with work itself.

However, they do acknowledge that sexuality is always present within the workplace. Others say that informal relations are as important as formal relationships in order to motivate employees and make the organization function. An awareness of the effects of sexuality in the workplace provides a new perspective on organizational behaviour and increases our ability to understand and manage it.

✓✓✓ **EMPLOYABILITY CHECK** (interpersonal skills, work ethic)

Your co-worker, Elizabeth, is a star salesperson of a 75-person software start-up. After a conference session, Brad the CFO of the company, asked her to join him for a drink at the hotel bar where they had flirted. A few days later, he asked her out on a real date. He was not her boss, neither appraising her performance nor setting her salary. He was in finance, she was in sales. They were more like peers. He wanted to get to know her and she had agreed. Despite their attempts to keep their relationship quiet, everyone in the office seemed to know. Her boss took her aside and explained that what they did privately was their own business, but that they should 'keep it out of the office'. What would you advise Elizabeth to do now? (Bearden, 2016)

Dating superiors in the workplace

Colleen Malachowski and her colleagues (2012) examined 212 organizational members' perceptions of and responses to workplace romances. They responded to hypothetical scenarios of a male or female co-worker dating a superior. When a co-worker was involved in a romance with a superior, as opposed to a person of another company status, they perceived them to be driven more by job motives rather than love motives. They believed that they were likely to enjoy unfair advantages due to the romance, a situation which subjects found threatening to themselves. They trusted them less because the co-worker's position in the organization could be compromised if privacy rule violations and information leakage occurred. The co-worker's privacy could be violated if the peer disclosed information about the co-worker to the superior that they were dating.

Organizational members were therefore likely to withhold, manipulate or provide ambiguous company-related information to a peer who was dating a superior as a means of self-protection. Communicating deceptively could be used to even the playing field. In addition, these perceptions led them to be less inclined to communicate accurate and honest personal information to that person. Controlling one's self-disclosure was a way to mask vulnerability and to protect oneself from breaches of privacy. There was a fear of personal information getting back to the superior. Employees could distort their self-disclosures as a means of organizational survival. It also led to a higher likelihood of workers actively deceiving those peers who were dating their superiors. Attributions of motives, judgements of fairness, and feelings of trust created by the workplace romances all appeared to drive the accuracy, honesty, quality, and quantity of information communicated between co-workers.

The authors conclude that workplace romances can affect information flow through the company. They impact negatively on an organization's psychological climate leading to lower job satisfaction and commitment, and higher absenteeism and turnover among employees. This being so, they recommend that it may be best for organizational members to strictly uphold the public–private split by refraining from engaging in workplace romances.

Roles in organizations

Role the pattern of behaviour expected by others from a person occupying a certain position in an organization hierarchy.

Roles are a central feature of every organization structure and are specified in the organization hierarchy. All organization structuring occurs through the specification of the roles that employees are expected to play. It follows that if individuals occupying different positions in the hierarchy have mutual and complementary expectations, then the patterning and predictability of their behaviour is increased. The formal positions identified on an organization chart of a company imply the expectation of certain behaviours from any person occupying that office. This becomes the person's **role**. Roles are thus associated with positions in the organization and are involved in interactions. A single person plays many different and sometimes conflicting roles in life, both sequentially and simultaneously (e.g., mother, team leader, union official).

Critical roles

Mike Barriere and his colleagues (2018) argued that every organization possessed roles whose successful performance was critical to its current operation and future growth. These critical roles fall into two categories. Value-creating roles generate revenue, lower operating costs and increase capital efficiency. Value-enabling roles perform indispensible work that allows value-creators to do their jobs e.g. support functions like cyber-security and risk management.

These critical roles were predominantly located below the level of the chief executive and could be in any of the functions – manufacturing, finance, human resources or design. Role importance is defined as the value that can be created or enabled by that role. Not all roles at the same hierarchical level are necessarily assigned the same importance. In the authors' experience, 60 per cent of these roles are located two levels below the chief execu-

tive, and 30 per cent are three levels below. Twenty per cent of critical roles were in counterintuitive places. The authors estimate that 25 to 50 critical roles in a company can represent the bulk of its potential value.

For this reason Barriere et al. say that companies need to identify which roles are critical to them and to objectively articulate each role's requirements so as to ensure that only the top performers who possess the appropriate skills and knowledge are recruited to fill them. The aim is to match employee talent to company value. They recommend that each business leader asks: Where does the value in this company department come from? Which roles are most critical to its success? Would a new company strategy create new critical roles? What disruptions might change current critical role responsibilities?

Source: based on Barriere et al. (2018)

● Critical role ■ New role

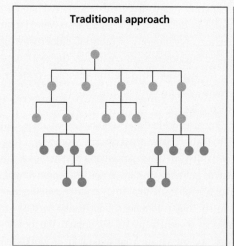

Traditional approach

Hierarchy heavily influences which roles are viewed as most important

Within a hierarchical level, roles are assigned similar levels of importance

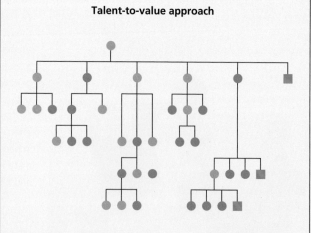

Talent-to-value approach

Role importance is linked to an explicit perspective on value that can be created or enabled by role

Not all roles in the same hierarchical level are assigned the same importance

People's roles in organizations are ranked by status. Individuals occupying the role of manager are generally accorded more status that those occupying that of cleaner. In other companies, the ranking of roles is less obvious. John van Maanen (1991) described the rank ordering of occupations at Disneyland:

1. Disneyland Ambassadors and Tour Guides. These were the upper class, prestigious, bilingual women in charge of ushering tourists through the park.

2. Ride operators who either performed skilled work such as live narration, or who drove costly vehicles such as antique trains, horse drawn carriages or the Monorail.

3. All the other ride operators.

4. Sweepers who kept the concrete grounds clean were designated as *proles*.

5. There was a still lower, fifth category of *sub-prole* or peasant status.

6. The 'lowest of the low' included food and concession workers, pancake ladies, peanut pushers, coke blokes, suds drivers and soda jerks.

Organizations are to a degree, cooperative arrangements that are characterized by give-and-take, mutual adjustment and negotiation. Their members get on with one another, often without explicit guidance, instruction or direction. The concept of role helps our understanding of this aspect of organizational life by stressing that employees monitor and direct their own work behaviour in the light of what they know is expected of them.

Many of the tasks involved in any job have been learned and assimilated so well by the employee that they become accepted as being part of the person. It raises the question of whether, in behaving in a certain way, we are ourselves or just conforming to what the organization (and society) expects of us. Role relationships therefore are the field within which behaviour occurs. People's behaviour at any given moment, is the result of:

- their personalities
- their perception and understanding of each other
- their attitudes to the behavioural constraints imposed by the role relationship
- the degree of their socialization with respect to constraints
- their ability to inhibit and control their behaviours

Prison experiment

Do our attitudes, values and self-image affect how we play roles in organizations (e.g. of a student, lecturer, doctor or doorman) or is it those organizational roles that determine our attitudes, values and self-image? In a classic experiment, Philip Zimbardo (2007) created his own prison at Stanford University to answer this question. He selected 21 young men who had responded to a newspaper advertisement, interviewing them to ensure they were mature, emotionally stable, normal, intelligent North American male students from middle-class homes with no criminal record. Each volunteer was paid $15 a day to participate in a two week study of prison life. A toss of a coin arbitrarily designated these recruits as either prisoners or guards. Hence, at the start of the study, there were no measurable differences between the two groups assigned to play the two roles (10 prisoners and 11 guards).

Those taking the role of guards had their individually reduced by being required to wear uniforms, including silver reflector glasses which prevented eye-contact. They were to be referred to as Mr Correction Officer by the prisoners, and were given symbols of their power which included clubs, whistles, hand-cuffs and keys. They were given minimal instructions by Zimbardo, being required only to 'maintain law and order'. While physical violence was forbidden, they were told to make up and improvise their own formal rules to achieve the stated objective during their eight-hour, three-man shifts.

Those assigned the role of prisoners were unexpectedly picked up at their homes by a city policeman in a squad car. Each was searched, hand-cuffed, finger-printed, booked in at the Palo Alto police station, blindfolded and then transferred to Zimbardo 'Stanford County Prison' in the basement of the university's

→

psychology building. Each prisoner's sense of unique-ness and prior identity was minimized. They were given smocks to wear and had nylon stocking caps on their heads to simulate baldness. Their personal effects were removed; they had to use their ID numbers; and were housed in stark cells. All this made them appear similar to each other and indistinguishable to observers. Six days into the planned 14-day study, the researchers had to abandon the experiment. Why?

In a matter of days, even hours, a strange relation-ship began to develop between the prisoners and their guards. Some of the boy guards began to treat the boy prisoners as if they were despicable animals and began to take pleasure in psychological cruelty. The prisoners in turn became servile, dehumanized robots who thought only of their individual survival, escape and mounting hatred of the guards. About a third of the guards became tyrannical in their arbitrary use of power, and became quite inventive in developing techniques to break the spirit of the prisoners and to make them feel worthless. Having crushed a prison rebellion, the guards escalated their aggression and this increased the prisoners' sense of dependence, depression and helplessness. Within 36 hours, the first 'prisoner' had to be released because of

uncontrolled crying, fits of rage, disorganized thinking and severe depression. Others begged to be paroled and nearly all were willing to forfeit their money if the guards agreed to release them.

Zimbardo attributed these changes to a number of causes. First, to the creation of a new environment within which the two groups were separated from the outside world. New attitudes were developed about this new 'mini-world' as well as what constituted appropriate behaviour within it. Second, within this new prison world, the participants were unable to differentiate clearly between the role that they were asked to play (prisoner or guard) and their real self. A week's experience of (tempor-ary) imprisonment appeared to undo a lifetime of learn-ing. Human values and self-concepts were challenged and the pathological side of human nature was allowed to surface. The prisoners became so programmed to think of themselves as prisoners, that when their requests for parole were refused, they returned docilely to their cells, instead of feeling capable of just withdrawing from an unpleasant university psychological research experiment.

Zimbardo concluded that individual behaviour is largely under the control of social and environmental forces, rather than being the result of personality traits, character or willpower. In an organizational context such as a prison, merely assigning labels to people and put-ting them in situations where such labels acquire validity and meaning appears sufficient to elicit a certain type of behaviour. The power of the prison environment was stronger than each individual's will to resist falling into his role. Zimbardo considered the relevance of the findings of his research, conducted in the 1970s with the behaviour of US soldiers in Abu Graib prison in Baghdad in 2004. A film, *The Experiment* (2010) was made, based on this research study.

 **STOP AND SEARCH**   YouTube for *Zimbardo Stanford Prison Experiment.*

CRITICAL THINKING   Zimbardo talks about 'bad apples', 'bad barrels' and 'bad barrel-makers'. In other words he says do not blame the individual, blame their environment and those who created that environment. Does Zimbardo's argument mean that employees, negligent bankers, brutal soldiers (even lazy students) no longer have to feel responsible for their own actions but can blame it on their organization's structure and the senior management who designed it?

Role conflict the simultaneous existence of two or more sets of role expectations on a person in such a way that compliance with one makes it difficult to comply with the others.

The roles that we play are part of our self-concept, and personality theory tells us that we come to know ourselves through our interactions with others. We play different roles throughout our lives. These require us to use different abilities, thereby adding more aspects to our self-image. Which roles we play and how successfully we play them during our adulthood affects our level of self-esteem. Thus the roles that we play inside and outside the organization affect both our self-image and self-esteem. In his research, Philip Zimbardo showed that people possess mental concepts of different roles and conform to them when asked or required to do so. The woman who is both a manager and a mother may experience role conflict when the expectations in these two important roles pull her in opposite directions.

✓✓✓   **EMPLOYABILITY CHECK** (self-management)

Identify any two roles that you currently occupy simultaneously in different social contexts, e.g. at work, home, leisure. Identify a role conflict that you regularly experience as a result of such multiple role occupancy. How do you deal with it?

Changing roles: master and servant?

Sharon Bolton and Carol Boyd (2003) studied the work of airline cabin crew. In an effort to gain a competitive advantage through superior customer service, international airlines have introduced highly selective recruitment programmes for cabin crew that identify those applicants who possess the particular qualities required for the job. However, contrary to popular belief, possessing the 'right' personality is not enough. Having been selected, successful candidates undergo intensive training and culture management programmes. They found that the airline went to great lengths to inculcate its values into its new hires. Interestingly, customer service training took the same amount of time as safety and emergency training; while training in areas related to the health and

well-being of crew (e.g. dealing with violence, manual handling) was minimal or did not take place at all.

The resounding message received by cabin crews was that what was most important was how they presented themselves to passengers. One respondent noted that over the years, the airline industry had taught its cabin crews to be very subservient. Flight attendants, like theatre or film actors, were asked to assume a particular identity that helps them to perform their work role more efficiently. In their case, they are asked to assume the status of servant in relation to the customer who was the master. One respondent stated that cabin crew encountered verbal abuse on a daily basis and that many passengers had no respect for them, seeing them as servants who were expected to carry their bags and place them in the overhead lockers. Another flight attendant with 21 years of experience who had had to suffer rudeness, said that the 'passenger is always right' and they are fully aware of this and take advantage of the situation. They know that they can say anything they like to cabin staff, usually do, and get away with it.

The airline required the work routines to be predictable and to correspond continually to predetermined standards. Temporal and spatial constraints meant that there was little room for any variation in routine. The airline needed to be able to rely on employees to give a homogeneous role performance on every occasion.

Home viewing

Erin Brockovich (2000, director Steven Soderbergh) is an unemployed single mother (played by Julia Roberts) with three children. After losing a car accident personal injury claim in court, she joins her attorney's law firm as a filing clerk. She discovers a systematic cover-up of the poisoning of a town's water supply by the Pacific Gas and Electric Company. The film demonstrates the sexualization of work. Brockovich makes her sexuality explicit in the way that she dresses and behaves. She wears her long blonde hair loosely, and dresses in tight, low-cut tops, short skirts, see-through blouses and high heels. Her sexuality and lack of self-control is shown as disrupting and threatening order in the office. She is on a 'prowl for papers'. Observe how she uses her sexual skills on a young male worker to obtain those documents (see Bell, 2008; Forbes and Smith, 2007).

Formalization

Rules procedures or obligations explicitly stated and written down in organization manuals.

Formalization the degree to which an organization has written rules, operating procedures, job descriptions, organizational charts and uses formal, written communication.

A defining characteristic of every bureaucratic organization structure are its **rules**. From the 1930s, senior managements in large organizations increasingly adopted systems of bureaucratic (rule-governed) control. **Formalization** refers to the degree to which an organization has written rules, operating procedures, job descriptions, organization charts and uses formal, written communication. Formalization complemented the control exercised through machinery, and replaced that exercised through supervisory commands. Rules serve to regulate and control what individuals do and, if employees comply with them, the rules ensure the predictability of employee behaviour within organizations. For example, as part of the routine process of monitoring its restaurant managers, McDonald's requires 72 safety protocols to be performed daily in each of its restaurants (Robbins and Judge, 2013, p. 221). Both parties can benefit. For employees, rational and fair rules avoid managers' personal biases. This is true despite the fact that the rules are devised and policed by management who can relax or ignore them at their discretion. Unions use rules to restrict the arbitrary power of employers and demarcation rules protect jobs. Although rules can cause frustration to employees, they also reduce role ambiguity.

Management also benefits from rules. It uses formal rules and procedures to coordinate the activities of different employees and to establish conformity. Bureaucratic structures create job hierarchies with numerous job titles, each with its own pay rate. Elaborate formal rules (based on purportedly 'objective' criteria) provide a basis for evaluating employee performance and determining rewards. Government rules on equality seek to stop discrimination at work based on race, sex, age, religion or national origin. Rules are part of management's attempt to 'routinize' tasks so as to remove the uncertainties involved in dealing with the environment. Provided that the environment is stable and unchanging, rules are likely to be an effective strategy to increase the predictability of employee behaviour.

"We only have a few rules around here, but we really enforce them."

Think of some of the rules that you have encountered in organizations to which you currently belong or used to belong. How effective are they in directing your behaviour and that of other members? What problems do they cause, what advantages do they offer and for whom?

Centralization versus decentralization

Centralization the concentration of authority and responsibility for decision-making power in the hands of managers at the top of an organization's hierarchy.

Decentralization the dispersion of authority and responsibility for decision making to operating units, branches and lower level managers.

A fundamental question faced by every chief executive is what kinds of decisions are to be made and by whom. The answer determines both the distribution of power within an organization (**see Chapter 22**) and the allocation of company resources. Some senior executives prefer to retain decision-making power in their hands and thus run highly centralized organizations. Centralization refers to the concentration of authority and responsibility for decision-making power in the hands of managers at the top of an organization's hierarchy. Others choose to delegate their power giving junior managers more individual autonomy; self-directed teams greater freedom; and introducing job enrichment for shop floor workers. Thus, their organizations are much more decentralized in their structure. Decentralization refers to the downward dispersion of authority and responsibility for decision making to operating units, branches and lower level managers.

New technology has facilitated this by making information easily available to all levels of employees, right down to the shop floor. The question of whether and how much to centralize or decentralize, has been one of the major topics discussed in organization structuring. Each approach has its own advantages:

Centralization advantages

- A greater uniformity in decisions possible.
- Fewer skilled (and highly paid) managers are required.
- Greater control and cost-effectiveness in company resources.
- Less extensive planning and reporting procedures are required.
- Senior managers' awareness of future plans ensures best decisions made for the organization.

Decentralization advantages

- Shop floor decisions can be made faster.
- Increases creativity, innovation and flexibility.
- Increased decision making by lower-level employees motivates them.
- Lower-level management problems can be dealt with quickly by junior staff.
- Junior managers have an opportunity to develop their decision-making skills.
- Spread of decision making workload allows senior managers time for strategic planning.

The balance between centralization and decentralization changes on an ongoing basis. It does so in response to changes in company size, market opportunities, developments in new technology, and not least, the quality of the existing decision making. Some cynics argue that whichever of the two is currently fashionable; it will be superseded by the other in due course. This may occur for no other reason than the incoming chief executive wishing to make a highly visible impact on his or her managers, employees, shareholders and financial analysts.

STOP AND SEARCH   YouTube for *centralization* and *decentralization*.

 **RECAP**

1. *Explain how organization structure affects human behaviour in organizations.*

   - The procedures employees are required to follow, and the rules by which they have to abide, all control and direct their behaviour in specified directions.

   - The roles that people play, and the expectations that others have of role holders, also direct the behaviour of employees. Indeed, in the long term, these may even lead to a change in the personality of the employee.

2. *List the main elements of organization structure.*

   - The main elements include: chain of command; hierarchical levels; line employees; rules; staff employees; role expectations; span of control; departmentalization; authority; and job description.

3. *Relate the concept of span of control to that of organization hierarchy.*

   - The narrower the span of control, the taller the organization hierarchy (and vice versa); and the greater the consequences for employee promotion opportunities.

4. *Identify line and staff relationships on an organization chart.*

   - Line relationships are depicted vertically on an organization chart, indicating that those above possess the authority to direct the behaviours of those below.

   - Seniors have responsibility for the work of the juniors, while the juniors are accountable for their work to their seniors.

   - Staff relationships are depicted horizontally on an organization chart, indicating that those who possess specific expertise e.g. Human Resources, IT, advise those in line positions.

5. *Distinguish between the formal and informal organization within a company.*

   - The formal organization refers to the collection of work groups that have been consciously designed by senior management to maximize efficiency and achieve organizational goals.

   - The informal organization refers to the unofficial, network of relationships that spontaneously establish themselves between individuals in an organization on the basis of their common interests and friendships.

   - The two forms consist of the same people, albeit arranged in different ways.

6. *Understand the nature and impact of sexuality on organizational behaviour.*

   - Sexuality refers to sex roles, sexual preferences, sexual attractiveness and notions of masculinity and femininity in organizations

   - Sexuality manifests itself in issues of sexual attractiveness; gender stereotyping; sex typing of jobs; the glass ceiling; the gender pay gap; work-life balance; office romances; and sexual harassment.

RECAP: What did they find?

- Cathcart et al. (2004) discovered a relationship between group span of control and the engagement of its members. As the number of members in a work group supervised by a nurse manager increased, their employee engagement scores declined. These findings were independent of demographic variables such as job tenure (years in post), work status (full or part time), union membership, role (management or not) and job type (patient care or not).

- The two points at which engagement scores dropped most noticeably was a span of control larger than 15:1, and then again, one larger than 40:1. What were reasons for this? For the sub-15:1 groups, the differentiating factors was whether their opinions were taken into account, and for the over-40:1 groups, the key issue was the presence of a person who encouraged their development. The findings demonstrated the organizational risk of increasing spans of control without first carefully analysing the possible negative effects on employee engagement.

- In this organization, senior nurse executives reviewed the work of nurse managers who were directly accountable for between 75 to 150 staff. They decided to add management positions in four patient care areas to decrease the manager's span of control and increase the engagement of the nursing staff within them. Before the change, each manager had 80 direct reports. The additions reduced their spans of control by between 30 and 50 per cent, and in these four areas, employee engagement rose by between 7 and 14 per cent. This healthcare system discovered that span of control did indeed matter.

Revision

1. Discuss the disadvantages of centralization and decentralization.

2. Why do organization structures differ? Is there a 'best' organization structure?

3. Suggest how a managers' role might be affected by the seniority of his or her position in the hierarchy, their industry sector and organizational size.

4. What are the costs and benefits for those involved in romances at work? Should a company ignore or actively discourage romantic relationships between its employees? What can senior management do to minimize the problems associated with workplace romances?

Research assignment

Interview a manager or supervisor about any of the seven elements of their organization's structure as shown in Table 15.1 (work specialization, hierarchy, span of control, etc). Do any of these prevent them from doing their job as they would like or force them to do it in a way that they do not like? Ask them what changes they would make; what aspect of their organization's structure would they change in order to improve it? Who would benefit from these changes?

Springboard

Robert Duncan (1978–79) 'What's the right organization structure?', *Organizational Dynamics,* 7(3): 59–73. This classic article provides a structured framework with which managers can determine which type of organization structure is most suitable for their particular company.

Bill McEvily, Giuseppe Soda and Marco Totoriello (2014) 'More formally: Rediscovering the missing link between formal organization and informal social structure', *Academy of Management Annals,* 8(1): 299–345. The authors attempt to bring together the studies into formal and informal structures which, in their view, have been considered separately.

Naomi Stanford (2018) *Organization Structure,* third edition, Abingdon: Routledge. The writer provides a detailed explanation of how to analyse and structure an organization.

Philip Zimbardo (2007) *The Lucifer Effect: How Good People Turn Evil,* London: Rider. The author describes how the organizational context in which individuals work (including the structure) affects their behaviour, irrespective of their individual attributes such as personality, learning or motivation.

OB cinema

Aliens (1986, directed by James Cameron). DVD track 14: 1:00:47-1:08:08 (8 minutes).

The second film in this science fiction series is set in the distant future on planet LV-426. The characters include Lieutenant Gorman, the senior officer of the space marines, Sergeant Apone, Corporal Hicks, Private Hudson and others. In addition to these military personnel, there is Burke, who represents the Weyland-Yutani Corporation which owns the facilities on the planet, and Ripley (played by Sigourney Weaver) who is employed by it. The scene begins with Ripley shouting at Gorman 'Get them out of there, do it now' and ends at the point at which Corporal Hicks says 'It's the only way to be sure. Let's do it!' Which elements of organizational structure are illustrated in this clip?

Chapter exercises

1: Invisible organization structure

Objectives 1. To make you aware of your existing experience of organization structures.

2. To allow you to consider how organization structures affects your behaviour.

Briefing Individually:

1. Think about the job that you currently have or have had in the past. If your work experience is limited, think about your 'job' as a pupil in school or a student at university. From this perspective, insert your answers to the questions below. Leave the concept column blank.

Item	Your answer	Concept
1 Write the job title of the person to whom you report.		
2 Write the job title of someone whose job in your organization is to make things or to provide a service to others.		
3 Write the job title of someone whose job it is to provide specialist advice or assistance to those people who make things or who provide a service to others.		
4 If you share one boss with others, how many other people does this one person supervise?		
5 Think of an instruction given to you by your boss, teacher or lecturer with which you complied.		
6 About how many levels of hierarchy are there between your position and the most senior person in the organization?		
7 Think of an organization rule that you have obeyed. What topic did it relate to?		
8 Think of one thing that you did because of the position that you hold in your organization, rather than because of your natural inclinations.		
9 At work or university, you are a member of a department. On what basis is that department organized?		
10 Do you have a piece of paper that describes the tasks that you are required to perform in your job, and what decisions you can make on your own?		

In groups:

1. Starting with the first item, compare the answers of the group members, highlighting the differences.

2. Move onto the second and later items as time allows.

2: Designing your organization's structure

Objectives 1. To translate an organization idea into a structural form depicted on an organization chart.

2. To understand the issues involved in designing organizations.

3. To examine structural alternatives when redesigning a company to deal with growth.

Briefing 1. Form into groups as directed by your instructor.

2. Read the exercise below.

3. Work with your group members to complete the task at the end of each stage.

Exercise You are eating a lunchtime sandwich and drinking a coffee. You realize that your mother could not do the same because she is gluten-intolerant. There must be many people like her. You decide to start your own bakery producing gluten-free bakery products in your town/city. You think of the range of different bakery products that people eat, as well as when, where and how they eat them.

Stage 1: Decide what gluten-free products your start-up bakery will sell and what services it will provide for customers. Will these be produced on-site, bought-in from outside, or a combination of both? What tasks need to be performed? What jobs need to be filled? Draw the organization chart of your start-up bakery. Each position on the chart will perform specific tasks or be responsible for particular outcomes. Your group should be prepared to justify the choice of its organization design.

Stage 2: Your bakery is in its third year of operation and is very successful. You decide to open a second bakery two miles away. What challenges would you face running your business at two locations? How do you intend to manage both bakeries at the same time? Draw an organization chart showing your two bakeries and justify your organization design choices.

Stage 3: Five years on and you are a successful entrepreneur. You now have five bakeries. Where have you opened these other bakeries? How do you keep in touch with what is going on in all of them? How do you deal with issues of human resources, control and information systems? What are your biggest problems? How have you dealt with them in terms of your structural design decisions? Draw an organization chart showing your five bakeries company and justify your organization design decisions.

Stage 4: Ten years further on and you have gone international. You have 80 bakeries spread around the five countries that are nearest to your own. What issues and problems that you have to deal with as a result of decision to enter foreign markets in terms of organization structure? Draw an organization chart showing your international bakery company and justify your organization design decisions.

Debrief
- Groups share, compare and justify their organization design choice at each of the stages of their bakery company's growth.
- In turn, spokespersons display their own groups' organizational charts, highlighting the similarities and differences with other groups, and justifying their own group's choices.
- The class pays particular attention decisions about organization structure which relate to the systems and mechanisms that facilitate information flow; co-ordination and control

Source: Exercise adapted from Harvey and Morouney (1998)

References

Albers, S., Wohlgezogen, F. and Zajac, E.J. (2016) 'Strategic alliance structures: an organization design perspective', *Journal of Management*, 42(3): 582–614.

Anderson, C. and Brown, C.E. (2010) 'The functions and dysfunctions of hierarchy', *Research in Organizational Behaviour*, 30: 55–89.

Anyangwe, E. (2018) 'Sexual harassment: the hidden costs for employers', *Financial Times*, 14 March.

Aquino, K., Sheppard, L. Watkins, M.B., O'Reilly, J. and Smith, A. (2014) 'Social sexual behaviour at work', *Research in Organizational Behaviour*, 34: 217–36.

Barriere, M., Owens, M. and Pobereskiln, S. (2018) 'Linking talent to value', *McKinsey Quarterly*, April.

Bearden, J.N. (2016) 'Case study: an office romance gone wrong', *Harvard Business Review*, 94(9): 109–13.

Bell, E. (2008) *Reading Management and Organization in Film*. London: Palgrave Macmillan.

Berebitsky, J. (2012) *Sex and the Office: A History of Gender, Power and Desire*, New Haven, CT: Yale University Press.

Bock, L. (2015) *Work Rules*, London: John Murray.

Boddy, D. (2016) *Management: An Introduction,* seventh edition, Harlow, Essex: Pearson.

Bolton, S. C. and Boyd, C. (2003) 'Trolley dolly or skilled emotion manager: moving on from Hochschild's managed heart', *Work, Employment and Society,* 17(2): 289–308.

Cathcart, D., Jeska, S., Karnas, J., Miller, S.E. Pechace, J. and Rheault, L.(2004) 'Span of control matters', *Journal of Nursing Administration,* 34(9): 395–99.

Chandler, A. D. (1988) 'Origins of the organization chart', *Harvard Business Review,* 66(2): 156–57.

Child, J. (2015) *Organization: Contemporary Principles and Practice,* second edition, Chichester: Wiley.

Duncan, R. B. (1979) 'What is the right organization structure? Decision tree analysis provides the answer', *Organizational Dynamics,* 7(3): 59–80.

Fleming, P. (2007) 'Sexuality, power and resistance in the workplace', *Organization Studies,* 28(2): 239–56.

Forbes, J.B. and Smith, J.E. (2007) 'The potential of Erin Brockovich to introduce organization behaviour topics', *Organization Management Journal,* 4(3): 207–18.

Foucault, M. (1979) *Discipline and Punish,* Harmondsworth, Middlesex: Penguin Books.

Fox, A. (1966) *Industrial Sociology and Industrial Relations, Research Paper 3,* London: Royal Commission on Trade Unions and Employers' Associations.

Gloor, P.A. (2016) 'What email reveals about your organization', *MIT Sloan Management Review,* 57(2): 8–11.

Grant, A.M., Berg, J.M. and Cable, D.M. (2014) 'Job titles as identity badges: how self-reflective titles can reduce emotional exhaustion', *Academy of Management Journal,* 57(4): 1201–25.

Gray, J. L., and Starke, F. A. (1984) *Organizational Behaviour: Concepts and Applications* (third edition), Columbus, OH: Merrill Publishing.

Harvard Business Review (2014) 'The chart that organized the 20th century', 92(9): 32–33.

Harvard Business Review (2016) 'Talent creative job titles can energize workers', 94(5): 24–25.

Harvey, C. and Morouney, K. (1998) 'Organization structure and design: The Club Ed exercise', *Journal of Management Education,* 22(3): 425–28.

Hearn, J.R., Sheppard, D.L., Tancred, P. and Burrell, G. (eds) (1989) *The Sexuality of Organization,* London: Sage Publications.

Jaques, E. (1990) 'In praise of hierarchy', *Harvard Business Review,* 68(1): 127–33.

Kanter, R.M. (1977) *Men and Women of the Corporation,* New York: Basic Books.

Knoche, H. and Castrogiovanni, G.J. (2015) 'The effects of informal social structures: a cognition-structure-action approach', *Organization Management Journal,* 12(3): 139–52.

Koontz, H. (1966) 'Making theory operational: the span of management', *Journal of Management Studies,* 3(3): 229–43

Lawler, E.E. (1988) 'Substitutes for hierarchy', *Organizational Dynamics,* 17(1): 5–15.

Leavitt, H.J. (1965) 'Applied organizational change in industry: structural, technological and humanistic approaches' in March J.G. (ed), *Handbook of Organizations,* Rand McNally: Stokie, IL, pp.1144–70.

Levitt, S.D. and Dubner, S.J. (2005) *Freakonomics,* London: Penguin Books

Levitt, S.D. and Venkatesh, S.A. (2000) 'An economic analysis of a drug-selling gang's finances', *Quarterly Journal of Economics,* 115(3): 755–89.

Lorsch, J.W. (1977) 'Organizational design: a situational perspective', *Organizational Dynamics,* 6(2): 2–14.

Malachowski, C., Chory, R. and Claus, C. (2012) 'Mixing pleasure with work: employee perceptions of and responses to workplace romance', *Western Journal of Communication,* 76(4): 358–79.

Nardi, H. (2008) *The Greenwood Encyclopedia of Love, Courtship and Sexuality Through History,* sixth edition, Westport, CT: Greenwood Press.

National Army Museum (2019) 'British army organization', https://www.nam.ac.uk.

Oakley, A. (1972) *Sex, Gender and Society.* London: Temple Smith.

Riach, K. and Wilson, F. (2007) 'Don't screw the crew: exploring the rules of engagement in organizational romance', *British Journal of Management,* (18)1: 79–92.

Robbins, S. P. and Judge (2013) *Organizational Behaviour,* fifteenth edition, Harlow: Pearson Education.

Robbins, S. P., Judge and Campbell, T.T. (2017) *Organizational Behaviour* (second edition), Harlow: Pearson Education.

Schmidt, E. and Rosenberg, J. (2017) *How Google Works* (second edition), London: John Murray.

Sweney, M. (2009a) 'Virgin ad prompts complaints of sexism', https://www.theguardian.com/media/2009/feb/09/virgin-atlantic-ad-sexist-ofcom [accessed January 2019]

Sweney, M. (2009b) 'Virgin ad not sexist, rules ASA', https://www.theguardian.com/media/2009/feb/09/virgin-atlantic-ad-not-sexist-rules-asa [accessed January 2019]

Theobald, N.A. and Nicholson-Crotty, S. (2005) 'The many faces of span of control: organization structure across multiple goals', *Administration and Society,* 36(6): 648–60.

Van Maanen, J. (1991) 'The smile factory: work at Disneyland' in Schein, E.H., Frost, P.J., Moore, L.F., Louis, M.R., Lundberg, C.C. and Martin, J. (eds.), *Reframing Organizational Culture,* Newbury Park, CA: Sage Publications, pp. 31–54.

Venkatesh, S.A. and Levitt, S.D. (2000) 'The financial activities of an urban street gang', *Quarterly Journal of Economics,* 115(3): 755–89.

Wilson, F. (2010) *Organizational Behaviour and Work: A Critical Introduction,* third edition, Oxford: Oxford University Press.

Withey, A. (2018) 'Pretentious 'executive' job titles were a Victorian invention', Exeter University, 12 February, https://www.exeter.ac.uk/news/research/title_639543_en.html [accessed January 2019]

Zimbardo, P.G. (2007) *The Lucifer Effect: How Good People Turn Evil,* London: Rider & Co.

CHAPTER 16

Organization design

Key terms

corporate strategy

organization design

legitimate authority

bureaucracy

managerial activities

management roles

contingency approach to organization structure

technological determinism

technological complexity

technological interdependence

mediating technology

long-linked technology

intensive technology

task variety

task analysability

environmental determinism

environmental complexity

environmental dynamism

mechanistic organization structure

organic organization structure

differentiation

integration

strategic choice

Learning outcomes

When you have read this chapter, you should be able to define those key terms in your own words, and be able to:

1. Relate corporate strategy to organization design.

2. State the main characteristics of a bureaucratic organization structure as specified by Max Weber.

3. Distinguish Fayol's six managerial activities and the main ideas of the classical management school.

4. Distinguish Mintzberg's ten management roles.

5. Identify the writers who comprise the early contingency approach and state their main individual contributions.

6. Discuss the strengths and weaknesses of bureaucratic organization structures.

7. Identify the influence of early organization design ideas on contemporary organizations.

Why study organization design?

A survey of global executives by the management consultancy McKinsey revealed that almost 60 per cent of them had experienced organizational re-design in the last two years, and a further 25 per cent had undergone it three or more years ago (Aronowitz et al., 2015). In contrast, past generations of employees could expect an organizational upheaval one or twice during their careers. It appears that companies are now in a state of near-permanent change. The design of an organization is the outcome of senior management's decision about its **corporate strategy** which refers to establishing the aims of a company and the means by which these will be achieved. Whenever a company changes its strategy, it alters the other variables including organization structure as depicted in Jay Galbraith's STAR model shown in Figure 16.1 (Galbraith, 2002; Kates and Galbraith, 2010).

Corporate strategy the aims of a company and the means by which these will be achieved.

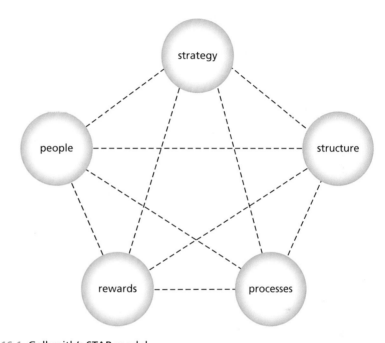

Figure 16.1: Galbraith's STAR model

Organization design the integration of structure, people, rewards and processes to support the implantation of an organization's corporate strategy.

Organization design refers to the integration of structure, people, rewards and processes to support the implantation of that corporate strategy. It is therefore not limited only to structural considerations but also affects and is affected by, the other variables. In this chapter however, we shall focus on the structural choices that managers make.

Designing organizations involves more than just deciding about which type of organization structure to adopt, choosing job titles and specifying reporting relationships on an organizational chart. It affects the employee roles and behaviours, simultaneously directing and constraining them. Organizational designers specify a formal structure of a company that enables a diverse set of roles, occupied by people with possibly divergent interests, to nonetheless accomplish organizational objectives. It contributes to company effectiveness and success by allowing individuals, groups and departments to achieve their intended goals. However, too much structure can stifle creativity and innovation (Sandhu and Kulik, 2018). Charles Handy (1993) stated that structures should be 'as simple as they can be, but as complex as they must'.

STOP AND SEARCH   YouTube for *What is organization design?*

Max Weber and bureaucracy

Legitimate authority based on formal, written rules that have the force of law, e.g. the authority of presidents, managers, lecturers.

Bureaucracy legal-rational type of authority underpinning a form of organization structure that is characterized by job specialization, authority hierarchy, formal selection, rules and procedures, impersonality, impartiality and recording.

Max Weber (1947), a German sociologist and philosopher writing at the start of the twentieth century, was the first to address the topic of the design of organization structures. If Frederick Taylor was interested in the one best way to perform a job, Weber was concerned with the one best way to structure an organization. He was interested in legitimate authority which was authority based on formal, written rules that had the force of law. This type of authority carries with it 'position power', that is, power deriving from the position occupied by an individual within an organization (e.g. the power of presidents, managers, lecturers). Power is used to refer to the capacity of individuals to overcome resistance on the part of others, to exert their will, and to produce results consistent with their interests and objectives.

Weber used the term bureaucracy to refer to the type of organization structure that is associated with the legitimate form of authority. Literally, bureaucracy means 'rule by office or by officials'. The six characteristics of bureaucracy are shown in Figure 16.2. Not every bureaucratic organization possesses all the characteristics that Weber identified. However, the more of them it has, the more bureaucratic it would be. For him, bureaucracy was a form of organization that emphasized speed, precision, regulation, clarity, reliability and efficiency. This was achieved through a fixed division of work tasks, detailed rules, regulations and procedures and the monitoring of employees by means of hierarchical supervision. It was this which, in his view, made it the most efficient form of organization structure.

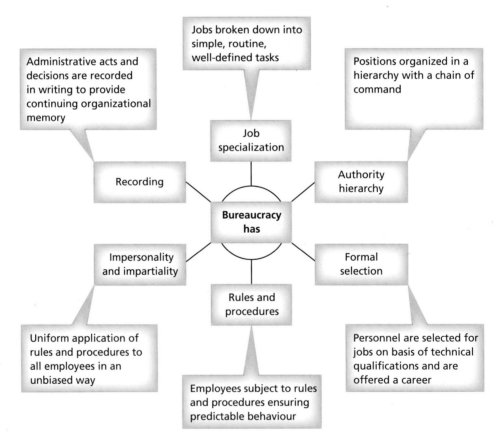

Figure 16.2: Characteristics of bureaucracy
Source: adapted from Robbins and Coulter (2017, p.71)

Benefits of bureaucracy

The strength of bureaucracy lies in its standardization. Employee behaviour is controlled and made predictable. In Weber's view this was achieved not through time-and-motion study, but through the application of rules, regulations and procedures. This ensures that different people in the same organization carry out their work in a similar way. Bureaucratic organizations have a reasonably consistent set of goals and preferences. They devote few resources to time-consuming information searches or the analysis of current activities to check if these are meeting stated goals. Instead, they rely on rules, tradition, precedent and standard operating procedures. Little time is spent on decision making since decisions follow from the established routines and few action alternatives are considered. The bureaucratic emphasis is on stability, fairness and predictability.

 **STOP AND SEARCH**   YouTube for *Max Weber Bureaucracy.*

Weber was struck by how the bureaucratic structure of a company routinized the processes of its administration, in a way similar to how a machine routinized production. His ideas developed independently, yet they neatly complemented those of Frederick Taylor. While Taylor focused on the worker on the shop floor measuring his output, Weber's interest was directed at the clerk at the office desk who was subject to administrative rules and the organizational hierarchy. Nevertheless, Weber would have approved of the disciplining, rational conditioning and training of workers proposed by Taylor. We can compare different organizations in terms of their degree of bureaucratization by measuring their job specialization, authority hierarchy, formal selection, rules and procedures, impersonality and impartiality and recording.

Problems of bureaucracy

In modern usage the term bureaucracy has acquired a negative connotation amongst the public and the media. For example, when people come up against obstructiveness in any aspect of organizational life, they complain about there being 'too much bureaucracy'. Employees complain about being bound by 'too much red tape' preventing them from doing their jobs. In response, governments and companies promise to remove or reduce it. Weber's view was in direct opposition to this. For him, bureaucracy was the most efficient form of social organization precisely because it was coldly logical and did not allow personal relations or emotions to get in the way of achieving goals.

Rules and bureaucratic procedures provide standard ways of dealing with employees that avoid favouritism and personal bias. Everyone knows what the rules are and receives equal treatment. However there is often frustration at having to follow what appear to be seemingly illogical rules and thereby experience delays. This change in the word's meaning has occurred because the principles of bureaucracy, originally designed to maximize efficiency, also resulted in inefficiencies. These negative aspects, costs or 'dysfunctions' of bureaucracy were the focus of debates in organizational behaviour during the 1950s and 1960s (Gouldner, 1954; Hall, 1963; Blau, 1966). The positive and negative consequences of bureaucracy are summarized in Table 16.1.

Today, these same negative consequences of bureaucracy continue to exist. Gary Hamel and Michele Zanini (2016, 2017a, 2017b) estimated that bureaucracy cost the US economy over $3 trillion in annual lost economic output while the figure for all 32 OECD countries was $9 trillion. These authors discuss a number of organizational processes which both they and

Table 16.1: Positive and negative consequences of a bureaucracy

Characteristic	Positive consequence	Negative consequences	
		For the individual	For the organization
1. Job specialization	Produces efficient, repetitive working.	Over specialization of employees' skills and knowledge prevents them recognizing or caring about problems not in their domain.	Inhibits job rotation and hence flexible use of personnel, and thus can reduce overall productivity.
2. Authority hierarchy	Clarifies who is in command.	Prevents employees contributing to decisions.	Allows errors to be hidden.
3. Formal selection	Most appropriate person appointed to a position and promoted.	Can restrict the psychological growth of the individual in their job.	Individuals throughout the company are promoted to their level of incompetence.
4. Rules and procedures	Employees know what is expected of them.	Introduces delays; stifles initiative and creativity.	Leads to individual and sub-unit goals replacing organization objectives; rules define *minimum* levels of acceptable performance.
5. Impersonality and impartiality	Fosters efficiency, reduces bias.	Dehumanizes those it purports to serve – officials are prevented from responding to unique features of clients who are treated as standard cases.	Creates a climate of alienation through the firm as employees come to see themselves as small cogs in a wheel.
6. Recording	Creates an organization history that is not dependent on individual memory.	Employees come to see record-keeping as an end in itself rather than a means to an end.	Recorded precedents stifle attempts at company innovation.Inhibits flexibility, adaptability and responsiveness.

their survey respondents refer to as bureaucratic 'chores' or 'drags'. They classify the costs of bureaucracy under seven headings:

1. *Bloat*: too many managers, administrators and management layers
2. *Friction*: too much busywork that slows down decision making
3. *Insularity*: too much time spent on internal issues
4. *Disempowerment*: too many constraints on autonomy
5. *Risk aversion*: too many barriers to risk taking
6. *Inertia*: too many impediments to proactive change
7. *Politics*: too much energy devoted to gaining power and influence

Hamel and Zanini (2017c) invited readers of the *Harvard Business Review* to complete their Bureaucracy Mass Index questionnaire (BMI), so as to gauge the extent of 'bureaucratic sclerosis' in their organizations. Over 7,000 readers volunteered to do this and they reported that (*Harvard Business Review*, 2017):

- *Company size:* large companies (over 5000 employees) contained more bureaucratic features than smaller ones (fewer than 100 employees).

- *Growth:* their companies had become more centralized, rule-bound and conservative in recent years, not less. Growth was highest in customer service and lowest in strategy and planning functions.

- *Perpetuates hierarchy:* their organization had not become flatter. The average respondent worked in a company with six management layers, some even had eight.

- *Time trap:* bureaucratic chores which created little or no value in their view took over a quarter of their work time. They felt that a significant reduction of head office staff would not affect or would even enhance their ability to deliver value.

- *Enemy of speed:* decision making had slowed down. Approval of unbudgeted expenditure took nearly twice as long in large companies than in small ones.

- *Produces parochialism:* just under half of their time was spent on internal organization issues, preventing them from focusing on external, strategic ones.

- *Undermines empowerment:* they were given little autonomy over decisions concerning the setting of their priorities, deciding work methods or participating in major company change initiatives.

- *Frustrates innovation:* new ideas in their companies were likely to encounter indifference, scepticism or outright resistance. Similarly, experimentation was found to be difficult.

- *Breeds inertia:* senior management only recognized the need for change once a problem was well advanced. Hence, change programmes inevitably focused on 'catching up' rather than 'breaking new ground'.

- *Politicises:* large, organizations with tall hierarchies were the settings for employee competition for influence and promotion. Politicking, in the form of blame-shifting, data hoarding and turf battles, was common.

CRITICAL THINKING   How reliable is the data from the Bureaucracy Mass Index? What are the problems with the way that it was collected? How confidently can you generalize from it?

The future of bureaucracy

Hamel and Zanini (2016) argue that the bureaucratic organization structure has passed its 'use by date'. It was once a new idea, even a blessing, which allowed organizations to achieve unprecedented levels of control and efficiency. However, despite the rhetoric about 'flatarchies' and 'holacracy' and case studies of companies such as Morning Star, Nucor, Zappos, Haier, and others which have attempted to move away from formal, hierarchical structures, it appears that bureaucracy, with all its positive and negative consequences, is here to stay. Several writers have suggested reasons for this (Magee and Galinsky, 2008; Halevy et al., 2011, 2012):

1. *Success:* For the most part, over the last 100 years, irrespective of technology, environment and people, and irrespective of whether it has been a manufacturing, medical, educational, commercial or military organization, it has worked.

2. *Large size:* Successful organizations survive and grow large and the bureaucratic form is most efficient with large size.

3. *Natural selection favours bureaucracy:* Bureaucracy's natural features, the six identified at the start of this chapter, are inherently more efficient than any others and thus allow the organizations to compete more effectively.

4. *Static social values:* The argument is that Western values favour order and regimentation and bureaucracy is consistent with such values. People are goal-oriented and comfortable with authoritarian structures. For example, workers prefer clearly defined job responsibilities.

5. *Familiarity:* Both managers, employees and customers are all familiar with bureaucracy having experienced it in various organizations all their lives. Prisons, hospitals, schools, railways all use it.

6. *Adaptability:* Bureaucracy has shown its ability to adjust to the knowledge revolution by modifying itself. The goal of standardization has been achieved in a different way among professional employees.

7. *Staff deficiencies:* Front line staff lack the information or skills to be autonomous and thus require bureaucratic direction from the top.

8. *Business complexity:* The speed of change both within and outside the organization creates a degree of business complexity that demands bureaucratic organization thereby making it inevitable.

9. *Eco-system consensus:* Every organization is embedded in a web of institutional relationships most of which are predicated on the belief that bureaucracy is essential.

10. *Bureaucracy maintains control:* It provides a high level of standardization, coupled with centralized power which is desired by those in command. For this reason senior managers who control large organizations favour the bureaucratic organization design.

 **STOP AND SEARCH**   YouTube for *Hamel: bureaucracy*

Harold Leavitt (2005) believed that the bureaucratic hierarchy in modern organizations was increasing rather than declining, and it was being helped by advances in technology. The authoritarian structures remain intact today but are cloaked by a veil of humanism. According to Leavitt, organizational hierarchies are particularly resilient, managing to change while retaining their basic nature. Hamel and Zanini's (2017b) survey respondents identified the main barriers to reducing bureaucracy to be senior management's reluctance to share power and the belief that bureaucracy was essential for control. As one would expect, fewer chief executives held this view than more junior managers. Nevertheless, attempts are being made to run large, complex organizations with a minimum of bureaucracy and these will be examined in the next chapter.

Home viewing

The film *Catch-22* (1970, director Mike Nicholls) is based on the classic novel of the same title by Joseph Heller, and provides a good introduction to it. It discusses management, hierarchy and organization. It tells the story of a US bomber group in World War II. One of the characters, Captain Yossarian wants to avoid flying any more bombing missions and requests to be grounded. But the only way to avoid combat duty is to be declared insane and, as anyone who wants to fly is crazy, not wanting to fly demonstrates your sanity. This is Catch-22. The film and book illustrate the many idiocies of a bureaucratic organization such as the military – individuals pursuing their own vested interests; the nonsensical top-down instructions given by superiors; and the struggle for promotion up the career ladder. The novel should be read for other examples of the dysfunctions of a bureaucracy (Skapinker, 2016).

Henri Fayol and managerial activities

Henri Fayol was a French mining engineer who in 1888 became general manager of the Commentary-Fourchambault Company and successfully turned around this failing company. By the time he retired in 1918, he had established financial stability in the organization. Fayol is credited with 'inventing' management, that is, with distinguishing it as a separate activity and defining its constituent elements. Interestingly, the word *management* is not translatable into all languages nor does the concept exist in all cultures. Managing of course occurs but is not always treated as anything special or separate.

It was in 1916, the year after Frederick Taylor died, that Fayol's book *General and Industrial Administration* was published. In it, Fayol put down in a systematic form, the experience that he had gained while managing a large organization. He stressed methods rather than personalities. This formed his theory of organization. While Taylor focused on the worker on the shop floor – a bottom—up approach, Fayol began from the top of the hierarchy and moved downwards. However, like Taylor, he too believed that a manager's work could be reviewed objectively, analysed and treated as a technical process which was subject to certain definite principles which could be taught.

Managerial activities activities performed by managers that support the operation of every organization and need to be performed to ensure its success.

Fayol identified six managerial activities that supported the operation of every organization and needed to be performed to ensure its success. Although his list of management activities was originally developed over 100 years ago, it continues to be used to this day. It is shown in Table 16.2.

The first managerial activity is *forecasting* the demand for a product or service. Once this has been done, the second activity is *planning*. For Fayol, planning involved 'making a programme of action to achieve an objective'. He collectively referred to forecasting and planning as *purveyance*. Because they are so closely related, many authors and books treat them as a single management activity.

Having made the plan, the third managerial activity is *organizing*. This involves breaking down the main task into smaller pieces and distributing them to different people. In a company structured along functional lines (accounting, production, marketing), the organizing of people may involve creating a temporary project team consisting of members from the different functions. This is the matrix structure to be discussed in a later chapter.

Fayol used the word *commanding* to describe his fourth managerial activity. It has been defined as 'influencing others towards the accomplishment of organizational goals'. Today, we would refer to it as *directing, motivating* or *leading*. Whichever term is chosen, performing this activity involves the manager ensuring that employees give of their best. To do this, managers must possess knowledge of both the work tasks to be performed and of the people who are to do them. This management activity is mainly, although not exclusively, performed in a face-to-face situation.

The fifth managerial activity *coordinating* involves ensuring that the various work tasks previously distributed to different employees through organizing, are being brought together

Table 16.2: Fayol's six managerial activities

Forecasting	Predicting what might happen in the future
Planning	Devising a course of action to meet that expected situation
Organizing	Allocating separate work tasks to different departments, units and individuals
Commanding	Providing direction to employees, now more commonly refereed to as *directing, motivating* or *leadership*.
Coordinating	Making sure that previously separated, assigned work tasks are integrated and people are working well together
Controlling	Monitoring progress to ensure that plans are being carried out properly

and synchronized with one another. Coordination can be achieved through emails, meetings and personal contacts between the people carrying out their unique work tasks.

The sixth and final managerial activity is *controlling*. This involves monitoring how the objectives set out in the plan are being achieved with respect to the limitations of time and budget that were imposed. Any deviations are identified and action taken to rectify them. It may be that the original plan will have to be amended.

Although Fayol's six managerial activities have been presented as a sequence, in reality they occur simultaneously in a company. However, forecasting and planning tend to be primary. There are also loops when original plans have to be changed because certain resources are found to be unavailable (when organizing) or when cost overruns are discovered (through controlling). Fayol's ideas mirror at the macro-organizational level, what scientific management offered at the micro-organization level. They are referred to as the *classical theory* of organizations or management because they promote the idea that there is one, best organization structure which would suit all organizations, irrespective of their size, technology, environment or employees. This structure is based on the application of certain key principles which reflected the 'logic of efficiency' which stressed:

- Functional division of work
- Hierarchical relationships
- Bureaucratic forms of control
- Narrow supervisory span
- Closely prescribed roles

 **STOP AND SEARCH**   YouTube for *Classical Management Theory*

Planning for doomsday

The brainchild of Cary Fowler, a scientist, conservationist and advocate of biodiversity, the Global Seed Vault is in Svalbard, a Norwegian archipelago in the Arctic Ocean off mainland Norway. It is 800 miles from the North Pole. It is located outside the village of Longyearbyen, one of the world's most northerly habitations and the farthest north that scheduled airline flights go. It opened in 2008, cost $9 million, and is the backup for the world's 1,750 country seed banks – the storehouses of agricultural biodiversity. It currently stores 4.5 million varieties of crops and has the capacity to hold 2.5 billion seeds.

The Philippines' national seed bank was made inoperable by fire in 2012 and those in Afghanistan have been destroyed in recent wars. In 2015, the Syrian war brought the first withdrawal from the seed vault. The seeds replaced those damaged in a gene bank near the war-torn city of Aleppo which was destroyed. The vault is designed to stand the test of time and the challenges of nature and man-made disasters. Made of concrete, it sits 120 metres above sea level to avoid flooding. It is sunk 160 metres into the permafrost, protected by two air locks and is maintained at a constant temperature of − 18°C. It is designed to last for 500 years. If the electricity were cut it would take 200 years to warm to freezing point.

The Seed Vault is the ultimate insurance policy for the world's food supply. It provides a backup service for the world's food and agriculture gene banks, by allowing them to store duplicates of their seeds, free-of-charge. Currently, the Seed Vault conserves almost 1 million different crop varieties, making it the largest collection of crop diversity in the world. Crop diversity is the raw material that farmers and scientists need to ensure there is enough nutritious food for a growing world population, in spite of challenges such as climate change.

✋ **STOP AND SEARCH**   YouTube for *Svalbard Global Seed Vault*.

Airbus 380: a challenge of coordination

The Airbus A380 is a wide-bodied, long range airliner. The plane is the first of its kind. It is built mainly from lightweight composite materials and is an assemblage of millions of parts governed by a million lines of computer code. A decade ago, a simple design miscalculation on the company's A380 superjumbo airliner required miles of wiring to be removed and reinstalled. The immediate cause of that problem was a breakdown in the snap-together, final assembly process in Toulouse. The A380's rear fuselages are made in Hamburg and were supposed to arrive in Toulouse with all their wiring ready to plug into the forward parts coming in from factories in north and west France. Each A380 contains 500 km of wiring, weighing 580 tonnes with 100,000 electrical connections, and this is woven through its walls and floor (see picture).

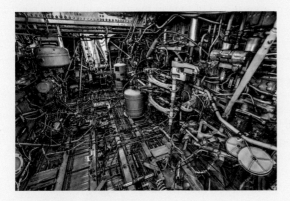

When the two halves of the airplane arrived, they did not match up. The wires were found to be too short to connect up with each other. Hamburg's failure to use the latest three-dimensional modelling software meant that nobody anticipated the effect of using lightweight aluminium wiring rather than copper. The aluminium made the bends in the wiring looms bulkier. Worse still, engineers who scrambled to fix the problem did so in different ways. So the early aircraft all had their own, one-of-a-kind wiring systems. This and engine supply problems, set production schedules for the A380 back two years, leading to $6 billion of losses.

This failure in coordination led to a company restructuring. Its Chief Executive reported that, 'We have changed our whole organization'. Airbus may look like a aircraft manufacturer but it more of an integrator. It develops the overall plan of the plane, but then outsources the design and manufacture of the parts, which it then fits together. The company has its own facilities in Toulouse (France), Broughton (Wales), Filton (England) and Hamburg (Germany). Over 7,000 engineers work on the A380, but only half of them are Airbus employees. To meet this co-ordination challenge, Airbus adopted standardized design software throughout the company. It also created a single, electronic rendering system of the airplane called 'digital mock up' (DMU) that every engineer working on the plane can use at any time. This allows any changes to be seen by everyone (*The Economist,* 2006)

✋ **STOP AND SEARCH**   YouTube for *Airbus A380 Production Problems, Part 2* (5:35).

✓✓✓   **EMPLOYABILITY CHECK** (leading and managing change)

Imagine that Britain has decided to drive on the right-hand side of the road to bring it into line with other continental European countries. How would you go about introducing the change over?

Work less, achieve more

In this podcast, Isabel Berwick, Andrew Hill and Emma Jacobs talk to Morten Hansen about his book *Great at Work: How Great Performers Work Less and Achieve More.* His work is based on a survey of 5,000 employees and managers. He tells us that working very long hours is unproductive, and suggests that the increasing use of technology in the office may not be helping our efficiency, either. Which of his points do you agree and disagree with? Give your reasons (25:07).

CRITICAL THINKING   From your personal experience of work and study of the subject, which managerial activities do you think Henri Fayol failed to mention which are particularly important in today's organizations?

Henry Mintzberg's management roles

Management roles

behaviours or work tasks that a manager is expected to perform because of the position that he or she holds within a group or organization.

While Henri Fayol focused on managerial activities, Henry Mintzberg investigated the different roles performed by managers. He researched how managers spent their time. His work led to a re-assessment of the nature of managerial work within organizations and a re-definition of the roles of the manager within organizational structures. Mintzberg (1973, 1975) studied chief executives in large- and medium-sized companies, categorizing the different behaviours associated with each of their positions. He distinguished ten management roles which he classified under the three headings of *interpersonal, informational* and *decisional* as shown in Table 16.3. Through their interpersonal roles managers acquired information; through their informational roles they determined the priority of information; and through their decisional roles they put it to use.

Mintzberg's research revealed a difference between what managers actually did and what they said they did. He showed that a manager's job was characterized by pace, interruptions, brevity and fragmentation of work tasks. In addition, managers preferred to communicate face to face, and spent a great deal of time in meetings and making contacts with others.

What did they find? Positive manager behaviours

David Garvin (2013) explained how since its early days, both the founders and the engineers at Google had questioned the value of managers. In 2002, the company eliminated all engineering managers and established a completely flat organization structure that recreated a college environment in an effort to encourage rapid idea development. They called it *dis-org* (Schmidt and Rosenberg, 2017). The experiment only lasted a few months. Larry Page was swamped with staff questions on anything and everything. They realized that managers made non-engineering contributions in the form of communicating strategy; helping staff prioritize projects; facilitating collaboration; supporting career development; and ensuring that company processes and systems were aligned with company goals. Google now has 5000 managers, 1000 directors and 100 vice presidents to manage 37,000 employees.

(photo credit: Russ Campbell)

David Garvin

However, if your highly skilled, hand-picked, newly hired engineers do not value management, how can you run your company effectively? How do you turn doubters into believers? Garvin describes how Google set out to prove management's worth by using the same analytical rigour and tools that it used to hire its engineers in the first place. Its people analytics group launched Project Oxygen which asked the question, 'Do managers matter?' This research programme measured key management behaviours and cultivated them through communication and training. It collected data from staff exit interviews, Googlegeist ratings, performance reviews and employee surveys. From these, the Project Oxygen team concluded that managers did indeed matter. Moreover, it identified eight positive behaviours shared by its high-scoring managers who led small and medium-sized teams at the first and second level of management.

What do you think these positive manager behaviours are? **(Answers in chapter Recap.)**

STOP AND SEARCH   YouTube for *The Top 8 Habits of Highly Effective Google Managers* (2:31).

Table 16.3: Mintzberg's ten management roles

Role	Description	Examples
Interpersonal roles arise directly from a manager's formal authority and concern relations with others.		
Figurehead	Performs symbolic, representative obligatory ceremonial, legal and social duties.	Greets visitors, presents retirement gifts, signs contracts, takes clients to lunch, opens premises, attends annual dinners.
Leader	Creates the necessary culture and structure to motivate employees to achieve organizational goals.	Increases productivity through hiring, staffing, developing, coaching, training and directing employees. Provides challenging assignments.
Liaison	Maintains a network of contacts with those inside and outside own unit or organization who provide information and favours.	Attends staff and professional meetings, lunches with customers, meets departmental managers. Also uses email and phone.
Informational roles concern how information is used in the manager's job, where it comes from and to whom it is communicated.		
Monitor	Scans environment for information to understand the working of own organization and its environment.	Questions subordinates and contacts, receives information from network contacts, reads business magazines, talks to customers and attends conferences.
Disseminator	Transmits information received from outsiders to the members of own organization (*internal* direction).	Makes phone calls, sends emails, writes reports, holds meetings with bosses, peers and subordinates.
Spokesperson	Transmits information to outsiders on organisation's views, policies, actions and results (*external* direction).	Gives press conferences; media interviews; speeches to external groups; prepares weekly status reports; conducts internal team briefings.
Decisional roles: their requirements are determined by the manager's role, seniority and availability of information.		
Entrepreneur	Searches the organization and its environment for new opportunities, and initiates planned, *voluntary* changes.	Develops new products, processes and procedures; reorganizes departments, and implements innovative employee payment systems.
Disturbance handler	Takes corrective action when organization has to react to important, *involuntary*, unexpected changes.	Intervenes to avoid a strike, deals with customer complaints, resolves personal conflicts between staff.
Resource allocator	Allocates resources to different departments by making approval decisions.	Budgets, schedules, programmes, assigns personnel, plans strategically, determines manpower load, sets targets.
Negotiator	Participates in sales or labour negotiations. Resolves inter-departmental arguments.	Negotiates merger details, supplier contracts, wage settlements and internal disputes.

Source: based on Mintzberg (1973, 1975)

The concept of role was introduced earlier in this chapter. One aspect of it is that any role-holder can choose how to carry it out their role. In the case of a manager, he or she can decide how they wish to blend the ten listed roles, taking into account organizational constraints and opportunities (Table 16.3). Mintzberg stated that all managerial work was encompassed by these ten roles. However, the prominence given to each role depended on the managerial level in the company hierarchy and the type of business. His study has provided the modern focus for all the subsequent research into debates about the nature of management.

> **CRITICAL THINKING**
>
> From your personal experience of work and study of the subject, which managerial roles do you think Henry Mintzberg failed to mention which are particularly important in today's organizations?

Home viewing

Watership Down (1978, director Martin Rosen) is based on the book by Richard Adams. The amorphous group of ten rabbits are united by having to flee their home warren. They encounter several difficult and dangerous situations before finally establishing a permanent warren on Watership Down. A major theme of the story is how a shrewd, buoyant, young rabbit, Hazel, becomes transformed into the great leader, Hazel-rah. As you watch the film, make a note of which of Mintzberg's ten management roles Hazel plays, and when in the story. Decide which roles he does not play himself and which he delegates to other rabbits. Which of his behaviours shows leadership? (Harris, 1989)

Michael Porter and Nitin Nohria (2018) repeated Mintzberg's study. Their 12-year investigation into how 27 chief executive officers managed their time was based on 60,000 hours of data. Examining their role, the authors describe it in terms of six *dimensions of influence* exercised by CEOs. Each dimension involves duality or a contradiction which has to be managed if the role is to be performed effectively. These are shown in Figure 16.3.

DIRECT	INDIRECT
The CEO is directly involved in numerous agendas and makes many decisions.	The CEO also exerts much influence over the work of others, using integrative mechanisms, processes, structures, and norms.
INTERNAL	**EXTERNAL**
The CEO works with the senior team and with employees at all other levels to get all the organization's work done.	The CEO also engages myriad external constituencies, serving as the face of the company, and must bring these external perspectives to the organization.
PROACTIVE	**REACTIVE**
CEOs' position and control of resources give them immense clout.	CEOs are constrained by the need to build buy-in, bring others along, and send the right message.
TANGIBLE	**SYMBOLIC**
The CEO makes many decisions about concrete things like strategic direction, structure, resource allocation, and the selection of key people.	Much of CEOs' influence proves to be intangible and symbolic; their actions set the tone, communicate norms, shape values, and provide meaning.
POWER	**LEGITIMACY**
CEOs hold formal power and authority in the company that is reinforced by their competence and track record.	CEOs' influence also rests on legitimacy that comes from their character and the trust they earn from employees through their demonstrated values, fairness and commitment to the organization.

Figure 16.3: Dimensions of CEO influence representing contradictions
Source: Porter and Nohria (2018, p.51)

 STOP AND SEARCH YouTube for *Time is the scarcest resource for CEOs: Harvard Business School study* (7:26).

> **CRITICAL THINKING** Compare Mintzberg's ten managerial roles with Porter and Nohria's six dimensions of CEO influence. In what ways are they similar and different?

Contingency approach

Contingency approach to organization structure a perspective which argues that to be effective, an organization must adjust its structure to take into account its technology, its environment, its size and similar contextual factors.

The contingency approach asserts that the appropriate solution in any specific, organizational situation depends (is *contingent* upon) the circumstances prevailing at the time. This approach has been influential in areas such as work design, leadership and, not least, in organization structuring. The contingency approach to organization structure argues that to be effective, a business must adjust its structure to take into account external factors. Managers need to analyse their own organizational circumstances, decide and implement the most appropriate structure for their situation at the time; and continually monitor the state of affairs as it changes, being ready to reorganize the structure as circumstances demand.

The contingency approach holds that:

- There is no one-best-way to design an organization.
- An organization's structure must 'fit' its circumstances.
- Employee needs are best met when a company is appropriately structured.
- The better the fit between an organization's structure and its circumstances, the more effective it will be.

From this perspective, organization design is an ongoing management task. Weber's bureaucratic organization structure described earlier in this chapter is said to be appropriate for (matches) a stable environment, while a turbulent company environment requires a more flexible or agile organization structure. The contingency approach was a reaction to management thinking in the first half of the twentieth century which was dominated by the search for the 'one best way'. Weber, Taylor and Fayol all recommended single, universal solutions to management problems, often in the form of laws or principles. Subsequent contributions to the contingency school came from many different researchers who studied wage payment systems, leadership styles and job design. They sought to identify the kinds of situations in which particular organizational arrangements and management practices appeared to be most effective.

Determinism versus strategic choice

The main debate within the contingency approach to organization structuring is between two of its sub-schools – the determinists and the strategic choice thinkers. The determinists assert that 'contextual' factors such as an organization's size, ownership, technology or environment, impose certain constraints on the choices that their managers can make about the type of structure to adopt. If the organization's structure was not adapted to suit its context, then opportunities would be lost; costs would rise; performance would be reduced; and the organization's existence could be threatened. They view the aforementioned variables as *determining* the organization's structure. Meanwhile, strategic writers contend that a company's structure is not pre-determined in this way. Instead they say that it is always the outcome of a *choice* made by those in positions of power.

CUTTING EDGE   Reorganization – restructure or reconfigure?

Stéphane Girod

Samina Karim

Stéphane Girod and Samina Karim (2017) asked what kind of reorganization companies needed to cope with ever-changing market conditions. They could either restructure, that is, create an entirely new organization structure or they could just reconfigure, i.e. tweak their existing one, modifying it slightly in some way. Organizational reorganization is a term that encompasses both change processes – restructuring and reconfiguration. Each seeks to boost innovation and financial performance and both can deliver value if pursued in the right way.

Restructuring involves changing the way in which resources and activities are grouped and coordinated. Companies commonly organize around functions, products, customer types or geography. In 2013, Microsoft changed from being structured by business lines to functions (e.g. Engineering, Marketing); and in 2015 Google restructured to became part of Alphabet. In contrast, *reconfiguration* involves adding, splitting, transferring, combining or dissolving business units without modifying the company's underlying structure. For example, transferring a department from one faculty or college into a different one within the same university.

Girod and Karim say that organizations should do both, in the right way, and at the right time. In 1995 with the demise of the mainframe computer, IBM switched to a 'services-and-solutions' strategy with an accompanying new organization structure (restructuring). The 'back end' of the company (Technology, Personal Systems, Server, and Software Technology Platforms) would henceforth develop solutions that the front-end, customer-facing part of the company (a new Worldwide Sales and Services group) would market. Then, during the 2000s, IBM used reconfiguration by shrinking its hardware business while upgrading its digital services. Today, it is back restructuring, prioritizing cognitive computing technologies that enable the 'internet of things'. The authors offer a four-part framework to help executives decide whether to scrap and replace an existing organizational structure or to modify it:

1. *Consider your circumstances:* Decide on your industry's level of turbulence and the need for a strategic reorientation. In dynamic industries which have new entrants and where market size fluctuates, restructurings are too slow and cumbersome. Hence, reconfigurations involving quick, small-scale changes that allow companies to seize fleeting opportunities are best. In dynamic industries such as retail, banking, and technology, companies tend to reconfigure more than those in more stable ones. However, when a firm is facing major industry disruption, piecemeal reconfigurations are insufficient and restructuring will be necessary.

2. *Pace yourself:* Remember to space out your reorganizations over time, restructure sparingly and reconfigure more frequently but not so often as to create chaos. To avoid confusion and faltering staff engagement, innovation and performance, restructurings should be limited. Since they can cause tension and take between four and five years to bear fruit, they should be limited to that time interval. With respect to reconfigurations, executives require sufficient practice in doing them well, but not so often as to create a dangerous inward focus and change fatigue within a company.

3. *Play to your strength and differentiate:* Use your reorganization to strengthen and differentiate your business from the competition. When restructuring or

reconfiguring, a company's activities and resources should be grouped and allocated in ways that play to its strengths and differentiates it from its competitors. Structural change works best when it reinforces a company's uniqueness rather than when it attempts to mimic competitors' strategies. Similarly, reconfigurations deliver better outcomes when they are explicitly designed to build on a company's strategic strong points.

4. *Determine which other systems need to change:* Clearly define the scope of change. A change in structure also usually means a change in management processes, IT systems, culture, incentives, rewards and leadership styles. These need to be made quickly and ideally simultaneously so as to avoid misalignments that can paralyze a company. In contrast, reconfigurations are successful when executives ensure that only the targeted unit is affected by the changes while the continuity of the remainder of the organization is maintained.

In related research, Girod and Whittington (2017) suggest that, in general, fundamental restructurings have positive consequences while incremental reconfigurations have negative consequences. However, the opposite becomes true in specifically dynamic environments where reconfigurations have positive financial outcomes while restructurings have negative ones. These authors conclude that relatively frequent reconfigurations help company adaptation in dynamic environments. Managers should choose forms of reorganization according to the rate of their industry's environmental change.

 **STOP AND SEARCH**   YouTube for *Restructure or reconfiguration (Girod)* and *VSI Introduction – Reconfiguration – Samina Karim and Laurence Capron* (4:28)

Contingency and technological determinism

Technological determinism the argument that technology can explain the nature of jobs, work groupings, hierarchy levels, values and attitudes found in an organization.

Joan Woodward, James Thompson and Charles Perrow are the leading figures in the school of technological determinism. They had an interest in the relationship between a company's structure and its technology. They all agreed that technology required that certain work tasks be performed, and that this in turn determined jobs, organization structures and attitudes and behaviours. However, they differed in both the way in which they classified technologies and in how they conceived of the relationship been technology and organization structure.

Joan Woodward and technological complexity

Joan Woodward was a British academic who worked in the 1950s. She studied 100 firms in south-east England and correlated their economic performance with different elements of organization structure which had been proposed by Weber, Fayol and other writers. These elements included the number of hierarchical levels, the span of control, and the level of written communication. She had expected her analysis to reveal a relationship between some of these elements of organization structure and the level of company performance, but it did not.

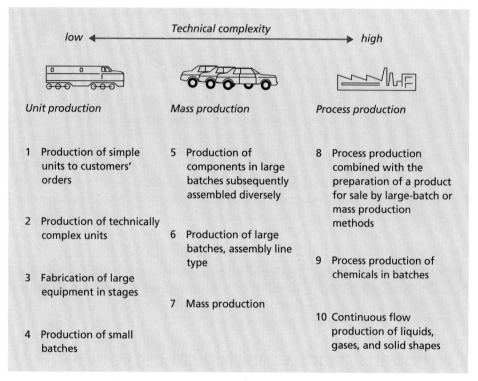

Figure 16.4: Woodward's classification of 100 British manufacturing firms according to their systems of production
Source: from Woodward (1958, p. 11). Crown copyright material reproduced under class Licence Number CO1W0000039 with the permission of the Controller of HMSO and the Queen's Printer for Scotland

Technical complexity
the degree of predictability about and control over the final product permitted by the technology used.

In her search for an alternative explanation, she noted that her firms used different technologies. She grouped their technologies into three main categories according to their systems of production – unit, mass and process. These were based on increasing technical complexity (1 = least complex; 10 = most complex) as shown in Figure 16.4. In unit production, one person works on a product from beginning to end, for example, a cabinet maker producing a piece of hand-built furniture. In mass production, the technology requires each worker to make an individual contribution to a larger whole, for example, fitting a windscreen on a car assembly line. In process production, workers do not touch the product but monitor machinery and the automated production processes, for example, in chemical plants and oil refineries. Technical complexity is related to the level of mechanization used in the production process.

> **CRITICAL THINKING**
>
> Woodward's classification of technologies is based on the manufacture of products. How well does it fit the provision of services? Consider services such as having your windows cleaned, buying a lottery ticket, insuring your car or having a dental check-up. What alternative classification system would you suggest for these service industries?

Woodward (1965) discovered that a firm's organization structure was indeed related to its performance but through an important additional variable – technology. The 'best' or most appropriate organization structure, that is, the one associated with highest company performance, depended (or was *contingent* upon), the type of technology employed by that firm. She introduced the concept of the 'technological imperative' – the view that technology determines an organization's structure. Specifically, she held that it was the *complexity of the technology* used that determined the structure.

Woodward found that as the technology became more complex (going from type 1 through to type 10) two main things occurred. First, the length of the chain of command increased with the number of management levels rising from an average of 3 to 6 .The proportion of managers to the total employed workforce rose, as did the proportion of indirect to direct labour. Her second major finding was that the increasing complexity of technology meant that both chief executives' and supervisors' spans of control increased. The span of control of first line supervisors was highest in mass production and lowest in process production. Span of control refers to the number of subordinates supervised by one manager and represents one of the ways of coordinating the activities of different employees.

Woodward argued that 'there was a particular form of organization most appropriate to each technical situation' (Woodward, 1965, p.72). In her view, the technology used to manufacture a product or provide a service, placed specific requirements on those who operated it in terms of controlling work or motivating staff, and these were reflected in the organization's structure. Each type of successful production system she argued called for its own characteristic organization structure.

For Woodward therefore, it was the *complexity* of a company's technology that determined the type of organizational structure that it should have

James Thompson, technology and interdependence

Technological interdependence the extent to which the work tasks performed in an organization by one department or team member, affect the task performance of other departments or team members. Interdependence can be high or low.

The second major contributor to technological determinist perspective school was a sociologist, James Thompson (1967). He was not interested in the complexity of technologies (as was Woodward), but in the characteristic types of technological interdependence that each technology created. His argument was that different types of technology create different types of interdependence between individuals, teams, departments and firms. These specified the most appropriate type of coordination required which, in turn, determined the type of structure needed (see Figure 16.5).

Type of technology	Form and degree of task interdependence	Main types of coordination used	Cost of coordination	Examples
Mediating	'Pooled' | | | | A B C D ↓ ↓ ↓ ↓ Low interdependence	*Categorization* standardization rules and procedures	low	Bank and branches University departments Baseball teams
Long-linked	'Sequential' A → B → C → D Medium interdependence	*Planning* scheduled meetings, committees	medium	Assembly line Fast food restaurants American football teams
Intensive	'Reciprocal' (A B C D reciprocal diagram) High interdependence	*Mutual adjustment* unscheduled meetings, face-to-face discussions, physical proximity, interdepartmental teams	high	Hospitals Airports Basketball teams

Figure 16.5: Thompson's typology of technology, interdependence and coordination

Mediating technology creates pooled interdependence

Mediating technology technology that links independent but standardized work tasks.

Mediating technology allows individuals, teams and departments to operate independently of each other. Pooled task interdependence results when each department or group member makes a separate and independent contribution to the company or team performance. The individual outputs are pooled. For example, lecturers running their own courses, secretaries

in a firm, sales representatives on the road, insurance claims units, and supermarket checkout operators. Since each individual's performance can be easily identified and evaluated, the potential for conflict between departments or individuals is low.

Thus, pre-determined rules, common forms and written procedures, all act to coordinate the independent contributions of different units and separate employees, while clearly defined task and role relationships integrate the functions. This produces a bureaucratic organization form in which the costs of coordination are relatively low.

Long-linked technology creates sequential task interdependence

Long-linked technology technology that is applied to a series of programmed work tasks performed in a predetermined order.

Long-linked technology requires specific work tasks to be performed in a pre-determined order. Sequential task interdependence results when one department, group or individual employee must perform their task before the next can complete theirs. For example, in an organizational behaviour course taught by three lecturers, sequential task interdependence means that the first one has to complete their sessions on individual psychology, before the second can teach

group psychology, who is then followed by the third who presents the material on organization structure. In a furniture factory, a cupboard has to be assembled before the handles can be attached. Sequential task interdependence means that a department's or group member's performance cannot be easily identified or evaluated as several individuals, groups or departments make their own contribution to a single product or service.

At the company level, coordination is achieved through planning and scheduling which integrates the work of different departments. At the group level, coordination is achieved by close supervision of workers, forming work

teams consisting of employees of similar levels of skills; and motivated by rewarding group rather than individual performance. The relative cost of coordination with this type of technology is medium.

Intensive technology creates reciprocal task interdependence

Intensive technology technology that is applied to work tasks that are performed in no predetermined order.

Intensive technology creates reciprocal interdependence, where all the activities of all the different company departments or all of the team members are fully dependent on one another. The work output of each, serves as the input for another. For example, in an organizational behaviour course which uses the group project method, a group of students can call upon different lecturers at different times, to provide them with knowledge or skill inputs to enable them to solve the project problems. Each lecturer would notice what the other had done and would contribute accordingly. For this reason, with reciprocal task interdependence, the sequence of required operations cannot be predetermined.

Thus, the mechanisms of coordination include unscheduled meetings, face-to-face contacts, project groups, task forces and cross-departmental teams. This in turn necessitates a close

physical grouping of reciprocally interdependent units so that mutual adjustment can be accomplished quickly. Where this is impossible, then mechanisms like virtual meetings, e-mail exchange and videoconferencing are needed to facilitate communication. The degree of coordination required through mutual adjustment is much higher than what is necessary for the other technologies discussed and is thus the most expensive of the three types.

For Thompson, it was the degree of *interdependence* that a company's technology created between individuals, groups and departments that determined the type of organizational structure that it should have.

Team game metaphors

Robert Keidel (2014) argued that by using the games of baseball, American football and basketball as metaphors, and placing them within an integrated framework, it was possible to understand many organizations and their problems. Each game has its own structures, processes and player behaviours. With respect to *task interdependencies,* baseball exhibits pooled interdependence (each player makes a discrete contribution to the whole); American football displays sequential interdependence (groups of players make serial, cumulative contributions), and basketball features reciprocal interdependence (in which all players interact in a back-and-forth manner). He gives examples of companies defined by each game: Salmon Brothers (*circa* 1986), the late financial powerhouse represents baseball; United Parcel Service (UPS) represents football; and Pixar Animation Studios represent basketball.

"From now on all corporate communications will be dominated by sports metaphors."

Keidal goes on to argue that each sport demonstrates its own key organizational variable. Baseball reflects the division of labour (autonomy); American football reflects hierarchy (control); and basketball reflects collaboration (cooperation). Nearly every complex organizational challenge, he says, calls for a particular blend of these three variables. He recommends *triangular thinking* which is the process of looking at organizational issues in terms of achieving a balance between these three variables. Together, these games and the variables they represent, form a coherent, logical system or 'trade-off space' which managers can use to aid their critical thinking and assist their decision making.

Charles Perrow, technology and predictability

Task variety the number of new and different demands that a task places on an individual or a function.

Charles Perrow (1970) is the third contributor to the technological determinist school. He saw technology's effect on organization structure as working through its impact on the predictability of providing a service or manufacturing a product. He considered two dimensions. The first he labelled task variety. This referred to the frequency with which unexpected events occurred in the transformation process (inputs to outputs). Task variety would be high if there were many such events and low if there were few. He labelled the second dimension task analysability. This refers to the degree to which the unexpected problems can be solved using readily available, off-the-shelf solutions. Task analysability would be low if individuals or departments had to search around for a solution and rely on experience, judgement, intuition and problems-solving skills, and high if they did not (see Figure 16.6).

Task analysability the degree to which standardized solutions are available to solve the problems that arise.

Types of technology

On the basis of these two dimensions, Perrow categorized technologies into four types, and discussed the effects of each one upon an organization's structure. He was particularly interested in coordination mechanisms, discretion, the relative power of supervisors and the middle managers who supervised them.

1. *Routine technology:* In cell 1 are work tasks which are simple and where variety is low (repetitive task). Task analysability is high (there are standard solutions available). Examples include supermarket checkout operations and fast food restaurants.

2. *Craft technology:* In cell 2 is craft technology, characterized by low task variety and low task analysability. The number of new problems encountered is small, but each requires some effort to find a solution. Examples include a plumber fitting a bath or shower; an accountant preparing a tax return.

3. *Non-routine technology:* In cell 3 are complex and non-routine work tasks, where task variability is high (with many new or different problems encountered); and task

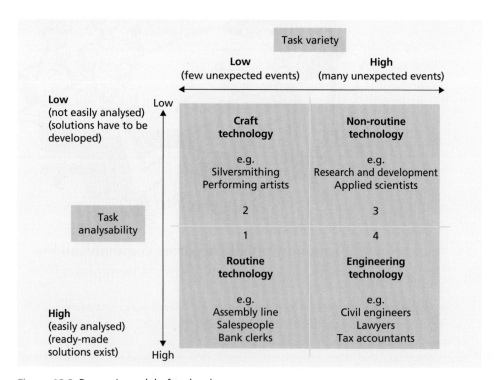

Figure 16.6: Perrow's model of technology

Source: Perrow (1970, p,78). Reprinted with permission of Wadsworth: a division of Thomson Learning

analysability is low (problem is difficult to solve). The tasks performed by research chemists, advertising agencies, hi-tech product designers and top management teams are all examples of non-routine technology.

4. *Engineering technology:* In cell 4, engineering technology is characterized by high task variety and low task analysability. Many new problems crop up, but each is relatively simple to solve. Civil engineering companies which build roads and bridges exemplify this type of technology as well as motor manufacturers producing customized cars.

Perrow argued that when an organization's work tasks and technology were routine, its structure would possess a tall hierarchy, channels of authority and formal, and standardized operating procedures which integrated the activities of individuals, groups and departments. In contrast, when a firm's tasks and technology become non-routine and complex, an organization would use a flatter hierarchy, more cross-functional teamworking and greater face-to-face contact to allow individuals, groups and departments to observe and mutually adjust to each other, and to engage in decision making and problem solving.

For Perrow, it was the degree of *predictability* that a company's technology created between individuals, groups and departments that determined the type of organizational structure that it should have.

Contingency and environmental determinism

Environmental determinism the argument that internal organizational responses are primarily determined by external environmental factors.

The second strand of determinism in organization structuring has been environmental. Several writers have had an interest in the relationship between a company's structure and its environment. Some of them argue that company success depends on securing a proper 'fit' or alignment between itself and its environment **(see Chapter 2)**. For them, environmental determinism means that the environment determines organization structure. One prominent environmental determinist, Paul Lawrence, even said, 'Tell me what your environment is and I shall tell you what your organization ought to be'. (Argyris, 1972, p.88)

Environmental complexity the range of external factors relevant to the activities of the organization; the more factors, the higher the complexity.

The environmental determinists see an organization as being in constant interaction with its environment (see Figure 16.7). That environment consists of 'actors' or 'networks' (e.g. competitors, investors, customers). It includes the general economic situation, the market, the competitive scene and similar factors. Each organization has its own unique environment. The greater the number of actors or networks that are relevant to a given company, the more complex its environment is said to be. Organizations vary in the relative degree of their environmental complexity (Duncan, 1972, 1973, 1974, 1979).

Environmental dynamism the pace of change in relevant factors external to the organization; the greater the pace of change, the more dynamic the environment.

Those same actors and networks in an organization's environment can also change a great deal or remain the same. They thus differ in their degree of environmental dynamism. Different industries vary widely in their degree of dynamism. At one extreme of stability is higher education where new players must confront the barriers of an entrenched set of historical standards. However, even here the creation of new private universities; the growth of online degree programmes; and establishment of overseas campuses by traditional institutions all add to market volatility (*The Economist*, 2018). Nevertheless, relatively speaking, higher education still represents environmental stability.

In the middle of the range, one finds businesses like branded consumer goods. Substitution ranges from medium to high, and new entrants can replace established ones but not overnight. Survival and success depend upon

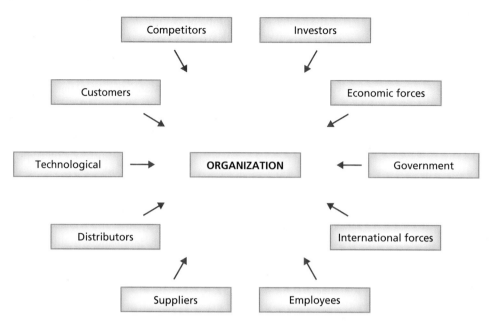

Figure 16.7: An organization depicted in its environment consisting of different actors, stakeholders and networks

capabilities and network relationships. Most industries are located in this middle ground. At the other extreme of turbulence, is a situation where customers can constantly and easily substitute. The environment consists of networks of players whose positions and prospects suddenly and unpredictably change. Many internet businesses are located at this end of the spectrum. For example, the popularity of the social networking website Facebook rapidly surpassed that of My Space which had previously been dominant.

Environmental determinists argue that because a company is dependent on its environment for its sales, labour and raw materials, that environment constrains the kind of choices an organization can make about how it structures itself. As the environmental situation changes, the organization–environment relationship also changes. Hence, to be effective, a company has to structure and re-structure constantly to maintain alignment (or 'fit'). The environmental determinists use the key concepts of environmental uncertainty and complexity in their explanations.

Mechanistic and organic organization structures

In the late 1950s, Tom Burns and George Stalker in Britain studied the behaviour of people working in a rayon mill. Rayon is a yarn or fibre produced by forcing and drawing cellulose through minute holes. They found that this economically successful company with contented staff was run using a management style which, according to contemporary wisdom about 'best' management practice, should have led to worker discontent and inefficiency. Some time later, the same authors studied an electronics company. Again it was highly successful, but used a management style completely different from that of the rayon mill studied earlier. This contradiction gave the authors the impetus to begin a large scale investigation to examine the relationship between management systems and the organizational tasks. They were particularly interested in the way management systems changed in response to changes in the commercial and technical work tasks of the firm (Burns and Stalker, 1961).

The rayon mill had a highly stable, highly structured character which would have fitted well into Weber's bureaucratic organizational model. In contrast, the electronics firm violated many of the principles of classical management. It discouraged written communications, defined jobs as little as possible, and the interaction between employees was on a face-to-face basis. Indeed, staff even complained about this uncertainty. Burns and Stalker gave the label mechanistic organization structure to the former and organic organization structure to the second (Table 16.4). These represented organization structures at opposite ends of a continuum. Most firms would be located somewhere in between.

Mechanistic organization structure one that possesses a high degree of task specialization, many rules, tight specification of individual responsibility and authority, and centralized decision making.

Organic organization structure one that possesses little task specialization, few rules, a high degree of individual responsibility and authority, and one in which decision making is delegated.

Table 16.4: Characteristics of mechanistic and organic organization structures

Characteristic	Rayon mill (Mechanistic)	Electronics (Organic)
Specialization	High – sharp differentiation	Low – no hard boundaries, relatively few different jobs
Standardization	High – methods spelled out	Low – individuals decide own methods
Orientation of members	Means	Goals
Conflict resolution	By superior	Interaction
Pattern of authority, control and communication	Hierarchical – based on implied contractual relation	Wide net based upon common commitment
Locus of superior competence	At top of organization	Wherever there is skill and competence
Interaction	Vertical	Lateral
Communication content	Directions, orders	Advice, information
Loyalty	To the organization	To project and group
Prestige	From the position	From personal contribution

Source: based on Litterer (1973, pp. 339)

Burns and Stalker argued that neither form of organization structure was intrinsically efficient or inefficient, but that rather that it all depended (was *contingent* on) the nature of the environment in which the firm operated. In their view, the key variables to be considered were the product market and the technology of the manufacturing process. These needed to be studied when the structure of a firm was being designed. Burns and Stalker argued, a mechanistic structure was most appropriate for an organization which used an unchanging technology and operated in relatively stable markets, while an organic structure was most suitable for a firm that has to cope with unpredictable new work tasks.

Differentiated and integrated organization structures

During the 1960s, Paul Lawrence and Jay Lorsch (1967) in the United States built on the work of Burns and Stalker using the concepts of differentiation and integration. First, consider **differentiation**. Differentiation refers to the process of a firm breaking itself up into sub-units, each of which concentrates on particular part of the firm's environment. A university differentiates itself in terms of different faculties and departments or colleges and schools. Such differentiation inevitably leads to the sub-units developing their own goals, values, norms, structures, time frames and inter-personal relations that reflect the job that they have to do, and the uncertainties with which they have to cope.

Differentiation the degree to which the work of individuals, groups and units are divided up within an organization.

Differentiation can take two forms. *Horizontal differentiation* is concerned with how work is divided up between the various company departments and who is responsible for which work tasks. *Vertical differentiation* is concerned with who is given authority at the different levels of the company's hierarchy. High horizontal differentiation creates many different departments producing a flat structure as shown on an organization chart. High vertical differentiation results in many hierarchical levels which creates a tall organization structure. Lawrence and Lorsch found that effective organizations increased their level of differentiation as their environment became more uncertain. These adjustments allowed staff to respond more effectively to their specific sub-environment for which they were responsible. On the other hand, the more differentiated the sub-units became, the more their goals would diverge and this could lead to internal conflicts.

Integration the required level to which units in an organization are linked together, and their respective degree of independence.

Turning next to integration, this refers to coordinating the work performed in the previously divided (differentiated) departments, so as to ensure that all are working together in sync and contributing to accomplishing the organizational goal. Thus, having divided the university into faculties/departments or colleges/ schools, there is the need to ensure that they all contribute to the goals of high quality research, teaching excellence and income generation. Lawrence and Lorsch found that as environmental uncertainty increased, and thus the degree of differentiation increased, organizations had to increase the level of integration (coordination) between their different departments and their staffs so as to ensure they worked together effectively towards the common goal. Coordination is achieved through the use of rules, policies and procedures; goal clarification and communication; temporary task forces; permanent project teams; and liaison and integrator roles.

When environmental uncertainty is low, differentiation too needs to be correspondingly low. Because the units share common goals and ways of achieving them, the hierarchy of authority in a company and its standard procedures are sufficient to integrate the activities of different departments, groups and individuals. However, as uncertainty increases, so too does the need for integration. While integration is expensive, using up the resources of time, money and effort, a failure to integrate can be equally problematic, leading to conflicts between departments which have to be resolved. Lawrence and Lorsch argued that the level of uncertainty in the environment that a firm had to cope with determined the organization structure that was most appropriate for it.

✓✓✓ **EMPLOYABILITY CHECK** (how organizations work)

How well or badly are the activities performed by your educational institution differentiated and integrated? What problems of coordination have you encountered as student? What solutions would you recommend to improve the situation for yourself and your colleagues?

 🖐 **STOP AND SEARCH**   YouTube for *contingency approach, organization design.*

Strategic choice

Strategic choice the view that an organization's environment, market and technology are the result of senior management decisions.

The determinists asserted that technology or environment determined the shape of the most appropriate organization structure. Their critics pointed to the neglect of *choice* in decisions about the design of organization structure. John Child (1972, 1997) rectified this omission. He disagreed with the contention that organization structures were *determined* by 'external, operational contingencies' such as technology or the environment. In his view, structures were *chosen*. He stressed the part played by powerful leaders and groups who exerted their influence to create organization structures which suited their particular values and preferences.

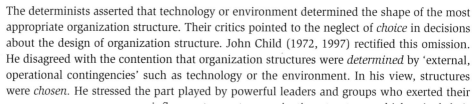

Strategic choice holds that senior executives who control an organization make a strategic choice about what kind of structure it will have. They also manipulate the context in which their company operates (e.g. which markets to enter) and how its performance is measured (e.g. market share, annual profit or shares price). Their decisions about the number of hierarchical levels, the span of control, and division of labour are ultimately based on their own personal beliefs and political manoeuvrings. Strategic choice researchers therefore focus on each company's particular situation, but ask how senior managers make the choices that link their firms' strategies to their organization structures. They have disagreed with deterministic researchers on a number of issues:

1. *The idea that an organization should 'fit' its environment.* That is, while there are choices about organization structure design, these will be relatively limited. Thus, for two similar companies operating in a stable environment to succeed, each would make similar choices about the shape of their organization structures. However, there are examples of companies making very different structural choices in the same circumstances and both succeeding.

2. *The idea that cause and effect are linked in a simple (linear) manner.* This ignores the fact that organizations are part of a larger, complex environmental system consisting of other organizations with which they interact. Managers can influence and shape their own company environments. The idea that organizations merely adapt to their environment is too simplistic a view.

3. *The assumption that the choice of organization structure is an automatic reaction to the facts presented.* Studies show that decisions are made by managers on the basis of the interpretations that they have made about the nature of their environment. The same environment can be perceived in different ways, by different managers who might implement different structures, which can be equally effective **(see Chapter 20)**.

4. *The view that choices of organization structure are not political.* Linked to the previous point, political factors will impinge on choices about structure as much as issues of perception and interpretation **(see Chapter 22)**.

The idea of choice also implies change. As circumstances change, existing organization structures will be modified to meet the new challenges in ways determined by senior management. For this reason, organizational reorganizations have become more common in companies. As the speed of change accelerates, so too does the frequency of both restructuring and reconfiguration. However, each one comes with its own costs and benefits and will have an impact upon the firm's employees.

Google restructures

In 2015, Google announced that it was changing the design of its organization. It restructured itself by creating a new, parent (holding) company called Alphabet Inc. which consists of a collection of different companies (Price and Nudelman, 2016). Google remains the biggest company and a subsidiary within Alphabet. It is shown down the left-hand side of the organization chart. It contains most of the internet products that people are most familiar with: *Google* (Ads, Search, Adwords, Adsense); *Cloud* (GSuite, Maps); *Android; YouTube; Hardware* (Home Pixel, Chromecast, ATAP); and *Infrastructure* (the back-end which powers other Alphabet units).

Those of its companies which were not primarily focused on the internet, and which were unrelated to each other, were spun off from Google, and become independent entities within Alphabet. They are called 'Bets' and are shown on the right hand side on the organization chart. Not all of these will be familiar to consumers: *X* (secretive R&D lab – robots, balloons, drones); *GV* (venture-capital fund); *Nest* (smart home devices); *Verily* (healthcare and disease prevention); *Calico* (life span research); *Jigsaw* (technology and geopolitical think tank); *Waymo* (autonomous vehicles); *Capital G* (investment company); *Chronicle* (cyber security firm); *Deep Mind* (artificial intelligence research lab); *Sidewalk Labs* (urban innovation); and *Access & Energy* (internet provider, includes Fiber).

→

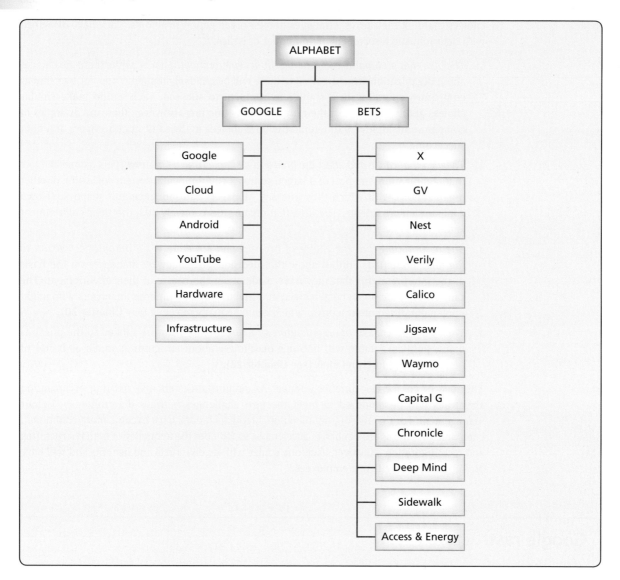

Companies need to periodically shake up their structures to reduce 'organizational cholesterol' which are the inertia, sticky routines, and fiefdoms that progressively undermine growth. They may also need to change strategic direction in the face of major industry transformation. Eric Schmidt and Jonathan Rosenberg (2017), two senior Google executives, explained the main reason behind Alphabet's restructuring. They wrote that it was primarily an attempt to keep the company 'nimble, uncomfortable and relevant'. In their view, the key to success are great products devised by 'smart creatives' who are able to work in an environment in which they can succeed. As the company increases in size, it becomes more difficult to produce this type of environment, so a restructuring becomes necessary.

Child argued (1997) that designing an organization structure was a political process in which power and influence were used to decide on the types of jobs, levels of hierarchy and spans-of-control that were to be adopted and, by implication, which markets to enter and with which companies to link up with. Figure 16.8 summarizes the different approaches to structuring organizations.

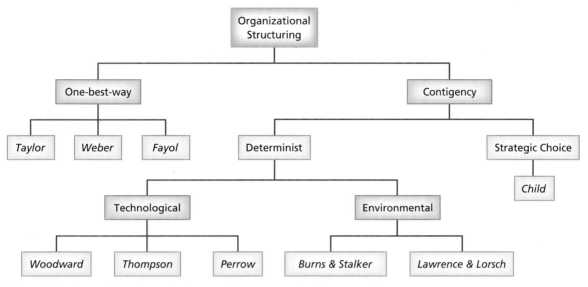

Figure 16.8: Contrasting theoretical approaches to organization structuring

CUTTING EDGE — Organizational reconfiguration and identification shifts

Marcia Lensges

Marcia Lensges and her colleagues (2016) examined employees' shifting identification perceptions during an internal organizational reconfiguration. This was a case of structural tweaking rather radical change. The researchers considered how employees moved from a state of de-identification with their former unit to identification with their new one. What were their experiences and expectations involving resources, justice and organization oneness? They interviewed academics from a Economics Department which was being relocated from the College of Arts to the College of Business within the same university. Prior to the change, the department had become very divided. Following a 'blow up', two staff camps had emerged. One prioritized research while the other emphasized meeting student needs. Both its culture and identity became fragmented. Some members identified with their existing college while others did not. To the annoyance of some and relief of others, the department's doctoral programme had also been suspended.

The researchers asked about the academics' perceptions of their old and new colleges as perceptions are important drivers of behaviours that can either support or impede reorganization efforts. The perception that emerged as most important was identification, that is, a feeling of 'oneness' with an entity. They discovered 'identification shifts' taking place at the individual level caused by certain triggers. Some of these triggers impacted on the de-identifying process through which an individual 'unhooks' his or her identification with an entity. These centred on the reality experienced by members in their former college. They included reduced resources (e.g. non-provision of teaching assistants for the doctoral students); injustice (e.g. the department 'getting the short end of the stick'); and lack of oneness with the college (e.g. the economics staff feeling underappreciated, 'picked on' and 'singled out').

The triggers identified as impacting the identifying process, resulting in identification with the new college, were focused on expected improved future experiences and included increased resources (e.g. getting their PhD programme back, recruiting more staff, chance of salaries going up, larger and better work space); anticipatory justice (e.g. wanting to be among other like-minded people); and anticipatory affinity with the new college (economics staff hoping that they would feel more 'part of the club'). Employees' anticipation of equitable treatment from their new college was what

→

actually triggered the identifying process. Subjects reported perceiving both anticipatory identification and anticipatory justice concurrently, suggesting that these two processes appeared to occur simultaneously rather than sequentially, suggesting a reciprocal relationship. Together, these triggers facilitated both their rapid de-identification with their old college and their identification with the new one.

Lensges et al. recommend that reorganizing leaders should use triggers to increase the speed of employee identification with the new unit, department or division to which the employees are moving. Before doing so, they should make explicit or implicit promises to staff about the future resources that they will receive in the new location. This will not only speed up identification shifts but will also shape employees' psychological contracts. The latter are the individuals' beliefs regarding the terms and conditions of the reciprocal exchange agreement between themselves and their organization.

 RECAP

1. *Relate corporate strategy to organization design.*

   - Corporate strategy refers to the aims of a company and organization design represents the means by which these will be achieved.

   - Organization design involves the integration of structure, people, rewards and processes to support the implantation of an organization's corporate strategy.

2. *State the main characteristics of a bureaucratic organization structure as specified by Max Weber.*

   - Job specialization, authority hierarchy, formal selection, rules and procedures, impersonality and impartiality and recording.

3. *Distinguish Fayol's six managerial activities and the main ideas of the classical management school.*

   - Fayol distinguished six managerial activities: forecasting, planning, organizing, commanding, coordinating and controlling.

   - The classical management school was based on the experience of managers and consultants rather than on the work of researchers.

4. *Distinguish Mintzberg's ten management roles.*

   - His ten management roles are figurehead, leader, liaison, monitor, disseminator, spokesperson, entrepreneur, disturbance handler, resource allocator and negotiator.

5. *Identify the writers who comprise the contingency approach and state their main individual contributions.*

   - Contingency writers challenged Max Weber and Henri Fayol's view that there was one best way to structure an organization.

   - They held that there was an optimum organization structure that would maximize company performance and profits, and that this structure would differ between firms.

   - Technological determinist contingency theorists Joan Woodward, Charles Perrow and James Thompson saw technology determining the most appropriate organization structure.

   - Environmental determinist contingency theorists Tom Burns, Graham Stalker, Paul Lawrence and Jay Lorsch saw the environment as determining the most appropriate organization structure.

6. *Discuss the strengths and weaknesses of bureaucratic organization structure.*

   - Bureaucracy provides a rationally designed, organizational model that allows complex work tasks to be performed efficiently. Persons who are best qualified to do it, carry out the work. It provides safeguards against personal bias and individual favouritism.

   - Bureaucracy creates dysfunctional consequences of members only interested in their own jobs; following rules obsessively; and being slow to respond to changes. Bureaucracies perpetuate themselves.

7. *Identify the influence of early organization design ideas on contemporary organizations.*

   - Modern organizations continue to possess the features first described by Weber and Fayol to this day.

   - Early design principles have been successful; have helped large organizations to survive and prosper; reflect the static social values of many nations and cultures; are capable of withstanding environmental turbulence; and allow senior management to retain power.

RECAP: What did they find?

Garvin (2013) reported what Project Oxygen team found what Google staff considered to be most positive management behaviours. For them, a good manager:

- is a good coach

- helps with career development

- is productive and results oriented

- has the technical skills to advise their team

- has a clear vision and strategy for their team

- empowers the team and does not micromanage

- is a good communicator, listener and information sharer

- expresses interest and concern for members' success and personal well-being

The project used data-driven decision making to pinpoint specific, desirable, measureable management behaviours, and translated these into detailed, hands-on guidance for company managers. The company discovered that data-driven cultures responded well to data-driven change.

Revision

1. Commentators argue that both too much and too little bureaucracy in an organization de-motivates employees and causes them stress. How can this be?

2. How does uncertainty affect the successful operation of rationally designed organization structures such as those proposed by Weber and Fayol?

3. Define and distinguish differentiation from integration. Using an example from your experience or reading, illustrate these two processes in operation, and the highlight some of the problems that can be encountered.

4. Explain how technology and environment might influence the structure of an organization. Consider their effect on coordinating activities.

Research assignment

Consider the organization design of your university or college. Focusing on the institution as a whole and using examples from your home department, assess its departmentalization, hierarchy, span of control, chain of command, formalization and centralization. Discover its purpose, mission or goals, and then decide how well its structure helps achieve these. Turning to your institution as a whole, assess its size, its level of technological complexity, and the degree of environmental uncertainty that it faces. Is your university or college predominantly mechanistic, organic or a mixture? What non-core services (e.g. catering, training, estate management) might be outsourced? Based on your assessments, write a report identifying the strengths and weakness of its current organization structure and recommend changes.

Springboard

Bret Sanner and Douglas Bunderson (2018) 'The truth about hierarchy', *MIT Sloan Management Review*, 59(2): 49–52. The authors consider the benefits of hierarchy found in groups within bureaucratic organizations and how it can contribute to creativity and innovation.

Elliot Jaques (1990) 'In praise of hierarchy', *Harvard Business Review*, 68(1): 127–33. A classic article that makes the case against 'flat organizations' and for a properly constructed hierarchical organization structures.

Henry Mintzberg (2009) *Managing,* Harlow, Essex: Financial Times Prentice Hall. The author develops his original ideas on managerial roles incorporating the research of others over the past thirty years and presents a general model of managing.

Nicolay Worren (2018) *Organization Design*, second edition, Abingdon: Routledge. The book provides tools and frameworks for understanding and re-designing organizations in order to improve effectiveness by simplifying complex roles, processes and structures.

OB cinema

Crimson Tide (1995, director Tony Scott). DVD track 04: 0:25:00-0.31.33 (7 minutes).

This is the story of how a global emergency provokes a power play onboard a US nuclear submarine between the battle-hardened Captain Frank Ramsay (played by Gene Hackman) who 'goes by the book' and his Executive Officer, Lieutenant Commander Ron Hunter (Denzil Washington). The captain regularly runs a weapons systems readiness drill in preparation for launching nuclear missiles. The clip begins with a loudspeaker announcement saying, 'Attention all hands, the fire has been contained', and ends with Ramsey saying to Hunter, 'We're here to defend democracy, not to practise it'.

As you watch this clip of the weapons test, identify an example of each of Weber's six principles of bureaucracy.

Bureaucratic principle	Examples
1. Work specialization	
2. Authority hierarchy	
3. Employment and career	
4. Recording	
5. Rules and regulations	
6. Impersonality and impartiality	

Chapter exercises

1: Debra's diary

Objectives
1. To contrast management roles with management activities.
2. To identify examples of each.

Briefing
1. Remind yourself of Mintzberg's ten management roles and Fayol's six managerial activities.

2. Form groups and nominate a spokesperson.

3. Read the case *Debra's Day* and then:

    a. Identify one example of each of the Mintzberg's ten roles (tasks 1–10).

    b. Identify one example of each of the Fayol's six managerial activities engaged in by Debra (tasks 11–16).

Debra's Diary
Debra is the chief executive of a large private hospital in London. In an effort to manage her time better, she kept a diary of the work tasks she performed during a couple of days.

	Mintzberg	Fayol
1 Held a meeting with all staff to inform them about the government's new requirements for the feeding and management of elderly patients.		
2 Closed the ward with patient infection (MRSA) problem; instigated a 'deep clean' procedure to ensure that this outbreak within the hospital had been contained; and introduced a new hygiene management code of conduct.		
3 Had the opportunity to buy a CAT scanner at a huge discount price, if we acted immediately. I called each of the board members to get them to agree to the investment. Some were unsure, but I managed to persuade them.		
4 Went to the local radio station to represent the hospital, to be interviewed about our work and answer listeners' calls.		
5 Gave a presentation to a training course which clarified hospital goals, and stressed the importance of staff's role in achieving them.		
6 Had lunch with our local Member of Parliament and obtained advanced information about future trends in government healthcare policy and funding.		
7 Spent two hours web surfing to discover how our hospital compares in terms of numbers of patients and staff as well as facilities, with our competitors here and abroad.		
8 Acted to resolve a dispute between a doctor in charge of the x-ray department and the union representative, concerning technicians.		
9 Finalized the budgets for all the hospital departments in line with our income and organizational objectives.		
10 Gave a speech at the Effective Healthcare Conference describing our hospital's approach to waste management.		
11 Held a meeting with the different department heads to ensure nursing staff were being efficiently allocated to the different wards.		
12 Reviewed the food purchase data to ensure that all foodstuffs had been obtained in accordance with procedures laid down by the hospital, and that the quantities of food supplied by vendors had been specified.		
13 Used internet to discover illness trends among the population so as to anticipate increases and decreases for our various medical services.		
14 Devised a new 'pay for performance' compensation system which ensured that those who had exceeded their targets were appropriately rewarded.		
15 In anticipation of the upcoming annual inspection, I compiled a list of tasks to be completed then assigned these to the various senior managers.		
16 Discussed with the board of directors how the expansion of our obesity care provision would be managed over the next five years.		

2: Simulating organizational design issues

Objectives
1. Understand how the organizational information-processing requirements and uncertainty are affected by the characteristics of tasks, environment and people.

2. Consider different ways of structuring an organization to deal with uncertainty, either reducing information processing needs or by enhancing information processing capabilities.

Instructions   Read the following scenario, and respond to the questions as directed by your instructor.

Step 1 (20 minutes)

Imagine that you are a member of a group of 12 students who are competing with other teams to prepare an advertising poster for a local shop. Your client requires that your team's poster should contain at least three colours; some artwork; and an impactful

→

phrase or caption that catches the attention of passers-by and is memorable. Your group has 20 minutes to decide how you will organize yourself to produce this poster. You have hired a management consultant to advise you. Your consultant recommends that:

- Your 'organization' should structure itself along functional lines. Dividing into three, equal-sized subgroups, each will specialize in a different aspect of poster production. The first will deal with poster layout (selection of poster size, shape, layout, colours, general arrangement); the second will focus on artwork (executing the drawings and lettering); while the third will decide on the choice of the written content.
- To avoid confusion about the different roles and responsibilities (and to avoid disruption) the three subgroups should be placed in separate but adjacent rooms.
- Each subgroup should appoint its own leader.
- Your 'organization' should also have an overall coordinator.

Which of your consultant's recommendations do you agree or disagree with? Give your reasons.

Step 2 (10 minutes)

After 20 minutes, each group submits a plan to the instructor describing how they have decided to organize themselves for their task. The plan can be in the form of an organization chart or a written statement. They indicate their areas or agreement and disagreement with the consultant's recommendations.

Step 3 (20 minutes)

The group(s) reform and discuss some of the following questions as directed by the instructor:

1. Consider the relationship between the nature of the task (poster production) and the consultant's proposed structure. Where does it match or mismatch? State its strengths and weaknesses.
2. Does the time pressure make the consultant's proposed structure more or less appropriate? Why?
3. Should the three sets of activities described be performed sequentially or concurrently? Give your reasons.
4. Is the hierarchical structure of the organization (three levels of coordination – workers, sub-group leaders, overall coordinator) and the physical separation of the three subgroups, likely to help or hinder the achievement of the task? Explain.
5. What inter-group communication needs must be met for the task to be achieved?
6. What is likely to be the role of the three subgroup leaders?
7. What aspects of the task contribute to its uncertainty?
8. What are the implications of such task uncertainty for the coordination of activities?
9. What are the possible trade-offs between task specialization by subgroup, and the coordination of the activities between them?

Source: French (1993)

References

Argyris, C. (1972) *The Applicability of Organizational Sociology,* London: Cambridge University Press.

Aronowitz, S., de Smet, A. and McGinty, D. (2015) 'Getting organizational redesign right', *McKinsey Quarterly,* June, pp. 1–11.

Blau, P. M. (1966) *The Dynamics of Bureaucracy,* second edition, Chicago, IL: University of Chicago Press.

Burns, T. and Stalker, G. M. (1961) *The Management of Innovation,* London: Tavistock Publications.

Child, J. (1972) 'Organizational structure, environment and performance: the role of strategic choice', *Sociology,* 6(1): 1–22.

Child, J. (1997) 'Strategic choice in the analysis of action, structure, organizations and environments:

retrospect and prospect', *Organization Studies,* 18(1): 43–76.

Crop Trust (2018) *Svalbard Global Seed Vault,* https://www.croptrust.org/our-work/svalbard-global-seed-vault/ [accessed January 2019].

Duncan, R. B. (1972) 'Characteristics of organizational environments and perceived environmental uncertainty', *Administrative Science Quarterly,* 17(3): 313–27.

Duncan, R. B. (1973) 'Multiple decision making structures in adapting to environmental uncertainty: the impact on organizational effectiveness', *Human Relations,* 26(3): 273–91.

Duncan, R. B. (1974) 'Modifications in decision making structures in adapting to the environment: some implications for organizational learning', *Decision Sciences,* 5(4): 705–25.

Duncan, R. B. (1979) 'What is the right organization structure? Decision tree analysis provides the answer', *Organizational Dynamics,* 7(3): 59–80.

French, J.W. (1993) 'Simulating organizational design issues', *Journal of Management Education,* 17(1): 110–13.

Galbraith, J. (2002) *Designing Organizations,* San Francisco: Jossey Bass.

Garvin, D.A. (2013) 'How Google sold its engineers on management', *Harvard Business Review,* 91(12): 75–80.

Girod, S.J.G. and Karim, S. and (2017) 'Restucture or reconfigure: designing the reorg that works for you?', *Harvard Business Review,* 95(2): 128–32.

Girod, S.J.G. and Whittington, R. (2017) 'Reconfiguration, restructuring and firm performance: dynamic capabilities and environmental dynamism', *Strategic Management Journal,* 38(5): 993–1190.

Gouldner, A. W. (1954) *Patterns of Industrial Bureaucracy,* New York: Free Press.

Halevy, N., Chou, E.Y, and Galinsky, A,D. (2011) 'A functional model of hierarchy: how, why and when vertical differentiation enhances group performance', *Organizational Psychology Review,* 1(1): 32–52.

Halevy, N., Chou, E.Y, Galinsky, A,D. and Murnghan, J.K. (2012) 'When hierarchy wins: evidence from the national basketball association', *Social Psychological and Personality Science,* 3(4): 398–406.

Hall, R.H. (1963) 'The concept of bureaucracy: an empirical assessment', *American Journal of Sociology,* 69(1): 32–40.

Hamel. G. and Zanini, M. (2016) *The $3 Trillion Prize for Busting Bureaucracy (and how to claim it), Human Management Network,* Research Paper Series no.28/16, https://papers.ssrn.com/sol3/papers.cfm?abstract_id = 2748842 [accessed January 2019]

Hamel. G. and Zanini, M. (2017a) 'Bureaucracy: where to liberate $3 billion', *London Business School Review,* 28(1): 6–9.

Hamel, G. and Zanini, M. (2017b) 'Assessment: do you know how bureaucratic your organization is?', 16 May, *Harvard Business Review,* https://hbr.org/2017/05/assessment-do-you-know-how-bureaucratic-your-organization-is [accessed January 2019].

Hamel, G. and Zanini, M. (2017c) *What we learned about bureaucracy from 7,000 HBR Readers,* 10 August, Harvard Business School Publishing Corporation, https://hbr.org/2017/08/what-we-learned-about-bureaucracy-from-7000-hbr-readers?referral = 03758&cm_vc = rr_item_page.top_right [accessed January 2019].

Handy, C. (1993) *Understanding Organizations,* fourth edition, London: Penguin.

Harris, C. (1989) 'Hazel to Hazel-RAH: Leadership on the Watership Down', *Journal of Management Education,* 13(3): 142–45.

Harvard Business Review (2017) 'Organizations: the costs of bureaucracy', 95(6): 30.

Kates, A. and Galbraith, J.R. (2010) *Designing Your Organization: Using the STAR Model to Solve 5 Critical Design Challenges,* San Francisco: Jossey Bass.

Keidel, R.W. (2014) 'Team sports metaphors in perspective', *Organizational Dynamics,* 43(4): 294–302.

Lawrence, P. R. and Lorsch, J. W. (1967) *Organization and Environment,* Boston, MA: Addison Wesley.

Leavitt, H.J. (2005) *Top Down: Why Hierarchies are Here to Stay and How to Manage Them More Effectively,* Boston, MA: Harvard Business School Press.

Lensges, M.L., Hollensbe, E.C. and Masterson, S.S. (2016) 'The human side of restructures: the role of shifting identification', *Journal of Management Inquiry,* 25(4): 382–96.

Litterer, J. A. (1973) *The Analysis of Organizations,* Chichester: John Wiley.

Magee, J.C. and Galinsky, A.D. (2008) 'Social hierarchy: the self-reinforcing nature of power and status', *Academy of Management Annals,* 2: 351–98.

Mintzberg, H. (1973) *The Nature of Managerial Work,* London: Harper Collins.

Mintzberg, H. (1975) 'The manager's job: folklore and fact', *Harvard Business Review,* 53(4): 49–61.

Perrow, C. (1970) *Organizational Analysis: A Sociological View,* Belmont, CA: Wadsworth.

Porter, M. and Nohria, N. (2018) 'How CEOs manage time', *Harvard Business Review,* 96(4): 42–53.

Price, R. and Nudeman, M. (2016) 'One chart that explains Alphabet, Google's parent company', *BusinessInsider,* 12 January.

Robbins, S. P. and Coulter, M. (2017) *Management* (fourteenth edition), Upper Saddle River, NJ: Pearson Education Inc.

Sandhu, S. and Kulik, C.T. (2018) 'Shaping and being shaped: how organizational structure and managerial discretion co-evolve in new managerial roles', *Administrative Science Quarterly* (published early online).

Sanner, B. and Bunderson, J.S. (2018) 'The truth about hierarchy', *MIT Sloan Management Review,* 59(2): 49–52.

Schmidt, E. and Rosenberg, J. (2017) *How Google Works* (second edition), London: John Murray.

Skapinker, M. (2016) 'Joseph Heller's *Catch-22* is the greatest of all business books', *Financial Times,* 9 February.

The Economist (2006) 'The airliner that fell to earth', 7 October.

The Economist (2018) 'Dreaming of new spires', 25 August, pp.17–18.

Thompson, J. D. (1967) *Organizations in Action.* New York: McGraw Hill.

Weber, M. (1947) *The Theory of Social and Economic Organization* (A. M. Henderson & T. Parsons, Trans.), Oxford: Oxford University Press.

Woodward, J. (1958) *Management and Technology,* London: HMSO.

Woodward, J. (1965) *Industrial Organization: Theory and Practice.* Oxford: Oxford University Press.

Key terms

meta-organization

organizational architecture

departmentalization

functional structure

divisional structure

matrix structure

team-based structure

cross-functional team

boundaryless organization

collaborative relationship structure

outsourcing

offshoring

reshoring

hollow organization structure

modular organization structure

virtual organization structure

co-opetition

user contribution system

agile organization structure

self-organization

holacracy

holacratic organization

distributed innovation system

distributed innovation

Learning outcomes

When you have read this chapter, you should be able to define those key terms in your own words, and you should also be able to:

1. Appreciate the reason for chief executives' need to design and redesign their organization's structure.

2. Distinguish eras of organizational design and what factors stimulated each.

3. Differentiate between functional, divisional, matrix and team-based organization structures.

4. Distinguish between an outsourcing relationship and hollow, modular and virtual organization structures.

5. Understand the trend towards companies' collaborative relationships with suppliers, competitors and users.

6. Compare current organization design experiments involving agile organizations, self-managing organizations and distributed innovation systems.

Why study organizational architecture?

Work has increasingly become 'net work', done in a self-organized way that relies on individual initiative and is performed in a collaborative, negotiated fashion, rather than through management fiat (Halgin et al., 2015). Dimitrina Dimtrova and Barry Wellman (2015) write that 'Changing social norms have resulted in new ways of organizing that in turn affect how people work with colleagues, use information technology, find information, advice and guidance, and where they set up shop'(p.443). Gulati et al. (2012) use the term meta-organization to refer to networks of firms or individuals not bound by authority relationships based on employment relationships but characterized by a system-level goal.

 **Meta-organization** networks of firms or individuals not bound by authority-based relationships based on employment relationships but characterized by a system-level goal.

Many companies have become networked as a result of challenges caused by the 'triple revolution' – the impact of social networks; the internet, and of mobile platforms (Rainie and Wellman, 2012). Networked organizations are judged to be able to respond rapidly to uncertainty. They have been described as 'choardic' – able to generate order out of chaos (Child, 2015). They can reshape the way that employees work and how they themselves function because they are coordinated by social networks and are better at exchanging information. All of these changes have affected companies' organization structures, authority relations and information flows. They are challenging the traditional, hierarchical organizational structures of today's companies.

> 🖐 **STOP AND SEARCH** YouTube for *RSA Animate: The Power of Networks* (10:58).

This 'beyond the organization' trend is changing the relationships between different organizations; between organizations and their owners; between their employees and their consumers; and is creating entirely new organizational forms (Miles et al., 2010). Traditional firms in sectors such as car manufacture, pharmaceuticals and media have begun collaborating with each other for mutual benefit. But what exactly constitutes a 'new' organizational form? Puranam et al. (2014) argue that an organization's structure can be conceptualized as offering solutions to four problems that all companies face:

- *Task division solutions:* new ways of converting company goals into individual and group tasks. How can one identify and arrange the performance of interrelated sub-tasks and their associated information transfers, to allow the achievement of organizational goals? For example, in a warehouse fulfillment centre, changing from a Pickers Find Items (PFI) system in which moving workers find stationary items, to a Items Find Pickers (IFP) one in which moving robots bring items to stationary pickers (Elliott and Long, 2016; Frey et al, 2016).

- *Task allocation solutions:* new ways of assigning employees to tasks, e.g. contributors self-select themselves to perform the tasks that they prefer rather than being assigned them by someone in authority. For example, in the Valve Corporation multidisciplinary teams (cabals) form organically using an open allocation procedure where employees themselves choose to join or initiate projects, recruit team members, allocate their time, establish budgets, set deadlines, and deliver products to customers (Felin and Powell, 2016).

- *Reward distribution solutions*: new ways of rewarding contributors, e.g. stress on intrinsic rewards based on the task itself; peer reputation enhancement; financial rewards beyond normal bonuses. For example, Google employees receive rewards based on their contribution to the company. Those whose efforts have had the greatest impact on the company can receive between two and ten times more than a colleague in the form of bonuses and shares (Bock, 2015).

- *Information provision solutions:* new ways of creating shared knowledge using IT to enable the coordination of activities of geographically dispersed contributors. This allows different individuals and groups to work independently but in parallel. For example, in

Zappos (an online retailer) enterprise software such GrassFrog and holaSpirit are used to codify the purpose, accountability and decision rights of every role and circle (team), and this information is accessible to everyone in the company (Bernstein et al., 2016).

Organizational architecture the framework of linked internal and external elements that an organization creates and uses to achieve the goals specified in its mission statement.

The term organizational architecture refers to the framework of linked internal and external elements that an organization creates and uses to achieve the goals specified in its mission statement. Thus it not only includes the internal arrangements that a firm makes to deploy its various business processes, but also includes linkages to outsiders (other individuals, groups and organizations) who come together to form a temporary system for mutual benefit. The first part of this chapter will focus on internal structural arrangements, while the second part will consider external linkages.

Organizational structures had been a way of institutionalizing and managing stability, but now they have had to become far more flexible and adaptive to accommodate uncertainty in the form of discontinuous, disruptive change. In the past, it was thought that an organizational arrangement whereby the company performed all its tasks internally was the best way to gain competitive advantage. Now, working with others has come to be seen as the best way to reduce costs and increase efficiency and productivity. Consequently, answers to the question of 'who does what' now extend beyond the organization's own boundary to encompass its partners, competitors, customers and other communities of interest. Meta-organizations address the question of how to organize relations between legally autonomous entities, whether firms in a network or individuals in a community, without recourse to the authority inherent in employment contracts (although other forms of contract may play a role).

Historically, the initial problem for management was building and maintaining large-scale production processes and the organizations that operated them. Then attention focussed on coordinating and controlling these large, complex organizations and facilitating their orderly growth. Most recently, the focus has shifted onto inter-organizational relationships. Building on the work of Robert Duncan (1979), Narasimhan Anand and Richard Daft (2007) traced the changes over time in the design of organization structures. They distinguish three eras of organizational design shown in Table 17.1. These show how management thinking about organization structure has changed from vertical organization to horizontal organization, and now to boundaryless hollow, modular, virtual and collaborative structures. In this chapter, we shall draw heavily on these authors' explanatory structure and use their framework to compare and contrast the changes that have occurred in the design of organizations.

Table 17.1: **Eras of organizational design**

Era 1	Era 2	Era 3	Era 4
Mid 1800s–late 1970s	1980–mid-1990s	Mid-1990s–present	Experiments
Self-contained vertical organization structures	Self-contained horizontal organization structures	Boundaryless organization structure, hollow, modular, virtual, collaborative	Self-managing organizations, holacracy, agile organizations, distributed innovation systems

Source: based on Anand and Daft (2007)

CRITICAL THINKING   Think of an example of a change to the structure of an organization with which you are familiar. How has it changed the way that you and others do your work? Has it improved or worsened it?

Era of self-contained organization structures

The first era identified by Anand and Daft (2007) lasted over a century from the mid 1800s to the late 1970s. During that time, the ideal organization was held to possess the following characteristics:

- being self-contained
- having clear boundaries between itself and its suppliers, customers and competitors
- transforming the inputs from suppliers into completed products or services
- meeting its transformation process requirements internally
- hierarchically based

Fjeldstad et al. (2012) stressed that these self-contained organizations were based on hierarchy which was used for both control and coordination. It involved setting goals, monitoring their fulfilment, allocating resources and managing interdependencies.

Their design emphasized the need to adapt to environmental conditions, and to maximize control through reporting relationships and a vertical chain of command (Galbraith, 1973). Anand and Daft (2007, p.335) list the underlying design principles of a self-contained organization structure as:

Departmentalization
the process of grouping together activities and employees who share a common supervisor and resources, who are jointly responsible for performance, and who tend to identify and collaborate with each other.

- Group people into functions or departments
- Establish reporting relationships between people and departments
- Provide systems to coordinate and integrate activities both horizontally and vertically

A department designates a distinct area or branch of an organization over which a manager has authority for the performance of specified activities. Thus job grouping or the departmentalization of jobs constitutes an important aspect of organizational design. During this era, the functional, divisional and matrix organization structures became popular. All three rely on vertical hierarchy and the chain of command.

Self-contained warships

Tommy Krabberød (2014), a lieutenant commander at the Royal Norwegian Naval Academy explained that a vessel at sea was perhaps the closest example of Anand and Daft's self-contained organization. Input arrives at the gangway and, when the vessel has left the quay, almost everything needed to produce its product – fighting power – is supplied internally. For this reason, a navy vessel must be self-reliant. Work on a vessel at sea is a continuous task. At all times the crew must be able to survive the forces of nature and internal threats such as fire and flooding regardless of whether the vessel is involved in warfare or not. The environment is inherently hostile and teamwork is required merely to survive.

While soldiers often report that their experiences of combat were 'unlike anything they had experienced before', sailors in contrast say that they found themselves doing virtually the same job in combat as in peacetime drills. A sailor describing the Falklands conflict said that it was 'just like Portsmouth' (a UK navy training facility). In

Krabberød's view, how a ship's organization functioned in peacetime was a good predictor of how it would function when at war.

"We're going to shrink your department even more."

Functional structure

Functional structure
an organizational design that groups activities and people according to the similarities in their work, profession, expertise, goals or resources used.

A functional structure groups its activities and people, from the bottom to the top, according to the similarities in their work, profession, expertise, goals or resources used, e.g. production, marketing, sales, finance (Figure 17.1). Each functional activity is grouped into a specific department. A university business school may group its staff into the main subject fields (finance, human behaviour; strategy, marketing, operations management).

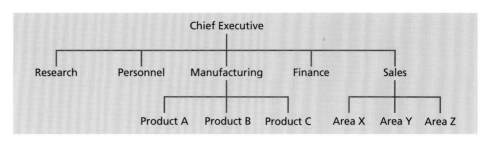

Figure 17.1: Functional organization structure

Divisional structure

Divisional structure
an organizational design that groups departments together based on the product sold, the geographical area operated in, or type of customer served.

A divisional structure divides an organization up into self-contained entities based on their organizational outputs – products or services provided; the geographical region operated in; or the customer groups served. Each division is likely to have its own functional structure replicated within it or receive functional support (e.g. marketing, human resources) from its headquarters. Each division operates as a stand-alone company, doing its own research, production, marketing, etc. (Chandler, 1962). British hospitals are increasingly divisionalized with surgery and medical diagnostics receiving support from finance and estates.

Product-based

A single motor company can organize around its different automotive brands. For example, Daimler's divisions include Mercedes-Benz and Smart, while BMW's include BMW and Mini. Most university business schools offer undergraduate, postgraduate and non-graduating courses. A product- or service-based organization structure is shown in Figure 17.2.

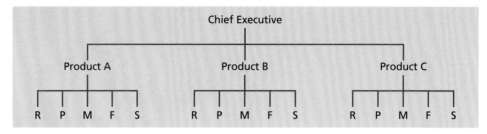

Figure 17.2: Product-based organization structure

Geography-based

Grouping on this basis is used where the product or service is provided within a limited distance. It meets customers' needs effectively and economically, and lets senior management check and control how these are provided. Hotels and supermarkets are organized in this way, so are ferry companies based on particular sea routes. A university business school may have a main campus, a city centre location and an out-of-town, residential (hotel) facility. A geography-based organization structure is shown in Figure 17.3.

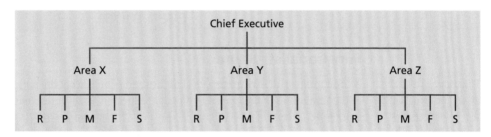

Figure 17.3: Geography-based organization structure

Customer-based

The company can be structured around its main customers or market segments. A large bank's departments may be personal, private, business and corporate. A university business school's clients include students, companies and research-funders. A customer-based organization structure is shown in Figure 17.4.

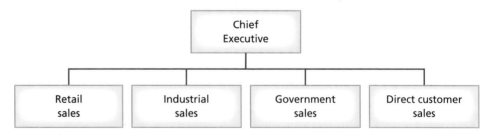

Figure 17.4: Customer-based organization structure

Matrix structure
an organizational
design that combines
two different types of
structure resulting in an
employee having two
reporting relationships
simultaneously.

Matrix structure

The matrix structure was pioneered by Philips, the Dutch electrical giant after the end of World War II. It combines a vertical structure with a strong horizontal overlay. The former provides downward control over the functional departments, and the latter allows inter-departmental coordination This structure comprises employees working in temporary teams composed of employees from different functions (e.g. marketing, human resources, production) contributing to specific projects. This structure has two lines of authority. Each team member reports to two bosses – their project team manager and their functional (department) manager, e.g. the head of production. There is thus a dual, rather than a single, chain of command. A matrix organization structure is shown in Figure 17.5.

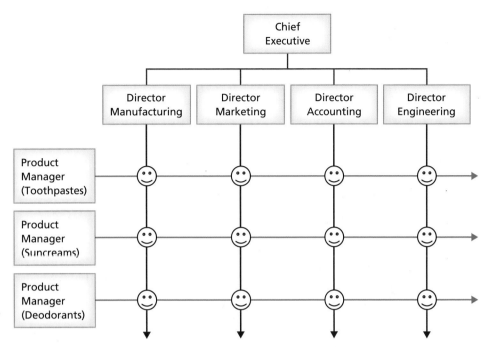

— The director of each functional department exercises line authority through the vertical chain of command.

— The product manager exercises authority through the horizontal chain of command, over those staff from the functional departments who have been assigned to work on the product.

☺ Employees at the intersections have two bosses. They report simultaneously to the director of their functional department (manufacturing, marketing, accounting, or engineering) as well as to their product manager (toothpastes, suncreams, or deodorants).

Figure 17.5: Matrix organization structure

As a student, the most likely place that you are likely to encounter a matrix structure is on your university course or module, if it is taught by lecturers from a number of different university departments. These contributing lecturers report to two different bosses. One of these is responsible for the function, in this case, their university academic department (e.g. Accounting, Economics, Law or Management). Their other 'boss' is the course or module coordinator responsible for the teaching, tutoring and assessments for the module.

Matrix structures can cause problems. Jon Katzenbach and Adam Michaels (2013) argue that when matrix organizations fail, it is often the result of a focus on structure to the exclusion of culture **(see Chapter 4).** The formal elements of organization design are normally addressed – the organization chart is altered, who reports to whom is specified, and decision making responsibilities are assigned. However, the cultural changes needed to support the newly created matrix structure are typically ignored. Changing structure is comparatively easy – roles, job titles, departments are concrete and visible. In contrast, the cultural norms, values and beliefs that form the web that connects people together and influences how they do their daily work, is intangible and difficult to define and map. They stress that in a matrix structure, collaboration between different departments requires a culture that encourages behaviours such as openness, a willingness to try new things, and an acceptance of mistakes.

CUTTING EDGE Same matrix problems, same solutions

Michael Bazigos and James Harter (2018) studied employees working in matrix organizations. Drawing upon a Gallup poll of 3,956 employees, they found that 48 per cent of them were matrixed to some degree. They could be slightly matrixed (serving in multiple teams on some days); matrixed (serving on multiple teams every day with different people, reporting to the same manager); or supermatrixed (reporting to different managers at work with different teams).

James Harter

The benefits reported by supermatrixed employees included good collaboration with co-workers; being able to do their best work and serve customers well; having their opinions taken into account; and facilitating bottom-up innovation. On the negative side, all classes of matrixed employees were not greatly involved in or enthusiastic about their work. They reported more time spent in responding to colleague requests and attending meetings. This slowed down decision making, blurred communication lines, stifled productivity, and hindered organizational responsiveness and agility.

However, the perennial 'elephant in the matrix room' continues to be role ambiguity. The majority of matrixed employees reported being unclear as to what was expected of them by other staff. They lacked clarity about their responsibilities, expectations and who was their boss. They sought more direction from their project leaders and wanted them to communicate better with their departmental manager. The found that these individuals were not greatly engaged with their jobs, i.e. involved in and enthusiastic about their work.

Consultants, in their turn, continue to offer role clarity – the traditional solution – to role ambiguity. They entreat matrix managers to help their subordinates be clear about the duties they are responsible for; to whom they report; set clear expectations aligned to the company business; have frequent conversations with them about their role in advancing company objectives; use a consultative rather than authoritarian leadership style; and provide them with regular feedback.

It appears that despite seventy years of its existence, the matrix organization continues to create the same problems for employees, and consultants continue to offer managers the same advice to address them. Nothing much appears to have changed!

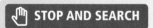 **STOP AND SEARCH** YouTube for *The Matrix Pyramid* (5:55) and *Global Business: Making The Matrix Work* (3:06).

Era of horizontal organization structures

The second era identified by Anand and Daft (2007) lasted from the 1980s to the mid-1990s. It promoted horizontal organization structures with a team- and process-based emphasis. It developed in response to the limitations of the earlier organization structures. These included difficulties of inter-departmental coordination; the ineffectiveness of vertical authority-based reporting systems; and the new opportunities offered by computers and networks to increase organizational information processing capacity. During this time, emphasis was placed on eliminating organizations' internal boundaries to improve horizontal coordination and communication. These ideas have currently been reintroduced in the form of agile teams and organizations. Anand and Daft (2007, p. 332) list the underlying design principles of a horizontal organization structure as:

- Organize around complete workflow processes rather than tasks
- Flatten hierarchy and use teams to manage everything
- Appoint team leaders to manage internal team processes and coordinate work
- Permit team members to interact with suppliers and customers facilitating quick adaptation
- Provide necessary expertise from outside the team as required

Team-based structure

Team-based structure an organizational design that consists entirely of project-type teams that focus on processes rather than individual jobs; coordinate their activities; and work directly with partners and customers to achieve their goals.

The above principles were predominantly implemented by means of a team-based structure which treats teams as the organizing units of work. These were pioneered in the 1950s by Eric Trist and his colleagues at the Tavistock Institute of Human Relations. Their research into the long wall mining method showed that multi-skilled, autonomous groups, interchanging roles and shifts with minimal supervision could substantially raise productivity in the coal mines (Trist and Bamforth, 1951). This organization design consists predominantly of project-type teams that focus on processes rather than individual jobs; coordinate their activities; and work directly with partners and customers to achieve their goals. The company uses teams to coordinate the activities within itself (Forrester and Drexler, 1999). Individual employees are assembled into teams in a way similar to being assigned to traditional, functional departments.

From relay to scrum to agile

During the 1980s, Takeuchi and Nonaka (1986) reported the difficulties that leading companies like Toyota and Canon were having with the traditional product development method. They dubbed it the *relay race approach* because each project went through the same sequence of six phases: concept development, feasibility testing, product design, development process, pilot production, and final production. As in the race, the baton for each phase was carried, in turn, by a different specialist functional department within the company. Marketing defined customer needs; R&D chose an appropriate design; and Production manufactured the product. The problem was that this approach was time-consuming and inflexible.

In an effort to reduce product development times from years to months, companies replaced the relay race with rugby. In this new approach, the 'ball' (project) was passed down between team members as it moved up the field. Instead of going through all the structured phases in sequence, flexibility was facilitated by the interplay between team members. For example, product development might be initiated before feasibility testing had been completed. The team engaged in a constant process of iterative experimentation. Takeuchi and Nonaka referred to this team approach as a rugby *scrum*. It possesses a number of distinct characteristics:

- A small number of members (3–9) are carefully chosen drawn from functions from across the company, so that the team collectively possesses all the skill and knowledge that it needs to complete its task.

- Senior management establishes priorities, provides money and moral support, but not a specific product concept or work plan.

- Acting like a start-up company, the scrum sets its own specific goals and develops its own agenda and way of working.

- It breaks down a problem into parts and develops solutions for each part.

- It works closely with its internal and external customers.

- Rapid prototyping and feedback is used and the different solutions are integrated into a coherent whole.

- Scrum team members work full time, are strictly accountable for all aspects of their work (growth, profitability, customer loyalty), and have start-to-finish responsibility for development project completion.

In 2001, in a similar development, 17 software developers calling themselves 'organizational anarchists' looked for an alternative to the traditional *waterfall* method of software development. This involves three basic work modes – individual work, team meetings and customer reviews. The problem was that software products were being released too slowly. By the time they were production-ready, they were already obsolete and customers' needs had changed.

They devised a new software development model which had its own set of values, principles and methodologies and was defined in the *Manifesto for Agile Software Development* (2001).

They called it a*gile software development* or *agile technology* but in many respects it resembled the earlier scrum approach. Rigby et al. (2016) summarized the four agile team values:

- *People priority:* ensure competent people work together effectively.
- *Working prototypes:* experiment with parts of the product with a few customers to learn what they find most useful and modify the product.
- *Customer collaboration:* since customers rarely know exactly what they want at the start, have rapid prototyping, frequent market testing and close customers collaboration, allowing specification requirements to evolve.
- *Respond to change:* project plans need to flexible enough to accommodate changes in technology, environment and stakeholders' priorities.

Both scrum and agile teams require solutions to problems to evolve through the collaborative efforts between a company's own self-organizing, cross-functional teams and its customers as end-users. These teams are characterized by horizontal communication; shared or rotated leadership; and delegated decision making that gives authority to junior staff to make decisions on their own. This team design advocates adaptive planning, evolutionary development, early delivery and continual improvement, encouraging a rapid and a flexible response to change. Once the goal has been achieved, the team moves onto a new project, perhaps reforming its membership before doing so. A true team-based structure is rarely found in organizations. Where it does exist, it tends to be in smaller organizations. A team structure is very flat, as shown in Figure 17.6.

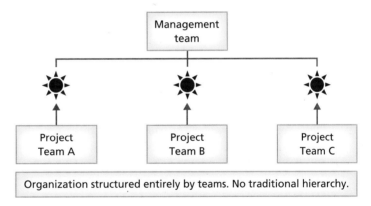

Figure 17.6: Team-based organization structure

Some chief executives have experimented with having a few agile teams but been reluctant to 'scale up' and create dozens or hundreds throughout the organization (Rigby et al., 2018). It is far more common for a traditional, vertically-structured company to just add various types of teams to the bottom of its hierarchy as shown in Figure 17.7.

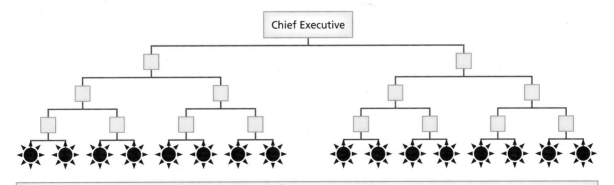

Figure 17.7: Traditional organization structure with teams at lowest level

Cross-functional team employees from different functional departments who meet as a team to complete a particular task.

This 'teams-at-the bottom' structure may use a cross-functional team approach in which a number of teams consisting of employees from various functional departments at about the same hierarchical level, are formed to complete particular tasks. As before, the benefits of this arrangement include access to the different expertise of members; improved horizontal communication and better inter-departmental coordination. Typical issues addressed by cross-functional teams are solving a problem; developing or launching a new product; or initiating a change programme. The development of the Ford Motor Company's Escape gas-electric hybrid sports utility vehicle involved cross-functional teamworking.

Home viewing

The Siege (1999, director, Edward Zwick) is an action thriller about terrorist bombings in New York City. How well or badly do the three organizations – the FBI, represented by Anthony 'Hub' Hubbard (played by Denzil Washington); the CIA by Sharon Bridger (Annette Bening) and the US Army by General William Deveraux (Bruce Willis) – work together to achieve their common goal of defeating the terrorists? What impedes their successful inter-organizational cooperation?

What did they find? Haier's microdivisionalization

Marshall Meyer and colleagues (2017) used a longitudinal, single-case approach to investigate how successfully Haier, a Chinese multinational $32 billion company with 60,000 employees, could reorganize itself into more than 2,000 teams called micro business units (MBUs). Was microdivisionalization on this scale possible? Like strategic business units (SBUs) of divisionalized firms, Haier's MBUs (also called 'self-ownership teams') were internally, focused on bottom-line financial performance and on customer results. However, unlike SBUs, they competed in an internal market for targets and were subject to takeover or dissolution if they set their targets too low or failed to achieve them. Essentially, this large operating company was divided up into thousands of business unit-like entrepreneurial teams, each responsible and accountable for its own performance.

Traditional SBUs are typically large; part of a single, divisionalized firm; self-contained; operate independently; have their own financial statements; and compete with other companies but not directly with each other. In contrast, Haier's MBU-teams are smaller; accountable for product, process improvement and financial performance; do not compete with other companies, but do complete with each other internally. Team members are encouraged to think and act as business owners.

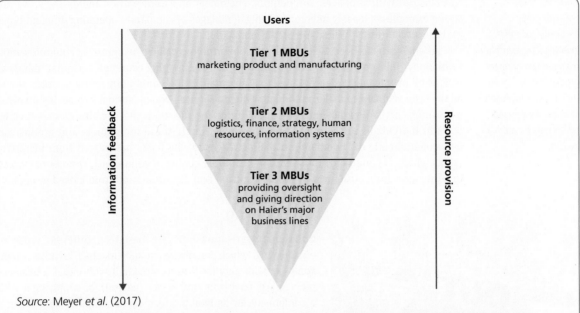

Users

Tier 1 MBUs
marketing product and manufacturing

Tier 2 MBUs
logistics, finance, strategy, human
resources, information systems

Tier 3 MBUs
providing oversight
and giving direction
on Haier's major
business lines

Information feedback

Resource provision

Source: Meyer *et al.* (2017)

The reorganization resulted in a new, three-level structure which took the form of an inverted triangle with the users at the top (see diagram). The first and highest level included marketing, product and manufacturing teams performing the core activities of the group. These teams comprised the majority of MBUs and were the focus of the research. The second tier comprised platform teams specializing in logistics, finance, strategy, human resources, information systems and purchasing. The third tier in the operating structure comprised MBUs having oversight and giving strategic direction to Haier's major business lines.

Each MBU-team has a leader and five to seven members who are product or marketing specialist. It receives baseline targets for sales and profitability which may be altered. These are posted within the company and are viewed by the other teams who compare them with their own and who can challenge them. Team performance is appraised using a combination of quantitative indicators and qualitative judgements. Individual compensation is based on a complicated formula. Each MBU team is a four-way matrix (geographic marketing, product, manufacturing and function. What do you think the researchers found to be the advantages and disadvantages of the new organization structure that Haier had created? **(Answers in chapter Recap.)**

 **STOP AND SEARCH**   YouTube for *Microdivisionalization* (1:33).

Era of boundaryless organization structures

Boundaryless organization one possessing permeable internal and external boundaries which give it flexibility and thus the ability to respond to change rapidly.

The third era identified by Anand and Daft (2007) began in the mid-1990s and continues to this day. It is characterized by the development of an architecture called the boundaryless organization. This concept views firms as possessing permeable boundaries, both internally and externally. The firm behaves like an organism encouraging better integration among its functional departments and closer partnerships with outsiders, so as to facilitate the free exchange of ideas and information, in order to maximize its flexibility and be able to respond rapidly to change.

Anand and Draft (2007) discussed the collaborative relationship structures used in boundaryless organizations. These involve a relationship between two or more organizations, sharing their ideas, knowledge, staff, production and technology for mutual benefit. They identified three types, all of which used the outsourcing principle – hollow, modular and virtual. Many organizations are adopting this approach in order to become more effective. Due to increasing costs and time pressures, companies now rarely innovate on their own. Instead, they seek partners with whom they can collaborate to share costs and speed up development. Adopting this type of organizational design involves establishing collaborative relationships with suppliers, competitors, customers and third parties. Increasingly, we are seeing examples of loosely interconnected assemblages of companies operating different types of these structures (Schilling and Steensma, 2001).

This approach has been facilitated by the opportunities created by improved communication technology (internet, mobile phones) and the rise of emerging economies (China, India), as well as by management's acceptance that an organization cannot efficiently perform alone, all the tasks required to make a product or offer a service. Organizational structuring involves translating company policy into practices, duties and functions that are allocated as specific tasks to individuals and groups. However, increasingly these individuals and groups can be located outside the company. In the last 20 years, the focus has moved from hierarchy (single chain of command) to heterarchy (multiple chains of command); from bureaucracy to adhocracy; from structures to processes; from real to virtual; and from closed to open.

Outsourcing

Collaborative relationships are based on different types of outsourcing, which describes a situation in which an organization contracts with another firm to provide it with either a business process, e.g. paying its staff wages (payroll); or supplying it with a component for its final product, e.g. a computer hard drive; a steering wheel or a packaging box, which it would have previously made itself. Figure 17.8 illustrates this relationship showing that outsourcers can supply both products and processes.

Companies have outsourced to cut costs, slim operations and to concentrate on their core strengths such as product development and marketing. When a business process or a product is acquired by an organization from a firm located in a different country, it is referred to as offshoring. Nike's factory in Vietnam is an example of offshoring. Outsourcing now accounts for 6 per cent of GDP in the United States, 11 per cent in France and the UK, and 16 per cent in the Netherlands (*The Economist*, 2018a).

However, outsourcing has become one of the most contentious inter-organizational arrangements. Commercially, companies are now rethinking their approach to outsourcing. Data shows a decline in outsourcing due to the reductions in savings obtained; the maturity of the market (much of what can be outsourced already has); the increasing problems with legal disputes; over-promising; sloppy contract writing; and injudicious sub-(sub)-contracting. Companies are rethinking outsourcing and supply chain strategies and some are bringing more work back in-house (called reshoring). Politically, in the United States, the export of jobs with the resulting local unemployment has become less acceptable, although many more jobs have been lost in the US due to technology than to offshoring.

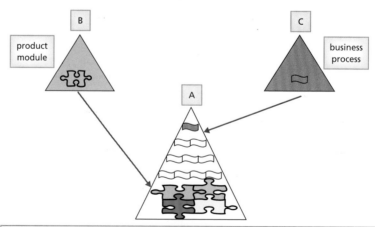

Firm B supplies Organization A with one of its product modules; Firm C provides it with one of its business processes.

Figure 17.8: Outsourcing relationship

The end of outsourcing?

Western multinationals like 3M have been outsourcing their production to low-cost countries such as China for at least 30 years. Indeed, 60 per cent of this company's $30 billion revenues and 40 per cent of its workforce are located outside the United States. However, 3M is now emphasizing 'localization' rather than globalization. In the last five years, it has increased its 20,000 US workforce by 10 per cent. Commentators note that this has coincided with a change policy in the White House. Instead of celebrating 'free trade', American executives are now calling for 'fair trade'.

However, the Boston Consulting Group noted that between 2012 and 2015 planned US company investment in China had already fallen, and that planned production in the US had increased. Amongst the reasons given were rising relative wage costs in China; falling US production costs caused by automation and cheap energy; and a realization of the political and logistical risks created by long supply chains. Jeff Immelt, chief executive of General Electric observed, 'The days of outsourcing are declining. Chasing the lowest labour costs is yesterday's model' (Tett, 2017).

Why executives are going local

In this video, Gillian Tett explains how automation, wage costs and political risk are driving businesses away from globalization. For the past three decades Western multinationals have been outsourcing production to low-cost countries such as China. But are executives turning to localization? (1:44)

Hollow organization structure

Hollow organization structure an organizational design based on outsourcing an organization's non-core processes which are then supplied to it by specialist, external providers.

Outsourcing the majority of a company's non-core *processes* such as human relations, payroll, purchasing, logistics and security (as opposed to the production of parts) creates a hollow organization structure. John Child (2015) explained that the removal of previously internally-provided processes or services 'hollows out' the organization, reducing its boundaries, size and workforce – hence the name. Specialist suppliers then provide these for the company as illustrated in Figure 17.9.

Some automobile manufacturers have even outsourced the assembly of their entire vehicles (*The Economist*, 2002). This leaves the company free to concentrate on those things which

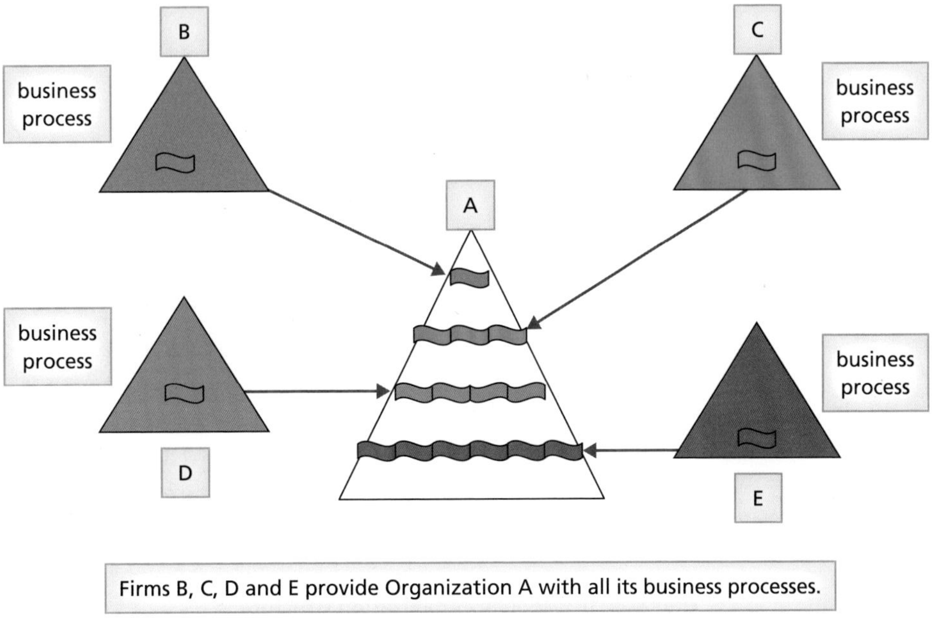

Firms B, C, D and E provide Organization A with all its business processes.

Figure 17.9: Hollow organization structure

represent the core of their activity; those that it does best; and those which lead to more value creation, e.g. research, design, marketing. Its remaining small number of core staff concentrate on strategic matters including the integration of the contributions of the multiple external providers that it has created.

Anand and Daft (2007, p. 335) list the underlying design principles of a hollow organization structure as:

- Determine the non-core processes that are not critical to business performance; that do not create current or potential business advantage; that are unlikely to drive growth or rejuvenation.
- Harness market forces to get non-core processes done efficiently.
- Create an effective and flexible interface.
- Align incentives between the organization and its outsourcing provider.

Nike, the sports goods company, considers its core competencies to be in marketing and distribution rather than in manufacturing. In consequence, the company relies on contract manufacturers located in low cost labour areas of the world which produce merchandise bearing Nike's well-known swoosh logo.

Modular organization structure an organizational design that involves assembling product chunks (modules) provided by internal divisions and external providers.

Modular organization structure

A modular organization structure is also based on outsourcing. However, unlike the hollow structure discussed earlier, in which outsourced processes such as logistics, payroll or warehousing are supplied by outsiders, a modular structure outsources the production of *parts* of the total product. Internal and external contractors supply component parts that the company then assembles itself. A company can break down its product's design into chunks that are then manufactured by either its internal divisions or external contractors. NASA, computer hardware and software companies, household appliances firms and aircraft manufacturers all organize themselves in this way. The analogy most often used is that of a Lego structure in which the different bricks are manufactured by a variety of different, external companies and then are fitted together (Schilling and Steensma, 2001). A modular organization structure is shown in Figure 17.10.

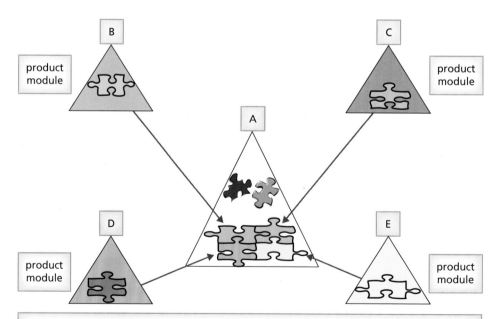

Firms B, C, D and E provide different product modules to Organization A, which produces its own as well, and assembles all of them.

Figure 17.10: Modular organization structure

Anand and Daft (2007, p.337) list the underlying design principles of a modular organization structure as:

- Break products into self-contained modules or chunks capable of stand-alone manufacture.
- Design interfaces to ensure different chunks work together.
- Outsource product chunks to external contractors who can make them more efficiently.
- Ensure that the company can assemble the chunks that are produced internally and those supplied by external providers.

Modular partners

In order to develop and manufacture its 787 Dreamliner model, Boeing Commercial Airplanes dramatically altered its usual approach. This organizational design involves a single large hub-company located at the network's centre, outsourcing chunks of its production functions to external providers while retaining those chunks deemed to be strategically vital and close to its core competence. Boeing's assembly plants are the final stage in a long and hugely complex global supply chain. This consists of about 1,300 'tier 1' suppliers, providing parts to Boeing from 5,400 factories in 40 countries. These in turn are fed by thousands of other 'tier two' suppliers which, in turn, receive parts from countless others.

This form of organizational structure did not work for Boeing. Steve Denning (2013a, 2013b) detailed the many problems the company encountered. Unfinished

Dreamliners had been scattered around its Everett plant due to a range of problems – a shortage of fasteners that hold the plane together; faulty horizontal stabilizers from an Italian supplier; parts not fitting together; suppliers failing to deliver their components on time; and Boeing having to take over some of its sub-contractors to stop them collapsing financially.

Jim Albaugh, head of Boeing's commercial airliner division admitted that too much of the Dreamliner's production had been contracted out. Some of that work has since been brought back in-house so that the company could check it more carefully. It established a 'war room' that monitored the outside parts and raw materials and sent out 'examiners' to visit suppliers to ensure that their production met Boeing's needs. In October 2011, the first Dreamliner, operated by ANA Airlines, made its inaugural commercial flight from Tokyo to Hong Kong. It was three years late and billions of dollars over budget. By 2015, the situation had recovered and by mid-year, the company had delivered 64 planes. However, in future, companies like Boeing will need to think long and hard as to how to employ outsourcing (*The Economist,* 2018b; *All Things 787,* 2015).

Virtual organization structure

Virtual organization structure an organizational design that uses technology to transcend the constraints of legal structures, physical conditions, place and time, and allows a network of separate participants to present themselves to customers as a single entity.

The **virtual organization structure** consists of a temporary network of nodes (entire organizations; parts of organizations, teams, specific individuals) linked by information technologies which flexibly co-ordinate their activities, and combine their skills and resources, in order to achieve common goals, without requiring traditional hierarchies of central direction or supervision. In this structure, the outsourcing company becomes primarily a 'network coordinate' and when supported by sophisticated technology – a virtual organization.

A virtual organization is viewed as a single entity from the outside by its customers despite consisting of a network of separate companies. McKinsey, a management consultancy, reported that a new class of company was emerging which used collaborative Web 2.0 technologies intensively to connect the internal efforts of employees and to extend the organization's reach to customers, partners and suppliers (Bughin and Chui, 2011). A virtual organization structure is shown in Figure 17.11.

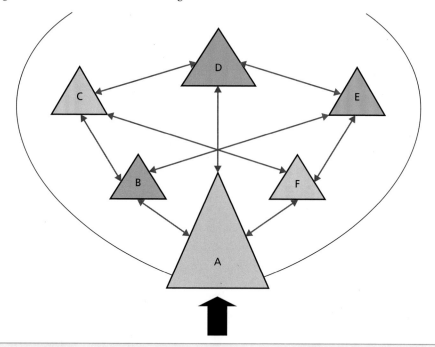

An organizational design that uses technology to allow a network of separate companies to present themselves as a single entity to customers

Figure 17.11: Virtual organization structures

Anand and Daft (2007, p.339) list the underlying design principles of a virtual organization structure as:

- Create boundaries around a temporary organization with external partners.
- Use technology to link people, assets and ideas.
- Each partner contributes their domain of excellence.
- Disband or absorb after opportunity ends.

Many observers see virtual organizations as a panacea for many of the current organizational problems. A virtual organization has the capacity to form and reform to deal with problems and (potentially) provide a flexible response to organizational needs and changing circumstances. The concept has generated considerable discussion and debate among managers, management consultants and business commentators, although they disagree about its nature. In the light of this, Warner and Witzel (2004) list the six features that nearly all virtual organizations possess (Table 17.2). These authors argue that organizations should not be classified into virtual or non-virtual categories. All firms can possess some degree of *virtuality* and that this can take different forms. They say that every organization is a mixture of virtual and tangible

Table 17.2: Features of virtual organizations

Feature	Description
1. Lack of physical structure	Less physical presence than conventional organizations. Fewer tangible assets such as offices or warehouses and those possessed are physically dispersed.
2. Reliance on communication technologies	Technology is used dynamically to link people, assets and ideas. Communication networks replace the physical structure of a conventional organization to define it and give a shape to its activities.
3. Mobile work	Communication networks reduce the importance of where work is physically located, meaning that individuals and team members no longer have to be physically co-located to work together on a common task.
4. Hybrid forms	Short- or long-term collaboration between agencies can take various forms, called hybrids, including networks, consortia, and webs, to achieve a mutual goal.
5. Boundaryless and inclusive	Not confined to legal entities, they but can encompass suppliers and distributors, working with producers, and even involving customers in the production process.
6. Flexible and responsive	Can be rapidly assembled from a variety of disparate elements, to achieve a certain business goal, and then, as required, can be dismantled or reconfigured.

Source. based on Warner and Witzel (2004, pp.3–5)

elements and they identify six dimensions along which companies can choose to organize their activities on a virtual or a tangible basis:

- Nature of product
- Nature of working
- Relationship with suppliers
- Relationship with customers
- Relationship between firm's elements
- Relationship between managers and employees

Collaborative organization structures

Collaboration between organizations has increased in recent years. Companies increasingly consist of a number of strategically aligned businesses which are closely linked where there are opportunities to create value by leveraging shared capabilities, but only loosely linked where the greater value lies in an undifferentiated focus. This implies that close and loose relationships will co-exist within and between organizations. Bob de Wit and Ron Meyer (2014) listed examples of inter-organizational, collaborative relationships. These included:

Co-branding alliance	R&D staff exchange
Learning communities	Licensing agreement
Shared payment system	New product joint venture
Joint reservation system	International marketing alliance

Albers et al. (2016) discussed the differences in how collaborative work was organized in strategic alliances among its partners. Currently, companies are seeking alliances for three main reasons (*The Economist*, 2015):

- Technological
    - *Industry fusions:* New technology brings previously separate industries together.
    - *Advances in collaborative technology:* videoconferencing, Skype, email, voicemail, social networks, wikis and blogs.

- Economic
  - *Knowledge economy*: The move towards a knowledge economy and a focus on the innovation of products and services.
  - *Rise of partnership strategies*: A change in perception away from seeing companies as competing for a piece of a finite cake and towards their making the cake bigger.
  - *Cross-border links*: Reciprocal relations between Western companies and those in developing countries to cut costs and enter new markets.
  - *Costs*: Technology costs are now so large that companies cannot fund them on their own.
- Social
  - *Working styles of Generation Y*: Generation Y (up to 30 years) is particularly adept at, and places value upon, collaborating with others.
  - *Consumer pressure*: The rise in online shopping has forced physical shop owners to work with others.

Companies are forming ever more complicated alliances. America's top 1,000 public companies now derive 40 per cent of their revenue from alliances compared with just 1 per cent in 1980 (*The Economist, 2016*). Renault and Nissan have been in a close alliance for 20 years and in 2016 they were joined by Mitsubishi. By 2017 the trio had overtaken Volkswagen as the world's biggest car maker. As *The Economist* (2018c, p.4) observed, ride-sharing is creating numerous alliances (see Figure 17.12):

> Carmakers, technology giants, start-ups and ride hailing firms are already engaged in a furious battle to dominate this emerging industry. The car makers understand metal-bashing, but know less about complex software. The tech firms know about machine learning and computer vision, but not making cars. The ride hailing firms, for their part, have their apps installed on millions of users' phones, providing the obvious route to market. The result has been a flurry of deals, much hedging of bets and a constantly evolving web of alliances.

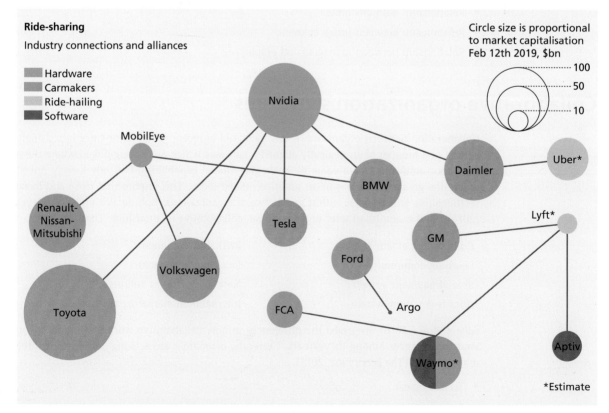

Figure 17.12: Ride sharing industry connections
Source: The Economist (2018c, p.4)

In 2018, Renault-Nissan-Mitsubishi announced a deal with Google to install technology into their cars that will provide services which would keep customers online irrespective of whether they were driving or out of their cars. The deal will allow motorists to use Google Maps, control music by speaking, and even predict breakdowns. This technology partnership between Google and the three-group alliance will be operational in vehicles from 2021 (Campbell, 2018).

Collaboration can take various forms:

Objectives of collaboration abroad

 In this video, Della Bradshaw talks to Andrea Sironi, rector of Bocconi University who discusses the reasons why business schools have been actively collaborating with each other in recent years. (4:34)

Collaboration with suppliers

Most inter-firm relationships in the early networks through the 1980s were managed by contracts. Some manufacturers realized that both upstream suppliers and downstream distributors possessed technical and market knowledge that was of value to them. They thus created cross-firm relationships with their suppliers and distributors that allowed such knowledge to be used to the mutual advantage of all supply chain members (Miles et al., 2010).

Collaboration with competitors

Co-opetition a form of cooperation between competing organizations which is limited to specified areas where both believe they can gain mutual benefit.

Collaboration with competitors can take the form of 'cooperative competition' or co-opetition. This occurs when two or more organizations decide that they do not possess an individual competitive advantage in a field; want to share common costs; or wish to innovate quickly but lack the necessary resources, knowledge or skill to do so (Brandenburger and Nalebuff, 2002). For instance, the cooperation between Peugeot and Toyota on shared components for a new city car for Europe. In this case, companies will save money on shared costs while remaining fiercely competitive in other areas.

The odd couple

If you are on a short flight, the chances are that your aircraft's engines were made by CFM International. CFM is an unusual yet durable joint venture between US-based General Electric (GE) the world's most successful conglomerate and standard bearer of raw Anglo-Saxon capitalism, and Snecma, a French firm owned by Safran. CFM's engines power 71 per cent of the world's fleet of single-aisle aircraft. They can be found in Boeing 737s, DC8s, Airbus A320s, and the

→

AWACs. It supplies 400 commercial and military customers worldwide. These are the workhorses of aviation and constitute the largest market for engines, much bigger than that for wide-bodied jumbos. The joint venture began in 1974 when both companies wanted to expand beyond their mostly military customers into the growing civilian business. At the time, this was dominated by Pratt & Whitney which had the best-selling engine for single-aisle planes. As the technological leader, it saw no need to collaborate with anyone. Snecma decided against linking up with Rolls Royce after a failed collaboration on Concorde engines. That left GE, which was anxious to get close to Airbus which was founded in 1970, and was then Europe's nascent aircraft consortium.

The European home of this odd pairing is an old military airfield on the edge of the forest of Fontainebleau outside Paris, while the American component is based within GE's aero-engine division in Cincinnati, Pennsylvania. Despite a huge disparity in size, the two firms operate their joint venture on a simple and equitable basis. In both factories, the core module of the CFM engine (a GE design originally developed for fighter aircraft) is married to a French front fan and low-pressure turbine. Each partner is responsible for the research, design and production of its modules. Many companies set up joint ventures and other forms of collaboration, but few have one that is so central to their entire business. GE and Snecma share nothing but engine parts and sales and they split the proceeds roughly 50–50. Jet engines may be awesomely complicated machines worth millions of dollars each, but the secret to making them successfully seems to be to keep it simple. The two companies have extended their partnership through to 2040 and are cooperating in the development of the new generation of LEAP engines (*The Economist,* 2007; **www.cfmaeroengines.com**, 2015).

Collaborating with users

User contribution system a method of aggregating people's contributions or behaviours in ways that is useful to others.

Amazon, eBay, Google, Wikipedia, You Tube, the Mozilla Foundation and Facebook are all examples of user contribution systems. These are methods of aggregating people's contributions or behaviours in ways that are useful to others, and these are responsible for much of their success. The contribution of users can be active, as when they donate their work, expertise or information; or it can be passive (and even unknowing), as in the case of behavioural data gathered from them automatically when they participate in a purchase transaction.

These companies regularly provide their super-customers with their latest products, asking them to recommend improvements. In this way, they benefit from free workers debugging their software and providing ideas for new products. Commercial companies are now developing ways in which unlimited numbers of outside people can volunteer their time, energy and expertise to improve things for themselves, and increase profits for the company. A user contribution structure is shown in Figure 17.13.

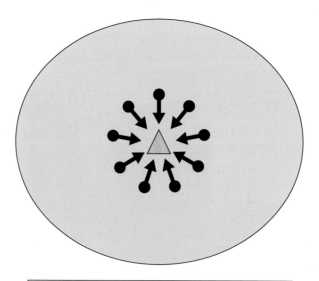

An organization uses the contributions of countless individual volunteers to help it achieve its goals.

Figure 17.13: User contribution system

Collaborating with super-consumers

Dubbed 'super-consumers', 'lead customers' or high-passion fans', these individuals provide valuable customer insights explains Eddie Yoon. They are defined by their attitude to the product whose consumption meets their emotional needs. Rather than treating these individuals as mere obsessives or ignoring them, Yoon advises companies to nurture them as these super-consumers come up with ideas for improving the products.

In the 1990s, LEGO® released a new product – a 727-part set called Mindstorms®. It contained a microchip that made a variety of movements possible. The product was a great success, selling 80,000 sets. However, to the company's surprise, it was being bought by adults for their own use, and not for children. Quite quickly, its users hacked the toy's code and created a variety of new applications from soda machines to blackjack dealers. The new programs spread quickly over the internet and were more sophisticated than those that Lego had itself developed. Over 40 guidebooks advised users on how to get the most out of this LEGO set. Initially, LEGO reacted negatively, feeling that customers were misusing their products. However, after a period of confusion and inaction, the company started to listen to their product's

'(ab)users' in an effort to discover what they were doing with it. Following discussions, the company decided that they were doing something interesting and important, even though it differed from LEGO's own business plan. The company discovered that this product's (re) creators formed a community around the LEGO brand and shared a passion for innovation. Companies should identify their super-consumers and reward them (*The Economist*, 2016; Kornberger, 2010; Guizzo and Cass, 2013; Yoon, 2016).

Experiments with agility and holacracy

Aghina et al. (2015) observed that companies faced a perfect storm of environmental change (rapidly evolving stakeholder demands); technological change (constant introduction of disruptive technology, accelerating digitization); social change (democratization of information); and human capital change (companies engaging in talent wars to attract and retain the best staff). While leaders know that to meet these mounting challenges they have to give their employees room to give of their best, they also want to retain control of a volatile situation.

This tension between employee freedom and management control says Ranjay Gulati (2018) 'ties companies up in knots'. This author discusses his concept of 'freedom within a framework'. 'Freedom' means trusting front line employees to think and act independently on behalf of the organization, and 'framework' refers to creating a structure that sets them boundaries, gives them direction, but goes not stifle their actions'. In their turn, Ethan Bernstein and colleagues (2016) discuss the tension between reliability and adaptability. Reliability means a company providing predictable returns for shareholders, stable employment for employees, and meeting customer expectations. Adaptability means making minor adjustments in production to meet local needs or introducing major changes in company strategy or capacities.

Foss and Klein (2014) argue that 'Managers need to move away from specifying methods and processes in favour of defining the principles they want people to apply or the goals they want people to achieve. In other words, executives can design the rules of the game without specifying the actions of the players' (p. 74). They give the example of Wikipedia. While its management does not control the content of its entries, it does design its structure, e.g. the format of entries, means of their revision and the dispute resolution process.

Hamel and Zanini (2017) argue that one of the obstacles to 'busting' bureaucracy and devolving authority and responsibility to front line staff has always been a lack of a single, step-by-step guide on how to do this successfully. However, we now have radically different, alternative models (in the form of agile and holacratic organizations) for disassembling a bureaucracy. A number of companies have attempted to achieve this difficult balancing act between freedom and control and between reliability and adaptability. Some of their experiments are elaborations of previous design models, while others break entirely new ground.

Agile organizations

Linda Holbeche (2015, p.11) described agility as a 'complex construct that can take multiple forms'. It captures an organization's ability to develop and quickly apply flexible, nimble and dynamic capabilities. Originally linked with software development, lean manufacturing, just-in-time supply chains and process improvements methodologies of the 1990s, agility theory is now informed by complexity science and encompasses more broadly an organization's capacity to respond, adapt quickly and thrive in a rapidly changing environment.

Like Trist's autonomous teams, agile has its roots in the 1950s in the work of Burns and Stalker (1961) and their distinction between mechanistic (bureaucratic, hierarchical) and organic (adaptable, agile) organization structures. Later, Rosabeth Moss Kanter (1983) relabelled these two constructs 'segmentalist' and 'integrative' arguing that the former stifled creativity while the latter stimulated innovation. The agile approach can be seen as a contemporary reworking of these earlier but well-established ideas. The new label comes from the engineers who, back in 2001, replaced the traditional waterfall software development method with an agile approach. Describing what are the common scrum and agile team features, Takeuchi and Nonaka (1986, p. 138) suggest that:

> this strategy for product development can act as an agent of change for the larger organization. The energy and motivation the effort produces can spread through the big company and begin to break down some of the rigidities that have set in over time.

Thus the original software product-focused and team-specific concept of the 1980s has morphed into a business-general, organization-wide approach of the twenty-first century. It is aimed at helping companies to respond effectively to a dynamic changing environment. A survey by McKinsey, a management consultancy, revealed that many companies also faced a 'waterfall problem' (McKinsey & Company, 2017a). They found that firms were reorganizing themselves every two years and each reorganization took an average of 18 months. Thus, just as one company redesign was completed, changes in the market or in customers' needs required them to start a new one. Rigby et al. (2018, p.90) note that 'In today's tumultuous markets, where established companies are furiously battling assaults from start-ups and other insurgent competitors, the prospect of a fast-moving, adaptive organization is highly appealing'.

Agile organization
one which allows an organization to quickly reconfigure strategy, structure, processes, people and technology toward value-creating and value protecting opportunities.

McKinsey defines an **agile organization** as a firm which is able to quickly reconfigure its strategy, structure, processes, people and technology toward value-creating and value-protecting opportunities (McKinsey & Company, 2017a, p.1). They contrast the old traditional company with the new agile one in the following way:

> The dominant 'traditional' organization (designed primarily for stability) is a static, siloed, structural hierarchy – goals and decisions rights flow down the hierarchy, with the most powerful governance bodies at the top (i.e., the top team). It operates through linear planning and control in order to capture value for shareholders. The skeletal structure is strong, but often rigid and slow moving.
>
> In contrast, an agile organization (designed for both stability and dynamism) is a network of teams within a people-centred culture that operates in rapid learning and fast decision cycles which are enabled by technology, and that is guided by a powerful common purpose to co-create value for all stakeholders. Such an agile operating model has the ability to quickly and efficiently reconfigure strategy, structure, processes, people, and technology toward value-creating and value-protecting opportunities. An agile organization thus adds velocity and adaptability to stability, creating a critical source of competitive advantage in volatile, uncertain, complex, and ambiguous (VUCA) conditions (McKinsey & Company, 2017b, p.3).

McKinsey's approach to creating an agile organization is to make it both stable and dynamic simultaneously. They measure a firm's level of agility by its possession of nine 'stable practices' which cultivate reliability and efficiency. These are the backbone elements that do not need to change frequently. In addition, there are nine 'dynamic practices' that allow companies to respond quickly to new challenges and opportunities. Both sets of practices are listed in Table 17.3.

Table 17.3: Stable and dynamic practices of an agile organization

Stable practices	Dynamic practices
Cohesive community	Role mobility
Entrepreneurial drive	Continuous learning
Performance orientation	Information transparency
Shared vision and purpose	Flexible resource allocation
Actionable strategic guidance	Technology, systems and tools
Shared and servant leadership	Sensing and seizing opportunities
Standardized ways of working	Active partnerships and ecosystem
Fit-for-purpose accountable cells	Rapid iteration and experimentation
Action-oriented decision architecture	Open physical and virtual environment

Source: based on McKinsey & Company (2017b, p.8)

 **STOP AND SEARCH**   YouTube for *Matthew Taylor, James Manyika: Seeking autonomous and flexible work [2 of 2]* (1:04).

Agile organizations resemble living organisms rather than machines (Figure 17.14). Like organisms responding to danger, agile organizations are nimble and their empowered staff are able to act quickly. Rigby et al. (2018) discussed the challenges of transforming a traditional hierarchical company into an agile organization. Could a firm scale up from having a limited number of agile innovation teams to having hundreds or even thousands of such teams? Are some functional departments potentially more suitable for 'agilification', e.g. product development, marketing, human resources than others, e.g. plant maintenance, purchasing, accounting (Cappelli and Tavis, 2018; Barton et al., 2018).

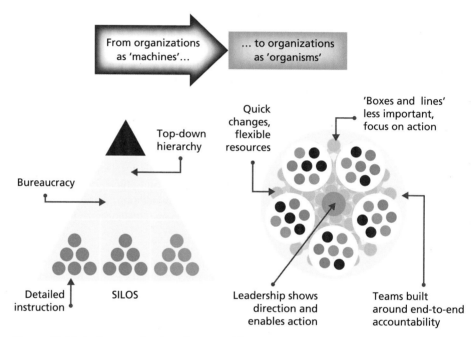

Figure 17.14: Agile organization: from machine to organism
Source: McKinsey & Company (2017a, p.5).

Commentators agree that company attempts at agile transformation have had mixed results. Success stories are matched with accounts of disappointments. Contemporary management literature is full of examples of company attempts at agile transformation (Bazigos et al., 2015; Baham et al, 2017; Birkinshaw 2018; Cadieux and Heyn, 2018). Some critics argue that agile practices are inefficient in large companies and inappropriate in certain contexts. Larman and Vodde (2008, 2009) listed a number of organizational obstacles which included bureaucratic company procedures; agile teams not being supported by non-agile company units; and individual rather than team performance evaluation. Rigby et al. (2016) list the market environment, customer involvement, innovation type and work modularity conditions which are more or less favourable to agile implementations. For many companies introducing an agile transformation is just too extreme a restructuring experiment. Instead, they have opted for hybrid approaches that mix elements of agile development with more traditionally driven approaches.

 **STOP AND SEARCH**   YouTube for *agile.*

For Holbeche (2015) organizational agility is not just a set of tools or activities but a state of being. She talks about having an agile mindset that is 'open, alert and flexible, that reframes change as the norm' (p.272) and which treats dynamic stability as an inevitable part of an organization's or individual's life journey. It involves the ability to live with ambiguity; make good decisions fast; bring people with you through change; remain true to your values; and lead from a shared purpose. As such, the agile concept can be applied not only to organizations but also to individual behaviour and other social arrangements such as families.

 **STOP AND SEARCH**   YouTube for *Bruce Feiler': Agile programming – for your family* (Ted Talk, 18:01).

Self-organization and the holacratic organization

Self-organization
a collective process of communication, choice and mutual adjustment in behaviour based on a shared goal among members of a given system which occurs when people and resources organize themselves without external planning into coordinated, purposeful activity.

This form of experimental organizational structure represents another less-hierarchical company response to the disappearance of organization stability. It emerges from the internal dynamics of the company rather than at the behest of top management. It is thus based on the principle of self-organization. Self-organization is a collective process of communication, choice, and mutual adjustment in behaviour based on a shared goal among members of a given system. It occurs when people and resources organize themselves without external planning to perform coordinated, purposeful activity (Comfort, 1994).

McCollum and Barber (2017) contrast traditional organizational characteristics with self-organization ones (Table 17.4). Self-organization involves groups of individuals spontaneously organizing themselves into a functioning system to accomplish a task. Its leaders emerge and recede based on who is available and who has the information. Self-organization can occur at both the organization and the group level.

Michael Lee

Michael Lee and Amy Edmondson (2017) discussed organization redesigns which involve the removal of managerial hierarchies; the radical decentralization of authority; and the creation of self-organizing and self-managing organizations. Some experiments have not simply adjusted the managerial hierarchy incrementally, but have severed entirely the reporting relationship between managers and their subordinates. The authors discuss three company studies – Valve, Morning Star, and Zappos.

Table 17.4: Comparison of traditional organization characteristics and self-organization characteristics

Traditional organization characteristics	Self-organization characteristics
Mechanistic	Organic, living
Linear, cause–effect relationships	Nonlinear
Rational analysis, problem solving	Patterns, socially constructed
Stable	Change, reorganize, grow
Control, predictable	Spontaneous, unpredictable
Order, rules	Adaptive, flexible, learning
Episodic, planned, managed change, organization-wide	Continuous, emergent change, self-organization, local

Source: McCollum and Barber (2017, p.167)

Valve (360 employees) is one of the largest and most successful makers of computer games was founded in 1996. It has developed its own organizational design in which employees form into *cabals* and have full flexibility and autonomy to choose the games on which they would like to work. Here, decentralization of authority involves replacing the practice of managers determining which games should be developed with an internal process of employees voting with their feet to decide which games the company should create. The company handbook explains to new employees that nobody reports to anybody else; that even the company founder or president is not your manager; that the company is theirs to steer towards opportunities and away from dangers; and that they have the power to green-light projects and ship products (Baldwin, 2015; Foss and Dobrajska, 2015).

STOP AND SEARCH   YouTube for *Valve, employees without managers.*

Morning Star (400 employees), a tomato processing company, developed its own self-management system in the 1990s. It changed from managers directing work to having individual employees voluntarily entering into bilateral contracts with fellow workers (Hamel, 2011). These contracts are called Colleague Letters of Understanding (CLOUs) and they outline individual responsibilities, activities, goals and metrics for evaluating performance. They are renegotiated annually and form the basis of work coordination. Additionally, elected committees settle salaries and also resolve conflicts between employees.

The company's goal is to foster an environment where employees 'will be self-managing professionals, initiating communications and the coordination of their activities with fellow colleagues, customers, suppliers, and fellow industry participants, absent directives' (Gino and Staats, 2014).

✋ **STOP AND SEARCH**   YouTube *Morning Star Company, self-management.*

Zappos (1,500 employees), an online retailer, is currently the company most closely associated with holacracy, a structure which it adopted in 2013 (Robertson, 2016). Holacracy is defined as a form of decentralized management and organizational governance that takes decision-making power away from managerial hierarchies and distributes it among self-organizing teams. It applies the concept of self-management over the *entire* company (Henshall, 2017). Holacracy aims at:

Holacracy a form of decentralized management and organizational governance that takes decision making power away from managerial hierarchies and distributes it among self-organizing teams.

- reducing the number of managers
- making decisions closer to the work
- responding to changing market needs
- harnessing individual and team initiative
- flattening managerial hierarchies replacing them with teams
- sensing market changes, seizing opportunities, reconfiguring existing assets and competences.

Holacratic organization a structure that is determined not through hierarchical planning but incrementally, responsively, and from the bottom up, that enables employees to self-organize and self-manage themselves to achieve organizational goals.

The holacratic organization has been described as 'a new kind of organization designed to enable 'whole' individuals (not narrow professional selves) to self-organize and self-manage to achieve an organic organizational purpose, determined not through hierarchical planning but incrementally, responsively and from the bottom up (Bernstein et al., 2016, p. 47).

By adopting holacracy, Zappos embraced an integrated set of detailed prescriptions that formally eliminated people managers and gave individual employees full autonomy over how they performed their roles. Rather than having managers directing individuals' work, staff individuals were directed by highly formalized, yet flexible, role definitions. They were formed into 'sub-circles' and 'super circles' (see Figure 17.15). The increased formalization of work into roles is demonstrated by the fact that, two years after adopting holacracy, the number of roles per employee at Zappos has grown from one per employee to 7.4 per employee (Bernstein et al., 2016). Such growth is less an indication of any drastic increase in workload and more a reflection of greatly refined and detailed staff role definitions.

Despite their increased formalization, the work roles are extremely flexible. Groups meet to define and revise roles in regular 'governance meetings'. In these, any member can propose changes to the way that the group is organized, such as changing any role's accountabilities, or proposing a new work group policy. All proposed changes are discussed and consented to by the group. As a result of this revision process, formal roles frequently evolve as new issues

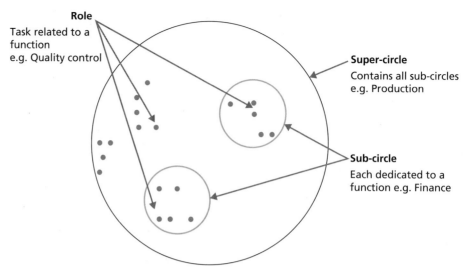

Figure 17.15: Holacracy – super-circle, sub-circle and role

emerged. Tony Hsieh, Zappos's CEO and founder, explained that he wanted to implement holacracy because productivity per employee had decreased as the company had grown. He believed that making the company more self-organizing might reverse that trend (*McKinsey Quarterly*, 2017).

 **STOP AND SEARCH**   YouTube for *Zappos Holacracy.*

A review of different companies' holacratic restructuring experiments reveals a number of common, recurring features relating to teams, work, roles and leadership.

- Teams
  - Company structure is based on many self-organizing teams.
  - These form and reform as company needs change and new goals, tasks and initiatives emerge.
  - Individual roles in teams are collectively defined and assigned to accomplish work.
  - Teams not only manage themselves, but also design and govern themselves.
- Work
  - Objectives are set by those who must make things happen.
  - Tasks and functions are organized through commitments.
  - Individual targets, tasks and commitments are made visible to others to facilitate cross-team integration.

- Individuals can transfer between teams or work in several teams simultaneously.
- Employees influence company governance by sharing accountability for they work, having authority over how goals are met, having discretion over resources, and ownership of work-related knowledge and information.

- Roles

  - Roles replace job descriptions.
  - They are shaped to match individual capabilities to achieve organizational goals.
  - They may be negotiated among employees or assigned by the organization.
  - Employees simultaneously perform multiple roles in various teams.
  - Individuals who are bad fit for a role are reassigned to other roles.

- Leadership

  - Distributed among roles not individuals.
  - Natural leadership defined by followership.
  - Changes as work changes, new teams are created, new roles defined.

Lee and Edmondson (2017) argue that the core element of all self-managing organizations is the radical decentralization of the authority typically granted to employees. They define radical decentralization as the elimination of the reporting relationship between managers and their subordinates. Employees in self-managing organizations no longer report to a manager who has the authority to allocate work, direct the execution of tasks, monitor performance, determine promotions or raises or fire employees. Indeed the notion of 'reporting to' someone who has 'authority over' you becomes an anathema in self-managing organizations. The authors list the six domains of decision authority that are held by managers in traditional organizational hierarchies:

1. *Work execution*: decisions as to how a given task or project is to be completed

2. *Managing and monitoring work*: assessing if work has been completed in a timely and satisfactory way

3. *Organization and work design*: decisions about tasks to be completed and how the organization is to be structured to complete them

4. *Work and resource allocation*: decisions as to how financial and human resources are be allocated to which parts of the organization

5. *Personnel and performance management*: evaluating individuals' roles performance, deciding the training required to improve performance, choosing whom to hire and fire

6. *Firm strategy*: decisions about the direction of the company, its goals, and how they are to be achieved

Figure 17.16 highlights how the three case study self-managing organizations discussed earlier deal with each decision-making domain compared to the typical managerial hierarchy. The domains are arranged according to those most and least likely to be decentralized.

There remains a question mark as to whether a holacratic organization structure is a feasible, long-term alternative to a traditional, bureaucratic organizational one. The development of holacracy offers a fully-specified model of radical decentralization that any company can adopt wholesale. While it is unlikely the majority of firms will rapidly transform into holacratic organizations, many companies are likely to adopt at least some of the holacratic features described above. Hundreds already have, and thus avoided the painful trial-and-error process of developing their own self-managing systems (Robertson, 2016).

Both agile and holacratic organization structures are not without their critics (*The Economist,* 2014). The former has been labelled a management fad that simply describes existing good practices under new jargon; promotes a 'one size fits all' mindset towards development strategies; and wrongly emphasizes method over results. Holacracy too has its

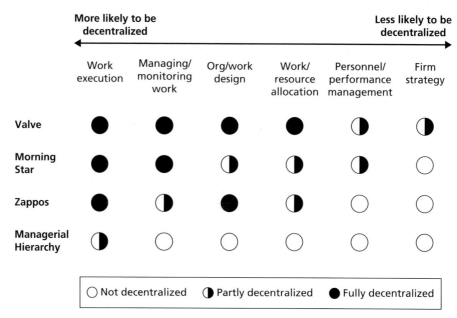

Figure 17.16: Patterns of decentralized authority in self-managing organizations
Source: Lee and Edmondson (2017, p. 47)

critics, Birkinshaw (2014) warns managers against being seduced by management fashions pioneered by their originating firm. He calls these organizations 'deviants' and distinguishes between 'upstarts' (Valve), 'certified weirds' (Morning Star) and 'dancing giants' (Haier). He recommends that senior management should extract the essential principle or logic underpinning an innovation; assess how closely their own company resembles the innovator; and then decide how beneficial it is likely to be for them. To help managers keep up with 'the 'language of self-management' Bernstein et al. (2016) provide a glossary of terms (Table 17.5).

✓✓✓   **EMPLOYABILITY CHECK** (how organizations work)

You have been asked by the campaigns organizers of *#Me Too* (anti-sexual harassment and assault) to advise them on converting their movement into a long-lasting organization. In the light of the Occupy Wall Street campaign's experience, how would you advise them to proceed? (Hill, 2018a; *The Economist,* 2018d).

One has to be careful not to be carried away by the 'brave new world' of organizational self-management. Zitek and Tiedens (2012) reported that employees found hierarchies to be predictable; easy to understand and remember; clarified who reported to whom; and identified those positions which offered the best pay and prospects. In contrast, flat structures were seen as messy and confusing. In a similar vein, Pfeffer (2013) claimed that the idea that companies were actually becoming less hierarchical and more egalitarian was a myth. He argued that power structures had not changed much over time because they were linked to 'survival advantages' and their associated beliefs and behaviours. Hierarchies:

- meet our psychological needs for order and security
- give us the chance to bask in the reflected glory of bosses who are 'winners'
- offer us opportunities for advancement and the possibility of more power and control of others

Pfeffer also says that people hang on to the illusion that as organizations flatten, so too will power and influence. They mistakenly believe that the emergence of inexpensive communication technologies, social networking and crowdsourcing will lead to the irrelevance of hierarchy and its disappearance. He concluded that it was easy to get diverted by the hype and by what everyone else says is the new order. In his view, you cannot play the organizational game by different rules.

Table 17.5: A glossary of self-management terms

	Term	Definition
ORGANIZATIONS	TEAL ORGANIZATION	A new kind of organization designed to enable 'whole' individuals (not narrow professional selves) to self-organize and self-manage to achieve an organic organizational purpose (determined not through hierarchical planning but incrementally, responsively, and from the bottom up).
	HOLACRACY	The most widely adopted system of self-management, developed in 2007 by Brian Robertson. Authority and decision making are distributed among fluid 'circles' (defined below) throughout the organization, and governance is spelled out in a complex constitution.
	PODULARITY	A system of self-management in which each basic unit, or 'pod', is treated as a microcosm of the whole business and acts on its behalf. Podularity has its roots in agile (defined below).
TEAMS	AGILE	A theory of management originating in software development. In an agile system of work, cross-functional, self-managed teams solve complex problems iteratively and adaptively – when possible, face-to-face – with rapid and flexible responses to changing customer needs.
	CIRCLE	In a holacracy, a group of 'roles' (defined below) working toward the same purpose; in essence, a team that forms or disbands as the organization's needs change.
	CABAL	At the video game developer *Valve*, a multidisciplinary project team that forms organically to work toward a major goal. 'Voting with their feet' employees create or join a cabal because they feel the work is important.
	ROLE	In a holacracy circle, a set of responsibilities for a certain outcome or process. Roles can be created, revised, or destroyed; individuals usually have more than one, in multiple circles.
INDIVIDUALS	LEAD LINK	In a holacracy circle, the role responsible for assigning other roles and allocating resources. A lead link has some characteristics of a traditional manager but is subject to the circle's governance process.
	CLOU	'Colleague letter of understanding' – at the tomato-processing company *Morning Star*, an agreement crafted by each employee in consultation with relevant colleagues, outlining the employee's roles along with detailed performance metrics.

Source: Bernstein et al. (2016, p.47)

Distributed innovation systems

Distributed innovation system an approach to organizing for innovation that accesses the knowledge that resides outside the boundaries of any one organization.

Martin Kornberger

Beyond the organization is the network or the system. Distributed innovation systems (DIS) represent an approach to organizing for innovation that accesses the knowledge that resides outside the boundaries of any one organization. DISs create value that transcends the boundaries of individual hierarchically organized firms.

Martin Kornberger (2017) argues that we need to shift our focus away from individual firms and towards networks and business ecosystems in order to organize crowds and innovation. The main function of a DIS is not to actually organize production or to innovate, but rather to provide the conditions in which distributed innovations can occur. This represents a very different concept of organization design. How do managers in organizations structure relationships between themselves and an unruly collection of producer-consumers? These include collectives (e.g. Wikipedia), crowds (e.g. TopCoder) and firms (e.g. Apple).

Distributed innovation decentralized problem solving involving self-selected participation, self-organizing coordination and collaboration, 'free' revealing of knowledge, and hybrid organizational models that blend community with commercial success.

Distributed innovation has been defined as 'decentralized problem-solving, self-selected participation, self-organizing coordination and collaboration, 'free' revealing of knowledge, and hybrid organizational models that blend community with commercial success' (Lakhani and Panetta, 2007, p. 98).

Within DISs, the main challenges are structuring interaction between actors; allowing different kinds of distributed actors to contribute; and evaluating the quality of the innovations produced. Three DIS design features address these issues:

Interface design

The design provides a 'go-between' function by structuring access to, and the exchange of information between, firms and external producers. Examples of interfaces include online forums, portals and websites that organize the flow of information and communication; and offline events such as conferences or innovation camps which link companies with communities. Facebook's interface design uses existing technology (the internet), existing hardware (computers, smartphones) and freely available programming languages (codes) combining these to create supposedly unique value for its users.

Participatory architecture design

The design has to allow for distributed actors, with varying degrees of motivation, skill, and commitment levels, to contribute to something that emerges without the planning of a managerial mastermind. This is achieved in three ways:

- *Modularity*: Products can be deconstructed into modular units and developed independently of each other allowing different people with different skills to work at different times at different speeds on different aspects of the same project.

- *Granularity*: Small-sized project modules attract people with different levels of motivation and commitment to participate. Wikipedia's contribution levels runs from entry rating with a click through to writing a new entry from scratch.

- *Low integration costs*: Integration can take the form of review-based quality control systems for peer-produced modular units. These normative systems can act as mechanisms of integration and quality control.

Evaluative infrastructure design

The design requires a way of judging the quality and value of products. In a DIS, there are just too many ideas, products, and experiences on offer. Quality control is achieved through rankings, ratings, reviews, tagging and bestseller lists. These can be produced by users (TripAdvisor or Facebook's *like* button), by experts (awards), or automatically through algorithms (Amazon's reference function or Google Search). All these devices grade DIS products. Nearly everything (downloads, citations, references, etc.) can be used for valuations. The 'click' plays a pivotal role because each one leaves a trace, providing the basis for evaluation. Evaluation performs two important functions. First, it makes trust visible, e.g. Airbnb's rating system creates a reputation for each user that makes exchange work and motivates members to contribute. Second, it bestows symbolic value on classes of products by relating them to one another, e.g. number of Twitter followers, grade scale (Airbnb) and seller rating (eBay).

 **RECAP**

1. *Appreciate the reason for chief executives' need to design and redesign their organization's structure.*

   - Organization structure is one of the ways of achieving organizational goals.

   - An organizations structure will be changed as a result of changes in its strategy, size, technology, environment, globalization and diversification.

2. *Distinguish eras of organizational design and what factors stimulated each.*

   - Era 1: mid-1800s to the late 1970s – self-contained organization structures.

   - Era 2: 1980s-mid to the 1990s – horizontal organization structures.

   - Era 3: mid-1990s to date – boundaryless organization structure (hollow, modular, virtual and collaborative).

   - Era 4: Experimental organizational structures.

3. *Distinguish between functional, divisional, matrix and team-based organization structures.*

   - A functional structure groups activities and people according to the similarities in their work, profession, expertise, goals or resources used.

   - A divisional structure split an organization up into self-contained entities based on their organizational outputs; geographical region operated in; or the customer groups served.

   - A matrix structure combines two different types of structure e.g. function and product.

- A team-based structure consists entirely of project-type teams that coordinate their activities and work directly with partners and customers to achieve their goals.

4. *Distinguish between an outsourcing relationship and hollow, modular and virtual organization structures.*

   - An outsourcing relationship involves contracting with external providers to supply the organization with the processes and products that were previously supplied internally.

   - A hollow organization structure is based on outsourcing an organization's non-core *processes* which are then supplied to it by specialist, external providers.

   - A modular organization structure involves assembling product chunks (modules) provided by internal divisions and external providers.

   - A virtual organization structure uses technology to transcend the constraints of legal structures, physical conditions, place and time, and allows a network of separate participants to present themselves to customers as a single entity.

5. *Understand the trend towards companies' collaborative relationships with competitors and users.*

   - Collaboration has become a matter of integrating activities rather than integrating organizations

- Factors contributing to increased collaboration include the rise of partnership strategies, the knowledge economy, the working style of generation Y and advances in collaborative technology.

- The increasing speed of change means that individual organizations lack the necessary resources, knowledge or skill to respond individually so have to collaborate with others.

6. *Compare the current organization design experiments involving agile organizations, self-managing organizations and distributed innovation systems.*

   - The structure of an agile organization allows it to quickly reconfigure strategy, structure, processes, people and technology toward value-creating and value-protecting opportunities.

   - The structure of a holacratic organization is not determined by hierarchical planning but by incremental bottom-up responses that enable employees to self-organize and self-manage themselves to achieve organizational goals.

   - The structure of a distributed innovation system is designed for a form of innovation that accesses the knowledge that resides outside the boundaries of any one organization

RECAP: What did they find?

- Meyer et al. (2017) found that Haier was managing its several thousand business units with varying degrees of success. Its MBU-teams structure produced both advantages and disadvantages.

- On the positive side, it found that it was able to measure each MBU-team's performance efficiently, reward its top performers, and reorganize or remove the underperformers. Replacing the bureaucratic organization structure through decentralization into separate team-focused business units allowed the firm to better serve its fragmented customer base This improved the firm's overall performance. Also, by creating an internal market for targets, it raised them without the need for management intervention.

- On the negative side, employees were rewarded using a complex formula which caused problems. By their nature, these MBU-teams were interdependent and needed to cooperate. However, the structure pitted thousands of teams in competition with each other, while attempting to maintain cooperation. Cross-team coordination suffered as business units failed to work together due to arguments and the competition that had sprung up between them. Conflict between product and manufacturing teams was particularly acute.

- Finally, some MBU-teams worked so closely with their customers that boundaries became blurred, and it was unclear whether the MBU-team was working for Haier or had created its own venture with its customer in competition with Haier. Can a single company really have 2000 chief executives?

Revision

1. Why might Max Weber and Henri Fayol be surprised by developments in contemporary organizational design arrangements?

2. Suggest how changes in organization structuring over the last fifty years have affected what workers and managers do and how they do it.

3. In the literature, inter-organizational collaboration is presented as the way forward. Consider the potential negative consequences of this arrangement for the companies involved and their employees and managers.

4. What are some of the similarities and differences between an agile and a holacratic organization?

Research assignment

Take the plot of any well-known novel, play, opera or film. Begin by rewriting it as a one- or two-sentence, business news story headline. Here are some examples: Shakespeare plays: *King Lear* – 'Torrid UK Succession Battle Ends With Deaths of Former Boss and Front-Runners for Top Job'; *Romeo and Juliet*, 'Inquiry Finds Significant Communication Failures Led To Death of Merger Between Two Great Houses'; a fairytale *Cinderella*: 'Underdog Domestic Services Provider Acquires A Royal Connection'; or Bizet's opera *Carmen*, 'Tobacco Worker Slain in Seville, Disrupting Production and Marring World-Famous Fiesta'. Continue by writing a newspaper style article summarizing the main plot from an organizational behaviour perspective, using relevant concepts, theories models and language from the book (Hill, 2018b, 2018c).

Springboard

Ethan Bernstein, John Bunch, Niko Canner and Michael Lee (2016) 'Beyond the holacracy hype', *Harvard Business Review,* 94(7): 38–49. The writers take stock of the new generation of self-management experiments involving both teams and organizations.

Catriona Burke and Michael Morley (2016) 'On temporary organizations: A review, synthesis and research agenda', *Human Relations,* 69(6):1235–58. With the growth of temporary organizations in many industries, the authors define and delineate the concept, document their evolution, assemble their bricolage, and consider their implications for management and organization behaviour research.

Stephen Denning (2018) *The Age of Agile: How Smart Companies are Transforming the Way Work Gets Done,* AMACOM. The author describes the principles and techniques of agile based on its three laws of the small team, the customer and the network.

Phanish Puranam, Oliver Alexy and Markus Reitzig (2014) 'What's 'new' about new forms of organizing?', *Academy of Management Review,* 39(20): 162–80. The authors consider the factors and processes which have created and shaped the organizational structures of the past, and those that are shaping them in the present.

OB cinema

The Godfather and *Godfather Part II* (1972, 1974, director Francis Ford Coppola) are considered to be among the greatest business films of all time. They deal with many aspects of management in organizations including corporate strategy, organization structure, start-up and entrepreneurship, geographic expansion, product development, finance, disruption, corporate communication, information security, government relations, executive succession, restructuring, leadership and beating your competitors. As you watch each film, make a note of the different 'lessons' about effective management that it suggests. Then compare what you have found with Scanati's (2002) list and those discussed by other commentators.

 **STOP AND SEARCH**   Google for *Lessons from the Godfather movie* and *Godfather business lessons.*

Chapter exercises

1: Fabulous Sports Enterprises

Objectives

1. To become acquainted with the advantages and disadvantages of functional and divisional forms of organizing.

2. To gain an understanding of the critical need for communication among groups in a multifaceted organization

3. To recognize the need for horizontal linking processes within organizations.

4. To appreciate how the acquisition of interpersonal affinity possible within one's own work group creates barriers with other groups that can affect performance.

Briefing

1. Form into groups as directed by your instructor.

2. Below are listed six events that can occur within a company. For each one, decide whether it would be easier for the company to deal with if it had a functional (F) or divisional (D) organizational structure. Give the reason for your decision.

3. With your instructor, discuss (a) how you rated each event, and (b) what effect organizational groupings (Accounting, HR, Sales & Marketing, Operations) have on interpersonal relations within and between groups and for company performance as a whole.

Functional organization structure

Divisional organization structure

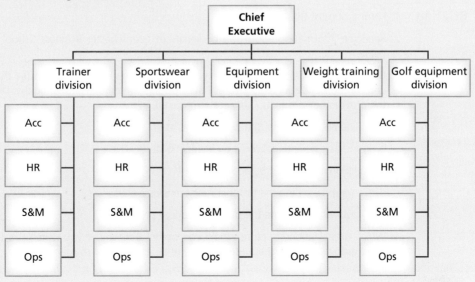

→

Event	Easier for		
	F	D	Reason
1. You just learned that a consulting firm is offering five-day training for accountants next week in Manchester. The £5,000 fee is being discounted to only £2,000 if registrations are submitted in the next 24 hours. Two accountants must be selected immediately to attend.			
2. A critical flaw has just been discovered in the operations/production process. It is imperative that production be shut down at all plants for at least 48 hours to discover the root cause of the problem before producing any more products.			
3. The corporate office has authorized a crash programme to develop a new line of children's products for Sportswear. This requires that the needed changes are worked out between Operations, Sales and Marketing, and HR managers who are associated with this product.			
4. Due to sagging corporate-wide sales, it has been announced that each division must increase profits by 10 per cent. This requires tight coordination among personnel in Operations, Sales, Human Resources and Accounting.			
5. One division is being sued for a Human Resources violation of highly complex employment laws. It is necessary to discover the cause of the violation and revise the offending policies across all product lines in the company as quickly as possible.			
6. A sales representative has found out that our largest competitor has piloted a drastic price reduction for their entry into our most important product line – trainers. Industry sources say that they are about to take this strategy into all of our other product lines (sportswear, equipment, etc.), requiring a response from each division.			

Source: adapted from Fairfield (2016)

2: University of Grantchester Business School

Objectives
1. To design alternative organization structures for a business school based on different criteria of departmentalization.

2. To assess their benefits to different stakeholders

Briefing
1. Form groups of three to five.

2. Read the information about the University of Grantchester Business School (UGBS) below.

3. Using the abbreviations shown, draw alternative organizational charts for the UGBS depicting organizational structures based on the five criteria shown below. Duplicate the provision of products / services as required.

   a. Academic subjects taught by academic staff

   b. Products / services delivered by academic staff

   c. Functions performed by academic staff

   d. Geography, where the product / service is delivered

   e. Clients who consume the product / service provided

4. Which organization structure would you prefer and why, if you were (a) a full-time undergraduate or postgraduate student (b) an academic staff member?

Information about the University of Grantchester Business School	a. *Academic subjects taught*: The 100 UGBS's academic staff are equally divided between the four main subject areas (equivalent to company functions): human behaviour (HB); financial management (FM); strategy and marketing (SM); and operations management (OM)

b. *Products offered*: The UGBS offers the following products:

   (U) Undergraduate teaching – BA full-time students who fund themselves, taught on the main campus

   (P1) Postgraduate teaching – MBA full-time students who fund themselves, taught on the main campus

   (P2) Postgraduate teaching – MBA part-time – working managers, funded by their companies, taught in the city centre campus

   (T) Together, these three constitute business school teaching (T=U+P1+P2)

   (R) Research conducted by academics funding by the research councils

   (D) Doctoral – supervision of conducted by doctoral (postgraduate) students who fund themselves, on the main campus

   (C) Consultancy – consultancy provided by academics for companies, bought by them, and provided on the companies' own premises

   (S) Short courses – short (non-graduating) courses, taught by academics for working managers, paid for by their companies, and run on company premises

c. *Services*: The school performs three major functions: teaching (T), research (R) and consultancy (C)

d. *Geography*: Academics can work in four locations; main campus (MC); city centre (CC); seaside residential facility (SRF); or on the company's own premises (COP).

e. *Customers*: The school has three classes of customers: non-managers (NM); research council-funders (RCF) and companies (COM)

References

Aghina, W., De Smet, A. and Weerda, K. (2015) 'Agility: it rhymes with stability', *McKinsey Quarterly*, December, 1: 58–69.

Albers, S., F. Wohlgezogen and E. J. Zajac (2016) 'Strategic alliance structures: An organization design perspective', *Journal of Management*, 42(3): 582–614.

All Things 787 (2015) '787 Dreamliner 2015 mid-year report', **http://nyc787.blogspot.co.uk** [accessed January 2019].

Anand, N. and Daft, R.L. (2007) 'What is the right organization design?', *Organizational Dynamics*, 36(4): 329–44.

Baham, C., Hirschheim, R., Calderon, A.A. and Kisekka, V. (2017) 'An agile methodology for the disaster recovery of information systems under catastrophic scenarios', *Journal of Management Information Systems*, 34(3): 633–63.

Baldwin, C. Y. (2015) 'In the shadow of the crowd: a comment on Valve's Way', *Journal of Organization Design*, 4(2): 3–5.

Barton, D., Carey, D. and Ram, C. (2018) 'One bank's agile team experiment', *Harvard Business Review*, 96(2): 59–61.

Bazigos, M., De Smet, A. and Gagnon, C. (2015) 'Why agility pays', *McKinsey Quarterly*, December, issue 4, pp.28–34.

Bazigos, M. and Harter, J. (2018) 'Revisiting the matrix organization', *McKinsey Quarterly*, January.

Bernstein, E., Bunch, J. Canner, N. and Lee, M. (2016) 'Beyond the holacracy hype', *Harvard Business Review*, 94(7): 38–49.

Birkinshaw, J. (2014) 'The big idea: Beware the next big thing', *Harvard Business Review*, 92(5): 50–57.

Birkinshaw, J. (2018) 'What to expect from agile', *MIT Sloan Management Review,* 59(2): 39–42.

Bock, L. (2015) *Work Rules: That Will Transform How You Live and Lead,* London: John Murray.

Brandenburger, A.M. and Nalebuff, B.J. (2002) *Co-opetition* (second edition), London: Profile Business Books.

Bughin, J. and Chui, M. (2011) 'The rise of the networked enterprise: Web 2.0 finds its payday', *McKinsey on Business Technology,* (4): 3–8.

Burns, T. and Stalker, G. M. (1961) *The Management of Innovation,* London: Tavistock Publications.

Cadieux, S. and Heyn, M. (2018) 'The journey to an agile organization at Zalando', *McKinsey Quarterly,* April.

Campbell, P. (2018) 'Renault Nissan Mitsubishi Alliance signs in-car tech deal with Google', *Financial Times,* 18 September.

Cappelli, P. and Tavis, A. (2018) 'HR goes agile', *Harvard Business Review,* 96(2): 46–52.

Chandler, A. D. (1962) *Strategy and Structure: Chapters in the History of American Industrial Enterprise.* Cambridge, MA: MIT Press.

Child J. (2015) *Organization: Contemporary Principles and Practice,* second edition, Chichester: Wiley.

Comfort, L. K. (1994) 'Self-organization in complex systems', *Journal of Public Administration Research and Theory,* 4(3): 393–410.

Denning, S. (2013a) 'Lessons every CEO must learn', *Forbes Magazine,* 17 January.

Denning, S. (2013b) 'What went wrong at Boeing', *Forbes Magazine,* 21 January.

De Wit, B. and Meyer, R. (2014) *Strategy Synthesis,* fourth edition, Andover, Hants: Cengage Learning EMEA.

Dimitrova, D. and Wellman, B. (2015) 'Networked work and network research: new forms of teamwork in the triple revolution', *American Behavioural Scientist,* 59(4): 443–56.

Duncan, R. B. (1979) 'What is the right organization structure?: Decision tree analysis provides the answer'. *Organizational Dynamics,* 7(3): 59–80.

Elliott, C.S. and Long, G. (2016) 'Manufacturing rate busters: computer control and social relations in the labour process', *Work, Employment and Society,* 19(1):153–74.

Fairfield, K.D. (2016) 'Understanding functional and divisional organizational structure: a classroom exercise', *Management Teaching Review,* 1(4): 242–51.

Felin, T. and Powell, T.C. (2016) 'Designing organizations for dynamic capabilities', *California Management Review,* 58(4): 78–96.

Fjeldstad, O.D., Snow, C.C., Miles, R.E. and Lettl (2012) 'The architecture of collaboration', *Strategic Management Journal,* 33(6): 734–50.

Forrester, R. and Drexler, A.B. (1999) 'A model of team-based organization performance', *Academy of Management Executive,* 13(3): 36–49.

Foss, N. and Dobrajska, M. (2015) 'Valve's way: Wayward, visionary, or voguish?', *Journal of Organization Design,* 4(2): 12–15.

Foss, N. and Klein, P.G. (2014) 'Why managers still matter', *MIT Sloan Management Review,* 56(1): 73–80.

Frey C.B., Osborne M., Holmes, C,, Rahbari E,, Garlick, R, Friedlander, G, McDonald, G. Curmi, E., Chua, J,, Chalif, P., Wilkie, M. (2016) *Technology at Work v2. 0: The Future is Not What It Used To Be,* CityGroup and University of Oxford, January https://www.oxfordmartin.ox.ac.uk/downloads/reports/Citi_GPS_Technology_Work_2.pdf [accessed January 2019]

Galbraith, J. (1973) *Designing Complex Organizations,* Boston, MA: Addison Wesley.

Gino, F. and Staats, B. (2014) *The Morning Star Company: Self-management at Work.* HBS No. 9-914-013. Boston, MA: Harvard Business School Publishing.

Guizzo, E. and Cass, S. (2013) 'Lego announces Mindstorms EV3, a more 'hackable' robotics kit', https://spectrum.ieee.org/automaton/robotics/diy/lego-announces-mindstorms-ev3-a-more-hackable-robotics-kit [accessed January 2019]

Gulati, R. (2018) 'Structure that's not stifling', *Harvard Business Review,* 96(3): 70–76.

Gulati, R., Puranam, P. and Tushman, M. (2012) 'Meta-organizational design: rethinking design in inter-organizational and community contexts', *Strategic Management Journal,* 33(6): 571–86.

Halgin, D.S., Gopalakrishnan, G.M., and Borgetti, S.P. (2015) 'Structure and agency in networked distributed work: the role of work engagement', *American Behavioural Scientist,* 59(4): 457–74.

Hamel, G. (2011) 'First, let's fire all the managers', *Harvard Business Review,* 89(12): 48–60.

Hamel, G. and Zanini, M. (2017) *What we learned about bureaucracy from 7,000 HBR Readers,* 10 August, Harvard Business School Publishing Corporation https://hbr.org/2017/08/what-we-learned-about-bureaucracy-from-7000-hbr-readers?referral = 03758&cm_vc = rr_item_page.top_right [accessed January 2019]

Henshall, A. (2017) 'How 4 top start-ups are reinventing organization structure', 13 October. http://www.process.st/organization-structure/ [accessed January 2019]

Hill, A. (2018a) 'Business school: leaderless groups, Honda, business school gifts', *Financial Times*, 3 April, https://www.ft.com/business-school/59 [accessed January 2019]

Hill, A. (2018b) 'Business school: Theranos, leadership at McAfee, Unilever's HQ Business school: Theranos, leadership at McAfee, Unilever's HQ', *Financial Times*, 19 March, https://www.ft.com/business-school/57 [accessed January 2019]

Hill, A. (2018c) 'Business school: book prize, engineering talent, cost of an MBA', *Financial Times*, 26 March, https://www.ft.com/business-school/58 [accessed January 2019]

Holbeche, L. (2015) *The Agile Organization: How to Build an Innovative, Sustainable and Resilient Business*, London: Kogan Page.

Kanter, R.M. (1983) *The Change Masters: Corporate Entrepreneurs at Work*. London: George Allen & Unwin.

Katzenbach, J. R. and Michaels. A. (2013), 'Life in the matrix', *Strategy + Business*, issue 72, Autumn.

Kornberger, M. (2010) *The Brand Society: How Brands Transform Management and Lifestyle*, Cambridge: Cambridge University Press.

Kornberger, M. (2017) 'The visible hand and the crowd: analyzing organization design in distributed innovation systems', *Strategic Organization*, 15(2): 174–93.

Krabberød, T. (2014) 'Mission command in a naval context', *Small Group Research*, 45(4): 416–34.

Lakhani K.R. and Panetta J.A. (2007) 'The principles of distributed innovation', *Innovations*, 2(3): 97–112.

Larman, C. and Vodde, B, (2008) *Scaling Lean & Agile Development: Thinking and Organizational Tools for Large-Scale Scrum*, Addison-Wesley Professional.

Larman, C. and Vodde, B. (2009) 'Top ten organizational impediments to large-scale agile adoption', 13 August, http://www.informit.com/articles/article.aspx?p=1380615 [accessed January 2019].

Lee, M.Y. and Edmondson, A.C. (2017) 'Self-managing organizations: exploring the limits of less-hierarchical organizing', *Research in Organizational Behaviour*, 17: 35–58.

McCollum, J. and Barber, C. R. (2017) 'It's a puzzle: a self-organizing activity', *Management Teaching Review*, 2(3): 166–178.

McKinsey Quarterly (2017) 'Safe enough to try: an interview with Zappos CEO Tony Hsieh', November, pp.112–22.

McKinsey & Company (2017a) *The 5 Trademarks of Agile Organizations*, McKinsey and Company, December, 20 pp.

McKinsey & Company (2017b) *How to Create an Agile Organization*, October, 23 pp https://www.mckinsey.com/business-functions/organization/our-insights/how-to-create-an-agile-organization [accessed January 2019]

Manifesto for Agile Software Development (2001). http://agilemanifesto.org/iso/en/manifesto.html [accessed January 2019]

Meyer, M.W., Lu, L., Peng, J. and Tsui, A.S. (2017) 'Microdivisionalizattion: using teams for competitive advantage', *Academy of Management Discoveries*, 3(1): 3–20.

Miles, R.E., Snow, C.C., Fjeldstad, Ø.D., Miles, G. and Lettl, C. (2010) 'Designing organizations to meet 21st-century opportunities and challenges', *Organizational Dynamics*, 39(2): 93–103.

Pfeffer, J. (2013) 'You're still the same: why theories of power hold over time and across contexts', *Academy of Management Perspectives*, 27(4): 269–80.

Puranam, P., Alexy, O. and Reitzig, M. (2014) 'What's 'new' about new forms of organizing?', *Academy of Management Review*, 39(2): 162–80.

Rainie, L. and Wellman, B. (2012) *Networked: The New Social Operating System*, Cambridge, MA: MIT Press.

Rigby, D.K., Sutherland, J. and Takeuchi, H. (2016) 'Embracing agile', *Harvard Business Review*, 94(5): 40–50.

Rigby, D.K., Sutherland, J. and Noble, A. (2018) 'Agile at scale', *Harvard Business Review*, 96(3): 88–96.

Robertson, B.J. (2016) *Holacracy: The Revolutionary Management System that Abolishes Hierarchy*, Portfolio Penguin.

Scanati, J.T. (2002) 'The Godfather theory of management: an exercise in power and control', *Management Decision*, 40(9): 834–41.

Schilling, M.A. and Steensma, H.K. (2001) 'The use of modular organizational forms: An industry level analysis', *Academy of Management Journal*, 44(6): 1149–69.

Takeuchi, H. and Nonaka, I. (1986) 'The new new product development game', *Harvard Business Review*, 64(1): 137–46.

Tett, G. (2017) 'Executives take a quiet turn away from globalization', *Financial Times*. 1 June.

The Economist (2002) 'Incredible shrinking plants', 23 February, pp. 99–101.

The Economist (2007) 'Odd couple', 5 May, pp.71–72.

The Economist (2014) 'Schumpeter: The holes in holacracy', 5 July, p. 62.

The Economist (2015) 'Schumpeter: Managing partners', 23 May, p.61.

The Economist (2016) 'Schumpeter: King customer', 3 December, p. 59.

The Economist (2018a) 'The good, the dumb and the desperate', 30 June, p.24.

The Economist (2018b) 'Sharing components', 17 March, pp. 59–60.

The Economist (2018c) 'Reinventing wheels', Special report, *Autonomous Vehicles,* 3 March, pp.3–4.

The Economist (2018d) 'Behind closed doors', 29 September, pp.59–61.

Trist, E. L., and Bamforth, K. W. (1951) 'Some social and psychological consequences of the longwall method of coal-getting', *Human Relations,* 4(1): 3–38.

Warner, M. and Witzel, M. (2004) *Managing in Virtual Organizations.* London: International Thomson Business Press.

Yoon, E. (2016) *Supercconsumers: A Simple, Speedy, and Sustainable Path to Superior Growth,* Boston MA: Harvard Business Review Press.

Zitek, E. M. and Tiedens, L. Z. (2012) 'The fluency of social hierarchy: the ease with which hierarchical relationships are seen, remembered, learned, and liked', *Journal of Personality and Social Psychology,* 102(1): 98–115.

Part 5 Leadership processes

PESTLE: The **P**olitical, **E**conomic, **S**ocial, **T**echnological, **L**egal, and **E**cological context

- **Individual** factors
- **Group** factors
- **Management and organization** factors
- **Leadership process** factors

- **Organizational effectiveness**
- **Quality of working life**

The organization's past,　　　present,　　　and future

CHAPTER 18

Leadership

Key terms

leadership

great man theory

consideration

initiating structure

contingency theory
of leadership

structured task

unstructured task

situational leadership

new leader

superleader

transactional leader

transformational leader

distributed leadership

Learning outcomes

When you have read this chapter, you should be able to define those
key terms in your own words, and you should also be able to:

1. Explain the apparent difference between the concepts of
   leadership and management.

2. Understand the relationships between personality traits and
   effective leadership.

3. Understand the challenges facing women who aspire to leadership
   roles, and the case for 'boardroom diversity'.

4. Understand why effective leaders either adapt their style to fit the
   organizational and cultural context in which they operate, or find
   contexts which fit their personal style.

5. Explain contemporary trends in this field concerning new
   leadership, distributed leadership, and the argument that leaders
   are unnecessary.

Why study leadership?

Gareth Southgate, England national football team manager, World Cup 2018

In 2018, for the first time since 1990, England reached the semi-finals of the football World Cup. The team manager, Gareth Southgate, describes his leadership style.

How well does his approach translate into 'normal' work organizations? Which parts of his leadership style do you think you should adopt?

'I like players to have responsibility, to think about what we are asking them to do, to have an opinion on the way we are asking them to play and the way we are asking them to train. I think if the players have some ownership of what's going on then that's going to help them make better decisions on the field and also buy into the way that we are trying to progress. My approach would be to have empathy with people. As a coach, you always have to be there to support the person – improving them as a player becomes secondary to a degree. But if a player feels that you respect them and you want to help them, then they are more likely to listen to you and follow you.

'I like the players to speak up in meetings – I like them to have an opinion on the game, because in the 85th minute they have got to make a decision that might win or lose the game and we can't make all those decisions from the sideline. When you have team meetings you are communicating certain messages to the team. But every meeting can be slightly different depending on what you want from it. There are meetings where you are delivering information, meetings where I am seeking opinion and looking for contribution from the players and times when I am looking to check their understanding of things. But for me, the most rewarding communication is one-to-one and that may be in a formal meeting or a very informal environment.

'I tend to prefer informal because it allows people to open up more and allows them to feel more comfortable expressing an opinion. I think it is important to listen and I think it is important to get a feel for what motivates the individual. Everybody is different and every player would like a slightly different approach and a slightly different style of communication and different buttons that need pressing. At the moment I don't know all of those things with all of the players, but the more you work with people the better you start to understand them. I think it is a great challenge for coaches to think about what is needed and what buttons need to be pressed for each individual player to try and help them to improve.' (*The FA Coach*, 2017)

Leadership the process of influencing the activities of an organized group in its efforts toward goal setting and goal achievement.

Leadership appears to be a key determinant of organizational effectiveness, whether we are discussing an army, an orchestra, a street gang, a political party, a mountaineering team or a multinational corporation. It is not surprising that leadership is a focus of intense interest. This focus is a recent phenomenon. In 1896, the United States Library of Congress had no books on leadership (Heller, 1997). The global literature on leadership is now vast.

CRITICAL THINKING

Consider those who you would call leaders, in business, politics, sport, music, the arts. What characteristics – skills, abilities, personality traits – do they have in common? Which of those leaders had a positive impact, and which had a negative impact? Do those whose impact was negative deserve the label of 'leader'? Compare your list of leaders with that of colleagues. How can the term 'leader' be applied to such different personalities, whose actions have led to different outcomes?

Leadership is a controversial topic. We hear the complaint that 'we need more leadership'. However, the organizational hierarchies and formal authority that underpin leadership positions are often challenged. We equate leadership with positions of power, influence and status, but leadership can be seen at all levels of an organization. Leaders have job titles and working conditions which symbolize their status. But flat structures, self-managing teams, knowledge work, and virtual and networked organizational forms, all weaken traditional leadership positions based on hierarchy and symbolism.

Ralph Stogdill (1950), an influential early commentator, defined leadership as an influencing process aimed at goal achievement. That definition has three components. First, it defines leadership as an *interpersonal process* in which one individual seeks to influence the behaviour of others. Second, it sets leadership in a *social context*, in which the other members of the group to be influenced are subordinates or followers. Third, it identifies a criterion for effective leadership – *goal achievement* – which is one practical objective of leadership theory and research. Most definitions of leadership share these processual, contextual and evaluative components.

Leadership in unusual situations: Archana Kumar, AK Bollywood Dance

'I teach Bollywood dancing to kids as young as three, and choreograph dancing for events. With the kids, you've got to get down to their level and be fun and active. They've got to know you're the teacher but, at the same time, you've got to be a very bubbly character. The children are always loud and excited, and you have to allow that to happen but then make sure they know when to focus. We try to give each of them an individual role and position – giving them that bit of independence. And we'll bring individual students forward to teach the others a few moves. We get a big mixture of people: some who are experienced, and some who've never danced before. I've just done a tutorial with a family of 25 adults who are doing a flashmob for a wedding – the bride and groom don't know about it. Some of them are really into it, while some have obviously been pushed into it by family members. You've got to create that fun vibe for them. You've got to be authoritative without feeling like you're telling them off' (Bain, 2016).

What advice does Archana Kumar offer that you think will be useful to you in your future career?

Traditionally, most leaders have been men. We will explore shortly the fact that there are low numbers of women in senior organizational roles. Given the benefits of diversity at all levels of an organization – especially the top team – male dominance is not just a problem for women seeking leadership careers. It raises wider social and organizational concerns. We need a better understanding of the forces that shape leadership stereotypes and biases in order to counter them, to achieve an appropriate gender balance.

This chapter explores six perspectives on leadership:

1. *Trait-spotting*: Identifies the personality traits and related attributes of the effective leader, in order to facilitate the selection of leaders.

2. *Style-counselling*: Characterizes different leadership behaviour patterns to identify effective and ineffective leadership styles, in order to improve the training and development of leaders.

3. *Context-fitting*: Contingency theories argue that leadership effectiveness depends on aspects of the organizational and cultural setting.

4. *New leadership*: 'Superleaders' and 'transformational leaders' are heroic, inspirational visionaries who give purpose and direction to others.

5. *Distributed leadership*: Leadership behaviour is not confined to those with formal senior roles, but can be seen at all organizational levels.

6. *Who needs leaders?* Transformational leaders can destabilize an organization by driving too much change too quickly, causing burnout; middle managers with change skills are more effective.

Trait-spotting was popular until the 1940s when inconsistent research findings led to the approach being largely abandoned. Style-counselling was then popular until the late 1960s, when it was overtaken by contingency theories which dominated thinking until the early 1980s. At that point, the 'new leadership' movement emerged. Towards the end of the twentieth century, the distributed nature of leadership attracted attention. In the twenty-first century, several commentators challenged the value of leadership, noting that 'celebrity bosses' often damaged organizational performance and reputation with rapid and radical changes. However, each shift in emphasis and approach has not replaced earlier thinking. All of those perspectives can be seen in today's research and practice.

Leaders under pressure: Bill McDermott

For Bill McDermott, his biggest challenge came not in the boardroom but as a result of an accident – in which he lost an eye. Andrew Hill of the *Financial Times* asks the SAP chief executive how this changed his leadership style (6.12 minutes).

Leadership versus management

What is the difference between leadership and management? Some commentators argue that leaders and managers make distinctly different contributions. Others argue that leadership is just one facet of a complex management role. Warren Bennis and Burt Nanus (1985) famously argued that 'managers do things right', while 'leaders do the right thing'. Leaders are thus often seen as visionaries who drive new initiatives. Managers simply maintain order and stability. The leader is prophet, catalyst, mover-shaker, strategist. The manager is technician, administrator, problem solver. The leader influences others to sign up to their vision, inspires them to overcome obstacles, and generates positive change. The manager establishes plans and budgets, designs and staffs the organization, monitors and controls performance, and delivers order and predictability.

Leadership in unusual situations: Jens Pagotto, Head of Mission, Médecins Sans Frontières

Jens Pagotto (photo credit: Diala Ghassan)

'I work for Médecins Sans Frontières as the head of mission in the central Mediterranean, where we have three boats doing rescues off the coast of Libya. I negotiate with authorities to make sure our teams can work safely and coordinate with the various civilian and military actors – which includes the marine rescue control centre in Rome, which coordinates most of the rescues, the Italian Navy and the European Union Naval Force, various coastguards and other vessels, Frontex [the EU's external border agency] and a number of NGOs. Recently, we had a particularly tragic rescue. Many people on board the boat had died. We had to recover 22 bodies, mostly women. Now our team is providing food and medical treatment to the people who survived, making sure everyone gets a chance to wash and put on clean clothes and is comfortable for the journey back to Italy. Something like this can be extremely difficult on a psychological level for the people rescued and for those carrying out the rescue. One of the most important things is to remember that you're not alone. There are always a lot of people out there who can support you. I've got a big team available: psychologists, my onshore team who can provide logistical support to make arrangements – it's about using all those assets. On a personal level it can be quite traumatic in some ways. It's important to know when to take a break and look after yourself, and to be able to separate the professional from the personal' (Bain, 2016).

What advice does Jens Pagotto offer that you think will be useful to you in your future career?

This is a 'good guys, bad guys' caricature: leaders exciting, managers dull. Noting that this is inaccurate and insulting, Julian Birkinshaw (2010) argues that leadership and management must be seen as complementary, as roles that the same person plays at different times. Another commentator, Henry Mintzberg (2009, pp.8–9), also challenges the distinction between leaders and managers:

> 'Frankly, I don't understand what this distinction means in the everyday life of organizations. Sure, we can separate leading and managing conceptually. But can we separate them in practice? Or, more to the point, should we even try? We should be seeing managers *as* leaders, and leadership as management practised well.'

CRITICAL THINKING

Henry Mintzberg asks: Would you like to be managed by someone who can't lead? Would you like to be led by someone who can't manage? How would you respond to those two questions?

Raffaella Sadun

Conventional thinking says that leaders set strategy, and managers handle the operational details. To be competitive, organizations must have a distinctive strategy. Operational effectiveness does not lead to sustainable competitive advantage, because this can be copied. Raffaella Sadun and colleagues (2017) argue that this reasoning is false. Management competence is just as important in determining corporate performance as strategic vision. The research team identified 18 core management practices in four categories:

- *Operations management*: use of lean techniques; reasons for adopting lean processes
- *Performance monitoring*: process documentation; use of key performance indicators (KPIs); KPI reviews; discussion of results; consequences for missing
- *Target-setting*: choice of targets; connection to strategy; extent to which targets cascade down to individual workers; time horizon; level of challenge; clarity of goals and measurement
- *Talent management*: talent mindset; stretch goals; management of low performance; talent development; employee value proposition; talent retention

They studied 12,000 companies in 34 countries, conducting 20,000 interviews. Companies were rated on their use of management practices. Ratings could be poor at one extreme; for example, monitoring performance using metrics that did not indicate whether business objectives were being met. A company that continuously tracked and communicated performance metrics, formally and informally, to all staff, using a range of visual tools, would get a high rating. Across the sample, 11 per cent of firms had low scores: weak performance monitoring, little effort to identify and fix problems, few targets for employees, promotions and rewards based on tenure and family connections. As for the 'superstars', 6 per cent of firms had high scores: rigorous performance monitoring, systems geared to ensure the flow of information, continuous improvement programmes linked to targets, performance systems that reward and promote talented employees and helped underperformers to improve.

They found that the best managed firms were more profitable, grew faster, and were less likely to go out of business. Moving a firm from the worst 10 per cent to the best 10 per cent on their ratings of management practices was linked to a US$15 million increase in profits, 25 per cent faster annual growth, and 75 per cent higher productivity. The best also attract more talented employees and encourage better employee well-being. Other findings included:

- Most organizations have difficulty in achieving operational excellence in management practices, despite the fact that these practices are well known.
- Differences in the use of core management practices were long-lasting.
- There were differences in the use of management practices in the same company, and especially large companies, as well as differences between organizations.
- Many managers have a false perception of how well their organizations are run.

Management matters. The researchers conclude that: '[T]he management community may have badly underestimated the benefits of core management practices – as well as the investment needed to strengthen them – by relegating them to the domain of "easy to replicate". One frequent suggestion in this era of flattened organizations is that everyone has to be a strategist. But we'd suggest that everyone also needs to be a manager' (Sadun et al., 2017, p.127).

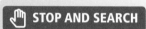 **STOP AND SEARCH**   YouTube for *How Much Does Management Matter? Raffaella Sadun* (3:44).

Trait-spotting

Great man theory a historical perspective which argues that the fate of societies, and organizations, is in the hands of powerful, idiosyncratic (male) individuals.

For the first half of the twentieth century, researchers assumed that they could identify the personality traits and other qualities of effective leaders. It would then be possible to select individuals with those characteristics, and give them leadership positions. This search for the qualities of good leaders was based on great man theory.

Great man theory focused on political figures, arguing that leaders reach positions of influence from which they dominate and direct the lives of others by force of personality. There is no equivalent 'great woman theory'. Great men are born leaders, and emerge to take power, regardless of the social, organizational or historical context. Research thus focused on identifying the traits of these special individuals. Ralph Stogdill reviewed hundreds of trait studies (1948; 1974) and compiled this list:

- Strong drive for responsibility
- Focus on completing the task
- Vigour and persistence in pursuit of goals
- Venturesomeness and originality in problem solving
- Drive to exercise initiative in social settings
- Self-confidence
- Sense of personal identity
- Willingness to accept consequences of decisions and actions
- Readiness to absorb interpersonal stress
- Willingness to tolerate frustration and delay
- Ability to influence the behaviour of others
- Capacity to structure social systems to the purpose in hand

It is difficult to challenge these qualities. Can we say that leaders should lack drive, persistence, creativity, and the ability to influence others? These are desirable qualities in many roles, however, and do not appear to be unique to leaders.

Research did not produce a consistent set of leadership traits, and as studies covered more settings, more qualities were identified. Almost 80 characteristics were reported from a review of 20 studies of leadership traits (Bird, 1940). More than half of these traits had been identified in only one study, very few appeared in four or more investigations, and only 'intelligence' was reported in at least half of the studies reviewed. In addition, many of these traits are vague. Willingness to tolerate delay? Capacity to structure social systems? Readiness to absorb stress? It is difficult to see how trait-spotting can be used in a leadership selection context, as originally intended.

The qualities of a good boss

Elena Lytkina Botelho
(© Matt Mendelsohn)

The idea that leaders have special characteristics, traits, or qualities is still popular. The CEO Genome Project is another attempt to identify these qualities. This was a ten-year study of the career histories, behaviours, and business results of 17,000 US executives, including 2,000 chief executive officers (CEOs). The leadership stereotype is of a visionary, charismatic, confident, extravert, six-foot-tall white man with a university degree, who makes perfect decisions under pressure. Elena Lytkina Botelho and colleagues (2017; 2018) found that very few successful leaders fit this profile. One of their interesting conclusions, for example, was that most successful CEOs are introverts. It seems that the qualities that appeal to interviewers are not actually related to the performance of CEOs in the job.

They found that, to be successfu, CEOs need to be:

Decisive   Making decisions quickly and with conviction

Engaging   Understanding stakeholders – including employees – and getting their backing

Flexible   Adapting to change, dealing with the unpredictable

Reliable   Predictable and consistent, rather than occasionally brilliant

The researchers ask: 'You might wonder, what about integrity and other "table stakes" qualities? Those are critical in screening out clearly unsuitable candidates, but they will not help you separate the best from the rest. Consider that 100 per cent of low-performing CEOs in our sample scored high in integrity, and 97 per cent scored high on work ethic' (Botelho et al., 2017, p.77). However, while there is no one 'perfect mix', this study suggests that focusing on these four behaviours will increase the chances of appointing a successful CEO.

By 1950 it appeared that there was little value in continuing to identify leadership traits, although some weak generalizations did emerge (Shaw, 1976; Fraser, 1978). On average, leaders score higher on measures of:

Ability   Intelligence, relevant knowledge, verbal facility
Sociability   Participation, cooperativeness, popularity
Motivation   Initiative and persistence

The trait-spotting approach was abandoned by most researchers who switched attention, first to leadership *styles*, and then to characteristics of *context*. However, it has been difficult to overcome the belief that effective leaders must have *some* traits in common, and the search for those personality markers and other attributes continues. Paradoxically, although dating from the 1940s, trait-spotting is a contemporary perspective, which can be seen in leadership competency models, such as the 'transformational leadership behaviours' approach discussed later in this chapter.

CUTTING EDGE   CEOs – are they worth it?

Herman Aguinis

Herman Aguinis and colleagues (2018) studied the extent to which CEOs deserve their pay. Chief executive pay is controversial. In some UK organizations, they are paid almost 400 times more than the lowest-paid front-line employees (equalitytrust.org.uk). Is this fair? Well, the job of CEO requires special talent, which is rare, and it is a complex and demanding role. One might expect, therefore, that CEOs in companies that were performing well would be paid more than those whose companies were not doing so well – that the top performers would also be the top earners. To see if this was the case, the researchers studied over 4,000 American CEOs in 22 industries. Their main measure of company performance was return on assets. And they looked at the total rewards for CEOs including their salaries, bonuses, and stock options.

The researchers found that only a very small number of CEOs were leading high-performing firms. They also found that an equally small proportion were very highly paid. Their most surprising finding, however, was that there was almost no overlap between the top performers and the top earners: 'CEOs who increasingly enjoy greater pay advantages relative to their peers as we move toward the top of the pay distribution are generally not the same CEOs as those who deliver the greatest value for their firms' (p.20). In other words, it looks as though CEO pay is not based on the performance of the organizations that they manage. Stars, this research suggests, are underpaid, and average performers are overpaid. These findings apply regardless of size of organization or sector. Executive search agencies (headhunters), the researchers note, can use these findings when looking for top performing CEOs that they may be able to tempt with an offer to move to another firm.

This study does not explain this anomaly in CEO remuneration. However, other research suggests that, 'CEOs' tenure-long pay patterns are established – essentially baked-in or hardwired – when CEOs first get hired. For various reasons, some CEOs receive ultra-grand pay packages at the outset of their tenures, and nothing – including mediocre performance – brings about subsequent diminishment of those sweet terms' (Hambrick, 2018, p.31). This suggests that CEOs who have been overpaid in one role are likely to be overpaid in their next position, while the opposite happens to those who have been underpaid. 'The rich get richer and the poor get poorer.'

Do women have the wrong traits?

For most of the twentieth century, it was assumed that leaders had to be *men*. Leadership research was mostly done by men whose subjects were men. Women were largely ignored in leadership research until the 1990s. Reinforcing traditional stereotypes, contemporary movies and television series rarely show women in positive, empowering, leadership roles (Ezzedeen, 2013; Davis, 2014).

Women today are under-represented in leadership and management roles, despite attempts to improve gender balance. In 2008, Norway set a mandatory target of 40 per cent for female representation on the boards of listed companies. Belgium, France and Italy followed with similar quotas, with sanctions for non-compliance. Germany, Spain and The Netherlands have quotas for female directors, but no sanctions. In 2011, the UK set a voluntary target of

25 per cent. Women are not just under-represented in senior roles. Research also shows that women are hired and promoted at lower rates than men at every level of the organization. This reduces the pipeline of female candidates who are then available for promotion at more senior levels. A study of over 1 million people working in financial services in America found a 'gender punishment gap': women were punished more severely than men in cases of misconduct such as contravening codes of conduct, customer disputes, and illegal acts (Egan et al., 2018). Women were more likely to be fired for misconduct than men, and a higher proportion of men than women found new jobs following misconduct.

The 30% Club was founded in the UK in 2010, and has branches in many other countries. Their goal was to achieve at least 30 per cent female representation on the boards of the FTSE 100 companies. When The 30% Club was formed, only 12.5 per cent of FTSE 100 board members were women. By 2018, that had risen to 28.9 per cent, and none of the FTSE 100 companies had all-male boards. However, only seven of those companies had a female chief executive in 2017 (Frean, 2017; Gordon, 2017). The 30% Club has a new goal: to achieve a minimum of 30 per cent female representation on the boards of FTSE 350 companies by 2020 (in 2018 this was 25.3 per cent).

 Mark Wilson explains why he signed up to The 30% Club's commitment, as Group Chief Executive Officer of Aviva plc – the first FTSE 100 CEO to join the campaign (5:58).

Inequality is also reflected in leaders' pay. In 2017, the highest paid executive in an FTSE 100 company was Sir Martin Sorrell, chief executive of the communications services company WPP, with an annual pay package of £48 million. The highest paid woman was Emma Walmsley, chief executive of the pharmaceutical company GlaxoSmithKline, with a package of £8.8 million. Only seven of the FTSE 100 companies had a female chief executive in 2017 (Donnellan, 2017).

Research by The 30% Club (2018, p.2) found that female and male managers describe their jobs differently: 'Female managers appear more attuned to managing relationship dynamics and more positive about diversity within their team. Male managers appear more attuned to managing performance dynamics and more positive about consistency within their team'. These findings came from a study of 114 'management trios' – each including a manager, a male report, and a female report. The gender differences in how women and men say that they manage are as follows:

Women	Men
Value individual differences on their team	Value core competence on their team
Adjust their management style to improve individual performance	Give constructive feedback to improve individual performance
Use their time to develop their people	Use organizational resources to develop people
Anticipate future shifts in management and leadership	Are optimistic about similar future management and leadership
Are risk alert for the individual	Are risk averse for the organization

Leadership in unusual situations: Captain Czarena Hashim, Royal Brunei Airlines

'As a captain of a Boeing 787 Dreamliner, I have a huge responsibility, although if I dwelled on the responsibility too much, I would never leave the ground. I understand that passengers expect to hear the captain, even if they don't get to meet me. When speaking to them over the passenger address system, it's important to give them assurance and to speak calmly and confidently, regardless of whether it's a smooth flight or not. There's nothing more important than trusting your team to do their jobs. With so many tasks to complete in-flight, our team needs to work smoothly. Every crew member is vital to the safe operation of the flight and everyone is different, so it's important to listen and encourage others to voice their opinions before making a decision. You have to have a friendly, positive attitude, remain calm under pressure and be confident in your own abilities' (Bain, 2016).

What advice does Captain Hashim offer that you think will be useful to you in your future career?

Øyvind Martinsen

Lars Glasø (photo credit: Linn de Lange)

Do women have the wrong personality traits for leadership roles? Research by Øyvind Martinsen and Lars Glasø (2014) suggests the opposite. They surveyed 2,900 Norwegian managers, male and female, from public and private sector organizations, measuring their personality traits, work motivation and commitment. The Big Five model of personality **(see Chapter 6)** suggests that effective leaders have the following characteristics:

1. Setting goals, being thorough, and following up (methodical).
2. Supporting, accommodating and including others (sociable).
3. Innovating, being curious and ambitious (open to new experiences).
4. Taking initiative, clearly communicating (extraverted).
5. Dealing with job-related pressure (emotionally stable).

Women scored higher than men on the first four characteristics. The researchers conclude, therefore, that women are better candidates than men for leadership roles. Women scored lower than men on emotional stability. This is not a disadvantage if it means that women are able to use levels of emotionality that are appropriate to the circumstances.

Based on research by the consulting firm McKinsey, Vivian Hunt and colleagues (2018) report that progress on inclusion and diversity has been slow. By 2018, the 346 UK and US companies involved in a 2015 study had increased average gender representation on their executive teams by only 2 per cent (to 14 per cent), and ethnic and cultural diversity by 1 per cent (to 13 per cent). Their more recent study, involving over 1,000 companies in 12 countries, reached the following conclusions:

- There is a statistically significant correlation between diverse leadership and corporate financial performance.
- Companies in the top 25 per cent for gender diversity on top teams were more likely to have above average profitability and value creation.
- The highest performing companies on profitability and diversity had more women in line (revenue-generating) roles than in staff roles on their executive teams.

CRITICAL THINKING

Given what we know about gender differences in approach to leadership and management, who would you prefer to be led by at work – a woman, or a man, and why?

Aspiring female leaders face unconscious as well as conscious bias

'What we're up against often is referred to as unconscious bias. It means that if I think kindergarten teacher, I don't think man. And if I think engineer, I don't think woman. Seeing really is believing.

'A powerful study demonstrating unconscious bias was actually run with orchestras. In the 1970s, some major US orchestras introduced blind auditions. They had musicians audition behind a curtain and then evaluated their performance. The interesting thing about this design feature, this curtain, is that it was introduced despite the fact that many of the orchestra directors thought that they of course didn't need curtains – that they of all people only cared about the quality of the music and not what somebody looked like.

'It turns out that curtains helped increase the fraction [of women] on these orchestras from about 5 per cent in the 1970s to almost 40 per cent now. That is the power of design. The curtain is important for me for two reasons. On the one hand, it is a real example showing the power of unconscious bias. But it is also important because it helps us understand that sometimes we have to make it easier for well-meaning people to do the right thing' (Kirkland and Bohnet, 2017, p.2).

Vivian Hunt

- Companies in the top 25 per cent for ethnic and cultural diversity on their executive teams were one third more likely to have industry-leading profitability.
- Companies in the bottom 25 per cent for gender, ethnic and cultural diversity were 29 per cent less likely to achieve above average profitability than all of the other companies in this study.
- Black women executives are underrepresented in line management roles, and find it difficult to move to chief executive positions; women in general hold a disproportionately small share of line roles on executive teams, and black, Latina and Asian women hold an even smaller share.

In many cultures, gender equality is seen as a goal worth pursuing in its own right. It is perhaps disappointing therefore, if not surprising, that debate has focused on 'the business case' for appointing more women to board positions. However, Hunt et al. (2018) conclude that inclusion and diversity can improve business performance in five ways:

- *Win the war for talent*: more diverse organizations have a wider talent pool from which to draw the capabilities that they need in order to compete.

- *Improve the quality of decision making*: research shows that diverse and inclusive groups make better quality decisions, faster, without bias or groupthink, than homogeneous groups.
- *Increase innovation and customer understanding*: diverse groups can be more creative than homogeneous groups, as they combine different experiences and perspectives, and understand diverse customer groups, including women, ethnic minorities, and LGBTQ+ communities.
- *Increase employee satisfaction*: a diverse and inclusive environment can be more attractive, especially to high performers, reduces conflict and improves collaboration.
- *Improve a company's global image*: companies with a strong record for diversity and inclusivity enjoy an enhanced reputation with employees, customers, suppliers, local communities, and the wider society.

 **STOP AND SEARCH**

 On YouTube, find *The Equality Lounge @ Davos 2018: Delivering Through Diversity* (26 minutes). Dame Vivian Hunt, Managing Partner, McKinsey UK and Ireland, speaks about the business impact of diversity and inclusivity.

The business case for gender diversity is controversial, but many studies suggest that board diversity improves corporate financial performance. Hedge funds that are run by women generate returns twice the size of their male counterparts. The HFRX Diversity Women index found that in 2017, female hedge fund managers returned 11.9 per cent on their investments compared with a 7.05 per cent return on the broader (male dominated) index. This is despite the under-representation of women in the hedge fund and asset management sector which has a reputation for being 'male, pale and stale'. Hedge funds run by women have higher failure rates than those managed by men, but only because female portfolio managers find it more difficult to raise capital. Only 10 per cent of UK fund managers are women, and only 184 of 7,000 US mutual funds are run by women (Mooney, 2017).

Jana Bukunina (2018) manages Silvergate Investments, a company that specializes in investing in innovative start-ups. When people – usually men – ask Bukunina if she prioritizes investment in female entrepreneurs because Silvergate is a charity, or a social impact fund, she replies that she invests in female entrepreneurs because she wants to make money.

Leaders under pressure: Ursula Burns

 Ursula Burns made history when she became the first African-American woman to run a Fortune 500 company – Xerox. Andrew Hill asks her how she dealt with a challenge from activist investor Carl Icahn (10.30 minutes).

There are obvious reasons for the small numbers of women in leadership roles, and there are more subtle explanations. Discrimination by male colleagues, and family responsibilities are the traditional explanations. Research by the Chartered Institute for

Personnel and Development (2015), based on the views of 2,000 working women, identified three other factors:

Self-confidence Women often lack the confidence to seek promotion, argue for a pay rise, or ask for development opportunities

Working the room Many women say that they lack networking skills, which limits their ability to get help from appropriate advisers and mentors

Embracing individuality Pressure to 'act like men' and to conform to the 'alpha female' stereotype holds many women back.

The Institute argues that, 'Organizations need to foster an environment in which women don't feel the pressure to act like men – or in any other contrived way – in order to succeed. In fact, our contributors emphasized that women have unique and natural advantages in leadership that need to be celebrated' (CIPD, 2015, p.6).

CRITICAL THINKING

What traits do women typically have that make them more suited than men to leadership roles?

CUTTING EDGE **Leadership lessons from African-American women**

Laura Morgan Roberts

Only 32 of the senior leaders of Fortune 500 companies are women. Three of those 500 leaders are African-American, and not one is an African-American woman. Laura Morgan Roberts and colleagues (2018) decided to find out why. They studied the careers of Harvard Business School alumni focusing on 532 African-American women who graduated between 1977 and 2015. They followed the careers of 67 who had been appointed as chair, chief executive, or to another C-suite (board level) executive post, and interviewed 30 of them in depth. How had these women beaten the odds? Qualifications from prestige institutions and personal abilities are part of the answer. However, others had been willing to recognize, support and develop those capabilities. So, what lessons can aspiring leaders take from the experiences of these successful African-American women?

One of the main challenges faced by this group is what the researchers call the visibility-invisibility conundrum – working under a microscope or feeling ignored. African-American women stood out in their organizations; they would often be the only black person in the room. This made many of them feel that they were 'on display', which was inhibiting but, as one said, 'It makes you work hard to make sure you're never misstepping'. Being hypervisible, however, often meant that others listened and paid attention. On the other hand, black women were often made to feel invisible, being mistaken for secretaries or members of the waiting staff when starting new jobs. However, some situations may be easier to access when one is not seen as a threat. One executive said, 'Senior executives would say, "Sure, you can come in", because they doubted me. If they had known that I was going to come in and get the jobs they wanted, they probably would have said no'.

→

The main lesson from this study, according to the researchers, concerns *resilience*. That is a well-known capability, but this group of extraordinary women relied on it heavily. They had faced obstacles and setbacks, often due to race and gender. But they bounced back, refused to be distracted, and continued to make progress. In particular, they displayed three skills key to their resilience:

- *Emotional intelligence*: they became expert at reading and managing the interpersonal and political dynamics of their organizations, regulating their feelings, and avoiding over-reacting to prejudice in ways that could damage their reputations and careers.

- *Authenticity*: they had deep self-awareness and were able to craft their own racial identities, which they revealed in ways that felt genuine, reinforced by candid self-disclosure and transparency about their motives and values.

- *Agility*: faced with the low expectations of colleagues, they confronted obstacles and turned them into opportunities to learn and develop, and to exploit their combination of race, gender, and professional identity to make an impact.

These abilities are useful for anyone's career, but are especially critical for members of historically disadvantaged groups. But personal attributes are not enough. The researchers conclude that:

'The success of the women we studied, like that of most people, depended on their having developed relationships with people who recognized their talent, gave them a safe space in which to make and learn from mistakes, provided candid and actionable feedback about their performance, and generally made it their business to support them and create opportunities for them to succeed. Many of the women pointed to managers, mentors, and sponsors who had helped them discover and actualize their best selves' (Roberts et al., 2018, p.131).

Glass ceiling, glass cliff

Michelle Ryan

Alexander Haslam

This discussion explains what is called the 'glass ceiling', which stops women reaching senior roles. Michelle Ryan and Alexander Haslam (2005, 2007) argue that women promoted to senior roles face another set of problems – concerning what they call the 'glass cliff'. Their research found that companies are more likely to change the composition of their boards of directors when performance drops, than when it is improving. Ryan and Haslam suggest that poor company performance can trigger the appointment of women to the board, because diversity leads to higher performance. They also observe that this means promoting women into positions that carry a high risk of failure. As women are a minority among senior managers, they are more visible, and their performance tends to be scrutinized more closely. The researchers conclude that women were being 'set up to fail', being placed on a glass cliff, in difficult organizational conditions, which made their positions precarious. Women may find that they are held responsible for poor performance caused by factors that were in place before they were promoted. Women may be under-represented in senior management ranks, but they may be over-represented in vulnerable senior positions. The traditional acronym TMTM (think management, think male) may have been replaced by TCTF (think crisis, think female).

Evidence for the glass cliff phenomenon is mixed. One study, based on Fortune 500 companies, found that women are more likely to be promoted to high-risk leadership positions than men, but lack the support to achieve their goals, and thus have shorter tenures compared to male colleagues (Glass and Cook, 2016). A study of 1,453 female directors, and 23,134 male directors of UK

FTSE All Share Index companies from 1996 to 2010 also found that women have shorter tenures than male colleagues (Main and Gregory-Smith, 2018). But this did not mean that female directors faced a glass cliff after their appointment. Women faced a higher risk of dismissal as they approached nine years of service on the board. The researchers argue that the appointment of a woman as an independent outside director is often symbolic, to satisfy public expectations. However, after nine years, following the UK corporate governance code, those appointments are no longer seen as independent, and have outlived their symbolic value.

Research into the appointment and tenure of 193 North American female chief executive officers between 1992 and 2014 confirmed the glass cliff hypothesis. This study found that women were indeed appointed as CEOs in situations where an organization was in financial difficulty. However, women in this study were *less* likely to lose their senior positions than male colleagues, who faced a higher risk of a shorter career (Elsaid and Ursel, 2018). These researchers conclude that labour market conditions have changed since the glass cliff phenomenon was first discovered. Companies now want to avoid the negative publicity that would follow the loss of a female chief executive. Perhaps the glass cliff is more secure than it once was.

CRITICAL THINKING	One of your well-liked and highly experienced female colleagues has just been passed over for promotion – which she expected to win. The job went to an equally well-liked but less-experienced male colleague. What advice can you give her?

Sodexo: champion of diversity

'Sodexo is an outspoken champion of diversity. Led by an enthusiastic CEO and board chairwoman, the global multinational services company has publicly committed to improving five dimensions of diversity: gender, people with disabilities, generations (age), cultures and origins, and sexual orientation and gender identity.

'For Sodexo, achieving gender balance was the starting point. The company's internal research revealed that greater representation of women in management positions – between 40 and 60% women – correlated with superior performance on measures such as customer satisfaction and employee engagement. The company pledged to boost the number of senior female executives to 40% by 2025. Management incentives – including 10% of bonuses – are correlated to achieving gender goals. Additionally, inclusivity and diversity initiatives are tailored to specific regional contexts and supported by a mix of global and local initiatives.

'These diversity efforts are already paying off. With women currently comprising half of the board, 32% of senior leaders and close to 50% of its total workforce, Sodexo is among the most gender-diverse companies in its industry group and home country. It is, notably, also among the most successful financially within our data set, with value creation that is 13% above the industry average.' (Hunt et al., 2018, p.9)

Style-counselling

The low numbers of women in senior leadership roles has little or nothing to do with 'female' traits and attributes. Going back to the 1950s, problems with the traits approach meant that the research focus switched to leadership, management and supervisory style. Instead of selecting leaders on the basis of personality traits, why not train and develop leaders to use appropriate behaviour patterns? This research tradition argues that a considerate, participative, democratic and involving leadership style is more effective than an impersonal, autocratic and directive style.

Two projects, known as the Michigan and Ohio studies respectively, underpinned the investigation of management style. Based on a study of foremen at the International Harvester Company, the work of the Survey Research Center in Michigan in the 1940s and early 1950s (Katz et al., 1950) identified two dimensions of leadership behaviour:

1. *Employee-centred behaviour*: focusing on relationships and employee needs

2. *Job-centred behaviour*: focusing on getting the job done.

Consideration a pattern of leadership behaviour that demonstrates sensitivity to relationships and to the social needs of employees.

Initiating structure a pattern of leadership behaviour that emphasizes performance of the work in hand and the achievement of product and service goals.

This work ran concurrently with the influential studies of Edwin Fleishman and Ralph Stogdill, at the Bureau of Business Research at Ohio State University (Fleishman, 1953a; 1953b; Fleishman and Harris, 1962; Stogdill, 1948; Stogdill and Coons, 1951). The Ohio results also identified two categories of leadership behaviour which they termed consideration and initiating structure. The considerate leader is relationships and needs orientated. The leader who structures work for subordinates is task or job-centred.

The considerate leader is interested in and listens to subordinates, allows participation in decision making, is friendly and approachable, and supports subordinates with personal problems. The leader's behaviour indicates trust, respect, warmth and rapport. This enhances subordinates' feelings of self-esteem and encourages the development of communications and relationships in a work group. The researchers first called this dimension 'social sensitivity'.

The leader who initiates structure decides how things will be done, structures tasks and assigns work, makes expectations clear, emphasizes deadlines, and expects subordinates to follow instructions. The leader's behaviour stresses the achievement of goals. This is the emphasis that the scientific management school (**Chapter 14**) encouraged, but task orientation in this perspective has a positive, motivating aspect. The researchers first called this leadership dimension 'production emphasis'.

 EMPLOYABILITY CHECK (leadership)

The job interviewer asks you to describe and justify your preferred team leadership style. How will you respond?

Consideration and structure are independent behaviour patterns. A leader can emphasize one or both. Job satisfaction is likely to be higher, and grievances and staff turnover lower, when the leader emphasizes consideration. Task performance, on the other hand, is likely to be higher when the leader emphasizes the initiation of structure. Inconsiderate leaders typically have subordinates who complain and who are more likely to leave the organization, but can have productive work groups if they are high on initiating structure. This theory is summarized in Figure 18.1.

Home viewing

Wonder Woman (directed by Patty Jenkins, 2017) tells the story of Diana of Themiscyra (Diana Prince), who finds herself in a leadership role in Europe during World War I (Urick and Sprinkle, 2018). This was one of the first superhero movies to feature a female superhero lead, played by Gal Gadot. Her team members include a fighter pilot, an actor, a sniper, and a smuggler. How could such a group work together and be successful? As you watch this movie, consider the following issues. What styles of leadership does Wonder Woman use? How does she respond to gender discrimination? How does she motivate this team to work together? Is Wonder Woman a transformational leader?
Can you identify examples of her acting as a role model for others to copy? To what extent is her leadership style consistent with a female stereotype: relationship building, open communication, positive influence tactics, collaboration? Why do you think she is a successful leader?

Beverly Alimo-Metcalfe and Margaret Bradley (2008; Alimo-Metcalfe and Alban-Metcalfe, 2010) also argue that a participative, engaging style improves performance. They studied 46 mental health teams involved in organizational change, and found that engaging leadership increases employee motivation, job satisfaction, and commitment while reducing stress. Each team had a designated leader, but as teams were on call around the clock, different members took the leadership role at different times. Engaging leadership had the following dimensions:

- Involving stakeholders early, to establish lasting relationships
- Building a collective vision, so the team 'owns' the work and the goals
- No team hierarchy, devolving leadership as appropriate
- Supportive culture, with informal support from colleagues, and formal support from supervision, so people can share problems, seek advice, and take risks
- Participation in change, as team members' views are taken into account.

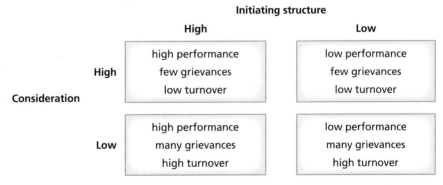

Figure 18.1: The Ohio State leadership theory predictions

Engaging with others was one of three dimensions of leadership identified in this study. The second was *visionary leadership*, which involves having clear goals, being sensitive to stakeholder interests, and inspiring them with determination. The third, *leadership capabilities*, involves understanding strategy, ensuring goal clarity, setting success criteria, commitment to high standards, and designing supportive systems and procedures. Of these three dimensions, engagement had the greatest impact on attitudes and performance, while leadership vision and capabilities had only limited impact. This study concludes that the development of leadership competencies should focus on encouraging a culture of engagement, at all levels of the organization.

Why do some leaders act like jerks?

"In his mysterious way, God has given each of us different talents, Ridgeway. It just so happens that mine is intimidating people."

Source: © Joseph Mirachi, reproduced with permission

Robert Sutton (2017a and b) argues that bullying and rudeness are widespread in our organizations. Bullying bosses – 'jerks' – are a problem, creating anxiety and distress with their intimidating behaviour. Jerks are expensive. Their rudeness and insults undermine the performance and productivity of others, weaken their decision-making capabilities, and reduce their willingness to put in extra effort and cooperate with others.

Sutton argues that the risks of turning into a jerk increase with seniority. In other words, this kind of behaviour is driven by the organizational context, and not just by individual personalities. He identifies seven factors that encourage leaders to act like jerks:

1. There are many other jerks around you

2. You wield power over others, but you once had little power yourself

3. You are very competitive, and feel threatened by smart subordinates

4. You work longer hours than anyone else and want to make sure that they know this

5. You don't get enough sleep

6. You have a high workload, too many things to think about, and never have enough time

7. You can't resist checking your smartphone even when you know you should exercise self-control.

The key to your self-awareness as a leader, Sutton argues, lies with how other people see you. He gives this example:

'The clueless (though well-meaning) CEO of one company I know was horrified when two female executive vice presidents pulled him aside and admonished him after a meeting. The women, who kept careful tallies, informed the CEO that he had interrupted each of them at least six times, but never interrupted the four male executive vice presidents. Stunned and embarrassed, the CEO begged for forgiveness and asked them to keep tracking his interruptions, vowing to halt his sexist ways. He didn't want to feel that self-loathing again' (Sutton, 2017b, p.106).

Sutton offers the following advice to avoid becoming a jerk. Don't catch the disease from others, use your power and influence with care, give credit to those who are less powerful, understand the risks of work overload and multitasking, and apologize when you get it wrong and offend someone. Finally, do some time travelling and ask how you want to feel about yourself when you look back from the future: 'When they are on their deathbed, no one ever says, I wish I had been meaner'.

Context-fitting

The Michigan and Ohio perspectives offer leaders 'one best way' to handle followers, by adopting the 'high consideration, high structure' ideal. This advice is supported by the fact that most people *like* their leaders to be considerate, even when they are performance orientated as well. The problem, however, is that one leadership style may not be effective in all settings. Several commentators have developed frameworks showing how leadership effectiveness depends on context.

Robert Tannenbaum and Warren Schmidt

Departing from 'one best way', Robert Tannenbaum and Warren Schmidt (1958) considered the autocratic-democratic choice of style as a continuum, from boss-oriented leadership at one extreme to follower-oriented leadership at the other. This is illustrated in Figure 18.2.

Tannenbaum and Schmidt gave their article a subtitle: 'Should a manager be democratic or autocratic – or something in between?'. The answer, they suggest, depends on three sets of forces:

Forces in the leader	Personality, values, preferences, beliefs about employee participation, confidence in subordinates
Forces in the followers	Need for independence, tolerance of ambiguity, knowledge of the problem, expectations of involvement
Forces in the situation	Organizational norms, size and location of work groups, effectiveness of teamworking, nature of the problem

Contingency theory of leadership a perspective which argues that leaders must adjust their style to take into account the properties of the context.

Having concentrated on 'forces in the leader', and challenged the notion of 'one best way' to lead, research now turned to consider the properties of the context in which the leader was operating. These properties included the people being led, the nature of the work they were doing, and the wider organizational setting. This perspective implies that leaders must be able to 'diagnose' the context, and then decide what behaviour will 'fit' best. As the best style is contingent (i.e. depends) on the situation, this approach is known as the contingency theory of leadership.

> **CRITICAL THINKING**
>
> Leadership theory seems to be consistent in arguing that a considerate, employee-centred, participative and democratic style is more effective.
>
> In what context would an inconsiderate, goal-centred, impersonal and autocratic leadership style be effective? **(See OB cinema, this chapter, for possible answers.)**

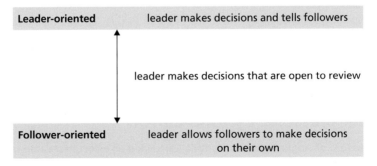

Figure 18.2: The Tannenbaum-Schmidt model of leadership behaviour
Source: Tannenbaum and Schmidt (1958)

Structured task a task with clear goals, few correct or satisfactory solutions and outcomes, few ways of performing it, and clear criteria of success.

Unstructured task a task with ambiguous goals, many good solutions, many ways of achieving acceptable outcomes, and vague criteria of success.

Fred Fiedler

Fred Fiedler developed one of the first contingency theories of leadership (1967; Fiedler and Chemers, 1974, 1984). From studies of basketball teams and bomber crews, he found that leadership effectiveness is influenced by three sets of factors:

1. The extent to which the task in hand is structured
2. The leader's position power, or formal authority
3. The nature of the relationships between the leader and followers.

This argument distinguishes between a structured task and an unstructured task.

CRITICAL THINKING   Would you describe the task of writing an essay for your organizational behaviour instructor as a structured or as an unstructured task? Would you prefer this task to be more or less structured, and how would you advise your instructor to achieve this?

Fiedler identified three typical sets of conditions in which a leader might have to work:

Condition 1	Condition 2	Condition 3
Highly structured task	Unstructured task	Unstructured task
High position power	Low position power	Low position power
Good relationships	Moderately good relationships	Poor relationships

In Condition 1, task-orientated leaders get better results, because they set targets and monitor progress. Relationships-orientated leaders get poor results because they want to maintain their relationships.

In Condition 2, relationships-orientated leaders get better results, as relationships are key to exerting influence. In this case, the task-orientated leader who lacks position power gets poor results.

In Condition 3, which is highly unfavourable, task-orientated leaders once again get better results, by structuring the situation, reducing uncertainty, and ignoring resistance. The relationships-orientated leader is reluctant to pressure subordinates, avoids confrontations, and pays less attention to the task.

Fiedler's theory confirms the importance of context in determining leader effectiveness, and supports the argument that there is no one best set of leadership traits or behaviours. But can leaders change style to fit the context? Fiedler felt that most managers and supervisors have problems in changing their styles. To be effective, he argued, *leaders have to change their context* (move to another organization), to find conditions in which their preferred style would be effective.

Leaders under pressure: Cynthia Carroll

As CEO of Anglo American, Cynthia Carroll led an effort to revamp safety standards and change the culture at the male-dominated multinational mining company. Andrew Hill asks her how she dealt with the backlash in this challenging context (8.12 minutes)

Paul Hersey and Ken Blanchard

Another influential contingency theory was developed by Paul Hersey and Ken Blanchard (1988). Like Fiedler, they argue that the effective leader 'must be a good diagnostician'. Unlike Fiedler, however, they believe that leaders can adapt their style to meet the demands of the situation in which they operate. Hersey and Blanchard call their approach situational leadership.

Their theory describes leadership behaviour on two dimensions. The first concerns 'task behaviour', or the amount of direction a leader gives to subordinates. This can vary from specific instructions, at one extreme, to delegation, at the other. Hersey and Blanchard identify two intermediate positions, where leaders either facilitate subordinates' decisions, or take care to explain their own. The second dimension concerns 'supportive behaviour', or the social backup a leader gives to subordinates. This can vary from limited communication, to considerable listening, facilitating and supporting. The model thus described four basic leadership styles:

S1   *Telling*: High amounts of task behaviour, telling subordinates what to do, when to do it and how to do it, but with little relationship behaviour.

S2   *Selling*: High amounts of both task behaviour and relationship behaviour.

S3   *Participating*: Lots of relationship behaviour and support, but little task behaviour.

S4   *Delegating*: Not much task behaviour or relationship behaviour.

Hersey and Blanchard argue that the willingness of followers to perform a task is also a key factor. At one extreme, we have insecure subordinates, reluctant to act. At the other, we have confident and able followers. Take into account subordinate readiness and you have a basis for selecting an effective leadership style. The view that insecure subordinates need telling, while willing groups can be left to do the job, is consistent with other theories. The strengths of this perspective thus lie with its emphasis on contextual factors, and on the need for flexibility in leadership behaviour.

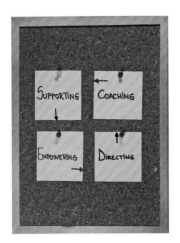

Daniel Goleman

Daniel Goleman (2000) reported research by the management consulting firm Hay McBer involving 4,000 executives from around the world. This identified six leadership styles which affect 'working atmosphere' and financial performance. The findings suggest that effective leaders use all of these styles, like an 'array of clubs in a golf pro's bag'. Each style relies on an aspect of *emotional intelligence* **(see Chapter 6)** which concerns skill in managing your emotions, and the emotions of others. Goleman's six styles are summarized in Table 18.1.

Table 18.1: Goleman's six leadership styles

Style	In practice	In a phrase	Competencies	When to use
Coercive	Demands compliance	'Do what I tell you'	Drive to achieve, self-control	In a crisis, with problem people
Authoritative	Mobilizes people	'Come with me'	Self-confidence, change catalyst	When new vision and direction is needed
Affiliative	Creates harmony	'People come first'	Empathy, communication	To heal wounds, to motivate people under stress
Democratic	Forges consensus	'What do you think?'	Collaboration, teambuilding	To build consensus, to get contributions
Pacesetting	Sets high standards	'Do as I do, now'	Initiative, drive to achieve	To get fast results from a motivated team
Coaching	Develops people	'Try this'	Empathy, self-awareness	To improve performance, to develop strengths

While coercion and pacesetting have their uses, the research showed that these styles can damage 'working atmosphere', reducing flexibility and employee commitment. The other four styles have a consistently positive impact on climate and performance. The most effective leaders, Goleman concludes, are those who have mastered four or more styles, particularly the positive styles, and who are able to switch styles to fit the situation. This is not a 'mechanical' matching of behaviour to context, as other contingency theories imply, but a flexible, sensitive and seamless adjustment.

Assessing contingency theories

Contingency theories argue that the most effective leadership style depends on the context. Organization structures, management skills, employee characteristics, and the nature of their tasks, are unique. No one style of leadership is universally best. There is, however, a large body of research which suggests that a considerate, participative or democratic style of leadership is generally more effective than a directive, autocratic style. There are two main reasons for this.

First, participative management is part of a long-term social and political trend in Western economies, which has raised expectations about personal freedom and quality of working life. These social and political values encourage resistance to manipulation by impersonal bureaucracies, and challenge the legitimacy of management decisions. Participation thus reflects democratic social and political values. Many commentators would note, however, that individual freedom, quality of working life, and genuine participation are still lacking in many organizations in different parts of the world.

Second, participative management has been encouraged by studies which have shown that this style is generally more effective, although an autocratic style can be effective in some contexts. A participative style can improve organizational effectiveness by tapping the ideas of those who have 'front line' knowledge and experience, and by involving them in a decision-making process to which they then become committed. This approach is encouraged by growing numbers of knowledge workers who expect to be involved in decisions affecting their work, and whose knowledge makes them potentially valuable contributors in this respect.

Leadership in unusual situations: Dr Haze, Circus of Horrors

'A lot of circuses these days don't have ringmasters. I'm proud to be keeping the tradition alive – it's a bit of a dying trade. The job of ringmaster is what the name says: you're in charge of that ring. I sing the songs and do all the compering, all the patter, as it was in Victorian times and before. And I make sure all the acts are in the right place at the right time and perform as well as they can. A lot of the acts are doing quite dangerous stuff and all sorts of things can go wrong. You always try and make sure the next act is ready in the ring doors. What you don't want is to announce the next act and they're not there. All the way through the show, I'm looking very closely at the acts as we go and taking mental notes, and the next day I'll come with a whole list of stuff. If something's gone wrong you say 'this wasn't right, we need to do this to rectify it' – the same way a football manager would. Some of the people I perform with have been in the show for years and years, so you've got to make sure they don't become complacent. They say a leopard never changes its spots – you've got to make sure it does change its spots. They say you can't teach an old dog new tricks – you've got to help them learn those tricks. You've got to keep people evolving, moving, changing' (Bain, 2016).

Which of Daniel Goleman's leadership styles does Dr Haze use?

What advice does Dr Haze offer that you think will be useful to you in your future career?

People who are involved in setting standards or establishing methods are more likely to experience 'ownership' of such decisions, and are therefore more likely to:

* accept the legitimacy of decisions reached with their help
* accept change based on those decisions
* trust managers who ultimately ratify and implement decisions
* volunteer new and creative ideas and solutions.

Autocratic management stifles creativity, ignores available expertise, and smothers motivation and commitment. However, there is no doubt that autocratic management can be effective:

* when time is short
* when the leader is the most knowledgeable person
* where those who participate will never agree with each other – but a decision must be made.

Contingency theories have attracted criticisms.

One criticism concerns the ability of leaders to diagnose the context in which they are operating, given the vague nature of the situational variables identified by different theories. In addition, contingency theories often overlook other key dimensions of context, such as the organization culture, degree of change and levels of stress, working conditions, external economic factors, organizational design and technology. All of these factors potentially influence the leadership process in ways not addressed by any of these theoretical accounts.

A second criticism concerns whether leaders can adapt their styles to fit the context in the ways the theories suggest. Personality may not be flexible enough. Inherent traits may inhibit managers from being participative in some circumstances and dictatorial in others. The manager who is motivated by affiliation, valuing friendship, may find it hard to treat others in an impersonal and autocratic way. The styles and expectations of other managers in an organization may also be influential.

New leader an inspirational visionary, concerned with building a shared sense of purpose and mission, creating a culture in which everyone is aligned with the organization's goals and is skilled and empowered to achieve them.

Superleader a leader who is able to develop leadership capacity in others, empowering them, reducing their dependence on formal leaders, stimulating their motivation, commitment and creativity.

New leadership

Transactional leader a leader who treats relationships with followers in terms of an exchange, giving followers what they want in return for what the leader desires, following prescribed tasks to pursue established goals.

Transformational leader a leader who treats relationships with followers in terms of motivation and commitment, influencing and inspiring followers to give more than mere compliance to improve organizational performance.

In the search for new ideas in the late twentieth century, the key role of heroic, powerful, visionary, charismatic leaders was recognized. Several new terms were invented to describe this role. We had the new leader, an inspirational figure motivating followers to higher levels of achievement. We also had the superleader who is able to 'lead others to lead themselves' (Sims and Lorenzi, 1992, p.295). These terms clearly overlap, and are closely related to the popular and influential concept of transformational leadership.

Transformational leadership

The new leadership movement began with the work of James McGregor Burns (1978), whose study of political leaders distinguished between the transactional leader and the transformational leader. Transactional leaders see their relationships with followers in terms of trade, swaps or bargains. Transformational leaders are charismatic individuals who inspire and motivate others to perform 'beyond contract'.

Noel Tichy and Mary Anne Devanna (1986) argue that transformational leaders have three main roles: recognizing the need for revitalization, creating a new vision, and institutionalizing change. Bernard Bass and Bruce Avolio (Bass, 1985a; 1985b; Bass and Avolio, 1990; Bass and Avolio, 1994) similarly claim that transformational leadership involves 'the Four Is':

* *Intellectual stimulation*: encourage others to see what they are doing from new perspectives.

- *Idealized influence*: articulate the mission or vision of the organization.
- *Individualized consideration*: develop others to higher levels of ability.
- *Inspirational motivation*: motivate others to put organizational interests before self-interest.

What did they find? Charismatic leadership

Jasmine Vergauwe and colleagues (2018) have been studying charismatic leadership. There are many books on this subject. You can learn how to become more charismatic. If charismatic leaders inspire others to perform well and encourage commitment, then more charisma is surely better.

For this research, charisma was defined in terms of four personality tendencies that make up 'the charismatic cluster': bold, mischievous, colourful and imaginative. In behavioural terms, charismatic leaders are likely to challenge the status quo, take risks, and be self-confident, captivating, expressive, extraverted, energetic, optimistic, inspirational and creative.

However, are charismatic leaders always effective? The researchers gathered information on 306 leaders in an international aerospace company. Each leader was assessed on their overall effectiveness by 14 raters, including subordinates, peers, and superiors. The leaders themselves completed a self-assessment based on the four dimensions of 'the charismatic cluster', and were each given a 'charisma score'.

Jasmine Vergauwe

What did they find? Were highly charismatic leaders more effective? Can a leader be too charismatic? **(Answers in chapter Recap.)**

 **STOP AND SEARCH**   YouTube for *Emma Jacobs: How to be charismatic* (3:20).

The Transformational Leadership Questionnaire developed by Beverly Alimo-Metcalfe and John Alban-Metcalfe (2002; 2003) identifies fourteen behaviours (competencies) in three categories:

Leading and developing others

- Showing concern
- Empowering
- Being accessible
- Encouraging change

Personal qualities

- Being transparent
- Acting with integrity
- Being decisive
- Inspiring others
- Resolving complex problems

Leading the organization

- Networking and achieving
- Focusing team effort

- Building shared vision
- Supporting a developmental culture
- Facilitating change sensitively

Research with public sector managers suggests that these behaviours can increase job satisfaction and motivation, and reduce stress. Metcalfe and Metcalfe also found that women were seen as more transformational than men on most of these behaviours, and were rated as better than men on decisiveness, focusing effort, mentoring, managing change, inspiring others and openness to ideas.

CRITICAL THINKING

Considering business and political leaders – past or present – with whom you are familiar, directly or through the media, which come closest to these definitions of new leader, superleader and transformational leader?

The new, super, transformational leader looks like a 'one best way' approach. Does this support trait-spotting and discredit contingency perspectives?

Transformational leaders make you sick

Karina Nielsen   Kevin Daniels

Transformational leadership has been associated with increased job satisfaction, employee well-being, and lower sickness absence. But does transformational leadership have a 'dark side'? Leaders who adopt a transformational style often put their followers under pressure to perform 'above and beyond the call of duty'. When this happens, are the outcomes for employee well-being always positive?

Karina Nielsen and Kevin Daniels (2016) studied the leadership of groups of postal workers in Denmark, looking at sickness absence rates over three years. They found that transformational leaders had groups with higher sickness absence, and that groups with higher levels of presenteeism **(see Chapter 9)** had even higher levels of sickness absence. Leaders with a transformational style may therefore increase sickness absence among healthy employees. Vulnerable employees may be encouraged to work when they are not well, and this self-sacrifice could lead to more sickness absence in the long run.

Distributed leadership

We need leadership to be distributed

'We observe that the need for leadership has changed following the global shifts in the ways we work today. While organizations are seen to be better at understanding leadership at the highest levels in the hierarchy, many are now seeking to devolve leadership down the line, expecting more junior managers and employees without managerial responsibility to treat the organizational agenda as their own. The need for leadership throughout the organization has only recently been acknowledged, mostly as front-line and middle managers have been asked to support continuous organizational change and generate discretionary effort by staff, as well as to apply informal leadership techniques in order to influence internal and external colleagues who do not report to them directly' (Zheltoukhova, 2014, pp.2–3).

Distributed leadership the exercise of leadership behaviours, often informally and spontaneous, by staff at all levels of an organization, with a group taking collective responsibility, or taking turns in leadership roles depending on circumstances.

Do we need visionary superheroes? Recent studies show how changes can be implemented by people at all levels of an organization, whether they have formal leadership positions or not. A number of terms have been used to describe this phenomenon: leadership in the plural, dispersed leadership, shared leadership and distributed leadership.

Leadership theory traditionally assumes that others will not act without 'strong and effective' leadership. We need leaders to generate the ideas and to provide the directions, the 'orders from above', which inspire followers, don't we? Peter Gronn (2002, 2009) contrasts this traditional idea of focused leadership, emphasizing the individual, with distributed leadership. Distributed leadership involves many people acting in concert, in formal and informal, spontaneous and intuitive roles. These roles may not be permanent. Leadership functions can be shared. The leadership role can sit with the group as a whole taking collective responsibility. The leadership role can also move from one person or group to another, as circumstances change. Leadership can thus involve role-sharing and turn-taking, rather than belonging to one person.

Distributed leadership is encouraged by flatter structures, teamwork, knowledge work, developments in communication technology, and 'network' organization forms. In turbulent economic conditions, many organizations are unstable and are evolving in novel ways. This often means creating new types of inter-organizational collaboration **(see Chapter 17)**. The scale and complexity of these changes involve more people, compared with change that only affects one part of an organization.

These trends combine with the fashion for empowerment and engagement **(Chapter 9)**. Debra Meyerson (2001) highlights the importance of behind-the-scenes, 'below the radar' change leadership of middle managers. Joseph Badaracco (2002) describes a 'quiet approach to change leadership', emphasizing 'small things, careful moves, controlled and measured efforts'. In appropriate conditions, motivated and capable staff can implement change covertly, quietly, by stealth, just as effectively as 'celebrity bosses', without destabilizing the organization and burning out colleagues.

One of the problems with distributed leadership is that the capabilities and contributions of those who are involved may not be recognized. Sylvia Ann Hewlett and colleagues (2005) note that members of ethnic minority groups, while holding junior posts in their organizations, often have major community leadership roles, with capabilities and talent that are neither recognized nor used by their main employer. These are the 'unsung heroes' who take personal responsibility, and risk, for driving change without always waiting patiently for others, or simply following directions.

David Buchanan et al. (2007) describe how complex changes to improve cancer services in a British hospital were implemented by a large number of people acting together to meet the same goals and targets, without formal management plans, structures and roles. Although four key people were involved at different stages, they were not senior managers, and the change process also involved 19 other individuals, and 26 managerial, administrative and clinical groups, patients' representatives, and other organizations. Their contributions were informal and fluid, and complemented each other. The researchers note how leadership responsibility for these changes 'migrated' around various groups and was shared by the individuals who were involved. They conclude that implementing change with 'nobody in charge' can be just as effective as traditional methods. This approach is not dependent on individuals or small teams, and survives the departure of the lone change leader.

Peter Gronn

| **CRITICAL THINKING** | When faced with the concept of distributed leadership, a common criticism is that there must always be *somebody* in charge. Must there? What is your view? |

Ksenia Zheltoukhova (2014) identifies four trends that are shaping leadership roles:

1. *Frequency and pace of change*: faster information sharing and aggressive competition means that decisions have to be taken faster, which means devolving responsibilities 'down the line'.

2. *Greater transparency and global consumer choice*: standards of business behaviour are now public and consumers can switch rapidly to competitors if they feel that an organization is breaching those standards.

3. *Collaborative working*: flat structures and external partnerships mean that people have to influence others over whom they have no line management authority.

4. *Workforce diversity*: need to address a wider range of different needs and motivations across the workforce – work has to appeal to a wider range of expectations than in the past.

These trends encourage a devolved, shared, distributed approach to leadership. Hierarchy, bureaucracy, a short-term focus, and individual reward systems undermine that approach. Distributed leadership does not imply a complete shift away from formal, senior figures who continue to exercise leadership functions. What is required is a 'twin track' approach in which visionary individual leaders, and a widely dispersed leadership decoupled from high office, work together.

Shared leadership in a global business context

Mansour Javidan

Companies seeking to expand their international markets need leaders who can work in global roles. Global business contexts are often more complex and competitive. Leaders thus need a 'global mindset', that enables them to work with people from different cultural, political, and institutional backgrounds. Are there gender differences in approaches to global leadership, and does that matter? Research has suggested that gender diversity in leadership teams can help an organization working across cultures. Mansour Javidan and colleagues (2016) studied over 1,000 managers, male and female, from 74 countries. These managers had completed the Global Mindset Inventory, created by the Thunderbird School of Global Management in the United States.

The researchers found significant differences between women and men with regard to their global leadership profiles. Women had stronger profiles in aspects of *building global relationships*. Men had stronger profiles in aspects of *contextual knowledge and exposure*:

Global leadership profile strengths

Women	Men
Building global relationships:	*Contextual knowledge and exposure*:
Passion for diversity	Global business savvy
Intercultural empathy	Cosmopolitan outlook
Diplomacy	Interpersonal impact

The researchers conclude that leadership should be shared between women and men in a global organization because their skills and knowledge complement each other. Senior leaders are unlikely to possess all of the knowledge and skills that are required to navigate a complex global business environment. Gender-diverse senior leadership teams are more likely to be effective. The men's profile suggests that they should be given lead roles 'when the context calls for pursuing global opportunities and negotiating contracts and agreements with the relevant parties from other countries' (p.68). In contrast, women should be given lead roles 'when the situation calls for an emphasis on relationships, or working and communicating effectively with individuals from other cultures' (p.68).

STOP AND SEARCH   YouTube for *Mansour Javidan: What is the global mindset?* (3:20).

Who needs leaders?

Most commentators accept that leadership is indispensable. But a novel perspective emerged in the early twenty-first century, challenging the enthusiasm for charismatic, visionary, transactional superleaders. Here is a perspective which argues that some leaders are *dangerous*.

Nick Morgan (2001, p.3) criticizes 'larger-than-life leaders and their grand strategies', arguing for 'a quieter, more evolutionary approach to change, one that relies on employee motivation instead of directives from on high'. Organizations should limit the amount of change, focus on incremental improvements, and 'above all lose the notion that you need heroic leaders in order to have meaningful, sustained change' (p.2). This is consistent Eric Abrahamson's (2004) approach to 'painless change' which is carefully staged and paced **(see Chapter 19)**.

Quy Huy (2001) also dismisses the role of visionary leadership, arguing that it is middle managers who achieve the balance between change and continuity, and that radical change imposed from the top makes this difficult. Jim Collins (2001) argues that 'larger than life' leaders are not always effective, and that the most powerful senior executives display what he calls 'level 5 leadership', combining humility with persistence. We have already met Meyerson's (2001) 'tempered radicals' who operate 'below the radar', and Badaracco's (2002) 'unglamorous, not heroic, quiet approach to leadership'. It is important to pay attention to these 'non-leadership' contributions to organizational change.

Rakesh Khurana (2002, p.62) is scathing in his assessment of transformational leaders. The popular stereotype is the charismatic individual who wins the confidence of investors and the business press, inspires employees, defeats overwhelming competition, and turns around dying companies. This is the white knight, the lone ranger, the heroic figure. Khurana has four criticisms of these characters:

1. They 'reject limits to their scope and authority, rebel against all checks on their power and dismiss the norms and rules that apply to others'. In other words, they are beyond the influence and control of senior colleagues.

2. They rely on 'the widespread quasi-religious belief in the powers of charismatic leaders'. This belief allows them to 'exploit the irrational desires of their followers'.

3. They encourage the attribution error of understanding success in terms of the actions of prominent leaders, while overlooking 'the interplay of social, economic, and other impersonal forces that shape and constrain even the most heroic individual efforts'.

4. New chief executives often deliberately destabilize their organizations, to foster revitalization. However, this can be harmful, if not disastrous, as corporate scandals illustrate.

Visionary leaders are expected to drive radical change, while managers maintain order and stability. However, Khurana regards the transformational leader as a 'dangerous curse'. This criticism has interesting implications. The views that we have just discussed take the debate back to the distinction between leadership and management. We discussed the perspective which says, 'leadership is good – management is bad'. This argument is now reversed, with the claim that leaders can be dangerously destabilizing while managers can drive organizational improvements more effectively. It seems that organizational effectiveness may depend on competent managers and not on charismatic visionaries.

CRITICAL THINKING
Identify examples of leaders – of organizations or countries – to whom Khurana's four criticisms apply. In your view, are those leaders successful or disastrous – and why?

RECAP

1. *Explain the apparent difference between the concepts of leadership and management.*

   - Leaders are typically portrayed as inspiring, change-oriented visionaries.

   - Managers are typically portrayed as planners, organizers and controllers.

   - In practice, the roles overlap, are complementary, and can be difficult to distinguish.

2. *Understand the relationships between personality traits and effective leadership.*

   - Many factors, besides personality traits, influence leadership effectiveness.

   - It has proved difficult to establish a consensus on specific traits.

   - The characteristics of the leader's role also influence behaviour and effectiveness.

3. *Understand the challenges facing women who aspire to leadership roles, and the social and business cases for 'boardroom diversity'.*

   - Women are traditionally powerless due to discrimination and exclusion by men.

   - Women have social and interpersonal leadership qualities, improve performance by widening management discussions, and are now more likely to be promoted on merit.

   - Board gender-diversity is seen in many countries as socially desirable for equality reasons, and the evidence suggests that board diversity is positively linked to corporate performance.

   - Women often hit a glass ceiling, preventing their progress into more senior management roles.

   - When organizations are in financial difficulty, they often appoint women to senior roles, where they are then vulnerable to failure; this has been described as a 'glass cliff'.

4. *Understand why effective leaders either adapt their style to fit the organizational and cultural context in which they operate, or else find contexts which fit their personal style.*

   - Considerate behaviour reduces labour turnover and improves job satisfaction.

   - Initiating structure improves performance but reduces job satisfaction.

   - Effective leaders combine consideration with initiating structure.

   - Contingency theory argues that leaders are more or less effective depending on how structured the task is, how powerful the leader is, and how good the relationships are.

   - Situational leadership advises the manager to use telling, selling, participating and delegating styles depending on the task, relationships, and employee readiness.

   - Some commentators argue that leaders cannot change their behaviour, and that to be effective they have to find organizational contexts that are suitable for their leadership style.

   - Most commentators argue that leaders can and should adapt their behaviour to fit the context and the culture in which they are operating.

5. *Explain contemporary trends in this field concerning new leadership, the dispersal of leadership, and the argument that leaders are unnecessary.*

   - One trend emphasizes charismatic, visionary, inspirational new leaders.

   - New leadership, superleader and transformational leadership are close synonyms.

   - Distributed or shared leadership can be observed at all organizational levels.

   - The new visionary leader helps to develop leadership capability in others.

   - The new leader has the right traits, and the right style, for the contemporary context, thus combining notions of trait-spotting, style-counselling, and context-fitting.

   - A more recent trend views charismatic, visionary leaders as dangerous because they can destabilize an organization; management capabilities are more important.

→

RECAP: What did they find? charismatic leadership

Vergauwe et al. (2017) found that:

- More experienced leaders saw themselves as more effective, and were perceived as more effective by subordinates and superiors.

- Leaders with higher charisma scores rated themselves as more effective.

- Leaders with low and high charisma scores were rated by others – subordinates, peers, and superiors – as less effective than leaders with moderate levels of charisma.

- These findings challenge the 'more is better' principle; charisma is a strength which can become a weakness, when bold, mischievous, colourful and imaginative, are seen by others as attempts to overwhelm, intimidate and manipulate.

- Too much charisma confirms the TMGT principle – 'too much of a good thing'.

Revision

1. What is the difference between leadership and management, and why is it difficult to separate these concepts in practice?

2. Why is trait-spotting such a popular theme in leadership research? What has trait-spotting told us about the qualities of successful leaders? What are the problems with this perspective?

3. Traditionally, leaders have been men with special qualities. Why are women now more likely to be considered as effective leaders?

4. What are the benefits and disadvantages of a charismatic leadership style?

Research assignment

The chief executives of private and public sector organizations are often in the news: online, blogs, Twitter, television. Sometimes, they attract media interest because their organization has been innovative and successful. When an organization has contributed to an accident, failure, or disaster, the media will report that, too. Find two chief executives who are in the news when you study this chapter. If possible, identify one male and one female chief executive. Search the internet for accounts – written and video – and note what they say about their personalities and other attributes. Can you identify examples of male–female stereotyping in those reports? How do the media reports link the personalities and attributes of those chief executives to the successes and failures that stimulated interest in them in the first place? From the evidence in this chapter, what feedback can you give to the media reporters on the accuracy and validity of their assessments of those two leaders?

Springboard

Elena Lytkina Botelho, Kim Powell and Tahl Raz (2018) *The CEO Next Door: The Four Behaviours that Transform Ordinary People into World Class Leaders.* London: Virgin Books. Shatters myths about what it takes to be a chief executive, and offers guidance for those who want to see themselves in that corner office.

Joanne Lipman (2018) *Win Win: When Business Works for Women It Works for Everyone.* London: John Murray. Describes how work and organizations are designed for men, and rigged against women. Also explores how women and men collaborate to end gender inequality.

Jeffrey Pfeffer (2015) *Leadership BS: Fixing Workplaces and Careers One Truth at a Time,* New York: Harper Business. Criticizes the 'leadership industry' for offering unhelpful advice based on wishful thinking that produces unrealistic images of leadership. Argues that leaders sometimes have to do bad things to achieve good results **(see Chapter 22).**

Hazel McLaughlin, JonSilvester, Diana Bilimoria, Sophie Jané, Ruth Sealy, Kim Peters, Hannah Möltner, Morten Huse, and Juliane Göke, (2017) 'Women in power: contributing factors that impact on women in organizations and politics; psychological research and best practice', *Organizational Dynamics,* October (published online). Reviews evidence showing that the challenges for women seeking positions of power are not just individual; women also face institiutional and social biases.

OB cinema

The Devil Wears Prada (2006, director David Frankel). DVD track 2: 0:03:20 to 0:09:47 (7 minutes). Track 2 begins with Andy coming out of the lift and heading for the office reception desk; clip ends when she is called back into the office as she is walking away.

Based on the novel by Lauren Weisberger, this movie tells the story of a naive, aspiring journalist, Andrea (Andy) Sachs (played by Anne Hathaway) who gets a job as assistant to the editor-in-chief of the fashion magazine *Runway.* The magazine's powerful and ruthless editor, Miranda Priestly (Meryl Streep) is a legend. We see Andy arriving for her job interview as 'second assistant' with Miranda's first assistant Emily Charlton (Emily Blunt). But Miranda decides to conduct the interview herself.

1. How would you describe Miranda Priestley's leadership style? Identify specific behaviours to support your conclusions.

2. What impact does Miranda's leadership style have on those around her? Identify specific employee behaviours to support your conclusions.

3. Good boss or bad boss: what is your assessment of this leadership style? Cite specific evidence of her impact on individual performance and organizational effectiveness to support your judgement.

4. To what extent does this leadership style apply in the real world, beyond Hollywood? Consider individual personality, organizational context, and industry sector in making this judgement.

5. Why do you think Miranda Priestly gave Andy the job?

Chapter exercises

1: Management and leadership

Objectives
1. To explore differences in the definition of the terms management and leadership.

2. To consider whether and how our understanding and use of these terms is changing.

Briefing
Are leadership and management different roles, or do they overlap? Look at this list of activities. Are these leadership activities, or management activities, or could they fall into both categories? Use the activities matrix to locate each of those activities depending on whether you feel they are management-oriented, leadership-oriented, or both (based on Gillen, 2004).

Activities list

1. Delegate tasks
2. Plan and prioritize steps to achieve task goals
3. Ensure predictability
4. Coordinate effort
5. Provide focus
6. Monitor feelings and morale
7. Follow systems and procedures
8. Provide development opportunities
9. Monitor progress
10. Appeal to rational thinking

11. Act as interface between team and others
12. Motivate staff
13. Inspire people
14. Coordinate resources
15. Give orders and instructions
16. Check task completion
17. Ensure effective induction
18. Unleash potential
19. Look 'over the horizon'
20. Be a good role model

21. Use analytical data to support recommendations
22. Explain goals, plans and roles
23. Appeal to people's emotions
24. Share a vision
25. Guide progress
26. Create a positive team feeling
27. Monitor budgets and tasks
28. Use analytical data to forecast trends
29. Take risks
30. Build teams

Activities matrix

Managerially oriented	Elements of management and leadership	Leadership oriented

Class discussion
Consider why you placed each of those activities in those categories:

1. What makes an activity a management activity?

2. What is distinctive about leadership activities?

3. If you put some activities in the middle, why did you do that?

4. Are there any current trends and developments which encourage managers to monitor and control rather than to exercise leadership?

2: Leadership in practice

Objectives
1. To relate the theory and concepts of leadership to practice.
2. To assess critically how leaders are typically seen and portrayed.

Briefing
1. Identify two business, sports or political leaders, one male and one female, past or present, with whom you are familiar through the media, or through movies based on their lives.
2. What traits and other characteristics do they have? To what extent do they conform with traditional female and male leadership stereotypes?
3. How are their leadership styles portrayed: participative, considerate, task-oriented, autocratic, transformational, for example? How do their styles influence their effectiveness?
4. What conclusions can you draw about leadership effectiveness, and about the way in which society sees leaders?

References

Abrahamson, E. (2004) *Change Without Pain: How Managers Can Overcome Initiative Overload, Organizational Chaos, and Employee Burnout.* Boston, MA: Harvard Business School Press.

Aguinis, H., Martin, G.P., Gomez-Mejia, L.R., O'Boyle, E.H. and Joo, H. (2018) 'The two sides of CEO pay injustice: a power law conceptualization of CEO over and underpayment', *Management Research: Journal of the Iberoamerican Academy of Management,* 16(1): 3–30.

Alimo-Metcalfe, B. and Alimo-Metcalfe, J. (2002) 'The great and the good', *People Management,* 8(11): 32–34.

Alimo-Metcalfe, B. and Alimo-Metcalfe, J. (2003) 'Under the influence', *People Management,* 9(5): 32–35.

Alimo-Metcalfe, B. and Alban-Metcalfe, J. (2010) 'Leadership: commitment beats control', *Health Service Journal,* 22 February, p.7

Alimo-Metcalfe, B. and Bradley, M. (2008) 'Cast in a new light', *People Management,* 14(2): 38–41.

Badaracco, J.L. (2002) *Leading Quietly: An Unorthodox Guide to Doing the Right Thing.* Boston, MA: Harvard Business School Press.

Bain, R. (2016) 'Management reinvented', *People Management* Online, 27 September, http://www2 .cipd.co.uk/pm/peoplemanagement/b/weblog/ archive/2016/09/27/management-reinvented.aspx [no longer available].

Bass, B.M. (1985a) *Bass and Stogdill's Handbook of Leadership: Theory, Research and Managerial Applications.* New York: Free Press, (third edn).

Bass, B.M. (1985b) *Leadership and Performance Beyond Expectations.* New York: Free Press.

Bass, B.M. and Avolio, B.J. (1990) 'The implications of transactional and transformational leadership for individual, team and organizational development', *Research and Organizational Change and Development,* 4: 321–72.

Bass, B.M. and Avolio, B.J. (1994) *Improving Organizational Effectiveness through Transformational Leadership.* Thousand Oaks, CA: Sage Publications.

Bennis, W.G. and Nanus, B. (1985) *Leaders: The Strategies for Taking Charge.* New York: Harper & Row.

Bird, C. (1940) *Social Psychology.* New York: Appleton-Century.

Birkinshaw, J. (2010) *Reinventing Management: Smarter Choices for Getting Work Done.* Chichester, West Sussex: Jossey-Bass.

Botelho, E.L., Powell, K. R., Kincaid, S. and Wang, D. (2017) 'What sets successful CEOs apart: the four essential behaviors that help them win the top job and thrive once they get it', *Harvard Business Review,* 95(3): 70–77.

Botelho, E.L., Powell, K. and Raz, T. (2018) *The CEO Next Door: The Four Behaviours that Transform Ordinary People into World Class Leaders.* London: Virgin Books.

Buchanan, D.A., Addicott, R., Fitzgerald, L., Ferlie, E. and Baeza, J. (2007) 'Nobody in charge: distributed change agency in healthcare', *Human Relations,* 60(7): 1065–90.

Bukunina, J. (2018) 'Investing in female founders is good business not charity', *Financial Times,* 18 September, p.13.

Burns, J.M. (1978) *Leadership.* New York: Harper & Row.

Chartered Institute for Personnel and Development (2015) *Breaking the Boardroom: A Guide for British Businesses on how to Support the Female Leaders of the Future.* London: Chartered Institute for Personnel and Development.

Collins, J. (2001) *Good to Great: Why Some companies Make the Leap and Others Don't.* New York: Harper Collins.

Davis, G. (2014) 'Addressing unconscious bias', *McKinsey Quarterly,* February: 1–4.

Donellan, A. (2017) 'Why we should all mind the pay gap', *The Sunday Times,* 23 July, p.5.

Egan, M.L., Matvos, G. and Seru, A. (2018) National Bureau of Economic Research Working Paper No. 23242, August.

Elsaid, E. and Ursel, N.D. (2018) 'Re-examining the glass cliff hypothesis using survival analysis: the case of female CEO tenure', *British Journal of Management,* 29(1): 156–70.

Ezzedeen, S.R. (2013) 'The portrayal of professional and managerial women in North American films: good news or bad news for your executive pipeline?', *Organizational Dynamics,* 42(4): 248–56.

Fiedler, F.E. (1967) *A Theory of Leadership Effectiveness.* New York: McGraw-Hill.

Fiedler, F.E. and Chemers, M.M. (1974) *Leadership and Effective Management.* Glenview IL: Scott, Foresman.

Fiedler, F.E. and Chemers, M.M. (1984) *Improving Leadership Effectiveness: The Leaders Match Concept.* New York: John Wiley, (second edn).

Fleishman, E.A. (1953a) 'The description of supervisory behaviour', *Journal of Applied Psychology,* 37(1): 1–6.

Fleishman, E.A. (1953b) 'The measurement of leadership attitudes in industry', *Journal of Applied Psychology,* 37(3): 153–58.

Fleishman, E.A. and Harris, E.F. (1962) 'Patterns of leadership behaviour related to employee grievances and turnover', *Personnel Psychology,* 15(1): 43–56.

Fraser, C. (1978) 'Small groups: structure and leadership', in Henri Tajfel and Colin Fraser (eds), *Introducing Social Psychology.* Harmondsworth: Penguin Books, pp.176–200.

Frean, A. (2017) 'Female chief executives pave way for more diversity in boardroom', *The Times,* 7 June, p.47.

Gillen, T. (2004) *Leadership or Management: The Differences.* London: Chartered Institute for Personnel and Development.

Glass, C. and Cook, A. (2016) 'Leading at the top: understanding women's challenges above the glass ceiling', *The Leadership Quarterly,* 27(1): 51–63.

Goleman, D. (2000) 'Leadership that gets results', *Harvard Business Review,* 78(2): 78–90.

Gordon, S. (2017) 'Little progress in women's battle to gain places on UK boards', *Financial Times,* 9 November, p.16.

Gronn, P. (2002) 'Distributed leadership as a unit of analysis', *Leadership Quarterly,* 13(4): 423–51.

Gronn, P. (2009) 'Leadership configurations', *Leadership,* 5(3): 381–94.

Hambrick, D.C. (2018) 'The fattest of the fat cats: observations on Aguinis and colleagues' findings on CEO pay', *Management Research: Journal of the Iberoamerican Academy of Management,* 16(1): 31–37.

Heller, F. (1997) 'Leadership', in Arndt Sorge and Malcolm Warner (eds), *The Handbook of Organizational Behaviour.* London: International Thomson, pp.340–49.

Hersey, P. and Blanchard, K.H. (1988) *Management of Organizational Behavior: Utilizing Human Resources.* Englewood Cliffs, NJ: Prentice-Hall International.

Hewlett, S.A., Luce, C.B. and West, C. (2005) 'Leadership in your midst: tapping the hidden strengths of minority executives', *Harvard Business Review,* 83(11): 74–82.

Hunt, V., Prince, S., Dixon-Fyle, S. and Yee, L. (2018) *Delivering Through Diversity.* London and New York: McKinsey & Company.

Huy, Q.N. (2001) 'In praise of middle managers', *Harvard Business Review,* 79(8): 72–9.

Javidan, M., Bullough, A. and Dibble, R. (2016) 'Mind the gap: gender differences in global leadership self-efficacies', *Academy of Management Perspectives,* 30(1): 59–73.

Katz, D., Maccoby, N. and Morse, N.C. (1950) *Productivity, Supervision, and Morale in an Office Situation.* Ann Arbor, MI: University of Michigan Institute for Social Research.

Khurana, R. (2002) 'The curse of the superstar CEO', *Harvard Business Review,* 80(9): 60–66.

Kirkland, R. and Bohnet, I. (2017) *Focusing on What Works for Workplace Diversity.* New York: McKinsey & Company.

Main, B.G.M. and Gregory-Smith, I. (2018) 'Symbolic management and the glass cliff: evidence from the boardroom careers of female and male directors', *British Journal of Management,* 29(1): 136–55.

Martinsen, O.L. and Glasø, L. (2014) 'Personality for leadership', Norwegian Business School Review, https://www.bi.edu/research/business-review/articles/2014/03/personality-for-leadership/ [accessed January 2019]

Meyerson, D.E. (2001) *Tempered Radicals: How People Use Difference to Inspire Change at Work.* Boston, MA: Harvard Business School Press.

Mintzberg, H. (2009) *Managing.* Harlow, Essex: Financial Times Prentice Hall.

Mooney A. (2017) 'Female hedge funds outperform those run by men', *Financial Times,* 18 September, p.25.

Morgan, N. (2001) 'How to overcome "change fatigue"', *Harvard Management Update:* 1–3.

Nielsen, K. and Daniels, K. (2016) 'The relationship between transformational leadership and follower sickness absence: the role of presenteeism', *Work & Stress,* 30(2): 193–208.

Roberts, L.M., Mayo, A., Ely, R. and Thomas, D. (2018) 'Beating the odds: leadership lessons from senior African-American women', *Harvard Business Review,* 96(2): 126–31.

Ryan, M.K. and Haslam, S.A. (2005) 'The glass cliff: evidence that women are over-represented in precarious leadership positions', *British Journal of Management,* 16(2): 81–90.

Ryan, M.K. and Haslam, S.A. (2007) 'The glass cliff: exploring the dynamics surrounding the appointment of women to precarious leadership positions', *Academy of Management Review,* 32(2): 549–72.

Sadun, R., Bloom, N. and Van Reenen, J. (2017) 'Why do we undervalue competent management?', *Harvard Business Review,* 95(5): 120–27.

Shaw, M.E. (1976) *Group Dynamics.* New York: McGraw Hill, (second edn).

Sims, H.P. and Lorenzi, P. (1992) *The New Leadership Paradigm.* Newbury Park, CA: Sage Publications.

Stogdill, R.M. (1948) 'Personal factors associated with leadership', *Journal of Psychology,* 25: 35–71.

Stogdill, R.M. (1950) 'Leadership, membership and organization', *Psychological Bulletin,* 47(1): 1–14.

Stogdill, R.M. (1974) *Handbook of Leadership: A Survey of Theory and Research.* New York: Free Press.

Stogdill, R.M. and Coons, A.E. (eds) (1951) *Leader Behaviour: Its Description and Measurement,* Research Monograph No.88, Columbus, OH: Ohio State University Bureau of Business Research.

Sutton, R. (2017a) *The Asshole Survival Guide: How to Deal With People Who Treat You Like Dirt.* New York: Penguin Portfolio.

Sutton, R. (2017b) 'Memo to the CEO: Are you the source of workplace dysfunction?', *McKinsey Quarterly,* 4 (September), pp. 102–11.

Tannenbaum, R. and Schmidt, W.H. (1958) 'How to choose a leadership pattern', *Harvard Business Review,* 36(2): 95–102 (reprinted in May–June 1973).

The FA Coach (2017) 'Southgate: "If a player feels you respect them, they are more likely to follow you"', *The Boot Room,* Issue 26, 6 June.

The 30% Club (2017) *Just About Managing: Men and Women Through the Executive Pipeline.* London: The 30% Club.

Tichy, N.M. and Devanna, M.A. (1986) *The Transformational Leader.* New York: Wiley.

Urick, M.J. and Sprinkle, T.A. (2018) 'Teaching leadership: using Wonder Woman to highlight the importance of gender diversity', *Management Teaching Review* (published online early): 1–9.

Vergauwe, J., Wille, B., Hofmans, J., Kaiser, R.B. and De Fruyt, F. (2018) 'The double-edged sword of leader charisma: understanding the curvilinear relationship between charismatic personality and leader effectiveness', *Journal of Personality and Social Psychology,* 114(1), 110–30.

Zheltoukhova, K. (2014) *Leadership: Easier Said Than Done.* London: Chartered Institute for Personnel and Development.

CHAPTER 19

Change

Key terms

triggers of change

transformational change

coping cycle

Yerkes–Dodson law

readiness for change

resistance to change

stakeholder

innovation

sustaining innovations

disruptive innovations

operational innovations

Learning outcomes

When you have read this chapter, you should be able to define those key terms in your own words, and you should also be able to:

1. Explain why effective change management is important, to organizations and to individuals.

2. Identify the main external and internal triggers of organizational change.

3. Explain the issues that management must take into account to ensure that change is successful.

4. Understand the typical characteristics of human responses to change.

5. Understand the nature of resistance to change and approaches to overcoming it.

6. Explain the advantages and limitations of participative methods of change management.

7. Understand the significance of innovation, and the distinction between sustaining, disruptive and operational innovations.

8. Explain the organizational properties that stimulate and stifle innovation respectively.

9. Recognize the challenges facing innovative change leaders.

Why study change?

Organizations must change, to keep up with economic and geopolitical developments, competitor behaviour, changing customer demands and expectations, new legislation and regulations, new materials, new technologies – and many other surprises. Failure to change, and to change rapidly, can threaten an organization's survival. You as an individual must also be able and willing to change. In order to 'future proof' your career, Carl Frey et al. (2016) argue that you will have to develop a whole new set of capabilities in order to be able to compete with increasingly smart machines **(Chapter 3).**

Managing change well, however, seems to be difficult. Most estimates put the failure rate of planned organizational changes at around 60 to 70 per cent. In a global survey conducted by the consulting company McKinsey, only 26 per cent of executives said that their change initiatives had been successful (Jacquemont et al., 2015). Hughes (2011) has previously criticized the methodology underpinning surveys of this kind, but no studies have yet reported a 70 per cent success rate.

CRITICAL THINKING

How would you respond to these 'true or false' questions?

People have a natural resistance to change.	True or False?
People get bored with routine and seek out new experiences.	True or False?
Older people are more resistant to change.	True or False?

Triggers of change disorganizing pressures that make current systems, procedures, rules, organization structures, processes, roles, and skills inappropriate and ineffective.

Did you answer 'true' to all three 'critical thinking' statements? These positive responses are inconsistent with each other, and contradict the evidence. For example, many people when they retire from work take up radically new activities and hobbies: painting, acting, community involvement, learning a musical instrument. We cannot have natural resistance to change and seek new experiences at the same time.

Change is a constant, and it is a constant challenge, for organizations, and for us as individuals. The need for organizational and personal change is prompted by many different triggers of change.

External triggers for organizational change include:

- Economic and trading conditions, domestic and global
- New technology and materials
- Demographic trends, silver tsunami, Gen Y, Gen Z, Gen Alpha

- Changes in consumers' demands and expectations
- Activities and innovations of competitors, mergers and acquisitions
- Legislation, regulation, government policies, corporate social responsibility demands
- Shifts in local, national and international politics
- Changes in social and cultural values.

Internal triggers for organizational change can include:

- Design of new products and services
- Low performance and morale, high stress and staff turnover
- Appointment of a new senior manager or top team
- Inadequate skills and knowledge base, triggering training programmes
- Office and factory relocation, closer to suppliers and markets
- Recognition of problems triggering redistribution of responsibilities
- Innovations in the manufacturing process
- New ideas about how to deliver services to customers.

Change is not simply a matter of reacting to triggers. Organizations and individuals can anticipate trends and opportunities, and be proactive as well.

One of the best known metaphors for change was developed by Kurt Lewin (1951) who argued for the need to *unfreeze* the current state of affairs, to *move* to a desired new state, then to *refreeze* and stabilize those changes (Cummings et al., 2016). Today, however, refreezing is not an option for most organizations. 'Repeat change' is the norm. 'Permanent thaw' is a better metaphor. The environment for most organizations seems likely to remain volatile, uncertain, complex, and ambiguous (VUCA), and change will be on the management agenda for some time. Change is thus a central issue, for managers concerned with organizational performance, adaptability and survival, and for individuals concerned about employability, their jobs, and their careers.

 EMPLOYABILITY CHECK (leading and managing change)

You know that the organization to which you have applied is experiencing a lot of change, and that you will be affected by this (but you don't know yet how you will be involved). The interviewer asks you about your attitude to change – organizational and personal. How will you answer this question?

 YouTube for *Unfreezing change as three steps* (7:37).

Making change happen

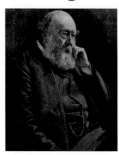

> *"Change? Change? Why do we need change? Things are quite bad enough as they are."*

Robert Gascoyne-Cecil, 3rd Marquess of Salisbury,
and UK Prime Minister to Queen Victoria, 1885–92

Organizational change takes many different forms, affecting structures, culture, working practices, information systems, and so on. Changes also vary in 'depth', from shallow to deep (Figure 19.1; Palmer et al., 2016, p.18). Some shallow change – 'small stuff' – may not be considered as change at all. At the top of the scale, we have radically new business models and working methods.

Off the scale	Transformational change Frame-breaking, mould-breaking Redraw dramatically organization and sector boundaries
Deeper	Strategic change New ways of thinking and solving problems, whole system change New ways of doing business
Deep change	Change the mission, vision, values, the organization's philosophy, in order to symbolize a radical shift in thinking and behaviour
	Change the organization's definition of success; create new goals, objectives, targets
Sustaining innovation	Improve business planning to symbolize a shift in thinking; tighten up on documentation, reporting, controls
	Reallocate resources; grow some departments, cut others, create new units
Shallow change	Fine-tuning: cut costs, improve efficiencies, constantly 'nibble away' making minor improvements
Not on the scale	'Sweat the small stuff' – quickly solve the minor annoying problems that nobody has bothered to fix; 'grease the wheels'

Figure 19.1: Assessing depth of change
Source: Palmer *et al.* (2016)

Minor, surface, or shallow changes may have limited impact on people and performance. Deep, penetrating changes are more wide-ranging in their effects. Faced with the geopolitical, economic, demographic, sociocultural, and technological trends and developments explored in **Chapters 2 and 3**, most organizations today appear to need deep transformational change. This is more difficult to implement than shallow change, as it is more costly and time-consuming, requires more management expertise, and affects more people in more significant ways.

In most organizations, many changes are likely to be under way at the same time, at different depths. We cannot argue that 'all change must be deep change'. Deep change is appropriate when dealing with 'deep problems', while fine tuning is an appropriate response to minor concerns. Surface and shallow changes can also provide critical support for deeper changes.

> **CRITICAL THINKING**
>
> If you want a high-flying, fast-track career, you are unlikely to get far if you focus your energies on shallow changes. Shallow changes do not contribute much to organizational performance, and will not improve your visibility or reputation. You would be advised to work on deep changes, as long as they are successful. What happens if all ambitious managers try to drive deep changes in the interests of progressing their careers?

The advice for managers on implementing change – on how to make it happen – is straightforward, with different commentators offering similar guidance, usually in the form of a checklist. One of the best-known sets of guidelines comes from John Kotter (2007; 2012). His research into over 100 American companies identifies the following eight steps to successful transformational change:

Transformational change large-scale change involving radical, frame-breaking, and fundamentally new ways of thinking, solving problems, and doing business.

1. Establish a sense of urgency for the proposed changes.
2. Create a powerful team to guide and drive the implementation.
3. Develop a vision to direct the change efforts, and a strategy to achieve the vision.
4. Communicate the new vision and strategy.
5. Empower others to help achieve the vision, removing obstacles, encouraging risk taking.

6. Plan for and create short-term wins, and recognize and reward those involved.

7. Consolidate improvements and develop new ideas and projects to support the vision.

8. Ensure that new approaches are embedded in the organization culture.

For successful change, Kotter suggested a careful planning process, working through these eight issues more or less in sequence, and not missing or rushing any of them. This takes time. Given the pace of change, perhaps many organizations try to take too many shortcuts to put change in place more quickly, and get it wrong as a consequence. Does this work in practice? Steven Appelbaum et al. (2012) reviewed the evidence relating to Kotter's model, and found support for most of the individual steps. However, despite Kotter's argument about integrating the eight stages, no studies have evaluated the framework as a whole. On the other hand, there was no evidence to challenge the practical value of the approach, which remains popular because it is easy to understand and to use.

Kotter (2012, p. 52) subsequently revised his framework, arguing that the eight steps should be seen as 'change accelerators', to speed up change. His new argument has three aspects. First, Kotter argues that the accelerators must operate concurrently, rather than in sequence. Second, change must not rely on a small core group, but on many change agents from across the organization. Third, traditional hierarchy must be complemented by flexible and agile networks.

Although Kotter focused his work on transformational change, his guidelines have been applied to the management of change in general. Reducing the task to these eight steps suggests that change, which is usually complex and untidy, can be controlled and managed effectively in a more or less logical and predictable manner. Also, having to handle such a small number of issues appears to lessen the scale of the management challenge. Success seems to be pretty much guaranteed. Why, then, is the failure rate of change so high? Have Kotter, and other commentators who have adopted similar 'change checklist' approaches, oversimplified the change management task?

CUTTING EDGE Ten steps to successful organizational change

Jeroen Stouten

Jeroen Stouten and colleagues (2018) reviewed the literature of organizational change (including Kotter's contribution), focusing on practical guidelines, and the underpinning theory. Noting that there is some agreement across practical and theoretical commentary, they developed an evidence-based approach to managing change effectively. Their approach suggests ten steps:

1. Diagnosis (1): gather the facts concerning the nature of the problem.
2. Diagnosis (2): assess the organization's readiness for change.
3. Identify solutions: implement evidence-based change interventions.
4. Develop effective change leadership throughout the organization.
5. Develop and communicate a compelling change vision.
6. Work with social networks and use their influence.
7. Use enabling practices – goal setting, learning, employee participation, transitional structures – to support implementation which should also be fair and just.
8. Encourage small-scale initiatives and experimentation, to allow local adjustments to broad change plans.
9. Assess change progress and outcomes over time.
10. Institutionalize the change to sustain its effectiveness.

Stouten et al. noted that managers do not use the available research evidence in making decisions concerning changes to organizational practices. Consequently, the failure rate of organizational change is high. The advice on offer here still has to be adapted to specific local circumstances, but the researchers argue that a rigorous evidence-based approach is more likely to succeed.

The acceleration trap

Is constant change 'the new normal'? Is rapid, 'accelerated' change necessary and desirable? Many commentators believe that it is. From a study of 4,900 US companies in 18 industries, Yong-Yeon Ji et al. (2014) note that some organizations ('hares') respond rapidly and aggressively to changing conditions – hiring or laying off parts of the workforce, for example. Others ('tortoises') try to maintain consistency, and make smaller adjustments. The study showed that employment instability lowered organizational performance. However, although very high instability was damaging, so was very low instability. Highly stable organizations may be too rigid and inflexible.

The researchers advise, therefore, a 'slow and steady' approach, changing in response to external conditions, but retaining talented employees. Change too slowly, and the organization's survival may be at risk. Change too quickly, and staff may be overloaded and demotivated – which could also threaten performance and survival. If the competition is changing rapidly, however, then 'slow and steady' could be a high-risk strategy.

Heike Bruch and Jochen Menges (2010) also argue that constant change leads to corporate burnout. In many organizations, intense market pressures encourage management to increase the number and speed of activities, raise performance goals, shorten innovation cycles, and introduce new systems and technologies. When the chief executive insists on this furious pace, the achievements turn into chronic overloading. Working constantly under time pressure, with priorities frequently changing, focus is scattered, staff become tired and demotivated, and customers get confused.

Bruch and Menges call this 'the acceleration trap'. They found that in companies that were 'fully trapped', 60 per cent of employees felt that they lacked the resources to get their work done, compared with only 2 per cent who felt that way in companies that were not 'trapped'. They also found three typical patterns:

- *Overloading*: staff have too many activities, but not enough time or resources.
- *Multiloading*: focus is reduced by asking employees to take on too many different activities.
- *Perpetual loading*: the organization operates close to capacity all the time, giving employees no chance to rest or retreat, but only to ask, 'When is the economizing going to come to an end?' (p.83).

If you answer 'yes' to five or more of the following statements, then your organization may have an 'acceleration culture' (p.85):

- Is it hard to get important things done because too many other activities diffuse focus?
- Is there a tendency to drive the organization to the limits of its capacity?
- Does the company value hard effort over tangible results?
- Are employees made to feel guilty if they leave work early?
- Do employees talk a lot about how big their workload is?
- Are managers expected to act as role models by being involved in multiple projects?
- Is 'no' a taboo word, even for people who have already taken on too many projects?
- Is there an expectation that people must respond to emails within minutes?
- After work, do staff keep their mobile phones on because they feel they need to be reachable?

Motown turnaround

The context

Detroit, in Michigan, has a population of over 4 million people. It was once the fourth largest city in America. In the early twentieth century, Henry Ford and other motor car manufacturers made Detroit famous as the automotive capital of the world; Detroit is also known as *Motor City* and *Motown*. But decades of decline, starting in the 1970s, have made Detroit famous as America's worst urban disaster story, as an iconic city in America's Midwestern rust belt.

The problem

Oil crises in the 1970s meant that customers wanted smaller, fuel-efficient vehicles, not the 'gas guzzlers' that Detroit made. In the late twentieth century, with falling employment in the motor industry, and with other businesses leaving, Detroit's population fell. As skilled

workers found employment elsewhere, the proportion of poor people in the city's population increased. These factors led to a smaller tax base, lower property prices, abandoned homes, and higher crime rates. The city administration was corrupt, and several officials (including the mayor) were imprisoned. In 2011, half of Detroit's property owners failed to pay their taxes.

By 2013, Detroit was bankrupt, and US$18.5 billion in debt. When the current mayor, Mike Duggan, was elected in 2013, 40 per cent of the city's street lights and 25 per cent of the fire hydrants were not working, and 40,000 properties were vacant. The city had stark racial, economic, and social divisions.

The solution

Duggan's priority was to reverse the decline. He describes his strategy as 'focusing on the boring': 'get the boring stuff right – street lights, fire hydrants, ambulance response times – and the rest falls into place. If each individual person says, OK my job is to get the grass cut in the parks; my job is to get the tractors repaired 20 per cent faster to get the grass cut in the parks – turnaround occurs. People get into public service because something in their heart wants them to help people, and over time the bureaucracy beats that idealism out of them. We are trying to bring idealism back'. Duggan has weekly meetings with residents, in their homes, where he asks them what he can fix next.

The outcomes

Bankruptcy brought some debt relief. Wealthy Detroit families invested in redevelopment which brought sports teams and businesses back to the city. Entrepreneurial start-ups came to Detroit for its low costs, light traffic, and because 'rust belt' became trendy. Now the street lights work, the fire hydrants have been repaired, and the city's population is growing again. In 2018, Duggan bid to host the new US headquarters for Amazon. 'Mike Duggan is an unremarkable guy who has done unremarkable things to achieve extraordinary results' (based on Hagen, 2018).

CRITICAL THINKING — Mike Duggan seems to be transforming Chicago without a 'management textbook' plan for change. Why do you think he has been so successful?

How can an organization escape from the acceleration trap? Be clear about strategy and goals. Stop less important work. Have a system that identifies more and less important initiatives. And 'declare an end to the current high-energy phase'. At one company studied by Bruch and Menges, the chief executive insisted that managers identify only three 'must-win battles', to concentrate attention and energy, instead of the 'ten top priority goals' with which they used to work.

✓✓✓   **EMPLOYABILITY CHECK** (self-management)

Your colleagues keep their mobile phones on all the time, evenings and weekends, just in case 'something comes up' at work. You want to have better work–life balance. But if something does come up, and you don't respond, this could damage your career. How will you manage this tension?

Change and the individual

David Schneider and Charles Goldwasser (1998) introduced 'the classic change curve' (Figure 19.2). In the middle of the curve, sits a 'valley of despair', suggesting that that change can mean loss and pain for those who are affected by it. Schneider and Goldwasser argue that this is probably inevitable in most cases of change, and that is useful to be aware of this and to weaken the impact if possible:

'A leader of change must anticipate employees' reactions, another key factor in the process. As shown [figure 19.2], these reactions occur along a 'change curve'. The blue line represents what is, unfortunately, typical. Unrealistically high expectations at the outset of a programme lead to a relatively deep 'valley of despair' when change doesn't come as quickly or easily as anticipated. Over time, employees do see a 'light at the end of the tunnel' and the change eventually produces some positive results. The red line illustrates what is possible with effective change management: a less traumatic visit to the valley and greater results as the programme reaches completion' (Schneider and Goldwasser, 1998, p.42).

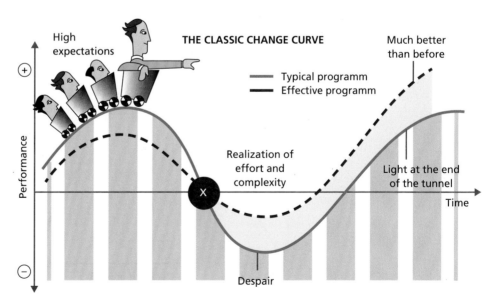

Figure 19.2: The classic change curve
Source: Elrod and Tippett (2002)

Coping cycle the emotional response to trauma and loss, in which we experience first denial, then anger, bargaining, depression, and finally acceptance.

The classic change curve draws on research concerning how individuals cope with traumatic personal loss, such as the death of a close relative. Elizabeth Kübler-Ross (1969) argued that we deal with loss by moving through a series of stages, each characterized by a particular emotional response. The coping cycle has since been used to help understand responses to major organizational changes.

The five stages in the Kübler-Ross coping cycle are defined in Table 19.1. This is an 'ideal' model. We may not all experience the same sets of responses. We may omit stages, revisit some, or pass through them more or less quickly than others. This can be a useful diagnostic tool. If we know where in the response cycle a person is, we could offer helpful support.

Yerkes–Dodson law a psychology hypothesis which states that performance increases with arousal, until we become overwhelmed, after which performance falls.

Just how much pressure can we take from organizational change? Psychology has long argued that the relationship between arousal, or sensory stimulation, on the one hand, and human performance, on the other, varies systematically, in the form of an 'inverted U' function. This is known as the Yerkes–Dodson law (Figure 19.3), named after Robert M. Yerkes and John D. Dodson (1908).

The Yerkes–Dodson law argues that task performance increases with arousal, stimulation, and pressure. This explains why the time you spend revising for an examination seems

Table 19.1: The coping cycle

Stage	Response
Denial	Unwillingness to confront the reality; 'this is not happening'; 'there is still hope that this will all go away'
Anger	Turn accusations on those apparently responsible; 'why is this happening to me?'; 'why are you doing this to me?'
Bargaining	Attempts to negotiate, to mitigate loss; 'what if I do it this way?'
Depression	The reality of loss or transition is appreciated; 'it's hopeless, there's nothing I can do now'; 'I don't know which way to turn'
Acceptance	Coming to terms with and accepting the situation and its full implications; 'what are we going to do about this?'; 'how am I going to move forward?'

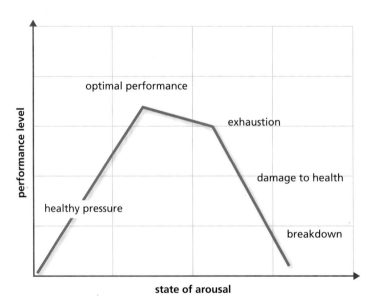

Figure 19.3: Pressure and performance – the inverted-U function

"So basically you are looking for books on changing everyone except yourself

to become more productive as the examination date draws closer. Here is the basis for the claim: 'I work better under pressure'. However, this hypothesis also says that, if the pressure gets too high, the individual will become stressed and exhausted, and performance will fall. This explains why, when you delayed all of your revision until the night before, you did badly the following day.

Performance may be low if a job is repetitive and boring, where arousal is low. Performance can sometimes be improved in such settings with background music, conversation, and job rotation. Now suppose that the job is enriched and becomes more interesting, responsible and demanding, making more use of the individual's skills and knowledge. As the level of pressure increases, performance is likely to increase. However, a point will eventually be reached where the pressure becomes so great that it is overwhelming rather than stimulating. At this point fatigue and stress set in, and eventually ill-health and breakdown can occur if the pressure continues to escalate.

The Yerkes–Dodson law applied to work settings is summarized in Table 19.2, which plots changes in response, experience and performance for escalating pressure levels. Deciding the optimal level of pressure is difficult, because this depends on the individual. Also, appropriate levels of stimulation depend on the difficulty of the task. If the task is easy, more stimulation can be applied. Music destroys our concentration during a chess game, but is enjoyable while backing up computer files.

As we have seen, organizational change can generate such pressure. How can we tell what levels of pressure people are experiencing, or when people are getting 'too close to the edge'? There are many proxy measures that show when people are suffering excess pressure: staff turnover, sickness rates, unexplained absences, accidents and mistakes, customer complaints, grievances. Physical appearance also changes as people become stressed, and interpersonal relationships can become strained.

Table 19.2: The pressure–performance relationship explained

Pressure level	Response	Experience	Performance
Very low	Boredom	Low levels of interest, challenge and motivation	Low, acceptable
Low to moderate	Comfort	Interest aroused, abilities used, satisfaction, motivation	Moderate to high
Moderate to high	Stretch	Challenge, learning, development, pushing the limits	High, above expectations
High to unrealistic	Stress	Overload, failure, poor health, dysfunctional coping behaviour	Moderate to low
Extreme	Panic	Confusion, threat, loss of self-confidence, withdrawal	Low, unacceptable

What did they find? Resourcing organizational change

Rene Wiedner and colleagues (2017) are interested in the support provided for organizational changes, which are known to fail when resources are inadequate. Confidence in and commitment to change, and experimentation with different options, can be encouraged by having access to the right financial and human resources. Experience shows, however, that the success of major changes is not guaranteed even where large amounts of resources are available.

The researchers studied links between available resources and the success of change in three healthcare settings in the UK National Health Service (NHS). These involved contracting for hospital services, contracting for community care, and contracting for mental health services. The NHS has been under pressure

Rene Wiedner

to cut costs, while maintaining quality, at a time when demand for health-care is rising. Changes to the hospital and community care practices were felt to be strategic priorities, so they were well resourced, and their change agents had a lot of freedom. In contrast, the mental health practice was not seen as a priority, and their budget and administrative support resources were cut. The researchers gathered information over four years, using a combination of observation, interviews, and a wide range of organizational documents.

What did they find? Which NHS organizations experienced the most profound changes, and why? **(Answers in chapter Recap.)**

Readiness and resistance

The American composer, John Cage, once said: 'I can't understand why people are frightened of new ideas. I'm frightened of the old ones.' (www.quotationspage.com)

From a practical change implementation perspective, it is usually useful to ask the question: are the conditions right, or do we have to do some preliminary work before we go ahead? One approach to preparing the ground is based on the concept of *readiness for change*.

Readiness for change
a predisposition to welcome and embrace change.

Readiness for change is a predisposition, perhaps even impatience, to welcome and embrace change. Where readiness is high, change may be straightforward. Readiness depends on understanding the need for change, knowing the direction and the goal, having a clear plan, and enough resources and capable people to implement it. Where the ingredients are in place, and readiness is high, resistance may be localized and weak. If readiness is low, implementation will be more difficult, and some 'groundwork' may be required in order to increase levels of readiness among those who are going to be affected. Readiness factors can potentially be managed. Timing can also be important. Some readiness factors may strengthen naturally, on their own, as events unfold.

🖐 **STOP AND SEARCH**   YouTube for *Can the aftermath of organizational change be positive?* (1:03).

Alannah Rafferty et al. (2013) view change readiness as an individual attitude which has both cognitive and emotional (or 'affective') dimensions. 'Collective readiness' for change, of a group or organization, is based on the shared beliefs which develop through social interaction and shared experiences. Underpinning an individual's change readiness, they argue, are five beliefs:

1. *Discrepancy*: the belief that change is needed.

2. *Appropriate*: the belief that the proposed change is an appropriate response.

3. *Efficacy*: the individual's perceived capability to implement the change.

4. *Principal support*: the belief that the organization (management, peers) will provide resources and information.

5. *Valence*: the individual's evaluation of the personal costs and benefits; no benefits, no overall positive evaluation of readiness.

Alannah Rafferty

CHANGE
HAPPENS
(but not to me)

Individual readiness is demonstrated through support for, openness towards, and commitment to change. These attitudes and behaviours can be influenced by three sets of factors. The first concerns external pressures, including industry and technology changes, new regulations, and professional group memberships. The second set of factors concerns 'internal context enablers', including change participation and communication processes and leadership. The third set of factors concern personal characteristics and include needs, values and traits such as self-confidence, risk tolerance, dispositional resistance to change and self-efficacy.

From a management perspective, therefore, individuals' readiness for change can be assessed, and can also be influenced. The research evidence points in particular to the power of the internal enablers. Individual readiness for change can be influenced by processes that are designed to enhance participation in decisions, by high-quality change communications, and by perceptions of the organization's history of change (previous experience, support for change, congruence of values). Again, there are practical steps that can increase the probability that a change initiative will be welcome and successful – and most of those steps involve little or no cost.

Readiness for change may of course be low. Past experience, and the perceived nature and impact of the proposed changes, may make it difficult to influence readiness levels. Those who are responsible for progress may therefore have to address resistance to change.

Resistance to change
an unwillingness, or an inability to accept or to discuss changes that are perceived to be damaging or threatening to the individual.

Change has positive and negative aspects. On the one hand, change implies experiment and the creation of something new. On the other hand, it means discontinuity and the dismantling of traditional arrangements and relationships. Despite the positive attributes, change can be resisted because it involves confrontation with the unknown, and loss of the familiar. It is widely assumed that resistance to change is natural. Many people find change both painful and frustrating.

There are many sources of resistance to change, but the main ones seem to be:

- *Self-interest*: We want to protect a status quo with which we are content and regard as advantageous. Change may threaten to push us out of our 'comfort zone'. We develop vested interests in organization structures and technologies. Change can mean loss of power, prestige, respect, approval, status and security. Change can also be inconvenient, disturbing relationships and other arrangements that have taken time and effort to establish. It may force an unwelcome move, and alter social opportunities. Perceived and actual threats to interests and values are likely to generate resistance. We have a personal stake in our knowledge and skills, and may not be willing to see these made redundant.

- *Misunderstanding*: We are more likely to resist change if we do not understand the reasons behind it, or its nature and consequences. Resistance can thus be reduced by improved understanding. However, if managers have little trust in employees, information about change may be withheld, or distorted. If employees distrust managers, information may not be believed. Incomplete and incorrect information create uncertainty and rumour, which increases the perception of threat, and also raises defensiveness. The way in which change is introduced can thus be resisted, rather than the change itself.

CUTTING EDGE Organizational change and insider threats

Rosalind Searle
(photo credit:
Adam Scott)

Charis Rice

Rosalind Searle and Charis Rice (2018) have been exploring the effect of organizational change on counterproductive work behaviour (CWB). CWB can be minor: time wasting, holding back information. But CWB can also be extremely damaging: destroying systems, removing confidential documents, passing information to malicious others, 'playing dumb'. Can this behaviour be predicted and avoided?

Searle and Rice studied a 'security critical' UK organization which was undergoing continual and significant physical and cultural changes. Some staff were engaged through these changes, but others became disengaged and behaved in deviant ways. As well as conducting a workforce survey, the researchers interviewed senior and middle managers, staff, and stakeholders who had been involved with insider threats. They found that the changes had four characteristics which had reduced trust in management, triggered cynicism and feelings of injustice, and encouraged CWB:

1. The changes created an unpredictable working environment, which was distracting.
2. There was inadequate communication – incomplete, inaccurate, or untimely.
3. Leadership at all levels was seen to be inconsistent.
4. The change processes were seen as poor or unfair, and this was felt most severely by those who lost power and influence.

The researchers identified four types of CWB perpetrators:

- *Omitters*: break rules unintentionally without realizing the implications of their actions
- *Slippers*: occasionally commit CWB – removing documents, being rude to others
- *Retaliators*: angry individuals who cause deliberate harm through small acts, as either

  Passive withdrawers: reducing effort, cooperation, and attention, or

  Active revengers: deliberately sabotaging organization systems

- *Serial transgressors*: disengaged individuals who routinely commit a range of CWB, undermining management and increasing security risks

Searle and Rice conclude that organizations can develop resilience and reduce the chance of CWB during change by:

- making sure that HR processes are fair and consistent
- encouraging the reporting of CWB as part of the organization's culture and values
- communicating change initiatives regularly, consistently and transparently
- assessing the vulnerability of individuals and teams affected by changes
- leaders acting as role models, demonstrating acceptable behaviours such as concern for others.

 **STOP AND SEARCH**   YouTube for *Rosalind Searle* (3:12).

Different assessments

We each differ in how we see and evaluate the costs and benefits of change. A major threat for me can be a stimulating challenge for you. Contradictory assessments are more likely to arise when communication is poor. As we have seen, communication is a component of effective change implementation, and this can be key to creating a common understanding of what is going to happen.

Low tolerance for change

We differ in our abilities to cope with change and uncertainty. Change that requires us to think and behave in different ways can challenge our self-concept. We each have ideas about our abilities and our strengths. One response to change may thus be self-doubt; 'can I handle this?'. Some people have a low tolerance for ambiguity and uncertainty. The anxiety and apprehension that they suffer may lead them to oppose even potentially beneficial changes.

How can resistance be managed? Different individuals and groups are likely to be affected in different ways, and are likely to react differently. To anticipate and manage these reactions, it helps to understand each **stakeholder**, or stakeholder group affected by a particular change.

Stakeholder anyone who is concerned with how an organization operates, and who will be affected by its decisions and actions.

Stakeholder mapping is a widely used method for deciding how to manage the different individuals and groups who are affected by change. This approach involves categorizing stakeholders on two dimensions. The first concerns power and influence. Can a particular individual or group give strong support or pose a serious threat to the initiative? Or perhaps they have little influence, and their views will not count for much. The second concerns what those individuals and groups expect to win or lose from the change; some may have high stakes, and others a low level of interest. Stakeholders can be plotted on the matrix shown in Figure 19.4.

Change leaders should thus pay close attention to influential stakeholders with a high level of interest in the outcomes of the change – those in quadrant 2. This group has the power to 'make or break' the change. However, degrees of power, and stakes in change, can themselves change. And such changes can be brought about by the way in which those stakeholders and the change process itself are managed. Those in quadrant 1, who are influential but with low interest, may find that their stakes in the outcomes are higher if components of the change are redesigned in ways that affect them. In this way, stakeholders in quadrants 1 and 4 can migrate to quadrants 2 and 3 respectively, creating either more support for the proposed changes, or greater resistance.

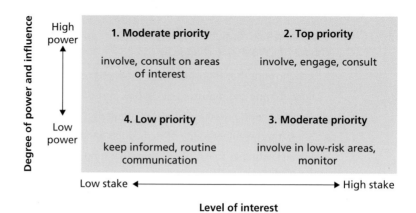

Figure 19.4: Stakeholder mapping matrix

> **CRITICAL THINKING**
>
> Your university has decided to scrap conventional written examinations. Assessments will now take place online. Students' answers to multiple choice questions will be computer graded and checked by administrative staff. Assignments and essays will be marked by artificially intelligent systems developed by the university's computing support unit, and programmed to detect plagiarism. Draw a stakeholder mapping matrix for this change. Does this matrix suggest any problems facing those who want to implement the change? What are the implications for stakeholder management in this case?

Methods for managing resistance

Different stakeholders must be managed differently. Allies need to be 'kept on side', while opponents need to be converted, or perhaps discredited and marginalized. John Kotter and Leo Schlesinger (2008) identify six methods for managing resistance. The advantages and disadvantages of each of these methods are summarized in Table 19.3. These methods can of course be used in combination. While education, participation and support are most likely to be the norm, there will be situations where negotiation, manipulation and coercion may be seen as appropriate.

Table 19.3: Methods for dealing with resistance to change

Method	Advantages	Disadvantages	Use when resistance is caused by
Education and communication	Increases commitment, merges opposing views	Takes time	Misunderstanding and lack of information
Participation and involvement	Reduces fear, uses individual skills	Takes time	Fear of the unknown
Facilitation and support	Increases awareness and understanding	Takes time and can be expensive	Anxiety over personal impact
Negotiation and agreement	Helps to reduce strong resistance	Can be expensive and encourage others to strike deals	Powerful stakeholders whose interests are threatened
Manipulation and cooptation	Quick and inexpensive	Future problems from those who feel they were manipulated	Powerful stakeholders who are difficult to manage
Explicit and implicit coercion	Quick and overpowers resistance	Change agent must have power; risky if people are angered	Deep disagreements and little chance of consensus

Resistance is not necessarily damaging. Donald Schön (1963) argued that resistance was not just desirable, but necessary, in order to prevent the implementation of weak ideas and ineffective proposals. In some settings, a difference of opinions can be constructive if this exposes the dimensions of an argument or the full range of consequences – positive and negative – of a change proposal. Rick Maurer (2010, p.23) argues that, 'Sometimes we need to hear the resistance in order to know that our plans are doomed to failure'.

CRITICAL THINKING Faced with resistance to a desirable change, would you ever recommend manipulation and threat, or would you regard these methods as unprofessional and unethical in all circumstances?

Jeffrey and Laurie Ford (2009, p.100) argue that, 'Even difficult people can provide valuable input when you treat their communication with respect and are willing to reconsider some aspects of the change you're initiating'. They identify five ways in which resistance can be used productively:

1. *Encourage dialogue*: keep the conversation alive, increase awareness of the change ideas, and allow those affected to think through the implications.

2. *Clarify the purpose*: help those affected to understand why their roles have to change.

3. *Consider new possibilities*: accept if useful the ideas of those resisting; the most outspoken are often closest to the operations affected, and care about getting it right.

4. *Listen to the voices*: encourage participation and engagement; people want to be heard, and noting concerns can generate novel and valuable options.

5. *Deal with the past*: current responses to change can be based on previous failures, in which today's managers were not involved; it may be necessary to resolve any 'leftover' issues before going ahead with new plans.

✓✓✓ **EMPLOYABILITY CHECK** (people management, leading and managing change)

You manage a team of six people in an open-plan office. Some minor changes to the office layout will make it much easier for people and visitors to move around. However, and to your surprise, your team is strongly resisting these changes. How will you deal with this?

Estée Lauder: time for a makeover

The context

Founded in 1946, and based in New York, Estée Lauder is a multinational cosmetics company, making skin-care, makeup, perfume and haircare products. The company owns several well-known brands including Aramis, Aveda, Bobbi Brown, Clinique, DKNY, Jo Malone, Smashbox, and Tommy Hilfiger.

The problem

When their president and chief executive, Fabrizio Freda, joined the company in 2008, the brand was dated and

→

the company's market value was shrinking. The company had a traditionally older customer base, and sales revenue was falling.

The solution

One of Freda's first challenges was to persuade younger customers to buy Estée Lauder products. Millennials were a key target customer group, because they buy more cosmetic products than their parents, and they are not loyal to particular brands. Freda made a number of changes:

- The company continued its strategy of brand acquisitions – including Smashbox, Becca and Too Faced – to broaden customer appeal and reduce the traditional dependence on skin care; online sales were introduced to complement the traditional focus on department stores.

- Selling to Asia and Latin America reduced the company's dependence on the US market.

- Freda set up a five-person in-house team called The Compass, to forecast beauty industry trends ten years ahead. This group's forecasts have been accurate, including predicting the growth in demand for new 'instant results' skincare products.

- He hired more Millennials, who now make up 67 per cent of the workforce.

- He set up a 'reverse mentoring' scheme, pairing senior leaders with younger colleagues. Freda's own mentor taught him how to use Facebook: 'She shows me what's new on Instagram or YouTube or the new retail model that she would shop in. Most importantly, I learn what's cool'.

The outcomes

By 2018, the company's market value had risen eightfold, from US$6.6 billion to $53 billion, and the share price had tripled since 2007 – outperforming the share price of their French rival L'Oréal by 165 per cent. These changes were made during and after the global financial crisis of 2008. Freda commented, 'You should never let a big crisis pass without taking advantage of doing all the changes, because during a normal period it's less clear to the people why they have to change, and there is more resistance' (based on Daneshkhu, 2018).

CRITICAL THINKING   Fabrizio Freda at Estée Lauder (see box above) exploited a crisis in order to weaken resistance to the organizational changes that he wanted to introduce. Do you think that is acceptable, ethical, leadership behaviour?

Participation and dictatorship

Taoist approach to change leadership

When it comes to change, Richard Pascale and Jerry Sternin (2005) argue that the leader should be a facilitator, not a 'path breaker'. This means encouraging the 'positive deviants' who are already doing things differently and better, and finding ways 'to engage the members of the community you want to change in the process of discovery, making them the evangelists of their own conversion experience' (p.74). To illustrate this approach, they quote the well-known Taoist poem written by Lao-tzu:

Learn from the people
Plan with the people
Begin with what they have
Build on what they know
Of the best leaders
When the task is accomplished
The people all remark
We have done it ourselves

The participative approach to organizational change was first made popular through the work of Lester Coch and John French (1948) at the Harwood Manufacturing Corporation in Marion, Virginia. The company made pyjamas, and employees complained about frequent changes in work methods and pay rates. Absenteeism was high, efficiency was low, output was restricted deliberately, and employees were aggressive towards supervisors. Most of the grievances concerned the fact that, as soon as they had learned a new job, and started to earn bonuses, they were moved to another task. This meant that they had to start learning all over again, during which time they lost the bonus.

Coch and French designed an experiment with three production groups, each with a different level of participation in changes. One group of 18 hand pressers had to accept changes imposed by the production department. A second group of 13 pyjama folders sent three representatives to discuss and approve new methods. In a third group of 15 pyjama examiners, everyone took part. The performance of the non-participating group did not improve, and hostility to management remained high. In contrast, the performance of the 'total participation' group rose to a level higher than before the experiment. Some months later, the initial non-participation group were brought together again for a new pressing job. This time, they participated fully in the changes, which resulted in a rapid increase in efficiency. This experiment confirmed that it was not the people involved but the way in which they were treated that affected resistance to or acceptance of change.

Since then, employee participation has been standard advice for managers seeking to encourage a welcoming and creative approach to change. However, participative methods have been challenged by the work of two Australian researchers, Doug Stace and Dexter Dunphy (Stace and Dunphy, 2001). They first define the scale of change, from incremental (fine tuning) to transformative (similar to our Figure 19.1). They then identify four styles of change:

Collaborative	Widespread employee participation in key decisions
Consultative	Limited involvement in setting goals relevant to areas of responsibility
Directive	The use of authority in reaching decisions about change and the future
Coercive	Senior management impose change on the organization

Plotting scale of change against style of change produces the matrix in shown in Figure 19.5. This identifies four strategies: participative evolution, charismatic transformation, forced evolution, and dictatorial transformation. Their approach is a contingency model which recommends using an approach which fits the context. Stace and Dunphy argue that participative strategies are time-consuming as they expose conflicting views that are difficult to reconcile. Where organizational survival depends on rapid and strategic change, dictatorial transformation is more appropriate:

'Perhaps the toughest organizational change program in Australia in recent years has been the restructure of the New South Wales Police Force. The person leading that restructure is Police Commissioner Peter Ryan. Ryan was appointed from the UK to stamp out corruption in the force and modernize it. In his own words, he initially adopted a management style that was 'firm, hard and autocratic, and it had to be that because that is what the organization understood' (Stace and Dunphy, 2001, p.185).

CRITICAL THINKING

Dictatorial transformation? Coercion? Surely these methods are more likely to generate hostility and resistance, and reduce organization performance? In what circumstances – if any – do you think it is appropriate to exclude others from participating in change that affects them?

	Incremental change strategies	Transformative change strategies
	Participative evolution	*Charismatic transformation*
Collaborative–consultative modes	Use when the organization needs minor adjustment to meet environmental conditions, where time is available, and where key interest groups favour change	Use when the organization needs major adjustments to environmental conditions, where there is little time for participation, and there is support for change
	Forced evolution	*Dictatorial transformation*
Directive–coercive modes	Use when minor adjustments are required, where time is available, but where key interest groups oppose change	Use when major changes are needed, with no time for participation, and no internal support for change, but where this is necessary for survival

Figure 19.5: The Stace–Dunphy contingency approach to change implementation

Do you want kale with that?

The context

The American fast food company McDonald's is based in Chicago, Illinois, and is one of the world's largest employers, with a global chain of 37,000 outlets. Despite the company's success, McDonald's faces criticism for its unhealthy menu (burgers and fries), its industrial-style food production methods, and low-skill, boring, low-wage jobs ('McJobs').

The problem

When Steve Easterbrook became global chief executive in 2015, customer tastes were changing, and sales had fallen for the first time in a decade. Millennials in particular wanted tastier and fresher food. The company had been slower than its competitors to recognize and respond to these trends. Easterbrook said, 'People's palates are getting broader and they're far more interested in where the food comes from, what's in it and how it gets there.'- Customers were going to rival chains, and McDonald's had to 'sharpen up' fast.

The solution

Easterbrook's turnaround strategy was radical. He replaced almost all of the global leadership team, many of whom were accustomed to working at a slower pace, and had a lower risk appetite. He also cut several layers of middle management, reducing overheads. This also streamlined the bureaucracy, allowing the company to introduce new products and services more quickly. The menu across the whole chain was revised, with healthier food, gourmet burgers, artisan buns, and locally sourced fresh beef rather than frozen. Customers placed their orders at touchscreen kiosks, food was cooked fresh, and delivered to their tables. A home delivery service was introduced.

The outcomes

Easterbrook's radical approach appears to have been successful. Profits have grown, returns to shareholders have increased, and McDonald's market value doubled, to US$140 billion, between 2015 and 2018. The chain now sells vegan burgers in Scandinavia and kale salad in California. These options are not yet available in the UK (based on Duke, 2018).

CRITICAL THINKING   Steve Easterbrook (see box above) changed almost the whole of the company's top leadership team and cut layers of middle managers. Should leaders be ruthless when implementing radical organizational change?

 **STOP AND SEARCH**   YouTube for *Steve Easterbrook: McDonald's CEO on Turnaround Plan, Customer Growth* (12:28).

Why change, when you can innovate?

'Anyone who has never made a mistake has never tried anything new'   *Albert Einstein*

'Trying is the first step towards failure'   *Homer Simpson*

Is 'change' an appropriate response to a fast-paced unpredictable world? To keep ahead of the competition, organizations must be creative and innovative. In the public sector, innovation is necessary in order to meet rising public expectations with regard to service cost and quality.

Innovation is not limited to new products. Most organizations also want to create new ways to organize, to develop new working practices, and to provide customers, clients or patients with innovative services. As a result, the term *innovation* is usually defined in broad terms, to mean the adoption of any device, system, process, programme, product, or service *new to that organization*. This definition means that an idea may have been developed and applied elsewhere, but if it is 'new in this setting', then it can be regarded as an innovation *here*.

Innovation and creativity are often seen as individual attributes, and inventors are sometimes seen as mavericks. However, innovation and creativity also have *organizational* dimensions. Despite commercial pressures, some organizational norms, systems, and practices are receptive to innovation, while others encourage risk avoidance. Creative people in the wrong organization are likely to be less creative. However, ordinary people in an organization that encourages innovation are more likely to become more creative in that environment.

The innovation process also has a *cultural* dimension. Some countries (e.g. United States, Germany) are considered to be more innovative than others (e.g. Britain, China). These differences are difficult to explain, and are influenced by social norms as well as by low investment in new technology, and weak training practices. The individual, organizational, and national cultural influences on creativity and innovation are summarized in Figure 19.6.

Clayton Christensen et al. (2000) distinguish between sustaining innovations, and disruptive innovations. Sustaining innovations improve existing products and processes: a more efficient motor car, a mobile phone with video capability. Disruptive innovations introduce wholly new processes and services: electric cars, social networking websites. Innovations that are disruptive do not necessarily mean chaos and upheaval; what is disrupted is often traditional ways of thinking and acting, and old business models. Truly disruptive innovations may be harder to manage, because they are riskier, and because there are no established routines for handling them.

Innovation the adoption of any device, system, process, programme, product, or service new to a particular organization.

Sustaining innovations innovations which make improvements to existing processes, procedures, services and products.

Disruptive innovations innovations which involve the development of wholly new processes, procedures, services and products.

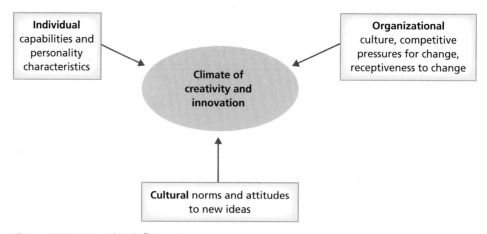

Figure 19.6: Innovation influences

CRITICAL THINKING

Identify three to five sustaining innovations that have affected you over the past year.

Identify three to five disruptive innovations that have affected you. Did you welcome these innovations because they were beneficial, or did you have cause to complain?

Christensen et al. (2015, p.46) have complained that disruptive innovation has been misunderstood. As we have done here, the term is often applied to any major or radical change. However, the original concept meant something more specific:

> '"Disruption" describes a process whereby a smaller company with fewer resources is able to successfully challenge established incumbent businesses. Specifically, as incumbents focus on improving their products and services for their most demanding (and usually most profitable) customers, they exceed the needs of some segments and ignore the needs of others. Entrants that prove disruptive begin by successfully targeting those overlooked segments, gaining a foothold by delivering more-suitable functionality – frequently at a lower price. Incumbents, chasing higher profitability in more-demanding segments, tend not to respond vigorously. Entrants then move upmarket, delivering the performance that incumbents' mainstream customers require, while preserving the advantages that drove their early success. When mainstream customers start adopting the entrants' offerings in volume, disruption has occurred.'

In other words, disruption is a *process* – not just a new product or service. Christensen et al. argue that we need to understand the nature of innovation in order to manage it effectively. Small competitors, for example, can often be ignored – unless they are on a 'disruptive trajectory', and then the incumbent has to act to counter the threat. This is different from head-on competition for an incumbent's traditional customers.

CRITICAL THINKING

Using the original definition of disruptive innovation as a process, is the transportation company Uber a disruptive innovator? How about Netflix – does it fit the growth pattern of a disruptive innovator?

Operational innovation inventing entirely new ways of working.

Commercial companies have always focused on innovations with new technology, products and services. Michael Hammer (2004) also advocates a focus on operational innovation finding new ways to lead, organize, work, motivate and manage.

Hammer (2004) describes a motor vehicle insurance company which introduced 'immediate response claims handling', operating 24 hours a day. This involved scheduling visits to customers by claims adjusters who worked from their vehicles, and would turn up within nine hours. Previously, when the adjusters were office-based, it could take over a week to inspect a damaged vehicle. Handling 10,000 claims a day, adjusters were empowered to estimate damage and write cheques on the spot. These operational innovations led to huge cost savings, with fewer staff involved in claims handling, better fraud detection, and reduction in payout costs. Customer satisfaction and loyalty also improved.

Not a good Kodak moment

Kodak invented the first digital camera in 1975, and the first megapixel camera in 1986. So why did the development of digital photography drive Kodak to bankruptcy in 2012? In 1975, the costs of this new technology were high, and the image quality was poor. Kodak believed that it could take at least another ten years before digital technology began to threaten their established camera, film, chemical, and photo printing paper businesses. That forecast proved to be accurate, but rather than prepare, Kodak decided to improve the quality of film, with sustaining innovations. With hindsight, it is easy to spot that mistake. But the market information available to management from the 1970s through the 1990s, combined with the company's financial performance, made the switch to digital appear risky. In 1976, Kodak accounted for 90 per cent of film and 85 per cent of camera sales in America. Kodak's annual revenues peaked in 1996, at $16 billion; profits in 1999 were $2.5 billion. However, success encouraged complacency, and reinforced confidence in the brand. Analysts noted that it might be unwise to switch from making 70 cents on the dollar with film, to 5 cents with digital. But by 2011, Kodak's revenues had fallen to $6.2 billion, and the company was reporting losses.

Kodak's competitor, Fuji, recognized the same threat, and decided to switch to digital while generating as

much return as possible from film, and developing new lines of business, including cosmetics based on chemicals used for film processing. Both companies had the same information, but came to different assessments, and Kodak was too slow to respond. By the time Kodak began to develop digital cameras, mobile phones with built-in digital cameras had become popular.

Kodak invented the technology, but did not recognize just how disruptive an innovation digital would prove to be, making their traditional business obsolete (Barabba, 2011; *The Economist,* 2012).

The best practices puzzle

Why do 'best practices' not spread more quickly? New ideas and methods that are developed and work well in one context are often not adopted elsewhere. This is known as 'the best practices puzzle, and it is not new. Don Berwick (2003) notes that the treatment for scurvy, first identified in 1601, did not become standard practice in the British navy until 1865, over 260 years later. Why the delay?

Everett Rogers (1995) argues that the probability of an innovation being adopted is increased when it is seen to have the following six properties:

1. Advantageous when compared with existing practice
2. Compatible with existing practices
3. Easy to understand

4. Observable in demonstration sites
5. Testable
6. Adaptable to fit local needs.

For innovations to diffuse effectively, Rogers argues that the perceptions of adopters, and properties of the organizational context, are as important as the innovation itself. Unless you believe that an innovation will help you to improve on current methods, you are unlikely to be persuaded. New ideas have to be adapted (sometimes significantly) to fit local conditions.

The stethoscope will never be popular

'That it [the stethoscope] will ever come into general use, notwithstanding its value, I am extremely doubtful; because its beneficial application requires much time, and it gives a good deal of trouble both to the patient and practitioner, and because its whole hue and character is foreign, and opposed to all our habits and associations. It must be confessed that there is something ludicrous in the picture of a grave physician formally listening through a long tube applied to a patient's thorax, as if the disease within were a living being that could communicate its condition to the sense without.'

(John Forbes, in the preface to his translation of *De L'Auscultation Mediate ou Traite du Diagnostic des Maladies des Poumons et du Coeur* [A Treatise on Diseases of the Chest and on Mediate Auscultation], by R.T.H. Laennec, T & G Underwood, London, 1821.)

Rogers also argues that the adoption of innovations follows a pattern. First, small numbers adopt, followed by 'take-off', then achieving a critical mass of adopters. Finally, saturation is reached, typically short of 100 per cent (you never convince everyone). The pattern of diffusion depends on local circumstances, and is influenced by the five groups in Table 19.4.

Table 19.4: From innovators to laggards

Innovators	Usually the first in their social grouping to adopt new approaches and behaviours, a small category of individuals who enjoy the excitement and risks of experimentation
Early adopters	Opinion leaders who evaluate ideas carefully, and are more sceptical and take more convincing, but take risks, help to adapt new ideas to local settings, and have effective networking skills
Early majority	Those who take longer to reach a decision to change, but who are still ahead of the average
Late majority	Even more sceptical and risk averse, wait for most of their colleagues to adopt new ideas first
Laggards	Viewed negatively by others, the last to adopt new ideas, even for reasons that they believe to be rational

How simple rules encourage innovation

'To illustrate how simple rules can foster innovation, consider the case of Zumba Fitness. That company's fitness routine was developed when Alberto Perez, a Columbian aerobics instructor, forgot to take his exercise tape to class and used what he had at hand – a tape of salsa music. Today, Zumba is a global business that offers classes at 200,000 locations in 180 countries to over 15 million customers drawn by the ethos, 'Ditch the workout. Join the party'.

'Zumba's executives actively seek out suggestions for new products and services from its army of over 100,000 licensed instructors. Other companies routinely approach Zumba with possible partnership and licensing agreements. In fact, it is deluged by ideas for new classes (Zumba Gold for baby boomers), music (the first *Zumba Fitness Dance Party* CD went platinum in France), clothing, fitness concerts, and video games, such as Zumba Fitness for Nintendo Wii. Zumba's founders rely on two simple rules that help them quickly identify the most promising innovations from the flood of proposals they receive. First, any new product or service must help the instructors – who not only lead the classes but carry Zumba's brand, and drive sales of products – to attract clients and keep them engaged. Second, the proposal must deliver FEJ (pronounced 'fedge'), which stands for 'freeing, electrifying joy' and distinguishes Zumba from the 'no pain, no gain' philosophy of many fitness classes' (Sull, 2015, pp.2–3).

Diffusion of a new idea relies initially on innovators and early adopters, and subsequently on the pace at which the early and late majority are swayed. These are not fixed categories. An individual may be an early adopter of one idea, but a late adopter of another. To be an innovator or a laggard depends as much on the context as on the individual. This perspective has two conclusions. First, diffusion is rarely a sudden event, but a protracted process, triggered and developed by contextual factors as well as individual perceptions and interpersonal communications. Second, there is no 'one best way' to influence people to change; interventions must consider individual needs and perceptions.

Building a creative climate

Rosabeth Moss Kanter (1983; 1989) contrasts what she calls *segmentalist* organization cultures from *integrative* cultures. A segmentalist culture is preoccupied with hierarchy, compartmentalizes its decision making, and emphasizes rules and efficiency. An integrative culture is based on teams and collaboration, adopts a holistic approach to problem solving, has no time for history or precedent, and emphasizes results. It is not surprising to find Kanter arguing that bureaucratic, mechanistic segmentalist cultures tend to be 'innovation smothering', and that adaptable, organic, integrative cultures are innovation stimulating.

Exploring how organizations smother and stimulate innovation, Göran Ekvall (1996; 1999) developed the concept of *creative organization climate*. Climate is a combination of attitudes, feelings, and behaviours, which exists independently of the perceptions and understandings of individual members (see box, 'How simple rules encourage innovation'). The ten dimensions of the creative climate are summarized in Table 19.5.

Table 19.5: Dimensions of the creative organization climate

Dimension	Promoting innovation	Inhibiting innovation
Challenge	People experience challenge, joy and meaning and invest high energy	People are alienated, indifferent, unchallenged, and are apathetic
Freedom	People make contacts, give and receive information freely, discuss problems, make decisions, take initiative	People are passive, rule-bound, anxious to remain within their well-established boundaries
Idea support	People listen to each other, ideas and suggestions are welcomed	Suggestions are quickly rejected as faults and obstacles are found
Trust and openness	High trust climate, ideas can be expressed without fear of ridicule	Low trust climate, people are suspicious of each other, afraid to make mistakes
Dynamism and liveliness	New things happening all the time, new ways of thinking and problem solving	Slow jog with no surprises, no new projects or plans, everything as usual
Playfulness and humour	Relaxed atmosphere with jokes and laughter, spontaneity	Gravity and seriousness, stiff and gloomy, jokes improper
Debates	Many voices are heard, expressing different ideas and viewpoints	People follow an authoritarian pattern without questioning
Conflicts	Conflict of ideas not personal, people behave in a mature manner, based on psychological insight	Personal and emotional tensions, plots and traps, gossip and slander, climate of 'warfare'
Risk taking	Rapid decisions and actions, experimentation rather than detailed analysis	Cautious, hesitant mentality, work 'on the safe side', 'sleep on the matter', set up committees before deciding
Idea time	Opportunities to test fresh ideas that are not part of planned work activity, and these chances are exploited	Every minute booked and specified, pressures mean that thinking outside planned routines is difficult

CRITICAL THINKING

Think of an organization with which you are familiar, perhaps one where you are currently employed, or one where you have worked recently. Assess that organization's climate on Ekvall's ten dimensions, in terms of how it promotes or inhibits innovation.

Where the organization inhibits innovation, what practical steps could management take to strengthen the creative climate, to promote innovation?

To be an innovator and lead change

Do you want to be a change leader, implementing new ideas? Being creative and driving change can be frustrating, as well as rewarding. The development of something new often involves such a high failure rate. (James Dyson's famous bagless vacuum cleaner went through over 5,000 prototypes to get to the winning design.) A lot of trial and error is necessary, to find out what works best. Despite corporate mission and values statements encouraging staff to be creative and to take risks in a 'no blame culture', management does not always look favourably on failure. In some cases, being innovative can jeopardize your job security and career.

Rosabeth Moss Kanter's (2002) rules for stifling innovation

1. Regard a new idea from below with suspicion, because it's new, and because it's from below.

2. Insist that people who need your approval to act first go through several other levels of management to get their signatures.

3. Ask departments or individuals to challenge and criticize each others' proposals. That saves you the job of deciding; you just pick the survivor.

4. Express criticism freely, and withhold praise. That keeps people on their toes. Let them know that they can be fired at any time.

5. Treat identification of problems as signs of failure, to discourage people from letting you know when something in their area isn't working.

6. Control everything carefully. Make sure people count anything that can be counted, frequently.

7. Make decisions to reorganize or change policies in secret, and spring them on people unexpectedly. That keeps people on their toes.

8. Make sure that requests for information are fully justified, and make sure that it is not given out to managers freely. You don't want data to fall into the wrong hands.

9. Assign to lower level managers, in the name of delegation and participation, responsibility for figuring out how to cut back, lay off, move people around, or otherwise implement threatening decisions you have made. And get them to do it quickly.

10. And above all, never forget that you, the higher-ups, already know everything important about this business.

Amy Edmondson (photo credit: Jenya Eliseeva)

Amy Edmondson (2011) argues that not all change failures are bad. She explores the reasons for failure on a spectrum ranging from blameworthy to praiseworthy (Table 19.6). At one extreme, deviance, breaking the rules deliberately, is blameworthy. At the other end of the spectrum, experiments to discover whether something new will work or not are praiseworthy. Do managers recognize this spectrum, and treat employees accordingly?:

'When I ask executives to consider this spectrum and then to estimate how many of the failures in their organization are truly blameworthy, their answers are usually in single digits – perhaps 2 per cent to 5 per cent. But when I ask how many are *treated* as blameworthy, they say (after a pause or a laugh) 70 per cent to 90 per cent. The unfortunate consequence is that many failures go unreported and their lessons are lost' (Edmondson, 2011, p.50).

Edmondson advises promoting experimentation, not blaming individuals when organizational circumstances have contributed to failure, and analysing carefully the reasons for failures, going beyond obvious and superficial reasons. In addition, the 'messengers' who speak out with bad news, awkward questions, concerns, or make mistakes, 'should be rewarded rather than shot'. Management should welcome the knowledge, and work out how to fix the problem. It is also necessary, she concludes, to be clear about which acts are blameworthy, and hold people accountable.

Table 19.6: Blameworthy and praiseworthy failures

Blameworthy	*Deviance*	Individual chooses to violate prescribed process or practice
	Inattention	Individual inadvertently deviates from specifications
	Lack of ability	Individual lacks skills, conditions, or training for the job
	Process inadequacy	Competent individual follows faulty or incomplete process
	Task challenge	Individual faces a task too difficult to be executed reliably
	Process complexity	A complex process breaks down under novel conditions
	Uncertainty	People take reasonable actions leading to undesired results
	Hypothesis testing	Failed experiment to see whether an idea will work
Praiseworthy	*Exploratory testing*	Experiment to expand knowledge leads to undesired result

Source: Edmondson (2011)

Who are your most capable strategic change leaders?

Research by the consultancy Pricewaterhouse Coopers (PwC) has found that only 8 per cent of senior managers have the strategic leadership capabilities required to drive organizational change (Lewis, 2015). From a survey of 6,000 managers in Europe, the highest proportion of strategic leaders were women over the age of 55 – a group which has traditionally been overlooked in the search for change leadership skills. PwC defines a strategic leader as someone who has 'wide experience of settings, people, and also of failure, which engenders humility or perspective and resilience, so that they know what to do when things don't work'. Women over 55 were more likely to:

- see situations from multiple perspectives
- think and work outside the existing system
- identify what needs to change
- be able to persuade or inspire others to follow them
- use positive language
- be open to frank and honest feedback
- exercise power courageously.

One consultant (female) at PwC said, 'Historically women over the age of 55 would not have been an area of focus, but as the research suggests, this pool of talent might hold the key to transformation and in some cases, business survival' (Lewis, 2015).

Change with Thai shrimps

The context

The seafood conglomerate, Thai Union, is the world's largest producer of canned tuna, and is based in Thailand. It is a global business, with revenues of US$4.5 billion and 50,000 employees. Half of the shareholders and 90 per cent of sales are outside Thailand. Most consumers have probably never heard of the company, but they will know its brands: John West in the UK, Chicken of the Sea in the US, Mareblu in Italy, Petit Navire in France.

The problem

In 2015, Associated Press (AP) issued a report accusing the company of exploiting slave labour in its shrimp peeling sheds. Migrant workers from Myanmar, including

children, were working long hours for low pay in dirty and cramped conditions, and were in debt to labour brokers. For Thai Union, this was a public relations disaster. Thirapong Chansiri, the company's chief executive, was shocked. Thai Union came under immediate pressure from British and American customers – Tesco, Sainsbury, Costco, Walmart – and faced criticism from human rights watchdogs and the environmental group Greenpeace. The US State Department downgraded Thailand's ranking on Trafficking in Persons to the lowest score. The European Union gave Thailand a 'yellow card' for fishing practices, and threatened to ban its exports.

The solution

Chansiri had to restore the company's reputation. Most importantly, the company culture had to change. He immediately cancelled contracts with shrimp processors, and brought the business in house. He developed a 'conduct and sustainability' code of practice, which applied to Thai Union and its suppliers. Thai Union was the first Thai seafood company to adopt a 'zero recruitment fee' policy, preventing labour brokers from exploiting migrant workers. A commitment to sustain-

ability changed labour and fishing practices on the company's boats. Thai Union introduced 'traceability' of all its tuna, and improved working conditions on its fishing fleet. In 2017, the company signed an agreement with Greenpeace to remove 'exploitative and unsustainable practices' from its supply chain, changing what had been an adversarial relationship with the environmental group.

The outcomes

Activists have continued to criticize the company. But Greenpeace and the International Labour Organization have supported the changes that have been introduced. Thai Union is listed on the Dow Jones Sustainability Index Emerging Markets, and the FTSE4Good Emerging Index. The company plans to increase sales to $8 billion by 2020. Reflecting the culture change that had taken place, the chief executive said, 'Sustainability and innovation became part of our business strategy. Because of the effort we have made so far, I want to turn it into a positive element for the company that differentiates us from the others in the industry' (based on Reed, 2018).

 **STOP AND SEARCH**   YouTube for *Thai Union Corporate Introduction* (2:12).

CRITICAL THINKING   What attributes do you think Thirapong Chansiri (see box above) has that make him an effective change leader?

Table 19.7: Trends in organizational change

Change in the twentieth century	Change in the twenty-first century
One theme among many	A management preoccupation
Importance of participation and involvement	Recognition of need for directive methods
Rational-linear model of change management	Messy, untidy change processes
Change driven by small elite groups	Change is everyone's responsibility
Focus on change agents	Focus on disruptive innovators
Implementation method is critical	Implementation must be tailored to context
Changes must be frequent and fast	Need to consider timing and pacing with care
Aimed at organizational effectiveness	Aimed at competitive advantage and survival

Why are some people more innovative than others, and make it look easy and effortless? It is often assumed that 'creatives' are special people with unique skills. However, Jeff Dyer, Hal Gregersen and Clayton Christensen (2011) argue that anyone can be innovative by using the right approach. Their research suggests that the best innovators have five habits:

Associating	Innovators are good at seeing connections between things that do not appear to be related, drawing ideas together from unrelated fields
Questioning	Innovators are always challenging what others take for granted, asking 'why is this done this way – why don't we do it differently?'
Observing	Innovators watch the behaviour of customers, suppliers, competitors – looking for new ways of doing things
Experimenting	Innovators tinker with products and business models, sometimes accidentally, to see what happens, what insights emerge
Networking	Innovators attend conferences and other social events to pick up ideas from people with different ideas, who may face similar problems, in other fields

Individuals can become more innovative by following this advice, and by collaborating with 'delivery-driven' colleagues. Dyer and colleagues argue that organizations also need to encourage these habits, stimulating employees to connect ideas, to challenge accepted practices, to watch what others are doing, to take risks and try things out, and to get out of the company to meet others.

The perceived need for rapid and continual adjustment to events and trends has made change management a key organizational issue. Change is no longer something which disturbs the stable fabric from time to time, but is an ever-present feature. However, some commentators argue that change is damaging when it is rapid and ongoing, and that the initiative stream should be carefully timed and paced. The significance of context, in shaping the opportunities for and directions of change, is now better understood and appreciated. Finally, the organizational capability to change rapidly and often is seen as contributing to competitive advantage and survival, and not just to performance improvement. These trends are summarized in Table 19.7.

Home viewing

Inside Job (2010, director Charles Ferguson, narrated by Matt Damon) examines the global financial crisis of 2008. Over the previous decade, deregulation allowed the finance industry to take risks that older rules would have discouraged. Identify the stakeholders (including academics), their competing interests, their relationships, and their efforts to conceal sensitive information. How did those interests, relationships, and 'information games' contribute to the crisis? The film concludes that, despite the crisis, the underlying system has remained much the same. How has the sector been able to avoid fundamental changes to financial regulation? What does this account reveal about the nature of organizational change in general?

↩ RECAP

1. *Explain why effective change management is important, to organizations and to individuals.*

   - Organizations that do not adapt to changing circumstances may see their performance deteriorate, and may go out of business.

   - The pace of organizational change means that individuals need to 'future proof' their careers by constantly gaining new knowledge and skills.

2. *Identify the main external and internal triggers of organizational change.*

   - Change can be triggered by factors internal and external to the organization, and can also be proactive by anticipating trends and events.

   - Change varies in depth, from shallow fine tuning, to deep transformational change.

   - The broad direction of change in most organizations is towards becoming less mechanistic and bureaucratic, and more adaptive, responsive and organic.

3. *Explain the issues that management must take into account to ensure that change is successful.*

   - The 'basics' of change implementation include clear benefits, strong leadership, powerful change agents, constant communication, employee engagement, short-term wins, and making sure that change is embedded in the culture.

   - The timing and pacing of change are also important: too slow, and organizational survival may be at risk, but too fast, and staff may be overloaded, and demotivated.

4. *Understand the typical characteristics of human responses to change.*

   - Emotional responses to traumatic changes differ, but the typical coping cycle passes through the stages of denial, anger, bargaining, depression and acceptance.

   - The Yerkes–Dodson Law states that the initial response to pressure is improved performance, and that increasing pressure leads to fatigue, and ultimately breakdown.

   - The evidence suggests that continuous organizational changes lead to work intensification, and burnout.

5. *Understand the nature of resistance to change and approaches to overcoming it.*

   - Resistance to change has many sources, including self-interest, lack of trust and understanding, competing assessments of the outcomes, and low tolerance of change.

   - One technique for addressing possible resistance to change, as well as identifying and strengthening support for change, is stakeholder analysis.

→

- The main prescribed approach for avoiding or dealing with resistance is participative management, in which those affected are involved in implementation.

- The use of manipulation and coercion to implement change are advocated by some commentators, but the 'political' role of management in change is controversial.

6. *Explain the advantages and limitations of participative methods of change management.*

- Participative methods can generate creative thinking and increase employee commitment to change, but this process is time-consuming.

- Some commentators argue that rapid and major corporate transformations are more successful when implemented using a dictatorial or coercive style.

7. *Understand the significance of innovation, and the distinction between sustaining, disruptive and operational innovations.*

- Innovation has become a strategic imperative in order to compete and to survive.

- Sustaining innovations are those which improve existing services and products.

- Disruptive innovations introduce completely new services and products.

- Operational innovations concern new ways of organizing, managing and working.

8. *Explain the organizational properties that stimulate and stifle innovation respectively.*

- A creative organizational climate is one which promotes lively and challenging debate, freedom of expression, trust and openness, humour, risk taking, giving people time to try out new ideas – and has a high level of receptiveness to new ideas.

- Organization properties that stifle innovation include rigid rules, suspicion of new ideas, low trust, criticism freely given, jokes seen as improper, aversion to risk, and tight time pressures.

- Creative individuals outside creative organizational climates are likely to stop innovating; anyone in a creative climate is capable of being creative, and will be encouraged to innovate.

9. *Recognize the challenges facing innovative change leaders.*

- The successful development of something new is exciting and challenging, but can involve a high rate of failure before the winning design is found.

- Organizations vary in their tolerance for and treatment of failure; even 'praiseworthy' failures can attract blame and punishment.

- We can become more innovative by practising the five habits of associating, questioning, observing, experimenting and networking.

RECAP: What did they find? resourcing organizational change

Wiedner et al. (2017) found that:

- Despite being very well-resourced, hospital and community care contracting practices were largely unchanged over the period of this study.

- Contracting mental health services changed and improved to such a degree that it became a local and national showpiece for strategic change initiatives.

- The practices that were prioritized and well-resourced attracted the attention of a wide range of powerful stakeholders, so these practices came under more intense scrutiny and challenge, and change agents had to devote time to managing all of the interested parties.

- Those working in mental health benefited from the lack of interest in what they were doing, as this allowed them to implement changes quickly, without becoming involved in lengthy negotiations.

Revision

1. What are the basic rules of change implementation? Although these appear to be simple, the failure rate of organizational changes is high. How can that failure rate be explained?

2. What are the main sources of resistance to organizational change, and how should resistance be managed?

3. Organizations are advised to change rapidly in order to compete to survive. What dangers come with this advice?

4. What are the main types of innovation, and how can an organization develop a climate that encourages individuals to be more creative?

Research assignment

Choose an organization that has experienced major change. Arrange to interview two managers who were involved in implementing this change. Using John Kotter's guide to corporate transformation, find out how the changes were managed. For each step, find out what was involved, how was it done, and how well did that work:

1. Establish a sense of urgency.
2. Form a guiding coalition.
3. Create a vision.
4. Communicate the vision.
5. Empower people to act on the vision.
6. Create 'short-term wins'.
7. Consolidate improvements to produce further change.
8. Embed new approaches in the organization's culture.

Finally, ask your managers for their assessment of these changes. Once you have discovered how the changes were managed, rate the organization on a 1 to 10 scale for each heading (1 = very poor; 10 = very good). A score of 8 suggests disaster; a score of 80 implies success. To what extent is your assessment consistent with that of the managers who you interviewed?

Now develop an assessment that answers the following questions:

- What should management have done differently in implementing these changes?
- What should management do differently the next time when implementing organizational change?

Springboard

Julia Balogun, Veronica Hope Hailey and Stefanie Gustafsson (2016) *Exploring Strategic Change*. Harlow: Pearson (fourth edition). Wide ranging theoretical and practical text on change management, advocating a contingent approach which tailors change implementation to the context, based on the 'change kaleidoscope' tool.

Alexa Clay and Kyra Maya Phillips (2015) *The Misfit Economy: Lessons in Creativity from Pirates, Hackers, Gangsters and Other Informal Entrepreneurs*. New York: Simon & Schuster. Argues that idealistic 'misfits' make the best innovators because they are tired of the discipline and obedience encouraged by most organizations – and they want to change that.

Robert Colvile (2016) *The Great Acceleration: How the World is Getting Faster, Faster*. London: Bloomsbury. Argues that almost everything that we do – walking, travelling, communicating, processing information, buying things, you name it – is getting faster. He also claims that this is beneficial, becasuse we are wealthier, and better informed, than we were. However, organizations that are not able to keep up with the pace of change will suffer (Borders, Blockbuster, Kodak), and many of us now feel overwhelmed by too much information.

Ian Palmer, Richard Dunford and David A. Buchanan (2016) *Managing Change: A Multiple Perspectives Approach*. Chicago: McGraw-Hill (third edition). Comprehensive text exploring need for change, what changes, managing resistance, implementation methods, sustainability, and the capabilities of change agents, managers or leaders.

OB cinema

Charlie's Angels (2000, director Joseph McGinty Nichol – 'McG' – 2000): DVD track 14: 0:35:57 to 0:38:10 (3 minutes). Clip begins outside the Red Star corporation headquarters; clip ends when Alex says, 'Better yet, can anyone show me?'.

Alex (played by Lucy Liu) masquerading as an 'efficiency expert' leads the Angels into the Red Star corporation headquarters building, in an attempt to penetrate their security systems. As you watch this three-minute clip, paying careful attention to details, consider the following questions:

1. Is this an organization that stimulates or smothers creativity and innovation?

2. How do you know? What are the clues, visual and spoken, that support your assessment of the organization culture?

Chapter exercises

1: Mis-managing change

Objectives
1. To identify tactics that can be used to delay, modify or sabotage organizational changes.

2. To establish how easy it is to disrupt organizational changes.

3. To identify 'best practice' guidelines for effectively managing change, by reversing the mis-management advice.

Briefing
This exercise involves 'reverse brainstorming': finding bad solutions to a problem rather than, as usual, looking at 'best practice' (Hagen et al., 2016). The problem is this. Senior management have announced plans for a radical organizational restructuring. The aims are to reduce hierarchy, streamline decision making, cut costs, and give customers a better service. You have seen the plans, and you don't like them. Some people will lose their jobs. Many people – including you – will have bigger workloads and will have to learn new skills. Customers will no longer have a named company contact. Response to customer queries will be slower than before.

Divide into groups of three or four to decide if there is anything that can be done about this. You may have personal experience – on which you can draw – of previous organizational changes that did not go well. What happened in those cases? Your team brief is as follows:

• Identify the tactics that you or others in the organization could use in order to delay, modify or sabotage management's reorganization plans.

- These tactics could involve *not* doing certain things, as well as taking active steps.
- Be creative: draw up as wide a range of spoiling tactics as possible – but they must be practical and realistic.
- Assess what the use of these tactics will cost, in financial terms.
- Assess the probability of these spoiling tactics having the desired result.

Present your findings to the whole class. If time allows, reverse the question, turning your thinking into positives: what should be the 'best practice' guidelines for effectively managing change?

2: Force-field analysis

Objective   1. To demonstrate the technique of force-field analysis in planning change.

Briefing   Force-field analysis is a method for assessing the issues supporting and blocking movement towards a given set of desirable outcomes, called the 'target situation'. The forces can be scored, say from 1 (weak) to 10 (strong), to calculate (approximately) the balance of forces.

If the driving forces are overwhelming, then the change can go ahead without significant problems. If the resisting forces are overwhelming, then the change may have to be abandoned, or delayed until conditions have improved.

If the driving and resisting forces are more or less in balance, then the force-field analysis can be used to plan appropriate action. The extent to which the force field is balanced is a matter of judgement. Used in a group setting, this method provides a valuable way to structure what can often be an untidy discussion covering a wide range of factors and differing perceptions.

For this analysis, your target situation is 'to double the time that I spend studying organizational behaviour'. In groups of three, complete the analysis using the following table as a guide. First identify as many driving and restraining forces as you can. Then, reach a group consensus on a score for each of those forces, from 1 (weak) to 10 (strong). Finally for this stage of the analysis, calculate the totals for each side of the force field.

Target situation: to double the time that I spend studying organizational behaviour

Scores	Driving forces >>>>>	<<<<< Restraining forces	Scores
	= Total driving forces score	Total restraining forces score =	

When you have completed this analysis, and added the scores, estimate the probability (high, medium or low) of reaching your target situation *if the force field stays the same*.

Now draw a practical action plan for managing the field of forces that you have identified in order to increase the probability of reaching the target situation. In devising your action plan, remember that:

1. Increasing the driving forces can often result in an increase in the resisting forces. This means that the current equilibrium does not change, but is maintained with increased tension.

2. Reducing the resisting forces is preferable as this allows movement towards the desired outcomes or target situation without increasing tension.

3. Group norms are an important force in shaping and resisting change.

References

Appelbaum, S.H., Habashy, S., Malo, J.-L. and Shafiq, H. (2012) 'Back to the future: revisiting Kotter's 1996 change model', *Journal of Management Development,* 31 (8): 764–82.

Barabba, V. (2011) *The Decision Loom: A Design for Interactive Decision-Making in Organizations,* Axminster, Devon: Triarchy Press.

Berwick, D.M. (2003) 'Disseminating innovations in health care', *Journal of the American Medical Association,* 289(15): 1969–75.

Bruch, H. and Menges, J.I. (2010) 'The acceleration trap', *Harvard Business Review,* 88(4): 80–86.

Christensen, C.M., Bohmer, R. and Kenagy, J. (2000) 'Will disruptive innovations cure health care?', *Harvard Business Review,* 78(5): 102–12.

Christensen, C.M., Raynor, M. and McDonald, R. (2015) 'Disruptive innovation', *Harvard Business Review,* 93(12): 44–53.

Coch, L. and French, J.R.P. (1948) 'Overcoming resistance to change', *Human Relations,* 1: 512–32.

Cummings, S., Bridgman, T. and Brown, K.G. (2016) 'Unfreezing change as three steps: rethinking Kurt Lewin's legacy for change management', *Human Relations,* 69(1): 33–60.

Daneshkhu, S. (2018) 'Estée Lauder chief Fabrizio Freda on winning over millennials', *Financial Times,* 12 March, p.24.

Duke, S. (2018) 'The wizard from Watford shaking up McDonald's, *The Sunday Times Business Section,* 7 January, p.6.

Dyer, J., Gregersen, H. and Christensen, C.M. (2011) *The Innovator's DNA: Mastering the Five Skills of Disruptive Innovators,* Harvard Business School Press, Boston, MA.

Edmondson, A. (2011) 'Strategies for learning from failure', *Harvard Business Review,* 89(4): 48–55.

Ekvall, G. (1996) 'Organizational climate for creativity and innovation', *European Journal of Work and Organizational Psychology,* 5(1): 105–23.

Ekvall, G. and Ryhammar, L. (1999) 'The creative climate: its determinants and effects at a Swedish university', *Creativity Research Journal,* 12(4): 303–10.

Elrod II, P.D. and Tippett, D.D. (2002) 'The "death valley" of change', *Journal of Organizational Change Management,* 15(3): 273–291.

Ford, J.D. and Ford, L.W. (2009) 'Decoding resistance to change', *Harvard Business Review,* 87 (4): 99–103.

Frey, C.B., Osbourne, M.A. and Homes, C. (2016) *Technology at Work v2.0: The Future Is Not What It Used To Be.* London and Oxford: Citigroup/University of Oxford, Oxford Martin School.

Hagen, N. (2018) 'Halting Detroit's decline', *Financial Times,* 8 January, p.24.

Hagen, M., Bernard, A. and Grube, E. (2016) 'Do it all wrong!: using reverse brainstorming to generate ideas, improve discussions, and move students to action', *Management Teaching Review,* 1(2): 85–90.

Hammer, M. (2004) 'Deep change: how operational innovation can transform your company', *Harvard Business Review,* 82(4): 84–93.

Hughes, M. (2011) 'Do 70 per cent of all organizational change initiatives really fail?', *Journal of Change Management,* 11 (4): 451–64.

Jacquemont, D., Maor, D. and Reich, A. (2015) *How to Beat the Transformation Odds.* New York: McKinsey & Company.

Ji, Y.-Y., Gutherie, J.P. and Messersmith, J.G. (2014) 'The tortoise and the hare: the impact of employee instability on firm performance', *Human Resource Management Journal,* 24 (4): 355–73.

Kanter, R.M. (1983) *The Change Masters: Corporate Entrepreneurs at Work.* London: George Allen & Unwin.

Kanter, R.M. (1989) *When Giants Learn to Dance: Mastering The Challenges of Strategy, Management, and Careers in the 1990s.* London: Unwin.

Kanter, R.M. (2002) 'Creating the culture for innovation', in Frances Hesselbein, Marshall Goldsmith and Iain Somerville (eds), *Leading For Innovation And Organizing For Results.* San Francisco: Jossey-Bass, pp.73–85.

Kotter, J.P. (2007) 'Leading change: why transformation efforts fail', *Harvard Business Review,* 85(1): 96-103 (first published 1995).

Kotter, J.P. (2012) 'Accelerate!', *Harvard Business Review,* 90 (11): 44–52.

Kotter, J.P. and Schlesinger, L.A. (2008) 'Choosing strategies for change', *Harvard Business Review,* 86(7/8): 130–39 (first published 1979).

Kübler-Ross, E. (1969) *On Death and Dying.* Toronto: Macmillan.

Lewin, K. (ed.) (1951) *Field Theory in Social Science: Selected Theoretical Papers by Kurt Lewin,* London: Tavistock Publications, (UK edition published 1952, edited by Dorwin Cartwright edn).

Lewis, G. (2015) 'Women over 55 best suited to lead transformational change, finds PwC', *People Management,* 18 May, http://www.cipd.co.uk/pm/peoplemanagement/b/weblog/archive/2015/05/18/

women-over-55-best-suited-to-lead-transformational-change-finds-pwc.aspx [accessed January 2019]

Maurer, R. (2010) *Beyond the Walls of Resistance.* Austin, TX: Bard Books (second edition).

Palmer, I., Dunford, R. and Buchanan, D.A. (2016) *Managing Organizational Change: A Multiple Perspectives Approach.* New York: McGraw Hill, (third edition).

Pascale, R.T. and Sternin, J. (2005) 'Your company's secret change agents', *Harvard Business Review,* 83 (5): 72–81.

Rafferty, A.E., Jimmieson, N.L. and Armenakis, A.A. (2013) 'Change readiness: a multilevel review', *Journal of Management,* 39(1): 110–35.

Reed, J. (2018) 'Cleaning up an abusive supply chain', *Financial Times,* 22 April, p.24.

Rogers, E. (1995) *The Diffusion of Innovation.* New York: Free Press, (fourth edition).

Schneider, D. M. and Goldwasser, C. (1998) 'Be a model leader of change', *Management Review,* 87(3): 41–45.

Schön, D.A. (1963) 'Champions for radical new inventions', *Harvard Business Review,* 41 (2): 77–86.

Searle, R. and Rice, C. (2018) *Assessing and Mitigating the Impact of Organisational Change on Counterproductive Work Behaviour: An Operational (Dis)trust Based Framework.* Coventry: Centre for Research and Evidence on Security Threats/Economic and Social Research Council.

Stace, D. and Dunphy, D. (2001) *Beyond the Boundaries: Leading and Re-creating the Successful Enterprise.* Sydney: McGraw Hill.

Stouten, J., Rousseau, D.M. and De Cremer, D. (2018) 'Successful organizational change: integrating the management practice and scholarly literatures', *Academy of Management Annals,* 1 (published online early): 1–93.

Sull, D. (2015) 'The simple rules of disciplined innovation', *McKinsey Quarterly,* May, pp.1–10.

The Economist (2012) 'The last Kodak moment?', 14 January, p.25.

Wiedner, R., Barrett, M. and Oborn, E. (2017) 'The emergence of change in unexpected places: resourcing across organizational practices in strategic change', *Academy of Management Journal,* 60(3): 823–54.

Yerkes, R.M. and Dodson, J.D. (1908) 'The relationship of strength of stimulus to rapidity of habit-formation', *Journal of Comparative Neurology and Psychology,* 18(5): 459–82.

CHAPTER 20

Decision making

Key terms

decision making

classical decision theory

rational model of decision making

rationality

rational decisions

descriptive model of decision making

behavioural theory of decision making

bounded rationality

maximizing

satisficing

prescriptive models of decision making

explanatory models of decision making

heuristic

bias

certainty

risk

uncertainty

routine decisions

adaptive decisions

innovative decisions

group polarization

risky shift

caution shift

groupthink

brainstorming

nominal group technique

escalation of commitment

evidence-based decision making

decision-based evidence making

Learning outcomes

When you have read this chapter, you should be able to define those key terms in your own words, and you should also be able to:

1. Distinguish between prescriptive, descriptive and explanatory models of decision making and provide an example of each.

2. Distinguish different decision conditions on the basis of risk and programmability.

3. Consider the advantages and disadvantages of group decision making.

4. Identify the factors used to decide whether to adopt individual or group decision making.

5. Match organizational conditions with the decision-making processes that favour them.

Why study decision making?

Decision making is the process of making a choice from among a number of alternatives. Why is the study of decision making important? Within organizations, decisions are made at all hierarchical levels, not just at the top. Both managers and non-managers make them. Herbert Simon (1957) believed that management theory should be based upon the question of choice, and that decision making was the very core of management. Henry Mintzberg (1989) concurred stating that decision making is one of the most important – if not the most important – of all managerial activities, and represents one of the most common and crucial work tasks of managers.

Behind each of the recent organizational scandals (e.g. 'dieselgate' car emissions manipulation; misselling of payment protection insurance (PPI); social media's misuse of personal data; patients dying prematurely in hospitals; and the manipulation of the Libor exchange rates) there was an organizational, group or individual decision. The people affected by those decisions experienced inconvenience, financial loss and death.

Decision making

the process of making choices from a number of alternatives.

Given the central role that decision making plays within organizations and the effect that it has on the lives of all organization members, it is not surprising that it has attracted the attention of practising managers, consultants and researchers. It can be analysed at a number of different levels as Table 20.1 shows. Each level focuses on its own key issues and possesses its own theoretical perspectives. However, the levels are interrelated with one affecting and being affected by the others.

Table 20.1: Levels of decision making

Level of analysis	Key issues	Theoretical perspectives
Individual	Limits to information processing Personal biases	Information processing theory Cognitive psychology
Group	Effects of group dynamics on individuals' perceptions, attitudes and behaviours	Groupthink, group polarization and group cohesiveness
Organizational	Effects of conflicts, power and politics	Theories of organization conflict, power, politics and decision making.

What did they decide? Decision making at Tham Luang

On the 23 June 2018, 12 boys (aged 11–17) and their football coach (25) became trapped in the Tham Luang cave complex in the Chiang Rai region of Thailand. They had entered the cave when it was dry, but sudden heavy rain flooded the cave and blocked their exit. To much rejoicing, the group was found alive and well nine days later on 2 July by two British rescue divers on a rock shelf 4 kilometres from the mouth of the cave. The trapped group received food and medical treatment.

What had been a race against time now became a race against water. Following a dry spell, a deluge was expected to force water levels up in the pocket where the group was taking refuge. The journey from the cave entrance to the group's location took 11 hours – six in and five back out. None of the boys could swim. The oxygen levels in the cave were dropping. The cave in which the

THAILAND CAVE RESCUE

Tham Luang

ENTRANCE

TEAM FOUND

4000 METERS

boys and coach were trapped was a snaking system of caverns. Some parts of the cave were 10 metres high while others were a tight squeeze for a grown man (see diagram). On the fifth day of rescue, a diver who was delivering supplies to the boys, died on his way back.

Once the monsoon rains start, they last until October, and make rescue efforts far more difficult. If the group did not dive, they would have to wait four months for the flood waters to recede. Food and other supplies were prepared for this eventuality. The group was huddled on a small rock ledge. To avoid hypothermia, they needed to keep warm and dry. Rock falls were a problem but the main danger was rising flood levels. The complicated access routes threatened air supplies into the underground chamber and hindered evacuation attempts. The boys had to remain calm and stay on the ledge otherwise they could fall down a crevice in the rock or get washed away by the water. About 1,000 people were involved in the rescue operation including navy divers, military personnel and civilian volunteers. Someone had to make the decision as to how to get them out. There were three options:

1. *Wait for waters to recede*: With food and other essential being delivered by regular diving supply trips, the group could wait for the water levels to drop. They could then leave safely on foot. This could take months and the place where they were living could become flooded.

2. *Drilling*: Boring a shaft down into the mountain to extract the group. The boys are 1 kilometre below the mountain top. This requires heavy equipment, new roads to get it to the drilling spot and a detailed cave survey. Groups are searching the mountain for unknown entrances.

3. *Diving*: The boys would be taught to swim and dive. They would be supplied with diving masks, wetsuits and fins. Dive lines and dive bottles of compressed air would be installed along the tunnels as well as glow sticks to light the path. The boys would swim and walk through the passages. Each boy would have a rescue diver accompanying him.

If the lives of 13 people had been in your hands, what would have been your decision? What did the authorities decide? **(Answers in chapter Recap.)**

Source: based on BBC Online News (2018a)

Models of decision making

Classical decision theory assumes that decision-makers are objective, have complete information and consider all possible alternatives and their consequences before selecting the optimal solution.

The traditional approach to understanding individual decision making is based upon classical decision theory and the rational model of decision making. These were originally developed in economics and they make certain assumptions about people and how they make decisions. The rational economic model of decision making is described in Figure 20.1.

Rational model of decision making assumes that decision making is and should be a rational process consisting of a sequence of steps that enhance the probability of attaining a desired outcome.

"What was the decision making process that led to hiring a cat?"

However, to understand the weaknesses of the rational model of decision making, it is necessary to list its assumptions and demonstrate how they fail to match up to reality. These are shown in Table 20.2.

Step	Example
Recognition of a problem or opportunity ↓	'I need to buy a new car'
Identifying choice criteria ↓	Price Engine (diesel, petrol, electric, hybrid) Reliability Cost per mile Brand image
Assigning weightings to the criteria ↓	Price ---------------------------- 10 Engine ------------------------- 9 Reliability --------------------- 6 Cost per mile ---------------- 8 Brand image ----------------- 4
Gathering data about alternatives ↓	Nissan Toyota Vauxhall Ford
Evaluation alternatives ↓	Nissan Toyota Vauxhall Ford
Selection from among the alternatives ↓	Nissan Toyota Vauxhall Ford
Implementation of preferred alternative	Buy the Ford

Figure 20.1: Rational model of decision making

Table 20.2: Rational model of decision-making assumptions and reality

Assumption	Reality
All alternatives will be considered	• Rarely possible to consider all alternatives since there are too many • Some alternatives will not have occurred to the decision maker
The consequences of each alternative will be considered	• Impractical to consider all consequences • Impractical to estimate many of the consequences considered. • Estimation process involves time and effort
Accurate information about alternatives is available at no cost	• Information available is rarely accurate, often dated, and usually only partially relevant to the problem • Information costs money to be generated or purchased • Decisions have to be made on incomplete, insufficient and only partly accurate information
Decision makers are rational	• Individuals lack the mental capacity to store and process all the information relevant to a decision • Frequently they lack the mental ability to perform the mental calculations required

Information

An information manager reported that on appointment to his job, he was told by his staff that:

The information you have is not what you want.

The information you want is not what you need.

The information that you need is not what you can obtain.

The information that you can obtain costs more than you want to pay.

What you are willing to pay will get you exactly the information you already have.

Source: Beske (2013)

 EMPLOYABILITY CHECK (self-awareness)

Think of some personal decision that you have recently made. How did you make it? Was the result good or bad for you?

Rationality the use of scientific reasoning, empiricism and positivism, along with the use of decision criteria that include evidence, logical argument and reasoning.

Rational decisions decisions that are made using evidence, logical argument and reasoning.

The rational view of decision making employs the concepts of rationality and rational decisions in its discussions and prescriptions. Rationality is equated with scientific reasoning, empiricism and positivism, as well as with the use of decision criteria of evidence, logical argument and reasoning. Rational decisions are decisions which are based on rationality, that is, on a rational mode of thinking rather than on feelings or emotions (Simon, 1986; Langley, 1989)

The rational decision-making model is now being challenged. It is no longer seen as providing an accurate account of how people typically make decisions (if it ever did). Moreover, its prescriptions for making better decisions have proved to be incorrect. Instead, contemporary cognitive research by psychologists has revealed the ways in which decisions are made based on heuristic models, judgements and tacit knowledge. Emotions now play a greater role in decision making. People are increasingly asked and explain not what they think but what they feel. University economics textbooks are being rewritten to match the new realities.

Descriptive model of decision making

Descriptive model of decision making a model which seeks to portray how individuals actually make decisions.

Descriptive models of decision making focus on how individuals actually make decisions. Each decision made by an individual or group is affected by a number of factors. Some of these include:

- Group relationships
- Decision to be made

- Organizational factors
- Individual personality
- Information availability
- Environmental pressures
- Power relationships and political behaviour

The aim of these models is to examine which of these factors are the most important, and how they interrelate to produce the decision that is to be made.

One of the earliest, and still among the most influential descriptive models, is the **behavioural theory of decision making**. It was developed by Richard Cyert, James March and Herbert (Simon, 1960; Cyert and March, 1963). It is called 'behavioural' because it treats decision making as another aspect of individual behaviour. For example, if a researcher interviewed brokers who bought and sold shares in the stock market to determine what factors influenced their decisions, it would be an example of a descriptive approach to decision making. It is also sometimes referred to as the 'administrative model' and it acknowledges that, in the real world, those who make decisions are restricted in their decision processes. Behavioural theory holds that individuals make decisions while they are operating within the limits of bounded rationality. Bounded rationality recognizes that:

- The definition of a situation is likely to be incomplete
- It is impossible to generate all alternatives
- It is impossible to predict all the consequences of each alternative
- Final decisions are often influenced by personal and political factors

The effect of personal and situational limitations is that individuals make decisions that are 'good enough' rather than 'ideal'. That is, they 'satisfice', rather than 'maximize'. When maximizing, decision makers review the range of alternatives available, all at the same time, and attempt to select the very best one. However, when satisficing, they evaluate one option at a time in sequence, until they alight on first one that is acceptable. The option chosen will meet all the minimum requirements for the solution, but may not be the very best (optimal) choice in the situation. Once an option is found, decision makers will look no further. The differences between the rational decision making described previously, and the bounded rationality discussed here are shown in Table 20.3.

Behavioural theory of decision making recognizes that bounded rationality limits the making of optimal decisions.

Bounded rationality a theory which says that individuals make decisions by constructing simplified models that extract the essential features from problems without capturing all their complexity.

Maximizing a decision-making approach where all alternatives are compared and evaluated in order to find the best solution to a problem.

Satisficing a decision-making approach where the first solution that is judged to be 'good enough' (i.e. satisfactory and sufficient) is selected, and the search is then ended.

Table 20.3: Rational decision making and bounded rationality contrasted

Rational decisions makers . . .	Bounded rationality decision makers . . .
Recognize and define a problem or opportunity thoroughly	Reduce the problem to something that is easily understood
Search for a extensive set of alternative courses of action, gathering data on each	Develop a few, uncomplicated and recognizable solutions, comparable to those currently being used
Evaluate all the alternatives at the same time	Evaluate each alternative as it is thought of
Select and implement the alternative with the most value (*maximize*)	Choose the first, acceptable alternative (*satisfice*)

Source: based on Simon (1979) and Kahneman (2003)

CRITICAL THINKING   When you chose your current partner did you maximize or satisfice? Is this distinction a useful way of explaining the decision-making process?

Prescriptive models of decision making

Prescriptive model of decision making

an approach that recommends how individuals should make decisions in order to achieve a desired outcome.

Prescriptive models of decision making recommend how individuals *should* behave in order to achieve a desired outcome. This makes the rational model described earlier, also a prescriptive one. Such models often also contain specific techniques, procedures and processes which their supporters claim will lead to more accurate and efficient decision making. They are often based on observations of poor decision-making processes where key steps may have been omitted or inadequately considered. They are developed and marketed by management consultants as a way of improving organization performance through improved decision making.

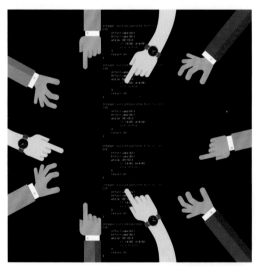

One of the best known prescriptive models of decision making was developed by Victor Vroom and Philip Yetton (1973) and later expanded by Vroom and Arthur Jago (1988). The focus is on decision-making *situations*. It uses seven factors to select the decision making style that is likely to be most effective in any given situation. It is concerned with *how* a leader decides rather than *what* a leader decides. It is concentrates on subordinate participation – the appropriate amount of involvement of the leader's subordinates in making a decision. The model consists of three main elements:

1. Decision participation styles
2. Diagnostic questions with which to analyse decision situations
3. Decision rules to determine the appropriate decision participation style

The model is underpinned by two key concepts – quality and acceptability. The quality of the decision relates to it achieving the aim; the cost of its implementation; and the time taken to implement it. The acceptability of the decision relates to subordinates and anyone else either affected by the decision or who has to implement it. Leaders and managers generally select the highest quality decision that is acceptable.

Decision participation styles

Five decision participation styles are identified: decide, consult individually, consult group, facilitate and delegate. These are shown ranging along a continuum (Table 20.4). These reflect differing amounts of subordinate participation in the leader's decision. As one moves from left to right on the continuum:

- The leader discusses the problem or situation more with others.
- Others' input changes from merely providing information to recommending solutions.
- Ownership and commitment to the decision increases.
- The time needed to arrive at a decision increases.

Diagnostic questions with which to analyse decision situations

It was found that leaders used different decision participation styles in different situations. All of these various styles could be equally effective depending on the situation. To determine which style is most suitable in a given situation Vroom asks seven diagnostic questions. The answers to these seven questions, in the form of 'high' (H) or 'low' (L), should determine the appropriate level of subordinate participation in the decision-making process.

Table 20.4: Participation in decision-making processes

	Leader-centred ←				→ **Group-centred**
Description	**(D) Decide** As leader, you feel your have the information and expertise to make the decision alone and then you either announce or 'sell' it to the group.	**(CI) Consult Individually** As leader, you lack the required information or expertise. You therefore obtain this from your group members individually, either telling them the problem or not. You then make the decision alone.	**(CG) Consult Group** As leader, you explain the situation and provide information to your group Together, solutions are generated and discussed. You then review these recommendations and make the decision alone.	**(F) Facilitate** As leader, you explain the situation and provide information to your group. Acting as facilitator, you reconcile differences and negotiate a solution acceptable to everyone. The final decision is made by you and your group together.	**(D) Delegate** As leader, you explain the situation, provide information, and set the boundaries for the decision to be made. You then delegate responsibility and authority for the final decision to the group who make it themselves. You accept and implement it.
Participants	Leader	Leader and others	Leader and others	Leader and others	Leader and others
Role of participants	Leader generates and evaluates solution alone.	Individuals provide leader with skill or information.	Group generates solutions or recommendations.	Group negotiates a solution with leader.	Group generates, evaluates and makes the decision.
Who makes the decision?	Leader	Leader	Leader (perhaps reflecting group inputs)	Leader and group together	Group

Source: based on Vroom (2000, p.84)

1. *Decision significance* How significant is this decision to the success of the project or organization? If significance is high, then the leader needs to be closely involved.

2. *Importance of commitment* How important is subordinate commitment in implementing the decision? If importance is high, then leaders should involve subordinates.

3. *Leader expertise* What is the level of the leader's information, knowledge or expertise in relation to the problem? If it is low, the leader should involve subordinates to obtain it.

4. *Likelihood of commitment* If the leader were to make the decision alone, would subordinates' commitment to it be high or low? If the answer is high, then subordinate involvement is less important.

5. *Group support for goals* What is the level of subordinate support for the team's or organization's goals with respect to this situation? If it is low, the leader should not allow the group to make the decision alone.

6. *Group expertise* What is the level of skill and commitment that group members have in working together as a team to solve the problem? If it is high, then more responsibility for the decision can be given to them.

7. *Team competence* What is the level of subordinates' skills and commitment in working together as a team to solve the problem? If their skill and desire to work together cooperatively is high, then more responsibility for the decision can be given to them.

Decision rules

The Vroom–Yetton–Jago model provides a set of decision rules in the form of a decision tree to allow the selection of the most appropriate decision-making style as shown in Figure 20.2.

 **STOP AND SEARCH**   YouTube for *Decision Making, Vroom.*

Prescriptive decision-making models are hugely popular in the managerialist literature since they offer executives a step-by-step guide as to how to make a decision. Modern ones combine vast amounts of data and increasingly sophisticated algorithms. Modelling has opened up new ways to improve company performance. These models can make very accurate predictions and guide difficult optimization choices. They also help firms to avoid the common biases that undermine judgements (Rosenzweig, 2014). Indeed big data analytics and machine learning are threatening to make many areas of decision making by managers redundant (**as discussed in Chapter 3**).

	1 — Decision significance: How significant is this decision to the success of the project or organization?	2 — Importance of commitment: How important is subordinate commitment in implementing the decision?	3 — Leader expertise: What is the level of the leader's information, knowledge, or expertise in relation to the problem?	4 — Likelihood of commitment: If the leader were to make the decision alone, would subordinates' commitment to it be high or low?	5 — Group support for goals: What is the level of subordinate support for the team's or organization's goals with respect to this situation?	6 — Group expertise: What is the level of skill and commitment that group members have in working together as a team to solve the problem?	7 — Team competence: What is the level of subordinates' skills and commitment in working together as a team to solve the problem?	
	H	H	H	H	–	–	–	Decide
	H	H	H	L	H	H	H	Delegate
	H	H	H	L	H	H	L	Consult group
P	H	H	H	L	H	L	–	Facilitate
R	H	H	H	L	L	–	–	Consult individually
O	H	H	L	H	H	H	–	Facilitate
B	H	H	L	H	H	L	–	Consult group
L	H	H	L	H	L	–	–	Decide
E	H	H	L	L	–	H	–	Facilitate
M	H	H	L	L	–	L	–	Consult individually
S T A T E	H	L	H	–	–	–	–	Decide
M E	H	L	L	–	–	H	H	Delegate
N	H	L	L	–	–	H	L	Facilitate
T	L	–	–	–	–	–	–	Decide

Figure 20.2: Time-driven model of leadership

Source: adapted from *Organizational Dynamics*, 28(4), Vroom, V.H. Leadership and decision making process, pp.82–94, Copyright 2000, with permission from Elsevier.

Home viewing

Thirteen Days (2001, director Roger Donaldson) is based on the true story of the Cuban Missile Crisis of October 1962, a diplomatic conflict between the United States and (the then) Soviet Union which nearly triggered a nuclear war. It stars Kevin Costner who plays an aide to President John F. Kennedy. What insights did you gain about the process of decision making as a result of watching this film? Make a list of these.

Explanatory model of decision making

Explanatory model of decision making an approach that accounts for how individuals, groups and organizations make decisions.

An explanatory model of decision making explains how a given decision was made. For example, there are studies of military fiascos which examine why generals took or failed to take certain actions. Often these explanations draw upon personality and leadership concepts and theories. The poor decisions made by teams have also been studied using concepts from the group level of analysis such as groupthink and group polarization. These will be examined later in this chapter. Finally, decisions such as whether to acquire or merge with another company have drawn upon the theories of conflict, power and politics and offer explanations at the organizational level.

Heuristic a simple and approximate rule, guiding procedure, shortcut or strategy that is used to solve problems.

Studies have highlighted the limits to rationality and introduced the concept of bounded rationality. What else might affect the individual who makes a decision? Decision making involves choice, and choice requires both careful thought and much information. Excessive information can both overload and delay us. Many managers believe that making the right decision late is the same as making the wrong decision on time. Hence we speed up the process by relying on judgement shortcuts called heuristics to cut through a large maze of information.

Bias a prejudice, predisposition or a systematic distortion caused by the application of a heuristic.

The developing field of behavioural economics considers the role of heuristics and their associated biases in our decision making and represents a further step away from the rational model. These are the mental shortcuts that we use to solve tricky problems and make difficult decisions. Heuristics are simple and approximate rules, guiding procedures, shortcuts or decision strategies; and biases are our prejudices, predispositions or systematic distortions that we apply when using a heuristic.

The leading authors in this field have been Daniel Kahneman, Amos Tversky and Richard Thaler. Human beings have two ways of processing information and making decisions (Kahneman, 2011; Kahneman and Tversky, 2000).

System 1 thinking	Fast, automatic, instinctive and emotional; relies on mental short-cuts; effortlessly generates intuitive answers to problems as they arise
System 2 thinking	Slow, logical and deliberate requiring much cognitive effort

System 1 – thinking fast – uses intuition and rules of thumb to take information and reach conclusions quickly. However, these shortcuts can cause errors, so System 2 – thinking slow – is needed to check whether our intuition is faulty or our judgement clouded by emotions. If our snap-judgements are not corrected by analysis and deliberation, problems of bias will result and poor decisions will be made. The biases in decision making operate at the subconscious level, are virtually undetectable, and have a powerful and immediate impact on individuals' judgement. Some of most common decision-making biases are listed in Table 20.5.

CRITICAL THINKING

Here are three questions. First think fast to obtain your answers: (1) A bat and ball cost £1.10 in total. The bat costs £1.00 more than the ball. How much does the ball cost?; (2) It takes five machines five minutes to make five widgets, how long would it take 100 machines to make 100 widgets? (3) In a pond is a patch of lily pads. Every day, the patch doubles in size. If it takes 48 days for the patch to cover the entire pond, how long would it take for the patch to cover half the pond? The answers to these three questions are *not* 10p, *not* 100 minutes and *not* 24 days, respectively. Now try again, this time think slow (Frederick, 2005, p.27).

Table 20.5: Common decision-making biases

Name of bias	Description
Anchor and adjustment	Judgement made by starting from an initial value or 'anchor', and then failing to adjust sufficiently from that point before making the decision
Availability	Judgement of probability made on the basis of information that is readily available
Bandwagon	Believing in certain outcomes because others believe the same
Confirmation	Placing extra value on information that supports our favoured beliefs; ignoring that which does not; failing to search for impartial evidence
Controllability	Believing we can control outcomes more than is the case leading us to misjudge the riskiness of our actions
Egocentrism	Focusing too narrowly on our own perspective, unable to imagine how others will be affected by our actions.
Loss aversion	Preferring to avoid losses to acquiring gains of the same amount, making us more risk averse than is rational
Optimism	Being excessively optimistic about the likelihood of positive outcomes from our planned actions and underestimating negative consequences
Overconfidence	Overestimating our skills and abilities, taking credit for past positive successes while ignoring the luck that might have been involved
Present	We value immediate rewards more highly than long-term gains
Representative	Basing judgements of probability on the basis of things with which one is familiar
Status quo	Preference for the status quo in the absence of pressure to change it
Sunk cost	Paying attention to unrecoverable, historic costs when considering future actions

Source: based on Kahneman (2011) and Beshears and Gino (2015)

 **STOP AND SEARCH**   You Tube for *Daniel Kahneman: Thinking fast and slow.*

Richard Thaler's contribution to behavioural economics has been to help us understand how one can use the findings of how humans actually think and make decisions to 'nudge' or push them in socially desirable ways e.g. to drive more safely, drink alcohol moderately (Thaler and Sunstein, 2008).

Richard Thaler: father of behavioural economics wins Nobel Prize

 In this video, Gemma Tatlow discusses behavioural economics, explains its relationship to rational decision making, and highlights the contribution of Professor Richard Thaler, 'Father of the Nudge' (3:34).

 **STOP AND SEARCH**   YouTube for *Cognitive biases.*

CRITICAL THINKING   Give an example of how social media and 'fake news' might affect the decision-making processes of customers, employees or managers?

Decision conditions: risk and programmability

Certainty a condition in which managers possess full knowledge of alternatives; a high probability of having these available; being able to calculate the costs and benefits of each alternative; and having high predictability of outcomes.

Table 20.6 distinguishes different types of environmental conditions faced by organizations and labels these 'stable equilibrium', 'bounded instability' (or chaos) and 'explosive instability'. The condition under which a decision is made affects both how it is made and its outcome. Decisions differ in terms of the degree of risk involved and programmability. Every decision is made under conditions of certainty, risk or uncertainty. We shall consider each in turn.

In a situation of **certainty**, no element of chance comes between the alternative and its outcome. All the outcomes are known in advance with 100 per cent certainty. In such circumstances, all that the individual has to do is to select the outcomes with the largest benefit. A situation of total certainty is so rare as to be virtually non-existent. In the past, government bonds which guarantee a fixed rate of interest over a period of time, which would be paid barring the fall of the government, represented an example of certainty. However, as financial instability around the world as shown, even government bonds carry an element of risk.

If decisions in organizations were constantly made in conditions of certainty, managers would not be needed. More junior, cheaper operatives, supplied with a rulebook could replace them. This is the area where AI is beginning to replace professionals in decision making. Managers are paid to make these types of decisions. In reality most organizational decisions are made under conditions of **risk**. Managers (and software) assess the likelihood of various outcomes occurring on the basis of their past experience, research and 'big data'.

Risk a condition in which managers have a high knowledge of alternatives; know the probability of these being available; can calculate the costs and know the benefits of each alternative; and have a medium predictability of outcomes.

Table 20.6: Environmental and decision-making conditions

Environmental condition	Decision-making condition	Characteristics	Example
Stable equilibrium is a state in which the elements are always in, or quickly return to, a state of balance.	Certainty	Alternatives and outcomes known and fully predictable	Fixed interest rate savings accounts
Bounded instability (or chaos) is a state in which there is a mixture of order and disorder, many unpredictable events and changes, and in which an organization's behaviour has an irregular pattern.	Risk	Known alternatives with only probable outcomes predictable	Tomorrow's weather
Explosive instability is a state in which there is no order or pattern whatsoever.	Uncertainty	Alternatives and outcomes poorly understood	Developing a new product

Uncertainty a condition in which managers possess little knowledge of alternatives; a low probability of having these available; can to some degree calculate the costs and benefits of each alternative; but have no predictability of outcomes.

Routine decisions decisions made according to established procedures and rules.

Adaptive decisions decisions that require human judgement based on clarified criteria and are made using quantitative decision tools.

Innovative decisions decisions which address novel problems and lack pre-specified courses of action.

Decisions made under uncertainty are the most difficult since the manager even lacks the information with which to estimate the likelihood of various outcomes and their associated probabilities and payoffs (March and Simon, 1958). Conditions of uncertainty prevail in new markets; those offering new technologies; and those aimed at new target customers. In all these cases there are no historical data from which to infer probabilities. In each case, the situation is so novel and complex that it is impossible to make comparative judgements.

Programmability of decisions

Organization members make many different decisions ever day. Some decisions are routine while others are not. Routine decisions are those which involve the use of pre-established organizational procedures or rules. Routine decision makers are given considerable guidance as to what to do and how to do it through a well-established process; clearly defined goals; and the provision of information sources and decision rules. Examples of routine decisions include the re-ordering of stock items which have fallen to a certain level; the efficient routing of delivery vans; and the scheduling of equipment maintenance. All these decisions tend to be repetitive and programmed. They are made by either low level employees on their own who rely on pre-determined courses of action or increasingly by computers.

Adaptive decisions typically require a form of judgement which is difficult for a computer to make. They involve a range of variables including values and ethical issues, which have to be weighted and compared. Quantitative decision tools such as break-even analysis or a pay-off matrix assist the managers who have to make these 'judgement calls'.

Finally, innovative decisions are made when a unique situation is confronted that has no precedent; when there are no off-the-shelf solutions; and when a novel answer has to be found. Innovative decisions are an outcome of problem solving and frequently deal with areas of the unknown. They are made mainly (but not exclusively) by company professionals or top managers. Within the organizational context, such decisions tend to be rare. Examples would include the decision whether or not to acquire another company, to invest in a new technology, or to adopt a new marketing approach. The differences between these types of decisions are summarized in Table 20.7.

Table 20.7: Routine, adaptive and innovative decisions

Decision type	Routine	← Adaptive →	Innovative
Goals	Clear, specific		Vague
Level	Lower level employees		Upper management
Problem	Well structured		Poorly structured
Process	Computational		Heuristic
Information	Readily available		Unavailable
Level of risk	Low		High
Involvement	Single decision maker		Group decision
Consequences	Minor		Major
Solution basis	Decision rule and procedures		Judgement, creativity
Decision speed	Fast		Slow
Time for solution	Short		Relatively long

Home viewing

Draft Day (2014, director Ivan Reitman) is the story of Sonny Weaver (played by Kevin Costner) who is the general manager of an American football team, the Cleveland Browns. He has the opportunity to rebuild his team, but personal problems intervene to affect the situation. The film illustrates the complicated process of decision making under pressure. As you watch the film, consider how his decisions are influenced time, money, personal motives and other people.

CRITICAL THINKING   In the case of the Tham Luang cave rescue situation in Thailand described at the start of the chapter, what *environmental condition* and *decision-making condition* did the director of the rescue operation face? What *type of decision* did he have to make?

Individual and group decision making

For a long time, organizational activities have been arranged around groups and teams on the assumption that group decisions are better than individual decisions (Hill, 1982). However, experimental research data show that while the average quality of a decision made by a *group* is higher than the average quality of a decision made by an individual, the quality of group decisions is consistently below that made by their *most capable individual* member (Rogelberg et al., 1992). The pros and cons of group decision making are summarized in Table 20.8.

Research has revealed that two main factors determine whether groups should be preferred to individuals. These are first, how structured the task is, and second, who the group members are (Table 20.9). If the task to be performed is structured (has a clear, correct solution) then groups are better, although they take longer (Weber, 1984). In the case of unstructured tasks (no single correct answer and creativity required), individuals are better. Hence the counter-intuitive finding that the performance of brainstorming groups is inferior to that of individuals.

Table 20.8: **Advantages and disadvantages of group decision making**

Advantages	Disadvantages
Greater pool of knowledge: A group can bring much more information and experience to bear on a decision or problem than an individual alone.	*Personality factors:* Traits such as shyness can prevent some members offering their opinions and knowledge to the group.
Different perspectives: Individuals with varied experience and interests help the group see decision situations and problems from different angles.	*Social conformity*: Unwillingness to 'rock the boat' and pressure to conform may combine to stifle the creativity of individual contributors.
Greater comprehension: Those who personally experience the give-and-take of group discussion about alternative courses of action tend to understand the rationale behind the final decision better.	*Diffusion of responsibility:* Members feel less responsibility for their actions believing it can be shouldered by the others present.
Increased acceptance: Those who play an active role in group decision making and problem solving tend to view the outcomes as 'ours' rather than 'theirs'.	*Minority domination:* The quality of the group decision can be is reduced when the group gives in to those who talk the loudest and longest.
Training ground: Less experienced members learn to cope with group dynamics by actually being involved in the decision.	*Logrolling:* Political wheeling and dealing can displace sound thinking when an individual's pet project or vested interest is at stake.
	Goal displacement: Secondary considerations such as winning an argument or defeating a rival displace the primary task of making a sound decision or solving a problem.
	Group brainstorming: Reduces rather than increases the quantity and quality of ideas compared to individual performance.
	Groupthink: Cohesive 'in-groups' let the desire for unanimity override the sound judgement when generating and evaluating alternative courses of action.
	Satisficing: Making decisions which are immediately acceptable to the group rather than the best ones.

Table 20.9: **Individual and group performance compared**

Factor	**Individuals when**	**Groups when**
Type of problem task	Creativity or efficiency is desired	Diverse skills and knowledge are required
Acceptance of decision	Acceptance is not important	Acceptance by group members is valued
Quality of the solution	'Best member' can be identified	Several group members can improve the solution
Characteristics of the individuals	Individuals cannot collaborate	Members have experience of working together
Decision-making climate	Climate is competitive	Climate is supportive of group problem solving
Time available	Relatively little time is available	Relatively more time is available

Source: Gordon, J.R. (1993) *Diagnostic Approach to Organization Behaviour*, (fourth edition) Prentice Hall, Inc., p. 253.

CUTTING EDGE · The wisdom of groups not crowds

Joaquin Navajas

Joaquin Navajas and his colleagues (2018) asked if you were visiting the Eiffel Tower and wanted to know its height, would it be better to ask 100 tourists around you and average their answers, or should you ask these individuals to come to a consensus? The view that the aggregation of many independent estimates can outperform the most accurate individual judgement is popularly known as the 'wisdom of crowds'. It has been applied to problems ranging from the diagnosis of cancer to financial forecasting. It is widely believed that social influence undermines collective wisdom by reducing the diversity of opinions within the crowd.

However, studies have found that crowds are not that wise. Human crowds may fail because human choices are affected by numerous systematic biases. Opinions in crowds are rarely independent because of the herd mentality – people talking to one another resulting in their opinions converging. However, letting the group come to a consensus is no better as research into groupthink demonstrates. Evidence suggests that the key to collective intelligence is to protect the independence of opinions within a group.

Navajas et al. advise taking the best from both approaches. By using individual opinions, group consensus and consensus averaging, one can benefit from the 'wisdom of groups'. They asked a crowd of 5,180 people about the height of the Eiffel Tower. Participants first answered individually, then deliberated and made consensus decisions in groups of five. The researchers then averaged the group consensus estimates. They found that average group consensus decisions were substantially more accurate than the aggregated initial independent opinions of individuals. Indeed, combining as few as four consensus choices outperformed the wisdom of thousands of individual crowd members.

Individual answers (100)	Group consensus answers (20)	Average of group consensus answers

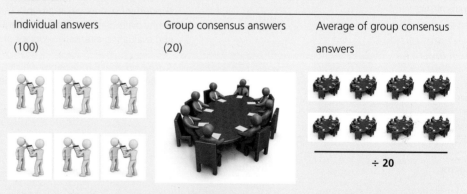

÷ 20

Navajas et al. noted that popular thinking says that if joint decisions are to be made, the best way to do it is to separate individuals as much as possible to avoid the herd mentality. However, this ignores the positive aspects of the group. They recommended their combined individual-group-consensus averaging procedure to overcome this deficiency.

STOP AND SEARCH YouTube for the TED talk *How can groups make good decisions* Mariano Sigman and Dan Ariely (8:37)

Problems with group decision making

Group polarization
a situation in which
individuals in a group
begin by taking a
moderate stance on
an issue related to a
common value but, after
having discussed it, end
up taking a more extreme
decision than the average
of members' decisions.
The extremes could
be more risky or more
cautious.

Risky shift the
tendency of a group to
make decisions that are
riskier than those which
individual members would
have recommended.

Caution shift the
tendency of a group
to make decisions
that are more risk
averse than those that
individual members of
the group would have
recommended.

Groupthink a mode of
thinking in a cohesive
in-group, in which
members' strivings for
unanimity override their
motivation to appraise
realistically the alternative
courses of action.

It is the very strengths of a group that are also its weaknesses. The cost of bringing individuals together in one place counters the benefits of getting contributions from supposedly independent minds. Four problems of group decision making will be examined here: group polarization, groupthink, brainstorming and escalation of commitment.

Group polarization

Group polarization refers to the phenomenon that occurs when a position that is held on an issue by the majority of group members is intensified (in a given direction) as a result of discussion (Lamm, 1988). This tendency can lead to irrational and hence to ineffective group performance. Social psychologists have documented the situation in which individuals in a group begin by taking a moderate stance on an issue related to a common value and then, after having discussed it, end up taking a more extreme stance. James Stoner conducted one of the earliest of these studies in the 1950s. He found that groups of management students were willing to make decisions involving greater risks than their individual preferences (Stoner, 1961). This phenomenon was referred to as the risky shift. However, the opposite can also occur, and is called the caution shift. Here a group can become more risk averse than the initial, average risk averse tendencies of its individuals members (Lamm and Myers, 1978; Isenberg, 1986).

Patricia Wallace (2001) believed that group polarization may be partly responsible for the extremism often found on the internet and the apparent absence of a temperate voice. An individual might hold a relatively moderate view about an issue initially. However, after exchanging views with others over the internet, they are likely to move away from the middle view towards one of the extremes. Factors that contribute to group polarization are present on the internet in abundance. First, people talk and talk endlessly. Second, members are selective about what they share with others and who those others are ('echo chamber effect'). As talk progresses, members become increasing reluctant to bring up items that might contradict the emerging group consensus. This creates a biased discussion where alternatives are insufficiently considered.

Groupthink

Groupthink is a mode of thinking that occurs when the members' strivings for unanimity override their motivation to appraise realistically the alternative courses of action. Groups and teams can develop a high level of cohesiveness. This is generally a positive thing but it also has negative consequences. Specifically, the desire not to disrupt the consensus can lead to a reluctance to challenge the group's thinking which in turn results in bad decisions. Irving Janis (1982) studied US foreign policy disasters including a failure to anticipate the Japanese attack on Pearl Harbour, the US invasion of Cuba's Bay of Pigs, and the escalation of the Vietnam War. More recently, groupthink it has been blamed for the decision to invade Iraq, and unwise lending leading to the global financial crisis of 2008–9. Janis named this phenomenon groupthink. He listed its symptoms and how it could be prevented. These are outlined in Table 20.10.

In the different historical examples quoted, groupthink led to a failure by the group to make the best decision. The group discussed a minimum number of alternatives, and the courses of action favoured by the majority of the group were not re-examined from the view of hidden risks and other alternatives. The group failed to use the expert opinion that it had, and when expert opinion was evaluated, it was done with a selective bias which ignored the facts and opinions which did not support the group view.

Table 20.10: **Groupthink: symptoms and prevention steps**

When groups become very cohesive, there is a danger that they will become victims of their own closeness.

Symptoms	Preventive action
1. *Illusion of invulnerability:* members display excessive optimism that past successes will continue and will shield them, and hence they tend to take extreme risks	(A) Leader encourages open expression of doubt by members
2. *Collective rationalization:* members collectively rationalize away data that disconfirm their assumptions and beliefs upon which they base their decisions	(B) Leader accepts criticism of his/her opinions
3. *Illusion of morality:* members believe that they, as moral individuals, are unlikely to make bad decisions	(C) Higher status members offer opinions last
4. *Shared stereotypes:* members dismiss disconfirming evidence by discrediting its source (e.g. stereotyping other groups and their leaders as evil or weak)	(D) Obtain recommendations from a duplicate group
5. *Direct pressure:* imposition of verbal, non-verbal or other sanctions on individuals who explore deviant positions express doubts or question the validity of group beliefs	(E) Periodically divide into sub-groups
6. *Self-censorship:* members keep silent about misgivings about the apparent group consensus and try to minimize their doubts	(F) Members obtain the reactions of trusted outsiders
7. *Illusion of unanimity:* members conclude that the group has reached a consensus because its most vocal members are in agreement	(G) Invite trusted outsiders to join the discussion periodically
8. *Mind-guards:* members take it upon themselves to screen out adverse, disconfirming information supplied by 'outsiders' which might endanger the group's complacency	(H) Assign someone to the role of devil's advocate
	(I) Develop scenarios of rivals' possible actions

Source: based on Janis (1982)

Research supports a link between the level of cohesion in a group and the occurrence of groupthink (Mullen et al., 1994; Turner and Pratkanis, 1998). However, an additional crucial variable is directive leadership. It appears that if the group leader is strong, states their position at the start, and appears to have a strong preference for a particular outcome, then there is more discouragement of dissent. The group is less likely to review a wide range of information; it will consider fewer solutions; and there will be more self-censorship by its members (Hill, 2018).

In the groups studied by Janis, while individual doubt may have been suppressed and the illusion of group unanimity and cohesiveness maintained, the groups paid a

"Today's theme is 'Getting Beyond Group Think'."

high price in terms of their effectiveness. The factors affecting group cohesiveness are listed in Table 20.11. Thus, while group cohesion can make a positive contribution to group effectiveness, it may also have negative consequences on the process of group decision making. Group loyalty, instilled through cohesion, may act to stifle the raising and questioning of controversial issues which in turn leads to the making of poor decisions. At the heart of groupthink is the tendency for groups to seek concurrence and the illusion of unanimity. To prevent groupthink occurring, individuals who disagree with the group's evolving consensus must be willing to make their voices heard and say 'no' is required.

 **STOP AND SEARCH**   YouTube for *Margaret Heffernan: Dare to disagree* (Ted Talk, 12.57)

Table 20.11: Factors affecting group cohesiveness

Size	Smaller groups are more cohesive than larger ones, partly because their members interact more frequently
Duration	The longer members are together, the more opportunity they have to find out about one another
Threats	An external threat can often (although not always) serve to harden the group against 'the enemy'
Isolation	Leads a group to feel distinct and hence special
Rewards	Group rewards can encourage cooperation to achieve the group goal
Restricted entry	Difficulty of attaining membership increases identification with the group
Similarities	When individuals share common goals and attitudes, they enjoy being in each others' company

Brainstorming and nominal group technique

Brainstorming a technique in which all group members are encouraged to propose ideas spontaneously, without critiquing or censoring others' ideas. The ideas so generated are not evaluated until all have been listed.

Brainstorming is usually presented as a technique that seeks to improve group decision-making, it can also be seen as a problem. Brainstorming asserts the superiority of a group's performance over that of an individual's. It was invented in 1939 by Alexander Osborn. He coined the term to mean using the *brain* to *storm* a problem creatively. The technique is based on the belief that under given conditions, a group of people working together will solve a problem more creatively than if the same people worked separately as individuals. The presence of a group is said to permit members to 'bounce ideas off each other' and to throw out half-formed ideas which others might turn into more practical suggestions.

The purpose of the technique is to produce creative, new ideas. Members of brainstorming groups are required to follow four main rules of procedure:

1. Avoid criticising others' ideas.

2. Share even fanciful or bizarre suggestions.

3. Offer as many comments as possible.

4. Build on others' ideas to create your own.

However, Taylor et al. (1958) showed Osborn to have been wrong. Their research showed that four-person groups following brainstorming instructions produced only half as many ideas as groups of four individuals working alone. This has been regularly confirmed (Furnham, 2000). On idea-generating tasks, nominal groups (i.e. a collection of individuals who generated ideas separately and whose ideas are subsequently added) outperformed interacting groups (i.e. groups of individuals working together in a room). In the five decades since then, a large body of research has confirmed the superiority of nominal groups methods. Eric Jones and John Lambertus (2014) explained that the gap between nominal groups and interacting groups could be ascribed to:

- *Production blocking:* In a brainstorming session, members interfere with each other's productivity. When people are generating ideas, many will be talking at the same time and others will be waiting their turn to speak (Kerr and Tindale, 2004; Nigstad and Stroebe, 2006).

- *Evaluation apprehension:* Brainstorming group members fear the negative appraisal of their contributions from others. This raises members' anxieties and leads to fewer ideas. This is despite explicit brainstorming instructions not to criticize ideas and to encourage the generation of wild ideas (Camacho and Paulus, 1995; Nemeth et al., 2004).

- *Social matching:* Occurs when members begin to match others' decreased efforts which is called social loafing (Paulus and Dzindolet, 1993). A related explanation is free-riding in a brainstorming group when some members decide that their efforts will not be needed and that others in the group will take up the slack (Harkins and Petty, 1982; Kerr and Bruun, 1983).

The continued popularity of brainstorming may be due partly to individuals' own beliefs that they are more productive when working in groups than alone, a tendency labelled the 'illusion of group productivity or effectiveness'. Group members may fail to contribute to brainstorming sessions for the reasons suggested above or because they are introverts; find the process artificial; or frequently end up with unremarkable solutions or unworkable ideas. However, brainstorming may be a good way for management to gain employee buy-in for decisions that it has already made (Furnham, 2000).

Modified brainstorming approaches

Marcia Hagen, Alan Bernard and Eric Grube (2016) recommend *reverse brainstorming* in which opposite or reverse solutions to problems are identified. Participants are given a scenario and, instead of solving the problem, they are asked to suggest ways of making it worse. They identify the likely undesirable outcomes; the potential repercussions; and rate the risks involved. They then turn each of their bad ideas into a good idea that the group can use to solve the initial problem.

Not all bad ideas can be turned into good ideas, but participants can be helped to turn some of the former into the latter. The key to this is encouraging the group to generate the largest and most diverse set of solutions possible, irrespective of how silly or untenable they seem. The technique has been used in marketing and product development (Williams and Smith, 1990) and to discover why some organizations foster collaboration while others do not (Evans, 2012). The rationale is that individuals find it easier and more engaging to identify negative elements, and the negative energy thus generated can spark creativity (Conrad, 2011; Wilson, 2007).

Hal Gregersen (2018) recommends *brainstorming for questions* instead of for answers. He argues that the best way to obtain great answers is to ask great questions which challenge deeply held assumptions **(see questioning techniques in Chapter 7)**. He offers an approach which he calls Question Burst that avoids the destructive group dynamics and biases that obstruct creative thinking. He offers five guidelines for great questions.

- Questions are most productive when they are open versus closed, short versus long, and simple versus complex.

- Descriptive questions (What's working? What's not? Why?) should precede speculative ones (What if? What might be? Why not?).

- Breakthrough thinking occurs when one moves from simple questions that require only recall to more cognitively complex ones that demand creative synthesis.

- Avoid questions that come from a group's deeply held convictions about what it wants to achieve as these can annoy and distract.

- Avoid posing questions aggressively, putting people on the spot, casting unwarranted doubt on their ideas, or cultivating a culture of fear.

 **STOP AND SEARCH**   YouTube for *How to ask the right question: Hal Gregersen* (9:33) and also *reverse brainstorming.*

Nominal group technique involves group members first working separately and then joining together in order to generate ideas or make decisions.

The nominal group technique (NGT) involves members coming together face-to-face in a traditional meeting. They are presented with a problem to solve or a decision to make. They then take the following steps:

1. On their own and silently, each person writes down their ideas about the problem.
2. When everyone has finished, they take turns to present one of their ideas to the group. Discussion is delayed until all the ideas have been presented and recorded.
3. The group then comes together and elaborates, synthesizes and debates the ideas.
4. Each group member independently rank-orders the ideas. The idea with the highest aggregate ranking is selected and becomes the group's choice.

The main benefit of NGT is that it does not restrict independent thinking. In the two-stage process, each member first generates ideas on their own before going on to have them evaluated by the group. Positive results have been obtained using this procedure with group members reporting higher levels of satisfaction and greater perceived group effectiveness in the form of superior group presentations and the implementation of their decisions (Van de Ven and Delbecq (1971, 1974). These outcomes are superior to those obtained from groups that brainstorm ideas together (Hegedus and Rasmussen, 1986).

Escalation of commitment

Escalation of commitment an increased commitment to a previously made decision despite negative information suggesting one should do otherwise.

Have you ever waited for a lift (elevator) that did not arrive, and the longer that you waited, the less inclined you were to use the stairs instead? Escalation of commitment refers to the tendency of individuals to increase their commitment to a course of action in the future, despite the evidence of negative outcomes from the past. It focuses on 'persistence in the face of failure'. In addition to waiting situations, this tendency has been noticed in interpersonal relations, gambling, economic investment and policy-making.

Barry Staw (1976, 1981) first demonstrated escalation of commitment as an individual phenomenon. Figure 20.3 shows the factors that Ross and Staw (1993) identified as contributing to commitment escalation by an individual or a group. Recent research has investigated many of these factors in greater detail (Sleesman et al., 2018, 2012; Hsieh et al., 2015).

Task factors

These concern the characteristics of the task itself – shooting a film or constructing a building. Task difficulty affects escalation (Lee et al., 2015) as it increases risk which in turn increases the chances of loss, which act to reduce the chances of escalation. A lack of clearly defined task goals and performance standards, coupled with inappropriate feedback contributes to escalation. Information about a task is critical. It provides a benchmark to assist the evaluation of past progress, helps predict future prospects, and reduces uncertainty. Negative feedback information needs to be unambiguous and come early. Perception of the project (e.g. as a long-term investment) are important. When the benefits of a task are delayed, decision makers are tempted to remain with it until the end.

Psychological factors

These concern the individual or group decision makers themselves. They include how familiar they already are with the task; how close they are to completing it; and their preference for a particular course of action. If responsible for initiating the task, they may be impelled to justify it by escalating their commitment to it. Emotions can influence the decision to escalate or terminate a course of action (Devigne et al., 2016). Self-confidence and self-justification affects selective perception as does over-optimism. Ego-involvement can threaten self-esteem and people wish to avoid regret. Once individuals become heavily involved in decisions and socially bound to them, they fear losing face (Steinkühler et al., 2014). Various kinds of decision errors can be made by both individuals (e.g. sunk cost effect) and by groups (e.g. risky shift).

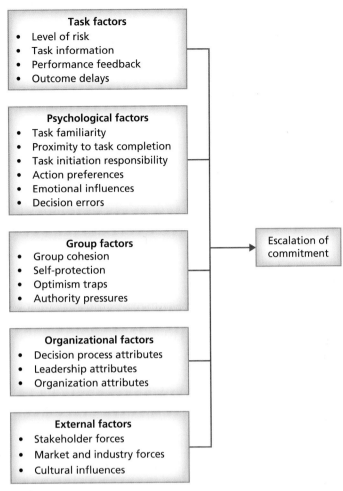

Figure 20.3: Model of escalation of commitment
Source: based on Sleesman et al. (2018, 2012) and Ross and Shaw (1993)

Group factors

The interactions of the group members and the group's decision-making process affect escalation. Cohesive groups exhibit member conformity of perception and judgement. Groups are more over-optimistic than individuals. They allow positive feedback to trump negative information. Having received the latter, they escalate rather than temper their commitment (Wieber et al., 2015). They use self-protection processes of idealization (tying success to the organization's image), splitting (separating evidence of failure from themselves) and blaming (other groups or projects), to maintain a collective fantasy that the task is progressing well. Authority pressures in the form of high-status individuals in leadership roles can suppress group dissent and influence group norms, forcing groups to escalate their commitment to unwise decisions.

Organizational factors

Escalation is reduced if the decision process is structured with goals or rules; if there is a role separation between task initiation and subsequent progress review; and if early unambiguous feedback signals problems. Executives who are overconfident and who obtain intrinsic motivation from their task can over-commit to a failing course of action. Organization culture can either exacerbate or attenuate escalation. A decision tied to company culture may be difficult to change if it is perceived to be inconsistent with that culture. Thus one successful, strong culture firm may ignore warning signs, while a different strong culture firm may be confident enough to terminate a failing project (Salter et al., 2013).

External factors

Factors outside the company including external stakeholders affect escalation inside it. Firms may escalate failing projects when they are embedded within their local community or when its costs are passed on to outsiders. The media can reinforce company decisions by publicizing them, making them difficult to reverse. Extensive and rapid market changes can discourage entrepreneurs, while a growing market encourages them to persevere in the face of setbacks.

Although escalation factors have been considered separately, a decision of whether to stop or continue a failing course of action is likely to be caused by a combination of a number of them. The problem for organizations and their managers is to decide when to exit or continue with a course of action.

Home viewing

The Age of Innocence (1993, director Martin Scorsese) is the story of an upper class, romantic triangle set in 1890s New York which vividly illustrates escalation theory. It portrays an escalation situation unfolding for an individual over a number of years and involves a commitment of the heart. As you watch the film, identify what psychological and external factors lead Newland Archer (played by Daniel Day-Lewis) to continue with a course of action that he really does not want to take (Ross, 1996).

Organizational decision making

Types of decisions

Aaron De Smet and his colleagues (2017) argue that growing organizational complexity and the proliferation of digital communications are contributing to poor decision making. The number of decision makers has risen and managers are less able to delegate decisions neatly. Many organizations are trying to streamline their decision making by becoming flatter and more agile and by linking decision authority and accountability more closely. The authors recommend improving organizational decision making by categorizing the type of decision to be made. They divide decisions according to their scope and impact, and to the level of an organization's familiarity with making them (Figure 20.4).

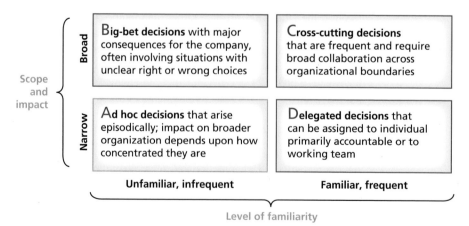

Figure 20.4: **The ABCDs of categorizing decisions.**
Source: from De Smet et al. (2017, p.3)

- *Big-bet decisions:* These infrequent and high-risk decisions have the potential to shape the future of the company. For example, decisions about major acquisitions and game-changing capital investment.

- *Cross-cutting decisions:* In these frequent and high-risk decisions, a series of small, interconnected decisions are made by different groups as part of a collaborative, end-to-end decision process. For example, decisions on pricing, sales or new-product launches. They require an input from a wide range of different constituents.

- *Delegated decisions:* These frequent and low-risk decisions are best handled by an individual or team, with limited input from others. For example, decisions about hiring, marketing or purchasing. Making staff who are closest to the work responsible for those decisions can result in better outcomes.

- *Ad hoc decisions:* The organization's infrequent, low-stakes decisions are deliberately ignored in this framework in order to focus on the other three areas where organizational ambiguity is most likely to undermine decision-making effectiveness.

By categorizing the decisions to be made in this way, De Smet et al. argue that companies can ensure that the right people make them in the right way at the right time. For each decision type, the authors specify the steps needed to avoid the previously discussed decision biases. For example, for big-bet decisions, they recommend appointing an executive sponsor; breaking the issue down and connecting the parts up again; employing a standard decision-making approach; and moving quickly without losing the commitment of those involved.

Decision-making processes

Junior-level individuals making delegated and ad hoc decisions usually have rules, procedures and precedents to help them determine what should be done in a particular case. In contrast, senior managers making their 'big bet' and 'cross cutting' decisions, do not. These decisions are 'unprogrammed' and involve discretion.

Sociologists have studied how power and politics impact on the decision-making process and prevent the operation of the rational decision making described at the start of this chapter. The more sources of uncertainty there are, the more possibility there is for individuals and groups to take up political positions. From this perspective, a particular decision is less an expression of an organization's goals, and more a reflection of the ability of a particular individual or group to impose their view or 'definition of the situation' and solution, onto others. The rational model of decision making ignores the internal politics of the organization system. It assumes that:

- Decision makers possess a consistent order of preferences.

- There is agreement among the stakeholders about the goals of the organization.

- Decision rules are known and accepted by everyone.

In contrast, the bounded rationality model introduced earlier, stresses that managers are prevented from making rational decisions for two reasons. First, there is ambiguity over which direction to take on an issue. People disagree about which goals to pursue or which problems to solve. Second, there is the issue of uncertainty. This concerns the degree to which people feel certain that a given action will produce a given outcome (cause-and-effect).

James Thompson and Arthur Tuden (Thompson and Tuden, 1959; Thompson, 1967) argued that any decision choice situation could be mapped along two dimensions:

- Degree of agreement or disagreement over goals to be achieved

- Degree of certainty that the outcome could be achieved by means of a given action

Using these two dimensions every decision situation could placed into one of four quadrants. The most suitable decision-making model for that quadrant was specified (Figure 20.5).

		Agreement on goals or problem definition?	
		agree	*disagree*
Certainty of outcome to be achieved by actions	*certainty*	I Computational strategy Rational model	III Compromise strategy Political model
	uncertainty	II Judgemental strategy Incremental model	IV Inspirational strategy Garbage can model

Figure 20.5: Conditions favouring different decision-making processes
Source: based on Thompson and Tuden (1959) and Thompson (1967)

I. Computational strategy–rational model

Participants agree on the outcome they desire (no ambiguity) and are certain about the consequences of their actions (high certainty). For example, as demand for ice cream increases in the summer, the company introduces an extra shift. The rational model can be applied in this situation. Since management knows the capabilities of their machines, the costs of extra manning and the income from extra sales, it can make the calculations using a *computational strategy*.

II. Judgemental strategy–incremental model

Participants agree on what outcome they desire (no ambiguity) but are uncertain about the consequences of their actions (low certainty) because information is inadequate. In the case of the ice cream makers, new equipment may need to be purchased whose performance is unknown. There is limited search for and evaluation of alternatives, so those that are offered differ only slightly (i.e. incrementally) from those which already exist. Thus current judgements are made on the basis of past decisions. They 'fix the past' by continually adjusting the present as it unfolds with problems being continually attacked. Lindblom (1959) referred to this process as *incrementalism* although it is more popularly referred to as the 'science of muddling through'.

III. Compromise strategy–political model

Participants disagree about what outcomes they desire (high ambiguity) but are sure that they can be achieved (high certainty). In this case, a *compromise strategy* is used. These unprogrammed decisions such as deciding on a company's future strategy are ultimately resolved through reasoning, judgement, influence and politics. Since there will always be disagreement, political behaviour is inevitable. Viewing an organization as a coalition of interests, a decision is not the result of the rational decision-making process, but something that is the outcome of horse-trading, and which is acceptable to all those involved.

Individuals, groups and departments unite their interests, propose alternatives, assess their power, join with others, negotiate and form coalitions. In conditions of high ambiguity decision makers look for alternatives that can accommodate the interests of all the parties involved.

IV. Inspirational strategy–garbage can model

Participants disagree about what outcomes they desire (high ambiguity). They are also uncertain about the consequences that their actions are likely to have (high uncertainty). When there is neither agreement on goals, nor certainty about cause and effect relationships, ambiguity and uncertainty prevail, and decision making becomes random. If there is no preference between high volume/low profits and low volume/high profits, or certainty about what will happen if they proceed, then the *inspirational strategy* is an inspired leap into the dark!

In such circumstances, Cyert and March's decision-making processes become 'uncoupled' from the decisions actually made. That is, a link ceases to exist between the problems identified and the solutions proposed or implemented. The garbage can model was developed by James March and Johan Olsen and turned the rational model on its head. Whereas both the rational and the bounded rationality models treated decisions as the outcomes of a reasoned approach of information-gathering and evaluation, the garbage can model contended that the elements that constituted decision problems were independent phenomena that came together in random ways (Cohen et al., 1972; March and Olsen, 1976; Einsiedel, 1983).

In their view, the various logical models of decision making had failed to recognize the amount of confusion that surrounded decision-making situations. They labelled these situations *organized anarchies* within which a decision 'occurred' rather than was consciously made. Thus, decision making involved streams of activities which sought to cope with uncertainty over time. It occurred when four separate but interdependent streams fortuitously met. These were:

Choice opportunities: Every organization has a stream of 'occasions' at which there is an expectation of a decision, e.g. weekly staff meetings, product review meetings, government cabinet meetings.

Participants: A stream of people who have an opportunity to make a choice.

Problems: A stream of problems which represent matters of concern for individuals both inside and outside the organization e.g. declining sales; need to recruit staff; increasing hospital waiting lists.

Solutions: The existence of a stream of solutions or answers, all seeking problems and questions, and all available from internal staff advisors or external consultants.

©Glasbergen
glasbergen.com

GLASBERGEN

"My team has created a very innovative solution, but we're still looking for a problem to go with it."

Decision making and evidence

Evidence-based decision making a situation in which a decision is made that follows directly from the evidence.

Peter Tingling and Michael Brydon (2010) defined evidence-based decision making as a situation in which a decision was made that followed directly from the evidence (Figure 20.6). They contrasted it with decision-based evidence making which involved marshalling facts and analysis to support a decision that had already been made elsewhere in the organization. They found that when making a decision, managers used evidence in three different ways:

- *To make* a decision: the decision arose directly from the evidence
- *To inform* a decision: the evidence was mixed in with intuition or bargaining, to lead to a decision
- *To support* a decision: the evidence was used simply to justify a decision already made

Decision-based evidence making marshalling facts and analysis to support a decision that has already been made elsewhere in the organization.

If decisions are allowed to trump the evidence, then it makes decision making ill-informed. In the best case, a decision that contradicts the evidence is an inspired hunch based on experience, while in the worst case, it is the product of ignorant bias. Moreover, once employees know that managers are more interested in finding evidence to fit their conclusions, rather than finding out the facts, then they become demoralized and the company is infected with destructive cynicism. However, historically some companies have collected data and have successfully ignored it, while in others, the cult of data-driven decision making leaves so little scope for personal beliefs and hunches that it results in employees just tailoring the evidence to fit pre-made decisions.

Not all decisions incorporate evidence in the same way, or intend to marshal it toward the same end. This chart shows three roles that evidence can play, depending on whether the aim is to make, inform, or support a decision.

ROLE OF EVIDENCE IN DECISION-MAKING	DESCRIPTION	ARCHETYPAL DECISION	RISKS
Make decision Evidence → Decision Process → Decision	Evidence forms the basis of the decision	Facilities location	Poor decisions due to misspecified models
Inform decision Evidence; Intuition, Experience, Bargaining, etc. → Decision Process → Decision	Evidence is one of several inputs to the decision process	Diagnosis, strategic planning	Mismatch between evidence and other inputs requires shift to 'make' or 'support' role
Support decision Intuition, Experience, Bargaining, etc. → Decision Process → Decision; Evidence	Evidence is created to support a decision made using other inputs	New product development, technology adoption	Demoralization of analysts; poor decisions due to decision biases and false consensus

Figure 20.6: **Role of evidence in decision making**
Source: from Tingling and Brydon (2010, p.73) © from MIT Sloan Management Review / Massachusetts Institute of Technology. All rights reserved. Distributed by Tribute Media Services

So what is to be done? Should one encourage the use of data, while leaving room for the occasional inspired decision? Tingling and Brydon offer managers four guidelines:

1. Understand the decision problem and assess the potential contribution of formal evidence to the quality of the decision-making process. For some problems (e.g. new product development), historical data is of little use and the decision is best made on instinct.

2. Use cost–benefit analysis. If the costs of obtaining evidence exceed the benefits, it may be necessary to make the decision on instinct and admit that this is what is being done.

3. Differentiate between internal and external decision audiences when engaging in decision-based evidence making. Some evidence can have ceremonial and signalling value, but internal stakeholders (employees) are seldom fooled by decision-based evidence making.

4. Ensure that the majority of decisions incorporate painstakingly gathered, objective evidence. If managers feel the necessity to feed manufactured evidence to internal audiences, it should be done rarely and sparingly, otherwise a disregard for evidence and analysis will become endemic throughout the organization.

 **RECAP**

1. *Distinguish prescriptive, descriptive and explanatory models of decision making and provide an example of each.*

   - Prescriptive models of decision making recommend how individuals should behave in order to achieve a desired outcome. The original prescriptive model is the rational model, while a later one was devised by Victor Vroom and Philip Yetton.

   - Descriptive models of decision making reveal how individuals actually make decisions. The behavioural theory of decision making is the earliest and most influential descriptive model and was developed by Herbert Simon, John March and Richard Cyert.

→

- Explanatory models of decision making look at what decisions were made and aim to provide an explanation of how they occurred. The heuristics and biases model developed by Kahneman, Tversky and Thaler, as well as Janis' groupthink, illustrate these.

2. *Distinguish different decision conditions on the basis of risk and programmability.*
   - Decision conditions can be classified as those involving: certainty, risk and uncertainty.
   - Decisions can be classified as routine, adaptive and innovative.

3. *Consider the advantages and disadvantages of group decision making.*
   - Groups offer the advantages of a greater pool of knowledge; different perspectives; greater problem comprehension; and increased acceptance of decisions.
   - Disadvantages of groups can be considered under the headings of personality factors; social conformity; diffusion of responsibility; minority domination;

logrolling; goal displacement; group brainstorming, groupthink and satisficing.

4. *Identify the factors used to decide whether to adopt individual or group decision making.*
   - Individual or group decision making has been made on the basis of the following factors: type of problem task; acceptance of decision; quality of the solution; characteristics of the individuals; and decision-making climate.

5. *Match organizational conditions with the decision-making-model that favour them.*
   - Combining a belief about the relationship between the causes and effects of a problem with the degree of consensus about the goals of actions can direct one to choose one of four strategies with its associated decision-making model – computational/rational; judgemental/incremental; compromise/political; or inspirational/garbage can.

RECAP: What did they decide?

Than Luang, Thailand:

- Taking advantage of the best cave conditions in days, the operation's chief decided on the diving option. At 03:00 GMT on the 8 July, 13 foreign divers and five from the Thai Navy entered the caves. Lowered water levels had made some of the previously flooded chambers walkable. The rescue process included a mixture of walking, wading, climbing and diving – all in complete darkness along guide ropes already installed.

- In the end, the boys were 'packaged'. They were heavily sedated to prevent them from panicking in the narrow, dark tunnels, and endangering themselves and their rescuers. Each semi-conscious boy was then strapped to a diver who manoeuvred him through the underwater passages and carried him through the tunnels. Each was accompanied by a second diver.

- The first four, boys were extracted on the Sunday. As the rains started, the next four were rescued on the Monday, and the remaining boys and their coach came out on Tuesday.

- After 17 days, what had been described by experienced cave rescue experts as 'mission impossible' had become, 'mission accomplished'. By going for the dive option the Thai director of the rescue had made the correct decision. In addition, the dive team, including the two British divers, were influential in that decision, and this illustrates the need for locally-informed decision making by someone with intimate knowledge of the prevailing conditions.

Source: based on BBC Online News (2018b, 2018c, 2018d)

Thai football team rescue underway

This video shows divers entering the flooded caves to rescue the young boys and their coach (1:28).

Revision

1. What are the strengths and weaknesses of the Vroom–Jago time-driven, decision-making model?

2. How does a 'satisficing' decision differ from a 'maximizing' one? Provide examples of each from your own experience. How have price comparison websites affected purchasing decisions?

3. 'No decision that is ever made by a manager is truly rational'. Do you agree or disagree with this statement. Support your view with arguments and examples.

4. Should decision making by groups be avoided or encouraged in organizations?

Research assignment

Talk to a manager from any organization and ask them for examples of decision-making or problem-solving situations that they have typically faced. Examples might include in which city to locate a new store; deciding on an advertising campaign; dealing with a sexual harassment complaint or deciding whether or not to fire an employee. Select one situation. Then use the internet to search for 'decision-making techniques' or 'problem-solving techniques'. These are examples of prescriptive models of decision making. Review what you find and choose a technique that is appropriate for your chosen situation. Apply the technique to the situation explaining how it can be used to arrive at the best decision or solve the problem.

Springboard

Eric Bolland and Carlos Lopes (2018) *Decision Making and Business Performance,* Edward Elgar Publishing. The authors examine how decisions and performance are connected for businesses of all sizes.

Chengwei Liu, Ivo Vlaev, Christina Fang, Jerker Denrell and Nick Chater (2017) 'Strategizing with biases: Making better decisions using the mindspace approach', *California Management Review,* 59(3): 135–61. The authors introduce the Mindspace framework which consists of nine behavioural interventions to eliminate decision-making bias.

Richard Thaler (2015) *Misbehaving: The Making of Behavioural Economics,* W.W. Norton, New York. The author charts the progress of behavioural economics, the way people actually makes decisions, and compares it with the traditional, rational model of economics.

Cass Sunstein and Reid Hastie (2014) 'Making dumb groups smarter', *Harvard Business Review,* 92 (12): 90–98. The authors review past research into group decision making.

OB cinema

Andrea Werner uses the film *Margin Call* (2011, director J.C. Chandler) to illustrate the *techniques of neutralization* (Heath, 2008) that people use to excuse and justify their decisions to themselves and others. In the film, the characters have to decide whether or not to sell vast numbers of risky assets that they know to be worthless to unsuspecting buyers, in a fire sale the next morning. They use language to rationalize their behaviour and distance themselves from the moral content of their actions. The six linguistic neutralization techniques they use are:

- *Denial of responsibility:* the perpetrator thinks that what happened was outside their control, that they had no choice.
- *Denial of injury:* the perpetrator denies that any harm was done by their actions.
- *Denial of the victim:* the perpetrator considers those harmed by their actions to be unworthy of concern.
- *Appeal to higher loyalty:* the perpetrator claims that their act was done out of a sense of moral obligation.
- *Everyone else is doing it:* the perpetrator assumes that it is unreasonable to expect legal/ethical behaviour because others are engaging in this practice too.
- *Claim to entitlement:* referring to a moral obligation or a misdeed perpetrated by the victim that entitles the perpetrator to act in a particular way.

The four key scenes in the film in which these techniques are found are the two night-time meetings at which the possibility of a fire sale is discussed (30:15–35:10; 43:20–52:44); John Tuld's interactions with Sam Rogers (53:00–55:00, 1:31:40–1:34:30); and Will Emerson's monologue about why bankers have the right to engage in such actions (1:13:42–1:14:55). As you watch each clip identify which of these neutralization techniques are being used.

Source: Werner (2014)

Chapter exercises

1: Decision types

Objectives
1. To allow you to distinguish between different types of decisions.
2. To make you aware of the requirements of each type of decision.

Briefing
This chapter defined and distinguished between routine, adaptive and innovative types of decisions. This exercise gives you the opportunity to identify and deal with each of the three types.

1. Class divides into groups. Each group represents the executive committee of a small manufacturing company which meets regularly to review and decide upon a list of problems. The list consists of items submitted by employees for decision. This week's list of issues is shown below.

2. Each group is to sort the items on the list into three decision categories – routine, adaptive and innovative.

3. Once all the items have been sorted into three piles, each group is to select one item from the routine pile and one item from the innovative pile, and develop an action plan for each. They should also select one adaptive decision issue and indicate what approach might be appropriate for working on that decision.

4. After 20–30 minutes, the executive committees/small groups reassemble in a class plenary session. Each group presents *one* of the decisions that it has worked on, and describes its conclusions.

5. Class discusses:

- Was a routine or innovative decision harder to deal with? Why?
- Did group members categorize the decision items in the same way?
- Over which items did group members disagree most?
- How were disagreements over categorization dealt with by the group?

List of decision items

1. An assembly worker wants the committee to decide on a more equitable method for allocating scarce parking spaces.

2. A departmental manager wants a decision as to whether one of his programmers can be given a special bonus for developing a popular software item.

3. The facilities manager wants to know if part-time employees are eligible to join the company health club.

4. A division manager wants a decision on whether to open a new office in Paris, Berlin or Moscow.

5. The cafeteria manager has asked for a decision on how to choose among suppliers of foodstuffs.

6. The marketing manager wants a decision on a new product that will not compete with other manufacturers' products but will be popular because it fills an unmet need.

7. A supervisor has asked whether overtime should be given to those who ask first or to those who have the most seniority.

8. A decision has to be made whether to purchase laptops or desktop computers during the next quarter.

9. The research department has developed an innovative and cheap memory chip which is capable of being incorporated in many devices. It has asked what direction your committee wants it to take in developing applications for this chip.

10. The board of directors has told your committee to consider whether it would better to open company-owned retail outlets in five major cities or to franchise the outlets.

Source: Sashkin and Morris (1987)

2: Which is better – brainstorming or NGT?

Objectives

1. Evaluate the brainstorming and the nominal group technique as alternative ways of generating creative ideas.

2. Identify the causes of any differences in group performance that are found.

3. Make proposals to management as to how best to stimulate creativity in groups.

Briefing

1. The instructor explains that half the class will use the brainstorming technique and the other half will apply the nominal group technique.

2. Students are divided into small groups of 4–5 members and placed in opposite parts of the same room or in different rooms.

3. The two groups are then given their respective instructions (see below). They generate their ideas and the results are recorded.

4. Once everyone understands the directions and is ready to begin, the timekeepers say 'Start' and make a note of the starting time. After 10 minutes, they shout 'Time up'.

→

5. After the stated time, the groups reform to compare the quantity of their ideas produced using the two techniques. They discuss possible reasons for any differences observed.

6. They consider how management might use these techniques to maximize creative idea generation in their teams and workgroups.

Instructions for brainstorming groups

- Nominate a timekeeper who will indicate 'Start' and 'Time up' after 10 minutes have elapsed.

- Nominate a recorder who will record the ideas generated by the group.

- Your group aim is to generate as many *uses of a brick* as possible in 10 minutes using the brainstorming technique which means that your group should:

  - Share your ideas with each other out loud.

  - Your goal is quantity. Try to come up with as many unusual ideas as possible.

  - Do not to criticize each other – a bizarre or impractical idea can form the basis for an excellent one.

  - Build on each other's ideas if possible.

  - Remember, the goal is quantity – your group should list as many brick uses as possible.

- Once 'Time up' is announced, count how many different brick ideas your group was able to generate.

  Insert the numbers on response sheet and return it to your instructor:

  a. Technique used (Brainstorming): ___

  b. Total number of brick uses generated: ___

  c. Number of group members: ___

  d. Average number of brick uses generated per group member: ___

Instructions for nominal groups

- Nominate a timekeeper who will indicate 'Start' and 'Time up' after 10 minutes have elapsed.

- Nominate a recorder who will record the ideas generated by the group at the end.

- Your group aim is to generate as many *uses of a brick* as possible in 10 minutes using the nominal group technique which means that:

  - Each group member will have 10 minutes to write down individually and quietly their own suggestions *without* interacting with other group members. Afterwards, you will have an opportunity to share your ideas with others.

  - Your goal is quantity so each person should list as many uses of a brick as they can.

- Once 'Time up' is announced, the group counts how many different brick use suggestions were generated. Because individuals worked separately, some suggestions will be duplicated. Hence, lists need to be read out loud, 'doublers' are removed, and the nominated recorder prepares a total for the whole of their particular NGT group.

  Insert the numbers on response sheet and return it to your instructor:

  a. Technique used (NGT): ___

  b. Total number of brick uses generated: ___

  c. Number of group members: ___

  d. Average number of brick uses generated per group member: ___

> **Debriefing** In the class, group members share information about:
>
> - Whether their group used brainstorming or NGT.
> - How many brick uses per person each group came up with.
> - Which three uses they thought were the most creative.
> - What helped and hindered the idea generation process for individuals and groups.
> - Whether their group outcome reflects the research findings on the use of brainstorming and NGT groups?
> - On the basis of your experience, what advice would you give management about organizing their work groups to solve problems creatively?

References

BBC Online News (2018a) 'Thailand cave: rescuers race against weather as rains close in', 6 July.

BBC Online News (2018b) 'Thailand cave rescue: first pictures emerge of boys in hospital', 11 July.

BBC Online News (2018c) 'Cave rescue: Key questions answered', 12 July.

BBC Online News (2018d) 'The full story of Thailand's extraordinary cave rescue', 14 July.

Beshears, J. and Gino, F. (2015) 'Leaders as decision architects', *Harvard Business Review,* 93(5): 51–62.

Beske, R. (2013) 'Letters: We ran circles round 'big data' with five simple maxims', *Financial Times,* 21 May, p.14.

Camacho, L.M. and Paulus, P.B. (1995) 'The role of social anxiousness in group brainstorming', *Journal of Personality and Social Psychology,* 68(6): 1071–90.

Cohen, M. D., March, J. G. and Olsen, J. P. (1972) 'Garbage can model of organizational choice', *Administrative Science Quarterly,* 17(1): 1–25.

Conrad, S. (2011, December 14) *How to solve problems with reverse-brainstorming.* http://www.halogensoftware .com/blog/how-to-solve-problems-with-reverse-brainstorming [accessed January 2019]

Cyert, R.M. and March, J.G. (1963) *A Behavioural Theory of the Firm,* Englewood Cliffs, NJ: Prentice Hall.

De Smet, A., Lackey, G. and Weiss, L.M. (2017) 'Untangling your organization's decision making', *McKinsey Quarterly,* June, pp. 1–12.

Devigne, D., Manigart, S. and Wright, M. (2016) 'Escalation of commitment in venture capital decision making: differentiating between domestic and international investors', *Journal of Business Venturing,* 31(3): 253–71.

Einsiedel, A. A. (1983) 'Decision making and problem solving skills: the rational versus the garbage can model of decision making', *Project Management Quarterly,* 14(4): 52–57.

Evans, N. (2012) 'Destroying collaboration and knowledge sharing in the workplace: a reverse brainstorming approach', *Knowledge Management Research & Practice,* 10(2): 175–87.

Frederick, S. (2005) 'Cognitive reflection and decision making', *Journal of Economic Perspectives,* 19(4): 25–42.

Furnham, A. (2000) 'The brainstorming myth', *Business Strategy Review,* 11(4): 21–28.

Gordon, J. (1993) *A Diagnostic Approach to Organizational Behaviour*, Boston, MA: Allyn.

Gregersen, H. (2018) 'Better brainstorming', *Harvard Business Review,* 96(2): 65–71.

Hagen, M., Bernard, A. and Grube, E. (2016) 'Do it all wrong! Using reverse-brainstorming to generate ideas, improve discussions, and move students to action', *Management Teaching Review,* 1(2): 85–90.

Harkins, S.G. and Petty, R.E. (1982) 'Effects of task difficulty and task uniqueness on social loafing', *Journal of Personality and Social Psychology,* 43(6): 1214–29.

Heath, J. (2008) 'Business ethics and moral motivation: a criminological perspective', *Journal of Business Ethics,* 83(3): 595–614.

Hegedus, D.M. and Rasmussen, R.V. (1986) 'Task effectiveness and interaction process of a modified nominal group technique in solving an evaluation problem', *Journal of Management,* 12(4): 545–60.

Hill, A. (2018) 'The many unhappy returns of group-think', *Financial Times,* 7 May, p.17.

Hill, G. W. (1982) 'Group versus individual performance: are N + 1 heads better than one?', *Psychological Bulletin,* 91(3): 517–39.

Hsieh, K. Y., Tsai, W. and Chen, M. J. (2015) 'If they can do it, why not us? Competitors as reference points for justifying escalation of commitment', *Academy of Management Journal,* 58(1): 38–58.

Isenberg, D. J. (1986) 'Group polarization: a critical review and meta-analysis', *Journal of Personality and Social Psychology,* 50(6): 1141–51.

Janis, I. L. (1982) *Victims of Groupthink,* second edition, Boston, MA: Houghton Mifflin.

Jones, E.E. and Lambertus, D.D. (2014) 'Expecting less from groups: a new perspective on shortcomings in idea generation groups', *Group Dynamics: Theory, Research and Practice,* 18(3): 237–50.

Kahneman, D. (2003) 'Maps of bounded rationality: psychology for behavioural economists', *American Economic Review,* 93(5): 1449–75.

Kahneman, D. (2011) *Thinking Fast and Slow,* London: Allen Lane.

Kahneman, D. and Tversky, A. (eds) (2000) *Choices, Values and Frames,* London: Cambridge University Press.

Kerr, N.I. and Tindale, R.S. (2004) 'Group performance and decision making', *Annual Review of Psychology,* 55(1): 623–55.

Kerr, N.I. and Bruun, S.E. (1983) 'Dispensability of member effort and group motivation losses', *Journal of Personality and Social Psychology,* 44(1): 78–94.

Lamm, H. (1988) 'A review of our research on group polarization: eleven experiments on the effects of group discussion on risk acceptance, probability estimation and negotiation positions', *Psychological Reports,* 62(3): 807–13.

Lamm, H., and Myers, D. G. (1978) 'Group induced polarization of attitudes and behaviour' in L. Berkowitz (ed.), *Advances in Experimental Social Psychology Vol.11,* New York: Academic Press, pp. 145–95.

Langley, A. (1989) 'In search of rationality: the purposes behind the use of formal analysis in organizations', *Administrative Science Quarterly,* 34(4): 598–631.

Lee, J. S., Keil, M. and Wong, K. F. E. (2015) 'The effect of goal difficulty on escalation of commitment', *Journal of Behavioural Decision Making,* 28(2): 114–29.

Lindblom, C. (1959) 'The science of muddling through', *Public Administration Review,* 34(4): 79–88.

March, J.G. and Simon, H.A. (1958) *Organizations,* New York: Wiley

March, J. G., and Olsen, J. P. (1976) *Ambiguity and Choice in Organizations,* Oslo: Universitetsforlaget.

Mintzberg, H. J. (1989) *Mintzberg on Management: Inside Our Strange World of Organizations,* New York: Free Press.

Mullen, B., Anthony, T., Salas, E., and Driskell, J. E. (1994) 'Group cohesiveness and quality of decision-making: an integration of tests of the groupthink hypothesis', *Small Group Research,* 25(2): 189–204.

Navajas, J., Niella, T., Garbulsky, G., Bahrami, B. and Sigman, M. (2018) 'aggregated knowledge from a small number of debates outperforms the wisdom of large crowds', *Nature Human Behaviour,* 2(2): 126–32.

Nemeth, C.J., Personnaz, B., Personnaz, M. and Goncalo, J.A. (2004) 'The liberating role of conflict in group creativity: a study in two countries', *European Journal of Social Psychology,* 34(4): 365–74.

Nigstad, B.A. and Stroebe, W. (2006) 'How the group affects the mind: A cognitive model of idea generation in groups', *Personality and Social Psychology Review,* 10(3): 186–213.

Paulus, P. B. and Dzindolet, M. T. (1993) 'Social influence processes in group brainstorming', *Journal of Personality and Social Psychology,* 64(4): 575–86.

Rogelberg, S. G., Barnes-Farrell, J. L., and Lowe, C. A. (1992) 'The stepladder technique: an alternative group structure facilitating effective group decision making', *Journal of Applied Psychology,* 77(5): 337–58.

Rosenzweig, P. (2014) 'The benefits and limits of decision models', *McKinsey Quarterly,* February, pp. 1–10.

Ross, J., and Staw, B. M. (1993) 'Organizational escalation and exit: lessons from the Shoreham nuclear power plant', *Academy of Management Journal,* 36(4): 701–32.

Ross, J. (1996) 'Scorsese's *The Age of Innocence*: an escalation interpretation', *Journal of Management Education,* 20(2): 276–85.

Salter, S. B., Sharp, D. J. and Chen, Y. (2013) 'The moderating effects of national culture on escalation of commitment', *Advances in Accounting,* 29(1): 161–69.

Sashkin, M. and Morris, W.C. (1987) 'Decision types', *Experiencing Management,* Addison Wesley, pp. 73–74.

Simon, H. (1957) *Administrative Behaviour,* second edition, New York: Macmillan.

Simon, H. (1960) *The New Science of Management Decision,* New York: Harper and Row.

Simon, H.A. (1979) 'Rational decision making in business organizations', *American Economic Review,* 69(4): 493–513.

Simon, H. (1986) 'Rationality in psychology and economics', *Journal of Business,* 59(4): 209–24.

Sleesman, D. J., Lennard, A. C., McNamara, G. and Conlon, D. E. (2018) 'Putting escalation of commitment in context: a multilevel review and analysis', *Academy of Management Annals,* 12(1): 178–207.

Sleesman, D.J., Conlon, D.E., McNamara, G. and Miles, J.E. (2012) 'Cleaning up the big muddy: a meta-analytic review of the determinants of escalation of commitment', *Academy of Management Journal,* 55(3): 541–62.

Staw, B. M. (1976) 'Knee deep in the big muddy: a study of escalating commitment to a chosen course of action', *Organizational Behaviour and Human Performance,* 16(1): 27–44.

Staw, B. M. (1981) 'The escalation of commitment to a course of action', *Academy of Management Review,* 6(4): 569–78.

Steinkühler, D., Mahlendorf, M. D. and Brettel, M. (2014) 'How self-justification indirectly drives escalation of commitment', *Schmalenbach Business Review,* 66(2): 191–222.

Stoner, J. A. F. (1961) *A Comparison of Individual and Group Decisions Involving Risk,* Unpublished Master's degree thesis, Massachusetts Institute of Technology, Boston, MA.

Taylor, D. W., Berry, P. C. and Block, C. H. (1958) 'Does group participation when using brainstorming facilitate or inhibit creative thinking?', *Administrative Science Quarterly,* 3(1): 23–47.

Thaler, R. and Sunstein, C. (2008) *Nudge: The Gentle Power of Choice Architecture,* New Haven, CT: Yale University Press.

Thompson, J. D. (1967) *Organizations in Action,* New York: McGraw Hill.

Thompson, J., and Tuden, A. (1959) 'Strategies, structures and processes of organizational decisions' in J. D. Thompson, P. B. Hammond, R. W. Hawkes, B. H. Junker and A. Tuden (eds.), *Comparative Studies in Administration* (pp. 195-216). Pittsburgh, PA: University of Pittsburgh Press.

Tingling, P. and Brydon, M. (2010) 'Is decision-based evidence making necessarily bad?', *Sloan Management Review,* 51(4): 71–76.

Turner, M.E. and Pratkanis, A.R. (1998) 'Twenty-five years of groupthink theory and research: lessons from the evaluation of theory', *Organizational Behaviour and Human Decision Processes,* 73(2-3): 105–15.

Van de Ven, A. and Delbecq, A.L. (1971)'Nominal versus interacting group processes for committee decision-making effectiveness', *Academy of Management Journal,* 14(2): 203–12.

Van de Ven, A. and Delbecq, A.L. (1974) 'The effectiveness of nominal, Delphi, and interacting group decision making processes', *Academy of Management Journal,* 17(4): 605–21.

Vroom, V.H. (2000) 'Leadership and the decision making process', *Organizational Dynamics,* 28(4): 82–94.

Vroom, V H., and Jago, A. G. (1988) *The New Leadership: Managing Participation in Organizations.* Englewood Cliffs, NJ: Prentice Hall.

Vroom, V. H., and Yetton, P. W. (1973) *Leadership and Decision Making,* Pittsburgh, PA: University of Pittsburgh Press.

Wallace, P. (2001) *The Psychology of the Internet.* Cambridge: Cambridge University Press.

Weber, C. E. (1984) 'Strategic thinking – dealing with uncertainty', *Long Range Planning,* 7(5): 60–70.

Werner, A. (2014) 'Margin Call: Using film to explore behavioural aspects of the financial crisis', *Journal of Business Ethics,* 22(4): 643–54.

Wieber, F., Thürmer, J. L. and Gollwitzer, P. M. (2015) 'Attenuating the escalation of commitment to a faltering project in decision-making groups: an implementation intention approach', *Social Psychological and Personality Science,* 6(5): 587–95.

Wilson, C. E. (2007) 'Inverse, reverse, and unfocused methods: variations on our standard tools of the trade', *Interactions,* 14(6): 54–55 and 63.

Williams, A. J. and Smith, W. C. (1990) 'Involving purchasing in product development', *Industrial Marketing Management,* 19(4): 315–19.

Key terms

conflict

frame of reference

unitarist frame of reference

pluralistic frame of reference

interactionist frame of reference

functional conflict

dysfunctional conflict

radical frame of reference

resistance

conflict resolution

negotiation

distributive bargaining

integrative bargaining

conflict stimulation

organizational justice

distributive justice

procedural justice

interactional justice

discretionary behaviour:
organizational citizenship
behaviour

counter-productive work
behaviour

Learning outcomes

When you have read this chapter, you should be able to define those key terms in your own words, and you should also be able to:

1. Identify the four major frames of reference on conflict.

2. Distinguish between functional and dysfunctional conflict.

3. Distinguish between different conflict levels and conflict causes.

4. Explain the mechanisms of group conflict contagion and how member differences can be revealed.

5. Explain the relationship between organizing, coordinating and conflict.

6. Distinguish different organizational coordination devices.

7. List Thomas' five conflict resolution approaches and Gelfand's four conflict resolution cultures.

8. Distinguish between distributive and integrative bargaining.

9. Contrast the three dimensions of organizational justice.

10. Distinguish four classes of counterproductive work behaviour.

11. Contrast employee counterproductive work behaviour with organizational citizenship behaviour.

Why study conflict?

Conflict a process that begins when one party perceives that another party has negatively affected, or is about to negatively affect, something that the first party cares about.

Conflict is defined as a process that begins when one party perceives that another party has negatively affected, or is about to negatively affect, something that the first party cares about.

It occurs when the interests of one party come up against the different interests of another, and when the achievement of one party's goals is blocked by another. Conflict:

- is a state of mind which has to be perceived by both the parties involved – if either of the parties is unaware of a conflict, then none exists

- possesses both a thinking and a feeling element

- triggers reactions in the form of conflict behaviours, directed at the other party

Organizational conflict occurs within companies, charities, educational institutions, churches, prisons, hospitals and government departments. The causes of these conflicts may be political, economic, social, technological, legal or ecological. Every day, the news media report the start of some new conflict or provide us with an update on an existing, unresolved one. A survey revealed that the average European worker spent the equivalent of a day a month dealing with conflicts of different kinds, although this varied between countries. Employees in the Netherlands spent 0.9 hours a week on conflict-related tasks; 1.8 hours in Denmark, France and Britain; rising to 3.3 hours in Ireland and Germany. Conflict can lead to project failure, absenteeism and even personal attacks (CIPD/OPP, 2008).

> **CRITICAL THINKING**
>
> Watch and listen to today's TV, radio or website news headlines. How many of the stories relate to some kind of conflict? Who are the parties involved in each conflict? What is cause of their disagreement? Why do the media like reporting conflicts?

Contrasting conflict frames of reference

Frame of reference a person's perceptions and interpretations of events, which involve assumptions about reality, attitudes towards what is possible, and conventions regarding correct behaviour.

A frame of reference refers to the influences which structure a person's perceptions and interpretations of events. These involve assumptions about reality, attitudes towards what is possible, and conventions regarding what is correct behaviour for those involved. The adoption of differing frames of references by opposing sides can impair the effective resolution of conflicts.

The literature distinguishes four different frames of reference on conflict based on the distinctions made by Alan Fox (1966). They are labelled *unitarist, pluralist, interactionist* and *radical.* These frames are neither 'right' nor 'wrong', only different.

- *Unitarist:* sees organizations as essentially harmonious and any conflict as bad.
- *Pluralist:* sees organizations as a collection of groups, each with their own interests.
- *Interactionist:* sees conflict as a positive, necessary force for effective performance.
- *Radical:* sees conflict as an inevitable outcome of capitalism.

Pronoun test

Robert Reich described the 'pronoun test' that he used to evaluate the nature of the employment relationship in the companies that he visited as US Secretary of Labour during the first Clinton Administration, in the following way: 'I'd say, 'Tell me about the company'. If the person said 'we' or 'us', I knew people were strongly attached to the organization. If they said 'they' or 'them', I knew there was less of a sense of linkage' (Rousseau, 1999).

The **unitarist frame of reference on conflict** views organizations as fundamentally harmonious, cooperative structures, consisting of committed, loyal, worker-management teams that promote harmony of purpose. The unitarist frame of reference:

1. Assumes workplace conflict to be unimportant.
2. Unquestioningly accepts the language, assumptions and goals of management.
3. Believes managers can sort out disagreements using conflict resolution techniques.
4. Asserts a commonality of interests between an organization's workers and managers.

Unitarist frame of reference on conflict
a perspective that regards management and employee interests as coinciding and which thus regards organizational conflict are harmful and to be avoided.

5. Sees conflict to be the result of communication failures, personality clashes or deviant individuals.
6. Thinks that economic, technological and political developments have now virtually eliminated non-sanctioned employee behaviour within organizations.

Pluralist frame of reference on conflict

The **pluralist frame of reference on conflict** views organizations as a collection of many separate groups, each of which have their own legitimate interests thereby making conflict between them inevitable as each attempts to pursue its own objectives. This frame of reference therefore rejects the view that individual employees have the same interests as the management, or that an organization is one big happy family.

The pluralist frame also recognizes that some of the time, the interests of the different groups will coincide, while at other times, they will clash and so cause conflict between them. These differences do not prevent an organization from functioning since all groups recognize that negotiation and compromise are essential if they are to achieve their goals even partially. Hence, the job of management becomes keeping a balance between different groups and their potentially conflicting goals and interests. Underlying the pluralist view is the belief that conflict can be resolved through compromise to the benefit of all.

Pluralist frame of reference on conflict
a perspective that views organizations as consisting of different, natural interest groups, each with their own potentially constructive, legitimate interests, which makes conflict between them inevitable.

Interactionist frame of reference on conflict

The **interactionist frame of reference on conflict** sees it as a requirement for improving decision making, avoiding poor performance, and stimulating creativity (to avoid stagnation and groupthink). The interactionist frame not only accepts the inevitability of conflict, but also contains the notion that there is an optimum level of it, neither too much nor too little. It sees the way to achieve that optimum conflict level is through the intervention of

Interactionist frame of reference on conflict a perspective that views conflict as a positive and necessary force within organizations that is essential for their effective performance.

managers. If there is excessive conflict, managers should resolve it, and if there is too little, they should stimulate it.

Some companies, as part of their organizational philosophy use conflict as a management tool to help generate and develop the best ideas, to retain the best employees, and thus to drive constant innovation within the organization. Staff members are encouraged to disagree and critically assess their colleagues' ideas (Contu, 2018). However, this managerially encouraged conflict has to be of the appropriate type. **Functional conflict** supports organization goals and improves performance, but **dysfunctional conflict** hinders organizational performance.

The relationship between the two is depicted on a bell-shaped curve shown in Figure 21.1. This is also referred to as the contingency model of conflict because it recommends that managers should increase or decrease the amount of conflict in their organizations depending (contingent) on the situation (Hatch and Cunliffe, 2006). Amongst the benefits of functional conflict are:

Functional conflict a form of conflict which supports organization goals and improves performance.

- Stimulating a sense of urgency
- Making underlying issues explicit.
- Discouraging engagement in avoidance behaviour
- Motivating energy to deal with underlying problems
- Preventing premature and often dangerous resolution problems
- Sharpening employees' understanding of real goals and interests
- Enhancing mutual understanding between different groups of employees.

Dysfunctional conflict a form of conflict which does not support organization goals and hinders organizational performance.

Condition	1	2	3
Conflict level	Too little	Optimal	Too great
Organizational performance	High ↑ ↓ Low		
	Low ← Level of conflict → High		
Organizational performance level	Low	High	Low
Organization's internal characteristics	• Apathy • Stagnation • Poor focus • Unmotivated • Few changes • Slow to adapt • Not integrated • Few new ideas	• Cohesive • Productive • Cooperation • Organizational goal focused • Innovative and changing • Solution searching • Creatively adapting to environment	• Chaotic • Disruptive • Distracted • Politicized • Uncooperative • Hostile to other groups
Probable impact on organization	Dysfunctional	Functional	Dysfunctional
Managerial action required	Stimulate conflict	Leave alone	Reduce conflict

Figure 21.1: Types of conflict, internal organizational characteristics and required management actions

Source: based on Robbins and Judge (2017, p.498)

Radical frame of reference on conflict

The radical frame of reference on conflict sees the workplace as an arena of conflict between managers (in their role as agents of the owners and controllers of the means of production) and the exploited employees. It holds that the logic of profit maximization involves managers relentlessly driving down the costs of production and controlling the production process. It sees conflict as an endemic, normal feature of capitalist employment relations that cannot be resolved by any management techniques.

Although much of the literature refers to 'conflict' in organizations, in reality, overt conflict is actually very rare. Carter Goodrich (1975) originally introduced the concept of the 'frontiers of control' and that of resistance. Management's attempt to exert control is met by employee resistance and that produces clashes over interests. While the term conflict suggests a single, visible, episode of disagreement (e.g. a strike), the notion of resistance carries with it the idea of something intermittent (occurring regularly but not continually), changing (the frontier being pushed forward and back) and covert (occurring below the surface).

Resistance thus refers to the more or less covert employee behaviour that counteracts and restricts management attempts to exercise power and control in the workplace. Employees resist if they believe that organizational practices are threatening or eroding their economic, social or ethical interests at work. Resistance prompts action because staff feel they have something to lose. It occurs at all organizational levels from shop floor employees working slower than they can, through to professionals like engineers, academics or hospital doctors obstructing the extension of managerialism which constrains their discretion. Employees who feel aggrieved and who resist will seek some form of organizational justice (see p.743) and are likely to engage in counter-productive work behaviours (see p.746). Contemporary views of resistance have been presented by Fleming (2005) and Mumby (2005). The four conflict frames of reference are summarized in Table 21.1.

Radical frame of reference a perspective that views organizational conflict as an inevitable consequence of exploitative employment relations in a capitalist economy.

Resistance more or less covert behaviour that counteracts and restricts management's attempt to exercise power and control in the workplace.

Table 21.1: **Conflict frames of reference**

Frame of reference	Beliefs	Assumptions	How to deal with conflict
Unitarist	Organizations are fundamentally harmonious, cooperative structures.	Accepts the internal management structure. Thinks of conflict as negative.	Humanistic approach to conflict resolution. Not interested in cause of conflict. Concentrates on resolution through communication. Managers able to change behaviour.
Pluralist	Organizations are made up of diverse groups with varying needs and interests.	Conflict is inevitable. Conflict serves as a regulation mechanism between the different groups. Acts as an early warning system to provide signs that system will break down if conflict not dealt with.	Conflict does not prevent organizations from functioning. Groups recognize that compromise and negotiation are necessary if they are to achieve common goals. Manager's job is to balance conflict between various groups.
Interactionist	Conflict is a positive and necessary force and essential for effective organizational performance.	Conflict should be institutionalized through systems of collective bargaining. Optimum level of conflict; too much or too little is dysfunctional and impairs performance.	Seen as beneficial in motivating energy to deal with underlying problems. Enhancing mutual understanding of goals and interests.
Radical	Organizational conflict is an inevitable consequence of exploitative employment relations, in a capitalist economy, based on Marxist critique.	Fundamental aim of capitalist enterprise is to expand capital and generate profit which is divided between managers and shareholders. Competition forces low production costs, forcing employees to earn less, which creates conflict.	Management deals with conflict by limited effects of worker resistance, walkouts, strikes, or conflict.

Source: Ashleigh and Mansi, (2012, p. 258)

Employee resistance that challenges corporate power has been expanded and facilitated by developments in social media (Upchurch and Grassman, 2016) and blogging (Fleming, 2016). Blogging offers a safety valve that provides emotional support for employees and allows them to share difficult experiences and tragedies. Courpasson (2016) reported that bloggers complain about management entrenching its power, defending its privileges and promoting a short-term vision of customer relationships. They identify their own injuries by communicating their own sufferings, bad jobs, suicides, and diseases, and articulate their grievances against their company and its management.

Looking through company glass doors

Launched in 2008, glassdoor.co.uk is the second most popular jobs website. Apart from job listings, it offers a forum for individuals to anonymously share salary information and post evaluations of their organizations. These include a five-star rating scale of companies and assessments of CEOs based on a percentage of those approving of their company's leadership. It contains 33 million reviews of more than 700,000 companies in almost 200 countries. glassdoor has changed the power dynamics between employees and employers in the same way that Ratemyprofessor.com has altered the power dynamics

between students and academics in universities. Beneath each company logo are accounts of inter-departmental feuds, managerial chaos, insecure bosses, toxic company cultures, building smells, employee confessions and pleas, as well as accounts of 'boys' club' dynamics (uncomfortable hugs and demands for sexual favours).

glassdoor has 'community guidelines' which include: no profanity or discriminatory language; no personal attacks; no sharing trade secrets; and no naming of individuals who are below the level of the most senior (C-suite) executives. Users have to supply data before they can access the website material. Data suggests that between 50 and 83 per cent of job seekers in the United States read its reviews and it has become increasingly common for job interviewees to ask interviewers 'I read this on glassdoor, how do you respond?' In 2017, 21 per cent of American workers changed jobs, and companies annually spend $200 billion on recruiting new people. It has been found that changes in company practices can drop a company from a four star to a one star rating overnight. glassdoor insists that the reviews and scores on the site are 'a mirror that reflects back on companies'. How objective and reliable are glassdoor reviews likely to be? (Widdicombe, 2018).

 **STOP AND SEARCH**   on YouTube for *glassdoor reviews*

CRITICAL THINKING   The glassdoor website (see box above) appears to offer a way of increasing employee resistance and company transparency. What are the challenges facing the website's owners, the companies being described, employee bloggers and individuals seeking information about an organization?

Conflict levels and causes

Our definition encompasses conflicts at all different levels within an organization:

- *Dyad:* This is conflict between two people (dyad) within an organization, e.g. between a manager and subordinate, two peers, or between a salesperson and a customer.

Table 21.2: Conflict levels and causes

Causes	Level		
	Dyad	Group	Organization
Relationship			
Task			
Process			

- *Group:* This is conflict that occurs between the members of a workgroup or a team (intra-group), e.g. in face-to-face or virtual teams.
- *Organization:* This is conflict that emanates from the way that the company is organized, e.g. inter-departmental conflict.

The causes of workplace conflicts are infinite but most of them can be classified under three broad headings:

- *Relationship:* Conflict over interpersonal issues, e.g. personality clash.
- *Task:* Conflict over the goals and content of work, e.g. describe or solve a problem.
- *Process:* Conflict over how a task is accomplished, e.g. task allocations.

The three causes of conflict can manifest themselves at any of the three levels of the organization (Table 21.2).

✓✓✓ **EMPLOYABILITY CHECK** (how organizations work)

Describe a workplace conflict situation that you have either been personally involved in or have heard about in the media Locate it on the conflict grid in Table 21.2. What was the level and cause? Explain who was involved, what was it about, whether it was resolved and how.

Dyad-level conflict

Dyadic conflict is a disagreement between two individuals in an organization which creates significant resentment and discontent between them. The two people involved may be a boss and a subordinate, two peers, or a staff member and a customer. It often arises out of personality clashes or emotionally-charged interactions. For example, between an extravert and an introvert, or between an optimist and a pessimist who share the same workspace. Major personality differences can prevent them from working together effectively. However, conflict can also be triggered by individuals' beliefs and perceptions. Roy and Judy Eidelson (2003) identified five such conflict domains:

- *Superiority:* an individual's belief that he or she is better than the other person in important ways. They have a sense of specialness, deservingness or entitlement.

- *Injustice:* an individual's perceived mistreatment by the other person. This results in their experiencing a feeling of unfairness which leads them to engage in retaliatory action.

- *Vulnerability:* an individual's belief that he or she is in state of danger created by the other person over which they have no control and thus is unable to feel safe.

- *Distrust:* an individual's perception that the other person is hostile and harbours malign intent towards them. This person is not trusted not to hurt, abuse, humiliate, cheat, lie, or take advantage of them.

- *Helplessness:* an individual's belief that despite their best efforts, correctly or incorrectly, they believe that they lack the ability to attain their goal. Their self-perception diminishes their motivation and can trigger a resentment of the other person.

✓✓✓ **EMPLOYABILITY CHECK (interpersonal skills)**

You are working on a project at work that is very important to you, but your supervisor makes you stop, requires you to put it away, and insists that you work on something else. This greatly frustrates you. How do you disagree effectively with your boss? What are going to do and say?

Workplace dyadic conflict

The Chartered Institute of Personnel and Development (CIPD, 2015) examined one-to-one (dyad) conflict which affected the relationships between employees and was caused by their personal incompatibilities. It resulted in tension and friction between staff and generated feelings of annoyance, frustration and irritation. The survey revealed that:

- Of the 2,195 respondents, 34 per cent reported either isolated disputes or ongoing difficult relationships with others – most commonly with their line manager (24 per cent); a team colleague (18 per cent); or a work colleague (14 per cent).

- The most common causes of such conflicts were differences in personality or working styles (44 per cent);

individual competence, performance and target setting (33 per cent); and the level of support or resources provided (23 per cent).

- The most common, perceived negative conflict behaviour reported was lack of respect (61 per cent); followed by bullying, intimation or harassment (33 per cent); and the refusal to work together or cooperate (33 per cent).

- The two consequences of conflict which clearly stood out were an increase in employee stress (43 per cent) and a reduction in motivation and commitment (39 per cent). Staff responded to conflict by discussing it

with their manager or a human relations department member (37 per cent); by discussing it informally with another person (26 per cent); or by talking about it with someone outside work – a family member or friend (23 per cent).

The researchers found that both informal discussion with another person, and the formal grievance, discipline or complaint procedure, were equally effective in resolving interpersonal conflict. However, the Institute recommended the use of alternative dispute resolution mechanisms such as mediation and what it called 'facilitated discussions' to complement the aforementioned formal approaches.

 **STOP AND SEARCH** YouTube for *How to disagree with your boss.*

Group-level conflict

Group (or intra-group) conflict exists when there are perceive interpersonal incompatibilities or differences between the individuals within a group or team. These can be the result of relationship, task or process causes.

- *Relationship* conflict relates to an awareness of interpersonal incompatibilities between group members. It includes emotional components such as feelings of tension and friction. These result in conflict over personal issues such as dislike of fellow members and feelings of annoyance, frustration and irritation.

- *Task* conflict relates to an awareness of differences between members in their ideas, viewpoints and opinions concerning the group task. Task conflicts generally lack the intense interpersonal negative emotions that are more commonly associated with relationship conflict.

- *Process* conflict relates to a group failing to agree on deadlines, task pacing, performance milestones or allocation of task responsibilities. Members can become dissatisfied with the uncertainty created and may express a desire to leave the group (Jehn and Mannix, 2001).

Collectively, these conflicts within a group increase the communication problems between its members, diminish their commitment to team decisions, and decrease their commitment to their organization.

Dysfunctional conflict can impede a team's performance and endanger its existence. How does conflict in a team begin and then spread to infect all of its members? Lindred Greer and her colleagues (2014) discovered three phases of conflict contagion within a group and three mechanisms by which it spreads (Table 21.3)

Table 21.3: Phases and mechanisms of group conflict contagion

Phase 1	
Meeting 1	Dyadic disagreement begins when team member A has an idea and member B disagrees with it.
Phase 2	
Meeting 2	Faction building follows as member C (a friend of member A) intervenes to support them. Member D, listens, weighs arguments, and sides with member B. Coalitions within the team begin to build.
Coalition forming is a conflict spreading mechanism	
Meeting 3	Other team members, not interested in the issue or unaware of the growing disagreement, remain uninvolved. Conflict begins to affect group performance. Those uncomfortable with the conflict withdraw either intellectually or physically. The created factions within the group address additional issues and the tensions increase.
Emotionally-charged behaviour is a conflict spreading mechanism	
Meeting 4	Negative emotions spread through the team, and previously uninvolved members engage in emotional outbursts. Resentment builds so that an issue of importance to only a few members begins to dominate the team agenda putting its entire output in jeopardy. Goal-focused members attempt to bring the high-jacked agenda back on track.
Threats to team outcome is a conflict spreading mechanism	
Phase 3	
	Full-blown conflict follows. The team's performance, efficiency and creativity all suffer. Since all members are now involved in the conflict, many of them will want to resolve it.

Source: based on Greer et al. (2014)

Greer et al. advise team leaders and managers to intervene before the initial dyadic conflict spreads to the rest of the team. They should keep attuned to possible dyadic disagreements which have the potential to escalate and to nip them in the bud. They should ensure that they understand the real issues underpinning the disagreement (e.g. personal antagonism, status envy) before intervening, and be aware of their own biases, perhaps delegating any required intervention to a neutral third party.

Lindred Greer

 **STOP AND SEARCH**   You Tube for *Lindred Greer: Managing Conflict in Teams* (7:59).

Ginka Toegel

Jean-Louis Barsoux

While intervening immediately *after* a leader is aware of a disagreement in their team is commendable, it still represents a reactive approach to team conflict. Waiting for a problem to arise before intervening risks frustration building up and trust being lost. Ginka Toegel and Jean-Louis Barsoux (2016) advocate a proactive approach to team conflict. They recommend surfacing team members' differences *before* a team starts work so as to pre-empt any destructive conflict later.

It involves a team and its leader coming together and sharing preferences and expectations in order to identify the most likely areas of future friction and suggesting ways in which differences can be accommodated. The focus is on team members' attitudes and behaviours rather than on the underlying sources of their differences (e.g. personality); and upon the process of the team's work rather than its content. The intention is to immunize members against unproductive future conflict. So how do you reveal group members' differences? The authors suggest exploring team members' respective world views using a Five Questions technique in which questions are used to start conversations between team members as shown in Table 21.4.

Table 21.4: **Five questions for revealing team members' world views**

Look Spotting the difference	Individuals quickly assess a peer's character, competence and status on the basis of how they look, dress, move and their tone of voice. Team-inappropriate clothing can also put colleagues off. Members reflect on how they want to come across to others compared with how they actually do. *Questions: In your world, what makes a good first impression, what do you notice first about another person, what do you value about and judge them on?*
Act Judging behaviour	Differing body language norms (e.g. gestures, interaction distances) can be a cause of group friction and disrupt communication especially if members are from different cultures. So too can their differing attitudes to work timekeeping, appropriate levels of assertiveness and expectations about helping one another. Members establish team norms around those issues. *Questions: In your world, how important are punctuality and time limits, what is a comfortable physical distance for interacting in the workplace, should members volunteer for tasks or wait to be assigned them?*
Speak Divided by language	Communication styles of team members with different native languages can cause controversy. The actual words chosen can cause misunderstanding since meanings differ – 'yes' can mean 'maybe', 'let's try it' or 'no way'. Members also differ in their tolerance for candour, humour, speaking pauses and being interrupted. Members establish guidelines on speaking up within the team. *Questions: In your world, is a promise an aspiration or a guarantee, do interruptions signal interest or rudeness, is unsolicited feedback welcome?*
Think Occupying different mindsets	Members' backgrounds and personalities affect how they think about their work, make decisions and solve problems. Some use methodical thinking, others employ intuitive thinking, some prefer experimentation and others value predictability. Members make themselves aware of each others' preferred cognitive styles and the value of each. *Questions: In your world, is uncertainty viewed as a threat or opportunity, is it better to be reliable or flexible, how do people respond to deviations from plan?*

Feel	How members display and manage their emotions in the face of disagree-ment can trigger conflict. Over-enthusiasm can fuel scepticism while displays of anger can be upsetting or intimidating. The team can discuss the dangers of 'telling it like it is' and bottling things up. Incivility in the form of withdrawal, sarcasm or private complaining, can be equally conflict-inducing. The aim is to establish ways of disagreeing productively.
Charting emotions	
	Questions: In your world, which positive and negative emotions is it acceptable and unacceptable to display in the workplace? How do people express anger and enthusiasm? How would you respond if a team mate had annoyed you?

Source: based on Toegel and Barsoux (2016, pp.81-84)

Organizational-level conflict

At the organizational level, a failure of coordination can trigger conflict. The process of organizing by senior managers acts to divide up work activities, and a conflict can thus be seen as a symptom of management's failure to adequately coordinate these same activities later on. A coordination–conflict four-stage model is shown in Figure 21.2. It organizes the diverse theoretical discussions and research findings into a framework that explains how conflict at the organizational level arises and how it might be managed. Such management may involve either the use of conflict resolution approaches (to reduce or eradicate conflict) or conflict stimulation approaches (to encourage and increase conflict).

Stage 1: Organizing

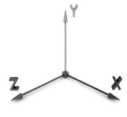

The first stage of the model consists of organizing, defined as the process of breaking up a single task and dividing it among different departments, groups or individuals. For example, a car company allocates the work involved in building a new vehicle to its different departments – human resources, accounting, production, sales and research. Such functional specialization is one of many bases on which to divide the total work involved. Specialization is rational because it concentrates specialists in departments, avoids duplication, allows performance goals to be established, and specifies practices.

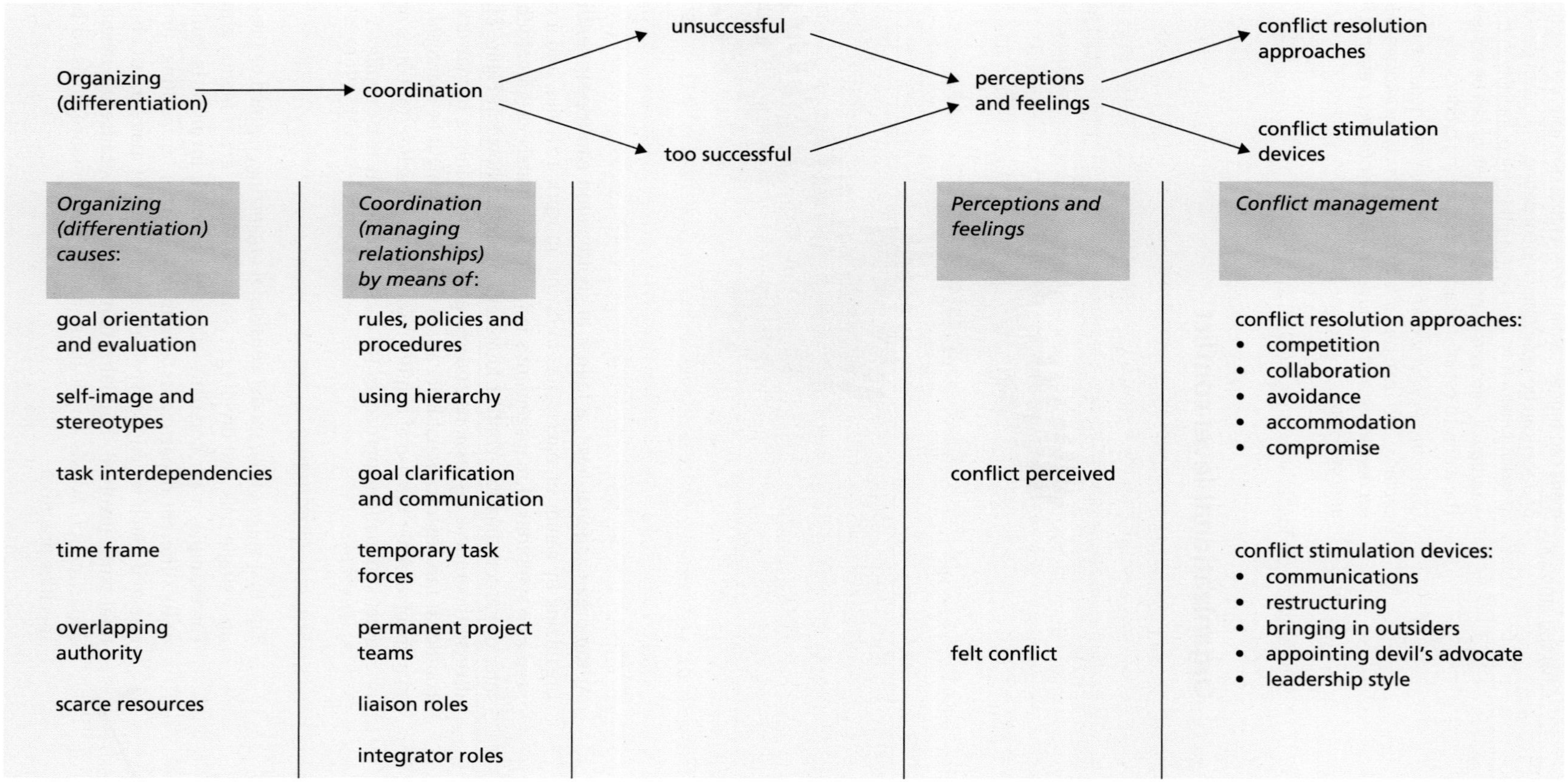

Figure 21.2: Coordination–conflict model

All forms of such horizontal specialization (divisions between departments) result in each sub-unit becoming concerned with its own particular part of the total objective and work process. The degree of such separation of tasks can vary, but it creates the conditions in which conflict can potentially arise. It does so because, by definition, each department, group or individual receives a different part of the whole task to perform. This differentiates them from the others in terms of their:

1. Goals orientation and evaluation
2. Self-image and stereotypes
3. Task interdependencies
4. Time perspective
5. Overlapping authority
6. Scarce resources

1. Goals orientation and evaluation

Each department is given its own goal and its members are evaluated in terms of how well they achieve it. Ideally, the goals of different departments, groups and individuals, although different should be complementary, but in practice this may not be so. Moreover, the measurement process can reinforce differences. Each department's unique goals and evaluation methods lead it to have its own view about priorities and how these are best achieved (see Table 21.5).

2. Self-image and stereotypes

Employees in each department become socialized into a particular perception of themselves and of the other departments in the company. A group may come to see itself as more vital to a company's operations than others, believing that it possesses higher status or greater prestige. Such an evaluation can engender an 'us-and-them' attitude. Whenever differences between groups and departments are emphasized, stereotypes are reinforced, relations deteriorate and conflict develops. Departments will often blame each other for problems and shortcomings.

3. Task interdependencies

The organizing process makes departments, groups and individuals dependent on each other to satisfactorily perform their own jobs and to achieve their own objectives. The degree of such interdependence varies and may be *pooled, sequential* or *reciprocal* (Thompson, 1967). Groups in sequential interdependence, and even more in reciprocal interdependence, require a high degree of coordination between their activities. If this is achieved then each group will perform effectively and its members will experience satisfaction. If it is not, the result can be conflict.

Table 21.5: Areas of potential goal conflict between marketing and manufacturing departments

Area	Marketing	Manufacturing
Product range	Many and complex	Few and simple
Product customization	Customer specific	Standard products
New products	Continual	Only if necessary
Production planning	Accept all orders	Assess order fit
Quality control	High standards	Reasonable, practical
Physical distribution	Immediate from large inventory	If possible, make to order

Source: Shapiro (1977)

4. Time perspective

Paul Lawrence and Jay Lorsch's (1967) study found that people's perceptions of how important various things were depended on the time frame that governed their work and their goal orientations. Groups with different time perspectives find it difficult to coordinate their activities, and this can result in greater inter-group conflict. These different time frames are often incompatible, hindering communication, impeding coordination and encouraging conflict.

5. Overlapping authority

Demarcation disputes ('who does what') have always caused difficulties and ambiguity over responsibility or authority is one example of this. Individuals or groups may be uncertain as to who is responsible for performing which tasks or duties, and who has the authority to direct whom. Each party may claim or reject responsibility and the result can be conflict. Groups may fight for the control of a resource while individual managers may attempt to seize each other's authority.

6. Scarce resources

Once a task is allocated to a department, group or individual, its recipient is allocated resources with which to achieve it. Since resources are finite, conflict can arise with respect to how personnel, money, space or equipment are shared out. From a win–lose perspective, one party's gain is another's loss. For this reason, conflicts often arise at times of budget cuts, reduced promotion opportunities and wage freezes.

CRITICAL THINKING

How complete is this list of organization-level conflict causes? Do they satisfactorily account for all conflicts at the organizational level? Are there other causes that you would add?

Stage 2: Coordinating

If organizing involved breaking up the task into bits, then coordinating is bringing the bits together again. Coordination involves ensuring that the previously divided tasks that were allocated between different departments, groups and individuals, are brought together in the right way and at the right time. Coordination entails synchronizing the different aspects of the work process. Organizations use coordination devices to manage the relationships between the different parties so to avoid conflict breaking out. There are seven such devices:

1. Rules, policies and procedures
2. Hierarchy
3. Goal clarification and communication
4. Temporary task forces
5. Permanent project teams
6. Liaison roles
7. Integrator roles

1. Rules, policies and procedures

All of these specify how one party is to interact with another. For example, a standardized operating procedure will specify when additional staff can be recruited to a department. Rules and procedures reduce the need for both interaction and information flow between parties. They are most useful when inter-party activities are known in advance; when they occur frequently enough to merit establishing rules and procedures to handle them; and when there is sufficient stability to make them relevant.

2. Hierarchy

Coordination of different parties' activities is achieved efficiently by referring any problems to a superior located higher up in the organizational chain-of-command. The supervisor uses his or her legitimate authority, based on their position in the hierarchy, to resolve a conflict. Team members who are unable to agree take their problem to their mutual boss who resolves their disagreement.

3. Goal clarification and communication

By specifying and communicating its goals to the others in advance, each party knows what the other is attempting to do. At the individual level this may mean clear job descriptions, while at the departmental level, it could be a statement of objectives. Parties can meet to ensure that they do not compete or interfere with each other's goals. Such discussions reduce the chances of each party misperceiving the others' intentions thereby avoiding conflict.

4. Temporary task force

This involves representatives from several different departments coming together on a temporary basis to form a task force. Once the specific problem they were created for is solved, the task force disbands, and members return to their usual duties and departments. During their membership, individuals come to understand the goals, values, attitudes and problems of their fellow members. This helps to resolve their differences effectively especially if more than two parties are involved.

5. Permanent project team

For complex tasks, a project team may be established consisting of cross-functional members (e.g. from Engineering, Marketing, Finance). This creates a matrix structure as each individual retains a responsibility both to the project team leader and to their functional department head. This solution allows coordination to occur and potential conflict to be avoided at the team level, thereby improving communication and decision making.

6. Liaison roles

If differences remain unresolved by senior management, then a liaison role may be created. It would be used most by departments which had the greatest potential for conflict. The occupant of this role has to be well informed about the needs and technology of the departments involved; be seen to be unbiased; and be interpersonally skilled. By holding meetings, supplying units with information, liaison personnel keep the employees in different sections in touch with each other.

7. Integrator roles

An individual or department may be tasked with integrating the activities of several, highly conflicting departments, e.g. production, sales and research (Figure 21.3) A scientist with financial and sales experience may be recruited to occupy an integrating role. By having a 'foot in each camp', this person can assist the departments to coordinate their activities. The integrator checks that the two departments' objectives complement each other; and that the output of one becomes a timely input to the other.

Home viewing

In the classic film, *Twelve Angry Men* (1957, director Sidney Lumet) a jury retires to decide on the guilt or innocence of a youth from a slum background. At the outset, eleven of the twelve jurors are convinced of the boy's guilt and are keen to find him guilty without further discussion. Only one member of the jury, played by Henry Fonda, has reservations and persuades the other members to take the time to review the evidence. The film can be broken down into a series of 'conflict episodes', each of which ends with a vote (conflict reduction) or a juror's change of mind. The film illustrates many aspects of conflict. In each episode, ask yourself how do the conflicts manifest themselves in the characters' behaviour? How does each vote become the basis for conflict for in the next episode? Watch Fonda's behaviour carefully. At first sight it appears that it is random. But then, you'll see a pattern. What is that pattern? (McCambridge, 2003)

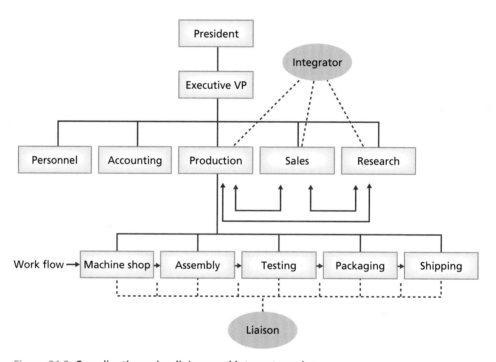

Figure 21.3: Coordinating using liaison and integrator roles

Stage 3: Perceptions and feelings

Unsuccessful coordination need not necessarily ignite a conflict. Perception plays an important part. It is only if one of the parties, department, group or individual becomes aware of, or is adversely affected by, the situation and cares about it, that potential conflict turns into perceived conflict. It occurs only when one party realizes that another is thwarting its goals. It is only at this stage that the conflict issue becomes defined and 'what it is all about' gets decided. Specifically, each party considers the origins of the conflict, why it emerged, and how the problem is being experienced by the other party. The way that the conflict is defined at this stage will determine the type of outcomes that the parties are willing to settle for in the later stages.

Not only must a party perceive a conflict, but it must also feel it. That is, it must become emotionally involved in experiencing feelings of anxiety, tension, frustration and hostility towards the other party. The emotional dimension of conflict shapes perceptions. For example, negative emotions result in an oversimplification of issues, reductions in trust, and negative interpretations of the other party's behaviour. Positive emotions, in contrast, increase the chances of the parties taking a broader view, seeing the issue as a problem to be solved, and developing more creative solutions.

Stage 4: Conflict management (resolution and stimulation)

The final stage is labelled conflict management. It involves not only resolving conflict once it has occurred, but also stimulating conflict where none exists. These issues are discussed below.

Conflict management

Conflict management is concerned with having a sufficient amount of conflict within an organization. Senior management may judge that there is too much or too little conflict.

In the case of the former, the existing coordination devices may be inadequate and cause too much conflict. In such a case, the company will manage the situation by implementing conflict resolution approaches to reduce or eliminate the immediate conflict, before adjusting the coordination mechanism to prevent it from occurring again in the future. Alternatively, they may consider that the coordination devices are working too well, thereby causing complacency and apathy. In this case, they may introduce conflict stimulation approaches to increase conflict. Thus, within organizations, conflict can be managed through a combination of conflict resolution and conflict stimulation approaches.

Conflict resolution approaches

Conflict resolution a process which has as its objective the ending of the conflict between the disagreeing parties.

Managers may judge that there is too much conflict, perhaps due to a failure in the coordination devices. If so, the company will manage the situation by implementing conflict resolution approaches to reduce or eliminate the immediate conflict. A manager or team leader can choose from a number of different conflict resolution approaches.

Kenneth Thomas (1976) distinguished five conflict resolution approaches based upon the two dimensions of:

- How assertive or unassertive each party is in pursuing its own concerns.

- How cooperative or uncooperative each is in satisfying the concerns of the other.

He labelled these approaches *competing* (assertive and uncooperative); *avoiding* (unassertive and uncooperative); *compromising* (mid-range on both dimensions); *accommodating* (unassertive and cooperative); and *collaborating* (assertive and cooperative). They are summarized in Figure 21.4 and defined in Table 21.6 in order of Competing, Avoiding, Compromising, Accommodating and Collaborating (CACAC).

In addition to Thomas' two behavioural orientation dimensions – assertiveness and cooperativeness, Callanan and Perri (2006) highlight three additional context factors to be considered when deciding on an appropriate conflict resolution approach:

- *Power congruity:* Your perception of differences in your own and the other's power, both formal power (boss-subordinate) and informal power (between peers). If you perceive your power as high and theirs low, you are likely to opt for a Competitive style, if the reverse, then you would choose Accommodation.

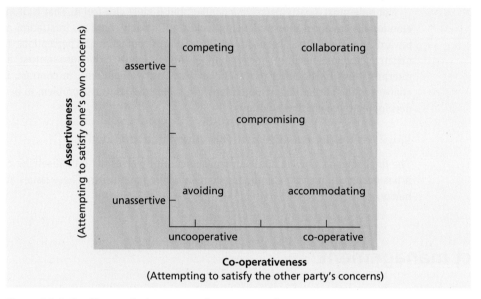

Figure 21.4: Conflict resolution approaches compared

Source: reprinted from *Organizational Behaviour and Human Performance*, vol.16, no.1, T.H. Ruble and K. Thomas, Support for a two-dimensional model of conflict behaviour, p.145. Copyright 1976 with permission from Elsevier.

Table 21.6: Conflict resolution approaches compared

Approach	Objective	Your posture	Supporting rationale	Likely outcome
1. Completing	Get your way	'I know what's right Don't question my judgement or authority.'	It is better to risk causing a few hard feelings than to abandon the issue.	You feel vindicated, but the other party feels defeated and possibly humiliated.
2. Avoiding	Avoid having to deal with conflict	'I'm neutral on that issue. Let me think about it. That's someone else's problem.'	Disagreements are inherently bad because they create tension.	Interpersonal problems don't get resolved, causing long-term frustration manifested in a variety of ways.
3. Compromising	Reach an agreement quickly	'Let's search for a solution we can both live with so we can get on with our work.'	Prolonged conflicts distract people from their work and cause bitter feelings.	Participants go for the expedient rather than effective solutions.
4. Accommodating	Don't upset the other person	'How can I help you feel good about this? My position isn't so important that it is worth risking bad feelings between us.'	Maintaining harmonious relationships should be our top priority.	The other person is likely to take advantage.
5. Collaborating	Solve the problem together	'This is my position, what's yours? I'm committed to finding the best possible solution. What do the facts suggest?'	Each position is important though not necessarily equally valid. Emphasis should be placed on the quality of the outcome and the fairness of the decision-making process.	The problem is most likely to be resolved. Both parties are committed to the solution and satisfied that they have been treated fairly.

Source: adapted from Whetton, D., Cameron, K. and Woods, M. (2000) *Developing Management Skills for Europe*, Pearson Education Ltd © 2000, p.345

"Aren't you glad we had this meeting
to resolve our conflict?"

 **STOP AND SEARCH**   YouTube for *Learning to Use Different TKI Modes* (2:26).

✓✓✓ **EMPLOYABILITY CHECK** (self-awareness)

What is your preferred conflict resolution style? Indicate your first (1) and second (2) preferences from among the following statements:

- I find conflicts challenging and exhilarating and enjoy the battle of wits that follows.
- Being at odds with other people makes me feel uncomfortable and anxious.
- I try to negotiate and adopt a give-and-take approach to problem situations.
- I may not get what I want but it's a small price to pay for keeping the peace.
- I explore issues with others so as to find solutions that meet everyone's needs.

The five statements above are arranged in the CACAC order, as listed in Table 21.6.

- *Issue criticality:* This is defined as the relative importance of a given conflict producing issue in terms of its impact on the individuals involved. The more important an issue is to you, the more Assertiveness you will use, and the more important it is to the other party, the more Cooperative behaviour they will use.

- *Aggressive intent attribution:* This concerns your judgement as to whether the other party will respond aggressively or non-aggressively. If an aggressive response is anticipated then the Competitive style will be selected, whereas if non-aggression is expected then the Accommodation style will be favoured.

Thomas showed that individuals had distinct ways of resolving workplace conflicts but do entire companies? Does the organizational context in which employees work define the expected and acceptable ways in which conflict should be resolved? In short, do companies possess distinct conflict resolution cultures? Understanding the ways in which the characteristics of the organization (rather than those of the individual or the group) affect the way conflict is resolved is important. The argument is that a company defines its own shared and acceptable way to resolve conflict. Ultimately, this minimizes individual and group variation in its conflict management resolution approaches that are employed.

"Why don't we enroll in a Conflict Resolution Program
where we can study the underpinnings of conflict dynamics
and implement strategies to foster sustainable peace?"

Conflict resolution cultures

Michele Gelfand

Michele Gelfand (2008) and her colleagues proposed a typology of organizational conflict resolution cultures based upon two dimensions. The horizontal dimension relates to whether conflict is managed in an agreeable and cooperative manner or a disagreeable and competitive manner. Agreeable norms prescribe behaviour that promotes group and organizational interests and reflects a collective attempt to move toward others when managing conflicts. Disagreeable norms prescribe behaviour that promotes self-interest and reflects collective attempts to move against others when managing conflicts (Figure 21.5).

The vertical dimension reflects the notion that organizations develop norms as to whether conflict is managed actively or passively Active norm management is characterized by open engagement, high agency, and low-situational constraint when managing conflicts, while passive norm management is characterized by a lack of open engagement, low agency, and high-situational constraint when managing conflicts. These two dimensions produce four distinct conflict cultures as shown in Figure 21.5. These closely echo Thomas' individual-level conflict resolution approaches:

- *Dominating* conflict cultures (active and disagreeable)
- *Collaborative* conflict cultures (active and agreeable)
- *Avoidant* conflict cultures (passive and agreeable)
- *Passive–aggressive* conflict cultures (passive and disagreeable).

Figure 21.5: Typology of conflict resolution cultures
Source: Gelfand et al., (2008, p.142)

The researchers then went on to investigate how leaders shaped their organization's conflict cultures (Gelfand et al., 2012). They obtained information from 862 employees who worked in 159 branches of the same American bank. They found that the different branches had their own, distinct, socially shared norms as to how conflict within them should be resolved. The researchers found three conflict cultures:

- *Collaborative*: Conflict norms stress active, cooperative discussion of conflict. The assumption is that cooperative behaviours and open conflict resolution is appropriate.

- *Dominating*: Conflict norms encourage active confrontation in order to publically win disputes. The assumption is that disagreeable or competitive behaviours are acceptable.

- *Avoidant*: Conflict norms stress passive withdrawal in cases of disagreement. The assumption is that conflict is dangerous, should be suppressed, and that harmonious relationships are essential.

Thus Gelfand et al. discovered that three of Thomas' individual conflict resolution approaches were reflected at the organizational level in the form of distinct company conflict resolution cultures in the various bank branches. But how did these different unit-level cultures develop?

They ascribed the causes to leaders' behaviours and employees' personality traits in the different branches. Thus leaders' cooperative conflict resolution styles were positively related to collaborative conflict cultures and negatively related to dominating cultures. Branch leaders with avoiding conflict resolution styles contributed to avoidant cultures. Branches with members high on the personality trait of agreeableness contributed to collaborative cultures while those who were disagreeable and extraverted helped to develop dominating cultures.

Negotiation

Negotiation a social process through which two or more interdependent parties make decisions, allocate resources, or resolve disputes.

Negotiation is a social process through which two or more interdependent parties make decisions, allocate resources or resolve disputes (Brett, 2014). The negotiators attempt to reach an agreement that works out the details of their interdependence while protecting and advancing their own interests. Wertheim et al. (2018) noted that organizations that are 'flatter, more decentralized, less hierarchical and less characterized by the top-down command and control model . . . where communication is more horizontal, place greater emphasis on interpersonal skills including persuasion, influence and negotiation' (p.2).

Negotiation can take place between individuals, groups, parts of companies, and between organizations. Richard Walton and Robert McKersie's (1965) classic research into negotiation behaviour distinguished distributive bargaining strategies from integrative bargaining strategies (Table 21.7).

Home viewing

There Will be Blood (2007, director Paul Thomas Anderson) is set in 1898 and tells the story of an oil man, Daniel Plainview (played by Daniel Day-Lewis), who is engaged in a ruthless quest for wealth during the oil boom. His son, HW has been injured in an accident leaving him profoundly deaf. In one scene, Plainview and his brother go into a meeting, shake hands, and sit down at a table. The brothers are going to negotiate with two investors who want to buy Plainview's oil wells. The investors appear to be offering lots of money. If Plainview accepts the deal, he will be a very rich man. The clip ends with Henry and his brother walking out of the meeting. Why does this negotiation session collapse into irreconcilable conflict? How could things have been handled better, by whom?

Table 21.7: Bargaining strategies

Bargaining characteristic	Integrative	Distributive
Outcomes	Pursuing own outcomes	Pursuing joint outcomes
Goal	Get as much of the pie as possible	Expand the pie so that both parties are satisfied
Motivation	Win–lose	Win–win
Focus	Positions ('I can't go beyond this point on this issue')	Interests ('Can you explain why this issue is so important to you?')
Interests	Opposed	Congruent
Information sharing	Low (Sharing information will only allow other party to take advantage)	High (Sharing information will allow each party to find ways to satisfy interests of each party)
Duration of relationship	Short term	Long term

Source: Robbins and Judge (2017, p.508)

Distributive bargaining a negotiation strategy in which a fixed sum of resources is divided up, leading to a win–lose situation between the parties.

 **STOP AND SEARCH**   YouTube for *Negotiation strategies.*

Integrative bargaining a negotiation strategy that seeks to increase the total amount of resources, creating a win–win situation between the parties.

Distributive bargaining operates under zero sum conditions. It seeks to divide up a fixed amount of resources creating a win-lose situation. Purchasing a new car exemplifies this. The more the buyer pays, the more profit the seller makes and vice versa. Here the pie is fixed and the parties bargain about the share each receives. Within an organization, distributive bargaining takes place between the trade (labour) unions and management. Issues involving wages, benefits, working conditions and related matters are seen as a conflict over limited resources.

Integrative bargaining seeks settlements that can create a win–win solution. A union-management agreement which increases productivity and profits, and wages in line with both, would be an example of integrated bargaining because the size of the total pie is increased. Integrative bargaining is preferable to distributive bargaining because the latter makes one party a loser. It can create animosities and deepen divisions between people who have to work together on an ongoing basis. Integrative bargaining makes both sides 'winners'.

✓✓✓   **EMPLOYABILITY CHECK** (interpersonal skills)

Negotiating effectively with those over whom you have no direct authority is now a key employability skill. Describe a situation when you had to persuade, influence or negotiate with someone senior to yourself. What was the outcome? What did you learn?

What did they find? Negotiation and culture

Jeanne Brett and her colleagues (2017) proposed a framework that explained cultural differences in the use and effectiveness of two differences negotiating strategies. The first was Questions and Answers (Q&A) which is an integrative, value-creating negotiation strategy. The negotiator's goal is focused upon creating value for both parties, and then claiming a sufficient portion of that joint value. The second is called Suggestions and Offers (S&O). It is a distributive, value-claiming negotiation strategy and the negotiator's goal is focused narrowly on claiming value for him or herself. It involves their making and substantiating offers to the other party. Brett et al.'s framework uses the cultural constructs of:

- *Trust*: This refers to a willingness to make oneself vulnerable to another during social interaction. At the cultural level, it is a judgement as to whether others are dependable. Trust in others can be high or low.

- *Cultural tightness*: This refers to norm strength. Cultural norms can either be strongly endorsed; conformity to them closely socially monitored and violations socially sanctioned (tight) or they are not (loose).

They classified national cultures into four regions of the world which shared similarities: West; East Asia; 'Latin cultures' (including Latin America, Spain, and Portugal); and the Middle East / South Asia. Examining the existing research literature, they categorized national cultures as being either Q&A or S&O strategy-using. This meant that negotiators from these cultures devoted relatively more of their negotiating time to either Q&A or to S&O.

In which region do you think people trust others the most? Which region had the tightest norms? Which regions used which Q&A and S&O negotiating strategies the most? **(Answers in chapter Recap.)**

 **STOP AND SEARCH**   YouTube for *Jeanne Brett, Secrets of cross-cultural communication* (4:40).

Conflict stimulation approaches

Conflict stimulation the process of engendering conflict between parties where none existed before, or escalating the current conflict level if it is too low.

Interactionists argue that too much harmony in the workplace breeds complacency which hinders achievement. In their view, the encouragement and intensification of conflict rather than its prevention or mitigation is more likely to enhance rather than hinder creativity, individual achievement, quality group decision making and organizational productivity. Conflict stimulation is required for performance enhancement and is defined as the process of engendering conflict between parties where none existed before or escalating the current conflict level if it is too low.

Walton (1969) recommended 'confrontation before integration'. Superior outcomes are achieved if individuals define and analyse an issue, offer alternative views and perspectives, and critically assess those offered by others, before arriving at a solution that all can agree on and commit to. This prevents a rush to the first acceptable but not necessarily the best solution. Limited conflict escalation can facilitate this process. Some of the stimulation techniques might include:

- Allowing a crisis to blow up or an error to occur
- Raising the perceived stakes of success or failure
- Tying a controversial issue to a previously conflict-free topic
- Setting targets so high that they cannot be reached by doing business as usual
- Choosing an issue at random, and circulating information that is threatening to one of the parties
- Creating mutual disagreement by drawing attention to differences of opinion the parties themselves were aware of before.

John Kotter (1996) also discussed the dangers of complacency and the need to drive employees out of their comfort zones. Various techniques can be used to stimulate conflict where none existed before, in order to encourage different opinions and engender new thinking and problem solving:

1. Communications

Managers can withhold information 'to keep them guessing' or send large amounts of inconsistent information ('we're expanding, we're going bust') to get people arguing. They might send ambiguous or anxiety-provoking messages.

2. Re-structuring a company

Re-aligning working groups and altering rules and regulations so as to increase or create interdependence between previously independent units. This can easily stimulate conflict, particularly if the goals of the newly interdependent departments are made incompatible, e.g. one department's objective being to minimize costs and another's is to maximize market share.

3. Bringing in outsiders

Adding individuals to a group whose backgrounds, values, attitudes or management styles differ from those of existing members, for example, by recruiting senior executives with career experience in automobile manufacture to manage healthcare organizations.

4. Devil's advocate method

Within an organization, a person is assigned the role of critic, to stimulate critical thinking and reality testing. For example, in deciding whether to embark on an e-commerce strategy, one team member might be assigned the devil's advocate role to focus on its pitfalls and dangers.

5. Dialectic method

This method explores opposite positions called 'thesis' and 'antithesis'. The outcome of the debate between the two is the 'synthesis' which in turn, becomes the new thesis to be opened up for debate. Before deciding on a take-over, a company may establish two teams giving them access to the same information, and requiring one of them to argue for the takeover and the other against the acquisition decision. The conflict of ideas throws up alternatives which can be synthesized into a superior final decision.

6. Leadership style

Organizations can appoint managers who encourage non-traditional viewpoints rather than authoritarian ones who might be inclined to suppress opposing viewpoints. Leadership style has been found to be a key element in organization change programmes and in particular those involving changes in organization culture.

Rahim (2002) noted that traditional conflict management approaches do not question whether the structure and processes of an organization are deficient and could be causing dysfunctional conflict. Instead he says, 'It tries to resolve or reduce conflict between parties at the micro-level within the existing system. Effective conflict management involves change at the macro-level in the organization so that substantive conflict is encouraged and affective conflict is minimized at the individual, group, intergroup and organizational levels' (p.215). He insists that this must involve changes in the leadership, culture and the design of an organization.

Organizational justice

Organizational justice a personal evaluation about the ethical and moral standing of managerial conduct.

Organizational justice is defined as the personal evaluation about the ethical and moral standing of managerial conduct (Cropanzano, et al., 2007, p. 35). It is employees' perception of whether their manager and their organization have acted fairly. There are three components of organization justice (Figure 21.6).

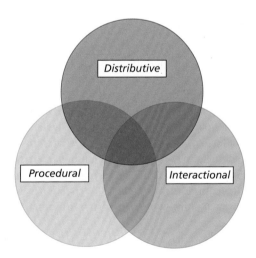

Figure 21.6: Components of organizational justice

Distributive justice employees' judgements about the fairness of outcomes.

Procedural justice employees' evaluations of the way in which decisions are made, irrespective of their outcome.

Distributive justice concerns employees' judgements about the fairness of outcomes, e.g. how company resources are distributed between departments.

Procedural justice concerns employees' evaluations of the way in which decisions are made, irrespective of whether the outcome is good or bad for them, e.g. chief executive allocates resources based on his friendship with departmental heads.

Table 21.8: Components of organizational justice

Distributive justice: Appropriateness of outcome fairness
- Equity: rewarding employees based on their contributions.
- Need: providing benefits based on one's personal requirements.
- Equality: providing each employee with roughly the same compensation.

Procedural justice: Appropriateness of the allocation process
- Consistency: all employees are treated the same.
- Ethics: norms of professional conduct are not violated.
- Accuracy: decisions are based on accurate information.
- Correction: an appeals process or other mechanism for rectifying mistakes.
- Lack of bias: no person or group is singled out for discrimination or ill treatment.
- Representation of all concerned: appropriate stakeholders have input into a decision.

Interactional justice: Appropriateness of treatment received from authority figures
- Informational fairness: sharing relevant information with employees.
- Interpersonal fairness: treating employees with dignity, courtesy, and respect.

Source: Cropanzano et al. (2007, p.36)

Interactional justice
employees' perceptions of the interpersonal treatment they receive from those in authority.

Interactional justice involves employees' perceptions of the interpersonal treatment they receive. It has two components: *informational justice,* which is the perceived truthfulness and adequacy of explanations offered; and *interpersonal justice,* which concerns being treated with dignity and respect, e.g. chief executive emails staff informing them that they have been made redundant; budget cuts after announcing increased annual profits to shareholders.

Each of the three components of organization justice can be further sub-divided as shown in Table 21.8.

Managers and employees place different amounts of weight on the three dimensions of justice when evaluating an action. Employees are typically attentive to all three dimensions of justice, but they do not necessarily give each dimension equal weight in their considerations (Greenberg, 1988). They prioritize the procedural and interactional ones (Colquitt et al., 2001). For example, performance appraisals give staff the chance to meet with their manager (procedural justice), exchange information and receive feedback (interactional justice). A well-organized and conducted appraisal meeting can increase employee perceptions of fairness, even if appraisees know that their comments have no effect on decisions about their rating, promotion or bonus (distributive justice).

In contrast, managers, believe that employees are much more concerned with outcomes, e.g. pay rises and promotions (distributive justice), than having an explanation of the process through which pay and promotion decisions are made (procedural justice) or with communicating those decisions to the staff affected (interactional justice). Managers' failure to recognize this difference inhibits their ability to be perceived as acting fairly.

CRITICAL THINKING   Suggest the different ways in which a company's staff appraisal system might break the principles of organizational justice.

Consequences of organizational justice

Evidence shows that many managers do not treat employees fairly (Cropanzano et al., 2007). This absence of fairness may be due either to a lack of desire or managerial inability. Since organizational justice refers to an employee's *perceptions* of fairness, managers need not only to make fair decisions and develop fair policies, but they also need to be perceived to be doing so. Research has studied the consequences of just and unjust treatment of employees by their organizations which has consequences not only for the employees themselves but also for their managers and for organizations as a whole (Viswesvaran and Ones, 2002).

Consequences for employees

- Justice builds trust and commitment – justly treated employees have higher morale, are more supportive of their managers, and are more committed to their organizations.
- Justice improves job performance – justly treated subordinates are motivated to higher job performance.
- Justice fosters employee organizational citizenship behaviour – justly treated employees show extra conscientiousness, comply with workplace policies and behave altruistically.
- Justice builds customer satisfaction and loyalty – the positive behaviour of justly treated employees 'spills over' to dealing with their customers and clients.
- Being fairly treated sends a message to employees – it shows they are valued and accepted which enhances their feelings of self-worth and is reflected in their reduced feelings of discrimination, lower stress levels and improved physical and mental health.

Consequences for managers

- Increased influence and power – bosses whose subordinates believe they treat them fairly strengthen their own power base. People admire those who are fair-minded and will comply with their requests to gain their approval.
- Increased status and credibility – being perceived as fair enhances a manager's standing among those with whom they interact. The person is judged to be trustworthy, consistent and lacking ulterior motives. This strengthens their ability to influence others.
- Increased employee trust – if a manager possesses a reputation for fairness, in ambiguous or novel situations when they have to make a decision based on information not available to subordinates, they can draw on their reputation and say to their staff 'trust me'.
- Reinforce identity and self-esteem – a manager's self-image as a fair person may be reinforced by employees who respond to the image of fairness that they portray (Greenberg, 1988, 2009).
- Fair treatment promotes similarly ethical behaviour in those receiving it, so fair managers can contribute to making their entire organization more just.

Consequences for the organization

- Increased influence and power – bosses whose subordinates believe they treat them fairly strengthen their own power base. People admire those who are fair-minded and will comply with their requests to gain their approval.

- Organization performance – the collective effect of improved individual employee job performance can result in improved overall organizational performance as measured in increased profits, customer satisfaction, reduced levels of absenteeism and theft.

- Corporate value – justice can be a core value that defines an organization's identity with both its internal and external stakeholders. A 'culture of justice' can be built if it is espoused as part of management philosophy and enacted internally by consistent management practices. Managerial fairness has become a topic of considerable public interest as a result of recent economic and legal concerns thereby exposing managers and their organizations to greater external scrutiny than ever before.

Organizational work behaviours

Discretionary behaviour freedom to decide how work is going to be performed; discretionary behaviour can be positive, such as putting in extra time and effort, or it can be negative, such as withholding information and cooperation.

Many different factors in the workplace including those concerning organizational justice, can trigger what managers would judge to be either a negative response from their employees (counter-productive work behaviour) or a positive reaction (organizational citizenship behaviour). They are both labelled discretionary behaviours and relate to employees' freedom to decide how work is going to be performed. Discretionary behaviour can be positive, such as putting in extra time and effort, or it can be negative, such as withholding information and cooperation. The causes and consequences of their two employee work behaviours have been extensively studied.

Organizational citizenship behaviour

Organizational citizenship behaviour employee behaviour that is discretionary, informal and which contributes to organizational effectiveness.

Organizational citizenship behaviour (OCB) is defined as an individual's behaviour that is discretionary, informal and which contributes to organizational effectiveness (Organ, 1997). Since it is performed by personal choice, these discretionary behaviours are not included in an employee's job description and therefore cannot be enforced by their manager. OCB is a facet of job performance and is discouraged by task and relationship conflict (de Wit et al., 2012).

Organizational citizenship behaviours are performed as a result of personal choice. They can be directed either at individuals or the organization as whole. Coleman and Borman (2000) identified three types of citizenship behaviour:

- *Personal support:* reflecting individually-oriented OCBs (e.g. altruism, courtesy) helping others who are experiencing work problems in the workplace.

- *Organizational support:* reflecting organizationally-oriented OCBs (e.g. conscientiousness) giving notice if unable to attend work; enhancing the company reputation.

- *Conscientious initiative:* reflecting persistence in the face of obstacles and proactive efforts beyond routinely assigned duties (e.g. supermarket staff picking up rubbish outside the store entrance which is not part of their job).

Counter-productive work behaviour

Counter-productive work behaviour any intentional employee behaviour viewed by the organization as being harmful to its legitimate interests.

Employees who perceive themselves to have been unfairly treated, that is, not received organizational justice, can engage in retaliatory and vengeful acts aimed at their bosses and their organizations (Flaherty and Moss, 2007). Collectively, these discretionary actions are termed counter-productive work behaviour (CWB) which is defined as any intentional employee behaviour viewed by the organization to be harmful to its legitimate interests. CWB is a facet of job performance and is stimulated by task and relationship conflict (de Wit et al., 2012).

Table 21.9: Examples of counter-productive work behaviour

Production deviance – behaviours that impede production	Inter-personal deviance – behaviours that involve other people	Political deviance – behaviours that involve deceit	Property deviance – behaviours that relate to physical items
Intentionally stopping or leaving work early	Verbal abuse and bullying	Showing favouritism	Sabotage of equipment
Wasting time (working slowly); wasting company materials	Sexual harassment	Revenge	Theft of company property
Taking extended work breaks; misuse of sick leave	Physical attacks on co-workers	Blaming others	Destruction or defacing of company property
Withdrawing; cyber-loafing	Incivility	Revealing confidential information to competitors	Fraud
Intentionally performing tasks incorrectly or poorly	Alcohol and substance abuse	Falsifying or restricting information	Misuse of employer discounts
Unexcused absenteeism	Arguing with customers	Gossiping, intentionally undermining co-workers	
Late-coming	Ignoring people's opinions	'Bad-mouthing' the company to others	
Unsafe working practices	Checking emails during meetings		

Research has identified a large number of different counter-productive work behaviours and writers have created various typologies of CWB (Marcus et al., 2016). These can be integrated into a single list which is shown in Table 21.9. Defining deviance as any behaviour that violates accepted norms, it is possible to distinguish four classes of deviance within the workplace context, each with its own associated behaviours. Each such deviant behaviour can either be focused on a person or on the organization. It can be considered as either a minor or a major infringement. Sackett et al. (2006) examined organizational citizenship behaviour (OCB) and counter-productive work behaviour (CWB) and concluded that they represented two distinct constructs instead of the opposite ends of a single continuum.

CUTTING EDGE Incivility in the workplace

Christine Porath (2016) researched incivility in the workplace that took the form of rudeness, bullying and similar counter-productive behaviours that resulted in employees becoming disengaged at work, undertaking acts of sabotage against the company, and taking their frustrations out on their families. Her recommendation was that victims of incivility should improve their own well-being in the office, rather than try to change the offender or the corrosive working relationship.

A common and natural response is to avoid the perpetrator, but in the workplace you may have no choice but to collaborate with that person. Another response is to tackle incivility head-on but this can make the dynamic worse. Porath reported that 85 per cent of people who used either avoidance or confrontation were dissatisfied

with the outcome, and of those who relied on institutional remedies, only 15 per cent were satisfied with how their employers handled incivility. However, for those wishing to manage incivility directly by confronting the workplace offender, she offers some advice.

Before confronting a colleague at work, Porath advises asking yourself three questions: Do you feel safe talking to this person? Was their rude behaviour intentional? Was it an isolated incident? Only if the answer to all these questions is yes, should you proceed to confront them. Otherwise just concentrate on your own effectiveness. She offers some confrontation tips (p.111):

- *Prepare for discussion*: choose a safe environment that is comfortable for both of you; decide whether to invite others as witnesses or mediators.

- *Rehearsal and feedback*: Ask a friend to role play the perpetrator, practise what you will say (your strategy and tactics) and how you will say it (body language) and obtain their feedback.

- *Issue not individual*: Focus your discussion on the issue that is the problem, not on the perpetrator him or herself; concentrate on how their behaviour affects both of your work performances.

- *Emotional response*: If the perpetrator responds emotionally, let them vent their anger. Neither agree nor disagree with them, but instead indicate that you hear and understand what they are saying, e.g. 'I can see why you might have been annoyed'.

- *Listen actively*: Paraphrase what you hear them say and repeat it back to them, so as to check that you have understood.

- *Establish norms*: Attempt to agree courteous interaction norms for the future so that neither of your work performances suffer.

 **STOP AND SEARCH** YouTube for *Christine Porath: How incivility shuts down our brains at work* (8:35) or Christine *Porath: Do Nice People Finish Last or Best?* (Ted Talk, 15:41).

 **RECAP**

1. *Identify the four major frames of reference on conflict.*

   - The unitarist frame sees organizations as essentially harmonious and any conflict as bad.

   - The pluralist frame sees organizations as a collection of groups, each with their own interests.

   - The interactionist sees conflict as a positive and necessary force for effective performance.

   - The radical frame sees conflict sees as an inevitable outcome of capitalism.

2. *Distinguish between functional and dysfunctional conflict.*

   - Functional conflict is considered by management to support organizational goals and improves organizational performance.

   - Dysfunctional conflict is considered to impede the achievement of organizational goals and reduces company performance.

3. *Distinguish between different conflict levels and conflict causes.*

   - Conflict can be studied at the level of the dyad (two people) e.g. between a manager and subordinate; at the level of the group (e.g. face-to-face or virtual team); or at the level of the organization (e.g. inter-departmental conflict).

   - Conflict can be caused by relationship differences (e.g. personality clashes); task differences (e.g. about the outcomes of tasks); or process differences (e.g. delegation of tasks or responsibilities).

4. *Explain the mechanisms of group conflict contagion and how member differences can be revealed.*

   - Coalition forming, emotionally-charged behaviour and threats to team outcomes have all been found to be conflict-spreading mechanisms within a work group.

   - The Five Questions technique helps a team identify how different members look, act, speak, think and display their emotions.

5. *Explain the relationship between organizing, coordinating and conflict.*

   - Organizing concerns dividing up a large task into sub-tasks, and assigning them to groups. Coordination brings those previously divided sub-tasks together to ensure that all activities are directed towards organizational goals. In the process of sub-division, departments acquire their own, subordinate goals and interests, which differ from organizational ones. Conflict ensues when these divergent interests and goals clash.

6. *Distinguish the different organizational coordination devices.*

   - Coordination devices include rules, policies and procedures; using hierarchy; goal clarification and communication; temporary task force; permanent project teams; liaison roles and integrator roles.

7. *List Thomas' five conflict resolution approaches and Gelfand's four conflict resolution cultures.*

   - Thomas' five conflict resolution approaches are avoidance, accommodation, compromise, collaboration and competition.

   - Gelfand's four conflict resolution cultures are dominating (active and disagreeable); collaborative (active and agreeable); avoidant (passive and agreeable); and passive-aggressive (passive and disagreeable).

8. *Distinguish between distributive and integrative bargaining.*

   - Distributive bargaining refers to a negotiation situation in which a fixed sum of resources is divided up. It leads to a win–lose situation between the parties.

   - Integrative bargaining, seeks to increase the total amount of resources and it creates a win–win situation between the parties.

9. *Contrast the three dimensions of organizational justice.*

   - Distributive justice concerns employees' judgements about the fairness of outcomes; procedural justice relates to employees' evaluations of the way in which decisions are made, irrespective of their outcome; and interactional justice involves employees' perceptions of the interpersonal treatment they receive from those in authority.

10. *Distinguish four classes of counterproductive work behaviour.*

   - Production deviance refers to employee behaviours that impede production (e.g. leaving work early); inter-personal deviance involves other people (e.g. verbal abuse and bullying); political deviance involves bias (e.g. showing favouritism); and property deviance are behaviours that relate to physical items (e.g. sabotage of equipment).

11. *Contrast organizational citizenship behaviour with employee counterproductive work behaviour.*

   • Organizational citizenship behaviour refers to employees' positive voluntary actions within an organization that are not part of their contracted role obligations, while counter-productive work behaviour is any intentional employee behaviour viewed by the organization to be harmful to its legitimate interests.

   • While intuitively appearing to be opposites, with employees who engage in the former not engaging in the latter, the research in fact suggests these represent two distinct constructs instead of the opposite ends of a single continuum.

RECAP: What did they find?

Brett et al.'s (2017) research answered the following questions:

• *In which region did people trust others the most?* The West (45 per cent) had the highest trust, followed by East Asia (39 per cent); then the Middle East/South Asia (19 per cent); with the Latin Countries at the bottom (14 per cent).

• *Which region had the tightest norms?* On a 15-point scale, The Middle East/South Asia (11) had the tightest norms; followed by East Asia (9); and the Latin Countries and the West (5) were equal third.

• *Which regions used which Q&A and S&O negotiating strategies the most?* Questions and Answers (Q&A) is an integrative, value-creating negotiation strategy which focuses upon creating value for both parties. Suggestions and Offers (S&O) is a distributive, value-claiming negotiation strategy which is focused narrowly on claiming value for only one side. On a six-point scale indicating frequency, the West (5) used Q&A most; East Asia (4) used S&O most; the Middle East/South Asia (2) also used S&O, but less so; and the Latin Countries used a combination of Q&A (1) and S&O (2).

Regions by trust, cultural tightness and frequency of strategy use			
		Trust	
		High trust	*Low trust*
Cultural tightness	*Tight*	East Asia (S&O)	Middle East / South Asia (S&O)
	Loose	West (Q&A)	Latin countries (Q&A or S&O)

Revision

1. Briefly describe each of Thomas' five conflict resolution approaches and give an example of an organizational situation in which each would be most appropriate.

2. 'Since every unit and department in an organization has its own goals and interests, conflict will always be a feature of organizational life'. Consider the costs and benefits of conflict for the various organization stakeholders. Give your reasons and illustrate your points with examples.

3. Discuss the ways that each of the three dimensions of organizational justice can benefit employees, managers and their organization.

4. How can a company discourage employee counterproductive work behaviour and encourage organizational citizenship behaviour among its staff?

Research assignment

Search Google for 'work blogs'. You will find reports of employees from different countries and different occupational groups (e.g. teachers, nurses, legal staff) talking about their jobs and their organizations. Also consult the *blogroll* (http://workblogging.blogspot.co.uk/). This is a list of blogs with hyperlinks. Employee bloggers frequently forge links with fellow bloggers, particularly those in similar jobs, occupations or professions. These hyperlinks are to other recommended or connected blogs. In addition, the *glassdoor* website (http://glassdoor.co.uk/) provides employee reviews about organizations. Analyse the contents of a selection of these work blogs and write a report answering the following questions:

- Identify recurring topics and themes found in your workblogs.
- What do these tell you about conflict and resistance in the workplace?
- Under what circumstances would you write a workblog?
- What do you see as the costs and benefits of work blogging for (a) the employee bloggers and (b) the company?

Source: based on Richards and Kosmala (2013)

Springboard

Alissa Contu (2018) 'Conflict and organization studies', *Organization Studies* (published early online). Provides a critically the various perspectives on conflict in organizations currently being taught in business schools.

Bernd Marcus, Anita Taylor, Stephanie Hastings, Alexandra Sturm and Oliver Weigelt (2016) 'The structure of counterproductive work behaviour: A review, a structural meta-analysis and a primary study', *Journal of Management*, 42(1): 203–33. The authors discuss the various forms that counterproductive work behaviour can take and discuss different ways of classifying them.

Elisabeth Mikkelsen and Stewart Clegg (2019) 'Conceptions of conflict in organizational conflict research: Toward critical reflexivity', *Journal of Management Inquiry*, 28(2): 166–79. The authors discuss the three distinct contested conceptions that frame discussion of conflict at work; recommend a more reflexive approach; and emphasize philosophical and political assumptions about conflict.

Dean Tjosvold, Alfred Wong and Nancy Chen (2014) 'Constructively managing conflicts in organizations', *Annual Review of Organizational Psychology and Organizational Behaviour 2014*, pp.545–68. The authors provide an overview of the main theories and research into conflict and its management spanning the last forty years.

OB cinema

Metallica: Some Kind of Monster (2004, directors Joe Berlinger and Bruce Sinofsky) is a documentary that shows the heavy metal band Metallica producing an album and the many conflicts that arise during the two-year process.

Clip 1: 0:29:10 to 0:31:40. After a long day of playing, the band listens to the resulting song. What is the key problem the band is discussing? What type of conflict is taking place?

Clip 2: 1:00:46 to 1:07:30. What was the issue the band discussed? What type of conflict is taking place? What unspoken assumptions do you think Lars and James have about working after 4 p.m.?

Clip 3: 1:38:11 to 1:39:47. What is different in how the band handles this disagreement over the ones before? Can you identify one good practice of conflict management in this clip?

Clip 4: 1:58:24 to 2:01:40. Are you surprised by Lars's strong defence of James's concerns? Can you identify one good practice of conflict management in this clip?

Source: Quijada (2016)

Chapter exercises

1: Counter productive work behaviours

Objectives
1. To find examples of counter productive work behaviours in organizations.
2. To suggest reasons for their occurrence in the workplace.
3. To propose management actions to prevent them.

Briefing
1. Make a list of employee misbehaviours that you have engaged in yourself while at work, observed others engaging in, or which you have read about.
2. Form into groups and discuss:
   a. What are the causes of such counter productive work behaviours?
   b. What options do employees have who either engage in counter-productive work behaviours themselves or see others doing it?
   c. What actions can senior management take to eliminate or reduce counter productive work behaviours?

Debriefing
1. Class reforms.
2. Categories of counter-productive work behaviours are charted up and students share examples of their CWBs indicating into which category they would best fit.

Production deviance	Inter-personal deviance	Political deviance	Property deviance
– behaviours that impede production	– behaviours that involve other people	– behaviours that involve deceit	– behaviours that relate to physical items

3. For each CWB, students discuss the causes of the behaviour, the options available to employees, and actions that management might take to eliminate or reduce such counter productive work behaviours.

2: Missed promotion

Objectives
1. To describe the importance of organizational justice
2. To distinguish between distributive, procedural and interactional justice
3. To understand how managers and subordinates can emphasize different aspects of justice which in turn influence their perceptions of fairness.

Briefing
This is a two-person role play in which one student takes the role of an employee who has just been passed over for promotion. The other takes the role of that employee's immediate supervisor. The two meet to discuss the promotion decision.

1. Students get into pairs with one taking the role of 'manager' and the other of the 'employee'.
2. Individually and separately, students read the scenario for their assigned role and write responses to the four questions which follow it.
3. The instructor provides a brief reminder of the key aspects of organizational justice.

4. Student pairs role play their meeting (10 minutes). Individuals can make up information as needed provided it is consistent with what is on their scenario sheet.

5. Following its conclusion, the students reflect on what has occurred. They make notes using their role-play reflection sheet. They do this individually without discussing their answers with their partner.

6. Students talk quietly with their partner about how their meeting went. They compare their experiences using their notes from their reflection sheets.

7. The instructor leads a debriefing of what happened in the students' meetings in terms of organizational justice theory. Students share their experiences and give examples from their own role-plays.

Scenario sheet information for manager role

You are a unit supervisor at Universidad Cable. Sam, one of your direct reports, has just sent you an email requesting a meeting. You know that Sam was expecting a promotion and was denied that promotion yesterday. The promotion decision is what you are meeting about.

Sam is a valuable employee, whom you definitely want to keep in your unit. To prepare for this meeting, you reviewed the minutes from the promotions committee meeting. There were six applicants for the position Sam wanted, and all six applicants were strong candidates. Sam was clearly qualified for the position, but the committee decided that one of the other applicants was a better choice.

You will be meeting with Sam in 10 minutes. To prepare, think about the issues involved in the meeting. There are four questions below. Please consider and write your answer to each of the questions in the space provided. Focus on the most important points in answering the questions.

1. Describe your goal for this meeting. What would make it successful?

2. What do you think Sam's goal for the meeting is?

3. How will you reach your goal? What approach will you use?

4. Describe any other issues or concerns you have about this meeting.

Scenario sheet information for employee role

You have been employed at Universidad Cable for two years. You will soon be meeting with your immediate supervisor, Chris. You sent an email requesting this meeting because you just found out that you did not receive a promotion you were expecting. You were surprised and disappointed when you learned that you did not get the promotion. You are definitely qualified. Moreover, your unique combination of skills and experience would have made you very effective in the new position.

You will be meeting with Chris in ten minutes. To prepare, think about the issues involved in the meeting. There are four questions below. Please consider and write your answer to each of the questions in the space provided. Focus on the most important points in answering the questions.

1. Describe your goal for this meeting. What would make it successful?

2. What do you think Chris's goal for the meeting is?

3. How will you reach your goal? What approach will you use?

4. Describe any other issues or concerns you have about this meeting.

Source: Caza et al., (2011)

References

Ashleigh, M. and Mansi, A. (2012) *The Psychology of People in Organizations,* Harlow, Essex: Pearson.

Brett, J. M. (2014) *Negotiating Globally: How to Negotiate Deals, Resolve Disputes, and Make Decisions Across Cultural Boundaries* third edition, San Francisco: Jossey-Bass.

Brett, J.M., Gunia, B.C. and Teucher, B.M. (2017) 'Culture and negotiation strategy: a framework for future research', *Academy of Management Perspectives,* 31(4): 288–308.

Callanan, G.A. and Perri, D.F. (2006) 'Teaching conflict management using a scenario-based approach', *Journal of Education for Business,* 81(3): 131–39.

Caza, A., Caza, B.B. and Lind, E.A. (2011) 'The missed promotion: An exercise demonstrating the importance of organizational justice', *Journal of Management Education,* 35(4): 537–63.

CIPD (2015) *Getting Under the Skin of Workplace Conflict: Tracing the Experiences of Employees,* London: Chartered Institute of Personnel and Development, April.

CIPD/OPP (2008) *Fight, Flight or Face IT?,* London: Chartered Institute of Personnel and Development/ OPP.

Coleman, V. L. and Borman,W. C. (2000) 'Investigating the underlying structure of the citizenship performance domain', *Human Resources Management Review,* 10(1): 25–44.

Colquitt, J. A., Conlon, D. E., Wesson, M. J., Porter, C. O. L. H. and Ng, K. Y. (2001) 'Justice at the millennium: a meta-analytic review of 25 years of organizational justice research', *Journal of Applied Psychology,* 86(3): 425–45.

Contu, A. (2018) 'Conflict and organization studies', *Organization Studies* (published early online).

Courpasson, D. (2016) 'Impactful resistance: the persistence of recognition politics in the workplace', *Journal of Management Inquiry,* 25(1): 96–100.

Cropanzano, R., Bowen, D. E. and Gilliland, S. W. (2007) 'The management of organizational justice', *Academy of Management Perspectives,* 21(4): 34–48.

De Wit, F.R.C., Greer, L.J. and Jehn, K.A. (2012) 'The paradox of intragroup conflict: a meta-analysis', *Journal of Applied Psychology,* 97(2): 360–90.

Eidelson, R.J. and Eidelson, J.I. (2003) 'Dangerous ideas: five beliefs that propel groups toward conflict', *American Psychologist,* 58(3): 182–92.

Flaherty, S. and Mossi, S.A. (2007) 'The impact of personality and team context on the relationship between workplace injustice and counterproductive work behaviour', *Journal of Applied Social Psychology,* 37(11): 2549–75.

Fleming, P. (2005) 'Metaphors of resistance', *Management Communication Quarterly,* 19(1):45–66.

Fleming, P. (2016) 'Resistance and the "post-recognition" turn in organizations', *Journal of Management Inquiry,* 25(1): 106–110.

Fox, A. (1966) *Industrial Sociology and Industrial Relations, Research Paper,* London: Royal Commission on Trade Unions and Employers' Associations.

Gelfand, M.J., Leslie, L.M. and Keller, K.M. (2008) 'On the etiology of conflict cultures', *Research in Organizational Behaviour,* 28, 137–66.

Gelfand, M.J., Leslie, L.M., Keller, K. and de Dru, C. (2012) 'Conflict cultures in organizations: how leaders shape conflict cultures and their organization-level consequences', *Journal of Applied Psychology,* 97(6): 1131–47.

Goodrich, C. L. (1975) *The Frontier of Control,* London: Pluto Press.

Greer, L.L., Jehn, K. and Rispens, S. and Jonsen, K. (2014) 'How conflict goes viral', Stanford University School of Business, 7 May. https://www.gsb.stanford.edu/insights/lindred-greer-how-conflict-goes-viral [accessed January 2019]

Greenberg, J. (1988) 'Cultivating an image of justice: looking fair on the job', *Academy of Management Executive,* 2(2): 155–57.

Greenberg, J. (2009) 'Everybody talks about organizational justice, but nobody does anything about it', *Industrial and Organizational Psychology,* 2(2): 181–95.

Hatch, M. J. and Cunliffe, A. L. (2006) *Organization Theory,* second edition, Oxford: Oxford University Press.

Jehn, K.A. and Mannix, E.A. (2001) 'The dynamic nature of conflict: a longitudinal study of intragroup conflict and group performance', *Academy of Management Journal,* 44(2): 238–51.

Kotter, J. (1996) 'Kill complacency', *Fortune,* 5 August 5, pp.122–24.

Lawrence, P. R. and Lorsch, J. W. (1967) *Organization and Environment,* Boston, MA: Addison Wesley.

Marcus, B., Taylor, O.A., Hastings, S.E., Sturm, A. and Weigelt, O. (2016) 'The structure of counterproductive work behaviour: a review, a structural meta-analysis and a primary study', *Journal of Management,* 42(1): 203–33.

McCambridge, J. (2003) '*12 Angry Men*: A study in dialogue', *Journal of Management Education,* 27(3): 384–401.

Mumby, D.K. (2005) 'Theorizing resistance in organization studies: A dialectical approach', *Management Communication Quarterly,* 19(1): 19–44.

Organ, D. W. (1997) 'Organizational citizenship behavior: it's construct cleanup time', *Human Performance,* 10(2): 85–97.

Porath, C. (2016) 'Managing yourself: an antidote to incivility', *Harvard Business Review,* 94(4):108–11.

Quijada, M.A. (2016) 'Heavy metal conflict management', *Management Teaching Review,* 1(3): 155–63.

Rahim, M.A.(2002) 'Toward a theory of managing organizational conflict', *International Journal of Conflict Management,* 13(3): 206–35.

Richards, J. and Kosmala, K. (2013) 'In the end, you can only slag off for so long: employee cynicism through work blogging', *New Technology and Employment,* 28(1): 66–77.

Robbins, S. P. and Judge, T.A. (2017) *Organizational Behaviour,* seventeenth edition, Harlow, Essex: Pearson Education.

Rousseau, D. M. (1999) 'Why workers still identify with organizations', *Journal of Organizational Behaviour,* 19(3): 217–33.

Ruble, T. T., and Thomas, K. (1976) 'Support for a two-dimensional model of conflict behaviour', *Organizational Behaviour and Human Performance,* 16(1): 143–55.

Sackett, P.R., Berry, C.M., Wiemann, S.A. and Laczo, R.M. (2006) 'Citizenship and counterproductive behaviour: clarifying relations between the two domains', *Human Performance,* 19(4): 441–464.

Thomas, K. W. (1976) 'Conflict and conflict management' in M. D. Dunette (ed.), *Handbook of Industrial and Organizational Psychology* Chicago, IL: Rand McNally, pp. 889–935.

Thompson, J. D. (1967) *Organizations in Action.* New York: McGraw Hill.

Toegel, G. and J-L. Barsoux (2016) 'How to pre-empt team conflict', *Harvard Business Review,* 94(6): 78–83.

Upchurch, M. and Grassman, R. (2016) 'Striking with social media: the contested (online) terrain of workplace conflict', *Organization,* 23(5): 639–56.

Viswesvaran, C. and Ones, D. S. (2002) 'Examining the construct of organizational justice: a meta-analytic evaluation of relations with work attitudes and behaviours', *Journal of Business Ethics,* 38(3): 193–203.

Walton, R. E. (1969) *Interpersonal Peacemaking: Confrontations and Third-party Consultation* Reading MA: Addison-Wesley.

Walton, R. E. and McKersie, R. B. (1965) *A Behavioural Theory of Labour Relations.* New York: McGraw Hill.

Wertheim, E., Glick, L. and Larson, B.Z. (2018) 'Teaching the basics of negotiation in one class', *Management Teaching Review* (published early online)

Whetton, D., Camerson, K. and Woods, M. (2000) *Developing Management Skills for Europe,* second edition, Harlow, Essex: Financial Times Prentice Hall.

Widdicombe, L. (2018) 'Rate your boss!', *The New Yorker,* 22 January, pp. 22–28.

Key terms

power	influence
power priming	organization politics
reward power	political skill
coercive power	need for power
referent power	Machiavellianism
legitimate power	locus of control
expert power	risk-seeking propensity
strategic contingencies theory	

Learning outcomes

When you have read this chapter, you should be able to define those key terms in your own words, and you should also be able to:

1. Appreciate the importance of power and politics in organizations.
2. Compare and contrast different perspectives on power.
3. Distinguish different bases of power.
4. Identify organizational factors which enhance the power of departments.
5. Differentiate between influencing techniques and the tactics of organization politics.
6. Identify the characteristics of individuals most likely to engage in political behaviour.
7. Explain how women use and are affected by organization politics.

Why study power and politics?

Leadership BS

Should leaders be 'squeaky clean' and avoid playing politics? Jeffrey Pfeffer (2016) notes that many famous leaders – including Nelson Mandela, Abraham Lincoln and John F. Kennedy, were pragmatists who were willing to use their power and political tactics to achieve what they believed were important objectives. This contradicts current leadership advice which emphasizes authenticity, telling the truth and building trust. Pfeffer claims that we often confuse what we believe ought to be true with what actually is. Citing a biography of the famous American President Abraham Lincoln, Pfeffer (2016, p.94) notes that:

'Sometimes, this approach to leadership required Lincoln to make deals he was initially uncomfortable with to gain the support of legislators, notably to win passage of the constitutional amendment that outlawed slavery. Sometimes, it required Lincoln to depart from the truth – for example, about precisely where a Southern peace delegation was as it approached Washington and when it might arrive, to give him an opportunity to negotiate privately with its members. Sometimes, it required him to display energy and confidence that he might not really have felt. The ability to do what is required in and by a situation, to behave in usefully inauthentic ways, characterized not only Lincoln but also, I would argue, many other great leaders.'

The popular view is that power corrupts, and that organization politics means underhand, cunning, manipulative 'dirty tricks' and backstabbing. While some of this may be true, leaders and managers who do not have power, and who are either unwilling or unable 'play the politics', have difficulty getting anything done. Inescapable features of organizational life, power and politics can be damaging, but can be also used in constructive ways, to solve problems, generate consensus and drive change.

We think of organizations as rational and orderly, with decisions based on evidence and reason, focusing on efficiency and effectiveness. But organizations are also political systems, and decisions are shaped by influence tactics designed to promote the interests of individuals or groups. As organizations become less hierarchical, and rely more on networks and teams, the use of power and influence becomes more important (Pfeffer, 2010). Power and politics are linked.

Power can be seen as the ability to get other people to do what you want them to do, and it is often necessary to use political tactics to achieve those ends. Politics is thus 'power in action'. Pfeffer (2010) also argues that management failures can often be attributed to lack of political skill.

An organization's members do not always share the same values and goals. Disagreements over the definitions of problems, and how best to solve them, can be expected. Disputes of this kind are often healthy, by exposing different perspectives and issues. What happens, however, when that open sharing of views fails to produce a consensus? Sometimes, those with the best ideas win. Often, the winners are those who are better able to exercise influence 'behind the scenes', by 'playing politics'. Good ideas do not always sell themselves, and rational arguments may not be effective on their own. As the American diplomat Henry Kissinger once said:

> 'Before I served as a consultant to [President John F.] Kennedy, I had believed, like most academics, that the process of decision-making was largely intellectual and all one had to do was to walk into the President's office and convince him of the correctness of one's view. This perspective, I soon realized is as dangerously immature as it is widely held' (Pfeffer, 1992, p.31).

CUTTING EDGE   Power corrupts – but powerlessness is a bigger threat

Dacher Keltner

Dacher Keltner (2017) argues that power is part of every relationship and every social interaction that we have. Power is not just something that applies to leaders and senior managers. He observes that we gain power by showing empathy, openness, fairness, and by collaborating with others. However, the behaviour of those who have achieved power often changes, and they become rude, selfish and unethical. This is what Keltner calls 'the power paradox'; our good qualities give us the power, which then allows our bad qualities to surface. Keltner describes a laboratory experiment in which one member of a group of three was given the leadership role, and they were all then given a writing task. While they were writing, Keltner brought them a plate with four cookies. In every case, each team member took a cookie and, being polite, left the extra one. Would anyone eventually take the extra cookie? In almost every case, those who had been named as leaders took the extra cookie, and were more likely to eat it with their mouths open, lips smacking, spraying crumbs on their clothes. Another study found that drivers of inexpensive cars always gave way to pedestrians at crossings, but drivers in BMWs and Mercedes gave way to pedestrians only half the time. The more expensive the vehicle, the more entitled its owner felt to break the law or to behave in an aggressive, arrogant way.

This evidence suggests that power does corrupt. Is power corrupting you? Keltner (2016, p.114) offers the following test questions:

> 'Are you interrupting people? Do you check your phone when others are talking? Have you told a joke or story that embarrassed or humiliated someone else? Do you swear at the office? Have you ever taken sole credit for a group effort? Do you forget colleagues' names? Are you spending a lot more money than in the past or taking unusual physical risks? If you answered yes to at least a few of these questions, take it as an early warning sign that you're being tempted into problematic, arrogant displays of power.'

Keltner argues that we can beat the power paradox by being more self-aware, and by showing more empathy, gratitude, and generosity towards others. However, Keltner (2017, p.10) introduces another paradox, arguing that *powerlessness* is a bigger problem. Powerless means having little control over one's life, which is caused by poverty, inequality, racism and gender bias. Why is this a problem?

> 'The costs of powerlessness, which are so often the result of others succumbing to the power paradox, are profound. Powerlessness amplifies the individual's sensitivity to threat; it hyperactivates the stress response and the hormone cortisol; and it damages the brain. These effects compromise our ability to reason, to reflect, to engage in the world, and to feel good and hopeful about the future. Powerlessness, I believe, is the greatest threat outside of climate change facing our society today.'

🖑 **STOP AND SEARCH**   YouTube for *Dacher Keltner: The Power Paradox UC Berkeley Executive Education* (2:14).

Management decisions are often the result of influence, bargaining, negotiation and jockeying for position. Leaders and managers who lack power, and who are not skilled in working with the politics of an organization, struggle to make things happen and to get things done. These capabilities make you more employable. After the job interviews, someone on the panel might say, 'this candidate is very well qualified . . . but . . . '. They are referring to lack of political skill: do not get caught by 'the but problem'.

An understanding of power and politics also allows us to assess the power of others, and to respond accordingly, regardless of whether we ourselves are power hungry or not. Psychologists use the term 'power tells' to describe the various signs and clues that indicate how powerful someone is – or how powerful they want to be (Collett, 2004). The power tells of dominant individuals include:

- Sitting and standing with legs far apart (men)
- Appropriating the territory around them by placing their hands on their hips
- Using open postures
- Using invasive hand gestures
- Smiling less, because a smile is an appeasement gesture
- Establishing visual dominance by looking away from the other person while speaking
- Speaking first, and dominating the conversation thereafter
- Using a lower vocal register, and speaking more slowly
- More likely to interrupt others, more likely to resist interruption by others

What did they find? The red sneakers effect

? Janneke Oostrom and Richard Ronay (2018) have been studying how the way that we dress can affect recruitment decisions. One of the first things that recruiters notice is what you wear to the interview. Dress can signal to others a number of your characteristics such as power, status and competence. For a job interview, we are expected to conform with social norms, so we adopt formal business dress in order to make a good impression. But what happens if we do not conform, if we turn up in, say, jeans and red sneakers?

The researchers recruited 80 participants in the Netherlands. They were shown a job advertisement for a human resources manager at a professional services company. They were also shown a curriculum vitae (CV) which outlined the candidate's education, work experience, knowledge, skills and abilities. The CVs included a picture of the applicant. (As norms regarding dress style differ for men and women, and are clearer for men, the applicants in this study were all male.) The quality of the candidates' CVs varied; some were weak, and some were strong. The photos showed candidates wearing different styles of clothing. Conforming candidates wore a black suit, black leather shoes, a white shirt, and a blue tie. Non-conforming applicants wore a grey jacket, striped sweater, white shirt, blue tie, dark blue jeans – and sneakers.

Janneke Oostrom

Richard Ronay

Participants were asked to rate the power of the applicant, based on four 'power statements': this person is influential; has a leadership position; is in charge of subordinates; enjoys considerable authority. They were also asked whether they would recommend hiring the candidate.

What did they find? Were non-conformists seen as less suitable for the job? **(Answers in chapter Recap.)**

The power tells of submissive individuals include:

- Modifying speech style to sound more like the person they are talking to
- More frequent hesitations, using lots of 'ums' and 'ers'
- Adopting closed postures
- Clasping hands, touching face and hair (self-comfort gestures)
- Blushing, coughing, dry mouth, heavy breathing, heavy swallowing, increased heart rate, lip biting, rapid blinking and sweating are 'leakage tells' which reveal stress and anxiety.

Knowledge of these tells means that we can 'read' the power signals of others. This also means that we can control our own tells so that we appear to be more (or less) powerful.

 EMPLOYABILITY CHECK (self-management, political awareness)

You have a job interview tomorrow. You want to appear professional, but you also want to appear independent-minded and creative, and not conventional or conformist. How will you dress?

Power in organizations

Power the capacity of individuals to overcome resistance on the part of others, to exert their will, and to produce results consistent with their own interests and objectives.

Power is a 'contested concept' because a number of competing perspectives have been developed. It is therefore useful to be able to view this concept from different angles, and to be aware of their respective strengths and limitations.

We will explore three perspectives. The first views power as something you possess, a property of the individual. The second sees power as a property of the relationship between one individual (or group) and another. The third sees power as embedded in social and organization structures.

Power as property of the individual

This perspective sees power as something that you possess, a set of resources that you accumulate. How much power do you have? Where did it come from? How can you acquire more power? Some of the main sources of power in an organization are shown in Table 22.1. Notice that some of these sources of power relate to the position that a manager holds in the organization (structural sources), while others relate to individual attributes (personal sources).

From this perspective, as power is something you can accumulate, you can take steps to strengthen both your structural and individual sources of power. Look for jobs in key departments, make friends with power brokers, join important networks and projects, develop your interpersonal and impression management skills, and emotional intelligence. Be aware, however, that others in the organization are also trying to accumulate power. You can win more power, but if you are not careful, you can lose it.

Table 22.1: **Power as property**

Structural sources	Personal sources
Formal position, job title	Energy, stamina
Access to and control over resources	Ability to focus energy
Centrality of department to the business	Sensitivity to and ability to read others
Degree of department unity	Flexibility in choice of means to achieve goals
Physical and social position in the organization's communication network	Resilience, toughness, willingness to engage in confrontation
Role in solving business-critical problems	Playing 'the subordinate' or the 'team member' in order to get support from others
Being irreplaceable	

Power priming

Research shows that we can feel and behave like a more powerful person by using a technique called **power priming** (Galinsky and Schwitzer, 2015; Cuddy, 2016; Cuddy et al., 2018). The method is simple: to become power-primed, think of a time in which you had power over others, and remember how that felt. You can also be powerless-primed, by thinking of a time when you lacked power. Power priming can be reinforced by adopting a power posture **(see Chapter 7)** and by listening to power anthems – a technique used by Serena Williams, who can often be seen wearing headphones when walking onto the tennis court.

In one experiment, students were first asked to write about a time when they either had power or lacked power. They were then asked to write an application letter for a job that had been advertised in a well-known newspaper. Another group of students was then asked to evaluate these application letters – some power-primed, and some powerless-primed – and to decide if they would appoint the person. The student judges were much more likely to hire the power-primed applicants.

In another experiment, business school graduates who wrote about a positive personal power experience before a job interview were accepted 68 per cent of the time, compared with a normal acceptance rate of 47 per cent. Only 26 per cent of the graduates who wrote about a time when they lacked power were selected; the power-primed applicants were rated as much more persuasive.

Power priming can help us to deal with experiences that are challenging and stressful. Cuddy describes a study which found that people who were asked to hold a power posture for a short time before a job interview were more likely to be offered the job than those who had been asked to sit in a 'weak' posture, hunched, holding their neck, with twisted legs. Galinsky describes a colleague who, when applying for university positions, was asked to make presentations to large audiences. She was interviewed by two prestigious universities, but neither offered her a job. She then wrote a power prime for herself, and got job offers from the next four top-tier universities to which she applied.

Power priming the process of making yourself feel more powerful, which in turn allows you to feel less stressed, and to behave as a more confident, persuasive and powerful person.

Reward power the ability to exert influence based on the other's belief that the influencer has access to valued rewards which will be dispensed in return for compliance.

Power as property of the relationship

John French and Bertram Raven (1958) identified five bases of power. If someone promises you promotion or money to act as they require, then they are using reward power. If they threaten you with demotion or redundancy, they are using

coercive power. When they rely on their charming personality, they are using referent power. If they rely on their formal organizational position to get you to comply, they are using legitimate power. When they can claim better knowledge and understanding of the situation, they are using expert power.

Referent power is also known as charisma (in German, *Ausstrahlung,* 'force of personality'). Legitimate power is also called position power, relying on formal organizational role and title. An individual may have access to rewards or possess expertise, but others will be less willing to comply if they do not believe that the individual has those resources (even if they do). Similarly, a person may lack expertise or the ability to reward, but will gain compliance from others because they are able to persuade them that they do have these. An individual can thus manipulate others' perceptions to gain compliance. Because two parties and their perceptions are involved, this perspective treats power as a *relational* concept, and not solely the personal property of an individual.

CRITICAL THINKING	While these power bases can help to influence others to do what you want them to do, they can have other consequences. For example, if your manager uses coercive power to get you to carry out a task, what longer term effects might this have? If your team leader uses expert power over the other team members, what consequences might this have, other than compliance with their immediate instructions?

Coercive power the ability to exert influence based on the other's belief that the influencer can administer unwelcome penalties or sanctions.

Referent power the ability to exert influence based on the other's belief that the influencer has desirable abilities and personality traits that can and should be copied.

Legitimate power the ability to exert influence based on the other's belief that the influencer has authority to issue orders which they in turn have an obligation to accept.

Expert power the ability to exert influence based on the other's belief that the influencer has superior knowledge relevant to the situation and the task.

Several different power bases, in different combinations, can be used at different times, depending on the context, and the target of the influence attempts. The American gangster Al Capone is reputed to have said, 'You can get a lot more done with a kind word and a gun than with a kind word alone' (McCarty, 2004). Managers work with different groups, and while particular power bases may be appropriate in some settings, other methods will be required in different circumstances. Traditionally, managers have relied on legitimate and coercive power. In the twenty-first century, expert and referent power are more appropriate, in most circumstances. However, an individual's power also depends on whatever resources are available to them at any given time.

Power as a property of social and organizational structures

This perspective explores how power controls our behaviour through less obvious means. Power is woven into the fabric of our society. We take many things for granted such as social and organization structures, the system of rules that we normally follow, the day-to-day 'natural order'. These routine features of our surroundings influence our behaviour in subtle ways, and we rarely challenge them, because they are 'normal'. It can be difficult to challenge 'the way things are' without appearing to be odd or extreme. We will explore the taken-for-granted nature of embedded power shortly, in our discussion of the work of Michel Foucault, and his concept of 'disciplinary power'.

Power that is *embedded* in social and organizational structures may be less visible (unless you pay attention), but can be just as powerful in controlling behaviour as more visible sources (such as Al Capone's gun). However, it is in the interests of those who can manipulate and exploit the unequal distribution of power and wealth that we do not challenge 'the way things are'. When power is embedded in this way, we simply accept the outcomes, in the same way that we accept that offices have desks, and bosses have bigger offices and bigger desks.

Tough at the top

Don't expect senior leaders to work well with other senior leaders. High-power individuals, it turns out, do not collaborate as well with each other as groups whose members have lower power. In a series of studies, John Hildreth and Cameron Anderson (2016) found that groups of otherwise capable leaders performed badly and were less creative when working together. They were accustomed to exercising power over those around them, and found it difficult to work with and to reach agreement with others who were equally powerful. They were more concerned to preserve their status, less concerned with the task in hand, and less willing to share information.

Strategic contingencies theory a perspective which argues that the most powerful individuals and departments are those best able to deal effectively with the issues that are most critical to the organization's survival and performance.

In most organizations, different sections or units have different levels of power. Why should this be the case? Groups or departments that are responsible for dealing with the issues that are key to the organization's performance and survival, or solving urgent problems, or dealing with a crisis, tend to be more powerful than those parts of the organization that are less critical. In one organization, at one period, research and development may be critical in terms of developing new products and getting ahead of the competition. In a recession, when consumer spending is low, marketing and sales may be more important. The finance function in most organizations is always a high priority, and they tend to have high levels of power and influence over key decisions.

This is known as the strategic contingencies theory of organizational power (Hickson et al., 1971; Salancik and Pfeffer, 1977; Mintzberg, 1983). Strategic contingencies are events that must take place if the organization is to survive and succeed. If your department handles these contingencies, then it will have more power and influence. A department's ability to deal with strategic contingencies depends on five factors; dependency creation, financial resources, centrality of activities, non-substitutability, and ability to reduce uncertainty. These five factors overlap, and the more of them a department possesses, the greater the power that it will exert in the organization.

✓✓✓   **EMPLOYABILITY CHECK** (self-management, how organizations work)

When applying as a graduate recruit for a position in an organization, how will you decide which of its departments to join?

1. Dependency creation

A department is powerful if other units and departments depend on it, for materials, information, resources and advice. The receiving department is always in an inferior power position.

2. Financial resources

A department's ability to control financial resources increases power. Departments thus compete with each other for new projects which have large budgets attached to them.

3. Centrality

Centrality concerns the degree to which a department's activities are critical to achieving the organization's goals. Departments such as training, payroll management, human resources, and advertising, can be outsourced, without jeopardizing the organization's performance.

4. Non-substitutability

A department is more powerful where its work cannot easily be done by another department. Individuals and sections increase power by handling specialized work that needs high levels of skill and knowledge.

5. Uncertainty reduction

Those with the ability to reduce uncertainty can gain significant reputations and positions of influence, by providing clear definitions of problems and solutions, thus restoring an otherwise confused situation.

CRITICAL THINKING   Given what you know about structural sources of power, can you explain why accountants tend to be more powerful and influential than human resource managers?

Three faces of power

Stephen Lukes (2005) argues that power may be visible and self-evident, or subtle and covert, or institutionalized, as we have seen, in organizational structures. Power, for Lukes, thus has three faces:

1. Visible power that is exercised to secure a decision in situations where there is observable conflict or disagreement.

2. Covert power that is exercised to keep issues off the decision-making agenda, so that potential conflicts or disagreements are avoided, and are therefore unobservable.

3. Institutional power, which defines reality and what is 'normal' for others, – if norms and meanings become internalized by an organization's members, they will then act in accordance with those norms, even if these work against their interests.

1. Visible power

The first face of power is the most obvious, and concerns a clash of interests between those making a decision and those who are likely to be affected by it. This face focuses on the *observable behaviours* that influence the form or content of a decision. For example, in the army, a sergeant threatens to put a private on a charge unless he completes an assigned task before midnight. The sergeant's words and actions, and their effect on the soldier's behaviours, can be observed.

2. Covert power

The second face of power concerns the manipulation of issues. The interests of certain groups can be excluded from a bargaining or decision-making arena: 'Sorry, that topic does not fall within the remit of this committee'. The focus here is on the non-observable behaviours that keep issues on or off an agenda. You may know that, if you bring a particular issue to a particular management group, you will not be thanked for raising that problem – so you keep quiet about it, even though there is no pressure on you to do this. This is known as *non-decision making* (Bachrach and Baratz, 1963), which those with power can use to avoid conflict and resistance. This prevents controversial issues from ever reaching the public domain, so discussion is prevented, and no decisions are taken. With the first face of power, at least you know what you are up against. With this second face, you are not invited to the conversation.

3. Institutional power

The third face of power involves shaping others' perceptions, cognitions and preferences, so that they accept their current situation, because they cannot see an alternative. Acceptance may be perceived as natural, unchangeable or divinely ordained, and also as beneficial, and can lead us to act against our objective interests. So we come to understand that maximizing profit through reducing waste and cutting costs are fundamental, unchallengeable features of reality (even though such actions may make working conditions more unpleasant or difficult). In this way, 'the powerful' define reality for 'the powerless', whose interests and grievances are obscured and silenced. Paradoxically, this face of power is characterized by harmony, as power is not exposed in public, those subjected to it are unaware of its presence and influence, and overt conflict is avoided.

Another distinguishing feature of institutionalized power is that it cannot be linked easily with the actions of any one particular individual. This contrasts with the first face of power where we can see individuals influencing a decision. And it may be seen with the second face of power, in the 'behind the scenes' manoeuvres of individuals who want to prevent

the open discussion of controversial issues. But if you can control indirectly the actions of others by getting them to accept particular norms and assumptions, in other words to 'internalize' those values and beliefs, not only is challenge stifled, but it is difficult to find individuals to blame for doing the stifling. Organizational culture **(see Chapter 4)** can be an effective source of this control. Institutional power sustains the dominance of the powerful by reducing the ability of the powerless to complain. This is simple to achieve: 'I'm afraid that my role does not give me responsibility for solving problems like that'; 'This committee does not deal with those issues.'

Disciplinary power

Michel Foucault, a French philosopher and historian, provides yet another perspective on power. His thinking relates to Lukes' third 'institutional' face of power focusing on the ways in which management remains dominant by defining reality and normality in ways that reduce the likelihood of challenge or resistance. Foucault (1979, p.93) observed that, 'power is everywhere, not because it embraces everything, but because it comes from everywhere'. The related concepts of *bio-power* and *disciplinary power* are central to understanding Foucault's thinking.

Bio-power

Bio-power is another term for power that operates by establishing what is normal or abnormal, or socially acceptable or deviant, in thought and behaviour. Bio-power is targeted at society as a whole, and is achieved through a variety of *discursive practices*: talk, writing, debate, argument, representation. The media play a major role in sustaining and altering what we conceive as socially normal. Bio-power exercises its control over us by 'constituting the normal' and operates through our individual cognition and understanding. If you accept without challenge 'the way things are', the way a situation is currently represented, ('the constitution of the normal' as Foucault puts it) then bio-power takes on a self-disciplining role with regard to your thinking and behaving:

> 'As you walk onto the street, you realize just how late it is. You can't believe that you have been at work for so long. You should be used to this by now. Most days you spend twelve hours in the office, with only a fading tourist photograph of an Indian village to remind you of what it was like to be free. There isn't anyone holding a gun to your head, is there? But long hours have their drawbacks. Even though you might want a family, you know that is impossible. Anyway, you have made your decision. You're out to achieve big things, and this requires a few small sacrifices.' (Fleming and Spicer, 2007, p.19)

There is no manager or supervisor telling you what to do. Procedures, instructions and controls are applied by individuals to themselves in pursuit of goals that they have been persuaded are their own, but which are set by self-interested elites. Rather than having individuals' behaviour regulated through external systems of monitoring and control (supervisors, technology, appraisals), these controls get inside the 'hearts and minds' of organization members, and work through self-regulation.

CRITICAL THINKING   How does bio-power affect your behaviour? Which goals do you accept as your own, and which have been 'given' to you by your university and/or its staff? In your work, current or past, which procedures and instructions have you accepted without criticism, and to which you have conformed without challenge? If you decided to challenge those goals, procedures, and instructions, how would you do that, and how would you estimate your chances of success in getting any of them changed?

Disciplinary power

Disciplinary power targets individuals and groups and works through the construction of social and organizational routines. Through this lens, Foucault sees power as a set of techniques, the effects of which are achieved through what he calls *disciplinary practices*. These practices include the tools of surveillance and assessment that are used to control and

regiment individuals, rendering them docile and compliant. The tools, or mechanisms that achieve compliance include (Hiley, 1987, p.351):

- The allocation of physical space in offices or factories, which establishes homogeneity and uniformity, individual and collective identity, ranks people according to status, and fixes their position in the network of social relations
- The standardization of individual behaviour through timetables, regimentation, work standards and repetitive activities
- The 'composition of forces', where individuals become parts of larger units, such as cross-functional teams, or production lines
- The creation of job ladders and career systems which, through their promises of future promotion and reward, encourage compliance with the organization's demands.

We do not normally consider office layouts, timetables, career ladders and work assignments to be manifestations of power. However, these normal features of organizational life help to shape and discipline our daily activities and interpersonal relationships, controlling us, and guaranteeing our compliance with social and organizational norms and expectations. It is precisely because they are 'micro techniques', so small, so unobtrusive, and so embedded in the organization's structure and processes, that they are hardly noticed. Foucault's concept of power is thus different from traditional concepts, as the contrasts in Table 22.2 indicate (Buchanan and Badham, 2008, p.296).

CRITICAL THINKING	How are disciplinary practices affecting your behaviour? Identify examples of practices to which you have been subjected, either in your educational institution or at work, which have shaped your routine daily activities and social interactions. So what? Is this a problem?

Table 22.2: Foucault and traditional concepts of power

Traditional concepts of power	Foucault's concepts of power
Power is possessed, accumulated, vested in the individual	Power is pervasive, a totality, reflected in concrete practices
Power is in the hands of social and organizational elites; resistance is futile	Power is found in the micro-physics of everyday social life; power depends on resistance
We are subject to the domination of those who are more powerful than us	We construct our own web of power by accepting current definitions of normality
Power is destructive, denies, represses, prevents, corrupts	Power is productive, contributes to social order, which is flexible and shifting
Power is episodic, visible, observable in action, deployed intermittently, absent except when exercised	Power is present in its absence, discreet, operating through taken-for-granted daily routines and ways of living
Knowledge of power sources and relationships is emancipatory, helping us to overcome domination	Knowledge maintains and extends the web of power, creating further opportunities for domination

Source: Buchanan and Badham (2008)

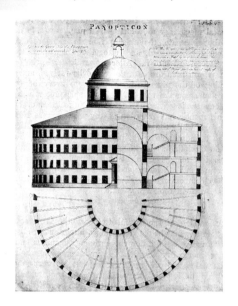

Foucault argues that we are trapped in a 'field of force relations', a web of power which we help to create, and which we are always recreating. We are creators of that web of power, and prisoners within it. At an organizational level, disciplinary practices condition employees' thought processes, leading them to treat taken-for-granted processes, such as performance-based pay, as 'natural', and beyond question. This 'force field', however, is neither stable nor inevitable. Challenge may be difficult, but is not impossible. As a consequence, this force field changes as points of resistance are encountered, networks of alliances change, fissures open up, old coalitions break up, and new ones are formed. Foucault also points out that resistance (by employees to management demands, for example) only demonstrates and reinforces the need for such disciplinary measures.

Foucault uses the metaphor of the *panopticon* for his image of disciplinary power. This is a circular prison designed by the eighteenth-century philosopher Jeremy Bentham, allowing all the prison inmates to be observed, in their cells, by one observer who cannot be seen by the prisoners. The prisoners cannot avoid the surveillance, but they do not know when they are being observed. They must therefore behave at all times *as if* they are being watched. They thus monitor themselves. As McAuley et al. (2007, p.263) argue: 'We are not necessarily compelled to act as we do by some external agency. Instead, through society's disciplines of schools, hospitals, prisons and military, we have internalized [*power*] to become self-governed or 'normalized'. A modern example of Bentham's panopticon principle is the wording on the back of delivery vehicles which reads, '*Well driven? Call 0800 11 22 33*'.

CUTTING EDGE — New power

Henry Timms and Jeremy Heimans (photo credit: Michael Creagh)

Jeremy Heimans and Henry Timms (2014; Timms and Heimans, 2018) argue that traditional concepts of power are being challenged by a new set of values and behaviours based on our desire for more participation, collaboration, and co-production. 'Old power', they argue, is like a *currency*: it is difficult to accumulate, few have large quantities, and they guard it jealously. 'New power', on the other hand, is like a *current,* which is generated by many, and is open, participative and peer-driven. New power is more dispersed, and is based on our growing desire and technological ability to participate. Heimans and Timms identify five ways in which participation is widening:

Sharing	Passing what one person has said or created on to others (e.g. Facebook)
Shaping	Adapting content or ideas to create a new message (e.g. Facebook)
Funding	Providing financial support for ideas (e.g. crowd-funding, peer-to-peer lending)
Producing	Creating content for a community of peers (e.g. YouTube, TaskRabbit)
Co-owning	Sharing ownership of something (e.g. Wikipedia, Linux)

New power is based on a distinct set of values. You are not just a passive user of YouTube; you can create your own content and share it with others. This 'peer-based collective action' means that collaboration is becoming the norm, and that traditional providers are becoming less influential. Participation has come to be regarded as a right, to shape and to create aspects of our lives. New power encourages 'DIO' or 'do it ourselves', solving social problems, for example, without the need for conventional bureaucracies. Traditional privacy is being replaced by permanent transparency as more people live on social media.

Heimans and Timms identify four types of organizations depending on their business models and their values. *Castles* are companies that have old power business models and old power values, such as Apple and the American National Security Agency. *Cheerleaders* combine old power models with new power values, such as the clothing companies Patagonia and Zappos. *Connectors* have new power models, but still work with old power values, such as Facebook and Uber. *Crowds* are peer-driven organizations that combine new power models and values, such as Wikipedia, Kickstarter, and HuffPost. New power, however, is not necessarily benign. Timms and Heimans (2018, p.53) argue:

> 'The future will be won by those who can spread their ideas better, faster, and more durably. In a world of fake news, climate change deniers, Holocaust deniers, anti-vaxers, and all manner of extremists, the stakes are high. Those on the side of the angels, who want to spread compassion, promote pluralism, or defend science, must first grapple with a painful reality: that new power can supercharge hate and misinformation. In fact, those darker forces often start at an advantage because their provocations compel our attention and our clicks. It isn't enough to simply have the facts on your side.'

 **STOP AND SEARCH**   YouTube for *Jeremy Heimans: What New Power Looks Like* (Ted Talk, 15:12)

CRITICAL THINKING   How are you affected by new power? How are you using new power? To see how Stefanie Sword-Williams uses new power, go to her self-promotion website at f***beinghumble.com.

Power and influence

Influence the process of affecting someone else's attitudes, beliefs or behaviours, without using coercion or formal position, such that the other person believes that they are acting in their own best interests.

How can we use power to get others to do what we want? Power is defined as exerting one's will and overcoming resistance to produce the results that we desire. Those over whom power is exercised may resent this. However, it is also possible to achieve the desired results in such a way that those affected are not aware, and only occasionally resentful, and may even be grateful. Andrzej Huczynski (2004) defines influence as one person's ability to

affect another's attitudes, beliefs or behaviours. Influence can be achieved without force or 'pulling rank'. When this is successful, the person who is influenced often believes that they have not been pressured into doing something, but are acting in their own best interests.

The use of influence tactics has attracted a lot of research interest, and we will consider two influential perspectives. One is based on the work of David Kipnis et al. (1984), who identified eight categories of influence tactic; assertiveness, ingratiation, rational appeal, sanctions, exchange, upward appeal, blocking and coalition (Table 22.3). Kipnis and colleagues note that managers do not exercise influence for self-interest and enjoyment, but in order to promote new ideas, encourage others to work more effectively, or introduce new working practices, for example.

From their study of American, Australian and British managers, Kipnis et al. (1984) identified four types of manager based on their patterns of use of these tactics:

- *Bystanders* rarely use any of these influence tactics, have low organizational power, have limited personal and organizational objectives, and are frequently dissatisfied.

- *Shotguns* use all of these influence tactics all the time, have unfulfilled goals, and are inexperienced in their job.

- *Captives* use one or two 'favourite' tactics, habitually, and with limited effectiveness.

- *Tacticians* use rational appeal frequently, make average use of other tactics, tend to achieve their objectives, have high organizational power, and are usually satisfied.

Discussing what he calls 'the science of getting what you ask for', Robert Cialdini (2008; 2013) identifies six principles of influence by observing the 'compliance professionals' who persuade other people for a living: salespeople, fund-raisers, advertisers, political lobbyists, cult recruiters, confidence tricksters. He shows how compliance professionals exploit the socialized responses that we automatically make to familiar cues. Anyone can learn these techniques.

1. *Reciprocity:* We are more likely to comply with a request from someone who has previously given us a gift, favour, or concession.

    We have a socially trained sense of obligation, to give 'something in return', even when the gift is unsolicited. Survey researchers include small payments to increase questionnaire response rates; restaurant staff increase tips by giving customers sweets with their bills.

Table 22.3: **Influence tactics**

Assertiveness	Order the person to do it. Point out that the rules demand it. Keep reminding them about what is required.
Ingratiation	Make the request politely and humbly. Act in a friendly way and be complimentary before asking. Sympathize with any hardships they may face.
Rational appeal	Write a detailed justification. Present relevant information in support. Explain the reasoning behind your request.
Sanctions	Threaten to get them fired. Threaten to block their promotion. Threaten them with a poor performance evaluation.
Exchange	Offer an exchange of favours – mutual backscratching. Remind them of favours you have provided them in the past.
Upward appeal	Get higher level management to intervene in your support. Send the person to speak to your boss.
Blocking	Threaten to stop working with the person. Ignore the person and stop being friendly. Withhold collaboration until they do what you want.
Coalition	Get the support of colleagues to support your request. Make the request at a formal meeting where others will support you.

2. *Social proof:* We are more likely to comply with a request, or to adopt a behaviour, which is consistent with what similar others are thinking or doing.

   If other people think it is correct, then we tend to agree. If others are doing it (driving fast on a stretch of road), then we feel justified in doing the same. Bartenders 'salt' their jar of tips to indicate that tipping is 'appropriate'. Church ushers use the same method, and evangelical preachers use 'ringers' who are briefed to 'spontaneously' come forward at predetermined moments during the service.

3. *Commitment/consistency:* We are more likely to comply with a request which leads to actions consistent with our previous acts and commitments.

   Consistency is linked to intellect, rationality, honesty and integrity, and tends to be valued. If I can get you to commit to something (meet me for coffee), then it will be easier to persuade you to do something else that is consistent with that prior commitment (join me for dinner).

4. *Friendship/liking:* We are more likely to comply with requests from friends, or from others whom we like.

   Charities recruit volunteers to collect donations in their local area. Compliance professionals as strangers, however, have to find ways to get us to like them. Attractive individuals are generally more persuasive, and we are more easily influenced by those who are similar to us in some way: opinions, background, lifestyle, personality, dress. In one study, a survey response rate was doubled by giving the person sending the questionnaire a name similar to that of the respondent: Bob Gregar and Cindy Johanson sent survey questionnaires to Robert Greer and Cynthia Johnson.

5. *Scarcity:* We are more likely to comply with requests that will lead to the acquisition of opportunities that are scarce.

   Opportunities tend to be more highly valued when they are less available, and items that are difficult to possess are 'better' than items that can be easily acquired, including information. Customers are told that products, services, membership opportunities are in short supply and will not last long, or 'offer available for one week only – hurry, buy now.'

6. *Authority:* We are more likely to comply with requests from those in positions of legitimate authority.

   Position power can be persuasive. The title 'doctor' often commands blind obedience to dangerous instructions, such as administering an unsafe level of a drug. People are more likely follow instructions from a security guard in uniform, and an expensive business suit has a similar effect.

CRITICAL THINKING   Who are the people that you need to influence most often? What influence techniques do you use? Which techniques work best, and which are less effective? How can you improve your use of these techniques, to become more influential?

Influencing from the middle: how to win support for new ideas

Susan Ashford

James Detert (© Tom Cogill)

Susan Ashford and James Detert (2015, p.73) argue that 'Organizations don't prosper unless managers in the middle ranks identify and promote the need for change'. However, when it comes to sharing those ideas, middle managers are often discouraged by the top leadership style ('if an idea was any good, we would have already thought of it'), and valuable opportunities are missed. Ashford and Detert asked middle managers to describe their experiences of selling three kinds of ideas: new products, processes or markets; improvements to existing products and processes; and better ways to meet

→

employees' needs. This helped them to identify seven influence tactics that middle managers use to attract senior executive attention and resources:

Tactic	Base your approach on these questions
Tailor your pitch	Where does my audience stand on this issue? What does my audience find most convincing or compelling?
Frame the issue	How can I connect my issue to organizational priorities? How can I best describe its benefits? How can I link it to other issues receiving attention? How can I highlight an opportunity for the organization?
Manage emotions	How can I use emotions to generate positive responses? How can I manage my audience's emotional responses?
Get the timing right	What is the best moment to be heard? Can I 'catch the wave' of a trend, or tap into what's going on outside? What is the right time in the decision-making process to raise my issue?
Involve others	Which allies from my network can help me sell my issue? Who are potential blockers, and how can i persuade them to support me? Who are fence-sitters, and how can I convince them that my issue matters?
Adhere to norms	Should I use a formal or a casual approach, or a combination?
Suggest solutions	Am I suggesting a viable solution? If not, am I proposing a way to discover one, instead of just highlighting the problem?

Ashford and Detert offer three other pieces of advice. First, choose your audience; your immediate boss may not be the best place to start. Second, use several tactics rather than just one or two; they are more powerful in combination. Finally, choose your battles; some ideas are too difficult to sell.

 **STOP AND SEARCH**   YouTube for *James Detert on Facilitating Upward Communication* (10:22).

Organization politics and political skill

Age and treachery

Bill Bratton is an American police chief known for his achievements in 'turning around' failing or problem forces.

'In 1980, at age 34 one of the youngest lieutenants in Boston's police department, he had proudly put up a plaque in his office that said: *Youth and skill will win out every time over age and treachery*. Within just a few months, having been shunted into a dead-end position due to a mixture of office politics and his own brashness, Bratton took the sign down. He never again forgot the importance of understanding the plotting, intrigue, and politics involved in pushing through change'. The advice is: know who the key players are, understand how they play the politics game, know their attitudes and positions in relation to change proposals (Kim and Mauborgne, 2003, p.68).

Gerald Ferris

Organization politics the ability to understand others at work, and to use that knowledge to influence others to act in ways that enhance one's personal and/or organizational objectives.

Political skill an interpersonal style that combines social astuteness with the ability to relate well, and to demonstrate situationally appropriate behaviour in a disarmingly charming and engaging manner that inspires confidence, trust, sincerity and genuineness

Organization politics are generally regarded as unsavoury and damaging, associated with back-stabbing and dirty tricks. 'Machiavellian' is an insult, not a compliment. Henry Mintzberg (1983) emphasizes the parochial, divisive and illegitimate nature of political behaviour. How could anyone be advised to use tactics such as these? However, research has also revealed the positive, constructive, 'pro-social' uses of political tactics, which can be used to pursue organizational as well as individual goals. This involves the exercise of **political skill**.

Gerald Ferris et al. (2000) argue that political skill ('savvy and street smarts') has four dimensions (Table 22.4). *Social astuteness* involves understanding the behaviour and motives of others. *Interpersonal influence* is the ability to influence others in a compelling way. *Networking ability* involves building relationships across and outside the organization. *Apparent sincerity* means being seen as forthright, open, honest and genuine (Ferris et al., 2005 and 2007; Brouer et al., 2006).

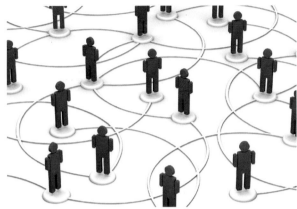

Studies using university staff and students as participants produced the following conclusions:

- Political skill correlates with measures of self-monitoring and emotional intelligence.
- Those who score high on political skill show less anxiety, and are less likely to perceive stressful events as threatening.
- Political skill is not correlated with general intelligence.
- Political skill predicts job performance and subordinate evaluations of leadership ability.
- The dimension of political skill related most strongly to performance rating is social astuteness.

Table 22.4: Dimensions of political skill

Dimension	Definition	Sample inventory items
Social astuteness	Attuned observers and good interpreters of behaviour, self-aware, sensitive to others, clever	I understand people very well. I pay close attention to people's facial expressions.
Interpersonal influence	Subtle and convincing style, calibrate actions to the situation, to the 'target', be flexible	I am able to make most people feel comfortable and at ease around me. I am good at getting people to like me.
Networking ability	Adept at using networks, develop friendships and build alliances easily, skilled in negotiation and conflict resolution	I spend a lot of time and effort at work networking with others. At work, I know a lot of important people and am well connected.
Apparent sincerity	Appear honest and open, and to have integrity, authenticity, sincerity, genuineness, no ulterior motives	It is important that people believe I am sincere in what I say and do. I try to show a genuine interest in other people.

Describing those who are highly skilled in politics, Ferris et al. (2005, p.128) observe that:

> 'Politically skilled individuals convey a sense of personal security and calm self-confidence that attracts others and gives them a feeling of comfort. This self-confidence never goes too far so as to be perceived as arrogance but is always properly measured to be a positive attribute. Therefore, although self-confident, those high in political skill are not self-absorbed (although they are self-aware) because their focus is outward toward others, not inward and self-centred. We suggest that people high in political skill not only know precisely what to do in different social situations at work but how to do it in a manner that disguises any ulterior, self-serving motives and appears to be sincere.'

The wider research evidence confirms that political skill can contribute to individual performance, leadership effectiveness, career success, and the ability to cope with workplace stress. The outcomes, however, depend on the organizational context, and on how political tactics are used (Kimura, 2015).

The main categories of political tactics are summarized in Table 22.5 (Buchanan and Badham, 2008). The use of these tactics is driven by four sets of factors: personal, decisional, structural and organizational change.

CRITICAL THINKING

What is your attitude towards organization politics and political skill? Are these behaviours unethical and to be avoided? Is a degree of political skill a requirement for success in your chosen career?

Table 22.5: **Political tactics**

Image building	We all know people who didn't get the job because they didn't look the part – appearance is a credibility issue; support for the right causes, adherence to group norms, self-confident manner
Information games	Withholding information, bending the truth, white lies, timed release of information, overwhelming others with complex technical details
Structure games	Creating new roles, teams, and departments, abolishing old ones, in order to promote supporters and sideline adversaries, and to signal new priorities
Scapegoating	Ensuring that someone else is blamed, that this is the fault of another department, or external factors, or my predecessor, or trading conditions, or a particular individual; avoiding personal blame
Alliances	Doing secret deals with influential others to form a critical mass, a coalition, to win support for and to progress your proposals
Networking	Friends in high places, 'wine and dine' them to get your initiatives onto the senior management agenda, improve your visibility, gather information
Compromise	Give in, all right, you win this time, I won't put up a fight and embarrass you in public – if you will back me next time
Rule games	Refuse requests because they have not followed correct procedures or are contrary to company policy; accept similar requests from allies on the grounds of 'special circumstances'
Positioning	Choose and move to roles that make you visible and appear successful; withdraw from failing projects; locate yourself appropriately in the building, sit in the 'right' place at meetings
Issue selling	Package, present, and promote your plans and ideas in ways that make them more appealing to your target audiences
Dirty tricks	Keep dirt files for blackmail, spy on others, discredit and undermine competitors, spreading false rumours, corridor whispers

Source: Buchanan and Badham (2008)

Personal drivers

Organizations hire people with ambition, drive, creativity, and ideas of their own. Recruitment, appraisal, training and promotion policies encourage political behaviour in those who are creative and ambitious, and who want to see their ideas implemented. The traits to look for include the *need for power, Machiavellianism, internal locus of control* and *risk-seeking propensity*.

Need for power (*n*Pow) the desire to make an impact on others, change people or events, and make a difference in life.

Need for power

David McClelland (1961) argues that three types of need are culturally acquired, or learned. These are need for power (*n*Pow), need for achievement (*n*Ach), and need for affiliation (*n*Aff). Some of us have a strong need to influence and lead others, and are thus more likely to engage in political behaviour. Since a desire to control others and events, and to have an impact on what is going on, is often associated with effective management, it is not surprising that selectors look for this trait in candidates for managerial jobs (McClelland and Boyatzis, 1982).

McClelland et al. (1976) distinguish between 'institutional managers' and 'personal power managers'. The latter seek personal gain at the expense of others and 'are not disciplined enough to be good institution builders' (McClelland and Burnham, 1995, p.130):

> '[They] exercise their power impulsively. They are more often rude to other people, they drink too much, they try to exploit others sexually, and they collect symbols of personal prestige such as fancy cars or big offices.'

Institutional managers, in contrast, combine power motivation with self-control, and represent 'the socialized face of power' (McClelland and Burnham, 1995, p.129):

> '[T]he good manager's power motivation is not oriented towards personal aggrandizement but toward the institution that he or she serves. [They] are more institution minded; they tend to get elected to more offices, to control their drinking, and have a desire to serve others.'

Good 'institutional' managers have the following profile:

- They feel responsible for developing the organizations to which they belong
- They believe in the importance of centralized authority
- They enjoy the discipline of work, and getting things done in an orderly way
- They are willing to sacrifice self-interest for organizational welfare
- They have a keen sense of justice, concerning reward for hard effort.

In other words, good managers use power in the interests of the organization, rather than in pursuit of self-interest. The use of power can therefore be acceptable, as long as it is subject to discipline, control, and inhibition. However, this viewpoint argues that institution building and personal career enhancement can be pursued at the same time.

✓✓✓ **EMPLOYABILITY CHECK** (self-management, political awareness)

You are being considered for promotion to a more senior management role. The role needs someone with ambition, with ideas of their own, and with the influence to implement those ideas. How will you persuade the promotions board that you are the right candidate for this job?

Machiavellianism

Machiavellianism
a personality trait or
style of behaviour
towards others which
is characterized by (1)
the use of guile and
deceit in interpersonal
relations, (2) a cynical
view of the nature of
other people; and (3)
a lack of concern with
conventional morality.

Machiavellianism is another trait which those who tend to engage in organization politics are likely to possess. Niccolò Machiavelli was a sixteenth-century Florentine philosopher and statesman who wrote a set of guidelines for rulers (princes in particular) to use in order to secure and hold on to power. These were published in *The Prince*, and suggested that the primary method for achieving power was the manipulation of others (Machiavelli, 1514). Since then, Machiavelli's name has come to be associated with opportunism and deceit in interpersonal relations.

Richard Christie and Florence Geis (1970) produced a famous study of Machiavellian personality characteristics. Those who score highly on their Machiavellian test – 'High Machs' – tend to agree with statements such as:

- The best way to handle people is to tell them what they want to hear.
- Anyone who completely trusts anyone else is asking for trouble.
- Never tell anyone the real reason you did something unless it is useful to do so.

'Low Machs' tend to disagree with those statements. High Machs prefer to be feared rather than to be liked. They manipulate others with their persuasive skills. They initiate and control interactions, are prepared to use deceit, engage in ethically questionable behaviour, and believe that the means justifies the desired end.

Internal locus of control

Locus of control an
individual's generalized
belief about internal
(self-control) versus
external control (control
by the situation or by
others).

A third trait that encourages political behaviour is an individual's **locus of control**. Some people believe that what happens to them in life is under their own control; they have an *internal* locus of control. Others believe that their life situation is under the control of fate or other people; they are described as having an *external* locus of control (Rotter, 1966). It is the 'internals', who believe that they control what happens to them, who tend to use more political behaviour than 'externals'. Internals are more likely to expect that their political tactics will be effective, and are also less likely to be influenced by others.

Political blunders

To develop a career, you need political skill, or 'savvy and street smarts'. Andrew DuBrin (2016) identifies the political blunders which can damage your reputation and career, and the mistakes which cause embarrassment:

Career-damaging blunders

1. Humiliating others in public (praise in public, criticize in private)
2. Violating the organization's code of ethics and standards of conduct
3. Uncontrolled greed, even if large sums of money are obtained legally
4. Sending negative messages through corporate emails, websites and social media

5. Bypassing the boss
6. Showing hostility and seeking revenge in an exit interview
7. Being indiscreet in one's private life
8. Conducting an improper office romance

Embarrassing blunders

1. Being politically incorrect
2. Displaying impatience for promotion
3. Gossiping about taboo subjects and sharing too much personal information
4. Attacking the organization's values and cherished customs – its 'sacred cows'

5. Refusing to take holidays

6. Showing insensitivity to cross-cultural differences

7. Rejecting business social invitations

8. Wearing sexually provocative clothes

9. Inappropriately consuming alcohol

10. Being insensitive to public opinion

DuBrin argues that you should avoid these political blunders. What do you think?

Risk-seeking propensity

Risk-seeking propensity an individual's willingness to choose options that involve risk.

A final trait that can determine whether a person engages in political behaviour is their risk-seeking propensity. Engaging in political behaviour is risky, and there are negative as well as positive outcomes for those who do it. They could be demoted, passed over for promotion, or given low performance ratings. Some people are naturally risk-averse, while others are risk-seekers. Risk-seekers are more likely to engage in political behaviour. For those who are risk-averse, the negative consequences of a failed influencing attempt may outweigh the possible benefits of a successful outcome.

The need for power, Machiavellianism, internal locus of control, and risk-seeking propensity – these personality characteristics are associated with a strong desire for career advancement. All organizations have a proportion of ambitious individuals who compete with each other, arguing and lobbying for their ideas, innovations, and projects. However, traditional organizational structures are hierarchical, and there are fewer positions available at each higher level. Those who are ambitious, therefore, are in constant competition to secure those scarce senior posts.

Decisional drivers

The extent to which politics affects the decision-making process depends on the type of decision. Some decisions are structured; others are unstructured. Structured decisions are programmable, and can be resolved using decision rules. Routine decisions, such as how much stock to order, are structured. If a decision is structured or programmed, and if there is no opposition to what a manager wants to do, then it will be less necessary to use politics.

The problem is, the number of management decisions that can be based simply on information, calculation and logic is small. Unstructured decisions also depend on judgement, experience, intuition, preference, values and 'gut feel'. Unstructured, or unprogrammable, decisions are more common, and virtually all senior management decisions are unstructured to some degree. Examples include:

- Should we maximize short term profitability, or develop our medium term market share instead?

- Should we develop our human resource management function, or outsource this to a specialist management services organization?

- Should we develop our social media strategy to focus on communications with customers and suppliers, or should we consider the employee engagement benefits of social media?

Home viewing

The film *Contact* (1997, director Robert Zemeckis) is about Dr Eleanor (Ellie) Arroway (played by Jodie Foster). It recounts humankind's first contact with aliens. The task of searching for extra-terrestrial life is fraught with personal, scientific, economic, political and ethical uncertainties. While she may be an excellent scientist, Ellie is not a good organizational politician. As you watch the film, answer the following questions. What organizational political mistakes does Ellie make? What political skills does Dr David Drumlin display? What mistakes does Ellie make in the President's advisory committee meeting? What tactics does Drumlin use to maintain his controlling position? What advice would you give Ellie if she wanted to become a more effective organizational politician?

With unstructured decisions, one can expect different managers with their own experiences, opinions, values, and preferences, to disagree. This debate is natural and valuable. Put another way, 'When two people always agree, one of them is unnecessary' (Pfeffer and Sutton, 2006, p.31). Since information, calculation and logic cannot help to reach an unstructured decision, what strategies are left? In these kinds of situations, those involved are more likely to use political tactics to gain the support of others, and to deflect resistance when necessary, to ensure that their preferred course of action is endorsed.

Structural drivers

Organization structures tend to be based on departments or functions, which compete with each other: purchasing, production, marketing, sales, finance, human resources. These functions have their own goals, priorities and perspectives: sales want to maximize revenue, finance want to cut costs. These functions are interdependent – they have to work together. This combination of factors can produce conflict, which results in the use of political tactics when the issues are important, resources are scarce, and power is distributed unevenly. In other words, political behaviour is an inevitable consequence of the way in which organizations are structured.

Organizational change drivers

Organizational change – especially major or strategic change **(Chapter 19)** – creates more unstructured decisions, particularly with regard to the direction and purpose of change, and also how the goals of change should best be achieved. The scope for political behaviour during periods of major change is therefore high. Change also generates uncertainty, and those who have the appropriate political knowledge and skill can exploit that uncertainty to their advantage, to influence decisions in their preferred direction, and to position themselves favourably in the new structure.

These four sets of drivers – personal, decisional, structural, and organizational change – present a powerful combination. Political behaviour in organizational settings is a naturally occurring phenomenon, and is highly resistant to management attempts to stifle or eradicate it.

Is it different for women?

Carly Fiorina was the first female chief executive of a Fortune 20 company, Hewlett-Packard. In her autobiography, she says that, 'Life isn't always fair, and is different for men than for women' (Fiorina, 2006, p.70). Women suffer from sex role stereotyping that associates management with masculinity: 'think manager – think male', and women's abilities are consequently underestimated.

Women are as likely to experience and to use organization politics as are men. However, there appear to be subtle differences between the sexes. Table 22.6 summarizes the evidence contrasting traditional female and male stereotypes with regard to attitudes to organization politics. This is the source of the cliché that, 'men are bad but bold, and women are wonderful but weak'. These are predispositions, broad patterns, and general tendencies, and must be treated with caution. Differences between the sexes must not be confused with individual differences. In addition, Buchanan and Badham (2008) emphasize that much of the research evidence is dated. Social norms and attitudes change rapidly, and these stereotypes may no longer apply in today's organizations.

What did she do? Not till the lady leaves

Carly Fiorina (2006) tells the following story about her early career:

You've just graduated from the company management development programme for 'high flying' university graduates, and you've been assigned to your first role, as a sales team member, in a successful division which provides government communications services. Your boss is not welcoming, and gives you a stack of paperwork which you are still reading at the end of the week. Talking to your new colleagues, you discover that your boss is having an affair with a colleague in another department, so he doesn't have much time for you. Marie, the only other woman on the team, is prepared to offer advice. David manages one of the team's largest clients, servicing a large national communications network. You are assigned to 'co-manage' this client with him. David thinks this is a bad idea. Two of the client's regional (male) managers, who decide on major purchases, are planning a visit. You ask if you can join them, and David agrees. However, the day before the meeting, David explains that you will not be able to join them after all, because the clients have specifically requested that they meet at their 'favourite restaurant'. You are confused, until Marie explains that this is a strip club, with table dancing during dinner. You know when and where they are meeting, and you are embarrassed and anxious.

Carly Fiorina

What would you do? Your options are: (1) This is just one meeting. It doesn't matter. Don't go; (2) Express outrage and insist that they hold the meeting somewhere else. (3) Tell David that you're coming anyway and that you'll meet them there. Which option would you choose, and why? Fiorina's answer is at the end of the chapter.

The evidence suggests, however, that women may not use political tactics to the same degree, or in the same manner, as men. This may be one explanation for the lack of women in senior management roles. Women have been shown to be less successful in acquiring organizational power and are more likely to suffer 'political skill deficiency' (Perrewé and Nelson, 2004). As political skill is more important at senior levels, women can struggle in the competition to secure

Table 22.6: Traditional gender stereotypes in approach to organization politics

Wonderful but weak female stereotype	Bad but bold male stereotype
Politically innocent, naive	Politically aware, skilled
Organizational power is difficult to acquire	Organizational power is readily acquired
Use passive or 'soft' influence tactics such as coalition forming	Use aggressive or 'hard' influence tactics such as threats and assertiveness
Use formal systems to get information	Use informal systems to get information
Uncomfortable with self-promoting behaviour	Self-promotion taken for granted
Career depends on doing a good job	Career depends on self-promotion

Source: Buchanan and Badham (2008)

top jobs, or struggle once they are in those positions. It is possible that women lack confidence and perceived competence in their ability to play organization politics (Arroba and James, 1998).

Reviewing the evidence on influence tactics, Ferris et al. (2002, p.103) found that:

- women tend to use fewer influence tactics than men
- the tactics most used by women tend to be consistent with female stereotypes
- organizational norms reward those who use traditional 'masculine' influence tactics
- women who use 'male' tactics may attract organizational rewards (promotion, pay rises) but may receive less social support from colleagues.

Marla Watkins and Alexis Smith (2011) studied 140 female law graduates working in American law firms, which were male-dominated. They used the measure of political skill developed by Gerald Ferris (described above). Those with high political skill scores were more likely to have been promoted to management roles than those with low political skill. The researchers conclude that women who are politically skilled, and who understand the gender-based interpersonal challenges they face in a male-dominated organization, will have an advantage over their less skilled peers in terms of advancing to more senior positions.

There are individual, social, and structural explanations for the apparent differences in the ways in which women and men approach organization politics.

The Joy of Tech™   by Nitrozac & Snaggy

YOU *QUIT?*

I JUST DON'T HAVE THE ENERGY TO *DRESS* FOR THIS JOB ANYMORE.

©2007 Geek Culture

joyoftech.com

He was luckier... the desk allowed him to work in his underwear.

Individual explanations

Personality

Variations in attitudes and behaviours may be attributable to innate personality traits and predispositions. Some psychologists argue that these are genetically acquired, while others believe that socialization, in the form of upbringing and cultural norms, have a major impact on personality **(Chapter 6).** Research has suggested that women are socialized to be more passive and accommodating than men. For example, Barbara Tannen (1995) argues that boys and girls acquire different linguistic and relational styles in childhood (boys are expected to be more competitive), which subsequently influence their working styles and career prospects.

Awareness

Women may not be aware of, or prefer to deny, the role of organization politics. Sandy Mann (1995) argues that women can be politically naive, adopting 'innocent' behaviours at work, putting their faith in rationality and fairness. They believe that they can mobilize the resources that they need through formal channels, and secure promotion by working hard without the need to influence others. From this standpoint, politics interferes with the process of getting the job done, and those who think this way are less likely to use informal relationships, friends or favours in order to achieve their goals.

Preference

Singh et al. (2002) found that, despite apparent gender differences, women understood as well as men the need to 'read' the organization and 'play the game' in order to become more visible and increase their promotion chances. However, women reported that they were uncomfortable in having to behave in a self-promoting manner, and that networking was not a natural female behaviour. Women in that study thus knew 'the rules of the game', but some chose deliberately not to play.

Authenticity

Women who seek or acquire a senior management position have the option of employing the 'take charge', 'dominant male' leadership stereotype. Alice Eagly (2005) noted that women who moderated their display of femininity, and who modelled confident, authoritative, masculine behaviours, were more likely to feel that they were inauthentic, unnatural and play-acting.

Motivation

A study of General Electric's 135,000 professional workers found that voluntary turnover among female staff was 8 per cent compared to 6.5 per cent among men. Also, 26 per cent of professional women who were not yet in senior posts said that they did not want those jobs. Of the 108 women who had appeared in the Fortune 500 lists of the most powerful women, at least 20 had left their prestige positions, most of them by their own choice. That study also found that women did not greet promotions to senior roles eagerly. Some did not actively seek promotion; some declined promotion outright; others replied to the invitation with the question, 'Are you sure?' The American politician Hillary Clinton suggested that many women pushed less strongly for promotion than men, not because they lacked ambition, but because they did not hang their egos on the next rung of the corporate ladder (Sellers, 2003).

Joanna Barsh and Lareina Yee (2011, p.4) found that women often turn down promotion in order to stay in a role that they find motivating, from which they derive a sense of meaning, and to avoid the 'energy-draining meetings and corporate politics at the next echelon'.

Social explanations

Women can copy the male leadership stereotype: aggressive, competitive, intense. It appears that certain behaviours are seen as being reserved for men, and that 'tough female managers are often labelled with epithets such as *battle axe, dragon lady, bitch* and *bully broad*':

> If a leadership role requires a highly authoritative or competitive behaviour that is perceived as masculine, the mere fact that a woman occupies the role can yield disapproval. [T]he more confidently a woman conveys those values, the less effective she may become because of her challenge to traditional gender norms and her overturning of the expected gender hierarchy' (Eagly, 2005, p.464).

Alice Eagly and Linda Carli (2007) suggest that women need to develop their 'social capital' – by building a network of professional colleagues. Women tend not to invest time in networking due to family responsibilities, and because they may not see this as important. Networking, however, is an important political skill. We each have our own network of relationships based on a variety of social, leisure, and work settings. Used effectively, these relationships can help us to find better jobs, and get promoted. Other people can also be a source of new ideas, and they can in turn pick up ideas from us. However, research by Herminia Ibarra (2015) shows that women and men build and use their networks in different ways. More importantly, women's approach to networking often puts them at a disadvantage in terms of influence and promotion.

Climbing the career ladder

Adrian Furnham (2015) argues that networking is key to career success:

'*Do serious networking*. You need a map of who's who; who holds power and influence; and who will be must useful to you. Job titles are poor indicators. Start mapping your environment; it is called social network analysis but all you need is a good eye and ear. Use those "elevator" and "water cooler" moments to introduce yourself. Build relationships by finding out what you have in common with people and how you might be able to help them. Accept all social invitations.'

The title of Keith Ferrazzi's (2014) guide to developing networking skills is *Never Eat Alone*.

Ibarra found that men tend to develop networks in which the people that they approach for work-related conversation and advice are those with whom they socialize outside work. Women, in contrast, have what Ibarra calls 'functionally differentiated' networks, with separate work-related and social groups. Men, whose work and social networks overlap, have more opportunities to share information and to develop influence. Ibarra puts it this way: 'They have more clout'. With their differentiated networks, women have less access to information, and are thus less influential.

Women are thus advised to be more calculating with regard to the friendships and relationships that they nurture. This means developing work-related networks that deliberately include people who can help them to achieve their goals, and who they may be able to help in return. Learning how to play golf is not essential, but may be useful in some circumstances.

✓✓✓   **EMPLOYABILITY CHECK** (self-management, political awareness, how organizations work)

As a female student, what steps can you take now to start building your professional network in preparation for when you graduate and start looking for work?

Structural explanations

Women can be rendered 'structurally powerless' by being limited to routine, low-profile jobs, and by having restricted access to line management roles early in their careers. Women face discrimination in what are often secretive promotion decisions, in organizations that are typically characterized by 'old boys' networks' and unequal power distribution (Oakley, 2000).

A male-dominated organization culture encourages long working hours. Men and women may have to choose between family responsibilities on the one hand, and attending breakfast meetings and evening drinks, on the other. Social expectations mean that this is often a more difficult decision for women, who are also faced with negative institutional mindsets: 'everybody "knows" you can't put a woman in that job'. The 'always on 24/7 executive lifestyle with travel' is the ultimate barrier, disrupting work-life balance. Barsh and Yee (2011) found that increasing numbers of men disliked this, too.

There are several explanations for women's apparent reluctance to use organization politics. This reluctance may in turn help to explain why there are so few women in senior management roles.

RECAP

1. *Appreciate the importance of power and politics in organizations.*

   - Organizations seem to be experiencing more change, uncertainty, ambiguity and discontinuity, creating a context that makes political skill more important.

2. *Compare and contrast different perspectives on power.*

   - Power can be considered from the 'power-as-property'; a 'faces of power'; and a 'disciplinary power' viewpoint.

   - The power-as-property viewpoint regards power as a characteristic of individuals, of relationships, and of the structures of society and organizations.

   - The faces of power viewpoint regards power as overt and observable, as covert and unobservable, and as internalized by employees.

   - Disciplinary power reduces employees' ability to dissent by creating and managing meanings for them.

3. *Distinguish different bases of power.*

   - The five bases of power are reward, coercion, referent, legitimate and expert.

4. *Identify organizational factors which enhance the power of departments.*

   - Factors enhancing the power of departments in organizations include dependency-creation, financial resources, centrality, non-substitutability, and uncertainty reduction.

5. *Differentiate between influencing tactics and political tactics.*

   - Influencing tactics include assertiveness, ingratiation, rational appeal, sanctions, exchange, upward appeal, blocking and coalition.

   - Political tactics include image building, information games, structure games, scapegoating, alliances, networking, compromise, rule games, positioning, issue selling and 'dirty tricks'.

6. *Identify the characteristics of individuals most likely to engage in political behaviour.*

   - Those who are most likely to engage in political behaviour have a high need for power (n*Pow*), a high Machiavellian score, an internal locus of control, and risk-seeking propensity.

7. *Explain how women use and are affected by organizational politics.*

   - Sex role stereotyping associates management with masculinity leading to a systematic underestimation of women's abilities.

   - Women appear to use power, influencing and impression management tactics differently from men; women tend to be less comfortable with self-promotion tactics which men use routinely.

   - Women can find it difficult to develop influence due to individual, social, and structural factors; women often do not develop useful professional networks in the way that men do.

RECAP: What did they find? the red sneakers effect

Oostrom and Ronay (2018) found that:

- Candidates dressed in a non-conformist way may be perceived more positively than those dressed in a more conforming manner; this is known as 'the red sneakers effect' – if you are confident enough to 'dress down', then you must be competent and highly regarded.

- Candidates with a strong CV were seen as powerful no matter how they dressed.

- Candidates with a weak CV were unlikely to be hired if they dressed in a non-conformist way.

- Deliberate non-conformity was seen as indicating that the candidate had the power, influence and status that allowed them to ignore social norms and behave as they liked; 'red sneakers' are a 'power tell' (which explains why Mark Zuckerberg can wear what he wants at work – 'I am successful so I can afford to dress in a nonconforming style' – but this also explains why he wore a formal business suit when he appeared before a congressional hearing in April 2018).

- This means that you will only get away with a non-conforming dress style – jeans and sneakers – if you have a strong CV which confirms your competence and qualifications for the job.

- A non-conforming dress style will backfire – you probably won't get the job – if you do not have strong evidence to demonstrate your capabilities.

Revision

1. How can someone low in the organizational hierarchy obtain more power?

2. Identify the costs and benefits to an organization of its members engaging in political behaviour.

3. 'Power is most potent when it appears to be absent.' What does this statement mean? Do you agree with it? Give reasons and examples to support your view.

4. What steps can women take in order to strengthen their organizational power and influence?

Research assignment

Interview three managers from the same or different organizations, ideally at junior, middle and senior manager levels. First, ask each one to give you a specific example of 'workplace politics in action'. Second, make three copies of the scoresheet from chapter exercise 2 below. Third, ask each manager to rank each type of decision according to the extent that they believe politics affected the outcome (1 = most political; 11 = least political). They should enter their ranking in column three. Finally, ask them what makes a decision 'political' in their organization.

Springboard

David A. Buchanan and Richard Badham (2008) *Power, Politics and Organizational Change.* London: Sage Publications (second edition). Considers the constructive use of power and political tactics in organizations.

Robert Cialdini (2016) *Pre-Suasion: A Revolutionary Way to Influence and Persuade.* London: Random House. Argues that the context in which an advertisement appears is more important than the selling strategy – illustrated with fascinating examples. The best per-suaders are the best 'pre-suaders', who work out how best to present a message in order to get agreement before the target audience has heard it.

Jeffrey Pfeffer (2010) *Power: Why Some People Have It – and Others Don't.* New York and London: Harper Business. An honest practical exploration of the skills involved in acquiring, holding on to, and using power to progress one's career – getting noticed by the right people, building networks, overcoming opposition, and building a reputation for getting things done.

Henry Timms and Jeremy Heimans (2018) *New Power: How It's Changing The 21st Century – And Why You Need To Know.* London and New York: Macmillan. Argue that the 'currents' of participative and open 'new power' are replacing the 'currency' of bureaucratic, closed old power. Offers examples of new power leaders, movements and organizations in action.

OB cinema

Dirty Rotten Scoundrels (1988, director Frank Oz). DVD track 2: 0:07:42 – 0:10:55 (4 minutes). Freddy Benson (played by Steve Martin) is a conman working on the French Riviera. This clip begins with a shot of Zurich railway station platform and ends with Benson's 'Thank you'. Benson persuades a woman on a train, a complete stranger, to buy him a meal. How does he achieve this?

1. What impression management techniques does he use?

2. What influencing tactics does he employ?

Chapter exercises

1: Power in a changing environment

Objectives

1. To introduce different types of power.

2. To explore the PESTLE change drivers in the environment which impact on the power of employees.

3. To understand how power in organizations is gained and lost as a result of these environment changes.

Briefing

1. Form groups and nominate a spokesperson. Read the description of your organization.

2. Read each of the five environmental change scenarios in order. For each one, decide:

   a. Which environment change driver is affecting your organization in this scenario?

   b. What types of activities are likely to increase/become more important in the company, as a result?

   c. Which five company employees' power bases will *increase* most in the light of this changed environmental condition?

   d. Why did you select these persons?

   Each scenario is separate from the others. Make any reasonable assumptions as you discuss the matter.

3. Each group's spokesperson presents and justifies their conclusions to the entire class.

Your organization

Your medium-sized company manufactures portable, petrol-driven, electric power generators that are sold to domestic and office customers, often for use in emergencies

Advertising expert (m)	Charted accountant (m)
Chief financial offer (f)	General manager (m)
Operations manager (f)	Marketing manager (f)
Industrial engineer (m)	Computer programmer (f)
Product designer (m)	Industrial chemist (m)
Public relations expert (m)	In-house legal advisor (m)
Company trainer (m)	Human resource manager (f)

Employees (m) = male; (f) = female

Five environmental change scenarios

1. The existing small batch production of generators will be replaced by a state-of-the-art, automated assembly line.

2. New laws about engine and factory emissions are being passed by the European Parliament.

3. Sales are greatly reduced, and the industrial sector seems to be shrinking.

4. The company is planning to go international in the next year or two.

5. The Equality Commission is pressing companies to establish better male-female balance in senior posts and is threatening to 'name-and-shame' companies.

Source: adapted from Barbuto (2000)

→

2: Politics in decision making

Objectives
1. To contrast perceptions about the use of politics in decision making.
2. To predict when and where politics will be used in organizations.
3. To contrast political with rational decision-making processes.

Briefing
1. Individually, using the worksheet, rank each of the 11 organizational decisions (a–k) in terms of the extent to which you think politics play a part. Rank the most political decision as '1' and the least political as '11'. Enter your ranking in the first column on your worksheet – 'Individual Ranking'.

2. Form groups of four to seven members. Rank the 11 items again, this time as a group. Use consensus to reach agreement, that is, listen to each person's ideas and rationale before deciding. Do not vote, bargain, average or toss a coin. Base your decision on the logical arguments made by group members rather than your personal preference. Enter your rankings in the second column on the scoresheet – 'Team Ranking'.

3. After all teams have finished, your instructor will read out the rankings produced by a survey of managers which indicates the frequency with which they believe that politics plays a part in each type of decision. As these are read out, enter them in column three on the scoresheet – 'Manager Ranking'.

4. Still in your groups:

   a. Compare the individual rankings (column 1) of group members. On which decisions did group members' perceptions differ significantly? Why might that be?

   b. Compare your group ranking (column 2) with the manager ranking (column 3). On which decisions did group and managers' perceptions differ significantly? Why might that be?

Scoresheet
'To what extent do you believe politics plays a part in the decision'

1 = most political   11 = least political

Decision	1 Individual ranking	2 Team ranking	3 Manager ranking
Management promotions and transfers			
Entry level hiring			
Amount of pay			
Annual budgets			
Allocation of facilities, equipment, offices			
Delegation of authority among managers			
Inter-departmental coordination			
Specification of personnel policies			
Penalties for disciplinary infractions			
Performance appraisals			
Grievances and complaints			

5. In plenary, answer the questions as directed by your instructor:

i. What distinguishes the most political decision items (ranked 1–4 in column 3) from the least political (ranked 8–11)?

ii. In what circumstances might a rational decision process be used in making a decision, and when would a political process be used?

iii. Research suggests that that political behaviour occurs more frequently at higher rather than lower levels in organizations. Why should this be so?

iv. How would you:

- apply rationality to those decisions currently possessing a large political element?
- politicize decisions currently made using rational processes?

v. How would you advise a manager who felt that politics was bad for the organization and should be avoided at all costs?

Source: based on Gandz and Murray (1980)

What did she do? The answer

Fiorina chose option 3. She wore a conservative business suit, and carried a briefcase. At the 'restaurant', in order to reach the client group, she had to walk in front of the stage, where about a dozen women were performing. She tried to sound relaxed and knowledgeable, ignoring the show, while David continued drinking and asking the women to come and dance on their table. All of the women who approached their table said, 'Sorry gentlemen. Not till the lady leaves'. The meeting lasted several hours. The client's business was secured. Fiorina concludes: 'After a few hours, having made my point, I left them all there. They heaved a sigh of relief, I'm sure, but the next day in the office, the balance of power had shifted perceptibly. I had shown David that I would not be intimidated, even if I was terrified. I truly cared about doing my job even when it meant working in difficult circumstances. Having tried to diminish me, David was himself diminished. He was embarrassed. And Bill [one of the other team members] decided that he would take me under his wing and help me succeed. We cannot always choose the hurdles we must overcome, but we can choose how we overcome them' (Fiorina, 2006, p.31).

References

Arroba, T. and James, K. (1998) 'Are politics palatable to women managers ? How women can make wise moves at work', *Women in Management Review,* 3(3): 123–30.

Ashford, S.J. and Detert, J. (2015) 'Get the boss to buy in', *Harvard Business Review,* 93 (1/2): 72–79.

Bachrach, P. and Baratz, M.S. (1963) 'Decisions and nondecisions: an analytical framework', *American Political Science Review,* 57(3): 641–51.

Barsh, J. and Yee, L. (2011) *Unlocking the Full Potential of Women in the US Economy.* New York: McKinsey & Company.

Brouer, R.L., Ferris, G.R., Hochwarter, W.A., Laird, M.D. and Gilmore, D.C. (2006) 'The strain-related reactions to perceptions of organizational politics as a workplace stressor: political skill as a neutralizer', in Eran Vigoda and Amos Drory (eds), *Handbook of Organizational Politics.* Thousand Oaks, CA: Sage Publications, pp.187–206.

Buchanan, D.A. and Badham, R. (2008) *Power, Politics, and Organizational Change: Winning the Turf Game* (second edition). London: Sage Publications.

Christie, R. and Geiss, F.L. (1970) *Studies in Machiavellianism.* New York: Academic Press.

Cialdini, R.B. (2008) *Influence: Science and Practice* (fifth edition). Boston, MA: Allyn and Bacon.

Cialdini, R.B. (2013) 'The uses (and abuses) of influence', *Harvard Business Review*, 91 (7/8): 76–81.

Collett, P. (2004) 'Show and tell', *People Management*, 10(8): 34–35.

Cuddy, A.J.C. (2016) *Presence: Bringing Your Boldest Self to Your Biggest Challenges.* London: Orion Publishing.

Cuddy, A.J.C, Schultz, S.J. and Fosse, N.E. (2018) 'P-curving a more comprehensive body of research on postural feedback reveals clear evidential value for power-posing effects: reply to Simmons and Simonsohn', *Psychological Science*, 29(4): 656–66.

DuBrin, A. (2016) 'Political blunders within organizations', in Eran Vigoda-Gadot and Amos Drory (eds), *Handbook of Organizational Politics: Looking Back and to the Future* (second edition). Cheltenham, UK: Edward Elgar Publishing, pp.172–92.

Eagly, A.H. (2005) 'Achieving relational authenticity in leadership: does gender matter?', *The Leadership Quarterly*, 16: 459–74.

Eagly, A.H. and Carli, L.L. (2007) 'Women and the labyrinth of leadership', *Harvard Business Review*, 85(9): 62–71.

Ferrazzi, K. (2014) *Never Eat Alone.* London: Portfolio Penguin.

Ferris, G.R., Perrewé, P.L., Anthony, W.P. and Gilmore, D.C. (2000) 'Political skill at work', *Organizational Dynamics*, 28(4): 25–37.

Ferris, G.R., Adams, G., Kolodinsky, R.W., Hochwarter, W.A. and Ammeter, A.P. (2002) 'Perceptions of organizational politics: theory and research directions', *Research in Multi-Level Issues Volume 1: The Many Faces of Multi-Level Issues*: 179–254.

Ferris, G.R., Treadway, D.C., Kolodinsky, R.W., Hochwarter, W.A., Kacmar, C.J., Douglas, C. and Frink, D.D. (2005) 'Development and validation of the Political Skill Inventory', *Journal of Management*, 31 (1): 126–52.

Ferris, G.R., Treadway, D.C., Perrewé, P.L., Brouer, R.L., Douglas, C. and Lux, S. (2007) 'Political skill in organizations', *Journal of Management*, 33 (3): 290–320.

Fiorina, C. (2006) *Tough Choices: A Memoir.* London and Boston: Nicholas Brealey Publishing.

Fleming, P. and Spicer, A. (2007) *Contesting the Corporation: Struggle, Power and Resistance in Organizations.* Cambridge: Cambridge University Press.

Foucault, M. (1979) *Discipline and Punish.* Harmondsworth, Middlesex: Penguin Books.

French, J.R.P. and Raven, B.H. (1958) 'The bases of social power', in D. Cartwright (ed.), *Studies in Social Power.* Ann Arbor, Michigan: Institute for Social Research, University of Michigan Press, pp.150–67.

Furnham, A. (2015) 'Seven steps to the stars: how to fly up the career ladder', *The Sunday Times Appointments Section*, 18 January, p.2.

Galinsky, A. and Schweitzer, M. (2015) *Friend and Foe: When to Cooperate, When to Compete, and How to Succeed at Both.* London: Random House Business.

Gandz, J. and Murray, V.V. (1980) 'The experience of workplace politics', *Academy of Management Journal*, 23 (2): 237–51.

Heimans, J and Timms, H. (2014) 'Understanding new power', *Harvard Business Review*, 92(12): 48–56.

Hickson, D.J., Hinings, C.R., Lee, C.A., Schneck, R.E. and Pennings, J.M. (1971) 'A strategic contingencies theory of intra-organizational power', *Administrative Science Quarterly*, 16(2): 216–29.

Hildreth, J.A.D. and Anderson, C. (2016) 'Failure at the top: how power undermines collaborative performance', *Journal of Personality and Social Psychology*, 110(2): 261–86.

Hiley, D.R. (1987) 'Power and values in corporate life', *Journal of Business Ethics*, 6(5): 343–53.

Huczynski, A.A. (2004) *Influencing Within Organizations.* London: Routledge, (second edn).

Ibarra, H. (2015) 'Friendships forged outside work can hold women back', *Financial Times*, 1 September, p.14.

Keltner, D. (2016) 'Managing yourself: don't let power corrupt you', *Harvard Business Review*, 94(10): 112–15.

Keltner, D. (2017) *The Power Paradox: How We Gain and Lose Influence.* London: Penguin Books.

Kim, W.C. and Mauborgne, R. (2003) 'Tipping point leadership', *Harvard Business Review*, 81(4): 60–69.

Kimura, T. (2015) 'A review of political skill: current research trends and directions for future research', *International Journal of Management Reviews*, 17(3): 312–32.

Kipnis, D., Schmidt, S.M., Swaffin-Smith, C. and Wilkinson, I. (1984) 'Patterns of managerial influence: shotgun managers, tacticians, and bystanders', *Organizational Dynamics*, 12(3): 58–67.

Lukes, S. (2005) *Power: A Radical View.* London: Macmillan, (second edn).

McAuley, J., Duberley, J. and Johnson, P. (2007) *Organization Theory: Challenges and Perspectives.* Harlow, Essex: Financial Times Prentice Hall.

McCarty, J. (2004) *Bullets Over Hollywood: The American Gangster Picture from the Silents to 'The Sopranos'.* Cambridge, MA: Da Capo Press.

McClelland, D.C. (1961) *The Achieving Society.* Princeton, NJ: Van Nostrand Reinhold.

McClelland, D.C., Atkinson, J.W., Clark, R.A. and Lowell, E.L. (1976) *The Achievement Motive*. New York: Irvington, (second edn).

McClelland, D.C. and Boyatzis, R.E. (1982) 'Leadership motive pattern and long term success in management', *Journal of Applied Psychology*, 67(6): 737–43.

McClelland, D.C. and Burnham, D.H. (1995) 'Power is the great motivator', *Harvard Business Review*, 73(1): 126–39 (first published 1976).

Machiavelli, N. (1514) *The Prince.*(George Bull, Trans.) London: Penguin Books 1961.

Mann, S. (1995) 'Politics and power in organizations; why women lose out', *Leadership and Organization Development Journal*, 16(2): 9–15.

Mintzberg, H. (1983) *Power in and Around Organizations*. Upper Saddle River NJ: Prentice Hall.

Oakley, J. (2000) 'Gender-based barriers to senior management promotions: understanding the scarcity of female CEOs', *Journal of Business Ethics*, 27(4): 323 34.

Oostrom, J.K. and Ronay, R. (2018) 'Dress to impress: the effects of nonconformist dress style in personnel selection contexts'. *Academy of Management Proceedings*: paper presented at the Academy of Management Annual Conference, August, Chicago.

Perrewé, P.L. and Nelson, D.L. (2004) 'Gender and career success: the facilitative role of political skill', *Organizational Dynamics*, 33(4): 366–78.

Pfeffer, J. (1992) *Managing With Power: Politics and Influence in Organization*. Boston, MA: Harvard Business School Press.

Pfeffer, J. (2010) 'Power play', *Harvard Business Review*, 88(7/8): 84–92.

Pfeffer, J. (2016) 'Getting beyond the BS of leadership literature', *McKinsey Quarterly*, 1(January), pp.90–95.

Pfeffer, J. and Sutton, R.I. (2006) *Hard Facts, Dangerous Half-Truths, and Total Nonsense: Profiting from Evidence-Based Management*. Boston, MA: Harvard Business School Press.

Rotter, J.B. (1966) 'Generalized expectations for internal versus external control of reinforcement', *Psychological Monographs*, 80(609; whole issue): 1–28.

Salancik, G.R. and Pfeffer, J. (1977) 'Who gets power – and how they hold on to it: a strategic contingency model of power', *Organizational Dynamics*, 5(3): 2–21.

Sellers, P. (2003) 'Power: do women really want it?', *Fortune*, 13 October, pp.58–65.

Singh, V., Kumra, S. and Vinnicombe, S. (2002) 'Gender and impression management: playing the promotion game', *Journal of Business Ethics*, 37(1): 77–89.

Tannen, D. (1995) 'The power of talk: who gets heard and why', *Harvard Business Review*, 73(5): 138–48.

Timms, H. and Heimans, J. (2018) *New Power: How It's Changing The 21st Century – And Why You Need To Know*. London and New York: Macmillan.

Watkins, M.B. and Smith, A.N. (2011) 'Importance of women's political skill in male-dominated organizations', *Journal of Managerial Psychology*, 29(2): 206–22.

Glossary

Accommodation stage of socialization: period during which newcomers learn about company norms, values, behaviours and expectations, and adjust themselves to them.

Accountability: the obligation of a subordinate to report back on their discharge of the duties for which they are responsible.

Action team: a team that executes brief performances that are repeated under new conditions. Its members are technically specialized, and need to coordinate their individual contributions with each other.

Activities: in Homans' theory, the physical movements, and verbal and non-verbal behaviours engaged in by group members.

Adaptive decisions: decisions that require human judgement based on clarified criteria and are made using quantitative decision tools.

Additive task: a task whose accomplishment depends on the sum of all group members' efforts.

Advice team: a team created by management to provide the latter with information for its own decision making.

Aggregate: a collection of unrelated people who happen to be in close physical proximity for a short period of time.

Agile organization: one which allows an organization to quickly reconfigure strategy, structure, processes, people and technology toward value-creating and value protecting opportunities.

Anticipatory stage of socialization: the expectations that a newcomer has about the job or organization before starting work.

Artificial intelligence: tasks performed by computer software that would otherwise require human intelligence.

Attribution: the process by which we make sense of our environment through our perceptions of causality.

Authority: the right to guide or direct the actions of others and extract from them responses that are appropriate to the attainment of an organization's goals.

Augmented reality: technology that superimposes digital information and images on the physical world through a screen, such as a smartphone, iPad, or television.

Balanced scorecard: an approach to defining organizational effectiveness using a combination of quantitative and qualitative measures.

Basic assumptions: invisible, preconscious, unspoken,'taken-for-granted' understandings held by individuals within an organization concerning human behaviour, the nature of reality and the organization's relationship to its environment.

Behaviour modification: a technique for encouraging desired behaviours and discouraging unwanted behaviours using operant conditioning.

Behavioural modelling: learning how to act by observing and copying the behaviour of others.

Behavioural theory of decision making: recognizes that bounded rationality limits the making of optimal decisions.

Behaviourist psychology: a perspective which argues that what we learn are chains of muscle movements; mental processes are not observable, and are not valid issues for study.

Bias: a prejudice, predisposition or a systematic distortion caused by the application of a heuristic.

Big data: information collected, often real-time, from sources such as internet clicks, mobile transactions, user-generated content, social media, sensor networks, sales queries, purchases.

The Big Five: consistent trait clusters that capture the main dimensions of personality: Openness, Conscientiousness, Extraversion, Agreeableness and Neuroticism.

Boundaryless organization: one possessing permeable internal and external boundaries which give it flexibility and thus the ability to respond to change rapidly.

Bounded rationality: a theory which says that individuals make decisions by constructing simplified models that extract the essential features from problems without capturing all their complexity.

Brainstorming: a technique in which all group members are encouraged to propose ideas spontaneously, without critiquing or censoring others' ideas. The ideas so generated are not evaluated until all have been listed.

Bureaucracy: legal-rational type of authority underpinning a form of organization structure that is characterized by job specialization, authority hierarchy, formal selection, rules and procedures, impersonality, impartiality and recording.

Caution shift: the tendency of a group to make decisions that are more risk averse than those that individual members of the group would have recommended.

Centralization: the concentration of authority and responsibility for decision-making power in the hands of managers at the top of an organization's hierarchy.

Certainty: a condition in which managers possess full knowledge of alternatives; a high probability of having these available; being able to calculate the costs and benefits of each alternative; and having high predictability of outcomes.

Chain of command: the unbroken line of authority that extends from the top of the organization to the bottom and clarifies who reports to whom.

Chronotype: a cluster of personality traits that can affect whether someone is more active and performs better in the morning or in the evening.

Classical decision theory: assumes that decision-makers are objective, have complete information and consider all possible alternatives and their consequences before selecting the optimal solution.

Cobots: collaborative robots that work alongside and help human workers.

Coding: the stage in the interpersonal communication process in which the transmitter chooses how to express a message for transmission to someone else.

Coercive power: the ability to exert influence based on the other's belief that the influencer can administer unwelcome penalties or sanctions.

Cognitive psychology: a perspective which argues that what we learn are mental structures; mental processes can be studied by inference, although they cannot be observed directly.

Collaborative relationship structure: one that involves a relationship between two or more organizations, sharing their ideas, knowledge, staff, production and technology for mutual benefit.

Communication climate: the prevailing atmosphere in an organization – *open* or *closed* – in which ideas and information are exchanged.

Communication network analysis: a technique that uses direct observation to determine the source, direction and quantity of oral communication between co-located members of a group.

Communication pattern analysis: a technique that uses analysis of documents, data, and voice mail transmission, to determine the source, direction and quantity of oral and written communication between the dispersed members of a group.

Communication pattern chart: indicates the source, direction and quantity of oral and written communication between the dispersed members of a group.

Communication process: the transmission of information, and the exchange of meaning, between at least two people.

Communigram: a chart that indicates the source, direction and quantity of oral communication between the members during a group meeting.

Compliance (in the context of a group): a majority's influence over a minority.

Compensatory mechanisms: processes that delay or reduce employment replacement effects, and which lead to the creation of new products, services, and jobs.

Computerization: job automation by means of computer-controlled equipment.

Concurrent feedback: information which arrives during our behaviour and which can be used to control behaviour as it unfolds.

Conflict: a process that begins when one party perceives that another party has negatively affected, or is about to negatively affect, something that the first party cares about.

Conflict resolution: a process which has as its objective the ending of the conflict between the disagreeing parties.

Conflict stimulation: the process of engendering conflict between parties where none existed before, or escalating the current conflict level if it is too low.

Conformity: a change in an individual's belief or behaviour in response to real or imagined group pressure.

Conjunctive task: a task whose accomplishment depends on the performance of the group's least talented member.

Consideration: a pattern of leadership behaviour that demonstrates sensitivity to relationships and to the social needs of employees.

Constructivism: a perspective which argues that our social and organizational worlds have no ultimate objective truth or reality, but are instead determined by our shared experiences, meanings and interpretations.

Contingency approach to organization structure: a perspective which argues that to be effective, an organization must adjust its structure to take into account its technology, its environment, its size and similar contextual factors.

Contingency theory of leadership: a perspective which argues that leaders must adjust their style to take into account the properties of the context.

Controlled performance: setting standards, measuring performance, comparing actual with standard, and taking corrective action if necessary.

Conversion: a minority's influence over a majority.

Co-opetition: a form of cooperation between competing organizations which is limited to specified areas where both believe they can gain mutual benefit.

Coping cycle: the emotional response to trauma and loss, in which we experience first denial, then anger, bargaining, depression, and finally acceptance.

Corporate social responsibility: the view that organizations should act ethically, in ways that contribute to economic development, the environment, quality of working life, local communities, and the wider society.

Corporate strategy: the aims of a company and the means by which these will be achieved.

Counter-productive work behaviour: any intentional employee behaviour viewed by the organization as being harmful to its legitimate interests.

Cross-functional team: employees from different functional departments who meet as a team to complete a particular task.

Cybernetic analogy: an explanation of the learning process based on the components and operation of a feedback control system.

Cybervetting: covertly gathering information from informal, non-institutional online sources via social media and search engines to help decide whom to recruit, hire, promote or fire.

Data analytics: the use of powerful computational methods to reveal and to visualize patterns and trends in very large sets of data.

Decentralization: the dispersion of authority and responsibility for decision making to operating units, branches and lower level managers.

Decision-based evidence making: marshalling facts and analysis to support a decision that has already been made elsewhere in the organization.

Decision making: the process of making choices from a number of alternatives.

Decoding: the stage in the interpersonal communication process in which the recipient interprets a message transmitted to them by someone else.

Deindividuation: an increased state of anonymity that loosens normal constraints on individuals' behaviour, reducing their sense of responsibility and leading to an increase in impulsive and antisocial acts.

Delayed feedback: information which is received after a task is completed, and which can be used to influence future performance.

Delegation: managers granting decision-making authority to employees at lower hierarchical levels.

Departmentalization: the process of grouping together activities and employees who share a common supervisor and resources, who are jointly responsible for performance, and who tend to identify and collaborate with each other.

Descriptive model of decision making: model which seeks to portray how individuals actually make decisions.

Differentiation: the degree to which the work of individuals, groups and units are divided up within an organization.

Differentiation perspective on culture: sees organizations as consisting of subcultures, each with its own characteristics, which differ from those of its neighbours.

Discretionary behaviour: freedom to decide how work is going to be performed; discretionary behaviour can be positive, such as putting in extra time and effort, or it can be negative, such as withholding information and cooperation.

Disjunctive task: a task whose accomplishment depends on the performance of the group's most talented member.

Disruptive innovations: innovations which involve the development of wholly new processes, procedures, services and products.

Distributed innovation: decentralized problem solving involving self-selected participation, self-organizing coordination and collaboration, 'free' revealing of knowledge, and hybrid organizational models that blend community with commercial success.

Distributed innovation system: an approach to organizing for innovation that accesses the knowledge that resides outside the boundaries of any one organization.

Distributed leadership: the exercise of leadership behaviours, often informally and spontaneous, by staff at all levels of an organization, with a group taking collective responsibility, or taking turns in leadership roles depending on circumstances.

Distributive bargaining: a negotiation strategy in which a fixed sum of resources is divided up, leading to a win–lose situation between the parties.

Distributive justice: employees' judgements about the fairness of outcomes.

Divisional structure: an organizational design that groups departments together based on the product sold, the geographical area operated in, or type of customer served.

Drive: an innate, biological determinant of behaviour, activated by deprivation.

Dysfunctional conflict: a form of conflict which does not support organization goals and hinders organizational performance.

Emotional intelligence: the ability to identify, integrate, understand and reflectively manage one's own and other people's feelings.

Employee engagement: being positively present during the performance of work by willingly contributing intellectual effort, experiencing positive emotions, and meaningful connections to others.

Employee voice: the ability of employees to express their views, opinions, concerns and suggestions, and for these to influence decisions at work.

Employment cycle: the sequence of stages through which all employees pass in each working position they hold, from recruitment and selection, to termination.

Empowerment: organizational arrangements that give employees more autonomy, discretion and decision-making responsibility.

Environment: issues, trends, and events outside the boundaries of the organization, which influence internal decisions and behaviours.

Environmental complexity: the range of external factors relevant to the activities of the organization; the more factors, the higher the complexity.

Environmental determinism: the argument that internal organizational responses are primarily determined by external environmental factors.

Environmental dynamism: the pace of change in relevant factors external to the organization; the greater the pace of change, the more dynamic the environment.

Environmental scanning: techniques for identifying and predicting the impact of external trends and developments on the internal functioning of an organization.

Environmental uncertainty: the degree of unpredictable turbulence and change in the political, economic, social, technological, legal and ecological context in which an organization operates.

Equity theory: a process theory of motivation which argues that perception of unfairness leads to tension, which motivates the individual to resolve that unfairness.

Escalation of commitment: an increased commitment to a previously made decision despite negative information suggesting one should do otherwise.

Ethics: the moral principles, values and rules that govern our decisions and actions with respect to what is right and wrong, good and bad.

Evidence-based decision making: a situation in which a decision is made that follows directly from the evidence.

Evidence-based management: systematically using the best available research evidence to inform decisions about how to manage people and organizations.

Expectancy: the perceived probability that effort will result in good performance, and is measured on a scale from 0 (no chance) to 1 (certainty).

Expectancy theory: a process theory which argues that individual motivation depends on the *valence* of outcomes, the *expectancy* that effort will lead to good performance, and the *instrumentality* of performance in producing valued outcomes.

Expert power: the ability to exert influence based on the other's belief that the influencer has superior knowledge relevant to the situation and the task.

Explanatory model of decision making: an approach that accounts for how individuals, groups and organizations make decisions.

External adaptation: the process through which employees adjust to changing environmental circumstances to attain organizational goals.

External work team differentiation: the degree to which a work team stands out from its organizational context in terms of its membership, temporal scope and territory.

External work team integration: the degree to which a work team is linked with the larger organization of which it is a part.

Extinction: the attempt to eliminate undesirable behaviours by attaching no consequences, positive or negative, such as indifference and silence.

Extrinsic feedback: information which comes from our environment, such as the visual and aural information needed to drive a car.

Extrinsic rewards: valued outcomes or benefits provided by others, such as promotion, pay increases, a bigger office desk, praise and recognition.

Feedback (communication): processes through which the transmitter of a message detects whether and how that message has been received and decoded.

Feedback (learning): information about the outcomes of our behaviour.

Feedforward interview: a method for improving employee performance by focusing on recent success and attempting to create the same conditions in the future.

Fordism: a form of work design that applies scientific management principles to workers' jobs; the installation of single purpose machine tools to manufacture standardized parts; and the introduction of the mechanized assembly line.

Formal group: one that has been consciously created by management to accomplish a defined task that contributes to the organization's goal.

Formal organization: the documented, planned relationships, established by management to coordinate the activities of different employees towards the achievement of the organizational goal.

Formal status: the collection of rights and obligations associated with a position, as distinct from the person who may occupy that position.

Formalization: the degree to which an organization has written rules, operating procedures, job descriptions, organizational charts and uses formal, written communication.

Fragmentation (or conflict) perspective on culture: regards it as consisting of an incompletely shared set of elements that are loosely structured, constantly changing and which are generally in conflict.

Frame of reference: a person's perceptions and interpretations of events, which involve assumptions about reality, attitudes towards what is possible, and conventions regarding correct behaviour.

Free rider: a member who obtains benefits from team membership without bearing a proportional share of the costs for generating that benefit.

Functional conflict: a form of conflict which supports organization goals and improves performance.

Functional relationship: one in which staff department specialists have the authority to insist that line managers implement their instructions concerning a particular issue.

Functional structure: an organizational design that groups activities and people according to the similarities in their work, profession, expertise, goals or resources used.

Fundamental attribution error: the tendency to explain the behaviour of others based on their personality or disposition, and to overlook the influence of wider contextual influences.

Gender: culturally specific patterns of behaviour which may be attached to either of the sexes.

Generalized other: what we think other people expect of us, in terms of our attitudes, values, beliefs and behaviour.

Gig economy: a system of employment in which freelance workers sell their skills and services, through online marketplaces, to employers on a project- or task-basis.

Globalization: the intensification of worldwide social and business relationships which link localities in such a way that local conditions are shaped by distant events.

Goal orientation: the motivation to achieve goals – *aggressive masculinity v passive femininity.*

Goal-setting theory: a process theory of motivation which argues that work motivation is influenced by goal difficulty, goal specificity, and knowledge of results.

Great man theory: a historical perspective which argues that the fate of societies, and organizations, is in the hands of powerful, idiosyncratic (male) individuals.

Group: two or more people in face-to-face interaction, each aware of their group membership and interdependence, as they strive to achieve common group goals.

Group cohesion: the number and strength of mutual positive attitudes between individual group members.

Group dynamics: the forces operating within groups that affect their performance and their members' satisfaction.

Group hierarchy refers to distinct differences in group members' status and power.

Group norm: an expected mode of behaviour or belief that is established either formally or informally by a group.

Group polarization: a situation in which individuals in a group begin by taking a moderate stance on an issue related to a common value but, after having discussed it, end up taking a more extreme decision than the average of members' decisions. The extremes could be more risky or more cautious.

Group process: the patterns of interactions between the members of a group.

Group sanction: a punishment or a reward given by members to others in the group in the process of enforcing group norms.

Group self-organization: the collective process of communication, choice and mutual adjustment in behaviour based on a shared goal among members of a given system.

Group socialization: the process whereby members learn the values, symbols and expected behaviours of the group to which they belong.

Group structure: the relatively stable pattern of relationships among different group members.

Groupthink: a mode of thinking in a cohesive in-group, in which members' strivings for unanimity override their motivation to appraise realistically the alternative courses of action.

Growth mindset: the belief that you can develop your capabilities through hard work, good methods and contributions from others.

Growth need strength: a measure of the readiness and capability of an individual to respond positively to job enrichment.

Habituation: the decrease in our perceptual response to stimuli once they have become familiar.

Halo effect: an overall assessment of a person which influences our judgement of their other specific characteristics.

Hawthorne Effect: the tendency of people being observed to behave differently than they otherwise would

Heuristic: a simple and approximate rule, guiding procedure, shortcut or strategy that is used to solve problems.

HEXACO model: a model of personality based on six trait clusters – honesty-humility, emotionality, extraversion, agreeableness, conscientiousness, and openness to experience.

Hierarchy: distinct differences between individuals in terms of their status and power.

Hierarchy of needs theory: a content theory of motivation which argues that we have innate needs for survival, safety, affiliation, esteem, and self-actualization, and that we pursue higher order needs only once our lower order needs have been met.

High context culture: a culture whose members rely heavily on a range of social and non-verbal clues when communicating with others and interpreting their messages.

High-performance work system: a form of organization that operates at levels of excellence far beyond those of comparable systems.

Holacracy: a form of decentralized management and organizational governance that takes decision-making power away from managerial hierarchies and distributes it among self-organizing teams.

Holacratic organization: a structure that is determined not through hierarchical planning but incrementally, responsively, and from the bottom up, that enables employees to self-organize and self-manage themselves to achieve organizational goals.

Hollow organization structure: an organizational design based on outsourcing an organization's non-core processes which are then supplied to it by specialist, external providers.

Human capital analytics: an HR practice enabled by computing technologies that use descriptive, visual and statistical analyses of data related to HR processes, human capital, organizational performance and external economic benchmarks to establish business impact and enable evidence-based, data-driven decision making.

Human Relations approach: a school of management thought which emphasizes the importance of social processes at work.

Human resource management: the function responsible for establishing integrated personnel policies to support organization strategy.

Hygiene factors: aspects of work which remove dissatisfaction, but do not contribute to motivation and performance, including pay, company policy, supervision, status, security and physical working conditions.

Idiographic: an approach to the study of personality emphasizing the uniqueness of the individual, rejecting the assumption that we can all be measured on the same dimensions.

Impression management: the processes through which we control the image or impression that others have of us.

Influence: the process of affecting someone else's attitudes, beliefs or behaviours, without using coercion or formal position, such that the other person believes that they are acting in their own best interests.

Informal group: a collection of individuals who become a group when they develop interdependencies, influence one another's behaviour, and contribute to mutual need satisfaction.

Informal organization: the undocumented relationships that arise spontaneously between employees as individuals interact with one another to meet their own psychological and physical needs.

Initiating structure: a pattern of leadership behaviour that emphasizes performance of the work in hand and the achievement of product and service goals.

Initiative and incentive system: a form of job design in which management gives workers a task to perform, provides them with the financial incentive to complete it, but then leaves them to use their own initiative as to how they will perform it.

Inner work life theory: a process theory of motivation which argues that our behaviour and performance at work are influenced by the interplay of our perceptions, emotions, and motives.

Innovation: the adoption of any device, system, process, programme, product, or service new to a particular organization.

Innovative decisions: decisions which address novel problems and lack pre-specified courses of action.

Instrumentality: the perceived probability that good performance will lead to valued rewards, and is measured on a scale from 0 (no chance) to 1 (certainty).

Integration: the required level to which units in an organization are linked together, and their respective degree of independence.

Integration (or unitary) perspective on culture: regards culture as monolithic, characterized by consistency, organization-wide consensus and clarity.

Integrative bargaining: a negotiation strategy that seeks to increase the total amount of resources, creating a win–win situation between the parties.

Intensive technology: technology that is applied to work tasks that are performed in no predetermined order.

Interaction Process Analysis: a technique used to categorize the content of speech.

Interactional justice: employees' perceptions of the interpersonal treatment they receive from those in authority.

Interactionist frame of reference on conflict: a perspective that views conflict as a positive and necessary force within organizations that is essential for their effective performance.

Interactions: in Homans' theory, the two-way communications between group members.

Internal integration: the process through which employees adjust to each other, work together and perceive themselves as a collective entity.

Internal work team differentiation: the degree to which a team's members possess different skills and knowledge that contributes towards the achievement of the team's objective.

Intrinsic feedback: information which comes from within, from the muscles, joints, skin, and other mechanisms such as that which controls balance.

Intrinsic rewards: valued outcomes or benefits which come from the individual, such as feelings of satisfaction, competence, self-esteem and accomplishment.

Japanese teamworking: use of scientific management principles of minimum manning, multi-tasking, multi-machine operation, pre-defined work operations, repetitive short cycle work, powerful first line supervisors, and a conventional managerial hierarchy.

Job definition: specification of the work task requirements of a job.

Job description: a summary statement of what an individual should do on the job.

Job specialization: the number of different work tasks that are combined within a single job.

Job diagnostic survey: a questionnaire which assesses the degree of skill variety, task identity, task significance, autonomy and feedback in jobs.

Job enrichment: a technique for broadening the experience of work to enhance employee need satisfaction and to improve motivation and performance.

Just-in-time system: managing inventory (stock) so that items are delivered when they are needed in the production process instead of being stored by the manufacturer.

Leadership: the process of influencing the activities of an organized group in its efforts toward goal setting and goal achievement.

Lean working: a systematic method for minimizing waste within a manufacturing or service providing system that does not sacrifice productivity.

Learning: the process of acquiring knowledge through experience which leads to a lasting change in behaviour.

Legitimate authority: based on formal, written rules that have the force of law, e.g. the authority of presidents, managers, lecturers.

Legitimate power: the ability to exert influence based on the other's belief that the influencer has authority to issue orders which they in turn have an obligation to accept.

Line employees: workers who are directly responsible for manufacturing goods or providing a service.

Line relationship: one in which a manager has the authority to direct the activities of those in positions below them on the same line.

Locus of control: an individual's generalized belief about internal (self-control) versus external control (control by the situation or by others).

Long-linked technology: technology that is applied to a series of programmed work tasks performed in a predetermined order.

Low context culture: a culture whose members focus on the written and spoken word when communicating with others and interpreting their messages.

McDonaldization: a form of work design aimed at achieving efficiency, calculability, predictability and control through non-human technology, to enhance organizational objectives by limiting employee discretion and creativity.

Machiavellianism: a personality trait or style of behaviour towards others which is characterized by (1) the use of guile and deceit in interpersonal relations, (2) a cynical view of the nature of other people; and (3) a lack of concern with conventional morality.

Maintenance activity: an oral input, made by a group member that reduces conflict, maximizes cohesion and maintains relationships within a group.

Management roles: behaviours or work tasks that a manager is expected to perform because of the position that he or she holds within a group or organization.

Managerial activities: activities performed by managers that support the operation of every organization and need to be performed to ensure its success.

Mass production: a form of work design that includes mechanical pacing of work, no choice of tools or methods, repetitiveness, minute subdivision of product, minimum skill requirements, and surface mental attention.

Matrix structure: an organizational design that combines two different types of structure resulting in an employee having two reporting relationships simultaneously.

Maximizing: a decision-making approach where all alternatives are compared and evaluated in order to find the best solution to a problem.

Mechanistic organization structure: one that possesses a high degree of task specialization, many rules, tight specification of individual responsibility and authority, and centralized decision making.

Mediating technology: technology that links independent but standardized work tasks.

Meta-organization: networks of firms or individuals not bound by authority-based relationships based on employment relationships but characterized by a system-level goal.

Modular organization structure: an organizational design that involves assembling product chunks (modules) provided by internal divisions and external providers.

Motivating potential score: an indicator of how motivating a job is likely to be for an individual, considering skill variety, task identity, task significance, autonomy and feedback.

Motivation: the cognitive decision-making process through which goal-directed behaviour is initiated, energized, directed, and maintained.

Motivator factors: aspects of work which lead to high levels of satisfaction, motivation and performance, including achievement, recognition, responsibility, advancement, growth, and the work itself.

Motive: a socially acquired goal activated by a desire for fulfilment.

Multigenerational workforce: an employee group which includes up to five different generations, each with potentially different expectations of work.

Need for achievement: a concern with meeting standards of excellence, the desire to be successful in competition, the motivation to excel.

Need for power (nPow): the desire to make an impact on others, change people or events, and make a difference in life.

Negative reinforcement: the attempt to encourage desirable behaviours by withdrawing negative consequences when the desired behaviour occurs.

Negotiation: a social process through which two or more interdependent parties make decisions, allocate resources, or resolve disputes.

Networked individualism: people functioning as connected individuals rather than embedded group members, moving between different sets of co-workers, using their ties to get jobs done; and relying on digital media to connect themselves with others.

Neuroplasticity: the ability of the human brain to keep learning and changing throughout an individual's life; also called brain plasticity.

New leader: an inspirational visionary, concerned with building a shared sense of purpose and mission, creating a culture in which everyone is aligned with the organization's goals and is skilled and empowered to achieve them.

Noise: factors outside the communication process which interfere with or distract attention from the transmission and reception of the intended meaning.

Nominal group technique: involves group members first working separately and then joining together in order to generate ideas or make decisions.

Nomothetic: an approach to the study of personality emphasizing the identification of traits, and the systematic relationships between different aspects of personality.

Non-verbal behaviour: the process of coding meaning through behaviours such as facial expressions, limb gestures and body postures.

Obedience: a situation in which an individual changes their behaviour in response to a direct command from another.

Offshoring: contracting with external providers in a different country to supply the organization with the processes and products that were previously supplied internally.

Operational definition: the method used to measure the incidence of a variable in practice.

Operational innovation: inventing entirely new ways of working.

Organic organization structure: one that possesses little task specialization, few rules, a high degree of individual responsibility and authority, and one in which decision making is delegated.

Organization: a social arrangement for achieving controlled performance in pursuit of collective goals.

Organization chart: a diagram outlining the positions in an organization's structure and the relationships between them.

Organization design: the integration of structure, people, rewards and processes to support the implantation of an organization's corporate strategy.

Organization hierarchy: differences in status and power in an organization reflected in the number of levels of authority shown on an organization chart.

Organization politics: the ability to understand others at work, and to use that knowledge to influence others to act in ways that enhance one's personal and/ or organizational objectives.

Organization structure: the formal system of task and reporting relationships that control, coordinate and motivate employees to work together to achieve organizational goals.

Organizational architecture: the framework of linked internal and external elements that an organization creates and uses to achieve the goals specified in its mission statement.

Organizational behaviour: the study of the structure and management of organizations, their environments, and the actions and interactions of their individual members and groups.

Organizational choice: the argument that work design and organization structure depend on decisions about how and why technology is used, and not by the technology itself.

Organizational citizenship behaviour: employee behaviour that is discretionary, informal and which contributes to organizational effectiveness.

Organizational culture: the shared values, beliefs and norms which influence the way employees think, feel and act towards others inside and outside the organization.

Organizational dilemma: how to reconcile inconsistency between individual needs and aspirations, and the collective purpose of the organization.

Organizational effectiveness: a multi-dimensional concept that can be defined differently by different stakeholders.

Organizational justice: a personal evaluation about the ethical and moral standing of managerial conduct.

Organizational socialization: the process through which an employee's pattern of behaviour, values, attitudes and motives is influenced to conform to those of the organization.

Organizational values: the accumulated beliefs held about how work should be done and situations dealt with, that guide employee behaviour.

Ostracism: an individual or a group failing to take actions that engage another organization member when it would be customary or appropriate to do so.

Outsourcing: contracting with external providers to supply the organization with the processes and products that were previously supplied internally.

Pavlovian conditioning: a technique for associating an established response or behaviour with a new stimulus.

Perception: the dynamic psychological process responsible for attending to, organizing and interpreting sensory data.

Perceptual filters: individual characteristics, predispositions and preoccupations that interfere with the effective transmission and receipt of messages.

Perceptual organization: the process through which incoming stimuli are organized or patterned in systematic and meaningful ways.

Perceptual set: an individual's predisposition to respond to people and events in a particular manner.

Perceptual threshold: a boundary point, either side of which our senses respectively will or will not be able to detect stimuli, such as sound, light or touch.

Perceptual world: the individual's personal internal image, map or picture of their social, physical and organizational environment.

Peripheral norms: socially defined standards relating to behaviour and beliefs that are important but not crucial to a group's objective and survival.

Person–group fit: the interpersonal compatibility between individuals and the members of their immediate groups.

Personality: the psychological qualities that influence an individual's characteristic behaviour patterns, in a stable and distinctive manner.

PESTLE analysis: an environmental scanning tool identifying Political, Economic, Social, Technological, Legal and Ecological factors that affect an organization.

Pivotal norms: socially defined standards relating to behaviour and beliefs that are central to a group's objective and survival.

Pluralist frame of reference on conflict: a perspective that views organizations as consisting of different, natural interest groups, each with their own potentially constructive, legitimate interests, which makes conflict between them inevitable.

Political skill: an interpersonal style that combines social astuteness with the ability to relate well, and to demonstrate situationally appropriate behaviour in a disarmingly charming and engaging manner that inspires confidence, trust, sincerity and genuineness.

Positive reinforcement: the attempt to encourage desirable behaviours by introducing positive consequences when the desired behaviour occurs.

Positivism: a perspective which assumes that the world can be understood in terms of causal relationships between observable and measurable variables, and that these relationships can be studied objectively using controlled experiments.

Power: the capacity of individuals to overcome resistance on the part of others, to exert their will, and to produce results consistent with their own interests and objectives.

Power orientation: the appropriateness of power / authority within organizations – *respect v tolerance*.

Power priming: the process of making yourself feel more powerful, which in turn allows you to feel less stressed, and to behave as a more confident, persuasive and powerful person.

Power tells: non-verbal signals that indicate to others how important and dominant someone is, or how powerful they would like us to *think* they are.

Predictive validity: the extent to which assessment scores accurately predict behaviours such as job performance.

Prescriptive model of decision making: an approach that recommends how individuals should make decisions in order to achieve a desired outcome.

Presenteeism: working for more hours than required, even when unwell, motivated by a sense of job insecurity, and the desire to appear enthusiastic and committed.

Procedural justice: employees' evaluations of the way in which decisions are made, irrespective of their outcome.

Process theory: an approach to explaining organizational behaviour based on narratives which show how several factors, combining and interacting over time in a particular context, are likely to produce the outcomes of interest.

Production team: a stable number of individuals who share production goals and who perform specific roles which are supported by a set of incentives and sanctions.

Project team: a collection of employees from different work areas in an organization brought together to accomplish a specific task within a finite time.

Projective test: an assessment based on abstract or ambiguous images, which the subject is asked to interpret by projecting their feelings, preoccupations and motives into their responses.

Provisional selves: the personal experiments that we carry out with regard to how we act and interact in new organizational roles, based on our observations of the behaviour of others.

Psychometrics: the systematic testing, measurement and assessment of intelligence, aptitudes and personality.

Punishment: the attempt to discourage undesirable behaviours by applying negative consequences, or withholding a positive outcome following the undesirable behaviour.

Quality circle: shop floor employees from the same department who meet for a few hours each week to discuss ways of improving their work environment.

Quality of working life: an individual's overall satisfaction with their job, working conditions, pay, colleagues, management style, organization culture, work–life balance, and training, development, and career opportunities.

Radical frame of reference on conflict: a perspective that views organizational conflict as an inevitable consequence of exploitative employment relations in a capitalist economy.

Rational decisions: decisions that are made using evidence, logical argument and reasoning.

Rational model of decision making: assumes that decision making is and should be a rational process consisting of a sequence of steps that enhance the probability of attaining a desired outcome.

Rationality: the use of scientific reasoning, empiricism and positivism, along with the use of decision criteria that include evidence, logical argument and reasoning.

Readiness for change: a predisposition to welcome and embrace change.

Referent power: the ability to exert influence based on the other's belief that the influencer has desirable abilities and personality traits that can and should be copied.

Replacement effects: processes through which intelligent machines substitute for people at work, leading to unemployment.

Reshoring: Returning to the home country the production and provision of products and services which had previously been outsourced to overseas suppliers.

Resistance (in conflict): more or less covert behaviour that counteracts and restricts management's attempt to exercise power and control in the workplace.

Resistance to change: an unwillingness, or an inability to accept or to discuss changes that are perceived to be damaging or threatening to the individual.

Responsibility: the obligation placed on a person who occupies a certain position in the organization structure to perform a task, function or assignment.

Responsibility time span: target completion time of the *longest* task, project or programme assigned to that role.

Reward power: the ability to exert influence based on the other's belief that the influencer has access to valued rewards which will be dispensed in return for compliance.

Risk: a condition in which managers have a high knowledge of alternatives; know the probability of these being available; can calculate the costs and know the benefits of each alternative; and have a medium predictability of outcomes.

Risk-seeking propensity: an individual's willingness to choose options that involve risk.

Risky shift phenomenon: the tendency of a group to make decisions that are riskier than those which individual members would have recommended.

Robots: Physical machines that move within an environment with a degree of autonomy.

Role: the pattern of behaviour expected by others from a person occupying a certain position in an organization hierarchy.

Role conflict: the simultaneous existence of two or more sets of role expectations on a person in such a way that compliance with one makes it difficult to comply with the others.

Role management stage of socialization: fine-tuning newcomers' learning and adding those responsibilities expected from fully fledged organizational members.

Role modelling: a form of socialization in which an individual learns by example, copying the behaviour of established organizational members.

Routine decisions: decisions made according to established procedures and rules.

Rules: procedures or obligations explicitly stated and written down in organization manuals.

Satisficing: a decision-making approach where the first solution that is judged to be 'good enough' (i.e. satisfactory and sufficient) is selected, and the search is then ended.

Scenario planning: the imaginative development of one or more likely pictures of the dimensions and characteristics of the future for an organization.

Schedule of reinforcement: the pattern and frequency of rewards contingent on the display of desirable behaviour.

Scientific management: a form of job design which stresses short, repetitive work cycles; detailed, prescribed task sequences; a separation of task conception from task execution; and motivation based on economic rewards.

Second machine age: a twenty-first century phenomenon based on computing developments which will affect tasks previously considered impossible to automate.

Selective attention: the ability, often exercised unconsciously, to choose from the stream of sensory data, to concentrate on particular elements, and to ignore others.

Self-actualization: the desire for personal fulfilment, to develop one's potential, to become everything that one is capable of becoming.

Self-categorization: perceiving ourselves as sharing the same social identity as other category members, and behaving in ways consistent with that category stereotype.

Self-concept: the set of perceptions that we have about ourselves.

Self-determination theory: a content theory of motivation which argues that we all have three equally important innate needs for autonomy, competence, and relatedness.

Self-esteem: that part of the self which is concerned with how we evaluate ourselves.

Self-fulfilling prophecy: a prediction that becomes true because someone expects it to happen.

Self-managing team: a group of individuals with diverse skills and knowledge with the collective autonomy and responsibility to plan, manage, and execute tasks interdependently to attain a common goal.

Self-organization: a collective process of communication, choice and mutual adjustment in behaviour based on a shared goal among members of a given system which occurs when people and resources organize themselves without external planning into coordinated, purposeful activity.

Sentiments: in Homans' theory, the feelings, attitudes and beliefs held by group members towards others.

Sex: the basic physiological differences between men and women.

Sexuality: the way someone is sexually attracted to another person, whether it is to the opposite or the same sex.

Shaping: the selective reinforcement of chosen behaviours in a manner that progressively establishes a desired behaviour pattern.

Shared frame of reference: assumptions held in common by group members which shape their thinking, decisions, actions and interactions, while being constantly defined and reinforced through those interactions.

Situational leadership: an approach to determining the most effective style of influencing, considering the direction and support a leader gives, and the readiness of followers to perform a particular task.

Skinnerian conditioning: a technique for associating a response or a behaviour with its consequence.

Social categorization: classifying the people we meet, on the basis of how similar or different they are, from the way that we see ourselves.

Social compensation: when group cohesion and evaluation are absent, a person who cares about the quality of the group's output will expend greater effort to compensate for others in the group who are performing inadequately.

Social facilitation: the effect of the presence of other people enhancing an individual's performance.

Social identity: that part of the self-concept which comes from our membership of groups and which contributes to our self-esteem.

Social influence: the process whereby attitudes and behaviours are altered by the real or implied presence of others.

Social inhibition: the effect of the presence of other people reducing an individual's performance.

Social intelligence: the ability to understand the thoughts and feelings of others and to manage our relationships accordingly.

Social loafing: the tendency for individuals to exert less effort when working as part of a group than when working alone.

Social matrix: an environment in which any online activity can be social, influencing actions, solving problems, innovating, and creating new types of organizations that are not constrained by traditional boundaries.

Social orientation: the relative importance of the interests of the individual versus the interest of the group – *individualism v collectivism.*

Social representations: the beliefs, ideas and values, objects, people and events that are constructed by current group members, and which are transmitted to its new members.

Social role: the set of expectations that others hold of an occupant of a position.

Social status: the relative ranking that a person holds and the value of that person as measured by a group.

Socialization: the process by which new members learn the value system, the norms, and the required behaviour patterns of the society, organization, or group which they are entering.

Sociogram: diagram showing the liking (social attraction) relationships between individual members of a group.

Sociometry: the measurement of interpersonal feelings and relationships within groups.

Socio-technical system design: an approach to job and organization design which tries to find the best fit between the social and technological dimensions.

Span of control: the number of subordinates who report directly to a single manager or supervisor.

Staff employees: workers who occupy advisory positions and who use their specialized expertise to support the efforts of line employees.

Staff relationship: one in which staff department specialists can recommend, advise or assist line managers to implement their instructions concerning a particular issue, but have no authority to insist that they do so.

Stakeholder: anyone who is concerned with how an organization operates, and who will be affected by its decisions and actions.

Stereotype: a category, or personality type to which we allocate people on the basis of their membership of some known group.

Strategic choice: the view that an organization's environment, market and technology are the result of senior management decisions.

Strategic contingencies theory: a perspective which argues that the most powerful individuals and departments are those best able to deal effectively with the issues that are most critical to the organization's survival and performance.

Strong culture: one in which an organization's core values and norms are widely shared among employees, intensely held by them, and which guide their behaviour.

Structured task: a task with clear goals, few correct or satisfactory solutions and outcomes, few ways of performing it, and clear criteria of success.

Superleader: a leader who is able to develop leadership capacity in others, empowering them, reducing their dependence on formal leaders, stimulating their motivation, commitment and creativity.

Surface manifestation of organizational culture: culture's most accessible forms which are visible and audible behaviour patterns and objects.

Sustaining innovations: innovations which make improvements to existing processes, procedures, services and products.

Synergy: the positive or negative result of the interaction of two or more components, producing an outcome that is different from the sum of the individual components.

Systematic soldiering: the conscious and deliberate restriction of output by operators.

Task activity: an oral input, made by a group member that contributes directly to the group's work task.

Task analysability: the degree to which standardized solutions are available to solve the problems that arise.

Task variety: the number of new and different demands that a task places on an individual or a function.

Team: a collection of individuals who exist to achieve a shared goal; are interdependent with respect to achieving that goal; whose membership is bounded and stable over time; and who operate within a system.

Team autonomy: the extent to which a team experiences freedom, independence and discretion in decisions relating to the performance of its tasks.

Team-based structure: an organizational design that consists entirely of project-type teams that focus on processes rather than individual jobs; coordinate their activities; and work directly with partners and customers to achieve their goals.

Team building: a set of techniques used to help team members to understand their own roles more clearly and improve their interaction and collaboration with other members.

Team performance: a measure of how well a team achieves its task, and the needs of management, customers or shareholders.

Team player: a person who works willingly in cooperation with others for the benefit of the whole team.

Team role: an individual's tendency to behave in preferred ways which contribute to, and interrelate with, other members within a team.

Team viability: a measure of how well a team meets the needs and expectations of its members.

Technical complexity: the degree of predictability about and control over the final product permitted by the technology used.

Technical feasibility: the potential that a given job task or work activity can be automated by adopting current technology.

Technological determinism: the argument that technology explains the nature of jobs, skill and knowledge requirements, and organization structure

Technological interdependence: the extent to which the work tasks performed in an organization by one department or team member, affect the task performance of other departments or team members. Interdependence can be high or low.

Thematic apperception test: an assessment in which the individual is shown ambiguous pictures and is asked to create stories of what may be happening in them.

Time-and-motion studies: measurement and recording techniques used to make work operations more efficient.

Time orientation: the time outlook on work and life – *short term v long term.*

Total quality management: a philosophy of management that is driven by customer needs and expectations and which is committed to continuous improvement.

Total rewards: All aspects of work that are valued by employees, including recognition, development opportunities, organization culture, and attractive work environment, as well as pay and other financial benefits.

Trait: a relatively stable quality or attribute of an individual's personality, influencing behaviour in a particular direction.

Transactional leader: a leader who treats relationships with followers in terms of an exchange, giving followers what they want in return for what the leader desires, following prescribed tasks to pursue established goals.

Transformational change: large-scale change involving radical, frame-breaking, and fundamentally new ways of thinking, solving problems, and doing business.

Transformational leader: a leader who treats relationships with followers in terms of motivation and commitment, influencing and inspiring followers to give more than mere compliance to improve organizational performance.

Triggers of change: disorganizing pressures that make current systems, procedures, rules, organization structures, processes, roles, and skills inappropriate and ineffective.

Type: a descriptive label for a distinct pattern of personality characteristics, such as introvert, extravert, neurotic.

Type A personality: a combination of emotions and behaviours characterized by ambition, hostility, impatience and a sense of constant time-pressure.

Type B personality: a combination of emotions and behaviours characterized by relaxation, low focus on achievement, and ability to take time to enjoy leisure.

Uncertainty: a condition in which managers possess little knowledge of alternatives; a low probability of having these available; can to some degree calculate the costs and benefits of each alternative; but have no predictability of outcomes.

Uncertainty orientation: the emotional response to uncertainty and change – *acceptance v avoidance*.

Unconditional positive regard: unqualified, non-judgemental approval and respect for the traits and behaviours of the other person (a term used in counselling).

Unitarist frame of reference on conflict: a perspective that regards management and employee interests as coinciding and which thus regards organizational conflict are harmful and to be avoided.

Unretirement: having retired, then later taking full-time work, or starting full-time work after partial retirement.

Unstructured task: a task with ambiguous goals, many good solutions, many ways of achieving acceptable outcomes, and vague criteria of success.

User contribution system: a method of aggregating people's contributions or behaviours in ways that is useful to others.

Valence: the perceived value or preference that an individual has for a particular outcome, and can be positive, negative, or neutral.

Variance theory: an approach to explaining organizational behaviour based on universal relationships between independent and dependent variables which can be defined and measured precisely.

Vertical loading factors: methods for enriching work and improving motivation, by removing controls, increasing accountability, and by providing feedback, new tasks, natural work units, special assignments and additional authority.

Virtual organization structure: an organizational design that uses technology to transcend the constraints of legal structures, physical conditions, place and time, and allows a network of separate participants to present themselves to customers as a single entity.

Virtual team: one that relies on technology-mediated communication while crossing boundaries of geography, time, culture and organization, to accomplish an interdependent task.

Weak culture: one in which there is little agreement among employees about their organization's values and norms, the way things are supposed to be, or what is expected of them.

Work design: the content and organization of an employee's work tasks, activities, relationships and responsibilities.

Work passion: a strong inclination towards a job that you like, and into which you invest your time and energy.

Yerkes–Dodson law: a psychology hypothesis which states that performance increases with arousal, until we become overwhelmed, after which performance falls.

Name index

Subject index